HUMAN BIOLOGY

HUMAN BIOLOGY

SANDRA S. GOTTFRIED, Ph.D.

Assistant Professor of Biology and Education
Departments of Biology and Educational Studies
University of Missouri—St. Louis

with 452 *illustrations*

 Mosby

St. Louis Baltimore Boston Chicago London Madrid Philadelphia Sydney Toronto

Mosby

Dedicated to Publishing Excellence

Editor-in-Chief: James M. Smith
Editor: Robert J. Callanan
Senior Developmental Editor: Jean Babrick
Project Manager: Carol Sullivan Wiseman
Production Editor: Catherine Schwent
Designer: Betty Schulz
Cover Photograph: © International Stock/George Ancona

Printed in the United States of America
Composition by The Clarinda Company
Printing/binding by Von Hoffman Press, Inc.

Mosby–Year Book, Inc.
11830 Westline Industrial Drive
St. Louis, MO 63146

Library of Congress Cataloging in Publication Data

Gottfried, Sandra S.
    Human biology / Sandra S. Gottfried.
        p.   cm.
    Includes index.
    ISBN 0-8016-7972-9
    1. Human biology.   I. Title.
    QP36.G66 1994   93-32916
    612—dc20   CIP

93 94 95 96 97 / 9 8 7 6 5 4 3 2 1

10%
TOTAL RECOVERED FIBER

Preface

Are you 18 or 80? . . .or somewhere in between? Are you an English major or an art major? Or are you studying to be an elementary school teacher? Perhaps you are a returning student, tackling college courses after being out of school for many years. You may not have studied science or biology for a long time; perhaps you're even "science shy" and are reluctant or afraid to take a science course. Hopefully, your fears will melt away as you begin to study the human body and find that you can understand, appreciate, and even enjoy a scientific approach to the study of "you" while you explore topics that are vital to your health and well-being.

Students take a course in human biology for a variety of reasons. Your classroom holds a group of students with a wide range of backgrounds, skills, motivations, and goals. I wrote *Human Biology* for you, the introductory student who is most likely majoring in a field other than biology. Having worked with a variety of students for over 20 years in biology education, I feel I am well aware of my audience—students like you—and their needs. My training in scientific research, biology, and education and my experience as a science writer and teacher enabled me to write this book so that it is understandable even though you may have no prior knowledge of biology. I have worked to make my writing style easy to read, and to develop scientific concepts by providing understandable descriptions that will be a solid basis for your learning and comprehension. In addition, I have used everyday situations or concerns you may have encountered in the media as examples whenever possible. I have also provided information about your own physiology to help you make informed decisions about life-style choices that will affect your body, such as choosing what foods to eat or whether or not to smoke.

Human Biology also contains eight case studies that raise bioethical questions, one at the beginning of each part of the book. These case studies are related to the scientific content of *Human Biology*. They offer situations that reflect the often-conflicting values of various groups and individuals as well as the ethical dilemmas raised by the application of current biological knowledge to medical treatment, reproductive choices, or consumer choices that may affect the environment. These dilemmas are as real as a government's decision to fund family planning clinics or a family's struggle to decide what medical care an elderly parent should receive. The decisionmaking framework that concludes each part of the book will help you focus on the bioethical questions each case addresses and devise a strategy for recognizing and analyzing similar bioethical dilemmas in your own life.

Organization

The 26 chapters of *Human Biology* are thematically grouped into eight parts. No parts are longer than five chapters, providing a manageable framework. However, the chapters are also designed to stand alone so that professors can use the text in the order in which it was written or in an alternative order. The chapter opening pedagogy provides "Highlights" for each chapter, which is a menu of the chapter's content. These Highlights will help professors determine the chapter order that best suits the organization of their courses. Page references to concepts previously defined and explained are noted throughout the chapters.

In general, the book is organized in a traditional fashion. Basic biological concepts are presented in the introduction, with chemistry, cell anatomy and physiology, and tissues comprising Part One. Parts Two to Four describe the systems of the human body. Parts Five and Six describe reproduction on the cellular and organismal levels, including a discussion of DNA, the hereditary material, and gene expression. The last part discusses human evolution and ecology.

Introduction

This short, introductory part consists of Chapter 1 (Biology: A Human Focus), which discusses scientific process as the unifying theme among all sciences. It gives an overview of research in human biology and describes how scientists build theories. The themes of biology are also discussed as a context in which to embed a study of human biology. The chapter closes with a discussion of principles of scientific classification.

Part One
Molecules, Cells, and Tissues

Part Two contains information about basic chemistry (Chapter 2, The Chemistry of Life) and cell structure (Chapter 3, Cell Structure and Function). Cell physiology is presented in Chapters 4 and 5 (The Flow of Energy Within Organisms and Cellular Respiration). The concluding chapter of this part describes the tissue level of organization of the human body in detail and gives an overview of organs and organ systems (Chapter 6, Levels of Organization in the Human Body).

Part Two
Maintenance Systems

The four chapters in this part include the systems of the body involved with: digesting food and absorbing nutrients (Chapter 7, Digestion), delivering oxygen to the lungs and eliminating the carbon dioxide from the body (Chapter 8, Respiration), transporting nutrients, oxygen, and other needed substances to cells and transporting wastes away from cells (Chapter 9, Circulation), and filtering the blood to maintain homeostasis, a "steady state" of the body (Chapter 10, Excretion).

Part Three
Communication and Regulatory Systems

The next four chapters describe both the "fast" communication system of the body, the nervous system, and the "slow" communication system, the endocrine system. Chapter 11 (Nerve Cells and How They Transmit Information) describes the structure of nerve cells and how impulses are conducted along their membranes and from nerve cell to nerve cell. This latter discussion provides the background and context for an explanation of how drugs cause their effects on the human brain. The next two chapters (Chapter 12, The Nervous System and Chapter 13, The Senses) look at the organ level of nervous system communication, describing the structure and function of the central and peripheral nervous systems as well as the sense organs. Chapter 14 (Hormones) describes the chemical messengers produced by cells and how they regulate other cells of the body, as well as describing the variety of endocrine glands and their specific roles.

Part Four
Protection, Defense, and Support

This part is made up of two chapters: Chapter 15, Protection, Support, and Movement and Chapter 16, Defense Against Disease. Chapter 15 discusses the integumentary, skeletal, and muscular systems and describes how the skin, bones, and muscles work together. Chapter 16 describes the nonspecific and specific defenses the body uses to combat foreign substances (including agents of infection, cancer cells, and foreign tissues) that enter the body.

Part Five
How Cells Pass on Biological Information

This unit discusses genetics, beginning with its molecular and cellular aspects in Chapter 17 (DNA, Gene Expression, and Cell Reproduction). Chapter 18 (Abnormal Cell Reproduction: Cancer) defines the term *cancer,* describes the molecular biology of this group of diseases, and discusses

factors that increase or decrease the risk of cancer. Chapter 19 (Patterns of Inheritance) covers classical Mendelian genetics. The part closes with a look at human inheritance patterns, including genetic disorders, in Chapter 20 (Human Genetics).

Part Six
How Humans Reproduce

Part 6 is made up of three chapters: Chapter 21, Sex and Reproduction; Chapter 22, Development Before Birth; and Chapter 23, Sexually Transmitted Diseases. Chapter 21 describes the anatomy and physiology of the male and female reproductive systems and also discusses various methods of birth control and how they work. Chapter 22 describes prenatal development. Chapter 23 gives an overview of viruses and bacteria before describing the sexually transmitted diseases they cause. Sexually transmitted diseases caused by other organisms, although not as prevalent, are included.

Part Seven
Human Evolution and Ecology

Three chapters comprise this part. Chapter 24 (Human Evolution) provides a summary of the evolution of all life as a prelude to the focus of this chapter: the evolution of humans. Chapter 25 (Human Population Concerns) describes how populations grow and explains the factors that influence the size of a population. The human population explosion is the focus of the last part of the chapter, which provides a natural transition to Chapter 26 (The Human Impact on the Environment). This last chapter explores current environmental issues affecting the land, water, and atmosphere, including topics such as species extinction, acid rain, air pollution, and the depletion of the ozone layer.

Features

Several pedagogical features make *Human Biology* easy to use. Students should find these features a great help when reading their assignments for class and reviewing for exams and quizzes.

Each chapter opens with a short "vignette" that is designed to spark student interest. Sometimes these vignettes explain something that may already be familiar to the student in a context that relates to the chapter material. For example, Chapter 14 (Hormones) opens with a vignette about the dangers of anabolic steroids. The vignette in Chapter 23 (Sexually Transmitted Diseases) discusses the debate on condom handouts in the New York City school district, the first school district in the country to distribute condoms to its students.

In addition to the vignettes, the chapter openers contain a list of chapter "Highlights", as mentioned previously,

Preface

that describe key concepts of the chapter. These highlights provide students with a content overview before they read the chapter. An "Outline" of the chapter accompanies the highlights, providing a topical summary of the chapter to help students organize chapter concepts.

Within each chapter are "Concept Summaries" that provide synopses at key points in the chapter. They help students identify the key ideas in the narrative and are valuable study aids.

"Boxed Essays," listed in boldface in the table of contents, are found in most chapters. Some link topics in human biology to students' everyday lives, highlighting the personal relevance of many biological concepts. Others highlight the links among human biology, technology, and societal issues. And lastly, some boxed essays describe the work of scientists in detail, often answering the question, "How do we know that?".

Each chapter closes with a "Summary" that lists all the key concepts in the chapter, a selection of "Review Questions" that test students' comprehension of the chapter content, and a few "Discussion Questions" designed to initiate class discussion and debate. Each chapter also has a short list of "Further Readings," chosen with the introductory student in mind. The articles are taken from periodicals such as *Scientific American, Science, Smithsonian,* and *National Geographic.*

At the back of the book, a glossary provides the pronunciation, definition, and derivation for each key term in the book and also gives the page reference for each term. An appendix provides answers to the review questions.

The art program

Human Biology uses its art program to help students visualize and understand concepts and processes. It accomplishes this task by following these principles:

- Illustrations and photographs should be used to make abstract concepts more concrete and to enhance student understanding.
- The content of the narrative and the art should match—concepts, processes, or structures should not be presented in the art that are not discussed in the narrative. Additionally, the narrative and the art should be integrated in a meaningful way.
- Illustrations that depict processes should use a clear, simple layout. For complex processes, numbered steps should be used.
- Legends should be a helpful guide to the illustration and should not introduce material that is not in the text.
- Art should be visually appealing so that students are prompted to "take a look."

We have followed these principles in *Human Biology,* with the result that the art program represents another important focus in the pedagogical program and is an element in itself.

Ancillaries

Carefully designed and executed, the ancillaries to *Human Biology* supplement, support, and enhance its student-oriented approach.

Instructor's Resource Guide

For the instructor, the *Instructor's Resource Guide* is a valuable teaching resource. Written by Elmer Kellman, a veteran teacher of biological sciences, each chapter contains a complete synopsis, suggested topics for class discussion, lecture outlines, and teaching ideas. In addition, the *Instructor's Resource Guide* provides complete instructor support for the bioethical essays and decisionmaking framework materials found as part openers and part closers in the textbook. The decisionmaking framework for each essay is discussed in detail. In addition, teaching strategies for using bioethical decisionmaking in the classroom are explained completely, providing an array of options for the instructor. This resource guide is also available on disk for IBM and Macintosh users.

A test bank of approximately 1000 questions, written by Margaret Foy Kelly, is also included in the manual. as are transparency masters of key illustrations in *Human Biology.*

Computerized Test Bank

The test bank questions are also available on Computest, a computerized test generation system for IBM users. It has many features that make it easy for the instructor to design tests and quizzes. The instructor can browse and select questions for inclusion on an examination using several different criteria, including question type and level of difficulty. A similar test-generating system is available for Macintosh and Apple users.

Transparency Acetates

Also available for the instructor is a set of full-color transparency acetates that reproduce the important illustrations in *Human Biology.* Labeling is clear, bold, and large enough for even students seated in the back of a large room to see.

Acknowledgments

Producing a textbook such as *Human Biology,* with a full-color art program, professional layout and design, and ancillaries cannot be accomplished by an author alone. A variety of highly-skilled professionals at Mosby have turned my manuscript for *Human Biology* into an attractive text-

videodisk ?

book program that will be a motivating learning tool for students and a useful teaching resource for instructors. Catherine Schwent, production editor, and Betty Schulz, book designer, worked long and carefully to make *Human Biology* an accurate, attractive teaching tool. *Human Biology* could not have been completed without the hard work of Jean Babrick, developmental editor. Jean has my deepest gratitude for her skillful editing and coordination of this project. In addition, Jean researched and acquired many of the outstanding photographs used in this book—a task that at times we thought was going to be impossible. Thank you, Jean, for your diligence, patience, talent, and caring in all aspects of your work. My thanks also go to Bob Callanan, acquisitions editor, for continuing to encourage innovation and excellence. His support of the bioethical decisionmaking feature in this textbook is only one example of his commitment to the production of books that are pedagogically sound and that incorporate features reflecting current goals in science education.

The Hastings Center of Briarcliff Manor, New York, and Bruce Jennings, an ethicist at that institute, played an important role in the development of the bioethical decisionmaking framework of *Human Biology*. Many of the bioethical essays used in *Human Biology* are adaptations of essays published in *The Hastings Center Newsletter*. In addi-

tion, the decisionmaking framework is adapted from a similar framework outlined in *New Choices, New Responsibilities*, a publication of the Center. Many thanks go to Bruce Jennings for acting as a consultant to this project.

I also want to thank some other important people who contributed their time and talents to the development of this book: Lucy Bradley-Springer, Harvey Friedman, Cris Hochwender, Peggy Foy Kelly, Eilene Lyons, Cynthia J. Moore, Wendy Schiff, Kathleen Scogna, and Carl Thurman.

SANDRA S. GOTTFRIED

Some of the bioethical decisionmaking case studies, and the decision making framework in *Human Biology*, have been adapted from Bruce Jennings, Kathleen Nolan, Courtney S. Campbell, and Strachan Donnelley, *New Choices, New Responsibilities: Ethical Issues in the Life Sciences*. Nutley, NJ: Hoffman-LaRoche, Inc., 1990. This teaching resource was developed by The Hastings Center with support from Hoffman-LaRoche, Inc.

An Introduction to Bioethical Decisionmaking

Scientific and technological advances have expanded our knowledge and given us new powers such as the ability to manipulate human genes, transplant organs, and keep profoundly sick or injured infants, children, and adults alive with specialized equipment and therapies. At the same time, science has been challenged to develop effective treatments for devastating diseases such as acquired immune deficiency syndrome (AIDS). Our new powers are awesome, and the need to confront these new medical challenges is urgent. Furthermore, both the powers and the challenges carry ethical responsibilities.

Many people use the terms ethics and morals interchangeably, but they have different meanings. *Morals* are the beliefs and standards of good and bad, right and wrong, upheld by a society. *Ethics* is the study of moral practices; it describes the theory or philosophy that underlies moral beliefs and behavior. The case studies presented at the beginning of each part of this text will challenge you to use one type of ethics: normative ethics. This field of ethics develops the ethical principles that spell out moral standards. *Normative ethics* offers answers to the questions, "What should I do?" and "How should I live?". It also offers reasons why a person should accept these answers. Normative ethics applied to decisionmaking and public policy in the areas of biology, medicine, and health care is *bioethics*. Bioethics is concerned with basic scientific research and with the social applications of biological knowledge and biomedical technology. This textbook offers a planned approach to bioethical decisionmaking that you can use by yourself to develop your critical thinking skills and decisionmaking strategies. As a part of classroom activities, the decisionmaking process will explore new dimensions of human biology as you, your classmates, and instructor discuss and debate bioethical issues.

The eight bioethical case studies that make up the part openers of this text are pertinent to a human biology course. A case is discussed at the beginning of each part of this book; it links in some way with the content of the chapters in that part. These cases require in-depth consideration of the often-conflicting values and the ethical dilemmas raised by the application of current biological knowledge. Each part ends with a bioethical decisionmaking framework. This framework consists of six basic questions that are repeated with each case along with in-depth questions that elaborate on these six questions. These questions will help you structure your thinking, focus it on the bioethical questions the case addresses, and devise a strategy for recognizing and analyzing similar bioethical dilemmas in your own life, be it reproductive choices, medical care for a family member, or choices as a consumer and citizen that affect your environment.

These case studies and the decisionmaking frameworks that accompany them will *not* offer clear-cut answers to the bioethical issues they raise. Ethical issues are rarely either neat or simple. Each of these cases contains questions of choice—understanding one's options—and questions of responsibility—what values are at stake in your choices and what moral principles should guide your decisions.

Contents in Brief

Contents

1 Biology:
A Human Focus

MAKING BIOETHICAL DECISIONS
The Bioethics of Controlled Experiments

A group of investigators at a major institution have developed a research proposal to test the effectiveness of a new drug for AIDS (acquired immune deficiency syndrome). They need funding to carry out this study and therefore have submitted this proposal to a federal agency that funds clinical research.

The agency's process for proposal approval is rigorous. At the first level, an initial review group composed of scientists examine the proposal and assign it a priority score based on its scientific merit. The review group that will consider this proposal deals only with AIDS research. The second level of the agency's review system is a national advisory council composed of both scientists and nonscientists. This council examines the recommendations of the first group, agrees with or modifies them, and evaluates the application. Evaluation is based on the agency's funding priorities and the research proposal's relevance. Finally, the council makes a recommendation to the agency concerning funding of the proposal.

The proposed research would actually be phase III of the research process for this drug. Phases I and II have already been completed. Phase I determined the dosage level that could be tolerated by AIDS patients and if the drug has any side effects. Phase II verified that the drug was active against the virus that causes AIDS. The present research proposal, Phase III, would use comparative trials to determine the usefulness of the drug in treating AIDS patients. In designing the trials, the researchers acknowledged that the drug may act differently on persons with different stages of the disease, and that their tolerance of the drug's side effects would differ. The researchers also acknowledged that the patients' age and manner of infection may affect how the disease progresses. Also, patients may have other diseases, such as hemophilia, to be considered in the research design. With these issues in mind, the researchers chose a methodology called a double-blind crossover study.

In such a study, half of the participants (all volunteers at a similar stage of AIDS) are randomly chosen to receive the new drug. This is the experimental group. The other half of the participants receive a placebo, a pill that resembles the drug but that contains no medication. This is the control group. The course of the disease in these groups is compared. Halfway through the study, the experimental group receiving the new drug "crosses over" to the placebo, and the control group crosses over to the actual drug. (Nobody involved in the study, including the researchers, knows which pill contains the drug and which contains the placebo; the pills are stamped with code letters by the drug company, and the code is revealed only after the study ends.) The researchers believe this "blinding" is necessary to remove any possible bias as they evaluate the drug's effects. (Placebos and a control group are necessary parts of the research design in a blinded study.)

The researchers believe that this cross-over design is the most ethical approach because they will be asking the study participants to stop taking all other medications. This is necessary if they are to determine the effects of the new drug alone and to avoid any drug interactions. By crossing over midway in the study, control group participants who might be doing badly would have a change in therapy and perhaps improve. However, the researchers also realize that the new drug's positive effects might not be revealed for a long time and that the crossing-over patients might not benefit if this is the case. The participants in the study, all volunteers, are fully informed about the use of placebos and have consented.

Based on the recommendations of both the initial review group and the advisory council, who found the proposal scientifically sound and ethically acceptable, the agency approved the research. After approval was announced, however, activists who publicize perceived or real injustices against people with AIDS began to picket the agency. The group claimed that withholding the new drug from some of the participants in the study, even for scientific research, is unethical because AIDS is a fatal disease. Using placebos for part of the experiment might worsen the disease or even lead to death, because the participants would be receiving no medication at all. The protestors charged that informed consent was irrelevant in this case. They demanded that the study design be changed and that the new drug be tested without the use of placebos.

If you were director of the agency, would you stand by the decision reached by the review process to approve this study?

1 Biology: A Human Focus

▼ Human biology is the scientific study of human life.

▼ All scientists study the natural world by using a process called the scientific method in which they ask questions, make predictions, and then test their predictions by means of experimentation.

▼ Rising out of the abundance of tested predictions are many themes, or accepted explanations, regarding all living things, including humans.

▼ Modern taxonomy, the classification of the diverse array of living things, categorizes organisms based on their common ancestry while taking into account their existing similarities and differences.

Scientific process: The unifying theme among all sciences
The pathway of thinking in the scientific method
Summarizing the steps in the scientific method
Research in human biology
Theory building

The unifying themes of biology
Living things display both diversity and unity
Living things are composed of cells and are hierarchically organized
Living things interact with each other and with their environments
Living things transform energy and maintain a steady internal environment
Living things exhibit forms that fit their functions
Living things reproduce and pass on biological information to their offspring
Living things change over time, or evolve

Classification: A reflection of evolutionary history

Humans can be studied from a variety of perspectives. Sociologists, for example, are interested in the values, beliefs, and cultures of humans, and study the structure of societies and the patterns of human interaction within them. Anthropologists are also interested in human cultures and social interactions, but with a wider scope. Anthropologists begin their study with the earliest humans who lived over a million years ago. Within this time frame, anthropologists often focus on how human social characteristics such as language, sexuality, or religion originated and developed. Biologists, however, study humans from a scientific perspective, placing our species in the context of all living things.

Biology, the study of life, is a multifaceted scientific discipline. Molecular biologists study life at the chemical level, probing the workings of the molecular "chain of command" within cells. Cell biologists study individual cells or groups of cells and ask questions about how cells interact with each other and the environment. At the organism level, some biologists focus on interactions within organisms, such as changes in female hormone levels during the reproductive cycle. Population biologists are interested in interactions among individuals of the same species that occur together at one place and time. Some biologists are interested in questions having worldwide impact such as the effects of rain forest destruction on global weather patterns and trends.

Scientific process: The unifying theme among all sciences

Science often seems a mysterious process to the nonscientist. White-coated men working in sterile laboratories and engaging in difficult-to-understand processes embody the stereotype of the typical scientist and *his* work. However, as you can see in Figure 1-1, scientists are both men *and* women and are a culturally and ethnically diverse group. In addition, not all scientists work in laboratories. In fact, the work of science can take place just about anywhere. Although scientists and "their" science may differ in focus, all scientists—biologists, chemists, physicists, and so forth—study the natural world and go about their work in a similar way. This similar way is referred to as the **scientific method.** The scientific method is a process, or series of steps, scientists use to answer the questions they ask. In fact, asking questions is part of the method. In addition, all scientists ask questions that can be investigated by means of experimentation. In other words, they ask questions that can be tested, producing results that are open to verification by others in their discipline. Scientists do not ask philosophical or religious questions such as "What is the meaning of life?" or "Does life exist after death?"

The scientific method, which is commonly used by various scientific disciplines, is a set of procedures used to answer questions.

The pathway of thinking in the scientific method

The scientific method usually starts with observations that lead to questions. In fact, one of the most important processes of science is observation, but observation alone does not constitute science. The predecessors of scientists—the ancient Greeks and Romans such as Plato, Aristotle, and Pliny—were skilled observers but were not scientists by today's definition. Rather, their science was called **natural history** and they were called **naturalists.** Until about the mid-1800s, biology continued to have a natural history perspective, focusing on descriptions and comparisons of organisms and providing explanations to questions based on observation alone. Although the scientific method had already taken hold in the physical sciences, it was not widely used in biology because many people believed that the living world transcended physical laws—experimentation could not answer questions regarding living things. A critical shift occurred during the nineteenth century, the shift that made biology a "true" science. A preoccupation with form moved to an investigation of function and process. Scientists went beyond observation to put forth **hypotheses,** or plausible answers to their questions, *testing them by experimentation.*

Hypothesis formation (often characterized as an educated guess that tentatively answers a question) and experimentation are key pieces in the scientific method. Before scientists formulate hypotheses, however, they gather information regarding their questions. Only after searching the scientific literature and synthesizing all the information they can find regarding their questions do scientists generate hypotheses. The hypothesis, therefore, is not just a guess but a well-thought-out prediction based on available knowledge and generalizations made from observations. This pattern of thought—developing generalizations from specific instances—is called **inductive reasoning.**

The scientific method usually starts with observations that lead to questions. Scientists then generate hypotheses, or plausible answers to their questions, by making generalizations based on their observations and the knowledge available to them. Scientists test their hypotheses by experimentation.

For example, you may observe that many of your friends grow houseplants that look healthy and robust. Because you struggle to keep yours alive, you might ask them their secrets. Many may answer that one key to growing healthy houseplants is giving them regular doses of Brand X fertilizer. You may have also read advertisements and other literature stating that Brand X fertilizer causes houseplants to grow 30% taller and produces healthier, greener plants. From these observations and testimonials, you might make the inductive generalization that Brand X fertilizer helps houseplants grow well. This generalization becomes a hypothesis when stated in an "If . . . then . . . " format.

FIGURE 1-1 Scientists are a diverse cultural and ethnic group.

Your hypothesis might be the following: "If houseplants are given Brand X fertilizer, then they will grow at least 30% taller and be greener than plants with no fertilizer." As you can see, a hypothesis is a *prediction*.

In analyzing the simplified hypothesis in our example (hypotheses can be much more complex), notice that the factor you are manipulating (the fertilizer) is stated after the "if" part of the hypothesis. This factor is called the **independent variable,** or manipulated variable. The word *variable* refers to a factor that changes, or varies. And, in fact, to test your hypothesis, you will need to add different amounts of Brand X fertilizer to houseplants to determine the effects on plant growth and color. Also notice that the factor stated after the "then" part of the hypothesis depends on the manipulated (independent) variable. This factor is called the **dependent variable,** or responding variable. It varies in response to changes in the independent variable.

Scientists test hypotheses by means of **controlled experiments.** An experiment tests a hypothesis by producing data that either support or refute the prediction made in the hypothesis. This testing process involves the use of deduction, or **deductive reasoning.** Deduction begins with a general statement (the prediction about Brand X fertilizer and its effects on houseplants) and proceeds to a specific statement (the effects of Brand X fertilizer on *your* houseplants).

In a controlled experiment the independent variable is manipulated and changes in the dependent variable are observed while all other possible variables are kept constant; that is, they are controlled. The variables to be kept constant include any factors in the experimental setup that can change. In this case, they include the type of soil, the amount of time the plants are exposed to the light, the temperature in which the plants are grown, and the type of plant tested. Can you think of any other possible variables that may need to be controlled?

As you design a controlled experiment to test your hypothesis, you should first outline the way in which you would manipulate the independent variable. In this case, you may decide to give one plant the "dose" of fertilizer suggested on its container and give some plants slightly more and others slightly less. If the suggested dose is one capful of liquid fertilizer, you may decide to give a second plant one-half capful, a third plant one and one-half cap-

fuls, and a fourth plant two capfuls. Each plant should be the same type of plant, such as all ivies, of approximately the same size. You should pot them all in the same soil in the same type and size of pot, place them near one another on the same windowsill, and water them all with the same amount of water at the same time. These plants will receive the **treatment,** in this case, the fertilizer. They are the experimental plants. A fifth plant should be the same as all the rest in every respect *except* that it will not receive the treatment (fertilizer). This plant serves as the **control** (Figure 1-2). The control is the standard against which the treatment plants can be compared. Any changes in the control are the result of factors other than the treatment.

Over a preselected time, you should observe your plants and **collect data** regarding leaf color and plant height or, in the case of ivies (vine-like plants), vine length. The data regarding the vine length of your ivies are called **quantitative data** because these data are based on numerical measurements (centimeters, for example). The data regarding leaf color are called **qualitative data** because these data are descriptive and not based on numerical measurements.

At the beginning of your experiment, you should measure the total length of the vines of each plant and record these data. At the end of your predetermined growing period, 6 weeks for example, you measure the vines again, recording these data. Your data table may look like this:

TOTAL VINE LENGTH IN CENTIMETERS (CM)

DOSE OF FERTILIZER	0 cf	½ cf	1 cf	1½ cf	2 cf
0 weeks	145	150	148	151	149
6 weeks	166	180	181	185	184
Increase in vine length	21	30	33	34	35

KEY: cf = capfuls of Brand X fertilizer

DESCRIPTION OF LEAF COLOR ON SELECTED VINES

DOSE OF FERTILIZER	0 cf	½ cf	1 cf	1½ cf	2 cf
0 weeks	mg	mg	mg	mg	mg
6 weeks	lg	mg	dg	dg	dg
Change in vine color	neg	nc	pos	pos	pos

KEY: y = yellow   mg = medium green
      lg = light green   dg = dark green
      neg = turned lighter (negative change)
      pos = turned darker (positive change)
      nc = no change

Independent variable

Dependent variable

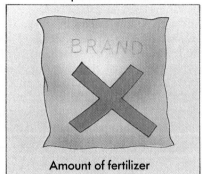
Amount of fertilizer

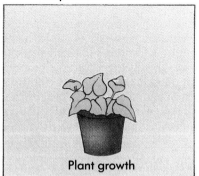
Plant growth

A

Constants

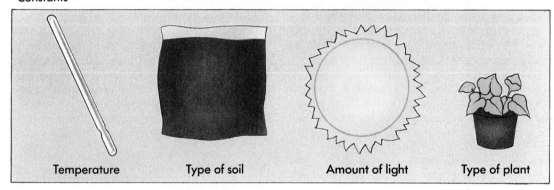

| Temperature | Type of soil | Amount of light | Type of plant |

B

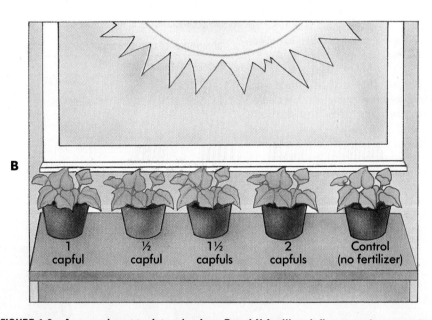

| 1 capful | ½ capful | 1½ capfuls | 2 capfuls | Control (no fertilizer) |

FIGURE 1-2 An experiment to determine how Brand X fertilizer influences plant growth.
A The variables in experiments are independent (manipulated) and dependent (responding). Other potential variables are held constant. In the plant experiment, the independent variable is the amount of fertilizer, the dependent variable is plant growth, and the constants are the type of soil, temperature, amount of light, and type of plant.
B The experimental set-up for the fertilizer-plant growth experiment.

Do your data support your hypothesis: If I add Brand X fertilizer to the soil of my houseplants, they will grow at least 30% taller and be greener than plants with no fertilizer? Looking at the qualitative data, the plants with fertilizer were greener than the control with no fertilizer. One capful to two capfuls, in this experiment, produced the greenest plants.

Looking at the quantitative data, can you determine if the vines were at least 30% longer than the control? First, let's compare the plant treated with one-half capful fertilizer to the control plant. The control plant grew 21 centimeters and the test plant grew 30 centimeters—9 centimeters more than the control. Is this difference at least 30% more (30% greater than the control growth)? This question is really asking "What percent of 21 is 9?" To find out, you divide 9 by 21, which yields 0.43. Multiplying by 100 to change this number into a percentage yields 43%. In other words, the vines of the plant receiving one-half capful of Brand X fertilizer grew 43% longer than the control. Using the same reasoning (1) the vines of the plant receiving one capful of Brand X fertilizer grew 57% longer, (2) the vines of the plant receiving one and one-half capfuls grew 62% longer, and (3) the vines of the plant receiving two capfuls grew 67% longer. In summary, these data do support your hypothesis; in fact, your test data suggest that Brand X fertilizer may help ivy plants grow greener and longer than the manufacturer suggests!

Why do you think the manufacturer of Brand X fertilizer is not making greater claims regarding this product? Your experiment certainly shows much greater than a 30% increase in growth. The answer lies in the limitations of your experiment. First, you experimented with one type of houseplant: ivy. Brand X fertilizer is probably sold for use on a variety of houseplants. Not all plants may grow as vigorously in response to the fertilizer as your ivies did. Second, you experimented on five plants. Scientists perform experiments over and over again, or make **repeated trials,** before drawing conclusions from their data. The Brand X fertilizer manufacturing company probably performs hundreds of experiments on a variety of houseplants before drawing conclusions from their data and generalizing to the population of houseplants grown throughout the United States (or possibly throughout the world).

Summarizing the steps in the scientific method

As you can see from this example, the scientific method is a procedure for problem solving that is appropriate for everyday use as well as for use by professional scientists. In fact, the scientific method is often referred to as *organized common sense*. In summary, the steps of the scientific method are:
• Posing a question
• Forming a hypothesis
• Testing the hypothesis by means of a controlled experiment
• Recording and analyzing the data
• Drawing a conclusion as to whether the data support the hypothesis
• Repeating the work

Evidence that contradicts the prediction of a hypothesis shows it to be false; that is, it disproves the hypothesis. However, evidence that is in keeping with the prediction a hypothesis makes does *not* prove that further testing will also produce supporting evidence. Factors may affect the outcome of a future experiment that may be unforeseen at the time. In your experiment, for example, the data collected using your plants supported your hypothesis. But data collected using other plants in someone else's home may not support your hypothesis. In summary, then, scientists cannot actually *prove* hypotheses; they can only *disprove* hypotheses or *support* hypotheses with evidence.

Research in human biology

Scientists study humans using research techniques similar to those used with the rest of the living world. Some scientists study tissue cultures, biochemical systems, and mathematical models to learn about the human body. These systems are useful when a problem must be studied under simplified, well-controlled conditions. However, such approaches are limited in their applications because nonliving systems cannot mimic the actual workings of a living organism. Often, therefore, animals are used as experimental models. The use of animals in biomedical research has helped scientists make advances in knowledge regarding a wide array of human diseases. For example, polio, a disease that can cause paralysis and that once reached near epidemic proportions, has been virtually wiped out by the use of vaccines developed through experimentation on monkeys. Likewise, the development of artificial joints was possible because of research on sheep. Today, animal models are used for AIDS (acquired immune deficiency syndrome) research in hopes of finding a cure for this deadly disease.

Biomedical researchers also conduct studies on humans. Research on human subjects follows the scientific method in its approach as does most scientific research, but the testing of a hypothesis may not involve experimentation. The study may be observational, in which investigators do not manipulate an independent variable (often called an intervention in biomedical research). Instead, the researchers may report observations that have biomedical importance, such as the numbers of persons receiving flu vaccinations during September of a particular year. Or, they may test a hypothesis by comparing two or more groups of subjects with regard to an intervention that occurs naturally, such as comparing the percent of unimmunized persons contracting the flu compared to the percent of immunized persons contracting the disease. When research involves a planned intervention, however, the investigator must be sure that it is ethical to conduct an experimental study to answer the research question and test the hypothesis. In other words, the researcher must be sure that persons are not subjected to undue risk, must be sure that the subjects are informed as to the possible benefits and risks of the experiment, and must have the written consent of the participants in the study. Using human subjects in research often raises many ethical questions that might not be raised when studying other forms of life such as bacteria or plants.

Medical research using human subjects often involves some degree of risk. Because scientists are concerned about the effect of drug treatments on fetal development, women of child-bearing age are often excluded from research studies. Such women could become pregnant before a study was completed, placing the pregnancy at risk and forcing the women to drop out of the trials. Such dropouts would reduce the size of the sample population, thus endangering the reliability of the study.

The reliability of a study might also be endangered by the normal hormonal changes experienced by premenopausal women during their menstrual cycles, or by the fact that the women were using oral contraceptives. Men, who do not experience such wide hormonal shifts, would seem to be a more convenient sample population for research.

However, if a drug is to be used by premenopausal women, it is important to know how its action is affected by varying hormone levels or by the use of oral contraceptives. Drug trials that exclude women may not provide all the information necessary for effective use of that drug by women.

Unfortunately, exclusion of women of childbearing age from research studies has often led, directly or indirectly, to exclusion of women of all ages. Both drug trials and studies investigating the cause of diseases, including such diseases as osteoporosis that often affect postmenopausal women in greater numbers than they

do men, have tended to use men for their sample populations.

In addition to women, men from minority groups are often excluded from research studies. However, this omission is not necessarily planned. Advocates for better health care claim that it is difficult to get members of minority groups to participate in research studies. There are several possible reasons for this difficulty. Many poor Hispanics and African-Americans lack access to health care providers and thus are not easily identified as possible participants. Members of minority groups may have had negative experiences with the available health care system and thus are suspicious of experimental care. Research studies may be located in inaccessible areas, such as suburban facilities with no public transportation. Research dollars are limited; there is not usually money to pay for subjects' transportation.

However, omitting any group of persons from a study means that its conclusions may not apply to that group. For example, early trials of the drug AZT for the treatment of AIDS (acquired immunodeficiency syndrome) included only white males. Later research indicated that this drug may be less effective for African-American men than for white men. The incidence of AIDS is increasing among minority groups (as well as among women). Using representative samples when studying the effects of new drugs for AIDS is thus essential for accurate results.

Under pressure from groups interested in health care issues for women and minorities, exclusionary practices in setting up research studies and drug trials are changing. In 1982 the National Institutes of Health (NIH), the health research wing of the United States Public Health Service (PHS), ruled that women and minorities must be included in any studies the NIH funds. This rule was not stringently enforced during the 1980s, but by 1991 Congress was pressuring the PHS to give more attention to women's health problems. An Office of Women's Health was established; one of its goals was to emphasize the earlier policy on the inclusion of women in NIH-funded studies. Researchers must now recruit women for clinical trials in the same percentages as they are affected by the disease under study. This means, for example, that women would not be included in studies of a drug developed to treat prostate infections; the prostate is a male organ. However, heart disease affects women as well as men. The makeup of the research sample used in studying this disease must reflect this fact. To date, the NIH has not paid as much attention to minority health care issues.

To be accurate, any research study or drug trial should include a representative sample. However, current economic conditions may mean that total federal revenues available for research will be less than in former years. For the present, the number of truly representative research samples may be reduced rather than expanded.

Theory building

As scientists repeat, or replicate, each other's work, their data may uphold a hypothesis again and again. As the explanations of such consistently supported and related hypotheses are woven together, "grand explanations" that account for existing data and that consistently predict new data are developed. Interwoven hypotheses upheld by overwhelming evidence over time are called **theories.** The word *theory* in a scientific context has a much stronger meaning than the everyday use of the term. A theory is a synthesis of hypotheses that have withstood the test of time and is therefore a powerful concept that helps scientists make dependable predictions about the world. Theories are sup-

ported by such an overwhelming weight of evidence that they are accepted as scientifically valid statements. The possibility always remains, however, that future evidence will cause a theory to be revised, since scientific knowledge grows and changes as new data are collected, analyzed, and then synthesized with information that came before.

Some theories are so strongly supported that the likelihood of their being rejected in the future is negligible. The theory of evolution, for example, is so broadly supported by different lines of inquiry that most biologists accept it with as much certainty as they do the theory of gravity. The theory of evolution provides the conceptual framework that unifies biology as a science.

The unifying themes of biology

Biology is often viewed by the nonscientist as an accumulation of facts, but it is much more than that. As the beginning of this chapter shows, biology (as well as all other sciences) is a way, or process, of understanding the world. As a result of observing living things, their environments, and the interactions between them, scientists have posed questions, have put forth hypotheses based on those observations, and have tested their predictions of the living world. Rising out of this abundance of tested predictions are the themes, or accepted explanations, that permeate the science of biology. Although the specific details of these themes may be updated or changed as biologists modify their hypotheses, the themes themselves transcend time. Since humans are a part of the living world described by these biological themes, the themes of biology are also the themes of human biology.

Living things display both diversity and unity

The diversity, or variety, of living things is astounding. Biologists estimate that from 5 million to 30 million *different* species exist on Earth. A **species** is a group of related organisms that share common characteristics and are able to interbreed, producing offspring that can reproduce. Only a sampling of the array of the species humans have seen and categorized is shown in Figure 1-3. Although these organisms are very different from one another and different from humans, each displays characteristics that are common among all species. Likewise, humans display characteristics that vary within the species *Homo sapiens*, but we all have characteristics in common. These characteristics of human anatomy, physiology, evolutionary history, and interactions with other organisms and the environment are the subject of *Human Biology*.

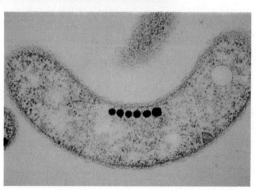

FIGURE 1-3   The diversity of species. Although scientists have categorized many species, there are still thousands of species that have yet to be seen or studied.
A Axolotl, an unusual amphibian.
B Stone plant. This unusual plant looks like a small stone.
C Bird's nest fungi.
D *Pyrocystis,* a bioluminescent single-celled organism.
E *Aquaspirillum magnetotaticum.* This bacterium contains crystals of magnetite (the small dark objects). With these crystals, the bacterium can orient itself in a magnetic field.

Living things are composed of cells and are hierarchically organized

Most cells are microscopic. All cells contain hereditary material and are membrane-bounded masses of protoplasm, a chemically active mixture of complex substances suspended in water. Until the invention of the microscope around 1600, naturalists could not probe this invisible level of organization of living things. And it was not until the mid-1800s when advances in the technology of the microscope allowed botanist Matthias Schleiden and zoologist Theodor Schwann to determine (through repeated lines of inquiry) that the unit of structure of all living things is the cell. Shortly thereafter, the German medical microscopist Rudolf Virchow argued that all cells can arise only from preexisting cells. The cells, he wrote, are "the last constant link in the great chain of mutually subordinated formations that form tissues, organs, systems, the individual. Below them is nothing but change."

Virchow's statement refers to the hierarchy, or levels, of organization seen in all living things. Living things, or **organisms,** are either multicellular (composed of many cells) as are humans, or are unicellular (composed of a single cell). Some organisms called **colonial organisms** are single-celled organisms that work and live together as a team. But whether unicellular, multicellular, or colonial, every organism has the cell as its lowest level of structure and function. Smaller units, such as atoms and molecules, make up cells but are not *living* units.

As shown in Figure 1-4, cells in multicellular organisms are organized to form the structures and perform the functions of the organism. The next highest, or more inclusive, level of organization is the tissue. **Tissues** are groups of similar cells that work together to perform a function. Grouped together, tissues form a structural and functional unit called an **organ.** An **organ system** is a group of organs that function together to carry out the principal activities of the organism—its highest level of organization. Interactions take place within an organism among its levels of organization. For example, when a fox sees, smells, and then chases a mouse, a complex series of events occur within the fox. The nerve *cells* embedded in the back wall of its eyes *(organs)* conduct impulses to its brain *(an organ)*. The vision center *(nervous tissue)* within the brain interprets these impulses, resulting in the fox seeing the mouse. Impulses speed to other brain centers *(nervous tissues),* which integrate this visual message with messages from olfactory *cells* in its nose. The brain coordinates these impulses, then sends out a response in the form of nerve impulses to the muscles *(organs)*. Skeletal muscles contract, allowing the animal to chase after its prey.

Living things interact with each other and with their environments

Interactions occur not only among the levels of organization within organisms but also between organisms and their external environments. Biologists usually classify the interactions between organisms and their environments into the following hierarchy of levels of organization: populations, communities, ecosystems, and the biosphere. These levels of organization build on the levels of organization of individual organisms and are depicted in Figure 1-4.

A population consists of the individuals of a given species that occur together at one place and at one time. To continue the example, the foxes living in a small forest make up a population. The foxes interact with one another in a variety of ways. Sometimes they compete for the same limited resources and for mates. Conversely, individuals within animal populations may also work cooperatively for common purposes. Foxes often hunt together, for example, working with one another to overtake and trap prey.

Populations of different species that interact with one another make up a community of organisms. A forest community may be made up of populations of bacteria, fungi, earthworms, plant-eating and animal-eating insects, mice, deer, salamanders, foxes, snakes, hawks, trees, and grasses. These populations within the forest community compete with one another for resources as do organisms within populations. The foxes, snakes, and hawks, for example, compete with one another to capture the mice for food. Other types of interactions may also exist within the community, such as mutualistic relationships in which two different species live in a close association for the benefit of both. Fungi and plants are often interdependent on one another. The fungi live near the roots of many plants, such as trees in a forest. The fungi envelop the roots and send billions of minute cell extensions into the soil. These microscopic "fingers" of fungus absorb water and nutrients better than the roots could alone, and they pass the substances to the plant. In turn, the fungus uses certain products that the plant makes by photosynthesis.

An ecosystem is a community of plants, animals, and microorganisms that interact with one another and their environments and that are interdependent on each other for their survival. The forest ecosystem includes all the organisms previously discussed as well as nonliving components of the environment such as air and water, which contribute substances needed for the ecosystem to function.

The biosphere is the part of the Earth where biological activity exists. Most people refer to the biosphere as simply "the environment." Within this global environment, living things interact with each other and with nonliving resources in a myriad of ways. Organisms other than humans use only renewable, or replaceable, resources. When they die, **decomposers**, which break down dead organisms, return the nutrients held within them to the soil and air. Humans, however, use many nonrenewable resources and fill the land with wastes. Scientists are testing and refining alternative renewable energy sources such as solar, wind, and water energy to help curb the use of nonrenewable energy sources such as coal, oil, and natural gas. The most severe crisis of natural resource destruction is occurring today in the tropical rain forests. Species are dying out as their rain forest habitats, or homes, are lost. In addition, humans are over-populating the land and polluting the water and the air. The destiny of future generations of all living things depends on our solving the problems humans have created and our learning to live on this planet without harming it and endangering everyone's future existence.

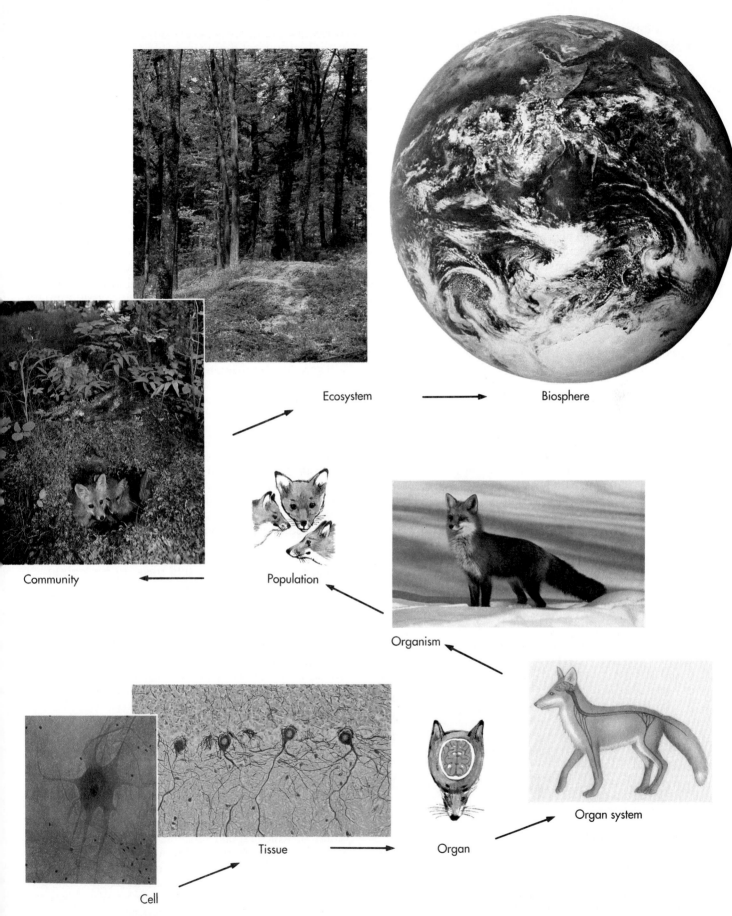

FIGURE 1-4 The levels of biological organization. Cells are the smallest living unit in an organism. The highest level of organization is the biosphere, which is the area on Earth where biological activity takes place.

Ecosystem

Biosphere

Population

Organism

Community

Organ system

Tissue

Organ

Cell

Living things transform energy and maintain a steady internal environment

Organisms need energy to do the work of living. This work involves many processes, such as movement, cell repair, reproduction, and growth. It also involves maintaining a stable internal environment despite a differing external environment. Energy drives the chemical reactions that underlie all of these activities.

What is the source of the energy that fuels life processes and helps organisms maintain an inner equilibrium? Ultimately, it comes from the sun. For example, certain organisms within our forest ecosystem such as the trees and grasses make their own food by capturing energy from the sun in a process called **photosynthesis.** These organisms are called **producers.** During photosynthesis, producers (primarily green plants) convert the energy in sunlight into chemical energy by locking it within the bonds of the food molecules they synthesize. Organisms that cannot make their own food, such as the insects, mice, deer, salamanders, foxes, snakes, and hawks in the forest, are called **consumers.** They feed on the producers and on each other, passing energy along that was once captured from the sun (Figure 1-5). Both the producers and the consumers release the stored energy in food by breaking down its molecules bit by bit. As food molecules are broken down, much of the

energy that is released is used to do work, but some of it is lost as heat and is therefore unusable. Consequently, organisms need a continual input of energy to fuel the chains of chemical reactions that move, store, and free energy needed to perform the activities of life. Decomposers such as the bacteria and fungi break down the organic molecules of dead organisms, serving as the last link in the flow of energy through an ecosystem and contributing to the recycling of nutrients within the environment.

Living things exhibit forms that fit their functions

Would it make sense to try to turn a screw with a hammer or eat soup with a knife? Of course not—tools and kitchen utensils are structured in specific ways to do specific jobs. Just as the shape and structure of a screwdriver or a spoon fits its function, the structures of living things fit their functions. Biologists sum up this idea with the phrase "form fits function." By analyzing form, inferences can be made regarding function. Conversely, knowing function gives insights into form.

For example, look at the variety of bird feathers shown in Figure 1-6. By analyzing their forms, determine which is used to insulate the bird against the cold. First, determine the characteristics of a good insulator from your everyday experience. Are you warmer in cold weather when you wear one thick sweater, or are you warmer when you wear many thinner layers that together may have the same thickness as the sweater? The answer is that many layers provide better insulation against the cold because they trap air between the layers. This trapped air is then warmed by the heat radiating from your body. In essence, you create a "blanket" of warm air around your body. Looking at the bird feathers, which feather might trap air within its structure?

Living things reproduce and pass on biological information to their offspring

All organisms reproduce, or give rise to, similar organisms. Reproduction may be sexual or asexual. Some organisms use both strategies at different times in their life cycles. In sexual reproduction, two parents give rise to offspring; in asexual reproduction, only one parent gives rise to offspring. In either case, genes—the units of heredity—are passed from one generation to the next.

Genes are made up of molecules of DNA, or deoxyribonucleic acid. In these molecules of DNA lies the "code of life," instructions that are translated into a working organism. Interestingly, these instructions take the form of molecular subunits of the DNA molecule called **nucleotides.** Using only four different nucleotides, DNA codes for all the structural and functional components of an organism. The secret to DNA's ability to carry information regarding the variety of structural and functional components lies in its code. The four nucleotides of DNA are used like code letters to produce code words, each composed of three letters. These code words are then sequenced to produce code sentences, which in a living organism are translated into the formation of a specific molecule designed to do a specific

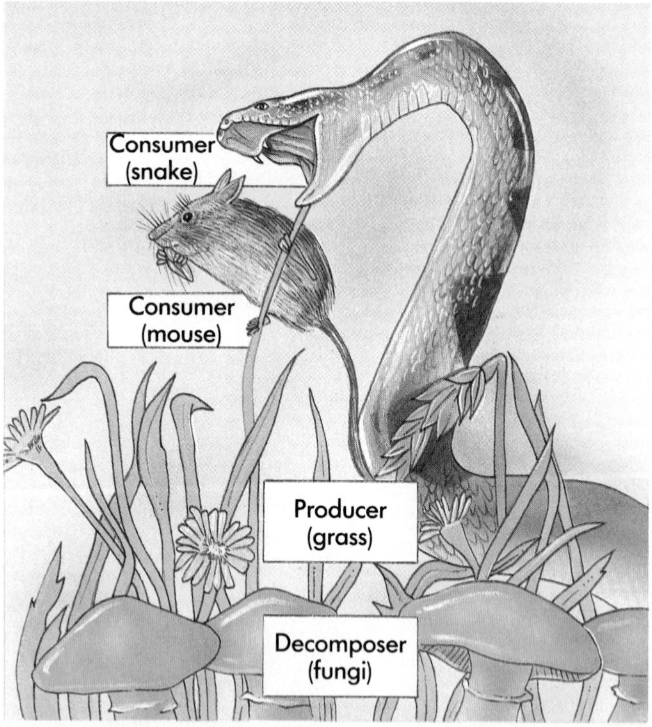

FIGURE 1-5 An energy pyramid in a forest ecosystem. Producers make their own food by means of photosynthesis. Consumers such as mice eat producers. Some consumers such as snakes eat other consumers. Decomposers, such as the fungi, decompose dead organisms and recycle their nutrients within the environment.

Introduction to Human Biology

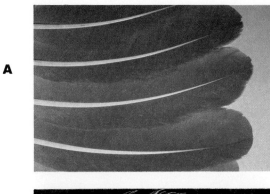

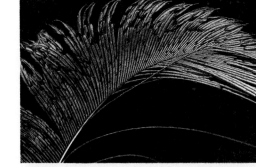

FIGURE 1-6 Different types of feathers: form fits function.
By examining the feathers shown here, can you determine which feather is the best insulator?
The feather in **A** is used for flight. The feather in **B** is a display feather used by the peacock to attract females (peahens). The feather in **C** is a down feather and used for insulation. Arranged in layers, these feathers trap air so that it can be warmed by the bird's body.

job. Thus the diversity of life is produced by the same code letters that produce code words and code sentences unique to each of the many species of organisms of the living world.

Living things change over time, or evolve

All organisms have common characteristics because they are related to one another. Just as you have a history and a family tree, so does the Earth's family of organisms. Yet all organisms have differences because as they changed over time, they diverged from one another. The Earth itself has changed from its beginnings some 4.6 billion years ago.

Scientists know very little about what "incubator Earth" was like nearly 4 billion years ago, but they do agree that it was a harsh environment different from today's environment. Under these conditions, many scientists think that the elements and simple compounds of the primitive atmosphere reacted with one another, forming complex molecules. In a way that scientists can only hypothesize, biochemical change took place over time and resulted in the appearance of single-celled organisms approximately 3.5 billion years ago. The remains of these early cells (and of any organisms) preserved in rocks are called **fossils.** Fossils provide scientists with a record of the history of life and document the changes in living things that have taken place over billions of years. By 1.4 to 1.2 billion years ago, the fossil record documents the existence of cells more complex than the first cells, and by 500 million years ago, an abundance of multicellular organisms—with members of groups similar to those that exist today—had appeared.

The fossil record is only one piece of evidence suggesting that living things have changed over time. Using this and other types of evidence, Charles Darwin, a nineteenth century English naturalist, developed what was then a hypothesis of organismal change over time or, as he put it, "descent with modification." He termed his hypothesis **evolution.** Darwin also proposed a mechanism by which evolution took place. Since Darwin's time, his hypothesis has been consistently supported by an overwhelming amount of scientific data and has therefore become a well-accepted theory. This theory embodies the ideas that organisms alive today are descendants of organisms that lived long ago and that organisms have changed and diverged from one another over billions of years. Scientists still ponder, examine, and develop hypotheses regarding details of the mechanisms of evolution but believe that evolution has been and is taking place.

Classification: A reflection of evolutionary history

As in any family tree, some organisms are more closely related than others. The species of the world are no exception. In the family trees of species, organisms having a common ancestor in the not-too-distant past are said to be *closely related*. Organisms having a common ancestor farther down the family tree are said to be *distantly related*. Modern **taxonomy,** the classification of the diverse array of species, categorizes organisms based on their common ancestry (their evolutionary history) while taking into account their existing similarities and differences. Therefore organisms that are close relatives and resemble one another in a variety of ways are placed in common groupings that reflect their similarities and closeness; organisms that are not closely related are placed in groupings separate from one another that reflect their differences.

Taxonomists group all living things into one of five broad categories called kingdoms: Monera, Protista, Plantae, Fungi, and Animalia (Figure 1-7). Kingdom Monera includes the bacteria. This kingdom differs from the other four kingdoms in that its cells lack membrane-bounded intracellular structures called **organelles.** In addition, the he-

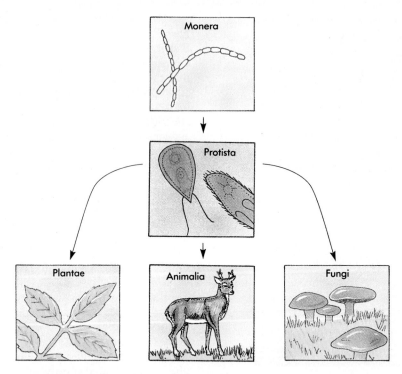

FIGURE 1-7 The five kingdoms of life. All life can be categorized into one of these five broad groups. The arrows indicate the direction of evolutionary development. The plants, animals, and fungi are thought to have evolved from ancestors of the protists. The protists evolved from moneran ancestors.

reditary material of the cell is not bounded by a membrane. Such cells are called **prokaryotes.** Finding these organisms is an easy task—bacteria live almost everywhere. If you take a moist cotton swab and draw it across any surface (except one that had been sterilized) you will collect an array of bacteria that is visible under a microscope. The organisms of the other four kingdoms are made up of cells that do have organelles and a membrane-bounded nucleus. Such cells are called **eukaryotes.**

Ancestors of the monerans gave rise to organisms in the kingdom Protista. The protist kingdom consists of primarily single-celled eukaryotes, whose cells are much more complex and much larger than the bacteria. By collecting a small amount of pond water and looking at it under a microscope, you can see some of the organisms in this kingdom. This kingdom also includes the algae, which encompass both multicellular and unicellular organisms that seem to be more closely related to the protists than to the plants, animals, or fungi.

The remaining three kingdoms originated from the protists. The plants are multicellular organisms that live on land and make their own food by using carbon dioxide from the air and light energy from the sun. Examples of plants are mosses, ferns, pine trees, and flowering plants. Animals are multicellular organisms that cannot make their own food and that obtain food by eating and digesting other organisms. Fungi are decomposers (as are the bacteria) and survive by breaking down substances and absorbing the breakdown products. Many of these multicelluar eukaryotes live off organisms that are no longer alive, such as fallen trees and leaves and dead animals. Some fungi, however, attack living organisms, causing human diseases or conditions such as athlete's foot and ringworm or plant diseases such as potato blight.

The kingdoms of organisms are further subdivided into groupings that reflect an increasing closeness in evolutionary history, as well as organisms' closeness in their existing behavioral (in the case of animals) and biochemical characteristics. Kingdoms Monera, Plantae, and Fungi are each subdivided into **divisions.** Kingdoms Protista and Animalia are each subdivided into **phyla** (singular, phylum). The animal kingdom, for example, has approximately 19 phyla,

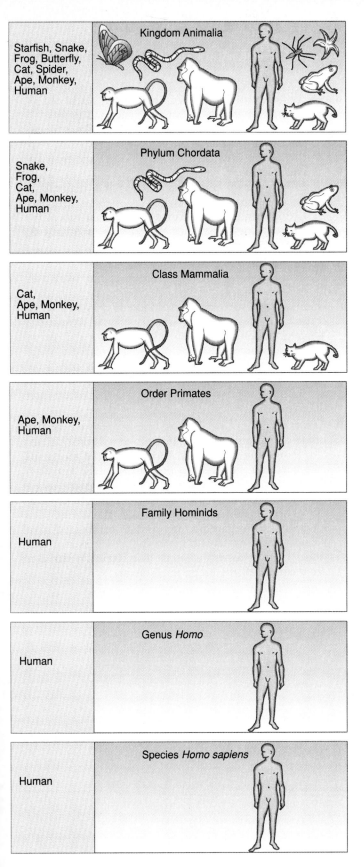

Kingdom Animalia

Starfish, Snake, Frog, Butterfly, Cat, Spider, Ape, Monkey, Human

Phylum Chordata

Snake, Frog, Cat, Ape, Monkey, Human

Class Mammalia

Cat, Ape, Monkey, Human

Order Primates

Ape, Monkey, Human

Family Hominids

Human

Genus *Homo*

Human

Species *Homo sapiens*

Human

FIGURE 1-8   Classification scheme for a human.
The classification of organisms reflects their evolutionary, behavioral, and biochemical closeness. Organisms of the same genus are the most closely related. No other living organisms share the genus *Homo.*

depending on the particular classification system that is referenced. Figure 1-8 shows some representatives of the animal kingdom. One of the phyla within this kingdom is the phylum Chordata: animals with a backbone. Notice that the starfish shown as a member of the kingdom Animalia is not included in phylum Chordata, yet all the other animals originally shown are included. These animals are more closely related to one another than to the starfish.

The next subcategory is **class.** The class Mammalia is a subgroup of phylum Chordata. The snake is no longer included in this group because it is not a mammal. Mammals are characterized by having skin with hair and by nourishing their young with milk secreted by mammary glands.

The next subcategory is **order.** One order of class Mammalia is the order Primates. Primates are mammals that have characteristics reflecting an arboreal, or tree-dwelling, lifestyle. Among these characteristics are hands and feet that are able to grasp objects, flexible limbs, and a flexible spine. Cats are not primates so are not included in this subgroup.

The last three subgroupings, in order of increasing relatedness, are **family, genus,** and **species.** Of all the organisms shown, which one is most closely related to humans?

The last two categories in the hierarchy of classification, genus and species, provide the scientific name of an organism. This system is known as **binomial nomenclature**—literally, "two-name naming." These names are usually Latin names that describe the organism. In this way, scientists worldwide have a common language and a reference for organisms that have been described and named. For example, humans are *Homo sapiens,* meaning "wise man." House cats are *Felis domesticus,* meaning "domesticated cat." Notice that the genus name is capitalized and the species name begins with a lowercase letter. Both are italicized.

Human biology and you

Throughout this chapter, the focus has been on humans in the context of all living things. Although humans share the characteristics of all living things, we differ from other living things in our level of intelligence and the development of culture. The word *culture* is a broad term and refers to the way of life of a people. It encompasses the manner in which persons interact with one another and with the environment. Culture is handed down from generation to generation, but each generation contributes in a unique way to that culture. As suggested in the opening paragraph, the study of the various human cultures is the domain of sociology and anthropology, not biology. However, just as the study of human biology implies the study of humans within the context of all living things, it cannot separate itself from the uniqueness of human intelligence and how culture affects humans' interactions with the rest of the living world. So studying human biology is more than learning scientific "facts" about your body. It also involves learning about your evolutionary roots and your connectedness to all organisms living on this Earth. In addition, it involves learning how to answer questions, solve problems, and make decisions about your body and about human concerns related to societal, technological, and environmental issues.

Summary

1. Human biology is the scientific study of human life and places humans in the context of all organisms. The study of human biology includes the study of human anatomy, physiology, development, and evolution, as well as the study of the interactions among humans, other organisms, and the environment.

2. All scientists study the natural world by using the scientific method. The scientific method is a process, or series of steps, scientists use to answer the questions they ask. Scientists ask questions that can be investigated by means of experimentation, producing results that are open to verification by others in their discipline.

3. To answer their questions, scientists develop hypotheses, or plausible answers to their questions, by generalizing from their observations of the world and information learned from scientific literature. Scientists then test their hypotheses by means of controlled experiments in which they keep all variables constant except the one being tested. An experiment tests a hypothesis by producing data that either support or refute the prediction made in the hypothesis.

4. As they weave together explanations of consistently supported and related hypotheses, scientists develop grand explanations that account for existing data and that consistently predict new data. Theories are interwoven hypotheses upheld by overwhelming evidence over time. Theories are powerful concepts that help scientists make dependable predictions about the world.

5. Although scientific knowledge grows and changes, certain themes, or accepted explanations, rise out of the abundance of tested predictions and permeate the science of biology. Although the specific details of these themes may be updated or changed as biologists modify their hypotheses, the themes themselves transcend time.

6. Seven themes of life are described in this textbook:
   a. Living things display both diversity and unity.
   b. Living things are composed of cells and are hierarchically organized.
   c. Living things interact with each other and their environments.
   d. Living things transform energy and maintain a steady internal environment.
   e. Living things exhibit forms that fit their functions.
   f. Living things reproduce and pass on biological information to their offspring.
   g. Living things change over time, or evolve.

7. Modern taxonomy, the classification of the diverse array of species, categorizes organisms based on their common ancestry (their evolutionary history) while considering their existing similarities and differences. Therefore organisms that are close relatives and resemble one another in a variety of ways are placed in common groupings that reflect their similarities and closeness. Organisms that are not closely related are placed in groupings separate from one another that reflect their differences.

8. Taxonomists group all living things into one of five broad categories, or kingdoms: Monera, Protista, Plantae, Fungi, and Animalia. Ancestors of the monerans (the bacteria) gave rise to organisms in the kingdom Protista (single-celled eukaryotes and the algae). Ancestors of the protists gave rise to the remaining three kingdoms of organisms: plants, animals, and fungi. The kingdoms of organisms are further subdivided into groupings that reflect an increasing closeness in evolutionary history as well as other characteristics. Humans are members of the kingdom Animalia.

1. What role does the scientific method serve in unifying the various scientific disciplines in the study of human biology? How do you think this may affect biologists doing research in different countries or time periods?

2. Distinguish between inductive and deductive reasoning. Give an example of each from your daily life.

4. The text states that scientists cannot actually prove hypotheses to be true. Explain this statement.

5. What is a theory? Can scientists state with certainty that a theory is true? Explain your answer.

6. Would you predict that damage to a person's pancreas (an organ) might be more or less life-threatening than damage to a few pancreatic cells? On what do you base your assessment?

7. Validate the seven themes of life as described in the text by using humans (*Homo sapiens*) as an example.

8. How do human beings' interactions with the biosphere differ from those of all other organisms?

9. From what ultimate source do you obtain the energy that keeps you alive? Explain how you obtain energy from that source.

10. Briefly state the theory of evolution. What are fossils, and how do they relate to this theory?

11. If you are told that two organisms are in the same taxonomic class, what can you hypothesize regarding their evolutionary history?

1. The text explains some of the reasons for and effects of animal research in the study of human biology. Animal right advocates assert that animals, like humans, have rights. Others assert that animals have no rights, for with rights come responsibilities. (For example, humans have the right to have as many children as they choose but have the responsibility to feed, clothe, educate, and meet the emotional needs of those children.) What implications do the concepts of rights and responsibilities cast on your view regarding the use of animals in medical research? Give your views on the following statement: "Humans have the right to use animals as 'model' systems in medical research but have the responsibility to treat those animals humanely."

2. If all living things are composed of one or more cells, it follows that a computer-driven machine cannot be alive. And yet such a machine can transform energy, do work, make copies of itself, and evolve over time to better suit the challenges of its environment. In a recent series of movies, such machines even attempt to replace humans as the world's dominant "lifeform." What is your opinion of whether machines can be alive? If you feel they can be, what *is* life?

Diamond, J. (1990, June). The cost of living. *Discover*, pp. 62-69.
This offers an interesting overview of the universal fact of aging and its use in nature as an evolutionary tool.

Gould, S. (1987, January). Darwinism defined: The difference between fact and theory. *Discover*, pp. 64-70.
This is a clear account of what biologists do and do not mean when they refer to the theory of evolution.

Gould, S. (1989). *Wonderful life: The Burgess Shale and the nature of history.* New York: W.W. Norton & Company, Inc.
This marvelous book is about the early evolution of animals and about evolution in general.

LaBarbera, M. (1991, September). Inner fluid. *The Sciences*, pp. 30-37.
This is an in-depth analysis of the fluid nature of most living beings, development of fluid-transport systems, and evolutionary effects.

Sapolsky, R. and Finch, C. (1991, March). On growing old. *The Sciences*, pp. 30-38.
This presents another discussion of the evolutionary advantage of aging and its effects on various lifeforms.

BIOETHICAL DECISIONMAKING
The Bioethics of Controlled Experiments

Consider the following questions as you think about the bioethical dilemma presented on page xviii:

1. What are the bioethical issues in this case?
   - What has to be decided?
   - Who are the decisionmakers?
   - Outline the decisionmaking process in this case as you understand it.

2. What factual information do the decisionmakers need?
   Consider the effects of the answers to the following questions on the decisionmaking process.
   - Have study participants who are currently taking medication improved as a result, or is their medication not effective against the disease? Is the medication making the disease worse?
   - Do the participants understand the implications of their consent? Do they know that discontinuing their present medication and participating in a study that involves the use of placebos might worsen their condition?
   - What reasons do the participants have for their decision to participate?
   - What risks are involved for human study participants in testing of other drugs for fatal diseases, such as diabetes? ...for nonfatal diseases, such as the common cold?
   - What other questions should the decisionmakers ask?
   - What additional factual information do the decisionmakers need?

3. Who are the "stakeholders" in this decision—those who stand to gain or lose as a result of the decision?
   - Are the study participants stakeholders? The researchers? Other persons who have AIDS? The scientific community, which relies on controlled experiments to probe scientific questions? What other persons or groups are stakeholders?

- Which stakeholders are decisionmakers? Which are not decisionmakers? Will individuals in the latter group be able to influence the decisionmaking process? Should they have influence?
- In what ways would each stakeholder be affected by the decision?

4. What are the values at stake in the decision? As you list and describe them, consider the following questions:
   - Is it possible to conduct a scientifically valid study without the use of controls? What kinds of information would such a study reveal? Would this be useful information? Would it tell the researchers what they need to know about the drug?
   - With a fatal disease such as AIDS, for which there is no cure and which threatens a large segment of the population, is it ethical to adjust research protocols to avoid putting human research participants at risk?
   - Do researchers have an obligation to protect the health of their study participants? What if such protection led to inaccurate or misleading research results?

5. What options are available to the decisionmakers? As you list these options, consider the following questions:
   - Which of these alternatives seem ethically feasible? Which seem administratively possible?
   - How would each alternative decision affect each of the stakeholders?
   - Is there a compromise solution that might give all parties the sense that they have come out the "winner" in the decision?

6. What are the values inherent to the decisionmaking process?
   - Is the decisionmaking process fair?
   - Do all stakeholders have equal resources to advocate their position?
   - What further steps might each group of stakeholders take if their views are disallowed?

PART ONE

Molecules, Cells, and Tissues

2 The Chemistry of Life

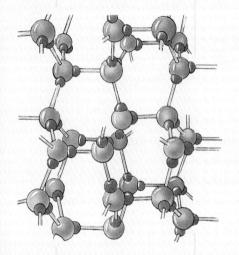

3 Cell Structure and Function

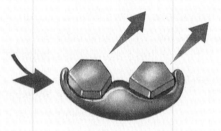

4 The Flow of Energy Within Organisms

5 Cellular Respiration

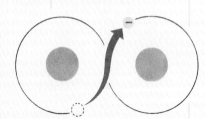

6 Levels of Organization in the Human Body

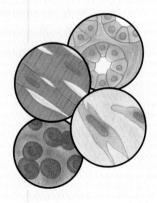

MAKING BIOETHICAL DECISIONS
Stem Cells and the Next Stage of Gene Therapy

Human gene therapy is presently one of the most promising areas of research in the fight against cancer and hereditary disorders. In this procedure, scientists insert genes (short segments of hereditary material [DNA] that specify the substances that cells manufacture) directly into the DNA of affected cells. Although the procedure is simple, it results in only one cell in 1000 to 100,000 integrating the "new" gene into its DNA.

The genes that are inserted into affected cells are specific for the disorder scientists are trying to treat. For example, the hereditary disorder called severe combined immunodeficiency (SCID) results from the lack of an important enzyme called adenosine deaminase (ADA). This enzyme is necessary for the immune system to function properly. Production of ADA is controlled by a specific gene. Without this enzyme, special lymphocytes called T cells, which play a key role in the immune system, self-destruct. Without T cells, the immune systems of ADA-deficient persons cannot defend the body against disease and even minor infections such as a common cold can be fatal.

In 1990, scientists successfully altered the T cells of a SCID patient by inserting the gene that directs the manufacture of ADA into some of that person's T cells. The results of this experiment are still being monitored and evaluated. Scientists are also attempting to develop gene therapy techniques to treat a variety of other disorders, including cystic fibrosis and Duchenne muscular dystrophy. The status of experimentation varies with the disorder; most work is in preliminary stages.

Scientists view gene therapy as a promising way to treat serious genetic aberrations. However, gene therapy does not provide a permanent cure; the patients must be treated periodically with infusions of modified cells. One way around this problem would be to insert genes into stem cells. These cells, found in red bone marrow, give rise to the various types of blood cells, including cells of the immune system. Inserting genes into stem cells would mean that the stem cells could give rise to blood and immune system cells that carry the new gene. Such an approach would work for disorders such as ADA deficiency that affect blood and immune cells; it would offer a permanent cure. However, medical researchers face an ongoing problem of poor gene expression—the inserted genes do not produce enough of the proteins they encode. Further research is needed.

The Recombinant DNA Advisory Committee of a national health research facility has received a proposal for an experiment that would insert the ADA gene into the stem cells of an ADA-deficient individual. This advisory panel is composed of experts who review each proposed human gene therapy experiment and decide whether or not to approve it. Many members of the panel voted to approve this proposal, but there was some opposition. Opponents to the experiment maintained that altering a human's stem cells constitutes changing that person's genome.(A genome is the complete set of genes that an individual possesses. It is his or her genetic "fingerprint" and is unique to the individual.) Although altering stem cells to cure a hereditary disease is certainly a worthwhile endeavor, these opponents ask whether it is right to start changing genomes, even for a good reason.

If you were on this advisory committee, would you approve or disapprove of the proposed experiment?

2 The Chemistry of Life

Water . . . without it you would die. In fact, life on Earth could not go on if deprived of this amazing liquid, and evolution could never have taken place without it. What is it about water that makes it so important to life?

The clues needed to answer this question lie in the chemical structure of water. Put another way, water is important because of its characteristics, which in turn depend on its parts and how they are put together. In the photo, you can easily observe some of these characteristics. Notice how the water sticks together to form droplets in the air. Notice, too, that its surface behaves like a thin film, caving in and bulging out in tiny waves as the airborne droplets fall on it. The story of how the parts of water relate to its characteristics, and the answer to why water is important to you, will soon be told—as you begin your study of the chemistry of life.

23

Atoms

Chemistry is the science of matter, the physical material that makes up everything in the universe. Matter is anything that takes up space and has a measurable amount of substance, or mass. All matter (including water) is made up of tiny parts called **atoms**. Although scientists know a great deal about atoms, a simplified explanation provides a good starting point in understanding their complex structures. One explanation was proposed in 1913 by the Danish physicist Niels Bohr. Bohr proposed that every atom is made up of particles tinier than the atom itself. These subatomic particles are of three types: **protons, neutrons,** and **electrons.** Protons and neutrons are found at the core, or nucleus, of the atom. Electrons orbit the nucleus.

Protons have mass and carry a positive (+) charge. Neutrons, although similar to protons in mass, are neutral and carry no charge. Electrons have very little mass and carry a negative (−) charge. They have so little mass, in fact, that they contribute only about one eyelash's worth of mass to your entire body! For this reason, the *atomic mass* of an atom is defined as the combined mass of all its protons and neutrons without regard to its electrons.

The number of protons in an atom, called the *atomic number*, is the same as the number of electrons in that atom. Atoms are therefore electrically neutral; the positive charges of the protons are balanced by the negative charges of the electrons. The number of neutrons in an atom, however, may not equal the number of protons. Atoms that have the same number of protons but different numbers of neutrons are called **isotopes** (Figure 2-1). Isotopes of an atom differ in atomic mass but have similar chemical properties because they have the same number of electrons. The properties of

an atom are determined by its electrons because atoms interact with one another by means of their electrons and not their protons or neutrons.

⯆⯆

An atom is a core (nucleus) of protons and neutrons surrounded by orbiting electrons. The electrons largely determine the chemical properties of an atom.

The key to the chemical behavior of atoms lies in the arrangement of their electrons. Although scientists cannot precisely locate the position of any individual electron at a particular time, they can predict where an electron is most likely to be. This volume of space around a nucleus where an electron is most likely to be found is called an **orbital** of that electron.

Atoms can have many electron orbitals. Some are simple spheres enclosing the nucleus like a wrapper, whereas others resemble dumbbells and other complex shapes. Each orbital of an atom contains one or two electrons. Atoms having more than two electrons have more than one orbital. These orbitals can be the same or a different distance from the nucleus. Orbitals at the same distance from the nucleus occupy the same shell.

In Figure 2-2, *A* the nucleus is shown as a small circle surrounded by concentric rings. These rings represent electron shells. In Figure 2-2, *B* the electrons are clustered to signify that they occupy different orbitals within that shell. The actual three-dimensional shapes of the orbitals are not shown. Notice that the atom of nitrogen pictured in Figure 2-2, *B* has electrons occupying two shells. The innermost shell has one orbital containing two electrons. The second shell has three orbitals; two of these orbitals have two electrons each and one orbital contains only one electron.

A

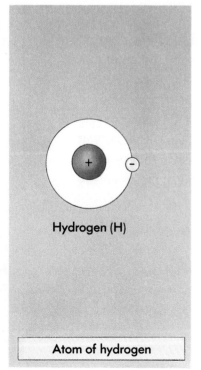

Hydrogen (H)

Atom of hydrogen

B

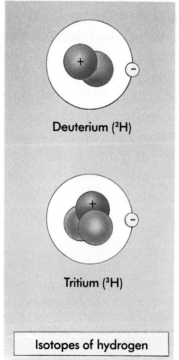

Deuterium (²H)

Tritium (³H)

Isotopes of hydrogen

FIGURE 2-1 Isotopes.
Isotopes of an atom differ in atomic mass but have the same chemical properties.
A The smallest atom is hydrogen. Its nucleus consists of a single proton.
B Two naturally occurring isotopes of hydrogen also exist. Both isotopes have a single proton in their nucleus (like hydrogen) but have different numbers of neutrons. Deuterium has one neutron, and tritium has two.

The Use of Isotopes in Medicine

Isotopes are elements that have the same number of protons and electrons but have different numbers of neutrons. For example, hydrogen (one proton and no neutrons) has two isotopes: deuterium (one proton and one neutron) and tritium (one proton and two neutrons) (see Figure 2-1, *B*). Because only the number of neutrons is different, all isotopes of an element have similar chemical properties. In fact, tritium can "substitute" for hydrogen in chemical reactions!

Some isotopes are unstable and can emit subatomic particles: neutrons, protons, or electrons. These unstable isotopes are termed **radioactive**. When a radioactive isotope emits subatomic particles, a new, more stable element is formed. This process is called **decay**.

Because of their radioactivity and the fact that isotopes are nearly indistinguishable to organisms, doctors use isotopes in many ways to detect and treat disease.

When used in diagnosis, isotopes are called **tracers** or **labels** because they can be used to follow the fate of certain substances in the body. For ex-

ample, suppose your doctor wants to investigate the rate at which your thyroid gland is using iodine, a substance in your diet that your body uses to make thyroid hormone. To determine this rate, your doctor injects you with a tracer—a solution of radioactive iodine, which your body will use in the same way it uses the "normal" iodine you acquire in your food. Equipment that counts the emission of particles from the nuclei of the radioactive iodine is placed over your thyroid gland and measures how fast the tracer iodine is entering your thyroid. The doctor can then see *exactly* how fast your thyroid is using iodine by simply reading the information on the detector (Figure 2-A).

Another way isotopes are used is in the treatment of cancer, especially those cancers (such as skin cancers) that are present on the surface of the body. A patch containing powerful radioactive isotopes is taped over the cancerous tumor. The particles emitted from the isotope bombard the tumor and destroy the cancerous tissue. Treatment with isotopes does have some drawbacks, however. Because the isotopes are radioactive, the pa-

tient receiving this type of treatment must be kept under strict quarantine. Isotope therapy also causes nausea and breakdown of the "normal" tissue surrounding the tumor. Unfortunately, treatment with isotopes is not a cure for cancer—the isotopes can only destroy localized tumors. Cancer cells that have migrated to other parts of the body are unaffected by isotope therapy. Still, treatment with isotopes offers hope to those in the early stages of cancer.

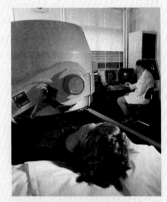

FIGURE 2-A Isotopes are used to diagnose and treat illness.

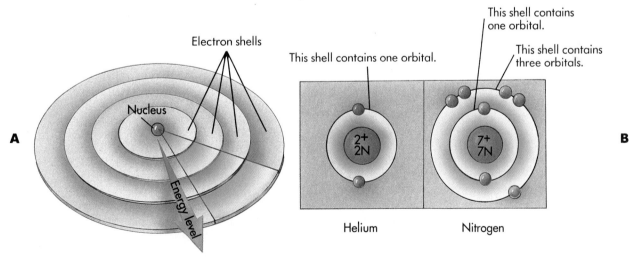

FIGURE 2-2 How atoms are organized.
A Electron shells, or energy levels, in an atom. Each concentric circle represents a different distance from the nucleus and thus a different electron energy level.
B Electron shells for helium and nitrogen. The electrons are indicated by orange dots. Within each shell, pairs of electrons occupy orbitals, which are not shown in this diagram because of their complex shapes. For example, the innermost shell of nitrogen has one orbital containing two electrons. The outermost shell has three orbitals—two of these orbitals have two electrons each, and one orbital has only one electron, for a total of five electrons in the outermost shell.

This outer shell of nitrogen, then, has a total of five electrons.

Because the energy of electrons increases as their distance from the attractive force of the nucleus increases, the various electron shells of atoms are also called **energy levels**. Electrons occupying increasingly distant shells from the nucleus have a stepwise increase in their levels of energy. The energy of electrons at the various energy levels is also influenced by the number of protons in the nucleus, since the attractive force of the nucleus increases as its number of protons increases.

 The farther an electron is from the nucleus, the more energy it has.

Molecules

The identity of an atom is determined by its number of protons and electrons. For example, an atom containing two protons and two electrons is helium, a gas you have probably seen used to blow up balloons. An atom possessing seven protons and seven electrons is nitrogen (Figure 2-2, B).

Elements are pure substances that are made up of a single kind of atom and that cannot be separated into different substances by ordinary chemical methods. The atoms of most elements interact with one another to form **molecules**, combinations of tightly bound atoms. Molecules can be made up of atoms of the same element or atoms of different elements.

The oxygen in the air consists of molecules made up of pairs of atoms of the same element—oxygen. These pairs are represented by the **chemical formula** O_2. A chemical formula is a type of "shorthand" used to describe a molecule. The atoms are represented by symbols, such as O for oxygen. (Chemical symbols are shown in Table 2-1 on p. 34.) A subscript shows the number of these atoms present in the molecule. Molecules made up of the atoms of two or more elements are called **compounds**. An example of a compound is water, which is H_2O. In this chemical formula the symbol H stands for the element hydrogen.

Three different types of chemical forces influence whether an atom will interact with other atoms to form molecules. In addition, these forces influence the type of interactions that are likely to take place. These forces are (1) the tendency of electrons to occur in pairs, (2) the tendency of atoms to balance positive and negative charges, and (3) the tendency of the outer shell, or energy level, of electrons to be full. This third chemical force is often called the **octet rule**.

The word *octet* means "eight objects" and refers to the fact that the outer electron shell of most atoms contains a maximum of eight electrons. The first energy level is an exception to this rule because it contains a maximum of two electrons. The octet rule states that an atom with an unfilled outer shell has a tendency to interact with another atom or atoms in ways that will complete this outer shell. Although the octet rule does not apply to all atoms, it does apply to all biologically important ones—those involved in

the structure, energy needs, and information systems of living things. These atoms and the molecules they make up are discussed later in this chapter.

 The identity of an atom is defined by its number of protons and electrons. Its interaction with other atoms is determined by chemical forces that are influenced by the number and arrangement of its electrons.

Atoms of elements that have equal numbers of protons and electrons, no unpaired electrons, and full outer-electron energy levels are the only ones that exist as single atoms. Atoms with these characteristics are called **noble gases**, or inert gases, because they do not react readily with other elements. Many stories explain the reason they are called noble, but they all center around the concept of nobility—those who have everything (in this case a full outer shell), need nothing, and interact little with others. Most of the noble gases—helium, neon, argon, krypton, xenon, and radon—are rare. In addition, they are relatively unreactive and unimportant in living systems. Helium and radon are probably the most well known and the least rare noble gases. Radon, in fact, has gained much notice in recent years. Formed in rock or soil particles from the radioactive decay of radium, radon gas can seep through cracks in basement walls and remain trapped in homes that are not well ventilated. Prolonged exposure to radioactive radon in levels greater than those normally found in the atmosphere is thought to lead to lung cancer.

Nature of the chemical bond

An atom having an incomplete outer shell can satisfy the octet rule in one of three ways:
1. It can gain electrons from another atom.
2. It can lose electrons to another atom.
3. It can share one or more electron pairs with another atom.

Such interactions among atoms result in **chemical bonds**, forces that hold atoms together. If the force is caused by the attraction of oppositely charged particles formed by the gain or loss of electrons, the bond is called **ionic**. If the force is caused by the electrical attraction created by atoms sharing electrons, the bond is called **covalent**. Other, weaker kinds of bonds also occur.

Ions and ionic bonds

Electrons stay in their orbits because they are attracted to the positive charge of the nucleus. However, electrons far from the nucleus are not held as tightly as electrons closer to the nucleus. The electrons more distant from the nucleus are said to be less stable than the electrons closest to the nucleus, and they interact with other atoms more easily than close, stable, tightly held electrons. Therefore atoms typically interact with other atoms by means of the electrons in their outermost (highest) energy levels, or shells. The types

FIGURE 2-3 The formation of an ionic bond.
A When a sodium atom donates an electron to a chlorine atom, the sodium atom, lacking that electron, becomes a positively charged sodium ion. The chlorine atom, having gained an extra electron, becomes a negatively charged chloride ion.
B and **C** Positive and negative ions cluster so that each charge is surrounded by ions of the opposite charge. This is what happens when Na^+ and Cl^- ions come together to form crystals of salt.

of interactions that occur tend to result in atoms with completed outer shells, thus satisfying the octet rule.

An atom tends to lose electrons if it has an outer shell needing many electrons to be complete. An atom tends to gain electrons if it has a nearly completed outer shell. Interestingly, one of these types of atoms tends to interact with the other type, resulting in a completed outer shell for each. The atom with a nearly completed outer shell tends to "take" enough electrons to complete its outer shell from an atom having only one or two atoms in an outer shell that needs eight for completion. Once these outer electrons are gone from the atom giving up electrons, the next shell in becomes its new, complete outer shell. As a result of this interaction, neither atom is electrically neutral; the number of protons no longer equals the number of electrons in either atom. The atom taking on electrons acquires a negative charge. The atom giving up electrons acquires a positive charge. They are not called atoms because they are no longer electrically neutral. Such charged particles are called **ions.**

Figure 2-3 illustrates the formation of ions with a specific example of electron "give and take." Sodium (Na) is an element with 11 protons and 11 electrons. It is a soft, silver-white metal that occurs in nature as a part of compounds. One familiar compound is sodium chloride, or table salt. Of sodium's 11 electrons, 2 are in its innermost energy level (full with 2 electrons), 8 are at the next level, and 1 is at the outer energy level. Because of this distribution of electrons, the outer electron is unpaired ("free") and has a strong tendency to form a pair. In addition, its outer energy level is not full, and therefore the octet rule is not satisfied.

Chlorine (Cl) is an element with 17 protons and 17 electrons. It is a greenish yellow gas that is poisonous and irritating to the nose and throat. In the compound sodium chloride, however, it does not have these characteristics. Of chlorine's 17 electrons, 2 are at its innermost energy level, 8 at the next energy level, and 7 at the outer energy level. Chlorine, like sodium, has an unpaired electron and an outer energy level that is not full. Sodium and chlorine atoms can interact with one another in a way that results in both having paired electrons and full outer energy levels.

When placed together, the metal sodium and the gas chlorine react explosively. The single, unpaired electrons in the outer energy levels of the sodium atoms fly off, lost to the sodium. These electrons pair with the unpaired electrons in the outer shells of the chlorine atoms. The result is the production of Na^+ and Cl^- ions. Ions, however, are unbalanced with respect to their positive and negative charges. This balance is achieved when these ions come together as their opposite charges attract one another. This type of attraction is called *electrostatic attraction* and results in ionic bonding of the sodium and chloride ions. As these ions are drawn to one another, they form geometrically perfect crystals of salt (Fig. 2-3, *B* and *C*).

An ionic bond is an attraction between ions of opposite charge.

The transfer of electrons between atoms is an important chemical event—one type of chemical reaction. In fact, this type of chemical interaction has a special vocabulary. When an atom loses an electron, it is said to be **oxidized.** The reaction is called an *oxidation,* a term that comes from the original meaning (an alternate definition still valid today), which is "to combine with oxygen." For example, when iron combines with oxygen in the presence of moisture, it becomes oxidized. The product of this oxidation is commonly known as *rust.* Conversely, when an atom gains an electron (or loses oxygen), it is said to be **reduced.** The reaction is called a *reduction.* Oxidations and reductions always occur together because an electron lost from an atom cannot exist by itself—it will be transferred to another atom. Therefore the shortened term **redox reaction** is often used to describe this paired transfer.

The loss of an electron by an atom is called an *oxidation.* **The gain of an electron is called a** *reduction.* **Together, these paired electron transfers between atoms are called redox reactions.**

Covalent bonds

Covalent bonds form when two atoms share electrons. Hydrogen is a simple example of an atom that usually shares electrons with other atoms. As you can see in Figure 2-4, a hydrogen atom has a single, unpaired electron and an unfilled outer electron shell. A filled outer shell at this energy level requires only two electrons. When hydrogen atoms are close enough to one another, an interesting thing happens. They form pairs, with each of their single electrons moving around the two nuclei. These paired atoms of hydrogen are called *diatomic molecules* and are represented by the chemical formula H_2.

As a result of this sharing of electrons, the diatomic hydrogen gas molecule is electrically balanced because it now contains two protons and two electrons. In addition, each

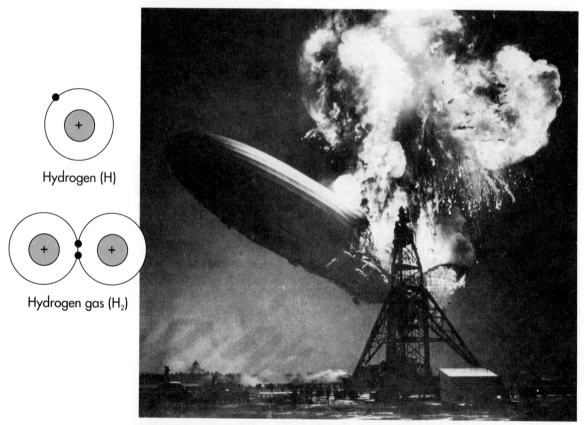

FIGURE 2-4 Covalent bonds.
Hydrogen gas is a diatomic molecule composed of two hydrogen atoms. Each hydrogen atom shares its electrons with another hydrogen atom. A more stable molecule is formed when two hydrogen atoms share their electrons with an oxygen atom, forming water. The flash fire that consumed the *Hindenburg* occurred when the hydrogen gas used to inflate the airship combined explosively with oxygen gas in the air to form water.

hydrogen atom has two orbiting electrons in its outer shell, completing this shell. This relationship also results in the pairing of two free electrons. Thus, by sharing their electrons, the two hydrogen atoms form a stable molecule.

▼▼▼
A covalent bond is formed by the sharing of one or more pairs of electrons.

Covalent bonds can be very strong, that is, difficult to break. **Double bonds,** those bonds in which two pairs of electrons are shared, are stronger than **single bonds,** covalent bonds sharing only one pair of electrons. As you might expect, **triple bonds,** those bonds in which three pairs of electrons are shared, are the strongest of these three types of covalent bonds. In chemical formulas that show the structure of covalently bonded molecules, single bonds are represented by a single line between two bonded atoms, double bonds by two lines, and triple bonds by three lines. For example, the structural formula of hydrogen gas is $H—H$, oxygen gas is $O=O$, and nitrogen gas is $N\equiv N$.

An atom can also form covalent bonds with more than one other atom. Carbon (C), for example, contains six electrons: two at the inner level and the other four in the outer shell. To satisfy the octet rule, it must gain four additional electrons by sharing its four outer-shell electrons with another atom or atoms, forming four covalent bonds. Because there are many ways that four covalent bonds may form, carbon atoms are able to participate in many different kinds of molecules in living systems, such as proteins and carbohydrates.

The strength of a covalent bond refers to the amount of energy needed to make or break that bond. The energy that goes into making the bond is held within the bond and is released when the bond is broken. Therefore covalent bonds are actually a storage place for energy as well as a type of chemical "glue" that holds molecules together. Living things store and use energy by means of making and breaking covalent bonds, thereby using molecules as a type of energy currency.

The cradle of life: Water

One covalently bonded molecule that plays a major role in living systems is water—H_2O. In fact, water is the most abundant molecule in your body, making up about two thirds of your body weight! Although it seems to be a simple molecule, water has many surprising properties. For example, of all the common molecules on earth, only water exists as a liquid at the earth's surface (Figure 2-5). When

FIGURE 2-5 Water takes many forms.
As a liquid, it fills our rivers and sometimes falls in great cascades. The penguins congregate on an iceberg formed in Antarctica from huge blocks of ice breaking away into the ocean. When water cools below 0° C, it forms beautiful crystals. Water is not always plentiful. In a dry creek bed, there is no hint of water except for the broken patterns of dry mud.

FIGURE 2-6 Water is the cradle of life.
Life most likely originated in the warm waters of ancient Earth. Many kinds of organisms, like these small frogs seen through the transparent walls of their eggs, begin life in water.

life on earth was beginning, this liquid provided a medium in which other molecules could move around and interact. Life evolved as a result of these interactions. And life, as it evolved, maintained these ties to water (Figure 2-6). Three fourths of the earth's surface is covered by water. Where water is plentiful, such as in the tropical rain forests, the land abounds with life. Where water is scarce, such as in the desert, the land seems almost lifeless except after a rain-

storm. No plant or animal can grow and reproduce without some amount of water.

The chemistry of life, then, is water chemistry. You might think that such an important molecule with such interesting properties would be complicated and hard to understand. Fortunately, this is not the case. Water has a simple atomic structure: one oxygen atom bonded by single covalent bonds to two hydrogen atoms. The resulting molecule is stable. It satisfies the octet rule and has no unpaired electrons, and its positive and negative charges are balanced.

This simple water molecule has one outstanding chemical property: it attracts other molecules and forms a special type of chemical bond with them. These bonds, called **hydrogen bonds,** have approximately 5% to 10% the strength of covalent bonds. The ability of water to form weak bonds with other molecules is the reason for much of the organization and chemistry of living things.

The story of water's ability to attract other molecules lies in its structure and in the movement of its electrons. The oxygen atom in a water molecule, like all oxygen atoms, contains eight protons in its core, or nucleus. Each hydrogen atom contains only one proton. As a result, the electron pair shared in each of the oxygen-hydrogen covalent bonds of a water molecule is more strongly attracted to the oxygen nucleus than to either of the hydrogen nuclei. Although the electron orbitals surround both the oxygen and hydrogen nuclei, the negatively charged electrons are far more likely to be found near the oxygen nucleus at a given moment than near one of the hydrogen nuclei. Because of this situation, the oxygen end of the water molecule acquires a partial negative charge. The hydrogen end acquires a partial positive charge (Figure 2-7). Molecules such as water that have opposite partial charges at different ends of the molecule are called **polar molecules.** Water is

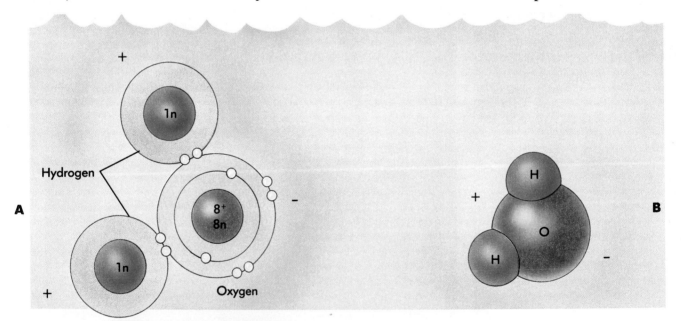

FIGURE 2-7 The structure of water.
A Each water molecule is composed of one oxygen atom and two hydrogen atoms. The oxygen atom shares a pair of electrons with each participating hydrogen atom.
B In this model the + and − represent the partial charges at opposite sides of the water molecule.

one of the most polar molecules known.

Polar molecules interact with one another. Hydrogen bonds form when the partial negative charge at one end of the molecule is attracted to the partial positive charge of another polar molecule. In fact, water forms bonds with other water molecules in just this way. Although hydrogen bonds are weak, these bonds are constantly made and broken. (Each lasts only 1/100,000,000,000 of a second!) The cumulative effect of very large numbers of hydrogen bonds is responsible for the many important physical properties of water (Figure 2-8) and is the answer why water sticks together as in the chapter opener photo.

▼▼▼

Much of the biologically important behavior of water results because its oxygen atom attracts electrons more strongly than its hydrogen atoms do. As a result, water molecules each have electron-rich (−) and electron-poor (+) regions, giving them positive and negative poles.

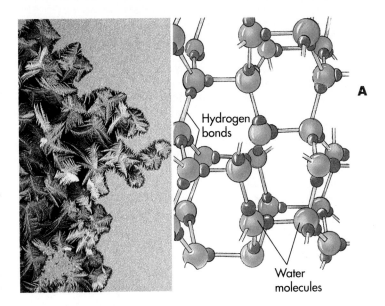

A

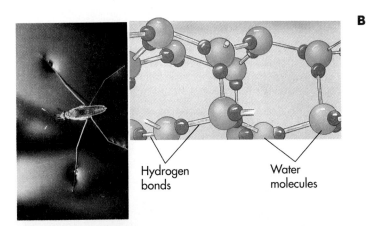

B

C

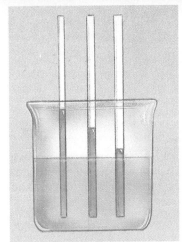

FIGURE 2-8 Many of the physical properties of water depend on hydrogen bonding.

A Ice formation. When water cools below 0° C, it forms a regular crystal structure in which the partial charges of each atom in the water molecule interact with opposite charges of atoms in other water molecules, forming H bonds.

B Surface tension. Some insects, such as the water strider, literally walk on water. In this photograph you can see the dimpling its feet make on the water as its weight bears down on the surface. The water strider does not sink because the surface tension of the water is greater than the downward force that the foot produces.

C Adhesion. Water droplets cling to this spider web due to the molecular attraction that exists between the surfaces of unlike bodies. The droplets remain intact, however, due to hydrogen bonding among the water molecules. Capillary action causes water within a narrow tube to rise above the surrounding fluid. Likewise, the adhesion of the water to the inner surface of a narrow glass tube, along with surface tension, draws it upward. This force, called capillary action, is stronger than the force of gravity drawing the water down. The narrower the tube, the higher it will rise above the surface of the water.

Water is a powerful solvent

Water molecules gather closely around any molecule that exhibits an electrical charge, such as ions and polar molecules. For example, sodium chloride (table salt) is made up of the positively charged sodium (Na^+) and negatively charged chloride (Cl^-) ions. These ions are attracted to one another and cluster in a regular pattern, forming crystals. When you put salt in a pot of boiling water, some ions break away from the crystals. Water molecules instantly form hydrogen bonds with these ions, surrounding each of them. This **hydration shell** prevents each ion from associating with other ions. The salt is said to be *dissolved* (Figure 2-9).

Similarly, hydration shells form around all polar molecules and ions. Molecules that dissolve in water this way are said to be **soluble** in water. Chemical interactions readily take place in water because so many kinds of molecules are water soluble and therefore move among water molecules as separate molecules or ions.

Water organizes nonpolar molecules

Remember the old saying that "oil and water don't mix"? This statement is true because oil is a nonpolar molecule and cannot form hydrogen bonds with water. Instead, the water molecules form hydrogen bonds with each other, causing the water to exclude the nonpolar molecules. It is almost as if nonpolar molecules move away from contact with the water. For this reason, nonpolar molecules are referred to as being **hydrophobic.** The word *hydrophobic* comes from the Greek meaning "water" (hydros) "fearing" (phobos). This tendency for nonpolar molecules to band together in a water solution is called **hydrophobic bonding.** Hydrophobic forces determine the three-dimensional shapes of many biological molecules, which are usually surrounded by water within organisms.

Water ionizes

The covalent bonds of water molecules sometimes break spontaneously. When this happens, one hydrogen atom nucleus (a proton) dissociates from the rest of the water molecule, leaving behind its electron. Because its positive charge is no longer balanced by an electron, it is a positively charged hydrogen ion, H^+. The remaining part of the water molecule now has an extra electron. It is therefore a negatively charged hydroxyl ion, OH^-. This process of spontaneous ion formation is called **ionization:**

$$H_2O \rightarrow OH^- + H^+$$

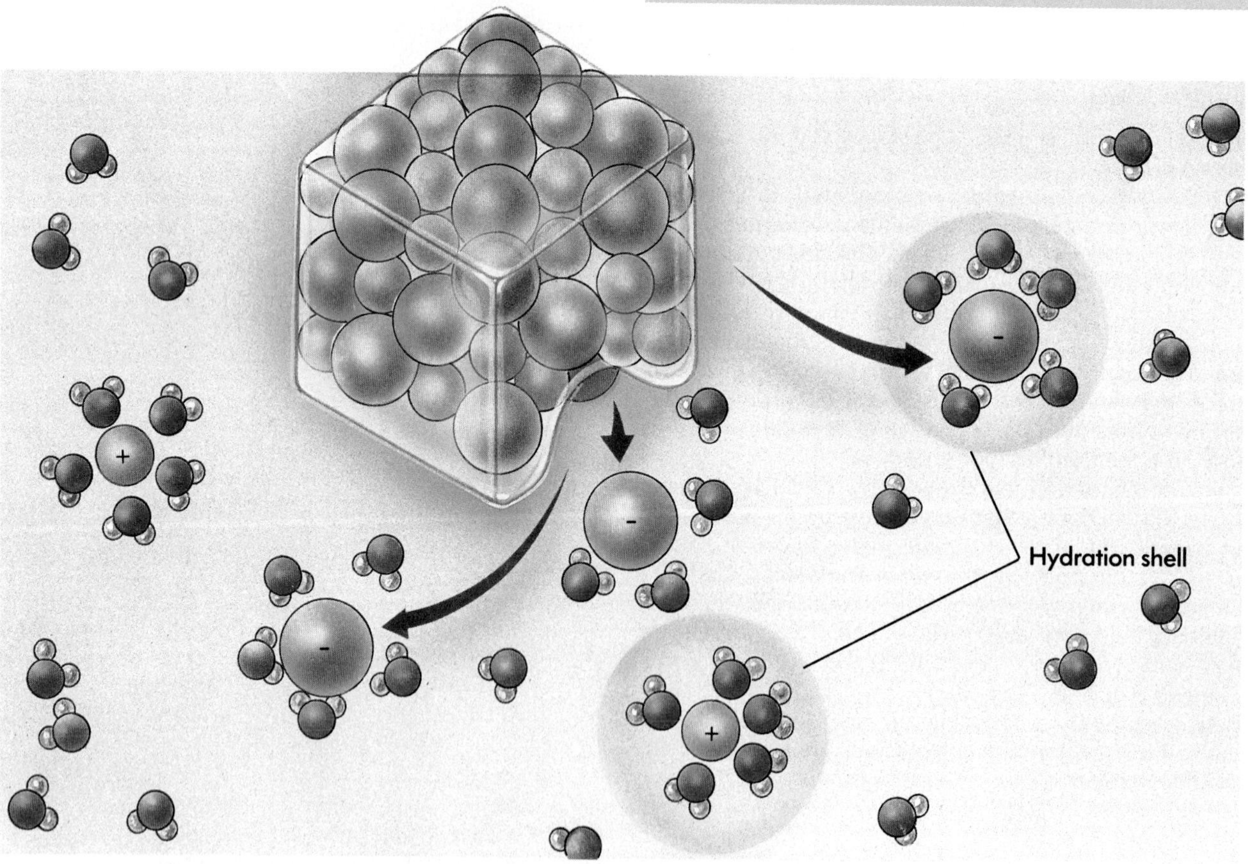

FIGURE 2-9 How salt dissolves in water.
The hydration shells formed by the hydrogen bonding between Na^+ and Cl^- ions prevents individual ions from associating. The salt is said to be *dissolved.*

Only very few water molecules are ionized at a single instant in time. Scientists calculate that the fraction of water molecules that dissociate (ionize) in pure water is 0.0000001. This tiny number can be written another way by using exponential notation. This is done by counting the number of places to the right of the decimal point. Because there are seven places, this number is written as 10^{-7}. The minus sign means that the number is less than 1.

To indicate the concentration of H^+ ions in a solution, scientists have devised a scale based on the slight degree of spontaneous ionization of water. This scale is called the **pH scale.** The pH values on this scale are expressed as positive numbers, 1 to 14. The pH of a solution is determined by taking the negative value of the exponent of its hydrogen ion concentration. For example, pure water has a hydrogen ion concentration of 10^{-7} and therefore a pH of 7. When water ionizes, hydroxyl ions (OH^-) are produced in a concentration equal to the concentration of hydrogen ions. In pure water the concentrations of H^+ and OH^- ions are equal at 10^{-7}. Because these ions join spontaneously, water, at pH 7, is neutral.

Any substance that dissociates to form H^+ ions when it is dissolved in water is called an **acid.** The more hydrogen ions an acid produces, the stronger an acid it is. Although an acid produces a higher concentration of H^+ ions than pure water (0.00001 as opposed to 0.0000001, for example), its pH is lower. Using the above numbers to illustrate: the first number (0.00001 or 10^{-5}) represents the hydrogen ion concentration of an acid. The negative value of its exponent results in a pH of 5. The second number (0.0000001 or 10^{-7}) represents the hydrogen ion concentration of water. The negative value of its exponent results in a pH of 7. Because pH is a logarithmic scale, a change of 1 reflects a tenfold change in pH. For example, an acid of pH 6 is ten times more acidic than neutral. An acid with pH 5 is 100 times more acidic than neutral.

Figure 2-10 shows many common acids and their pH values. The pH of champagne, for example, is about 4. This low pH is due to the dissolved carbonic acid that causes champagne to bubble. Some bodies of water are acidic, such as peat bogs (pH 4 to 5). The hydrochloric acid (HCl) of your stomach ionizes completely to H^+ and Cl^-. It forms a strong acid with a pH of 2 to 3. Stronger acids are rarely found in living systems.

▼▼

pH refers to the relative concentration of H^+ ions in a solution. Low pH values indicate high concentrations of H^+ ions (acids), and high pH values indicate low concentrations.

Any substance that combines with H^+ ions, as OH^- ions do, is said to be a **base.** Any increase in the concentration of a base lowers the H^+ ion concentration. Bases therefore have pH values higher than water's neutral value of 7. For example, the environment of your small intestine is kept at a basic pH of between 7.5 and 8.5. Strong bases such as sodium hydroxide (NaOH) have pH values of 12 or more. As with acids, a change of 1 in the pH value of a base reflects a tenfold change in pH.

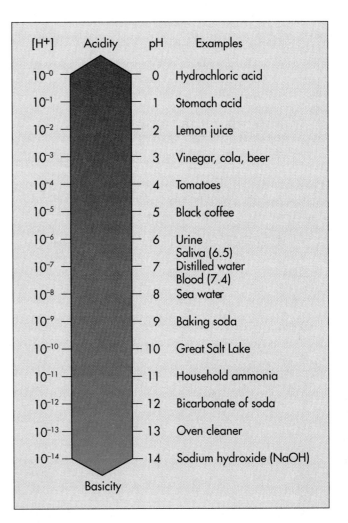

FIGURE 2-10 The pH scale.
A fluid is assigned a value according to the number of hydrogen ions present in a liter of that fluid. The scale is logarithmic, so a change of only one means a tenfold change in the concentration of hydrogen ions. Lemon juice is 100 times more acidic than tomato juice, and seawater is 10 times more basic than pure water.

Inorganic versus organic chemistry

With the exception of water, most molecules that are formed by living organisms and that make up their structures contain the element carbon. This fascinating element lends itself to being the basis of living material because of its ability to form four bonds with other atoms and therefore interact with other molecules in a myriad of ways. It is also an extremely abundant element, more so than silicon –an atom with similar bonding properties. However, silicon is used by some organisms in building outer skeletons or shells. An example of a group of such organisms is the diatoms, one of the most abundant protists on this planet.

The carbon-containing molecules that make up living things are called **organic molecules.** Organic molecules are often very large and usually interact with each other by means of covalent bonding. The study of organic molecules and their interactions is called *organic chemistry*. The study of molecules and substances not containing carbon is called *inorganic chemistry*. Inorganic molecules are often quite small and usually interact with one another by means of ionic bonding.

Although carbon is the underlying component of biological molecules, 10 other elements are common in living organisms. These elements are listed in Table 2-1 and are compared according to their frequency in the earth's crust. Notice that the great majority of atoms in living things (96.3% in fact) are either nitrogen, oxygen, carbon, or hydrogen. Another representation of these data is shown in Figure 2-11, the periodic table of the elements. Elements in the periodic table are arranged according to their atomic numbers (see right).

| TABLE 2-1 | The most common elements on Earth and their distribution in the human body |

ELEMENT	SYMBOL	ATOMIC NUMBER	APPROXIMATE PERCENT OF EARTH'S CRUST BY WEIGHT	PERCENT OF HUMAN BODY BY WEIGHT	IMPORTANCE OR FUNCTION
Oxygen	O	8	46.6	65.0	Necessary for cellular respiration, component of water
Silicon	Si	14	27.7	Trace	—
Aluminum	Al	13	6.5	Trace	—
Iron	Fe	26	5.0	Trace	Critical component of hemoglobin in the blood
Calcium	Ca	20	3.6	1.5	Component of bones and teeth, trigger for muscle contraction
Sodium	Na	11	2.8	0.2	Principal positive ion bathing cells, important in nerve function
Potassium	K	19	2.6	0.4	Principal positive ion in cells, important in nerve function
Magnesium	Mg	12	2.1	0.1	Critical component of many energy-transferring enzymes
Hydrogen	H	1	0.14	9.5	Electron carrier, component of water and most organic molecules
Manganese	Mn	25	0.1	Trace	—
Fluorine	F	9	0.07	Trace	—
Phosphorus	P	15	0.07	1.0	Backbone of nucleic acids, important in energy transfer
Carbon	C	6	0.03	18.5	Backbone of organic molecules
Sulfur	S	16	0.03	0.3	Component of most proteins
Chlorine	Cl	17	0.01	0.2	Principal negative ion bathing cells
Vanadium	V	23	0.01	Trace	—
Chromium	Cr	24	0.01	Trace	—
Copper	Cu	29	0.01	Trace	Key component of many enzymes
Nitrogen	N	7	Trace	3.3	Component of all proteins and nucleic acids
Boron	B	5	Trace	Trace	—
Cobalt	Co	27	Trace	Trace	—
Zinc	Zn	30	Trace	Trace	Key component of some enzymes
Selenium	Se	34	Trace	Trace	—
Molybdenum	Mo	42	Trace	Trace	Key component of many enzymes
Tin	Sn	50	Trace	Trace	
Iodine	I	53	Trace	Trace	Component of thyroid hormone

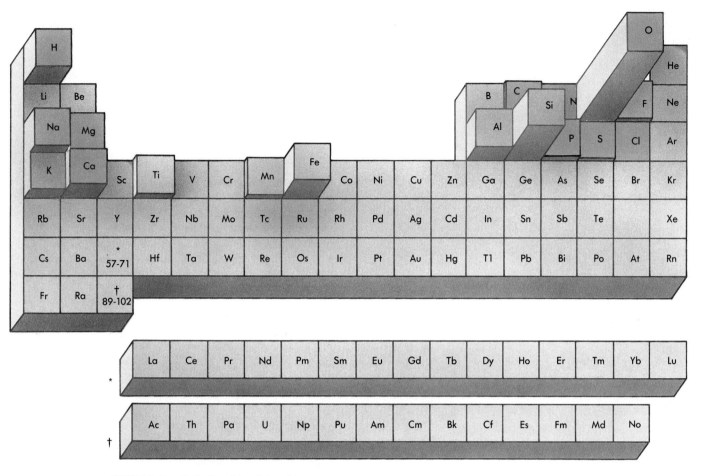

FIGURE 2-11 Periodic table of the elements.
In this representation the frequency of elements that occur in the Earth's crust in more than trace amounts is indicated in the vertical dimension. Thus the most frequent element, oxygen, rises the farthest above the plane of the page, whereas iron, not as common, does not rise as far. Elements found in significant amounts in living organisms are shaded in green.

The chemical building blocks of life

It is often helpful to think of an organic molecule as a carbon-based core with other special parts attached. Each of these special parts is really a group of atoms called a **functional group** and has definite chemical properties. A hydroxyl group (—OH), for example, is a functional group. The most important functional groups are illustrated in Figure 2-12. These groups are important because most chemical reactions that occur within organisms involve the transfer of a functional group from one molecule to another. Other frequent chemical reactions involve the breaking of carbon-carbon bonds.

Some of the molecules of living things are simple organic molecules, often having only one functional group. Other molecules are far larger with many functional groups and are called **macromolecules.** Most of these giant molecules are **polymers,** macromolecules that are built by forming covalent bonds between similar building blocks, or **monomers,** to form long chains. Four major groups of biologically important macromolecules are polymers: complex

carbohydrates, lipids, proteins, and nucleic acids. Lipids are different from the rest, however, because they are made up of two types of monomers rather than just one. For this reason, lipids are also termed **composite molecules.** The four major classes of macromolecules are presented in Table 2-2.

Although the four major classes of macromolecules are each composed of different building blocks, the process by which these building blocks are put together is the same. **Dehydration synthesis** is the process by which monomers are put together to form polymers. During dehydration synthesis, one molecule of water is removed (dehydration) from each two monomers that are joined (synthesis). One monomer loses its hydroxyl group (—OH), and the other loses an atom of hydrogen (H). Having lost electrons they were sharing in covalent bonding, both monomers bond covalently with one another (see Figure 2-22). The process of dehydration synthesis uses energy, which is stored in the bond that is made, and takes place with the help of special molecules called *enzymes* (see Chapter 4).

Polymers are disassembled in an opposite process called **hydrolysis** (see Figure 2-22). During hydrolysis the bonds

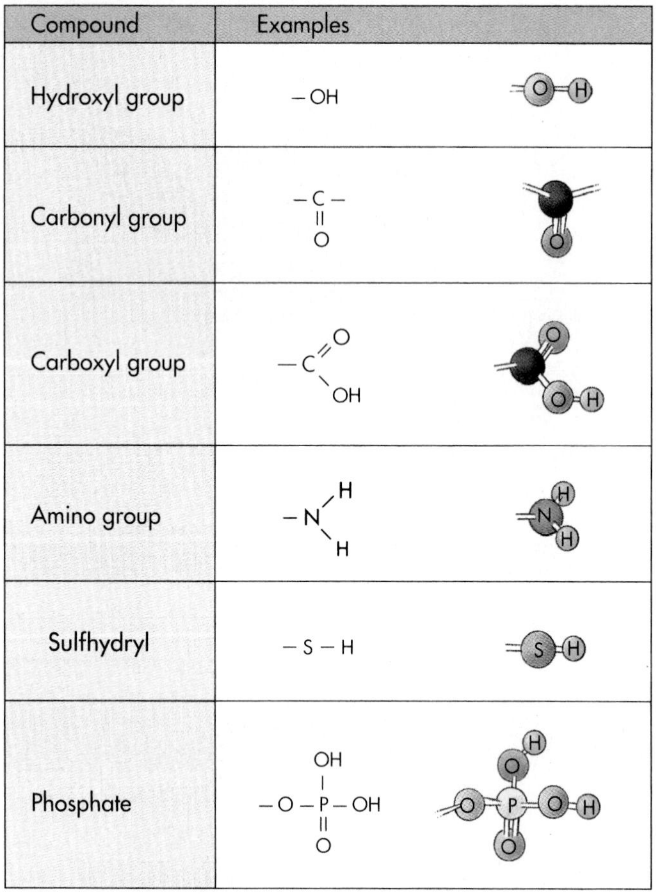

Compound	Examples	
Hydroxyl group	– OH	
Carbonyl group	$-\overset{\displaystyle |}{\underset{\displaystyle \underset{\displaystyle O}{\|}}{C}}-$	
Carboxyl group	$-C\overset{\displaystyle O}{\underset{\displaystyle OH}{}}$	
Amino group	$-N\overset{\displaystyle H}{\underset{\displaystyle H}{}}$	
Sulfhydryl	– S – H	
Phosphate	$\overset{\displaystyle OH}{\underset{\displaystyle \underset{\displaystyle O}{\|}}{-O-\overset{\displaystyle |}{P}-OH}}$	

FIGURE 2-12 The principal functional chemical groups.
These groups tend to act as units during chemical reactions. They also confer specific chemical properties on the molecules that possess them. Hydroxyl groups make a molecule more basic, for example, because this group forms OH⁻ ions when the molecule is dissolved in water. Carboxyl groups make a molecule more acidic because this group forms H⁺ ions.

TABLE 2-2	Macromolecules

MACROMOLECULE	SUBUNIT	FUNCTION	EXAMPLE
CARBOHYDRATES			
Starch, glycogen	Glucose	Stores energy	Potatoes
Cellulose	Glucose	Makes up cell walls in plants	Paper
Chitin	Modified glucose	Makes up the exterior skeleton in some animals	Crab shells
LIPIDS			
Fats	Glycerol + 3 fatty acids	Store energy	Butter
Phospholipids	Glycerol + 2 fatty acids + phosphate	Make up cell membranes	All membranes
Steroids	4 carbon rings	Act as chemical messengers	Cholesterol, estrogen
PROTEINS			
Globular	Amino acids	Help chemical reactions take place	Hemoglobin
Structural	Amino acids	Make up tissues that support body structures and provide movement	Muscle
NUCLEIC ACIDS			
DNA	Nucleotides	Helps code hereditary information	Chromosomes
RNA	Nucleotides	Helps decode hereditary information	Messenger RNA

are broken between monomers with the addition of water (and in the presence of enzymes). In fact, the term *hydrolysis* literally means "to break apart" (lysis) "by means of water" (hydro). The hydroxyl group of a water molecule bonds to one monomer, and the hydrogen atom bonds to its neighbor. The energy held in the bond is released.

Carbohydrates

Carbohydrates are molecules that contain carbon, hydrogen, and oxygen, with the concentration of hydrogen and oxygen atoms in a 2:1 ratio. Abundant energy is locked in their many carbon-hydrogen bonds. Plants, algae, and some bacteria produce carbohydrates by the process of photosynthesis. Most organisms use carbohydrates as an important fuel, breaking these bonds and releasing energy to sustain life.

Among the least complex of the carbohydrates are the simple sugars or **monosaccharides.** This word comes from two Greek words meaning "single" (monos) and "sweet" (saccharon) and reflects the fact that monosaccharides are individual sugar molecules. Some of these sweet-tasting sugars have as few as three carbon atoms. The monosaccharides that play a central role in energy storage, however, have six. The primary energy-storage molecule used by living things is glucose ($C_6H_{12}O_6$), a six-carbon sugar with seven energy-storing carbon-hydrogen bonds. Notice in Figure 2-13 that glucose, like other sugars, exists as a straight chain or as a ring of atoms.

▼▼
Sugars are among the most important energy-storage molecules in living things.

Glucose is not the only sugar with the formula $C_6H_{12}O_6$. Other monosaccharides having this same formula are fructose and galactose. Because these molecules have the same molecular formula as glucose but are put together slightly differently, they are called **isomers,** or alternative forms, of glucose (Figure 2-14). Your taste buds can tell the difference: fructose is much sweeter than glucose.

In living systems, two of these three sugars are often found covalently bonded to one another. Two monosaccharides linked together form a **disaccharide.** Many organisms, such as plants, link monosaccharides together to form disaccharides that are less readily broken down while being transported within the organism (Figure 2-15). Sucrose (table sugar) is a disaccharide formed by linking a molecule of glucose to a molecule of fructose. It is the common transport form of sugar in plants. Lactose, or milk sugar (glucose + galactose), is a disaccharide produced by many mammals to feed their young.

Not only do organisms unlock, use, and transport the energy within carbohydrate molecules, they can store this energy. To do this, however, organisms must convert soluble sugars such as glucose to an insoluble form to be stored. Sugars are made insoluble by joining them together into long polymers called **polysaccharides.** To store energy, plants use glucose to form polysaccharides called **starches.** The starch amylose, for example, is made up of hundreds of glucose molecules linked together in long, unbranched chains. Most plant starch is a branched version of amylose called *amylopectin*. Animals store glucose as highly branched chains called **glycogen** (Figure 2-16).

▼▼
Starch and glycogen, both types of polysaccharides, are storage forms of glucose. Plants store sugar as starch, whereas animals store sugar as glycogen.

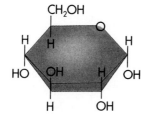

FIGURE 2-13 Structure of a glucose molecule.
Glucose exists as a linear six-carbon molecule or as a ring of atoms. In the ring structure on the right, carbon atoms are located at each point in the hexagon except where the oxygen atom is shown.

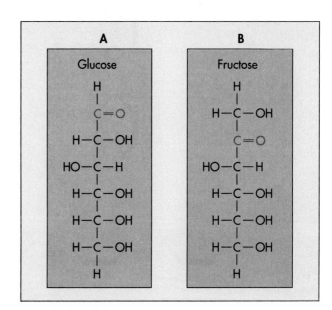

FIGURE 2-14 Isomers.
A structural isomer of glucose (A), such as fructose (B), has identical chemical groups bonded to different carbon atoms.

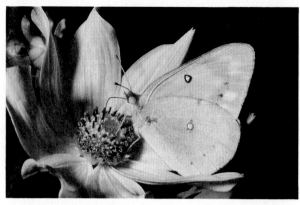

A

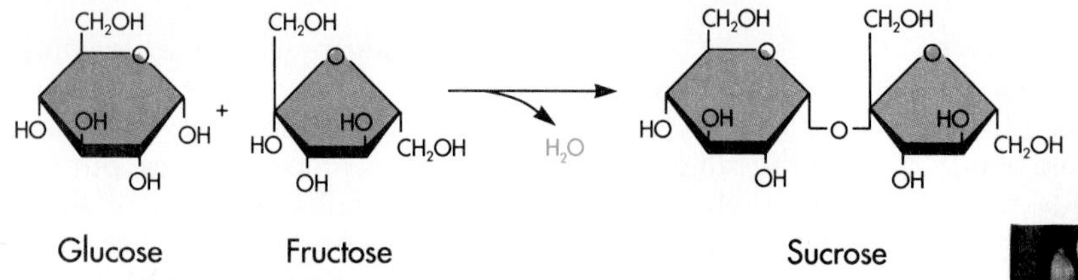
CH₂OH
HO
OH
OH
OH
+
CH₂OH
HO
HO
CH₂OH
OH
H₂O
CH₂OH
CH₂OH
HO
OH
O
HO
CH₂OH
OH
OH
Glucose
Fructose
Sucrose

B

FIGURE 2-15 Disaccharides.
A The disaccharide shown here, sucrose, is formed by linking the two monosaccharides glucose and fructose.
B Sucrose is the most common transport form of sugar in plants. This butterfly has extended its uncoiled mouthparts into a sugar solution, which it is sucking from a flower.

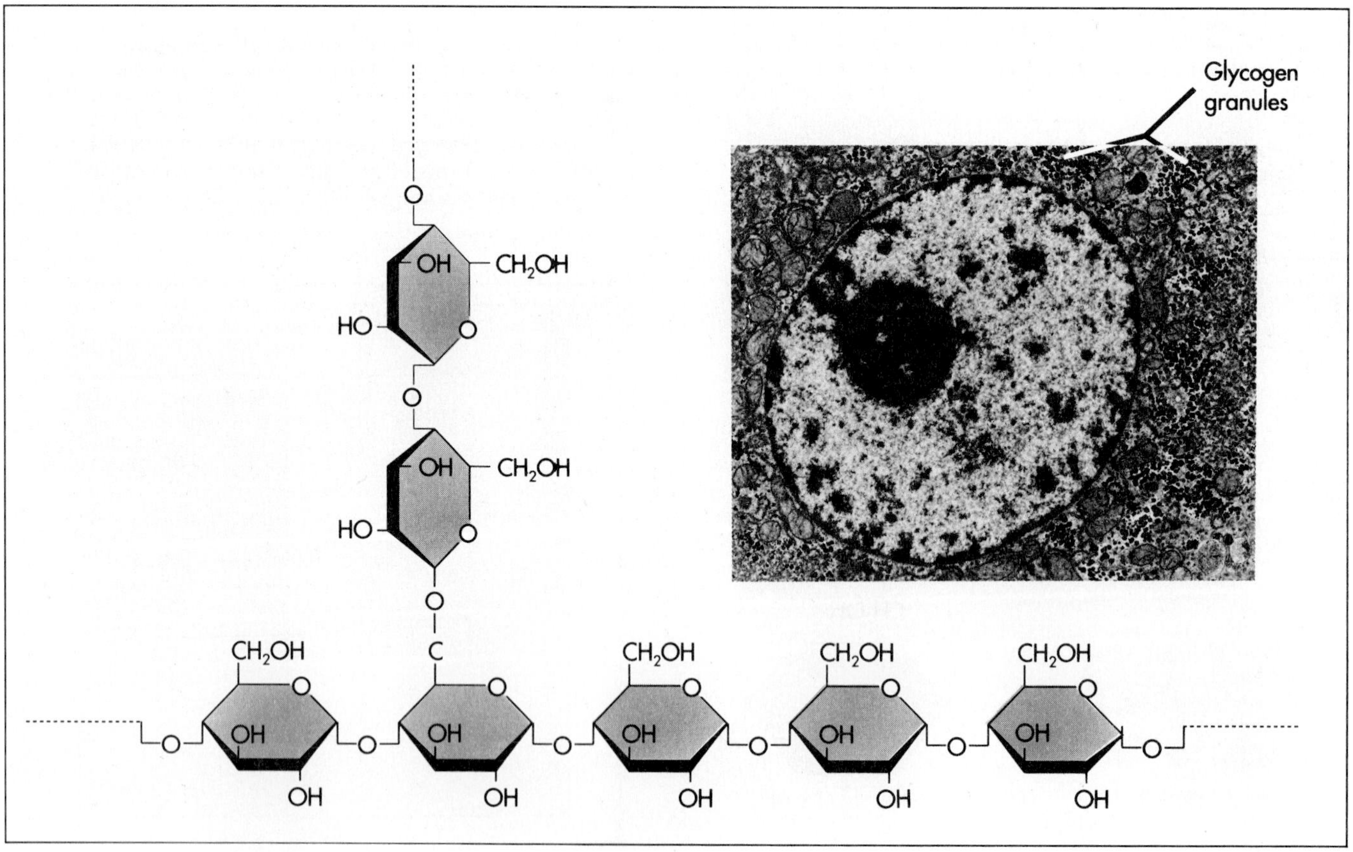
Glycogen granules
O
OH
CH₂OH
HO
O
O
OH
CH₂OH
HO
O
O
C
CH₂OH
OH
OH
O
OH
OH
O
CH₂OH
OH
OH
O
CH₂OH
OH
OH
O
CH₂OH
OH
OH
O

FIGURE 2-16 Glycogen.
The nuclear membrane of the liver cell in the micrograph is surrounded by glycogen, a highly branched polysaccharide. Plants store glucose as starch, whereas animals store it as glycogen.

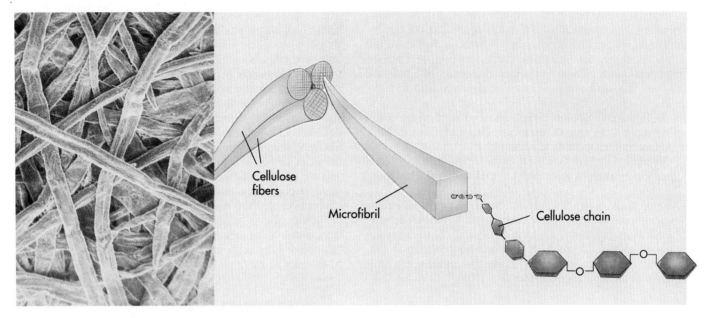

FIGURE 2-17 A journey into wood.
The jumble of cellulose fibers *(left)* is from a ponderosa pine. Each fiber is composed of microfibrils, which are bundles of cellulose chains. Cellulose fibers can be very strong, which is one reason wood is such a good building material.

FIGURE 2-18 Chitin.
Chitin is the principal structural element in the external skeletons of many invertebrates, such as this lobster.

The chief component of plant cell walls is a polysaccharide called **cellulose.** Cellulose is chemically similar to amylose but is bonded together in a way that most organisms cannot digest (Figure 2-17). For this reason, cellulose works well as a biological structural material and occurs widely in this role in plants. The structural material in insects, many fungi, and certain other organisms is a modified form of cellulose called **chitin** (Figure 2-18). Chitin is a tough, resistant surface material that is also relatively indigestible.

Fats and lipids

When organisms store glucose molecules for long periods, they usually store them as **fats** rather than as carbohydrates. Fats are large molecules made up of carbon, hydrogen, and oxygen, as are the carbohydrates, but their hydrogen-to-oxygen ratio is higher than 2:1. For this reason, fats contain more energy-storing carbon-hydrogen bonds than carbohydrates. In addition, fats are nonpolar, insoluble molecules, so they work well as storage molecules.

Fats are only one kind of **lipid**. Lipids include a wide variety of molecules, all of which are soluble in oil but insoluble in water. This insolubility is because almost all the bonds in lipids are nonpolar carbon-carbon or carbon-hydrogen bonds. Three important categories of lipids are (1) oils, fats, and waxes; (2) phospholipids; and (3) steroids.

Lipids are composite molecules: that is, they are made up of more than one component. Oils and fats are built from two different kinds of subunits:

1. Glycerol: Glycerol is a three-carbon molecule with each carbon bearing a hydroxyl (—OH) group. The three carbons form the backbone of the fat molecule.
2. Fatty acids: Fatty acids have long **hydrocarbon** chains (chains consisting only of carbon and hydrogen atoms) ending in a carboxyl (—COOH) group. Three fatty acids are attached to each glycerol backbone (Figure 2-19). Because there are three fatty acids, the resulting fat molecule is called a **triglyceride:**

```
          H
          |
   H — C — Fatty acid
          |
   H — C — Fatty acid
          |
   H — C — Fatty acid
          |
          H
```

The difference between fats and oils has to do with the number of double bonds in their fatty acids. As Figure 2-20 shows, a fatty acid with only single bonds between its carbon atoms can hold more hydrogen atoms than a fatty acid with double bonds between its carbon atoms. A fatty acid that carries as many hydrogen atoms as possible, such as the fatty acid in Figure 2-20, *A*, is saturated. Fats composed of fatty acids with double bonds are unsaturated because the double bonds replace some of the hydrogen atoms. If a fat has more than one double bond, it is polyunsaturated. Polyunsaturated fats (Figure 2-20, *B*) have low melting points and are therefore liquid fats, or oils. The fatty acids of most plant triglycerides such as vegetable oils are unsaturated. (Exceptions are the tropical oils.) Animal fats, in contrast, are often saturated and occur as hard fats. Human diets with large amounts of saturated fats appear to upset the normal balance of fatty acids in the body, a situation that can lead to diseases of the circulatory system.

▼▼▼

Fats are important energy-storing molecules. They are made up of three fatty acid chains attached to a glycerol backbone.

Waxes, which are used by land plants and some animals as a waterproofing material, differ from fats and oils by having a chemical backbone slightly different than glycerol. Phospholipids are also similar to oils except that one of their fatty acids is replaced by a phosphate group attached to a

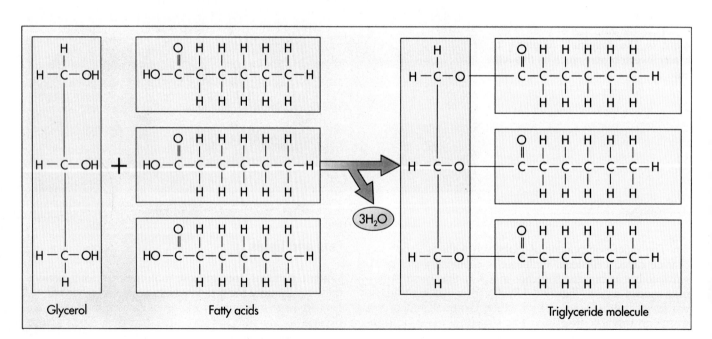

FIGURE 2-19 Structure of a triglyceride.
Triglycerides are composite molecules, made up of three fatty acid molecules bonded to a single glycerol molecule.

Imagine eating all the french fries, ice cream, and cake you wanted without ever putting on an extra pound. What makes these foods fattening, and thus avoided by many people, is their fat content. Excess dietary fat has also been identified as a factor in some forms of heart disease. So finding a safe substitute for dietary fats has been a research goal for a number of food manufacturers.

Fats are composed of fatty acid molecules attached to a backbone of glycerol. These molecules are the body's form of long-term storage for the components of glucose. When the body needs more energy than is supplied in the everyday diet, these components can be reassembled into glucose, and the glucose processed to provide energy. However, when more food (including fats) is consumed than is needed to meet the body's energy requirements, the excess can accumulate in the bulges that many of us have.

In addition to producing those bulges, excess fats have been implicated in a higher incidence of heart disease and in some cancers. Nutritional experts currently recommend that no more than 25% to 30% of total calories in the diet of a healthy person of normal weight come from the various kinds of fats. But 37% of the typical American diet consists of calories from fat. Clearly, Americans need to find ways to reduce their fat consumption.

One way to reduce fat intake while still eating some of the familiar foods most of us enjoy so much is to eat foods made with fat substitutes. A fat substitute already available is marketed under the brand name Simplesse. This fat substitute is used in the manufacture of such foods as ice cream, salad dressings, and cheese products. Simplesse has a fat-like consistency and texture because it is composed of protein microspheres that mimic the "mouth feel" of real fat molecules, and that smooth, creamy texture is a large part of what we enjoy in a chocolate bar or a scoop of ice cream. Because Simplesse is made from protein, however, it provides the fat-like texture without the dietary disadvantages.

Simplesse has one drawback. It does not retain its fat-like consistency and taste when it is heated. Olestra, which is not yet on the market, is a fat substitute that can withstand heat. Olestra is a sucrose molecule to which six, seven, or eight fatty acid chains are attached. Triglycerides, or natural fats, are also composed of fatty acids, so Olestra comes closer than Simplesse to mimicking their molecular structure. Fat-digesting enzymes do not break down Olestra, so it bypasses the body's digestive and absorptive mechanisms. This ability, combined with Olestra's textural resemblance to natural fat, make it a very convincing and effective fat substitute. Studies are presently underway to test Olestra's safety, and the preliminary reports are positive.

Figure 2-B Ice cream made with a fat substitute allows users to reduce fat intake while enjoying a favorite dessert.

Some nutritionists argue that the best way to lower fat consumption is to develop a taste for foods that are naturally low in fat, rather than searching for substitutes for fatty foods. The manufacturers of Olestra caution that it should not be used to replace a balanced diet low in natural fat. Rather, fat substitutes offer the opportunity to eat a once-forbidden treat occasionally without increasing fat consumption above healthy levels. They are also useful for those on no-fat diets for health reasons.

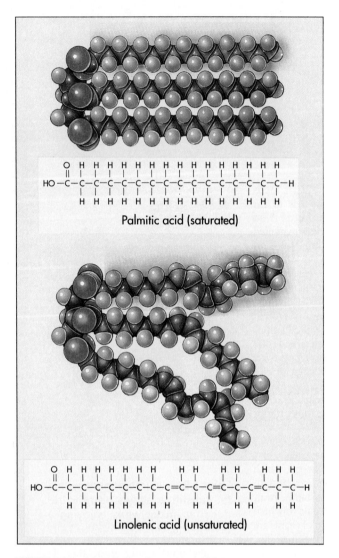

FIGURE 2-20   Saturated and unsaturated fats.
A Palmitic acid, with no double bonds and thus a maximum number of hydrogen atoms bonded to the carbon chain, is a saturated fatty acid.
B Linolenic acid, with three double bonds and thus fewer than the maximum number of hydrogen atoms bonded to the carbon chain, is an unsaturated fatty acid.

nitrogen-containing group. Phospholipids play a key role in the structure of cell membranes (see Chapter 3). Membranes often contain steroids, a lipid having a structure very different from oils. Steroids are composed of four carbon rings. Most of your cell membranes contain the steroid cholesterol. Male and female sex hormones (discussed in Chapter 21) are also steroids.

Proteins

Proteins are the third major group of macromolecules that make up the bodies of organisms. Proteins play diverse roles in living things. Perhaps the most important proteins are **enzymes,** proteins capable of speeding up specific chemical reactions. Other short proteins called **peptides** are used as chemical messengers within your brain and throughout your body. Collagen, a structural protein, is an important part of bones, cartilage, and tendons. Despite their varied functions, all proteins have the same basic structure: a long chain of amino acids linked end to end.

Amino acids are small molecules containing an amino group ($-NH_2$), a carboxyl group ($-COOH$), a hydrogen atom, a carbon atom, and a functional group that differs among amino acids. In a generalized formula for an amino acid, the functional group is shown as R. The identity and unique chemical properties of each amino acid are determined by the nature of the functional (R) group.

$$H_2N-\underset{\underset{H}{|}}{\overset{\overset{R}{|}}{C}}-COOH$$

Only 20 different amino acids make up the diverse array of proteins found in living things. Each protein differs according to the amount, type, and arrangement of amino acids that make up its structure. These 20 "common" amino acids are illustrated in Figure 2-21. They are grouped according to the chemical nature of their functional groups.

When ionized, each amino acid has a positive (amino, or $-NH_3^+$) group at one end and a negative (carboxyl, or $-COOH^-$) group at the other end. During dehydration synthesis, each of these groups on separate amino acids loses a molecule of water between them, forming a covalent bond that links the two amino acids (Figure 2-22, A). This bond is called a **peptide bond.** A long chain of amino acids linked by peptide bonds is a **polypeptide.** Proteins are long, complex polypeptides. The great variability possible in the sequence of amino acids in polypeptides is perhaps the most important property of proteins, permitting tremendous diversity in their structures and functions.

The sequence of amino acids that makes up a particular polypeptide chain is termed the **primary structure** of a protein (Figure 2-23). This sequence determines the further levels of structure of the protein molecule resulting from bonds that form between these groups. Having the proper sequence of amino acids, then, is crucial to the functioning of a protein. Put simply, if the protein does not assume its correct shape, it will not work properly or at all. Because different amino acid functional groups have different chemical properties, the shape of a protein may be altered by a single amino acid change.

The functional groups of the amino acids in a polypeptide chain interact with their neighbors, forming hydrogen bonds. In addition, portions of a protein chain with many nonpolar functional groups (see Figure 2-21) tend to be

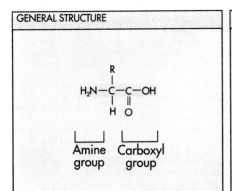

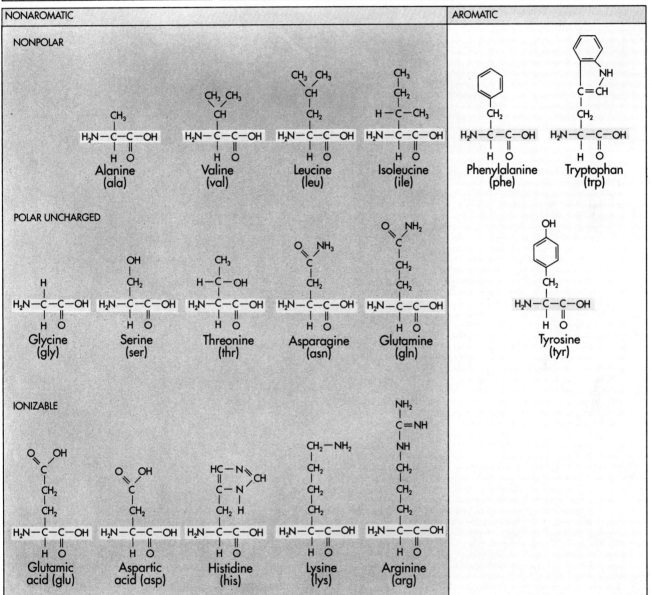

FIGURE 2-21 The 20 common amino acids.
Each amino acid has the same chemical backbone but differs from the others in the side, or R, group. Six of the amino acid R groups are nonpolar. The ones containing ring structures are called *aromatic amino acids*. Another six are polar but uncharged; these differ from one another in their polarity. Five more are polar and capable of ionizing to a charged form; under typical conditions some of these five are acids, others bases. The remaining three have special chemical (structural) properties that play important roles in forming links between protein chains or forming kinks in their shapes.

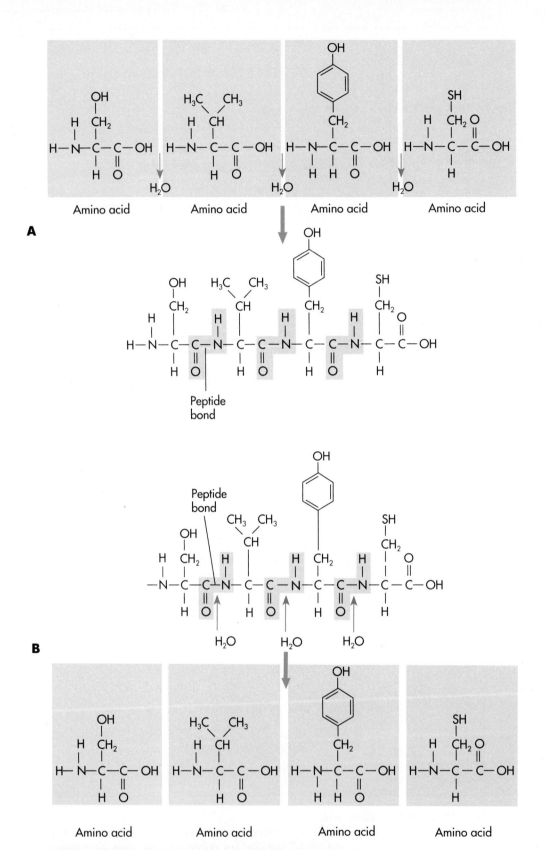

FIGURE 2-22 How a polypeptide chain is formed and broken.
A During dehydration synthesis a peptide bond is formed between two amino acids. A chain of amino acids is called a *polypeptide.*
B During hydrolysis, a molecule of water is added to each peptide bond that links adjacent amino acids, breaking the bonds between them.

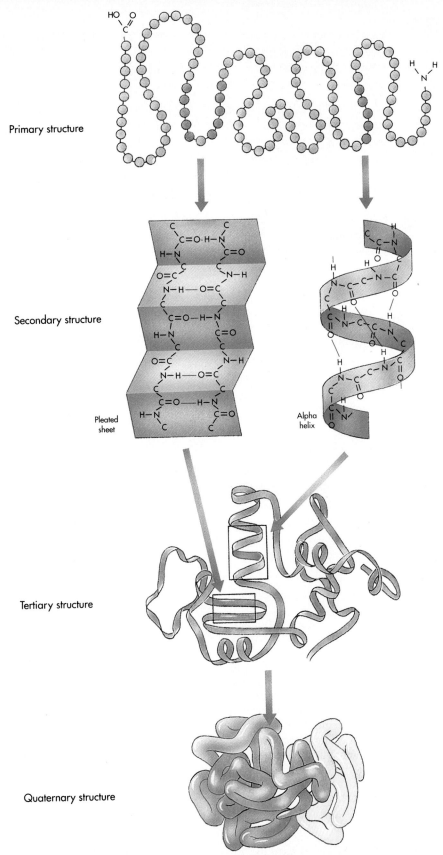

Primary structure

Secondary structure

Pleated
sheet

Alpha
helix

Tertiary structure

Quaternary structure

FIGURE 2-23   How primary structure determines a protein's shape.
The amino acid sequence of the enzyme protein lysozyme, called its *primary structure,*
encourages the formation of hydrogen bonds between nearby amino acids, producing
coils and foldbacks called the *secondary structure.* The lysozyme protein assumes a
three-dimensional shape; this is called its *tertiary structure.* Many proteins (not lysozyme) aggregate in clusters called the *quaternary structure* of the protein.

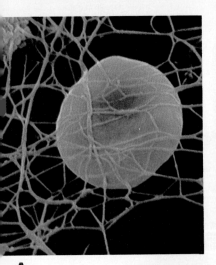

A

B

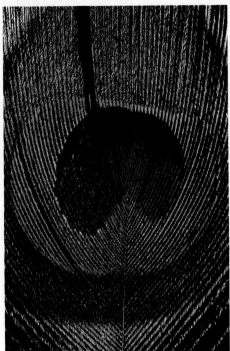

C

D

E

shoved into the interior of the protein because of their hydrophobic properties. Because of these interactions, polypeptide chains tend to fold spontaneously into sheets or wrap into coils. This folded or coiled shape is called its **secondary structure.** The primary structure of a protein also determines its three-dimensional shape, or **tertiary structure.** Proteins made up largely of sheets often form fibers (Figure 2-24). Proteins that have regions forming coils frequently fold into globular shapes. When two polypeptide chains associate to form a functional unit, the chains are termed *subunits,* and the functional unit is the protein. For proteins that consist of subunits, the way these subunits are assembled into a whole is called the **quaternary structure.**

Approximately 20 different amino acids are used in various sequences and combinations to make up a wide variety of proteins. These amino acids have different properties from one another. These differences and the sequence in which the amino acids are arranged determine the shape of a protein, which is crucial to its proper functioning.

FIGURE 2-24 Many proteins play structural roles.
A Fibrin—electron micrograph of a blood clot.
B Collagen—strings of a tennis racket.
C Keratin—a peacock feather.
D Silk—a spider's web.
E Keratin—a woman's hair.

Nucleic acids

Organisms store information about the structures of their proteins in macromolecules called **nucleic acids.** Nucleic acids are long polymers of repeating subunits called **nucleotides.** Each nucleotide is made up of three smaller building blocks (Figure 2-25):
1. A five-carbon sugar
2. A phosphate group ($-PO_4^{\equiv}$)
3. An organic nitrogen-containing molecule called a *base*

To form the nucleic acid chain, the sugars in nucleotides are linked together in a line by means of the phosphate and hydroxyl groups. A nitrogenous base protrudes from each sugar (Figure 2-26). The order in which the nucleotides are linked together forms a code that ultimately specifies the order of amino acids in a particular protein.

Organisms store and use hereditary information by coding the sequence of the amino acids of each of their proteins as a sequence of nucleotides in nucleic acids.

Organisms have two forms of nucleic acid. One form, deoxyribonucleic acid (DNA), stores the information for making proteins. The other form, ribonucleic acid (RNA), directs the production of proteins. Details of the structure of DNA and the ways it interacts with RNA are presented in Chapter 17.

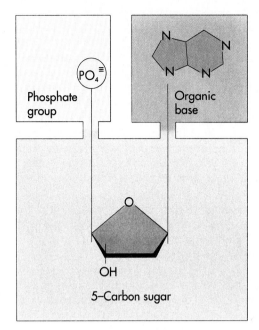

FIGURE 2-25 The structure of a nucleotide.
A nucleotide is made up of three elements: a five-carbon sugar, a phosphate group, and an organic nitrogen-containing molecule called a *base*.

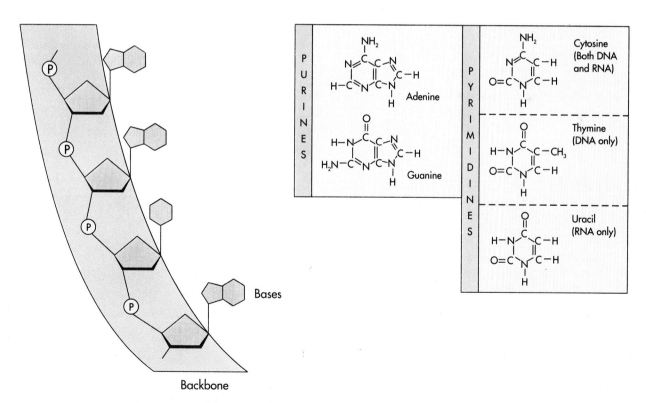

FIGURE 2-26 The five nitrogenous bases of nucleic acids.
Only four of these bases occur in DNA and four in RNA. In DNA the base thymine replaces the base uracil found in RNA. Adenine, cytosine, and guanine are found in both DNA and RNA.

Summary

1. Atoms make up all matter and are composed of three types of subatomic particles: protons, neutrons, and electrons. Protons and neutrons are found at the core of the atom, and electrons orbit this core.

2. The chemical behavior of an atom is largely determined by the distribution of its electrons, particularly the number of electrons in its outermost energy level. Atoms are most stable when their outer energy levels are filled. Electrons are lost, gained, or shared until this condition is reached.

3. The atoms of most elements interact with one another to form molecules, combinations of tightly bound atoms. Compounds are molecules made up of the atoms of two or more elements.

4. Water is an extremely important molecule for living things. It has one outstanding chemical property: it attracts other charged particles to its positive and negative ends. For this reason, water is a polar molecule.

5. Water dissolves polar substances and excludes nonpolar substances. Chemical interactions readily take place in water because so many kinds of molecules are water soluble and therefore move among water molecules as separate molecules or ions.

6. The chemistry of life is concerned with the interactions among biological molecules, or organic molecules. Organic molecules have a carbon core with various functional groups attached to the carbon atoms.

7. Most organisms use carbohydrates as an important fuel. The most important of the energy-storing carbohydrates is glucose, a six-carbon sugar.

8. Certain lipids—the fats—are important in the long-term storage of energy. Phospholipids are a major component of cell membranes.

9. Proteins are linear polymers of amino acids. Because the 20 amino acids that occur in proteins have functional groups with very different chemical properties, the shape and therefore the functioning of a protein are critically affected by its particular sequence of amino acids.

10. Hereditary information is stored as a sequence of nucleotides in the nucleotide polymer DNA. A second form of nucleic acid, RNA, directs the production of proteins.

1. a. Draw a diagram of an atom with an atomic number of 1. Label the nucleus and the subatomic particles, and show the electrical charge of each particle.
   b. Draw an isotope of the same atom.

2. Explain the three types of chemical forces that influence how an atom interacts with other atoms. What is the significance of the octet rule?

3. Nitrogen gas is formed via a triple bond between nitrogen molecules. What kind of bonding is this? What does this bond have in common with the bonds forming water molecules?

4. What characteristics of water make it so unusual? How do these traits make life on earth possible? Relate these properties to water's molecular structure.

5. After an oil spill in the ocean, why is it necessary to clean up the water?

6. Distinguish between organic and inorganic molecules. Which would you study if you wanted to learn more about the human body?

7. The pH of the material within the human small intestine is between 7.5 and 8.5. How would you describe this environment? Would the concentration of H^+ ions in this material be high or low?

8. Both carbon and water are discussed in this chapter as the essential components of life on earth. How are the bonding characteristics of each an important aspect of its biological importance?

9. Distinguish among monosaccharides, disaccharides, and polysaccharides. To what group do they belong, and why are they important?

10. Why do plants and animals not store glucose as it is for future use? What forms of storage are most common in plants and animals?

11. Explain the role that your intake of lipids has in nutrition. How does your body use lipids? What role do lipids play in energy storage in our bodies?

12. While doing your grocery shopping, you find this label on a product:
    Nutritional Information Per Serving

% of calories from fat	100%
Polyunsaturated fat	2 grams
Saturated fat	2 grams
Protein	0 grams
Carbohydrates	0 grams

    Explain the difference between polyunsaturated and saturated fats. What type(s) of macromolecules does this product contain?

13. What structural features distinguish the different proteins in our bodies? Explain the different levels of protein structure.

14. What do human RNA and DNA have in common? In what ways are they different?

15. Discuss the three classes of macromolecules taken in as food energy by humans. Which chemical process, dehydration synthesis or hydrolysis, do you think is essential in human digestion of food?

1. A long-distance runner stopping for a quick break may drink orange juice, a liquid high in fructose. A skier preparing for a long day of activity may choose a high carbohydrate breakfast with a number of starches. How does the form of the carbohydrate fuel affect the human body's short- or long-term energy needs?

2. All life on earth is based on the chemistry of water and the chemistry of carbon molecules. All living organisms are composed of only 20 different amino acids! How might these facts support the relatedness of all life on earth?

Cox, T. (1990, February 3). The origin of the chemical elements. *New Scientist*, pp. 1-4.
The heavier elements making up most of the Earth—and you—were created through the birth and death of the stars.

Fitzgerald, J., & Taylor, G. (1989, May). Carbon fibres stretch the limits. *New Scientist*, pp. 48-53.
This is a fascinating discussion of the ways in which the principles discussed in this chapter are used to produce modern, synthetic materials.

Noonan, D. (1990, February). Dr. Doolittle's question. *Discover*, pp. 35-44.
This article clearly details the study of one human protein, fibrinogen, and its possible evolution from more primitive organisms.

Sutton, C. (1989, February). Subatomic forces [supplement]. *New Scientist*, pp. 1-4.
This article is a contemporary review of the interactions between particles within the atom.

Trefil, J. (1990, June). Seeing Atoms. *Discover*, pp. 54-60.
A unique article that reveals the ability of the latest technology to reveal the nature of the atom. New supermicroscopes open the atomic world to scientists.

3 Cell Structure and Function

The illustration may not look like any highway you've ever seen, but that's exactly what it is. This highway, and billions more like it, make up a transportation network within your body. The threads, called microtubules, shuttle particles within your body's cells. Amazingly, they can move particles in two directions at the same time!

Microtubules are only one type in a myriad of structures found within cells. Many other subcellular structures do jobs such as providing energy, manufacturing molecules, and directing the activities of cells. But what are these complex structures called "cells"?

Cells are much more than the empty "boxes" seen by the British microscopist Robert Hooke in the mid-1600s. Scientists today know that cells are the smallest unit of life that can exist independently. Cells can take in nutrients, break them down to release energy, and get rid of wastes. They can reproduce, react to stimuli, and maintain an internal environment different from their surroundings. In multicellular organisms such as humans, cells work together to maintain life. In single-celled organisms such as the paramecium in Figure 3-1, each cell survives independently. This chapter will help you become familiar with the structure of cells and how they work. By studying their structure and function, you will also see their tremendous diversity and complexity (Figure 3-1) and will begin to understand the cellular level of organization of the human body.

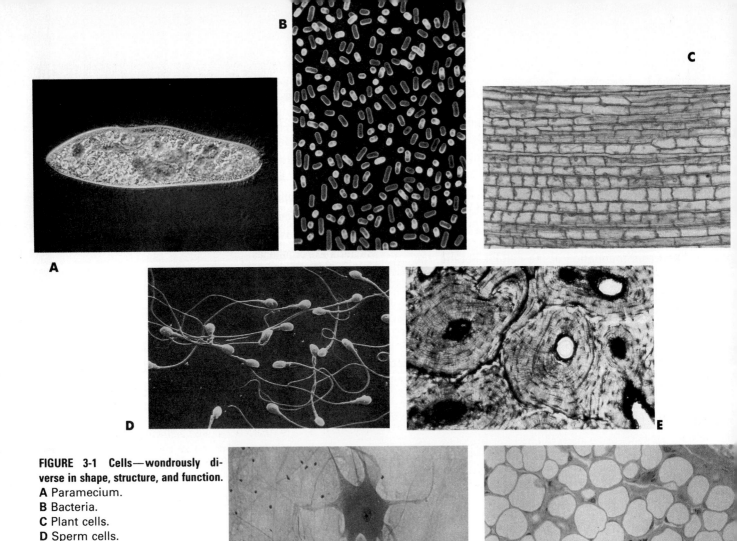

FIGURE 3-1 Cells—wondrously diverse in shape, structure, and function.
A Paramecium.
B Bacteria.
C Plant cells.
D Sperm cells.
E Bone cells.
F Nerve cell.
G Fat cells.

The cell theory

In 1839 botanist Matthias Schleiden and zoologist Theodor Schwann formulated the theory that all living things are made up of cells. In other words, they realized that cells make up the structure of such things as houseplants and people—but not of rocks or soil. It took another 50 years and the work of Rudolf Virchow for scientists to understand another basic concept about cells. Living cells can only be produced by other living cells. As Virchow put it, "all cells from cells." Together, these concepts are called **the cell theory.**

The cell theory is a profound statement regarding the nature of living things. It includes three basic principles:
1. All living things are made up of one or more cells.
2. The smallest *living* unit of structure and function of all organisms is the cell.
3. All cells arise from preexisting cells.

When these statements were formulated in the mid-1800s, scientists discarded the idea of **spontaneous generation:** that living things could arise from the nonliving. This theory suggested that frogs could be born of the mud in a pond and that rotting meat could spawn the larvae of flies. After the development of the cell theory, scientists recognized that life arose directly from the growth and division of single cells. Today, scientists believe that life on earth represents a continuous line of descent from the first cells that evolved on Earth.

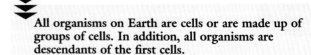

All organisms on Earth are cells or are made up of groups of cells. In addition, all organisms are descendants of the first cells.

Why aren't cells larger?

Most animal cells are extremely small, ranging in diameter from about 10 to 30 microns. To help you understand this size, there are 1000 microns in 1 millimeter (mm)—the width of a paper clip's wire. As you might expect, most cells are invisible to the naked eye without the aid of a microscope. Your red blood cells, for example, are so small that it would take a row of about 2500 of them to span the diameter of a dime. Only a few kinds of cells are large. Individual cells of the marine alga *Acetabularia,* for example, are up to 5 centimeters long (Figure 3-2). If you had eggs for breakfast, you were eating single cells! Other kinds of cells are long and thin, such as nerve cells that run from your spinal cord to your toes or fingers. But very few cells are as large as a hen's egg or as long as a nerve cell.

To understand why cells are so small, you must first realize that most cells are constantly working, doing such jobs as breaking down molecules for energy, producing substances that cells need, and getting rid of wastes. Each cell must move substances in and out across its boundary—the cell membrane—quickly enough to meet its needs. Therefore the amount of membranous surface area a cell has in relationship to the volume it encloses is crucial to its survival.

To illustrate, suppose that a cell is a cube like the one pictured in Figure 3-3. Each side of the "cell" is 1 centimeter (cm) in length. The surface area of the membrane of each "side" of the cell is 1 cm × 1 cm, or 1 cm^2. Therefore the total area of the six surfaces or sides is 6 cm^2. The volume of this cell is calculated by multiplying length × width × height. Its volume is therefore 1 cm × 1 cm × 1 cm, or 1 cm^3. The ratio, or relationship between the surface area and volume of this cell, can be expressed as 6:1.

What happens as the cell grows? As Figure 3-3 shows, as the cell grows to 2 centimeters on a side, the total surface area is 24 cm^2. The volume increases to 8 cm^3 (2 cm

FIGURE 3-2 The marine green alga *Acetabularia*
The marine green alga *Acetabularia* is a large, single-celled organism with clearly differentiated parts, such as the stalks and elaborate "hats" visible here. Each cell is a different individual several centimeters tall.

× 2 cm × 2 cm). This surface-to-volume ratio is 24:8, or 3:1. As the cell grew, it went from having 6 cm^2 of surface area for each 1 cm^3 of volume, to only 3 cm^2 for each 1 cm^3. The diagram also illustrates that this ratio only gets smaller as the cell continues to grow to 4 centimeters on a side.

FIGURE 3-3 Cells maintain a large surface-to-volume ratio.
As the cell increases in volume, the ratio of its surface area to volume gets smaller. Multicellular organisms are made up of many microscopic cells. This organization increases the total surface area of the cell membranes within living things.

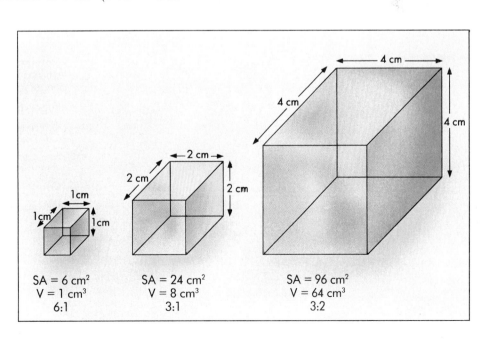

Therefore one reason that cells are microscopic is that they must maintain a large surface area-to-volume ratio or they cannot move substances in and out (across their membranes) fast enough to meet their needs.

Another reason that cells generally do not grow large has to do with their controlling centers, or **nuclei.** Scientists think that a nucleus could not control all the activities of an active cell if it grew too large. In fact, some large complex cells, such as the unicellular paramecia, have two nuclei. Large cells with only one nucleus, such as unfertilized egg cells, are usually inactive cells.

Most cells are microscopically small so that substances can move in and out of them, across their cell membranes, quickly enough to meet their needs.

Two kinds of cells

All cells can be grouped into two broad categories: **prokaryotic cells** and **eukaryotic cells.** Cells are placed into one of these categories based on their types of structure. Prokaryotic cells, or prokaryotes, have a simpler structure than eukaryotes and were the first type of cell to exist as

life arose on Earth billions of years ago. Eukaryotic cells evolved from these simpler cells.

You know the prokaryotes as *bacteria.* The cells of organisms within the other four kingdoms of life—plants, animals, protists, and fungi—are eukaryotes. Although the structure of cells in either group may vary among species, prokaryotes and eukaryotes each have distinctive features common to each group. In addition, because members of both groups are living cells, they also have some of the same features. Almost all cells have the following four characteristics:

1. A surrounding membrane
2. A thick fluid enclosed by this membrane that, along with the other cell contents, is called *protoplasm*
3. Organelles, or "little organs," located within the protoplasm (of eukaryotes) that carry out certain cellular functions
4. A control center called a *nucleus* (in eukaryotes) or *nucleoid* (in prokaryotes) containing the hereditary material DNA

The structure of bacterial cells is discussed in Chapter 23, but Table 3-2 located on p. 66 will help you clarify and classify the differences among three cell types: plant cells and animal cells (both eukaryotes) and bacterial cells (prokaryotes). Also, Figures 3-4 (an animal cell) and 3-5 (a plant cell) will help you visualize eukaryotic cell structures.

FIGURE 3-4   An animal cell.
This diagram shows the major eukaryotic organelles. Membranes and membranous organelles create anatomical and functional compartments, including a complex system of transport channels. Organelles found in eukaryotic cells include the true nucleus, mitochondria, endoplasmic reticula, and Golgi bodies.

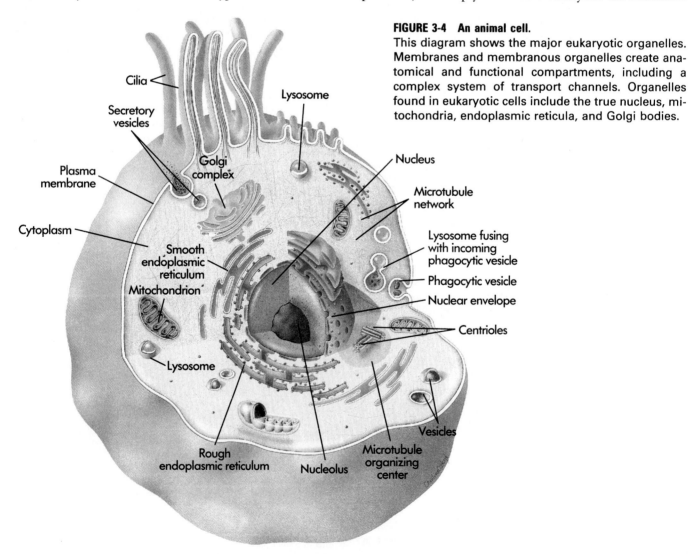

Cilia
Secretory vesicles
Plasma membrane
Cytoplasm
Golgi complex
Smooth endoplasmic reticulum
Mitochondrion
Lysosome
Rough endoplasmic reticulum
Nucleolus
Microtubule organizing center
Lysosome
Nucleus
Microtubule network
Lysosome fusing with incoming phagocytic vesicle
Phagocytic vesicle
Nuclear envelope
Centrioles
Vesicles

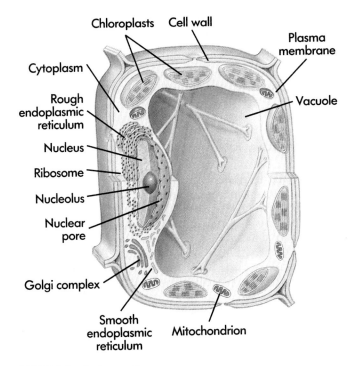

Chloroplasts Cell wall
Cytoplasm
Rough endoplasmic reticulum
Nucleus
Ribosome
Nucleolus
Nuclear pore
Golgi complex
Smooth endoplasmic reticulum
Plasma membrane
Vacuole
Mitochondrion

FIGURE 3-5 A plant cell.
Many plant cell organelles are similar to those in animal cells, since both are eukaryotic. But the typical plant cell has chloroplasts that carry out photosynthesis, has a rigid cellulose cell wall, and frequently has large water-filled vacuoles occupying a major part of the cell volume.

Eukaryotic cells: An overview

Although eukaryotic cells are quite a diverse group, they share a basic architecture. Since humans are eukaryotes, their cells have the eukaryotic features described in this chapter. However, like all animals, human cells do not have the eukaryotic cell structures characteristic of plants, which are also described here. Table 3-2 lists the characteristics of human cells under the heading "animal."

All eukaryotic cells are bounded by a membrane called the **plasma membrane.** This membrane encloses a semifluid material called the *cytosol,* which is crisscrossed with a supporting framework of protein called a **cytoskeleton.** All eukaryotic cells also possess many organelles (Table 3-1). These organelles are of two general kinds: (1) membranes or organelles derived from membranes and (2) bacteria-like organelles. The organelles found in human cells are printed in red in Table 3-1.

Most biologists agree that the bacteria-like organelles in eukaryotes were derived from ancient **symbiotic bacteria.** The word **symbiosis** means that two or more organisms live together in a close association. An organism that is symbiotic within another is called an **endosymbiont.** The major endosymbionts that occur in eukaryotic cells are mitochondria, which occur in all but a very few eukaryotic organisms, and chloroplasts, which occur in algae and plants.

TABLE 3-1	Eukaryotic cell structures and their functions		
STRUCTURE	**DESCRIPTION**		**FUNCTION**
STRUCTURAL ELEMENTS			
Cell wall	Outer layer of cellulose or chitin, or absent		Protection, support
Plasma membrane	Lipid bilayer in which proteins are embedded		Regulation of what passes in and out of cell, cell-to-cell recognition
Cytoskeleton	Network of protein filaments		Structural support, cell movement
Flagella (cilia)	Cellular extensions with 9 + 2 arrangement of pairs of microtubules		Motility of moving fluids over surfaces
ORGANELLES			
Endoplasmic reticulum	Network of internal membranes		Formation of compartments and vesicles
Ribosomes	Small, complex assemblies of protein and RNA, often bound to ER		Sites or protein synthesis
Nucleus	Spherical structure bounded by double membrane, site of chromosomes		Control center of cell, directing of protein synthesis and cell reproduction
Chromosomes	Long threads of DNA associated with protein		Sites of hereditary information
Nucleolus	Site on chromosome of rRNA synthesis		Assembly of ribosomes
Golgi complex	Stacks of flattened vesicles		Packaging of proteins for export from cell
Lysosomes	Membranous sacs contain digestive enzymes		Digestion of worn-out mitochondria and cell debris, role in cell death
Mitochondria	Bacteria-like elements with inner membrane highly folded		"Power plant" of the cell
Chloroplasts	Bacteria-like elements with vesicles containing chlorophyll found in plant cells and algae		Site of photosynthesis in plant cells and algae

The plasma membrane

All eukaryotic cells are bounded by a membrane called the *plasma membrane*. It gets this name because it encloses the protoplasm, the semifluid cell contents, and cell organelles. Although the plasma membrane is a thin, nonrigid structure, in many cells it is molded into a specific shape. Human red blood cells, for example, look like a round pillow that has been punched in the center (Figure 3-6, *A*). The muscle cells of the stomach have tapered ends and bulging middles. In cells such as these, which have no rigid, supporting cell walls as do most bacterial and plant cells, cell shapes are determined by a protein network lying beneath the plasma membrane. Were it not for this protein network, or cytoskeleton, these cells would look like shapeless blobs.

The plasma membrane has two main components: phospholipids and proteins. Lipids, as you may recall from Chapter 2, are made up of glycerol and fatty acids. The phospholipids of plasma membranes are composed of two fatty acids bonded to a glycerol backbone. A polar, nonlipid molecule is also attached to the glycerol backbone by means of a phosphate group. In the plasma membrane, these molecules form a double layer (Figure 3-6, *B*).

Nothing can enter or leave the cell without passing across the plasma membrane. Interestingly, very little does cross the lipid layer itself. Instead, a variety of proteins penetrates the lipid layer and controls the interactions of the cell with its environment. Some of these proteins, called *channels,* act as doors that let specific molecules into and out of the cell. Other proteins, called *receptors,* recognize certain chemicals such as hormones that signal cells to respond in particular ways (see Chapter 14). Receptor proteins cause changes within the cell when they come in contact with such chemical "messengers" or signals. A third type of protein works to identify a cell as being of a particular type. These cell surface markers help cells identify one another, an ability that helps cells in a multicellular organism (such as your body) function correctly. This model of the cell membrane is widely accepted today. It is called the **fluid mosaic model**, a name that describes the fluid nature of a lipid bilayer studded with a mosaic of proteins.

The plasma membrane is a thin, nonrigid structure that encloses the cell and regulates interactions between the cell and its environment.

The cytoplasm and cytoskeleton

The **cytoplasm** of the cell is a viscous fluid containing all cell organelles except the nucleus. The word *cytoplasm* literally means "living gel" (plasm) "of the cell" (cyto). The major components of the cytoplasm are (1) a gel-like fluid, (2) storage substances, (3) a network of interconnected filaments and fibers, and (4) cell organelles. The fluid part of the cytoplasm is made up of approximately 75% water and 25% proteins. The proteins, mostly enzymes and structural proteins, make the cytoplasm viscous—much like thickening gelatin. Nonprotein molecules involved in the various chemical reactions of the cell, such as ions and ATP (an important energy-storing molecule), are also dissolved in this fluid.

Storage substances vary from one type of cell to another. For example, the cytoplasm of liver cells contains large molecules of glycogen, a storage form of glucose. Fat cells contain a large lipid droplet.

The cytoplasm also contains a cytoskeleton—a network of filaments and fibers that do many jobs. The cytoskeleton is made up of three different types of fibers: **microfilaments, microtubules,** and **intermediate filaments.** The microfilaments are the thinnest—a twisted double chain of protein—and are not visible with an ordinary light microscope. The microtubules, a chain of proteins wrapped in a spiral to form a tube, are the thickest members of the cytoskeleton. As the name suggests, the intermediate filaments are an in-between size. These are thread-like protein molecules that wrap around one another to form "ropes" of protein (Figure 3-7).

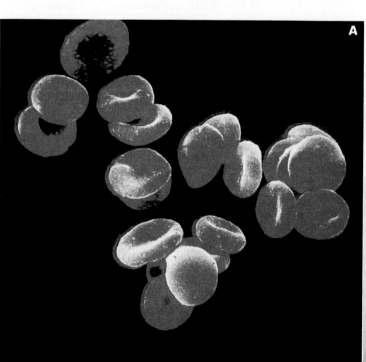

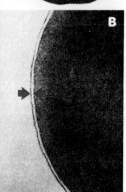

FIGURE 3-6 Red blood cells.
A The human red blood cell is a disk with a concave depression on both sides.
B This electron micrograph of a thin section of a red blood cell (×200,000) clearly shows the double-layered plasma membrane, which is indicated by *arrows.*

The microfilaments and intermediate filaments provide the protein network that lies beneath the plasma membrane to help support and shape the cell (Figure 3-8). This network of proteins extends into the cytoplasm and looks something like the web of proteins shown in Figure 3-9. Microtubules are also part of this "skeleton" of the cytoplasm. Together, these three types of protein fibers provide the cell with mechanical support and help anchor the organelles. They also help move substances from one part of the cell to another. The filaments forming the highway in the chapter opener photo are microtubules found within nerve cells.

The cytoskeleton is a network of filaments and fibers within the cytoplasm that helps maintain the shape of the cell, move substances within cells, and anchor various structures in place.

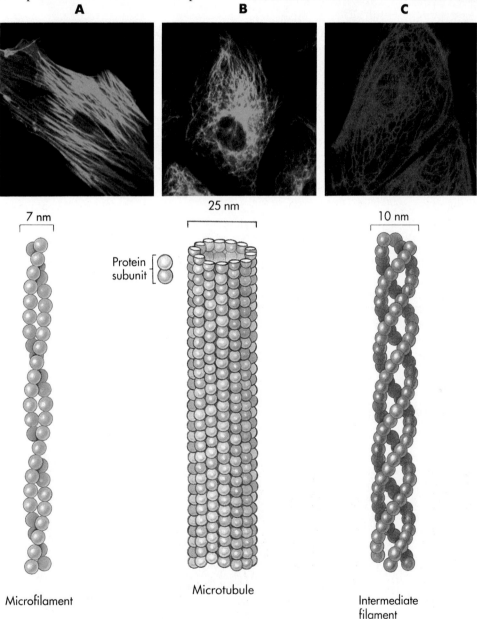

FIGURE 3-7 Molecules that make up the cytoskeleton.
A Microfilaments run parallel to the cell membrane in bundles.
B Microtubules are composed of a spiral array of protein subunits. The microtubules in the micrograph radiate from an area near the nucleus (the dark region in the center). Microtubules provide intracellular support in the nondividing cell.
C Intermediate filaments are probably made up of three subunits that are wound together in a coil, interrupted by uncoiled regions. In a skin cell, such as the one shown, intermediate filaments form thick, wavy bundles that probably provide structural support.

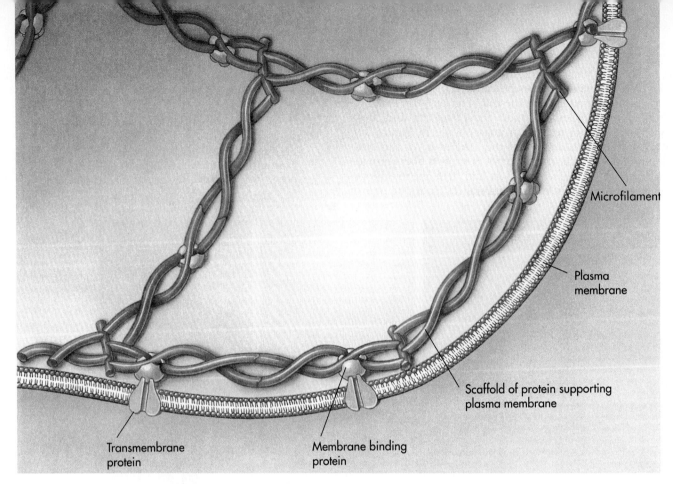

Microfilament

Plasma
membrane

Scaffold of protein supporting
plasma membrane

Transmembrane
protein

Membrane binding
protein

FIGURE 3-8   Membrane support.
Cell membranes are reinforced by a network of protein fibers. Here you can see a portion of the network, attached to the inside of the plasma membrane by proteins inserted into the lipid bilayer.

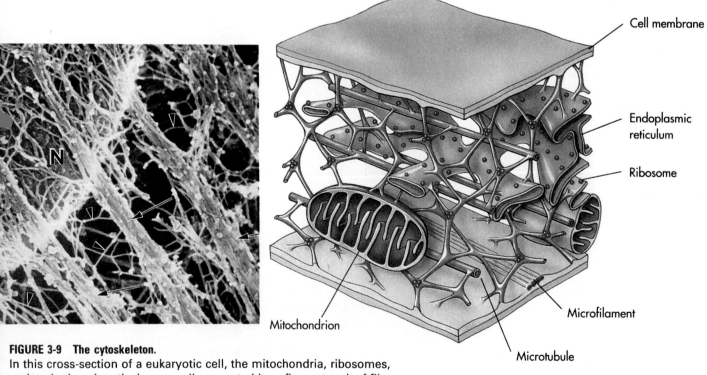

Cell membrane

Endoplasmic
reticulum

Ribosome

Microfilament

Microtubule

Mitochondrion

FIGURE 3-9   The cytoskeleton.
In this cross-section of a eukaryotic cell, the mitochondria, ribosomes, and endoplasmic reticulum are all supported by a fine network of filaments. Microtubules run through the filaments, linking various portions of the cell. In the micrograph, the *arrows* point to the intermediate filaments that anchor the nucleus (N) to the cytoplasm.

Membranous organelles

Enmeshed within the cytoskeletal fibers, the cell organelles constantly work, each contributing in a special way to the life and well-being of the cell. Most organelles of eukaryotic cells are bounded by membranes. Many different enzymes—molecules that help specific chemical reactions take place—are attached to these membranes. In this way, these subcellular structures form organized compartments within the cytoplasm and make the cell an efficiently running living machine.

The endoplasmic reticulum

The **endoplasmic reticulum,** or ER, is an extensive system of interconnected membranes that forms flattened channels and tube-like canals within the cytoplasm, almost like a cellular subway system. The channels are used to help move substances from one part of the cell to another. The name *endoplasmic reticulum* may sound very strange. It is, however, descriptive of its location and appearance. The word *endoplasmic* means "within the cytoplasm." The word *reticulum* comes from a Latin word meaning "a little net." And that is exactly what the ER looks like—a net within the cytoplasm.

There are two types of endoplasmic reticula in cells: **rough ER** and **smooth ER.** The *rough* refers to the minute, spherical structures called **ribosomes** covering the surface of one type of endoplasmic reticulum. With ribosomes dotting their surfaces, rough ER membranes look much like long sheets of sandpaper (Figure 3-10).

Ribosomes are the places where proteins are manufactured. Some ribosomes are attached to the rough ER, but others float in the cytoplasm bound to cytoskeletal fibers.

The cytoplasmic ribosomes help produce proteins for use in the cell, such as those making up the structure of the cytoskeletal fibers or certain organelles. The proteins made at the ribosomes of the rough ER are most often destined to leave the cell. Cells specialized for secreting proteins, such as the pancreatic cells that manufacture the hormone insulin, contain large amounts of rough ER. After the proteins are manufactured at the ribosomes on the surface of the ER, they enter the inner space of the ER. Within this channel the proteins may be changed by enzymes bound to the inner surface of the ER membrane. Carbohydrate molecules are often added to them.

When the proteins reach the end of their journey in the ER, they are encased in tiny membrane-bounded sacs called **vesicles.** These vesicles are formed by sections of smooth ER continuous with the rough ER. "Buds" of the smooth ER pinch off as the newly formed proteins reach them. These vesicles eventually fuse with the membranes of another organelle called the **Golgi body.**

Smooth ER has no ribosomes attached to its surfaces. Therefore it does not have the grainy appearance of rough ER and does not manufacture proteins. Instead, smooth ER has enzymes bound to its inner surfaces that help build carbohydrates and lipids. Cells specialized for the synthesis of these molecules, such as animal cells that produce male or female sex hormones, have abundant smooth ER.

> The endoplasmic reticulum (ER) is an extensive system of membranes that divides the interior of eukaryotic cells into compartments and channels. Rough ER makes and transports proteins destined to leave the cell. Smooth ER helps build carbohydrates and lipids.

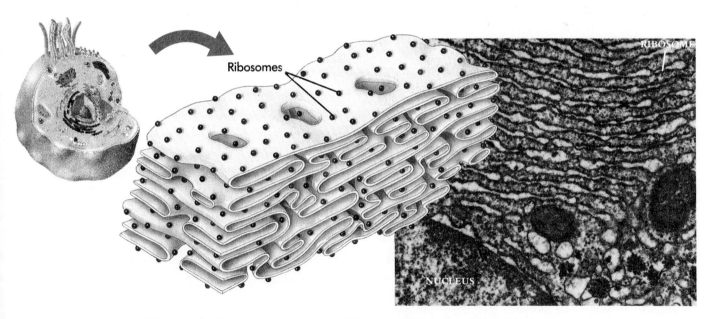

FIGURE 3-10 Rough endoplasmic reticulum (ER).
The electron micrograph is of a rat liver cell, rich in ribosomes attached to ER. As the drawing indicates more clearly, you can see that the ribosomes are associated with only one side of the rough ER. Proteins are synthesized at the ribosomes along the rough ER, secreted into the ER channel, and may be either transported to other parts of the cell or secreted outside the cell.

Golgi bodies

First described by the physician Camillo Golgi in the last half of the nineteenth century, Golgi bodies look like microscopic stacks of pancakes in the cytoplasm. Animal cells each contain 10 to 20 sets of these flattened membranes. Plant cells may contain several hundred because the Golgi bodies are involved in the synthesis and maintenance of plant cell walls (a structure animal cells do not have). Collectively, the Golgi bodies are referred to as the **Golgi complex.**

Molecules come to a Golgi body in vesicles pinched off from the ER. The membranes of the vesicles fuse with the membranes of a Golgi body. Once inside the space formed by the Golgi membranes, the molecules may be modified by the formation of new chemical bonds or by the addition of carbohydrates. For example, mucin, which is a protein with attached carbohydrates that forms a major part of the mucous secretions of the body, is put together in its final form in the Golgi complex. This refining of molecules occurs in stages in the Golgi complex, with different parts of the stack of membranes containing enzymes that do specific jobs. When molecular products are ready for transport, they are sorted and pinched off in separate vesicles (Figure 3-11). Each vesicle travels to its destination and fuses with another membrane. The vesicles containing those molecules that are to be secreted from the cell fuse with the plasma membrane. In this way the contents of the vesicle are liberated from the cell (Figure 3-12). Other vesicles fuse with the membranes of organelles such as lysosomes, delivering the new molecules to their interiors.

The Golgi complex is the delivery system of the eukaryotic cell. It collects, modifies, packages, and distributes molecules that are made at one location within the cell and used at another.

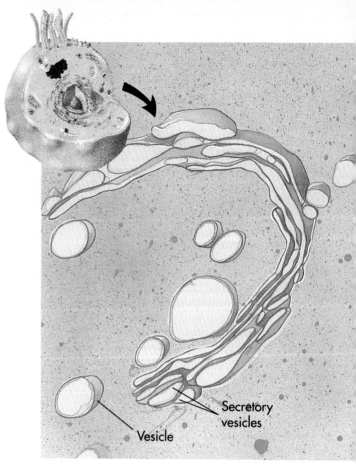

FIGURE 3-11   A Golgi complex.
The Golgi complex is a structure that collects, modifies, packages, and distributes molecules, particularly proteins made at the rough ER and lipids made at the smooth ER. These molecules accumulate in the Golgi vesicles, where they may be modified by chemicals into glycoproteins or glycolipids. When ready, the molecules are sorted and pinched off in separate secretory vesicles.

FIGURE 3-12   How a molecule is packaged for transport in a Golgi body.
Molecules, in this case proteins, are synthesized at the ribosomes attached to the ER. A protein can either move out into the cytoplasm for use by the cell, or it can be packaged for export by the Golgi body. The proteins destined for export move through the Golgi body, are modified by other chemicals, and are finally encased in secretory vesicles. These vesicles then fuse with the cell's plasma membrane, liberating the proteins from the cell.

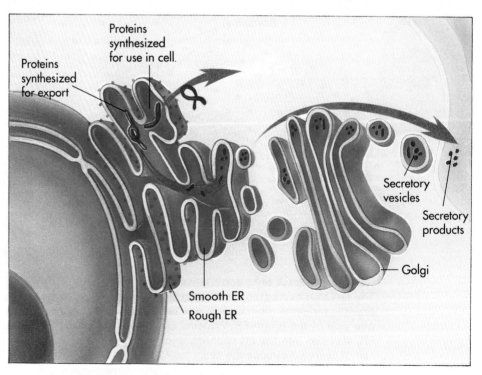

Lysosomes

The new molecules delivered to **lysosomes** are digestive enzymes—molecules that help break large molecules into smaller molecules. Lysosomes are, in fact, membrane-bounded bags of many different digestive enzymes (Figure 3-13). Several hundred of these organelles may be present in one cell alone.

Lysosomes and their digestive enzymes are extremely important to the health of a cell. They help cells function by aiding in cell renewal, constantly breaking down old cell parts as they are replaced with new cell parts. During development, lysosomes help remodel tissues, such as the reabsorption of the tadpole tail as the tadpole develops into a frog. In some cells, lysosomes also break down substances brought into the cell from the environment. For example, one job of certain white blood cells is to get rid of bacteria invading the body. The cytoplasm of these cells flows around their prey, engulfing them in a membrane-bounded sac called a **vacuole.** A lysosome then fuses with this vacuole, and digestion of the invader begins. In the past, lysosomes were thought to be active during the aging process, breaking open and destroying whole cells. Scientists now know this idea to be false, since lysosome enzymes work only in the acid environment of the lysosome and become inactive at the relatively neutral pH of the cytoplasm.

What happens to the digestion products of lysosomes? Substances such as parts of bacteria are packaged in a vesicle, transported to the plasma membrane, and exit the cell. Other molecules, such as the breakdown products of old cell parts, may simply be released into the cytoplasm. These cellular building blocks can be recycled—used once again to build new cell parts.

Lysosomes are vesicles that contain digestive enzymes. These enzymes break down old cell parts or materials brought into the cell from the environment.

Vacuoles

The word *vacuole* comes from a Latin word meaning "empty." However, these membrane-bounded storage sacs only look empty. Within them can be found such substances as water, food, and wastes. Their number, kind, and size vary in different kinds of cells.

Vacuoles are most often found in plant cells. These giant water-filled sacs play a major role in helping plant tissues stay rigid. In a mature plant cell the vacuole is often so large that it takes up most of the interior of the cell. Certain single-celled eukaryotes (protists) and some yeasts also contain vacuoles. Some fresh water protists contain contractile vacuoles. These organelles take up extra water that tends to flow into these organisms. Periodically, these vacuoles fuse with the plasma membrane and expel their contents, keeping the cell from swelling and bursting. Many protists have food vacuoles, places where food is stored and eventually digested by fusion with lysosomes.

The nucleus

The **nucleus,** or control center of the cell, is made up of an outer, double membrane that encloses the chromosomes and one or more nucleoli. In fact, the word *eukaryote* means "true nucleus" and refers to the fact that the nucleus is a closed compartment bounded by a membrane. Other than large fluid-filled vacuoles in plants, this compartment is the largest in eukaryotic cells.

The outer, double membrane of the nucleus is called the **nuclear envelope.** The inner of the two membranes actually forms the boundary of the nucleus, and the outer membrane is continuous with the endoplasmic reticulum. At various spots on its surface, the double membrane fuses to form openings called **nuclear pores.** Figure 3-14 shows the surface of the nuclear membrane of a cell that was frozen and then cracked during a special type of preparation for the electron microscope. The pores look like pockmarks on the surface of the membrane. These ring-like holes are lined with proteins and serve as passageways for molecules entering and leaving the nucleus.

Within the nucleus is the hereditary material deoxyribonucleic acid, or **DNA.** DNA determines whether your hair is blonde or brown or whether a plant flowers in pink or white. It controls all activities of the cell. To accomplish these amazing feats, DNA performs one job: it directs the synthesis of ribonucleic acid, or RNA, which in turn directs the synthesis of proteins. (The structure, interactions, and roles of both DNA and RNA are discussed further in Chapter 17.)

DNA is bound to proteins in the nucleus, forming a complex called *chromatin.* In a cell that is not dividing, the chromatin is strung out, looking like strands of microscopic

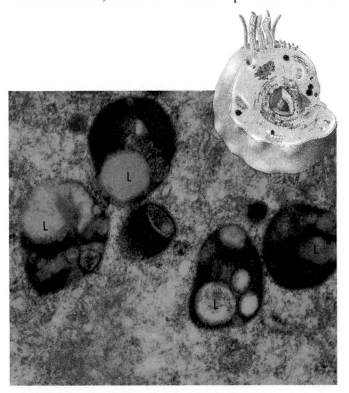

FIGURE 3-13 Lysosomes and their digestive enzymes.
Lysosomes *(L)* are membrane-bounded vesicles that contain powerful digestive enzymes. The enzymes are the blackened areas within the lysosomes in this electron micrograph.

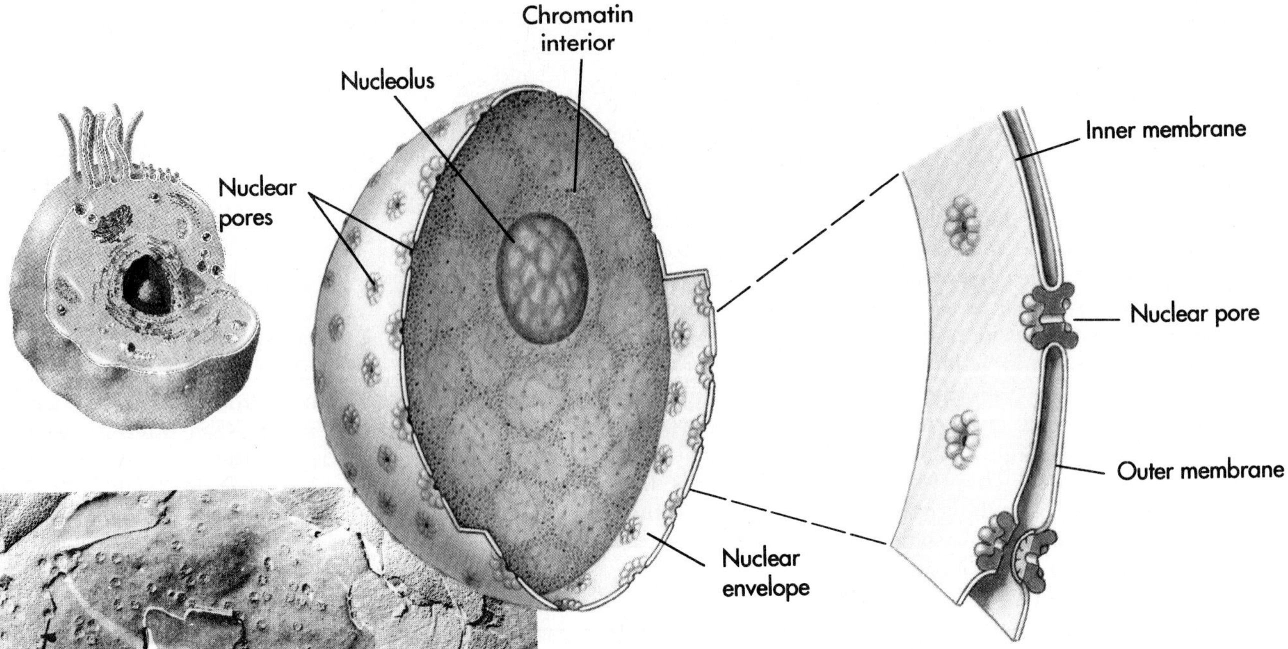

A

Nucleolus

Chromatin interior

Nuclear pores

Inner membrane

Nuclear pore

Outer membrane

Nuclear envelope

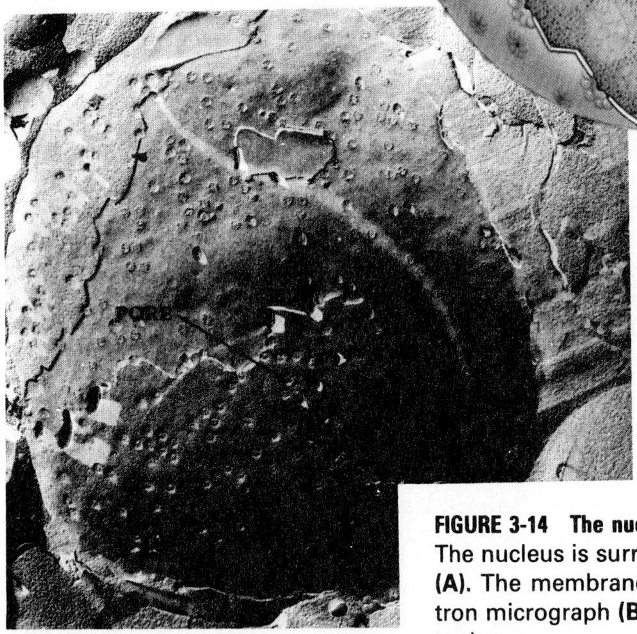

B

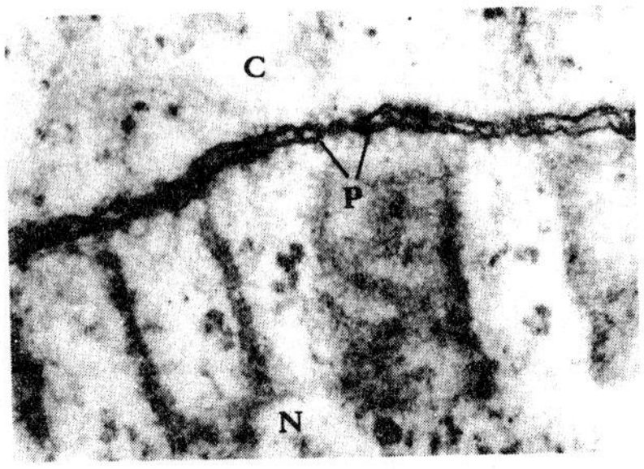

POREW

C

C

P

N

FIGURE 3-14   The nucleus.
The nucleus is surrounded by a double membrane called the nuclear envelope **(A)**. The membrane is covered with pores, visible as depressions in the electron micrograph **(B)**. These pores are visible in **C,** designated by *P. C* is the cytoplasm.

FIGURE 3-15   Eukaryotic chromosomes within an onion root-tip cell.
As a cell begins to divide (a process called *mitosis*), long strands of DNA and protein thicken, shorten, and condense into chromosomes *(arrow).*

pearls. But as a cell begins to divide, the DNA coils more tightly around the proteins, condensing to form shortened, thickened structures called **chromosomes** (Figure 3-15).

The **nucleolus** (plural nucleoli) is a darkly staining region within the nucleus (Figure 3-16). Most cells have two or more nucleoli. Making up the bulk of the nucleolar material is a special area of DNA that directs the synthesis of ribosomal ribonucleic acid, or **rRNA.** As rRNA is made at this DNA, it forms clumps of molecules that are structural components of ribosomes. Proteins, another component of ribosomes, can also be found in the nucleolus. They are brought into the nucleus from the cytoplasm. After the ribosomes are manufactured (or partly manufactured) in the nucleolus, they move through the pores in the nuclear membrane and pass into the cytoplasm.

⮛

The nucleus of a eukaryotic cell contains the hereditary material, or DNA. When the cell divides, the DNA condenses into compact structures called *chromosomes.*

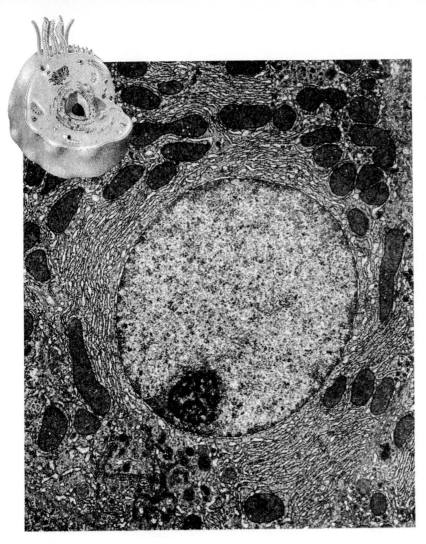

FIGURE 3-16 The nucleolus.
Appearing as a darkly stained region within the nucleus, the nucleolus is the site of ribosomal RNA synthesis and consists of ribosomal RNA plus some ribosomal proteins.

Bacteria-like organelles

The idea of the symbiotic origin of mitochondria and chloroplasts has had a controversial history, and a few biologists still do not accept it. The endosymbiotic hypothesis is, however, the most widely agreed-on model at this time.

Mitochondria

The **mitochondria** that occur in most eukaryotic cells are thought to have originated as symbiotic bacteria. According to this hypothesis the bacteria that became mitochondria were engulfed by eukaryotic cells early in their evolutionary history. Before they had acquired these bacteria, the host cells were unable to carry out chemical reactions necessary for living in an atmosphere that had increasing amounts of oxygen. The engulfed bacteria were able to carry out these reactions and are considered to be the precursors to mitochondria.

Mitochondria are oval, sausage-shaped, or thread-like organelles about the size of bacteria. They are bounded by a double membrane. The outer of the two membranes is smooth and defines the shape of the organelle. The inner membrane, however, has many folds called **cristae** that dip into the interior of the mitochondrion. These cristae resemble the folded membranes that occur in various groups of bacteria. Notice in Figure 3-17 that this arrangement of membranes forms two mitochondrial compartments.

The job of the mitochondria is to break down fuel molecules, releasing energy for cell work. The two most important fuels of cells are glucose and fatty acids. Some organisms, such as plants, make their fuel (glucose) using the raw materials of carbon dioxide, water, and sunlight. Other organisms, such as animals, eat food and digest it to produce glucose and fatty acids, which can then be transported to the cells. In both plants and animals, these fuels are broken down by cells, releasing energy by means of a series of oxygen-requiring reactions called **cellular respiration.** The energy released during these reactions is stored for later use in special molecules called ATP. (See Chapter 5 for a detailed description of cellular respiration and ATP.) Using chemical symbols, the reactions of cellular respiration can be summarized as follows:

$$C_6H_{12}O_6 \; + \; 6O_2 \; \rightarrow \; 6CO_2 \; + \; 6H_2O \; + \; \text{Energy}$$

Glucose   Oxygen   Carbon dioxide   Water

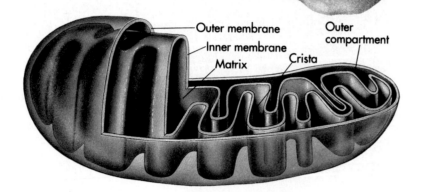

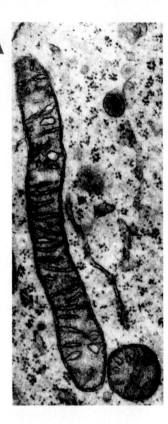

FIGURE 3-17   The mitochondrion.
Mitochondria have a smooth outer membrane and an extensively folded inner membrane. The drawing reveals the intricate structure of the cristae and the inner and outer compartments. The similarity of the electron micrograph to a rod-shaped bacterium is striking.

Outer membrane
Inner membrane
Matrix
Crista
Outer compartment

Cellular respiration begins in the cytoplasm, but most of the energy from the breakdown of glucose and fatty acids is generated in the mitochondria. The enzymes that are used in this breakdown are bound to the membranes of the mitochondrion. Within this closed compartment, the complex series of reactions needed to break apart glucose and to capture the liberated energy and store it are accomplished in an orderly and efficient way separated from the rest of the cell.

 The mitochondria apparently originated as endosymbiotic bacteria. In a complex series of reactions using oxygen, cell fuel is broken down to release the energy within mitochondria.

Chloroplasts

Symbiotic events similar to those postulated for the origin of mitochondria also seem to have been involved in the origin of **chloroplasts.** They are thought to be derived from symbiotic photosynthetic bacteria. *These energy-producing organelles are found in the cells of plants and algae.* In these organelles the energy in sunlight is used to power the reactions that make the cellular fuel—glucose—by using molecules of carbon dioxide from the air. Together, the complex series of chemical reactions that perform these tasks is known as **photosynthesis.** Using chemical symbols, this series of reactions can be summarized as follows:

$$6CO_2 + 6H_2O + \text{Sun's energy} \rightarrow C_6H_{12}O_6 + 6O_2$$
Carbon   Water   Glucose Oxygen
dioxide

The glucose can then be broken down in the mitochondria to release its energy to ATP for immediate use or short-term storage, or the glucose can be stored as complex carbohydrates for later use.

Chloroplasts have a structure similar to the mitochondria. Like mitochondria, chloroplasts are bounded by a double membrane. In addition, the inner of these membranes forms folds, invading the interior of the organelle. In chloroplasts, however, these membranes are extensive and form sacs called **thylakoids.** These sacs, stacked one on another, are called **grana** (Figure 3-18). Chlorophyll, a chemical that can absorb light energy from the sun and that allows photosynthesis to take place, is found within the grana. As with the mitochondria, chloroplasts provide an orderly, closed compartment within the cell in which a series of reactions can occur.

Chloroplasts, which are located within the cells of plants and algae, apparently originated as endosymbiotic photosynthetic bacteria. Within chloroplasts, carbon dioxide, water, and light energy are used to produce the cell fuel glucose during a series of reactions called *photosynthesis.*

Cilia and flagella

Single-celled eukaryotic cells are often motile—able to move within their environments. One way in which these cells move is by means of cell extensions that look somewhat like hairs. These structures, called **cilia,** are short and often cover a cell. In human cells, cilia are found only on

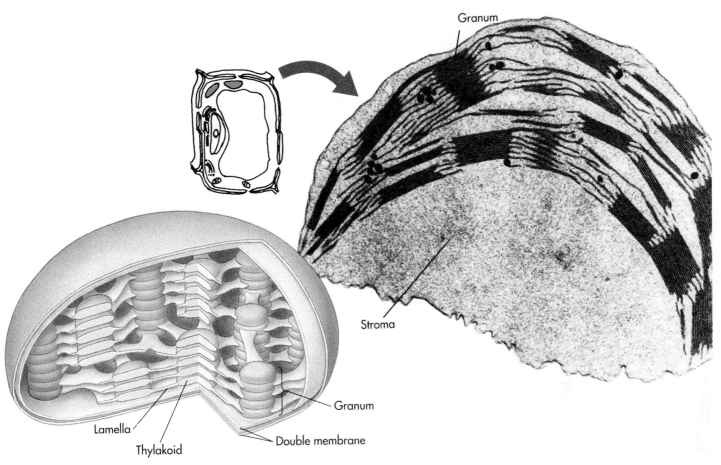

FIGURE 3-18   The chloroplast.
Chloroplasts have a double outer membrane and a system of interior membranes that form sacs called *thylakoids.* A stack of thylakoids is called a *granum.* Chlorophyll and the other light-gathering pigments for photosynthesis are embedded in the numerous grana.

sections of certain cells and are used to move substances across their surfaces. Figure 3-19 shows the cilia that line the trachea, or windpipe. They help sweep invading particles and organisms up the trachea and away from the lungs. Some cells have whip-like extensions called **flagella.** Used strictly for movement, these structures are longer than cilia, but fewer are usually present on a cell. Sperm are the only human cells that have flagella. Normal human sperm have a single flagellum, as you can see in Figure 3-1,*D.*

Although cilia and flagella differ in length, they have the same structure: they are bundles of microtubules covered with the plasma membrane of the cell. As you can see in Figure 3-20, nine pairs of microtubules surround a single, central pair. As these microtubules dip into the cell beneath the level of the plasma membrane, they connect with another structure called the *basal body.* Also composed of microtubules, a basal body serves to anchor a cilium or flagellum to the cell.

Cilia and flagella are whip-like organelles of motility that protrude from some cells.

FIGURE 3-19   Cilia lining the trachea, or windpipe.
These cilia, coated with mucus, help move particles and bacteria away from the lungs and upward to the oral cavity.

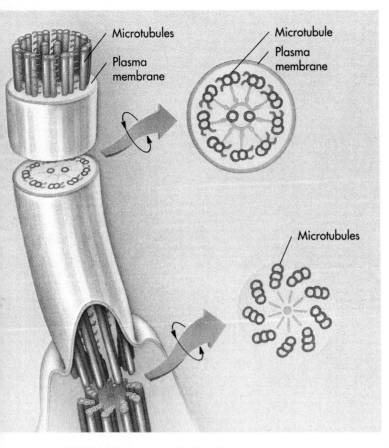

Cell walls

Many plants, algae, and fungi have a rigid structure called a **cell wall** that surrounds the plasma membrane. (Human cells do not have cell walls.) Almost all plant cell walls are made up of cellulose, large molecules formed by the linking of glucose units. Many single-celled eukaryotes have a similar type of cell wall. However, other single-celled eukaryotes, such as *Paramecium* and *Euglena* species, have an outer structure called a *pellicle* that is made up of protein. Fungi have cell walls that contain chitin, the same substance that is found in the shells of organisms such as grasshoppers and lobsters.

Cell walls perform many jobs for cells. In plants and fungi, they help impart a stiffness to the tissues. They also provide some protection from a drying environment. In single-celled organisms, cell walls give shape to the organisms and help protect them. Pellicles are even more specialized in their function, often serving as anchors for defense mechanisms.

Summing up: How bacterial, animal, and plant cells differ

Table 3-2 summarizes the differences among bacterial, animal (including human), and plant cells. As the table shows, prokaryotes (bacterial cells) and eukaryotes (plant and animal cells) differ greatly in structure and complexity. The most distinctive difference between these two cell types is the extensive subdivision of the interior of eukaryotic cells by membranes. (Prokaryotic cells are described in more detail in Chapter 23.) The rest of this chapter will explain how the substances cells use move across their plasma membranes.

FIGURE 3-20 Structure of a flagellum.
A eukaryotic flagellum is composed of a ring of nine pairs of microtubules, with two microtubules in its core. Anchoring the flagellum to the cell is a basal body of nine microtubule triplets. Cilia have the same pattern of microtubules.

TABLE 3-2	A comparison of bacterial, animal, and plant cells		
	BACTERIUM	**ANIMAL**	**PLANT**
▼ **EXTERIOR STRUCTURE**			
Cell wall	Present (protein-polysaccharide)	Absent	Present (cellulose)
Cell membrane	Present	Present	Present
Flagella	Sometime present (one strand)	Sometimes present	Absent except in sperm of a few species
▼ **INTERIOR STRUCTURE**			
ER	Absent	Usually present	Usually present
Microtubules	Absent	Present	Present
Centrioles	Absent	Present	Absent
Golgi bodies	Absent	Present	Present
▼ **ORGANELLES**			
Nucleus	Absent	Present	Present
Mitochondria	Absent	Present	Present
Chloroplasts	Absent	Absent	Present
Chromosomes	A single circle of naked DNA	Multiple units, DNA associated with protein	Multiple units, DNA associated with protein
Ribosomes	Present	Present	Present
Lysosomes	Absent	Usually present	Present
Vacuoles	Absent	Absent or small	Usually a large single vacuole in mature cell

How substances move into and out of cells

Cells usually live in an environment where they are bathed in water. When you consider that bacteria live on your body, or that protists live in the soil, this fact may not seem to be true. However, all cells must move substances across their membranes to survive, and water is the liquid in which their molecules are dissolved. In addition, water provides a fluid environment within which molecules can move. Therefore water must surround cells, even in microscopic amounts that may not be readily apparent.

How do molecules get where they are going? To answer this question, you must first understand that molecules cannot move *purposefully* from one spot to another. Molecules move randomly. All molecules and small particles have a constant, inherent "jiggling" motion called *Brownian movement*. And because molecules are always jiggling, they tend to bump into things, such as other molecules. A bump may push a molecule in a particular direction until it bumps into another molecule and gets pushed again. This random motion in all directions often results in a net movement of molecules in a particular direction in response to differences in concentration, pressure, or electrical charge. These differences are referred to as a **gradient.** The term *net movement* means that although individual members of a group of molecules are moving in different directions, the resulting movement of the group is in one direction. This movement results in a uniform distribution of molecules.

Movement that does not require energy

The net movement of molecules often requires no input of energy. In this type of movement, molecules move from regions of high concentration to low concentration or from regions of high pressure to regions of low pressure. Ions, because they each carry an electrical charge, move toward unlike charges or away from like charges.

As molecules or ions move from regions of high concentration to regions of low concentration, they are referred to as going *down* a concentration, pressure, or electrical gradient. Some molecules move into and out of cells as they move down gradients. Molecular movement down a gradient but across a cell membrane is called **passive transport.** There are three types of passive transport: diffusion, osmosis, and facilitated diffusion.

Diffusion

Everyone has had experience with molecules in the air moving down a concentration gradient. Did you ever wake up to the smell of fresh brewed coffee? Did you ever spill a bottle of a liquid that had a strong odor, such as ammonia or perfume? The molecules that reached the smell receptors in your nose moved from an area of high concentration (the spill) to an area of low concentration (your nose). They moved down the concentration gradient, eventually becoming evenly spread.

You can perform a simple experiment to demonstrate diffusion. Take a small jar, fill it with ink to the brim, and cap it. Place the jar at the bottom of a full bucket of water, and gently remove the cap. The ink molecules will slowly diffuse out of the jar until there is a uniform concentration of ink in the bucket and in the jar. This process is illustrated in Figure 3-21 with a lump of sugar.

> Diffusion is the net movement of molecules from a region of higher concentration to a region of lower concentration, eventually resulting in a uniform distribution of the molecules. This movement is the result of random, spontaneous molecular motions.

Osmosis

Osmosis is a special form of diffusion in which water molecules move from an area of higher concentration to an area of lower concentration across a differentially permeable membrane. A **differentially permeable membrane** allows only certain types of molecules to pass through it, or permeate it, freely. Cell (plasma) membranes are differentially permeable membranes (and are also called *semipermeable* or *selectively permeable membranes*). In fact, most types of molecules that occur in cells cannot pass freely across the plasma membrane. Small organic molecules such as sugars and amino acids, for example, can dissolve in water but not in lipids, so they are unable to move among the lipid molecules of the bilayer to traverse it. Water molecules, however, are small molecules that are able to pass through slight

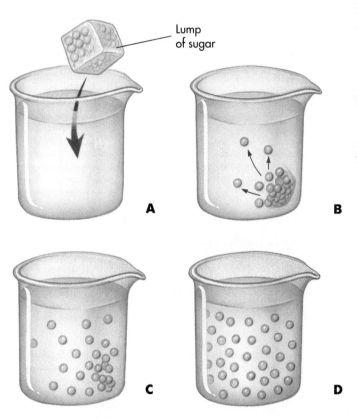

FIGURE 3-21 Diffusion.
If a lump of sugar is dropped into a beaker of water **(A)** its molecules dissolve and diffuse **(B and C)**. Eventually, diffusion results in an even distribution of sugar molecules throughout the water **(D).**

imperfections in the lipid bilayer and diffuse across the membrane.

The cytoplasm of a cell consists of many different types of molecules and ions dissolved in water. The mixture of these molecules and water is called a **solution.** Water, the most common of the molecules in the mixture, is called the **solvent.** The other kinds of molecules dissolved in the water are called **solutes.**

Because of diffusion, both solvent and solute molecules in a cell move from regions where the concentration of each is greater to regions where the concentration of each is less. When two regions are separated by a membrane, however, what happens depends on whether the molecule can pass freely through that membrane.

Osmosis is the diffusion of water molecules across a differentially permeable membrane.

The cytoplasm of living cells contains approximately 1% dissolved solutes. If a cell is immersed in pure water, interesting things begin to happen. Because the water has a lower concentration of solutes than the cell, water molecules begin to move into the cell. The reason is simple: water moves down the concentration gradient, or from a region of higher concentration of water molecules to a region of lower concentration of water molecules. The pure water is said to be **hypotonic** (Greek *hypo,* "under") with respect to the cytoplasm of the cell because its concentration of solutes is less than the concentration of solutes in the cell.

As you can see in Figure 3-22, a cell in a hypotonic solution begins to blow up like a balloon. Likewise, if a cell is placed in a **hypertonic** (Greek *hyper,* "over") solution, one with a solute concentration higher than the cytoplasm of the cell, water will move out of the cell, and the cell will shrivel. If a cell is placed in a solution with the same concentration of solutes as its cytoplasm, an **isotonic** (Greek *isos,* "equal") solution, water will move into and out of the cell, but no net movement will take place.

A solution with a solute concentration lower than that of another fluid is said to be *hypotonic* to that solution. A solution with a solute concentration higher than that of another fluid is said to be *hypertonic* to that solution. Solutions having equal solute concentrations are *isotonic* to one another.

Intuitively you may think that as "new" water molecules diffuse into a cell placed in a hypotonic solution, the pressure of the cytoplasm pushing against the cell membrane builds. This is indeed what happens. At the same time, however, the water molecules that continue to diffuse into the cell also exert a pressure—**osmotic pressure.** Because the pressure of the cytoplasm within the cell opposes osmotic pressure in this case, diffusion of water molecules into the cell will not continue indefinitely. The cell will eventually reach an equilibrium—a point at which the osmotic force driving water inward is counterbalanced exactly by the pressure outward of the cytoplasm. However, the pressure within the cell may become so great that the cell bursts like an overinflated balloon. The cell is said to **lyse.**

Red blood cells in hypotonic solution

Red blood cells in hypertonic solution

Red blood cells in isotonic solution

FIGURE 3-22 Osmosis in a red blood cell.
When the outer solution is hypotonic with respect to the cell, water moves into the cell and causes the cell to eventually burst, or lyse. When the outer solution is hypertonic, water moves out of the cell, and the cell shrinks. Arrows show the direction of net movement of the water.

Water moves into cells placed in hypotonic solutions and out of cells placed in hypertonic solutions.

Single-celled and multicellular organisms have various mechanisms that work to keep their cells from swelling and bursting or shriveling like prunes. Single-celled organisms that live in fresh water, for example, battle a constant influx of water. Some of these organisms have one or more organelles that collect water from the cell's interior and transport it to the cell surface. Plant cells have cell walls that support their membranes, so plant cell membranes press outward against cell walls in hypotonic solutions and pull in away from cell walls in hypertonic solutions.

Many multicellular animals, such as humans, circulate a fluid through their bodies that bathes cells in isotonic liquid. By controlling the composition of its circulating body fluids, a multicellular organism can control the solute concentration of the fluid bathing its cells, adjusting it to match that of the cells' interiors. The blood in your body, for example, contains a high concentration of a protein called *albumin*, which serves to elevate the solute concentration of the blood to match that of your tissues so that the movement of water molecules is regulated.

Facilitated diffusion

One of the most important properties of any cell is its ability to move substances necessary for survival into its interior and to get rid of unnecessary or harmful substances. Your cells, for example, move glucose into the cytoplasm from the bloodstream to be used for fuel. Without the ability to move glucose into your cells, you would die.

Cells can perform these feats because they have differentially permeable membranes. The cell membrane can select which molecules are to enter and leave and in which concentrations because most molecules must enter or leave the cell through protein doors, or channels. These doors are not open to every molecule that presents itself; only a particular molecule can pass through a given kind of door. Some of the channels in the cell membrane help certain molecules and ions enter or leave the cell and speed their movement by providing them with a passageway. These passageways are most likely transport proteins that extend from one side of the membrane to the other. After the transport protein binds with a solute molecule, its shape changes, and the molecule moves across the membrane. This type of transport process, in which molecules move down the concentration gradient without an input of energy by the cell, is called **facilitated diffusion** (Figure 3-23). Facilitated diffusion helps rid the cell of certain molecules present in high concentrations and moves molecules into the cell that are present on the outside in high concentrations.

Facilitated diffusion is the movement of selected molecules across the cell membrane by specific transport proteins along the concentration gradient and without an expenditure of energy.

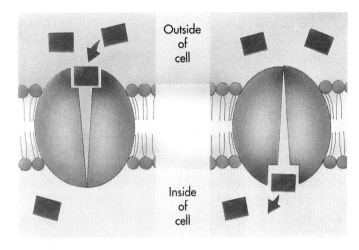

FIGURE 3-23   Facilitated diffusion.
Facilitated diffusion moves molecules across the cell membrane by means of protein channels *(purple oval shapes)*. It is a passive process because the molecules move in the direction of lower concentration.

Facilitated diffusion has two essential characteristics: (1) it is *specific*, with only certain molecules being able to traverse a given channel, and (2) it is *passive*, the direction of net movement being determined by the relative concentrations of the transported molecule inside and outside the membrane.

Movement that does require energy

Cells often move substances into or out of the cell *against* the gradients of concentration, pressure, and electrical charge. A cell uses energy to move molecules against a gradient much like you might use energy to move something against gravity. For example, if you are driving downhill, you can put your car into neutral and coast (although that is not the safest way to drive downhill). The car will continue to move without a push from the engine. As soon as you come to a hill, however, you must put the car in gear and press on the accelerator or the car will soon come to a stop. Cells, too, need to use energy to move molecules "uphill," or against a gradient. Cells also need to expend energy to move large molecules or particles into the cell that cannot move across the cell membrane.

Active transport

There are many molecules that a cell takes up or eliminates against a concentration gradient. Some, such as sugars and amino acids, are molecules the cell needs to use for energy or to build new cell parts. Others are ions such as sodium and potassium that play a critical role in such functions as the conduction of nerve impulses. These many kinds of molecules enter and leave cells by way of a variety of selectively permeable transport channels. In all these cases, a cell must expend energy to transport these molecules against the concentration gradient and maintain the concentration difference. This type of transport is called **active transport.** Active transport is one of the most important functions of

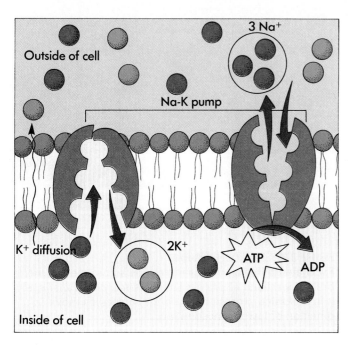

 K+

Na+

FIGURE 3-24 The sodium-potassium pump.
The pump is represented by the *purple shapes,* which show the two states of one protein. The molecules move in the direction of higher concentration.

Endocytosis

Certain types of cells transport particles, small organisms, or large molecules such as proteins into their cells. In humans, for example, white blood cells police the body fluids and ingest substances as large as invading bacteria. In nature, some single-celled organisms often eat other single-celled organisms whole. How can cells move such large substances into their interiors?

Cells such as these ingest particles or molecules that are too large to move across the membrane by a process called **endocytosis,** which literally means "into the cell." Even if the substance is not being transported against a concentration gradient, the cell must use energy for this process to occur. During endocytosis a cell envelops the particle with finger-like extensions of the membrane-covered cytoplasm (Figure 3-25). The edges of the membrane eventually meet on the other side of the particle. Because of the fluid nature of the lipid bilayer, the membranes fuse together, forming a vesicle around the particle.

> **Endocytosis is a process in which cells engulf large molecules or particles and bring these substances into the cell packaged within vesicles.**

If the material that is brought into the cell contains an organism (Figure 3-25, *A* and *C*) or some other fragment of organic matter, the endocytosis is called **phagocytosis** (Greek *phagein,* "to eat," and *cytos,* "cell"). If the material brought into the cell is liquid—contains dissolved molecules as in Figure 3-25, *B*—the endocytosis is referred to as **pinocytosis** (Greek *pinein,* "to drink"). Pinocytosis is common among the cells of multicellular animals. Human egg cells, for example, are "nursed" by surrounding cells that secrete nutrients that the maturing egg cell takes up by pinocytosis.

Virtually all animal cells are constantly carrying out endocytosis, trapping extracellular fluid in vesicles and ingesting it. Within the cell, these vesicles fuse with lysosomes, tiny cellular bags of digestive enzymes, to break down these large particles into molecules usable to the cell. Rates of endocytosis vary from one cell type to another but can be surprisingly large. Some types of white blood cells, for example, ingest 25% of their cell volume each hour!

any cell. Without it, the cells of your body would be unable to maintain the proper concentrations of substances that they need for survival.

> **Active transport is the movement of a solute across a membrane against the concentration gradient with the expenditure of chemical energy. This process requires the use of a transport protein specific to the molecule(s) being transported.**

More than one third of all the energy expended by a cell that is not dividing is used to actively transport sodium (Na^+) and potassium (K^+) ions. The type of channel by which *both* ions are transported across the cell membrane *in opposite directions* is a **coupled channel,** which has binding sites for both molecules on one membrane transport protein. This remarkable coupled channel is called the **sodium-potassium pump,** and it uses energy to move these ions across the cell membrane. Sodium ions are moved out of the cell to maintain a low internal concentration relative to the concentration outside of the cell. Conversely, potassium ions are moved into the cell to maintain a high internal concentration relative to the concentration outside the cell (Figure 3-24). (Three sodium ions are moved out for every two potassium ions that are moved in by the channel.) This transport mechanism is important in most cells of the human body but is particularly important for the proper functioning of muscle and nerve cells.

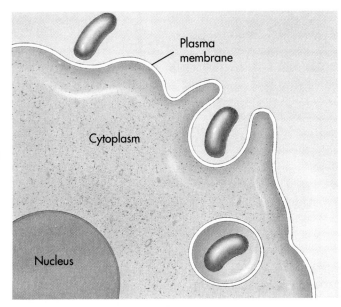

Phagocytosis

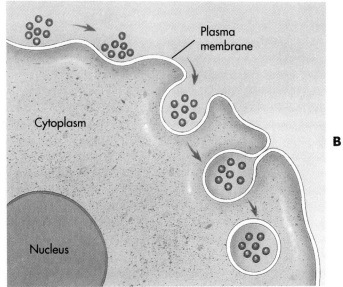

Pinocytosis

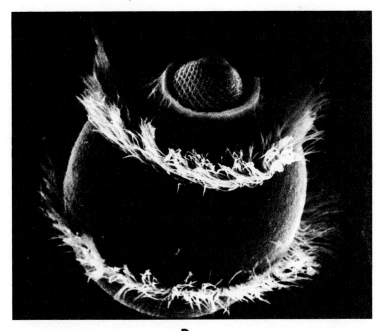

FIGURE 3-25 A cell ingests particles or organisms by endocytosis.
A Phagocytosis is the ingestion of an organism or particulate matter.
B Pinocytosis is the ingestion of dissolved materials (liquids).
C This large protist *(Didinium nasutum)* has begun to phagocytize a smaller protist (*Paramecium* species).
D The paramecium is almost completely ingested.

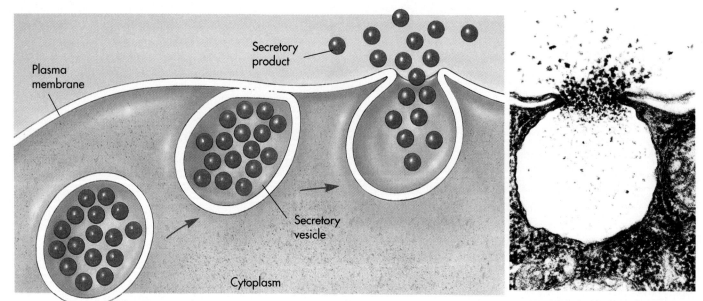

FIGURE 3-26 Exocytosis.
Proteins and other molecules are secreted from cells in small pockets called *vesicles,* whose membranes fuse with the cell membrane. When this fusion occurs, the contents of the vesicles are released to the cell surface.

Exocytosis

The reverse of endocytosis is **exocytosis.** As with endocytosis, a cell must expend energy for exocytosis to occur. During exocytosis, a cell discharges material by packaging it in a vesicle and moving the vesicle to the cell surface. The membrane of the vesicle fuses with the cell membrane, and the contents are expelled (Figure 3-26). In plants, exocytosis is the main way that cells move the materials from the Golgi body and out of the cytoplasm to construct the cell wall. In animals, many cells are specialized for secretion using the mechanism of exocytosis, such as cells that produce and secrete digestive enzymes or hormones.

Summary

1. A cell is a membrane-bounded unit containing hereditary material and cytoplasm. It can release energy from fuel and use that energy to grow and reproduce.

2. The cell theory was first formulated in the mid-1800s. It states that all living things are made up of cells, the smallest unit of life. In addition, all cells arise from the growth and division of other cells.

3. Most cells divide before they grow too large, maintaining a large surface area-to-volume ratio. In this way, cells are able to move substances across their cell membranes quickly enough to meet their needs.

4. All cells can be classified as either prokaryotic or eukaryotic. Prokaryotic cells are the bacteria and have a relatively simple structure. Eukaryotic cells are more complex than prokaryotes and evolved from ancestors of today's prokaryotes. Eukaryotic cells make up the bodies of plants, animals, protists, and fungi.

5. Eukaryotic cells represent a highly diverse group. However, all eukaryotic cells are bounded by a plasma membrane and contain membrane-bounded organelles. The cytoplasm of eukaryotic cells also contains a network of filaments and fibers that provide support and help shape cells having no outer, rigid wall. Ribosomes, which are small, spherical organelles located in the cytoplasm, are the sites of protein synthesis.

6. Cilia and flagella are composed of microtubules and help propel cells. In some eukaryotic cells, cilia are used to move substances across surfaces.

7. Lipid bilayers allow only certain molecules to pass across them. Membrane proteins facilitate the movement of many types of molecules into and out of the cell.

8. Molecules move randomly with a constant jiggling motion. However, molecules and ions undergo net movement in response to differences, or gradients, in concentration, pressure, and electrical charge, resulting in an equal distribution of these molecules and ions. Movement down a gradient requires no added energy to take place.

9. Molecular movement down a gradient but across a cell membrane is called *passive transport.* Three types of passive transport are diffusion, osmosis, and facilitated diffusion.

10. When cells move substances against a gradient, energy is required. This movement is called *active transport.*

11. The transport of particles or molecules into the cell that are too large to move across the membrane takes place by a process called *endocytosis.* The reverse of endocytosis is exocytosis. These processes require energy to take place.

1. Humans are multicellular organisms. Explain what this means and discuss some of the tasks performed by the cells of your body.

2. Some of the skeletal muscle cells that allow you to move your legs can be as long as 30 to 40 centimeters. These cells have many nuclei. Explain why.

3. Trace the path by which a nutrient outside a cell passes into the interior of a cell. Which parts of the plasma membrane act as channels or receptors?

4. A human liver cell has produced a protein product to be used outside of the cell. Using what you know about the endoplasmic reticulum and Golgi complex, trace the path of protein from production to removal from the cell. What was the role of the smooth ER in this process?

5. Cigarette smoking reduces the effectiveness of cilia lining the respiratory tract in humans. What is the role of these cilia and what would you hypothesize might be a result of smoking for many years?

6. What would happen inside your cells if the lysosomes stopped working?

7. Make a table that briefly describes each of the following and lists its function(s): plasma membrane, flagella (cilia), cytoskeleton, endoplasmic reticulum, ribosomes, nucleus, chromosomes, nucleolus, Golgi complex, lysosomes, mitochondria, and chloroplasts.

8. You're examining three cells. You know that one is a bacterium, one is from a plant, and the third is from an animal. From their structures, how can you tell which is which?

9. Many scientists theorize that chloroplasts and mitochondria evolved from ancient bacteria living within the cells of host organisms. Does this mean that the mitochondria in your cells are endosymbionts?

10. Identify the type(s) of molecular movement involved in each of the following. Which are active and which are passive?
   a. Glucose molecules leave your bloodstream (where they are usually in higher concentrations) and enter your cells by attaching to specialized carrier proteins.
   b. You lounge in a bathtub full of warm tap water until your skin looks swollen and "puckered."
   c. You dissolve a spoonful of instant coffee crystals in a mug of hot water.
   d. Your cells "import" amino acids by transporting them against the concentration gradient.

11. In question 10c, identify the solute, solvent, and solution.

12. When a patient is suffering from dehydration, the physician may recommend that an isotonic saline solution be added to the patient's bloodstream. Explain why it is essential that the infusion be isotonic and not hypertonic or hypotonic as compared to the blood.

13. What characteristics do diffusion and facilitated diffusion have in common? In what ways do they differ?

14. Though Americans tend to eat too much table salt (NaCl), sodium and potassium are essential elements necessary for the body's normal function. What role do these elements play in cell function?

15. Draw a diagram of a cell engaging in endocytosis. Give an example of this process in the human body.

1. The DNA in our cells determines the function and structure of every cell in the body. What might the advantage be in nature to have so much hereditary material repeated in every cell?

2. Before the nineteenth century, most people assumed that living things could arise from nonliving material. This theory, called "spontaneous generation," was proven false by the improvement of scientific equipment and development of the cell theory. How might these changes have altered the study of science and understanding of life on earth?

3. A typical person drinks liquids in rather large volumes a few times each 24 hours, rather than sipping continuously all through the day and night. How does the blood stay isotonic at all times if it is diluted by water so irregularly?

De Duve, C. (1986). *A guided tour of the living cell*. Vols. 1 and 2. New York: Scientific American Books.
This review has excellent illustrations and presents a wide variety of the techniques used to study cells.

Kiester, E. (1991, February). A bug in the system. *Discover*, pp. 70-76.
Recent studies of human mitochondria reveal that genetic abnormalities in these organelles may cause some human diseases. A fascinating twist on the endosymbiont origin of mitochondria.

McDermott, J. (1989, August). A biologist whose heresy redraws Earth's tree of life. *Smithsonian*, pp. 71-81.
This is an engaging account of the scientific approach taken by Lynn Margulis, leading contemporary advocate of the endosymbiotic theory of the origin of some organelles.

Murray, M. (1991, March). Life on the move. *Discover*, pp. 72-75.
An interesting survey of the microfilaments and microfibers of human cells and their role in cell movement.

Symmons, M., Prescott, A., & Warn, R. (1989, February). The shifting scaffolds of the cell. *New Scientist*, pp. 44-47.
New findings show that the microtubules of which cells are built are constantly appearing and disappearing.

4 The Flow of Energy Within Organisms

Did you know that your body takes constant "rollercoaster rides" that you can't even feel? At the beginning of a rollercoaster ride, the cars are pulled up a high hill by a cable. For the cable to pull the cars, it must be run by an engine that supplies energy for the cable to do its work. Energy is, in fact, the ability to do work. In the case of the rollercoaster, energy is needed to pull the cars up the hill, otherwise they would go nowhere. After the cars reach the top and are freed of the cable, they swoop down the hill, releasing this input of energy and coasting around the rails at breakneck speed.

All the chemical reactions within your body—your metabolism—take place in a similar way. Chemical reactions are changes in molecules in which one substance is changed into another. However, for chemical reactions to take place, they need an input of energy to get started. This input of energy helps molecules "climb" an energy "hill" and interact with one another.

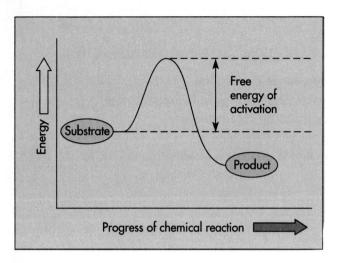

FIGURE 4-1 A chemical reaction.
Before a chemical reaction occurs, energy must be supplied to the substrates to destabilize existing chemical bonds. This energy is called the *free energy of activation.*

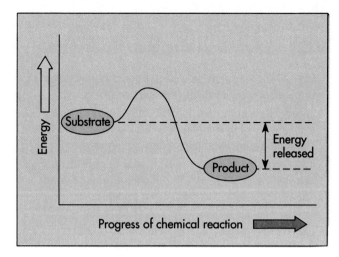

FIGURE 4-2 An exergonic reaction.
In an exergonic reaction the products contain less energy than the reactants. The excess energy is released.

Starting chemical reactions

Figure 4-1 is a graph of the varying energy states of the molecules in a chemical reaction. Doesn't this graph look like the beginning hill of a rollercoaster? The **substrates** are the molecules entering into the chemical reaction—the rollercoaster cars. The energy needed to pull the substrates up the energy hill is called the **free energy of activation**. This energy input destabilizes the bonds of the substrates. Molecules with unstable bonds interact with one another more easily than molecules with stable bonds do. In this way, the free energy of activation allows the chemical reaction to "go." The substrates undergo a chemical change resulting in new bonding arrangements between the molecules. This chemical change may involve the breaking of bonds and the making of new bonds. The changed substrates are called **products**.

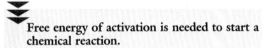

Free energy of activation is needed to start a chemical reaction.

Sometimes substrates are chemically broken down to yield products. When a substrate is broken down, energy is released from the chemical bonds that were holding it together. This type of reaction is called **exergonic**, meaning "energy out." In an exergonic reaction the products contain less energy than the substrate. The excess energy is released (Figure 4-2). Exergonic reactions happen *spontaneously;* that is, they absorb free energy from their surroundings and occur with no additional input of energy from another chemical reaction.

You may have seen an example of an exergonic reaction if you have ever used baking soda and water to remove the light-blue substance that can build up on the terminals of a car's battery. This substance is formed when battery acid seeps from inside the battery and reacts with the lead on the battery terminals. As you pour a baking soda solu-

tion onto the battery, it fizzes and bubbles and the material that has built up disappears. What happened? The baking soda and acid reacted to form two new substances: carbon dioxide gas and water. In addition, energy was released as heat (Figure 4-3). Exergonic reactions take place in your body, too. In fact, a series of exergonic reactions break down the glucose in your cells to supply your body with energy. The heat released from these reactions helps keep your body warm. Reactions such as this, which release energy by breaking down complex molecules into simpler molecules, are called **catabolic reactions.**

In some chemical reactions, substrates are chemically joined to yield a product. When substrates are joined, energy is used to build the chemical bonds holding the product together. This type of reaction is called **endergonic**, meaning "energy in." In an endergonic reaction, the product contains more energy than the substrates (Figure 4-4). Endergonic reactions *do not occur spontaneously;* that is, they require more free energy of activation to drive the reaction than the substrates are able to absorb from their surroundings. Endergonic reactions play important roles in your body, such as putting molecules together to build muscles and bones. Reactions such as this, which use energy to build complex molecules from simpler molecules, are called **anabolic reactions.**

In living things, exergonic and endergonic reactions are **coupled reactions,** meaning that they occur in conjunction with one another. In this way the energy released when molecules are split (exergonic reactions) is used to power the combining of molecules (endergonic reactions) (Figure 4-5).

Reactions that break apart substrates release energy. These reactions are *exergonic*. Reactions that bond substrates together store energy. These reactions are *endergonic*. In living systems, exergonic reactions are coupled with endergonic reactions, supplying the energy for endergonic reactions to take place.

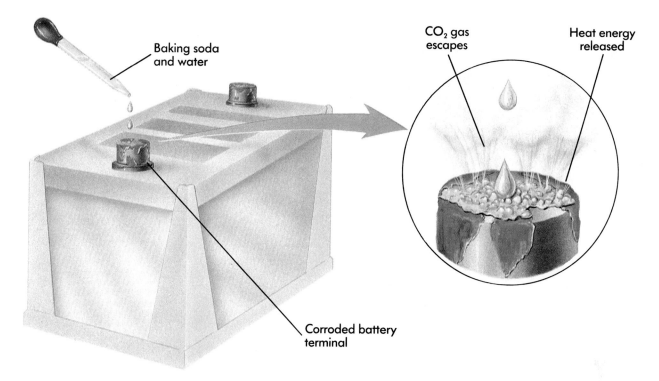

FIGURE 4-3 An example of an exergonic reaction.
When you clean your car battery with baking soda and water, these two substances react with the acid on the battery terminals, releasing carbon dioxide gas and water. Energy in the form of heat is also released.

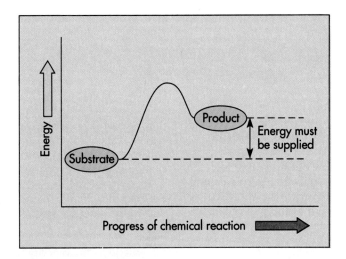

FIGURE 4-4 An endergonic reaction.
In an endergonic reaction the products of the reaction contain more energy than the reactants, so the extra energy must be supplied for the reaction to proceed.

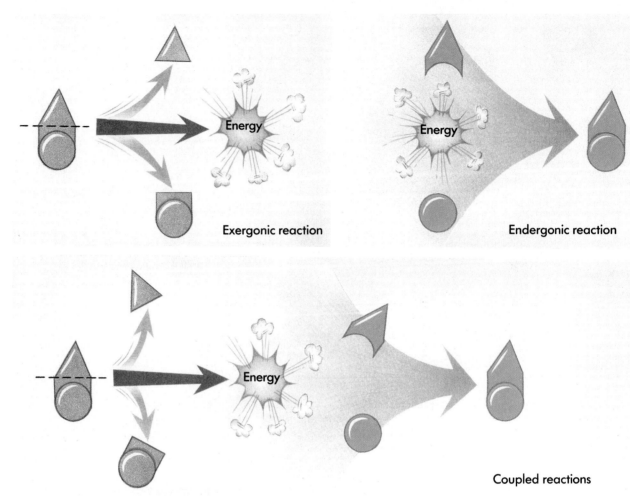

Energy

Exergonic reaction

Energy

Endergonic reaction

Energy

Coupled reactions

FIGURE 4-5 A coupled reaction.
In a coupled reaction the energy released in an exergonic reaction is used to drive an endergonic reaction.

Energy flow and change in living systems

Life can be viewed as a constant flow of energy that is channeled by organisms to do the work of living. As you learned at the beginning of this chapter, energy is the ability to do work, and work is many things, such as the pull of a cable on a rollercoaster car or the swift dash of a horse. It is also heat, such as the blast from an explosion or a warming fire. Energy can exist in many forms, including mechanical force, heat, sound, electricity, light, radioactivity, and magnetism. All these forms of energy are able to create change—to do work.

Energy exists in two states. Energy not actively doing work but having the capacity to do so is called **potential energy.** The rollercoaster cars perched atop that first hill, for example, possess this type of stored energy. They have the capacity to roll downhill, having stored the energy from their pull up the hill. Then, as the cars roll down the hill,

they are actively engaged in doing work. This form of energy is called **kinetic energy,** or the energy of motion. Much of the work performed by living organisms involves changing potential energy to kinetic energy (Figure 4-6). The exergonic reactions that supply your body with energy, for example, change the potential energy stored in the food you eat to kinetic energy for cellular work.

⯯
Energy is the capacity to do work, or bring about change. It can exist in many forms, such as mechanical force or heat. Energy actively doing work is called *kinetic energy;* stored energy is called *potential energy.*

All of the changes in energy that take place in the universe, from nuclear explosions to the buzzing of bees, are governed by two laws called the **laws of thermodynamics.** The **first law of thermodynamics** states that energy can

FIGURE 4-6 The energy of motion.
Transforming potential energy into kinetic energy, this athlete has just jumped to make a basket.

FIGURE 4-7 All the energy that powers life is captured from sunlight.
These trees in a Michigan forest absorb sunlight and use it in the process of photosynthesis.

change from one form to another and from one state to another, but it can never be lost. Nor can any new energy be made. The total amount of energy in the universe remains constant.

The first law of thermodynamics states that energy cannot be created or destroyed; it can only be changed from one form or state to another.

The **second law of thermodynamics** states that all objects in the universe tend to become more disordered and that the disorder in the universe is continually increasing. Stated simply, disorder is more likely than order. You can relate to this concept as you try to keep your personal environment in order. Your bedroom continually becomes messy, for example, unless you make an effort to keep it neat. Interestingly, molecules also become increasingly disordered.

Disorder with respect to molecules refers to their random motion. As you may recall from Chapter 3, this random motion, or disorder, is an inherent jiggling that is characteristic of all molecules and small particles. Their disor-

der increases as energy is added to molecules in the form of heat. This heat is the energy that is lost as energy transfers are made between molecules during chemical reactions. This lost heat energy is often called the *kinetic energy of molecular motion*. Although the total amount of energy in the universe does not change, the amount of useful energy available to do work decreases as progressively more energy is degraded to heat. With the addition of this heat, molecules move more quickly, becoming more disordered.

The second law of thermodynamics states that disorder in the universe constantly increases. Energy spontaneously converts to less organized forms.

The energy lost to disorder is referred to as **entropy.** In fact, entropy is a measure of the disorder of a system. Sometimes the second law of thermodynamics is simply stated as "entropy increases." So although energy cannot be destroyed, the universe is constantly moving toward increasing entropy. Eventually, the universe will have wound down like a forgotten clock. Scientists speculate that this will occur approximately 100 billion years from now.

Although energy cannot come into or go out of the universe, the Earth is constantly receiving "new" energy from the sun. Much of this energy heats up the oceans and continents. Some of it is captured by photosynthetic organisms such as green plants (Figure 4-7). In photosynthesis, the energy from sunlight is changed to chemical energy, combining small molecules into more complex molecules by means of endergonic reactions. This stored energy can be shifted to other molecules by forming different chemical bonds. In addition, this stored energy can be changed into kinetic energy: motion, light, electricity—and heat. Thus energy continuously flows into and through the biological world, with new energy from the sun constantly flowing in to replace the energy that is lost as heat.

> ⯆ Photosynthetic organisms such as green plants change energy from the sun to other forms of energy that drive life processes. This energy is never destroyed, but as it is exchanged in chemical reactions, much of it is changed to heat, a form of energy that is not useful for performing work.

Regulating chemical reactions

The flow of energy within an organism such as you consists of a long series of coupled reactions. Energy is moved from one molecule to the next by means of exergonic and endergonic reactions. Some of this energy is stored in the bonds of the molecules that make up the structure of your body. Some is freed to do cellular work. And some is lost as heat. These chains of reactions that move, store, and free energy are called **metabolic pathways.** Metabolic pathways accomplish jobs such as obtaining energy from the food you eat and repairing tissues that are worn out or damaged. By means of such pathways, your body and the bodies of all living things work to maintain order and avoid increasing entropy. Put simply, all the metabolic pathways in your body work to help you survive. But for these chemical reactions to occur, they must be pushed over the hill of activation energy. In addition they must be controlled so that they occur on schedule.

Enzymes: Biological catalysts

As you read earlier in this chapter, chemical reactions require activation energy to get started. This energy is needed for various reasons. In some chemical reactions, it is used to help break old bonds so that new bonds can be formed. In others, it is used to excite electrons—to help them achieve a higher energy level or orbit—so that they will pair up in covalent bonds. And in others, this energy helps molecules overcome the mutual repulsion of their many electrons so that they can get close enough to react. In any chemical reaction the free energy of activation performs one or more of these jobs.

If molecules are moving very quickly and bump into one another forcefully, the kinetic energy of the bump can provide enough energy for activation. This situation rarely occurs in living organisms, however, because the chemical reactions of living things take place in the moderate temperatures of living cells. But living systems contain proteins called **enzymes** that lower (or lessen) the free energy of activation that is needed, allowing chemical reactions to take place.

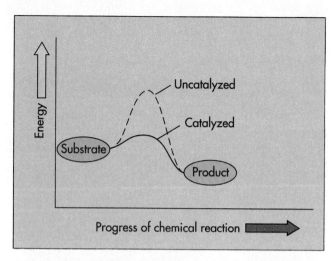

FIGURE 4-8   The function of enzymes.
Enzymes are able to catalyze particular reactions because they lower the amount of activation energy required to initiate the reaction.

Enzymes are proteins that act as **catalysts.** A catalyst is a substance that increases the rate of a chemical reaction but is not chemically changed by the reaction. It lowers the barrier of the free energy of activation—reduces the amount of energy needed for the reaction to occur—by bringing substrates together so that they can react with one another or by placing stress on the bonds of a single substrate, making it more reactive (Figure 4-8). Enzymes are biological catalysts and control all the chemical reactions making up the metabolic pathways in living things. Life is therefore a process regulated by enzymes.

> ⯆ Enzymes are biological catalysts that reduce the amount of free energy of activation needed for a chemical reaction to take place, thus speeding up the reaction.

How enzymes work
Enzymes are proteins that have one or a few grooves or furrows on their surfaces (Figure 4-9), much like the deep creases in a prune. These surface depressions are called **active sites** and are determined by the side groups of the amino acids making up the protein. Nonpolar side groups of amino acids, for example, tend to be shoved into the interior of the protein because of their hydrophobic (water-fearing) interactions, thereby imparting a particular shape to that portion of the protein (see Chapter 2).

The active sites are the locations on the enzyme where a reaction is catalyzed—where **catalysis** takes place. For catalysis to occur, a substrate must fit into the surface depression of an enzyme so that many of its atoms nudge up against atoms of the enzyme. The fit between a substrate and an enzyme is much like putting your foot into a tight-fitting shoe. However, the binding of a substrate in some cases causes the enzyme to adjust its shape slightly, allowing a better fit called an *induced fit.* Just as your feet will

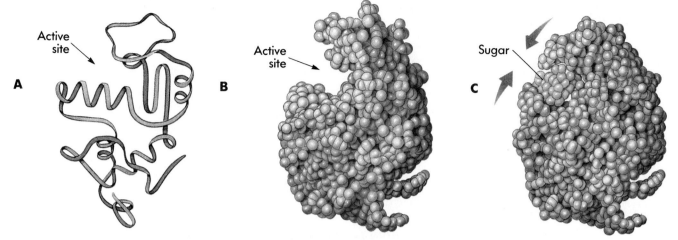

FIGURE 4-9   How the active sites in the enzyme lysozyme work to break apart bacterial cell walls. The tertiary structure of the enzyme lysozyme, shown as a ribbon in **A** and a three-dimensional model in **B** and **C,** forms a groove called the *active site* through the middle of the protein. This groove fits the shape of a substrate such as chains of sugars within bacterial cell walls. A chain of sugars, indicated in *yellow* in **C,** slides into the groove, its entry inducing the protein to alter its shape slightly and embracing the substrate more intimately. This *induced fit* positions a glutamic acid in the protein right next to the bond between two adjacent sugars in the substrate, causing stress to be put on the bond. The bond between the two sugars eventually breaks, releasing the individual sugars. In this way, the enzyme lysozyme breaks apart bacterial cell walls, killing the bacteria.

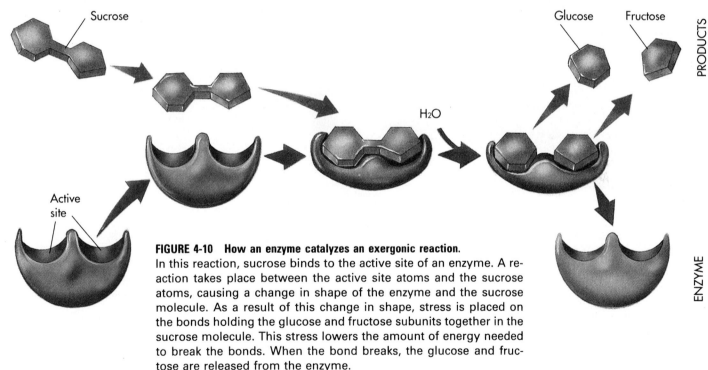

FIGURE 4-10   How an enzyme catalyzes an exergonic reaction. In this reaction, sucrose binds to the active site of an enzyme. A reaction takes place between the active site atoms and the sucrose atoms, causing a change in shape of the enzyme and the sucrose molecule. As a result of this change in shape, stress is placed on the bonds holding the glucose and fructose subunits together in the sucrose molecule. This stress lowers the amount of energy needed to break the bonds. When the bond breaks, the glucose and fructose are released from the enzyme.

only fit into certain shoes, substrates can only fit into, or bind with, the active site of certain enzymes. Therefore enzymes typically catalyze only one or a very few different chemical reactions. Because of this specificity, each cell in your body contains from 1000 to 4000 different types of enzymes.

Enzymes catalyze both endergonic and exergonic reac-

tions. Figure 4-10 shows how an enzyme catalyzes an exergonic reaction. In this example, a molecule of sucrose binds to the active site of an enzyme. After binding takes place, certain atoms within the active site of the enzyme chemically interact with the sucrose. This interaction causes a slight change in the shape of both the enzyme and the sucrose molecule. This change in shape places stress on the

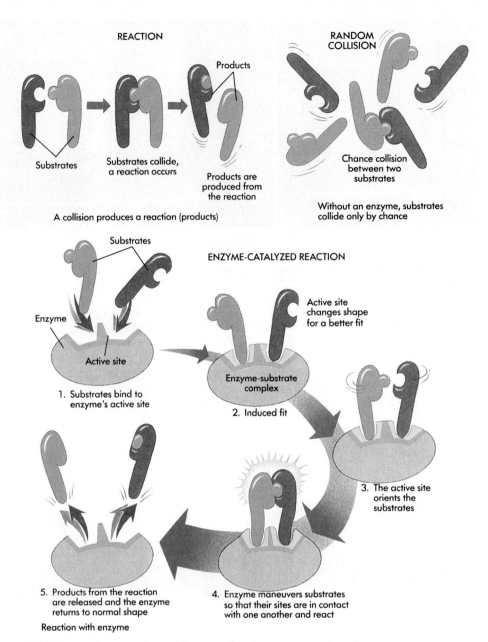

REACTION

Products

Substrates

Substrates collide,
a reaction occurs

Products are
produced from
the reaction

A collision produces a reaction (products)

RANDOM COLLISION

Chance collision
between two
substrates

Without an enzyme, substrates
collide only by chance

ENZYME-CATALYZED REACTION

Substrates

Active site
changes shape
for a better fit

Enzyme

Active site

Enzyme-substrate
complex

1. Substrates bind to
enzyme's active site

2. Induced fit

3. The active site
orients the
substrates

5. Products from the reaction
are released and the enzyme
returns to normal shape

4. Enzyme maneuvers substrates
so that their sites are in contact
with one another and react

Reaction with enzyme

FIGURE 4-11 Enzymes also catalyze reactions between two substrates.
A A collision between two substrates causes a reaction to occur, resulting in products.
B Without an enzyme, substrates only collide by chance.
C With an enzyme, a reaction is more likely to occur. The binding of the substrates to
the active site of the enzyme weakens their chemical bonds so that less energy is needed
for a reaction to occur. The enzyme also orients the substrates in the best possible position for a productive reaction.

bonds joining the glucose and fructose subunits, reducing
the amount of free energy of activation needed to be absorbed by the molecules for them to react. The bond then
breaks, and the products are released from the enzyme.

Enzymes also catalyze reactions that bind two substrates together (Figure 4-11). Both substrates bind at the
active site on the enzyme. The binding of the substrates to

the enzyme distorts and weakens their chemical bonds. In
addition, their interaction with the enzyme orients the substrates so that their reactive sites are in contact with one
another and react. Put simply, the enzyme is like a dating
service. It gets the substrates together so that their meeting
does not simply occur by chance. Interestingly, the Chinese
characterize enzymes in a similar way, calling them *tsoo mei,*

or "marriage brokers". Moreover, enzymes do not get used up after one interaction takes place. They are only intermediaries in chemical reactions and are then released, available to catalyze yet another reaction.

Enzymes work by bringing substrates together so that they react more easily and by placing stress on bonds, which lowers the amount of free energy of activation that must be absorbed by the substrates for them to react.

Factors that affect enzyme activity

The activity of an enzyme is affected by anything that changes its three-dimensional shape. If it loses its shape, or is denatured, an enzyme cannot bind with a substrate. Three environmental conditions that can affect enzyme activity in this way are temperature, pH, and the binding of specific chemicals. You can see the protein in an egg become denatured when you cook it. The heat of the cooking process permanently changes the shape of the egg proteins, which results in the egg becoming firmer and more opaque.

Most human enzymes function best between 36° C and 38° C, close to body temperature. Likewise, the enzymes of other living things work best at temperature ranges specific to the organism. Bacteria that live in hot springs, for example, have enzymes that function at temperatures between 74° C and 76° C (Figure 4-12, *A*). At temperatures colder or warmer than the enzyme's optimum range, the bonds between the amino acids that are responsible for the enzyme's three-dimensional shape become weak or rigid, changing the shape of the active site and causing chemical reactions to stop.

Enzymes also work best within a particular range of pH values. As previously stated, pH is a measure of the acidity or alkalinity of a solution (see Chapter 2). Most enzymes work best within the range of pH 6 to 8. Some enzymes, however, function in very acidic environments. For example, the enzyme pepsin digests proteins in your stomach at pH 2, a very acidic level (Figure 4-12, *B*).

The activity of an enzyme is sensitive not only to temperature and pH, but also to the presence of specific chemicals that bind to the enzyme and cause changes in its shape. By means of these specific chemicals, a cell is able to turn enzymes on and off. When the binding of a chemical changes the shape of the protein and the active site so that it can catalyze a chemical reaction, the chemical is called an *activator*. When the binding causes a change in the active site that shuts off enzyme activity, the chemical is called an *inhibitor*. Enzymes usually have special binding sites for the activator and inhibitor molecules that affect them, and these binding sites are different from their active sites.

Enzyme action is often regulated by inhibitors in a process called **negative feedback**. In this process the enzyme catalyzing the first step in a series of chemical reactions has an inhibitor binding site to which the end product of the pathway binds. As the concentration of the end product builds up in the cell, it begins to bind to the first enzyme in the metabolic pathway, shutting off that enzyme. In this way, the end product is feeding information back to the first enzyme in the pathway, shutting the pathway down when additional end product is not needed (Figure 4-13). Such

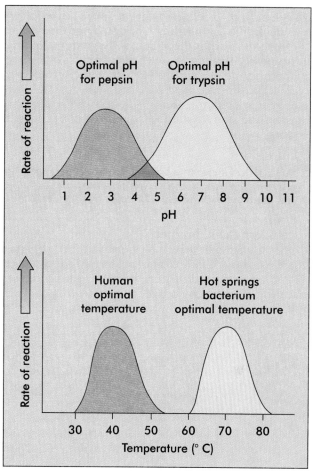

FIGURE 4-12 Enzymes are sensitive to the environment.
The activity of an enzyme is influenced both by pH **(A)** and temperature **(B)**. Human enzymes tend to work best within a pH range of 6 to 8 and at temperatures of about 37° C.

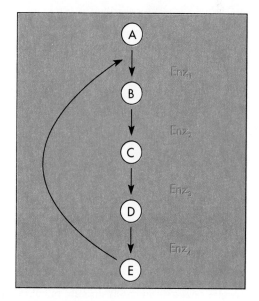

FIGURE 4-13 End-product inhibition.
Product *E* controls the rate of its own synthesis by acting on Enz_1, the enzyme that catalyzes the first reaction in the pathway.

end-product inhibition is a good example of the way many enzyme-catalyzed processes within cells are self-regulated. For example, the enzyme threonine deaminase catalyzes the first reaction in a series that converts the amino acid threonine to another amino acid, isoleucine. The cells of the body need both amino acids in proper concentrations to make proteins. The presence of an adequate amount of isoleucine for protein manufacture shuts off the enzyme threonine deaminase and stops any further conversion of threonine to isoleucine.

> The activity of enzymes is regulated by changes in enzyme shape; these changes result when activator and inhibitor molecules bind to specific enzymes.

Cofactors and coenzymes

Enzymes often have additional parts in their structures that are made up of molecules other than proteins (Figure 4-14). These additional chemical parts are called **cofactors**. Cofactors help enzymes catalyze chemical reactions. For example, many enzymes have metal ions such as zinc, iron, or copper locked into their active sites. These ions help draw electrons from substrate molecules. One of your digestive enzymes, carboxypeptidase, breaks down proteins in foods by using a zinc ion to draw electrons away from the bonds being broken in the food. Many trace elements necessary for your health, such as manganese, help enzymes in this way. When the cofactor is a nonprotein organic (carbon-containing) molecule, it is called a **coenzyme.** Many of the vitamins that your body requires, such as members of the B-vitamin complex, are used to synthesize coenzymes to maintain health. These coenzymes perform many jobs in the body, playing key roles in the reactions of cellular respiration, amino acid synthesis, and protein metabolism.

> Special nonprotein molecules called *cofactors* help enzymes catalyze chemical reactions. Cofactors that are nonprotein organic molecules are called *coenzymes.*

Storing and transferring energy

Many metabolic pathways in your body break down complex substances into simpler substances, releasing energy in the process. What happens to the energy that is released in these exergonic reactions? If your body could only use this energy when it was released, you might run out of energy a few hours after lunch, leaving you without enough energy to eat another meal. Obviously, living things could not survive under such circumstances. They have evolved ways to capture energy when it is released so that it can be used to do cell work.

ATP: The energy currency of living things

One way your body stores energy is by converting it to fat. In fact, many of us think we have too much of this stored energy. Fat, however, cannot serve our cells' immediate energy needs. It is used for long-term storage.

Glycogen is another molecule used by the body to store energy. Although glycogen can be more readily converted into energy than body fat can, it is still unable to meet immediate energy demands. The primary molecule used by cells to capture energy and supply it at a moment's notice is a molecule called **adenosine triphosphate,** or **ATP.**

Each ATP molecule is made up of three subunits (Figure 4-15):
1. A five-carbon sugar called *ribose*
2. A double-ringed molecule called *adenine*
3. Three phosphate groups (PO_4) linked in a chain called a *triphosphate group*

Together, the ribose sugar and the adenine rings are called *adenosine.* The "working end" of the molecule, however, is the triphosphate group.

Notice in the diagram that the bonds linking the phosphate groups in ATP are shown as wavy lines. These symbols stand for special bonds called **high-energy bonds.** As their name suggests, high-energy bonds require a lot of energy to form. These bonds are also special in another way:

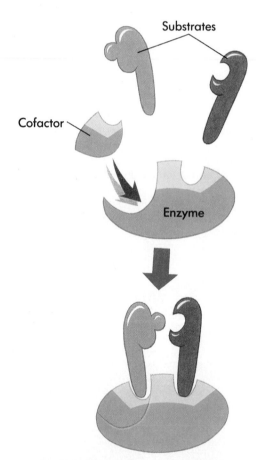

FIGURE 4-14   Cofactors.
Cofactors assist enzymes in catalyzing chemical reactions. An example of a cofactor is zinc, which helps a digestive enzyme break down food by drawing electrons away from the bonds being broken in the food.

they are fairly unstable and require very little free energy of activation to be broken.

ATP is often referred to as the energy currency of the cell because it is used much like money. When cells break down molecules in exergonic reactions, the energy that is released can be captured in molecules of ATP and carried there until it is needed. Likewise, when cells need energy to drive endergonic reactions, the cell can "spend" ATP to provide this energy.

▼▼ ATP, the universal energy currency of all cells, can capture energy in its high-energy bonds and later release this energy.

Carrying and transferring energy using ATP

When ATP is used to drive an endergonic reaction, the bond that links the last phosphate group to the rest of the ATP molecule is broken, releasing needed energy (Figure 4-16). The molecule that remains is called **adenosine diphosphate,** or **ADP.** In addition, the phosphate group (often symbolized as P_i, or inorganic phosphate) exists on its own. Thus ATP → ADP + P_i + energy.

Cells always contain a pool of ATP, ADP, and phosphate. ATP is constantly being cleaved into ADP and phosphate to drive the endergonic, energy-requiring processes of the cell by means of coupled reactions. In addition, however, ATP is continually being made from ADP, phosphate, and energy during coupled exergonic reactions. This recycling happens quickly. In fact, if you could mark every ATP molecule in your body at one instant in time and then watch them, they would be gone in a flash. Most cells maintain a particular molecule of ATP for only a few seconds before using it.

▼▼ ATP, ADP, and phosphate are continually being recycled within living cells, thus capturing, carrying, and releasing energy.

ATP is used to fuel a variety of cell processes. It is used, for example, when fireflies and deep water fishes produce light. It is used to build larger, more complex molecules like proteins from smaller, simpler molecules like amino acids. It also provides energy for you to move, fueling the reactions that take place in your muscles that cause muscle fibers to contract. Cells also use ATP to help move substances

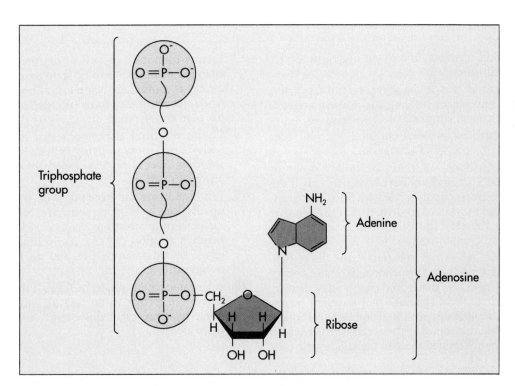

FIGURE 4-15 ATP is the primary energy currency of the cell.
ATP has three subunits: a five-carbon sugar called *ribose,* a double-ringed structure called *adenine,* and three phosphate groups called a *triphosphate group.* The phosphate groups are linked together by high-energy bonds.

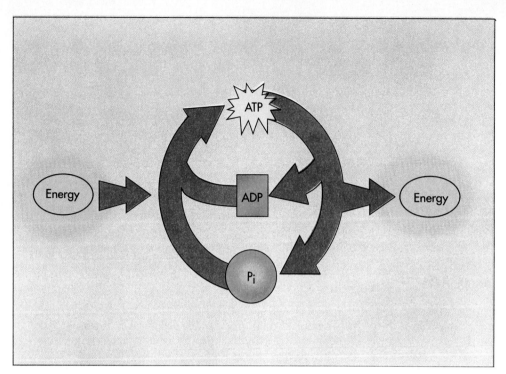

FIGURE 4-16 The ATP-ADP cycle.
When ATP is used to drive the energy-requiring activities of living things, the high-energy bond that links the last phosphate group to the ATP molecule is broken, releasing energy. Cells always contain a pool of ATP, ADP, and phosphate (symbolized by P_i), so ATP is continually being made from ADP, phosphate, and the energy released from exergonic reactions.

against a gradient—it is the fuel of active transport. Finally, the energy in ATP is changed into electrical energy primarily in nerves.

Where does the energy come from that is captured in molecules of ATP? The ultimate source of energy, of course, is the energy of the sun that is captured by plants during the process of photosynthesis. Plants and the animals that eat them are food sources for other animals. Your body breaks down the food you eat into molecules such as glucose that are usable for fuel by your cells. Your cells break down these fuel molecules, releasing energy that is then captured in molecules of ATP.

Summary

1. All the chemical reactions in a living organism are referred to as its *metabolism*.

2. Chemical reactions involve changing one substance into another. The substances entering the reaction are substrates. The changed substrates are products.

3. Energy is needed to initiate a chemical reaction. This energy is the free energy of activation.

4. In exergonic reactions, substrates are broken down to yield products. The products have less energy than the substrates; the excess energy is released. So little free energy of activation is needed to drive these reactions that this energy is absorbed from the environment and the reaction occurs spontaneously.

5. In endergonic reactions, substrates are chemically joined to yield a product. The product has more energy than the substrates. So much free energy of activation is needed to drive these reactions that it cannot be absorbed from the surroundings. In living systems, endergonic reactions are coupled with exergonic reactions to provide the energy needed to drive the endergonic process.

6. Energy exists in two states. Stored energy, or energy not actively doing work, is potential energy. Energy of motion, or energy actively doing work, is kinetic energy. Energy can be changed from one form to another during chemical reactions.

7. Energy cannot be created or destroyed; it can only be changed from one form or state to another. However, energy is continually being lost as heat during chemical reactions. Heat is a form of energy that is not useful for performing work.

8. Chains of chemical reactions that move, store, carry, and release energy in living systems are called *metabolic pathways*. Special proteins called *enzymes* regulate these series of reactions.

9. Enzymes lower the free energy of activation and speed up reactions by bringing substrates together so that they can react or by stressing chemical bonds that must break before a reaction can take place. Enzyme activity is affected by temperature, pH, and the binding of certain chemicals.

10. Adenosine triphosphate, or ATP, is the energy currency of the cell in that it can capture energy from an exergonic reaction, carry this energy, and then "spend" it when needed.

1. What is the role of free energy of activation in a chemical reaction?

2. Cells within your bone marrow are continuously producing blood cells for the body. Reactions occur that involve creating complex molecules from simple molecules. Are these processes dependent on anabolic or catabolic reactions? Bone marrow cells also receive nutrients, such as glucose, to fuel the cell. What type of reaction would you hypothesize occurs as glucose is broken down, releasing energy?

3. We have studied how the body stores lipids for later use as a fuel source. Similarly, glycogen is the human short-term storage form of sugars. The liver stores glycogen until energy is needed and it is converted to glucose for quick use. What form of energy is represented by these lipid and glycogen stores?

4. What are the first and second laws of thermodynamics?

5. When asked about his messy room, a friend who's studied science simply replies, "Entropy increases." Explain what this means.

6. Explain the role played by photosynthetic organisms in the biological flow of energy. Why is it important?

7. What are metabolic pathways? Explain their significance.

8. If a catalyst is not changed by a reaction, what purpose does it serve? Why do the cells of your body require so many enzymes (1000-4000 per cell)?

9. What do enzyme activators and inhibitors have in common? Which plays a key role in the process of negative feedback?

10. What are cofactors and coenzymes? Name a biologically important example of each.

11. ATP has been called the "energy currency of the cell." Explain what this means.

12. Our cells exhibit a continual cycle of ATP build-up and breakdown involving exergonic and endergonic reactions. What do you think might be the biological advantage of such a simple, universal energy exchange system?

13. Industrial pollution can change the pH of a pond or river to make the water more acidic. How can this affect the metabolic pathways of the plants that live in the water?

1. The chapter states that "life is a process regulated by enzymes." What might be the sources of these enzymes? If a particular enzyme is not available in a person's cells, what sequence of events might result to produce it?

2. The cellular cycle of ATP → ADP + P_i + energy is occurring continuously in all of our cells. However, since energy is neither created nor destroyed, why is the input of fuel (food energy) needed to run this cycle?

Hinkle, P.C., & MacCarty, R.E. (1978, March). How cells make ATP. *Scientific American*, pp. 104-123.
This article describes how cells use electrons stripped from foodstuffs to make ATP.

Lehninger, A.L. (1961, September). How cells transform energy. *Scientific American*, pp. 62-73.
Written more than 25 years ago, this article still provides one of the clearest explanations of how cells channel energy through metabolism.

Raloff, J. (1990, January 20). Women and alcohol: A gastric advantage. *Science News*, p. 39.
A new study is discussed which reveals an enzyme in many women which is less capable of degrading alcohol than the corresponding enzyme in males.

Revkin, A. (1989, April). Sleeping beauties. *Discover*, pp. 62-65.
A scientist studies hibernating bears to uncover the processes of metabolism. Potential uses of information include medical applications for humans.

5 | Cellular Respiration

Did you know that you and the cars in the photo have a lot in common? Both you and cars speeding down a highway are complex machines that burn fuel for energy. But you and a car burn fuel in ways that have important differences.

In the car's engine, gasoline is burned in the presence of oxygen. During exergonic reactions, molecules of gasoline are broken down to carbon dioxide and water, releasing energy as heat. Explosive bursts of heat produce pressure that moves the pistons in the engine, propelling the car. When the driver presses down on the accelerator and gives it the gas, the rate of these exergonic reactions increases. Because a car has no way to store the energy liberated from these reactions, this energy is used immediately, and the car speeds ahead.

In the engines of each of your cells—the mitochondria—the products of glucose breakdown are burned in the presence of oxygen. During a series of exergonic reactions, molecules of glucose are broken down to carbon dioxide and water, releasing energy. Most of this energy is released as heat and helps maintain your body temperature. But about 38% of it is captured in molecules of ATP—the energy currency of your cells. In fact, you do a better job of converting the energy in food to useful energy for your body—a car can convert only about 25% of the energy in gasoline into useful energy. And by using ATP, your body can capture, carry, and spend energy when it is needed, an ability that even a car of the future will not have.

Using chemical energy to drive metabolism

All the activities that organisms perform—bacteria swimming, a cat purring, you reading these words—use energy. These activities require energy because endergonic chemical reactions underlie all life activities. For example, energy-requiring chemical reactions cause muscles to contract and are involved in the active transport of molecules across nerve cell membranes, maintaining the crucial balance of various ions necessary for their functioning. In addition, living things constantly use energy to build larger molecules from smaller ones. Chains of reactions move, store, and free the energy needed to perform these activities of life. As you may recall from Chapter 4, such chains of reactions are called *metabolic pathways*.

In metabolic pathways, exergonic reactions—those that release energy—occur spontaneously with the help of enzymes, absorbing enough free energy as heat from their surroundings to "go." Endergonic reactions—those that require an input of energy—do not occur spontaneously because they are unable to absorb enough free energy from their environment to drive the reaction. So where does the energy come from to drive endergonic reactions? All living things get this energy in the same way: they *couple* endergonic reactions with exergonic reactions—those that release energy from molecules such as ATP. In this way, the energy of ATP is spent to enable an endergonic reaction to go (Figure 5-1).

Chemical energy powers metabolism by driving endergonic reactions. Chemical energy from exergonic reactions is captured in molecules of ATP, and the splitting of ATP is coupled to endergonic reactions, providing the energy necessary to drive them.

How cells make ATP: Variations on a theme

The energy used to make ATP is actually energy from the sun, captured by plants, algae, and certain bacteria in a process called **photosynthesis.** During this process, the energy from the sun powers the synthesis of glucose molecules, using the raw materials of carbon dioxide and water (Figure 5-2). Glucose is a sugar that plants use as a source of energy and as building blocks to construct larger molecules such as the cellulose found in plant cell walls. Plants also manufacture starch from glucose, a food that can be stored in plant cells and then converted to glucose when energy is needed. By eating plants and by eating animals that eat plants, humans and other animals can harvest the energy from the sun that was originally captured and stored by plants.

Living things, including photosynthetic organisms, make ATP by breaking down nutrient molecules such as glucose to release the energy stored in its bonds. The complex series of chemical reactions during which ATP is made from nutrient molecules in the presence of oxygen is known as **cellular respiration.** The term *cellular* refers to this process taking place in the cells of living things. The term *respiration* describes the process: the breakdown of fuel molecules in the presence of oxygen, with a resulting release of energy. Cellular respiration is called an **aerobic** process because this series of reactions is oxygen-dependent. Do not confuse this process with the breathing of oxygen gas that your body carries out, which is also called respiration. However, the process of cellular respiration does depend on the oxygen you breathe. *All* organisms that take in oxygen—including plants, which produce oxygen as a by-product of photosynthesis—break down nutrient molecules by means of cellular respiration.

Organisms that do not "breathe" oxygen, such as certain microorganisms, make ATP by a process known as **fer-**

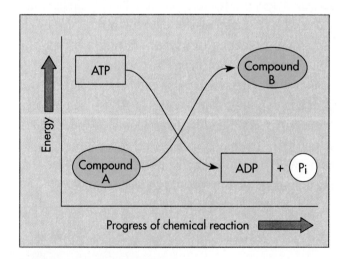

FIGURE 5-1   A coupled reaction.
The energy that is released from the conversion of ATP to ADP + P$_i$ (an exergonic reaction) is used to drive the conversion of compound A to compound B (an endergonic reaction).

FIGURE 5-2   Photosynthesis.
These vigorously growing corn plants capture energy from the sun, producing glucose from carbon dioxide and water.

mentation. This process consists of glycolysis (an initial series of reactions of cellular respiration) and one or two additional reactions that take place **anaerobically**—literally, "without" (an) "oxygen" (aerobically). Baker's yeast, for example, can generate ATP by fermentation. During this process the yeast produces carbon dioxide gas, an end product that causes bread dough to rise. Certain yeasts produce alcohol during fermentation and are used in the production of beers, wines, and other alcoholic beverages.

All organisms use either cellular respiration or fermentative pathways to generate ATP, suggesting a strong evolutionary relationship among all living things. The only organisms that use neither of these two ATP-generating processes are single-celled parasites called *chlamydia*. One species of chlamydia causes certain diseases of the eyes and also one of the most prevalent sexually transmitted diseases in the United States: nongonococcal urethritis. Another species causes diseases in animals. These organisms, among the smallest of the bacteria, can grow only within other cells and obtain their ATP from the cells they infect. For this reason, scientists call chlamydia "energy parasites." Chlamydia are thought to have lost the ability to generate ATP during their evolution.

⩔ **All cells, with few exceptions, make ATP by the process of cellular respiration or by the process of fermentation.**

How oxygen-using organisms release ATP from food molecules

An overview of cellular respiration

The process of cellular respiration is described chemically in the following formula:

$$36 \text{ ADP} + 36 \text{P}_i \longrightarrow 36 \text{ ATP}$$

$$C_6H_{12}O_6 + 6O_2 \longrightarrow 6CO_2 + 6H_2O$$
Glucose + Oxygen → Carbon dioxide + Water

Although the above formula is stated as if glucose were broken down to carbon dioxide and water in a single step, this is not the case. The formula is a summary of a complex series of reactions, much as you might summarize the details of a book in a single paragraph. This simplified formula shows that as cellular respiration occurs, the net effect is the breakdown of one molecule of the substrate glucose in the presence of six molecules of oxygen to yield end products of six molecules of carbon dioxide and six molecules of water. During this process, enough energy is liberated from the glucose as it is being cleaved to power 36 endergonic reactions: 36 molecules of ADP are bonded to 36 atoms of inorganic phosphate—an energy yield of 36 ATPs! Therefore the breakdown of glucose during cellular respiration releases energy (is exergonic), which helps to produce molecules of ATP, a type of endergonic reaction.

⩔ **Cellular respiration is a series of chemical reactions that captures energy in molecules of ATP. During cellular respiration, glucose is broken down in the presence of oxygen, yielding carbon dioxide and water and capturing energy in molecules of ATP.**

The complex series of reactions of cellular respiration can be divided into three parts: **glycolysis,** the **Krebs cycle,** and the **electron transport chain.** The word *glycolysis* comes from Greek words meaning "to break apart" (lysis) a "sugar" (glyco). Glycolysis takes place in the cytosol of the cell and is the first stage of extracting energy from glucose. No oxygen is needed for it to take place. It is a metabolic pathway in which ATP is generated, but the total yield of ATP molecules is small—only two ATPs for each original glucose molecule. When glycolysis is completed, the six-carbon glucose has been cleaved in half, yielding two three-carbon molecules called **pyruvate,** or pyruvic acid. The two pyruvate molecules still contain most of the energy that was present in the one original glucose molecule.

The Krebs cycle takes place in the mitochondria of the cell and is the second stage of extracting energy from glucose. Named after the biochemist Sir Hans Krebs, this cycle of reactions begins with a two-carbon molecule that is produced by the removal of a molecule of carbon dioxide (CO_2) from each pyruvate of glycolysis. Each of these two-carbon molecules combines with a four-carbon molecule to form a six-carbon molecule called *citric acid*. For this reason, the Krebs cycle is also often called the **citric acid cycle.** For every two pyruvate molecules entering the Krebs cycle as the result of the glycolytic breakdown of one glucose molecule, two more ATP molecules are made and a large number of electrons are removed from the substrates in the cycle. These electrons are passed to special molecules, also located in the mitochondria, called *electron carriers*. These electron carriers are part of the electron transport chain. By means of chemical reactions and processes that take place along the chain, 32 ATPs are produced. The process of cellular respiration is summarized in Figure 5-3. You may not fully understand this summary illustration now; refer to Figure 5-3 as you continue reading this chapter.

Three series of reactions make up the process of cellular respiration: glycolysis, the Krebs cycle, and the electron transport chain.

Oxidation-reduction

As chemical reactions take place in metabolic pathways such as cellular respiration, energy stored in chemical bonds is transferred to new chemical bonds, with the electrons shifting from one energy level to another. In some (but not all) chemical reactions, electrons actually pass from one atom or molecule to another. As explained in Chapter 2, this class of chemical reaction is called an **oxidation-reduction reaction.** Oxidation-reduction reactions are critically important to the flow of energy through living systems and essential to the flow of energy in cellular respiration.

When an atom or molecule gives up an electron, it is **oxidized.** The process by which this occurs is called **oxidation.** The name reflects that in biological systems, oxygen, which strongly attracts electrons, is the most frequent electron acceptor.

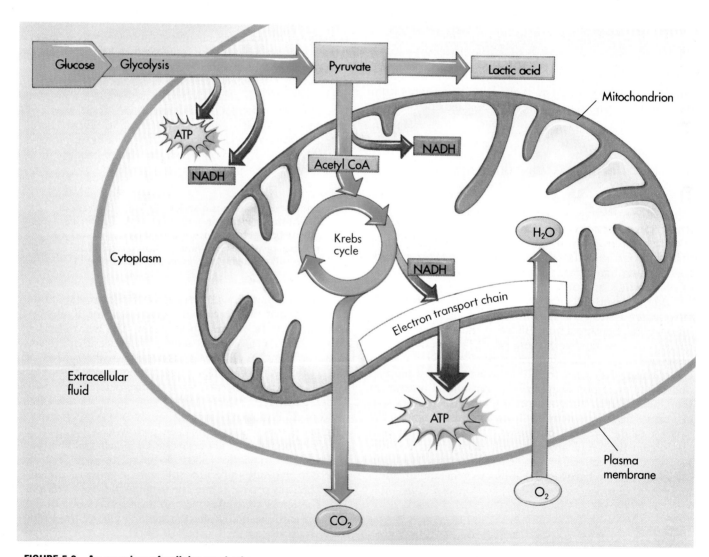

FIGURE 5-3 An overview of cellular respiration.
Living things, including plants, use cellular respiration to make ATP.

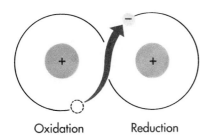

FIGURE 5-4 Oxidation-reduction.
Oxidation is a loss of an electron; reduction is the gain of one.

When an atom or molecule gains an electron, it becomes **reduced.** The process is called **reduction.** This name reflects that the addition of an electron *reduces* the charge by one. For example, if a molecule had a charge of +2, the addition of an electron (-1) would reduce the molecule's charge to +1.

Oxidation and reduction always take place together because every electron that is lost by one atom (oxidation) is gained by some other atom (reduction) (Figure 5-4). Together they are therefore called **redox reactions.** In a redox reaction the charge of the oxidized atom is increased, and the charge of the reduced atom is lowered.

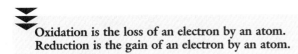

Oxidation is the loss of an electron by an atom.
Reduction is the gain of an electron by an atom.

Electron carriers

In biological systems, electrons often do not travel alone from one atom to another, but instead take along a proton. As you may recall from Chapter 2, a proton and an electron together make up a hydrogen atom. In living things,

special electron carriers transfer electrons as hydrogen atoms from one molecule to another. One such carrier is the molecule nicotinamide adenine dinucleotide, or NAD^+, a molecule synthesized from the vitamin niacin. The + sign indicates that NAD is the oxidized form of the molecule. It can accept two electrons and one proton (H^+) to become reduced to NADH. Notice that this molecule no longer bears a positive charge because it has been reduced. In addition, the extra H^+ and electron (hydrogen atom) are shown by the addition of one H to NAD.

Flavine adenine dinucleotide, or FAD, is another special electron carrier. It can accept *two* electrons and *two* protons to be reduced to $FADH_2$. The subscript *2* indicates the number of hydrogen atoms that FAD has accepted.

Both NADH and $FADH_2$ can pass on the electrons and protons they accept to other carriers. They are key players in the electron transport chain, one of the three series of reactions in cellular respiration. By passing electrons and protons in a series of redox reactions, the molecules in this chain create a flow of energy that works in special ways to produce most of the ATP of cellular respiration (Figure 5-5).

A more detailed look at cellular respiration

Food is a complex mixture of sugars, lipids, proteins, and other molecules. The first thing that happens in food's journey toward ATP production is that digestive system enzymes break down complex molecules to simple ones. Complex sugars like those found in vegetables and pasta, for example, are split into simple sugars such as glucose or into sugars that are changed to glucose. Proteins, which are found in foods such as meats and nuts, are broken down to amino acids. Complex lipids like those found in oil-based salad dressings are split into fatty acids and glycerol. These steps taken by the digestive system yield no usable energy, but they change a diverse array of complex molecules into a small number of simpler molecules that can be used by your cells as fuel.

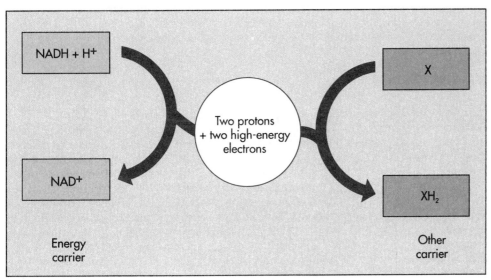

FIGURE 5-5 NADH$_2$, an electron carrier.
The high-energy electrons carried by NADH$_2$ are transferred to proton pumps or other energy-requiring components (indicated by *X*).

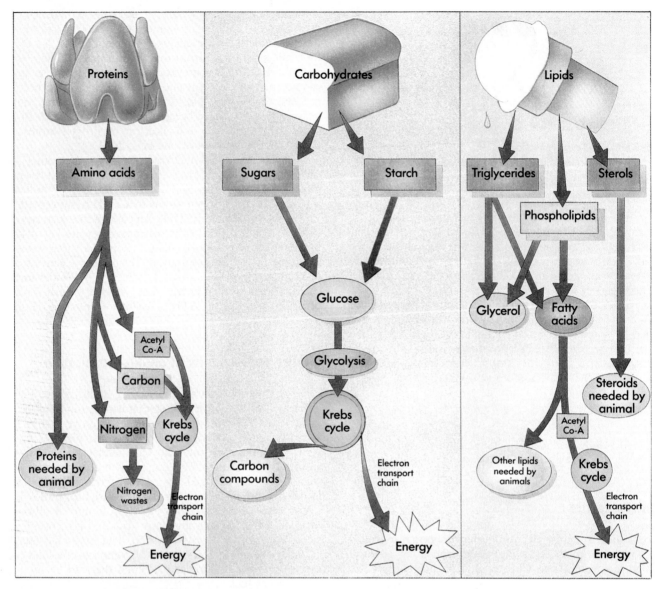

FIGURE 5-6 The complex molecules in food must be broken down into simpler molecules before they can be used by cells as fuel.
Proteins are broken down into amino acids. Carbohydrates are broken down into simpler sugars. Lipids are broken down into fatty acids and glycerol. Note that proteins and lipids, once broken down into their simpler subunits, enter the Krebs cycle without undergoing glycolysis.

The primary metabolic pathways in your body that break apart these simple molecules to release their stored energy and capture it in molecules of ATP are glycolysis, the Krebs cycle, and the electron transport chain. Once they are changed to glucose, carbohydrates are completely metabolized this way. After the digestion of proteins to amino acids, their carbon portions are chemically modified and are then metabolized by the Krebs cycle and the electron transport chain, skipping over glycolysis. Likewise, some of the breakdown products of the fats in your diet are converted to substances that can also be metabolized by these two series of reactions (Figure 5-6).

Glycolysis

Scientists think that glycolysis was one of the first metabolic processes to evolve. One reason is that this process uses no molecular oxygen and therefore occurs readily in an environment devoid of oxygen—a characteristic of the atmosphere of the primitive earth. In addition, all of the reactions of glycolysis occur free in the cytoplasm; none are associated with any organelle or membrane structure. "Early" cells most certainly had no specialized structures such as organelles, so metabolic processes that evolved independently of membrane systems are probably evolutionarily older than those associated with membrane systems.

All living things (except the chlamydia) possess glycolytic enzymes. However, most present-day organisms are able to extract considerably more energy from glucose molecules than glycolysis does. For example, of the 36 ATP molecules you obtain from each glucose molecule that you metabolize, only 2 are obtained by glycolysis. Why, then, is glycolysis still maintained even though its energy yield is comparatively meager?

This simple question has an important answer: evolution is a step-by-step process. Change occurs during evolution by improving on past successes. In catabolic metabolism, glycolysis was an improvement. A **catabolic process** is one in which complex molecules are broken down into simpler ones. Cells that could not carry out the catabolic reactions of glycolysis were at a competitive disadvantage; cells that were capable of glycolysis survived the early competition of life. Later improvements in catabolic metabolism built on this success. Glycolysis was not discarded during the course of evolution but rather was used as the starting point for the further extraction of chemical energy.

The catabolic pathway of glycolysis is shown in Figure 5-7. Its reactions can be divided into four stages:
1. Stage A—**Glucose mobilization:** During reactions 1 and 2, glucose is changed into a compound that can be split into two molecules. During two of these reactions, ATP molecules have their outermost phosphate groups enzymatically removed. The bonds holding these phosphate groups release a high amount of free energy when broken. The energy in this case is used to attach the phosphate group to the glucose molecule. Before energy can be released from glucose, your body must spend two ATP to prime the glucose pump.
2. Stage B—**Cleavage:** During reaction 3, the six-carbon product of glucose mobilization is split into two three-carbon molecules.
3. Stage C—**Oxidation:** During reaction 4, one H^+ and two electrons are removed from each three-carbon molecule and are donated to NAD^+. NAD^+ acts as an electron carrier, forming two molecules of NADH for each original glucose molecule. As this chemical change takes place, an inorganic phosphate molecule is bonded to each resulting three-carbon molecule (DPG) by means of high-energy bonds.
4. Stage D—**ATP generation:** During reactions 5 through 7, the two high-energy phosphate groups on each three-carbon molecule (DPG) are removed by enzymes and bonded to two ADP molecules, producing four ATP molecules for each original glucose molecule and two 3PG molecules. A molecule of water is removed from each 3PG molecule producing two PEP molecules. The end product of these reactions after the removal of two high-energy phosphate groups is two three-carbon molecules called pyruvate.

Because each glucose molecule is split into *two* three-carbon molecules, the overall net reaction sequence yields two ATP molecules as well as two molecules of pyruvate:

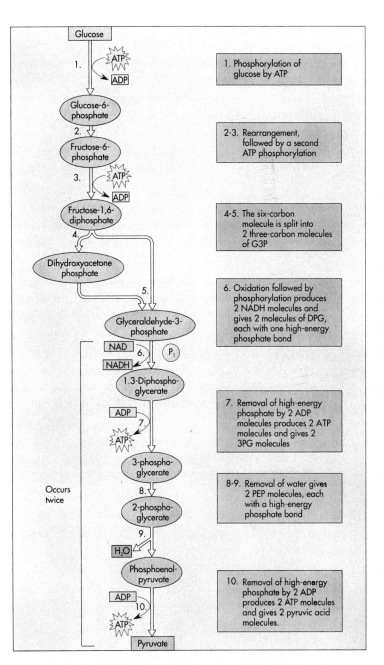

−2ATP	Stage A
+ 2(2ATP)	Stage D
+2 ATP	

FIGURE 5-7 Glycolysis.
Glycolysis produces a net yield of two ATP molecules for each original glucose molecule, as well as two molecules of NADH and two molecules of pyruvate.

Although this is not a great amount of energy (only 2% of the energy in the glucose molecule), glycolysis does generate ATP. During the first anaerobic, or airless, stages of life on Earth, this reaction sequence was the only way for living things to extract energy from food molecules.

▼▼
The sequence of reactions of glycolysis generates a small amount of ATP by reshuffling the bonds of glucose molecules. Glycolysis is a very inefficient process, capturing only about 2% of the available chemical energy of glucose.

Three changes take place during glycolysis:
1. Glucose is converted to pyruvate.
2. ADP + P_i is converted to ATP.
3. NAD^+ is converted to NADH.

These three products can continually be formed as long as the substrates that are used to produce them are available. The glucose is supplied by the food you eat. ADP and P_i continually become available as ATP is broken down to do cellular work. But cells contain only a small amount of NAD^+, and the supply is quickly depleted unless NADH passes along its hydrogen atom to another electron carrier. In this way NADH is oxidized to form NAD^+ once again.

Cells recycle NADH in one of two ways:
1. *Aerobic metabolism:* In the presence of oxygen gas, NADH passes its hydrogen atom to another electron carrier in the electron transport chain. The oxygen, an excellent electron acceptor, forms the last link in the chain. Each atom of oxygen accepts two H atoms to form one molecule of water. In addition, three molecules of ATP are formed during various chemical processes that take place (see p. 98).
2. *Anaerobic metabolism:* When oxygen is not available, another organic molecule must accept the hydrogen atom—

instead. This process occurs when organisms such as bacteria or yeast grow without oxygen and is called *fermentation* (Figure 5-8). Fermentation is described in more detail later in this chapter.

In all aerobic organisms—like you—the oxidation of glucose continues with the further oxidation of the product of glycolysis, which is pyruvate. In eukaryotic organisms, aerobic metabolism takes place in the mitochondria. Glycolysis, however, takes place in the cytoplasm outside the mitochondria. Therefore the cell must spend two ATPs (for each original molecule of glucose) to move the two NADH molecules produced during glycolysis into the mitochondrion. So, although the entire process of aerobic cellular respiration produces 38 ATPs, the net result is 36 ATPs for each molecule of glucose. Pyruvate, which is in high concentration in the cytoplasm, simply diffuses into the mitochondrion.

Before entering the reactions of the Krebs cycle, each pyruvate molecule is cleaved into a two-carbon molecule called an **acetyl group.** The leftover carbon atom from each pyruvate is split off as carbon dioxide gas (CO_2). In addition, one H^+ and two electrons reduce NAD^+ to NADH. In the course of these reactions the two-carbon acetyl fragment removed from pyruvate is added to a carrier molecule called *coenzyme A,* or CoA, forming a compound called **acetyl-CoA.** This process is summarized in Figure 5-9.

These reactions produce a molecule of NADH, which is later used to produce ATP molecules. Of greater importance, however, is the acetyl-CoA. Acetyl-CoA is important because it is the first substrate in the Krebs cycle, which generates many more molecules of NADH. It is produced not only during the breakdown of glucose but also during the metabolic breakdown of proteins, fats, and other lipids. This molecule is the point at which many of the catabolic processes of eukaryotic cells converge (see Figure 5-6).

The Krebs cycle
The Krebs cycle, which oxidizes acetyl-CoA, consists of nine enzyme-mediated reactions. These reactions are shown in Figure 5-10. The cycle has two stages:
1. Stage A—**Preparation reactions:** These three reactions set the scene. In the first reaction, acetyl-CoA joins a four-carbon molecule from the end of the cycle to form the six-carbon molecule citric acid. In the next two reactions, chemical groups are rearranged.

FIGURE 5-8 Fermentation.
In the absence of oxygen, yeast metabolizes pyruvate to ethyl alcohol. This process takes place naturally in grapes left to ferment on vines and artificially in fermentation vats of crushed grapes. As the concentration of ethyl alcohol in the vats rises to about 12%, further growth of the yeast is inhibited. What is left is wine.

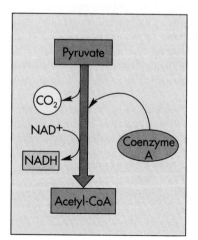

FIGURE 5-9 How pyruvate enters the Krebs cycle.
First, a carbon atom from each pyruvic acid molecule is split off as carbon dioxide gas, and a molecule of NADH is formed. Coenzyme A, a carrier molecule, is added to what is left of the pyruvic acid molecule, forming acetyl-CoA. Acetyl-CoA is the starting compound for the Krebs cycle.

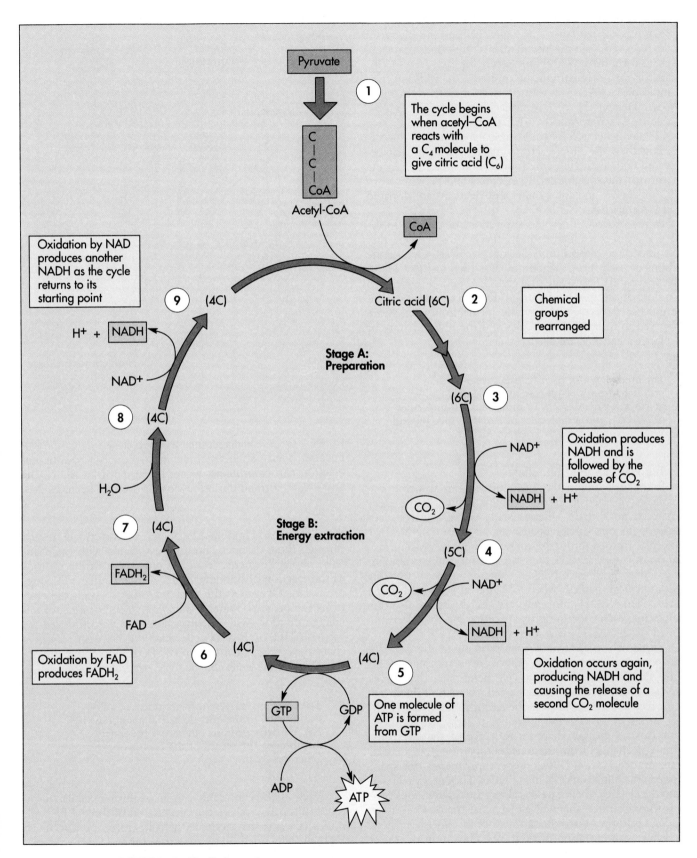

FIGURE 5-10 The Krebs cycle.
The Krebs cycle yields three molecules of NADH, one molecule of FADH$_2$, and one molecule of ATP for each acetyl-CoA molecule that enters the cycle.

2. Stage B—**Energy extraction:** Four of the remaining six reactions are oxidations in which H ions and electrons are removed from the intermediate compounds in the cycle to form three NADH molecules for each acetyl-CoA, six for each original glucose molecule. In addition, one molecule of $FADH_2$ is formed, two for each original glucose. During the cycle a molecule called *GTP* is produced, which is quickly used to produce an ATP; two ATP are generated for each original molecule of glucose.

Together, the nine reactions make up a cycle that begins and ends with the same four-carbon molecule. At every turn of the cycle, acetyl-CoA enters and is oxidized to CO_2 and H_2O, and the H ions and electrons are donated to electron carriers.

In the process of aerobic respiration the glucose molecule has been consumed entirely. Its six carbons were first split into three-carbon units during glycolysis. One of the carbons of each three-carbon unit was then lost as CO_2 in the conversion of pyruvate to acetyl-CoA, and the other two were lost during the oxidations of the Krebs cycle. Part of the glucose molecule's energy and its electrons, which are preserved in four ATP molecules and the reduced state of 12 electron carriers, are all that is left.

▼▼
The breakdown of the two pyruvate molecules produced from one glucose molecule during glycolysis generates 2 ATP molecules, 10 molecules of NADH, and 2 molecules of $FADH_2$. NADH and $FADH_2$ can be used to generate ATP.

The electron transport chain

Embedded within the inner mitochondrial membrane is a series of electron carrier proteins known as the **electron transport chain** (Figure 5-11). Here, electrons are passed from one carrier protein to another. The NADH molecules formed during glycolysis and the subsequent oxidation of pyruvate carry their electrons to this membrane. As you may recall, each NADH contains a pair of electrons and a proton gained when NADH was formed from NAD^+. The $FADH_2$ molecules are already attached to this membrane, each containing two protons and two electrons gained when $FADH_2$ was formed from FAD.

Three of the electron carrier proteins in the electron transport chain act as proton pumps. A proton pump is an active transport mechanism in cell membranes that forces hydrogen ions (protons) out of a cell. As each of these carriers accepts electrons in turn, the electrons fall to lower energy levels, releasing energy in the process. In addition, these carriers change shape as they accept the electrons, forming a channel from the inner compartment, or matrix, of the mitochondrion to the outer compartment—the space between the mitochondrial membranes. The energy released from the electrons being passed along the chain pumps protons through these channels and against the concentration gradient into the outer compartment of the mitochondrion. As a high concentration of protons builds up in the outer compartment, they begin to diffuse back across the membrane. But the only way they can get back in is through special channels called **respiratory assemblies,** visible in electron micrographs as projections on the inner surface of

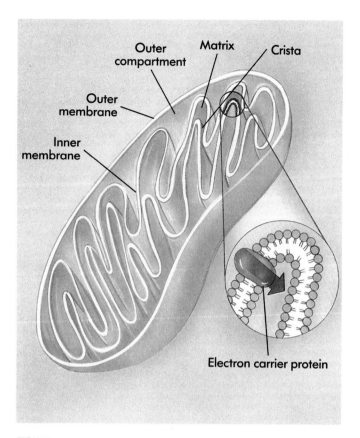

FIGURE 5-11   Site of the electron transport chain.
Located deep within the inner mitochondrial membrane, electron carrier proteins accept electrons from the NADH and $FADH_2$ formed during glycolysis and the Krebs cycle.

the membrane (Figure 5-12). As the protons travel inward through these channels, proteins associated with the channels couple the energy from the movement of the protons to the reaction of bonding P_i to ADP, forming ATP (Figure 5-13). Oxygen is the final acceptor for both the electrons and protons. Water is therefore an end product of cellular respiration, with one molecule of water produced for each NADH or $FADH_2$. Because the electron transport chain uses oxygen as its terminal electron acceptor, this series of reactions is also termed the *respiratory chain*.

▼▼
The electrons harvested from glucose and transported to the mitochondrial membrane by NADH drive protons out across the inner membrane. The return of the protons by diffusion generates ATP.

Each NADH molecule produced during cellular respiration ultimately causes the production of three ATP molecules, because its electrons activate three pumps. Each $FADH_2$, which activates two of the pumps, leads to the production of two ATP molecules. However, eukaryotes carry out glycolysis in the cytoplasm and the Krebs cycle within the mitochondria. This separation of the two processes within the cell requires transporting the electrons of the

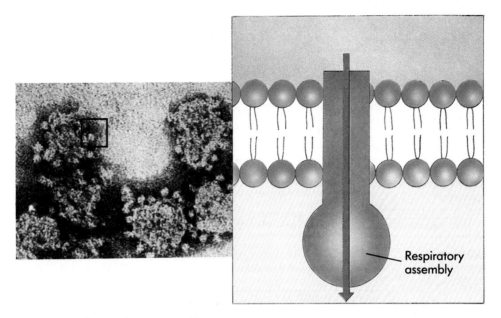

FIGURE 5-12 The respiratory assembly.
Protons in the outer compartment of a mitochondrion pass back into the inner compartment through special channels called *respiratory assemblies.* Each passage of a proton back into the inner compartment through a respiratory assembly is coupled to the synthesis of an ATP molecule.

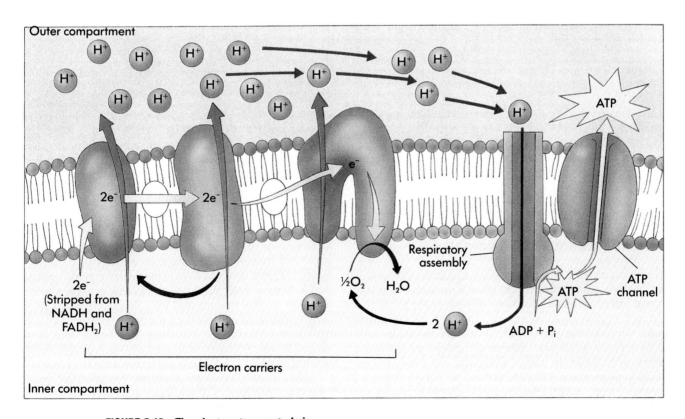

FIGURE 5-13 The electron transport chain.
The NADH and FADH$_2$ formed during the Krebs cycle pass their electrons to electron acceptors located in the inner membrane of the mitochondrion.

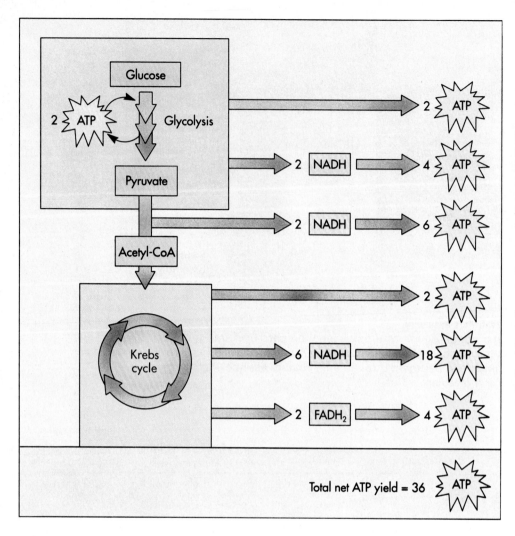

FIGURE 5-14 An overview of the energy extracted from the oxidation of glucose.
During glycolysis, each NADH actually produces three ATP molecules. However, because eukaryotes carry out glycolysis in the cell cytoplasm and the Krebs cycle in their mitochondria, it takes energy to transport their electron-carrying NADH molecules into the mitochondrion—one ATP molecule per NADH, a total of two ATPs per molecule of glucose. Therefore each NADH molecule produced during glycolysis yields only two molecules of ATP instead of three.

NADH created during glycolysis across the mitochondrial membrane, using one ATP molecule per NADH. Thus each glycolytic NADH produces only two ATP molecules instead of three in the final total. Figure 5-14 describes the total energy yield from the aerobic metabolism of one molecule of glucose.

How organisms release ATP from food molecules without using oxygen

Aerobic metabolism cannot take place in the absence of oxygen because a final electron acceptor is missing from the electron transport chain. Not only will the reactions of the electron transport chain come to a halt, the Krebs cycle reactions will not take place because NADH molecules will not be recycled to NAD^+ molecules, needed electron acceptors in the cycle. In such a situation, cells must rely on glycolysis to produce ATPs. However, they must regenerate NAD^+ from NADH for use in the glycolytic pathway. During aerobic respiration, cells accomplish this task by means of the reactions of the electron transport chain. During anaerobic respiration, bacteria and yeasts produce an organic molecule from pyruvate that will accept the hydro-

gen atom from NADH and thus re-form NAD^+. These reactions, including the glycolytic pathway, are termed **fermentation**. The end products of fermentation depend on the organic molecule that is produced from pyruvate.

Bacteria and yeasts carry out many different sorts of fermentations. In fact, more than a dozen fermentative processes have evolved among bacteria, each process using a different organic molecule as the hydrogen acceptor. Often the resulting reduced compound is an acid. In some organisms, such as yeasts, an organic molecule called *acetaldehyde* is formed from pyruvate and then reduced, producing an alcohol (Figure 5-15, *A*). This particular type of fermentation is of great interest to people because it is the source of the ethyl alcohol in wine and beer. However, ethyl alcohol is an undesirable end product for yeast because it becomes toxic to the yeast when it reaches high levels. That is why natural wine contains only about 12% alcohol—12% is the amount it takes to kill the yeast fermenting the sugars.

Muscle cells undergo a similar fermentative process when they produce ATP without sufficient oxygen (Figure 5-15, *B*). During strenuous exercise, muscle cells break down large amounts of glucose to produce ATP. However, because muscle cells are packed with mitochondria, the pace of glucose breakdown far outstrips the blood's ability to de-

A

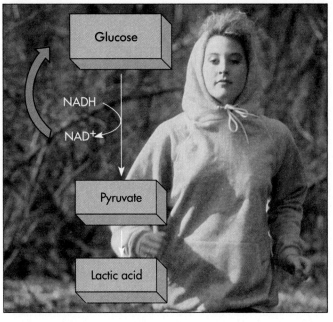

B

FIGURE 5-15 Anaerobic metabolism.
A Yeasts use acetaldehyde as the hydrogen acceptor. The result is the ethyl alcohol of wine and beer.
B When animal cells do not have sufficient oxygen, pyruvate accepts the hydrogen atom from NADH to reform the NAD^+ needed to continue glycolysis. This converts pyruvate into lactic acid, which builds up in the muscles until oxygen becomes available. This is what happens when you exercise strenuously. The ache in your muscles as you run is the result of a buildup of lactic acid.

liver oxygen for aerobic respiration. Therefore the muscle cells switch from aerobic respiration to fermentation. Muscle cells do not change pyruvate to another organic molecule to be reduced as the bacteria and yeasts do but instead directly reduce pyruvate to lactic acid. This acid builds up in the muscle and tends to produce a sensation of muscle fatigue. Gradually, however, the lactic acid is carried by the blood to the liver, where it is broken down aerobically. This need for oxygen to break down the lactic acid produces what is termed an **oxygen debt** and is the reason a person continues to pant after completing strenuous exercise.

In fermentations, which are anaerobic processes, pyruvate molecules or organic compounds produced from pyruvate are reduced, accepting the electrons of NADH generated in the glycolytic breakdown of glucose. These last reactions of the fermentative process produce the NAD^+ needed for the anaerobic breakdown of glucose to continue.

Summary

1. All the activities performed by living things involve chains of reactions that use, move, carry, store, and free energy. These chains of reactions are called *metabolic pathways*. In metabolic pathways, organisms couple exergonic reactions that release energy from molecules such as ATP with endergonic reactions to enable them to take place.

2. Almost all living things, including photosynthetic organisms, make ATP by a process called *cellular respiration*. Certain organisms make ATP by an anaerobic process called *fermentation*.

3. Cellular respiration is composed of three series of chemical reactions: glycolysis, the Krebs cycle, and the electron transport chain. During these reactions, glucose is broken down in the presence of oxygen, capturing energy in molecules of ATP. The by-products of this process are carbon dioxide and water.

4. The energy stored in chemical bonds can be transferred from one atom or molecule to another. In some chemical reactions, electrons pass from one atom or molecule to another. This class of chemical reaction is called an *oxidation-reduction reaction*.

5. NAD^+ and FAD are important electron carriers in living systems. Both become reduced by accepting electrons and protons and can then pass on the electrons and protons they accept to other carriers. Such carriers play important roles in the production of ATP.

6. In the human body, most carbohydrates are changed to glucose and completely metabolized by cellular respiration. Parts of protein and lipid molecules are also metabolized by part of this metabolic pathway.

7. Cellular respiration yields 36 ATP molecules from glycolysis, the Krebs cycle, and the electron transport chain.

8. Organisms that metabolize nutrient molecules anaerobically by the process of fermentation use pyruvate or a molecule derived from pyruvate to accept the electrons produced during the glycolytic breakdown of glucose. This process produces end products that are frequently acids or alcohols.

1. What is ATP, and why is it important to life?
2. Distinguish between cellular respiration and fermentation. What purpose do they serve?
3. Explain what this formula means. What process does it describe?

$$C_6H_{12}O_6 + 6O_2 \rightarrow 6CO_2 + 6H_2O + energy$$

4. Give your analysis of how the process of glucose breakdown during cellular respiration has both endergonic and exergonic elements.
5. Does oxidation always involve the acceptance of an electron by oxygen?
6. What do NAD^+ and FAD have in common? How do they differ?
7. You stop at a fast-food restaurant to eat a burger and fries. Explain how your body converts these foods into usable energy.
8. Summarize the changes that occur during glycolysis.
9. The chapter says that glycolysis is inefficient; explain why. If it is inefficient, why do our cells still carry out the process?
10. Summarize what happens during the Krebs cycle.
11. Create a table that summarizes the output of aerobic metabolism for glycolysis, the oxidation of pyruvate, and the Krebs cycle.
12. We have discussed before how the chemistry of life is integrally involved with the nature of water. Analyze the link between water and the electron transport chain, also called the "respiratory chain."

13. By filling in the diagram below, summarizes the stages, products, and by-products of cellular respiration. Show which events occur outside the mitochondrion and which take place inside the organelle. Include the number of ATP molecules produced at each stage.

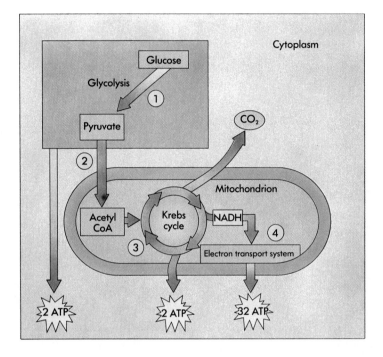

1. When a person falls into water and stays submerged for long lengths of time without breathing air, the person usually drowns. However, if the water is very cold, a submerged individual can sometimes survive as long as half an hour under water. Why do you think the temperature of the water plays such a critical role?
2. Scientists theorize that the environment of the very primitive earth, billions of years ago, was oxygen deficient. Given this restriction, what process do you hypothesize the first cellular organisms used to generate ATP? Why do you suppose almost all living organisms exhibit either fermentive or cellular respiraton?

Dickerson, R. (1980, March). Cytochrome *c* and the evolution of energy metabolism. *Scientific American*, pp. 136-154.
This is a superb description of how the metabolism of modern organisms evolved.

Hinkle, P. & McCarty, R. (1978, March) How cells make ATP. *Scientific American*, pp. 104-123.
This is a good summary of oxidative respiration, with a clear account of the events that happen at the mitochondrial membrane.

Levine, M., Muirhead, H., Stammers, D., & Stuart, D. (1978). Structure of pyruvate kinase and similarities with other enzymes: possible implications for protein taxonomy and evolution. *Nature, 271,* 626-630.
This advanced article recounts how the enzymes of oxidative metabolism may have evolved and is well worth the effort of reading it.

6 Levels of Organization in the Human Body

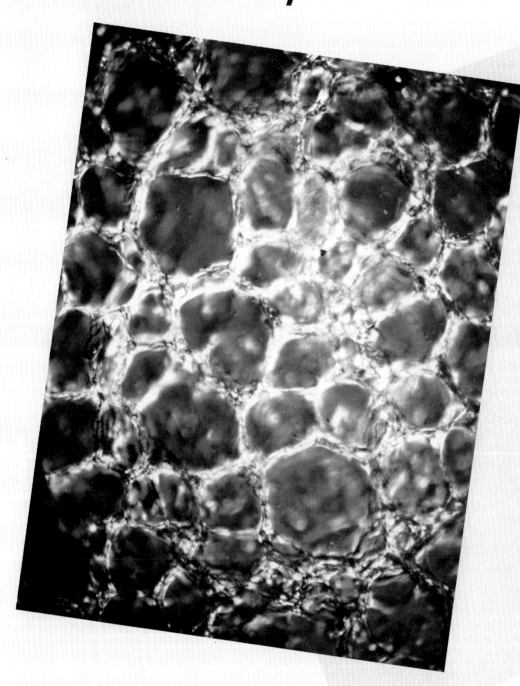

Did you ever blow soap bubbles through a straw when you were a child, or see a bubble-blowing machine at a science museum? The bubbles form one on top of the other, looking much like the pattern in the photo. But although the "bubbles" in the photo are filled with air, they are not bounded by soap. They are enclosed by cells and are filled with the air in your lungs. In fact, these bubbles are not bubbles at all. They are microscopic air sacs that help deliver the oxygen in the air you breathe to your bloodstream.

Although several hundred million air sacs can be found in each of your lungs, your lungs are not made up solely of air sacs. They include many other structures, such as blood vessels and air passageways. Together, these structures and others help the lungs do their job—transporting oxygen to the bloodstream and ridding the blood of the waste gas carbon dioxide. A complex structure such as the lung is called an *organ* and forms only one of the levels of organization in the human body.

How the human body is organized

The human body, like the bodies of all other multicellular animals, is made up of many different types of cells. In fact, the human body contains over 100 different kinds of cells! These cells are not distributed randomly but are organized to form the structures and perform the functions of the human body, just as workers in a factory may be organized to manufacture a product.

The cells of the body are organized into **tissues**. Tissues are groups of similar cells that work together to perform a function. Traditionally, tissues are divided into four basic types based on their function: **epithelial, connective, muscle,** and **nervous** (Figure 6-1). For example, the cells making up the walls of the air sacs of your lungs are a type of epithelial tissue—tissue that covers body surfaces and lines its cavities. All four tissue types are described later on in this chapter.

Two or more tissues grouped together to form a structural and functional unit are called **organs.** Your heart is an organ. It contains cardiac muscle tissue wrapped in connective tissue and "wired" with nerves. All of these tissues work together to pump blood through your body. Other examples of organs are the stomach, skin, liver, and eyes.

An **organ system** is a group of organs that function together to carry out the principal activities of the body. For example, the digestive system is composed of individual organs concerned with the breaking up of food (teeth), the passage of food to the stomach (esophagus), the storage and partial digestion of food (stomach), the digestion and absorption of food and the absorption of water (intestine), and the expulsion of solid waste (rectum). The human body contains 11 principal organ systems (Table 6-1), which are discussed in later chapters.

The organ systems are all encased in the human body (Figure 6-2), which is an incredible living machine. The human body has the same general body architecture that all

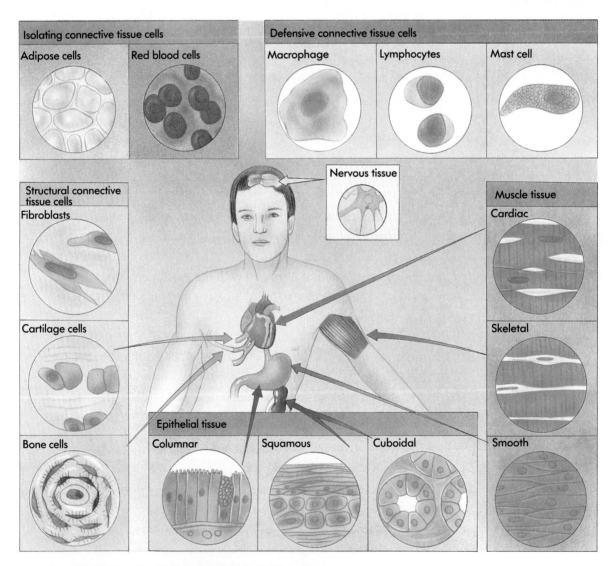

FIGURE 6-1 The basic tissue types and their cells.
The tissues in the body are divided into four basic types according to their function: epithelial, connective, muscle, and nervous.

TABLE 6-1 The major human organ systems

SYSTEM	FUNCTIONS	COMPONENTS	CHAPTER
Digestive	Breaks down food and absorbs breakdown products	Mouth, esophagus, stomach, intestines, liver, and pancreas	7
Respiratory	Supplies blood with oxygen and rids it of carbon dioxide	Trachea, lungs, and other air passageways	8
Circulatory	Brings nutrients and oxygen to cells and removes waste products	Heart, blood vessels, blood, lymph, and lymph structures	9
Urinary	Removes wastes from bloodstream	Kidney, bladder, and associated ducts	10
Nervous	Receives and helps body respond to stimuli	Nerves, sense organs, brain, and spinal cord	11, 12, 13
Endocrine	Coordinates and regulates body processes and functions	Pituitary, adrenal, thyroid, and other ductless glands	14
Skeletal	Protects the body and provides support for locomotion and movement	Bones, cartilage, and ligaments	15
Muscular	Produces body movement	Skeletal, cardiac, and smooth muscles	15
Integumentary	Covers and protects the body	Skin, hair, nails, and sweat glands	15
Immune	Helps defend body against infection and disease	Lymphocytes, macrophages, and antibodies	16
Reproductive	Produces sex cells and carries out other reproductive functions	Testes, ovaries, and other associated reproductive structures	21

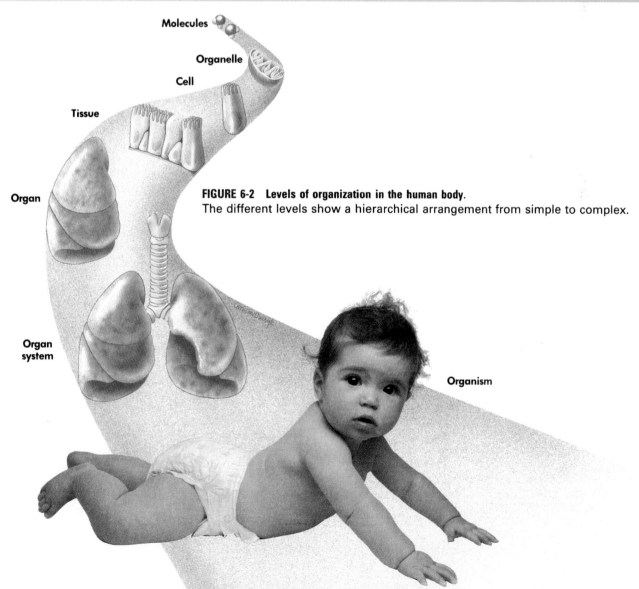

Molecules

Organelle

Cell

Tissue

Organ

Organ system

Organism

FIGURE 6-2 Levels of organization in the human body.
The different levels show a hierarchical arrangement from simple to complex.

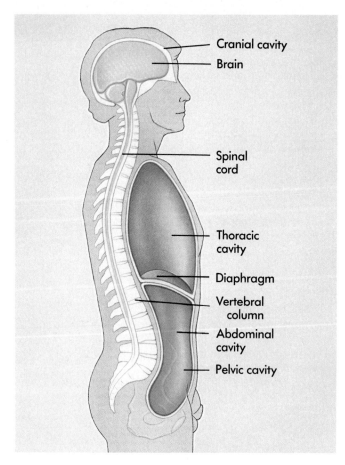

FIGURE 6-3 Architecture of the human body.
Humans, like all vertebrates, have a spinal cord and brain enclosed in the vertebral column and skull. In mammals a muscular diaphragm divides the coelom into the thoracic cavity and the abdominal cavity.

animals with a backbone have (Figure 6-3). It includes a long tube that travels from one end of the body to the other, from mouth to anus. This tube is suspended within an internal body cavity called the **coelom.** In human beings the coelom is divided into two main parts: (1) the thoracic cavity, which contains the heart and lungs, and (2) the abdominal cavity, which contains organs such as the stomach, intestines, and liver. The lower portion of the abdominal cavity is often referred to as the *pelvic cavity*. The body is supported by an internal scaffold, or skeleton, made up of bones that grow as the body grows. A bony skull surrounds the brain, which is located in a cavity separate from the coelom, called the *cranial cavity*. In addition, a column of bones called the *vertebral column* forms the backbone, or spine, of the human body. These bones surround a nerve cord, the spinal cord, that relays messages between the brain and other parts of the body.

Tissues

Epithelial tissue

Epithelial cells guard and protect your body; these cells are really the doors to the inner you. Put simply, epithelial cells cover and line the surfaces of the body, both internal and external. Remember, you can think of your body as a tube, with your skin forming the outside of the tube and your digestive system forming the inside of the tube. Therefore the surfaces of your inner tube as well as your skin are made up of epithelial cells. And, because epithelial cells cover the surfaces of the body, they determine which substances enter and which do not.

All epithelial cells, collectively called the **epithelium,** are broadly similar in form and function. The epithelial layers of the body function in six different ways:

1. **Protection:** They protect the tissues beneath them from drying out, mechanical injury, and invasion by microorganisms.
2. **Absorption:** They provide a barrier that can help or hinder the movement of materials into the tissue beneath. Because epithelium encases all of the body's surfaces, every substance that enters or leaves the body must cross an epithelial layer.
3. **Sensation:** Many sensory nerves end in epithelial cell layers. The epithelium therefore provides a sensory surface.
4. **Secretion:** Certain epithelial cells are specialized to produce and discharge substances; they are called *glands*. Glands may be single cells, such as the mucus-secreting cells lining the intestine. Most glands, however, are multicellular structures, such as the thyroid gland located in your neck or the pituitary gland that hangs like a tiny pea from the underside of your brain. Even your sweat glands are made up of many cells. Because many glands lie deep within your body and do not cover or line a surface, they may seem inappropriately described as being composed of epithelial tissue. However, glands form during embryological development from infoldings of epithelial cell layers and do fit in this category.
5. **Excretion:** Specialized epithelial cells in the kidney excrete waste products during the formation of urine. Also, the epithelium forming the air sacs of the lungs excretes the waste gas carbon dioxide.
6. **Surface transport:** Some epithelial cells have hair-like projections called *cilia*. These cilia beat in unison, causing a wave-like movement in the thin film of mucus that bathes the cells' surfaces, sweeping particles along in the process. The cells lining parts of your respiratory passageways, for example, use this technique to keep foreign particles from entering the lungs. Cigarette smoking damages these cilia, resulting in accumulations of mucus in the throat and respiratory passageways that leads to "smoker's cough" and, over time, to serious upper respiratory problems.

Structurally, epithelial tissues share some common characteristics. Epithelial tissues are usually only one or a few cells thick (with the exception of the skin), are packed together and stacked very tightly, and have very few blood vessels running through them. The circulation of nutrients,

| TABLE 6-2 | Epithelial tissue |

TISSUE	LOCATION	FUNCTIONS	DESCRIPTION
Simple squamous epithelium	Lining of blood vessels, air sacs of lungs, kidney tubules, and lining of body cavities	Diffusion, filtration, and passage of materials where little protection is needed	The simplest of all epithelial tissues, simple epithelium consists of a single layer of thin, flat cells.
Cuboidal epithelium	Kidney tubules, glands and their ducts, terminal bronchioles of lungs, and surface of ovaries and retina	Secretion, absorption, or movement of substances	The structure is a single layer of cube-shaped cells. Some have microscopic extensions called *microvilli*. Some have cilia that protrude from their surfaces.
Columnar epithelium	Lining of the digestive and upper part of respiratory tracts, auditory and uterine tubes	Secretion of mucus	The structure is a single layer of tall, narrow cells. Some have microvilli or cilia.

Continued.

gases, and wastes in epithelial tissue occurs by diffusion from the capillaries of neighboring tissue. In addition, although the chemical reactions of many types of epithelial cells take place at a very slow rate, many have amazing regenerative powers. Your skin cells, for example, are continually being replaced throughout your lifetime. Your liver, a gland having epithelial tissue on its absorptive and secretory surfaces, can readily regenerate substantial portions of tissue if parts are surgically removed or are damaged by certain diseases.

There are three main shapes of epithelial cells: **squamous, cuboidal,** and **columnar** (Table 6-2). Squamous

cells are thin and flat. They are found in places such as the air sacs of the lungs, the lining of blood vessels, and the skin. Cuboidal cells have complex shapes, but look like cubes when the tissue is cut at right angles to the surface. These cells are found lining tubules in the kidney and the ducts of glands. Columnar cells look like tiny columns (as their name suggests) when viewed from the side. Much of the digestive tract is lined with columnar epithelium.

The various types of epithelial cells may also be arranged in various ways. Epithelial tissue that is only one cell thick is referred to as **simple epithelium.** It is usually found in areas where substances diffuse through the tissue and

TABLE 6-2 Epithelial tissue—cont'd

TISSUE	LOCATION	FUNCTIONS	DESCRIPTION
Stratified squamous epithelium	Skin, mouth, and throat lining; vaginal lining; anal lining; and cornea	Protection, hard outer layer continuously removed by friction and replaced from below	The structure has several layers of cells. The lower layers are columnar and active. The upper layers are flattened at the surface.
Pseudostratified epithelium	Nasal cavity and sinuses, ducts of some glands, and some ducts of the male reproductive system	Protection and secretion of mucus	The structure is a single layer of cells. It is similar to columnar epithelium, but all cells are not the same height. Some reach the surface and others do not. Some have cilia, and some may have microvilli.
Transitional epithelium	Lining of urinary bladder and ureters	Stretches easily to accommodate fluid fluctuations in an organ or tube	There are several layers of columnar cells beneath layers of surface cells. Cells are flattened when tissue is stretched.

where substances are secreted, excreted, or absorbed. The cells lining your blood vessels are simple squamous epithelium, for example, whereas much of your digestive tract is lined with simple columnar epithelium. **Stratified epithelium** is made up of two or more layers. These layers are usually protective. The surface of your skin is stratified squamous epithelium. **Pseudostratified epithelium** only looks as though it is layered. In reality, this tissue is made up of only one layer of cells—some tall, some short. The sides of the top portions of the tall cells rest on top of the shorter cells, looking like two or more layers of cells. Some of your airways are lined with pseudostratified epithelium. **Transitional epithelium** is tissue that can stretch. The cells of transitional epithelium are cube-like; when stretched, the cells appear thin and flat. Transitional epithelium is found in the bladder and ureters of the urinary tract, an organ and tubes that accommodate fluid fluctuations.

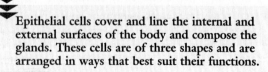

Epithelial cells cover and line the internal and external surfaces of the body and compose the glands. These cells are of three shapes and are arranged in ways that best suit their functions.

Connective tissue

The cells of connective tissue provide the body with structural building blocks and potent defenses. In addition, connective tissue joins the other tissues of the body. Connective tissue performs an assortment of important jobs for the body. The varied composition of the different types of connective tissue reflects this diversity. However, connective tissue is generally made up of cells that are usually spaced well apart from one another and are embedded in a nonliving substance called a **matrix.** In fact, connective tissue is made up of a great deal more matrix than cells. This matrix varies in consistency among the different types of connective tissue—from a fluid to a gel to crystals.

The different types of connective tissues and cells are categorized in many different ways. One way to group them is by function: **defensive, structural,** and **isolating connective tissue.** Defensive cells, those that protect the body from attack, float in a matrix of blood plasma. They roam the circulatory system, hunting invading bacteria and foreign substances. An example of this type of cell is the lymphocyte, a special type of white blood cell (Figure 6-4). Structural connective tissue cells, such as bone and cartilage cells, stay in

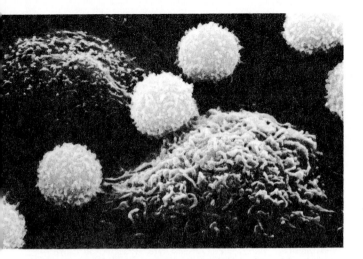

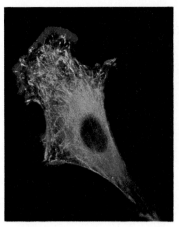

FIGURE 6-5 A fibroblast.
Note the flat, irregular, branching shape. Fibroblasts secrete fibers of protein, constructing a web that supports other fibroblasts.

FIGURE 6-4 Lymphocytes and macrophages.
The lymphocytes are small and spherical; the macrophages are larger and more irregular in form. Both types of cells play key roles in the body's defense against infection.

one place, secreting proteins into the empty spaces between them. These proteins provide structural connective tissue with a fibrous matrix, giving it the strength it needs to support the body and provide connections among tissues. Isolating connective tissue cells act as storehouses, accumulating specific substances such as fat, the skin pigment melanin, and hemoglobin.

Connective tissue and its cells provide a framework for the body, join its tissues, help defend it from foreign invaders, and act as storage sites for specific substances.

Cells that defend

The three principal defensive cell types are **lymphocytes** (see Figure 6-4), **macrophages**, and **mast cells.** All of these cells are dispersed throughout the body either in the blood or among other tissues.

Lymphocytes are a type of white blood cell that circulates in the blood or resides in the organs, vessels, and nodes of the lymphatic system. Both these cells and the lymphatic system itself play complex, key roles in the body's defense against infection. Your body has an amazing trillion or so lymphocytes ready to attack foreign cells or viruses that enter the body or to produce specific antibodies that can act against specific substances. (How lymphocytes and antibodies function in the body's defense against disease is described in Chapter 16.)

Macrophages are abundant in the bloodstream and also in the fibrous mesh of many tissues, such as the lungs, spleen, and lymph nodes. They develop, or differentiate from, white blood cells called *monocytes*. Usually macrophages move about freely, but sometimes they stay in one place, attached to fibers. These cells may be thought of as the janitors of the body, cleaning up cellular debris and invading bacteria by a process known as *phagocytosis*—an engulfing and digesting of particles.

Mast cells produce substances that are involved in the body's inflammatory response to physical injury or trauma. One important substance produced by mast cells is histamine, a chemical that causes blood vessels to dilate, or widen. As more blood then flows through the vessels, it brings added oxygen and nutrients and dilutes any toxins, or poisons. The increased blood flow also aids the movement of defensive leukocytes coming to the area. Mast cells, although important in the inflammation response, also play a role in allergic reactions (see Chapter 16).

Protective connective tissue cells defend the body against foreign invaders. Lymphocytes attack foreign cells or viruses that enter the body or produce specific antibodies that can act against specific substances. Macrophages then engulf and digest the invader. Mast cells enlarge the blood vessels in response to trauma, speeding the healing process.

Cells and tissues that shape and bind

The three principal types of cells found in structural connective tissue are **fibroblasts**, cartilage cells (**chondrocytes**), and bone cells (**osteocytes**). These cells produce substances that cause the tissues of which they are a part to have distinctive characteristics.

Fibroblasts. Of all the connective tissue cells, fibroblasts are the most numerous. They are flat, irregular, branching cells that secrete fibers into the matrix between them (Figure 6-5). These fibers are of three basic types: collagen, reticulin, and elastic.

Both the collagen fibers and the reticulin fibers are made up of the protein collagen, the most abundant protein in the human body (Figure 6-6). Collagen fibers are strong and wavy. These properties allow the connective tissues that they make up to be somewhat flexible and stretchy, without the fibers themselves stretching. **Dense fibrous connective tissue** is primarily made up of collagen fibers. In Table 6-3 you can see bundles of collagen fibers with widely spaced rows of fibroblasts. This type of connective tissue is very strong and is found as tendons connecting muscles to bones, making up the lower layer of the skin, and making strong attachments between organs.

TABLE 6-3 | Connective tissue

TISSUE	LOCATION	FUNCTIONS	DESCRIPTION
Dense fibrous connective tissue	Tendons (attach muscle to bone) and ligaments (attach bones to bones), attachments between organs and dermis of the skin	Support, ability to withstand great pulling forces in the direction in which the fibers are oriented	Structure consists of mostly collagen fibers with occasional rows of collagen-producing cells.
Reticular connective tissue	Liver, lymph nodes, spleen, and bone marrow	Support	The structure is intertwined reticular fibers.
Elastic connective tissue	Lung tissue, arteries	Strength with stretching and recoil	The structure consists of elastic fibers dotted with cells.
Loose connective tissue	Widely distributed throughout body; packing between glands, muscles, and nerves; attachments between the skin and underlying tissues	Support, loose packing	The structure consists of cells within a fine network of fibers (mostly collagen), which they produce. The cells and fibers are separated from each other by fluid-filled spaces.
Hyaline cartilage	Ends of long bones, joints, respiratory tubes, costal cartilage of ribs, nasal cartilage, and embryonic skeleton	Flexible support, reduction of friction between movable bones	Cartilage cells are found in lacunae within a rigid, transparent matrix. Collagen fibers are small and not visible.

TABLE 6-3 | Connective tissue—cont'd

TISSUE	LOCATION	FUNCTIONS	DESCRIPTION
Elastic cartilage	Auditory tube, external ear, epiglottis	Rigidity with flexibility, returning to original shape after being stretched	The structure resembles hyaline cartilage but has elastic fibers
Fibrocartilage	Connection between pubic bones, intervertebral disks	Support, connection, shock absorption, ability to withstand considerable pressure	The structure resembles hyaline cartilage but has thick bundles of collagen fibers.
Bone	Bones of skeleton	Strength, support, and protection of internal organs; storage of calcium; attachment for muscles	Bone-making cells (osteocytes) are found in lacunae. In compact bone (as shown) the lacunae are arranged in circles around the Haversian canals, which contain blood vessels and nerves. The structure is a hard, mineralized matrix.
Adipose connective tissue	Found under the skin, insulation of organs such as the heart, kidneys, and breasts	Storage, insulation, energy, support of organs	The structure consists of lipid-filled, ring-shaped cells packed together.
Blood	Blood vessels, heart	Protection of body from infections; transportation of oxygen, nutrients, wastes, and other materials; regulation of body temperature	The structure consists of blood cells in a fluid matrix.

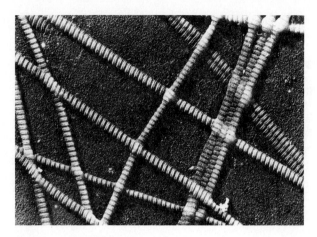

FIGURE 6-6 Collagen fibers.
Each fiber is composed of many individual collagen strands and is very strong.

Reticulin is a fine branching fiber that forms the framework of many glands such as the spleen and the lymph nodes. It also makes up the junctions between many tissues. The tissue formed by fibroblasts and reticulin alone is called **reticular connective tissue** (see Table 6-3). Elastic fibers, as the name suggests, act much like rubber bands. They are not made of collagen but of a protein called *elastin,* a "stretchy" protein. **Elastic connective tissue** is made up of branching elastic fibers with fibroblasts interspersed throughout (see Table 6-3). This type of tissue is found in structures that must expand and then return to their original shape, such as the lungs and large arteries.

Loose connective tissue contains various connective tissue cells and fibers within a semifluid matrix (see Table 6-3). Fibroblasts and macrophages are the most common cells in loose connective tissue. It also contains loosely packed elastic and collagen fibers, so it is therefore a somewhat strong but very flexible tissue. Loose connective tissue is distributed widely throughout the body and is found wrapping nerves, blood vessels, and tissues; filling spaces between body parts; and attaching the skin to the layers beneath it. If you've ever skinned chicken before cooking, for example, you've seen the loose connective tissue that binds the skin to the muscle beneath.

Cartilage cells. Chondrocytes are the cells that produce cartilage, a specialized connective tissue that is hard and strong. It is found in many places such as the ends of long bones, the airways of the respiratory system, and the spaces between the vertebrae. Cartilage is made up of cells that secrete a matrix consisting of a semisolid gel and fibers. The fibers are laid down along the lines of stress in long parallel arrays (groups or arrangements). The result of this process is a firm and flexible tissue that does not stretch.

As the cartilage cells secrete the matrix, they wall themselves off from it and eventually come to lie in tiny chambers called **lacunae.** In Table 6-3, you can see that although there are three different types of cartilage—**hyaline cartilage, elastic cartilage,** and **fibrocartilage**—they all have cartilage cells within lacunae. Their differences lie in the matrix.

Hyaline cartilage has very fine collagen fibers in its matrix that are almost impossible to see under the light microscope. During your development before birth, most of your skeleton was composed of hyaline cartilage. As an adult, you have hyaline cartilage on the ends of your long bones, cushioning the places where these bones meet. Hyaline cartilage also rings the windpipe, keeping this airway propped open, and makes up parts of your ribs and nose. Elastic cartilage, as the name suggests, has elastic fibers embedded in its matrix. It is found where support with flexibility is needed, such as in the external ear. Fibrocartilage has collagen fibers embedded in its matrix. It is therefore a very tough substance and is used in places of the body where shock absorbers are needed. It is found, for example, as discs between the vertebrae and in the knee joint.

Bone cells. Osteocytes are the cells that produce bone. As in cartilage, these cells are isolated in lacunae. They lay down a matrix of collagen fibers that become coated with small, needle-shaped crystals of calcium. The calcium makes the bone rigid, whereas the fibers keep the bone from being brittle. Bone makes up the adult skeleton, which supports the body and protects many of the organs. Bone is also a storehouse for calcium.

The bones of your skeleton have two types of internal structure: **spongy bone** and **compact bone.** Spongy bone makes up the ends of long bones and the interiors of long bones, flat bones, and irregular bones (Figure 6-7). It is composed of an open lattice of bone that supports the bone just as beams support a building (Figure 6-8). It also helps keep bones somewhat lightweight. The spaces within the latticework of bone are filled with red bone marrow, the substance that produces most of the body's blood cells.

Compact bone is denser than spongy bone and gives the bone the strength to withstand mechanical stress. In compact bone, the cells lay down matrix in thin concentric rings, forming tubes of bone around narrow channels or canals (see Table 6-3). These canals run parallel to the length of the bone, are interconnected, and contain blood vessels and nerves. The blood vessels provide a lifeline to the bone-forming cells, and the nerves control the diameter of the blood vessels and thus the flow through them.

The three different types of structural connective tissue cells each produce substances that cause the tissues of which they are a part to have distinctive characteristics. Fibroblasts produce fibers of different types that are found in dense and loose connective tissue, reticular connective tissue, and elastic connective tissue. Cartilage cells lay down a matrix of gel and fibers. Bone cells lay down a matrix of fibers that become coated with calcium.

FIGURE 6-7 Structure of a long bone.
A long bone, such as the bone located in your upper leg, is composed of spongy bone and compact bone. Spongy bone adds support and (along with the hollowed-out shaft) keeps the bone somewhat lightweight. Compact bone adds strength.

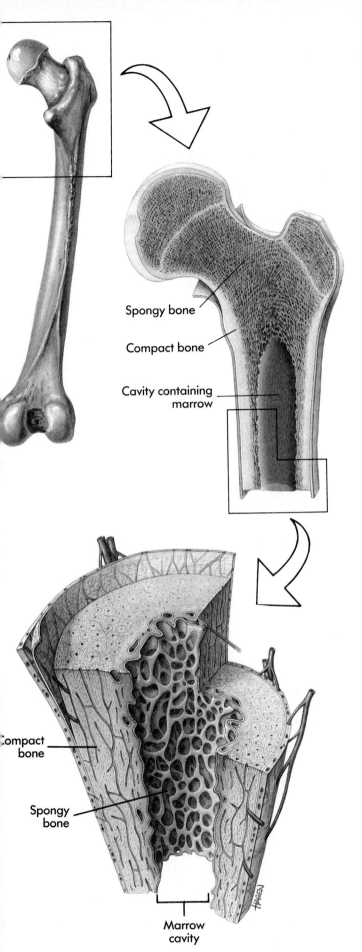

Spongy bone

Compact bone

Cavity containing marrow

Compact bone

Spongy bone

Marrow cavity

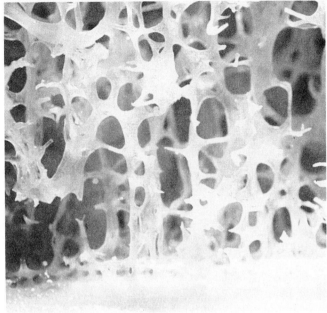

FIGURE 6-8   Spongy bone.
Although you may think of bone as hard and solid, spongy bone is composed of a delicate latticework. Bone, like most tissues in your body, is a dynamic structure, constantly renewing itself.

Cells and tissues that isolate

The third general class of connective tissue is composed of cells that specialize in accumulating and transporting particular molecules. Isolating connective tissues include the fat cells of adipose tissue as well as pigment-containing cells.

As you can see in Table 6-3, groups of fat cells as seen under a microscope bear a striking resemblance to chicken wire. The "wire" is really the cytoplasm and nucleus of each cell pushed against the cell membrane by a large fat droplet. The fat takes up much of the cell and is released when the body needs it for fuel. Although many people feel that they have more fat cells than they need for fuel emergencies, fat serves other purposes too. Adipose tissue helps shape and pad the body and insulates against heat loss.

Possibly the most important "isolating" cells are red blood cells, one of the solids that float in the fluid connective tissue called blood. Blood cells are classified according to their appearance (Figure 6-9), either as **erythrocytes** (red blood cells) or **leukocytes** (white blood cells). Some types of white blood cells were described earlier in this chapter; they include the macrophages and lymphocytes that defend the body. The role of red blood cells is very different. They act as mobile transport units, picking up and delivering gases. Cell fragments called *platelets* are also present in the blood. These cell pieces play an important role in the clotting of blood.

Red blood cells are the most common of the blood cells. There are about 5 billion in every milliliter of blood. During their maturation in the red bone marrow, they lose their nuclei and mitochondria and their endoplasmic reticula dissolve. As a result of these processes, red blood cells are rela-

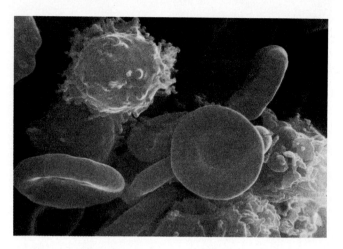

FIGURE 6-9 Blood cells.
White blood cells, or leukocytes, are roughly spherical and have irregular surfaces. Red blood cells, or erythrocytes, are disks with depressed centers.

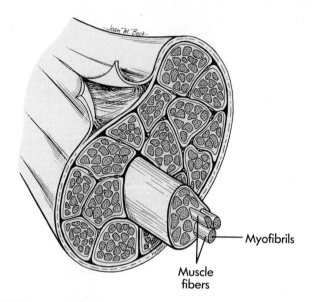

Myofibrils

Muscle fibers

FIGURE 6-10 A skeletal muscle fiber.
Muscle fibers (cells) are composed of many myofibrils. Myofibrils, in turn, are made up of microfilaments, which are responsible for muscle contraction.

tively inactive metabolically, but they still perform the life-sustaining job of carrying oxygen to your tissues. This oxygen is carried by the iron-containing pigment hemoglobin. This pigment imparts the color to red blood cells. Hemoglobin is produced within the red bone marrow as the red blood cells are formed. An amazing 300 million molecules of hemoglobin become isolated within each red blood cell.

Blood cells float in a fluid intercellular matrix, or plasma. This fluid is both the banquet table and the refuse heap of your body because practically every substance used and discarded by cells is found in the plasma. These substances include the sugars, lipids, and amino acids that are the fuel of the body, as well as the products of metabolism such as the waste gas carbon dioxide. The plasma also contains minerals such as calcium used to form bone; fibrinogen, which helps the blood to clot; albumin, which gives the blood its viscosity; and antibody proteins produced by lymphocytes. Every substance secreted or discarded by cells is also present in the plasma.

Many connective tissues are specialized for accumulating particular classes of molecules, such as fats and pigments. Red blood cells accumulate the oxygen-carrying pigment hemoglobin.

Muscle tissue

Muscle cells are the workhorses of your body. The distinguishing characteristic of muscle cells is the abundance of special thick and thin microfilaments. These microfilaments are highly organized to form strands called **myofibrils.** Each muscle cell is packed with many thousands of these myofi-

bril strands (Figure 6-10). The myofibrils shorten when the microfilaments slide past each other, causing the muscle to contract. Table 6-4 shows the three different kinds of muscle cells of the human body: **smooth muscle, skeletal muscle,** and **cardiac muscle.**

Smooth muscle

Smooth muscle cells are long, with bulging middles and tapered ends and a single nucleus. The cells are organized into sheets, forming smooth muscle tissue. This tissue contracts involuntarily—you cannot consciously control it. Because it is found in the organs, or viscera, smooth muscle tissue is also often called *visceral muscle tissue.*

Some smooth muscle contracts when it is stimulated by a nerve or hormone. Examples of smooth muscle that contract in this way are the muscles found lining your blood vessels and those that make up the iris of your eye. But nerves do not reach each muscle cell. In many cases, impulses may be able to pass directly from one smooth muscle cell to another so that a wave of contraction can pass through a layer of some kinds of smooth muscle all by itself. In other smooth muscle tissue such as that found in the wall of the intestines, individual cells may contract spontaneously when they are stretched, leading to a slow, steady squeeze of the tissue.

Skeletal muscle

Skeletal muscles are attached to your bones and allow you to move your body. These muscles are called *voluntary muscles* because you have conscious control over their action. They are also called striated muscles because the tissue has "stripes"—microscopically visible bands, or striations (see Table 6-4). These striations result from the organization of thick and thin microfilaments within the myo-

TABLE 6-4 Muscle tissue

TISSUE	LOCATION	FUNCTIONS	DESCRIPTION
Smooth muscle	Walls of hollow organs, pupil of eye, skin (attached to hair), and glands	Regulation of size of organs, forcing of fluid through tubes, control of amount of light entering eye, and production of "gooseflesh" in the skin; functioning under involuntary control	The tissue is not striated. The spindle-shaped cells have a single, centrally located nucleus.
Skeletal muscle	Attachment to bone	Movement of the body, functioning under voluntary control	The tissue is striated. Cells are large, long, and cylindrical with several nuclei.
Cardiac muscle	Heart	Pumping of blood, functioning under involuntary control	The tissue is striated. Cells are cylindrical and branching with a single centrally located nucleus.

fibrils and the alignment of the myofibrils with one another. The myofibrils are organized so that all the myofibrils within a single cell contract at the same time when the muscle cell is stimulated by a nerve.

Striated muscle cells are extremely long. A single muscle cell, or **fiber,** may run the entire length of a muscle. Each fiber has many nuclei that are pushed to the edge of the cell and lie just under the cell membrane. Bundles of these muscle cells are wrapped with connective tissue and joined with other bundles to form the muscle itself.

Cardiac muscle

The heart is composed of striated muscle fibers, but these fibers are arranged differently from their arrangements in skeletal muscle. Instead of very long cells running the length of the muscle, heart muscle is composed of chains of single cells. These chains of cells are organized into fibers that branch and interconnect, forming a latticework (see Table 6-4). This lattice structure is critical to how heart muscle functions, and it allows an entire portion of the heart to contract at one time.

Muscle cells contain microfilaments that are capable of contraction. Smooth muscle contracts involuntarily and is located in the walls of certain internal structures such as blood vessels and the stomach. Skeletal muscle is connected to bones and allows you to move your body. Cardiac muscle makes up the heart, acting as a pump for the circulatory system.

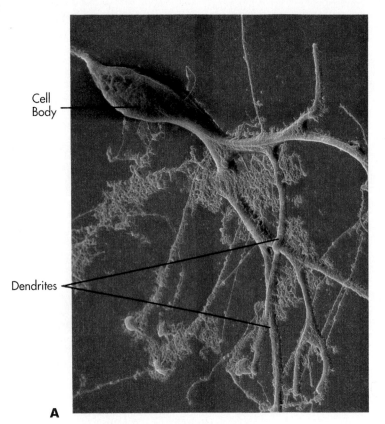

Cell Body

Dendrites

A

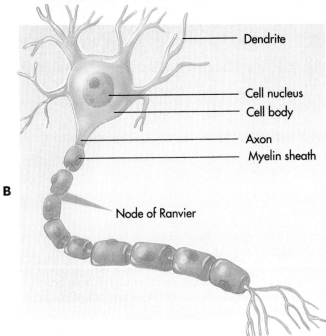

B

Dendrite

Cell nucleus
Cell body

Axon
Myelin sheath

Node of Ranvier

FIGURE 6-11 A human neuron.
A The cell body is at the upper left, with the axon extending up out of view. The branching network of fibers extending down from the cell body is made up of dendrites, which carry signals to the cell body.
B This diagram illustrates the generalized structure of a vertebrate neuron.

Nervous tissue

The fourth major class of tissue in humans is nervous tissue. It is made up of two kinds of cells: (1) **neurons,** which transmit nerve impulses, and (2) **supporting cells,** which nourish and protect the neurons.

Neurons are cells specialized to conduct an electrical current (Figure 6-11). The cell body of a neuron contains the nucleus of the cell. Two different types of projections extend from the cell body. One set of projections, the **dendrites,** act as antennae for the reception of nerve impulses and conduct these impulses toward the cell body. A single projection called an **axon** conducts impulses away from the cell body. When axons or dendrites are long, they are referred to as **nerve fibers.** Some nerve fibers are so long, in fact, that they can extend from your spinal cord all the way to your fingers or toes. Single neurons over a meter in length are common.

The **nerves,** which appear as fine white threads when they are viewed with the naked eye, are actually composed of clusters of axons and dendrites. Like a telephone trunk cable, they include large numbers of independent communication channels—bundles of hundreds of axons and dendrites, each connecting a different nerve cell with a different muscle fiber or sensory receptor. In addition, the nerve contains numerous supporting cells bunched around the nerve fibers. In the brain and spinal cord, which together make up the central nervous system, these supporting cells are called **glial cells.** The supporting cells associated with nerve fibers of all other nerve cells, which make up the peripheral nervous system, are called **Schwann cells.**

⯬⯬⯬ Neurons are cells that are specialized to conduct electrical signals. Nerve tissue is made up of these cells and supporting cells.

Organs

The four major classes of tissues that we have discussed in this chapter (see Figure 6-1) are the building blocks of the human body. These tissues form the organs of the body. Each organ contains several different types of tissue coordinated to form the structure of the organ and to perform its function. A muscle, for example, is composed of muscle cells that together make up the muscle tissue. Bundles of this tissue are wrapped in connective tissue and wired with nervous tissue. Muscles can help you walk, pump your blood, and help you digest your food. Different combinations of tissues are found in different organs that perform different functions.

Organ systems

An organ system is a group of organs that function together to carry out the principal activities of the body. Figure 6-12 shows the 11 major organ systems of the human body. The skeletal system supports and protects your body. It is moved by the large, voluntary muscles of the muscular system. Other muscles in this system help move internal fluids

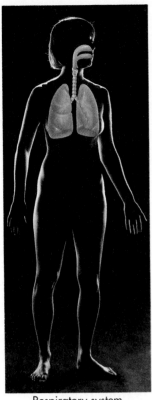

Respiratory system

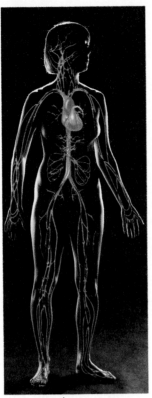

Circulatory system

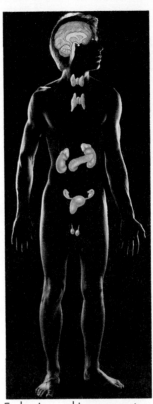

Endocrine and immune systems

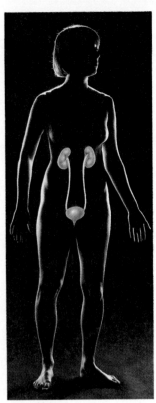

Urinary system

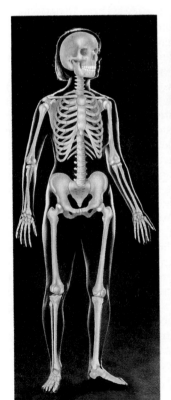

Skeletal and integumentary systems

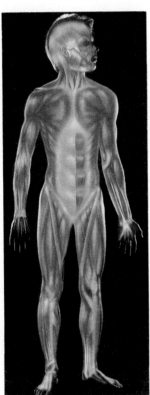

Muscular system

Reproductive system—male

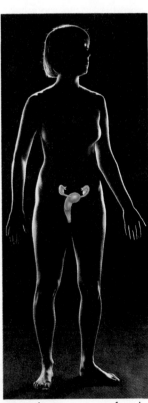

Reproductive system—female

FIGURE 6-12 The major organ systems of vertebrates. The body is composed of combinations of the four types of tissue, assembled in various ways. The many organs working together to carry out the principal activities of the body are traditionally grouped together as organ systems.

Continued.

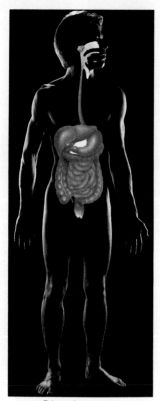

Digestive system

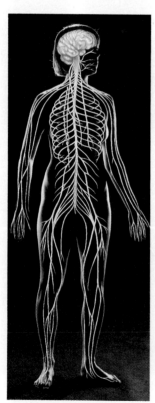

Nervous system

FIGURE 6-12. cont'd.

throughout your body. The nervous system regulates most of the organ systems. It can sense conditions in both your internal and external environment and help your body respond to this environmental information. The organs of your endocrine system secrete chemicals called *hormones* that also regulate body processes and functions. The circulatory system is the transportation system of the body. It brings nutrients and oxygen to your cells and removes the waste products of metabolism. Along with the immune and integumentary (skin) systems, it also helps defend the body against infection and disease. The respiratory system works hand in hand with the circulatory system, supplying the blood with oxygen and ridding it of the waste gas carbon dioxide. The food you eat is broken down by the digestive system and is absorbed through the intestinal walls into the bloodstream. Solid wastes are also eliminated from the body by this organ system. Liquid wastes are eliminated by the urinary system after it collects waste materials and excess water from the bloodstream. And to ensure the continuance of the human race, the reproductive system produces gametes, or sex cells, that can join in the process of fertilization to produce the first cell of a new individual.

The organism: Coordinating it all

As you can see from their descriptions, the organ systems interact with one another to keep the organism—you—alive and well. This state of "wellness" is called **homeostasis.** Put another way, homeostasis is the maintenance of a stable internal environment despite what may be a very different external environment. To maintain this internal equilibrium, all your molecules, cells, tissues, organs, and organ systems must work together.

Your body maintains a steady state by means of feedback systems or **feedback loops.** Feedback loops are mechanisms by which information regarding the status of a physiological situation or system is fed back to the system so that appropriate adjustments can be made. The thermostat in your house or apartment works by means of a feedback loop and is a good analogy to use to understand feedback loops in your body. If you set the temperature in your house at 68° F, for example, the furnace will run until that temperature is reached. A sensor in the thermostat monitors the temperature in the room, and this information triggers the electrical stimulation of the furnace. As soon as the temperature near the thermostat reaches 68° F, the thermostat sends an electrical signal to the furnace to turn off. In this way the temperature fluctuates within a small range. Such a feedback loop is called a **negative feedback loop** because the change that takes place is negative—the furnace turns off—to counter the rise in temperature. In other words, the response of the regulating mechanism (the thermostat turning off the furnace) is negative with respect to the output (the heat of the furnace). Figure 6-13 shows examples of negative feedback loops.

Most regulatory mechanisms of your body work by means of negative feedback loops. The secretion of hormones is regulated in this way (see Chapter 14). Sufficient levels of specific hormones in the blood trigger mechanisms that result in the shutdown of their secretion. Likewise,

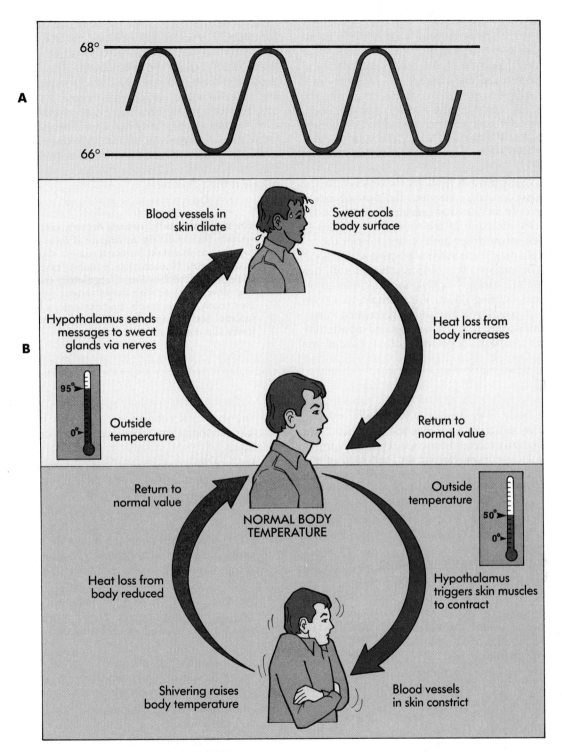

FIGURE 6-13 A negative feedback loop.
A In a negative feedback loop, the response is negative with respect to the output. Heat generated by the furnace (the output) triggers it to shut off (a negative response) when the temperature reaches a setpoint (68° F, for example). The temperature falls with no output until it reaches another point (66° F, for example), a point at which the furnace is triggered to go on. (Turning on is negative with respect to no output.) A similar process occurs in your body and is described in **B**.

your body temperature is maintained by means of negative feedback, much as the temperature of your home is maintained. When your body temperature rises too high, your thermostat (a special portion of the brain called the *hypothalamus*) senses this rise and counters it. Messages race along your nerve fibers to your sweat glands, triggering the release of sweat, which evaporates and cools the body. Blood vessels near the surface of the skin dilate, or widen, bringing blood near the surface, where the heat is dissipated. Likewise, when your body temperature falls, the hypothalamus triggers tiny muscles under the skin to contract, causing a shiver that generates heat. Blood vessels near the surface of the skin constrict, lessening the flow of blood there and the amount of heat that radiates from the body.

Very few body mechanisms are regulated by means of **positive feedback loops.** In positive feedback loops the response of the regulating mechanism is positive with respect to the output. You can see the problems inherent with this type of regulatory mechanism—a situation continues to intensify rather than shutting down. For example, in a positive feedback loop, your furnace would be stimulated to stay on when the temperature in the house reached a particular setting. Positive feedback loops most often disrupt the steady state and can even lead to death. In circulatory shock, for example, a severe loss of blood can result in such a decreased blood volume that the body cannot compensate—homeostasis cannot be maintained. The blood pressure drops and the blood flow is reduced so much that the heart and brain do not receive enough oxygen. As the heart weakens, the blood flow decreases more, weakening the heart even further. As the body becomes damaged from the loss of oxygen and nutrients, the shock worsens and can result in death. There are, however, some examples of and good uses for positive feedback in the body, including oxytocin release during childbirth.

The molecules, cells, tissues, organs, and organ systems that make up an organism must all work together to maintain homeostasis—a stable internal environment. Homeostasis is maintained by means of negative feedback loops, regulatory mechanisms that slow down or shut down output systems when they reach certain levels. For example, a high internal body temperature triggers mechanisms that lower the temperature.

Summary

1. The human body is organized hierarchically; that is, small units of structure and function together form larger units of structure and function, eventually forming the whole organism. Specifically, the cells of the body are organized into tissues. Several different tissues grouped together in a structural and functional unit make up an organ. Organs that work together to carry out particular body activities are called *organ systems.* The human body is an organism made up of 11 major organ systems.

2. The four basic types of tissue are epithelial tissue, connective tissue, muscle tissue, and nerve tissue.

3. Epithelium covers the surfaces of the body. The lining of the major body cavities is composed of simple epithelium, whereas the exterior skin is composed of stratified epithelium. The major gland systems are also derived from epithelium.

4. The defensive connective tissue cells are macrophages, which engulf foreign bacteria and antibody-coated cells or particles; lymphocytes, certain of which produce antibodies; and mast cells, which release inflammation-producing chemicals at sites of trauma.

5. The structural connective tissue cells include cartilage cells (chondrocytes), bone cells (osteocytes), and fibroblasts.

6. The isolating connective tissue cells include fat cells and pigment-accumulating cells, such as red blood cells.

7. Muscle contraction provides the force for mechanical movement of the body. There are three kinds of muscle tissue: smooth muscle, which is found in internal organs; skeletal muscle, which moves the body parts; and cardiac muscle, which makes up the heart—the pump of the circulatory system.

8. Nerve cells provide the body with a means of rapid communication. There are two kinds of nerve cells: neurons and supporting cells. Neurons are specialized for the conduction of electrical impulses.

9. Organs are body structures composed of several different tissues grouped into a structural and functional unit. An organ system is a group of organs that function together to carry out the principal activities of the body.

10. The human body is organized so that its parts form an integrated whole. These parts work together at each level of organization to maintain homeostasis—a stable internal environment within the human organism.

1. Distinguish among cells, tissues, organs, and organ systems. Given an example of each.

2. What are the four basic types of tissue in the human body? Give an example of each.

3. Draw and label the three shapes of epithelial cells. Give an example of where each is found in your body.

4. What do lymphocytes, erythrocytes, and fibroblasts have in common? How do they differ?

5. Your cat scratches your finger, and the skin surrounding the scratch turns reddish and feels warm. Explain why.

6. The text states that connective tissues are generally made up of cells spaced well apart in a nonliving matrix. Using your knowledge of cells and tissues, develop hypotheses regarding functions of the matrix.

7. Red blood cells provide the life-sustaining role of carrying oxygen to your body cells. For what cellular process is this oxygen necessary?

8. Our bones generally have reached their full growth and mature length by age 20. How then is the femur, a leg bone, of a 30-year-old man able to heal fully when broken in an accident?

9. Everybody hates fat cells. Do they serve a purpose, and if so, what purpose(s)?

10. Which type of muscle tissue is under voluntary control and may be specifically strengthened by exercise? Which type may be indirectly strengthened by aerobic exercise?

11. What sort of signals are carried on nerve fibers? Does this system work more quickly or slowly than a negative feedback hormonal loop?

12. Create a table that lists the major function(s) and at least two components of each of the principal organ systems in your body.

13. What is homeostasis? How is it achieved?

1. Certain tissues in your body do not repair themselves if damaged (nervous tissue within the brain and spinal cord is a good example), whereas other tissues like skin rapidly repair themselves. Why do you think nerve tissue in your central nervous system does not repair itself as readily as skin?

2. Hair and cilia are often present in human organ systems and their role is primarily protective or sensory. These may be damaged, causing loss of proper function in an organ. Discuss the following items and make hypotheses as to normal function of the structure, possible causes of damage, and probable results.
   a. the cilia of the inner ear
   b. nasal hairs
   c. respiratory cilia

3. Normal red blood cells are short-lived and quickly replaced by new red blood cells manufactured in the red bone marrow. Because of this, blood can be donated to others with little effect on the donor. Discuss in small groups your experience with blood donation, uses of donated blood, and present-day attitudes toward blood donation.

Caplan, A. (1984, October). Cartilage. *Scientific American*, pp. 84-97.
 This is an interesting account of the many roles played by cartilage in the vertebrate body.

Diamond, J. (1991, August). The athlete's dilemma. *Discover*, pp. 78-83.
 Many of today's top athletes may have reached the limits of human metabolism. This is an interesting look at body systems and endurance.

Houk, J.C. (1988, February). Control strategies in physiological systems. *FASEB Journal*, p. 97.
 This discussion of control systems is written for a general audience.

Montgomery, G. (1990, June). A brain reborn. *Discover*, pp. 48-57.
 Unlike the situation in some animals, some human nerve tissue doesn't regenerate when damaged. This is a study of body tissues, especially nerve tissue.

National Geographic Society: *The incredible machine*, National Geographic Society, Washington, D.C., 1986.
 This series of outstanding articles on the human body focuses on its major organ systems. It is beautifully illustrated and fun to read.

BIOETHICAL DECISIONMAKING
Stem Cells and the Next Stage of Gene Therapy

Consider the following questions as you think about the bioethical dilemma presented on page 21:

1. What are the bioethical issues in this case?
   - What has to be decided?
   - Who are the decisionmakers?
   - Outline the decisionmaking process in this case as you understand it.

2. What factual information do the decisionmakers need? Consider the effects of the answers to the following questions on the decisionmaking process.
   - What information on gene therapy has been obtained from animal studies?
   - What is the current status of other gene therapy research? Aside from the patient with SCID, have other human clinical trials taken place? If so, what are the results of this experimentation?
   - What are the possible detrimental effects of inserting new genes into stem cells? Is there anyway to predict all the detrimental effects?
   - What other therapies are used to treat ADA-deficient individuals? Are they effective?
   - What is the advantage of altering stem cells instead of T cells? Are these advantages crucial to the life of the ADA-deficient individual? Would a patient be completely cured with either therapy?
   - What other questions should the decisionmakers ask?
   - What additional factual information do the decisionmakers need?

3. Who are the "stakeholders" in this decision—those who stand to gain or lose as a result of the decision?
   - Is the ADA-deficient individual participating in the experiment a stakeholder? All ADA-deficient individuals? What other persons or groups are stakeholders?
   - Which stakeholders are decisionmakers? Which are not decisionmakers? Will individuals in the latter group be able to influence the decisionmaking process? Should they have influence?
   - In what ways would each stakeholder be affected by the decision?

4. What are the values at stake in the decision? As you list and describe them, consider the following questions:
   - Is it ethical to subject patients to highly experimental gene therapies if alternative therapies exist?
   - Is it ethical to alter the genome of a human being even to cure a previously incurable disease?
   - What religious or spiritual questions are raised by this dilemma? Do the values reflected in these questions have a place in scientific endeavors?
   - Should scientists be allowed to conduct experiments of this nature without the input of a board such as the Recombinant DNA Advisory Committee? Does the committee foster or impede scientific creativity?
   - If this experiment is approved, what other types of stem cell manipulation experiments should be approved? What about an experiment inserting a gene into a stem cell, changing a person's rare blood type to a more common type, so that if the person needs a blood transfusion, the correct blood type will always be available?
   - This technology can alter the genetic makeup of sex cells, creating new genetic traits that could be passed on to future generations. Should scientists be allowed to conduct experiments of this nature? In what ways are the issues regarding sex cell therapy the same as or different from the issues regarding somatic (body) cell therapy?

5. What options are available to the decisionmakers? As you list these options, consider the following questions:
   - Which of these alternatives seem ethically feasible? Which seem administratively possible?
   - How would each alternative decision affect each of the stakeholders?
   - Is there a compromise solution that might give all parties the sense that they have come out the "winner" in the decision?

6. What are the values inherent to the decisionmaking process?
   - Is the decisionmaking process fair?
   - Do all stakeholders have equal resources to advocate their position?
   - What further steps might each group of stakeholders take if their views are disallowed?

P A R T T W O

Maintenance Systems

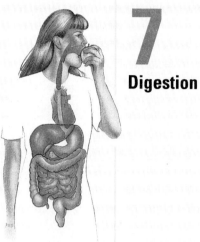

7
Digestion

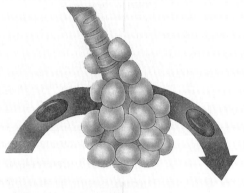

8
Respiration

9
Circulation

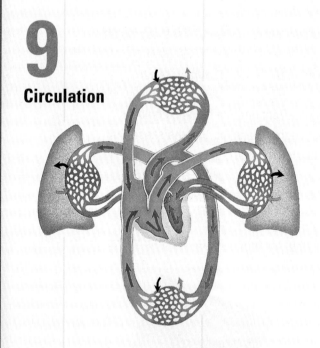

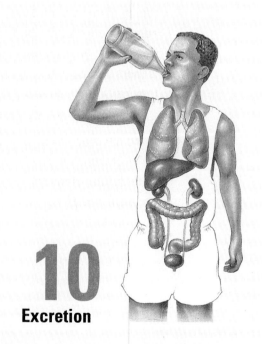

10
Excretion

BIOETHICAL DECISIONMAKING
Family Wishes and Patient Autonomy

A 75-year-old man was admitted to the intensive care unit of a hospital in acute respiratory distress, gasping for breath. He had suffered from chronic obstructive pulmonary disease (see page 160) for the past 15 years. Although he had stopped smoking 6 years ago, his condition had deteriorated and he had been confined to his home. Before this hospital visit his condition had been diagnosed as emphysema, in which many of the alveoli, the tiny air sacs in his lungs, had lost their elasticity and could no longer expel air.

Tests showed that the man now had bilateral pneumonia, in which both lungs are infected with a bacterium that causes inflammation of the lung tissue. He was given antibiotics and put on a mechanical respirator with supplemental oxygen. Within 2 weeks the pneumonia was largely cleared, and his physician began to try to wean him from the respirator. Unfortunately, he had become "respirator dependent" because of damage to his lungs in addition to the emphysema caused by the infection, weakened respiratory muscles, and fear of breathing on his own. Despite a slow, cautious approach and much reassurance, the weaning attempts repeatedly failed. Short of breath and terrified, the patient would demand to be placed back on the respirator.

The physician rated the chances of successfully weaning the patient from the respirator at "maybe 20 percent." Meanwhile, the patient became more and more discouraged because of his lack of progress and the painful medical procedures he had to undergo, such as constant intravenous feeding, frequent needle punctures to check the level of oxygen in his blood, and frequent suctioning of his respiratory passageways. After 3 weeks of unsuccessful weaning efforts, the man refused to cooperate with further attempts. His wife and son became concerned that he had given up the will to live. They begged the medical staff to "do something to save him." Although he had become less communicative, the patient remained alert and aware. In the opinion of the staff, he was fully competent. He told his physician that he wanted the respirator disconnected. "I want to die," he said.

If you were the physician, what would you do?

7 | Digestion

▼ Carbohydrates, fats, and proteins supply the body with energy and the raw materials to build the substances it needs.

▼ Vitamins and minerals help the chemical reactions of the body take place; water provides the medium for these reactions.

▼ Digestion breaks down the energy nutrients—carbohydrates, fats, and proteins—into smaller molecules that can be used to produce ATP by means of cellular respiration.

▼ Parts of the digestive system are specialized to perform both the mechanical and chemical processes of digestion.

What's wrong with this picture? Take a critical look at the photograph and solve this nutrition puzzle. Fish is certainly a healthy choice, you might be thinking, and you are correct. In fact, evidence suggests that a group of substances in fish oil protects the human body against heart attack. In addition, fish is generally lower in calories than beef or poultry and has other healthy qualities. The problem is that the typical American dinner usually contains double, triple, or sometimes quadruple the amount of protein needed for the entire day! The half-pound of fish here is too hefty a portion of protein.

Vegetables and a potato are also healthy food choices. However, the butter that is saturating these foods is not a good choice. This fat, plus the fat in the salad dressing and ice cream, means that at least half the calories in this meal come from fat—far too many when you realize that one tablespoon of vegetable oil satisfies your daily requirement.

The sugary soda and dessert probably caught your eye. As you may know, refined sugar, or sucrose, is a relatively simple carbohydrate that provides only calories—something most Americans already consume in excess. Sugar is therefore often called a source of "empty" calories, and it also promotes tooth decay.

How would you change the composition of this meal to make it healthier? Do you know which types of foods to add and which to cut down on or omit? To do this task, you may need to know the answers to a few questions. What are nutrients? Why do we need them to survive? What amounts and types of nutrients do we need? And how do our bodies get these nutrients from the food we eat? The answers to some of these questions begin the story of digestion. By the time you finish reading this chapter, you should be able to answer all the questions.

The nutrition-digestion connection

Humans are heterotrophs, organisms that cannot produce their own food. Heterotrophs must ingest, or take in, food. At least 95% of the species of organisms on Earth—all animals, all fungi, and most protists and bacteria—are heterotrophs. Food provides these "other-feeders" with two things: (1) energy and (2) the raw materials to build the substances they need. The energy in food is described in units called **calories,** or more properly kilocalories (thousands of calories, or kcal). The raw materials are called **nutrients.**

There are six classes of nutrients: **carbohydrates, fats** (lipids), **proteins, vitamins, minerals,** and **water.** These are the substances, in fact, that make up most of your body. Assuming that you are a proper weight for your height, your body is made up of about 60% water and about 20% fat. The other 20% is mostly protein, carbohydrate, combinations of these two substances, and two major minerals found in your bones: calcium and phosphorus. Other minerals and vitamins make up less than 1% of you.

As you may recall from Chapter 2, carbohydrates, lipids, and proteins are organic (carbon-containing) compounds and are used by your body as a source of energy, or kilocalories. They are therefore often referred to as the energy nutrients. (Proteins, however, are not a preferred energy source.) In addition, these three organic compounds are used as building blocks for growth and repair as well as to produce other substances your body may need.

Your body does not obtain energy from vitamins, minerals, or water. Vitamins are organic molecules that perform functions such as helping your body to form red blood cells and to unlock the energy in carbohydrates, fats, and proteins. Although required only in small amounts, each of the 13 different vitamins plays a vital role in your body (Table 7-1). Many, such as the B vitamins, are used for the synthesis of coenzymes, small molecules that help enzymes work. For example, niacin and riboflavin, two of the B vitamins, are used to make the coenzymes NAD and FAD , which function in cellular respiration (see Chapter 5). The roles and interactions of some other vitamins, such as vitamin C, are not as well understood.

| TABLE 7-1 | Major vitamins and minerals |

VITAMINS AND MINERALS	MAJOR FUNCTION	RICH FOOD SOURCES	RDA* (MG)	SIGNS AND SYMPTOMS	
				DEFICIENCY	TOXICITY
VITAMINS					
A	Formation of visual pigments, maintenance of epithelial cells	Green or yellow fruits and vegetables, milk products, liver	0.8-1.0	Night blindness, dry skin, growth failure	Headache, nausea birth defects
Thiamin	Coenzyme in CO_2 removal during cellular respiration	Pork, whole grains, seeds and nuts	1.1-1.5	Mental confusion, loss of muscular coordination	None from food
Riboflavin	Part of coenzymes FAD and FMN	Liver, leafy greens, dairy products, eggs, meats	1.3-1.7	Dry skin, cracked lips	None from food
Niacin	Part of coenzymes NAD^+ and $NADP^+$	Wheat bran, tuna, chicken, beef, enriched breads and cereals	15-19	Skin problems, diarrhea, depression, death	Skin flushing
Pantothenic acid	Part of coenzyme A, energy metabolism	Widespread in foods	4-7†	Rare	None from food
B_6	Protein metabolism	Animal proteins, spinach, broccoli, bananas	1.6-2.0	Anemia, headaches, convulsions	Numbness, paralysis
B_{12}	Coenzyme for amino acids and nucleic acid metabolism	Animal foods	0.002	Pernicious anemia	None from food

*Recommended Dietary Allowances (1989) values are for adults.
†Estimated minimum requirement for adults (no RDA established).
‡Estimated safe and adequate daily dietary intake for adults (no RDA established).

TABLE 7-1 | Major vitamins and minerals—cont'd

VITAMINS AND MINERALS	MAJOR FUNCTION	RICH FOOD SOURCES	RDA* (MG)	SIGNS AND SYMPTOMS	
				DEFICIENCY	TOXICITY
Biotin	Coenzyme in carbohydrate and fat metabolism, fat synthesis	Liver, peanuts, cheese, egg yolk	0.03-0.10†	Rare	Rare
Folate	Nucleic acid and amino acid synthesis	Green leafy vegetables, orange juice, liver	0.18-0.20	Anemia, embryonic neural tube defects	None from food
C	Collagen synthesis, antioxidant	Citrus fruits, broccoli, greens	60	"Scurvy"-poor wound healing, bruises	Diarrhea, kidney stones
D	Absorption of calcium and phosphorus, bone formation	Vitamin D fortified milk, fish oils	0.005-0.010	"Rickets"-bone deformities	Calcium deposits in soft tissues, growth failure
E	Antioxidant	Vegetable oils	8-10	Rare	Muscle weakness, interferes with vitamin K metabolism
K	Synthesis of blood clotting substances	Green leafy vegetables, liver	0.06-0.08	Hemorrhage	Anemia
▼ **MAJOR MINERALS**					
Calcium (Ca)	Component of bone and teeth, blood clotting, nerve transmission, muscle action	Dairy products, canned fish	800-1200	Osteoporosis	Kidney stones
Phosphorus (P)	Component of bone and teeth, energy transfer (ATP), component of nucleic acids	Dairy products, meat, soft drinks	800-1200	None	Bone loss if calcium intake is low
Magnesium (Mg)	Bone formation, muscle and nerve function	Wheat bran, green vegetables, nuts	280-350	Weakness, muscle pain	Rare
Sodium (Na)	Osmotic pressure, nerve transmission	Salt, seafood, processed food	500‡	Nausea, vomiting, muscle cramps	Possible hypertension
Chlorine (Cl)	HCl synthesis, osmotic pressure, nerve transmission	Salt, processed food	700‡	Rare	Possible hypertension
Potassium (K)	Osmotic pressure, nerve transmission	Fruits and vegetables	2000‡	Heart irregularities, muscle cramps	Slowed heart rate
Iron (Fe)	Hemoglobin synthesis, oxygen transport	Liver, meat, enriched breads and cereals	10-15	Anemia	Constipation, death from overdose of children's Fe supplements

Continued.

TABLE 7-1 Major vitamins and minerals—cont'd

VITAMINS AND MINERALS	MAJOR FUNCTION	RICH FOOD SOURCES	RDA* (MG)	SIGNS AND SYMPTOMS	
				DEFICIENCY	TOXICITY
Zinc (Zn)	Component of many enzymes including those involved in growth, sexual development, and immune function	Seafood, liver, meats, whole grains	12-15	Skin rash, poor growth, hair loss	Diarrhea, depressed immune function
Iodine (I)	Thyroid hormone production	Iodized salt, seafood	0.15	Goiter	Interferes with thyroid function
Fluorine (F)	Strengthens teeth	Fluoridated water, tea	1.5-4.0	Increased risk of dental caries	Teeth become stained during development
Copper (Cu)	Iron metabolism, component of many enzymes	Liver, cocoa, whole grains	1.5-3.0†	Anemia	Rare, vomiting

Minerals are inorganic substances and are transported around the body as ions dissolved in the blood and other body fluids. Your body uses a variety of minerals, and they perform a variety of functions (see Table 7-1). Calcium, for example, does many jobs, including making up a part of the structure of your bones and teeth and helping your blood to clot. Sodium plays a key role in regulating the fluid balance within your body. Magnesium is an important player in the process of releasing energy from carbohydrates, fats, and proteins.

Water provides the medium in which all the body's reactions take place. Along with dissolved substances and (sometimes) suspended solids, it bathes your cells, makes up much of the cytosol within your cells, and courses through your arteries and veins. It even lubricates your joints and cushions organs such as the brain and spinal cord. The atoms that make up water molecules are also held within the bonds of the energy molecules. These atoms are key players when bonds are broken (by hydrolysis) or formed (by dehydration synthesis) in these molecules. (See Chapter 2 for a description of the processes of hydrolysis and dehydration synthesis.)

Your body obtains the energy and raw materials it needs to survive from six classes of nutrients. Carbohydrates, fats, and proteins provide energy and building blocks. Vitamins, minerals, and water help body processes take place. Some minerals are also incorporated into body structures.

To obtain these nutrients and energy from the food you ingest, your body must first digest the food. **Digestion** is a process in which food particles are broken down into small molecules that can be absorbed by the body. Digestion is also carried out mechanically in the mouth as food is crushed by the teeth and in the stomach as food is churned by the stomach's muscular walls. Digestion is carried out chemically in three ways: (1) by hydrochloric acid (HCl), which denatures, or unfolds, protein molecules and disrupts the protein glue that holds cells together; (2) by bile salts, which emulsify, or separate, large lipid droplets into much smaller lipid droplets; and (3) by a variety of highly specific enzymes that help cleave certain chemical bonds (Table 7-2). As you read in Chapter 4, enzymes are proteins that speed up the rate of chemical reactions in living things. In fact, without enzymes, you would die before needed chemical reactions took place!

The enzymes that help digest the energy nutrients—proteins, carbohydrates, and lipids—are of three basic types:

1. **Proteases,** which break down proteins to smaller polypeptides and polypeptides to amino acids.
2. **Amylases,** which break down starches and glycogen to sugars. (Both starch and glycogen are storage forms of polysaccharides.)
3. **Lipases,** which break down the triglycerides in lipids to fatty acids and glycerol.

Proteins, carbohydrates, and lipids, along with their breakdown products, are described in Chapter 2.

During digestion, proteins are unfolded by hydrochloric acid and are then cleaved into peptides and individual amino acids by protease enzymes. Starch and glycogen are digested to sugars by amylases. Triglycerides are digested to fatty acids and glycerol by lipases.

TABLE 7-2 | Digestive enzymes

SOURCE	ENZYME	SUBSTRATE	DIGESTION PRODUCT
Salivary gland	Amylase	Starch, glycogen	Disaccharides
Stomach	Pepsin	Proteins	Short polypeptides
Small intestine	Peptidases	Short peptides	Amino acids
	Lactase ⎫		
	Maltase ⎬ disaccharidases	Disaccharides	Glucose, monosaccharides
	Sucrase ⎭		
Pancreas	Pancreatic amylase	Starch, glycogen	Disaccharides
	Trypsin	Proteins	Polypeptides
	Chymotrypsin		
	Carboxypeptidase		

Where it all begins: The mouth

Does your mouth ever water when you think about your favorite food? Does the smell of some of your favorite foods also evoke this reaction? Do you know why this reaction occurs?

The water in your mouth is really a secretion from a set of glands called **salivary glands.** The locations and names of each of these glands are shown in Figure 7-1. Their secretion, **saliva,** is a solution that consists primarily of water, mucus, and the digestive enzyme **salivary amylase.** Other substances can be found in smaller amounts, such as antibodies and a bacteria-killing enzyme.

Salivary amylase breaks down starch into molecules of the disaccharide maltose. During this reaction, the starch is broken down on the addition of water—a process called **hydrolysis.**

Starch + Water $\xrightarrow{\text{Salivary amylase}}$ Maltose

Enzymes that break down substances by hydrolysis are called *hydrolyzing enzymes.* Along with playing this role in digestion, the saliva also moistens and lubricates food so that it is swallowed easily and does not scratch the tissues of the throat.

The secretions of the salivary glands are controlled by the nervous system. Although the nervous system works to maintain a constant secretion of saliva in the mouth, it speeds up the secretion when it is stimulated by the presence (or sometimes the sight, smell, or thought) of food. When food is in the mouth, nerve endings called *chemoreceptors,* which are sensitive to the presence of certain chemicals, send a signal to the brain, which responds by stimulating the salivary glands. Did you ever suck on a slice of lemon? Then you know that the most potent stimuli are acid solutions; lemon juice can increase the rate of salivation eightfold.

Mechanical digestion begins when the teeth tear food apart into tiny pieces. In this way the surface area of the food is increased, allowing the digestive enzymes to mix

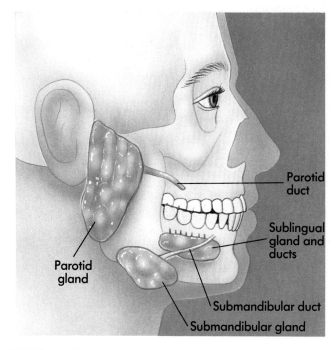

FIGURE 7-1 The salivary glands.
Saliva, the solution that these glands secrete, contains salivary amylase, an enzyme that breaks down starch into maltose.

with the food and break it down more quickly and completely. The teeth of humans as well as those of other organisms are specialized in different ways. This specialization depends on the type of food an organism eats and how it obtains its food. Human beings are **omnivores.** An omnivore eats both plant and animal foods. As a result, human teeth are structurally intermediate between the pointed, cutting teeth characteristic of **carnivores,** or meat eaters, and the flat, grinding teeth characteristic of **herbivores,** or plant eaters. In fact, the teeth of humans are like carnivores in the front and herbivores in the back.

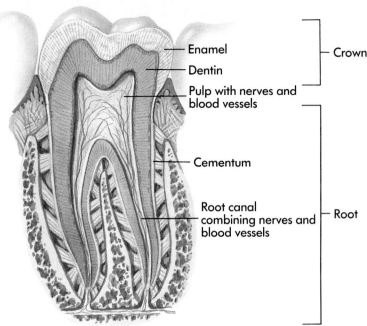

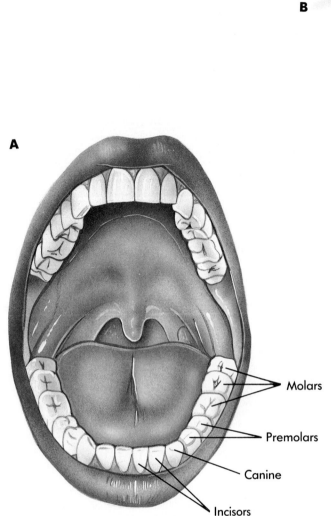

FIGURE 7-2 Teeth in humans.
A The four front teeth are incisors, used for biting. Canines are used for tearing food. The premolars and molars are used for grinding and crushing.
B Although you may forget until you are in the dentist's chair, each tooth in your mouth is alive and contains nerves and blood vessels.

The four front teeth in the upper and lower jaws of humans are **incisors** (Figure 7-2, *A*). These teeth are sharp and chisel shaped and are used for biting. On each side of the incisors are pointed teeth called **canines,** which are used in tearing food. Behind each canine, on each side of the mouth and along both top and bottom jaws, are two **premolars** and three **molars,** all of which have flattened ridged surfaces for grinding and crushing food. In early childhood, however, humans do not have these 32 adult teeth but only 20 "baby teeth." These first teeth are lost during childhood and are replaced by the 32 adult teeth.

Each tooth is alive and is rooted in the bones of the upper and lower jaw. The gums cover this bone; the portion of the tooth protruding above the gumline is called the **crown** (Figure 7-2, *B*). The portion of the tooth that extends into the bone is called the **root.** Inside lies a central, nourishing **pulp** containing nerves, blood vessels, and connective tissue. The nerves and blood vessels pass out of the tooth through holes at the root. The actual chewing surface of the tooth is made up of enamel—the hardest substance in the body. It is layered over the softer dentin that forms the body of the tooth.

Teeth shred and grind the plant and animal material that humans ingest as food. Saliva secreted into the mouth moistens the food, which aids its journey into the rest of the digestive system and begins its enzymatic digestion.

The journey of food to the stomach

As food is chewed and moistened, the tongue forms it into a ball-like mass called a **bolus** and pushes it into the **pharynx.** The pharynx is the upper part of the throat (Figure 7-3). As this happens, the soft palate raises up, sealing off the nasal cavity and preventing any food from entering this chamber. The soft palate is the tissue at the back of the roof of the mouth. The pressure of the food in the pharynx stimulates nerves in its walls that begin the swallowing reflex, an involuntary action. As part of this reflex action, the voice box, or **larynx,** raises up to meet the **epiglottis,** a flap of tissue that folds back over the opening to the larynx. With this action the epiglottis acts much like a trapdoor, closing over the **glottis,** the opening to the larynx and trachea (your windpipe) so that food will not go down the wrong way. If you place your hand over your larynx (Adam's apple), you can feel it move up when you swallow.

After passing into the pharynx and then bypassing the windpipe, the food enters the **esophagus,** a food tube that connects the pharynx to the stomach (Figure 7-4). The esophagus, which is about 25 centimeters long (a bit less than a foot), pierces the diaphragm before it connects to the stomach. The diaphragm is a sheet-like muscle that forms the floor of the chest cavity; it is a muscle of breathing (see Chapter 8). The opening in the diaphragm that allows the esophagus to pass is called the *esophageal hiatus* (opening). Sometimes the stomach, intestine, or other abdominal organ pushes through this opening up into the chest, resulting in occasional heartburn. Such a condition, called a *hiatal hernia,* is quite common, especially in people over 50 years of age, but it can be treated with a bland diet, antacids, and sleeping with the head elevated.

The esophagus ends at the door to the stomach. This door is called the **cardiac opening** and is ringed by a circular muscle called the **lower esophageal sphincter.** When the ring of muscle contracts, or tightens, it closes the cardiac opening. When it relaxes, or loosens, it opens this stomach door. Although it is in the abdominal cavity, the cardiac opening is located very close to the heart, which lies just above it in the thoracic cavity. Have you ever had heartburn? This distress is caused when the acid contents of the stomach splash back into the esophagus at the cardiac opening. The acid burns the esophagus—but it feels like your heart is on fire!

The esophagus does not take part in digestion but instead acts like an escalator, moving food down toward the stomach. The sets of longitudinal and circular muscles in its walls work in tandem to produce successive waves of contractions called **peristalsis** (Figure 7-5). The movement of food to the stomach is therefore not dependent on gravity, so even astronauts in zero gravity—or you standing on your head—can swallow without difficulty.

> When the tongue pushes food into the pharynx, nerves stimulate the swallowing reflex. The food then enters the esophagus, or food tube, and is moved to the stomach by rhythmic muscular contractions called peristalsis.

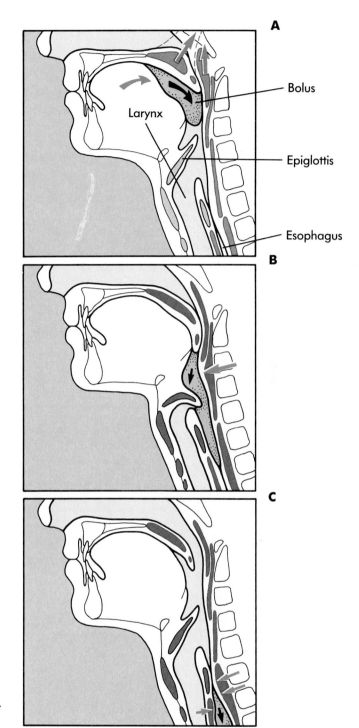

FIGURE 7-3 How humans swallow.
As food passes the rear of the mouth **(A)**, muscles raise the soft palate against the back wall of the pharynx, sealing off the nasal passage. In addition, a flap of tissue called the *epiglottis* folds down **(B)**, sealing the respiratory passage. After the food enters the esophagus, the soft palate lowers and the epiglottis is raised **(C)**, opening the respiratory passage between the nasal cavity and the trachea.

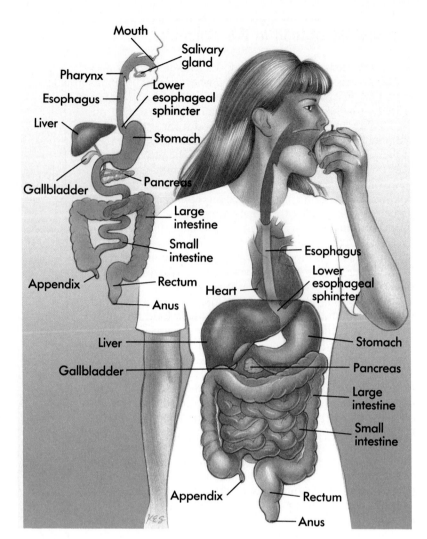

FIGURE 7-4 The human digestive system. Note the location of the cardiac opening, which acts as a door to the stomach. The pain of heartburn is caused when acid in the stomach splashes through this opening, burning the esophagus.

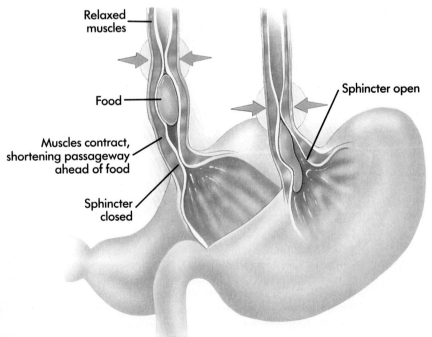

FIGURE 7-5 Peristalsis. Successive waves of contraction move food down the esophagus to the stomach.

Preliminary digestion: The stomach

The lower esophageal sphincter relaxes when food reaches it, allowing food to enter the **stomach.** The stomach is a muscular sac in which the food is collected and partially digested by hydrochloric acid and proteases (Figure 7-6). The stomach then "feeds" this food, little by little, to the primary organ of digestion, the small intestine.

The stomach and intestinal tract have the same basic structural plan (Figure 7-7). Their interiors are lined with a layer of tissue called the **mucosa.** The mucosa consists of epithelial cells, blood and lymph vessels, and a thin layer of muscle. It covers a deeper, thicker layer of connective tissue, the **submucosa,** which is rich in blood vessels and nerves. Surrounding the connective tissue are layers of smooth muscle tissue—three in the stomach and two in the intestines. An envelope of tough connective tissue called **serosa** serves as the outer covering of the digestive tract (as well as the other abdominal organs). Thin sheets of connective tissue called **mesentery** are attached to the serosa along most of the intestinal tract, holding it in place and serving as a highway for blood vessels and nerves.

The inner surface of the stomach is dotted with **gastric glands** that extend from the epithelium but dip deeply into the mucosa. Two different kinds of cells in these glands secrete a gastric juice made up of hydrochloric acid and the protein pepsinogen. After the secretion of both, the acid chemically interacts with the pepsinogen, converting it to the protein-hydrolyzing enzyme **pepsin.** The hydrochloric acid also softens the connective tissue in foods; denatures, or unfolds, large protein molecules; and kills most bacteria that may have been ingested with the food. The pepsin digests only proteins, breaking them down into short polypeptides. Other epithelial cells are specialized for the secretion of mucus. This mucus, produced in large quantities, lubricates the stomach wall and protects the stomach from digesting itself.

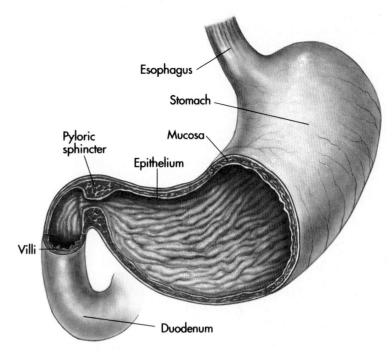

FIGURE 7-6   The stomach.
The stomach stores food, partially digests it with hydrochloric acid and proteases, and moves the food to the small intestine.

The stomach controls the production of gastric juice by means of a digestive hormone called **gastrin** (Table 7-3). Hormones are regulating chemicals that are made at one place in the body and work in another. Gastrin is produced by endocrine (hormone-secreting) cells that are scattered throughout the epithelium of the stomach. Some stomachs greatly overproduce gastrin, however, which results in excessive acid production. The causes of this overproduction include such factors as stress, heredity, diet, and smoking.

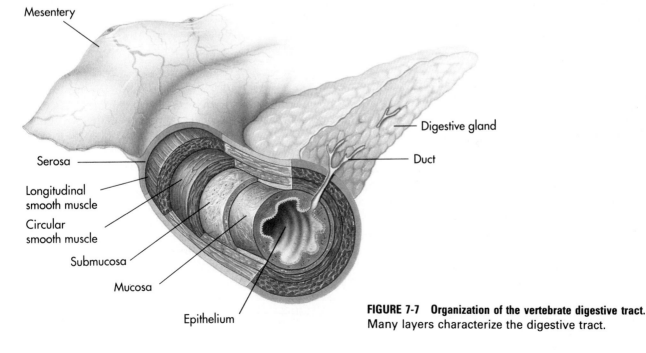

FIGURE 7-7   Organization of the vertebrate digestive tract.
Many layers characterize the digestive tract.

| TABLE 7-3 | Hormones of digestion |

HORMONE	SOURCE	STIMULUS	ACTION	NOTE
Gastrin	Stomach	Entry of food into stomach	Regulates secretion of HCl	Unusual in that it acts on same organ that secretes it
Cholecystokinin (CCK)	Duodenum	Arrival of food in small ingestine	Stimulates gallbladder contraction and therefore the release of bile salts into intestine, stimulates secretion of digestive enzymes by pancreas	CCK bears a striking structural resemblance to gastrin
Secretin	Duodenum	HCl in duodenum	Stimulates pancreas to secrete bicarbonate, which neutralizes stomach acid	The first hormone to be discovered (1902)

This extra acid may attack the walls of the first portion of the small intestine, or duodenum, burning holes through the wall. These holes are called **duodenal ulcers** (see box on p. 139). Because the contents of the small intestine are not normally acidic, this organ is much less able to withstand the disruptive actions of stomach acid than the wall of the stomach is. For this reason, over 90% of all ulcers are duodenal, although other ulcers sometimes occur in the stomach.

Food stays in the stomach for approximately 2 to 6 hours. During this time the contractions of the muscular wall of the stomach churn the food, mixing it with the gastric juice and mucus. By the time the food is ready to leave the stomach as a substance called **chyme,** it has the consistency of pea soup. The gate to the small intestine, the **pyloric sphincter,** opens to allow just a bit of the chyme to pass through. When the acid in this chyme is neutralized and the food is digested, the pyloric sphincter is signaled by the nervous system to open again, allowing the next bit of chyme to pass.

▼▼ In the stomach, concentrated acid breaks up connective tissue and unfolds proteins. These proteins are digested by pepsin into short polypeptides. Starches and lipids are not digested in the stomach.

Terminal digestion and absorption:The small intestine

Most of the digestion of food takes place in the small intestine. Within this organ, starches and glycogen are broken down to sugars, proteins to amino acids, and lipids to fatty acids and glycerol. These products of digestion then pass through the cells of the intestinal mucosa and diffuse into the blood in underlying blood vessels. The triglycerides move into the lymph in neighboring lymphatic vessels.

All of this activity takes place in the **small intestine,** the tube-like portion of the digestive tract that begins at the pyloric sphincter and ends at its **T**-shaped junction with the large intestine. Although the small intestine is approximately 6 meters long—long enough to stretch from the ground to the top of a two-story building—only the first 25 centimeters (8 inches) is actively involved in digestion. This initial portion of the small intestine is called the **duodenum.** The other portions of the small intestine, the **jejunum** and the **ileum,** are highly specialized (along with the duodenum) to aid in the absorption of the products of digestion by the blood and lymph.

Accessory organs that help digestion

Some of the enzymes necessary for digestion are secreted by the salivary glands, epithelial cells of the stomach, and epithelial cells of the duodenum. The others are secreted by the **pancreas,** a long gland that lies beneath the stomach and is surrounded on one side by the curve of the duodenum (see Figure 7-4). A tiny duct runs from the pancreas to the small intestine and serves as the passageway for the pancreatic juice. As you can see from Table 7-2, this secretion of the pancreas includes a number of digestive enzymes.

The **liver** is another organ that works with the duodenum to digest food. This organ, which weighs over 3 pounds, lies just under the diaphragm (see Figure 7-4). It is one of the most complex organs of the body and performs over 500 functions! Although the liver produces no digestive enzymes, it does help in the digestion of lipids by secreting a collection of molecules called **bile.** One of the many components of bile is bile pigments, breakdown products of the hemoglobin from old, worn-out red blood cells. These pigments give bile its greenish color. The bile also contains bile salts, which are substances that act much like detergents, breaking lipids up into minute droplets of triglycerides, similar to droplets of cream suspended in milk. The liver manufactures bile salts from cholesterol. Excess

Everyone has seen the portrayal of the hard-hitting executive who barks orders, has no time for relaxation and is the proud owner of a "bleeding" ulcer. Unfortunately, this portrayal is no longer confined to business people who thrive on stress. Many people now have ulcers, and sufferers are from all walks of life, including children and college students. In addition, the incidence of ulcers among women is on the rise.

What is an ulcer? Basically, an ulcer is a hole that develops in the lining of the digestive tract (Figure 7-A). These holes or sores develop because of an excess of hydrochloric acid secretion in the digestive tract that literally burns a hole through the protective mucus in the tract. Ulcers are divided into two types: peptic and duodenal. Peptic ulcers occur in the lining of the stomach itself. Duodenal ulcers are more common and, as their name implies, are located in the duodenum, the first segment of the small intestine that leads from the stomach. The duodenum is especially sensitive to acid, since it is essentially a basic environment. Acid mixed with the stomach contents, if it is not neutralized before it leaves the stomach and enters the small intestine, can irritate the duode-

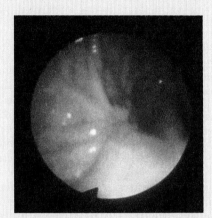

FIGURE 7-A View of an ulcer from the end of an endoscope.

num and cause ulcers. Duodenal ulcers are more likely than peptic ulcers to perforate (punch through) the lining of the tract, causing bleeding and potential infection of the surrounding organs by the contents of the stomach.

The most common symptom of ulcers is pain. The classic symptom of an ulcer is a boring pain in the stomach that occurs 1 to 2 hours after eating. The pain is relieved when the affected individual eats again. The pain is caused by excess acid irritating the

ulcer; when food is introduced into the stomach again, the acid is neutralized and the pain subsides.

The factors contributing to ulcers are numerous. Smoking seems to be linked to ulcers, since cigarette smoke stimulates acid production in the stomach. In fact, experts think that the increase in smoking among women is a prime factor in their increase in ulcers. Prolonged aspirin intake has also been implicated in the incidence of ulcers. Of course, stress and emotional tension have always been linked to ulcers. Recently, researchers have discovered that a bacterium called *Heliobacter pylori* might cause ulcers. This bacterium is extremely common and enters the body through human contact or dirty water. Researchers estimate that as many as 50% of all Americans harbor this bacteria in their stomachs. The good news is that once diagnosed, the patient can be treated with antibiotics, which destroy the bacteria and cure the ulcers.

You can do a lot to prevent ulcers. First, don't smoke. Watch your intake of aspirin, and if it is a problem for you, learn to deal more effectively with stress. By protecting your digestive tract with common sense, you can avoid the pain of ulcers.

---

bile is stored and concentrated in the **gallbladder** on the underside of the liver. A bile duct brings bile from the liver and gallbladder to the small intestine.

The liver and pancreas, although not organs of the digestive system, help digestion take place. The pancreas secretes a number of digestive enzymes. The liver produces bile as one of its numerous and diverse functions. One component of bile, bile salts, aids in lipid digestion.

Digestion

As the food enters the small intestine, some of it has already been partially digested. Salivary amylase has broken some of the bonds in the starches and glycogen, producing the disaccharide maltose. However, much starch and glycogen remains undigested. In the small intestine, **pancreatic amylase** breaks down these carbohydrates to maltose. Maltose, sucrose (table sugar), and lactose (milk sugar) are digested to the monosaccharides glucose, fructose, and galac-

tose by enzymes called **disaccharidases** that are produced by specialized epithelial cells of the small intestine. Some people do not produce the enzyme to digest lactose, however, and are therefore unable to digest milk. These persons cannot drink milk without experiencing cramps and, in some cases, diarrhea.

Some of the proteins in the food entering the small intestine have also been partially digested. The hydrochloric acid of the stomach has unfolded these proteins, and pepsin has cleaved some of them to shorter polypeptides. Three other enzymes produced by the pancreas complete the digestion of proteins: **trypsin, chymotrypsin,** and **carboxypeptidase.** These enzymes work as a team with **peptidases** produced by cells in the intestinal epithelium, breaking down polypeptides into shorter chains and then to amino acids. These enzymes are secreted in an inactive form and become active in the presence of a particular enzyme secreted by cells in the intestinal epithelium. This way, they do not digest their way down the pancreatic duct to the small intestine.

The lipids are not digested until they reach the small intestine. Because they are insoluble in water, they tend to enter the small intestine as globules. Before these lipids can be digested, they are emulsified, or made soluble, by bile salts. When the lipid globules are in the form of triglycerides, **pancreatic lipase** cleaves them into fatty acids and glycerol.

▼
▼

In the first part of the small intestine, the duodenum, digestion is completed. Undigested starch and glycogen are digested to disaccharides and then to monosaccharides. Undigested proteins and other polypeptides are digested to shorter peptides and then to amino acids. Triglycerides are made soluble and are then digested to fatty acids and glycerol.

As you can see, the digestion of food involves so many players that the digestive team could use a manager! In fact, the key players in digestion—the liver, gallbladder, pancreas, stomach, and small intestine—have more than one manager. These managers of digestion are hormones (see Table 7-3). Earlier in this chapter you read how the hormone gastrin controls the release of hydrochloric acid in the stomach. Two other hormones, **secretin** and **cholecystokinin** (CCK), control digestion in the small intestine (Figure 7-8).

When chyme enters the small intestine, the acid in it stimulates cells in the intestinal mucosa to produce secretin. This hormone does two things: first, it stimulates the release of an alkaline fluid called *sodium bicarbonate* from the pancreas. This solution neutralizes the acid in the chyme so that it will not damage the wall of the small intestine and produces the proper pH in which the pancreatic and intestinal enzymes will work. In addition, secretin increases the rate of bile secretion in the liver.

The presence of fatty acids and partially digested proteins in the chyme stimulates the mucosa to produce CCK. This enzyme signals the gallbladder to contract and pour its contents into the small intestine. It is also a stimulus to the pancreas to release its digestive enzymes.

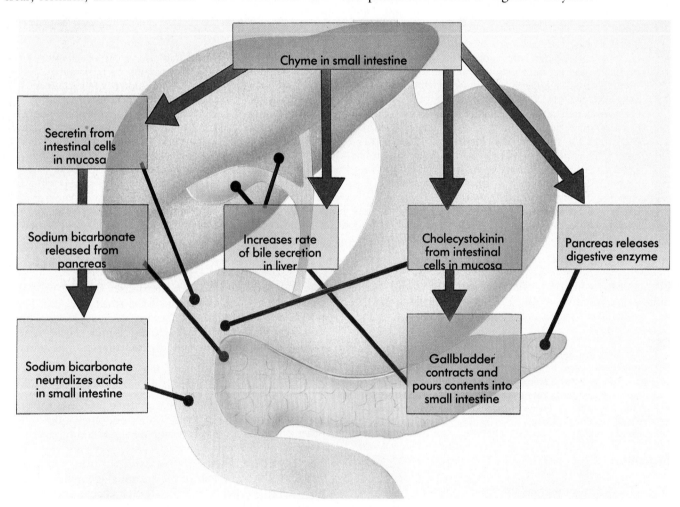

FIGURE 7-8 Digestive hormones manage many digestive enzymes. Secretin and cholecystokinin control and integrate digestive processes in the small intestine. The boxes describe events that take place during digestion. A line from each box shows the approximate location of the events. The arrows indicate how one event triggers another in the digestive process.

Absorption

The amount of material passing through the small intestine is startlingly large. An average person consumes about 800 grams of solid food and 1200 milliliters of fluid each day, for a total volume of about 2 liters, or a little more than 2 quarts. To this amount is added about 7 liters of fluid secreted by the salivary glands, stomach, pancreas, liver, and the small intestine itself. The total is a remarkable 9 liters, or almost 2 1/2 gallons! Of the 800 grams of solid food and 9 liters of liquid that enter the digestive tract, only about 50 grams of solid and 100 milliliters of liquid leave the intestinal tract as waste, or **feces.** The small intestine absorbs the 750 grams of nutrients per day and most of the water; the large intestine absorbs the remaining water—approximately 750 milliliters.

To aid in the absorption of nutrients, the internal surface area of the small intestine increases dramatically in three ways. First, the mucosa and submucosa of the small intestine are thrown into folds; they do not have a smooth in-

ner surface like a garden hose. This folded surface, in turn, is covered by fine finger-like projections of the epithelium. These projections are called **villi** (singular villus) and are so small that it takes a microscope to see them (Figure 7-9). In addition, the epithelial cells of the villi are covered on their exposed surfaces by cytoplasmic projections called **microvilli.** The infoldings, the villi, and the microvilli provide the small intestine with a surface area of about 300 square meters, or 2700 square feet, an area greater than the floor space in many homes!

Within each villus is a network of capillaries and a lymphatic vessel called a **lacteal.** Although the nutrients from digested food do not have far to travel—through a single layer of epithelial cells and a single layer of cells forming the wall of the capillary or lacteal—a great deal of work must be done. Each monosaccharide and amino acid must catch a ride on a carrier molecule to get into an epithelial cell. Energy is needed to ferry many of these molecules across cell membranes—a process called *active transport* (see Chapter 3). Others are taken up by facilitated diffusion.

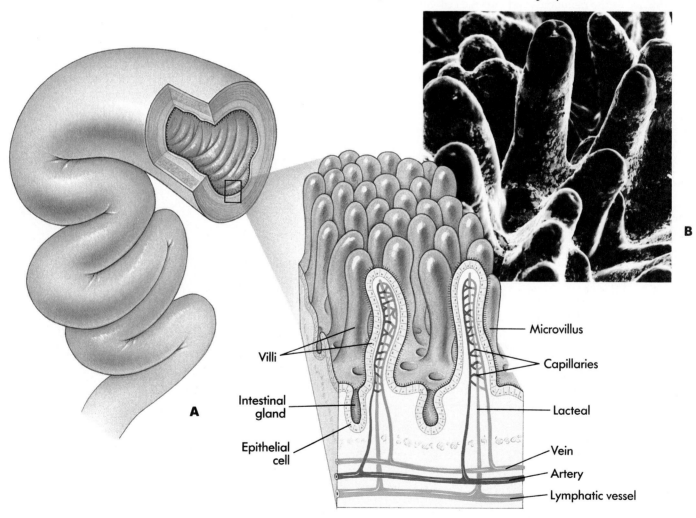

B

— Microvillus

— Capillaries

Villi —

Intestinal gland —

Epithelial cell —

— Lacteal

— Vein

— Artery

— Lymphatic vessel

A

FIGURE 7-9   Structure of villi.   A Villi are finger-like projections of tissue located on the inner surface of the small intestine. The villi, and microvilli on the surface of the villi, greatly increase the surface area of the small intestine, providing more room for absorption.
B Electron micrograph of intestinal villi.

Once the monosaccharides and amino acids are in the epithelial cells, however, they accumulate and eventually diffuse through the base of the cell and into the blood. When in the bloodstream, they are quickly swept away to the liver for processing and storage. When blood levels of glucose are sufficient to supply all your cells with this fuel of cellular respiration (see Chapter 5), the liver stores glucose as glycogen. When more glucose is needed, such as between meals, the liver readily converts the glycogen back to glucose. In this way, the liver is your metabolic bank, accepting deposits and withdrawals in the currency of glucose molecules.

The absorption of lipids takes place somewhat differently. After lipids are broken down into fatty acids and glycerol, they become surrounded by bile salts. Packaged in this way, they move to the cell membranes of the villi. As you may recall from Chapter 3, one of the main ingredients in cell membranes is lipid. Therefore when the fatty acids and glycerol from digestion come into contact with these cell membranes, they discard their shell of bile salts and easily move across the membrane and into the cell. Short-chained fatty acids are absorbed directly into the bloodstream. Longer-chained fatty acids are reassembled into triglycerides by the endoplasmic reticulum and are then encased in protein. After this processing, they pass out of the epithelial cells and into the lacteal. These protein-coated triglycerides are then transported in the lymphatic fluid through a system of vessels that drains the lymph into the blood at the left subclavian vein, a major blood vessel at the base of the neck.

The internal surface area of the small intestine is increased by the presence of inner folds and projections, which results in a more efficient absorption of nutrients and water. Monosaccharides and amino acids are absorbed into the intestinal epithelium by means of facilitated diffusion and active transport and then diffuse into the bloodstream. Epithelial cells re-form fatty acids and glycerol to triglycerides and shuttle them to the blood by means of the lymphatic system. Water is absorbed by osmosis.

Concentration of solids: The large intestine

The large intestine, or **colon,** is much shorter than the small intestine—only about a meter and a half, or 5 feet, long. It is wide, however, having a diameter slightly less than the width of your hand. In contrast, the small intestine has a diameter only slightly larger than the width of two of your fingers. The small intestine joins the large intestine about 7 centimeters up from its end, creating a blind pouch out of the beginning of the large intestine (Figure 7-10). Hang-

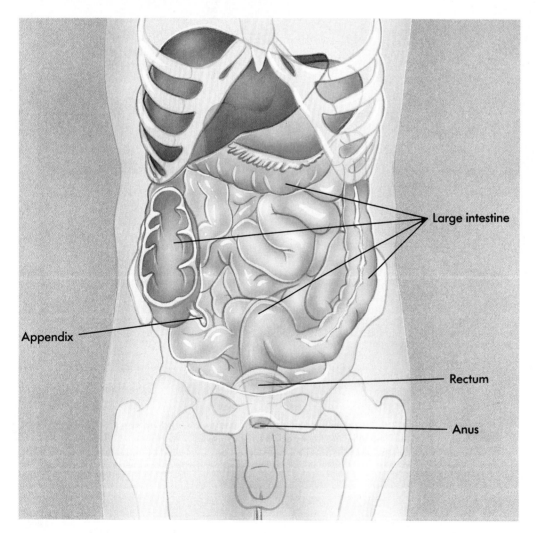

FIGURE 7-10 Location of the large intestine.
The large intestine, or colon, terminates at the rectum. The appendix hangs from a blind (dead-end) pouch where the small intestine meets the colon. The appendix serves no function in humans.

ing from this pouch is the **appendix,** a structure that serves no essential purpose in humans. An infection of the appendix is called *appendicitis* and can be quite serious and painful. In certain animals the blind pouch is more fully developed and is called the *cecum*. It serves as a place where the cellulose of plant cell walls is digested by the activity of intestinal bacteria and other microorganisms. Humans cannot digest cellulose, so it becomes a digestive waste. This waste, however, is important to the regular movement of the feces through the large intestine. Also called **dietary fiber,** undigested plant material provides bulk against which the muscles of the large intestine can push.

The junction of the small and large intestines is in the lower right side of the abdomen. From there the large intestine goes up the right side of the abdomen to the liver. It then turns left, crossing the abdominal cavity just under the diaphragm. On the left side of the abdominal cavity, it turns downward, ending at a short portion of the colon called the **rectum.** The rectum terminates at the **anus,** the opening for the elimination of the feces.

No digestion takes place within the large intestine. Its job is to absorb sodium and water, to eliminate wastes, and to provide a home for friendly bacteria. These bacteria help keep out disease-causing microbes and produce certain vitamins, especially vitamin K.

Waste materials move slowly along the smooth interior of the large intestine as water and sodium are slowly reabsorbed. As they move along, the wastes become more compacted. If the wastes move too slowly through the colon, too much water may be reabsorbed, leading to a difficulty in elimination called constipation. Conversely, if the wastes move too quickly, as happens with certain intestinal illnesses, not enough water may be removed, resulting in diarrhea. Eventually, the solids within the colon pass into the rectum as a result of the peristaltic contractions of the muscles encasing the large intestine. From the rectum the solid material passes out of the anus through two anal sphincters. The first of these is composed of smooth muscle. It opens involuntarily in response to a pressure-generated nerve signal from the rectum. The second sphincter, in contrast, is composed of skeletal muscle. It is subject to voluntary control from the brain, thus permitting a conscious decision to delay **defecation,** or the elimination of waste.

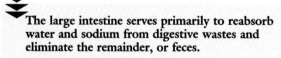

The large intestine serves primarily to reabsorb water and sodium from digestive wastes and eliminate the remainder, or feces.

Diet and nutrition

The digestion of food yields no usable energy but changes a diverse array of complex molecules into a small number of simpler molecules that can be used by your cells as fuel for cellular respiration. During cellular respiration, ATP molecules are produced—the energy currency of your body. As you read in Chapter 5, glucose is completely broken down by the processes of glycolysis, the Krebs cycle, and the electron transport chain to yield 36 usable molecules of ATP. In addition, the carbon portions of amino

acids and the glycerol backbones of triglycerides are converted to substances that can also be metabolized by two of these pathways. Fatty acids are metabolized by another metabolic pathway to yield ATP molecules.

Any intake of food in excess of that required to maintain the blood sugar (glucose) level and the glycogen reserve in the liver results in one of two consequences. Either the excess glucose is metabolized by the muscles and other cells of the body or it is converted to fat and stored within fat cells. Only when all the body's energy needs have been met—including the energy needed to run chemical reactions, move muscles, and digest food—will kilocalories be stored as fat. Think of your body as a giant scorecard, keeping track of kilocalories eaten and kilocalories used. If you eat more than you use, you will gain weight. Unfortunately, 10% to 25% of all teenagers and 25% to 50% of all adults in the United States are obese. In other words, they weigh at least 20% more than the average weight for their height (Figure 7-11).

As the digestive process breaks down food into molecules usable in cellular respiration, it also unlocks the vitamins and minerals from these foods. Vitamins fall into two general categories: water soluble and fat soluble (see Table 7-1). The water-soluble vitamins enter the cells of the in-

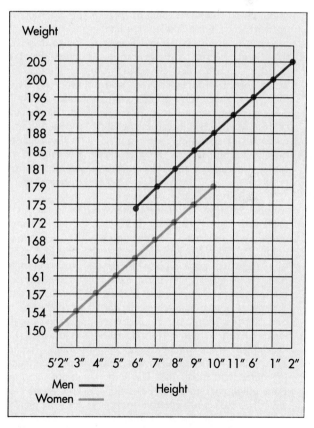

FIGURE 7-11 Obesity ranges for men and women.
Obesity is usually characterized as the state of being more than 20% heavier than the average person of the same sex and height. The graph charts height versus weight, showing the lowest weights at which a person of an indicated height is considered obese by most physicians.

Today, more Americans than ever before are concerned about nutrition. This interest in a healthy diet has caught the attention of advertisers and the media, and food fads and fashions have proliferated. Oat bran, fish oils, and "good" cholesterol have all received acclaim for their healthy nutritional properties, but it seems that as soon as one food or nutrient is hailed as the key to a healthy diet, another quickly takes its place. Given all the conflicting studies and claims about what we should and should not eat, how can we be sure that our diet is really nutritious?

A practical approach is to use a food guide, an easy-to-use chart developed by nutritionists to help people monitor the quality of their diets. A food guide groups foods of similar nutrient composition together. Guides also recommend how much of each food should be eaten to meet nutrient needs. For example, the guide presently in use in the United States, the Food Pyramid, groups fruits together because they contribute a major portion of vitamins A, C, and folate to the diet. This guide recommends eating two to four servings of fruit daily. And because not all foods in a grouping are equally nutritious, nutritionists recommend eating a variety of foods from each group.

In 1943, in an effort to promote nutrition education, the United States Department of Agriculture (USDA) introduced the Basic Seven food guide. This plan remained in use until 1956, when it was replaced by the Basic Four guide. The Basic Seven guide divided foods into seven groups: (1) green and yellow vegetables; (2) oranges, tomatoes, and raw salads; (3) potatoes; (4) milk and cheese; (5) meat, poultry, fish, and eggs; (6) bread, flour, and cereals; and (7) butter and margarine. The Basic Four guide combined the Basic Seven's three fruit and vegetable groupings into one group, and eliminated the butter and margarine group. The Basic Four plan was not revised for over 20 years, and it formed the basis for most nutrition education during that time.

By the late 1970s critics charged that the Basic Four guide did not reflect current scientific findings about

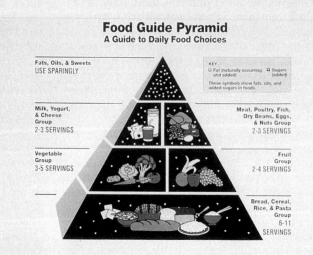

FIGURE 7-B The food guide pyramid is the latest attempt to reflect healthy eating habits.

the role of such nutrients as fats in the development of such diseases as heart disease, and some cancers. Responding to these concerns, the USDA presented the Hassle-Free Guide to a Better Diet in 1979. This guide, sometimes referred to as the Basic Five, added a fifth food group (fats, sweets, and alcoholic beverages) and recommended limiting intake of foods rich in these substances. Critics still were not satisfied, however, that these recommendations went far enough. For instance, recent studies have shown that a diet high in fiber was instrumental in the prevention of colon cancer. Other researchers had uncovered a link between a diet high in fat with an increased incidence of breast cancer. Nutritionists wanted a food guide that stressed the necessity of including high fiber foods and limiting fat intake.

Again, the USDA responded with a revised food guide. The Food Wheel—A Daily Pattern for Food Choices recommended eating more fiber-rich fruits, vegetables, and whole grains, and limiting dairy products and meats—foods that are high in fat—in the diet. By this time the development and use of food guides had become a political and economic issue in addition to one of health. Meat and dairy producers, for example, were not pleased with the latest food guide that recommended the limitation of their products from the American diet. The USDA realized that on this issue, it could not yield to the concerns of

these producers and still present a scientifically valid food guide.

The latest food guide was introduced in 1992. Called the Food Pyramid, this guide continues to reflect health concerns. In some ways it is a return to the Basic Seven concept with more food groups, but it also adds recent recommendations on healthy eating by providing a visual model of the optimal diet. Grouped together at the base of the pyramid are cereals and other grain products. These foods have the highest number of recommended servings. Fruits and vegetables, grouped separately, form the next tier. Fewer servings of these foods are needed for a healthy diet, so the tier is smaller. Because they include dietary fat, meats, meat alternatives, and dairy products form the next, still smaller tier. And at the top are high-sugar or fat foods and alcoholic beverages, which offer few vitamins and minerals in relation to calories.

Food guides can bea convenientway to assess the nutritional quality of one's diet, but they are not perfect. Combination foods such as casseroles and ethnic foods such as Oriental or Mexican dishes may still be difficult to classify without checking recipes. As scientificresearch uncovers new information, food guides will continue to change,and nutrition educators will have to revise their teachings. It seems unlikely that any new food guide will be used as long as the now obsolete "Basic Four."

testinal mucosa and move into the bloodstream. The fat-soluble vitamins are carried across the membranes of the intestinal cells associated with the fatty acids and glycerols. They are also transported to the bloodstream by means of the lymphatic system. Minerals are absorbed into the bloodstream as ions. (The recommended dietary allowances of the various vitamins and minerals are listed in Table 7-1.) Most people who eat a sufficient amount and variety of foods get the vitamins they need in the food they eat.

Proteins, lipids, and carbohydrates provide more than energy for the diet—they provide the raw materials to build the substances the body needs. In fact, proteins are used primarily as building blocks and not as a source of energy. Of the 20 different amino acids that make up proteins, humans can manufacture only 12. Therefore 8 of the amino acids, called **essential amino acids,** must be obtained by humans from proteins in the food they eat (Figure 7-12). Protein foods that contain the essential amino acids in amounts proportional to the body's need for them are called high-quality, or complete proteins. Unfortunately, many high-quality protein foods such as meat, cheese, and eggs are high in animal fat and cholesterol as well. A high percent of an-

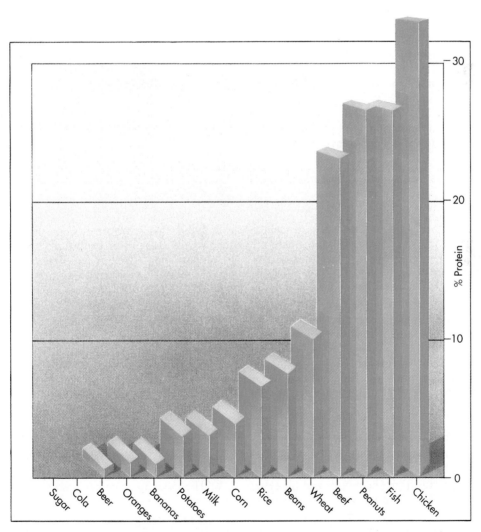

FIGURE 7-12 The protein content of a variety of common foods. Eight of the essential amino acids humans need must be obtained from high-quality proteins in the diet.

imal fat and cholesterol in the diet has been shown to result in weight gain and increase the risk of heart attack because of the clogging of blood vessels with cholesterol deposits. To reduce fat intake yet get the amino acids you need, you should combine any legume (dried peas, beans, peanuts, or soy-based food) with any grain, nut, or seed or you should combine any grain, legume, nut, or seed with small amounts of milk, cheese, yogurt, eggs, red meat, fish, or poultry.

So how much protein, fat, and carbohydrate *should* you have in your diet? The U.S. Senate Select Committee on Nutrition and Human Needs recommends that 12% of your daily intake of kilocalories come from proteins, 30% *or less* come from fats, and 58% from carbohydrates (Figure 7-13). You may want to approximate the number of kilocalories in the meal shown at the beginning of the chapter. How many of its kilocalories come from proteins, fats, and carbohydrates? Although you may not be analyzing all of its nutritional aspects, what recommendation can you make for it to be a healthier meal?

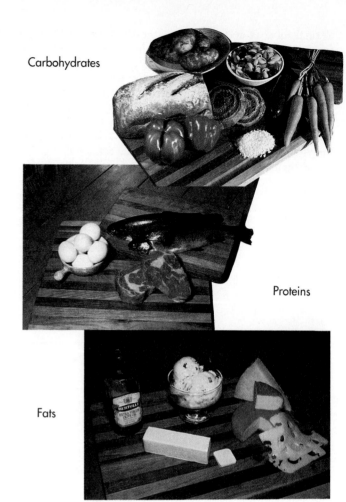

Carbohydrates

Proteins

Fats

FIGURE 7-13 What proportion of the energy nutrients should you eat?
Experts agree that 12% of your total daily intake of kilocalories should be from proteins, 30% or less from fats, and 58% from carbohydrates. Most Americans, however, eat too much protein and fat and not enough carbohydrates. How does your diet compare to the experts' recommendations?

Summary

1. Nutrients are substances in food that are used to help the body grow and repair and sustain itself. There are six classes of nutrients: carbohydrates, fats (lipids), proteins, vitamins, minerals, and water.

2. Digestion is the process whereby food is broken down into a form that is usable by the body's cells. Carbohydrates are digested to monosaccharides, lipids to fatty acids and glycerol, and proteins to amino acids. Amino acids are primarily used as building blocks. Monosaccharides and glycerol are primarily used as the fuel of cellular respiration and other metabolic pathways that produce ATP molecules, the energy currency of the body.

3. Vitamins and minerals are not broken down during digestion but are released from the food of which they are a part. These nutrients help various chemical reactions and bodily processes take place.

4. The digestive tract leads from the mouth and pharynx, through the esophagus, to the stomach. The digestion of carbohydrates begins in the mouth with the action of salivary amylase. The stomach juices contain a concentrated acid in which the protein-digesting enzyme pepsin is active.

5. Food passes from the stomach to the small intestine where the pH is neutralized. A variety of enzymes, many synthesized in the pancreas, acts to complete digestion. Most digestion occurs in the first 25 centimeters of the small intestine, a portion called the *duodenum*.

6. The products of digestion are absorbed across the walls of the small intestine, which possess numerous villi and achieve a large surface area. Amino acids and monosaccharides pass into the bloodstream. Fatty acids and glycerols pass into the lymphatic system and, coated with proteins, are transported to the bloodstream.

7. Glucose and other metabolic products of digestion do not enter the general circulation directly but instead flow to the liver. The liver removes and stores any excess metabolic products and maintains blood glucose levels within narrow bounds.

8. The large intestine has little digestive or absorptive activity; it functions principally to absorb water from the waste that is left over and eliminate it from the body.

9. The U.S. Senate Select Committee on Nutrition and Human Needs recommends that 12% of the daily intake of kilocalories come from proteins, 30% or less from fats, and 58% from carbohydrates.

1. Name the six classes of nutrients, and explain why you need each one in your diet.

2. Describe the digestive fates of proteins, lipids, and carbohydrates. What three types of enzymes are involved?

3. Where does the process of human digestion begin?

4. While on a hike, a student finds the dry skull of a small mammal. How could he determine if that animal ate only plant products?

5. You bite off a mouthful from a crunchy apple and chew it thoroughly. Describe the role(s) played by each type of tooth in your mouth.

6. Is the muscle activity of peristalsis under voluntary control or is it an involuntary process? Does digestion occur in the esophagus as peristalsis is occuring?

7. What important tasks does the hydrochloric acid in the human stomach accomplish? What protects the stomach wall from potential damage by this chemical product?

8. What is the duodenum? Summarize the digestive activities that take place there.

9. Why do you think that the liver and pancreas are not called organs of the digestive system although they serve important accessory roles in digestion?

10. Identify and give a function for each of the following: gastrin, secretin, and cholecystokinin. What do they have in common?

11. For years, baking soda (sodium bicarbonate) has been a popular home remedy for indigestion and heartburn. Explain why.

12. Discuss the features of the small intestine that increase its internal surface area. Why is this increase important?

13. Summarize how your body produces ATP from glucose, amino acids, triglycerides, and fatty acids.

14. Keep a record of everything you eat and drink for 3 days. Then (this could be painful!) analyze your diet. Compare it to the recommendations in Figure 7-13. How could you improve your nutritional intake?

1. Many people of other countries live a vegetarian life-style. This has become more common in the United States in recent years also. Discuss how a vegetarian could create a balanced diet while eliminating meat and animal products.

2. Many diseases are found to be closely related to nutrition; cancer and heart disease are especially linked to diet. Gather in small groups to exchange ideas and information regarding change in diet as a healthy preventative to disease.

Harris, A.R. (1988). Why do more women get ulcers? *Chatelaine, 61,* 32.
This article discusses the link between ulcers in women and risk factors such as smoking, alcohol, and stress.

McAuliffe, K. (1990, August). In the belly of the bug. *Omni,* pp. 20, 72.
Scientists have discovered a microorganism that is responsible for most stomach ulcers and are designing new antibiotic treatment.

Moog, F. (1981, November). The lining of the small intestine. *Scientific American,* pp. 154-176.
This is a clear description of the most important absorptive surface in the human body.

Sapolsky, R. (1989, September). Health matters. *Discover,* pp. 48-52.
An enterprising scientist has studied a baboon troop that has been eating a typical American diet for a decade, with worrisome results.

8 Respiration

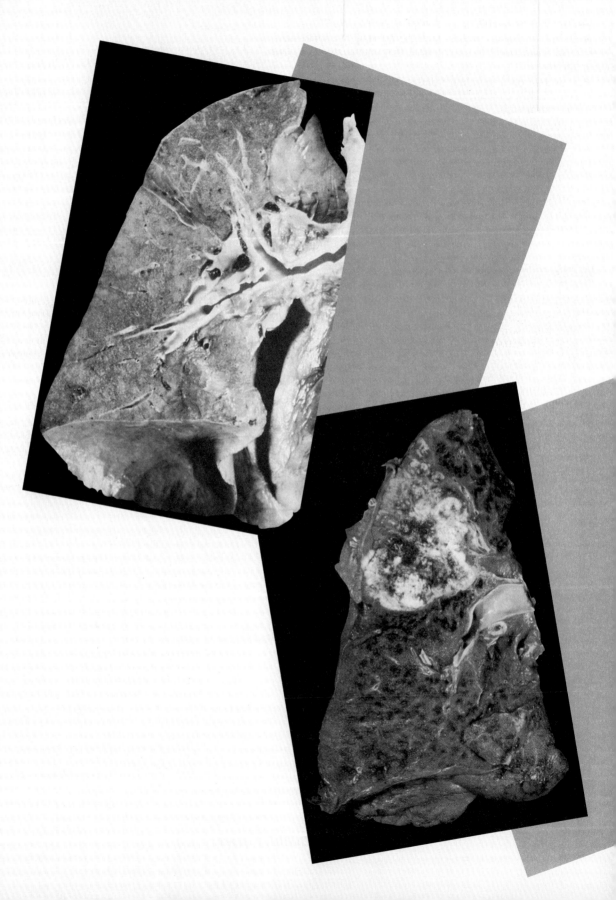

▼ In its journey to the lungs, air passes through the nostrils, nasal cavities, pharynx, larynx, trachea, bronchi, and bronchioles..

▼ In the process of breathing, a negative pressure within the thoracic cavity causes air to be pulled into the lungs; a positive pressure causes air to be pushed out of the lungs.

▼ Oxygen diffuses into the blood and carbon dioxide diffuses out of the blood at the lungs; the reverse exchange of gases occurs at the body cells.

▼ Cigarette smoking damages respiratory structures and can lead to such disorders as lung cancer, chronic bronchitis, and emphysema.

Respiration

The pathway of air into and out of the body

   Nasal cavities

   The pharynx

   The larynx

   The trachea

   The bronchi and their branches

   The alveoli: Where gas exchange takes place

The mechanics of breathing

   Inspiration

   Expiration

   Deep breathing

   Lung volumes

Gas transport and exchange

   External respiration

   Internal respiration

Choking: A common respiratory emergency

Chronic obstructive pulmonary disease

Which lung would you choose? Probably the healthy, red lung in the top photo. Unbelievably, however, over 50 million Americans choose to have lungs similar to that in the bottom photo. Why? Because these people choose to smoke cigarettes.

When people smoke cigarettes, they inhale many particles and gases. Carbon monoxide is one of the colorless, odorless gases present in cigarette smoke (and in your car's exhaust). It binds to the oxygen-carrying molecules of hemoglobin in your blood, reducing their oxygen-carrying capability by as much as 15%. Tobacco also contains nicotine, a drug that is physically addicting. In addition, nicotine stimulates the nervous system in a way that causes the heart to race and the blood pressure to rise. The blood vessels also narrow—including the arteries that supply the heart with blood. Both the nicotine and carbon monoxide work in different ways to decrease the amount of oxygen that can get to the heart. If the decrease is severe, a part of the heart muscle can die, an experience commonly referred to as a heart attack.

Tar is another substance found in cigarette smoke. It is the residue of smoke—what is left over after the nicotine and moisture have been removed. In the bottom photo, you can easily see how tar blackens lung tissue. The whitish areas are no longer functional—they are cancerous tumors caused by the tar. This person did not survive the addiction to cigarettes.

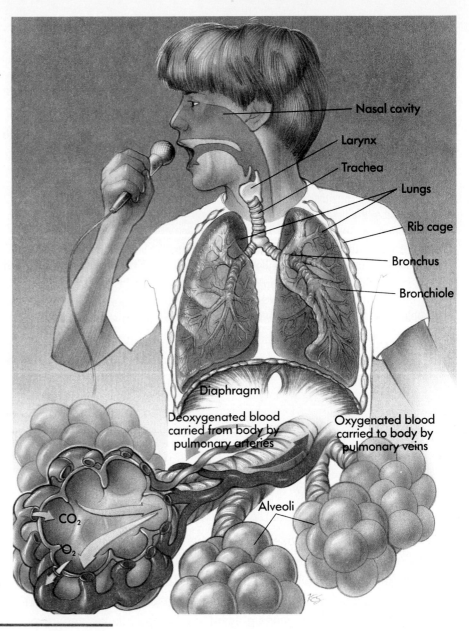

FIGURE 8-1 The human respiratory system. A section of the lung is enlarged to show the alveoli.

Nasal cavity

Larynx

Trachea

Lungs

Rib cage

Bronchus

Bronchiole

Diaphragm

Deoxygenated blood carried from body by pulmonary arteries

Oxygenated blood carried to body by pulmonary veins

Alveoli

CO_2

O_2

Respiration

Your lungs play an important role in the process of **respiration** (Figure 8-1). The term *respiration* is used in many ways when speaking about the processes of the human body, so its definition can be confusing. Used alone, respiration refers to gas exchange—the uptake of oxygen (O_2) and the release of the waste gas carbon dioxide (CO_2) by the whole body. The phrase *cellular respiration* uses the term respiration in a more specific way: it is the chemical process by which cells break down fuel molecules to release energy, using oxygen and producing carbon dioxide. Cellular respiration is a process that uses the oxygen you breathe in and produces the carbon dioxide you breathe out. (This process is described in detail in Chapter 5.)

At the millions of tiny air sacs, or **alveoli,** that make up most of your lungs, oxygen enters the blood and carbon dioxide leaves. The exchange of these gases between the blood and the alveoli is known as **external respiration.** The movement of air into and out of the lungs is **breathing.**

After the blood picks up oxygen at the lungs and gets rid of carbon dioxide, it travels to the heart and gets a push out to the rest of the body. The cells of the body receive the oxygen they need and get rid of the waste gas carbon dioxide as the blood moves past the cells within microscopic blood vessels. At the cells, carbon dioxide moves by diffusion from the tissue fluid into the blood. Tissue fluid (also called *interstitial fluid* or *intercellular fluid*) is a water-like fluid derived from the blood that bathes all the cells of the body. Oxygen moves in the opposite direction—from the blood into the tissue fluid. This process is called **internal respiration,** the exchange of oxygen and carbon dioxide between the blood and the tissue fluid.

▼▼
Respiration is the uptake of oxygen and the release of carbon dioxide by the body. The processes of cellular respiration, internal respiration, and external respiration are all part of the general process of respiration.

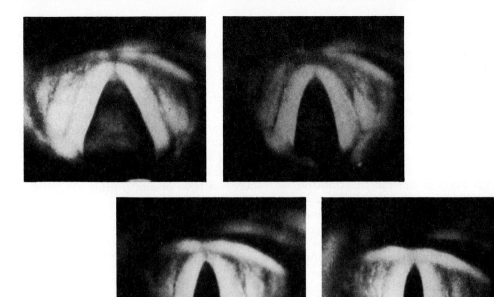

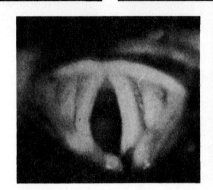
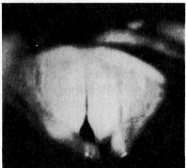

FIGURE 8-2 Movement of the vocal cords.
The space between the two folds of tissue in the glottis. In this series of photographs, the vocal cords are shown in the process of closing off the glottis.

The pathway of air into and out of the body

How many times per minute do you breathe? A breath consists of taking air into the lungs, or **inspiration,** and expelling air from the lungs, or **expiration.** Try to breathe normally, count the number of breaths you take in 15 seconds, and multiply by four. Is your breath rate within the average of 14 to 20 breaths per minute?

Nasal cavities

As you breathe in, air first enters your body through the nostrils. The nostrils are lined with hairs that filter out dust and other particles from the air. The air is warmed and moistened as it swirls around in the **nasal cavities.** These cavities, located above your oral cavity and behind your nose, are bordered by projections of bone covered with epithelial tissue. This tissue stays moist with mucus secreted by its many mucous glands. This sticky fluid helps trap dirt and dust that you breathe in. The epithelium is also covered with tiny hair-like projections called **cilia** (see Figure 8-3). The word *cilia* comes from a Latin word meaning "eyelashes." These "cell eyelashes" beat in unison, creating a current in the mucus that carries the trapped particles to-

ward the back of the nasal cavity. From here, the mucus drips into the throat and is swallowed—at a rate of over a pint per day!

As air moves about within the nasal cavities, it is warmed and moistened.

The pharynx

After passing through the nasal cavities, air enters the **pharynx,** or throat. The pharynx extends from behind the nasal cavities to the openings of the esophagus and larynx. The esophagus, as you may recall from Chapter 7, is the food tube, a passageway for food to the stomach. The **larynx,** or voice box, lies at the beginning of the trachea. The **trachea** is the air passageway that runs down the neck in front of the esophagus and that brings air to the lungs.

The larynx

The larynx is a cartilaginous box shaped somewhat like a triangle. Stretched across the upper end of the larynx are the **vocal cords** (Figure 8-2). The vocal cords are two pieces of elastic tissue covered with a mucous membrane. Muscles within the larynx pull on the cartilage, which in turn pulls or relaxes the tension on the vocal cords. When the vocal cords are stretched tightly, the space between them—the **glottis**—is closed. In this way the vocal cords provide a "backup" for the epiglottis that flaps over the glottis during swallowing. Both structures work to prevent food and drink from going down the wrong way. The vocal cords also produce the sounds you make as air rushes by and causes them to vibrate. You can illustrate this principle by stretching a rubber band between your fingers. Have someone repeatedly pluck the band. At the same time increase and then decrease the stretch on the band. What happens? Your vocal cords work in much the same way to produce a variety of pitches of sound. But you also have a mouth with lips and a tongue to form the sounds into words. Your lungs add a power supply and volume control to your personal musical instrument—your voice.

The trachea

Put your hand on your larynx, or Adam's apple, and then picture about 4 or 5 inches of garden hose attached to its bottom end. A garden hose is about the diameter of your trachea, or windpipe, which extends downward from your larynx toward your lungs. The trachea has thin walls, similar to the thickness of those in the hose. Garden hoses are reinforced with materials such as rubber or vinyl to keep them from collapsing; your trachea is reinforced with rings of cartilage. The cartilage wraps around the trachea only part way, forming C shapes that begin and end where the windpipe lies next to the esophagus. Press gently on your windpipe just below your Adam's apple and you can feel some of these cartilaginous rings.

The inner walls of the trachea are lined with ciliated epithelium (Figure 8-3). Certain cells in the epithelium secrete mucus. Together, the cilia and the mucus provide your

windpipe with an up escalator for any particles or microbes you may have inhaled. This escalator brings substances up to the pharynx where they are swallowed and eliminated through the digestive tract. In the trachea of a cigarette smoker, however, action of the cilia is impaired, causing mucus to build up in the airway. The result is that the tars in cigarettes are not caught and expelled with the action of cilia. They move easily into the lungs and settle there. A chronic cough, often called *smoker's cough*, is triggered by accumulations of mucus below the larynx.

▼▼
Air passes from the nasal cavities and into the throat, or pharynx. From the pharynx, it passes over the vocal cords that are stretched across the larynx. From this voice box, air moves into the trachea, or windpipe, on its way to the lungs.

The bronchi and their branches

If you could look down your trachea as in Figure 8-4, the two black holes you would see would be your **primary bronchi**. These airways are structured much like the trachea but are smaller in diameter. One bronchus goes to each lung, branching into three right and two left **secondary bronchi** serving the three right and two left lobes of the lungs. The heart is nestled into the left side of the lungs, taking up some of the space that a third left lobe might occupy.

The secondary bronchi divide into smaller and smaller branches, looking much like an upside-down tree (Figure 8-5), until they end in thousands of passageways called **respiratory bronchioles**. These airways have a diameter less than that of a pencil lead. Their walls have clusters of tiny pouches that, along with the respiratory bronchioles, are the sites of gas exchange. These pouches, or air sacs, are called **alveoli**.

FIGURE 8-3 Cilia such as these line the trachea.
Cilia sweep trapped particles out of the respiratory tract.

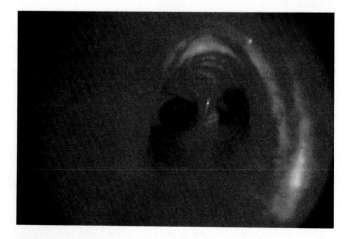

FIGURE 8-4 The trachea.
The two holes that you see are the primary bronchi. One bronchus leads to each lung.

Air moves from the trachea into the two bronchi that supply each lung. The bronchi divide into smaller and smaller branches ending in respiratory bronchioles having outpouchings called alveoli, the sites of gas exchange.

The alveoli: Where gas exchange takes place

The alveoli provide a perfect place for carbon dioxide and oxygen to diffuse between the air in the lungs and the blood. These clusters of microscopic air sacs are bounded by membranes made up of a single layer of epithelial cells. A network of capillaries tightly clasps each alveolar sac. The capillary walls are also only one cell thick and press against the alveolar epithelium. These two adjacent membranes provide the thinnest possible barrier between the blood in the capillaries and the air in the alveoli.

The alveoli also provide another important component of efficient gas exchange: a large surface area. In fact, if the epithelial membrane of all your alveoli was spread out flat, it would cover a tennis court! The capillaries cover this enormous surface, creating patterns much like tightly woven spider webs, providing nearly a continuous sheet of blood over the alveolar surface.

Large white blood cells called *macrophages* are also found at the alveoli. These cells work to remove any particles or microbes that have escaped the other defenses of the airways. The macrophages transport the invaders to the bronchioles or to the lymphatic system. Sometimes the job is too big, however, and particles remain in the lungs. In smokers the action of the macrophages is impaired, making the lungs more susceptible to disease and injury.

The alveoli provide a thin, enormous surface area over which gas exchange can take place.

The mechanics of breathing

Air moves into and out of your lungs as the volume of your thoracic cavity is made larger and smaller by the action of certain muscles. The **thoracic cavity,** or chest cavity, is within the trunk of your body above your diaphragm and below your neck. The **diaphragm** is a sheet of muscle that forms the horizontal partition between the thoracic cavity and the abdominal cavity. Various blood vessels and the esophagus puncture it as they traverse these two body cavities. The position of the diaphragm is shown in Figure 8-6.

The diaphragm is assisted by other muscles of breathing. These muscles extend from rib to rib—from the lower border of each rib to the upper border of the rib below—and are called **intercostal muscles.** The word *intercostal* literally means "between" (inter) "the ribs" (costal). You have two sets of intercostals: the **internal intercostals** and the **external intercostals.** The internal intercostals are those that lie closer to the interior of the body (as their name suggests) and that have fibers extending obliquely downward

FIGURE 8-5 Secondary bronchioles.
Secondary bronchi divide into smaller and smaller branches, resembling an upside-down tree or a system of roots.

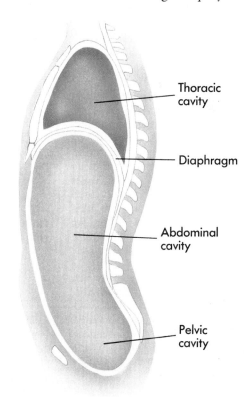

FIGURE 8-6 Location of the diaphragm.
The diaphragm forms a partition between the thoracic and abdominal cavities.

Of the 2.2 million people who died in the United States last year, one-fourth died of cancer and 25% of these—106,000 people—died of lung cancer. About 150,000 cases of lung cancer were diagnosed each year from 1980 to 1992, and 90% of these persons died or will die within 3 years. Of those who die, 96% will be cigarette smokers.

Smoking is a popular pastime in the United States. Almost one third of the U.S. population smokes. American smokers consumed over 550 billion cigarettes in 1991. These cigarettes emit smoke tars and other chemicals in their tobacco that are potent mutagens, and these cancer-causing chemicals are introduced to your lungs when you inhale cigarette smoke. Absorbed by the cells lining your lungs, these chemicals lead to cancer as surely as if you had smoked powerful radioisotopes. Cigarette smoke also contains nicotine, a chemical mimic of the neurotransmitter acetylcholine that is powerfully addictive. That is why it is so difficult to stop smoking once you have started—your body becomes addicted. Smoking is drug abuse with a very dangerous drug.

Among cigarette manufacturers, it has been popular to argue that the causal connection between smoking and cancer has not been proven, that somehow the relationship is coincidental. Look carefully at the data presented in Figure 8-A and see if you agree. The upper graph presents data collected on the incidence of smoking and lung cancer for American males from the turn of the century until now. Note that as late as 1920, lung cancer was a rare disease. With a lag of some 20 years behind the increase in smoking, it became progressively more common.

Now look at the lower graph, which presents data on American females. Significant numbers of American females did not smoke until after World War II, when many social conventions changed. As late as 1963, when lung cancer among males was near current levels, this disease was still rare in females. In the United States that year, only 6588 females died of lung cancer. But as their smoking increased, so did their incidence of lung cancer, with the same inexorable lag of about 20 years. American females today have achieved equality with their male

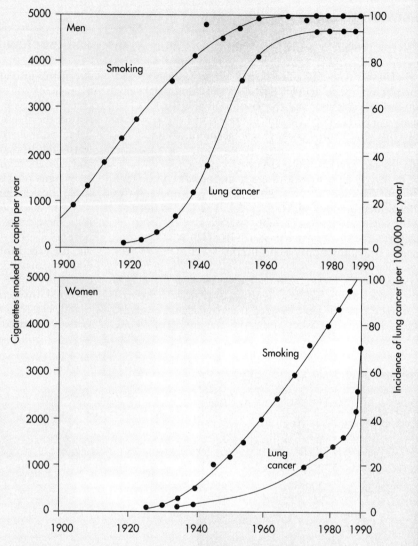

FIGURE 8-A Correlation of smoking to lung cancer, for men *(top graph)* and women *(lower graph).*

counterparts in the numbers of cigarettes that they smoke—and their lung cancer death rates are now approaching those of males. In 1991, more than 49,000 fe-males died of lung cancer in the United States.

Among smokers, the current rate of death from lung cancer is 180 per 100,000 or about 2 of every 1000 smokers each year. Life insurance companies have computed that, on a statistical basis, smoking a single ciga-

rette lowers your life expectancy 10.7 minutes. (That is more time than it takes to smoke the cigarette!) Every pack of cigarettes bears an unwritten label: *The price of smoking this pack of cigarettes is 3½ hours of your life.*

If you don't smoke, don't start. If you do smoke, quit now. Your body gradually replaces its tissues, and your chance of getting lung cancer will fall until it eventually is no greater than that of nonsmokers.

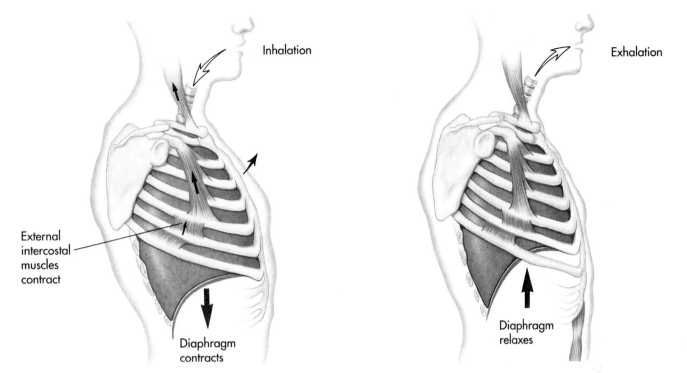

FIGURE 8-7 How a human breathes. *Inhalation:* The diaphragm flattens and the ribs are raised, increasing the volume of the chest cavity. As a result of the larger volume, air is pulled in through the trachea.
Exhalation: The diaphragm resumes its dome-like shape and the ribs fall, reducing the volume of the chest cavity and forcing air outward through the trachea.

and backward (from front to back). The **external intercostals** extend from back to front, having fibers that are directed downward and forward.

Inspiration

When you are breathing quietly—not exerting yourself physically—your diaphragm and external intercostals alone are responsible for the change in the size of your thoracic cavity. This change in size results in the movement of air into and out of your lungs. During **inspiration** the dome-shaped diaphragm contracts, flattening somewhat and thereby lowering the floor of the thoracic cavity. The external intercostals contract, raising the rib cage. Notice in Figure 8-7 how these two actions increase the size of the thoracic cavity.

The interior walls of the thoracic cavity are lined with a thin, delicate, sheet-like membrane called the **pleura.** The pleura folds back on itself to cover each lung. These two parts of the membrane are close to one another, separated only by a thin film of fluid. As the volume of the thoracic cavity increases during inspiration, the lungs also expand, held to the wall of the thoracic cavity by cohesion of the water molecules between the two membranes. Put simply, the lungs stick to the thoracic wall and move with it.

As the lungs expand in volume, the air pressure within the lungs decreases because there are fewer air molecules per unit of volume. As a result, air from the environment outside the body is pulled into the lungs, equalizing the pressure inside and outside the thoracic cavity. By means of this process, you breathe in 13,638 liters (more than 3000 gallons) of air every day!

Expiration

The lungs contain special nerves called *stretch receptors.* When the lungs are stretched to their normal inspiratory capacity, these receptors send a message to a respiratory center in the brain. This respiratory center is located in parts of the brainstem called the *medulla* and the *pons* (see Chapter 12). The respiratory center stops sending "contract" messages to the muscles of breathing, which causes them to relax—a passive process in contrast to the active process of inspiration. As the diaphragm relaxes, it assumes its dome-like shape, reducing the volume of the thoracic cavity. Likewise, as the external intercostals relax, the rib cage drops, reducing the volume of the thoracic cavity further. The volume of the lungs, in turn, decreases, aided by the recoil action of the lungs' elastic tissue. The reduced volume of the lungs results in an increase in the air pressure within them. Air is forced out of the lungs, equalizing the pressure outside and inside the thoracic cavity. The cycle of

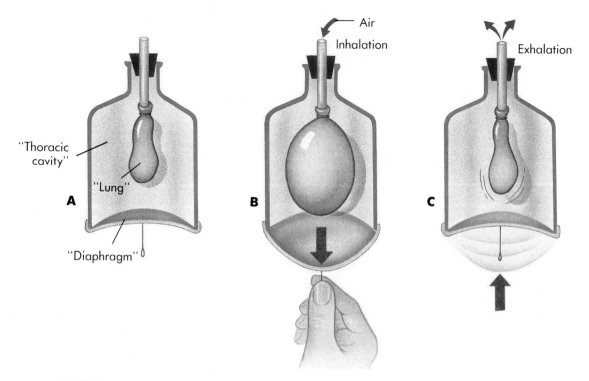

"Thoracic cavity"

"Lung"

A

Air

Inhalation

B

Exhalation

C

"Diaphragm"

FIGURE 8-8   A simple experiment that shows how you breathe.   In the jar is a balloon **(A).** When the diaphragm is pulled down, as shown in **B,** the balloon expands. When it is relaxed **(C),** the balloon contracts. In the same way, air is taken into your lungs when your diaphragm contracts and flattens, expanding the volume of your chest cavity. When your diaphragm relaxes and resumes its dome-like shape, the volume of your chest cavity decreases and air is expelled.

inspiration and expiration is shown in Figure 8-8.

The brainstem also contains areas sensitive to changes in the levels of carbon dioxide in the blood that control the rate of the cycle of inspiration and expiration. Hydrogen ions (H^+) that are produced from a series of chemical reactions involving carbon dioxide also play an extremely important role in influencing the activity of the respiratory center (see Internal respiration, p. 158). So when you have a high level of carbon dioxide in your blood, the level of hydrogen ions in your blood increases (blood pH decreases), and your breathing rate is "stepped up."

Deep breathing

When you breathe deeply, such as during physical exercise, the internal intercostals as well as other muscles in the chest and abdomen help out the muscles of respiration. During inspiration, certain muscles attached to the breastbone—the bone in the center of your chest to which your ribs are attached—pull up on it. In addition, other muscles pull up on the first two ribs. This action increases the volume of the chest cavity more than during quiet breathing, so more air flows into the lungs. By deep breathing and increasing the rate of breathing, world champion runners have been shown to increase their air intake fifteenfold.

Expiration, a passive process during quiet breathing,

becomes an active process during deep breathing. The internal intercostals pull down on the rib cage. Abdominal muscles also contract, pulling down on the lower ribs and compressing the abdominal organs, which results in a push up on the diaphragm. These actions additionally decrease the volume of the thoracic cavity and cause more air to be expelled than during quiet breathing.

> **Inspiration occurs when the volume of the thoracic cavity is increased and the resulting negative pressure causes air to be pulled into the lungs. Expiration occurs when the volume of the thoracic cavity is decreased and the resulting positive pressure forces air out of the lungs.**

Lung volumes

How much air do you move into and out of your lungs during inspiration and expiration? You can find out by performing this simple procedure: Fill a large jar with water and invert it in a pan of water. Be careful not to let any of the water seep out of the jar while you are turning it upside down. Mark the level of the water in the jar with tape or a wax pencil. Take a piece of rubber tubing or garden hose about a foot long and put one end up into the jar.

Put the other end into your mouth and exhale normally. The air you breathe out will displace the water. Mark the new level of the water. Remove the jar from the water and fill it to this line with water. Now measure the volume of the water between the two lines with a measuring cup or a graduated cylinder. Its volume equals the volume of air you breathed out. The average adult male breathes out 500 milliliters of air during quiet breathing, or slightly more than 1 pint. This volume of air—the amount inspired or expired with each breath—is called the **tidal volume.**

Of the 500 milliliters of air you normally breathe in, only about 350 milliliters reaches the alveoli. The other 150 milliliters is either on its way into or out of the lungs, occupying space in the nose, pharynx, larynx, trachea, and bronchial tree. This space is called **dead air space** because it serves no useful purpose in gas exchange. Some of this air, in fact, will never reach the lungs. And some air, called **residual air,** remains in the lungs—even during deep breathing.

Gas transport and exchange

The transport of gases throughout the body is assisted by the circulatory system. Without the help of a "highway" of blood, scientists estimate that it would take a molecule of oxygen 3 years to diffuse from your lung to your toe! Humans could not survive if gas transport were this slow.

Although the pathway of blood throughout the body will be described in detail in the next chapter, it is helpful to understand the basic routing of blood when discussing gas transport. Notice in Figure 8-9 that the upper right chamber of the heart collects incoming blood from the upper and lower body. This blood has given up its supply of oxygen to the tissues, so it is oxygen poor. Along its route, however, it collected the waste product of cellular respiration, which is carbon dioxide. Deoxygenated blood such as this (more carbon dioxide than oxygen) is shown as blue in the diagram. The deoxygenated blood passes from the upper to the lower right chamber of the heart, where it is pumped to the lungs. Some of this blood goes to the right lung, and some goes to the left lung.

At the lungs, carbon dioxide within the blood of the capillaries surrounding the alveoli and the oxygen in the air of the alveoli are exchanged. External respiration, the exchange of gases at the lungs, works by the process of diffusion. It converts deoxygenated blood to oxygenated blood (more oxygen than carbon dioxide). This blood is shown as red in Figure 8-9. The oxygenated blood flows from the lungs to the left side of the heart, where the lower left chamber pumps it out to other parts of the body.

⯆⯆ The circulatory system aids in respiration by transporting gases throughout the body.

External respiration

Air is made up of many different kinds of molecules, such as oxygen, nitrogen, and carbon dioxide. Each of these gases exerts a pressure that depends on the number of molecules of the specific gas present per unit of volume. Molecules of a gas in a liquid (such as blood) also exert a pressure. Differences in pressures of a particular gas in two adjoining locations within a living system produce a *pressure gradient*. Molecules of a gas such as oxygen or carbon dioxide tend to move from an area of higher pressure to an area of lower pressure, or down the pressure gradient. Each gas moves according to its own pressure gradient, unaffected by the pressure gradients of other gases with which it might be mixed. This movement is a type of diffusion.

As deoxygenated blood (blue in Figure 8-9) arrives at the lungs, the pressure of the carbon dioxide in the blood is greater than the pressure of carbon dioxide in the air within the alveoli. Therefore carbon dioxide diffuses out of the blood and into the alveoli. Likewise, the pressure of the oxygen in the air within the alveoli is greater than the pressure of the small amount of oxygen in the blood. Therefore oxygen diffuses out of the alveoli and into the blood.

Most of the carbon dioxide (70%) in the blood travels around bound to water molecules in the fluid portion of the blood. The carbon dioxide and water combine chemically to form molecules of carbonic acid (H_2CO_3) but quickly break apart, or dissociate, into bicarbonate ions (HCO_3^-) and hydrogen ions (H^+). About one fourth (23%) of the carbon dioxide is carried in the red blood cells, bound to the oxygen-carrying molecule **hemoglobin** (Hb). It is carried, however, by a different portion of the molecule than oxygen is. A small amount (7%) of the carbon dioxide is simply dissolved in the blood. At the alveoli, the dissolved carbon dioxide first moves out of the blood. This decrease in its concentration triggers a reversal of the chemical reactions described above:

$$H^+ + HCO_3^- \rightarrow H_2CO_3 \rightarrow H_2O + CO_2$$

Carbon dioxide also dissociates from hemoglobin, and the freed carbon dioxide molecules diffuse into the alveoli.

As oxygen diffuses from the alveoli, very little of it (3%) dissolves in the fluid portion of the blood. Instead, it combines with hemoglobin within the red blood cells. When the pressure gradient is high, as in the alveoli, hemoglobin binds with large amounts of oxygen. When oxygenated, hemoglobin turns bright red, which makes blood look red. You will notice, however, that the blood vessels on the underside of your wrists look blue. These blood vessels are veins carrying deoxygenated blood. Deoxygenated blood is dark red but appears blue through layers of skin.

At high altitudes, such as in mountainous regions, the air is thinner and the pressure of the oxygen molecules within the air is lower than at sea level. Therefore less of a pressure gradient is created at the alveoli. As a consequence, less oxygen diffuses into the blood, causing shortness of breath, nausea, and dizziness. This condition is referred to as **high altitude sickness.** Mountain climbers, athletes working out or playing at high altitudes (such as Mile High Stadium in Denver, Colorado), and tourists visiting an area of high altitude (such as Mexico City, Mexico) need to slowly work up to their normal levels of activity to give their bodies time to adjust to the lower oxygen pressure.

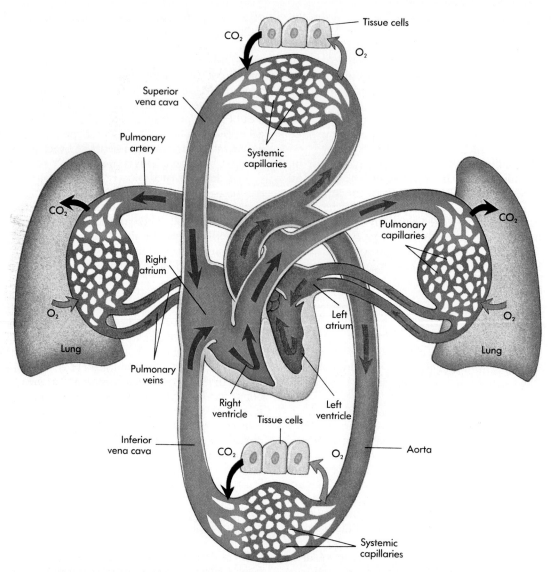

FIGURE 8-9 The route of blood during gas transport. As blood moves through the body, it gives up its supply of oxygen (O_2) to the tissues and collects carbon dioxide (CO_2). This deoxygenated blood is then pumped through the heart to the lungs, where the CO_2 in the blood and O_2 in the alveoli are exchanged. The reoxygenated blood flows to the heart and is pumped to the rest of the body tissues.

During external respiration, carbon dioxide moves down a pressure gradient, diffusing from the blood in capillaries surrounding the alveoli to air in the alveoli. Likewise, oxygen moves down a pressure gradient, diffusing from the alveolar air to the blood in the capillaries surrounding the alveoli. Carbon dioxide is carried in the fluid portion of the blood primarily as bicarbonate ions; oxygen is carried within the red blood cells by the oxygen-carrying molecule hemoglobin.

Internal respiration

Oxygenated blood is pumped out to the body by the left ventricle, or lower left chamber, of the heart. It travels through the aorta to other large arteries that soon branch into smaller and smaller arteries. Eventually the blood vessels become so small that only one red blood cell at a time can pass. These vessels are the capillaries and are the sites of internal respiration.

Internal respiration is the exchange of oxygen and carbon dioxide between the blood within capillaries at the tis-

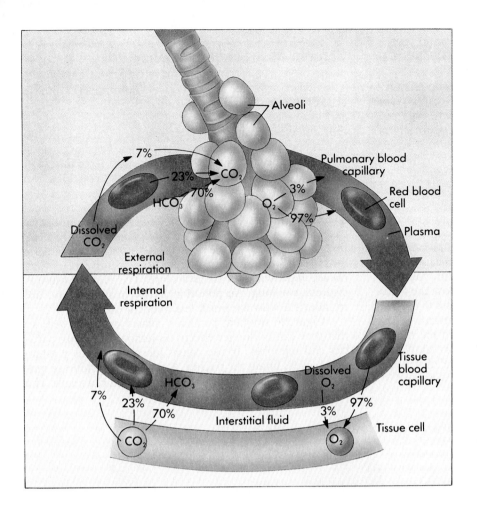

FIGURE 8-10 How gases are transported during external and internal respiration. External respiration takes place in the lungs, as red blood cells exchange CO_2 for O_2. During internal respiration, oxygenated blood travels to the tissues distributing O_2 and collecting CO_2.

sues and the tissue fluid that bathes the cells. As this exchange takes place, oxygenated blood becomes progressively deoxygenated. In essence, the processes of internal respiration are the reverse of the processes of external respiration. As the blood begins its journey from the lungs around the body, it is oxygen rich. The oxygen molecules in the blood exert a higher pressure than those in the cells because oxygen is continuously being used by the cells in the process of cellular respiration. Consequently, oxygen molecules begin to dissociate from the hemoglobin, diffuse into the tissue fluid, and from there diffuse into the cells. Conversely, the levels of carbon dioxide are higher in the cells than in the blood because carbon dioxide is continuously being produced during cellular respiration. Consequently, carbon dioxide diffuses from the cells into the tissue fluid and then into the blood.

As gas exchange at the capillaries continues, an interesting thing happens. The oxygen supply of the blood decreases, thereby decreasing the pressure of oxygen in the blood. Diffusion of oxygen into the tissue fluid does not slow down, however, because the pH at the capillaries lowers as carbon dioxide diffuses into the blood. Remember, carbon dioxide is carried in the blood primarily as bicarbonate ions. As these ions are formed, hydrogen ions are also produced. The buildup of these hydrogen ions makes

the blood increasingly acidic as more carbon dioxide diffuses in. (See Chapter 2 for a discussion of the relationship between hydrogen ions and pH.) This acid environment helps split more oxygen from hemoglobin, thereby enhancing oxygen's diffusion into the tissue fluid. (Figure 8-10 shows the processes of internal and external respiration.)

Temperature also helps split oxygen from hemoglobin. During exercise or any type of exertion, your body needs more oxygen delivered to its cells. However, active cells also produce more carbon dioxide and heat, thereby helping to split oxygen from hemoglobin and meet their own needs. This is one example of how your body works to maintain homeostasis, a state of internal equilibrium.

▼
During internal respiration, carbon dioxide moves down a pressure gradient, diffusing from the tissue fluid surrounding the body cells to the blood. Likewise, oxygen moves down a pressure gradient, diffusing from the blood within capillaries to the tissue fluid. As carbon dioxide diffuses into the blood, the resultant increase in hydrogen ions increases the dissociation of oxygen from hemoglobin.

Choking: A common respiratory emergency

Have you ever been eating with someone who started to choke? Did you know what to do? Choking is caused when food or a foreign object becomes lodged in the windpipe. When you are with someone who is choking, first notice whether the person can talk, breathe, or cough. If so, stay with the person until the airway is cleared by coughing. Do not try to slap the person on the back. The slapping may only cause the food to become more deeply lodged in the windpipe.

If a person cannot talk or cough and appears not to be breathing, administer several short, quick abdominal thrusts. This technique is called the *Heimlich maneuver,* after Dr. Henry Heimlich who developed the procedure. First, stand behind the choking victim. Put your arms around the person, placing your fists just below the breastbone. The proper placement is shown in Figure 8-11. Then give a series of quick, sharp, upward and inward thrusts. These thrusts push in on the diaphragm and the thoracic cavity, suddenly decreasing its volume. This sudden decrease creates a surge in air pressure below the obstruction, which usually projects it forcefully from the windpipe.

Chronic obstructive pulmonary disease

The term **chronic obstructive pulmonary disease (COPD)** is used to refer to disorders that block the airways and impair breathing. COPD affects 25 million people in the United States alone and is responsible for at least 50,000 deaths per year. Most doctors agree that it is one of the fastest growing health problems in this country. Two disorders commonly included in COPD are **chronic bronchitis** and **emphysema.**

The term *chronic* refers to something that occurs over an extended time. Chronic bronchitis, then, does not refer to an isolated, one-time infection or inflammation. It refers to an inflammation of the bronchi and bronchioles that lasts for at least 3 months each year for 2 consecutive years with no accompanying disease as a cause. The primary cause is cigarette smoking. Air pollution and occupational exposure to industrial dust are much less frequent causes.

Cigarette smoking paralyzes ciliated epithelial cells so that they can no longer effectively remove incoming particles and microbes. It also causes increased mucus production by cells lining the trachea. A continued buildup of mucus provides food for bacteria, and infection can result. The

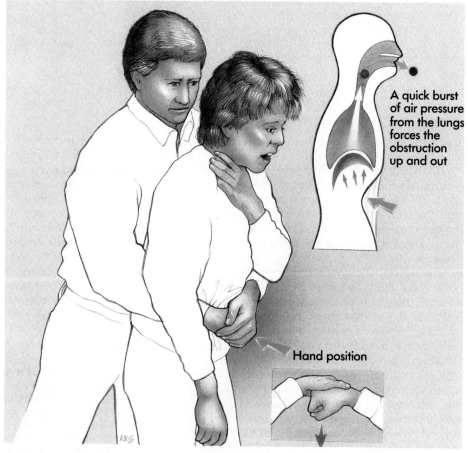

FIGURE 8-11 The Heimlich maneuver. Learning the Heimlich maneuver could save someone you know from choking.

A quick burst of air pressure from the lungs forces the obstruction up and out

Hand position

mucus also plugs up the respiratory "plumbing."

Normally, bronchioles widen, or dilate, during inspiration; they narrow, or constrict, during expiration. If mucus is plugging various bronchioles, some air may therefore be able to get to the alveoli beyond the plugged bronchioles but may not be able to get out. Coughing spells produce pressure within these continuously inflated alveoli that ruptures their walls, decreasing the surface area over which gas exchange can take place (Figure 8-12). In addition, the lungs lose their elasticity and the ability to recoil during exhalation, staying filled with air. This disorder is aptly called *emphysema*, meaning "full of air." A person with emphysema has to work voluntarily to exhale.

People with COPD find that they have more respiratory infections than they did before the disorder and that these infections last longer. They have a morning cough or may cough all day. They may also tire easily and become short of breath with minimal physical exertion. Some people with COPD feel as though they cannot breathe at times. As the disorder progresses, some find it difficult to do a day's work or accomplish the daily activities of living. Periods of breathlessness increase. Some persons suffer bouts of respiratory failure and must be hospitalized. COPD is serious and deadly—but in most cases, it is avoidable.

FIGURE 8-12   Alveoli ruptured as a result of emphysema. Emphysema permanently damages lungs and, along with cancer, is one of the dangerous risks of smoking.

Asthma—It Doesn't Have to Control Your Life

Asthma is a chronic lung disease affecting about 10 million people in the United States. "Chronic" means that a person with asthma usually has the disease for his or her entire life, although some people affected with asthma in childhood may "outgrow" it. So far there is no cure. However, new drugs and preventive measures can lessen the severity of asthma attacks and allow sufferers to lead normal lives.

The underlying cause of asthma attacks is hypersensitive airways. The airways (bronchi and bronchioles) of a person with asthma are much more sensitive to certain stimuli, such as dust, pollen, or animal dander, than the airways of other people. In an asthma attack or episode, the lining of the airways swell. The bronchial muscles contract. Mucus production increases. This combination of swelling, increased mucus production, and muscle contraction narrows the airways. The person with asthma then has trouble bringing air into the lungs and also has trouble getting air out. Forcing air through the narrowed airways can produce a whistling or wheezing sound.

It was once thought that asthma was a psychosomatic illness, with no physical cause. Some physicians believed that the symptoms were all in a person's mind, or that he or she could somehow control the attacks. Others believed that asthma was a bad habit, like a temper tantrum, that showed a person's extreme need for attention. Today, the physiological mechanism of asthma is well known. It is understood that asthma is indeed a physical illness, although emotions can influence the frequency and severity of asthma attacks. Stimuli or triggers that are known to cause asthma attacks include allergens such as pollen, dust, or certain foods; physical factors such as coughing, sneezing, rigorous exercise, or cold temperatures; viral infections; and chemical irritants such as cigarette smoke.

Asthma is treated by teaching the asthma patient to recognize the triggers that bring on attacks and to prevent attacks before they can occur. Asthma patients are encouraged to measure their lungs' vital capacity by exhaling into a device called a peak flow meter. The measurements shown by this device can help the physician

and the patient to develop an individualized treatment plan.

Treatment can involve several types of drugs. *Antiinflammatory agents* lessen the swelling of the airways—these drugs are taken to prevent an attack. *Bronchodilators* that are inhaled are taken during an attack—these fast-acting drugs work to open constricted airways. However, bronchodilators must be used sparingly. Recent studies have shown that overuse of bronchodilator inhalers can lead to a worsening of asthma and even to death in a few cases. The inhaler itself does not cause the death. Instead, the asthma patient comes to rely on the fast-acting nature of the drug and does not notice that his or her asthma might be worsening. A severe attack of asthma can take such a person by surprise, leading to serious complications and death. That is why asthma patients must participate as much as possible in monitoring and treating their condition. This participation can lessen the severity of the disease, giving asthma patients some control over the episodes and the opportunity to lead a normal life.

Summary

1. Respiration is the uptake of oxygen and the release of carbon dioxide by the body. It includes the processes of cellular respiration, internal respiration, external respiration, and breathing.

2. Breathing consists of taking air into the lungs, or inspiration, and expelling air from the lungs, or expiration. The average rate of breathing is 14 to 20 breaths per minute.

3. Air passes through many respiratory structures on its way to the lungs. The nasal cavities, located behind the nostrils, warm and moisten incoming air. The air then passes down the throat, or pharynx, and into the larynx. The larynx, or voice box, sits on top of the windpipe, or trachea. The trachea divides into two bronchi, which further divide into smaller and smaller bronchioles, ending in microscopic air sacs called *alveoli*.

4. The epithelium of the trachea, the bronchi, and some of the bronchioles produce mucus that helps trap foreign particles. In addition, cilia beat to produce a current in the mucus that brings particles up to the throat to be swallowed.

5. During inspiration, the diaphragm, a sheet-like muscle that forms the floor of the thoracic cavity, flattens somewhat as it contracts, increasing the volume of the thoracic cavity. Muscles between the ribs pull up on the rib cage, also increasing this volume. The negative pressure that is created pulls air into the lungs. During expiration, these muscles relax, decreasing the volume of the thoracic cavity. The positive pressure that is created pushes air out of the lungs.

6. Oxygen in the air and carbon dioxide in the blood are exchanged at the alveoli. This exchange is called *external respiration*.

7. Deoxygenated blood from the body is pumped by the heart to the lungs. Here it is oxygenated during external respiration and is then returned to the heart to be pumped to the rest of the body.

8. At the capillaries in the body tissues, oxygen in the blood diffuses out of the blood and into the tissue fluid surrounding the cells and then into the cells for use during cellular respiration. The waste of cellular respiration, carbon dioxide, diffuses out of the cells, into the tissue fluid, and then into the blood. This process is called *internal respiration*.

9. To assist a person who is choking and cannot talk or breathe, administer several short, quick, abdominal thrusts with your arms around the victim and your fists just below the breastbone.

10. *Chronic obstructive pulmonary disease (COPD)* refers to disorders that impair movement of the air in the respiratory system. Chronic bronchitis and emphysema are two common COPD disorders that are most frequently caused by cigarette smoking.

1. Distinguish among respiration, cellular respiration, internal respiration, and external respiration.

2. Your biology instructor poses a problem in class, and you suggest a solution. Explain how you produced the necessary sounds.

3. Hiccups occur when the diaphragm begins to contract spasmodically, causing a sudden inhalation. What do you theorize causes the sound effect that results?

4. After an aerobic exercise class, you may feel winded and out of breath. What voluntary practices (breathing exercises) could you do to increase your lung capacity and air intake overall?

5. Explain how differences in air pressure help you to breathe.

6. How does the circulatory system assist the process of respiration? Why is this help important?

7. While on vacation in the mountains, you find that you feel light-headed and short of breath. Explain why.

8. Explain what happens during gas exchange at the alveoli. What gases are exchanged, and what forces "drive" this exchange?

9. A normal hemoglobin level is an essential circulatory function. What is carried by the hemoglobin?

10. Deoxygenated blood appears blue while in the veins. Why then, when you cut a vein and look at your injury, does your blood appear red as it leaves the wound?

11. Explain the process of gas exchange at the capillaries. What gases are exchanged, and why does an exchange of gases occur?

12. What symptoms indicate that a person is choking and it would be essential to apply the Heimlich maneuver to the person?

13. Why do you think that people with COPD and emphysema tire easily?

1. The U.S. Surgeon General reports that heart disease killed over 800,000 Americans in 1990, making it the single largest cause of death. Of these deaths, one third are directly attributable to smoking cigarettes. Why do you think smoking increases the risk of heart disease?

2. There is much discussion in the media these days about the rights of nonsmokers and the possibly harmful effects of "passive smoke," the smoke-filled air breathed in by nonsmokers in the presence of a smoker. Discuss, in small groups, your experiences with "passive smoke" and opinions on the rights of smokers and nonsmokers in public settings.

3. In the James Bond spy novel *Goldfinger*, a woman is murdered by painting her body with gold paint so that all of her skin is covered. Agent 007 states knowingly that if even a small square of skin had been left uncovered at the base of her skull, she would have lived but that painting over *all* of her skin caused her to suffocate. What do you think of this possibility?

Perutz, M.F. (1978, December). Hemoglobin structure and respiratory transport. *Scientific American*, pp. 92-125.
This is an account of how hemoglobin changes its shape to facilitate oxygen binding and unloading by the man who won a Nobel Prize for unraveling the structure of hemoglobin.

Raloff, J. (1991, March). Air pollution: a respiratory hue and cry. *Science News*, p. 203.
This disturbing article links air pollution to serious respiratory tract damage in some Los Angeles youths.

Stone, R. (1992, July). Bad news on secondhand smoke. *Science*, p. 607.
This is a discussion of the recent EPA study linking passive smoking and lung cancer.

9 | Circulation

History was made in 1982 when a 61-year-old dentist from Seattle, Washington, had his diseased heart replaced with a total artificial heart (TAH) in an operation similar to the one in the photo. This bridge to life—the Jarvik-7—was named for the doctor who designed it. A product of over three decades of research on mechanical replacements for the heart, the Jarvik-7 was constructed primarily of polyurethane and a Dacron polyester mesh and was actually held together by Velcro!

Since 1982, the Jarvik-7 has been implanted in approximately 180 patients, but it is no longer approved for use by the Food and Drug Administration. Air tubes that supplied strong pulses of air to the artificial heart, "pushing" the blood from its chambers, caused problems; the place where they entered the body became infected easily. Also, the artificial heart often produced blood clots that traveled to the brain, resulting in strokes. Now, however, history is being made again with a new Jarvik heart—the Jarvik 2000.

Called a *left ventricular assist device,* this new design helps a person's diseased heart; it does not replace it. The small egg-shaped pump sits in the left lower chamber of the patient's heart. It connects to a battery pack worn outside the body and is regulated by microprocessors (computer chips). As amazing as these "high tech" replacements and assist devices are, scientists still have not been able to duplicate the body's own remarkable pump—the heart.

Functions of the circulatory system

Your circulatory system is made up of three components: (1) the **heart,** a muscular pump; (2) the blood vessels, a network of living tube-like vessels that permeate the body; and (3) the blood, which circulates within these vessels (see Figure 9-3). Together, the heart and blood vessels—the "plumbing" of the circulatory system—are known as the **cardiovascular system.** The prefix *cardio* refers to the heart, and the suffix *vascular* refers to blood vessels. However, the terms *cardiovascular system* and *circulatory system* are often used interchangeably.

Your circulatory system is like a roadway that connects the various muscles and organs of your body with one another. It serves four principal functions:
1. Nutrient and waste transport
2. Oxygen and carbon dioxide transport
3. Temperature maintenance
4. Hormone circulation

In addition, proteins and ions in the fluid portion of the blood regulate the movement of water between the blood and the tissues. Specialized cells defend the body against invading microorganisms and other foreign substances. (These two functions are discussed later in the chapter.) Many biologists argue that the functions of the circulatory system are truly functions of the blood alone; however, the blood cannot perform these functions without circulating throughout the body within vessels, pushed by a powerful pump.

Nutrient and waste transport

The nutrient molecules that fuel cell metabolism are transported to the cells of the body by the circulatory system. Sugars and amino acids pass into the bloodstream at the small intestine, diffusing into a fine net of blood vessels below the mucosa. Most fatty acids are absorbed by the epithelial cells lining the small intestine. After being resynthesized into fats and packaged for transport, these fats pass into lymphatic vessels and are transported to the blood by the lymphatic system. The blood takes all these digestive products to the liver for processing. There, some of these molecules are converted to glucose, which is released into the bloodstream. Others, such as essential amino acids and vitamins, pass through the liver unchanged. Still others, such as excess energy molecules and excess amino acids, are used for the synthesis of glycogen and body fat and are stored for later use.

From the liver, the blood carries glucose and other energy molecules to all the body's cells. In addition, the blood also brings molecules such as amino acids to the cells, which are used as building blocks to produce other substances. The cells, in turn, release the waste products of metabolism into the bloodstream. The blood carries most of these wastes to a cleansing organ, the kidney, which captures and concentrates them for excretion in the urine (see Chapter 10). The cleansed blood then passes back to the heart.

Oxygen and carbon dioxide transport

The cells of the body carry out cellular respiration and need oxygen for this series of reactions to take place. Oxygen is transported to the cells of the body by the circulatory system. Within the lungs, oxygen molecules diffuse into the circulating blood through the walls of capillaries, which are very fine blood vessels (see Chapter 8). This oxygen passes into red blood cells suspended in the liquid portion of the blood. From the lungs the blood carries its cargo of oxygen to all cells of the body. At the same time, it picks up a waste product of cellular respiration, carbon dioxide. The blood then returns to the lungs where the carbon dioxide is released and a fresh supply of oxygen is captured.

Temperature maintenance

As you read in Chapter 4, energy is continuously being lost as heat during the chemical reactions that take place in the cells of your body. The blood distributes this heat as it circulates, helping to maintain your body temperature. As the blood circulates, it passes through delicate, microscopic networks of blood vessels that lie under your skin. As the blood passes through these vessels, it gives up heat because the environment is usually cooler than the body's temperature of 98.6° F. The body works to balance the amount of heat produced and the amount of heat lost to maintain a stable internal temperature.

To maintain this balance, a regulatory center in the brain, the hypothalamus, acts like your own personal thermostat, constantly monitoring body temperature and stimulating regulatory processes. If your body temperature drops, for example, signals from this center cause surface blood vessels to narrow, or constrict. Constriction of these blood vessels limits blood flow to the surface of the skin and lessens heat loss. Conversely, if your body temperature rises, signals from this center cause surface blood vessels to widen, or dilate. Dilation increases blood flow to the surface of the skin and increases heat loss (Figure 9-1).

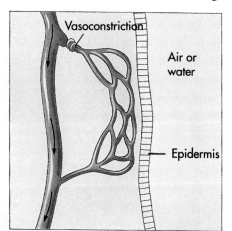

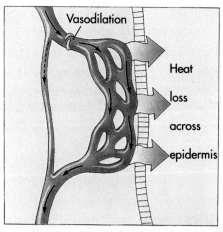

FIGURE 9-1 Regulation of heat loss. The amount of heat lost at the body's surface can be regulated by controlling the flow of blood to the surface. Constriction of the surface blood vessels limits flow and lessens heat loss. Dilation of the surface blood vessels increases blood flow and thus increases heat loss.

Hormone circulation

The chemical reactions and other activities of the body are coordinated by nerve signals and hormones. Hormones are the body's chemical messengers; they are produced in one place and produce an effect in another. The circulatory system is the highway within which hormones travel throughout the body from their site of production and, in this way, reach the target tissues that are capable of responding to them.

The circulatory system transports oxygen and nutrients to cells, transports carbon dioxide and metabolic wastes away from cells, helps maintain a stable internal temperature, and carries chemical messengers called *hormones* throughout the body. Substances within the blood regulate the movement of water between the blood and the tissues and defend the body against disease.

The heart and blood vessels

As the blood is pushed along by the heart to begin its journey throughout the body, it leaves the heart within vessels known as **arteries** (Figure 9-2). From the arteries, the blood passes into a network of **arterioles,** or small arteries. From these, it eventually is forced through the **capillaries,** a fine latticework of very narrow tubes, which get their name from the Latin word *capillus,* meaning "a hair." As blood passes through these capillaries, gases are exchanged between the blood and the tissues, nutrients are delivered to the tissues, and wastes are picked up from the tissues. After its journey through the capillaries, the blood passes into a third kind of vessel: the **venules,** or small **veins.** A network of venules and larger veins collects the circulated blood and carries it back to the heart.

FIGURE 9-2 The human circulatory system.
The circulatory system is composed of the heart, blood vessels, and blood.

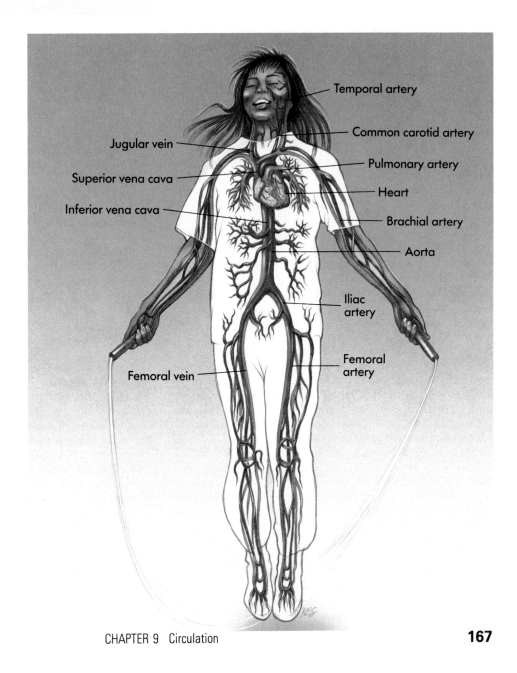

Temporal artery

Common carotid artery

Pulmonary artery

Heart

Brachial artery

Aorta

Iliac artery

Femoral artery

Jugular vein

Superior vena cava

Inferior vena cava

Femoral vein

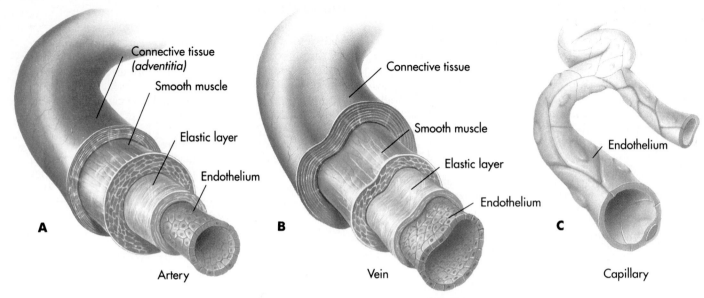

FIGURE 9-3 The structure of some important blood vessels. Blood leaves the heart through arteries **(A)** and returns to the heart through veins **(B)**. The capillaries **(C)** are the tubes through which the blood is forced in the tissues, exchanging gases, delivering nutrients, and collecting wastes.

Arteries and arterioles

Arteries are vessels that carry blood away from the heart. The adult human heart pumps about 70 milliliters of blood—a little over 2 ounces—into the arteries with each beat. On average, your heart beats about 75 times per minute, pumping over 5 liters, or 5 1/2 quarts, of blood into your arteries each minute of your life. The vessels leading out from the heart expand slightly in diameter and then recoil before the next heartbeat in response to the pressure of blood surging into them.

The walls of the arteries are made up of three layers of tissue (Figure 9-3, *A*) and have a hollow core called the *lumen* through which blood flows. *Endothelial cells* (the inner epithelium of blood vessels and the heart) line arteries and are in contact with the blood. Surrounding these cells is a thick layer of smooth muscle and elastic fibers. The elastic tissue allows the artery to expand and recoil in response to the pulses of blood. The steady contraction of the muscle layer strengthens the wall of the vessel against overexpansion. This muscle and elastic layer is encased within an envelope of protective connective tissue.

Arterioles differ from arteries in that they are smaller in diameter. The walls of the largest arterioles are constructed very much like those of arteries. However, as arterioles near the capillaries, their diameter decreases until they consist of nothing but a layer of endothelium wrapped with a few scattered smooth muscle cells.

The muscle cells within the walls of arterioles tighten or relax in response to messages from nerves and hormones. When these muscles relax, the arteriole dilates and the blood flow through it increases. This response is exactly what is happening when you blush. When you are embarrassed (or when you become overheated), signals from the nerve fibers connected to muscles surrounding the arterioles are inhibited, which relaxes the smooth muscle and causes the arterioles in the skin to dilate. The increased blood flow brings heat to the surface for escape and causes you to have a red face. Conversely, when you are scared or cold, the muscles in the walls of the arterioles in your skin contract. When the muscles contract, the arteriole constricts and the blood flow through it decreases, conserving your body heat. When you are scared, the body constricts these vessels to route more blood to other tissues such as your skeletal muscles.

Capillaries

Capillaries are microscopic blood vessels that connect arterioles with venules. They have a simple structure (Figure 9-3, *C*) and are little more than tubes with walls one cell thick and with a length that would barely stretch across the head of a pin. The internal diameter of the capillaries is about the same as that of red blood cells, causing these cells to squeeze through the capillaries single file (Figure 9-4). The closeness between the walls of the capillaries and the membranes of the red blood cells facilitates the diffusion of gases, nutrients, and wastes between them—a swap of oxygen and nutrients for carbon dioxide and other metabolic waste products.

Your entire body is permeated with a fine mesh of capillaries, networks that amount to several thousand kilometers in overall length. In fact, if all the capillaries in your body were laid end to end, they would extend across the United States! These networks of capillaries are called **cap-**

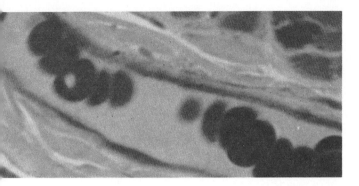

FIGURE 9-4 Red blood cells in a capillary passing along in single file.
Many capillaries are even smaller than those shown here from the bladder of a monkey. Red blood cells will even pass through capillaries narrower than their own diameter, pushed along by the pressure generated by a pumping heart.

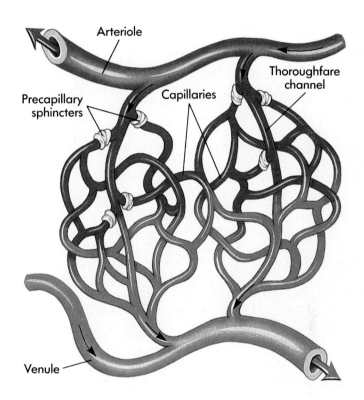

Arteriole

Thoroughfare channel

Precapillary sphincters

Capillaries

Venule

FIGURE 9-5 The capillary bed connects arteries with veins.
The most direct connection is via thoroughfare channels that connect arterioles directly to venules. Branching from these thoroughfare channels is a network of finer capillary channels. Most of the exchange of gases, nutrients, wastes, and ions between body and red blood cells occurs while the red blood cells are in this capillary network.

illary beds. In a capillary bed, some of the capillaries connect arterioles and venules directly (Figure 9-5) and are called **thoroughfare channels.** From these channels, loops of true capillaries—those not on the direct flow route from arterioles to venules—leave and return. Almost all exchanges between the blood and the cells of the body occur through these loops. The entry to each loop is guarded by a ring of muscle that, when contracted, blocks flow through the capillary. Restricting blood flow in capillary beds near the surface of the skin is a powerful means by which the

body can limit heat loss in addition to the constriction of surface arterioles. The body can also cut down on the flow within a capillary bed when heavy flow is not needed—to your muscles, for example, when you are resting. Likewise, the body can increase the flow within a capillary bed when the need increases—to your small intestine, for example, after a meal. Interestingly, you do not have enough blood to fill all your capillary beds if they were all open at the same time. If such a situation occurred, you would faint because of lack of sufficient blood to the brain.

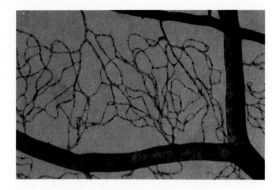

FIGURE 9-6   Venules.
Venules collect blood from the capillary bed and deliver it to the larger veins.

FIGURE 9-8   A one-way valve in a vein.
These valves assist the blood in its movement back toward the heart by preventing the blood from moving backwards.

Veins and venules

Venules are small veins that collect blood from the capillary beds and bring it to larger veins (Figure 9-6) that carry it back to the heart. The force of the heartbeat is greatly diminished by the time the blood reaches the veins, so these vessels do not have to accommodate pulsing pressures as arteries do. Therefore the walls of veins, although similar in structure to those of the arteries, have much thinner layers of muscle and elastic fiber (Figures 9-3, *B* and 9-7). Lacking much of this supportive tissue, the walls of veins collapse when they are empty (although this situation would never occur in the living body). Empty arteries, on the other hand, stay open like tiny pipes. In addition, the lumen of veins is larger than that of arteries. This difference in size is related to the lower pressure of blood flowing within veins back toward the heart—large vessels present less resistance to the flow than smaller vessels do.

The pathway of blood back to the heart from much of the body is an uphill struggle. The pressure pushing the blood upward in the veins of your legs, for example, approximately equals the force of gravity pulling it down. As skeletal muscles contract, they press on veins and help move blood along. In addition, many veins have one-way valves that help blood move back toward the heart by preventing its backflow (Figure 9-8). If some of the valves in a vein are weak, however, gravity can force blood back through these valves, overloading a portion of a vein and pushing its walls outward. These "stretched out" veins, called *varicose veins,* are often seen in the legs at the surface of the skin.

Arteries and veins are the major vessels of the circulatory system and have walls composed of three layers: (1) an innermost, thin layer of endothelial tissue that is in contact with the blood; (2) a layer of elastic fibers and smooth muscle serviced by nerves; and (3) a layer of protective connective tissue. The walls of arteries have more elastic tissue and smooth muscle than veins do, which helps them accommodate pulses of blood pumped from the heart. Capillaries are microscopic blood vessels that have walls only one cell thick. The exchange of substances between the cells and the blood takes place at the capillaries.

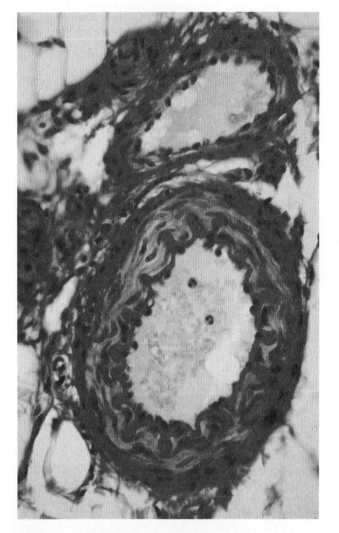

FIGURE 9-7   A closer look at blood vessels.
The vein *(top)* has the same general structure as an artery *(bottom)* but has much thinner layers of muscle and elastic fiber. An artery will retain its shape when empty, but a vein will collapse.

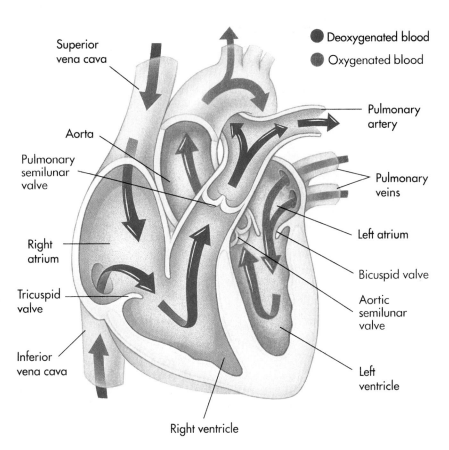

Superior
vena cava

Aorta

Pulmonary
semilunar
valve

Right
atrium

Tricuspid
valve

Inferior
vena cava

Right ventricle

● Deoxygenated blood
○ Oxygenated blood

Pulmonary
artery

Pulmonary
veins

Left atrium

Bicuspid valve

Aortic
semilunar
valve

Left
ventricle

FIGURE 9-9   The path of blood through the human heart.

Oxygenated blood from the lungs enters the left atrium by way of the pulmonary veins and flows through the bicuspid valve to the left ventricle, from which it enters the general circulatory system by way of the aorta. Deoxygenated blood enters the right atrium by way of the superior and inferior venae cavae and flows through the tricuspid valve to the right ventricle. The blood then moves through the pulmonary semilunar valve to the pulmonary artery and lungs.

The heart: A double pump

The human circulatory system is referred to as a *closed circulatory system* because blood flows throughout the body confined within blood vessels. The blood is therefore separated from the rest of the body's fluids and does not mix freely with them. The plumbing of a closed circulatory system requires not only a system of vessels through which the blood can continuously flow throughout the body but also a pump to push the blood along. The pump of the human circulatory system is the heart, but it is two pumps in one. Figure 9-9 is a diagram of a frontal section through the heart and shows the organization of this double pump. The left side (one pump) has two connected chambers, as does the right side (the other pump). But the two sides, or pumps, of the heart are not directly connected with one another.

Circulatory pathways

The journey of blood around the body starts with the entry of oxygenated blood into the heart from the lungs. Oxygenated blood from the lungs enters the left side of the heart, emptying directly into the upper left chamber of the heart, the **left atrium,** through large vessels called the **pulmonary veins.** These veins are unusual in that they carry

oxygenated blood; other veins, since they carry blood back to the heart from the body tissues, carry deoxygenated blood. The word *pulmonary* refers to the lungs. The circulation of blood to and from the lungs is therefore called the **pulmonary circulation** (Figure 9-10).

From the left atrium of the heart, blood flows through a one-way valve, the **bicuspid valve,** into the lower, adjoining chamber, the **left ventricle.** Most of this flow (roughly 80%) occurs while the heart is relaxed. The atrium then contracts, pushing the remaining 20% of its blood into the ventricle. After a slight delay the ventricle contracts. The walls of the ventricle are far more muscular than those of the atrium, and as a result, this contraction is much stronger. It forces most of the blood out of the ventricle in a single strong pulse. The blood is prevented from going back into the atrium by the bicuspid valve, whose flaps are pushed shut as the ventricle contracts. Strong fibers that prevent the flaps from moving too far when closing are attached to their edges. If the flaps did move too far, they would project out into the atrium.

Prevented from reentering the atrium, the blood takes the only other way out of the contracting left ventricle: an opening that leads into the largest artery in the body—the **aorta.** The aorta is closed off from the left ventricle by a one-way valve, the **aortic semilunar valve.** It is oriented to permit the flow of the blood out of the ventricle. As the blood is pushed forcefully out of the left ventricle to make

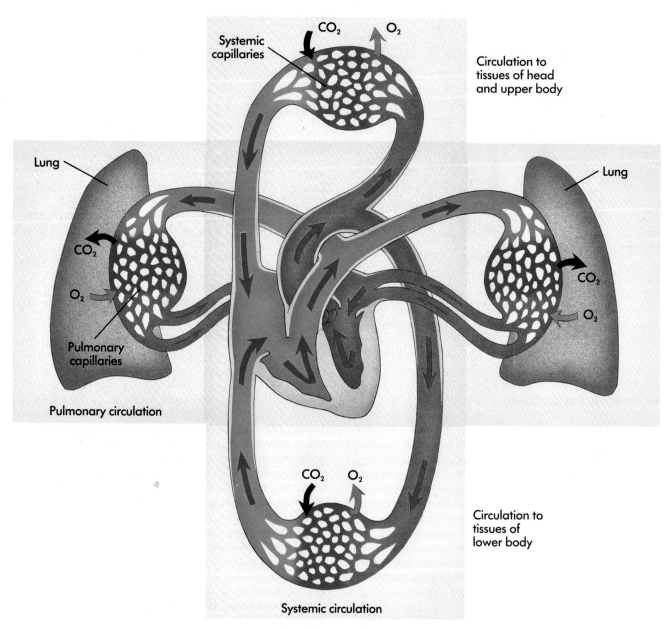

FIGURE 9-10 Pulmonary circulation versus systemic circulation. The circulation of the blood to and from the lungs is called the *pulmonary circulation.* The circulation of the blood to the body regions and organs other than the lungs is called the *systemic circulation.*

Infectious diseases like AIDS are not the greatest killers of Americans. Every year over 80% of those who die in the United States (some 1.5 million people in 1991) die from one of five chronic diseases—what you often think of as the disorders of middle age. The top five causes of death in 1991 were the following:

1. Heart disease
2. Cancer
3. Stroke
4. Accidents
5. Chronic obstructive pulmonary disease

The most striking thing about this list is the preponderance of preventable illness. One fourth of the deaths are from cancer, and most of them are due to smoking. Even more striking, over 900,000—60% of all deaths—are due to heart disease and stroke. This carries a very important message to everyone because deaths from these chronic illnesses are influenced greatly by individual living habits. In fact, it is possible to predict in large measure how a person will die from how that person lives. As many as 70% of the deaths from these "top killers" could be prevented by altered living habits.

Heart disease is the greatest killer in the United States today. It is not, however, an inevitable result of being alive. A few simple changes in lifestyle can drastically lower an individual's risk of heart disease. Strokes, which are caused by a stoppage of blood flow to part of the brain, share many of the same risk factors as heart disease. The three principle risk factors are the following:

1. *Smoking:* About 29% of Americans smoke, leading to one third of heart disease deaths because smoking elevates cholesterol levels and thus blood vessel blockage, according to the U. S. Surgeon General. Smokers also run a 20% to 60% greater chance of stroke. It is not easy to quit smoking—nicotine has been declared an addictive drug—but the best way for smokers to avoid death by heart disease and stroke is to throw their cigarettes away.
2. *High cholesterol levels:* If your blood cholesterol level is high—over 200 for adults—it should be lowered by eating fewer saturated fats (eggs,

FIGURE 9-A This unhealthy meal with its large doses of salt and fats and the cigarette beside it are major contributors to heart attacks.

meat, and tropical oils) (Figure 9-A). If the blood cholesterol level is over 240, many physicians recommend cholesterol-lowering drugs.

3. *High blood pressure:* Hypertension (high blood pressure) is a killer, causing up to one half of all strokes. If your blood pressure exceeds 140 over 90 mm, it should be lowered with a low-fat, low-salt diet.

its trip around the body, it rushes into the aorta, causing the elastic, muscular walls of this artery to bulge slightly outward. Quickly, however, the aorta walls recoil as a stretched elastic band does when let go. This recoil action pushes on the blood; some of it is pushed backward against the valve. The valve is constructed in such a way that it snaps shut in response to this backflow. The other oneway valves found in the heart and blood vessels are constructed in a similar manner, preventing the backflow of blood.

Many arteries branch from the aorta, carrying oxygen-rich blood to all parts of the body. The pathway of blood vessels to the body regions and organs other than the lungs is called the **systemic circulation** (see Figure 9-10), with the aorta being the first and largest vessel in the circuit. The first arteries to branch off the aorta are the coronary arteries, which carry freshly oxygenated blood to the heart itself; the muscles of the heart do not obtain their supply of blood from directly within the heart. From the arch of the aorta, the carotid arteries branch off and bring blood to networks of vessels in the neck and head. The subclavian arteries bring blood to the shoulders and arms. The aorta then descends down the trunk of the body, with arteries branching off to supply various organs such as the kidneys, liver, and intestines. The aorta divides into two major vessels at the level of the lower back, one traveling to each leg.

The blood that flows into the arterial system eventually returns to the heart after delivering its supply of oxygen

to the cells of the body and picking up the waste gas carbon dioxide. This exchange takes place at the capillaries. In returning, blood passes through a series of veins, eventually entering the right side of the heart. Two large veins collect blood from the systemic circulation. The **superior vena cava** drains the upper body, and the **inferior vena cava** drains the lower body. These veins dump deoxygenated blood into the right atrium.

The right side of the heart is similar in organization to the left side. However, the muscular walls of the right ventricle are not as thick as those of the left. Blood passes from the right atrium into the right ventricle through a one-way valve, the **tricuspid valve.** It passes out of the contracting right ventricle through a second valve, the **pulmonary semilunar valve,** into a single **pulmonary artery,** which subsequently branches into two pulmonary arteries that carry deoxygenated blood to the lungs. The blood then returns from the lungs to the left side of the heart, replenished with oxygen and cleared of much of its load of carbon dioxide. (The human circulatory system as a whole is outlined in Figure 9-2.)

▼▼▼
The circulation of the blood to and from the lungs is called the pulmonary circulation. The circulation of the blood through the parts of the body other than the lungs is called the systemic circulation.

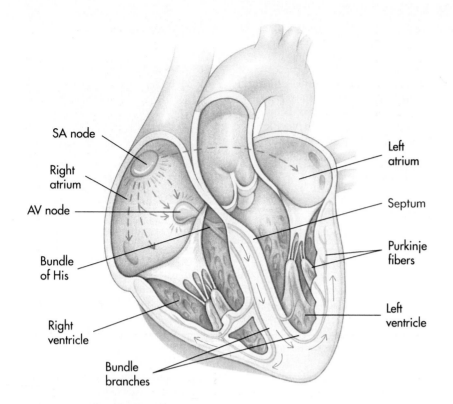

FIGURE 9-11 How the heart contracts. Contraction of the human heart is initiated by an impulse that begins at the SA node. After passing over the right and left atria and causing their contraction, the impulse reaches the AV node. From there it passes through the bundle of His, which has a bundle branch to each ventricle. From the tips of the ventricles, the depolarization is conducted rapidly over their surfaces by the branches of the Purkinje fibers.

Labels in figure: SA node; Right atrium; AV node; Bundle of His; Right ventricle; Bundle branches; Left atrium; Septum; Purkinje fibers; Left ventricle

How the heart contracts

The contraction of the heart depends on a small cluster of specialized cardiac muscle cells that are embedded in the upper wall of the right atrium (Figure 9-11). This cluster of cells, called the **sinoatrial (SA) node,** automatically and rhythmically sends out impulses that initiate each heartbeat. The SA node is therefore nicknamed the pacemaker of the heart.

The impulse initiated by the SA node causes both atria to contract simultaneously and also excites a bundle of cardiac muscle cells located at the base of the atria. These cells are known as the **atrioventricular (AV) node.** The AV node conducts the impulse to a strand of specialized muscle in the **septum,** the tissue that separates the two sides of the heart. This strand of impulse-conducting muscle, known as the **bundle of His,** has branches that divide to the right and left. On reaching the apex (lower tip) of the heart, each branch further divides into conducting fibers called **Purkinje fibers,** which initiate the almost simultaneous contraction of all the cells of the right and left ventricles. The conduction of the impulse from the atria to the ventricles takes approximately 0.2 seconds. During this delay the atria finish emptying their contents into the corresponding ventricles before the ventricles start to contract.

▼
An excitatory impulse is initiated in the SA node of the heart, which causes the atria to contract and the impulse to be passed along to other specialized groups of cardiac cells: the AV node, bundle of His, bundle branches, and Purkinje fibers. The passage of this excitatory impulse causes the almost simultaneous contraction of all cells of the right and left ventricles.

Monitoring the heart's performance

The heartbeat is really a series of events that occur in a predictable order. A physician can gain information about the health of the heart and events occurring during the heartbeat by making several different kinds of observations. The simplest is to listen to the heart at work.

The first sound heard, a low-pitched *lubb,* is caused by the turbulence in blood flow created by the closing of the bicuspid and tricuspid valves at the start of ventricular contraction. A little later a higher-pitched *dupp* can be heard, signaling the closing of the pulmonary and aortic semilunar valves at the end of ventricular contraction. If the valves are not closing fully or if they open too narrowly, a slight backflow of blood occurs within the heart. This backflow can be heard as a sloshing sound; this condition is known as a *heart murmur.*

A second way to examine the events of the heartbeat is to monitor the blood pressure, the force exerted by the blood on blood vessel walls. During the first part of the heartbeat the atria are filling and contracting. At this time the pressure in the arteries leading from the left side of the heart out to the tissues of the body decreases slightly because blood is not being forced into them by the left ventricle. This period of relaxation (with respect to the ventricles) is referred to as the **diastolic period.** The force the blood exerts on the blood vessels at this time is the diastolic pressure. During the contraction of the ventricles, a pulse of blood is forced into the systemic arterial system by the left ventricle, immediately raising the blood pressure within these vessels. This period of contraction (with respect to the ventricles) ends with the closing of the aortic semilunar valve and is referred to as the **systolic period.** The force the blood exerts on the blood vessels at this time is the systolic pressure.

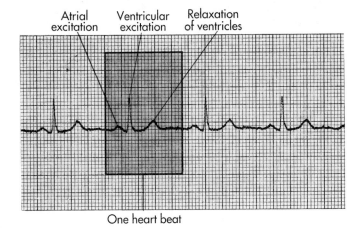

Atrial excitation   Ventricular excitation   Relaxation of ventricles

One heart beat

FIGURE 9-12   An electrocardiogram.
An electrocardiogram records the electrical impulses made throughout the body as the heart contracts.

Blood pressure is measured in units called millimeters (mm) of mercury (Hg). These units refer to the height to which a column of mercury is raised in a tube by an equivalent pressure. Using this system of measurement, normal blood pressure values are 70 to 90 (mm of Hg) diastolic and 110 to 130 systolic. Blood pressure is expressed as the systolic pressure over the diastolic pressure, such as 110 over 70. When the inner walls of the arteries accumulate fats, as they do in the condition known as **atherosclerosis,** the diameters of the passageways are narrowed. Such narrowing is one cause of elevated systolic and diastolic blood pressures.

A third way to monitor the events of a heartbeat is to measure the electrical changes that take place as the heart's chambers both contract and relax. Because so much of the human body is made up of water, it conducts electrical currents rather well. Therefore as the impulses initiated at the SA node pass throughout the heart as an electrical current, this current passes in a wave throughout the body. Although the magnitude of this electrical pulse is tiny, it can be detected with sensors placed on the skin. A recording made of these impulses (Figure 9-12) is called an **electrocardiogram,** or **ECG.**

Three successive electrical pulses are recorded in a normal heartbeat. The first pulse occurs when the atria contract. There is a much stronger pulse 2/10 of a second later, reflecting both the contraction of the ventricles and the relaxation of the atria. Finally, a third pulse occurs caused by the relaxation of the ventricles.

▼
The heartbeat is a series of events that occurs in a predictable order. A physician can gather data about the health of the heart by monitoring the heartbeat in various ways: by listening to the sounds the heart makes, by monitoring the blood pressure, and by measuring the electrical changes that take place as it contracts and relaxes.

The blood

Your blood makes up about 8% of your body. It is a viscous, or thick, fluid made up of two parts: a liquid portion called **plasma** and a portion consisting of **formed elements**—several different kinds of cells and cell parts suspended within the plasma.

Blood plasma

Blood plasma is a straw-colored liquid made up of water and dissolved substances. The dissolved substances can be grouped into three categories:
1. Nutrients, hormones, respiratory gases, and wastes: These substances can be thought of as the traffic on the highway of blood. Dissolved within the plasma are substances that move from one place to another in the body and that are used or produced by the metabolism of cells. These substances include glucose, lipoproteins (a soluble form of lipid), amino acids, vitamins, hormones, and the respiratory gases.
2. Salts and ions: Plasma is a dilute salt solution. Chemically, the word *salt* refers to more than just table salt. It is a general term applied to any substance composed of positively and negatively charged ions. In water, salts dissociate into their component ions. An ion is a charged particle—an atom that has an unequal number of protons and electrons (see Chapter 2).

   The chief plasma ions are sodium (Na^+), chloride (Cl^-), and bicarbonate (HCO_3^-). In addition, there are trace amounts of other ions, such as calcium (Ca^{2+}), magnesium (Mg^{2+}), copper (Cu^{2+}), potassium (K^+), and zinc (Zn^{2+}). In living systems these ions are called *electrolytes*. Electrolytes serve three general functions in the body. First, many are essential minerals. Second, they play a role in the movement of water—osmosis—between various compartments within the body. Third, they help maintain the acid-base (pH) balance required for normal cellular activities.
3. Proteins: Blood plasma is approximately 90% water. As the plasma circulates past the cells of the body, water moves between the tissue fluid and the blood from an area of higher concentration of water to an area of lower concentration of water. Blood contains a concentration of proteins that balances that of the cells, thereby balancing the concentration of water between the cells and the blood. For this reason, water is not osmotically sucked out of the blood.

   The types of proteins in blood vary. Some of these proteins are antibodies and other proteins are active in the immune system. Others are fibrinogen and prothrombin, key players in blood clotting. Taken together, however, these proteins make up less than half of the amount of protein that is necessary to balance the protein content of the other cells of the body. The rest consists of a protein called *serum albumin,* which circulates in the blood as an osmotic counterforce.

Blood cell		Life span in blood	Function
Erythrocyte		120 days	O_2 and CO_2 transport
Neutrophil	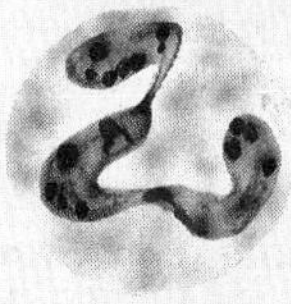	7 hours	Immune defenses
Eosinophil	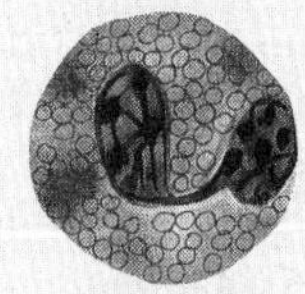	8-12 days	Defense against parasites
Basophil	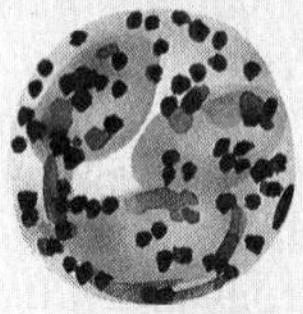	A few hours to a few days	Inflammatory response
Monocyte	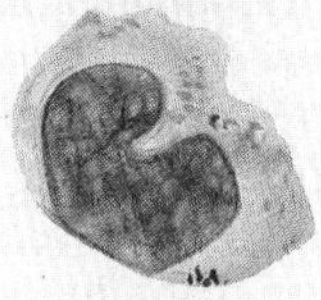	3 days	Immune surveillance (precursor of tissue macrophage)
B-lymphocyte		Memory cells may survive for years	Antibody production (precursor of plasma cells)
T-lymphocyte	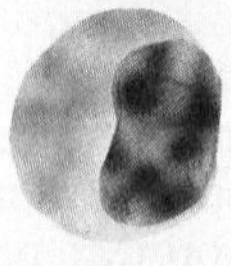	Memory cells may survive for years	Cellular immune response
Platelets	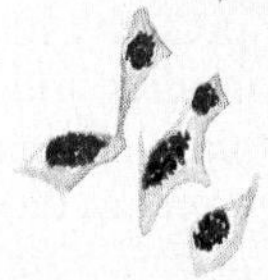	7-8 days	Blood clotting

FIGURE 9-13 Types of blood cells.
Different blood cells perform different functions and have varying lifespans, as this chart shows.

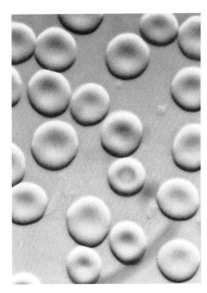

FIGURE 9-14 Human erythrocytes, magnified 1000 times.
Mature human erythrocytes have a characteristic collapsed appearance, like a pillow on which someone has sat.

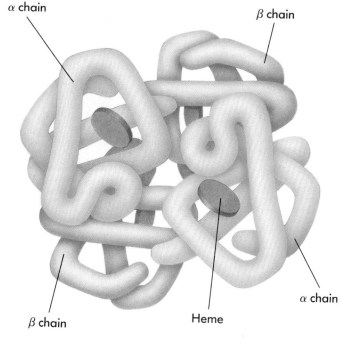

α chain   β chain

β chain   Heme   α chain

FIGURE 9-15 A hemoglobin molecule.
The interior of a red blood cell is packed with hemoglobin. Each hemoglobin molecule is composed of four polypeptide chains. At the center of each chain is a heme group that contains iron. Oxygen binds to the iron for transport.

Blood plasma contains nutrients, hormones, respiratory gases, wastes, and a variety of ions and salts. It also contains high concentrations of the protein serum albumin, which functions to keep the blood plasma in osmotic equilibrium with the cells of the body.

Types of blood cells

Although blood is liquid, 45% of its volume is actually occupied by cells and pieces of cells, collectively called *formed elements*. There are three principal types of formed elements in the blood: erythrocytes, leukocytes, and platelets (Figure 9-13).

Erythrocytes
In only one teaspoonful of your blood, there are about 25 billion **erythrocytes,** or **red blood cells.** Each erythrocyte is a flat disk with a central depression (Figure 9-14), something like a doughnut with a hole that does not go all the way through. Almost the entire interior of each cell is packed with the oxygen-carrying molecule hemoglobin (Figure 9-15). One estimate, in fact, is that each erythrocyte can carry 280 million molecules of hemoglobin!

Mature erythrocytes do not have nuclei or the ability to manufacture proteins. Red blood cells are therefore unable to repair themselves and consequently have a rather short life span. Erythrocytes live only about 4 months. Old, worn-out erythrocytes are processed by macrophages in the spleen, liver, and bone marrow. New erythrocytes are con-

stantly being synthesized and released into the blood by cells within the soft interior marrow of bones at the amazing rate of 2 million per second!

Leukocytes
Less than 1% of the cells in human blood are **leukocytes,** or **white blood cells.** In fact, there are only about 1 or 2 leukocytes for every 1000 erythrocytes. Leukocytes are larger than red blood cells; they contain no hemoglobin, have nuclei, and are essentially colorless. There are several kinds of leukocytes, and each has a different function. All functions, however, are related to the defense of the body against invading microorganisms and other foreign substances (see Chapter 16).

There are two major groups of leukocytes: **granulocytes** and **agranulocytes.** Granulocytes are circulating leukocytes and get their name from the tiny granules in their cytoplasm. In addition, they have lobed nuclei (see Figure 9-13). The granulocytes are classified into three groups by their staining properties. About 50% to 70% of them are **neutrophils,** cells that migrate to the site of an injury and stick to the interior walls of the blood vessels. They then form projections that enable them to push their way into

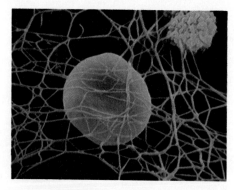

FIGURE 9-16 Fibrin threads have caught a red blood cell. Eventually, many red blood cells will become caught in this net, forming a clot.

the infected tissues, where they engulf, or *phagocytize,* microorganisms and other foreign particles. The term *phagocytosis* comes from a Latin word meaning "cell eating." **Basophils,** a second kind of granulocyte, contain granules that rupture and release chemicals that enhance the body's response to injury or infection. They play a role in causing allergic responses. The third kind of granulocyte, the **eosinophils,** are also believed to be involved in allergic reactions. In addition, they act against certain parasitic worms.

Agranulocytes have no cytoplasmic granules, nor are their nuclei lobed. One group of agranulocytes, the **monocytes,** circulate as the granulocytes do. Monocytes are attracted to the sites of injury or infection where they are converted into **macrophages**—enlarged, amoeba-like cells that entrap microorganisms and particles of foreign matter by phagocytosis. They usually arrive after the neutrophils and clean up any bacteria and dead cells. **Lymphocytes,** the other type of agranulocyte, recognize and react to substances that are foreign to the body, sometimes producing a protective immunity to disease. Occasionally, however, these cells produce an inflammation or an allergic response (see Chapter 16).

Platelets

Certain large cells within the bone marrow called *megakaryocytes* regularly pinch off bits of their cytoplasm. These cell fragments, called **platelets,** enter the bloodstream and play an important role in controlling blood clotting, or coagulation. The clotting of blood is a complicated process initiated by damage to blood vessels or tissues.

When an injury occurs, platelets clump at the damaged area, temporarily blocking blood loss. The damaged tissues and platelets release a complex of substances called *thromboplastin.* The release of this complex begins a cascade of events, one dependent on the other. A simplified explanation is as follows: thromboplastin interacts with calcium ions, vitamin K, and other clotting factors to form an enzyme called *prothrombin activator.* Prothrombin activator brings about the conversion of prothrombin to thrombin. Thrombin converts fibrinogen, a soluble protein, to fibrin, an insoluble thread-like protein. Fibrin threads, along with

trapped red blood cells (Figure 9-16), form the clot—a plug at the damaged area so that blood cannot escape.

⬇⬇

The three principal types of formed elements in the blood are erythrocytes, leukocytes, and platelets. Erythrocytes, or red blood cells, carry oxygen; leukocytes, or white blood cells, defend the body against invading microorganisms and other foreign substances; and platelets play an important role in blood clotting.

The lymphatic system

Although the blood proteins and electrolytes help maintain an osmotic balance between the blood and the tissues, the blood loses more fluid to the tissues than it reabsorbs from them. Of the total volume of fluid that moves from the blood into and around the tissues, about 90% reenters the cardiovascular system. Where does the other 10% go? The answer is to the body's one-way, passive circulatory system, the **lymphatic system** (Figure 9-17). This system counteracts the effects of net fluid loss from the blood.

By osmosis and diffusion, blind-ended lymphatic capillaries (see Figure 9-17) fill with tissue fluid (including small proteins that have diffused out of the blood). From these capillaries, the tissue fluid—now called **lymph**—flows through a series of progressively larger vessels to two large lymphatic vessels, which structurally resemble veins. These vessels drain into veins of the circulatory system near the base of the neck through one-way valves. Although the lymphatic system has no heart to pump lymph through its vessels, the fluid is driven through them when the vessels are squeezed by the movements of the body's muscles. The lymphatic vessels contain a series of one-way valves (Figure 9-18) that permit movement only in the direction of the neck.

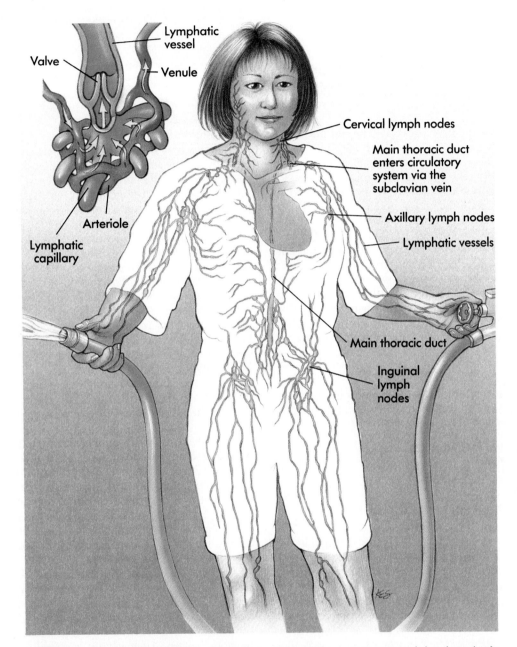

Valve

Lymphatic vessel

Venule

Arteriole

Lymphatic capillary

Cervical lymph nodes

Main thoracic duct enters circulatory system via the subclavian vein

Axillary lymph nodes

Lymphatic vessels

Main thoracic duct

Inguinal lymph nodes

FIGURE 9-17 The human lymphatic vessels and nodes. Other organs containing lymphatic tissue include the spleen, thymus, appendix, tonsils, and bone marrow. The enlarged diagram at the upper left shows the path of the excess fluid that leaves the arteriole end of a capillary bed, enters the adjacent tissue spaces, and is absorbed by lymphatic capillaries.

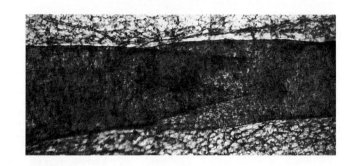

Figure 9-18 A lymphatic vessel magnified 25 times.
Flow from left to right is not impeded because this flow tends to force open the valve. Flow from right to left is prevented because "backward" flow tends to force the one-way valve closed.

Small, ovoid, spongy structures called **lymph nodes** are located in various places of the body along the route of the lymphatic vessels. They are clustered in areas such as the groin, armpits, and neck, filtering the lymph as it passes through. Some lymphocytes, the cells that activate the immune response, reside in the lymph nodes. (These cells are discussed in more detail in Chapter 16.) In addition, the lymphatic system has two organs: the **spleen** and the **thymus.** The spleen stores an emergency blood supply and also contains white blood cells. Specific types of white blood cells in the spleen destroy old red blood cells, filter microorganisms out of the blood as it passes through, or initiate an immune response against the foreign microbes. The thymus plays an important role in the maturation of certain lymphocytes called *T cells,* which are an essential part of the immune system.

 Approximately 10% of the fluid that moves out of the blood and into the cells and cell spaces at the capillaries does not return to the blood directly. It is collected and then returned to the blood by a system of one-way, blind-ended vessels called the lymphatic system.

Diseases of the heart and blood vessels

Cardiovascular diseases are the leading cause of death in the United States. More than 42 million people in this country have some form of cardiovascular disease—about one person in five.

Heart attacks, the most common cause of death in the United States, result from an insufficient supply of blood reaching an area of heart muscle. Heart attacks may be caused by a blood clot forming in one of the vessels that supplies the heart with blood, thereby blocking its blood supply. They may also result if a vessel is blocked sufficiently by fatty deposits, especially cholesterol and triglycerides. Recovery from a heart attack is possible if the segment of damaged heart tissue is small enough that other blood vessels in the heart can supply the damaged tissues. *Angina pectoris,* which literally means "chest pain," occurs for reasons similar to those that cause heart attacks, but it is not as severe. In this case, a reduced blood flow to the heart muscle weakens the cells but does not kill them. The pain may occur in the heart and often also in the left arm and shoulder.

The amount of heart damage associated with a small heart attack may be relatively slight and thus difficult to detect. It is important that such damage be detected, however, so that the overall condition of the heart can be evaluated properly. Electrocardiograms are very useful for this purpose because they reveal abnormalities in the timing of heart contractions, abnormalities that are associated with the presence of damaged heart tissue. Damage to the AV node, for example, may delay as well as reduce the second, ventricular pulse. Unusual conduction routes may lead to continuous disorganized contractions called *fibrillations.* In many fatal heart attacks, ventricular fibrillation is the immediate cause of death.

Many factors contribute to heart disease and heart attacks. One factor is heredity. You may inherit the predisposition to heart disease from your parents. Other factors involve eating too much saturated fat and cholesterol, not exercising, and being overweight. Cigarette smoking greatly increases a person's risk for heart attacks and strokes, although the physiological mechanisms involved are not totally understood at this time.

Strokes are caused by an interference with the blood supply to the brain and often occur when a blood vessel bursts in the brain. A stroke may also be caused by a blood clot, or *thrombus,* that forms in these vessels or by a blood clot that has traveled to the brain from another location. This type of clot is called an **embolus.** Blood clots may be caused by cancer or other diseases. The effects of strokes depend on the severity of the damage and the specific location of the stroke.

Arteriosclerosis is a thickening and hardening of the walls of the arteries. Blood flow through such arteries is restricted, and they lack the ability to dilate and so have difficulty accommodating the volume of blood pumped out by the heart. The narrowing of these vessels forces the heart to work harder. *Atherosclerosis* is a form of arteriosclerosis in which masses of cholesterol and other lipids build up within the walls of large and medium-sized arteries (Figure 9-19). These masses are referred to as **plaque.** The accumulation of plaque impairs the arteries' proper functioning. When this condition is severe, the arteries can no longer dilate and constrict properly and the blood moves through them with difficulty. The accumulation of cholesterol is thought to be the prime contributor to atherosclerosis, and diets low in cholesterol are now prescribed to help prevent this condition. Atherosclerosis contributes to both heart attacks and strokes.

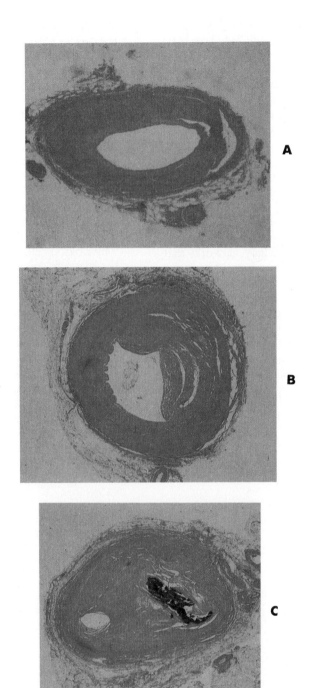

Figure 9-19 The path to a heart attack.
A The coronary artery shows only minor blockage.
B The artery exhibits severe atherosclerosis—much of the passage is blocked by buildup of cholesterol and other lipids on the interior walls of the artery.
C The coronary artery is almost completely blocked.

Summary

1. The *circulatory system* is made up of three components: the heart, the blood vessels, and the blood. Together, the heart and blood vessels—the "plumbing" of the circulatory system—are known as the *cardiovascular system*. These terms are often used interchangeably.

2. The circulatory system transports nutrients, wastes, respiratory gases, and hormones and plays an important role in temperature maintenance of the body.

3. The heart is a double pump, pushing both pulmonary (lung) circulation and systemic (general body) circulation. Because the two circulations are kept separate within the heart, the systemic circulation receives only fully oxygenated blood.

4. The general flow of blood circulation through the body is a circuit starting from the heart, which pumps blood out via muscled arteries to the capillary networks that interlace the tissues of the body; the blood returns to the heart from these capillaries via the veins.

5. The contraction of the heart is initiated at the SA node, or pacemaker, as a periodic spontaneous impulse. The impulse spreads across the surface of the two atrial chambers, causing all of these cells to contract.

6. The passage of the impulse to the ventricles is briefly delayed by tissue that insulates the two segments of the heart from one another. Only a narrow channel of specialized conducting cells is able to carry the impulse from the atria to the ventricles. The delay in the passage of the impulse permits the atria to empty completely into the ventricles before ventricular contraction occurs.

7. The heartbeat can be heard, or monitored, by tracking changes in blood pressure through the period of filling and contracting of the atria (the diastolic period) and the contraction of the left ventricle (the systolic period). The impulses can also be measured directly as an electrical current that passes in a wave throughout the body. A recording of this electrical wave is called an *electrocardiogram*.

8. The liquid portion, or plasma, of the circulating blood contains the proteins and ions that are necessary to maintain the blood's osmotic equilibrium with the surrounding tissues.

9. The formed elements of the blood are the red blood cells (erythrocytes), white blood cells (leukocytes), and platelets. The red blood cells transport oxygen, the white blood cells defend the body against disease, and the platelets are essential to the process of blood clotting.

10. The lymphatic system gathers fluid from the body that has been lost from the circulatory system by diffusion and returns it via a system of lymphatic capillaries, lymphatic vessels, and two large lymphatic ducts to veins in the lower part of the neck.

11. Cardiovascular diseases, diseases of the heart and blood vessels, are the leading cause of death in the United States. Heart attacks, strokes, and atherosclerosis are all serious cardiovascular diseases.

1. What are the principal functions of the circulatory system?

2. You've just finished a great lunch. Discuss what happens to the molecules of the food after they pass into your bloodstream.

3. It's a hot summer day, and as you ride your bike you start feeling very warm. Explain how your circulatory system helps to keep you from overheating.

4. Distinguish between the circulatory system and the cardiovascular system. What are the component(s) of each?

5. What significant change occurs in the blood from the time it exits the capillaries until it enters the venules?

6. Mystery novels sometimes describe people who "turn pale with fear." Describe the circulatory reason for this.

7. How can the body regulate blood flow within the capillary beds? Why is this important?

8. Compare the structure of arteries, capillaries, and veins. Relate any differences to their respective functions.

9. The text states that the heart is actually two pumps in one; explain this duality. Can you make a hypothesis as to why these two sides do not make contact?

10. The explanation of heart function indicates the tremendous muscular strength of this organ. Do you recall the type of muscle found in the heart? Do you think that this muscle can be strengthened voluntarily?

11. Why are valves necessary in heart function?

12. What are the SA node and the AV node? Explain their significance.

13. What is a normal blood pressure for you? Have you ever experienced high blood pressure? How was it treated?

14. Explain how a high-fat diet could place you at risk for cardiovascular disease.

1. Why does atherosclerosis raise blood pressure? Won't a narrowing of an artery's diameter simply cause the blood to move faster through it, like closing down the nozzle on a garden hose?

2. In small groups, discuss the following issues after having written for yourself a few notes on your family history of heart disease, personal exercise and eating habits, and stress level at this point in your life:
   a. Do you think that your family history and life-style predispose you toward cardiovascular disease?
   b. Why do you think that despite medical evidence so many people are unable to alter their life-style to a more heart-healthy one?

Fackelman, K. (1991, October). The African gene? *Science News,* pp. 254-255.
Scientists are searching through family histories to trace the genetic origin of the dangerously higher rates of hypertension (high blood pressure) in African-Americans.

Goldstein, G., & Belz, A.L. (1986, September). The blood-brain barrier. *Scientific American,* pp. 74-83.
Many chemicals will not pass from the bloodstream to the cells of the brain. This article explains that this "barrier" is the result of the structure of brain capillaries, which possess an unusual array of membrane channels.

Robinson, T., Factor, S., & Sonneblink, E. (1986, June). The heart as a suction pump. *Scientific American,* pp. 84-91.
Between birth and death your heart beats millions of times. These authors argue that the heart is aided greatly in this Herculean task by a very clever trick: contraction compresses elastic elements within the heart muscles, which then bounce back to expand the ventricles.

10 Excretion

The story of excretion is primarily a story about water and salt. And that story is the reason this sea turtle is crying. Animals (like you and the sea turtle) live not only on land but in salt water, in fresh water, in marshes . . . in many environments. In any environment, an animal needs water to live. Water bathes its cells and helps move substances within its body. Water is the medium in which substances are dissolved and in which chemical reactions take place. The amount of water in the body is crucial to survival—having too much water can cause as many problems as having too little.

In animal bodies, water is separated within compartments. Cells themselves are compartments, as are such structures as the interiors of the blood vessels and the heart. Water moves among body compartments by osmosis, moving from areas of a high concentration of water to areas of a lower concentration of water. The concentration of salts affects the concentration of water in the various body compartments and therefore water's movement. To regulate the water in the various body compartments, animals must regulate the amount of salt as well—a balancing act of sorts.

Animals have evolved various mechanisms that deal with their water and salt problem. The production of salt water "tears" is only one mechanism. Because the turtle lives in a salty environment, water tends to leave its less salty body. To compensate, the turtle drinks a lot of seawater but then needs to get rid of the salt and keep the water. Interestingly, the sea turtle has evolved excretory organs located in the corners of its eyes that eliminate salt. So shedding salty tears is really one way of accomplishing its balancing act. Animals that live on land, such as humans, do not have the problem of water moving into or out of their bodies through the skin in response to the concentration of water in their environments. Therefore land animals can regulate the balance of water and salt in their bodies without shedding a sea of salty tears.

What substances does the body excrete?

Although the story of **excretion** is, to a large extent, a story about water and salt balance, this process also regulates the concentrations of other ions and molecules and removes metabolic wastes from the body. The metabolic wastes of excretion, however, are not the wastes of the digestive process removed during **elimination.** Unabsorbed digestive wastes are not involved in cellular metabolism—the chemical reactions of the body. Technically, they never pass *into* the body's cells or blood but remain outside as they pass down the pipeline of the digestive tract. Metabolic wastes, on the other hand, are substances produced within the body by various chemical processes such as cellular respiration.

The only true excretory products that are removed from the body during elimination are bile pigments and the salts of certain minerals. **Bile pigments** are produced by the liver from the breakdown of old, worn-out red blood cells. These pigment molecules are combined with other substances to form bile, which is carried by a duct from the liver, to the gallbladder (bile's storage pouch), and then to the small intestine. You may recall from Chapter 7 that bile plays a role in the emulsification of fat globules during the digestion of food. The bile pigments leave the body mixed with the digestive wastes and are the cause of the characteristic color of the feces. Because of its role in the excretion of the bile pigments, the liver is considered an organ of excretion. The large intestine is also considered an organ of excretion because cells lining its walls excrete the salts of some minerals such as calcium and iron (Figure 10-1).

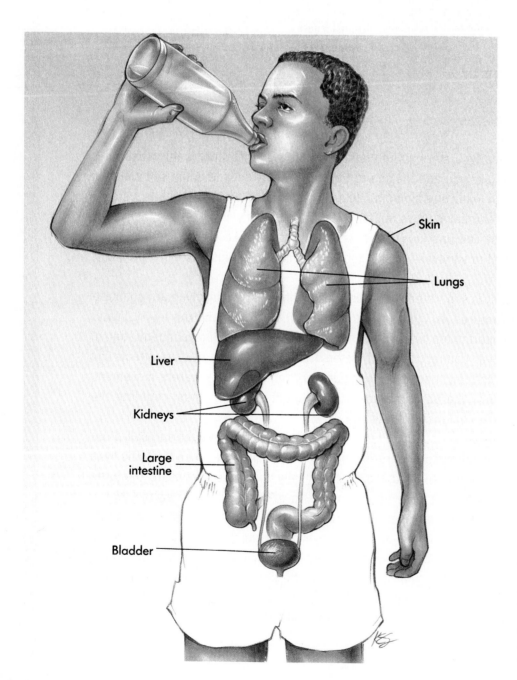

Skin

Lungs

Liver

Kidneys

Large intestine

Bladder

FIGURE 10-1 Organs that carry out excretion.
In addition to the kidneys, the skin, lungs, liver, and large intestine all play a role in the excretion of metabolic waste from the body.

Bile pigments excreted by the liver and the minerals excreted by the large intestine make up only a tiny fraction of the excretory products of the human body. The major products of excretion are water, salts (primarily NaCl—table salt), carbon dioxide, and nitrogen-containing molecules. Carbon dioxide (CO_2) is a gas produced during cellular respiration and is excreted primarily by the lungs (see Chapter 8). The lungs also excrete water in the form of water vapor—which is the reason you can see your breath on a cold day as the water vapor condenses to droplets. A small amount of salt and often a large amount of water also leave the body by means of glands in the skin (see Chapter 15).

Nitrogen-containing molecules, or **nitrogenous wastes,** are produced from the breakdown of proteins and nucleic acids. As discussed in Chapter 7, humans need to take in protein as a source of amino acids. These amino acids are used to construct body-building proteins. The liver breaks down any extra amino acids you may eat—those not needed for building new body parts or repairing old ones. In the liver, enzymes break down these amino acids by removing their amino groups (NH_2), a process called **deamination.** The molecules that result can then be used to supply the body with energy. The amino group is a leftover that cannot be used.

▼▼
The primary metabolic waste products of the human body are carbon dioxide, water, salts, and nitrogen-containing molecules.

In the liver, amino groups ($-NH_2$) are chemically converted to ammonia (NH_3). Ammonia is quite toxic, or poisonous, to all cells, and the body must get rid of it quickly, not allowing its concentration to increase. A bit of chemical reshuffling takes care of this problem, as the ammonia combines with carbon dioxide to form **urea,** the primary excretion product from the deamination of amino acids. In fact, approximately 90% of all nitrogenous wastes are eliminated from the human body in the form of urea. Two other nitrogenous wastes found in small amounts in the urine are uric acid and creatinine. **Uric acid** is formed from the breakdown of nucleic acids (DNA and RNA) found in the cells of the food you eat and from the metabolic turnover of your nucleic acids and ATP. **Creatinine** is derived primarily from a nitrogen-containing molecule called *creatine* found in muscle cells.

▼▼
In humans, most nitrogenous (nitrogen-containing) waste products are excreted as urea.

The organs of excretion

The skin, liver, and large intestine play a minor role in the excretion of metabolic wastes from the body. The primary organs of excretion are the lungs (see Chapter 8) and the **kidneys** (see Figure 10-1). As mentioned previously, the lungs excrete carbon dioxide and water vapor. The kidneys excrete the ions of salts, such as Na^+ (sodium), K^+ (potassium), Cl^- (chloride), Mg^{2+} (magnesium), and Ca^{2+} (calcium). In addition, they excrete the nitrogenous wastes urea, creatinine, and uric acid along with small amounts of other substances that may vary depending on diet and general health. These substances, together with water, form the excretion product called **urine.**

The kidneys produce urine by first filtering out most of the molecules dissolved in the blood, then selectively reabsorbing useful components, and finally secreting a few other waste products into this remaining filtrate, which becomes urine. As the kidneys process the blood in this way, they regulate its chemical composition and water content and, in turn, the chemical and fluid environment of the body. For example, although almost no amino acids are removed from the blood by the kidneys, almost half its urea is removed and then excreted. In addition, the kidneys maintain the concentrations of all ions within narrow boundaries. This strict maintenance of specific levels of ion concentrations keeps the blood's pH at a constant value, maintains the proper ion balances for nerve conduction and muscle contraction, and affects the amount of water reabsorbed into the bloodstream from the filtrate.

▼▼
The primary organs of excretion are the lungs and the kidneys. The kidney is a regulatory as well as an excretory organ.

An overview of how the kidney works

Your body has two kidneys, each about the size of a small fist, located in the lower back region and partially protected by the lower ribs (see Figure 10-1). Each is a living filtration plant that balances the concentrations of water and salts (ions) in the blood and, at the same time, excretes wastes. Put simply, kidneys work in the following way: As blood flows through the millions of microscopic filtering systems, or **nephrons,** within each kidney, the fluid portion of the blood is forced through capillary membranes into the nephron tubules. The formed elements of the blood (red blood cells, white blood cells, and platelets), along with most proteins, stay within the blood. Much of the fluid portion of the blood, including ions and molecules other than large proteins, passes through the membrane. The fluid that passes through the membrane is called the **filtrate.** Most of the water as well as selected ions and molecules is then reabsorbed from the filtrate back into the blood as the filtrate passes through the rest of the nephron.

▼▼
The human kidney maintains the proper balance of water in the body, retains substances the body needs, and eliminates metabolic wastes by first filtering most substances out of the blood and then reabsorbing what is needed.

The fluid that passes through the membrane filters of each nephron contains many molecules that are of value to

FIGURE 10-2 **Freshwater fishes produce large quantities of dilute urine.**
Because these fish live in fresh water, they take on water by osmosis. To maintain a proper water balance, they drink very little and do not reabsorb water in the nephron.

the body, such as glucose, amino acids, and various salts and ions. Humans (and all vertebrates) have evolved a means of selectively reabsorbing these valuable molecules without absorbing the waste molecules that are also dissolved in the filtered waste fluid, or urine. Such selective reabsorption gives the vertebrates great flexibility, since the membranes of different groups of animals have evolved specific transport channels that reabsorb a variety of different molecules. This flexibility is a key factor underlying the ability of different vertebrates to function in many diverse environments. They can reabsorb small molecules that are especially valuable in their particular habitat and not absorb wastes. In all vertebrates the kidney carries out the processes of filtration, reabsorption, and excretion. It can function with modifications in fresh water, in the sea, and on land (Figures 10-2 and 10-3).

FIGURE 10-3 **Kangaroo rats produce small quantities of concentrated urine.**
In contrast to freshwater fishes, the kangaroo rat can concentrate urine to a high degree by reabsorbing water. As a result, it avoids losing any more moisture than necessary. Because kangaroo rats live in dry or desert habitats, this feature is extremely important to them.

A closer look at how the kidney works

The anatomy of the kidney

The kidneys look like two gigantic reddish brown kidney beans. Substances enter and leave the kidneys through blood vessels that pierce the kidney near the center of its concave border. If you were to slice a kidney vertically, dividing it into front (ventral) and back (dorsal) portions, you would see an open area called the **renal pelvis** near the concave border. The urine produced by the nephrons within the kidneys is carried by **collecting ducts** that empty into this space. From here, urine exits the kidney via a tube called a **ureter.**

The kidney itself is made up of outer, reddish tissue called the **cortex** and inner reddish brown tissue called the **medulla.** Lined up within the medulla are triangles of tissue called the **renal pyramids** (Figure 10-4). (The word *renal* means "kidney.") The cortex and pyramids are made up of approximately one million nephrons, their collecting ducts, and the blood vessels that surround them.

Figure 10-5 shows the plan of the major blood vessels within a kidney. Blood enters each kidney via the right and left **renal arteries.** Branches split off these major arteries, travel up the sides of the pyramids, and meet at the interface of the cortex and medulla. Smaller branches extend into the cortex, giving rise to the arterioles that enter each individual nephron. The total volume of blood in your body passes through this network of blood vessels every 5 minutes!

The kidney is made up of two main types of tissue: an outer cortex and an inner medulla. These tissues are composed of microscopic filtering units called nephrons, *their collecting ducts, and blood vessels.*

The workhorse of the kidney: The nephron

Each nephron (Figure 10-6) is a tubule that is structured in a special way to accomplish three tasks:
1. **Filtration:** During filtration the blood is passed through membranes that separate blood cells and proteins from much of the water and molecules dissolved in the blood. Together the water and dissolved substances are referred to as the **filtrate.**
2. **Selective reabsorption:** During reabsorption, desirable ions and metabolites and most of the water from blood plasma are recaptured from the filtrate, leaving nitrogenous wastes, excess water, and excess salts behind for later elimination. The filtrate is now called *urine.*
3. **Tubular secretion:** During secretion the kidney *adds* materials such as potassium and hydrogen ions, ammonia, and potentially harmful drugs to the filtrate from the blood. These secretions rid the body of certain materials and control the blood pH.

Filtration
At the front end of each nephron tube is a filtration apparatus called **Bowman's capsule.** The capsule is shaped

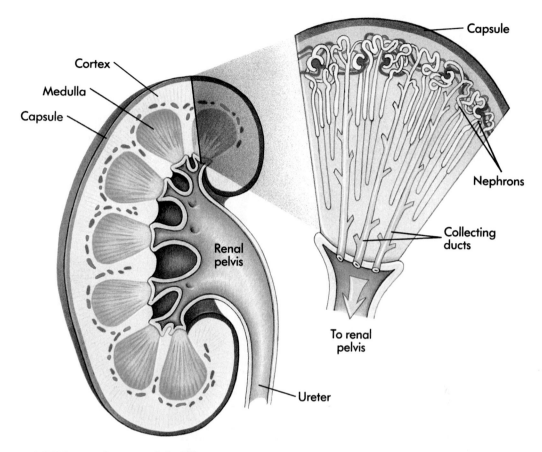

FIGURE 10-4 Structure of the kidney.
The enlarged portion of the diaphragm shows a detailed section of a renal pyramid and the cortex above. The renal pyramids are composed of nephrons, their collecting ducts, and surrounding blood vessels.

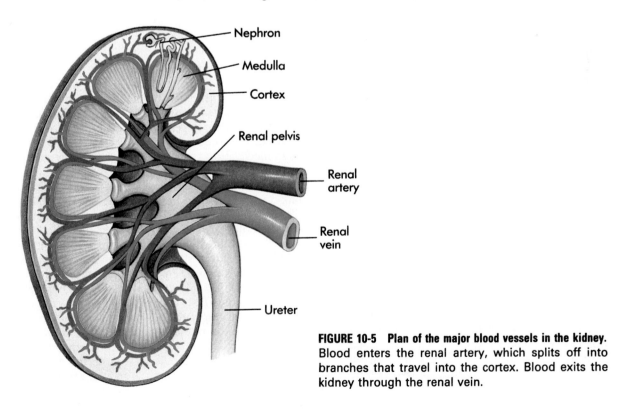

FIGURE 10-5 Plan of the major blood vessels in the kidney.
Blood enters the renal artery, which splits off into branches that travel into the cortex. Blood exits the kidney through the renal vein.

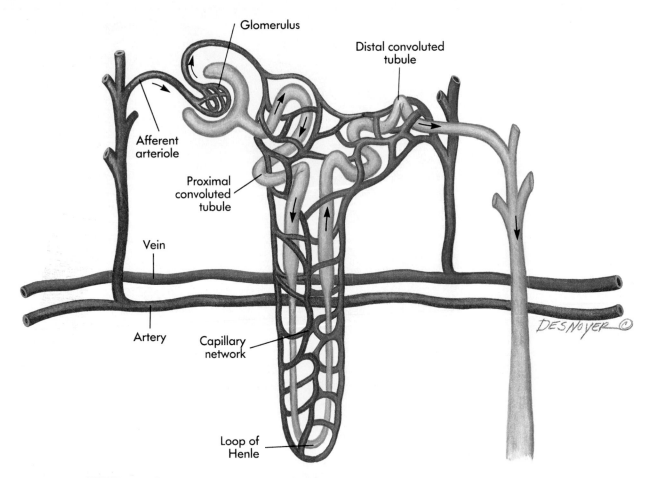

FIGURE 10-6 Structure of a nephron. Part of the nephron is located in the cortex, and part is located in the medulla. Nephrons filter the blood, reabsorb substances to the blood from the blood filtrate, and secrete certain ions and potentially harmful substances into the filtrate. These processes take place along specific portions of the nephron tubule.

much like a caved-in tennis ball and surrounds a tuft of capillaries called the **glomerulus.** The glomerular capillaries branch off an entering arteriole termed the **afferent arteriole** (named after the Latin verb *affero,* which means "going toward"). The walls of the glomerular capillaries, along with specialized cells of the capsule, act as filtration devices. The pressure of the incoming blood forces the fluid within the blood through the capillary walls and through spaces between capsular cells that surround the capillaries. Capillary walls are made up of a single layer of cells having differentially permeable membranes. These walls do not allow large molecules such as proteins and the formed elements of the blood to pass through. Water and smaller molecules such as glucose, ions, and nitrogenous wastes pass through easily.

This filtrate passes into the tubule of the nephron at Bowman's capsule. From there, it passes into a coiled portion of the nephron called the **proximal convoluted tubule.** This name describes the coiled (convoluted) tubule as that portion closest to (proximal to) Bowman's capsule. Both these structures lie in the cortex of the kidney. As the filtrate passes through the proximal tubule, reabsorption begins.

Selective reabsorption

Reabsorption is carried out by the epithelial cells throughout the length of the tubule. During this extremely discriminating process, specific amounts of certain substances are reabsorbed depending on the body's needs at the time. Substances are reabsorbed by both active and passive transport mechanisms (see Chapter 3). In the proximal convoluted tubule, glucose and small proteins are put back into the blood. These substances move out of the tubule and into the blood within surrounding capillaries (Figure 10-7).

The filtrate moves from the proximal convoluted tubule to the descending arm of the loop of Henle. The loop of Henle is the part of the tubule that dips into the medulla of the kidney. The part that dips down from the cortex (where Bowman's capsule and the proximal convoluted tubule are) into the medulla is called the **descending arm of the loop of Henle.** The tubule then extends in the opposite direction, back up into the cortex. This portion of the nephron is called the **ascending arm of the loop of Henle.** The walls of the descending arm are impermeable to salt and urea. Put simply, the cells making up the walls of the descending arm do not permit salt and urea to pass out of the tubule. However, the walls of the descending arm are

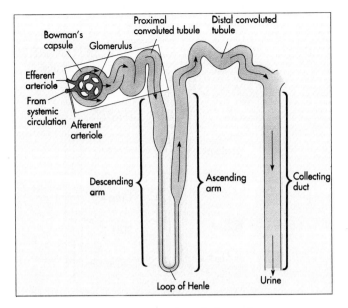

FIGURE 10-7   Path of the filtrate through the nephron.
In this figure and the five that follow here and on page 192, the filtrate will be traced through the nephron. In the first stage of filtration, the filtrate passes into the nephron at Bowman's capsule. The filtrate then enters the proximal convoluted tubule, where glucose and small proteins are reabsorbed by the blood.

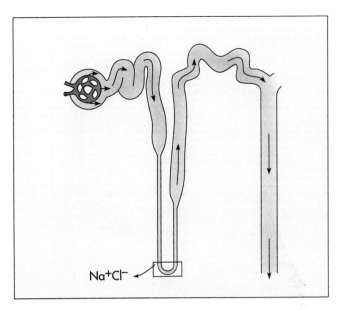

FIGURE 10-9   The turn of the loop of Henle.
At the turn of the loop of Henle, the walls of the tubule become more permeable to salt (Na^+ and Cl^- ions) but less permeable to water. As the concentrated filtrate moves through the turn of the loop, salt diffuses out of the tubule into the surrounding tissues. The area surrounding the bottom of the loop, then, acquires a high concentration of salt.

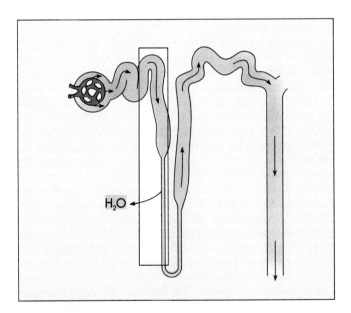

FIGURE 10-8   The descending loop of Henle.
In the descending loop of Henle, water moves out of the tubule into the surrounding tissue, leaving a more concentrated filtrate.

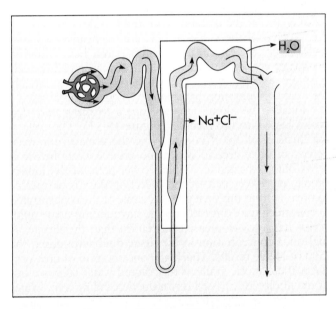

FIGURE 10-10   The ascending loop of Henle.
In the ascending loop, channels in the cell membranes of the tubule cells actively pump salt (Na^+ and Cl^-) out of the kidney tubule. At the distal convoluted tubule, water diffuses out of the filtrate. The filtrate now contains only some water and urea.

freely permeable to water. Water moves out of the tubule by osmosis, passing into the surrounding tissue fluid and then into the blood within surrounding capillaries. As water passes out of the descending arm, it leaves behind a more concentrated filtrate (Figure 10-8).

At the turn of the loop, the walls of the tubule become permeable to salt but much less permeable to water (Figure 10-9). Therefore as the filtrate (which became quite con-

centrated as it moved down the descending arm) passes up the ascending arm, salt passes out into the surrounding tissue fluid by diffusion. This movement of salt produces a high concentration of salt in the tissue fluid surrounding the bottom of the loop.

Higher in the ascending arm, the walls of the tubule contain active transport channels that pump even more salt out of the filtrate within the kidney tubule (Figure 10-10).

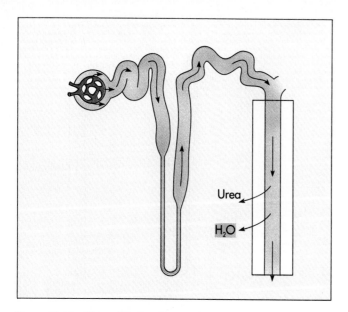

Figure 10-11   The collecting duct.
In the collecting duct, urea and water pass out of the filtrate. The filtrate, or urine, moves out of the collecting duct to the renal pelvis, in which urine collects before it flows from the kidney.

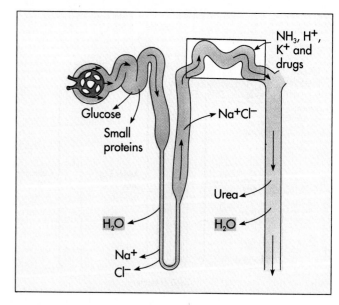

Figure 10-12   The distal convoluted tubule.
Another important function of the kidney is tubular secretion. The distal convoluted tubule secretes substances such as ammonia, drugs, and ions into the filtrate. This illustration also summarizes the process of selective reabsorption.

This active removal of salt from the ascending arm causes water to diffuse outward from the filtrate just above the ascending arm at the **distal convoluted tubule.** The walls of this portion of the kidney tubule are permeable to water, which is not the case in the ascending arm. Left behind in the filtrate are some water and the urea that initially passed through the glomerulus as nitrogenous waste; eventually the urea concentration becomes very high in the tubule.

Finally, the filtrate empties into a *collecting duct* that passes back into the medulla (Figure 10-11). The collecting ducts of all the nephrons bring the urine to the renal pelvis, an open area in which the urine collects before it flows out of the kidney. Unlike other parts of the kidney tubule, the lower part of the collecting duct is permeable to urea. During this final passage, some of the concentrated urea in the filtrate diffuses into the surrounding tissue fluid, which has a lower urea concentration than the filtrate. A high urea concentration in the tissue fluid surounding the loop of Henle results. This high concentration of urea produces the osmotic gradient that caused water to move out of the filtrate as it passed down the descending arm. Water also passes out of the filtrate as it moves down the collecting duct. This movement occurs as a result of the osmotic gradient created by both the movement of urea out of the collecting duct and the movement of salt out of the ascending arm. The water is then collected by blood vessels in the kidney, which carry it into the systemic circulation.

In summary, the human kidney achieves a high degree of water reabsorption by using the salts and urea in the glomerular filtrate to increase the osmotic concentration of the tissue fluid surrounding the nephron. This high concentration of salts and urea creates an osmotic gradient that pulls water from the filtrate out into the surrounding tissue fluid. It is collected there by blood vessels impermeable to the high urea concentration but permeable to water.

Tubular secretion

A major function of the kidney is the elimination of a variety of potentially harmful substances that you may eat, drink, or inhale or that may be produced during metabolism. The human kidney has evolved the ability to detoxify the blood through the process of tubular secretion. During this process the cells making up the walls of the distal convoluted tubule take substances from the blood within surrounding capillaries and from within the surrounding tissue fluid and put them into the filtrate (urine) within the kidney tubule (Figure 10-12). Ammonia (NH_3) from the deamination of amino acids that have not been converted to urea is removed from the blood by tubular secretion. Certain prescription drugs such as penicillin are also removed by this process. In addition, the body rids itself of harmful drugs such as marijuana, cocaine, heroin, and morphine by tubular secretion. These drugs are processed by the liver and their breakdown products are secreted into the filtrate within the kidney tubules. Specific tests for the breakdown products of these drugs can be performed on urine samples to determine whether a person has particular drugs in the body. Testing the urine in this way, or **drug testing,** has become a controversial topic among groups of people such as athletes and employees involved in certain types of work, for example, airline pilots.

Tubular secretion can also be thought of as a fine-tuning mechanism. By removing specific amounts of hydrogen ions (H^+) from the blood and secreting them into the filtrate, the kidney can keep the pH of the blood at a constant level (7.35 to 7.45). (See Chapter 2 for an explanation of pH.) Likewise, the potassium ion (K^+) concentration of the blood is fine tuned by tubular secretion. The proper concentration of potassium ions is important to the

In the late 1960s, the National Institute on Drug Abuse in Washington, DC, began to develop ways of monitoring heroin use among people at treatment centers to learn which therapies worked and which did not. They settled on analysis of urine, finding that telltale traces of heroin use cound be detected in urine for days after drug use. Recall that substances such as drugs are removed from the blood during tubular secretion. These substances become part of the filtrate that eventually leaves the body as urine.

After 20 years, urine testing has become quite a sophisticated industry. In the last few years in particular, there has been a revolution in the industry because of the improved quality of test procedures.

The major improvements have come with the introduction of tests that use recombinant DNA techniques to amplify trace chemicals in urine. The Enzyme-Multiplied Immunoassay Technique (EMIT) has become the standard approach for screening large numbers of urine samples. EMIT can be used in a robot tester that employs a light sensor to read urine samples and prints out a value for each of five or six drugs present—it can churn out 18,000 results an hour. Traces of marijuana, cocaine, opiates, and amphetamines can be detected for days and even weeks after use using EMIT. The test is more than 98% accurate, with error biased toward nondetection.

Because EMIT responds to a broad range of opiate and amphetamine compounds, it sometimes kicks out a "positive" for harmless prescription

FIGURE 10-A This laboratory technician is preparing a urine sample for drug testing.

drugs like ibuprofen and foods like poppy seeds. For this reason, samples that come up positive on EMIT are then retested by more cumbersome but 100% accurate procedures (gas chromatography-mass spectrometry). For example, eating poppy seeds may trigger a positive signal on EMIT, but the confirmation test tells that a key heroin breakdown product (6-0-acetylmorphine) is not present.

Enlistees in the armed services are routinely tested for evidence of drug use. The biggest use of urine testing, however, is in courts and prisons. There is strong evidence that heavy drug use is linked with criminal activity. In drug monitoring surveys carried out by the Department of Justice in ten major cities in 1988, for exam-

ple, half of all arrestees, and in most cities three-quarters of them, tested positive for drugs.

Drug use by the drivers of public transportation (bus, train, subway, and airplane) has sometimes resulted in tragic accidents or near-accidents, and there has been considerable public pressure for mandatory urine testing of such key employees. Congress has not yet decided how broadly to impose this surveillance or whether the loss in privacy would be worth the gain in public safety. Thousands of private companies already test new job applicants—in 1990, over 40% of 1000 companies surveyed were using some sort of drug screening. In today's world, testing urine for evidence of drug use is becoming part of everyday life (Figure 10-A).

A summary of urine formation

The roughly two million nephrons that form the bulk of the two human kidneys receive a flow of approximately 2000 liters of blood per day—enough to fill about 20 bathtubs! The nephron first filters the blood—removing most of its water and all but its largest molecules and its cells. The nephron then selectively reabsorbs substances back into the blood. This process is driven by two factors: (1) the development of a high osmostic gradient surrounding the loop of Henle and (2) the varying permeability of the membranes of the cells lining the kidney tubule.

Because of the varying permeability of kidney tubule cells, substances move from the filtrate back into the blood by diffusion and active transport mechanisms at specific places along the length of the tubule. Each substance will only be reabsorbed to a particular threshold level, however, with the rest remaining in the filtrate. For example, glucose is reabsorbed at the proximal convoluted tubule to a threshold level of 150 milligrams per 100 milliliters of blood. Any glucose above this threshold will be excreted in the urine. The amount of glucose in the blood of a healthy person does not normally exceed this limit. However, persons with diabetes mellitus (sugar diabetes) excrete glucose because they fail to produce a hormone called *insulin* that promotes glucose uptake by the cells. Urea, on the other hand, has a very low threshold that is reached quickly. Therefore most urea stays in the filtrate (except the urea that diffuses from the collecting duct, adding to the osmotic gradient surrounding the loop of Henle).

The high osmotic gradient surrounding the loop of Henle causes most of the water filtered from the blood to be reabsorbed, or conserved, in the descending arm of the loop. Water conservation is, in fact, the job of this loop. Vertebrates that do not need to conserve water have no loop. For example, a freshwater fish drinks little water and produces large amounts of urine. Because the body fluid of a freshwater fish is hyperosmotic (contains more dissolved substances and therefore has a lower concentration of water) to the water in which it lives, water is not reabsorbed in its nephrons. The excess water that enters its body passes instead through the relatively straight nephron tubes to be excreted as urine (Figure 10-13). In general, the longer the loop of Henle, the more water can be reabsorbed. Animals such as desert rodents that have highly concentrated urine have exceptionally long loops of Henle.

The nephron also controls blood pH, fine tunes the concentrations of certain ions and molecules, and removes potentially harmful drugs from the blood by the process of tubular secretion. In these ways the kidney contributes to the chemical and water balance of the body, thus functioning as a major organ of internal equilibrium, or homeostasis. The resulting fluid is urine, a waste that is excreted from the body.

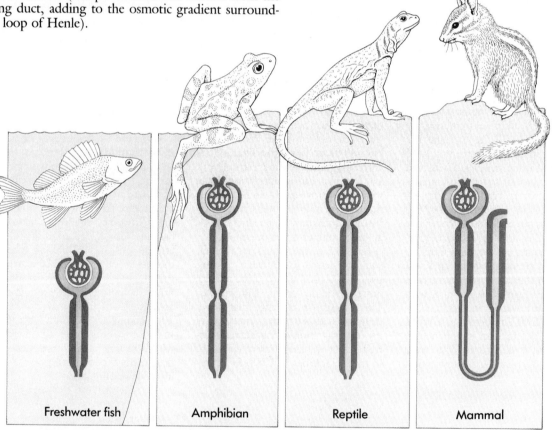

| Freshwater fish | Amphibian | Reptile | Mammal |

Figure 10-13 The function of the loop of Henle is the conservation of water.
Animals that do not need to conserve water such as fresh water fishes do not have loops of Henle. Only birds and mammals have a loop in the nephron tubule that allows the reabsorption of water.

The urinary system

The kidneys are only one part of the **urinary system**—a set of interconnected organs (Figure 10-14) that not only remove wastes, excess water, and excess ions from the blood but store this fluid, or urine, until it can be expelled from the body. The urine exits each nephron by means of the collecting duct. From there, it flows into the renal pelvis (see Figure 10-4). This area narrows into a tube called the ureter that leaves the kidney on its concave border, near where the renal artery and vein enter and exit. By means of muscular contractions **(peristalsis),** these muscular tubes—one from each kidney—bring the urine to a storage bag called the **urinary bladder.**

The urinary bladder is a hollow muscular organ that, when empty, looks much like a deflated balloon. As the bladder fills with urine, it assumes a pear shape. On the average, the bladder can hold 700 to 800 milliliters of urine, or almost a quart. However, when less than half this amount is in the bladder, special nerve endings in the walls of the bladder, called *stretch receptors,* send a message to the brain that results in the desire to urinate.

The urinary bladder empties into a tube called the **urethra.** This tube leads from the underside of the bladder to the outside. The urethra in men plays a role in the reproductive system, carrying semen to the outside of the body during ejaculation. However, the urinary and reproductive systems have no connection in women. In addition, the urethra in women is much shorter than the urethra in men. For this reason, women contract urinary infections more easily than men.

The kidney and homeostasis

The kidney is an excellent example of an organ whose principal function is homeostasis, the maintenance of constant physiological conditions within the body. It is concerned with both water balance and ion balance. To maintain homeostasis, however, the urinary system depends in part on the endocrine (hormone) system.

A **hormone** is a chemical messenger sent by a gland to other cells of the body. Hormones are produced in one part of the body and have an effect in another (see Chapter 14). The hormone that regulates the rate at which water is lost or retained by the body is **antidiuretic hormone,** or **ADH.** It is secreted by the pituitary gland at the base of the brain. Its effect on the excretion of water is easy to remember if you know that a **diuretic** is a substance that helps remove water from the body. Because ADH is an *anti*diuretic, it works to conserve, or retain, water.

ADH works by controlling the permeability of the distal convoluted tubules and collecting ducts to water (Figure 10-15, *A*). When ADH levels increase, the permeability of the collecting ducts to water increases. Water therefore moves out of the ducts by osmosis and back into the blood within surrounding capillaries. When ADH levels decrease, the permeability of the collecting ducts to water decreases. Therefore less water is reabsorbed from the urine (filtrate). Instead, it remains in the ducts and is excreted from the body. Alcohol inhibits the release of ADH, resulting in decreased reabsorption of water and therefore increased urination, which causes dehydration.

Another hormone regulates the level of sodium ions (Na^+) and potassium ions (K^+) in the blood. This hormone is called **aldosterone** (Figure 10-15, *B*). When aldosterone levels increase, the kidney tubule cells increase their reabsorption of sodium ions from the filtrate and decrease their reabsorption of potassium ions. Put simply, aldosterone promotes the retention of sodium and the excretion of potassium. In addition, because the concentration of sodium in the blood affects the reabsorption of water, the increase in sodium in the blood causes water to move by osmosis from the filtrate into the blood.

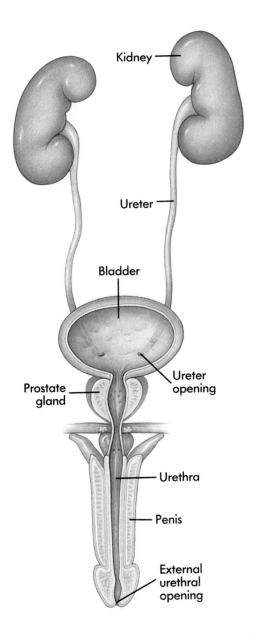

Kidney

Ureter

Bladder

Prostate gland

Ureter opening

Urethra

Penis

External urethral opening

Figure 10-14 The human urinary system
The urinary system in males and females includes the kidneys, ureters, urinary bladder, and urethra. This diagram shows the male urinary system.

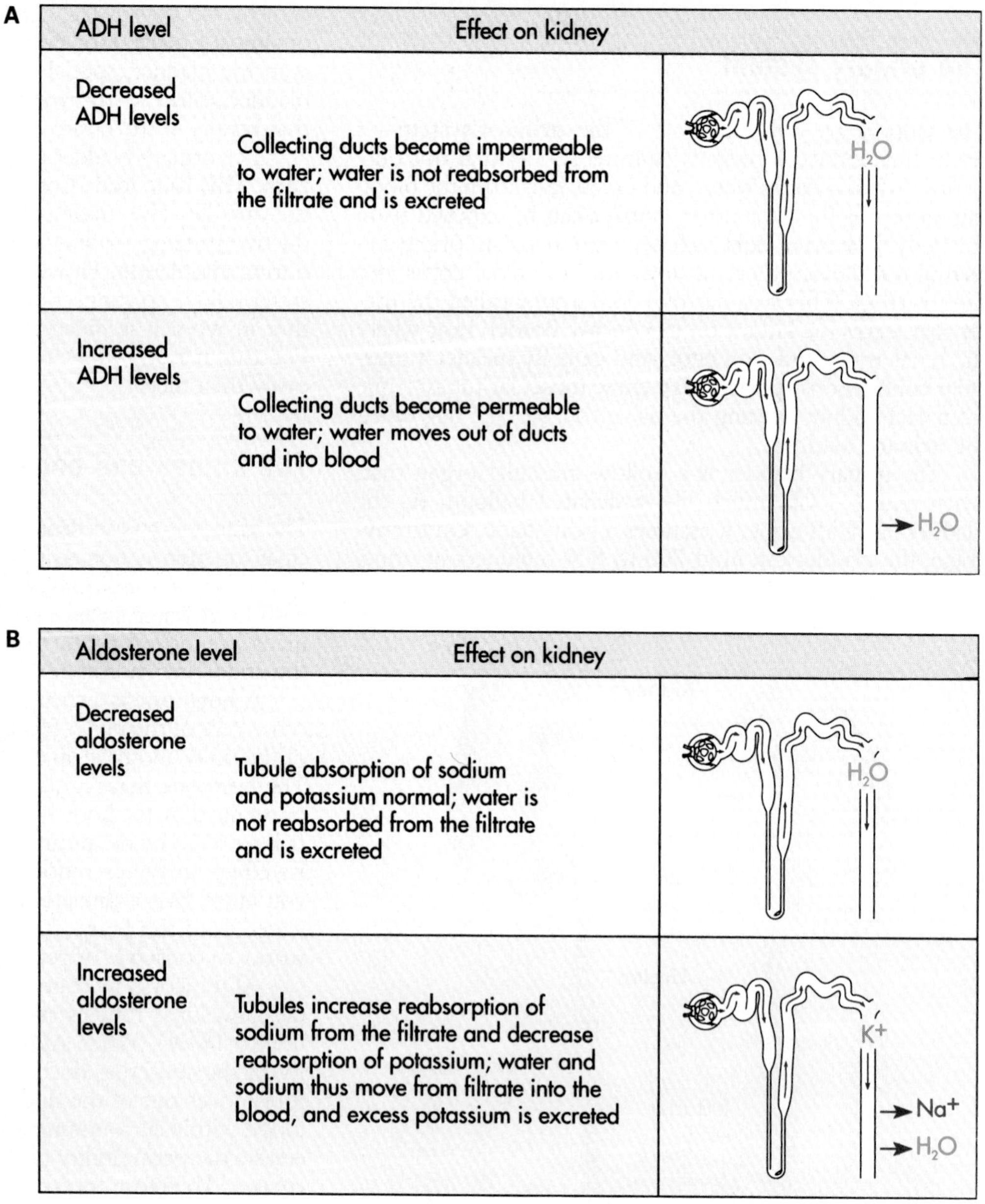

Figure 10-15 How hormones regulate kidney function.
A ADH is a hormone that helps the body conserve water by acting on the permeability of the distal convoluted tubules and collecting ducts to water. When ADH levels decrease, more water is excreted from the body. When ADH levels increase, more water is conserved. **B** Aldosterone regulates the levels of sodium and potassium in the body by acting on the permeability of the distal convoluted and collecting tubule to these ions and water. When Na^+ levels are low and K^+ levels are high, aldosterone acts on the nephron tubules to correct the imbalance. Aldosterone causes Na^+ and water to be reabsorbed in the blood and excess K^+ to be excreted.

A

ADH level	Effect on kidney	
Decreased ADH levels	Collecting ducts become impermeable to water; water is not reabsorbed from the filtrate and is excreted	H_2O
Increased ADH levels	Collecting ducts become permeable to water; water moves out of ducts and into blood	$\rightarrow H_2O$

B

Aldosterone level	Effect on kidney	
Decreased aldosterone levels	Tubule absorption of sodium and potassium normal; water is not reabsorbed from the filtrate and is excreted	H_2O
Increased aldosterone levels	Tubules increase reabsorption of sodium from the filtrate and decrease reabsorption of potassium; water and sodium thus move from filtrate into the blood, and excess potassium is excreted	K^+ $\rightarrow Na^+$ $\rightarrow H_2O$

The principal function of the kidney is homeostasis—the maintenance of a constant internal environment. Two hormones help the kidney maintain homeostasis. The hormone ADH regulates the amount of water reabsorbed at the collecting duct. The hormone aldosterone promotes the conservation of sodium, and therefore water, and promotes the excretion of potassium.

Problems with kidney function

Kidney stones

During the formation of urine, salts and other wastes to be excreted from the body are normally dissolved in the water of the filtrate and pass with it out of the kidney as urine. Sometimes, however, certain salts do not stay dissolved—most notably calcium salts or uric acid—but instead form crystals called **kidney stones.** Each year more than 300,000 Americans form these stones for reasons such as diminished water intake, diets high in protein and calcium, genetic disorders, infections, and the misuse of medications. Kidney stone attacks are excruciatingly painful; the stone moves through the kidney and then blocks the flow of urine. Small stones—those with diameters less than 5 millimeters (about 1/5 inch)—pass through the ureters, bladder, and urethra within a few days. Larger stones require certain medical procedures to remove them.

Since 1984, a treatment for kidney stones called *shock-wave lithotripsy* has been available. Before this time, surgery was the only means of relief. Surgery is still used, however, to remove stones larger than 2 centimeters in diameter or stones that are causing infection. During one form of sur-

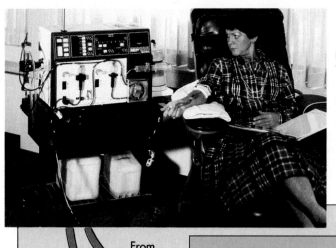

Figure 10-16 Dialysis
The dialysis procedure uses a semipermeable membrane to imitate the nephron of the kidney. Blood from the patient on dialysis is separated from the dialysate by this membrane. Wastes and excess ions diffuse across the membrane into the dialysate. Although dialysis is a life-saving measure, it is no substitute for the selective reabsorption of the human kidney.

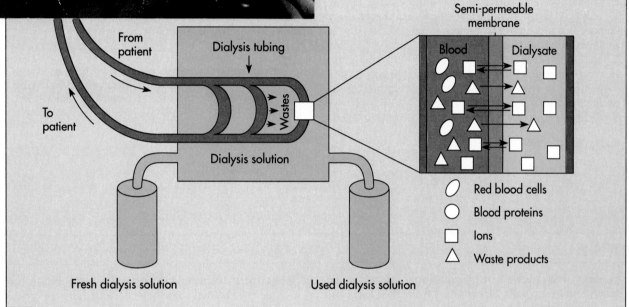

gery a tube is inserted into the renal pelvis. An ultrasonic probe within the tube first bombards the stone with sonic waves, crushing it. Tiny forceps then protrude from the tube and are used to collect the pieces of the stone. In another type of surgical procedure the kidney is cut open and forceps are used to remove the stones.

Shock-wave lithotripsy involves a procedure quite different from these two. The patient is lowered up to the neck into a tank of water. Guided by x-ray monitors, intense sound waves are directed at the stone, shattering it. Once the stone is broken apart, the pieces are excreted in the urine.

 Kidney stones are crystals of certain salts that develop in the kidney and block urine flow. They may be surgically removed or broken apart with shock-wave therapy.

Renal failure

Renal failure occurs when the filtration of the blood at the glomerulus either slows or stops. In acute renal failure, filtration stops suddenly. Acute renal failure can have many causes, such as a decreased flow of blood through the kid-

neys caused by problems with the heart or blockage of a blood vessel, damage to the kidney by disease, or the presence of a kidney stone blocking urine flow.

In chronic renal failure, the filtration of the blood at the glomerulus slows gradually. Unfortunately, this condition is usually irreversible, since it is most commonly caused by injury to the glomerulus. These injuries have many causes, such as the deposit of toxins, bacterial cell walls, or molecules produced by the immune system within the glomerulus; the coagulation of the blood within the glomerulus; or the presence of a disease such as diabetes.

Treatments for renal failure

If the kidneys become unable to excrete nitrogenous wastes, regulate the pH of the blood, and regulate the ion concentration of the blood because of renal failure, the individual will die unless the blood is filtered. This job is accomplished by a machine called an **artificial kidney.** The process of filtering blood in this way is called **dialysis.** During dialysis, small amounts of the patient's blood are pumped through tubes to one side of a selectively permeable membrane (Figure 10-16). This membrane is a derivative of cellulose, very similar to material that makes up the cell walls of plants. On the other side of the membrane is a fluid called the *dialysate*. The dialysate contains the same concentration of ions as that normally found in the bloodstream. Because small molecules can pass across the membrane, any extra ions in the patient's blood move by diffusion into the dialysate until their concentrations on both sides of the membrane are equal. In addition, the dialysate contains no wastes, so the wastes in the patient's blood also diffuse into the dialysate. Unfortunately, dialysis is a slow process, usually taking 6 to 8 hours. Recently, however, researchers have created a new synthetic membrane made of a plastic copolymer said to be 25% more efficient than cellulose membranes. Other scientists are also currently developing tailor-made artificial cells to replace or help kidney cells. The artificial cells currently being developed are designed to change the toxic urea and ammonia that build up in patients with renal failure into useful amino acids.

In the United States, approximately 7000 renal failure patients receive kidney transplants per year. During a transplant operation a patient's nonfunctioning kidney is removed and a donor kidney is implanted. Although two thirds of these transplant patients suffer serious problems of organ rejection, many of their problems are alleviated with the use of immunosuppressive drugs. Recently, treating patients with monoclonal antibody therapy has been shown to reverse rejection in a significant number of patients.

Monoclonal antibodies are special proteins produced in the laboratory that are all descendants of a single cell. These proteins are therefore all alike. In addition, they are antibodies and will attack a specific antigen (see Chapter 16). The monoclonal antibodies developed for use with kidney transplant patients target the specific immune cells involved in the rejection of the donor kidney. The use of monoclonal antibodies and new drug therapies hold much promise for kidney transplant patients.

Renal failure is a reduction in the filtration rate of blood in the glomerulus. This condition has many possible causes and may be treated by dialysis or with a kidney transplant.

Summary

1. Excretion is a process whereby metabolic wastes, excess water, and excess salts are removed from the blood and passed out of the body. Elimination is a process that takes place as digestive wastes leave the body during defecation.

2. The excretory products of the body are bile pigments, nitrogen-containing molecules (nitrogenous wastes), carbon dioxide, water, and salts. The bile pigments are excreted by the liver and passed out of the body by means of the digestive system. Most carbon dioxide is excreted by the lungs. The kidneys excrete most of the nitrogenous wastes along with excess water and salts.

3. The kidneys excrete wastes as urine. Urine is formed within microscopic tubular units of the kidney called *nephrons*. During the formation of urine, most of the water and other small molecules are first filtered out of the blood. These substances are called the *filtrate*.

4. As the filtrate flows through the nephron tubule, substances are selected for reabsorption into the blood within surrounding capillaries. Various substances are reabsorbed along sections of the tubule because the permeability of its walls varies along its length. In addition, most of the water removed from the blood is reabsorbed from the filtrate because of a high osmotic gradient that surrounds certain sections of the tubule.

5. Different groups of vertebrates can function in a wide variety of environments because of adaptations in their nephrons allowing selective reabsorption of molecules valuable to their particular habitat.

6. By means of tubular secretion, the kidney also excretes the breakdown products of a variety of potentially harmful substances from the blood, such as marijuana, cocaine, heroin, morphine, and prescription drugs. The breakdown products of these substances can be detected in the urine.

7. The kidney is made up of an outer region called the *cortex* and an inner region called the *medulla*. Certain portions of the nephron lie in the cortex, and another portion dips into and out of the medulla. Because of the high osmotic gradient created within the medulla, the reabsorption of water takes place there.

8. Urine leaves the kidneys by means of muscular tubes called *ureters*. It is conveyed to a storage pouch called the *urinary bladder*. A tube called the *urethra* brings urine to the outside. These interconnected organs make up the urinary system.

9. The principal function of the kidney is homeostasis. Two hormones help the kidneys control the balance of water and ions in the blood, thus helping maintain homeostasis.

10. Crystals of salts that sometimes form within the kidney are called *kidney stones*. If these stones do not pass out of the body on their own, they may need to be removed. Surgery and shock-wave lithotripsy are two ways in which kidney stones are removed.

11. When the filtration of the blood at the glomerulus is seriously impaired, the blood must be filtered by means of dialysis. In severe cases of renal failure, a patient may require a kidney transplant.

1. What is excretion? Explain its importance to life.

2. What are the primary metabolic waste products that you excrete?

3. What do urea, urine, and uric acid have in common? How do they differ?

4. Where do you think the carbon dioxide used in the formation of urea comes from? Where does the remainder of excess carbon dioxide go to be excreted?

5. The kidneys are integrally linked to blood pressure control in the body by their regulation of water and dissolved salts. What part of the blood contains these components?

6. How are our muscles dependent on the kidney for proper function?

7. Draw a diagram of a human kidney showing the location of the renal pelvis, collecting ducts, ureter, cortex, medulla, renal pyramids, and renal arteries.

8. Summarize how your kidneys help your body to conserve water.

9. Explain why urine can reveal the use of certain drugs.

10. Do you think people's urine should ever be tested for drug use? Do you feel it would be justified in some cases more than others? Explain your answer.

11. Briefly summarize the process by which urine is formed.

12. What is homeostasis? Explain how ADH and aldosterone are important in maintaining homeostasis.

13. Describe two problems that can occur with kidney function.

14. The text states that over two-thirds of kidney transplants are somewhat unsuccessful because of organ rejection. What system is involved in such rejection?

1. Imagine you are the sole survivor of a ship that sank in the ocean, and you have managed to crawl onto a raft containing nothing but bottles of whiskey. After several days, you are very thirsty. Without water you may die. Should you drink the whiskey, the ocean water, or neither?

2. Among the many ways in which Americans can improve their diets is to decrease their intake of salt. What is unhealthy about a high-salt diet?

Beeuwkes, R. (1982). Renal countercurrent mechanisms, or how to get something for (almost) nothing. In Taylor, C.R., et al, editors. *A companion to animal physiology*. New York: Cambridge University Press.
This is a clearly presented summary of current ideas about how the human kidney works.

Heatwole, H. (1978). Adaptations of marine snakes. *American Scientist*, 66, 594-604.
Several groups of snakes are able to live in the sea by clever adaptations that modify salt and water balance.

BIOETHICAL DECISIONMAKING
Family Wishes and Patient Autonomy

Consider the following questions as you think about the bioethical dilemma presented on page 127:

1. What are the bioethical issues in this case?
   - What has to be decided?
   - Who are the decisionmakers?
   - Outline the decisionmaking process in this case as you understand it.

2. What factual information do the decisionmakers need? Consider the effects of the answers to the following questions on the decisionmaking process.
   - In similar cases, have alternate approaches to weaning been used that have not been tried in this case?
   - Is the patient's wish to die a temporary depression in reaction to pain or sleepless nights, or a clear, considered decision?
   - Is his wish based on fears arising from misperception or misinformation about the course of his treatment?
   - What is the basis for the family's wishes? Can they distinguish their own needs from those of the patient?
   - What other questions should the decisionmakers ask?
   - What additional factual information do the decisionmakers need?

3. Who are the "stakeholders" in this decision—those who stand to gain or lose as a result of the decision?
   - Is the patient a stakeholder? His family? His physician? What other persons or groups are stakeholders?
   - Which stakeholders are decisionmakers? Which are not decisionmakers? Will individuals in the latter group be able to influence the decisionmaking process? Should they have influence?
   - In what ways would each stakeholder be affected by the decision?

4. What are the values at stake in the decision? As you list and describe them, consider the following questions:
   - Does a patient have the right to refuse medical treatment, even if such refusal will result in death?
   - What rights does a patient's family have to overrule the patient's requests in regard to treatment?
   - To whom does the physician have an obligation? Must the physician always follow the patient's wishes, or must the family's wishes be taken into consideration, even when they contradict the patient's wishes?
   - Should a patient's wishes be honored immediately, or should his motivations be evaluated?

5. What options are available to the decisionmakers? As you list these options, consider the following questions:
   - Which of these alternatives seem ethically feasible? Which seem administratively possible?
   - How would each alternative decision affect each of the stakeholders?
   - Is there a compromise solution that might give all parties the sense that they have come out the "winner" in the decision?

6. What are the values inherent to the decisionmaking process?
   - Is the decisionmaking process fair?
   - Do all stakeholders have equal resources to advocate their position?
   - What further steps might each group of stakeholders take if their views are disallowed?

PART THREE

Communication and Regulatory Systems

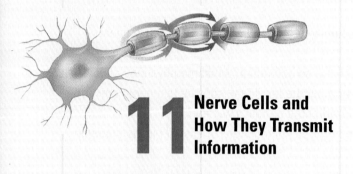

11 Nerve Cells and How They Transmit Information

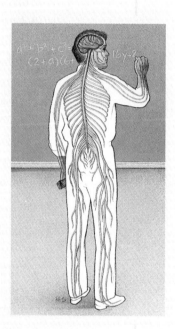

12 The Nervous System

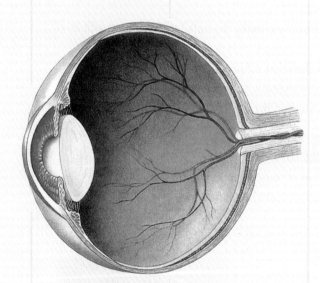

13 The Senses

14 Hormones

BIOETHICAL DECISIONMAKING
Mental Competence to Refuse Treatment

A 56-year-old farmer and his wife came to the neurology department of a veteran's hospital because he had been having memory difficulty. For the past 2 years he had also had increasing difficulty with the technical aspects of farming. Recently, he had begun talking about a deceased brother as if he were still alive.

On examination, the man gave his age as 48 and was unsure of the year. He walked with an unnatural gait, a sign of a brain abnormality, and other tests indicated that he had decreased cerebral function. (Persons with decreased cerebral function have difficulty with memory, certain thought processes, and the identification and expression of emotions because the cerebrum is the part of the brain that controls these "higher" cognitive activities.) However, the man had no difficulty with coin problems and could accurately repeat a list of numbers recited to him. Although these data were difficult to interpret, the physicians concluded that his left cerebral hemisphere, which controls mathematical ability, was probably not involved. They suggested that the problem most likely involved the right side of his cerebrum, which controls the understanding of spatial relationships and the expression of emotions.

The man refused hospitalization to determine the cause of his decreasing cerebral function. His wife tried unsuccessfully to persuade him, but when a resident suggested that she assume guardianship for her husband through court action she refused.

Six months later the man's condition had worsened. He now leased most of his farmland to neighbors and did no work. His gait had become so abnormal that people thought he was drunk. He sometimes suffered urinary incontinence but seemed not to care. Although he watched television all day, he paid no attention to the programs.

A second examination showed that he was alert, had no apparent speech difficulty, but had experienced considerable mental deterioration. This deterioration included confusion not only about his age and the year but about his location as well. Although he could recite the months of the year and give fairly long quotations from the Bible when asked, he was unable to subtract 20 cents from a dollar. Based on their observations and the wife's description of her husband's behavior and attitude at home, the physicians concluded that the involvement of the right cerebral hemisphere was increasing and that the left hemisphere was now also affected. They again urged hospitalization so that he could be evaluated for treatable causes of mental deterioration and mental deficit. His abnormal gait and urinary incontinence, in association with his dementia, made it seem likely that he had occult hydrocephalus. The physicians explained that this disorder was caused by a malfunction in the brain's blood vessels, in which they did not absorb excess cerebrospinal fluid (CSF), resulting in a buildup of this fluid with resultant pressure on the cerebrum.

Occult hydrocephalus is treated by placing a plastic tube in the skull to drain the excess CSF from the brain into the circulatory system. This procedure was explained to the patient, using diagrams. The patient immediately rejected surgery. His wife again tried to persuade him to accept hospitalization and possible surgery. When he again refused, the attending physician told the wife that her husband was not competent to decide his own fate and that she should now become his legal guardian to force hospitalization. The wife rejected this idea, saying that in their family the husband made all important decisions.

At this point the resident and the attending physician disagreed. The resident observed that although the man's mental abilities had decreased, he still retained enough intelligence to decide his own fate. The resident suggested that the patient should be treated as an outpatient, with the hope that he might change his mind. The attending physician thought that court action to make the patient the ward of one of his other relatives or, if necessary, the temporary ward of the hospital to force hospitalization and therapy was appropriate.

With whom do you agree, the resident or the attending physician?

11 Nerve Cells and How They Transmit Information

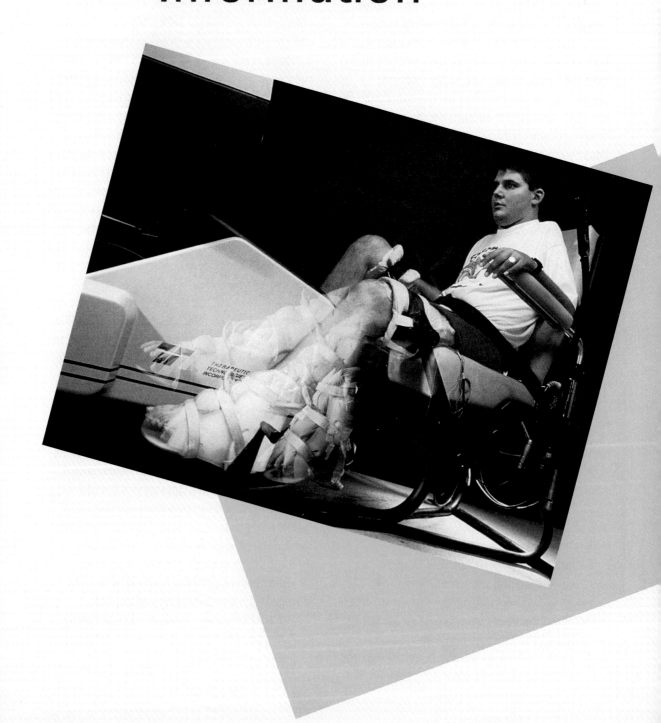

You won't find this machine among the Nautilus equipment at your local health club. It wasn't designed for physical fitness buffs but for paraplegics and quadriplegics—people who cannot move their legs. Impossible as it sounds, this machine can take over the job of nerves that tell leg muscles to move.

Nerves bring messages from the brain to other parts of the body by means of electrical impulses that sweep along their membranes. This stationary bicycle with its attached computer mimics this nervous activity. The computer generates pulses of electrical current and sends them to the patient's hamstrings, quadriceps, and buttocks by means of electrodes. These electrical pulses "fire" each leg muscle for an instant and in a specific order. The result is what you see in the photo—a pedaling motion that helps keep a patient's muscles, metabolism, and even mood in shape.

In the past decade, remarkable information has been learned about the nervous system. Scientists have discovered that cells in the peripheral nervous system—those outside the spinal cord and brain—are capable of limited regeneration. Some researchers are now experimenting with ways to enhance this process. For example, researchers in California have designed computer chips riddled with microscopic holes through which they are trying to get the severed ends of nerve cells to grow. They hope that the chips will not only help cut nerve cells reconnect but also relay messages along damaged nerve cells.

Scientists have had a more difficult time finding ways to encourage cells in the central nervous system (the brain and spinal cord) to repair themselves. Within the past decade, researchers have learned ways to stimulate nerve cell growth and regeneration in the brains of rats. Unfortunately, these techniques do not work in humans; the regeneration of human brain and spinal cord tissue is merely science fiction at this time. However, science and technology are entering arenas in which many paralysis victims, like the one in the photo, may be able to take a walk—or pedal—in ways they never before thought possible.

The communication systems of your body

The cells of your body communicate with one another in several ways. Your nervous system is only one means of communication. A simple way in which cells communicate with one another is by direct contact: open channels between adjacent cells allow ions and small molecules to pass freely from one cell to another. This method of communication allows cells to interact with their neighbors but is too slow and inefficient a method for interactions among cells that are far apart, like those in your toes and those in your fingers. It can be likened to running a large corporation with only face-to-face interactions between the people who sit next to each other! It would be better, in terms of distant communication, if managers of the various departments within a corporation sent memos to their staff members, instructing them what to do.

The varied tissues within the body communicate in a similar way by means of chemical instructions called **hormones.** The hormone "memos" are produced by one of several different **endocrine glands,** secreted into the bloodstream, and are carried around the body by the circulatory system. Each hormone, however, only interacts with certain target tissues, just as a memo that is sent through interoffice mail is delivered only to those persons to whom it is addressed. (Hormones are discussed in more detail in Chapter 14.)

Although hormones are an important means of communication within your body, they do not serve all the communication needs. For example, if the message to be delivered to your leg muscles is "Contract quickly, we are about to be hit by a car," hormones are too slow a message system. That is, a person in an emergency does not send a memo to the police but uses the telephone to get help quickly. That, in effect, is what your nervous system does.

The quick message system of your body is the **nervous system.** Your nervous system, as well as the nervous systems of all complex animals, is made up of nerve cells, or **neurons.** Neurons are specialized cells that transmit signals throughout the body (Figure 11-1). Bundled in groups, the long cell extensions of neurons make up nerves. Their message signals are called **nerve impulses.** Like the dots and dashes of Morse code, all nerve impulses are the same, differing only in their frequencies, their points of origin, and their destinations.

The command center of your nervous system is the **brain,** a precisely ordered but complicated maze of interconnected neurons—a large biological computer. The brain is connected by a network of neurons to both the hormone-producing glands and the individual muscles and other tissues. This dual channel of command permits great flexibility: the signals can be slow and persistent (hormones), fast and transient (nerve signals), or any combination of the two.

Two forms of communication integrate and coordinate body functions in humans, as well as in all other vertebrate animals and some invertebrates. Neurons are specialized cells that transmit rapid signals called nerve impulses, reporting information or initiating quick responses in specific tissues. Hormones are chemical messengers that trigger widespread prolonged responses, often in a variety of tissues.

The nerve cell, or neuron

Despite the fact that individual neurons vary widely in size and shape, all neurons have the same basic parts: a cell body and cell extensions called **dendrites** and **axons.** Some neurons have only a few cell extensions; others are bushy with these projections. Many of the neurons in your body, such as those extending from the base of your spinal cord to your toes, have extensions that are a meter or more long!

Figure 11-2 illustrates some of the structural differences that exist among neurons. These differences are intimately related to the varying functions of nerve cells. **Sensory neurons** transmit information to the central nervous system (Figure 11-2, *A*). Each of these neurons has one long dendrite bringing messages from all parts of the body. The cell bodies of sensory neurons lie near the central nervous system. **Motor neurons** transmit commands away from the central nervous system (Figure 11-2, *B*). Each of these neurons has one long axon bringing messages to muscles and glands. The cell bodies of most motor neurons lie in or near the central nervous system. Axons carry messages from the cell body and are usually quite long. Many axons, for example, extend from the spinal cord to muscles or glands. As mentioned previously, the axons that control the muscular activity in your legs and feet can be more than a meter long (depending on your height). Even longer axons occur in larger mammals. In a giraffe, single axons extend from the toes in its front legs all the way to the neck and from the toes in its back legs all the way to the pelvis, each spanning a distance of several meters (Figure 11-3). **Interneurons,** those located within the brain or spinal cord, integrate incoming with outgoing messages (Figure 11-2, *C*). These neurons usually have a highly branched system of dendrites, which is able to receive input from many different neurons converging on a single interneuron.

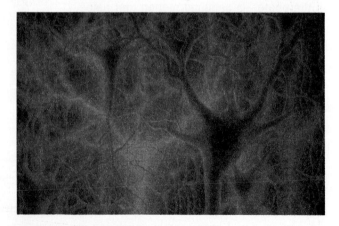

FIGURE 11-1   A network of neurons.
Nerve cells, or neurons, transmit nerve impulses throughout the body. Highly specialized, neurons are extremely sensitive to conditions within the body and to external conditions to which the body is subjected.

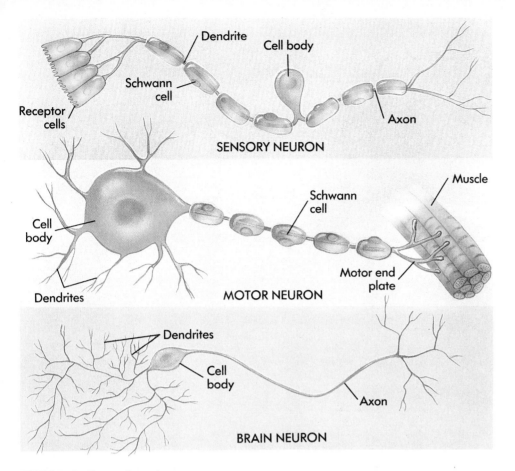

FIGURE 11-2 Types of vertebrate neurons.
A Sensory neurons carry signals from sense organs to the brain and spinal cord.
B The axons of motor neurons carry commands from the brain to muscles and glands.
C Interneurons within the brain and spinal cord often have extensive, highly branched dendrites.

The **cell body** of a neuron has the structures typical of a eukaryotic cell, such as a membrane-bound nucleus. Surrounding the nucleus is cytoplasm, which contains the various cell organelles. The cell body is responsible for producing substances that are necessary for the nerve cell to live. The rough endoplasmic reticulum, for example, makes proteins that are used for the growth and regeneration of the nerve cell processes, or extensions. Substances such as these are able to leave the cell body and travel down the cell processes of the neuron, riding on "currents" within the cytoplasm or along "tracks" made by microtubules and microfilaments (see p. 204). In addition, some materials travel back to the cell body to be degraded or recycled.

FIGURE 11-3 Some nerve cells are quite long.
From the neck of this giraffe, axons of neurons extend all the way to the toes of the front legs—a distance of about 5 meters.

⮟⮟

A nerve cell, or neuron, is made up of a cell body that contains a nucleus and other cell organelles and two types of cellular projections: axons and dendrites. Dendrites bring messages to the nerve cell body; axons carry messages from the nerve cell body. Structural differences exist among neurons; these differences relate to functional differences among neurons.

Most neurons do not exist alone but have companion cells nearby. These companion cells are called **neuroglia** and provide nutritional support to neurons. Special neuroglial cells called **Schwann cells** are wrapped around many of the long cell processes of sensory and motor neurons of the peripheral nervous system. Such long cell extensions are nerve fibers. The fatty wrapping created by multiple layers of many Schwann cell membranes is called the **myelin sheath**. The myelin sheath insulates the axon; however, the Schwann cells are wrapped around the axon in such a way that uninsulated spots occur at regular intervals (Figure 11-4). These uncovered spots are called **nodes of Ranvier**. These nodes and the myelin sheath (discussed in more detail later in this chapter) create conditions that speed the nerve impulse as it is conducted along the surface of the axon.

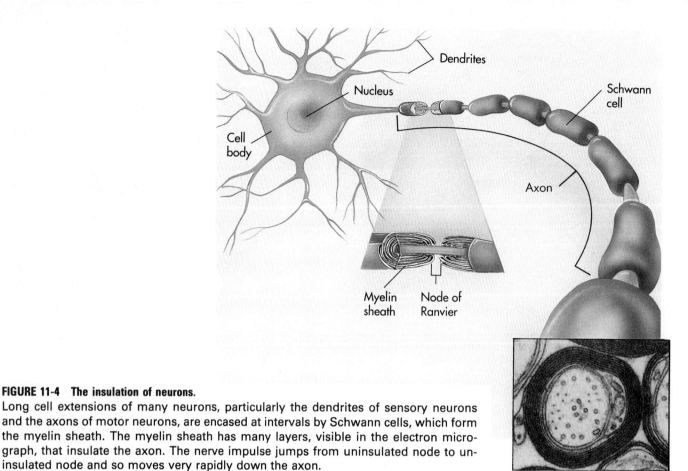

FIGURE 11-4 The insulation of neurons.
Long cell extensions of many neurons, particularly the dendrites of sensory neurons
and the axons of motor neurons, are encased at intervals by Schwann cells, which form
the myelin sheath. The myelin sheath has many layers, visible in the electron micrograph, that insulate the axon. The nerve impulse jumps from uninsulated node to uninsulated node and so moves very rapidly down the axon.

The nerve impulse

How do nerve cells conduct nerve impulses? The answer is
not obvious from examining the amazingly complex network of nerve cells that extends throughout the body. Looking at this network and trying to understand how the nervous system operates is a little like gazing at a telephone
wire and trying to understand how it transmits your voice
to a receiver far away—nothing can be seen moving along
the wires. The key to understanding how your telephone
(and your nerve cells) transmit information is an understanding of the abstract concept of electricity.

Electricity is a form of energy—an invisible form—and
you can only see, hear, or feel its effects. Electricity is invisible because it is a flow of electrons, subatomic particles so
minute that they cannot be visualized even with a high-
powered microscope. In a telephone line a flow of electrons
carries information from your telephone to the receiver of
the person whom you called. The telephone changes the
sound energy of your voice into electrical energy, transmits
it over the telephone lines, and then changes it back to
sound energy when it reaches its destination.

Neurons carry information in a similar way. The job of
nerve cells is to transmit information from the environment
to the spinal cord and brain, from one cell to another within
the brain, and from the brain and spinal cord to other parts
of the body. Nerve cells transmit this information in the
form of electrical signals. The stimulation of specialized receptor cells, such as the rods and cones in your eyes, or specialized receptor endings of nerve cells, such as pressure receptors in your skin, causes electrical signals to be generated in these cells. Once an electrical signal is generated in
a receptor, it can travel in the nervous system.

The neuron at rest: The resting potential

How do neurons conduct electricity? The story begins with
the neuron at rest—a neuron not conducting an impulse.
A resting neuron, interestingly, is electrically charged. This
electrical charge has been measured in the laboratory (by
means of microelectrodes) to be approximately -70 millivolts (mV) (Figure 11-5, *A*). The negative charge means
that the inside of the cell (near the membrane where the
microelectrode is placed) is negatively charged relative to
extracellular fluid along the outside of the membrane (where
a reference electrode is placed). A millivolt is one-
thousandth of a volt, the unit measure of electrical potential. The term *electrical potential* refers to the amount of potential energy created by a separation of positive and negative charges (in this case, along the inside and outside of
the cell membrane of the neuron). This potential energy
comes from the work that is done to separate these charges.

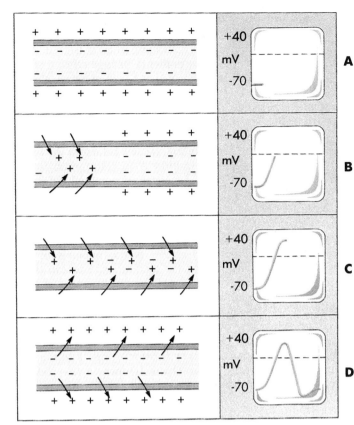

FIGURE 11-5 The stages of membrane depolarization.
A When a neuron is at rest, there is a net negative charge along the inside of the nerve cell membrane of −70 mV.
B When a neuron is sufficiently stimulated, Na$^+$ ions enter the cell, abolishing the voltage difference.
C Enough positive ions enter to establish a net interior positive charge.
D The exit of K$^+$ ions then returns the interior to a net negative charge.

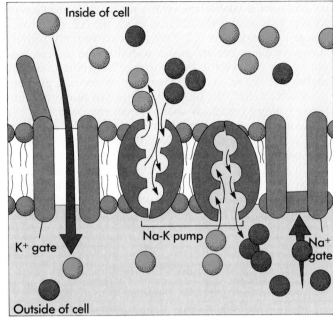

FIGURE 11-6 The sodium-potassium pump helps maintain the resting potential in a neuron.
The sodium-potassium pump consists of enzymes that are embedded in the cell membranes of neurons. The pump maintains the interior negative charge and exterior positive charge of the neuron as it pumps Na$^+$ ions outside the cell and K$^+$ ions inside the cell. However K$^+$ ions are constantly diffusing back out of the cell and Cl$^-$ ions remain within the cell, blocked from diffusing out because the nerve cell membrane is only slightly permeable to them. Due to these events, the interior of the cell becomes slightly negative. This separation of negative and positive charges across the cell membrane of a neuron is called *polarization.* Polarization characterizes the resting potential of the neuron.

For example, work is necessary to roll a boulder up a hill. Some of the actively working energy (kinetic energy) used to roll the boulder uphill is stored in the boulder (potential energy) as it sits at the top of the hill. In the same way, positive and negative charges that are separated from one another possess potential energy. The energy it takes to separate these oppositely charged particles is released if they rejoin.

The charges that are separated from one another along the nerve cell membrane are carried as ions—atoms with unequal numbers of protons and electrons (see Chapter 2). The ions that play the principal role in the development of the electrical potential along the membrane of the neuron (and that are also important to many other body processes) are sodium ions (Na$^+$) and potassium ions (K$^+$).

Embedded within the cell membranes of neurons are enzymes called **sodium-potassium pumps** that actively transport these ions across the cell membrane (see Chapter

3 and Figure 11-6). These transmembrane proteins (enzymes) use the energy stored in molecules of ATP to move potassium ions into the neuron at the same time that they move sodium ions out of the neuron. However, the potassium ions can simply diffuse back out of the cell through channels or tunnels open to them. Put simply, potassium ions actively enter the cell through one type of "door" but then exit by another. The situation with the sodium ions is different. These ions *cannot* move back into the cell even though they would normally do so by diffusion. There are no open inward channels in the neuron membrane through which the sodium ions can pass. In other words, they have no open door to get back into the cell. Sodium specific channels exist, but they are closed at −70 millivolts (the resting potential).

As a result of constantly pumping sodium ions out, the cell lowers the concentration of positively charged sodium ions within its interior. In this way a chemical gradient of sodium ions is established, with a higher concentration of sodium ions outside the cell than inside the cell. Negatively charged chloride ions (Cl⁻) are attracted to the positively charged sodium but are unable to follow the sodium ions out of the cell because the neuron cell membrane is only slightly permeable to them. Therefore an electrical gradient is also established; the inside of a nerve cell along its membrane is more negatively charged than the outside of the cell along the membrane. The membrane of the neuron is said to be **polarized**; there is a difference in charge on the two sides of the membrane. Resting neurons—ones not conducting an impulse—have this difference in electrical charge on either side of the membrane. The difference in charge is called the **resting potential**. This electrical potential difference across the membrane is the basis for the transmission of signals by nerves.

The action of sodium-potassium transmembrane pumps and ion-specific membrane channels produces conditions that result in the separation of positive and negative ions along the inside and outside of the nerve cell membrane. This separation of charged particles creates an electrical potential difference, or electrical charge, along the membrane of the resting neuron. This electrical potential difference is defined as the resting potential.

Conducting an impulse: The action potential

A neuron transmits a nerve impulse when it is excited by an internal or external environmental change called a **stimulus** (pl. stimuli). Examples of stimuli are pressure, chemical activity, sound, and light. Specialized **receptors** detect stimuli. For example, the rods and cones in the retina of your eye are sensitive to light, pressure receptors in your skin allow you to feel a hug, and certain cells in your nose allow you to smell your favorite dessert baking in the oven.

Stimuli cause a nerve impulse to be transmitted by initiating events that change the electrical potential difference of the receptor cell or nerve cell membrane. This change in electrical potential difference is called **depolarization**. The first event to occur when a neuron is sufficiently stimulated, depolarizing the membrane to a level called the **threshold potential** (see Figure 11-5, B), is the opening of the sodium-specific channels in the membrane. You can think of these channels as being operated by electricity. A change in voltage across the nerve cell membrane opens and closes them. What actually happens is that the sudden change in voltage changes the shape of the proteins forming the channels. As their shape changes, these channels become permeable to sodium ions and allow them to diffuse into the cell.

As the sodium-specific channels open, a few sodium ions move rapidly into the cell, diffusing from where there

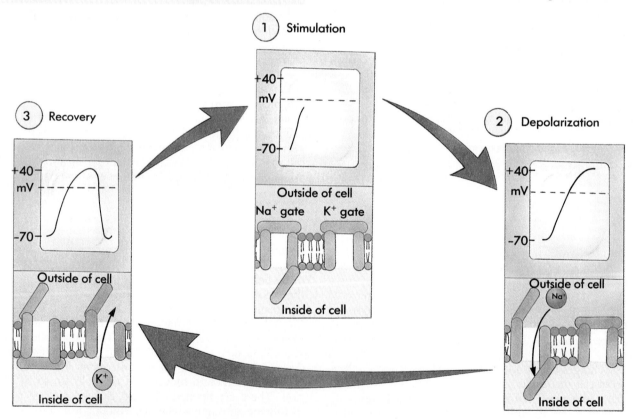

FIGURE 11-7 The action potential.
The stages of the action potential are *(1)* stimulation of a neuron, which causes Na⁺ gates in the neuron to open; *(2)* depolarization, in which the Na⁺ ions flood into the neuron, depolarizing the electrochemical gradient established during the resting potential; and *(3)* recovery, in which K⁺ gates open, allowing K⁺ ions to leave, thus repolarizing the membrane.

are more sodium ions (outside the cell) to where there are fewer (inside the cell). This permeability for sodium ions across the cell membrane wipes out the local electrochemical gradient (the polarization) and further depolarizes the nerve cell membrane. Amazingly, although only about 1 in 10 million ions actually moves across the membrane, the interior of the cell develops a positive charge relative to the outside of approximately +40 millivolts (see Figure 11-5, C), a 110 millivolt electrical difference from the −70 millivolts resting potential. This electrical difference occurs because a new electrical potential develops when the inwardly directed permeability for sodium ions develops across the cell membrane. This rapid change in the membrane's electrical potential is called the **action potential.**

Although it may seem hard to believe, the depolarization of the cell membrane (the action potential) lasts for only *a few thousandths of a second* (milliseconds) because the sodium channels close quickly. They cannot reopen until after the resting potential is reestablished and another depolarization occurs, triggering them again. During this inactive state of the sodium channels, a nerve impulse cannot be conducted. This period, which is only milliseconds long, is called the **refractory period.**

When the sodium channels close, potassium ions move outward as they usually do through potassium channels. Many neurons contain voltage-sensitive potassium channels that open as the membrane depolarizes and the sodium channels shut down. It is this event—the movement of potassium ions out of the cell—that repolarizes the membrane (Figure 11-5, D). The sodium-potassium pump (Figure 11-6) works to maintain the resting potential on a more long-term basis. The whole process of stimulation, depolarization, and recovery happens in the blink of an eye (Figure 11-7). In fact, 500 such cycles could occur in the time it takes you to say the words "nerve impulse."

Transmission of the nerve impulse: A propagation of the action potential

An action potential at one point on the nerve cell membrane is a stimulus to neighboring regions of the cell membrane. The change in membrane potential causes sodium channels to open, depolarizing the adjacent section of membrane. Put simply, depolarization at one site produces depolarization at the next. In this way the initial depolarization passes outward over the membrane, spreading out in all directions from the site of stimulation (Figure 11-8). Like a burning fuse, the signal is usually initiated at one end and travels in one direction, but it would travel out from both directions if it were lit in the middle. The self-propagating wave of depolarization that travels along the nerve cell membrane is the nerve impulse.

⟱

A nerve impulse arises when a receptor is stimulated. This stimulation results in a rapid change in the electrical potential difference along the nerve cell membrane. This transient disturbance, or depolarization, has electrical consequences to which nearby transmembrane proteins respond, spreading the depolarization in wave-like fashion.

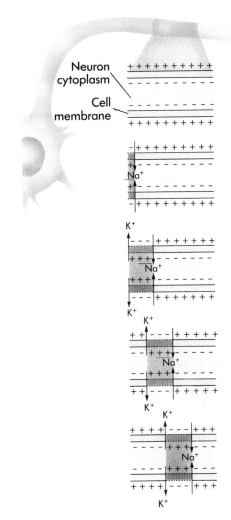

FIGURE 11-8 Transmission of a nerve impulse.
Depolarization moves laterally along a neuron in a self-propagating wave. The process of depolarization can be compared to the burning of a fuse because the signal usually starts at one end and travels in one direction. However, if the signal were able to start in the middle of the neuron, depolarization would travel in both directions outward.

The nerve impulse is an **all-or-nothing response.** The amount of stimulation applied to the receptor or neuron must be sufficient to open enough sodium channels to generate an action potential. Otherwise, the cell membrane will simply return to the resting potential. For any one neuron the action potential is always the same. But any stimulus intense enough to open a sufficient number of sodium channels will depolarize the membrane to the threshold level and initiate an impulse. The neuron is said to have fired. This wave of depolarization has a constant amplitude (the height or strength of the wave). The speed at which impulses are conducted, however, varies among nerves.

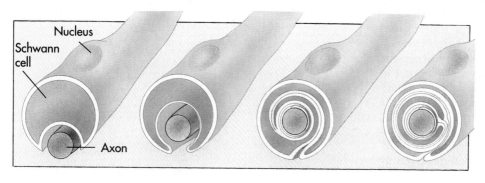

FIGURE 11-9 Schwann cells.
Schwann cells wrap around nerve cell processes forming stacks of lipid-rich layers. The progressive growth of the Schwann cell membrane around the process contributes the many membrane layers characteristic of myelin sheaths. These layers act as an excellent electrical insulator.

FIGURE 11-10 Saltatory conduction.
A In a fiber without Schwann cells, each portion of the membrane becomes depolarized in turn, like a row of falling dominoes.
B In neurons of the same diameter as in **A**, the nerve impulse moves faster along a myelinated fiber because the wave of depolarization jumps from node to node without ever depolarizing the insulated membrane segments between nodes.

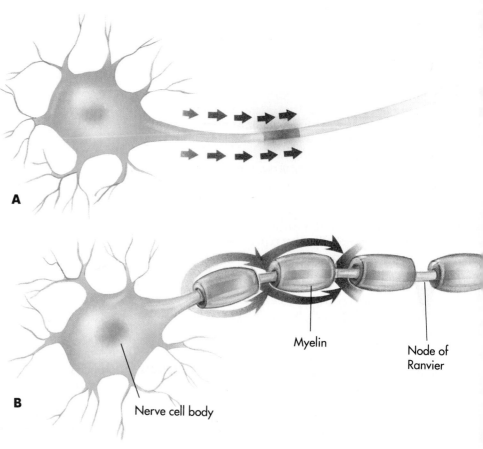

Myelin

Node of Ranvier

Nerve cell body

Speedy neurons: Saltatory conduction

As mentioned earlier, many neurons have axons and axon-like dendrites that are covered by neuroglial Schwann cells. These cells envelop many of the long cell processes of sensory and motor neurons and certain interneurons as well (Figure 11-9), wrapping their cell membranes around them so many times that they form stacks of lipid-rich layers. In fact, some neurons have as many as 100 membrane layers surrounding them! This "cell wrapper" is the myelin sheath.

Schwann cells wrap around the length of an axon or axon-like dendrite, one after the other, with spaces separating one from the next (Figure 11-10). These spaces, the nodes of Ranvier, are critical to the propagation of the nerve impulse in myelinated cells. The myelin sheath is an insulator; it prevents the transport of ions across the neuron mem-

brane beneath it. However, within the small gaps between Schwann cells, the surface of the axon is exposed to the intercellular fluid surrounding the nerve. An action potential can be generated only at these gaps. In fact, the pumps and channels that move ions across the neuron membrane are concentrated at the nodes of Ranvier, enhancing ion movements at these spots.

The action potential moves along the nerve cell membrane differently in myelinated cells than in unmyelinated cells. The wave of membrane depolarization that travels down the axon of unmyelinated neurons is impossible in myelinated axons due to the myelin sheath, which acts as an electrical insulator. Instead, the action potential jumps from one node to the next (much as mountain climbers rappel down a cliff [Figure 11-11]), causing a depolarization there. This depolarization opens the voltage-sensitive sodium channels at that node, resulting in the production of

FIGURE 11-11 A mountain climber rappelling down a cliff. The way in which a mountain climber rappels down a cliff–pushing off the rock face, landing a distance away, and then pushing off again–is analogous to saltatory condition, the movement of ions from node to node along a myelinated nerve fiber.

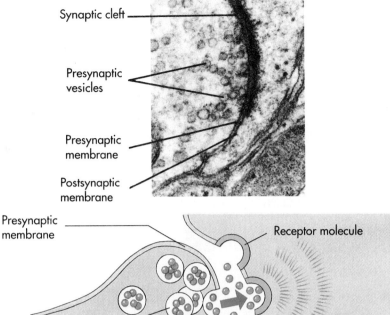

FIGURE 11-12   A synaptic cleft between two neurons. Nerve signals cross the gap between neurons by changing from an electrical signal to a chemical signal.

an action potential. This very fast form of nerve impulse conduction is known as **saltatory conduction,** from the Latin word *saltare,* meaning "to jump."

Impulses conducted by myelinated neurons travel much faster than impulses conducted by nerve fibers of the same diameter without this insulation. In fact, impulses conducted in large-diameter myelinated neurons travel up to 270 miles per hour (120 meters per second). These myelinated neurons can transmit a signal from your toes to your brain in less than half a second!

Multiple sclerosis (MS), one of the leading causes of serious neurological disease in adults, affects approximately one out of every 2000 people in the United States. This disease results in the destruction of large patches of the myelin sheath around neurons of the brain and spinal cord. Left behind are hardened scars (scleroses) that interfere with the transmission of nerve impulses. The resulting slowed transmission of signals in the nervous system results in a gradual loss of motor activity. Although the cause of MS is unknown, evidence strongly suggests that proteins within the myelin sheath are attacked by certain enzymes or by cells from the body's immune system.

▼
Not all nerve impulses propagate as a continuous wave of depolarization spreading along the neuronal membrane. Along myelinated neurons, impulses travel by jumping along the membrane, leaping over insulated portions. Impulses travel much more quickly along these myelinated neurons than along unmyelinated ones.

Transmitting information between cells

When the nerve impulse reaches the end of an axon, it must be transmitted to another neuron or to muscle or glandular tissue. Muscles and glands, because they effect (or cause) responses when stimulated by nerves, are called **effectors.** This place—where a neuron communicates with another neuron or an effector cell—is called the **synapse.**

Most neurons do not actually touch other neurons or cells with which they communicate. Instead, there is a minute space (*billionths* of a meter across) separating these cells (Figure 11-12). This space or gap is called the **synaptic cleft.** The nerve impulse must cross this gap and does so by the direct passage of electrical current or by changing an electrical signal to a chemical signal. Chemical synapses are the prevalent type of synapse in humans (and all vertebrates).

The membrane on the axon side of the synaptic cleft is called the **presynaptic membrane.** In chemical synapses, when a wave of depolarization reaches the presynaptic

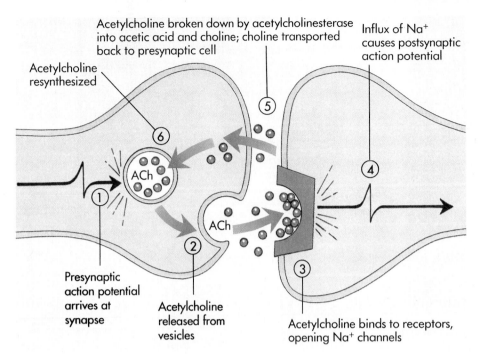

Acetylcholine resynthesized

Acetylcholine broken down by acetylcholinesterase into acetic acid and choline; choline transported back to presynaptic cell

Influx of Na⁺ causes postsynaptic action potential

Presynaptic action potential arrives at synapse

Acetylcholine released from vesicles

Acetylcholine binds to receptors, opening Na⁺ channels

FIGURE 11-13   The sequence of events in synaptic transmission at a neuromuscular junction.
This diagram demonstrates how a nerve impulse causes muscle cells to contract. *ACh* is an abbreviation for acetylcholine.

membrane, it stimulates the release of organic molecules called **neurotransmitters** into the cleft. These molecules are stored in thousands of small membrane-bound sacs located at the tips of the axon. Each sac contains from 10,000 to 100,000 molecules of neurotransmitter. These chemicals diffuse to the other side of the gap. Once there, they combine with receptor molecules in the **postsynaptic membrane** (associated with either a dendrite or a cell body) of the target cell. When they do, they cause ion channels to open.

▼▼
A synapse is a junction between an axon tip and another cell, usually including a narrow gap separating the two cells. Passage of the impulse across the gap is by an electrical current or, more likely in vertebrates, a chemical signal from the axon.

Chemical junctions between neurons and other neurons or effector cells have a distinct advantage over direct electrical connections—flexibility. The chemical transmitters can be different in different junctions. Just as you might take an aspirin to stop headache pain or cough syrup to subdue a cough, different neurotransmitters result in different kinds of responses. In fact, more than 60 different chemicals have been identified that act as neurotransmitters or that act to modify the activity of neurotransmitters.

Neuron-to-muscle cell connections

Synapses between neurons and skeletal muscle cells are called **neuromuscular junctions.** The neurotransmitter found at neuromuscular junctions is **acetylcholine.** Passing across the gap, the acetylcholine molecules bind to recep-

tors in the postsynaptic (muscle cell) membrane, opening sodium channels. This influx of sodium ions depolarizes the muscle cell membrane, which initiates a wave of depolarization that passes down the muscle cell (Figure 11-13). This wave of depolarization releases calcium ions, which in turn trigger muscle contraction.

▼▼
At a neuromuscular junction, acetylcholine released from an axon tip depolarizes the muscle cell membrane, releasing calcium ions that trigger muscle contraction.

After an impulse has been transmitted across the synaptic cleft, the neurotransmitter must be broken down or the postsynaptic membrane will remain depolarized. The breakdown products of the neurotransmitter then diffuse or are actively transported from the postsynaptic cell. In general, some or all of the breakdown products are transported back to the presynaptic cell to be reused. For example, the neurotransmitter acetylcholine is broken down to acetic acid and choline by an enzyme called **acetylcholinesterase.** Choline is transported back to the presynaptic cell, where it is used to make molecules of acetylcholine. Acetylcholinesterase is one of the fastest-acting enzymes in the body, breaking down one acetylcholine molecule every 40 microseconds. The fast work of acetylcholinesterase permits as many as 1000 impulses *per second* to be transmitted across the neuromuscular junction. Interestingly, nerve gases and the agricultural insecticide parathion work by blocking the action of acetylcholinesterase. These chemicals can cause death because they produce continuous neuromuscular transmission, which results in a continuous muscular contraction of vital muscles such as those involved in breathing and the circulation of blood. Many drugs work by affecting synapses

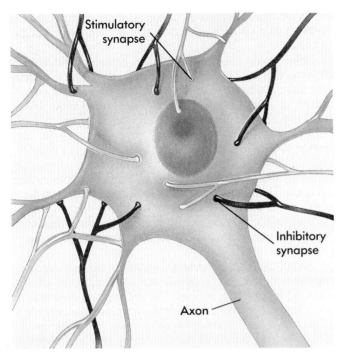

Stimulatory synapse

Inhibitory synapse

Axon

FIGURE 11-14 Integration of nerve impulses takes place on the neuron cell body.
The synapses made by some axons are inhibitory, tending to counteract depolarization of the postsynaptic membrane; these axons are indicated in *red*. The synapses made by other axons are stimulatory, tending to depolarize the postsynaptic membrane; these axons are indicated in *blue*. The summed influences of these inputs determine whether the postsynaptic membrane will be sufficiently depolarized to initiate a nerve impulse.

also. For example, cocaine, local anesthetics, and some tranquilizers work by destroying the control of neurotransmitter release. (See "How drugs affect neurotransmitter transmission.")

Neuron-to-neuron connections

Impulses are transmitted from one neuron to another by a variety of neurotransmitters. Some neurotransmitters depolarize the postsynaptic membrane, which results in the continuation of the nerve impulse. This type of synapse is called an **excitatory synapse**. Other neurotransmitters have the reverse effect, reducing the ability of the postsynaptic membrane to depolarize. This type of synapse is called an **inhibitory synapse**. A single nerve cell can have *both* kinds of synaptic connections to other nerve cells. And, as you might expect, excitatory signals cancel out inhibitory signals, modifying each other's effects. The postsynaptic neuron keeps score as the impulses reach its dendrites and cell body and it responds accordingly. For this reason the postsynaptic neuron is called an **integrator** (Figure 11-14).

The dendrites and cell body of a postsynaptic neuron integrate the information they receive from presynaptic neurons. The summed effect of both excitory and inhibitory signals either facilitate depolarization or inhibit it.

Within your body, synapses are organized into functional units with definite patterns, like electrical circuits. Just as your house is wired in a definite pattern to provide electricity to various appliances and light fixtures, your body is wired in a specific manner. But the manner in which your body is wired is much more complex than that in your home, allowing you to maintain internal homeostasis as well as to adapt to the outside environment.

How drugs affect neurotransmitter transmission

Drugs are substances that affect normal body functions. Although the specific actions of drugs vary, they all work by interfering with the normal activity of neurotransmitters. In this way, drugs affect communication between neurons, or between neurons and muscles or glands.

One way in which drugs work is to decrease the amount of neurotransmitter that is released from a presynaptic neuron. Some drugs directly block neurotransmitter release. Other types of drugs work more indirectly, causing neurotransmitter molecules to leak out of their storage vesicles and then to be degraded by enzymes. Reserpine, a tranquilizer that also lowers blood pressure, is such a drug. It interferes with the storage of the neurotransmitter norepinephrine (also called noradrenaline). This neurotransmitter is one of two active in the sympathetic nervous system, a branch of the autonomic nervous system that controls involuntary body functions (see p. 236). Among norepinephrine's functions within the sympathetic nervous system, it acts to constrict blood vessels, which increases blood pressure. So decreasing the amount of norepinephrine decreases the constriction of the blood vessels and lowers the blood pressure.

Some drugs increase the amount of a neurotransmitter or its effects at the synapse. These types of drugs either enhance the release of neurotransmitter molecules, inhibit the action of enzymes that degrade neurotransmitter molecules at the postsynaptic neuron, or chemically resemble the neurotransmitter and mimic its effects at the postsynaptic neuron. In all cases, the postsynaptic neuron becomes or remains stimulated by the neurotransmitter or its mimic. *Amphetamines*, drugs that stimulate the brain, are of this type and are described in more detail below.

Some drugs that chemically resemble specific neurotransmitters act in still another way. These mimics occupy receptor sites but do not stimulate postsynaptic neurons. They simply block the neurotransmitter molecules from the sites. Therefore these drugs block the effects of the neurotransmitter.

Drugs are substances that affect normal body functions by interfering with the normal activity of neurotransmitters.

Drug addiction

Psychoactive drugs are chemical substances that affect neurotransmitter transmission in specific parts of the brain. Some psychoactive drugs are used medically to alter moods or to treat diseases or disorders. For example, the drug diazepam, commonly known as Valium, is used to control anxiety. Imipramine is a psychoactive drug that works as an antidepressant. Morphine is sometimes used to control pain after surgery. However, many psychoactive drugs (like morphine) are abused. That is, they are used for nonmedical reasons, are taken in doses that may cause damage to the body, and often result in personally destructive, antisocial, and crime-related behaviors.

The chronic use of psychoactive drugs results in **drug addiction**: a compulsive urge to continue using the drug, physical and/or psychological dependence on the drug, and a tendency to increase the strength (dosage) of the drug. Persons physically dependent on a drug show symptoms of this dependence when they stop taking the drug. These symptoms are called *withdrawal symptoms*; their effects are usually opposite to the effects caused by the drug. For example, if a drug relieves pain, those physically addicted to it become hypersensitive to pain when they stop taking the drug. Drugs that cause euphoria, a feeling of intense well-being, will result in depression on withdrawal. Unfortunately, these feelings are often the ones addicts try to relieve by taking the drug in the first place. Symptoms of withdrawal become a new stimulus for the drug-taking response, resulting in a cycle of addiction that is hard for the addict to break.

Chronic drug users also tend to increase the dosage of the drug they take because they become drug tolerant. **Drug tolerance** is a decrease in the effects of the same dosage of a drug in a person who takes the drug over time. Therefore, the chronic user of a drug must take increasingly higher dosages of a drug for it to continue to elicit the same response. One reason behind the phenomenon of drug tolerance is that the chronic use of a drug stimulates liver enzymes to degrade, or break down, a drug with increasing swiftness. Another metabolic reason for drug tolerance is that brain cells become less responsive to a drug over time. As drug users increase the amount of the drug they take, dangerous side effects appear more often and become stronger.

Compulsive drug-seeking behavior and psychological dependence have sociological and psychological dimensions. Unfortunately, the biological factors involved in drug addiction, other than those already mentioned, are not clear. However, recent research on alcoholism (an addiction described below) points to the conclusion that this addiction is a disease. Twin and adoptive studies, animal studies, and physiological studies of addicts all provide evidence supporting the hypothesis that a gene may exist that predisposes those inheriting this gene to alcohol addiction. Hopefully, future research will reveal further information and understanding regarding drug addiction that could lead to more effective treatments and preventive measures.

TABLE 11-1	Major classes of psychoactive drugs		
CLASS	**TYPE**	**EXAMPLES**	**STREET NAMES**
Depressants	Sedative hypnotic	Barbiturates (Seconal, Nembutal, Phenobarbital) Benzodiazepines (Valium)	Downers, dolls
		Methaqualone	Ludes, sopors
	Alcohol	Beer, wine	
Opiates		Opium	
		Morphine	Mexican brown, Black tar
		Codeine	
		Heroin	
Stimulants		Amphetamines	Uppers, speed, bennies
		Cocaine	Crack, ice
		Nicotine	
		Caffeine	
Hallucinogens		LSD	
		Marijuana (cannabis)	Pot, weed, grass
		PCP (phencyclidine)	Angel dust, trank
		Psychedelic mushrooms	

Psychoactive drugs and their effects

Table 11-1 lists the major classes of psychoactive drugs. Their actions relate to the neurotransmitters to which they are chemically similar and to the parts of the brain or spinal cord that have receptors for those neurotransmitters. Just as neurons communicate with skeletal muscles by secreting acetylcholine at neuromuscular junctions, neurons in specific parts of the brain and spinal cord communicate using specific neurotransmitters. After reading Chapter 12, which will help you understand brain anatomy, you may choose to reread this discussion of drugs.

Depressants

Depressants are drugs that slow down the activity of the central nervous system (brain and spinal cord). The **sedative-hypnotics** are central nervous system depressants that induce sleep (sedatives) and reduce anxiety (hypnotics). This group of drugs interacts with gamma-aminobutyric acid (GABA), an inhibitory brain neurotransmitter. The interaction takes place at receptor sites found close together on postsynaptic neurons located in the amygdala of the limbic system and throughout the cerebral cortex. When GABA binds to these postsynaptic neurons, it slows the neurons' rate of firing. When a sedative-hypnotic drug binds to the postsynaptic neurons, it enhances GABA's inhibitory effects and results in calmness. Scientists are unsure, however, why the binding of benzodiazepine reduces anxiety while the binding of a barbiturate produces sedation. However, barbiturates and benzodiazepines bind at separate sites near the GABA receptor site.

Sedative-hypnotics are used to treat sleep disorders, epileptic convulsions, and anxiety and are sometimes used as anesthetics for dental surgery. However, they are addictive drugs that can have dangerous side effects from either large single doses or prolonged use. Some of these side effects are the inability to think clearly, regression of the personality to child-like characteristics, emotional instability and irritability, unsteadiness when walking, and an indifference to personal hygiene. Because they suppress body functions, a sedative-hypnotic drug overdose can be fatal.

Another type of depressant drug is **alcohol** (ethanol). The amount of ethanol in an alcoholic beverage is designated by the word "proof"; the percentage of alcohol in the beverage is half that of the proof. Eighty-proof whiskey, for example, is 40% ethanol. About 20% of the alcohol a person consumes is absorbed from the stomach. It immediately enters the bloodstream and travels all over the body. The rest passes into the small intestine and is then absorbed. Once in the bloodstream, ethanol, like other psychoactive drugs, is able to pass through the cells that make up the walls of the blood vessels within the brain. These cells, because of the way they are joined together, screen out many substances harmful to the brain. However, lipid-soluble drugs (all psychoactive drugs) are able to pass through the cells themselves. Once in the brain, ethanol acts at the same binding site as barbiturates and has sedating effects as do barbiturates. These close interactions may account for the potentially lethal interactions of alcohol or barbiturates and benzodiazepines. In other words, it is extremely dangerous to take benzodiazepines (such as Valium) with alcohol or a barbiturate (sleeping pill) because one enhances the activity of the other and at relatively low doses the combination can lead to death.

The effects of alcohol include increased heart rate, loss of alertness, blurred vision, and decreased coordination. Persons who use alcohol on a regular basis can proceed through the stages of addiction (use/tolerance/dependency/ abuse) and display the characteristics of addicts described previously. Long-term use of alcohol can result in liver damage, ulcers, inflammation of the pancreas, nutritional disorders (due to both the behavior of the alcoholic and metabolic changes that result from alcoholism), heart disease, and, in pregnant women, children who exhibit fetal alcohol syndrome (see the boxed essay in Chapter 22).

Opiates

The **opiates** are compounds derived from the milky juice of the poppy plant *Papaver somniferum* or their synthetic (human-made) derivatives. These drugs are *narcotic analgesics*. An analgesic is a drug that stops or reduces pain without causing a person to lose consciousness. A narcotic is a drug that produces sedation and euphoria; originally it referred only to the opiates. Today, however, the term narcotic is used more loosely and refers to any addictive drug that produces narcosis, a deadened or dazed state. It is used incorrectly when referring to stimulant drugs, which are described later in this chapter.

The opiates work by mimicking naturally occurring morphine-like neurotransmitters called *endorphins* (*endogenous morphine*-like substances). Endorphins help us cope with pain and help modulate our response to emotional trauma. They bind to opiate receptors concentrated in areas of the central nervous system that include: (1) the portion of the thalamus that conveys sensory input associated with deep, burning, aching pain; (2) portions of the midbrain and spinal cord involved in integrating pain information; (3) portions of the limbic system that govern the emotions; and (4) portions of the brainstem that control respiratory reflexes, pupil constriction, cough suppression, and gastric secretion and motility. This distribution of opiate receptors is shown in a guinea pig brain in Figure 11-15.

Some opiates have therapeutic uses. Dextromethorphan, an ingredient in some cough medicines, is a synthetic opiate that stimulates brainstem receptors that control coughing. Paregoric, a drug given to infants and small children to control diarrhea and accompanying cramps, contains a small amount of opium that acts to control pain and decrease gastric secretion and motility. Codeine is sometimes prescribed for the control of pain. Taken in an uncontrolled way, however, the opiates are highly addictive and dangerous drugs.

Stimulants

Stimulants include the *amphetamines* and *cocaine*. Stimulant drugs enhance the activity of two neurotransmitters: norepinephrine and dopamine. These neurotransmitters function in brain pathways that regulate emotions, sleep, attention, and learning. The alerting, stimulating effects produced by these drugs relate to their action in the cerebral cortex and the action of norepinephrine in the sympathetic division of the autonomic nervous system (see p. 236). The euphoria users feel relates to the action of these neurotransmitters in the limbic area of the brain. Stimulant drugs act by moving into presynaptic neurotransmitter storage vesicles, which causes norepinephrine and dopamine to move into the synaptic cleft. The drugs then block the breakdown and recycling of the neurotransmitter molecules, causing a depletion of the neurotransmitters. When their supply of neurotransmitters is gone, drug users must take more and more of the stimulant to achieve their "high." In fact, the nervous system eventually becomes so depleted of neurotransmitter that drug users cannot get through a day without the stimulant because their nervous systems are no longer working properly.

If a user begins to ingest large amounts of a stimulant drug such as cocaine, the drug can cause a schizophrenia-like mental disorder characterized by paranoia, the hearing of voices, and irrational thought. This disorder appears to be caused by an overstimulation of dopamine receptors. Chronic cocaine use can also lead to long-lasting and severe physical changes in the brain, as well as severe damage to the tissues of the nose and the lungs, heart disease, epileptic seizures, and respiratory failure.

Despite the fact that cocaine and other stimulants can be extremely dangerous drugs, they have important therapeutic uses. The drug ritalin (methylphenidate) is used in the treatment of attention deficit disorder. The seemingly paradoxical effects of this drug (hyperactive children are slowed down) are attributed to the drug's attention-focusing effects, allowing hyperactive children to focus their attention for longer periods of time and, therefore, resulting in their not moving quickly from one activity or place to the next. Another important therapeutic use of stimulant drugs is the use of cocaine as a local anesthetic. When injected into peripheral nerves, cocaine blocks the conduction of nerve fibers that transmit sensation. Most dental and eye surgery uses synthetic cocaine derivatives as local anesthetics.

Nicotine is also a stimulant drug, although it produces much milder effects than the amphetamines and cocaine. Along with stimulating the release of norepinephrine and dopamine, nicotine also affects the nicotinic receptors of the autonomic nervous system by affecting the release of acetylcholine in the presynaptic neurons. Depending on the dosage of nicotine, it may either increase or decrease the release of this neurotransmitter. Nicotinic receptors are found in both divisions of the autonomic nervous system. Because the divisions of the autonomic nervous system oppose one another in their activities and because the effect on acetylcholine release is variable, the effects of nicotine are often variable. For example, nicotine may cause the heart rate to increase or decrease. The result is that the heart rhythm becomes somewhat irregular. But the effects of nicotine on the brain and body are only one reason not to smoke cigarettes. The carbon monoxide in cigarette smoke replaces some of the oxygen in a smoker's red blood cells, thus interfering with the delivery of oxygen to the heart, brain, and other vital organs. In addition, smoking impairs the functions of the respiratory system. Cigarette smoke also contains a number of known cancer-causing agents and has been directly linked to cancers of the lungs, throat, and mouth. Cigarette smoking may also result in heart disease, high blood pressure, ulcers, earlier onset of menopause, excessive wrinkling of the skin, and sleep problems.

Hallucinogens

Hallucinogens, or psychedelic drugs, cause sensory perceptions that have no external stimuli; that is, a person hears, sees, smells, or feels things that do not exist. These drugs bear a close chemical resemblance to the neurotransmitters norepinephrine, dopamine, and serotonin (a transmitter involved with mood, anxiety, and sleep induction). However, scientists have not been able to pinpoint the exact mechanisms by which psychedelic drugs might affect the transmission of these neurotransmitters. The best hypothesis at this time is that hallucinogenic drugs act on two small nuclei in the brainstem (containing serotonin, norepinephrine, and dopamine neurons) that act as filtering stations for incoming sensory stimuli. These two nuclei are part of the reticular formation. Although small, these two nuclei give rise to axons that branch out to interact with billions of neurons in the cerebral cortex and cerebellum. Scientists think that hallucinogens may disrupt the sorting process and allow a surge of sensory data to overload the brain.

Hallucinogens can have devastating effects. Regular use of marijuana, the psychoactive plant *Cannabis*, can result in impaired eye-hand coordination, increased heart rate, panic attacks, anxiety, paranoia, depression, immune system impairment, upper respiratory system damage, and decreased levels of sex hormones. Regular use of this drug can also result in two syndromes: (1) *acute brain syndrome*, a condition marked by perceptual distortions, sleep and memory problems, disorientation with regard to time and place, and the inability to concentrate or sustain attention to important stimuli in the environment, and (2) *amotivational syndrome*, characterized by apathy, fatigue, poor judgment, loss of ambition, and diminished ability to carry out plans. Other hallucinogens such as LSD, PCP, peyote, and mescaline can result in psychotic behavior (derangement of the personality and loss of contact with reality). These episodes can trigger chronic mental health problems or can result in suicide.

The only hallucinogen shown to have possible therapeutic effects is marijuana. It has been found to relieve nausea in some patients undergoing chemotherapy treatment for cancer. The courts have approved the use of this drug in specific cases of this nature.

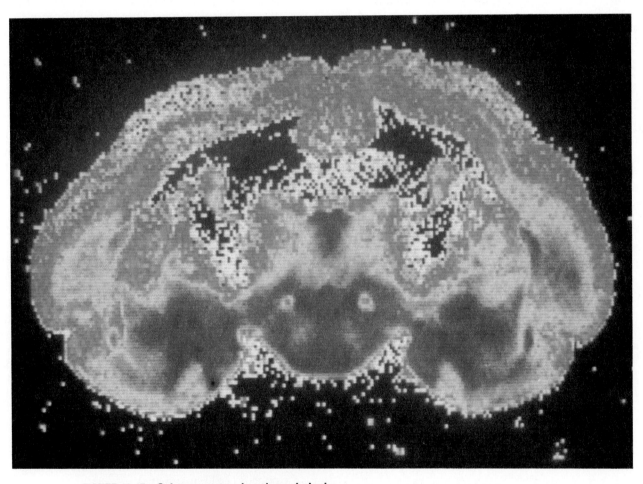

FIGURE 11-15   Opiate receptors in guinea pig brain.
This scan of guinea pig brain shows the concentration of opiate receptors; the highest density is indicated in red; yellow indicates moderate density; blue indicates low density; purple and white indicate very low densities.

Summary

1. The human body has two primary means of internal communication: hormones and nerve impulses. Nerve impulses are quick and transient electrical signals. Hormones are slower, persistent chemical signals.

2. Nerve cells are called *neurons*. These cells have a cell body containing structures typical of a cell and cellular extensions called *axons* and *dendrites*. Dendrites receive incoming messages and bring them toward the cell body. Axons carry messages from the cell body.

3. Nerve cells transmit information in the form of electrical signals. A resting neuron (one not conducting an impulse) has an electrical potential difference across its cell membrane. This electrical potential, or resting potential, occurs because of the separation of positively and negatively charged ions along the inside and outside of the nerve cell membrane.

4. A neuron transmits an impulse when it is excited by an environmental change, or stimulus. Specialized receptors detect stimuli and can initiate events that change the electrical potential difference along the nerve cell membrane. This change in electrical potential is called *depolarization*.

5. If a neuron is depolarized to a certain threshold, sodium channels in the membrane open. This permeability for sodium ions across the cell membrane wipes out the local electrochemical gradient and further depolarizes the nerve cell membrane. This rapid change in the membrane's electrical potential is called the *action potential*.

6. Within a few thousandths of a second, the sodium channels close. When these channels close, ion permeabilities are changed once again, and potassium tends to move out of the cell. This change in the electrochemical gradients at the cell membrane changes the electrical potential of the membrane once again, resulting in a return to the resting potential.

7. An action potential at one point on the nerve cell membrane causes depolarization of the adjacent section of membrane. A "wave" of depolarization continues along the nerve membrane. This self-propagating wave of depolarization is the nerve impulse.

8. The long cell processes of many neurons are wrapped in cells in which lipid-rich membranes act as insulation. Spaces between the cells making up the neuron cell wrapper help speed the nerve impulse as the action potential jumps from one node to the next. This very fast form of nerve impulse conduction is known as *saltatory conduction*.

9. When a nerve impulse reaches the axon tip of most vertebrate nerve cells, it causes the release of chemicals called *neurotransmitters*. These chemicals pass across a space called the *synaptic cleft* to the next cell. In neuron-to-muscle cell connections the neurotransmitter triggers muscle cell contraction. In neuron-to-neuron connections the neurotransmitter may cause either an excitatory response or an inhibitory response.

10. The integration of nerve impulses occurs on the cell body membranes of individual neurons, which receive both excitatory and inhibitory signals. These signals tend to cancel each other out, with the final amount of depolarization depending on the mix of the signals received.

11. Drugs affect body functions by interfering with the normal activity of neurotransmitters. In this way, drugs affect communication between neurons, or between neurons and muscles or glands.

12. Psychoactive drugs are chemical substances that affect neurotransmitter transmission in specific parts of the brain. Some psychoactive drugs are used medically to alter the mood or to treat diseases or disorders. However, many psychoactive drugs are used for nonmedical reasons, are taken in doses that may cause damage to the body, and often result in personally destructive, antisocial, and crime-related behaviors. The chronic use of psychoactive drugs results in drug addiction, which is a compulsive urge to continue using the drug, physical and/or psychological dependence on the drug, and a tendency to increase the strength (dosage) of the drug.

13. Major classes of psychoactive drugs are depressants (sedative-hypnotics, alcohol), opiates (opium, morphine), stimulants (amphetamines, cocaine), and hallucinogens (LSD, marijuana).

1. What do neurons and hormones have in common? How are they different?

2. If you spill hot coffee on your hand, you quickly jerk your hand away. What type of neuron responded to the hot coffee first?

3. Is the nerve impulse a chemical reaction? Explain the nature of such an impulse as you understand it.

4. Explain the term *resting potential*. What creates it, and why is it important?

5. Explain how a nerve impulse travels through the body.

6. What is saltatory conduction? Explain how it works and what advantages it offers.

7. You decide to move your finger, and it moves. Explain how your nervous system communicated your decision to the muscles in your finger.

8. In question 7, explain why your finger muscles stopped contracting when you wanted them to stop.

9. Why are neurons of the central nervous system called *integrators*? What do they integrate?

10. A drug may cause decreased communication between neurons or between neurons and muscles or glands. By what common action do drugs cause such varied effects?

11. Why do you think that psychoactive drugs are among the most commonly abused type of drug?

12. Can you hypothesize a link between drug tolerance and increased criminal or antisocial behavior among long-term addicts?

13. Susan takes sleeping pills regularly with no ill effects. She assumes that having a few drinks at a party is not overly dangerous either and plans to still use her regular bedtime sedative. Do you agree with her logic?

14. How do cocaine and amphetamines affect neurotransmitters, such as norepinphrine and dopamine?

15. Some people claim that marijuana is not an addicitve psychoactive drug since it does not cause physical addiction to the substance. How might you refute this argument?

1. If you take an addictive drug like heroin or cocaine, your nervous system soon becomes addicted to it. When the brains of addicts are examined closely, it is found that the brain neurons have greatly increased numbers of protein receptors for the addcitive drug. What does the number of drug-specific receptors in neuron membranes have to do with addiction?

2. There has been much debate in the last decade regarding the legalization of drugs to remove the criminal element present in the cycle of drug abuse. This has been tried in some countries, the Netherlands, and parts of Switzerland for example. In small groups, gather and discuss the following points:

   a. Are all antisocial and criminal behaviors linked to drug abuse due merely to difficulty in drug acquisition?

   b. Alcohol is a legally available psychoactive drug. What antisocial and criminal effects are still seen due to its abuse?

   c. What problems do you find in our society's reaction to drug abuse? What course of action do you feel might help curb drug abuse in future generations?

Dunant, Y., & Israel, M. (1985, April). The release of acetylcholine. *Scientific American*, pp. 58-66.
This article challenges the accepted theory that acetylcholine is emitted by synaptic vesicles.

Kuffler, S.W., & Nicholls, J.G. (1984). *From neuron to brain: A cellular approach to the function of the nervous system.* ed2, Sunderland, Mass: Sinauer Associates, Inc.
This is a superb overview of the mechanisms of nerve excitation and transmission.

Morell, P., & Norton, W.T. (1980, May). Myelin. *Scientific American*, pp. 88-118.
This article still reflects current thought. It describes the composition of myelin, its synthesis, and how myelination increases the conduction velocity.

Reynolds, B.A., & Weiss, S. (1992, March 27). Generation of neurons and astrocytes from isolated cells of the adult mammalian central nervous system. *Science*, pp. 170-1710.
The development of mammalian neurons is believed to end just after birth. New research, however, shows that some neurons can be grown in vitro (in a test tube) with the help of epidermal growth factor.

12 The Nervous System

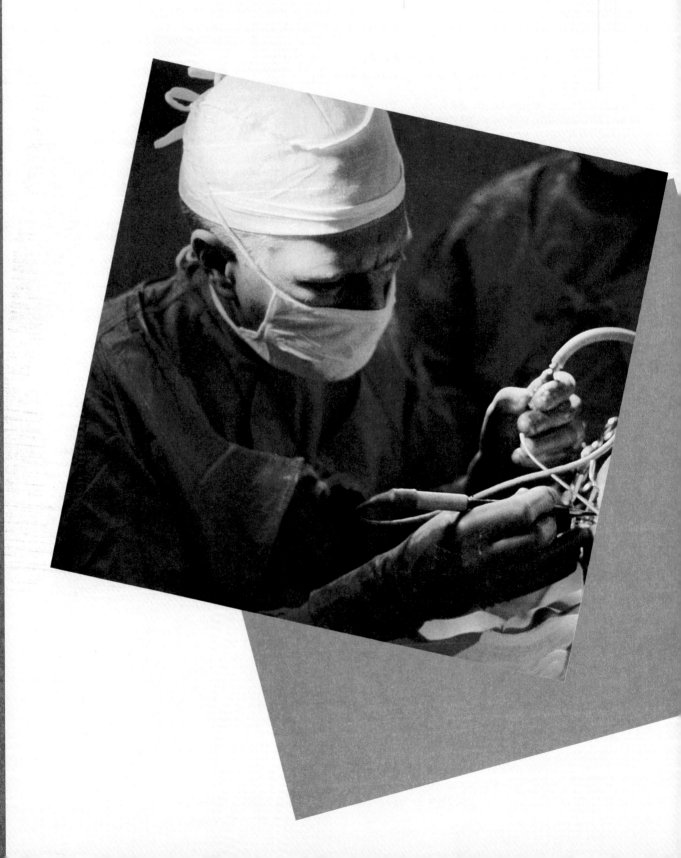

A brain transplant? Science fiction, of course. But scientists are performing types of experimental brain surgery today that would have seemed like science fiction only a decade ago. One of these intricate procedures is a tissue transplant called *brain grafting.*

Brain grafting involves taking tissue from another part of the body, like adrenal tissue found atop the kidneys, and surgically implanting it in part of the brain. This tissue takes over the function of brain tissue that is not working properly. One example of the use of this procedure is in patients with Parkinson's disease.

Parkinson's disease is a progressive disorder of the nervous system that affects approximately 50,000 Americans each year. It develops when one part of the brain does not produce enough of a neurotransmitter called *dopamine.* The disease first causes muscle tremors, resulting in uncontrolled movement such as shaking of the hands or arms. After awhile the muscles become rigid, and the victim can no longer write, eat, or perform other similar tasks. Medications help some persons but are not a cure.

In their search for alternative therapies, researchers transplanted minute bits of tissue from the adrenal glands into a part of the brain that helps coordinate movement. The adrenal glands, interestingly, manufacture dopamine as an intermediate in the production of other hormones. Early results of this transplant therapy have shown near-miraculous improvement in patients with Parkinson's. Scientists are now studying these first transplant patients to collect long-term data on the positive and negative effects of this procedure.

The organization of the nervous system

The brain is only one part of the complex network of neurons known as the **nervous system** (Figure 12-1). One job of the nervous system is to gather information about the body's internal and external environments. The nervous system then performs its other job—processing and responding to the information it has gathered. These nervous system responses are nerve impulses—commands sent out to the body's muscles and glands, directing them to react in an appropriate way.

Structurally, the nervous system can be divided into two main parts (Figure 12-1): (1) the **central nervous system**—the site of information processing within the nervous system, which is made up of the **brain** and **spinal cord,** and (2) the **peripheral nervous system**—an information highway made up of nerves that bring messages to and from the brain and spinal cord. The nerves of the peripheral nervous system are made up of the long cell processes of nerve cells (nerve fibers), support cells (see Chapter 11), connective tissue, and blood vessels. The nerves of the peripheral nervous system contain the nerve fibers of two different types of neurons: **sensory neurons,** which transmit information to the central nervous system, and **motor neurons,** which transmit commands away from the central nervous system (Figure 12-2). Sensory neurons are also called **afferent neurons,** from the Latin prefix *affero* meaning "going toward." Motor neurons are also called **efferent neurons,** from the Latin prefix *effero* meaning "going away from."

FIGURE 12-1 The human nervous system.
The central nervous system is shown in green and the peripheral nervous system in gold.

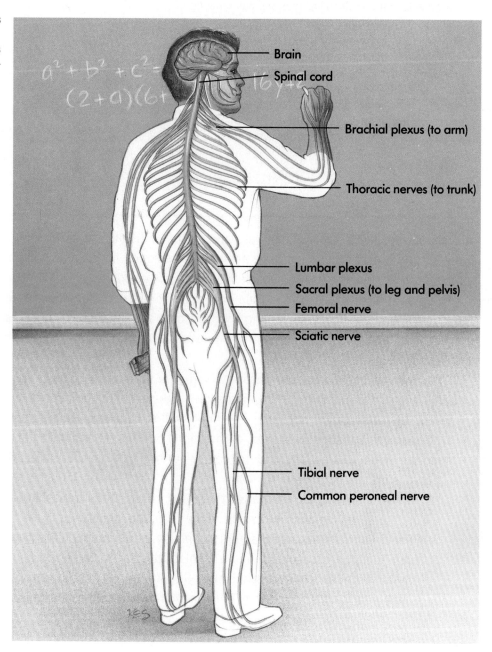

Brain

Spinal cord

Brachial plexus (to arm)

Thoracic nerves (to trunk)

Lumbar plexus

Sacral plexus (to leg and pelvis)

Femoral nerve

Sciatic nerve

Tibial nerve

Common peroneal nerve

▼▼The human nervous system is made up of the central nervous system, consisting of the brain and the spinal cord, and the peripheral nervous system. Within the peripheral nervous system, sensory pathways transmit information to the central nervous system, and motor pathways transmit commands from it.

One group of motor neurons controls **voluntary responses,** such as coordinating the movement of muscles in your legs so that you can cross the street. These responses are called voluntary because you consciously choose whether or not to do this activity. Motor neurons that control voluntary responses make up the **somatic nervous system.** The word *somatic* means "body" and refers to the fact that these neurons carry messages to your skeletal muscles—those that move the parts of your body. In addition, certain voluntary activities that may seem somewhat out of your control, such as blinking and breathing, are also directed by the somatic nervous system. Such activities are actually **reflexes,** automatic responses to stimuli that are mediated by the spinal cord or lower portions of the brain—those closest to the spinal cord.

Another group of motor neurons carries messages that control **involuntary responses.** These responses include such activities as mixing the food in your stomach with acid and enzymes after a meal, and pumping adrenaline into your bloodstream when you dodge an oncoming car. Motor neurons that carry messages about involuntary activities make up the **autonomic nervous system.** The word *autonomic* comes from Greek words meaning "self" (*auto*) "governing"

(nomos). This portion of the nervous system, then, literally takes care of you—by itself! In general, it works to promote homeostasis (a "steady state") within your body. The autonomic nervous system accomplishes this feat by carrying messages that speed up or slow down the activities of your glands, heart muscle, and smooth muscles such as those found in the digestive, excretory, and circulatory systems. In fact, these opposing messages are carried on separate neurons, dividing the autonomic nervous system functionally into two parts: the sympathetic and parasympathetic systems. (The effect of nerve impulses from each of these systems on various organs is shown in Figure 12-13.) An overview of the relationships of the various parts of the nervous system is shown in Figure 12-2.

▼▼One group of motor neurons makes up the somatic nervous system and controls voluntary responses. Another group of motor neurons makes up the autonomic nervous system and controls involuntary responses.

The central nervous system

In many ways, your central nervous system can be compared to the central processing unit (CPU) of your computer. Without your CPU, input (what you type on the keyboard, for example) is not processed by any of the programs in your computer. Therefore you will have no output either

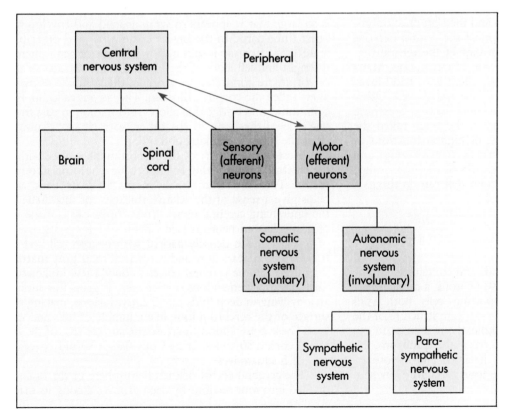

FIGURE 12-2 The organization of the human nervous system.
The nervous system is divided into two parts: the central nervous system and the peripheral nervous system. The central nervous system is composed of the brain and spinal cord. The peripheral nervous system is composed of sensory pathways that transmit information to the central nervous system and motor pathways that transmit information away from the central nervous system.

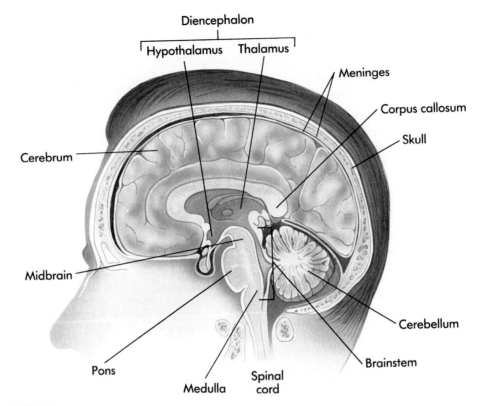

FIGURE 12-3 The human brain.
The brain has four main parts, each with different functions: the cerebrum, the cerebellum, the diencephalon, and the brainstem.

on your monitor or from your printer. In a similar but much more complex way, your brain and spinal cord make sense of incoming sensory information and then produce outgoing motor impulses. This function of the central nervous sytem is called **integration.** Each part of the central nervous system plays its own unique role in integration. Many simple nervous reactions, such as pulling your hand away from a hot stove, are integrated in the spinal cord. Other more complex nervous system reactions such as breathing are controlled in a lower portion of the brain called the *brainstem.* And the most complex or highest functions of the nervous system, such as thinking, remembering, and feeling, are all integrated in a portion of the brain called the *cerebrum* . . . a part of the brain that can do things a computer will *never* be able to do!

The brain

Your brain weighs about 3 pounds and contains an amazing 100 billion (100,000,000,000) neurons, a number that does not include neuroglial (supporting) cells. Both types of cells work together to form the intricate structure of the brain. Although a complicated whole, the human brain can be described as having four main parts: the **cerebrum,** the **cerebellum,** the **diencephalon** (thalamus and hypothalamus), and the **brainstem.** These four parts are shown in Figure 12-3.

The cerebrum

The cerebrum, the dominant part of the human brain, is so large that it appears to wrap around and envelop the other three parts. In the brains of humans (and other primates) the cerebrum is split into two halves, or hemispheres, the right and left sides of the brain. These two sides of the cerebrum are connected by a single, thick bundle of nerve fibers called the **corpus callosum.** The corpus callosum is a communication bridge that allows information to pass from one side of the brain to the other, so each side "knows" what the other is thinking and doing.

Most of the activity of the cerebrum takes place within the **cerebral cortex,** a thin layer of tissue that forms its outer surface. The word *cortex* actually means "rind" or "bark" and helps give a sense of the relative thickness of this tissue to the underlying cerebral tissue. Your cortex cap is made up of unmyelinated neurons (see Chapter 11 for a discussion of myelin) and is densely packed with neuron cell bodies. It therefore appears gray and is referred to as **gray matter.**

Although the cerebral cortex is only a few millimeters thick, it has a tremendous surface area. It gains this surface area by lying in deep folds called **convolutions,** making the surface of the cerebrum look like a jumble of hills and valleys. These convolutions increase the surface area of the cerebral cortex 30 times. If laid out flat, it would cover an area of 5 square feet!

The cerebral cortex of each hemisphere of the brain is divided into four sections by deep grooves among its many

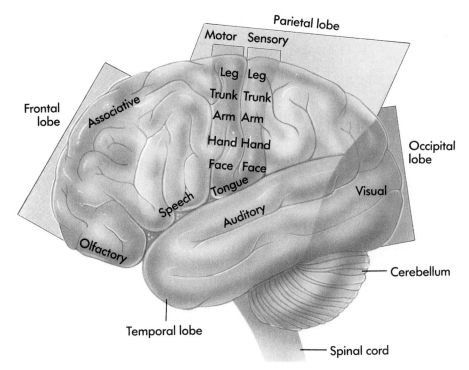

FIGURE 12-4 The cerebral cortex. The cerebral cortex has four sections: the frontal, parietal, temporal, and occipital lobes. Each of these lobes is responsible for various motor, sensory, and associative activities.

convolutions. These four sections are called the **frontal, parietal, temporal,** and **occipital lobes** (Figure 12-4). By examining the effect of injuries to particular sites on the cerebrum, scientists were first able to determine the approximate location of the various activities of each lobe of the cerebral cortex. More recently, using positron emission tomography (PET) scans, researchers have been able to determine more specifically the areas of the cerebral cortex that are used during various activities. Figure 12-5 shows a series of PET scan photos of the brain of a person performing a series of intellectual tasks related to words. These photos show the increase in blood flow that occurs at the part of the brain performing the task.

There are three major types of activities that take place within the lobes of the cerebral cortex: motor, sensory, and association activity (see Figure 12-4). The **motor area,** the part of the brain that sends messages to move your skeletal muscles, straddles the rearmost portion of the frontal lobe. Each point on its surface is associated with the movement of a different part of the body (Figure 12-6). Right behind the motor area, on the leading edge of the parietal lobe, lies the **sensory area.** Each point on the surface of the sensory area represents sensory receptors from a different part of the body, such as the pressure sensors of the fingertips and the taste receptors of the tongue. Other sensory areas are located on other lobes. For example, the auditory area lies within the temporal lobe; different surface regions of this area correspond to different tonal patterns and rhythms.

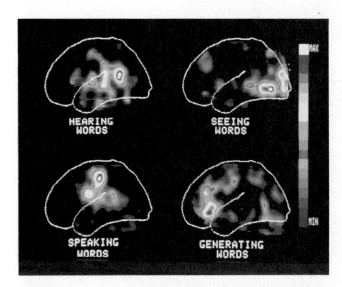

FIGURE 12-5 Visualizing brain activity. These PET scans show the areas of the brain that are most active during varied intellectual tasks related to words. Red indicates the most intense activity; blue the least.

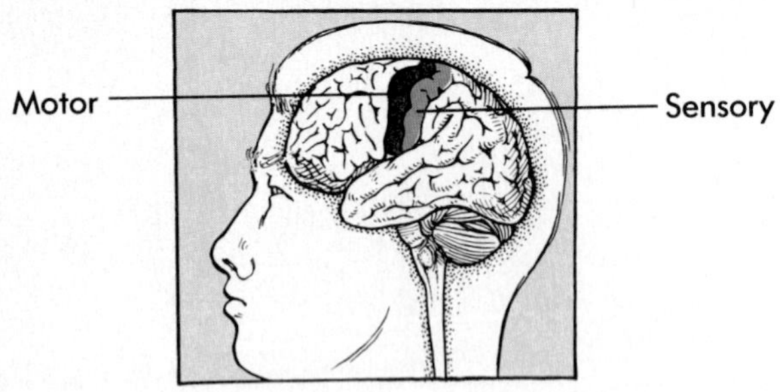

FIGURE 12-6 Motor and sensory regions of the cerebral cortex. Each region of the cerebral cortex is associated with a different part of the human body.

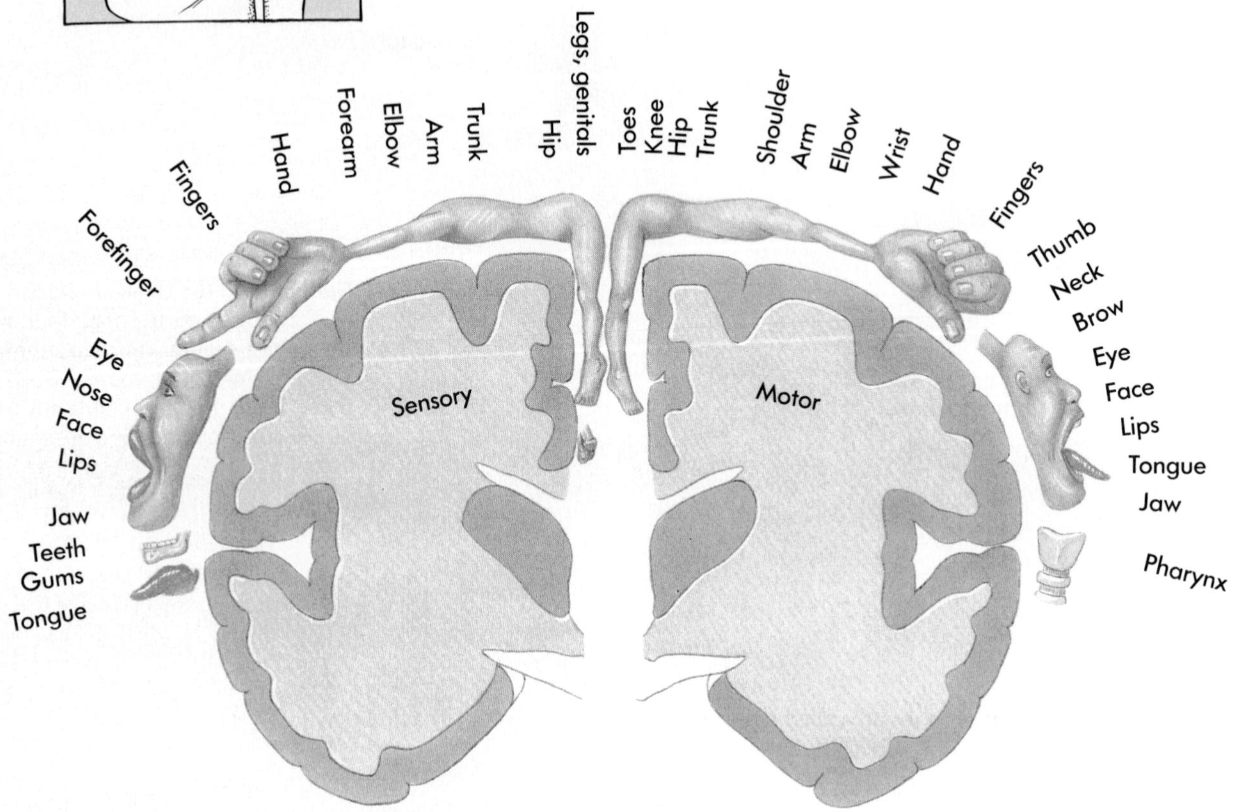

The visual area lies on the occipital lobe, with different sites corresponding to different positions on the retina.

The remaining areas within the cerebral cortex are referred to as **association areas.** These areas appear to be the site of higher cognitive activities, such as planning and contemplation. The associative cortex represents a far greater portion of the total cortex in primates than it does in any other mammals and reaches its greatest extent in human beings. In a mouse, for example, 95% of the surface of the cerebral cortex is occupied by motor and sensory areas. In humans, only 5% of the surface is devoted to motor and sensory functions; the remainder is associative cortex.

The cerebral cortex is the major site of higher cognitive processes such as sense perception, thinking, learning, and memory. It makes up a thin layer on the surface of the cerebrum, the largest and most dominant part of the brain.

Although each hemisphere of the cerebrum contains motor, sensory, and association areas, the hemispheres are responsible for different associative activities. The right side of the cerebrum controls spatial relationships, musical and artistic ability, and expression of emotions. You might think of it as your "artistic" and "visual" side. The left side controls speech, writing, logical thought, and mathematical ability. It is your "logical" or "verbal" side. Injury to the left hemisphere of the cerebrum, for example, often results in the partial or total loss of speech, but a similar injury to the right side does not. Also, several speech centers control different aspects of speech. An injury to one speech center produces halting but correct speech; injury to another speech center produces fluent, grammatical, but meaningless speech; and injury to a third center destroys speech altogether. Injuries to other sites on the surface of the brain's left hemisphere result in impairment of the ability to read, write, or do arithmetic. Comparable injuries to the right hemisphere have very different effects, resulting in impairment of three-dimensional vision, musical ability, and the ability to recognize patterns and solve inductive problems. The significance of this clustering of associative activities in different areas of the brain is not clear and remains a subject of much interest.

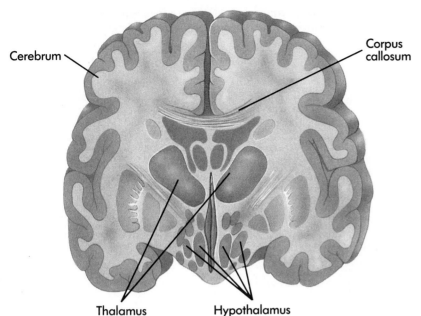

Cerebrum

Corpus callosum

Thalamus

Hypothalamus

FIGURE 12-7 The basal ganglia.
The basal ganglia, shaded in bright green and olive green, are groups of nerve cell bodies. The ganglia are connected to the thalamus and hypothalamus and play a part in controlling many subconscious behaviors.

▼▼ The right side of the cerebrum controls spatial relationships, musical and artistic ability, and expression of emotions. The left side controls speech, writing, logical thought, and mathematical ability.

In addition to the gray matter of the cerebral cortex, other masses of gray matter are located deep within the cerebrum. These islands of gray matter, shown in Figure 12-7, are often collectively referred to as the **basal ganglia.** Ganglia are groups of nerve cell bodies; these areas of gray matter are therefore described by their name as groups of nerve cell bodies located at the base, or lowest level, of the cerebrum. (Generally, however, groups of nerve cell bodies having a similar function are called **nuclei** when they are located within the central nervous system, and are called **ganglia** when they are located within the peripheral nervous system.) The basal ganglia are connected to one another, to the cerebral cortex, and to parts of the brain not yet described—the thalamus and the hypothalamus—by bridges of nerve fibers. These ganglia play important roles in the control of large, subconscious movements of the skeletal muscles, such as swinging the arms while walking. Injury to the basal ganglia can result in an array of uncontrolled muscular activity, such as shaking, aimless movements, sudden jerking, and muscle rigidity. Parkinson's disease is associated with the degeneration of parts of the basal ganglia.

▼▼ The cerebral nuclei, also called the *basal ganglia*, are groups of nerve cell bodies located at the base of the cerebrum that control large, subconscious movements of the skeletal muscles.

The cerebral cortex, or gray matter, covers an underlying solid white region of myelinated nerve fibers. These nerve fibers are the highways of the brain, bringing messages from one part of the brain to another. These highways, like the message highways in all parts of the nervous system, are composed of individual axons and long dendrites all bundled together like the strands of a telephone cable. Within the central nervous system, bundles of nerve fibers are called **tracts.** In the peripheral nervous system, they are called **nerves.** The tracts that make up the white matter of the cerebrum run in three principal directions: (1) from a place in one hemisphere of the brain to another place in the same hemisphere, (2) from a place in one hemisphere to a corresponding place in the other hemisphere, and (3) to and from the cerebrum to other parts of the brain and spinal cord.

▼▼ The cerebral white matter, which lies beneath the cerebral cortex, consists of myelinated nerve fibers that send messages from one part of the central nervous system to another.

The thalamus and hypothalamus

At the base of the cerebrum but not part of it, lying close to the basal ganglia, are paired oval masses of gray matter called the **thalamus.** A view of these nuclei in Figure 12-7 shows them connected by a bridge of gray matter and indicates how the thalamus—meaning "inner chamber"—got its name. This structure acts as a relay station for most sensory information. This information comes to the thalamus from the spinal cord and certain parts of the brain. The thalamus then sends these sensory signals to appropriate areas of the cerebral cortex. In addition, the thalamus interprets certain sensory messages such as pain, temperature, and pressure.

The **hypothalamus,** located beneath the thalamus (*hypo* means "under"), controls the activities of various body organs. Its position is shown in Figure 12-7. The hypothalamus works to maintain homeostasis, a steady state within the body, by means of its various activities such as the control of body temperature, respiration, and the heartbeat. It also directs the hormone secretions of the pituitary, which is located at the base of the brain.

The hypothalamus is linked by a network of neurons to the cerebral cortex. This network, together with the hypothalamus, is called the **limbic system.** The term *limbic* is derived from a Latin word meaning "border." As shown in Figure 12-8, the neurons of the limbic system form a ring-like border around the top of the brainstem. The operations of the limbic system are responsible for many of the most deep-seated drives and emotions of vertebrates, including pain, anger, sexual drive, hunger, thirst, and pleasure.

The thalamus and hypothalamus are masses of gray matter that lie at the base of the cerebrum. The thalamus receives sensory stimuli, interprets some of these stimuli, and sends the remaining sensory messages to appropriate locations in the cerebrum. The hypothalamus controls the activities of various body organs and the secretion of certain hormones.

Solving the Mystery of Alzheimer's Disease

Alzheimer's disease was first described in 1901 by a Swiss psychiatrist, Dr. Alois Alzheimer. One of Dr. Alzheimer's patients, aged 51, was having substantial memory difficulties. She continued to deteriorate, forgetting words and losing her ability to reason. She died 4 years later. At the autopsy, the woman's brain was found to be riddled with lesions, spaces where nerve cells had died.

The disease currently affects an estimated 2 million Americans. It is characterized by a gradual loss of memory and reasoning. Affected individuals cannot remember things that they heard or saw just a few minutes previously. They have trouble finding their way around and eventually forget how to talk, to feed themselves, even to swallow. There is no treatment.

Because Alzheimer's is most common among old people, doctors at first believed Alzheimer's to be a normal part of old age, as the brain simply wore out. Evidence soon mounted, however, that it was a genetic disorder—Alzheimer's showed up most often in particular families, for example. Studying how it is inherited, researchers soon focused on two human chromosomes, 19 and 21. Many if not all Alzheimer's cases could be linked to one of these two chromosomes.

In 1991, researchers identified the "Alzheimer's gene" on chromosome 21. They found that a single point mutation in this gene can lead to Alzheimer's disease. The same mutation identified was identified in two unrelated families who have Alzheimer's and does not occur in people who do not have the disorder. Although other genes (such as the one on chro-mosome 19) may also cause Alzheimer's, this gene offers the first clear look at the cause of the disorder.

What is the normal function of this gene? The gene at fault encodes a component of nerve cell membranes called *amyloid protein.* Amyloid is found in every nerve cell, but in Alzheimer's patients its synthesis goes awry, spitting out pieces of amyloid that pile up in sticky masses on the cell surface and eventually kill the nerve cell. The mutation appears to make the amyloid protein more fragile and liable to be chopped into fragments that accumulate in the brain.

As the population ages and people begin to live long enough for defective amyloid genes to begin their deadly work, Alzheimer's disease is becoming more common (Figure 12-A). It now affects 20% of the population that reaches age 85. Researchers are now focusing their efforts on finding ways to block the formation of amyloid fragments or their attachment to the surface of brain cells. For example, researchers are searching for ways to inhibit the enzyme that chops off the amyloid fragments. A cure will not be available tomorrow, but researchers finally seem to be on the road to success.

FIGURE 12-A The number of people over age 65 is steadily increasing. Therefore Alzheimer's disease will affect an increasing number of people unless a cure is found.

The cerebellum

The cerebellum is a relatively large part of the brain, weighing slightly less than half a pound. It is located below the occipital lobes of the cerebrum, as shown in Figure 12-3. Although its name means "little cerebrum," the cerebellum does not perform cerebral functions. Instead, it coordinates subconscious movements of the skeletal muscles. Sensory nerves bring information to the cerebellum about the position of body parts relative to one another, the state of relaxation or contraction of the skeletal muscles, and the general position of the body in relation to the outside world. These data are gathered in the cerebellum and synthesized. The cerebellum then issues orders to motor neurons that result in smooth, well-coordinated muscular movements, contributing to overall muscle tone, posture, balance, and equilibrium.

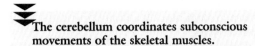

The cerebellum coordinates subconscious movements of the skeletal muscles.

The brainstem

If you think of the brain as being shaped somewhat like a mushroom, the cerebrum, thalamus, and hypothalamus would be its cap. The brainstem would be the mushroom's stalk (see Figure 12-3). Its 3 inches of length consist of three parts—the midbrain, pons, and medulla. Each part makes up about an equal length of the brainstem and contains tracts of nerve fibers that bring messages to and from the spinal cord. In addition, each portion of the brainstem contains nuclei that govern important reflex (automatic) activities of the body. Many of the cranial nerves, nerves that enter the brain rather than the spinal cord, enter at the brainstem. These cranial nerves bring messages to and from the regulatory centers of the brainstem or use the brainstem as a relay station. These nerves can be seen in Figure 12-9 and are discussed in more detail later in the chapter.

At the top of the brainstem sits the **midbrain**, extending down from the lower portion of the thalamus and hypothalamus about an inch—approximately the distance from the tip of your thumb to its first knuckle. If you were

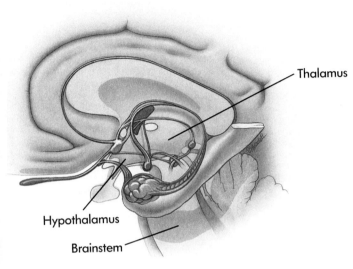

FIGURE 12-8 The limbic system.
Shaded in blue in this diagram, the limbic system is responsible for many of your most deep-seated drives and emotions.

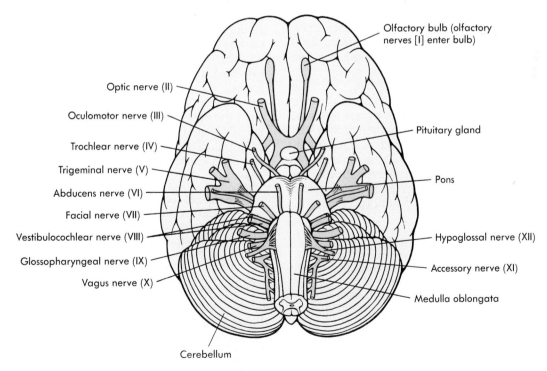

FIGURE 12-9 A view of the brain from its underside.
In this view, the origins of the cranial nerves can be clearly seen.

to cut open the midbrain, you would see both white and gray matter. The white matter consists of nerve tracts that connect the upper parts of the brain (cerebrum, thalamus, and hypothalamus) with lower parts of the brain (pons and medulla). In addition, the midbrain contains nuclei that act as reflex centers for movements of the eyeballs, head, and trunk in response to sights, sounds, and various other stimuli. For example, if a plate falls off the counter behind you, you probably turn around quickly and automatically. That is your midbrain at work.

The term **pons** means "bridge," and it is actually two bridges. One bridge consists of horizontal tracts that extend to the cerebellum, connecting this part of the brain to other parts and to the spinal cord. The other bridge consists of longitudinal tracts that connect the midbrain and structures above to the medulla and spinal cord below. In addition, the gray matter of the pons contains nuclei that work with certain nuclei in the medulla to help control respiration.

The **medulla,** the lowest portion of the brainstem, is continuous with the spinal cord below. Because of its location, a large portion of the medulla consists of tracts of neurons that bring messages up from the spinal cord and others that take messages down to the spinal cord. Interestingly, most of these tracts cross over one another within the medulla. Therefore sensory information from the right side of the body is perceived in the left side of the brain and vice versa. Likewise, the right side of the brain sends messages to the left side of the body; the left side of the brain controls the right side. In addition to these tracts, the medulla contains reflex centers that regulate heartbeat, control the diameter of blood vessels, and adjust the rhythm of breathing. Centers there also control less vital functions such as coughing, sneezing, and vomiting.

Throughout the entire length of the brainstem, but concentrated in the medulla, weaves a complex network of neurons called the **reticular formation.** All of the sensory systems have nerve fibers that feed into this system, which serves to "wiretap" all of the incoming and outgoing communications channels of the brain. In doing so, the reticular formation monitors information concerning the incoming stimuli and identifies important ones. The reticular formation also plays a role in consciousness, increasing the activity level of many parts of the brain when aroused and decreasing in activity during periods of sleep. Interestingly, this is the part of the brain that causes a knockout during boxing. When the head is twisted sharply and suddenly during a punch to the jaw, the brainstem (and reticular formation) is twisted, resulting in unconsciousness.

⏷⏷

The brainstem, consisting of the midbrain, pons, and medulla, contains tracts of nerve fibers that bring messages to and from the spinal cord. In addition, nuclei located in various parts of the brainstem control important body reflexes such as the rhythm of the heartbeat and rate of breathing.

The spinal cord

The central nervous system also includes the brain's extension, the spinal cord. The spinal cord runs down the neck

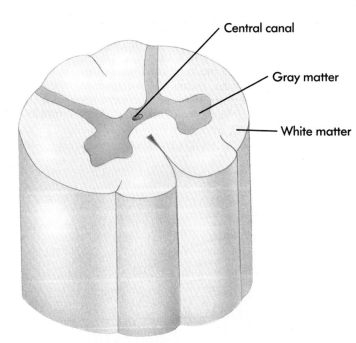

FIGURE 12-10 Section through the spinal cord. The location of the gray matter, the white matter, and the central canal is shown here.

and back within an inner "tunnel" of the vertebral column, or spine. This tunnel is created by the stacking of vertebrae one on another, with their central spaces, or **foramina** (singular **foramen**), in alignment with one another. This bony casing protects the spinal cord from injury, just as the bones of the skull protect the brain.

The spinal cord receives information from the body by means of **spinal nerves** (see Figure 12-1). It carries this information to the brain along organized tracts of myelinated nerve fibers (white matter) and similarly sends information from the brain out to the body. In addition, the gray matter of the spinal cord integrates responses to certain kinds of stimuli. These integrative pathways are called **reflex arcs** and are discussed in more detail later in the chapter.

⏷⏷

The spinal cord, the part of the central nervous system that runs down the neck and back, receives information from the body, carries this information to the brain, and sends information from the brain to the body.

The white matter tracts of the spinal cord, unlike the white matter of the brain, are located on the exterior of the spinal cord with gray matter in the center (Figure 12-10). (The brain, as discussed earlier, is covered with gray matter, which surrounds the white matter hidden below.) In addition, the spinal cord has a tiny central canal that pierces its length. This tube-like space is filled with **cerebrospinal fluid** and is continuous with fluid-filled spaces, or **ventri-**

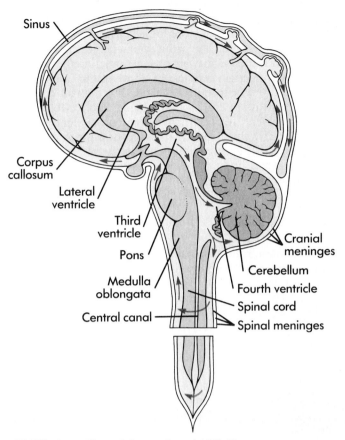

FIGURE 12-11 Flow of the cerebrospinal fluid.
Arrows indicate the direction of flow. Notice that the fluid travels around the cerebrum and into the ventricles within the brain. The cerebrospinal fluid acts like a shock absorber for the brain and is also the medium in which gases such as CO_2 dissolve. The amount of gases in the cerebrospinal fluid triggers the cells in the brain to adjust such factors as the heartbeat and breathing rates.

Labels on figure:
Sinus
Corpus callosum
Lateral ventricle
Third ventricle
Pons
Medulla oblongata
Central canal
Cranial meninges
Cerebellum
Fourth ventricle
Spinal cord
Spinal meninges

cles, in the brain. (The arrows in Figure 12-11 show the direction of flow of this fluid.) The cerebrospinal fluid is a filtrate of the blood, formed by specialized structures in the ventricles. This fluid acts as a shock absorber, cushioning the brain and the spinal cord. In fact, your brain is actually *floating* in this fluid, although its volume would barely fill an average-sized glass. In addition, the cerebrospinal fluid brings nutrients, hormones, and white blood cells to different parts of the brain.

As well as being encased in the skull and vertebrae and cushioned by the cerebrospinal fluid, both the brain and spinal cord are protected by three layers of membranes called the **meninges.** The outermost of these layers is called the *dura mater,* from the medieval Latin meaning "tough mother." Surrounding the brain, the dura mater is made up of two parts: one that adheres to the inner side of the bones of the cranium and another that lies closer to the brain. Surrounding the spinal cord, however, the dura mater is only a single layer. In between it and the bones of the vertebrae is a space filled with fat, connective tissue, and blood ves-

sels called the *epidural* (outside the dura) *space.* At the level of the lower back, the epidural space is where anesthetics are injected to numb the lower body for certain operations or childbirth. Another space exists between the middle (arachnoid layer) and inner (pia mater) membranes of the meninges. The cerebrospinal fluid circulates within this space, called the *subarachnoid space.* The subarachnoid space is continuous with the central canal of the vertebral column and the ventricles of the brain (see Figure 12-11).

> The brain and spinal cord are protected by a cushion of fluid called the *cerebrospinal fluid,* layers of membranous coverings called the meninges, and bones of the skull and vertebral column.

The peripheral nervous system

Just as your central nervous system can be compared to the CPU of your computer, your peripheral nervous system can be compared to the cables that connect the CPU to the other pieces of hardware—the peripherals—that make up your computer. In your computer, connector cables carry information to the monitor to be visualized on the screen or to the printer to be printed. So too the nerve "cables" of your peripheral nervous system bring information to your muscles, instructing them to contract and relax in patterns that result in the integrated and flowing movements of your body. For example, food in your stomach (the input) sends signals along your peripheral nervous system to the medulla to be interpreted, resulting in the release of gastric juice and the churning of the muscular stomach walls (the output). These are only two examples of how the peripheral nervous system works to connect the integrative portion of your nervous system with its **receptors** (structures that detect stimuli) and **effectors** (muscles and glands that respond to that stimuli).

Sensory pathways

Seeing a sunset, hearing a symphony, experiencing pain—all these stimuli travel along sensory neurons to the central nervous system and arrive there in the same form—as nerve impulses. Put simply, every nerve impulse is identical to every other one. How, then, does the brain distinguish between pleasure and pain or sight and sound? Interestingly, the information that the brain derives from sensory input is based solely on the source of the impulse and its frequency. Thus if the auditory nerve is artificially stimulated, the central nervous system perceives the stimulation as sound. If the optic nerve is artificially stimulated in exactly the same manner and degree, the stimulation is perceived as a flash of light. Increasing the intensity of the stimulation of either receptor will result (within limits) in an increase in the frequency of nerve impulses and therefore produce a perception of a brighter light or a louder noise.

Many kinds of receptors have evolved among vertebrates, with each receptor sensitive to a different aspect of the environment. Sensory receptors are able to change specific stimuli into nerve impulses by having low thresholds for specific types of stimuli and high thresholds for others. Receptors in the retina of your eye, for example, have a low threshold for light. Appropriate stimuli open ion channels within the membrane of the receptor cell, thus depolarizing it (see Chapter 11). This depolarization is called a **generator potential.** When the generator potential reaches the threshold level, it initiates an action potential in the sensory neurons with which the receptor synapses. Simple receptors, such as pain receptors in the skin, may be simply the dendrite endings of sensory neurons. The generator potential then initiates an action potential along that same neuron.

Sensory nerve fibers that travel directly to the brain are axons, not dendrites as in the spinal nerves. The cell bodies and dendrites of these sensory neurons are located outside the brain in the sense organ. Their axons are bundled into groups with other sensory nerve fibers arising from the same area to form certain **cranial nerves.** The cranial nerves that conduct only sensory stimuli are those associated with sight, sound, smell, and equilibrium, such as cranial nerve I (see Figure 12-9); the olfactory nerve, which brings in "smell" messages from your nose; cranial nerve II, the optic nerve, which brings in "sight" messages from your eyes; and cranial nerve VIII, which brings impulses from your ears regarding hearing and balance. Other cranial nerves called **mixed nerves** are made up of both sensory (incoming or afferent) and motor (outgoing or efferent) nerve fibers, such as cranial nerve VII, which shuttles messages to and from your salivary and tear glands, and cranial nerve X (the vagus nerve), which regulates the function of your heart rate, respiration rate, and digestive activities. The motor nerve fibers of cranial nerves are also axons; the cell bodies of these motor neurons are located within the brain. Cranial nerve XII, which stimulates movement in your tongue, carries outgoing (motor) messages only.

Sensory and motor nerve fibers that travel directly to the spinal cord make up the spinal nerves (Figure 12-12). Nerve fibers that serve the same general area of the body, whether of sensory or motor neurons, are bundled together to form these nerves (see Figure 12-1). Thus all spinal nerves are mixed nerves. Close to the spinal cord, however, motor and sensory fibers separate from one another. The sensory (afferent) fibers are myelinated axon-like dendrites that extend from the source of stimulation (your fingers or toes, for example) to a swelling near their entrance to the dorsal (back) side of the spinal cord. This swelling is a ganglion containing the nerve cell bodies of these sensory neurons. The short axons of these neurons extend from this ganglion to the gray matter of the spinal cord. Here, the axon ends of these sensory neurons synapse with neurons that play a role in integrating incoming messages with outgoing responses.

Integration

"Integrating" neurons, or **interneurons,** receive incoming messages and send appropriate outgoing messages in response. Interneurons extend from the spinal cord to the brain, make up part of the brain tissue itself, and in the case of certain reflex pathways, are located within the gray matter of the spinal cord. The pathway of a nerve impulse from stimulus to response may involve a single interneuron, as in the case of certain reflexes. In a few of the simplest reflexes, a sensory neuron may synapse directly with a motor neuron, with no interneuron(s) playing a role. Most pathways, however, involve many interneurons that, in sequence, receive the incoming message, direct it to other interneurons for interpretation (such as specific areas of the cerebrum), and bring the outgoing message to the appropriate motor neurons.

Motor pathways

The short dendrites of spinal motor neurons, located in anterior portions of the gray matter of the spinal cord, synapse with interneurons. These dendrites then conduct the impulses picked up from the interneurons to their cell bodies located within the same area of gray matter of the spinal cord. The nerve impulse sweeps along the membrane of the axon of each motor neuron to effectors: muscles or glands that produce a response. Motor pathways to skeletal muscles contain a single motor neuron; motor pathways to smooth and cardiac muscles and to glands are made up of a series of two motor neurons.

The bundles of axons leaving the spinal cord join with the dendrites of sensory neurons entering the same level of the cord, forming spinal nerves. A total of 31 pairs of spinal nerves brings messages to and from specific areas of the body. Figure 12-1 shows the approximate location of the spinal nerves and, in general, the areas of the body that they serve.

Sensory receptors change stimuli into nerve impulses. The nerve fibers of sensory neurons then bring this information to the brain or spinal cord where, except in the case of very simple reflexes, interneurons interpret them and send appropriate outgoing messages. The axons of motor neurons conduct these impulses to muscles and glands, the structures that effect a response.

The somatic nervous system

The central nervous system directs different types of responses in different ways. Movements of the skeletal muscles are controlled by messages from the brain and spinal cord via pathways containing a single motor neuron. These motor pathways are referred to as the *somatic nervous system.* Messages along these pathways coordinate your fingers when you grasp a pencil, spin your body when you dance, and outstretch your arms when you hug a friend. These muscular movements are primarily subject to conscious control by the associative cortex of the cerebrum. However, not all movements of the skeletal muscles are conscious. Blinking your eyes, putting one foot in front of the other when you walk, and breathing can be consciously controlled but most often take place without conscious thought.

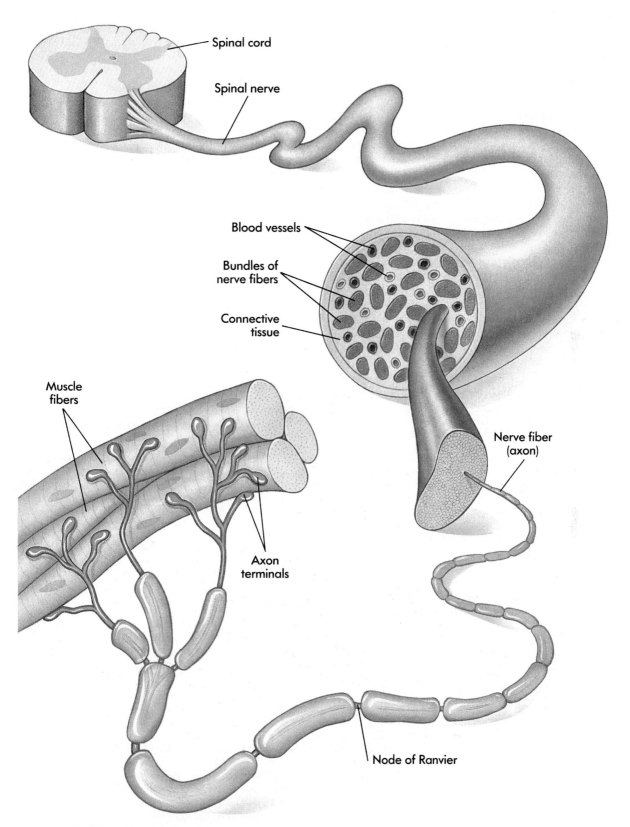

Spinal cord

Spinal nerve

Blood vessels

Bundles of
nerve fibers

Connective
tissue

Muscle
fibers

Axon
terminals

Nerve fiber
(axon)

Node of Ranvier

FIGURE 12-12 Structure of a nerve.
A nerve is composed of bundles of nerve fibers and various layers of connective tissue.

The somatic branch of the peripheral nervous system consists of motor fibers that send messages to the skeletal muscles.

A *reflex* is an automatic response to nerve stimulation. Very little, if any, integration (and certainly no thinking) takes place during reflex activity. The knee jerk is one of the simplest types of reflexes in the human body; a sensory neuron synapses directly with a motor neuron (Figure 12-13). This pathway—the pathway an impulse follows during reflex activity—is called a *reflex arc*. Simple reflex arcs such as the knee jerk are called **monosynaptic reflex arcs** (literally, "one synapse"). A monosynaptic reflex arc is not subject to control by the central nervous system. Most voluntary muscles within your body possess such monosynaptic reflex arcs, although usually in conjunction with other more complex reflex pathways. It is through these more complex paths that voluntary control is established. In the few cases in which the monosynaptic reflex arc is the only feedback loop present, its function can be clearly seen, such as in the knee jerk reaction. If the ligament just below the kneecap is struck lightly by the edge of your hand or by a doctor's rubber mallet, the resulting sudden pull stretches the muscles of the upper leg, which are attached to the ligament. Stretch receptors in these muscles immediately send an impulse along afferent nerve fibers to the spinal cord, where these fibers synapse directly with motor neurons that extend back to upper leg muscles, stimulating them to contract and the leg to jerk upward. Such reflexes play an important role in maintaining posture.

A reflex is an automatic response to nerve stimulation. The pathway of nervous activity in a reflex is called a *reflex arc*. Impulses travel along sensory neurons to the spinal cord, which sends a message out via motor neurons without involving the brain.

The autonomic nervous system

When you enter a dark movie theater, the pupils of your eyes dilate, or become larger. When you are frightened, adrenaline is pumped into your bloodstream and your heart beats faster. Neither of these reactions is governed by conscious thought—they occur automatically and involve the action of smooth muscle, cardiac muscle, or glands. The motor pathways that control such involuntary and automatic responses of the glands and nonskeletal muscles of the body are referred to as the *autonomic nervous system*. The autonomic nervous system takes your temperature, monitors your blood pressure, and sees to it that your food is properly digested. The body's internal physiological condition is thus fine tuned within relatively narrow bounds, a regulatory process called *homeostasis*.

The autonomic nervous system is made up of two divisions, the **parasympathetic nervous system** and the **sympathetic nervous system,** that act in opposition to each other, speeding up or slowing down certain bodily processes (Figure 12-14). Each of these motor pathways consists of a series of two motor neurons. In the parasympathetic system the axons of the motor neurons leaving the spinal cord extend to ganglia located near the muscles or organs they affect. In the sympathetic system the axons leav-

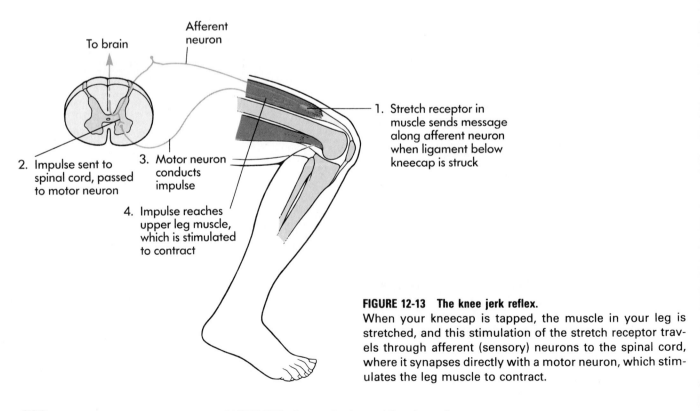

To brain

Afferent neuron

1. Stretch receptor in muscle sends message along afferent neuron when ligament below kneecap is struck

2. Impulse sent to spinal cord, passed to motor neuron

3. Motor neuron conducts impulse

4. Impulse reaches upper leg muscle, which is stimulated to contract

FIGURE 12-13   The knee jerk reflex.
When your kneecap is tapped, the muscle in your leg is stretched, and this stimulation of the stretch receptor travels through afferent (sensory) neurons to the spinal cord, where it synapses directly with a motor neuron, which stimulates the leg muscle to contract.

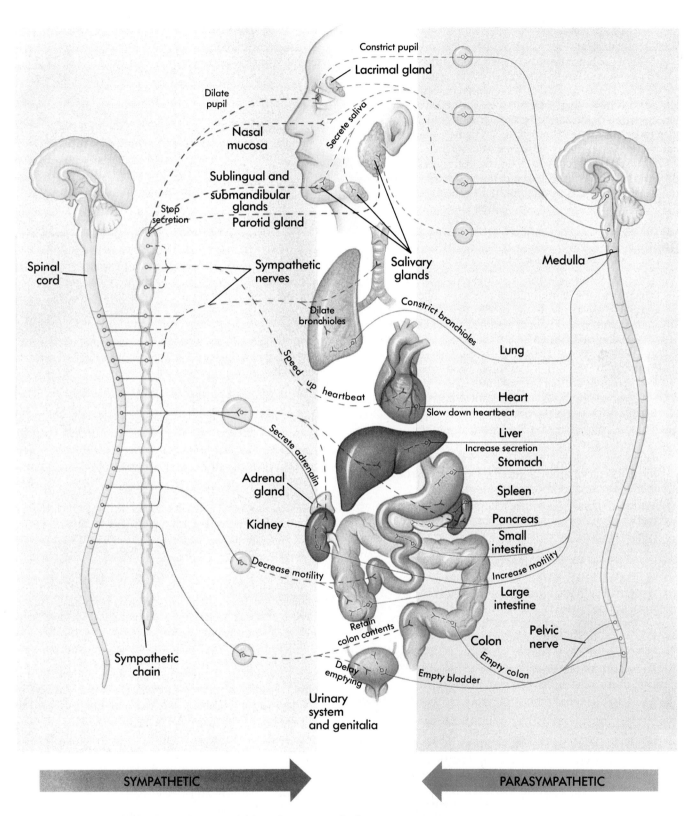

FIGURE 12-14 The sympathetic and parasympathetic nervous systems.
The ganglia of sympathetic nerves are located near the spine, and the ganglia of parasympathetic nerves are located far from the spine, near the organs they affect. A nerve
runs from both of the systems to every organ indicated, except the adrenal gland.

CHAPTER 12 The Nervous System

ing the spinal cord are much shorter and extend only to ganglia located near the vertebral column. The axons of second motor neurons in each system extend from these ganglia to their targets.

The neurotransmitters used by each of these two branches of the autonomic nervous system differ at the axon ends of the second motor neuron—at the synapse with the target organ. The actions of these different neurotransmitters oppose each other. Thus because each gland (except the inner portion of the adrenal gland), smooth muscle, and cardiac muscle is "wired" to *both* the systems, an arriving signal will either stimulate or inhibit the organ. For example, the sympathetic system speeds up the heart and slows down digestion, whereas the parasympathetic system slows down the heart and speeds up digestion. In general, the two opposing systems are organized so that the parasympathetic

system stimulates the activity of normal body functions such as the churning of the stomach, the contractions of the intestine, and the secretions of the salivary glands. The sympathetic system, on the other hand, generally mobilizes the body for greater activity, as in increased respiration or a faster heartbeat. The "decision" to stimulate or inhibit a muscle, organ, or gland is "made" by the central nervous system.

The autonomic nervous system is a branch of the peripheral nervous system that consists of two antagonistic sets of motor fibers. Messages sent along these fibers control smooth and cardiac muscle as well as glands.

Summary

1. The nervous system consists of the peripheral nervous system and the central nervous system. The peripheral nervous system, made up of the nerves of the body, gathers information about the internal and external environments and brings it to the central nervous system via sensory nerve cells. The central nervous system, made up of the brain and spinal cord, then processes and responds to that information. These responses are sent out to the body via the motor nerve cells of the peripheral nervous system.

2. The cerebrum, the dominant part of the human brain, is split into two hemispheres connected by a nerve tract called the *corpus callosum*. Each hemisphere is divided further by deep grooves into four lobes: the frontal, parietal, temporal, and occipital lobes.

3. Various cognitive activities take place in the outer gray matter of the cerebrum, or cerebral cortex. Specific sensory areas are located in the various lobes of the cortex. One large sensory area lies on the leading edge of the parietal lobe. Other sensory areas, the auditory and visual areas, lie within the temporal and occipital lobes, respectively. The motor region is mostly a part of the frontal lobe. Association areas connect all parts of the cerebral cortex and govern such functions as memory, reasoning, intelligence, and personality.

4. The cerebral white matter, myelinated nerve fibers that lie beneath the cerebral cortex, send messages from one part of the central nervous system to another.

5. The basal ganglia, groups of nerve cell bodies located at the base of the cerebrum, control large, subconscious movements of the skeletal muscles. Additional groups of nerve cell bodies also located near the base of the cerebrum but not part of it are the thalamus and the hypothalamus. These parts of the brain receive and interpret certain sensory stimuli and control the activities of various body organs and glands, respectively.

6. The cerebellum is the part of the brain that coordinates unconscious movements of the skeletal muscles.

7. The brainstem consists of three parts: the midbrain, pons, and medulla. All three parts contain nerve fibers that bring messages to and from the spinal cord. In addition, the brainstem contains groups of nerve cell bodies that control important body reflexes.

8. The spinal cord brings messages to the brain and sends messages from the brain out to the body. It also integrates the incoming and outgoing information of reflex arcs, with the exception of certain simple reflexes.

9. In the peripheral nervous system, sensory receptors change stimuli into nerve impulses. These impulses travel along the nerve fibers of sensory neurons to the brain or spinal cord. There, integrating neurons called *interneurons* interpret this sensory information and send appropriate outgoing messages. The axons of motor neurons conduct these impulses to muscles and glands, the structures that effect a response.

10. No matter what the stimulus, a nerve impulse takes the same form: depolarization of a nerve fiber membrane.

11. The motor pathways are divided into somatic pathways, which relay commands to skeletal muscles, and autonomic pathways, which stimulate the glands and other muscles of the body. The autonomic pathways consist of nerve pairs having antagonistic neurotransmitters, one of which stimulates while the other inhibits. In general, the parasympathetic nerves stimulate the activity of normal internal body functions and inhibit alarm responses, and the sympathetic nerves do the reverse.

1. Distinguish among the nervous system, central nervous system, and peripheral nervous system. What are the functions and components of each?

2. Distinguish between the somatic and autonomic nervous systems. What type of response does each control? Give an example of each type.

3. A friend accidentally steps on your foot and you quickly pull it away. Where in the nervous system do you think that this reflex is integrated?

4. A sentimental movie makes you remember your beloved grandparents. Where in the nervous system would the connection between the movie (visual) and emotional reaction be integrated?

5. Which animal would you hypothesize to have a larger portion of the cerebral cortex devoted to association areas: a chimpanzee or a dog? Why?

6. Looking at Figure 12-6, can you create a hypothesis explaining why a greater proportion of the sensory and motor area of the cerebral cortex is devoted to hands and facial structures rather than an equal distribution according to body parts? Use your own body as a model.

7. Doctors have warned parents to avoid applying their own low-fat diet to small toddlers, since a higher fat level is essential for the body's production of myelin. Why do you think this may be so important in prenatal care and in the diet of infants and toddlers?

8. Which would you hypothesize to be more similar in function; the limbic systems of a human and a lion or the associative cerebral cortex of these vertebrates? Why?

9. What is the brainstem? Name its three major components and summarize its functions.

10. If the spinal cord is severed in an injury, the closer the point of damage to the brain the more severe the disability. For example, a break near the neck may result in paralysis from the neck down. Why do you think this occurs?

11. You're studying in a quiet library. Suddenly someone drops an armful of books; you hear the loud crash and turn your head toward the noise. Explain how your sensory and motor pathways allowed you to detect and respond to this stimulus.

12. In question 11, why did you perceive this stimulus as a loud noise (rather than, say, as a bright light)?

13. Compare the effects of the parasympathetic and sympathetic nervous systems on your body. Why is this important?

1. The organs of your body are controlled by two branches of the autonomic nervous system, the sympathetic and parasympathetic. Each organ is reached by neurons from each system. Why *two* systems? Why use two neutrons to communicate with an organ rather than one?

2. People often use phrases such as "nervous person," "high strung" or "hypersensitive" to refer to others with a seemingly higher level of emotional or sensory sensitivity. Do you think that there is wide variation in levels of human nervous function? Do you have examples from your experience? How might increased sensitivity such as to cold or loud noises have been an evolutionary advantage in the survival of primitive humans? How might such sensitivity have been disadvantageous? Do you think there are similar variations between the sexes? Why?

Allport, S. (1986). *Explorers of the black box: The search for the cellular basis of memory.* New York: W.W. Norton & Co.
This is a vivid account of the pioneering studies of Eric Kandel and others in their efforts to demonstrate how we remember. Easy to read, this book shows scientists in action, gathering data and disputing among themselves about what the data mean.

Corina, D.P., Vaid, J., & Bellugi, V. (1992). The linguistic basis of left hemisphere specialization. *Science, 255,* 1258-1261.
The left hemisphere of the human brain seems to specialize in linguistics (spoken language) but not in sign language or symbolic (pantomime) language.

Kalaska, J.F., & Crammond, D.J. (1992, March 20). Cerebral cortical mechanisms of reaching mechanisms. *Science,* pp. 1517-1523.
This article reports on the role of the central nervous system in the planning and execution of a reaching movement.

Winter, P., & Miller, J. (1985, April). Anesthesiology. *Scientific American,* pp. 124-131.
This article is a clear description of how certain drugs act to block consciousness.

13 The Senses

Can the mind block out pain? These firewalkers appear not to feel the hot coals they are walking on. In 1965, Ronald Melzack and Patrick Wall described a means by which the body could short-circuit its own warning system. They called this revolutionary idea the *gate-control theory of pain*. Melzack and Wall hypothesized that signals coming down from the brain could put a stop to signals going up the spinal cord. In this way, the "gate" was shut to certain incoming sensory messages before they got to the brain. In the same way, they explained, people tune out background noise to focus on a task, or football players continue to play the game with a broken leg, not realizing their situation. Current physiological research supports the idea that various parts of the brain exert control over the perception of pain. In fact, psychologists who treat chronic pain sufferers use the brain's ability to focus on certain sensory information and screen out other data to help patients develop strategies for the control of pain.

Pain receptors are distributed widely throughout the body and are very important to your well-being; they are the body's way of knowing when it is in danger of being harmed. Simple in structure, pain receptors are the branching ends of dendrites of certain sensory neurons. These neurons bring the pain message to the spinal cord, where it is transferred to tracts of neurons that travel up the cord to the brain.

The nature of sensory communication

Pain is not a type of environmental stimulus itself but can be caused by various types of stimuli such as heat, cold, and pressure. Sensory receptors can change environmental stimuli such as these into nerve impulses. Some receptors are composed of nervous tissue; others are not but are capable of initiating a nerve impulse in an adjacent neuron. Many kinds of receptors have evolved among vertebrates with each receptor sensitive to a different aspect of the environment (Figure 13-1).

For you to be aware of, or to sense, your internal or external environment, certain events must take place. First, a change in the environment (the stimulus) must be of sufficient magnitude to open ion channels within the membrane of the receptor cell, thus depolarizing it (see Chapter 11). This depolarization is called a *generator potential*. When the generator potential reaches the threshold level, it initiates an action potential—a nerve impulse—in the sensory neurons with which the receptor synapses. In simple receptors (the dendrite endings of sensory neurons) the generator potential initiates an action potential along that same neuron. The impulse is conducted by nerve fibers to either the spinal cord or the brain.

Impulses conducted to specific sensory areas of the cerebral cortex produce conscious sensations (see Chapter 12). Only the cerebral cortex can "see" a flower, "hear" a symphony, or "feel" a paper cut. Although not a part of the cortex, the thalamus can sense pain, but it is unable to distinguish its source or intensity. Impulses that end at the spinal cord or brainstem do not produce conscious sensations. They may, however, result in reflex activity such as the rhythmic contraction of the muscles of breathing or the

FIGURE 13-1 Types of sensory information processed by sensory receptors.
A A person who feels sick is relying on information about the body's internal environment. A headache, for example, causes pain because of the activation of pain receptors located within the body.
B This dancer maintains a proper stance by using information about his position in space.
C This person is reading, using her eyes to perceive patterns of light. In this way, the reader is sensing information about the external environment.

turning of your head toward a startling noise.

Receptors provide the body with three types of information:

1. Information about the body's internal environment
2. Information about the body's position in space
3. Information about the external environment

Receptors that sense the internal environment are located deep in the body within the walls of blood vessels and organs. They tell you when you are hungry, thirsty, sick, or tired. Receptors sensitive to stimuli ouside the body are located at or near the body surface. They allow you to see, hear, taste, and feel various stimuli in the environment. Receptors that provide information about body position and movement are located in the muscles, tendons, joints, and inner ear. They tell you whether you are lying down or standing up and where the various parts of your body are in relationship to one another.

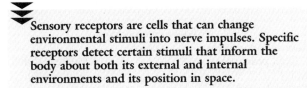

Sensory receptors are cells that can change environmental stimuli into nerve impulses. Specific receptors detect certain stimuli that inform the body about both its external and internal environments and its position in space.

Sensing the body's internal environment

Many of the neurons that monitor body functions are simply nerve endings that depolarize in response to direct physical stimulation—to temperature, to chemicals such as carbon dioxide diffusing into the nerve cell, or to a bending or stretching of the neuron cell membrane. Among the simplest of these neurons are those that report on changes in body temperature and blood chemistry.

Temperature-sensitive neurons in the hypothalamus, a tiny portion of the brain that lies above the brainstem, act as your body's thermostat. These neurons constantly take your temperature by monitoring the temperature of your blood. If the temperature of the blood rises, such as when you are sick or vigorously exercising, neurons in the hypothalamus trigger your body's heat loss mechanisms. Such mechanisms include dilating, or widening, the blood vessels closest to the skin so that excess heat can be lost to the environment. Likewise, if the temperature of the blood drops, such as when you are in a cold environment, neurons in the hypothalamus trigger your body's heat production mechanisms. Such mechanisms include shivering, a cycle of contraction and relaxation of your skeletal muscles producing body heat as a waste product of the cellular respiration that generates ATP for muscle contraction.

Other receptors are sensitive to the levels of carbon dioxide and oxygen in your blood, as well as its pH. These receptors are embedded within the walls of your arteries at several locations in the circulatory system. Bathed by the blood that flows through the arteries, these chemical receptors provide input to respiratory centers in the medulla and pons, which use this information to regulate the rate of respiration. When carbon dioxide and pH levels in the blood rise and the oxygen level falls, the respiratory centers respond by increasing the respiration rate.

Various other receptors that sense the environment within your body have membranes whose ion channels open in response to mechanical force. Put simply, twisting, bending, or stretching these nerve endings results in depolarization of their membranes, causing these nerves to "fire." These receptors differ from one another primarily in their locations and in the way that they are oriented with respect to the stimulus. Pain receptors, for example, are widely distributed throughout the body. They respond to many different types of stimuli when these stimuli reach a level that can endanger the body. Pain receptors deep within the body detect such internal environmental stresses as inadequate blood flow to an organ, excessive stretching of a structure, and spasms of muscle tissue.

Specialized mechanical receptors sensitive to pressure changes are attached to the walls of three major arteries of your body (the carotids and the aorta) and constantly monitor your blood pressure. These highly branched networks of nerve endings detect the stretching of the walls of these arteries caused by the "push" of the blood as it is pumped out of the heart. These neurons fire at a low rate at all times, sending a steady stream of impulses to the cardiac (heart) center in the medulla. A rise in blood pressure stretches the walls of these vessels, resulting in a higher frequency of nerve impulses, which inhibits the cardiac center. A drop in blood pressure lessens the stretch, resulting in a lower frequency of nerve impulses, which stimulates the cardiac center.

Receptors that sense the body's internal environment are located within the walls of blood vessels and organs.

Sensing the body's position in space

Your body uses receptors called **proprioceptors** to sense its position in space. The term *proprioceptor* comes from a Greek word meaning "self." Proprioceptors tell you how much your arms and legs are bent, where they are in relationship to your body, and where your head is relative to the ground even if you cannot see! They also tell you whether your body is moving.

Proprioceptors buried deep within your muscles keep track of the degree to which your muscles are contracted (Figure 13-2). These receptors are actually specialized muscle cells called *muscle spindles*. Wrapped around each spindle is the end of a sensory neuron called a **stretch receptor.** When a muscle is stretched, the muscle spindle gets longer and stretches the nerve ending, repeatedly stimulating it to fire. Conversely, when the muscle contracts, the tension on the fiber lessens and the stretch receptor ceases to fire. The frequency of stretch receptor discharges along the nerve fiber tells the body the degree to which a muscle is contracted at any given moment. The central nervous system uses this information to control those movements that involve the combined action of several muscles, such as those involved in breathing and walking. Other proprioceptors are found in your tendons, which is the connective tissue that joins your muscles to your bones, and in the tissue surrounding

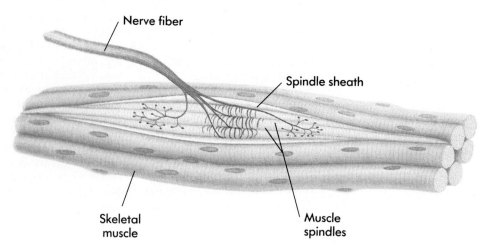

FIGURE 13-2 A stretch receptor embedded within skeletal muscle.
Stretching of the muscle elongates the spindle fibers, which deforms nerve endings, causing them to fire and send a nerve impulse out along the nerve fiber.

Nerve fiber

Spindle sheath

Skeletal muscle

Muscle spindles

your joints. These receptors are also stimulated when they are stretched and help protect your muscles, tendons, and joints from excessive tension and pulling.

Gravity and motion receptors are other types of proprioceptors. These receptors, both located in the inner ear, help you maintain your equilibrium, or balance. They are discussed later in the chapter.

▼▼ Receptors called proprioceptors, located within the skeletal muscles, tendons, and inner ear, give the body information about the position of its parts relative to each other and to the pull of gravity.

Sensing the external environment

Various receptors are located at or near the body surface that sense changes in the external environment. Many types of simple, microscopic receptors are located within the skin. These receptors detect touch, pressure, pain, and temperature—the so-called general senses. Other, more structurally complex receptors are located in specific places at or near the body surface. These receptors detect smell, taste, sight, and hearing and help you keep your balance. They are your special senses.

The general senses

The body has a mosaic of mechanical receptors in the skin for touch, pressure, and pain. These receptors are the same as those found deeper in the body, but because they are located close to the surface of the skin, they provide information about the external rather than the internal environment. Figure 13-3 is a diagram of a cross section of human skin showing these specialized nerve endings.

Disk-shaped dendrite endings called *Merkel's disks* and egg-shaped receptors called *Meissner's corpuscles* are two types of touch receptors. (The word *corpuscle* means "little body.") Both are widely distributed in the skin but are most numerous in the hands, feet, eyelids, tip of the tongue, lips,

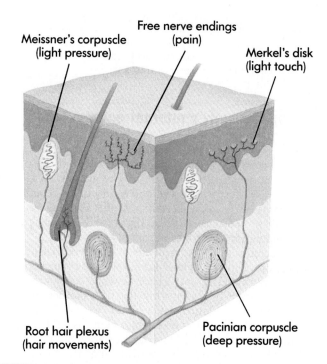

Meissner's corpuscle (light pressure)

Free nerve endings (pain)

Merkel's disk (light touch)

Root hair plexus (hair movements)

Pacinian corpuscle (deep pressure)

FIGURE 13-3 Receptors in the human skin.
These receptors, although they are found within the body, sense the external environment because they are located close to the surface of the skin.

nipples, clitoris, and tip of the penis. In addition, free nerve endings wrap around the roots of hairs and detect any stimulus, such as the wind or an insect, that moves body hair. Pressure receptors called *pacinian corpuscles* are located deeper within the skin. As shown in Figure 13-3, pacinian corpuscles look layered, much like an onion. The layers are made up of connective tissue with dendrites sandwiched between. These receptors are most numerous in the nipples and external genitals of both sexes. Pacinian corpuscles are also a part of the body's internal sensing system because of their locations around joints and tendons, in muscles, and in certain organs.

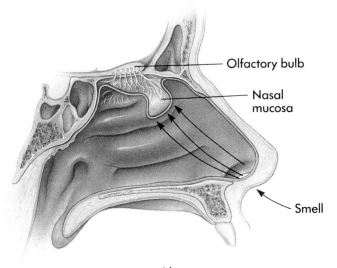

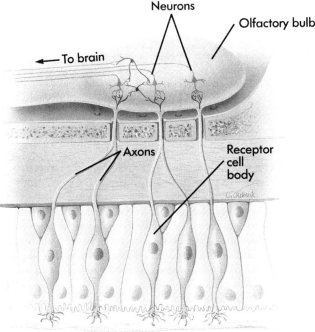

FIGURE 13-4 The sense of smell.
Human beings smell by means of olfactory receptor cells located in the lining of the nasal cavity. The receptor cells are neurons. Airborne gases combine with chemicals within the cilia on each neuron's dendrites, and the neuron is depolarized. Axons from these sensory neurons carry the impulse back through the olfactory nerve directly to the cerebral cortex in the brain.

Two populations of nerve endings in the skin are sensitive to changes in temperature. One set is stimulated by a lowering of temperature (the cold receptors) and the other by a raising of temperature (the heat receptors). Scientists are unsure how these receptors work. However, evidence suggests that changes in the temperature cause changes in the shapes of the proteins that make up the sodium channels of their cell membranes, leading to the depolarization and firing of these neurons.

Various receptors in the skin sense touch, pressure, pain, and temperature stimuli from the external environment.

The special senses

The special senses—smell, taste, sight, hearing, and balance—have receptors that are much more specialized and complex than the receptors for the general senses. Smell and taste receptors sense chemicals, whereas hearing receptors sense sound waves. Other receptors in the ears detect motion and the effect of gravity on the body. Sight receptors sense wavelengths of electromagnetic energy known as *visible light*.

Smell
Although smell receptors are structurally the simplest of your special senses, they can distinguish several thousand different odors. Smell receptors are also called **olfactory receptors,** a name derived from Latin words meaning "to make" *(facio)* "a smell" *(oleo)*. They are *not* located (surprisingly) in your nostrils, but in a 1/2- inch square of tissue in the roof of the nasal cavity—just behind the bridge of your nose (Figure 13-4).

Olfactory receptors consist of neurons whose cell bodies are embedded in the nasal epithelium, the tissue that lines the nasal cavity. Dendrites extend from these cell bodies. Cilia, microscopic projections of the dendrites, poke out of the epithelium like minute tufts of hair and are bathed by the mucus that covers this tissue. Gases in the air dissolve in the mucus and come into contact with the cilia.

Scientific evidence suggests that the olfactory receptors detect different smells because of specific binding of airborne gases with receptor chemicals located within the cilia. This interaction opens ion channels within the membrane of the receptor so that a generator potential is developed, firing the neuron when it reaches a particular threshold. From here, the nerve impulse travels to the olfactory area of the cerebral cortex to be interpreted. On its way, it travels through the brain's limbic system (see Chapter 12), the area of the brain responsible for many drives and emotions. Does the odor of baking cookies please you? Does the smell of rotting garbage cause you to turn your head in disgust? That is your limbic system at work—in conjunction with your cerebrum and your sense of smell.

The smell, or olfactory, receptors are located in the nasal epithelium and detect airborne chemicals as they bind with receptor chemicals.

Taste
Taste receptors, or **taste buds,** detect chemicals in the foods you eat. Human beings have four kinds of taste buds located on the tongue that each respond to a different class of stimulus: salty, sweet, sour, and bitter. Each type of taste bud is concentrated on different areas of the tongue, with sweet and salty on the front, sour on the sides, and bitter

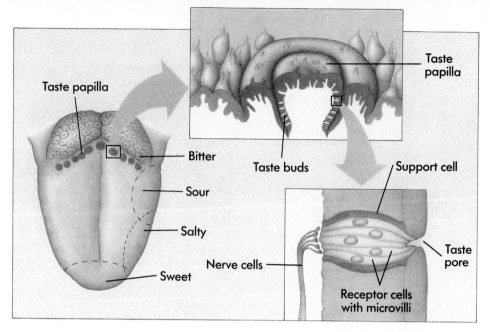

FIGURE 13-5 Taste.
Human beings have four kinds of taste buds (bitter, sour, salty, and sweet) located on different regions of the tongue. Groups of taste buds are typically organized in sensory projections called papillae. Individual taste buds are bulb-shaped collections of chemical receptor cells that open out into the mouth through a pore.

at the back (Figure 13-5). Humans, of course, perceive a rich and diverse array of tastes that are much more complex than simply salty, sweet, sour, and bitter. Interestingly, these tastes are composed of different combinations of impulses from just these four types of chemoreceptors. In addition, the sense of taste interacts with the sense of smell to produce the taste sensation, as you may have noticed when you had a "stuffy nose" and could perceive only the four basic tastes—those not dependent on smell for their perception.

Nearly 9000 taste buds are packed within the short projections on your tongue known as *papillae*. Figure 13-5 shows a drawing of a typical papilla on the tongue and points out the location of taste buds deep within the papilla. Taste buds are microscopic structures shaped like tiny onions. Each is made up of 30 to 80 receptor cells bound together by support cells. Hair-like projections of the receptor cells poke through an opening in the taste bud called a *taste pore*. The receptor cells are stimulated by the various chemicals in food as these chemicals dissolve in the saliva and come into contact with the cellular "hairs." A certain threshold of stimulation produces generator potentials within the receptor cells, firing neighboring sensory nerve fibers. These nerve fibers travel from the tongue and throat to the cerebrum, medulla, and thalamus. Some of these nerve fibers also travel to the reticular formation (see Chapter 12), the part of the brain that monitors incoming stimuli, identifying important information.

▼▼
The taste receptors, or taste buds, are microscopic chemoreceptors embedded within the papillae of the tongue. They work with the olfactory receptors to produce the taste sensation.

Sight

The eye is the only human sense organ that can detect wavelengths of electromagnetic energy, or radiation, known as *visible light*. Visible light is only a part of the full range of electromagnetic radiation, which is called the electromagnetic spectrum (Figure 13-6). Electromagnetic energy is repeating disturbances in electrical and magnetic fields in the atmosphere and can be thought of as a wave, much like the repeating disturbances or tiny waves caused by a stone thrown in a still pond.

The electromagnetic waves coming from the sun vary in length. Their lengths are measured from the crest of one wave to the crest of the next and are expressed in meters or in billionths of meters (nanometers, or nm). The shortest wavelengths are gamma rays; the longest are radio waves. Visible light has wavelengths in between these two extremes, but it, too, is made up of many different wavelengths. Remember the last rainbow you saw? Its array of colors was caused by the separation of the various wavelengths of visible light as they passed through tiny droplets of water in the air.

The receptors of the eye sensitive to the various wavelengths of visible light are called **rods** and **cones.** These receptors are located in the back of the eye and act somewhat like film in a camera. Light that falls on the eye is focused by a lens onto these receptors, just as the lens of a camera focuses light on film.

It is important to discuss how the eye's sensory receptors work before discussing the structure of the eye in greater detail. A primary event is the absorption of a **photon** of light by a pigment. Photons are units or packets of electromagnetic energy. One complexity of electromagnetic energy is that it travels as waves but also behaves like indi-

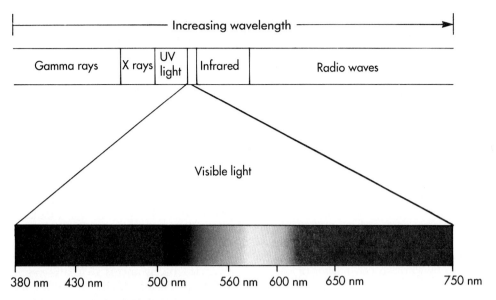

FIGURE 13-6 The electromagnetic spectrum.
Light is a form of electromagnetic energy and is conveniently thought of as a wave. The shorter the wavelength of light, the greater the energy. Visible light represents only a small part of the electromagnetic spectrum, that between 380 and 750 nanometers.

vidual units. In the eye, photons of light are absorbed by the pigment **rhodopsin.** This pigment is located in the tips of rod and cone cells that make up tissue at the back of the eye called the **retina** (Figure 13-7). Rhodopsin consists of **retinal,** a derivative of vitamin A, coupled to a membrane protein called **opsin.** As each rhodopsin complex absorbs a photon of light, the molecular shapes of both retinal and opsin change. As a result, retinal separates from opsin. The activated opsin triggers a series of events that are responsible for *closing* sodium channels. As discussed in Chapter 12, stimuli usually lead to an *opening* of sodium channels, allowing sodium ions to rush into the cell, *depolarizing* the receptor membrane. Sodium channels close in rod and cone cells when they are stimulated. The result is **hyperpolarization**—the interior of the rod becomes even more negatively charged than before. Hyperpolarization of the cell in turn activates a mechanism that *lowers* the amount of neurotransmitter released by the cell. This decrease in neurotransmitter release lessens the frequency of firing in adjacent neurons—nerve signals that eventually reach the brain and are interpreted as patterns of light and dark.

▼
Light receptors are rod and cone cells located within the retina at the back of the eye. The pigment within these cells absorbs photons of light, which causes a series of events leading to a hyperpolarization of the receptor cells and a subsequent firing of adjacent neurons.

Rod cells are able to detect low levels of light because even one photon can stimulate a rod cell. In addition, they detect only white light, so vision with rod cells alone is black, white, and shades of gray. Did you ever try to see color in extremely dim light? Your rods alone are at work,

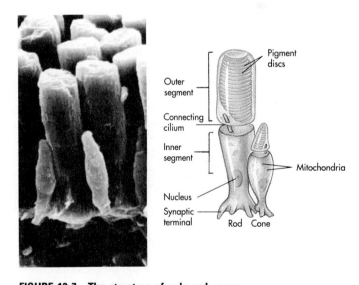

FIGURE 13-7 The structure of rods and cones.
Although not obvious from the electron micrograph, light-absorbing pigment is contained in the outer segments of these cells.

and they cannot see color. Color vision is achieved by your cone cells, which function in bright light. There are three kinds of cone cells (although they all look the same under the electron microscope). Each type of cone cell possesses rhodopsin molecules that have slightly different shapes from one another because they have different types of opsin. These differences determine which wavelengths of light the pigment (and therefore the cone cell) will absorb. One type absorbs wavelengths of light in the 455-nanometer (blue-absorbing) range. Another type absorbs in the 530-nanometer (green-absorbing) range, and the third in the 625-nanometer (red-absorbing) range. The color you perceive depends on how strongly each group of cones is stimulated by a light source. The pigment in rod cells, on the other hand, absorbs in the 500-nanometer range. As shown in Figure 13-8, this range encompasses the three primary colors (blue, green, and red), which together make up white light.

▼▼▼
Rod cells function in dim light and detect white light only, whereas cone cells function in bright light and detect color.

The basic structure of the human eye is shown in Figure 13-9. Your eyes are each about 1 inch in diameter and are covered and protected by a tough outer layer of connective tissue called the **sclera.** The front of the eye is transparent, allowing light to enter the eye. This portion of the eye's outer layer is called the **cornea.** Because the cornea is rounded, it not only allows light to enter the eye but bends it as well. This bending, or refraction, of light occurs as the light waves slow down as they move from the air and pass through the tissue of the cornea. You can see this phenomenon if you put a straw in a glass of water. The parts of the straw both outside and inside the water do not appear connected. If the cornea were flat, the light waves or rays would exit the cornea traveling in a path parallel to their original path. However, the cornea is rounded; the light waves that enter above, below, or to the side of the center of the cornea are bent slightly toward one another. Therefore the cornea is the first structure of the eye that begins to focus incoming light onto a point at the rear of the eye.

A chamber behind the cornea is filled with a watery fluid called the **aqueous humor.** The word *humor* refers to "fluid within the body," and the word *aqueous* means "water." Fresh aqueous humor is continually produced as old fluid is drained into the bloodstream. This fluid nourishes both the cornea and the lens, since neither structure has a supply of blood vessels. In addition, the aqueous humor (along with fluid further back in the eye called the *vitreous* [Latin for "glass"] *humor*) creates a pressure within the eyeball that maintains the eyeball's shape and keeps the retina pressed properly against the back of the eyeball.

The **lens** lies just behind the aqueous humor and plays a major role in focusing the light that enters the eye onto the retina at the back of the eye. It looks much like a lemon drop candy or a somewhat flattened balloon. If you were to cut a lens in half, it would look similar to an onion, since it is made up of layer upon layer of protein fibers. The lens is encircled by ligaments that suspend it within the eye. These ligaments are attached to a tiny circular muscle called the **ciliary muscle** that, by contracting or relaxing, slightly changes the shape of the lens. The greater the curve of the lens, the more sharply it bends light rays toward one another.

In persons with normal vision, this bending of the light results in its being focused on the retina. Some people, however, may have an elongated eyeball or a thickened lens. In either case, the light is focused on a spot in front of the retina. Such people are nearsighted. As Figure 13-10 shows, this condition can be corrected with a lens that spreads the light rays entering the eye so that they focus on the retina. Some people are farsighted, having either a shortened eyeball or a thin lens. Light is focused on a spot behind the retina. This condition can be corrected with a lens that converges entering light rays so that they focus on the retina.

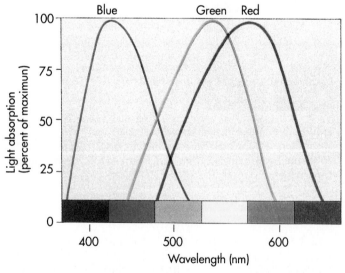

FIGURE 13-8 **The absorption spectrum of human vision.**
The wavelength of light absorbed by the visual pigment of cone cells depends on the opsin proteins to which the pigment is bound. There are three such proteins, producing cones that absorb at 455 nanometers (blue), 530 nanometers (green), and 625 nanometers (red).

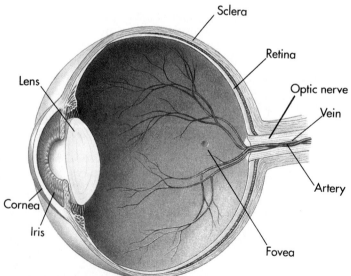

FIGURE 13-9 **Structure of the human eye.**
Light passes through the transparent cornea and is focused by the lens on the retina at a particular location called the *fovea.* The retina is rich in rods and cones.

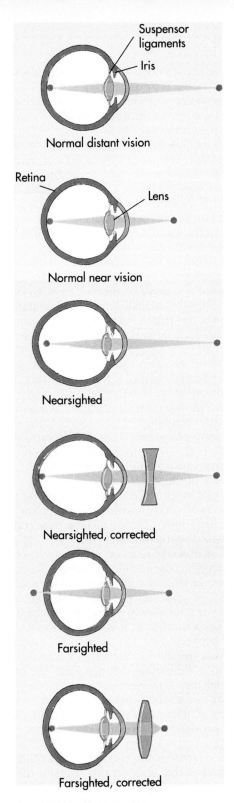

FIGURE 13-10 Focusing the human eye.
Contraction of ciliary muscles pulls on suspensory ligaments and changes the shape of the lens, which alters its point of focus forward or backward. In nearsighted people the ciliary muscles place the point of focus in front of the retina rather than on it. The problem can be corrected with glasses or contact lenses, which extend the focal point to where it should be. In farsighted people, the ciliary muscles make the opposite error, placing the point of focus behind the retina. Corrective lenses can shorten the focal point.

The amount of light entering the eye is controlled by a diaphragm called the **iris,** which lies between the cornea and the lens. The iris reduces the size of the transparent zone, or **pupil,** of the eye (what you see as a black dot) through which the light passes. Together, the ciliary muscle and the iris make up two of the structures of the middle layer of the eye. The third structure is the **choroid.** As shown in Figure 13-9, the choroid extends toward the back of the eye as a thin, dark-brown membrane that lines the sclera. It contains vessels carrying blood that nourishes the retina and a dark pigment that absorbs light rays so that they will not be reflected within the eyeball.

The inner layer of the eye is the retina. The retina lines the back of the eye and contains the rods and cones. The human retina contains about 7 million cones, most of which are located at a central region of the retina called the **fovea.** The lens focuses incoming light on this spot, the area of sharpest vision because of this high concentration of cones. There are no rods in the fovea. Some are located just outside the fovea and increase in concentration as the distance from it increases.

Each foveal cone cell makes a one-to-one connection with a special kind of neuron called a *bipolar cell* (Figure 13-11). Each of the bipolar cells is connected in turn to a ganglion cell, whose axon is part of the **optic nerve.** The bipolar cells receive the hyperpolarization stimulus from the cone cells and transmit a depolarization stimulus to the ganglion cells. The axons of the ganglion cells transmit the impulses to the brain. The frequency of pulses transmitted by any one receptor provides information about light intensity. The pattern of firing among the different foveal axons provides a point-to-point image. The different cone cells provide information about the color of the image.

The relationship of receptors to bipolar cells to ganglion cells is one-to-one-to-one within the fovea. Put simply, each receptor (cone) cell in the fovea synapses with its own bipolar cell that in turn synapses with its own ganglion cell. Outside the fovea, however, the output of many receptor cells is channeled to one bipolar cell. Many bipolar cells, in turn, synapse with one ganglion cell. In fact, in the outer edge of the retina, more than 125 receptor cells feed stimuli to each ganglion cell in the optic nerve. In this outer, or peripheral, region, many additional neurons cross-connect the ganglion cells with one another and carry out extensive processing of visual information. As a result, this portion of the retina does not transmit a point-to-point image as the fovea does but transmits instead a processed version of the visual input that may be interpreted simply as movement. Think of the periphery of your retina as a detector, whereas your fovea is an inspector.

Light enters the pupil of the eye, and the lens focuses it on the back of the eye, on an area of the retina that is rich in cone cells. These cells, along with surrounding rod and cone cells, initiate nervous impulses that travel to the cerebrum via the optic nerve.

The positioning of your two eyes on each side of the head sends two slightly different sets of information to the

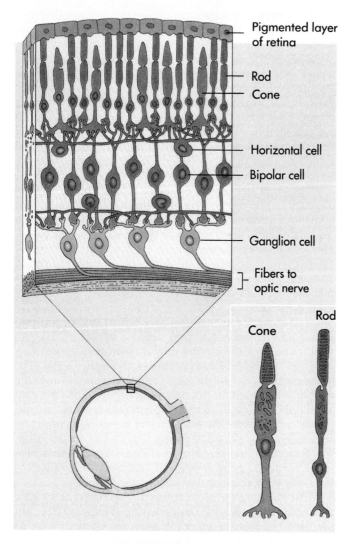

Pigmented layer of retina

Rod

Cone

Horizontal cell

Bipolar cell

Ganglion cell

Fibers to optic nerve

Cone   **Rod**

FIGURE 13-11   Structure of the retina.
Note that the rods and cones are at the rear of the retina, not the front. Bipolar cells receive the hyperpolarization stimulus from the cone cells and transmit a depolarization to the ganglion cells. The ganglion cells, whose axons are part of the optic nerve, transmit the impulse to the brain.

brain about what you are seeing. Each set of information is slightly different because each eye views an object from a slightly different angle. This slight displacement of images gives **depth perception**—a three-dimensional quality—to your sight.

Hearing

Sound is a type of mechanical energy resulting from the vibration of an object. This vibration disturbs the air around the object, pushing the molecules in the air closer to one another, compressing them. These areas of compression are followed by areas of molecules that are not compressed. If you could visualize these disturbances, they would look much like the concentric circles of waves on the surface of water that occur when you throw a pebble into a still pond. Sound waves are these wave-like disturbances of molecules

in the air (or in certain other substances such as water, glass, iron, or wood) caused by a vibrating object. Two parts of the ear—the outer and middle ear—work together to transmit sound waves to the inner ear, where sound stimuli are changed into nerve impulses.

The flaps of skin on the outside of the head that are called ears are only one part of the **outer ear.** Each flap, or **pinna,** funnels sound waves into an **auditory canal.** The auditory canal, which is about 1 inch long, leads directly to the eardrum. The eardrum, or **tympanic membrane,** is a thin piece of fibrous connective tissue that is stretched over the opening to the **middle ear.** On its external side the eardrum is covered with skin. On its internal side the eardrum is connected to one of the smallest bones in the body—the *hammer,* or **malleus.** The malleus is connected to another tiny bone called the *anvil,* or **incus.** The anvil, in turn, is connected to a third bone called the *stirrup,* or **stapes.** These three bones are the structures of the middle ear that pick up sound vibrations from the outer ear and transfer them to the inner ear.

Sound waves entering the outer ear beat against the tympanic membrane, causing it to vibrate like a drum. Vibrations of this membrane cause the malleus to move with a rocking motion, since it is attached to the internal surface of the tympanic membrane. This rocking is transferred, in turn, to the incus and stapes. These three bones are hinged to one another in a way that produces a lever system, a mechanism that causes them to act like an amplifier and increase the force of the vibrations.

Also located in the middle ear is an opening to the eustachian tube (a structure named after an Italian physician who lived in the 1500s). The **eustachian tube** connects the middle ear with the nasopharynx (the upper region of the throat). Its function is to equalize air pressure on both sides of the eardrum when the outside air pressure is not the same as the pressure in your middle ear. You have probably had the experience of your ears popping while you were driving up or down a mountain, taking off and landing in an airplane, or deep-sea diving; it is the result of the pressure equalization between these two sides of the eardrum.

The stirrup, the third in the series of middle ear bones, is attached to a membrane that separates the middle ear from the inner ear. This membrane covers the **oval window,** the entrance to the **inner ear,** the part of the ear in which hearing actually takes place. In addition, other parts of the inner ear detect motion and the effect of gravity on the body.

The oval window is the entrance to the fluid-filled **cochlea**—the part of the inner ear that contains the organ of hearing. To understand the cochlea's structure and function, imagine a tapering blind-ended tube (Figure 13-12) having two membrane-covered holes at its wider end. The upper hole is the oval window, and the lower hole is called the **round window.** Also imagine that another, smaller membranous tube runs down its center, serving as a partition between the oval and round windows and bisecting the large tube into upper and lower channels, or canals. The upper channel is called the **vestibular canal;** the lower channel is called the **tympanic canal.** The inner tube stops short of the blind, tapered end of the outer tube, however, so the two canals connect with one another there. Imagine this

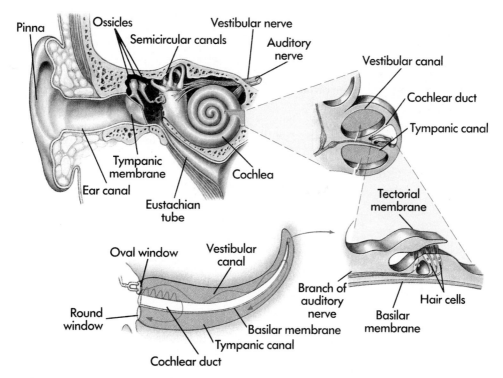

FIGURE 13-12 Structure of the human ear.
The human ear is composed of outer, middle, and inner sections. The outer ear extends from the pinna to the tympanic membrane. The middle ear contains the ear ossicles, or bones that transmit sound vibrations from the tympanic membrane to the cochlea. The cochlea contains the organ of hearing and makes up part of the inner ear.

tube rolled up like a jellyroll, and you have the basic structure of the cochlea. In fact, the word *cochlea* comes from a Latin word meaning "snail" and describes the rolled-up shape of this structure extremely well.

The inner tube of the cochlea is called the **cochlear duct,** and it contains specialized cells that are the receptors of hearing. These cells are called *hair cells* and are embedded in the floor of the inner tube, the basilar membrane. The hairs that project from the hair cells stick up into the cochlear duct and are covered by a roof called the **tectorial membrane.** Together, the hair cells with supporting cells of the basilar membrane and the overhanging tectorial membrane are called the **organ of Corti**—the organ of hearing.

How does the organ of hearing detect sound? As the stapes rocks in the oval window, it sets the fluid within the vestibular canal in motion. As the oval window membrane rocks inward, it pushes on the fluid in the vestibular canal. This fluid moves forward in waves that pass into the tympanic canal. When the waves reach the membrane-covered round window, it bulges outward. Meanwhile, the stapes rocks backward in the oval window, setting up an opposite motion of the fluid. As the waves then flow backward through the tympanic canal on the way to the vestibular canal, they push on the basilar membrane. The basilar membrane bends, causing the hairs of the receptor cells to be pressed against the tectorial membrane. As the hairs bend, they develop generator potentials that fire adjacent neurons. These impulses then pass to the brain to be interpreted. The brain is able to interpret pitch (the highness or lowness of a sound) because sounds of different pitches produce sound waves of different frequencies (numbers of waves per second). These differences set up differing wave patterns within the fluid of the inner ear that cause specific regions of the basilar membrane to vibrate more intensely than others. In addition, louder sound waves cause greater vibrations of the basilar membrane than can be interpreted by the brain. Repeated exposure to extremely loud noises such as gunshots, jet engines, and loud music can damage the hairs of the receptor cells and cause partial but permanent hearing loss.

The ear has three parts: the outer, middle, and inner ear. The outer ear funnels sound waves in toward the eardrum, which changes these waves into mechanical energy. This energy is then transmitted to the bones of the middle ear, which increase its force. The inner ear, a complex of fluid-filled canals, contains the organ of hearing. The receptor cells of this organ change the mechanical sound energy into nerve impulses.

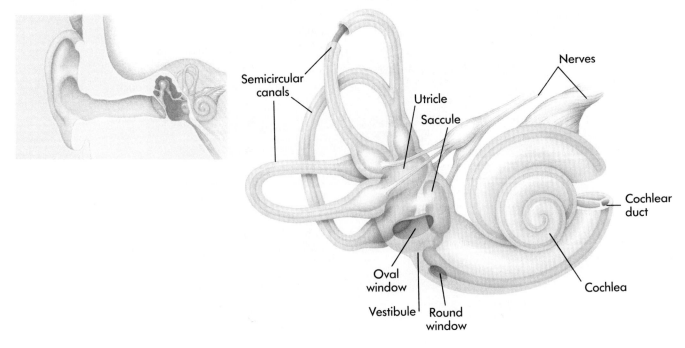

FIGURE 13-13 Structure of the inner ear.
The inner ear contains the organs of hearing and the organs that are responsible for maintaining the body's equilibrium.

Balance

The inner ear has two other portions that are each structured as a fluid-filled tube within a tube like the cochlea, but their shapes are different from that of the cochlea. As shown in Figure 13-13, the cochlea makes up one side of the inner ear. The bulge in the midsection of the inner ear is called the **vestibule,** and it contains structures that sense whether you are upside down or right side up. In other words, it detects the effects of gravity on the body.

Inside this bulge are two sacs called the **utricle** and the **saccule** (both words mean "a little bag or sac"). Within each of these sacs is a flat area composed of both ciliated and nonciliated cells. Spread over the surfaces of these cells is a layer of jelly-like material. Embedded within the jelly are small pebbles of calcium carbonate called **otoliths** (literally, "ear stones"). The ciliated cells are the receptor cells and have long cilia and thin cell extensions that stick up into the jelly-like microscopic tufts of hair (Figure 13-14). When the head is moved, the otoliths slide within the jelly just as a hockey puck slides on ice. As the otoliths move, they pull on the jelly, which pulls on the cilia, bending them. Any shift in the position of the otoliths results in different cilia being bent and cilia being bent to a specific degree and in a specific direction (Figure 13-15). These stimuli initiate generator potentials that are transmitted to neurons that make

up a branch of cranial nerve VIII (see Chapter 12). The brain interprets these messages, resulting in your perception of "up" with respect to the pull of gravity.

Positioned above the saccule and utricle are three fluid-filled **semicircular canals** (see Figure 13-13). These loops are oriented at right angles to one another in three planes. At the base of each loop is a group of ciliated sensory cells that are connected to neurons. Lying above these cells is a mass of jelly-like material. When the head moves, the fluid within the semicircular canals moves and pushes the jelly (and the cilia) in a direction opposite to that of the motion. (You have experienced this phenomenon when you accelerate suddenly in your car and your head is thrown backward.) This movement initiates the depolarization of the cell membrane, which triggers a nerve impulse. Because the three canals are each oriented differently, movement in any plane is sensed by at least one of them. Complex movements are analyzed in the brain as it compares the sensory input from each canal.

The vestibule of the inner ear detects your position with respect to gravity, whereas the semicircular canals detect the direction of your movement.

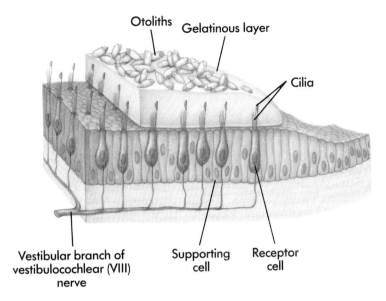

Otoliths Gelatinous layer

Cilia

Vestibular branch of
vestibulocochlear (VIII)
nerve

Supporting
cell

Receptor
cell

FIGURE 13-14   The structure of the interior of the utricle and saccule.
Movement of the otoliths pulls on the cilia attached to the receptor cells, initiating a nerve impulse that is sent through a nerve to the brain. The utricle and saccule provide sensory information necessary to maintain your body's orientation relative to the ground and provide information regarding acceleration and deceleration.

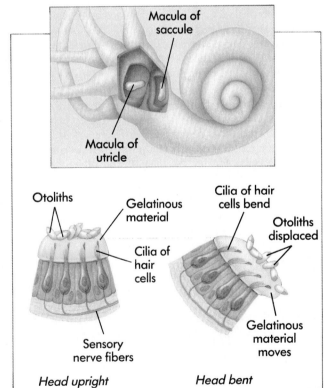

Macula of
saccule

Macula of
utricle

Otoliths

Gelatinous
material

Cilia of
hair
cells

Sensory
nerve fibers

Cilia of hair
cells bend

Otoliths
displaced

Gelatinous
material
moves

Head upright

Head bent

FIGURE 13-15   Balance is maintained by the semicircular canals.
At the base of each semicircular canal is a group of ciliated cells connected to neurons. The cells are covered with a jelly-like material studded with otoliths. A sudden movement of the head causes the otoliths to be displaced, depolarizing the neurons and initiating a nerve impulse that is sent to the brain. Because each semicircular canal is oriented in a different plane in space, movement in any plane can be detected by at least one of the canals. The brain interprets complex movements by comparing information sent from each canal.

Summary

1. Sensory receptors change environmental stimuli into nerve impulses. These stimuli, or changes in the environment, must be of a sufficient magnitude to open ion channels within the membranes of receptor cells, depolarizing them. This initial depolarization is called a *generator potential* and initiates an action potential, or nerve impulse, that is carried to either the spinal cord or brain.

2. Some sensory receptors monitor body functions. Temperature-sensitive neurons in the hypothalamus, for example, monitor the temperature of the blood and trigger mechanisms to regulate this temperature. Other receptors embedded in the walls of certain arteries are sensitive to the carbon dioxide, oxygen, and pH levels of the blood and provide input to respiratory centers in the medulla and pons. Still others monitor the blood pressure and provide feedback to a cardiac center that regulates heartbeat.

3. Sensory receptors called *proprioceptors* gather information about the body's position in space. Proprioceptors buried deep within the muscles keep track of the degree to which they are contracted. Gravity is detected by structures in the inner ear called the *utricle* and *saccule*. Motion is sensed by the semicircular canals, also located in the inner ear. Together, these two structures help you maintain your balance and know which way is up.

4. Various receptors located at or near the body surface sense changes in the external environment. Many simple receptors located in the skin detect general environmental stimuli such as touch, pressure, pain, and temperature. More specialized senses—smell, taste, sight, hearing, and balance—have more complex receptors located only at certain locations.

5. The olfactory receptors, which are located in the nasal epithelium just behind the bridge of the nose, detect various smells. Scientific evidence suggests that the olfactory receptors detect these different smells because of specific binding of airborne gases with receptor chemicals located within the cilia of the olfactory receptor cells.

6. Taste receptors, or taste buds, are located within the short projections on the tongue known as *papillae*. The receptor cells of the taste buds detect sweet, sour, salty, and bitter tastes in food as food molecules dissolve in the saliva and come into contact with cellular "hairs" that poke out of the taste pores.

7. The human eye detects wavelengths of electromagnetic energy known as *visible light*. Electromagnetic energy is generated by charged subatomic particles moving through space emitting waves of electrical and magnetic energy. The human eye contains receptor cells called *rods* and *cones* that contain pigments capable of absorbing units of electromagnetic energy of certain wavelengths. The absorption of light causes a change in the shape of the pigment, which in turn triggers a series of events resulting in a hyperpolarization of the receptor cell membrane. This hyperpolarization leads to an adjustment in the frequency of the firing of adjacent neurons—nerve signals that eventually reach the brain and are interpreted as patterns of light and dark.

8. Structurally, the human eye is similar to a camera. Light entering the eye is focused by a lens onto the receptors located at the back of the eye, which act like film in a camera.

9. Sound waves are disturbances of molecules in the air (and in certain other substances) that result from the vibration of an object. The ear collects sound waves and changes them into other forms of mechanical energy that stimulate the organ of hearing within the inner ear. The receptor cells of this organ propagate nerve impulses that are carried to the cerebral cortex.

1. The text states that the perception of pain involves an individual's reaction to particular sensory stimuli. Would you consider pain, therefore, an objective or subjective state of being?

2. Explain the events that occur at the cellular level that allow you to "sense" something.

3. Which type of receptor would be most highly stimulated by an experience of riding on an amusement park ride, such as a roller coaster? Why?

4. Researchers have found the hypothalamus to be very involved in the sense of satiation or "feeling full" after a meal and thus integrally involved in weight control. What type of information would you theorize is being sent to the hypothalamus?

5. John has chronic allergies that cause him to suffer from constant sinus congestion. What special senses may be highly affected by this condition?

6. Explain how you can smell the difference between your favorite perfume and your least favorite food.

7. You may have noticed that certain smells are able to evoke specific memories and emotions—both good and bad. Explain why.

8. What are taste buds? Explain their role in allowing you to taste the flavors in your favorite ice cream. What other sense (besides taste) is involved?

9. How are you able to see different colors?

10. Explain the process that allows you to see objects.

11. Draw a diagram of the human eye. Label the sclera, cornea, aqueous humor, lens, iris, pupil, and fovea.

12. Is there any difference in the manner in which you see in a well-lit environment as compared to your vision in a darkened room? What type of cells are involved specifically?

13. Mr. Garcia undergoes minor eye surgery and must wear a patch over his left eye for 3 days. During this time, he finds that he has trouble grasping things because he keeps underreaching and overreaching. Explain why.

14. You switch on the radio to your favorite program. Explain how your ears enable you to hear the sounds.

15. Even with your eyes closed, you can tell when your head tilts to one side. Explain how.

1. In *The Silence of the Lambs* and many other movies, you see people using "snooper-scopes," devices that allow them to literally see in the dark. How might such a device work?

2. In a very interesting series of experiments, migrating song birds were placed in a cage lined with carbon paper similar to that used in credit card slips. The birds would peck at the wall of the cage, attempting to get out, but not at random—by far the greatest density of pecks is in the direction they were migrating when captured! Now when a large magnet is placed in the room, they peck in the direction of the magnet, even though they cannot see it. What sort of sensory system do you imagine the birds possess that lets them orient in this way?

3. There is presently much interest in the medical and research community on the effects of "biofeedback," a process whereby people are taught to focus thought and relax in order to exert conscious control over certain body functions. For example, pain may be reduced by learning to focus on consciously lowering sensation in an area. Cardiac patients have been able to voluntarily relax and reduce their blood pressures. Discuss as a class the merits of such patient-controlled treatments and possible problems.

Finke, R. (1986, May). Mental imagery and the visual system. *Scientific American*, pp. 84-92.
The article explains the theory that the way in which visual information is perceived and carried to the brain has a strong influence on mental imagery.

Gibbons, B. (1986, September). The intimate sense of smell. *National Geographic*, pp. 324-361.
This detailed account of the human sense of smell is interesting and well illustrated.

Miller, J.A. (1990). A matter of taste. *BioScience, 40*(2), pp. 78-82.
Innovative methods and materials have made possible new insights into the way your sense of taste works.

14 Hormones

HIGHLIGHTS

- Hormones are chemical messengers produced by cells; they regulate other cells of the body.
- Hormones produced by glands and transported to cells via the bloodstream are known as endocrine hormones, whereas hormones that are secreted into the tissue fluid to affect nearby cells are known as local hormones.
- Hormones affect cells in one of four ways: by regulating their secretions and excretions, by helping them to respond to changes in the environment, by controlling activities related to reproductive processes, and by influencing their proper growth and development.
- The production of hormones is controlled by a feedback mechanism that works in much the same way as a thermostat in a house.

Shooting up with anabolic steroids has been the downfall of many winners. These controversial drugs are really synthetic hormones, chemicals that affect the activity of specific organs or tissues. The various hormones of the body all affect their "target" tissues in unique ways. Anabolic steroids affect the body in ways similar to the male sex hormone testosterone and stimulate the buildup of muscles. But along with building a championship body, anabolic steroids strikingly change the body's metabolism.

Female athletes on steroids experience side effects such as shrinking breasts, a deepening voice, and an increase in body hair. Male athletes find that their testicles shrink. Some users also experience life-threatening kidney and liver damage. Youngsters who take these drugs risk stunting their growth because anabolic steroids cause bones to stop growing prematurely. And a great deal of controversy still surrounds claims that anabolic steroids can cause psychological effects such as "steroid rage," a state of mind in which users attack people and things around them.

Today, scientists still lack solid scientific data regarding all aspects and consequences of anabolic steroid use. However, it is clear that their use is risky at the least—and may put users in the cemetery rather than in the winner's circle.

FIGURE 14-1 The human endocrine system.
The endocrine glands pictured in this diagram secrete chemical "messengers" that travel through the bloodstream to affect other cells in the body.

Endocrine glands and their hormones

A **hormone** is a chemical messenger sent by a gland to other cells of the body. Traditionally, animal hormones have been described by scientists as the chemical products of glands that travel within the bloodstream to all parts of the body, causing an effect on specific cells, or target organs, far removed from that gland. Glands are individual cells or groups of cells that secrete substances. Their secretory portions are made up of specialized epithelial cells. The glands that secrete hormones spill these chemicals directly into the bloodstream and are called **endocrine,** or ductless, **glands.** Glands that secrete other substances such as digestive enzymes or sweat route their secretions to specific destinations by means of ducts. For example, the digestive enzyme pancreatic amylase flows directly from the pancreas to the small intestine and goes nowhere else. Glands having this kind of associated ductwork are called **exocrine glands.**

Today, most scientists have expanded their definition of hormones to include any chemical produced by one cell that causes an effect in another. Included in this description, then, are substances such as neurotransmitters—chemicals produced by the axon end of a nerve cell that travel to and bind with the dendrite end of an adjacent nerve cell, contributing to the propagation of the nerve impulse along that neuron (see Chapter 11). Such chemicals are often called **local hormones** because they affect neighboring target cells. The human body produces many local hormones; they are described later in this chapter.

▼▼▼
Hormones are chemical messengers secreted by cells that affect other cells. Hormones that travel within the bloodstream and affect cells in another part of the body are called *endocrine hormones*. Hormones that do not travel within the bloodstream but only affect cells lying near the secretory cells are called local hormones.

The 10 different endocrine glands of the human body make over 30 different hormones. Together, these glands are called the **endocrine system** (Figure 14-1). The endocrine system works with the nervous system to integrate the functioning of the various tissues, organs, and organ systems of the body. The nervous system sends messages to muscles and glands, regulating muscular contraction and glandular secretion. The hormones of the endocrine system, on the other hand, carry messages to virtually any type of cell in the body. The messages of the endocrine hormones are varied but can be grouped into four categories:

1. **Regulation:** Hormones control the internal environment of the body by regulating the secretion and excretion of various chemicals in the blood, such as salts and acids.
2. **Response:** Hormones help the body respond to changes in the environment and cope with physical and psychological stress.
3. **Reproduction:** Hormones control the female reproductive cycle and other reproductive processes essential to conception and birth and control the development of sex cells, the reproductive organs, and secondary sexual characteristics (those that make men and women different) in both sexes.
4. **Growth and development:** Hormones are essential to the proper growth and development of the body from conception to adulthood.

Once molecules of a hormone are released into the bloodstream, they travel throughout the body. Although hormone molecules may pass billions of cells, specific hormones only affect specific cells called **target cells.** Hormones recognize target cells because they bind to receptor molecules embedded within the cell membrane or located within the cytoplasm of the cell. The binding of a hormone molecule to a receptor molecule activates a chain of events in the target cell that results in the effect of the hormone being expressed.

Two major classes of endocrine hormones work within the human body: **peptide hormones** and **steroid hormones.** Peptide hormones are made of amino acids, but the

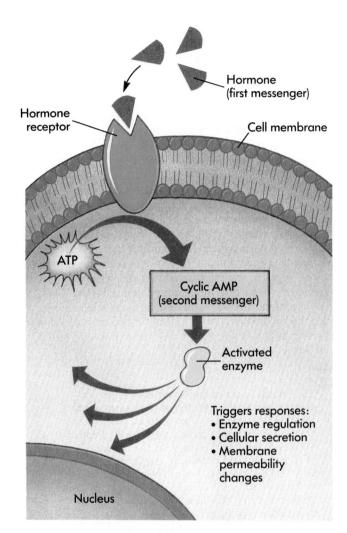

FIGURE 14-2 How peptide hormones work.
Once inside the cell, peptide hormones bind to the cell membrane and trigger an increase of second messenger compounds within the cell, such as cyclic AMP. The second messenger in turn activates enzymes that alter the cell's function in response to the hormonal message.

amino acid chain length varies greatly from hormone to hormone. The smallest are actually modifications of the single amino acid tyrosine. Somewhat larger are short peptide hormones that are several amino acids in length. Polypeptide hormones have chain lengths of several dozen or more amino acids, such as the hormone insulin. Even larger are protein hormones that may have over 200 amino acids with carbohydrates attached at several positions.

Unable to pass through the cell membrane, peptide hormones bind to receptor molecules embedded in the cell membrane of target cells. The binding of a hormone to a receptor triggers an increase in that cell's production of a compound referred to as a **second messenger.** A second messenger triggers enzymes that cause the cell to alter its functioning in response to the hormone (Figure 14-2). For example, prolactin stimulates cells of the mammary glands to produce milk. Target cells respond as enzymes go into action catalyzing reactions that produce the components of mother's milk. Other types of hormone responses include the secretion of substances from target cells and the closing or opening of certain protein doors within target cell membranes. Cyclic adenosine monophosphate (cyclic AMP for short), a cousin of ATP (see Chapter 4), acts as a second messenger to many cells. Besides cyclic AMP, other second messenger molecules have been discovered.

Steroid hormones are all made from cholesterol, a lipid synthesized by the liver. You know cholesterol as that dietary devil present in certain foods such as eggs, dairy products, and beef. A characteristic of steroid hormones is their set of carbon rings. Steroid hormones, being lipid soluble, pass freely through the lipid bilayer of the cell membrane. Once inside a cell, these hormones bind to receptor molecules located within the cytoplasm of target cells. Together, the hormone-receptor complex moves into the nucleus of the cell, causing the cell's hereditary material, or DNA, to trigger the production of certain proteins (Figure 14-3). In response to the sex hormones estrogen or testosterone, for example, the proteins produced are those involved in such processes as the development and maintenance of female or male sexual characteristics.

> Two main classes of endocrine hormones are peptide hormones and steroid hormones. Both travel within the bloodstream to all parts of the body but affect only certain target cells. Peptide hormones bind to receptors on the cell membrane of target cells and ultimately trigger enzymes that alter cell functioning. Steroid hormones bind to receptors within the cytoplasm of target cells and ultimately cause the hereditary material of the cell to produce specific proteins.

The production of hormones is regulated by a mechanism called a *feedback loop*. In general, hormonal feedback loops work in the following way: endocrine glands are initially stimulated to release hormones. Stimulation of an endocrine gland occurs in one of three ways:

1. *Direct stimulation by the nervous system:* The sensation of fear, for example, can cause the autonomic nervous system to trigger the release of the hormone adrenaline from the adrenal medulla.
2. *Indirect stimulation by the nervous system by means of releasing hormones:* The hypothalamus is a specialized portion of the brain that produces and secretes releasing hormones. Some releasing hormones stimulate the release of other hormones; some prevent the release.
3. *The concentration of specific substances in the bloodstream:* The blood level of a substance such as glucose or calcium, for example, may signal an endocrine gland to turn on or turn off.

After an endocrine gland secretes its hormone into the bloodstream, the hormone travels throughout the body via the circulatory system and interacts with target tissues. The target tissues cause the desired effect to be produced. This effect acts as a new stimulus to the endocrine gland (Figure 14-4). Put simply, the body feeds back information to each

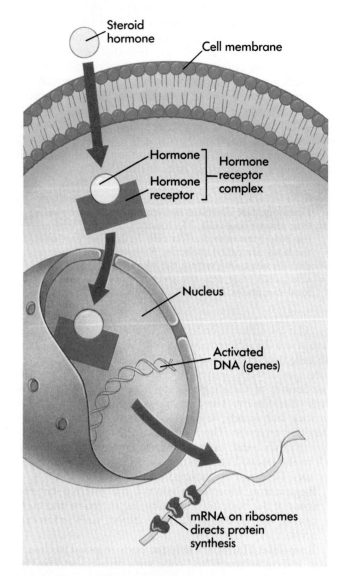

FIGURE 14-3 How steroid hormones work.
Steroid hormones are able to pass through the cell membrane without the aid of a receptor molecule. Inside the cell, they bind with receptor molecules. The hormone-receptor complex then enters the nucleus of the cell, where it acts on DNA to produce proteins. These proteins control physiological processes such as growth and development.

endocrine gland after it releases its hormone. In a positive feedback loop, the information that is fed back causes the gland to produce more of its hormone. In a **negative feedback loop,** the feedback causes the gland to slow down or to stop the production of its hormone. Most hormones work by means of negative feedback loops. (Specific examples of feedback mechanisms and interactions are discussed throughout this chapter.)

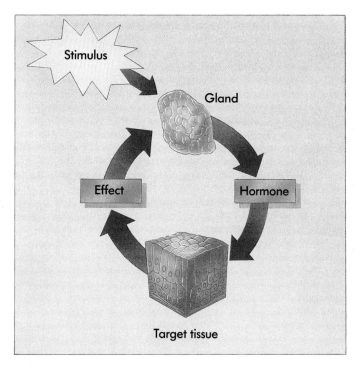

FIGURE 14-4 A simple feedback loop.
In response to a stimulus, an endocrine gland releases a specific hormone that acts on a specific target tissue. The effect of the hormone on the target tissue either causes the gland to release more of the hormone (positive feedback) or causes the gland to slow or stop its production of the hormone (negative feedback).

The pituitary gland

The **pituitary** is a powerful gland that secretes nine different hormones. Although it secretes so many hormones, it is amazingly tiny—about the size of a marble. The pituitary gland hangs from the underside of the brain, supported and cradled within a bony depression of the sphenoid bone.

Controlling the pituitary: The hypothalamus

The pituitary secretes seven major hormones from its larger front portion, or lobe, the anterior pituitary. It secretes two from its rear lobe, the posterior pituitary. The secretion of these hormones is regulated by a mass of nerve cells that lies directly above the pituitary, making up a small part of the floor of the brain. This regulatory nervous tissue, the **hypothalamus,** is connected to the pituitary by a stalk of tissue (Figure 14-5, *A*). The hypothalamus uses information it gathers from the peripheral nerves and other parts of the brain to stimulate or inhibit the secretion of hormones from the anterior pituitary. In this way, the hypothalamus acts like a production manager, receiving information about the needs of the company's customers and regulating the production of products to satisfy those needs. The hypothalamus accomplishes its management job by

producing **releasing hormones** that affect the secretion of specific hormones from the anterior pituitary. The hypothalamus also produces two hormones that do not regulate hormonal release in the pituitary. When they are needed by the body, the hypothalamus signals the pituitary to release them.

The pituitary is a tiny gland that hangs from the underside of the brain. The secretion of its many diverse hormones is controlled by a mass of nerve cells lying directly above it called the *hypothalamus.* The hypothalamus stimulates or inhibits the secretion of hormones from the pituitary by means of releasing hormones. In addition, the hypothalamus produces two hormones that it stores in the pituitary.

The anterior pituitary

The seven hormones produced by the anterior pituitary regulate a wide range of bodily functions (Figure 14-5, *B*). Four of these hormones are called **tropic hormones.** The word *tropic* comes from a Greek word meaning "turning" and refers to the ability of tropic hormones to turn on or stimulate other endocrine glands. Of the four tropic hormones, two are **gonadotropins.**

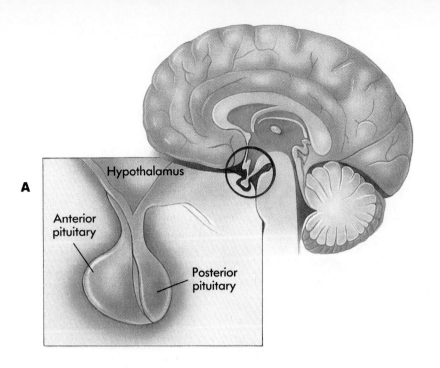

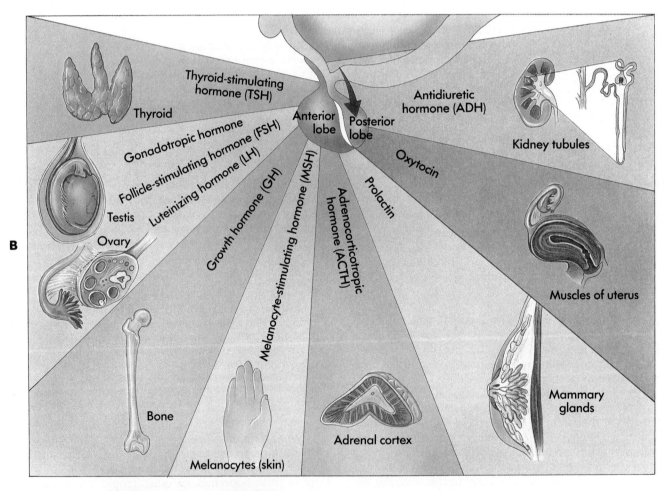

FIGURE 14-5   The role of the pituitary.
A In this diagram, the stalk of connecting tissue between the hypothalamus and the pituitary can be clearly seen.
B The hormones secreted by the pituitary can be divided into anterior pituitary hormones and posterior pituitary hormones.

The gonads are the male and female sex organs, the testes and the ovaries. The gonadotropins are hormones that affect these sex organs (considered endocrine glands because they secrete sex hormones). The two gonadotropins are **follicle-stimulating hormone (FSH)** and **luteinizing hormone (LH).** In females, FSH targets the ovaries and triggers the maturation of one egg each month. In addition, it stimulates cells in the ovaries to secrete female sex hormones called *estrogens.* In men, FSH targets the testes and triggers the production of sperm. LH stimulates cells in the testes to produce the male sex hormone testosterone. In females, a surge of LH near the middle of the menstrual cycle stimulates the release of an egg. In addition, LH triggers the development of cells within the ovaries that produce another female sex hormone—progesterone. (See Chapter 21 for a description of the organs and processes of the reproductive system.)

The two other tropic hormones are **adrenocorticotropic hormone (ACTH)** and **thyroid-stimulating hormone (TSH).** ACTH triggers the adrenal cortex to produce certain steroid hormones. The adrenal glands are located on top of the kidneys (see Figure 14-1). Each of these two glands has two distinct parts: an outer cortex and an inner medulla. ACTH stimulates the adrenal cortex to produce hormones that regulate the production of glucose from noncarbohydrates such as fats and proteins. Others regulate the balance of sodium and potassium ions in the blood. Still others contribute to the development of the male secondary sexual characteristics. TSH triggers the thyroid gland to produce the three thyroid hormones. This endocrine gland is located on the front of the neck, just below the voice box (see Figure 14-1). Its hormones control normal growth and development and are essential to proper metabolism. (Further discussion of ACTH is on p. 268, and further discussion of TSH is on p. 264.)

The front portion of the pituitary, the anterior pituitary, secretes seven hormones. Of these seven, four stimulate other endocrine glands and are called tropic hormones.

Growth hormone (GH) is produced by the anterior pituitary and works with the thyroid hormones to control normal growth. GH increases the rate of growth of the skeleton by causing cartilage cells and bone cells to reproduce and lay down their intercellular matrix. In addition, GH stimulates the deposition of minerals within this matrix. GH also stimulates the skeletal muscles to grow in both size and number. In the past, children who did not produce enough GH did not grow to an average height; this condition is called *hypopituitary dwarfism.* However, in the past decade, scientists have been able to use the techniques of genetic engineering to insert the human GH gene into bacteria to produce human GH. Currently, this laboratory-made hormone is being used successfully for treating growth disorders caused by hyposecretion (underproduction) of GH in children. The opposite problem may also occur: during the growth years, some children produce too much GH. This hypersecretion (overproduction) can cause the long bones to grow unusually long (Figure 14-6) and result in a con-

FIGURE 14-6 The world's tallest woman.
Sandy Allen is shown here with her mother, brother, and dog. Giantism is caused by the oversecretion of growth hormone.

dition known as *giantism.* In adults, hypersecretion of GH causes the bones of the hands and face to thicken, resulting in a condition known as *acromegaly* (Figure 14-7).

Prolactin is another hormone secreted by the anterior pituitary. Prolactin works with estrogen, progesterone, and other hormones to stimulate the mammary glands in the breasts to secrete milk after a woman has given birth to a child. During the menstrual cycle, milk is not produced and

FIGURE 14-7 Effects of acromegaly.
These photographs of a woman with acromegaly, at ages 16 and 33, show the thickening of the facial bones that results from the oversecretion of growth hormone.

secreted because prolactin levels in the bloodstream are very low. Late in the menstrual cycle, however, as the levels of progesterone and estrogen fall, the pituitary is stimulated by the hypothalamus to secrete some prolactin. This rise in prolactin, although not sufficient to cause milk production, does cause the breasts of some women to feel sore before menstruation. After menstruation, estrogen levels begin to rise, and prolactin secretion is once again inhibited.

Melanocyte-stimulating hormone (MSH) acts on cells in the skin called *melanocytes*, which synthesize a pigment called *melanin*. This pigment is taken up by epidermal cells in the skin, producing skin colorations from pale yellow (in combination with another pigment called *carotene*) to black. Variations are caused by the amount of pigment the melanocytes produce; this variation is genetically determined and is an inherited characteristic.

The posterior pituitary

The posterior lobe of the pituitary stores and releases two hormones that are produced by the hypothalamus: **antidiuretic hormone (ADH)** and **oxytocin.** ADH helps control the volume of the blood by regulating the amount of water reabsorbed by the kidneys. For example, receptors in the hypothalamus can detect a low blood volume by detecting when the solute concentration of the blood is high. When the hypothalamus detects such a situation, it triggers its specialized neurosecretory cells to make ADH. This hormone is transported within axons to the posterior pituitary, which releases the hormone into the bloodstream. ADH binds to target cells in the collecting ducts of the nephrons of the kidneys, increasing their permeability. More water then moves out of these ducts and back into the blood, resulting in a more concentrated urine. ADH also acts on the smooth muscle surrounding arterioles. As these muscles tighten, they constrict the arterioles, an action that helps raise the blood pressure. Alcohol suppresses ADH release, which is why excessive drinking leads to the production of excessive quantities of urine and eventually to dehydration.

Oxytocin is another hormone of the posterior pituitary: it is produced in the hypothalamus and transported within axons to the posterior pituitary for secretion. In women, oxytocin is secreted during the birth process, triggered by a stretching of the cervix of the uterus at the beginning of the birth process. Oxytocin binds to target cells of the uterus, enhancing the contractions already taking place. The mechanism of oxytocin secretion is an example of a **positive feedback loop** in which the effect produced by the hormone enhances the secretion of the hormone. For this reason, oxytocin is used by physicians to induce uterine contractions when labor must be brought on by external means. Oxytocin also targets muscle cells around the ducts of the mammary glands, allowing a new mother to nurse her child. The suckling of the infant triggers the production of more oxytocin, which aids in the nursing process and helps contract the uterus to its normal size.

▼
▼
▼
The rear lobe of the pituitary, or posterior pituitary, stores and releases two hormones, ADH and oxytocin, which are produced by the hypothalamus.

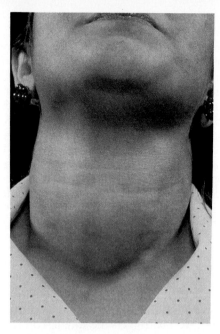

FIGURE 14-8   A goiter.
The thyroid gland becomes enlarged when the diet lacks iodine. Iodine is used in the production of the thyroid hormones; when not enough iodine is available, the thyroid cannot produce thyroid hormones, and the thyroid swells from overstimulation by the anterior pituitary.

The thyroid gland

Sitting like a large butterfly just below the level of the voice box, the thyroid gland can be thought of as your metabolic switch. This gland secretes hormones that determine the rate of the chemical reactions of your body's cells. Put simply, thyroid hormones determine how fast bodily processes take place.

The thyroid hormones are **thyroxine (T_4)** and **triiodothyronine (T_3).** These hormones are called *amines:* single, modified amino acids. They are not considered to be true peptide hormones, however, because they act on the DNA of target cells as steroid hormones do. They are also unique because an inorganic ion—iodine—is part of their structures.

Your body uses iodine in the food you eat to help make the thyroid hormones; the *3* or *4* in each hormone name refers to the number of atoms of iodine in each hormone. Foods such as seafood and iodized salt are good sources of dietary iodine. If the diet contains an insufficient amount of iodine, the thyroid gland enlarges. This condition is called a **hypothyroid goiter** (Figure 14-8).

The hypothalamus and the thyroid gland work together to keep the proper level of thyroid hormone circulating in the bloodstream. This level is detected by the hypothalamus. A low level of thyroid hormones stimulates the hypothalamus to secrete a releasing factor—a chemical message—to the anterior pituitary. This message tells the pituitary to release more TSH. The thyroid responds, thereby raising the blood level of T_3 and T_4 back to normal (Figure 14-9). This mechanism of action is an example of a negative feedback loop in which the effect produced by stimulation of a gland shuts down the stimulus. Shutdown occurs when a suffi-

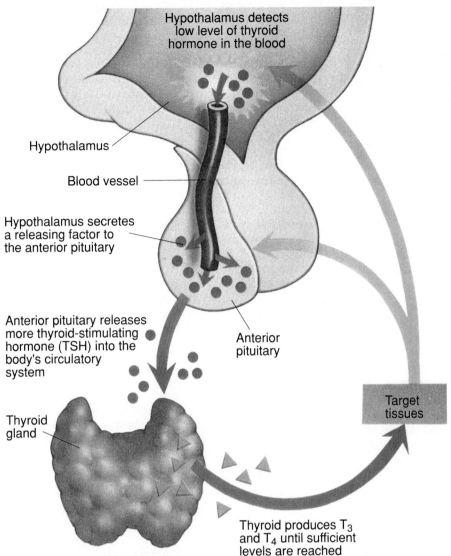

Hypothalamus detects
low level of thyroid
hormone in the blood

Hypothalamus

Blood vessel

Hypothalamus secretes
a releasing factor to
the anterior pituitary

Anterior pituitary releases
more thyroid-stimulating
hormone (TSH) into the
body's circulatory
system

Anterior
pituitary

Thyroid
gland

Target
tissues

Thyroid produces T$_3$
and T$_4$ until sufficient
levels are reached

FIGURE 14-9 A negative feedback loop is used in the release of thyroid hormone. When enough thyroid hormone has been produced, the hypothalamus stops producing thyroid-releasing hormone.

cient effect has been produced, similar to the mechanism of a thermostat. In your home, your furnace is triggered to go on when the temperature goes below the thermostat setting. The furnace stays on until the house heats up to the desired level. The thermostat then signals the furnace to turn off.

In certain disease conditions the amount of thyroid hormones in the bloodstream cannot be regulated properly. If the thyroid produces too much of the thyroid hormones, a person may feel as though the "engine is racing," with such symptoms as a rapid heartbeat, nervousness, weight loss, and protrusion of the eyes (Figure 14-10). This condition is called **hyperthyroidism.** On the other hand, if the thyroid produces too little of the thyroid hormones, a person may feel run down, with such symptoms as weight gain and slow growth of the hair and fingernails. This condition is

called **hypothyroidism.** Various factors can be the underlying cause of such problems; often medication or surgery can correct the situation.

In addition to secreting the thyroid hormones, the thyroid gland secretes a hormone called **calcitonin,** or **CT.** This hormone works to balance the effect of another hormone called **parathyroid hormone,** or **PTH.** PTH regulates the concentration of calcium in the bloodstream. Calcium is an important structural component in bones and teeth and aids in the proper functioning of nerves and muscles.

The thyroid gland, located in the neck near the voice box, produces hormones that regulate that body's metabolism.

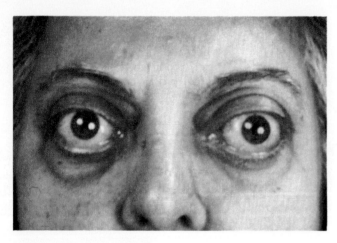

FIGURE 14-10 Hyperthyroidism.
One of the few symptoms of an overactive thyroid is protrusion of the eyes.

The parathyroid glands

Embedded in the posterior side of the thyroid are the **parathyroid glands.** Most people have two parathyroids on each of the two lobes of the thyroid, as shown in Figure 14-11. These are the glands that secrete PTH, which works antagonistically to CT to help maintain the proper blood levels of various ions, primarily calcium. Two of the many problems related to abnormal calcium levels in the blood are kidney stones and osteoporosis. If calcium levels in the blood remain high, tiny masses of calcium may develop in the kidneys. These masses, called *kidney stones,* can partially block the flow of the urine from a kidney. If calcium levels in the blood remain low, calcium may be removed from the bones, a disorder known as *osteoporosis.* Osteoporosis is most common in middle-aged and elderly women, who have stopped secreting estrogen at menopause (see Chapter 21). Estrogen stimulates bone cells to take calcium from the blood to build bone tissue.

PTH and CT work in the following way to keep calcium at an optimum level in the blood: If the calcium level is too low, PTH stimulates the activity of osteoclasts, or bone-destroying cells. These cells liberate calcium from the bones and put it into the bloodstream. PTH also stimulates the kidneys to reabsorb calcium from urine that is being formed and stimulates cells in the intestines to absorb an increased amount of calcium from digested food. CT acts antagonistically to PTH. When the level of calcium in the blood is too high, less PTH is secreted by the parathyroids and more CT is secreted by the thyroid. The CT inhibits the release of calcium from bone and speeds up its absorption, decreasing the levels of calcium in the blood. These interactions of PTH and CT are an example of a negative feedback loop that does not involve the hypothalamus or pituitary gland. The level of calcium in the blood directly stimulates the thyroid and parathyroid glands (Figure 14-12).

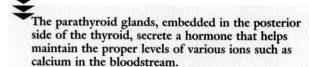

The parathyroid glands, embedded in the posterior side of the thyroid, secrete a hormone that helps maintain the proper levels of various ions such as calcium in the bloodstream.

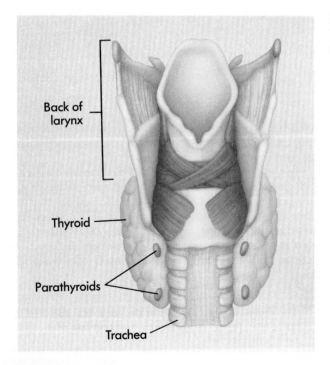

FIGURE 14-11 Location of the parathyroid glands.
These glands are embedded in the underside of the thyroid and secrete parathyroid hormone.

Back of larynx

Thyroid

Parathyroids

Trachea

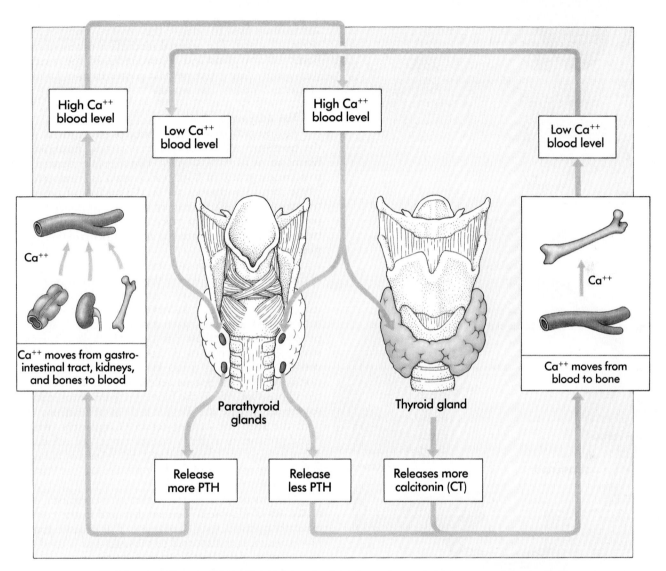

High Ca⁺⁺
blood level

Low Ca⁺⁺
blood level

High Ca⁺⁺
blood level

Low Ca⁺⁺
blood level

Ca⁺⁺

Ca⁺⁺ moves from gastro-
intestinal tract, kidneys,
and bones to blood

Ca⁺⁺

Ca⁺⁺ moves from
blood to bone

Parathyroid
glands

Thyroid gland

Release
more PTH

Release
less PTH

Releases more
calcitonin (CT)

FIGURE 14-12   How parathyroid hormone and calcitonin work to maintain proper calcium levels in the blood.
Parathyroid hormone stimulates the removal of calcium from the bones, the reabsorp-
tion of calcium from the urine, and the absorption of calcium from digested food when
calcium levels are low. When calcium levels in the blood are high, calcitonin works to
inhibit calcium release from bone and speed up its absorption.

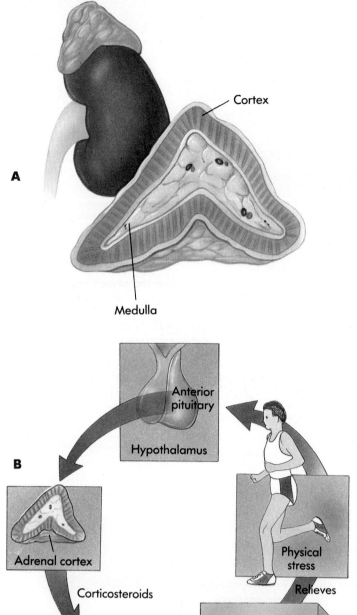

The adrenal glands

The two **adrenal glands** are named for their position in the body: above (*ad* meaning "near") the kidneys (*renal* meaning "kidney"). Each of these triangular glands has two parts with two different functions (Figure 14-13). The **adrenal cortex** is the outer, yellowish portion of each adrenal gland. The word *cortex* comes from a Latin word meaning "bark" and is often used to refer to the outer covering of a tissue, organ, or gland. The **adrenal medulla** is the inner, reddish portion of the gland and is surrounded by the cortex. Not surprisingly, the word *medulla* comes from a Latin word meaning "marrow" or "middle."

The adrenal cortex

As you may recall, the anterior pituitary gland secretes the hormone ACTH, adrenocorticotropic hormone. This hormone, as its name implies, stimulates the adrenal cortex to secrete a group of hormones known as **corticosteroids.** These steroid hormones act on the nucleus of target cells, triggering the cell's hereditary material to produce certain proteins. The two main types of corticosteroids produced by the adrenal cortex are the **mineralocorticoids** and the **glucocorticoids.**

The mineralocorticoids are involved in the regulation of the levels of certain ions within the body fluids. The most important of this group of hormones is **aldosterone.** It affects tubules within the kidneys, stimulating them to reabsorb sodium ions and water from the urine that is being produced, putting these substances back into the bloodstream. The secretion of aldosterone is triggered when the volume of the blood is too low, such as during dehydration or blood loss. Special cells in the kidneys monitor the blood pressure. When the blood pressure drops, these cells secrete an enzyme that begins a chain of reactions ending with the secretion of aldosterone. Conversely, when the blood pressure is within a normal range, the cell detectors in the kidneys are not stimulated, the release of aldosterone is not triggered, and the kidney tubules are not stimulated to conserve sodium and water.

The glucocorticoids affect glucose metabolism, causing molecules of glucose to be manufactured in the body from noncarbohydrates such as proteins. This glucose enters the bloodstream, is transported to the cells, and is used for energy as part of the body's reaction to **stress.**

Almost everyone is familiar with the term *stress.* And almost everyone can give examples of stressful situations: their boss "chewing them out" in front of co-workers, their kids fighting constantly with one another, or their sustaining a physical injury. The stress reaction was first described in 1936 by Hans Selye, a researcher who has since become the acknowledged authority on stress. Dr. Selye explained how the body typically reacted to stress—any disturbance that affects the body—and called this reaction the **general adaptation syndrome.** Over a prolonged period of stress, the body reacts in three stages: (1) the alarm reaction, (2) resistance, and (3) exhaustion. Contrary to maintaining homeostasis within the body, the general adaptation syndrome works to help the body gear up to meet an emergency.

During the alarm reaction the body goes into quick ac-

FIGURE 14-13 Structure and function of the adrenal glands.
A The adrenal glands are located on top of each kidney. Each gland has a cortex (the outer portion) and a medulla (the inner portion).
B The adrenal cortex plays a role in stress reduction. When the body is under stress, the hypothalamus, through the action of releasing hormone, induces the anterior pituitary to secrete ACTH. ACTH stimulates the adrenal cortex to produce corticosteroids. These corticosteroids cause the body to make glucose from noncarbohydrates such as protein, providing extra energy and thus reducing stress.

tion. Imagine entering your place of work and having your boss confront you, accusing you—in front of the office staff—of making a costly mistake. Your body reacts with a quickening pulse, increased blood flow, and an increased rate of chemical reactions within your body. Why does your body react in this way? Although the adrenal cortex is involved in the stress reaction, the beginning of the story lies in an understanding of the middle section of the adrenal glands, the adrenal medulla.

The adrenal medulla

The adrenal medulla is different from most other endocrine tissue in that its cells are derived from cells of the peripheral nervous system and are specialized to secrete hormones. These cells are triggered by the autonomic nervous system, which controls involuntary or automatic responses. The other major nervous tissues with direct endocrine function are the secretory portion of the hypothalamus in the brain and the posterior pituitary just under the hypothalamus.

The two principal hormones made by the adrenal medulla are **adrenaline** and **noradrenaline** (also called *epinephrine* and *norepinephrine*). These two hormones are primarily responsible for the alarm reaction. The hypothalamus is responsible for sending the alarm signal (via the autonomic nervous system) to the adrenal medulla. The hypothalamus picks up the alarm signal as it monitors changes in the emo-

tions and carries it as nerve signals on tracts of neurons that connect the hypothalamus with the emotional centers in the cerebral cortex. It can therefore sense when the body perceives an emotional stress. It can also sense physical stress, such as cold, bleeding, and poisons in the body. The hypothalamus reacts to stress by readying the body for fight or flight; it first triggers the adrenal medulla to dump adrenaline and noradrenaline into the bloodstream. These hormones cause the heart rate and breathing to quicken, the rate of chemical reactions to increase, and glucose (stored in the liver) to be dumped into the bloodstream. In general, the actions of adrenaline and noradrenaline increase the amounts of glucose and oxygen available to the organs and tissues most used for defense: the brain, heart, and skeletal muscles. (A summary of the stress reaction is shown in Figure 14-14.)

The adrenal glands, located on top of each kidney, are divided into two secretory portions: an outer cortex and an inner medulla. The hormones of the adrenal cortex, the corticosteroids, primarily regulate the level of sodium and consequently water in the bloodstream and stimulate the liver to produce glucose from stored carbohydrates. The hormones of the adrenal medulla, adrenaline and noradrenaline, ready the body to react to stress.

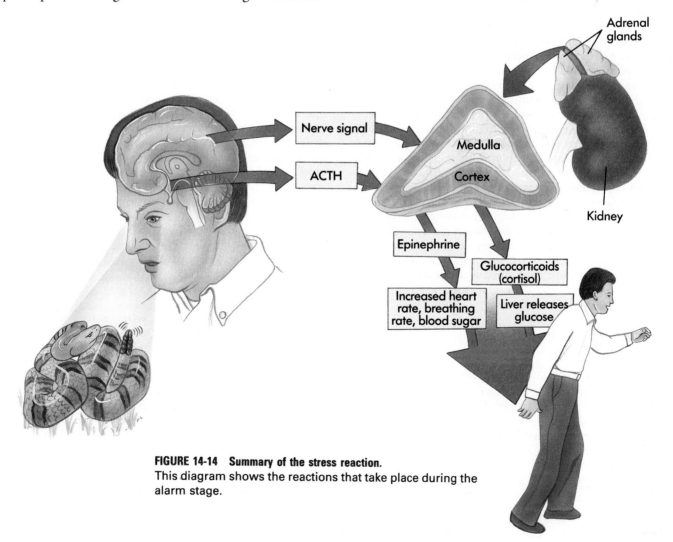

FIGURE 14-14   Summary of the stress reaction.
This diagram shows the reactions that take place during the alarm stage.

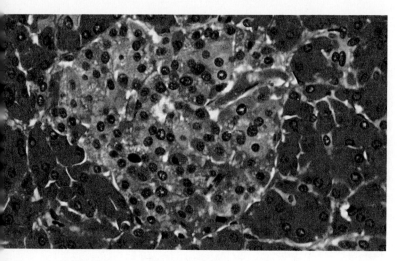

FIGURE 14-15 Islets of Langerhans.
Glucagon and insulin are produced by the islets of Langerhans, which are more lightly stained in this preparation.

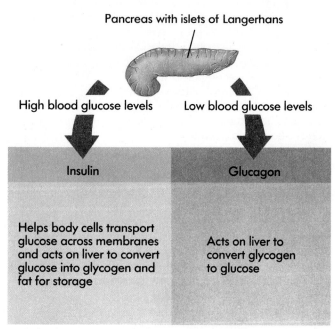

Pancreas with islets of Langerhans

High blood glucose levels   Low blood glucose levels

Insulin   Glucagon

Helps body cells transport glucose across membranes and acts on liver to convert glucose into glycogen and fat for storage

Acts on liver to convert glycogen to glucose

FIGURE 14-16 Functions of insulin and glucagon.
Glucagon and insulin work antagonistically. Insulin helps cells transport glucose across their membranes and acts on the liver to convert the excess glucose to glycogen and fat. These activities lower blood glucose levels. When blood glucose levels are low, glucagon triggers the liver to convert glycogen to glucose.

During the second stage of stress, the resistance stage, the hypothalamus triggers continuing responses by releasing regulating factors. These factors stimulate the pituitary to release ACTH, GH, and TSH. TSH stimulates the thyroid to secrete T_4, which stimulates the liver to break down stored carbohydrates (glycogen) to glucose. GH also stimulates the liver to produce glucose from glycogen, providing the body with an abundant energy source. ACTH stimulates the adrenal cortex to secrete both mineralocorticoids and glucocorticoids. The mineralocorticoids cause the body to retain sodium and water, raising the blood pressure and providing more blood volume in the case of blood loss. The glucocorticoids also promote the production of glucose.

If a person continues to be highly stressed over a long time, the body may lose the fight and enter the third stage of the stress reaction: exhaustion. This stage is serious and can cause death. One cause of exhaustion is the loss of potassium ions, which are excreted when sodium ions are retained. This loss severely affects the cells' ability to function properly. Another cause is depletion of the glucocorticoids, resulting in a sharp drop in the blood glucose level. The organs also become weak and may cease to function. To combat chronic stress, people can learn ways in which to psychologically handle their stress and can work toward a level of health and fitness that will help their bodies cope with the physical effects of stress.

The pancreas

The pancreas, located alongside the stomach (see Figure 14-1), is two glands in one: an exocrine gland and an endocrine gland. As an exocrine gland, it secretes the digestive enzymes discussed in Chapter 7. As an endocrine gland, it secretes the hormones **insulin** and **glucagon.**

The endocrine portion of the pancreas consists of separated clusters of cells that lie among the exocrine cells. For this reason, these cells are called *islets*—the **islets of Langerhans** (Figure 14-15). Separate types of cells within

the islets produce insulin and glucagon. These hormones act antagonistically to one another to regulate the level of glucose in the bloodstream. Glucagon increases the blood glucose level by triggering the liver to convert stored carbohydrates (glycogen) into glucose and to convert other nutrients such as amino acids into glucose. Insulin decreases the blood glucose level by helping body cells transport glucose across their membranes. In addition, insulin acts on the liver to convert glucose into glycogen and fat for storage (Figure 14-16).

Diabetes mellitus is a set of disorders in which a person tends to have a high level of glucose in the blood. There are many variations of the disorder and many causes. The underlying cause is the lack or partial lack of insulin, or the inability of tissues to respond to insulin, which leads to increased levels of glucose in the blood. The high levels of glucose in the blood result in water moving out of the body's tissues by osmosis. The kidneys remove this excess water through increased urine production, which causes excessive thirst and dehydration.

The primary types of diabetes mellitus are termed *type I* and *type II diabetes*. Persons with type I diabetes, or juvenile onset diabetes, have no effective insulin of their own. This type of diabetes usually develops in people younger than age 20. These persons must take injections of insulin as well as maintain an appropriate diet. Their deficiency of insulin causes the body to act as though it does not have enough glucose to fill its energy needs. Therefore it breaks down its fat reserves, resulting in the production of acids

When you think of dread diseases, the ones that come to mind are AIDS, cancer, Alzheimer's, multiple sclerosis, muscular dystrophy, and the like. Few would think to add diabetes to this list. However, untreated diabetes eventually leads to serious complications, doubling the risk of heart attack and stroke. It is the leading cause of blindness in adults and accounts for one third of all cases of kidney failure. Because of these many ill effects, diabetes is now the seventh leading cause of death in the United States.

Diabetes is a disorder in which the pancreas does not produce adequate amounts of the hormone insulin or the body becomes insensitive to it. As a result, muscles, fat, and liver cells are prevented from absorbing sugar from the blood; the sugar is excreted in urine, while the undernourished cells literally starve. Diabetes is treated by adding insulin directly to the bloodstream by injection (a protein, it would be destroyed in the stomach if administered as a pill), usually twice a day (Figure 14-A).

Over 100 million people worldwide have diabetes. Because initial symptoms are usually mild (fatigue and frequent urination), half the 12 million Americans with diabetes do not realize they have it.

There are two kinds of diabetes. In type I diabetes, which chiefly strikes in childhood, the body loses its ability to produce insulin. Affecting about 10% of diabetics, type I diabetes is a hereditary autoimmune disease in which the body's immune system attacks the pancreas, destroying its ability to produce insulin. Glucose builds up in the bloodstream to a three times normal level, while the cells starve. The high levels of blood glucose cause the thickening of capillary and artery walls, constricting blood flow and damaging critical organs. Affected individuals

FIGURE 14-A
The father of this boy with diabetes is testing his son's blood-sugar level with a pocket-sized machine.

must take two insulin shots a day all their lives to avoid disaster. Researchers are working hard to uncover a way to prevent the immune system from attacking the pancreas.

In type II diabetes, which primarily affects adults over the age of 40, the body becomes resistant to the effects of insulin, requiring the pancreas to produce ever-larger amounts until it is unable to produce enough insulin to meet its needs and the same symptoms that ravage type I patients set in. In the United States, 90% of those who develop type II diabetes are obese. Cells, sated with food, adjust their appetite for glucose downward by reducing their sensitivity to insulin. To compensate, the pancreas pumps out ever more insulin. In most obese people, the pancreas is able to keep up with the work load, but in individuals carrying particular recessive genes for type II diabetes, obesity overloads the system and insulin-producing cells begin to stop functioning. These cells also make a protein called *amylin*, and some researchers believe that amylin deposits in the pancreas lead to type II diabetes, much as amyloid protein deposits in the brain lead to Alzheimer's disease. Fortunately, type II diabetes can usually be treated by diet and exercise, and most affected individuals do not need daily injections of insulin.

---

called *ketones*. These acids lower the pH of the blood (make it more acidic), a situation that can result in death.

Persons with type II diabetes, or maturity onset diabetes, have some effective insulin but not enough to meet their needs. Others have sufficient insulin, but the cells in many parts of the body lack enough insulin receptors. These persons can often treat their disorder with diet alone. Research on the possibility of transplanting islets of Langerhans for persons who do not produce enough insulin holds much promise as a lasting treatment for this disease.

The pancreas secretes two hormones, insulin and glucagon, that act antagonistically to one another, regulating the level of glucose in the bloodstream.

The pineal gland

The **pineal gland** gets its name because it looks like a tiny pine cone embedded deep within the brain (see Figure 14-

TABLE 14-1   Endocrine glands and their hormones

ENDOCRINE GLAND AND HORMONE	TARGET TISSUE	PRINCIPAL ACTIONS
▼ **HYPOTHALAMUS**		
Releasing hormones	Other endocrine glands	Stimulate the release of hormones by other endocrine glands
▼ **POSTERIOR PITUITARY**		
Oxytocin	Uterus Mammary glands	Stimulates contraction of uterus and milk production
Antidiuretic hormone (ADH)	Kidneys	Stimulates reabsorption of water by the kidneys
▼ **ANTERIOR PITUITARY**		
Follicle-stimulating hormone (FSH)	Sex organs	Stimulates ovarian follicle, spermatogenesis
Luteinizing hormone (LH)	Sex organs	Stimulates ovulation and corpus luteum formation in females
Adrenocorticotropic hormone (ACTH)	Adrenal cortex	Stimulates secretion of adrenal cortical hormones
Thyroid-stimulating hormone (TSH)	Thyroid	Stimulates secretion of T_3 and T_4
Growth hormone (GH)	Cartilage and bone cells, skeletal muscle cells	Stimulates division of cartilage and bone cells, growth of muscle cells, and deposition of minerals
Prolactin	Mammary glands	Stimulates milk production
Melanocyte-stimulating hormone (MSH)	Melanocytes	Stimulates production of melanin
▼ **THYROID GLAND**		
Thyroxine (T_4) and triiodothyrone (T_3)	General	Regulates metabolism
Calcitonin	Bone	Regulates calcium levels in the blood
▼ **PARATHYROID GLAND**		
Parathyroid hormone (PTH)	Bone, kidney, small intestine	Regulates calcium levels in the blood

1). Although a great deal of research has been conducted regarding the workings of this gland, it still remains somewhat of a mystery. Interestingly, the pineal is the possible site of your biological clock, the control center that regulates your daily rhythms, such as sleeping and waking. It may also stimulate such activity as the onset of puberty.

The thymus gland

The thymus gland is a small gland located in the neck a few inches below the thyroid (see Figure 14-1). In the thymus, certain immune system cells called *T lymphocytes* develop the ability to identify invading bacteria and viruses (see Chapter 16). The thymus produces a variety of hormones to promote the maturation of these cells. This gland is quite active during childhood but is replaced by fat and connective tissue by the time a person reaches adulthood.

The ovaries and testes

The ovaries produce female sex cells, or eggs, and the testes produce male sex cells, or sperm. In addition, the ovaries produce the hormones estrogen and progesterone, and the testes produce testosterone. The detailed structure of these endocrine glands and the specific roles their hormones play are discussed in Chapter 21.

Nonendocrine hormones

The principal endocrine glands and their hormones are listed in Table 14-1. However, certain cells in the body produce chemical messengers that regulate nearby cells without traveling in the bloodstream and are therefore not considered endocrine hormones. These intercellular chemical messengers are often called *local hormones* and include a wide

TABLE 14-1	Endocrine glands and their hormones—cont'd

ENDOCRINE GLAND AND HORMONE	TARGET TISSUE	PRINCIPAL ACTIONS
▼ **ADRENAL CORTEX**		
Aldosterone	Kidney	Increases sodium and water reabsorption and potassium excretion
Glucocorticoids	General	Stimulate manufacture of glucose
▼ **ADRENAL MEDULLA**		
Adrenaline and noradrenaline	Heart, blood vessels, liver, fat cells	Regulate "fight or flight" response: increase cardiac output, blood flow to muscles and heart, conversion of glycogen to glucose
▼ **PANCREAS (ISLETS OF LANGERHANS)**		
Insulin	Liver, skeletal muscle, fat	Decreases blood glucose levels by stimulating movement of glucose into cells
Glucagon	Liver	Increases blood glucose levels by converting glycogen into glucose
▼ **OVARY**		
Estrogens	General, female reproductive organs	Stimulate development of secondary sex characteristics in females; control monthly preparation of uterus for pregnancy
Progesterone	Uterus	Completes preparation of uterus for pregnancy
	Breasts	Stimulates development
▼ **TESTIS**		
Testosterone	General	Stimulates development of secondary sex characteristics in males and growth spurt at puberty
	Male reproductive structures	Stimulates development of sex organs, spermatogenesis

variety of substances. Certain cells in the walls of the stomach and small intestine, for example, secrete hormones that regulate the release of digestive juices by various cells. The ends of axons secrete a variety of transmitter substances that stimulate the dendrites or cell body of a neighboring neuron, allowing a nerve impulse to be conducted from neuron to neuron. Cells throughout the body secrete substances called **prostaglandins** that are derived from the cell membranes. These local hormones accumulate in regions of tissue injury or disturbance. They stimulate smooth muscle contraction and the dilation and constriction of blood vessels. Overproduction of prostaglandins swells cerebral blood vessels, so their walls press against nerve tracts in the brain, causing pain. Aspirin relieves this pain, commonly known as a headache, because it inhibits prostaglandin production.

In recent years, a group of local hormones has been identified within the brain. The most commonly known local brain hormones are the **enkephalins** and **endorphins.** Both have pain-killing properties similar to the drug morphine. It has been suggested that these chemical messengers are the body's natural painkillers, and they have been linked to a feeling of well-being referred to as *runner's high* experienced by some joggers.

Certain cells in the body produce hormones such as prostaglandins, enkephalins, and endorphins that regulate nearby cells. Because these chemicals do not travel in the bloodstream, they are not considered endocrine hormones.

Summary

1. Hormones are the chemical products of cells, used as messengers to affect other cells within the body. Hormones that are secreted into the bloodstream are called *endocrine hormones*. The 10 different endocrine glands make over 30 different hormones. Together, the glands that secrete the endocrine hormones are known as the *endocrine system*.

2. Hormones that are not secreted into the bloodstream but move within the tissue fluid to affect cells near their sources are called *local hormones*. These intercellular chemical messengers include a wide variety of substances.

3. Hormones affect cells in one of four ways: by regulating their secretions and excretions, by helping them to respond to changes in the environment, by controlling activities related to reproductive processes, and by influencing their proper growth and development.

4. The two primary types of endocrine hormones are the peptide hormones and the steroid hormones. Peptide hormones work by binding to receptor molecules embedded in the cell membranes of target cells and ultimately triggering enzymes that cause cells to alter their functioning. Steroid hormones work by binding to receptor molecules within the cytoplasm of cells and ultimately causing the hereditary material to produce certain proteins.

5. The production of hormones is regulated by feedback mechanisms in the following way: an endocrine gland is initially stimulated directly or indirectly by the nervous system or by the concentration of various substances in the bloodstream. The gland secretes a hormone that interacts with target cells, and the effect produced by the target cells acts as a new stimulus to increase or decrease the amount of hormone produced.

6. The pituitary gland, which hangs from the underside of the brain, secretes nine different hormones: seven from its anterior lobe and two produced by the hypothalamus that are stored in its posterior lobe. The hypothalamus is a small mass of brain tissue lying above the pituitary. The hypothalamus controls the pituitary by means of releasing hormones.

7. Four of the hormones produced by the anterior pituitary control other endocrine glands. In addition, the anterior pituitary secretes growth hormone, which works with the thyroid hormones to control normal growth; prolactin, which works with other female sex hormones to stimulate the mammary glands to secrete milk after childbirth; and melanocyte-stimulating hormone, which affects certain pigment-producing cells of the body.

8. The posterior pituitary secretes two hormones produced by the hypothalamus. Antidiuretic hormone helps control the volume of the blood by regulating the amount of water reabsorbed by the kidneys. Oxytocin is secreted during the birth process and enhances uterine contractions.

9. The parathyroids, located on the underside of the thyroid gland in the neck, secrete parathyroid hormone. This hormone works with one of the thyroid hormones, calcitonin, to help maintain the proper blood levels of various ions, primarily calcium.

10. The adrenal glands, located on top of the kidneys, have two different secretory portions: the outer cortex and the inner medulla. The cortex secretes a group of hormones known as *corticosteroids* that regulate the levels of certain mineral ions, water, and glucose in the bloodstream. The adrenal medulla secretes the hormones adrenaline and noradrenaline, which ready the body for action during times of stress.

1. What are hormones, and why are they important?

2. How do the "messages" sent by the endocrine system differ from those carried by the nervous system?

3. Why is cyclic AMP required to act as a "second messenger" in peptide hormone–related processes?

4. Puberty is the physiological period when adolescents quickly mature and develop secondary sex characteristics (facial hair, breast development, menses, etc.). This is a period of great increase in hormonal levels. What class of hormones would you hypothesize are responsible for many of the physiological changes in puberty?

5. Describe how a feedback loop regulates the production of a hormone. What is the difference between a negative feedback loop and a positive feedback loop?

6. If the fluid content of the blood is low, where would this information initially be received and processed? What hormone would be released and from which endocrine gland would it be released?

7. Explain the term *tropic hormone*. Identify the four tropic hormones produced by the anterior pituitary and summarize the function(s) of each.

4. In the past, people living in remote inland areas often suffered from goiter. Can you assess the reasons for increased goiter problems in such places?

5. After playing softball on a hot sunny day, you are sweating hard and feeling very thirsty. A friend suggests getting a beer. Will the beer help your body replace the fluids it has lost? Explain.

6. Describe two hormones that together regulate calcium levels in your blood and discuss how they do it.

7. Describe the three stages of the general adaptation syndrome. What hormones are involved?

8. Doctors may prescribe vitamin B$_6$ as a dietary supplement to relieve stress and enhance glucose metabolism. What gland do you think may be affected by this vitamin? Give a descriptive summary of a stress reaction that you have experienced recently.

9. Chronic emotional stress has been linked to a greater than normal risk of various diseases. How might this link be explained?

10. Which hormones regulate the level of glucose in your blood? Describe how they do this. Where are they produced?

DISCUSSION QUESTIONS

1. There is no question that athletes using steroids gain a competitive advantage from the extra muscle the steroids induce. Why do you think the use of steroids is universally banned?

2. We know that hormones provide a slower and different system of communication between body tissues than the nervous system. What might be some advantages of the slower system? Why is hormonal interaction significant?

3. It has often been speculated that the pineal gland is involved with the body's rhythms. How would you test this hypothesis?

FOR FURTHER READING

Cantin, M., & Genest, J. (1986, February). The heart as an endocrine gland. *Scientific American*, pp. 76-81.
This is a good example of how your body self-regulates its activities; in addition to pumping blood, the heart secretes a hormone that fine tunes the control of blood pressure.

Cohen, D. (1992, July). Zen and the art of dealing with stress. *American Scientist*, pp. 28-32.
A study of the complex relationships between physical exertion, stress, and mind-body effects of hormones.

Davis, J. (1984). *Endorphins: New waves in brain chemistry*, New York: Doubleday & Co., Inc.
This article provides a popular account of research on brain hormones.

Perry, H.M. and Hughes, G.W. (1992, December). A case of affective disorder associated with use of anabolic steroids. *British Journal of Sports Medicine*, pp. 219-221.
A clinical discussion of the abuse of anabolic steroids by athletes.

BIOETHICAL DECISIONMAKING
Mental Competence to Refuse Treatment

Consider the following questions as you think about the bioethical dilemma presented on page 203:

1. What are the bioethical issues in this case?
   - What has to be decided?
   - Who are the decisionmakers?
   - Outline the decisionmaking process in this case as you understand it.

2. What factual information do the decisionmakers need? Consider the effects of the answers to the following questions on the decisionmaking process.
   - Do the patient's mental incapacities make him unable to understand the full implications of refusing surgery?
   - Did the patient express any positive or negative feelings about medical procedures (and brain surgery in particular) before the onset of his mental deterioration?
   - Is the wife agreeing with her husband because she respects his authority, or because she knows what her husband would decide if he were not mentally impaired?
   - Is the patient's behavior a threat to society? Could his behavior become antisocial and threatening?
   - Will the patient eventually die if his condition is not treated?
   - What other questions should the decisionmakers ask?
   - What additional factual information do the decisionmakers need?

3. Who are the "stakeholders" in this decision—those who stand to gain or lose as a result of the decision?
   - Is the patient a stakeholder? His wife? The resident? The attending physician? What other persons or groups are stakeholders?
   - Which stakeholders are decisionmakers? Which are not decisionmakers? Will individuals in the latter group be able to influence the decisionmaking process? Should they have influence?
   - In what ways would each stakeholder be affected by the decision?

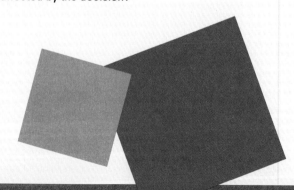

4. What are the values at stake in the decision? As you list and describe them, consider the following questions:
   - Does a patient have the right to determine his or her own fate? If so, does that right still exist when his or her mental abilities are impaired?
   - Do physicians have the right to compel patients to accept treatment when they believe it is in the patient's best interest? Under what circumstances is such compulsion acceptable?
   - Does the patient's refusal of treatment have implications for society at large? (For example, without treatment he will eventually be hospitalized for an extended period of time, which will be costly to both his family and society.) Should such implications affect the physicians' decision?

5. What options are available to the decisionmakers? As you list these options, consider the following questions:
   - Which of these alternatives seem ethically feasible? Which seem administratively possible?
   - How would each alternative decision affect each of the stakeholders?
   - Is there a compromise solution that might give all parties the sense that they have come out the "winner" in the decision?

6. What are the values inherent to the decisionmaking process?
   - Should the resident and the attending physician alone make this decision? Is this decisionmaking process fair?
   - Can the hospital impose its physicians' decisions on its patients?
   - Do all stakeholders have equal resources to advocate their position?
   - What further steps might each group of stakeholders take if their views are disallowed?

PART FOUR

Protection, Support, and Defense

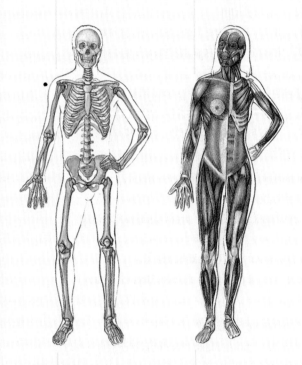

15

Protection, Support, and Movement

16

Defense Against Disease

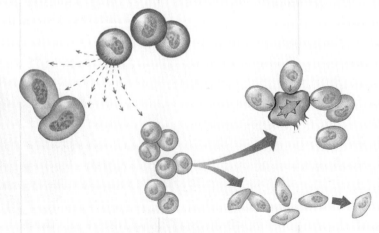

BIOETHICAL DECISIONMAKING
Organ Donation and Consent

Senate Bill 428 was introduced by two state senators to reduce the difficulty of obtaining organs for transplant in their state. Many citizens in these senators' constituencies had expressed frustration with the way that organs were made available for transplant. They knew that in other states in the United States, the family of a deceased person could donate that person's organs for transplantation. Presently, in their state, individuals who needed vital organs that could not be donated by a living person had to wait until a healthy person died suddenly, such as in an automobile accident. That person had to have signed the consent to organ donation form on the back of his or her driver's license. Only then could organs be removed for donation.

An organ recipient must wait until an organ from a compatible donor is available; the immune system will reject incompatible donor organs. This situation arises because each body cell is marked with a chemical "name tag" that denotes "self." These name tags are a group of cell surface antigens called the major histocompatibility complex (MHC). When a microbe or other foreign cell or group of cells, such as from a donated organ, invades the body, roving immune system cells detect the presence of "nonself" cells. The immune system then sets into motion chemical machinery that will track and destroy the "nonself" cells. Although the "self" name tags on cells are highly individualistic, scientists have identified certain types of name tags, similar to the way in which blood has been typed. The challenge in organ donation is to find a donor who has the same type of name tag on his or her cells as the waiting recipient. The procedure in which the name tag is identified is called a pretransplant crossmatch. Even with crossmatching,

however, organ rejection occurs, although the advent of drugs that suppress the activity of the immune system have lowered the rate of rejection.

The senators' bill can do nothing about compatibility, but it can broaden the pool of possible organ donors and thus increase the probability of providing compatible matches for recipients. Presently, the organ donation consent form appears on the back of an individual's driver's license. It is up to the individual to sign the form. Bill 428 states that in the absence of a certain objection or certain evidence of objection, an individual is presumed to have consented to the donation of the individual's organs. The bill outlines the following qualifications:

1. The next of kin (spouse, children, parents, or siblings) must be notified that organs are to be donated.

2. In the absence of a specific objection expressed by the individual in life or objection by the next of kin immediately following the individual's death, the individual is deemed to have consented to organ donation.

3. An individual who is known to have adhered to a religion that specifically forbids organ donation is deemed to have objected to organ donation.

4. If the individual has expressed written (in a form available to the health care provider) or oral consent (directly to the health care provider) to organ donation, this consent overrides any objection by the next of kin.

If you were a member of the Senate, how would you vote on this bill?

15 Protection, Support, and Movement

Fashioning faces using computers is one type of medical miracle taking place at Johns Hopkins Children's Facial Rehabilitation Center in Baltimore, Maryland. Erin Williams, born with a genetic disorder called Treacher Collins syndrome, knows all about this medical miracle. She was born without a jaw, cheekbones, or fully formed ears. Although she still faced surgery at the time this photo was taken, Erin does not look like a child who had to struggle just to eat and breathe during her infancy.

Doctors at the Children's Center performed "phantom surgery" to plan the reconstruction of Erin's face. Using three-dimensional computer images of her skull, doctors simulated Erin's surgery before they actually operated on her. Phantom surgery can be used to experiment with cutting and fitting bone pieces from other parts of a patient's body, or the computer can be used to design an artificial bone. This technology is called computer-aided design, or CAD for short. CAD has been used for years by engineers to design such products as cars and airplanes, but researchers are now applying this concept to medicine. To help Erin, doctors recreated her skull as a computer graphic using a stack of computerized tomography (CT) scan images. Each CT scan image pictures a thin slice of the body. A CAD computer stacks these images to produce a three-dimensional graphic that can be rotated and viewed from any angle. Using this image, doctors designed prostheses—artificial bones—for Erin. The instructions to build these prostheses were put on tape and then fed into a computer specialized in computer-aided manufacturing (CAM). CAM computers produce the mold necessary to make a prosthesis. In Erin's case, one company used a CAM computer attached to a milling machine to make Erin a plastic jaw. During surgery, a real jaw was fashioned for Erin using the plastic model as a template. To do this, physicians used bits of Erin's ribs and pieces of a chemically treated South Pacific coral that mimics human bone. Another company used CAD/CAM to construct titanium cheekbones for her. This lightweight, durable, biocompatible metal will hold bone grafts that will be added to Erin's face as she grows. After her teenage years, Erin will no longer need reconstructive surgery. The growth and development of her face, fashioned with modern technology, will be complete.

How skin, bones, and muscles work together

Bones not only give shape to the body and protect its delicate inner structures but also help you move. Your skeletal muscles are attached to your bones, pulling on one while anchored to another. Rigid yet flexible, bones are able to bear a considerable amount of weight. If you have ever tried to lift a heavy object, you are familiar with this basic problem of movement: gravity exerts a force, or "pull," on objects. For any motion to take place, the force exerted on an object—including your body parts—must be greater than the opposing force of gravity. The manner in which muscles are attached to bones allows bones to be used as levers to increase the strength of a movement, similar to the way a claw hammer increases the force you can exert on a nail to pull it out of a piece of wood.

To supply the force needed for movement, your body uses the chemical energy of adenosine triphosphate, or ATP (see Chapter 4). By splitting an ATP molecule into adenosine diphosphate (ADP) and inorganic phosphate (P_i), energy is made available to do the work of movement. Your body uses this energy to move certain microfilaments within your muscle cells, resulting in the shortening of those cells. When a large group of muscle cells shortens all at once, the muscle cells exert a great deal of force. For a muscle to use this force to produce movement, it must direct its force against an object. In humans, muscles pull on bones, so, for example, muscle contraction results in the lifting of a

leg or the bending of a finger. And although your movement is determined largely by your muscles and their attachments to bones, your skin plays an important role, too. It is a soft and flexible covering, stretching to accommodate the myriad of movements of which your body is capable.

Movement results from the contraction of skeletal muscles anchored to bones. These muscles use bones like levers to direct force against an object. When a body part is pulled to a new position, the skin stretches to accommodate the change.

Skin

Your skin is far more than simply an elastic covering of epithelial cells encasing your body's muscles, blood, and bones. Instead, it is a dynamic organ that performs many functions:

1. Skin is a protective barrier. It keeps out microorganisms that would otherwise infect the body. Because skin is waterproof, it keeps the fluids of the body in and other fluids out. Skin cells also contain a pigment called *melanin*, which absorbs potentially damaging ultraviolet radiation from the sun.
2. Skin provides a sensory surface. Sensory nerve endings in skin act as your body's pressure gauge, telling you how gently to caress a loved one and how firmly to hold a

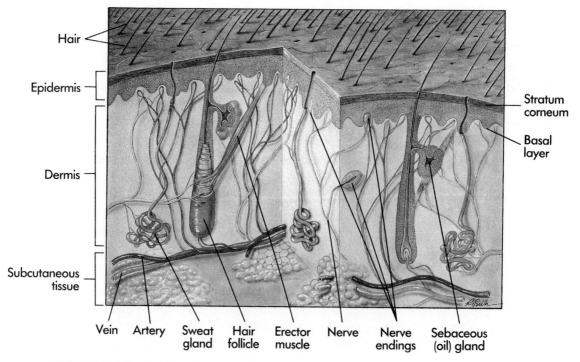

FIGURE 15-1 The structure of human skin.
Human skin is composed of three layers: the epidermis, the dermis, and the subcutaneous layer. Within these layers are specialized tissues and cells that perform many specialized functions.

pencil. Other sensors embedded in the skin detect pain, heat, and cold (see Chapter 13). Skin is the body's point of contact with the outside world.

3. Skin compensates for body movement. Skin stretches when you reach for something and contracts quickly when you stop reaching. It grows when you grow.
4. Skin helps control the body's internal temperature. When the temperature is cold, the blood vessels in the skin constrict, so less of the body's heat is lost to the surrounding air. When it is hot, these same vessels dilate, giving off heat. In addition, glands in the skin release sweat, which then absorbs body heat and evaporates, cooling the body surface.

Your skin is the largest organ of your body. In an adult human, 15% of the total body weight is skin. Much of the multifunctional role of skin reflects the fact that its tissues are made up of a myriad of specialized cells. In fact, one typical square centimeter of human skin contains 200 nerve endings, 10 hairs with accompanying microscopic muscles, 100 sweat glands, 15 oil glands, 3 blood vessels, 12 heat receptors, 2 cold receptors, and 25 pressure-sensing receptors (Figure 15-1). Together with the hair and nails, the skin is called the **integument** (meaning "outer covering") or the **integumentary system.**

⮟ The skin is the largest organ of the body and is made up of a myriad of specialized cells. It covers the surface of the body, protecting it while helping to control the body's internal temperature, providing a sensory surface, and compensating for body movement.

Bones

Bone is a type of connective tissue (see Chapter 6) consisting of widely separated bone cells embedded in a matrix of collagen fibers and mineral salts. The bones' mineral salts are needle-shaped crystals of calcium phosphate and calcium carbonate. The collagen fibers (see Figure 6-6) are coated and surrounded by these mineral salts. Interestingly, these two components give bone a structure strikingly similar to that of fiberglass, producing bones that are rigid yet flexible. You can see this interplay of flexibility and hardness by soaking a chicken bone in vinegar overnight. The acetic acid of the vinegar dissolves the mineral salts in the bone. Without the hardness of the mineral salts, the collagen fibers leave the bone so flexible that you can tie it in a knot!

Living cells are as important a component of bone as the collagen fibers and mineral salts are. New bone is formed by cells called **osteoblasts.** These cells secrete the collagen fibers on which the body later deposits mineral salts. The osteoblasts lay down bone in thin, concentric layers called **lamellae** (Figure 15-2), like layers of insulation wrapped around an old pipe. You can think of the osteoblasts as being within the insulation and the open tube of the pipe as a narrow channel called the **haversian canal.** Haversian canals run parallel to the length of the bone and contain blood vessels and nerves. The blood vessels provide a lifeline to living bone-forming cells, whereas the nerves

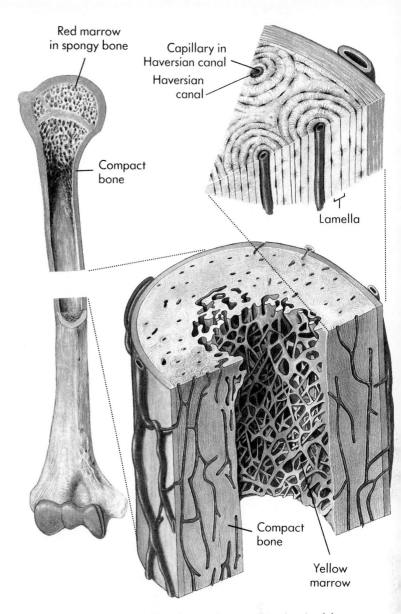

FIGURE 15-2 The organization of bone, shown at three levels of detail.
Some parts of bone are dense and compact, giving the bone strength. Other parts are spongy, with a more open lattice; it is here (within red bone marrow) that most red blood cells are formed. The microscopic structure of bone is shown in the upper right illustration.

control the diameter of the blood vessels and thus the flow through them. Nutrients and oxygen diffuse from the bloodstream into thin cellular processes of the osteoblasts, and metabolic wastes diffuse out.

⮟ Bone is a type of connective tissue made up of widely separated living cells that secrete collagen fibers into their surrounding matrix. The body deposits mineral salts on these fibers. The salts give bone hardness, whereas the collagen fibers contribute flexibility. This bone tissue appears under the light microscope as concentric rings surrounding a central canal containing blood vessels and nerves.

The bones of the human skeleton are composed of spongy bone and compact bone. Microscopically, **compact bone** has the concentric ring structure described previously. As shown in Figure 15-2, it runs the length of long bones, such as those in your arms and legs. However, if bones were completely made up of compact bone, your body would be very heavy, and your arms and legs would be nearly impossible to move! Instead, the central core of long bones is a hollow cylinder, and this cavity is filled with a soft, fatty connective tissue called **yellow marrow.**

Spongy bone makes up most of the ends of long bones and most of the bone tissue of short bones (like your wrist and ankle bones), flat bones (like your ribs), and irregularly shaped bones (like some of your facial bones). Spongy bone is an open latticework of thin plates, or bars, of bone. Microscopically, its structure does not show a regular concentric ring structure like compact bone; it has a somewhat more irregular organization. The spaces within its bony latticework are filled with **red bone marrow.** Here, most of the body's blood cells are formed. Surrounding the spongy bone tissue are layers of compact bone (see Figure 15-2). The compact bone gives bones the strength to withstand mechanical stress, and spongy bone provides some support and a storage place for the red bone marrow while helping to lighten bones.

The bones of the skeleton contain two kinds of tissue: spongy bone and compact bone. Compact bone runs the length of long bones and has no spaces within its structure visible to the naked eye. Spongy bone is found in the ends of long bones and within short, flat, and irregularly shaped bones. It looks like interweaving bars of bone with the intervening spaces filled with red bone marrow.

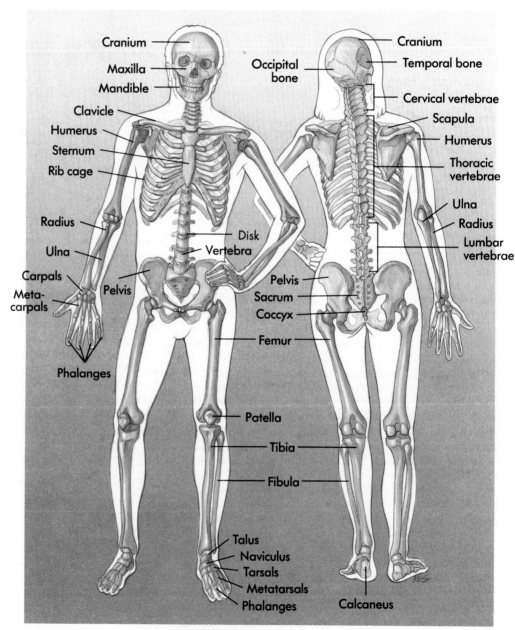

FIGURE 15-3 The human axial and appendicular skeletons.
The axial skeleton is made up of the bones of the head, face, rib cage, and vertebral column. The appendicular skeleton includes the bones of the legs and feet, arms and hands, clavicles, scapula, and pelvis.

The skeletal system

The 206 bones of the body make up a working whole called the *skeleton,* or *skeletal system.* Together, the bones of the skeleton perform many important functions, some of which have already been mentioned. To summarize: (1) The skeletal system provides support for the body—otherwise you would be a shapeless blob of skin-covered tissues and organs. (2) It also provides for movement, with individual bones serving as points of attachment for the skeletal muscles and acting as levers against which muscles can pull. (3) Delicate internal structures are protected by the skeleton. The brain, for example, lies within a strong, bony casing called the *skull;* the rib cage surrounds and protects the heart and lungs. (4) The bones of the skeleton are a storehouse for minerals such as calcium and phosphorus. Amazingly, bone tissue is continually broken down and re-formed, the mineral salts being transported to other parts of the body on demand. In fact, scientists have estimated that your body completely replaces your skeleton over a period of 7 years! (5) Lastly, certain inner portions of bones contain red marrow and are your internal factory of blood cells. Without this factory you would die because red blood cells have a short life span of approximately 120 days. Without these cells your body would have no efficient means to transport life-giving oxygen to your tissues. White blood cells are also produced in the red bone marrow. One of the main jobs of certain classes of these cells is to ingest bacteria and debris. White blood cells also form the cells of your immune system (see Chapter 16). It is essential to your survival that the red marrow continue to manufacture these cells, which have varying life spans and help protect your body from infection and disease.

Scientists divide your internal scaffolding of bones into two parts: the axial skeleton and the appendicular skeleton (Figure 15-3). The **axial skeleton** is your axis, or central column, of bones off which the appendages (arms and legs) of your **appendicular skeleton** hang. The appendicular skeleton also includes the bones that serve to attach the appendages to the axial skeleton.

The axial skeleton

The 80 bones of the axial skeleton include the bones of the skull, vertebral column, and rib cage. The **skull** contains 8 cranial and 14 facial bones. Find the following skull bones in Figure 15-4: 1 frontal bone that forms the forehead, 2 parietal bones that form a large portion of the sides and top of the skull, 2 temporal bones that form the sides of the skull toward the back, and 1 occipital bone that forms the lower back portion of the skull. The irregularly shaped ethmoid and sphenoid bones are not easy to locate in a diagram because only a tiny portion of these bones lies on the surface of the skull. The ethmoid bone sits between the eyes; only a fraction of it can be seen forming a part of each orbit, or eye socket. The rest of this bone forms part of the nasal cavity and the floor of the cranial cavity. The sphenoid bone makes up part of the back and sides of the eye sockets. Looking somewhat like wings, it extends from one side of the skull to the other, forming the middle portion of the base of the skull.

Some of the 14 facial bones are easy to see in Figure 15-4: 1 mandible, or lower jawbone; 2 maxillae, which unite to form the upper jawbone; 2 nasal bones, which form the bridge of the nose; and 2 zygomatic bones, or cheekbones. Look below the part of the ethmoid bone that forms part of the nasal septum to find the vomer. Along with the ethmoid and cartilage, the vomer helps divide the nose into right and left nostrils. The paired lacrimal bones are tiny, therefore difficult to see, and are located at the inner corners of the orbits near the nose. Each of these bones has a

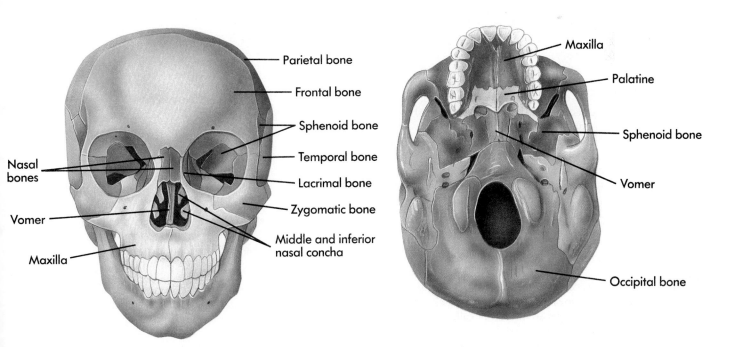

FIGURE 15-4 Frontal view of the human skull.
The skull contains 8 cranial and 14 facial bones.

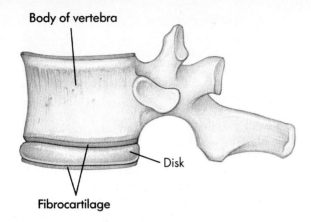

FIGURE 15-5 A vertebra with disk attached.
The vertebral column is composed of 26 vertebrae. Between each vertebra and the next is a disk composed of an outer layer of fibrocartilage and an inner, more elastic layer.

groove forming part of the tear ducts, canals that drain excess fluid bathing the eyes. The two L-shaped palatine bones are hidden from view because they form the back portion of the roof of your mouth and extend upward to form part of the floor and sides of the nasal cavity. The two inferior nasal conchae are "swirled" bones and project into the nasal cavity. The structure of these bones causes the air that enters the nose to be circulated and warmed before being breathed into the lungs.

The **vertebral column** is made up of 26 individual bones called *vertebrae* (Figure 15-5). Stacked one on top of the other, these bones act like a strong yet very flexible rod that supports the head. In addition, some of the vertebrae serve as points of attachment for the ribs. Each vertebra has a central hole, or foramen. Lined up, the vertebrae form a bony canal protecting the spinal cord, which runs down much of its length.

The 7 vertebrae closest to the head are the cervical (neck) vertebrae. Next are 12 thoracic (chest) vertebrae. Following these are 5 lumbar (lower back) vertebrae. The sacrum and the coccyx, or tailbone, are the last vertebrae in the column. Positioned between the vertebrae (except the sacrum and coccyx) are disks of fibrocartilage called **intervertebral disks.** These disks act as shock absorbers, provide the means of attachment between one vertebra and the next, and permit movement of the vertebral column.

Attached to the 12 thoracic vertebrae are 12 pairs of ribs. The ribs curve around to the front of the thoracic (chest) cavity, producing a bony cage that protects the heart and lungs. The upper 7 pairs of ribs directly connect to a flat bone that lies at the midline of the chest called the *breastbone,* or sternum. These 14 ribs each connect to the sternum by means of a strip of hyaline cartilage and are therefore called *true ribs.* The remaining five pairs of ribs, called *false ribs,* do not directly connect to the sternum. Instead the cartilages of ribs 8 through 10 attach to each other, and then to the cartilage of the seventh ribs pair. Ribs 11 and 12 do not attach to the sternum but hang free, supported by muscle tissue. These ribs are therefore called *floating ribs.*

The remaining bone of the axial skeleton is the **hyoid bone,** a name that means "U-shaped." This bone is supported by ligaments in the neck. It is the only bone in the body that does not form a joint with other bones. The

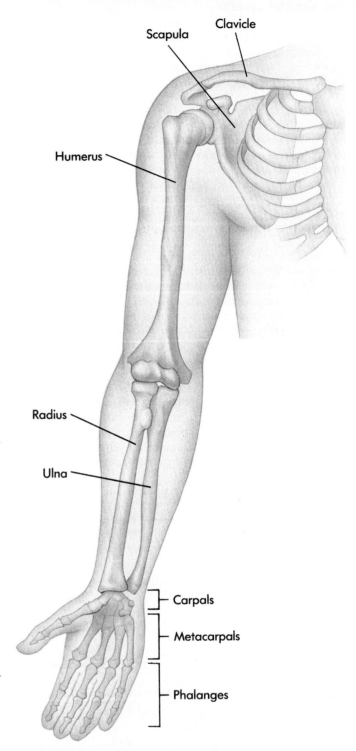

FIGURE 15-6 Bones of the pectoral girdle and arm, wrist, and hand.
Notice that the bones of the pectoral girdle support and form joints with the bones of the arm.

tongue is attached to the hyoid bone. Because this bone is often broken when a person is strangled, the hyoid can provide important evidence in certain murder cases.

The appendicular skeleton

The appendicular skeleton is made up of the bones of the appendages (arms and legs), the **pectoral (shoulder)**

girdle, and the **pelvic (hip) girdle.** The pectoral girdle is made up of two pairs of bones: the clavicles, or collarbones, and the scapulae, or shoulder blades. Find these bones in Figures 15-3 and 15-6, and then locate the edges of your own clavicles and scapulae. The bones of the pectoral girdle support and articulate with (form joints with) the arms. Both arms, or upper extremities, contain 60 bones.

As shown in Figure 15-6, the bone of the upper arm is called the *humerus*. This bone articulates with both the clavicle and the scapula. The other end of this long bone articulates with the two bones of the forearm: the radius and the ulna. The wrist is made up of eight short bones called *carpals*, lined up in two rows of four. These bones are held together by ligaments and articulate with the bones of the hand, or metacarpals. The five metacarpals articulate with the bones of the fingers, or phalanges (singular phalanx). Each finger has three phalanges; the thumb has only two.

The pelvic girdle is made up of two bones called *coxal bones*. You know these bones as pelvic bones or hipbones. Find these bones in Figures 15-3 and 15-7. Male and female skeletons can be distinguished from one another by looking at their pelvic bones. Females have a wider pelvis with a large, oval opening in the center for giving birth. The male pelvic girdle, in contrast, is narrower and has a smaller, heart-shaped opening in the center.

The bones of the pelvis support and articulate with the legs. Together, both legs, or lower extremities, contain 60 bones as the arms do. As shown in Figure 15-7, the bone of the upper leg, or thigh, is called the *femur*. This bone has a rounded, ball-shaped head that articulates with a depression, or socket, in the hipbone. The femur, the longest and heaviest bone in the body, articulates at its lower end with the two bones of the lower leg: the tibia and the fibula. The tibia is the bone commonly referred to as the *shinbone* and can be felt at the front of the lower leg. If you have ever had shin splints, you are well aware of this bone. Shin splints are an inflammation of the outer covering of the tibia caused by repeated tugging by muscles and tendons. Vigorous walking, running, or other types of exercise can sometimes result in shin splints, which can be very painful.

The patella, or kneecap, is a small triangular bone that sits in front of the joint formed by the femur, tibia, and fibula. The patella is a sesamoid bone, one that is formed within tendons where pressure develops.

Each ankle is made up of seven short bones called *tarsals*. One of these bones forms the heel, and is the largest and strongest ankle bone. The tarsals are held together by ligaments and articulate with the bones of the foot, or metatarsals. The five metatarsals articulate with the bones of the toes, or phalanges. Like the fingers, each toe has three phalanges; like the thumb, the "big toe" has only two.

⌄⌄
The 206 bones of the body make up the skeletal system, which can be divided into the axial skeleton and the appendicular skeleton. The axial skeleton includes your central axis—the skull, vertebral column, and rib cage. The appendicular skeleton is made up of the appendages (arms and legs) and the bones that help attach the appendages to the axial skeleton.

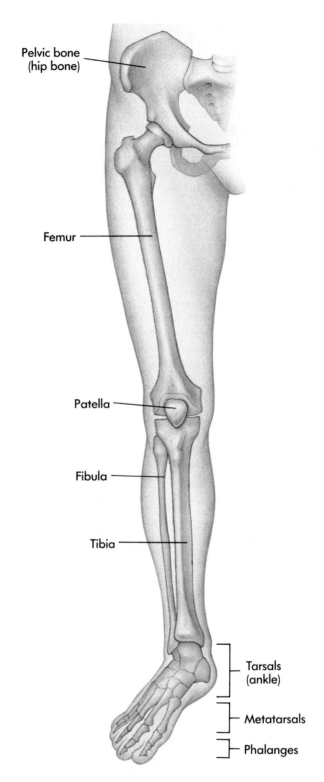

FIGURE 15-7 Bones of the pelvic girdle and leg, ankle, and foot. The two pelvic bones (also called *coxal* or *hip bones*) articulate with the head of each femur, or thigh bone.

Joints

If you have ever broken a leg or an arm and had a cast covering a joint, you have learned firsthand just how important joints are to movement. A **joint,** or **articulation,** is a place where bones or bones and cartilage come together. All joints are not alike; some permit little or no movement (immovable joints); some permit limited movement (slightly movable joints); and some permit a considerable amount of movement (freely movable joints). The amount of movement afforded by a joint is a direct result of how tightly the bones are held together at that location.

The bones of the skull articulate with one another in a type of immovable joint called a **suture.** The edges of each skull bone are ragged but fit tightly with the ragged edges of adjoining bones—just as puzzle pieces fit together (see Figure 15-3). A layer of dense connective tissue helps keep the bones from separating (see Chapter 6). Another example of immovable joints is the articulation of your teeth with the mandible and maxillae. Here, peg-shaped roots fit into cone-shaped sockets in the jawbones. A ligament lies between each tooth and its socket, holding each tooth in place. **Ligaments** are bundles, or strips, of dense connective tissue that hold bones to bones. A third example of an immovable joint is the articulation between the first pair of ribs and the breastbone. Each of these two ribs is connected to the sternum by a strip of hyaline cartilage, connections that change to bone during adult life.

As you twist your forearm to the right and left or twist your lower leg in the same manner, imagine the movement taking place between the shafts of the radius and ulna or between the tibia and fibula at their lower ends. Dense connective tissue is present at these locations, holding these bones together while permitting some flexibility. These two articulations are examples of slightly movable joints. The articulation between one vertebra and the next is also an example of a slightly movable joint. Here, a broad, flat sheet of fibrocartilage covers the top and bottom of each intervertebral disk (see Figure 15-5), which is sandwiched between adjacent vertebrae creating a somewhat flexible connection.

In slightly movable and immovable joints, there is no space between the articulating bones. The bones forming these joints are held together by dense connective tissue or cartilage. In freely movable joints, there is a space between the articulating bones. Such joints are common in your body and are called **synovial joints.** Figure 15-8 diagrams the components of a synovial joint. Hyaline cartilage covers the ends of the articulating bones, which are separated by a fluid-filled space, or joint cavity. The entire joint is encapsulated in a double layer of connective tissue, with the joint cavity and its fluid lying in between these two layers. The outer layer of the capsule is made up of dense connective tissue that holds the bones of the joint together. Some of the connective tissue fibers are arranged in bundles forming strips of tissue, or ligaments. Although this outer capsule holds the bones of the joint in place, it permits a wide range of motion. The inner layer of the capsule is made up of loose connective tissue, including elastic fibers and adipose tissue, or fat. This inner layer of tissue secretes the fluid of the joint cavity, called *synovial fluid.* In fact, the synovial joint gets its name from this "egg white-like" fluid; the word

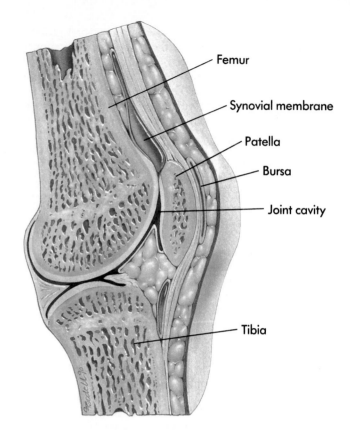

FIGURE 15-8 A synovial, or freely movable, joint.
The articulation of the kneecap (patella) with the femur and tibia is an example of a synovial joint. In the knee joint a sac filled with synovial fluid (a bursa) lies on top of the kneecap, providing a cushion between the bone and skin.

synovial comes from a Greek word and a Latin word meaning "with" *(syn)* "an egg" *(ovum).* Synovial fluid lubricates the joint, provides nourishment to the cartilage covering the bone, and contains white blood cells that battle infection. Table 15-1 summarizes the types of movements possible at synovial joints and gives other examples of joints.

Although synovial joints permit a wide range of movement, this movement is limited by several factors, including the tension, or tightness, of the ligaments and muscles surrounding the joint and the structure of the articulating bones. You can see the various types of movement of synovial joints on your own body. For example, move your hand at the wrist or your foot at the ankle. During this movement the carpals or tarsals slide over one another to produce gliding movements. Other joints allow angular movements, which as the name suggests increase or decrease the angle between two bones. When body builders flex their biceps, for example, they bring their forearms closer to their upper arms, decreasing the angle between the radius/ulna and the humerus. The elbow joint permits this movement and is called a **hinge joint.** A hinge joint allows movement in one plane only, similar to how a door opens and closes by means of its hinges. Another type of movement is rotation, the movement of a bone around an axis. You see this type of movement when a pitcher winds up and throws a baseball or when you move your head from side to side.

TABLE 15-1 **Locations and motions of various joints in the human body**

TYPE OF JOINT	LOCATION	TYPE OF MOVEMENT
Hinge joint	Elbow, knee	Hinge movement
Ball and socket joint	Shoulder, hip	Wide range of movement in almost any direction
Pivot joint	Joint between first two vertebrae	Rotational movement
Plane or gliding joint	Processes (projections) between vertebrae	Sliding in many different directions
Saddle joint	Thumb	Movement in right angles
Ellipsoid joint	Joint between skull and first vertebra	Nearly hinge movement; rotation restricted

The type of joint the pitcher is using at the shoulder is called a **ball-and-socket** joint. In this joint the rounded head or ball of the humerus articulates with the concavity or socket formed by the ends of the clavicle and scapula. When you move your head from side to side, the type of joint you are using is a **pivot joint,** formed by the first two vertebrae, the atlas and the axis. Your skull rests on the ring-like atlas (named after the mythological Greek god who could lift the Earth) and pivots on a projection of the axis, rising from below.

A joint is a place where bones and cartilage come together. The amount of movement allowed between two bones depends on how tightly the bones are held together. Freely movable joints, those in which a space exists between articulating bones, are common in the body and include such joints as the elbow and knee.

Muscles

Bones and joints are of no use in movement unless muscles are attached to the bones. Muscles provide the power for movement and are made up of specialized cells packed with intracellular fibers capable of shortening. Your body has three different kinds of muscle tissue: smooth muscle, cardiac muscle, and skeletal muscle (see Table 6-4). Each type is found in certain locations within the body and performs specific functions. Smooth muscle tissue is made up of sheets of cells that are found in many organs, doing such jobs as mixing food in your stomach and narrowing the interior of your arteries to restrict blood flow. Cardiac muscle tissue makes up the heart—the pump of your circulatory system. Skeletal muscle tissue makes up the muscles that are attached to bones, allowing you to move your body; these muscles are the nearly 700 muscles of the muscular system.

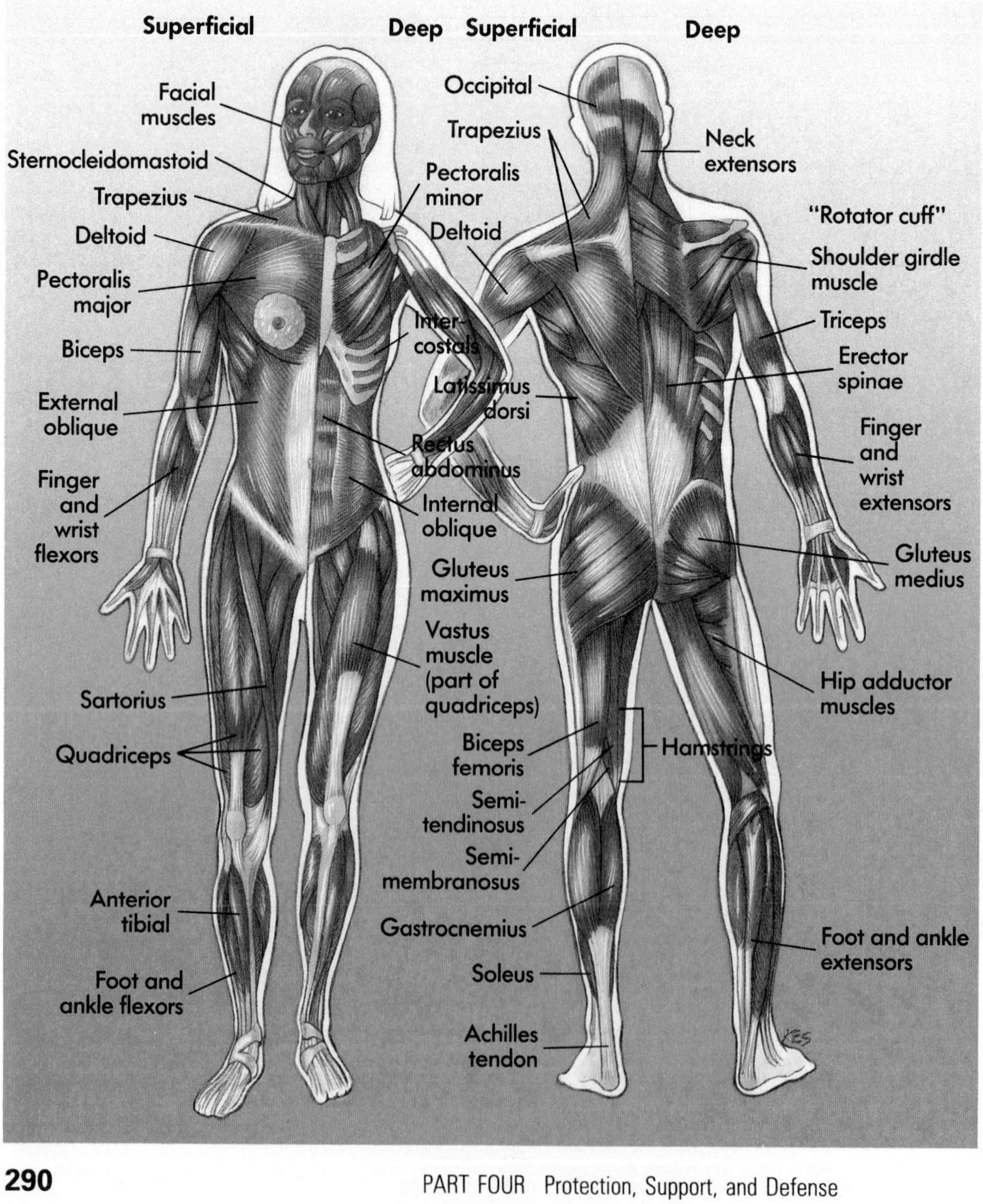

FIGURE 15-9 The human muscular system. Body movements are accomplished by the contraction of the skeletal muscles, which are attached to the bones.

The muscular system

The muscular system is shown in Figure 15-9. Its muscles are attached to bones by means of cords of dense connective tissue called **tendons.** One end of a skeletal muscle is attached to a stationary bone; this attachment is called the **origin.** The other end is attached to a bone that will move; this attachment is called the **insertion.** The origin serves to anchor the muscle as it pulls at the insertion. As an example, Figure 15-10 shows the biceps and triceps muscles and their origins and insertions. The biceps brachii is located on the front of the upper arm. In fact, the word *brachii* means "arm." This muscle has two upper ends, or heads (hence, *biceps,* meaning "double headed"). These two heads have origins on the edges of the scapula near the front side of the humerus. Their tendons pass from the scapula over the upper end of the humerus and then blend into the fattened midsection, or belly, of the biceps. The insertion of the biceps is by means of flattened tendons into the radius. When the biceps shortens, the insertion is brought closer to the origin of the muscle, an action that pulls the forearm to the upper arm. To lower the forearm, the triceps brachii goes

into action. Skeletal muscles oppose each other in this way; such opposing muscle pairs are called **antagonists.** In this case the action of the triceps opposes the action of the biceps. The triceps sits on the back of the arm with one of its three heads originating on edges of the scapula near the back side of the humerus. Another head originates along the upper half of the back side of the humerus and the third along the lower half of the back side of the humerus. The triceps inserts on the ulna near the elbow. When the triceps shortens, its insertion is brought closer to its origin and the forearm is brought downward. The distance between the origin and insertion is measured as the length of the muscle and tendons, not as a straight line between the two points.

> The nearly 700 muscles of the skeletal system are attached to bones by means of connective tissue called *tendons.* One end of a muscle is attached to a stationary bone (the origin) and the other to a movable bone (the insertion). The origin anchors the bone as it pulls at the insertion.

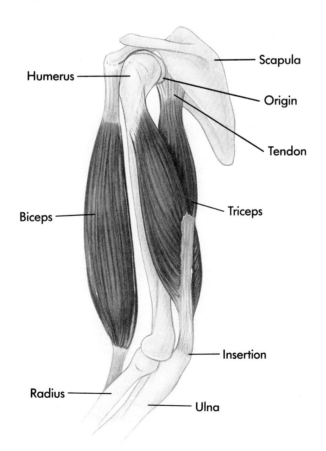

FIGURE 15-10 The attachments of skeletal muscles to bones.
The bicep is attached to the stationary scapula at the origin and to the movable radius at the insertion with straps of tissue called *tendons.* The origin anchors the muscle as it pulls at the insertion.

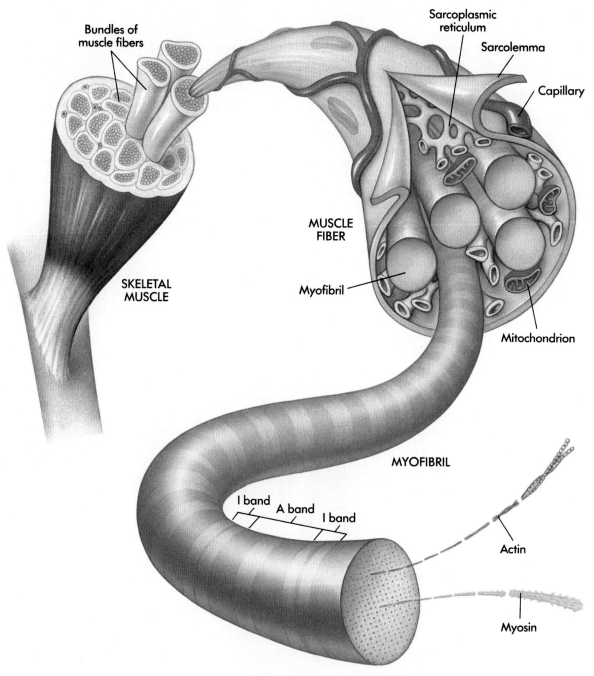

Bundles of
muscle fibers

Sarcoplasmic
reticulum

Sarcolemma

Capillary

SKELETAL
MUSCLE

MUSCLE
FIBER

Myofibril

Mitochondrion

MYOFIBRIL

I band   A band   I band

Actin

Myosin

FIGURE 15-11   Structure of a skeletal muscle.
This diagram shows progressively magnified views of a skeletal muscle.

How skeletal muscles contract

Skeletal muscles are also called **striated muscles** because their cells appear marked with striations, or lines, when viewed under the light microscope (see Figure 15-12, *A*). These striations are caused by an orderly arrangement of microfilaments within skeletal muscle cells. Special groupings of these microfilaments are the contractile units of muscle cells.

Skeletal muscle cells are extremely long cells formed by the end-to-end fusion of shorter cells during embryonic development. These long muscle cells are called **muscle fibers.** Each muscle fiber contains all the nuclei of the fused cells pushed out to the periphery of the cytoplasm (Figure 15-11). To see the relationship between muscle fibers and muscles, study Figure 15-11, noting that a muscle is made up of bundles of muscle fibers, bound together with connective tissue, and nourished by blood vessels. As you study the diagram, you will notice that the names of certain parts of muscle cells have the prefix *sarco,* which comes from a Greek word meaning "flesh." Table 15-2 lists these differences in terminology.

Each muscle fiber is packed with **myofibrils,** which are cylindrical, organized arrangements of special thick and thin microfilaments capable of shortening the muscle fiber (see Chapter 3). In muscle cells, microfilaments are called **myofilaments** (*myo* means "muscle"). The so-called thin

TABLE 15-2	Muscle cell terminology

CELL COMPONENT	MUSCLE CELL COMPONENT
Cell membrane (or plasmalemma)	Sarcolemma
Cytoplasm	Sarcoplasm
Endoplasmic reticulum	Sarcoplasmic reticulum

myofilaments are made up of the protein **actin.** The thick myofilaments are made up of a much larger protein, **myosin.** All the myofilaments within a muscle fiber are lined up in such a way that the cells appear to have interior bands of light and dark lines, a feature readily observable in Figures 15-11 and 15-12.

Figure 15-12 is a close-up view of the banding pattern in a muscle fiber as shown in an electron micrograph. This pattern is repeated throughout each muscle fiber. Below the electron micrograph in Figure 15-12, the diagram shows

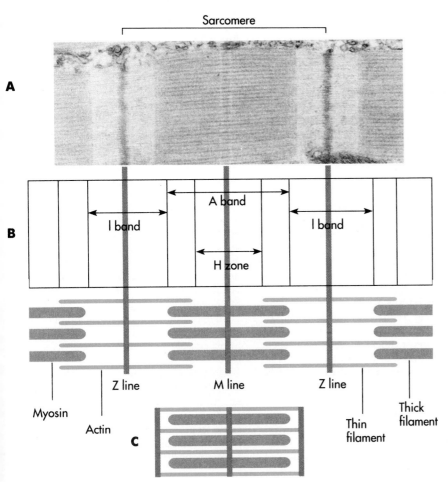

FIGURE 15-12 Structure of a sarcomere.
A The micrograph shows the banding patterns of the thick and thin filaments in a sarcomere, the contractile unit of muscles.
B Actin filaments (thin filaments) are attached to the Z line. Myosin filaments (thick filaments) interdigitate with actin filaments. The different zones of the muscle are also illustrated in this diagram; the I band contains thin filaments and the Z line, the A band contains some thin filaments and the thick filaments, and the H zone contains only thick filaments that have been anchored in place by the M line.
C In a contracting sarcomere, the thick and thin filaments move toward the center. As this movement occurs, the I band disappears.

how the actin and myosin filaments are arranged, forming this banding pattern. The thin actin filaments are attached to plates of protein that appear as dark lines called *Z lines*. The actin filaments extend from the Z lines (plates) equally in two directions, perpendicular to the plates. In a resting muscle the actin filaments that extend from two sequential Z lines are not long enough to reach each other. Instead, they are joined to one another by interdigitating myosin filaments, similar to the way your fingers interlock when you fold your hands. This arrangement of protein plates and myofilaments produces the banding patterns shown in Figure 15-12. The I band contains the Z line and the thin actin filaments. The A band contains a portion of the thin filaments and the thick myosin filaments. The H zone appears as a light zone running down the center of the A band; it contains only thick filaments held in place by a series of fine threads called the *M line*. The part of the myofibrils lying between adjacent Z lines is called the **sarcomere,** the contractile unit of muscles.

▼
▼▼

Skeletal muscle cells are long, multinucleated cells called *muscle fibers*. A muscle is made up of bundles of muscle fibers. Each muscle fiber is packed with organized arrangements of microfilaments that are capable of contracting.

Molecularly, each actin filament (that is, thin filament) consists of two strings of proteins wrapped around one another, like two strands of loosely wound pearls. The result is a long, thin, helical filament. Myosin has an unusual shape: one end of the molecule is a coil of two chains that forms a very long rod, whereas the other end consists of a double-headed globular region. In electron micrographs a myosin molecule looks like a two-headed snake. The contraction of myofilaments occurs when the heads of the myosin filaments change shape. This causes the myosin filaments to slide past the actin filaments, their globular heads "walking" step by step along the actin (Figure 15-13).

Bulking Up

Most body builders will tell you that the most important nutrient needed to produce a body bulging with muscles is protein. For years these and other athletes have believed that a diet abundant in protein-rich foods such as meat and eggs was essential to success. And if some is good, they reasoned, more would be better. Recent advances in food technology have made it possible to increase consumption of protein or protein components (amino acids) beyond the protein available from dietary sources. Health food stores and the ads in body builder magazines offer protein or amino acid–containing powders, drinks, and wafers made from milk, soy, yeast, or gelatin proteins.

Do body builders and other athletes benefit from such additional sources of protein? Can too much protein be harmful? Are claims that these supplements increase muscle size and strength true, or just hype intended to attract people in search of perfect bodies?

Certainly, proteins are an important class of nutrients. Our bodies disassemble the proteins in our food into their component amino acids by the process of digestion. Eventually, these amino acids are reassembled into human proteins such as enzymes, hormones, or antibodies that fight infection. Protein is needed for a healthy body, but will protein supplements produce a healthier, more muscular body than can be attained by a normal diet alone?

The protein needs for most healthy people have been well-documented by research. The Recommended Dietary Allowance (RDA) for adults is 0.8 gram of protein/kilogram of body weight. That means that the RDA for a 138-pound adult is about 50 grams/day. Protein needs do increase during growth periods, pregnancy, and while a woman is breast-feeding her infant. If additional protein is needed during these periods, then it might seem that athletes such as body builders would need additional protein to enlarge their muscles. However, researchers disagree as to whether athletes' needs are significantly greater than those of other healthy adults.

Some researchers believe that because athletes already eat more food than most other people to meet their energy needs, their protein intake is already likely to be adequate. Others suggest that athletes need to double their protein intake to meet actual increases in need. Studies demonstrate, however, that eating extra protein does not stimulate muscle cells to divide and make more muscle. Instead exercise, together with the normal recommended intake of protein, increases the size of individual muscle cells.

Other studies indicate that most Americans already consume about twice the recommended amount, about 100 grams of protein per day. By supplementing their diets with extra protein, athletes may be consuming 125 grams or more of protein each day. And it is possible that too much may not be better than just enough.

This is because when protein molecules are broken down during digestion, a portion is either used for energy or converted to body fat and stored for future energy needs. The remainder of the molecule is a waste product, and elimination of these wastes makes additional metabolic work for the body. This may not be much of a problem for healthy people, but it can be an additional strain for those with liver or kidney disease. Even in healthy people, elimination of unneeded protein wastes often leads to increased loss of calcium and body water.

Most nutrition experts agree that body builders and other athletes do not need protein supplements. Instead, during training they should exercise appropriately and follow the same dietary guidelines recommended for everyone.

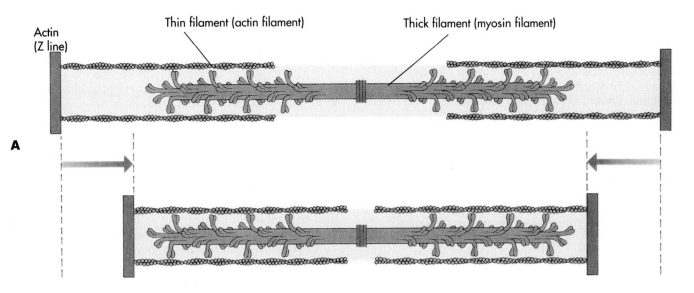

Actin
(Z line)

Thin filament (actin filament)

Thick filament (myosin filament)

A

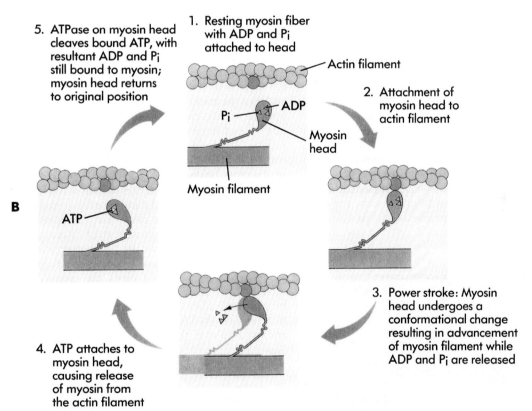

5. ATPase on myosin head cleaves bound ATP, with resultant ADP and P_i still bound to myosin; myosin head returns to original position

1. Resting myosin fiber with ADP and P_i attached to head

Actin filament

2. Attachment of myosin head to actin filament

P_i

ADP

Myosin head

Myosin filament

B

ATP

3. Power stroke: Myosin head undergoes a conformational change resulting in advancement of myosin filament while ADP and P_i are released

4. ATP attaches to myosin head, causing release of myosin from the actin filament

FIGURE 15-13   How the myofilaments move during muscle contraction.
A The sliding of myosin filaments past the actin filaments pulls the actin filaments toward the center.
B An illustration of a microscopic model of how myosin slides past actin. Myosin moves along the actin filament by first binding to it and then moving forward as the result of a change in the shape of the myosin head.

How does myofilament sliding lead to muscle contraction? Because actin myofilaments are anchored to the Z lines, the Z lines are pulled closer to one another when actin slides along the myosin, contracting the sarcomere. All the sarcomeres of a myofibril contract simultaneously, shortening the myofibril. In addition, all the myofibrils of a muscle fiber usually contract at the same time. However, all the muscle fibers within a muscle *do not* contract simultaneously. The forcefulness, speed, and degree of a muscle contraction depend on the number of muscle fibers that contract, their position in relation to one another, and the frequency of nerve stimuli.

▼▼ **Muscle cells contract as a result of the sliding of actin and myosin filaments past one another. Changes in the shape of the ends of the myosin molecules, which are located between adjacent actin filaments, cause the myosin molecule to move along the actin, producing contraction of the myofilament.**

How nerve impulses signal muscle fibers to contract

The contraction of skeletal muscles is initiated by a nerve impulse that causes a series of events ultimately resulting in the interaction of actin and myosin. The nerve impulse arrives as a wave of depolarization along the nerve fiber (see Chapter 11). The end of the nerve fiber, the **motor endplate,** is microscopically close to the surface of the muscle fiber, forming a **neuromuscular junction** (Figure 15-14). When the wave of depolarization reaches the motor endplate, it causes the release of the neurotransmitter acetylcholine from the nerve cell into the junction. The acetylcholine passes across to the muscle fiber membrane and opens the ion channels of that membrane, depolarizing it. Infoldings of the membrane of the muscle fiber called **transverse (T) tubules** carry this action potential deep into the muscle fiber, reaching each myofibril. In turn, the depolarization of the muscle fiber membrane opens calcium

ion channels in the membrane of the **sarcoplasmic reticulum,** which is a tubular, branching latticework of endoplasmic reticulum that wraps around each myofibril like a sleeve (see Figure 15-11). In resting muscle, calcium ions are actively pumped through these channels, concentrating calcium ions within the spaces or sacs of the sarcoplasmic reticulum and thus polarizing the sarcoplasmic reticulum membrane with respect to calcium ions. When the ion channels of the sarcoplasmic reticulum membrane open, calcium ions stored within the sarcoplasmic reticulum move across its membrane and into the sarcoplasm (cytoplasm) (Figure 15-15). The presence of calcium ions triggers the series of chemical reactions of contraction.

In resting muscle, myosin filaments are not free to interact with actin because the myosin binding sites on the actin (called **cross bridge binding sites**) are not available. These binding sites are blocked by a thread-like molecule called **tropomyosin** (see Figure 15-15). Along this tropomyosin thread lie other globular proteins called **troponin.** The troponin molecules bind the calcium molecules when they are released from their storage sacs in the sarcoplasmic reticulum. When this binding occurs, the troponin molecules change their shape. With this change the tropomyosin thread is repositioned to a new location where it does not interfere with myosin interaction. The globular heads of the myosin filament bind to the actin, forming cross bridges that exert tension on the actin threads, pulling them toward the center of the sarcomere. As in a chain reaction, the myosin then cleaves a molecule of ATP (see Chapter 4) and uses the energy that is released to break the cross bridge. Spontaneously, the now-freed head of the myosin forms a new cross bridge at another actin binding site, once again pulling the actin thread closer to the center of the sarcomere. This cycle of formation, breaking, and re-formation of the cross bridges results in the speedy and simultaneous contraction of the sarcomeres within a muscle fiber. After the passage of the stimulating nerve impulse, the membrane's calcium channels close. The sarcoplasmic reticulum repolarizes by the active transport of calcium ions back out of the cytoplasm and into the reticular spaces. As the level of calcium in the cytoplasm decreases, the tropomyosin-troponin complexes again block the myosin binding sites on actin, and the muscle relaxes. Thus the release of calcium by the nerve fiber's stimulation of the sarcoplasmic reticulum releases the troponin that, together with an input of energy, results in the contraction of the myofibril.

▼▼ **In skeletal muscle, contraction is initiated by a nerve impulse. Acetylcholine passes across the neuromuscular junction from the nerve to the muscle, initiating the process that causes the muscle to contract. This process is driven by the energy from ATP.**

FIGURE 15-14 A neuromuscular junction.
The thick central portion is the body of an axon, with small branches each terminating in a motor endplate. This special synapse between a motor nerve fiber and a muscle fiber is the neuromuscular junction.

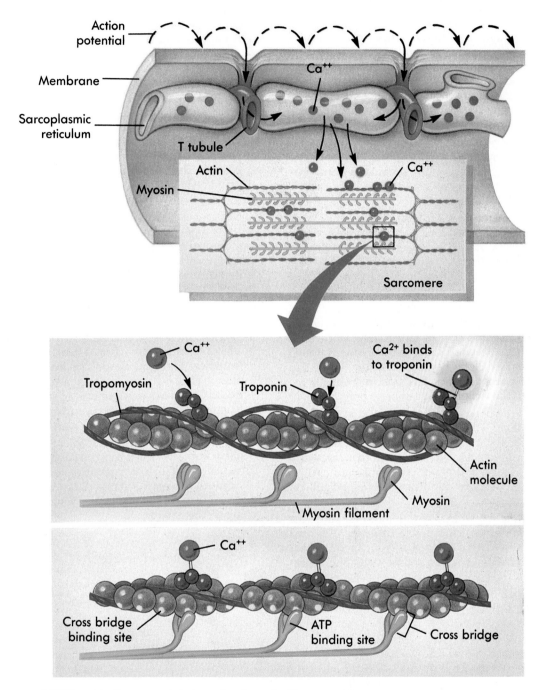

FIGURE 15-15 How nerve impulses signal muscle fibers to contract.
When a nerve impulse reaches a motor endplate, acetylcholine causes a depolarization
in the muscle fiber membrane. The T tubules in the membrane transmit this action potential to each myofibril, causing calcium ions to be released from their storage sites in
the sarcoplasmic reticulum. For muscle contraction to occur, myosin must be able to
bind to the actin at specific sites called *cross bridge binding sites.* However, in resting
muscle, these sites are obstructed by tropomyosin threads. When a muscle is signaled
to contract, the calcium ions released from the sarcoplasmic reticulum bind to troponin, a molecule that studs the tropomyosin threads. This binding causes the tropomyosin to move out of the way so that myosin can bind to actin at the cross bridge binding sites.

Summary

1. The human body is able to move from place to place because it is supported by a rigid internal framework of bones powered by skeletal muscles. The skeletal muscles are attached to the bones and use them as levers to move the body itself or other objects. The skin provides a flexible covering for the body, accommodating each movement, no matter how large or small.

2. In addition to providing an elastic covering for the body, the skin serves as a protective barrier against water loss and invading microbes, provides a surface by which you sense your environment, and helps control the body's internal temperature.

3. Although bones may not look like living tissue, they contain living cells embedded in a matrix of collagen fibers and mineral salts. The collagen provides flexibility, whereas the mineral salts provide hardness. Bone is nourished by blood that flows in blood vessels permeating its interior.

4. Not all bone is made up of solid, or compact, bone. Compact bone is found along the length of long bones, surrounding a central core of fatty yellow marrow. A lighter, bony latticework called *spongy bone* is found within the ends of long bones and within short, flat, and irregularly shaped bones. Red bone marrow fills the spaces within the latticework of spongy bone.

5. Together, all the bones of the body make up the skeletal system. Along with providing support for the body and places for the attachment of skeletal muscles, the skeletal system protects delicate internal structures such as the heart, lungs, and brain; stores minerals such as calcium and phosphorus; and produces blood cells in its red marrow.

6. Scientists divide the skeletal system into two parts: the axial skeleton and the appendicular skeleton. The axial skeleton is your central column of bones and consists of the skull, vertebral column, and rib cage. The appendicular skeleton consists of the bones of the appendages (the arms and legs), and the bones off which the appendages hang (the collarbones, shoulder blades, and pelvic bones).

7. A joint, or articulation, is a place where bones or bones and cartilage come together. At places where bones are held tightly together, such as in the skull, little or no movement is possible at the joint. At places where bones are held together less tightly, such as between the two bones of the forearm, slight movement is possible at the joint. At places where a space exists between articulating bones, such as between your upper leg and your pelvic bone, somewhat free and varied movement is possible. Such joints are common in your body and are called *synovial joints*.

8. There are three kinds of muscle tissue: smooth muscle tissue, which is found in many body organs and contracts spontaneously; cardiac muscle tissue, which makes up the heart and may initiate contraction spontaneously; and skeletal muscle tissue, which is organized into trunks of long fibers and contracts only when stimulated by a nerve. Skeletal muscles are attached to bones and move the body. These are the muscles of the muscular system.

9. Skeletal muscles move bones by pulling on one while anchored to another. They are made up of bundles of extremely long muscle cells called *muscle fibers*. Each muscle fiber is packed with myofibrils, which are cylindrical, organized arrangements of special thick and thin filaments called *myofilaments,* capable of shortening the muscle fiber as they slide past one another.

10. The contraction of skeletal muscles is initiated by a nerve impulse, which causes a series of events that ultimately result in the interaction of actin and myosin. Acetylcholine passes across the neuromuscular junction from the nerve to the muscle, triggering the events leading to this interaction.

1. You raise your hand to answer a question in class. Explain the roles played by your bones and skeletal muscles in this movement.

2. Your skin is covered with varying amounts of hair in various areas. What physiological functions of skin do you think are enhanced by the presence of this hair?

3. Human babies learn extensively by touching and manipulating toys and objects. What physiological role does skin serve in this process?

4. What is bone, and what are its functions? Explain its importance.

5. Leukemia patients sometimes receive red bone marrow transplants as treatment for their disease. From what kind of bone tissue would this marrow be obtained?

6. What type of bone tissue composes most of the bones of the axial skeleton?

7. What do you hypothesize happens to excess calcium taken in by the body yet not needed at the moment?

8. Mrs. Gorman has injured her back; her doctor tells her she has a "slipped disk." What type of "disk" is involved, and what is its function?

9. What is an articulation? Describe the three main categories of articulations, and give an example of each. On what factor are these categories based?

10. What do hinge, pivot, and ball-and-socket joints have in common? How are they different?

11. What connective tissue connects muscles to bones? What connects muscles to each other?

12. Many older people suffer from osteoarthritis, which causes painful inflammation and decreased mobility in the knees, fingers, shoulder, or elbows. What skeletal structures seem, therefore, to be the targets for this disease?

13. Define actin, myosin, and myofilament. Explain their roles in the contraction of a muscle fiber.

14. Explain how a nerve impulse can lead to a muscle contraction.

15. What changes to the skin and bone tissues have you noticed occur as we age?

1. When an adult begins to jog, doctors warn about the importance of building up slowly, starting with short distances and building up to longer ones only over periods of months. Individuals who ignore this warning often come down with painful stress fractures, tiny spiral cracks along the length of the leg bones. Why does building up slowly prevent such stress fractures?

2. In recent years, there has been tremendous progress made in the development and use of metallic artificial joints and bone replacement. What activities and bone functions would be easily served by such artificial structures? Are there functions of the bone that could not be filled by such replacements? Discuss the restrictions and limits to replacing organic tissues with artificial parts.

Carafoli, E., & Penniston, J. (1985, November). The calcium signal. *Scientific American*, pp. 70-78.
This article discusses how the release of calcium ions is the only known way in which the electricity of the nervous system is able to produce changes in the body. Nerves regulate all muscle contractions and hormone secretions by controlling the level of calcium ions.

Fackelman, K. (1990, March). Myelin on the mend. *Science News*, pp. 218-220.
An encouraging treatment for multiple sclerosis, a nerve and muscle disorder that is one of the most common crippling diseases in the United States.

Fackelman, K. (1990, July). Hormone may restore muscle in elderly. *Science News*, p. 23.
The use of human growth hormone to build muscle and increase skin thickness as we age is discussed.

Smith, K., & Kiev, W. (1989, January). Trunks, tongues and tentacles; moving with skeletons of muscle. *American Scientist*, pp. 28-35.
An interesting discussion of how, in many cases, muscles provide not only movement but unique skeletal support.

16 Defense Against Disease

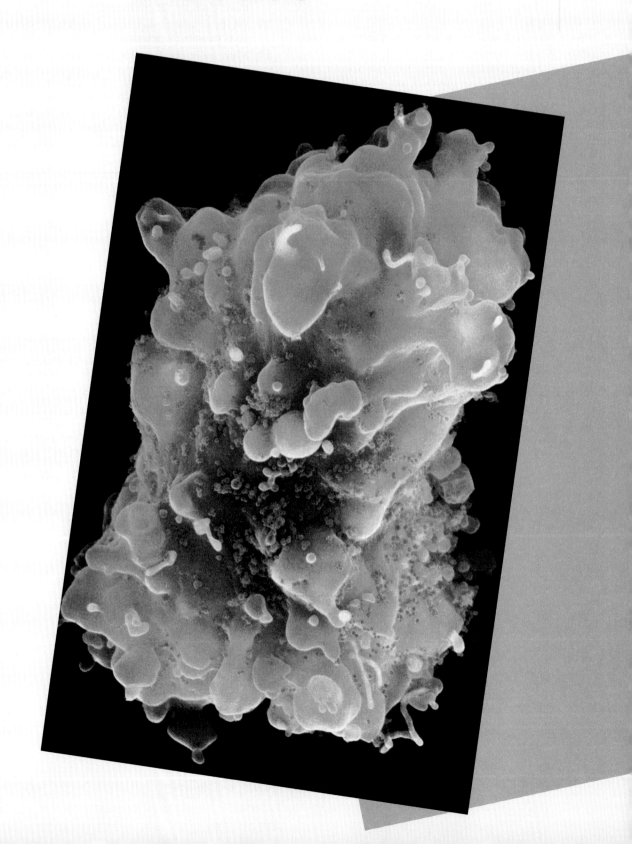

Every day you fight for your life. Some of your attackers swarm over your skin. Some enter your mouth, nose, eyes—any place where they may be able to gain a foothold in your tissues and spread. The battles between you and these invaders are silent and deadly. The fighting is one on one; chemical warfare is commonplace.

It is your immune system that fights and wins these thousands of battles, yet the war within you rages on continually. Each day thousands of people lose their inner wars, succumbing to invasions of the body by viruses, bacteria, fungi, or protists. People whose immune system is impaired, such as those infected with the deadly AIDS virus, have the hardest time winning the battle because the AIDS virus attacks the immune system itself, lowering its defenses.

Looking at the photo, you can see the AIDS virus doing some of its dirty work, attacking one of the most important cells of the immune system—a helper T cell. Helper T cells identify foreign invaders and stimulate the production of other cells to fight an infection. Although thousands of times larger than the AIDS virus particles (colored blue for this photograph), the helper T cell is inactivated and sometimes killed by this virus. The body is then an easy mark for other invaders to enter—unnoticed—and win the war between life and death.

Nonspecific versus specific resistance to infection

Your body works in many ways to keep you healthy and free of infection. An **infection** results when microorganisms or viruses enter the tissues, multiply, and cause damage. Your body has one set of defenses against infection called **nonspecific defenses.** These defenses work to keep out *any* foreign invader, just as the walls and roof of your home protect you from any of the elements of the environment— rain, hail, wind, the sun's rays, insects, or the neighbor's dog, for example. But your body has another set of defenses, too. This set of defenses is called **specific defenses** because they work against *each particular type* of microbe that may invade your body. A specific defense in your home, for example, may be a certain chemical you use to rid your kitchen of ants in the summer. Your nonspecific defenses consist of mechanical and chemical barriers and cells that attack invaders in general. Your specific defense is called **immunity,** and it consists of cellular and molecular responses to particular foreign invaders.

>>> The defenses of the body are both nonspecific— acting against any foreign invaders—and specific—acting against particular invaders.

Nonspecific resistance

Unbroken skin is an effective mechanical barrier to any foreign substance entering the body. Most microorganisms cannot penetrate the skin of a healthy individual. However, if the skin is injured, many types of microorganisms will grow and multiply at the injured site, causing an inflammation or infection.

An **inflammation** occurs when cells are damaged by microbes, chemicals, or physical injuries. Characterized by redness, pain, heat, and swelling, an inflammation consists of a series of events that removes the cause of the irritation, repairs the damage that was done, and protects the body from further invasion and infection. During this nonspecific response, blood vessels dilate, or widen, bringing an increased supply of blood to the injured area. This increased flow brings defensive substances to the site of injury as fluid and phagocytic white blood cells pass out of the capillaries. Lymphatic drainage removes dissolved poisonous substances that may accumulate there. Blood clots wall off the area, preventing the spread of microbes or other injurious substances to other parts of the body. Phagocytes, both neutrophils and monocytes, migrate to the area and ingest microbes and other foreign substances. Nutrients stored in the body are also released to the area to support these defensive cells.

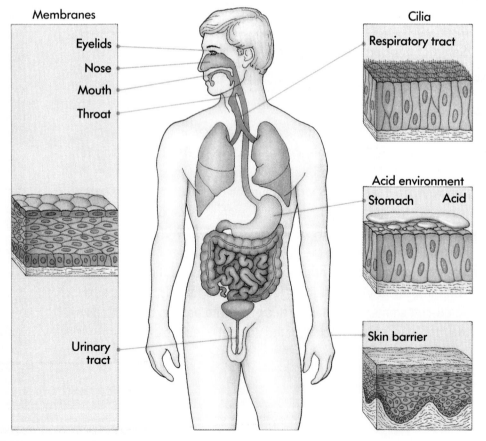

FIGURE 16-1 Nonspecific defenses in the human body.
These nonspecific defenses are the body's first line of defense against foreign invaders.

Membranes

Eyelids
Nose
Mouth
Throat

Urinary tract

Cilia
Respiratory tract

Acid environment
Stomach   Acid

Skin barrier

The mucous membranes of the body, such as those lining your mouth, nose, throat, eyelids, urinary tract, and genital tract, also defend the body against invaders. These membranes are sticky and trap microbes and foreign particles much as flypaper traps flies. Some of the mucous membranes of the body also have other physical or chemical aids for combating infection. For example, the membranes covering the eyes and eyelids are constantly washed in tears, a fluid that contains a chemical called lysozyme, which is deadly to most bacteria. The ciliated mucous membranes of the respiratory passageways have a comparatively thick coating of mucus that not only traps invaders but efficiently moves them from the respiratory passageways to be swallowed by the digestive system. In the digestive system, microorganisms are killed by the acid environment of the stomach. The environments of the urinary and genital tracts are somewhat acidic, too—an unfavorable situation for many foreign bacteria. Foreign bacteria are also kept from invading the body by bacteria that are normal inhabitants of the body, colonizing such areas as the mouth, throat, colon, vagina, and skin. Figure 16-1 summarizes some of the nonspecific defense mechanisms of the body.

The nonspecific defenses of the body include the skin and mucous membranes, chemicals that kill bacteria, and the inflammatory process.

Specific resistance

Sometimes invaders get by your nonspecific defenses. This situation may occur if your body is invaded by many organisms at one time or if the invaders are extremely **virulent,** that is, if they are good at establishing an infection and damaging the body. In addition, the defenses of a person ill with certain diseases, such as diabetes mellitus or cancer, may not be as strong as those of persons who are free of disease.

Invaders that get into the blood, lymph, or tissues encounter a second line of defense—the **immune system,** your body's specific defense. Have you ever had measles, chickenpox, or mumps? All these infections are caused by specific viruses that enter the body through the respiratory system, invade cells, multiply, and spread. As you may know from experience, the body is usually effective in combating these diseases. In addition, having had one of these diseases confers an immunity, or resistance, to getting that same disease again. The mechanism that provides you with this resistance is the immune system—the backbone of your health—protecting you not only from measles, mumps, and chickenpox but also from a myriad of other diseases. And although the immune system is not always able to protect a person from infection, the immune system of a healthy person staves off most infections and usually overcomes those that take hold.

The specific defense of the body is the immune response.

Discovery of specific resistance: The immune response

In 1796 an English country doctor named Edward Jenner (Figure 16-2) carried out experiments that marked the beginning of immunology, the study of the responses of the body when it is challenged by molecules foreign to it. His experiments had to do with a disease called *smallpox,* a common and frequently deadly disease in Jenner's day. Although thousands died from smallpox, many survived. Jenner noted that these survivors were now immune from becoming reinfected. The only other group of people immune to smallpox were milkmaids who had caught another, much milder form of the pox called *cowpox.* Jenner hypothesized that cowpox somehow conferred protection against smallpox.

To test his hypothesis, Jenner deliberately infected healthy people with fluid he removed from the pox vesicles of sick milkmaids, causing the healthy people to develop cowpox. Many of the people Jenner infected with cowpox became immune to smallpox, just as he had predicted. Scientists now know that smallpox is caused by the variola virus and that cowpox is caused by a different but similar virus called the *vaccinia virus.* The word vaccinia is derived from the Latin *vacca* meaning "cow." Jenner's patients injected with fluid containing cowpox virus mounted a defense against the cowpox infection, a defense that was also effective against infection by the similar smallpox virus. Jenner's procedure of injecting a harmless microbe into a person or animal to confer resistance to a dangerous one is called **vaccination.**

It was a long time after Jenner's experiments before scientists understood how one microbe conferred resistance to another. Further important information was added about 85 years after Jenner by Louis Pasteur of France. Pasteur

FIGURE 16-2 The birth of immunology.
Edward Jenner is shown here inoculating patients with cowpox in the 1790s and thus protecting them from the disease smallpox. The underlying principles of vaccination were not understood until more than a century later.

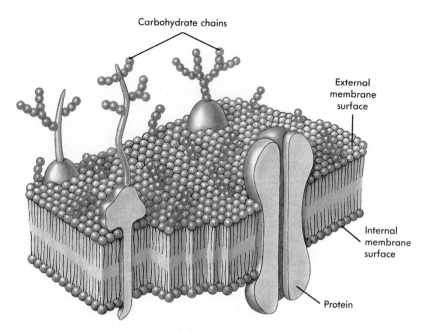

Carbohydrate chains

External membrane surface

Internal membrane surface

Protein

FIGURE 16-3   The outer surface of a cell is imbedded with proteins, carbohydrates, and lipids. The glycoproteins (carbohydrate-protein complexes) often serve as highly specific cell surface markers that identify specific cell types and also identify the cell as "self."

was studying fowl cholera, a serious bacterial disease of chickens. From diseased chickens, Pasteur isolated bacteria that brought on the disease when injected into healthy birds. These birds became seriously ill and died.

During a period of experimentation, Pasteur injected healthy birds with an old culture of fowl cholera—one that had sat on his benchtop for several weeks—because he had no fresh cultures. Interestingly, the injected birds became only slightly ill and then recovered. Pondering this outcome, Pasteur reasoned that the culture had become weakened as it sat for many days at room temperature. Trying to get his experiment to work, he then injected the recovered birds with massive doses of fresh cultures—active virulent fowl cholera bacteria. These birds did *not* develop fowl cholera! Chickens receiving the same injections but that had not previously recovered from a mild form of the illness all died. Pasteur began to realize that his old culture acted on the birds in a unique way. Clearly, these old, weakened bacteria possessed something that could confer resistance yet not cause the chickens to become seriously ill. Scientists now know what that "something" was: molecules protruding from the surface of the bacterial cells.

Every cell has proteins, carbohydrates, and lipids on its surface (Figure 16-3). It was the presence of molecules on the surface of the cholera bacteria—molecules different from any of the birds' own—to which the chickens were responding. Nonself or foreign molecules such as these are

called **antigens.** Chickens injected with weakened or killed fowl cholera bacteria are immune to later infection because the bacterial antigens cause the chickens to produce proteins called **antibodies.** These antibodies are able to recognize any future cholera invaders, weakened or normal, and prevent them from causing disease (Figure 16-4). The body's response to foreign molecules, such as the production of antibodies directed against a specific antigen, is called an **immune response.** The immune response is a result of the complex activities of recognition and defense carried out by the immune system.

FIGURE 16-4   Immunity to smallpox.
The immunity to smallpox that Jenner's patients acquired was a direct result of their cowpox inoculation. The cowpox inoculation caused Jenner's patients to develop antibodies to the antigen. An exposure to smallpox later stimulated them to produce large amounts of the antibody in much larger amounts than before, resulting in immunity to smallpox.

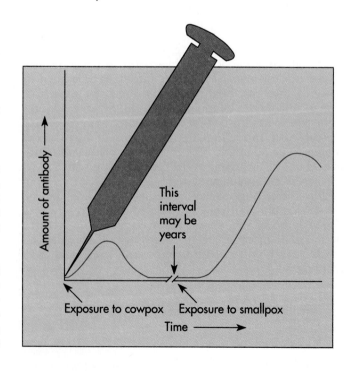

Amount of antibody →

This interval may be years

Exposure to cowpox   Exposure to smallpox

Time →

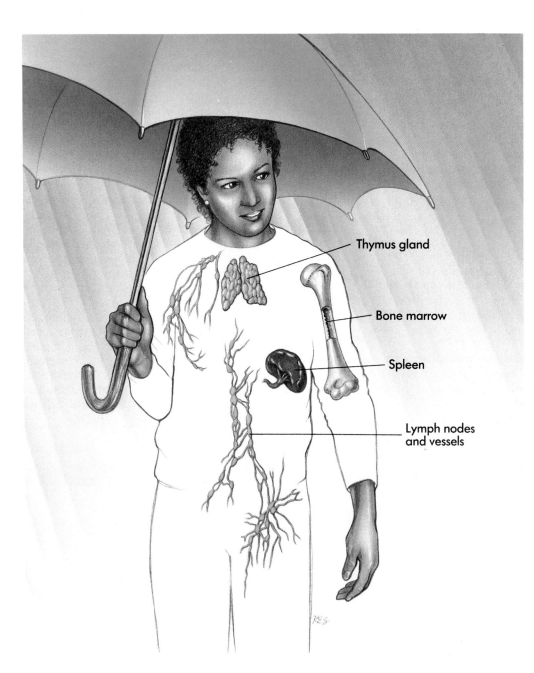

FIGURE 16-5 Organs in which immune cells reside.
The principal organs in which the cells of the immune system mature and reside include the thymus, bone marrow, spleen, lymph nodes, and lymph vessels.

Thymus gland

Bone marrow

Spleen

Lymph nodes and vessels

The cells of the immune system

The immune system is different from the other body systems in that it cannot be identified by interconnected organs. In fact, the immune system is not a system of organs, nor does it have a single controlling organ. The immune system is, instead, made up of cells that are scattered throughout the body but have a common function: reacting to specific foreign molecules.

The cells of the immune system are white blood cells, or leukocytes (see Chapter 9). Two types of white blood cells are involved in the immune system: **phagocytes** and **lymphocytes.** Three classes of lymphocytes play roles in

specific resistance: T cells, B cells, and **natural killer (NK) cells.** These cells arise in the bone marrow, circulate in the blood and lymph, and reside in the lymph nodes, spleen, liver, and thymus (Figure 16-5). Although not bound together, these white blood cells exchange information and act in concert as a functional, integrated system—your "army" of 200 billion defenders—that is called into action when antigens invade your body.

> The immune system is composed of white blood cells, or leukocytes. Two types are involved: phagocytes and lymphocytes (T cells, B cells, and natural killer cells).

The immune response: How it works

The immune system responds in several ways to defend your body against foreign invaders. Some of the cells of the immune system react immediately to invasion by foreign antigens. Other cells work to protect your body against future attack. The immune response is a complex yet coordinated effort, and it involves several types of immune protection. An overview of the alarm sounding activation of the immune response is shown in Figure 16-6.

Sounding the alarm

Constantly patrolling your body are roving armies of white blood cells called *phagocytes*. A phagocyte is a cell that destroys other cells by engulfing and ingesting them. This process is called **phagocytosis.** Two types of white blood cells are phagocytes: neutrophils and macrophages. **Macrophages** are the phagocytes that play a key role in the body's immune response.

Large, irregularly shaped cells, the macrophages act as the body's scavengers. Macrophages phagocytize anything that is not normal, including cell debris, dust particles in the lungs, and invading microbes. When the body is not under attack, only a small number of macrophages circulate in the body's bloodstream and lymphatic system. In response to infection, precursors of macrophages called **monocytes** develop into mature macrophages in large numbers.

When macrophages encounter foreign microbes in the body, they attack and engulf them and then display parts of these microbes on their surfaces. This display, as well as proteins secreted by the macrophages, is important in activating the immune response.

The macrophages secrete many different proteins. Some of these proteins trigger the maturation of monocytes into macrophages, thereby increasing their numbers. Another protein, **interleukin-1,** signals the brain to raise the body temperature, producing a **fever.** The higher temperature aids the immune response and inhibits the growth of invading microorganisms.

At the onset of the infection, immune system cells other than the monocytes also go to work. Reacting to cell surface changes that occur on cancer cells or virally infected cells, *natural killer cells* attack them, breaking them apart. Rather than ingesting infected or diseased cells as macrophages do, natural killer cells secrete proteins that create holes in the membranes of the cells they attack. In addition, natural killer cells secrete toxins that poison these cells. The cells under attack burst open and die. This initial defense

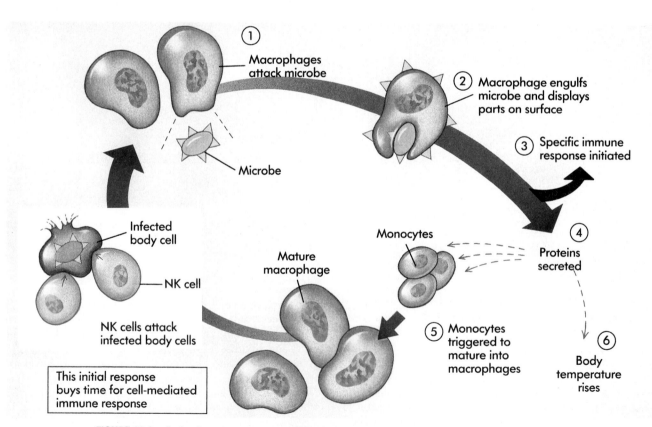

FIGURE 16-6 Activation of the immune response.
As macrophages encounter microbes (1), they initiate a local inflammation. Macrophages engulf and display parts of microbes on their surfaces (2), causing an activation of the specific immune response (3) and the secretion of proteins (4). Some proteins stimulate the maturation of monocytes (5); others cause fever (6).

by macrophages and natural killer cells peaks within a day or two of the infection. This response buys time for the immune system to respond.

The two branches of the immune response

In addition to its other interactions mentioned previously, interleukin-1 activates helper T cells that have been presented with antigens by the macrophages, triggering the immune response. **T cells,** or **T lymphocytes,** develop in the bone marrow but then migrate to the thymus. The thymus, a small gland located in the neck, is the place where T (thymus) cells mature. In the thymus, T cells develop the ability to identify invading bacteria and viruses by the foreign molecules (antigens) on their surfaces. Tens of millions of different T cells are produced, each specializing in recognizing one particular foreign antigen. No invader can escape being recognized by at least a few T cells. There are four principal kinds of T cells:

1. **Helper T cells,** which initiate the immune response
2. **Cytotoxic T cells,** which break apart cells that have been infected by viruses and break apart foreign cells such as incompatible organ transplants
3. **Inducer T cells,** which oversee the development of T cells in the thymus
4. **Suppressor T cells,** which limit the immune response

When they are triggered by interleukin-1 and the presentation of antigens, the helper T cells can stimulate both branches of the immune response: the **cell-mediated immune response** and the **humoral immune response.**

The cell-mediated immune response

The activation of helper T cells by interleukin-1 and the binding of antigen to these activated helper T cells unleash a chain of events known as the *cell-mediated immune response.* The main event of this response is that cytotoxic T cells ("cell-poisoning" cells), also called *killer cells,* recognize and destroy infected body cells.

When a helper T cell has been activated, it produces a variety of chemical substances collectively called **lymphokines.** One type of lymphokine attracts macrophages to the site of infection, and another inhibits their migration away from it. Another of the lymphokines stimulates T cells that are bound to foreign antigens to undergo cell division many times. This cell division produces enormous quantities of T cells capable of recognizing the antigens specific to the invader. Each type of activated T cell does a specific job.

The activated inducer T cells trigger the maturation of immature lymphocytes in the thymus into mature T cells. Activated cytotoxic T cells kill the body's own cells that have been infected with fungi, some viruses, and bacteria that produce slowly developing diseases such as tuberculosis. In addition, they act to kill cells that have become cancerous. Cytotoxic T cells bind to these infected or abnormal cells by means of molecules on their surfaces that specifically fit antigens, much as a key fits a lock. Because the entire cell binds to the abnormal cells (by means of specific cell-surface proteins), this response is called *cell-mediated.* The cytotoxic T cells then secrete a chemical that breaks apart the foreign cell (Figure 16-7). Unfortunately for organ transplant patients, cytotoxic T cells also recognize foreign body cells in a similar way. Because of this, the immune system attacks transplanted tissue, leading to the rejection of transplanted organs.

After the cytotoxic cells and macrophages do their jobs, the cell-mediated immune response begins to shut down. The cells in charge of shutdown are the suppressor T cells. The number of suppressor T cells slowly begins to rise after activation by the helper T cells. However, it takes about 1 to 2 weeks for their numbers to increase to a point where they are able to suppress the cytotoxic T cell response.

After suppression, or shutdown, a population of T cells persists, probably for the life of the individual. Referred to as **memory T cells,** these helper and cytotoxic T cells provide an accelerated and larger response to any later encoun-

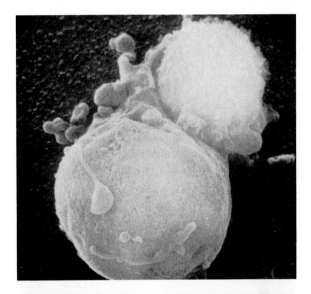

FIGURE 16-7 Cytotoxic T cell: a killer cell.
The cell-mediated response induces cytotoxic T cells to bind to antigens on the surface of an infected cell and secrete a chemical that breaks the infected cell apart. The top photo shows a cytotoxic T cell binding with a tumor cell; at bottom, the tumor cell is disintegrating.

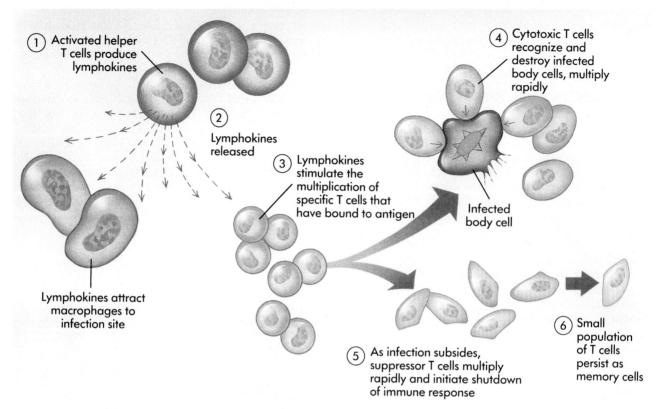

① Activated helper T cells produce lymphokines

② Lymphokines released

③ Lymphokines stimulate the multiplication of specific T cells that have bound to antigen

④ Cytotoxic T cells recognize and destroy infected body cells, multiply rapidly

Infected body cell

Lymphokines attract macrophages to infection site

⑤ As infection subsides, suppressor T cells multiply rapidly and initiate shutdown of immune response

⑥ Small population of T cells persist as memory cells

FIGURE 16-8 Summary of the cell-mediated immune response.
The cell-mediated response involves three stages: activation and attack by T cells, proliferation of suppressor cells that eventually shuts down the immune response, and the persistence of memory cells.

ter with the same antigens. A summary of the cell-mediated immune response is shown in Figure 16-8.

T cells carry out the cell-mediated immune response, during which cytotoxic T cells recognize and destroy body cells infected with certain bacteria, viruses, and fungi. In addition, they destroy transplanted cells and cancer cells. Helper T cells initiate the response, activating cytotoxic T cells, macrophages, inducer T cells, and, as the infection subsides, suppressor T cells.

The humoral immune response

When helper T cells are stimulated to respond to foreign antigens, they activate the cell-mediated immune response as described and activate a second, more long-range defense called the **humoral,** or antibody, **response.** Depending on the types of antigens present, the helper T cells may stimulate either or both of these branches of the immune response. The key players in humoral immunity are lymphocytes called **B cells** or **B lymphocytes.** The B cells are named after a digestive organ in birds called the *bursa of Fabricius* in which these lymphocytes were first discovered. However, B cells mature in the bone marrow of humans, which may be a convenient way for you to remem-

ber these cells. The term *humoral response* refers to the fact that B cells secrete antigen-specific chemicals into the bloodstream—one of the body fluids called "humours" long ago.

On their surfaces, B cells each have about 100,000 copies of a protein receptor that binds to antigens. Because different B cells bear different protein receptors, each recognizes a different, specific antigen. At the onset of a bacterial infection, for example, the receptors of one or more B cells bind to bacterial antigens. The B cells may bind to either free bacteria or bacterial antigens displayed by macrophages. These antigen-bound B cells are detected by helper T cells, which then bind to the antigen-B cell complex (Figure 16-9). After binding, the helper T cells release lymphokines that trigger cell division in the B cell.

After about 5 days and numerous cell divisions, a large clone of cells is produced from each B cell that was stimulated to divide. A **clone** is a group of identical cells that arise by repeated mitotic divisions from one original cell. (See Chapter 17 for a discussion of mitosis.) After these clones are formed, most of the B cells stop dividing but begin producing and secreting copies of the receptor protein that responded to the antigen. These receptor proteins are called *antibodies,* or **immunoglobulins.** The secreting B cells are called **plasma cells.** After B cells become plasma cells, they live for only a few days but secrete a great deal of antibody

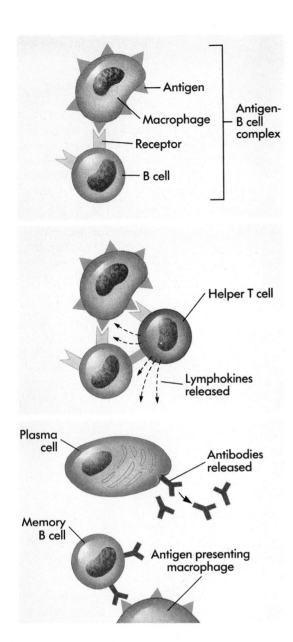

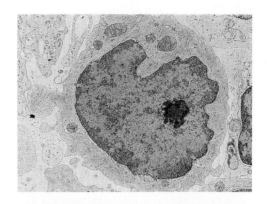

FIGURE 16-10   A B cell *(top)* and a plasma cell *(bottom)*. The plasma cell contains a large amount of rough endoplasmic reticulum, on which antibodies are made.

FIGURE 16-9   Summary of the humoral immune response. The humoral immune response involves the participation of three immune cell types: B cells, helper T cells, and antigen-presenting macrophages. The humoral response imparts a more long-range defense than the cell-mediated response through the production of antibodies.

during that time (Figure 16-10). In fact, one plasma cell will typically secrete more than 2000 antibodies per second!

Antibodies do not destroy a virus or bacterium directly but rather mark it for destruction by one of two mechanisms (Figure 16-11):

1. *Complement:* **Complement** are proteins that kill foreign cells by creating a hole in their membranes. Water floods the cell through these holes, causing the cell to swell and burst.
2. *Macrophages:* The activity of these phagocytes is enhanced by the binding of both antibodies and complement to the antigen.

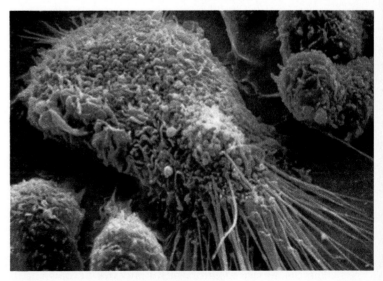

FIGURE 16-11   A macrophage ingesting cells. Macrophages engulf "marked" antigens by phagocytosis.

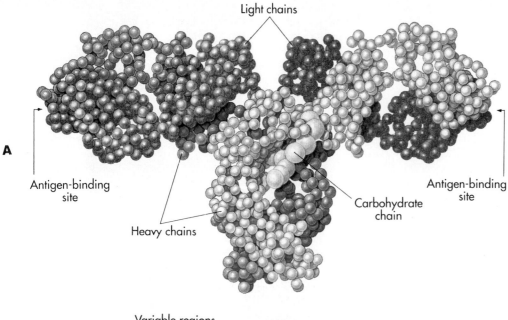

Light chains

Antigen-binding
site

A

Antigen-binding
site

Heavy chains

Carbohydrate
chain

FIGURE 16-12 The structure of an antibody molecule.
A A molecular model of an antibody. Each amino acid is represented by a small sphere. The heavy chains are colored blue, the light chains, red. The four chains wind around one another to form a Y shape, with two identical antigen-binding sites at the arms of the Y.
B A schematic drawing of an antibody molecule. Each molecule is composed of two identical light chains and two identical heavy chains. Disulfide bonds hold the chains together.

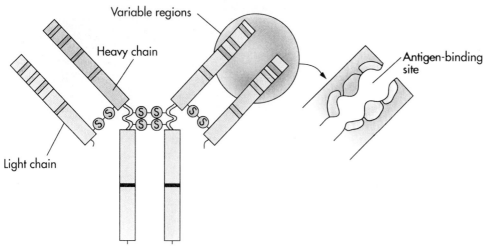

Variable regions

Heavy chain

B

Light chain

Antigen-binding
site

The B cell clones that did not become plasma cells live on as circulating lymphocytes called **memory B cells.** These cells provide an accelerated response to any later encounter with the stimulating antigen. This is why immune individuals are able to mount a prompt defense against infection. As in the case of the cell-mediated immune response, the antibody response is shut down after several weeks by suppressor T cells.

> ▼▼ B cells carry out the humoral immune response in which B cells recognize foreign antigens and, if activated by helper T cells, produce large quantities of antibody molecules directed against the antigen. The antibodies bind to the antigens they encounter and mark them for destruction.

How immune receptors recognize antigens

The cell surface receptors of lymphocytes (T cells and B cells) can recognize specific antigens with great precision. Even single amino acid differences between proteins can often be discriminated, with a receptor recognizing one form

and not the other. This high degree of precision is a necessary property of the immune system, since without it the identification of foreign antigens would not be possible in many cases; the differences between self and foreign (nonself) molecules can be very subtle.

A typical antibody, or immunoglobulin molecule, consists of four polypeptide chains. A polypeptide is a chain of amino acids linked end-to-end by peptide bonds (see Chapter 2). There are two identical short strands, called **light chains,** and two identical long strands, called **heavy chains.** The four chains are held together by disulfide (-S-S-) bonds, forming a Y-shaped molecule (Figure 16-12, *A*). The two "arms" of the Y determine which antigen will bind to the antibody. Antibodies recognize, or lock onto antigens by means of special binding sites in their arms (Figure 16-12, *B*). These binding sites are made up of specific sequences of amino acids that determine the shape of the site. The specificity of the antibody molecule for an antigen depends on this shape. An antigen fits into the binding site on the antibody like a hand into a glove. Changes in the amino acid sequence of an antibody can alter the shape of this region and, by doing so, change the antigen that can bind to that antibody, just as changing the size of a glove will alter which hand can fit into it.

⯆
An antibody molecule recognizes a specific antigen because it possesses binding sites into which an antigen can fit, much as a key fits into a lock. Changes in the amino acid sequence at the binding sites alter the antibody's shape and thus change the identity of the antigen that is able to fit into them.

The stem of the Y determines what role the antibody plays in the immune response. An antibody can have one of five different stems and therefore be a member of one of the five classes of antibodies. For example, the antibodies produced in the first week of an infection are primarily class M antibodies and are called *IgM* (immunoglobulin M). After the first week, IgG antibodies are primarily produced.

Immunization: Protection against infection

Although scientists have unraveled many of the mysteries of the immune response since Jenner's day, scientists still use the same basic idea of vaccination that Jenner used to help people become resistant to specific diseases. A vaccine is made up of disease-causing microbes or toxins (poisons) that have been killed or changed in some way so as not to produce the disease. Injection with these antigens causes an antibody (B cell) response, with the production of memory cells. A booster shot induces these memory cells to differentiate into antibody-producing cells and more memory cells. So vaccination causes your body to build up antibodies against a particular disease without getting the disease. This type of immunity is called **active immunity.**

Scientists can now use the techniques of genetic engineering to produce vaccines. Instead of growing cultures of an agent of infection such as a bacterium or a virus, scientists can, in the laboratory, produce large quantities of antigenic proteins from disease-causing microbes. These antigens can then be used as vaccines.

Vaccination to produce active immunity works well for many diseases but is a somewhat slow process. After the injection of the antigen, it takes weeks for the body to develop sufficient antibodies and memory cells to combat the disease. However, another type of immunity, **passive immunity,** can be used when protection is needed quickly. One example is the use of **antitoxin** when a person has been bitten by a snake.

When a poisonous snake bites a person or other animal, it injects a toxin (poison) into the body. This toxin circulates in the bloodstream. Certain toxins damage the nerve cells they reach and may result in death. An antitoxin is a preparation of antibodies specific for a toxin. These antibodies are injected into the victim and they bind with the toxin, preventing the toxin from causing damage. Although effective, this type of borrowed immunity lasts for only a short time. The body soon uses or eliminates these antibodies, so they will not be available if another snake bite occurs.

Newborn babies have a type of passive immunity borrowed from their mothers. Antibodies that pass from mother to fetus through the placenta provide babies with a short-term immunity that subsides by the time the baby has produced its own system of antibodies. In addition, if a mother nurses her baby, antibodies in the mother's milk may provide the baby with some protection.

Defeat of the immune system: AIDS

Helper T cells are the key to the entire immune response because they initiate the proliferation of both T cells and B cells (Figure 16-13). Without helper T cells, the immune system is unable to mount a response to foreign antigens. The AIDS virus, called **human immunodeficiency virus,**

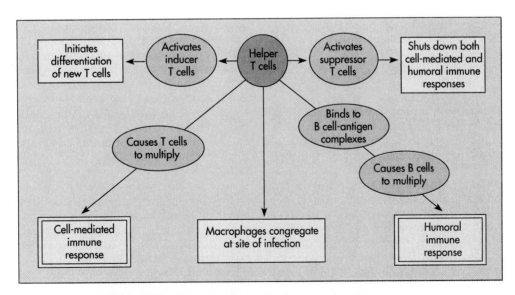

FIGURE 16-13 Helper T cells are the key to the immune response.
This diagram outlines the many roles of the helper T cell.

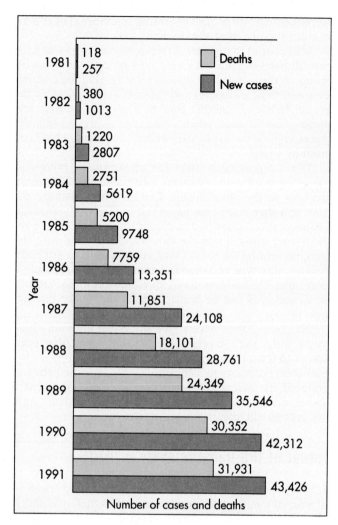

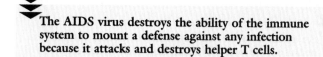

FIGURE 16-14 AIDS cases and deaths since 1981.
The U.S. Centers for Disease Control reports that by the end of 1991, there were 206,392 AIDS cases in the United States and 133,232 deaths. Over 1 million other individuals are thought to have been infected with HIV. By August 1989, 8 years into the epidemic, 100,000 AIDS cases had been reported; the next 100,000 cases took just 26 months.

The AIDS virus destroys the ability of the immune system to mount a defense against any infection because it attacks and destroys helper T cells.

Although the AIDS virus was discovered to be a cause of human disease only within the past decade, it is clear that it is a serious disease. The fatality rate of AIDS is virtually 100%; of the earliest identified AIDS patients, only a few are still alive. The disease is *not* highly infectious; that is, it is not transmitted from person to person by casual contact. It is only transmitted by the direct transfer of body fluids, typically in semen or vaginal fluid during sexual activity, and in blood during transfusions or by contaminated hypodermic needles. It also crosses the placenta to infect babies within the womb of an infected mother. Not all individuals exposed to AIDS (as judged by antibodies in their blood directed against the AIDS virus) have yet come down with the disease, but scientists expect between 95% and 100% of all HIV-positive people to develop AIDS.

Efforts to develop a vaccine against AIDS continue, both by splicing portions of the AIDS surface protein gene into a harmless virus (Figure 16-15) and by attempting to develop a harmless strain of AIDS. These approaches have not yet proved successful and are limited by the fact that different strains of AIDS virus seem to possess different surface antigens. Drugs that inhibit specific genes of the AIDS virus or that block the operation of enzymes critical to the synthesis of its genetic material are also being investigated, with a notable lack of success at this time.

Allergy

Although the human immune system provides very effective protection against viruses, bacteria, parasites, and other microorganisms, sometimes it does its job too well, mounting a major defense against a harmless antigen. Such immune responses are called **allergic reactions.** Hay fever, the sensitivity that many people exhibit to proteins released from plant pollen, is a familiar example of an allergy. Many other people are sensitive to proteins released from the feces of a minute house-dust mite (Figure 16-16). This microscopic insect lives in the house dust present on mattresses and pillows and eats the dead epithelial tissue that everyone sheds from their skin in large quantities daily. Many people sensitive to feather pillows are actually allergic to the feces of mites that are residents of the feathers.

What makes an allergic reaction uncomfortable and sometimes dangerous is involvement of class E (IgE) antibodies. The binding of antigens to these antibodies initiates an inflammatory response; powerful chemicals cause the dilation of blood vessels and a host of other physiological changes. Sneezing, runny nose, and fever often result. In some instances, allergic reactions can be far more dangerous, resulting in anaphylactic shock, a severe and life-threatening response of the immune system. The chemicals that dilate blood vessels are released suddenly into the

or **HIV,** is deadly because it mounts a direct attack on T lymphocytes, mainly targeting the helper T cells. The HIV particles kill helper T cells by entering them, using the cells' own machinery to produce more virus particles, and then bursting open the cells to release the new viruses (see p. 000). These viruses infect other helper T cells until the entire population is destroyed. In a normal individual, helper T cells make up 60% to 80% of circulating T cells; in AIDS patients, helper T cells often become too rare to detect. Because the immune response cannot be initiated, any of a variety of infections proves fatal. This is the primary reason that AIDS is a particularly devastating disease (Figure 16-14).

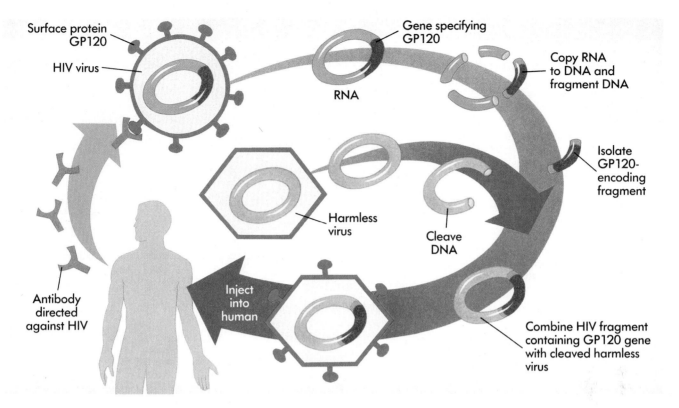

FIGURE 16-15 **How scientists are attempting to construct a vaccine for AIDS.**
Of the several genes of the human immunodeficiency virus (HIV), one is selected (GP120) that directs the synthesis of a certain surface feature on the virus. All of the other HIV genes are discarded. This one gene is not in itself harmful to humans. This one gene or fragment of it is inserted into the DNA of a harmless vaccinia cowpox virus, resulting in a harmless virus whose surface imitates the AIDS virus. Persons injected with the vaccinia virus do not become ill, but they do develop antibodies directed against the infecting virus surface. However, the AIDS virus mutates, or changes rapidly. For this reason an effective vaccine against HIV has not yet been developed.

bloodstream, causing many vessels to widen suddenly. Their widening causes the blood pressure to fall. In addition, the muscles of the trachea, or windpipe, may contract, making breathing difficult.

Not all antigens are **allergens,** initiators of strong immune responses. Nettle pollen, for example, is as abundant in the air as ragweed pollen, but few people are allergic to it. Nor do all people develop allergies; the sensitivity seems to run in families. Allergies require both a particular kind of antigen and a high level of class E antibodies. The combination of an appropriate antigen on the one hand and inappropriately high levels of IgE antibodies on the other hand produces the allergic response.

FIGURE 16-16 **The house-dust mite *Dermphagoides*.**
Believe it or not, mites like this live in the dust in your house. Many people are allergic to the proteins released in these mites' feces.

The acquired immunodeficiency syndrome known as AIDS was first recognized in the United States in 1981. We now know that AIDS is the final phase of a chronic, long-term, immune function disorder caused by the human immunodeficiency virus (HIV). The typical course of HIV infection follows the pattern shown in Figure 16-A.

SPECTRUM OF HIV INFECTION

Initial infection with HIV causes an immune reaction during which HIV-specific antibodies are produced. These antibodies are measurable at a median of 2 months after infection, although some people will demonstrate antibody as early as 3 weeks and others may take as long as 6 months. Some people have a flu-like syndrome of fever, nausea, and diarrhea during this time, but others have no symptoms.

The median time between HIV infection and a diagnosis of AIDS is 10 years. This is called the asymptomatic phase, but vague symptoms, including fatigue, headaches, low-grade fevers, and night sweats may occur. During this phase, people are usually able to continue their normal routines. Many people who are in the asymptomatic phase are not aware that they are infected. Because they have no obvious symptoms, their infection often goes undetected.

Toward the end of the asymptomatic phase and before AIDS is diagnosed, early symptomatic disease develops. Some early symptoms are constitutional, including persistent fevers, night sweats, and fatigue severe enough to interrupt normal routines. Localized infections may also occur. The most common is thrush, a mouth infection caused by a fungus that rarely causes problems in people with healthy immune systems. Other infections that can occur at this time include shingles (*Varicella zoster* virus), persistent vaginal yeast infections, and outbreaks of oral or genital herpes.

AIDS occurs when the immune system becomes severely compromised. Severe immune system deterioration is documented by helper T cell counts of less than 200 (normal is 800 to 1200). As the immune system deteriorates, health problems including infections (such as *Pneumocystis carinii* pneumonia), cancers (such as Kaposi's sarcoma), wasting syndrome (a loss

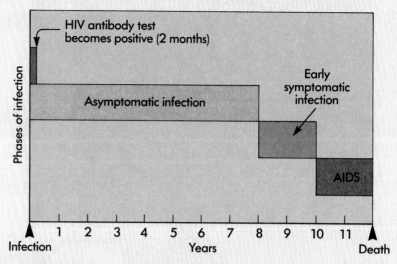

FIGURE 16-A The spectrum of HIV infection: Median times for progression of HIV disease.

of 10% or more of ideal body mass), and dementia syndromes occur. An individual with HIV is not diagnosed with AIDS until at least one of these additional conditions is present.

The median time for survival after a diagnosis of AIDS is 2 years but this varies greatly. Some people with AIDS live for 6 or more years; others survive for only a few months. Advances in the treatment and diagnosis of HIV infection have increased survival times, but there is no indication that AIDS fatality rates will decrease. In other words, people will continue to die, but it may take them longer.

HIV AND WHAT IT DOES

HIV is an RNA virus that was discovered in 1983. Like all viruses, HIV is an obligate parasite. That means that it must live inside a host cell to survive and replicate. HIV can enter a cell when it binds to a specific (CD4) receptor site on the cell's surface (see Figure 16-B). In the cell, viral RNA is transcribed into DNA. The viral DNA then splices itself into the host cell DNA where it becomes part of the cell's genetic material, causing permanent HIV infection of the cell and all of its daughter cells. HIV can remain quiescent in the nucleus of infected cells for many years.

Although HIV can infect several types of cells, immune dysfunction results from destruction of helper T lymphocytes, which are targeted because they display a large number of CD4 receptor sites on their surfaces. Remember that helper T cells play a pivotal role in the ability of the immune system to recognize and defend against foreign invaders. When HIV actively replicates within an infected helper T cell, the newly formed viruses bud out from the cell's membrane. This process not only releases new viruses to infect other cells, it also kills the host cell by punching holes in the cell membrane. Destruction of helper T cells eventually reaches a point where there are not enough of these lymphocytes to direct needed immune responses.

IMPACT OF HIV

Between 1981 and December, 1992, over 253,000 cases of AIDS and over 171,000 AIDS-related deaths were reported in the United States. HIV is estimated to infect over 1 million people in this country. The fastest growing groups of people with HIV and AIDS in the United States are women and adolescents. According to the Centers for Disease Control and Prevention, of the approximately 27,000 cases of AIDS reported in women, 44% were reported between 1990 and 1992. Also, during those years, 32% of the over 10,000 AIDS cases in people aged 13 to 25 were reported. The face of AIDS in the United States is not only changing along the lines of gender and age, it is also becoming an increasing problem for people of color and people who live in poverty. Globally, HIV is even more devastating, with a worldwide estimate of 8 to 10 million infected people.

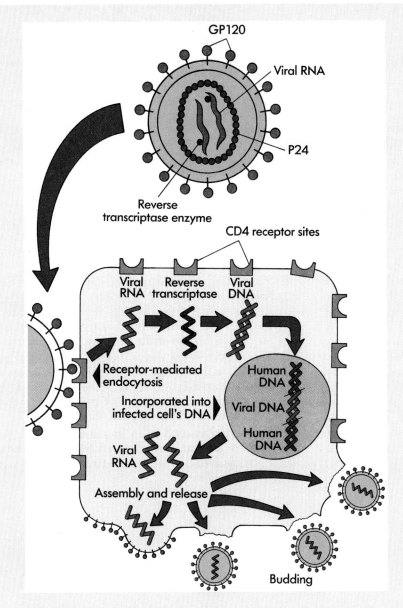

GP120

Viral RNA

P24

Reverse
transcriptase enzyme

CD4 receptor sites

Viral   Reverse   Viral
RNA   transcriptase   DNA

Receptor-mediated
endocytosis

Incorporated into
infected cell's DNA

Human
DNA

Viral DNA

Human
DNA

Viral
RNA

Assembly and release

Budding

FIGURE 16-B   How HIV replicates within a cell.

TRANSMISSION

HIV is transmitted between humans through infected blood, semen, vaginal secretions, and breast milk. If these infected fluids are introduced into a person's body, the potential for transmission occurs. The good news is that behaviors which create a risk for transmission of HIV have been clearly identified and are avoidable. Sexual contact with an HIV-infected partner is the most common method of transmission. Sexual activity allows contact with semen, vaginal secretions, and/or blood. Although male homosexuals were the initial targets of HIV in this country, heterosexual transmission is becoming more prevalent and is a common method of infection for women. Sharing contaminated equipment to inject drugs is the leading cause of transmission among women and is a major means of transmission to both sexes in many large metropolitan areas. HIV transmission through blood products is now rare in the United States because of donor screening, blood testing, and heat or chemical treatment of hemophilia clotting factor products.

Transmission from HIV-infected mothers to infants can occur during pregnancy, at the time of delivery, or after birth through breast feeding. Studies have found that 14% to 30% of infants born to HIV-infected women will be infected. This means that 70% to 86% of these infants will *not* be infected. Despite this, 86% of pediatric cases of AIDS in this country occur through perinatal transmission. Infants born to HIV-infected mothers pose a number of problems. A major problem is that all infants born to HIV-infected mothers will be positive on the HIV antibody test because maternal antibodies cross the placental barrier. It may take 15 months before it is known if an infant is infected with HIV or not. An additional problem is that these infants, even if they are not infected, are likely to be orphaned as AIDS claims the lives of their parents. In addition, breast feeding from an HIV-infected woman is a rare, but well-documented, risk. Because of this, HIV-infected mothers in the United States are encouraged not to breast feed.

PREVENTION

Although advances are being made, there is still no evidence that a cure or a vaccine will be developed soon. The only absolute defense against HIV is prevention through education about risky behaviors and risk reduction.

Risk related to injecting drugs can be *eliminated* by not using drugs or by only using equipment that is never shared with anyone. Risk *reduction* during drug use involves cleaning used equipment with bleach and rinsing with water prior to use. Individuals who use drugs of any kind (including alcohol and drugs that are smoked, snorted, or swallowed rather than injected) may put themselves at risk of sexual transmission if they make unwise sexual decisions while under the influence of a drug.

Elimination of risk related to sexual activity includes abstinence or involvement in a mutually monogamous relationship where neither partner is infected. Risk *reduction* includes correct and consistent use of condoms, decreasing the number of sex partners, and refraining from unprotected anal intercourse, the most risky form of sexual activity.

CONCLUSION

By all accounts, HIV infection will continue as a worldwide epidemic for the foreseeable future, bringing with it untold suffering and early death. Education and prevention are the only known ways to decrease the devastation caused by HIV, but these efforts are often hampered by social, cultural, and governmental policies that restrict the presentation of information about risk reduction measures. If ways to surmount these barriers are not developed, HIV will continue to cause escalating losses of life and health care resources.

Lucy A. Bradley-Springer Ph.D., R.N.
The University of New Mexico

Summary

1. Although immunity was discovered almost 200 years ago, it has only recently been understood that resistance to disease is achieved by populations of white blood cells, collectively called the *immune system*.

2. The human body has both nonspecific and specific defenses against disease. The nonspecific defenses, those acting against any foreign invader, include the skin and mucous membranes, chemicals that kill bacteria, and the inflammatory process. The specific defense of the body is the immune response, a complex series of processes carried out by the cells of the immune system.

3. There are two types of white blood cells involved in the immune system: phagocytes and lymphocytes. Three classes of lymphocytes play roles in specific resistance: T cells, B cells, and natural killer cells. These lymphocytes are capable of recognizing specific foreign substances (usually proteins) called *antigens*.

4. Lymphocytes recognize specific antigens by means of receptor proteins on the lymphocyte cell surface.

5. The immune response is initiated by groups of T cells called *helper T cells*. When stimulated by macrophages and antigens, helper T cells can activate the two branches of the immune response: the cell-mediated immune response (T cell response), and the humoral immune response (B cell response).

6. In the cell-mediated immune response, cytotoxic T cells attack infected body cells. In the humoral immune response, a longer-range defense than the T cell response, B cells are converted to plasma cells that secrete proteins called *antibodies*. These antibodies specifically bind circulating antigen and mark cells or viruses bearing antigens for destruction.

7. The exquisite specificity of an antibody for a particular antigen is caused by the three-dimensional shape of the ends of the arms, or antigen binding sites, of the molecule. Slight changes in the amino acid sequence alter the shape of these sites and thus the identity of molecules able to fit into it.

8. Vaccination, which is an injection with disease-causing microbes or toxins that have been killed or changed in some way so as to be harmless, causes the body to build up antibodies against a particular disease. Scientists can now use laboratory-made antigenic proteins as vaccines.

9. The AIDS virus is deadly because it primarily attacks helper T cells, the key to the entire immune response. Because helper T cells are no longer present to initiate the immune response, any of a variety of otherwise commonplace infections prove fatal.

10. An allergic reaction is an immune response against a harmless antigen. It is produced by the combination of a particular kind of antigen and a high level of a certain class of antibody.

1. Distinguish between nonspecific and specific defenses. Which could be considered the first line of defense and why?

2. Name your body's nonspecific defenses, and summarize how each protects you against infection or injury.

3. How is your immune response involved if you get a particle of foreign matter, such as dust, in the mucus membranes of your eyelid?

4. How is the immune system different from other body systems discussed so far?

5. In earlier chapters, we discussed how a cell membrane may have proteins or carbohydrates on its surface to act as "cell markers." How do you think these would be interpreted if this cell were placed in the tissues of another organism?

6. Why do you think it is important that there are phagocytes constantly circulating in the bloodstream and in body tissues?

7. What are the four principal types of T cells? Summarize the function(s) of each.

8. Summarize the events of the cell-mediated immune response. What cells are involved?

3. You had measles as a child. Now your younger brother has measles, but you don't catch it from him. Explain why.

4. Summarize the events of the humoral immune response. What cells are involved?

5. How is an antibody molecule able to discriminate between millions of cells in a tissue and bind only to one specific antigen?

6. Pediatricians often encourage mothers to breast-feed infants since maternal antibodies circulate in milk and provide the baby with some protection against infection. What sort of immune response is involved here?

7. A nurse vaccinates a child against the tetanus bacterium. Later, the child receives a booster shot. Describe how these two vaccinations affect the child's immune response during subsequent exposures to tetanus.

8. Which virus is responsible for AIDS? Explain why this virus is so deadly.

9. Many people—including you, perhaps—are allergic to something. Explain what an allergic reaction is and why it occurs. What causes its uncomfortable symptoms?

1. When your body is fighting an infection, your immune system causes your body to raise its temperature. In severe infections the rise in temperature can be high enough to produce serious body damage and even death. Why do you think the body does not regulate the maximum rise in temperature during a fever it induces to fight an infection?

2. In 1796, Edward Jenner vaccinated patients with cowpox to prevent later infection with smallpox. He was successful and these patients did not develop the potentially deadly disease. In present times, however, medical research is more stringently controlled and scientists may work for years on a medical advance, using animals or cell culture, before they receive approval to try experimental medicine or treatments on humans. Many patients, especially AIDS sufferers, have complained that this caution may prevent their potential for improvement or even survival. Get into small groups and discuss the issue of medical caution versus rapid advancement by means of voluntary involvement by patients.

Caldwell, M. (1992, April). The transplanted self. *Discover*, pp. 62-68.
Organ transplant donors in the future might donate their immune cells along with their organs to prevent organ rejection by the recipient.

Gallo, R.C., & Montagnier, L. (1987, October). AIDS in 1988. *Scientific American*, p. 40.
In their first collaboration the two investigators who established the cause of AIDS describe how HIV was isolated and linked to AIDS, the current status of AIDS research, and the prospects for an AIDS therapy.

Jaret, P. (1986, June). Our immune system: the wars within. *National Geographic*, pp. 702-736.
This is a very readable account of current progress in the study of the human immune system, with striking photographs by Lennart Nilsson.

Smith, K.A. (1990, March). Interleukin-2. *Scientific American*, pp. 50-57.
The first hormone of the immune system to be recognized, it helps the body to mount a defense against microorganisms by triggering the multiplication of only those cells that attack an invader.

BIOETHICAL DECISIONMAKING FRAMEWORK
Organ Donation and Consent

Consider the following questions as you think about the bioethical dilemma presented on page 279:

1. What are the bioethical issues in this case?
   - What has to be decided?
   - Who are the decisionmakers?
   - Outline the decisionmaking process in this case as you understand it.

2. What factual information do the decisionmakers need? Consider the effects of the answers to the following questions on the decisionmaking process.
   - Will complete understanding of the biological issues of organ transplant rejection help the decisionmakers? If so, in what ways?
   - In what ways could the present system of consent be improved so that more donors could give written consent?
   - What other questions should the decisionmakers ask?
   - What additional factual information do the decisionmakers need?

3. Who are the "stakeholders" in this decision—those who stand to gain or lose as a result of the decision?
   - Are the persons waiting for organs stakeholders? The citizens of the state? What other persons or groups are stakeholders?
   - Which stakeholders are decisionmakers? Which are not decisionmakers? Will individuals in the latter group be able to influence the decisionmaking process? Should they have influence?
   - In what ways would each stakeholder be affected by the decision?

4. What are the values at stake in the decision? As you list and describe them, consider the following questions:
   - Should the next of kin be allowed to override an individual's stated wish that his or her organs be donated?
   - Should the fact that a person never stated opinions about organ donation during life be equated with consent to such donation?
   - Will everyone in the state understand the bill? What about those who are mentally incapacitated and do not have guardians or next of kin? Is it ethical to use these individuals' organs when they did not know about the bill or understand its implications?

5. What options are available to the decisionmakers? As you list these options, consider the following questions:
   - Which of these alternatives seem ethically feasible? Which seem administratively possible?
   - How would each alternative decision affect each of the stakeholders?
   - Is there a compromise solution that might give all parties the sense that they have come out the "winner" in the decision?

6. What are the values inherent to the decisionmaking process?
   - Is the decisionmaking process fair?
   - Do all stakeholders have equal resources to advocate their position?
   - What further steps might each group of stakeholders take if their views are disallowed?

PART FIVE

How Cells Pass on Biological Information

17 DNA, Gene Expression, and Cell Reproduction

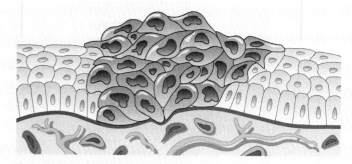

18 Abnormal Cell Reproduction: Cancer

19 Patterns of Inheritance

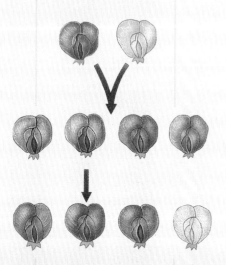

20 Human Genetics

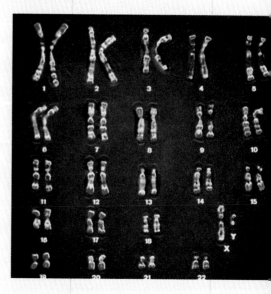

BIOETHICAL DECISIONMAKING
Nuturing a Newborn with a Genetic Aberration

A baby girl was born 4 weeks prematurely, after an uncomplicated pregnancy. At birth the baby breathed spontaneously but shortly afterward had an episode in which her respiration stopped. She was given oxygen, and her breathing resumed. This baby also had unusual facial features and hands, and showed little spontaneous motor activity. For these reasons she was transferred to a neonatal intensive care unit where physical examination showed findings consistent with trisomy 18, a serious genetic aberration. The baby continued to have occasional episodes of apnea (cessation of breathing) and needed the assistance of a respirator. Physicians then discovered that the baby exhibited signs of early heart failure, a condition normally treated with a variety of medications.

Thirty-six hours after the birth, the parents, who had not yet seen their child, met with the pediatrician and geneticists caring for her, who described the baby's primary problem (trisomy 18) and her immediate difficulties. These difficulties included the episodes of apnea and heart failure that were probably caused by an opening between the major artery to the body and the large artery that serves the lungs. The parents were told about the characteristics of a child with trisomy 18: small size, unusual facial features, and deformed hands. The parents were also informed that the child would be profoundly retarded and would probably die before her first birthday.

Within the next day or two, decisions needed to be made:

1. Should the baby be resuscitated the next time she stops breathing?
2. Should a respirator be used to keep her alive?
3. Should medications be given to control the potentially life-threatening heart failure? Should surgery be performed to repair the arterial abnormality?
4. Should other routine care be given?

Before any of these decisions are made, however, should the parents see the baby? Should the physician encourage or discourage them from touching and holding the baby?

17 DNA, Gene Expression, and Cell Reproduction

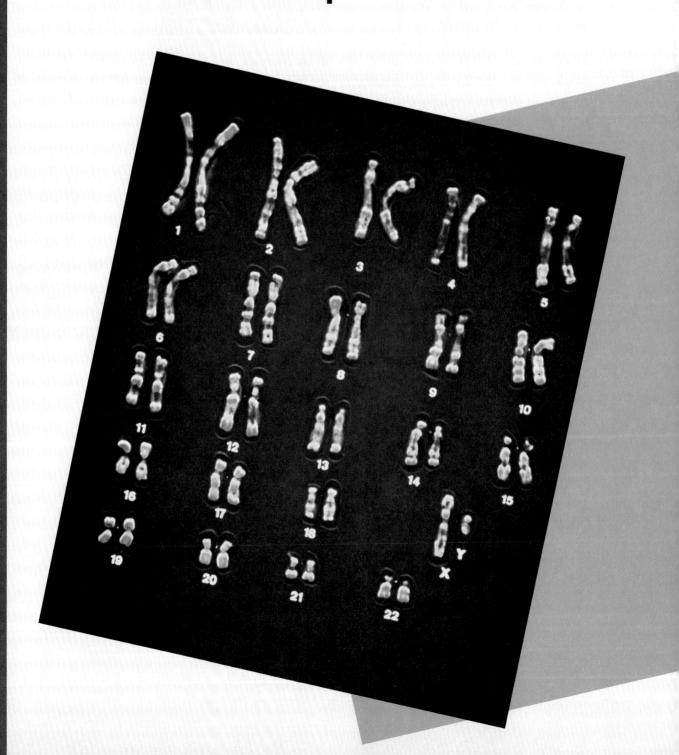

▾ Most traits reflect the action of enzymes; the hereditary message is a molecular code in DNA, located in the nucleus of eukaryotic cells, which results in the production of these enzymes.

▾ RNA plays key roles in the translation of the hereditary message of DNA.

▾ Before cell division, the hereditary material of cells condenses to form chromosomes; in this form, the hereditary material can be distributed in an orderly fashion during cell division.

▾ Mitotic cell division produces new cells during the growth and repair of human cells; meiotic cell division produces sex cells in humans.

When you were born, did you come with instructions? You may not know it, but you did. The brightly stained bodies in the photo are human "instructions" called **chromosomes,** but they can't be read in the usual way. Instead, using a special code that can be understood by other special molecules, they direct all the chemical reactions that take place in your body. Instructions in the chromosomes determine such things as whether your hair is red or brown and whether you are male or female. But, most importantly, they hold the key to the mystery of what makes *you*.

Chromosomes

The chapter opening photo is a **karyotype,** a particular array of chromosomes that belong to an individual. Scientists make this type of picture by specially treating a cell just as it is about to divide. The cell is then photographed, and the chromosomes are cut out of the photograph and arranged on a piece of paper. Each chromosome has a mate, so they are paired up and then arranged in order of decreasing size.

In the century since the discovery of chromosomes, scientists have learned a great deal about their structure and function. Scientists know that the chromosomes of eukaryotes are made up of a complex of deoxyribonucleic acid (DNA) and protein. This complex is called **chromatin.** The DNA is the part of the chromatin that contains hereditary information, commonly called the *code of life.* DNA exists as one very long, double-stranded molecule that extends unbroken through the chromosome's entire length. The relationship of the amount of DNA to protein in a single chromosome can be seen in Figure 17-1.

To fit into cells, DNA strands are coiled, much as you might coil up your garden hose. The coiling of DNA within cells, however, is much more complicated. Figure 17-2 shows how this coiling is accomplished to provide organization and orderliness. First, the double strand of DNA winds like thread on a spool around groups of tiny proteins called **histones.** In this form the DNA looks similar to a string of pearls (Figure 17-3). This string of pearls then wraps up into larger coils called **supercoils.** These supercoils are looped and packaged with other proteins to form chromatin. And as Figure 17-2 shows, the chromatin can be condensed by further coiling to form the chromosomes, a process that takes place just before and during cell division. (Cell division is described later in this chapter.)

▼▼

Proteins and the hereditary material, DNA, make up the chromatin material of the cell. When coiled and condensed, chromatin material forms chromosomes.

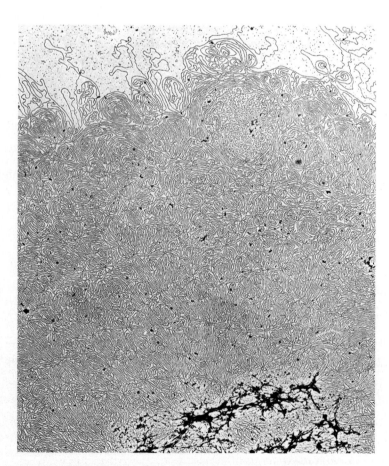

FIGURE 17-1   A human chromosome contains an enormous amount of DNA.
The dark element at the bottom of the photograph is the protein component of a single chromosome. All of the surrounding material is the DNA of that chromosome.

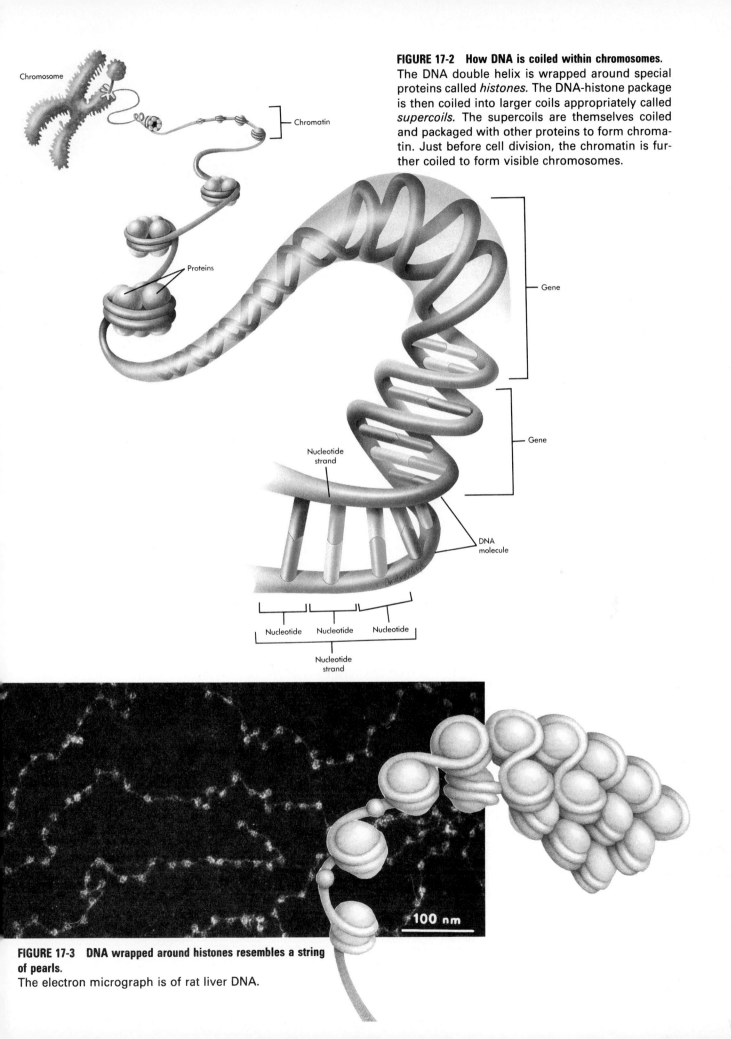

Chromosome

Chromatin

FIGURE 17-2 How DNA is coiled within chromosomes.
The DNA double helix is wrapped around special proteins called *histones.* The DNA-histone package is then coiled into larger coils appropriately called *supercoils.* The supercoils are themselves coiled and packaged with other proteins to form chromatin. Just before cell division, the chromatin is further coiled to form visible chromosomes.

Gene

Proteins

Gene

Nucleotide strand

DNA molecule

Nucleotide   Nucleotide   Nucleotide

Nucleotide strand

100 nm

FIGURE 17-3   DNA wrapped around histones resembles a string of pearls.
The electron micrograph is of rat liver DNA.

The location of the hereditary material, DNA

Today, scientists understand (in considerable detail) the way that information in the DNA of a developing organism is translated into its eyes, arms, and brain. However, this understanding is the result of over a half century of work by a succession of scientific investigators. Gregor Mendel's work, done in the late 1800s, suggested that traits are inherited as discrete packets of information. At the turn of the century, Walter Sutton suggested that these packets of information were on the chromosomes, but he had no direct evidence to support this hypothesis. In 1910, however, Thomas Hunt Morgan's experiments provided the first clear evidence upholding Sutton's theory. (The work of Mendel, Sutton, and Morgan is described in Chapter 19.) Beginning in the 1930s, experiments by biologists like Joachim Hammerling further probed the question of where the hereditary information is stored within the cell.

Hammerling chose a single-celled organism on which to focus his experiments—the long, slender alga *Acetabularia* (Figure 17-4, *A*). Although unicellular, *Acetabularia* is visible to the naked eye; it is about half as long as your little finger. This huge cell has three distinct parts: a foot, a stalk, and a cap.

FIGURE 17-4   The marine green alga *Acetabularia* has been the subject of many experiments in biology.
A, Although *Acetabularia* is a large organism with clearly differentiated parts, individuals are actually single cells.
B, Hammerling's *Acetabularia* graft experiment.
To the foot of each species, Hammerling grafted a stalk of the other. In each case, the cap that eventually developed was dictated by the foot, the location of the nucleus, and not the stalk.

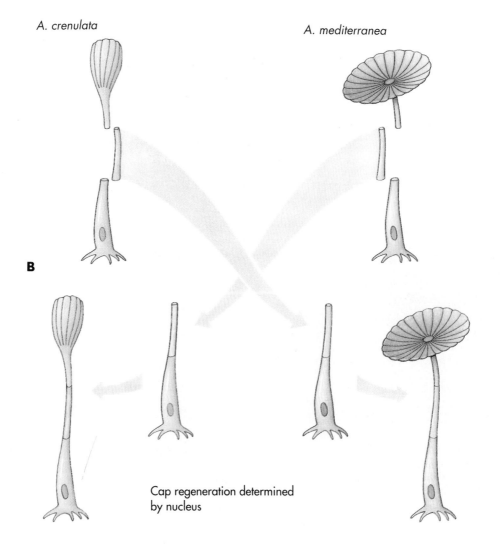

A. crenulata

A. mediterranea

B

Cap regeneration determined by nucleus

Hammerling amputated the caps from some *Acetabularia* cells and the feet from others. He found that when the cap was amputated, a new cap regenerated from the remaining portions (foot and stalk) of the cell. When the foot was amputated, however, a new foot was *not* regenerated from the cap or the stalk. After analyzing these data, Hammerling hypothesized that the hereditary information resides in the nucleus within the foot of *Acetabularia* and is necessary for the regeneration of amputated parts of the cell.

To test this hypothesis, Hammerling used two different species of *Acetabularia*: *A. mediterranea*, which has a disk-shaped cap, and *A. crenulata*, which has a branched, flower-like cap. He cut the stalk and cap away from a disk-capped cell, and grafted a stalk from a flower-capped cell to its remaining foot (Figure 17-4, *B*). The new cap that formed had characteristics of both types of caps. However, when Hammerling cut off this regenerated cap, a disk-shaped one—exactly like that of *A. mediterranea*—grew in its place and in every regeneration thereafter.

From this experiment and others producing similar results, Hammerling concluded that the instructions specifying the type of cap are stored in the foot of the cell—probably in the nucleus. The data suggested that these instructions must pass from the foot through the stalk to the cap. In his regeneration experiments, the initial blended cap was formed as a result of flower-shape instructions remaining in the transplanted stalk and disk-shape instructions transported from the nucleus. All the subsequent caps used new information from the nucleus.

⏷⏷ **Gregor Mendel's work suggested that traits are inherited as discrete packets of information. Walter Sutton's and Thomas Hunt Morgan's work suggested that these packets might be located on the chromosomes. The experiments of Joachim Hammerling provided firm evidence that the hereditary information is located within the nucleus of the cell.**

Identifying the nucleus as the most likely source of hereditary information again focused attention on the chromosomes, which are located within the nucleus. Scientists had been studying the chromosomes since the late 1800s and had suspected them to be the vehicles of inheritance. In 1869 a German chemist named Friedrich Miescher isolated the DNA contained within the chromosomes of various types of cells. He did not call it DNA (this designation would not come until the 1920s). Miescher called this chromosomal material **nucleic acid** because it seemed to be specifically associated with the cell nucleus and was slightly acidic.

The chemical nature of the hereditary material: Nucleic acids

In the 1920s the American biochemist P.A. Levene discovered that two types of nucleic acid were located within cells. Today scientists understand that one type of nucleic acid contains the hereditary message, whereas the other type helps express that message. Levene found that both types

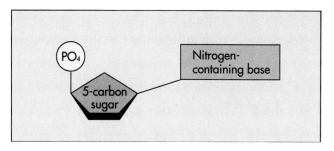

FIGURE 17-5 Structure of a nucleotide.
A nucleotide contains three different molecular components: a phosphate group (PO_4), a five-carbon sugar, and a nitrogen-containing base.

were nearly identical in their structures and contained three molecular parts (Figure 17-5): (1) phosphate (PO_4) groups, (2) 5-carbon sugars, and (3) four types of nitrogen-containing bases. Although nucleic acids as a whole are acidic and tend to form hydrogen ions when in solution, the nitrogen-containing bases tend to accept hydrogen ions. For this reason, these portions of nucleic acids are called bases.

The nucleic acids: DNA and RNA

Levene found that nucleic acids are composed of roughly equal portions of these three molecular parts. He concluded (correctly) from this information that these three molecular parts, bonded together, form the unit of structure of nucleic acids. Each unit, a five-carbon sugar bonded to a phosphate group and a nitrogen-containing base, is called a **nucleotide** (see Figure 17-5). One of the two types of nucleic acids found in cells is composed of units containing the 5-carbon sugar, ribose. It is therefore called **ribonucleic acid**, or **RNA** for short. The other type of nucleic acid is composed of units containing a 5-carbon sugar similar to ribose but having one less oxygen atom. This sugar is called *deoxyribose*, and the nucleic acid is called **deoxyribonucleic acid**, or **DNA**. Figure 17-6 shows the structure of both ribose and deoxyribose sugars. Can you find the difference between them? How do their names reflect this difference?

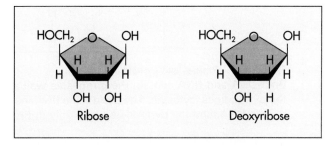

FIGURE 17-6 Comparison of ribose and deoxyribose.
Both sugars have five carbons, but deoxyribose has one less oxygen atom. Ribose is found in RNA and deoxyribose is found in DNA.

TABLE 17-1	Chargaff's analysis of DNA nucleotide base compositions

ORGANISM	BASE COMPOSITION (MOLE PERCENT)			
	A	T	G	C
Escherichia coli	26.0	23.9	24.9	25.2
Streptococcus pneumoniae	29.8	31.6	20.5	18.0
Mycobacterium tuberculosis	15.1	14.6	34.9	35.4
Yeast	31.3	32.9	18.7	17.1
Sea urchin	32.8	32.1	17.7	18.4
Herring	27.8	27.5	22.2	22.6
Rat	28.6	28.4	21.4	21.5
Human	30.9	29.4	19.9	19.8

There are two types of nucleic acids located within cells: deoxyribonucleic acid (DNA) and ribonucleic acid (RNA). Both types of nucleic acid are composed of units called nucleotides, which are made up of three molecular parts: a sugar, a phosphate group, and a base.

Each nucleotide making up the structure of DNA and RNA contains one of four different bases. DNA and RNA both contain the bases adenine and guanine, which are double-ring compounds called **purines** (Figure 17-7). DNA also contains the bases thymine and cytosine, which are single-ring compounds called **pyrimidines.** RNA contains the pyrimidine cytosine as well but contains the single-ring base uracil instead of thymine.

In the late 1940s, the experiments of Erwin Chargaff showed that the proportion of bases varied in the DNA of different types of organisms, as is shown in Table 17-1. This evidence suggested that DNA had the ability to be used as a molecular code. Its base composition varied as its code varied from organism to organism.

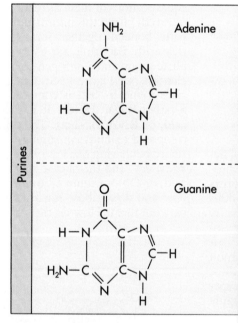

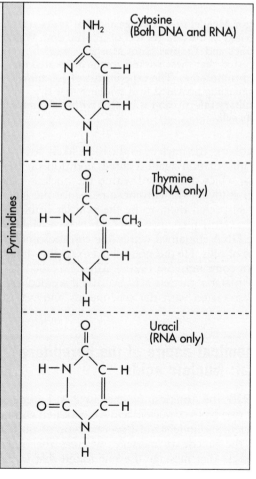

FIGURE 17-7 Purines and pyrimidines.
Both DNA and RNA contain the purines as well as one of the pyrimidines, cytosine. The pyrimidine thymine is found only in DNA, and the pyrimidine uracil only in RNA.

Along with the variations among the DNA molecules of different organisms, Chargaff also noted an important similarity: the amount of adenine present in DNA molecules is always equal to the amount of thymine, and the amount of guanine is always equal to the amount of cytosine (A = T and G = C). (Notice the roughly equal percentages of A and T, and G and C in each organism listed in Table 17-1.) Therefore DNA molecules always have an equal proportion of purines (A and G) and pyrimidines (C and T).

A major scientific breakthrough: The structure of DNA

In 1952 Alfred Hershey and Martha Chase performed now-famous experiments showing that the DNA in chromatin, not chromatin protein, is the hereditary material. They reasoned that if DNA carried hereditary information, then bacteria infected with viruses would contain viral DNA inside their cells, which would direct the formation of new virus particles. If, on the other hand, the protein carried the hereditary message, then virally infected bacteria would contain viral proteins within their cells. The experiments of Hershey and Chase showed clearly that viral DNA, not viral protein, was inside the infected bacteria.

The next puzzle to solve was how the nucleotides of DNA were put together. The significance of the regularities in the proportion of pyrimidines and the proportion of purines in DNA pointed out by Chargaff became clear through the work of two later experiments.

Two British biophysicists, Rosalind Franklin and Maurice Wilkins, carried out x-ray diffraction analysis of fibers of DNA. In this process the DNA molecule is bombarded with an x-ray beam. When individual rays encounter atoms, each ray's path is bent or diffracted; the pattern created by these diffractions can be captured on photographic film. With careful analysis of the diffraction pattern, it is possible to develop a three-dimensional image of the molecule causing the diffractions of the x-rays. The diffraction patterns that Franklin and Wilkins obtained (Figure 17-8) suggested that the DNA molecule was a helical coil. Put simply, this complex molecule was shaped like a spring.

Learning informally of Franklin and Wilkins' results before they were published in 1953, James Watson and Francis Crick (Figure 17-9), two young scientists at Cambridge University in England, quickly worked out a likely structure of the DNA molecule. They built models of the nucleotides, assembled them into molecular structures, and then tested each to see whether its structure fit with what they knew from Chargaff's and Franklin and Wilkins' work. They finally hit on the idea that the molecule might be a double helix (two springs twisted together) in which the bases of the two strands pointed inward toward one another (Figure 17-10). Pairing a purine (which is large) with a pyrimidine (which is small) resulted in a helical "ladder" with "rungs" of uniform length (Figure 17-11). In fact, always pairing adenine with thymine, and cytosine with guanine yielded a molecule in which A = T and C = G—a molecule consistent with Chargaff's observations. In their model, the sugar and phosphate units linked in an alternating fashion to form the sides of this twisted ladder (the springs in the earlier analogy). For their groundbreaking work, Watson and Crick shared the Nobel Prize in 1962.

Chargaff determined that although the proportion of the bases in DNA varied among organisms, the amount of adenine always equalled the amount of thymine and guanine always equalled cytosine. This information, coupled with the work of Rosalind Franklin, Maurice Wilkins, James Watson, and Francis Crick, led to the determination that the DNA molecule is a double-stranded, helical, molecular ladder. The bases of each strand of DNA form rungs of uniform length and alternating sugar-phosphate units form the ladder uprights.

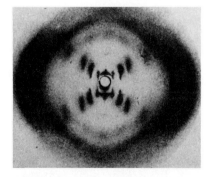

FIGURE 17-8 Evidence for the helical structure of DNA.
This x-ray diffraction photograph of crystals of DNA was made in 1953 by Rosalind Franklin in the laboratory of Maurice Wilkins. It suggested to Watson and Crick that the DNA molecule was a helix, like a winding staircase.

FIGURE 17-9 Watson and Crick and the double helix.
Watson and Crick examine their first model of the DNA double helix.

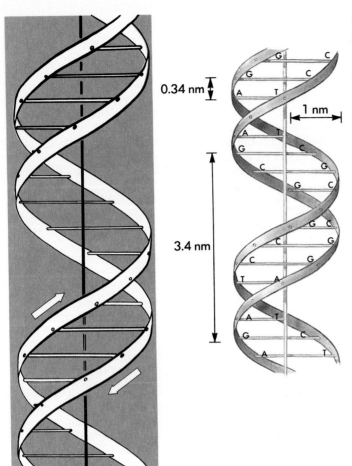

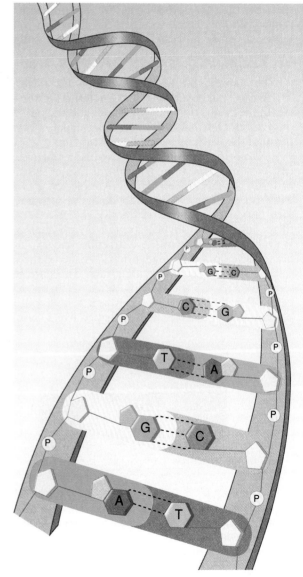

FIGURE 17-10   Diagram of DNA.
On the left is a reproduction of the original diagram of the double-helical structure of DNA presented in the 1953 paper by Watson and Crick. The diagram on the right shows the location of the nucleotide bases. This diagram also points out that the helix has a radius of 1 nanometer (nm) and completes a 360-degree turn every 3.4 nm. The base pairs are 0.34 nm apart. The arrows indicate the direction of replication of the DNA strands, which run in opposite directions. The vertical line shown in both diagrams is not part of the molecule—it is the imaginary axis.

FIGURE 17-11   Base pairing.
In a DNA molecule, only two base pairs are possible: adenine *(A)* with thymine *(T),* and guanine *(G)* with cytosine *(C).* A G-C base pair has three hydrogen bonds, and an A-T base pair has only two hydrogen bonds.

How DNA replicates

The Watson-Crick model immediately suggested that the basis for copying the genetic information is the complementarity of its bases. One side of the DNA ladder may have any base sequence, resulting in a particular code that the body understands. This sequence of bases then determines the sequence of bases making up the other side of the ladder. If the sequence on one side is ATTGCAT, for example, the sequence of the other side would have to be TAACGTA—its complementary image.

Scientists have also learned how DNA replicates, or makes more DNA. Before a cell divides, the bonds between the complementary bases break in short sections of the double-stranded DNA molecules, and the complementary strands separate from one another. This process is commonly referred to as *unwinding* or *unzipping*. Each split in the molecule is called a **replication fork.** At these forks, each separated strand serves as a template for the synthesis of a new complementary strand. Figure 17-12 shows a diagram of the replication fork of DNA during the replication process. Notice the Y-shaped replication point. In a process directed by enzymes, free nucleotide units that are present in the nucleus link to complementary bases on each of the DNA strands. The sugars and phosphates of the new nucleotides bond together to form the backbones of both new strands. Thus the process of DNA replication begins with one double-stranded DNA molecule and ends with two double-stranded DNA molecules. Each double strand contains one strand from the parent molecule plus a new complementary strand assembled from free nucleotides. Each of the new double-stranded molecules is identical to the other and is also identical to the original parent molecule.

 DNA begins replication by unwinding at intervals along its helix before cell division. In a process initiated and coordinated by enzymes, free nucleotides bond to the exposed bases, producing two new DNA strands, each identical to one another and to the original double strand from which they were replicated.

Genes: The units of hereditary information

Just before the scientific discovery of Watson and Crick, scientists were also working to determine how DNA directs the growth and development of an organism. They asked the question, "What is the hereditary message that DNA carries?" This question was answered by means of experiments conducted in the 1940s and early 1950s by two geneticists—George Beadle and Edward Tatum. These researchers officially marked the beginning of molecular genetics as they studied biochemical characteristics as the expression of genes. They worked with the common red bread mold *Neurospora.*

At the same time Beadle and Tatum were doing their work, various biochemists were also studying the manufac-

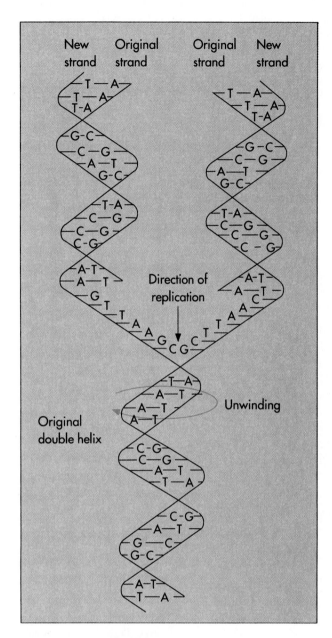

FIGURE 17-12 A replication fork.
The double-stranded DNA molecule separates at its bases, forming a split, or fork. At this fork, each separated strand acts as a template for the synthesis of a new complementary strand.

ture and breakdown of organic molecules within cells. They determined that cells build and degrade molecules by sequences of steps in which each step is catalyzed by a specific enzyme. These enzymatically controlled sequences of steps are called biochemical pathways.

Beadle and Tatum studied mold cultures they had exposed to x-rays. The x-rays induced mutations, or changes, in the DNA of the organism, resulting in a variety of mutants, each unable to manufacture certain amino acids. Using known information about the biochemical pathways of *Neurospora*, they hypothesized that specific enzymes must be involved in the manufacture of these amino acids and that

More than 4000 diseases are known to result from failure or abnormality of a gene, ranging from cystic fibrosis to epilepsy. However, only 164 of these disease-related defects have been pinpointed to specific locations on the human chromosomes. In fact, only 1700 genes of any sort have been located precisely on the human chromosomes, out of an estimated total of 100,000 genes. This lack of a precise map of genes is a matter of some importance now that gene transfer therapy offers hope of curing genetic defects. The problem is that doctors cannot transfer a healthy copy of a gene into an individual lacking it unless researchers have first isolated that gene from a normal individual and located the disease-related gene's position on the chromosomes. If gene transfer therapy is going to be applied to a wide range of genetic defects, a far more detailed map of the human chromosomes is needed.

The preparation of this map is now well underway. The initial stage involved identifying the positions of a variety of short nucleotide sequences. Used as recognition sites by DNA-cutting enzymes, these sequences are scattered around the chromosomes (much as the sequence of letters "en" is scattered about at various locations on this page). Each kind of enzyme has a different recognition site, called a *restriction site*. By looking at many different enzymes, researchers can identify restriction sites all over the chromosome. By looking to see how the sites are inherited in families with hereditary disorders, it becomes possible to quickly associate a genetic defect with a particular restriction site and thus to locate the gene's position. Scientists hope to have such "sign

FIGURE 17-A Maynard Olson (left) and Eric Green review DNA sequences. Olson was instrumental in developing key technologies that have made the Human Genome Project possible.

posts" positioned every million nucleotides along the chromosomes by 1995 (Figure 17-A).

At the same time, efforts are underway to determine the full nucleotide sequence of all the chromosomes—the Human Genome Project. This is a mammoth task because there are some 3×10^9 nucleotide base pairs in the human chromosomes—a complete map, printed in the same size type as this text, would stretch from St. Louis to Anchorage! Two recent key developments have made this gargantuan project possible. The first is the polymerase chain reaction (PCR), which makes it possible for a scientist to obtain millions of copies of any small segment of DNA. Researchers can use PCR to test for the presence of a particular gene in large numbers of chromosome fragments. The second key development is a method of combining human DNA with pieces of yeast chromosomes. The yeast artificial chromosomes, or YAKs, enable scientists to isolate and clone far larger pieces of DNA than had been possible before. This is greatly speeding the sequencing of the human genome because it eliminates the need to sort through tiny bits of DNA that often contain only parts of a gene. Although scientists have a long way to go in meeting their goal of sequencing the entire human genome, no one believes it an impossible task.

some or all of the enzymes in each biochemical pathway must not be doing their jobs. To test their hypothesis, Beadle and Tatum chose mutants unable to synthesize the amino acid arginine. They supplied each mutant with various compounds intermediate in the arginine pathway and observed whether or not the mutant was then able to synthesize arginine. Using this method, Beadle and Tatum were able to infer the presence of defective enzymes in this biochemical pathway (Figure 17-13).

From these studies, Beadle and Tatum proposed the **one gene–one enzyme theory,** which states that the production of a given enzyme is under the control of a specific gene. If the gene mutates, the enzyme will not be synthesized properly or will not be made at all. Therefore the re-

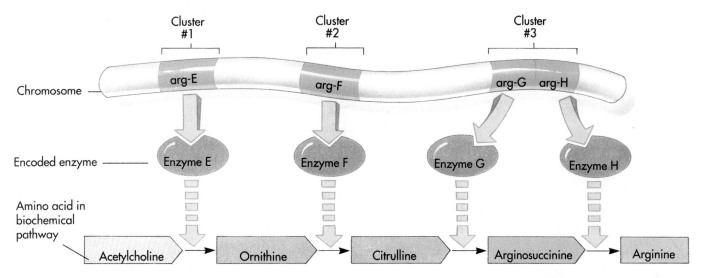

FIGURE 17-13 The one gene – one enzyme theory.
This theory states that the production of a given enzyme is under the control of a specific gene. This theory was postulated by Beadle and Tatum after their work with *Neurospora.*

action it catalyzes will not take place, and the product of the reaction will not be produced. Today scientists have refined this hypothesis to say that the production of a given polypeptide (a portion of an enzyme or other protein) is under the control of a single gene. In addition, their conclusions have been upheld by other biochemical evidence. For their groundbreaking work, Beadle and Tatum were awarded the Nobel Prize in Physiology and Medicine in 1958.

These experiments and other related ones have finally brought a clear understanding of what the unit of heredity is. A unit of heredity—a **gene**—is a sequence of nucleotides that codes for (scientists say encodes) the amino acid sequence of an enzyme or other protein. Although most genes code for a string of amino acids (polypeptides), there are also genes devoted to the production of special forms of RNA, which play important roles in protein synthesis.

⌄
⌄

DNA carries a code that directs the synthesis of polypeptides—pieces of enzymes and other proteins that orchestrate and regulate the growth, development, and daily functioning of cells. Each hereditary unit, or gene, codes for one polypeptide.

Gene expression: How DNA directs the synthesis of polypeptides

An overview

Interestingly, polypeptides are not made in the nucleus where DNA is located. Instead, they are made in the cytoplasm at the **ribosomes.** These complex polypeptide-making factories contain over 50 different proteins in their structure. Along with proteins, ribosomes are also made up of RNA—a hint that RNA molecules play an important

role in polypeptide synthesis. In fact, as shown in Figure 17-14, cells contain three types of RNA, and each plays a special role in the manufacture of polypeptides.

The type of RNA found in ribosomes is called **ribosomal RNA,** or **rRNA.** A second type of RNA, called **transfer RNA,** or **tRNA,** is found in the cytoplasm. During polypeptide synthesis, tRNA molecules transport amino acids (used to build the polypeptide) to the ribosomes. In addition, tRNA molecules position each amino acid at the correct place on the elongating polypeptide chain. A third type of RNA, called **messenger RNA,** or **mRNA,** brings information from the DNA (within the nucleus) to the ribosomes (in the cytoplasm) to direct which polypeptide is assembled.

Transcribing the DNA message to RNA

The first step in the process of polypeptide synthesis and gene expression is the copying of the gene into a strand of messenger RNA. Scientists call this copying process **transcription.** Transcription begins when a special enzyme, called an **RNA polymerase,** binds to a particular sequence of nucleotides on a single DNA strand. This sequence of nucleotides is located at the beginning of the gene that is being expressed. You can think of such a sequence of nucleotides as an enzyme code that says, "Start here." Scientists call this place on a DNA strand a **promoter site.**

First, the DNA base-pair bonds break, no longer holding the double-stranded helix together. As the DNA strands separate, one strand begins to function as a template as RNA polymerase binds to a promoter site on the DNA molecule. RNA nucleotides bind with the now-exposed DNA bases in a sequence complementary to that of the DNA. For example, RNA nucleotides having the base adenine pair with DNA nucleotides having the base thymine. Likewise, RNA nucleotides having the base uracil pair with DNA nu-

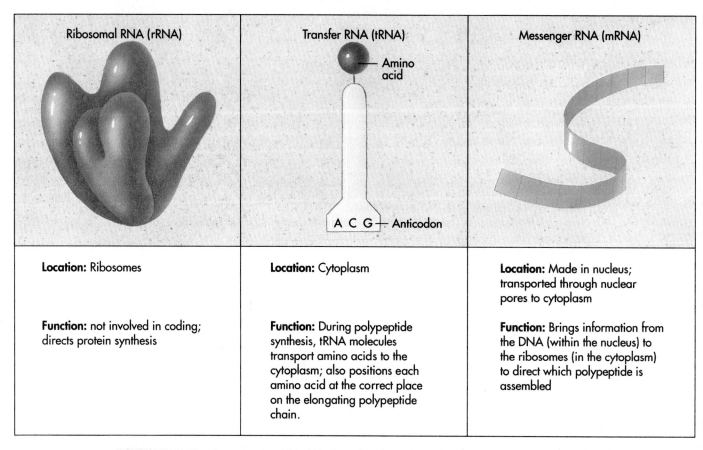

Ribosomal RNA (rRNA)	Transfer RNA (tRNA)	Messenger RNA (mRNA)
Location: Ribosomes	**Location:** Cytoplasm	**Location:** Made in nucleus; transported through nuclear pores to cytoplasm
Function: not involved in coding; directs protein synthesis	**Function:** During polypeptide synthesis, tRNA molecules transport amino acids to the cytoplasm; also positions each amino acid at the correct place on the elongating polypeptide chain.	**Function:** Brings information from the DNA (within the nucleus) to the ribosomes (in the cytoplasm) to direct which polypeptide is assembled

FIGURE 17-14   The three types of RNA with their locations and functions.
The illustrations are diagrammatic representations of the shapes of these molecules and are used to depict each type of RNA throughout this chapter.

cleotides having the base adenine. Figure 17-15 shows a representation of the process of RNA transcription. Which DNA nucleotides bond with RNA nucleotides having the base guanine?

As the RNA polymerase moves along the DNA strand encountering each DNA nucleotide in turn, it adds the corresponding complementary RNA nucleotide to the growing single strand of mRNA. When the enzyme arrives at a special stop sequence (frequently a loop in the DNA) located at the end of the gene, it disengages from the DNA and releases the newly assembled mRNA strand. A processing step then removes segments of RNA from the original transcript that are not used in polypeptide synthesis. These extra sequences of nucleotides that intervene between the polypeptide-specifying portions of the gene are called **introns** (they *intrude* into the gene but are not expressed).

The remaining segments of the gene—the nucleotide sequences that encode the amino-acid sequence of the polypeptide—are called **exons** (expressed portions of a gene). Cutting out introns and splicing together exons results in the final mRNA strand. After cutting and splicing, the mRNA strands leave the nucleus through the nuclear pores and travel to the ribosomes in the cytoplasm of the cell (Figure 17-16).

▼▼▼
In the first step of polypeptide synthesis, mRNA is constructed from free RNA nucleotides by using a single strand of DNA as a template. After noncoding sequences are removed from the mRNA strand, it leaves the nucleus and travels to the ribosomes where polypeptide synthesis takes place.

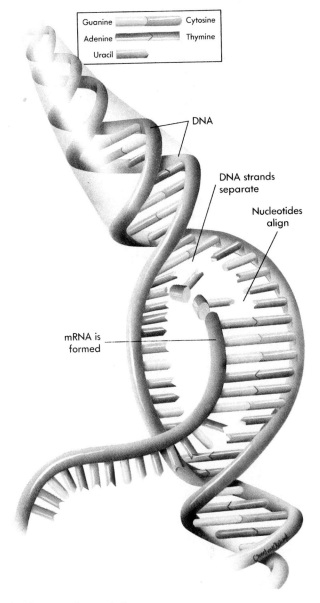

Guanine — **Cytosine**
Adenine — **Thymine**
Uracil

DNA

DNA strands
separate

Nucleotides
align

mRNA is
formed

FIGURE 17-15   Transcription.
One of the strands of DNA functions as a template on which nucleotide building blocks are assembled by RNA polymerase (not shown here) into RNA.

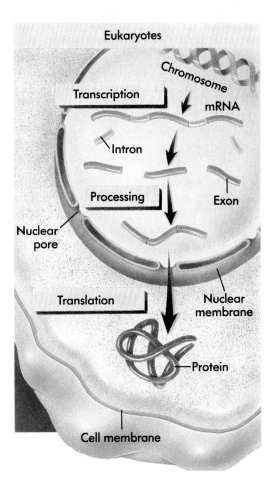

Eukaryotes

Chromosome

Transcription

mRNA

Intron

Processing

Exon

Nuclear pore

Translation

Nuclear membrane

Protein

Cell membrane

FIGURE 17-16   Polypeptide synthesis in eukaryotes.
Genes in eukaryotes are long and contain extra sequences of nucleotides called *introns,* which are not used in protein synthesis. These introns must be cut out of the mRNA transcript of the gene, leaving exons, before protein synthesis can proceed.

Translating the transcribed DNA message into a polypeptide

In the second step of gene expression, the mRNA—using its *copied* DNA code—directs the synthesis of a polypeptide. Scientists call this decoding process **translation.** In 1961, as a result of experiments led by Francis Crick (one of the researchers who worked out the structure of DNA), scientists learned that the DNA code is made up of sequences of three nucleotide bases. These triplet-nucleotide code words, as they appear on the transcribed mRNA, are called **codons.** Researchers soon broke the code and learned which codons stand for which amino acids, the building blocks of polypeptides.

Table 17-2 is a list of the mRNA codons and the amino acids for which they stand. The table is structured so that every triplet-base sequence of the four mRNA bases is listed. As you can see from the table, using a three-base sequence of four different bases produces 64 possible codon combinations ($4 \times 4 \times 4$ or 4^3). Approximately 20 amino acids are used in polypeptide production, so extra codons exist, providing alternate code words for many of the amino acids. Also notice that certain codons do not code for amino acids but act as stop signals for the process of translation.

During the process of translation the genetic code (the sequence of codons) is deciphered. First, the initial portion of the mRNA transcribed from DNA in the nucleus binds to an rRNA molecule interwoven in the ribosome (Figure 17-17). The mRNA lies on the ribosome in such a way that only the three-nucleotide portion of the mRNA molecule—the codon—is exposed at the polypeptide-making site. As each bit of the mRNA message is exposed in turn, a molecule of transfer RNA, or tRNA, binds to the mRNA.

TABLE 17-2 | The genetic code

FIRST LETTER	SECOND LETTER				THIRD LETTER
	U	C	A	G	
U	Phenylalanine	Serine	Tyrosine	Cysteine	U
	Phenylalanine	Serine	Tyrosine	Cysteine	C
	Leucine	Serine	Stop	Stop	A
	Leucine	Serine	Stop	Tryptophan	G
C	Leucine	Proline	Histidine	Arginine	U
	Leucine	Proline	Histidine	Arginine	C
	Leucine	Proline	Glutamine	Arginine	A
	Leucine	Proline	Glutamine	Arginine	G
A	Isoleucine	Threonine	Asparagine	Serine	U
	Isoleucine	Threonine	Asparagine	Serine	C
	Isoleucine	Threonine	Lysine	Arginine	A
	(Start); Methionine	Threonine	Lysine	Arginine	G
G	Valine	Alanine	Aspartate	Glycine	U
	Valine	Alanine	Aspartate	Glycine	C
	Valine	Alanine	Glutamate	Glycine	A
	Valine	Alanine	Glutamate	Glycine	G

A codon consists of three nucleotides on mRNA read in the sequence shown above. For example ACU codes threonine. The first letter, A, is read in the first column; the second letter, C, from the second letter column; and the third letter, U, from the third letter column. Each of the mRNA codons is recognized by a corresponding anticodon sequence on a tRNA molecule. Most amino acids are encoded by more than one codon. For example, threonine is encoded by four codons (ACU, ACC, ACA, and ACG), which differ from one another only in the third position.

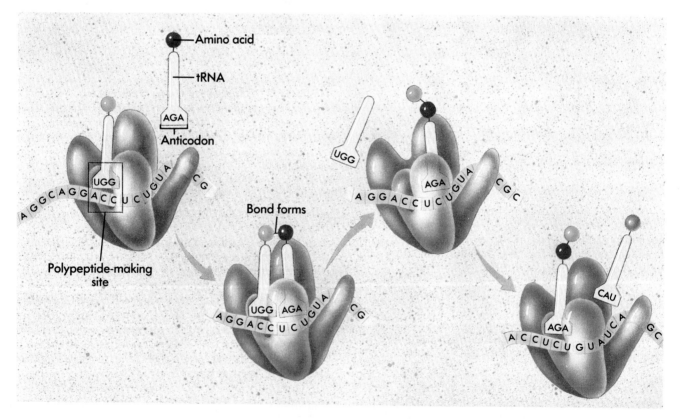

FIGURE 17-17 Translation.
The steps of translation are as follows:
1. mRNA binds to rRNA.
2. tRNA with an attached amino acid approaches the mRNA-rRNA complex.
3. The tRNA attaches to the mRNA at a special binding site. The amino acid at the end opposite to the anticodon loop forms a bond with the amino acid attached to the adjacent tRNA molecule.
4. The adjacent tRNA molecule breaks its bond with the mRNA and falls from its site.
5. The rRNA moves along the mRNA, exposing the next codon of mRNA.

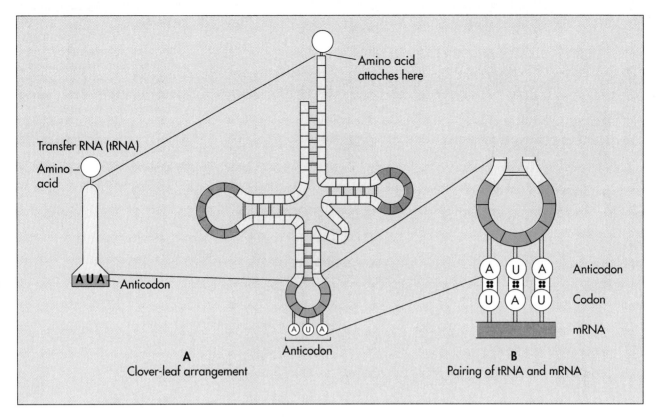

FIGURE 17-18   Structure of a tRNA molecule.
A A tRNA molecule is shaped like a cloverleaf. The anticodon is at the bottom of the cloverleaf, and the amino acid specific to the anticodon is at the top. The cloverleaf structure is not shown throughout this chapter; instead a more simplified tRNA molecule is used. It is symbolized by a bar as shown above.
B The anticodon pairs with a complementary codon on the mRNA molecules.

tRNA molecules each have an **anticodon** loop—a portion of the molecule with a sequence of three base pairs complementary to a specific mRNA codon (Figure 17-18). On the opposite end of the anticodon loop, each transfer RNA molecule carries an amino acid specific to its anticodon sequence. For example, a tRNA molecule having the anticodon AGA carries the amino acid serine. A special family of enzymes links the amino acids to the tRNA molecules. Using the information in Table 17-2 and your understanding of the relationship between codons and anticodons, can you determine which amino acid a tRNA molecule with the anticodon GGG carries?

One by one, as tRNA molecules bind to codons at the mRNA, amino acids are lined up in an order determined by the sequence of codons. As each amino acid is added to the chain, a bond is formed. When an amino acid bonds to the forming polypeptide, its bond to its carrier tRNA molecule breaks. The tRNA falls from its site on the ribosome, leaving that site vacant. The ribosome then moves along the mRNA strand, exposing the next codon of the mRNA.

When a tRNA molecule that recognizes this next codon appears, its anticodon bonds to the codon, adding a new amino acid to the growing chain. When a stop codon is encountered (Figure 17-19), no tRNA exists to bind to it. Instead, it is recognized by special release factors, proteins that bring about the release of the newly made polypeptide from the ribosome. Figure 17-20 shows an overview of protein synthesis.

Polypeptide synthesis takes place at the ribosomes. Ribosomes bind to sites at one end of a mRNA strand and then move down the strand, exposing the codons one-by-one. At each step of a ribosome's progress, it exposes a codon to binding by a tRNA molecule having a three-base sequence complementary to the exposed mRNA codon. The amino acid carried by that particular tRNA molecule is then added to the end of the elongating polypeptide chain.

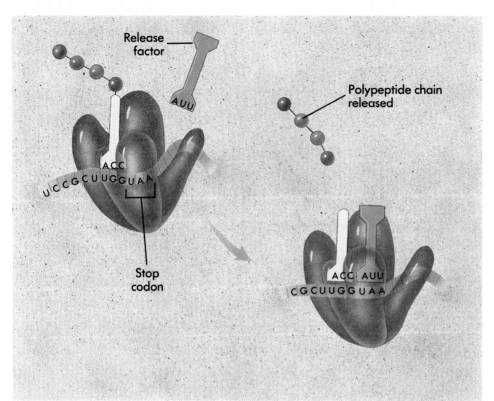

FIGURE 17-19 Termination of protein synthesis.
There is no tRNA with an anti-codon complementary to any of the three stop codons, such as UAA. When a ribosome encounters a stop codon, it stops moving along the mRNA. The anticodon, however, *is* recognized by a special release factor that brings about the release of the newly made polypeptide from the ribosome.

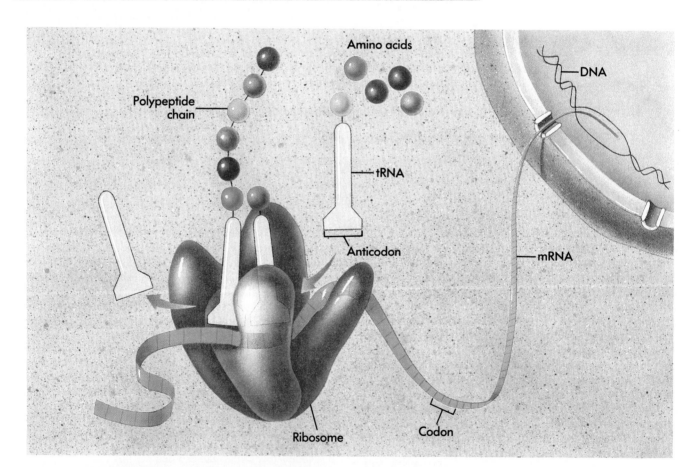

FIGURE 17-20 Overview of protein synthesis.
This diagram presents a summary of protein synthesis, beginning in the nucleus where DNA is transcribed into mRNA. mRNA leaves the nucleus and enters the cytoplasm where it binds with a ribosome. The ribosome exposes codons on the mRNA so that tRNA molecules with complementary anticodons can bind. These tRNA molecules carry amino acids. In this manner, a chain of amino acids—a polypeptide—is formed.

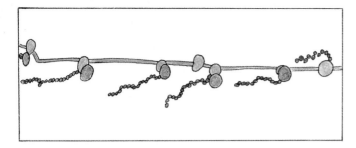

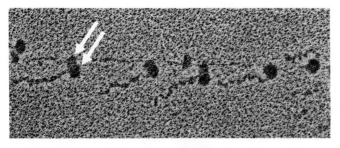

FIGURE 17-21 Protein synthesis in a fly.
These ribosomes are reading along an mRNA molecule of the fly *Chironomus tentans* from left to right, assembling polypeptides that dangle behind them like tails. Clearly visible are the two subunits *(arrows)* of each ribosome translating the mRNA.

Figure 17-21 shows that more than one ribosome at a time reads and translates the mRNA message to synthesize a polypeptide. Here, a group of many ribosomes (called a *polyribosome*), are reading along an mRNA molecule taken from a cell of a fly. The polypeptides being made can be seen dangling behind each ribosome.

Regulating eukaryotic gene expression

Cells not only know how to make particular polypeptides but also when to make them. For example, during your fetal development, specific enzymes played crucial roles at certain times, directing the series of biochemical reactions that resulted in your growth. As this growth and development took place, your genes were transcribed in a specific order, each gene for a specified time. Likewise, the cells in your body that produce digestive enzymes know when to manufacture these enzymes. Your red blood cells—not other types of cells—synthesize hemoglobin to carry oxygen to all parts of your body. How are these specific genes activated?

Molecular geneticists are only now beginning to understand these mechanisms in eukaryotic cells. Interestingly, cells have gene switches. These switches are really proteins that interact with specific nucleotide sequences called **regulatory sites.** Regulatory sites control the transcription of genes. Control can be positive and result in turning a gene on, or it can be negative and result in turning a gene off. In eukaryotes, control is generally positive because eukaryotic genes are usually inactive—so genes must be turned on. In one type of gene switch, steroid hormones along with

protein receptor molecules from the cytoplasm activate transcription by binding to regulatory sites on the DNA. Scientists are probing the details of this regulatory process.

Eukaryotic cells also regulate gene expression by the number of identical genes they transcribe at one time. This use of multiple copies of genes is a way to control the amount of a particular protein that is produced at a particular time. Some genes have related, but not identical, nucleotide sequences. Transcribing these genes at the same time produces related products. Such multiple copies of genes in eukaryotes, called **gene families,** are derived from a common ancestral gene and are a reflection of the evolutionary process.

> Organisms control the expression of their genes by selectively inhibiting the transcription of some genes and facilitating the transcription of others. Regulatory proteins control the transcription process.

Cell division, growth, and reproduction

This highly ordered and orchestrated process of DNA replication, transcription, and translation results in the expression of your heredity — the expression of the uniqueness of you. The fact that DNA is packaged neatly in chromosomes not only allows a tremendous amount of information to reside in each cell of your body but also allows your cells to separate this genetic material in an organized way during cell division so that each cell receives the appropriate complement of DNA.

Cell division occurs in your body (as well as in other eukaryotes) as a means of cellular growth, repair, and reproduction. To illustrate, look at the human life cycle diagrammed in Figure 17-22. A **life cycle** is the progression of stages an organism passes through from its conception until it conceives another similar organism. The human life cycle is representative of the life cycle of all animals. The baby in the diagram represents that part of the life cycle during which a new individual has been produced by the fusion of **gametes,** or sex cells, from a male and a female of the same species. The female gamete is the egg, and the male gamete is the sperm.

After a person (or other animal) grows to sexual maturity, the sex organs within its body begin to produce gametes by a type of cell division called **meiosis.** During meiosis, one parent cell produces four sex cells, but these cells are *not* identical to the parent cell. Each sex cell is **haploid;** that is, it contains *half* the amount of hereditary material of the original parent cell. It is a single set of the genetic information. Because of this reduction in chromosome number, one sex cell from each of two parent organisms can join together in a process called **fertilization** to form the first cell of a new individual that has a full complement of hereditary material. This new cell is **diploid.** That is, it contains double the haploid amount—a double set of the genetic information. This type of reproduction, which involves the fusion of gametes to produce the first cell of a new individual, is called **sexual reproduction.**

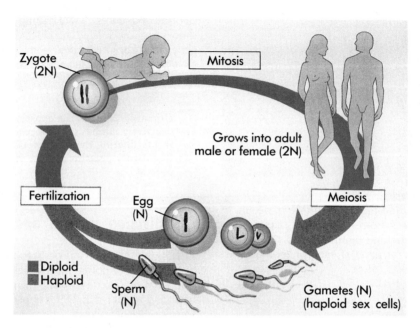

FIGURE 17-22 The human life cycle.
Mitosis, which produces two identical diploid daughter cells, is responsible for the growth of a human being into an adult. Meiosis, on the other hand, produces four haploid gametes (sex cells) that are *not* identical—each gamete contains half the hereditary material of the original cell. Meiosis in human females produces one functional gamete and three nonfunctional gametes. During fertilization, one gamete from each of the two parents comes together to form a new individual.

The first cell of any multicellular organism divides, and those cells divide, and so on. This type of cell division is called **mitosis** and produces two daughter cells from one parent cell. These daughter cells have genetic information that is identical with one another and with the original parent cell. As the growth and development of the individual continues, certain cells are triggered by other developmental processes to begin to differentiate, or become different, from one another while continuing to divide. The animal life cycle begins again when the growth and development of the individual is complete and sexual maturity is reached.

Mitosis is a process of cell division that produces two identical cells from an original parent cell. Meiosis is a process of cell division that produces four cells from one parent cell. Each of these four cells has one set of genetic information rather than two sets like the parent cell.

Plants and animals are similar in that they both use the process of mitosis to grow. Also, the life cycles of both plants and animals have two phases: a haploid phase and a diploid phase. In animals, however, the diploid phase of the life cycle predominates. The haploid phase consists only of single-celled gametes. In most organisms, these gametes live only 1 or 2 days after meiosis is complete unless fertilization takes place. During fertilization, two haploid gametes join to form the first cell in the diploid phase of the life cycle. Plant life cycles differ from animal life cycles because most plants have distinct *multicelled* haploid as well as diploid phases. One phase usually dominates over the other, but both phases are always present.

Single-celled eukaryotes (such as many of the protists) generally reproduce by mitosis; this process plays no role in the growth of single-celled organisms but plays a role in the growth of populations of single-celled organisms. During reproduction, a parent organism divides by mitosis, producing two identical organisms. This type of reproduction is called **asexual reproduction.** Some simple animals such as the hydra pictured in Figure 17-23 and many plants are also capable of reproducing asexually by mitosis.

FIGURE 17-23 Asexual reproduction.
Many organisms, such as this hydra, are capable of reproducing asexually by mitosis. Hydra also reproduce sexually.

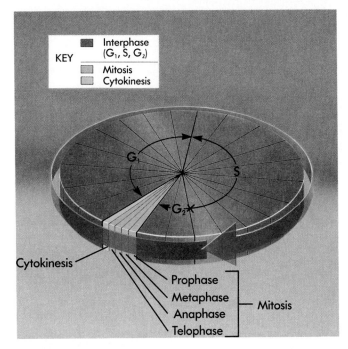

FIGURE 17-24 The cell cycle
In this diagram, each wedge represents 1 hour of the 22-hour division cycle of human liver cells. Actual cell division makes up a very small part of the cycle.

Mitosis

Notice in Figure 17-24 that only a small portion of a cell's "life," called the **cell cycle,** is involved with mitosis. The activities of **interphase** occupy the majority of the cell cycle.

In the past, interphase was nicknamed the resting stage. Scientists now know that a cell in interphase is far from resting. In fact, it doubles its size and replicates its DNA as well as carrying out its normal life functions. During the G_1 stage of interphase (the time gap between the last mitosis and the start of DNA synthesis), the cell is growing. For many organisms, this growth period occupies the major portion of the cell's life span—possibly days, months, or years. During the S (synthesis) stage of interphase, a complete replica of the cell's DNA is synthesized. The cell now contains two complete, identical copies of hereditary information. These two copies of hereditary information can be seen as sister chromatids when the chromosomes later become visible.

During the G_2 stage of interphase (the time gap between the end of DNA synthesis and the beginning of mitosis), the supercoils of DNA, normally somewhat diffuse or strung out within the cell nucleus, begin the long process of **condensation.** During this process the complex of DNA and proteins coil into more tightly compacted bodies that will become visible as chromosomes during mitosis. In addition, during the G_2 phase the cell begins to assemble the "machinery" (microtubules that make up the spindle) that it will later use to move and divide the chromosomes. In animal cells, for example, the **centrioles** replicate. These organelles are surrounded by microtubule-organizing centers that play a key role in the mitotic process; most plants and fungi lack centrioles.

⬇⬇ Interphase is the portion of the cell cycle in which the cell grows and carries out normal life functions. During this time the cell also produces an exact copy of the hereditary material, DNA, as it prepares for cell division.

Mitosis is a continuous sequence of events that occurs just after interphase, and that results in the division of the chromosomes duplicated during its S phase. To more easily understand this process, scientists divide its events into the following phases: prophase, metaphase, anaphase, and telophase (Figure 17-25).

Prophase

The first stage of mitosis, **prophase,** begins when the chromosomes have condensed to the point where they become visible under a light microscope. As prophase continues, the chromosomes continue to shorten and thicken, looking much bulkier at the end of prophase than at its beginning. The nucleolus, which was previously conspicuous, disappears. This disappearance is due to the nucleolus being unable to make ribosomal RNA (rRNA) when the part of the chromosome bearing the rRNA genes is condensed. And it is rRNA that makes up most of the substance of the nucleolus (see Chapter 3).

⬇⬇ Prophase is the stage of mitosis characterized by the appearance of visible chromosomes.

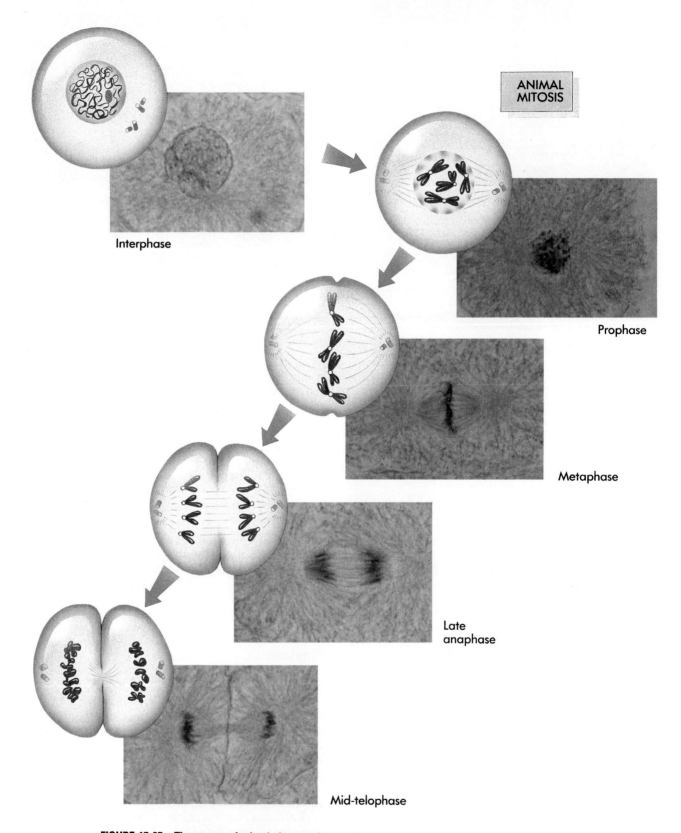

Interphase

Prophase

Metaphase

Late
anaphase

Mid-telophase

FIGURE 17-25   The stages of mitosis in an animal cell.
The stages of mitosis are shown here in photographs and drawings of a dividing white-fish cell. Although they are barely noticeable in the photographs, centrioles play a key role in animal cell mitosis. Although interphase is shown here to complete the cell cycle, it is not a stage of mitosis.

While the chromosomes are condensing, another series of equally important events is also occurring: special microtubules (thin, tube-like, protein structures [see Chapter 3]) called the **spindle fibers** are being assembled. In animal cells, these spindle fibers extend from a pair of related microtubular structures called *centrioles* (see Figure 17-25). Although the centrioles were once thought to play a role in forming the spindle, recent evidence suggests that this is not the case. Instead, the microtubules of the spindle appear to form from granules surrounding the centrioles, called the *microtubule organizing center,* or MTOC. Interestingly, plant cells do not contain centrioles, but spindle fibers form in plant cells.

In early prophase the centrioles of animal cells begin to move away from one another. By the end of prophase, each member of the pair has moved to an opposite end, or pole, of the cell. As the spindle fibers form, the nuclear envelope breaks down, forming small vesicles that disperse in the cytosol. Without the nucleus in the way, the spindle fibers form a bridge between the centrioles, spanning the distance from one pole to the other. Some spindle fibers extending from each pole attach to their side of the centromere of each sister chromatid. By this time, each chromatid has developed a **kinetochore** at its centromere. A kinetochore is the structure to which several pole-to-centromere microtubules will attach. The effect is to attach one sister chromatid to one pole and the other sister chromatid to the other pole. During later stages of mitosis the sister chromatids separate and move to opposite poles of the cell, pulled by the spindle fibers. The proper attachment of each spindle fiber to the kinetochore is therefore critical to the process of mitosis; a mistake is disastrous. The attachment of two sister chromatids to the same pole, for example, results in their not separating, so they end up in the same daughter cell. Such a situation can result in a cell with an extra chromosome. Depending on the type of cell, it may be abnormal or it may die.

> By the end of prophase, spindle fibers that radiate from opposite poles of the cell attach to each kinetochore at the centromere.

When the centrioles reach the poles of the cell in animal mitosis, they radiate an array of microtubules outward (toward the cell membrane) as well as inward (toward the chromosomes). This arrangement of microtubules is called an **aster.** The function of the aster is not well understood. Evidence suggests that the aster probably acts as a support during the movement of the sister chromatids.

Metaphase

The second phase of mitosis, **metaphase,** begins when the chromatid pairs line up in the center of the cell. In reality, the chromosomes are not in a line but form a circle. They only appear to form a line when viewed two dimensionally with a light microscope as in Figure 17-25, *C.* Figure 17-26 is a diagram of a three-dimensional view of an animal cell

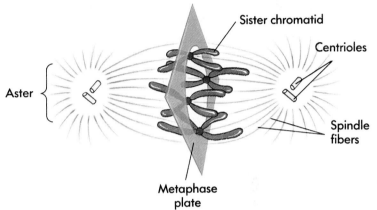

FIGURE 17-26 The metaphase plate.
In metaphase, the chromosomes array themselves around the spindle midpoint.

at metaphase. As you can see, the chromosomes form a circle perpendicular to the direction of the spindle fibers. Positioned by the microtubules attached at their centromeres, all the chromosomes are equidistantly arranged between the two poles at the "equator" of the cell. The region of this circular arrangement, called the **metaphase plate,** is not a physical structure but indicates approximately where the future axis of cell division will be.

> Metaphase is the stage of mitosis characterized by the alignment of the chromosomes in a ring, equidistant from the two poles of the cell.

Anaphase

At the beginning of anaphase the sister chromatids separate at the centromere, freeing them from their attachment to one another. Before this split, the chromatids are tugged in two directions at once by opposing microtubules—somewhat like a cellular tug-of-war. With the separation of the chromatids (now called chromosomes), they move rapidly toward opposite poles of the cell, each pulled at its kinetochore by attached, shortening microtubules.

> Anaphase is the stage of mitosis characterized by the physical separation of sister chromatids and their movement to opposite poles of the cell.

Telophase

The separation of the sister chromatids in anaphase equally divides the hereditary material that replicated just before mitosis. Therefore each of the two new cells that are forming receive a complete, identical copy of the chromosomes. This partitioning of the genetic material is the essence of the process of mitosis.

The events of this last phase of mitosis, **telophase,** ready the cell for **cytokinesis,** or division of the cytoplasm. The spindle fibers are chemically disassembled and therefore disappear. The nuclear envelope re-forms around each set of what were sister chromatids, now chromosomes in their own right. These chromosomes begin to uncoil, returning to their normally strung out, more diffuse state. The DNA of the nucleolus begins making ribosomal RNA once again; this rRNA is visible, resulting in the reappearance of the nucleolus. In summary, the events of telophase are very much like the reverse order of the events of prophase.

Telophase is the stage of mitosis during which the mitotic apparatus assembled during prophase is disassembled, the nuclear envelope is reestablished, and the normal use of the genes present in the chromosomes is reinitiated.

Cytokinesis

At the end of telophase, mitosis is complete. The eukaryotic cell has divided its duplicated hereditary material into two nuclei that are positioned at opposite ends of the cell. While this process has been going on, the cytoplasmic organelles, such as the mitochondria have been somewhat equally distributed to each side of the cytoplasm. These organelles replicate throughout interphase.

At this point the process of cell division is still not complete. The division of the cytoplasm—that portion of the cell outside the nucleus—has not yet begun. The stage of the cell cycle at which cell division actually occurs is called *cytokinesis.* Cytokinesis generally involves the division of the cell into approximately equal halves.

Cytokinesis is the physical division of the cytoplasm of a eukaryotic cell into two daughter cells.

Cytokinesis in animal cells

In human cells and in the cells of other eukaryotes that lack cell walls, cytokinesis occurs by a pinching of the cell in two. This pinching is accomplished by a belt of microfilaments that encircles the cell at the metaphase plate. These microfilaments contract, forming a **cleavage furrow** around the circumference of the cell (Figure 17-27). As contraction proceeds, the furrow deepens until the opposing edges of the membrane make contact with one another. Then the membranes fuse, separating the one cell into two new cells. In plants and some algae, a rigid wall surrounds the cell. Therefore cytokinesis involves the laying down of a new cell

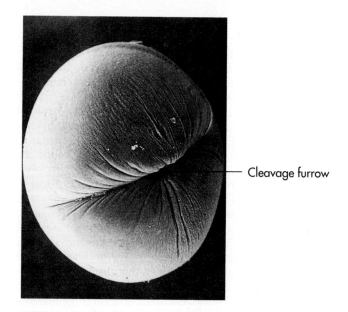

— Cleavage furrow

FIGURE 17-27 Cytokinesis in an animal cell. A cleavage furrow is forming around this dividing sea urchin egg.

wall between the two daughter cells rather than a pinching in of the cytoplasm.

Meiosis

Most animals, plants, algae, fungi, and certain protists reproduce sexually. In sexual reproduction, gametes of opposite sexes or mating types (sometimes just termed + *cells* and − *cells*) unite in the process of fertilization, producing the first cells of new individuals (see Figure 17-22).

Humans have 46 chromosomes in all of their body cells—the diploid amount. If the two cells that joined in fertilization each contained 46 chromosomes, however, the first cell of the future offspring would have 92 chromosomes. An individual born after 10 generations would have more than 47,000 chromosomes! Such a continuing addition of chromosomes to each new individual is obviously an unworkable situation. Even early investigators realized that there must be some mechanism during the course of gamete formation to reduce the number of chromosomes. They reasoned that if sex cells were formed with half the number of chromosomes characteristic of the cells of that species, then the fusion of these cells during fertilization would produce cells of new individuals with the proper number of chromosomes. Investigators soon oberved this special type of cell division and named it *meiosis,* from a Greek word meaning "less."

During meiosis the diploid number of chromosomes is reduced by half, forming haploid cells. For this reason, meiosis is often called **reduction-division.** Four daughter cells result from two divisions of one original parent cell, although in human females, only one of the four cells is functional (see Chapter 21). In animals, meiosis occurs in the cells that produce gametes.

Meiosis is a process of nuclear division in which the number of chromosomes in cells is halved, forming gametes in most animals and spores in plants.

The stages of meiosis

Although meiosis is a continuous process, scientists describe it by dividing it into stages, just as is done in describing the process of mitosis. The two forms of cell division have much in common. They are both special forms of nuclear division, although these processes are often referred to as forms of cell division for convenience. Meiosis consists of two sets of divisions called **meiosis I** and **meiosis II.** Each set is divided into prophase, metaphase, anaphase, and telophase, just as in mitosis. In meiosis, however, prophase I is much more complicated.

Meiosis is preceded by an interphase that is similar to the interphase of mitosis. During interphase the chromosomes are replicated, resulting in each chromosome consisting of two genetically identical sister chromatids held together at the constricted centromere. The centrioles also replicate.

Meiosis I

In prophase I, the individual chromosomes condense as their DNA coils more tightly, thus becoming visible under a light microscope. Because this DNA replicated before meiosis, each chromosome consists of two sister chromatids joined at the centromere.

Chromosomes, as you can see in the chapter opener photo, come in pairs. Each pair is formed during fertilization as an egg and sperm fuse. Each of these gametes contributes one chromosome to each pair of chromosomes. Thus, you received half your chromosomes (one set of genetic information) from your father, and half (a second set of genetic information) from your mother. Likewise, all organisms produced by sexual reproduction receive half their chromosomes from one parent organism and half from the other. These pairs of chromosomes are called **homologous chromosomes** or **homologues** (Figure 17-28).

Homologous chromosomes each contain genes that code for the same inherited traits, such as eye color or hair color. During prophase I, homologous chromosomes line up side-by-side in a process called **synapsis.** Because each chromosome is made up of two sister chromatids, the paired homologous chromosomes together have four chromatids. These synapsed homologues are therefore called **bivalents** (meaning "two strong"), or **tetrads** (meaning "groups of four").

The process of synapsis begins a complex series of events called **crossing over.** During crossing over, homologous *nonsister* chromatids actually cross over one another. These crossed over pieces break away from the chromatids to which they are attached and reattach to the non-sister chromatid—literally exchanging parts (Figure 17-29). Once crossing over is complete, the nuclear envelope dissolves and the homologues begin to move apart. These four chromatids cannot separate from one another, however, because (1) the sister chromatids are held together at their cen-

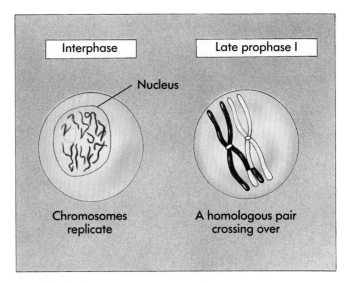

FIGURE 17-28 Interphase and late prophase in meiosis I. Chromosomes are replicated during interphase. Each chromosome is paired (homologous chromosomes). During prophase I, they line up side by side (called *synapsis*) and exchange genetic material (called *crossing over*).

tromeres and (2) the paired homologues are held together at the points where crossing over occurred. However, as the chromosomes move apart somewhat, the points of crossing over can be seen (under a light microscope) as **X**-shaped structures called **chiasmata** (Figure 17-30). Crossing over is a significant event in meiosis because it produces new combinations of genes. This process provides one way in which offspring have a different genetic makeup than either of its parents.

Early in prophase I of meiosis, homologous chromosomes pair up in a process called *synapsis.* Synapsis initiates the process of crossing over. During this process, homologous chromosomes exchange genetic material, which produces new combinations of genes.

In metaphase I of meiosis I, the microtubules have formed a spindle, just as in mitosis. A crucial difference exists, however, between this metaphase and that of mitosis: the chromosomes line up with their homologues double-file in meiosis, not single-file as in mitosis. For each pair of homologues, however, the orientation on the metaphase plate is random; which homologue is oriented toward which pole is a matter of chance.

After spindle attachment to the kinetochore of each homologous pair is complete, the homologues begin to move toward opposite poles of the cell. As this movement occurs, the homologues pull apart at their cross over points. By the end of anaphase I, each pole has one member of each chromosome pair. Each chromosome still has two sister chromatids. These chromatids are no longer perfectly identical, however, due to crossing over. During the last stage of meiosis I (telophase I) the two groups of chromosomes gather

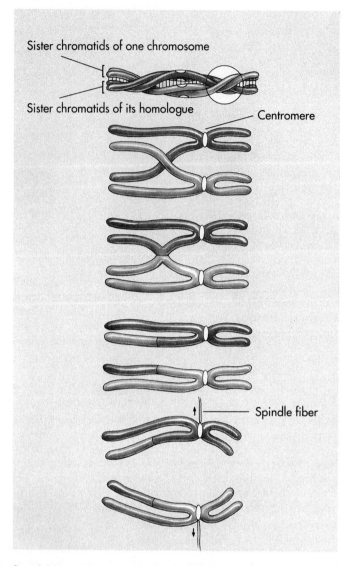

Sister chromatids of one chromosome

Sister chromatids of its homologue

Centromere

Spindle fiber

FIGURE 17-29 Crossing over.
The *circle* highlighting the upper chromosome indicates one region where homologous chromosomes are being held together tightly. Crossing over occurs when the paired chromosomes exchange genetic material at such locations.

together at their respective poles, forming two chromosome clusters. A nuclear membrane forms around each group of chromosomes.

An interphase-like period of variable length often occurs between meiosis I and meiosis II. During this time, *there is no replication of DNA*. In some cells, cytokinesis occurs and the cells separate completely. In cells in which cytokinesis does not occur, telophase I simply merges with prophase II.

The first meiotic division is traditionally divided into four stages as well as interphase:
1. Prophase I—Homologous chromosomes pair and exchange pieces of genetic material.
2. Metaphase I—Homologous chromosomes align on a central plane.
3. Anaphase I—Homologous chromosomes move toward opposite poles. Chromatids do *not separate.*
4. Telophase I—Individual chromosomes gather together at the two poles and the nuclear membranes re-form.
5. Interphase—The haploid cells separate completely.

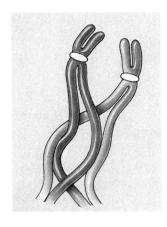

FIGURE 17-30   Chiasmata.
Chiasmata are the points of crossing over, where genetic material has been exchanged.

Meiosis II

At the end of anaphase I, each pole of the original cell has a haploid complement of chromosomes. That is, each pole has *half* the normal amount of chromosomes—only one member of each homologous pair. Each chromosome, however, still has two sister chromatids. Meiosis II separates these sister chromatids. Because of crossing-over in the first phase of meiosis, these sister chromatids are *no longer identical* to one another.

The two haploid cells formed during meiosis I divide during meiosis II. The nuclear envelopes disappear, and the spindle fibers form. The chromosomes line up, their sister chromatids separate, and they move to the opposite poles of each cell. At this point the nucleoli reorganize and nuclear envelopes form around each set of chromosomes (Figure 17-31).

Meiosis II results in the production of four daughter cells, each with a haploid number of chromosomes. The cells that contain these haploid nuclei function as gametes for sexual reproduction in most animals and as spores in plants. A comparison of mitotic and meiotic cell division is shown in Figure 17-32.

During meiosis II, four haploid daughter cells are produced from the two haploid daughter cells of meiosis I. These two haploid cells were produced during meiosis I from one original diploid parent cell.

The importance of meiotic recombination

The reassortment of genetic material that occurs during meiosis generates variability in the hereditary material of the offspring. To understand why this is true, remember that most organisms have more than one chromosome. Human beings, for example, have 23 different pairs of homologous chromosomes, one of each pair from the father and one of each pair from the mother. Each human gamete receives one of the two copies of each of the 23 different chromosomes, but which copy of a particular chromosome it receives is random. For example, the copy of chromosome 14 that a particular human gamete receives has no influence on which copy of chromosome 5 that it will receive. Each of the 23 pairs of chromosomes goes through meiosis independently of all the others, so there are 2^{23} (more than 8 million) different possibilities for the kinds of gametes that can be produced, and no two of them are alike. In addition, crossing over adds even more variability to the random assortment of chromosomes. The subsequent union of two gametes thus creates a unique individual, a new combination of the 23 chromosomes that probably has never occurred before and probably will never occur again. And when you study evolution in Chapter 24, you will see that variability within species is essential to the process of evolution by natural selection.

Prophase I

Metaphase I

Anaphase I

Telophase I

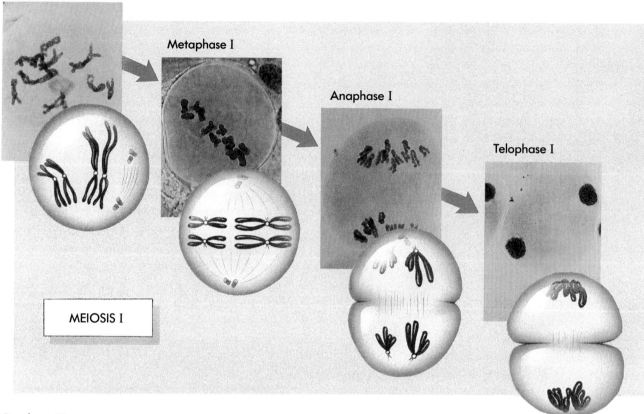

MEIOSIS I

Prophase II

Metaphase II

Anaphase II

Telophase II

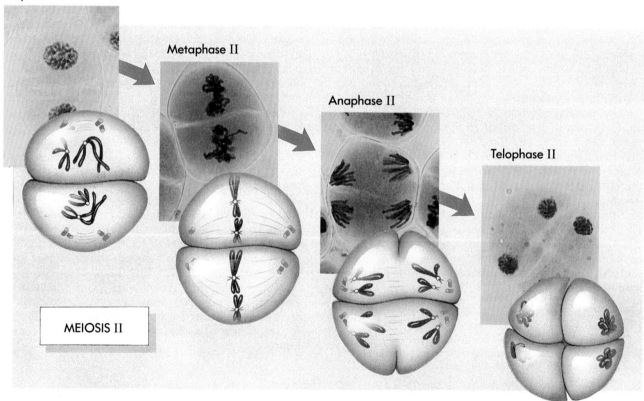

MEIOSIS II

FIGURE 17-31 Meiosis. Meiosis ensures the reassortment of genetic material. It is preceded by interphase, during which the chromosomes are replicated. An interphase-like period of variable length often occurs between meiosis I and meiosis II. During this time there is no replication of chromosomes (DNA).

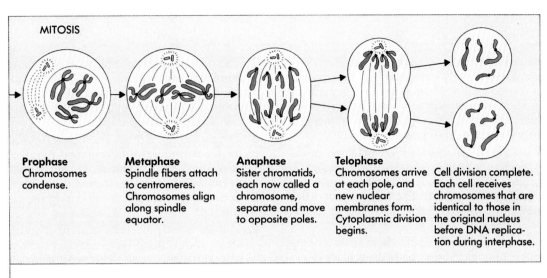

MITOSIS

Prophase
Chromosomes condense.

Metaphase
Spindle fibers attach to centromeres. Chromosomes align along spindle equator.

Anaphase
Sister chromatids, each now called a chromosome, separate and move to opposite poles.

Telophase
Chromosomes arrive at each pole, and new nuclear membranes form. Cytoplasmic division begins.

Cell division complete. Each cell receives chromosomes that are identical to those in the original nucleus before DNA replication during interphase.

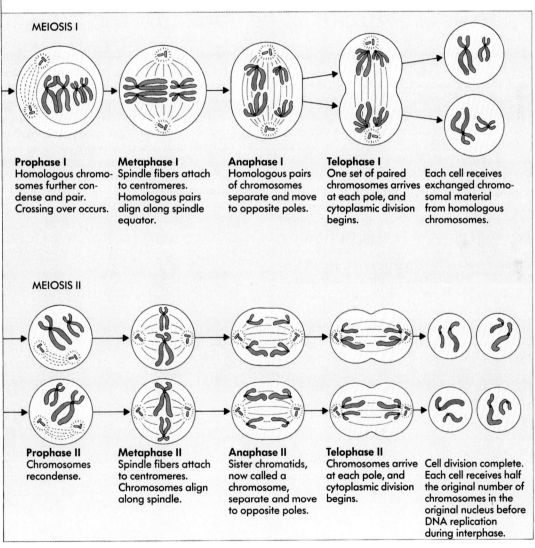

MEIOSIS I

Prophase I
Homologous chromosomes further condense and pair. Crossing over occurs.

Metaphase I
Spindle fibers attach to centromeres. Homologous pairs align along spindle equator.

Anaphase I
Homologous pairs of chromosomes separate and move to opposite poles.

Telophase I
One set of paired chromosomes arrives at each pole, and cytoplasmic division begins.

Each cell receives exchanged chromosomal material from homologous chromosomes.

MEIOSIS II

Prophase II
Chromosomes recondense.

Metaphase II
Spindle fibers attach to centromeres. Chromosomes align along spindle.

Anaphase II
Sister chromatids, now called a chromosome, separate and move to opposite poles.

Telophase II
Chromosomes arrive at each pole, and cytoplasmic division begins.

Cell division complete. Each cell receives half the original number of chromosomes in the original nucleus before DNA replication during interphase.

FIGURE 17-32   A comparison between mitosis and meiosis.
Meiosis involves two nuclear divisions with no DNA replication between them. Meiosis therefore produces four daughter cells, each with half the original amount of DNA. Mitosis produces two identical daughter cells, each with the same number of chromosomes as the orginal mother cell.

CHAPTER 17   DNA, Gene Expression, and Cell Reproduction

349

Summary

1. The hereditary material is deoxyribonucleic acid, or DNA. In eukaryotes, DNA is combined with protein to form a complex called *chromatin*. DNA is made up of nucleic acids. Ribonucleic acid, or RNA, plays key roles in the translation of the hereditary message of DNA. It, too, is made up of nucleic acids.

2. The nucleic acids of all organisms are made up of nucleotides. Each nucleotide contains three molecular parts: one phosphate group, one 5-carbon sugar, and one nitrogen-containing base. The relative proportion of the bases found in DNA varies from species to species.

3. DNA has the structure of a double helix, two molecular "chains" held to each other by hydrogen bonds between its nucleotides. Its four bases are adenine (A), thymine (T), cytosine (C), and guanine (G). The nucleotide A always bonds with T and G with C. These bases are complementary to one another.

4. Before cell division, DNA replication is orchestrated by a battery of enzymes that "unzip" the DNA, cause it to unwind, and then use each of the single strands as a template to assemble a complementary new strand.

5. The hereditary message of DNA is actually a code within its sequence of bases. A gene, or unit of heredity, is a sequence of bases that codes for a specific polypeptide, or portion of an enzyme. Most hereditary traits reflect the actions of enzymes.

6. The expression of hereditary information in all organisms takes place in two stages. First, in the process of transcription, a portion of the DNA message is copied onto a single strand of mRNA by using the DNA as a template. Second, in the process of translation, an amino acid chain is assembled by a ribosome and tRNA, using the mRNA base sequence to direct the sequence of amino acids.

7. The control of gene expression is exercised largely by regulating transcription. Cells have "on" and "off" gene transcription switches. Generally, in eukaryotic cells, control is positive; cellular signals are required before transcription can start.

8. The packaging of DNA into chromosomes allows a tremendous amount of information to reside in each cell of a eukaryote and also allows this hereditary material to be separated in an organized way during cell division. Eukaryotic cells divide during the growth, repair, and reproduction of organisms.

9. Mitosis is the process of nuclear division that distributes a complete, identical set of chromosomes to each of two daughter cells. This type of nuclear division is used in the growth and repair of multicellular organisms and in the asexual reproduction of single-celled eukaryotes and some simple animals. It produces cells that are identical to the parent cell.

10. Meiosis is the process of nuclear division that distributes half the complement of chromosomes to each of four daughter cells. This type of nuclear division is used to produce gametes for sexual reproduction in humans.

11. Crossing over is an essential element of meiosis. This process produces sister chromatids that are not identical with each other. Crossing over and the reassortment of genetic material that occurs during meiosis provides for new combinations of hereditary material during sexual reproduction.

1. Explain how a unique characteristic of yours, such as your hair color, is a result of specific chemical instructions. Where do these instructions originate?

2. What are the two types of nucleic acids found in your cells? Describe the structures of each.

3. Explain the term *double helix,* and describe its structure.

4. What characteristics of DNA did Chargaff's experiments reveal? Why was this significant?

5. What do you hypothesize might occur if there is an error made in base arrangement during DNA transcription? Suggest a possible sequence of subsequent events.

6. Bob is unable to digest milk because he lacks an enzyme that breaks down milk molecules in the human digestive tract. How many genes are probably involved in this problem?

7. Distinguish among rRNA, tRNA, and mRNA. What does each abbreviation stand for, and what are their respective functions?

8. Is mitosis or meiosis responsible for the tremendous genotypic and phenotypic variation among human beings? Explain.

9. Place these steps in the correct sequence and label each stage. What process is being described?
   a. The chromosomes line up in a ring in the center of the cell.
   b. The nuclear envelope forms and the chromosomes uncoil.
   c. The chromosomes grow shorter and thicker, and spindle fibers form.
   d. The sister chromatids separate and move to opposite poles of the cell.

10. Place these steps in the correct sequence and label each stage. What process is being described?
    a. Homologous chromosomes move toward opposite poles of the cell; chromatids do not separate.
    b. Chromosomes gather together at the two poles of the cell and the nuclear membranes re-form.
    c. Homologous chromosomes pair and exchange segments.
    d. Homologous chromosomes align on a central plane.
    e. The haploid cells separate completely.

11. Compare the cells that result from mitosis with those that result from meiosis. How are they different?

12. Explain the importance of the genetic recombination that occurs during meiosis.

13. Compare the cells resulting from meiosis to their mother cell. What functions do these cells serve?

14. There is often a tremendous amount of repetition in genetic code for enzyme production. Why do you suppose such a backup system is necessary to an organism?

1. There is much excitement about the possibility of curing cystic fibrosis with somatic cell gene therapy by using a virus as the gene carrier. Doctors will attempt a cure by placing a "healthy" copy of the CF gene into the DNA of a common cold virus (adenovirus) and having the patient inhale the engineered virus. Infecting the cells of the patient's lungs, the adenovirus will introduce the working copy of the CF gene into these cells, curing the disorder. What do you think the limitations of such an approach might be? What other human genetic disorders might be candidates for similar treatment?

2. One of the first steps in cell division is the condensation of the DNA into compact chromosomes. What drives this process—where does the energy required to wrap up so much DNA come from?

McElfresh, K. (1993, March). DNA-based testing in forensic science. *Bioscience,* pp. 149-157.
A clear study of the role of DNA testing in identity study and familial chromosome markers.

Murray, A., & Kirschner, M. (1991, March). What controls the cell cycle? *Scientific American,* pp. 56-63.
This article is a modern look at how cell division is controlled.

Ptashne, M. (1989, January). How gene activators work. *Scientific American,* pp. 41-47.
This is a lucid overview of how genes are turned on and off.

Radetsky, P. (1990, November). Genetic heretic. *Discover,* pp. 78-84.
An interesting look at new roles that RNA seems to play in our bodies; it is no longer seen solely as a messenger for DNA.

Rosen, J. (1992, December). Genetic surprises. *Discover,* pp. 82-88.
An amusing but complete overview of the rapidly expanding role we now know that DNA plays in human development.

18 Abnormal Cell Reproduction: Cancer

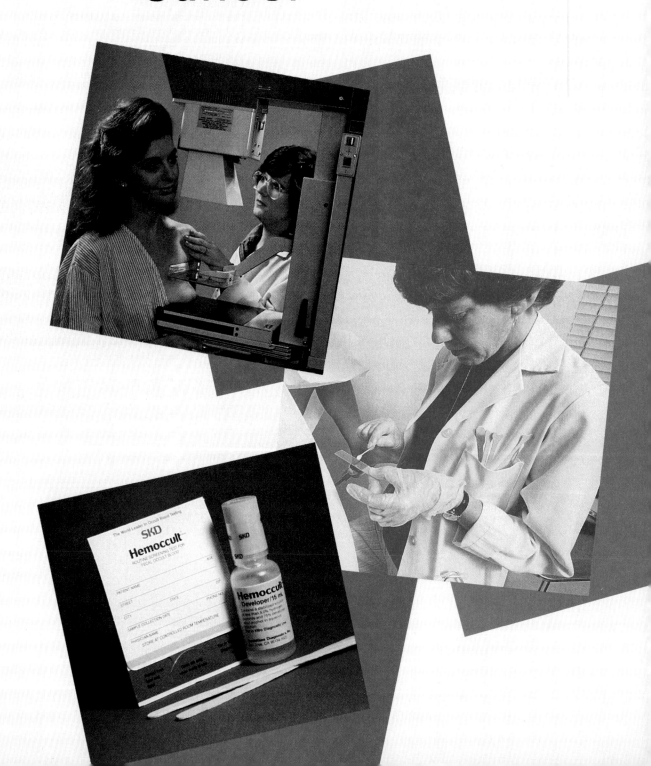

▼ Cancer is a variety of diseases characterized by the development of cells that grow in an uncontrolled manner, become less differentiated, invade normal tissues, and spread to multiple sites in the body.

▼ Cancer cells arise through a series of stepwise, progressive mutations to the DNA of normal body cells; these mutations can be inherited or are caused by certain viruses, chemicals, or types of radiation.

▼ To reduce your risk of cancer, avoid cancer-causing agents, watch for the cancer danger signs, follow the recommendations of the American Cancer Society (ACS) regarding diagnostic tests, and follow the ACS dietary guidelines.

▼ The key to future progress in dealing with the variety of diseases called cancer is research in prevention, detection, and treatment.

We are still *losing* the war against cancer. Each year in the United States, one million people are diagnosed as having some form of this disease. Of those persons, 50% die within 5 years, making cancer the second most common cause of death in this country. (Heart disease is the first.) Unfortunately, the incidence of cancer is increasing at a rate of 1% annually. Something must be done to change these statistics, and you can play a role in that change.

The opening photos contain messages about what we all can do to effect a change in these devastating statistics. Each photo shows a means of cancer detection or prevention. Can you identify the cancer tests? Do you know if you should have any or all of these tests ? Do you know when and how often these tests should be performed?

Although early detection of cancer improves the probability of survival for those who are diagnosed, many public health experts feel that prevention is the key to winning the war against cancer. As you learn more about cancer by reading this chapter, you will also learn about these diagnostic tests as well as cancer prevention. Think about applying what you read to help you live a long, cancer-free life.

What is cancer?

Cancer is not a single disease. In fact, this term refers to over 200 diseases! All cancers have four commonalities, however; they are characterized by (1) uncontrolled cell growth, (2) loss of cell differentiation (specialization), (3) invasion of normal tissues, and (4) **metastasis**, or spread, to multiple sites. Uncontrolled cancer eventually causes death because the cancer cells continually increase in number while spreading to vital areas of the body, occupying the space in which normal cells would reside and carry out normal body functions.

The molecular biology of cancer

Cancer cells arise through a series of step-wise, progressive mutations, or changes, in the DNA of normal body cells. (DNA mutation is described in Chapter 20.) The first set of changes may involve proto-oncogenes and/or tumor suppressor genes. *Proto-oncogenes* are latent (dormant) forms of cancer-causing genes, or **oncogenes**, that are present in all people. (The word "oncogenes" is derived from the Greek word "onkos" meaning mass or tumor.) Proto-oncogenes become oncogenes when some part of their DNA undergoes mutation. Oncogenes can be thought of as "on" switches in the development of cancer, signaling cells to speed up their growth and decrease their levels of differentiation.

Tumor suppressor genes are a separate class of genes that can be thought of as "off" switches in the development of cancer, signaling cells to slow their growth and increase their levels of differentiation. The expression of tumor suppressor genes is required for the normal functioning of a cell; they appear to allow normal cells to differentiate into mature cell types with reduced or no growth potential. These genes are inactivated when they undergo mutation.

Mutations in proto-oncogenes or in tumor suppressor genes may be inherited or may be caused by three types of agents: viruses, chemicals, and radiation. These agents are referred to as *initiators* and the process of proto-oncogene or tumor suppressor gene mutation as *initiation*. Unfortunately, initiation may occur after only brief exposure to an initiator. Initiation does not directly result in cancer. It results in a mutated cell that may or may not look abnormal and that gives rise to other initiated cells when it divides.

> Cancer cells arise through a series of progressive mutations to the DNA of normal body cells. These initial mutations may be inherited or may be caused by certain viruses, chemicals, or types of radiation; they activate proto-oncogenes (dormant cancer-causing genes) and/or inactivate tumor suppressor genes.

Initiation

Initiated cells (also called transformed cells) are *precancerous cells*. As mentioned previously, some types of initiated cells

are inherited, such as the cells that make up moles. Moles should be watched for changes in appearance, which is an indication that they may have become cancerous (Figure 18-1). Another example is the condition neurofibromatosis. Persons with this hereditary disorder develop numerous neurofibromas, which are growths resulting from an increased production of Schwann cells that surround nerve fibers (see Chapter 11). Persons having neurofibromatosis are at greater risk for developing many cancers such as brain tumors. Several childhood cancers, such as retinoblastoma (eye cancer) and osteosarcoma (bone cancer), have been linked to inherited defects in tumor suppressor genes.

The viruses that have been shown to cause initiation are the hepatitis B virus (cancer of the liver), human T lymphotropic/leukemia virus (cancer of white blood cells), human papillomavirus (cancers of the cervix and skin), human cytomegalovirus (Kaposi's sarcoma, a cancer of the skin), and Epstein-Barr virus (cancers of the lymph nodes and nasopharynx) (see Table 18-1). These viruses are called *tumor viruses*. They increase the risk of developing the particular types of cancers listed in parentheses but do not *definitely* lead to cancer. Tumor viruses change the DNA of a host cell by either integrating their genetic information (containing proto-oncogenes) into the host cell's DNA or

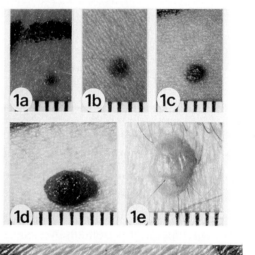

A

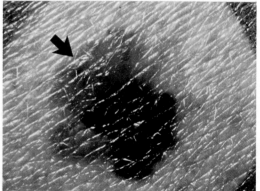

B

FIGURE 18-1 Moles.
A Examples of normal moles.
B A mole that has become cancerous. The arrow points to the region of the mole that has changed in appearance and has become a dangerous skin cancer called *malignant melanoma*.

by activating or modifying proto-oncogenes within the host DNA. (How viruses enter and replicate within cells is described in Chapter 23.)

A wide array of chemicals are initiators, such as certain chemicals used in the manufacture and processing of various products as well as the chemicals found in cigarette smoke. In general, chemicals capable of initiation have electrically charged regions within their molecules that react with electrically charged portions of other molecules. When such a reaction occurs with the DNA of a cell, mutation results.

Two types of radiation are especially dangerous because they can modify DNA: ultraviolet (UV) radiation (which comes to us in sunlight) and ionizing radiation. UV radiation can be absorbed by the bases in DNA and can produce chemical changes in them. Ionizing radiation, such as x-rays and nuclear radiation, transfers energy to electrons in the outer shells of the atoms it encounters, raising them to a still higher energy level and ejecting them from their orbitals. The result is the breaking of covalent bonds and the formation of charged fragments of molecules with unpaired electrons. The charged molecular fragments, or **free radicals**, are highly reactive. They may interact with DNA, producing chromosomal breaks or changes in the nucleotide structure.

The cells of the body are continually bombarded by chemicals and radiation capable of causing damage to DNA. However, cells also have repair mechanisms that continually work to undo this damage. Unfortunately, these cellular repair mechanisms are not 100% effective (or we would never develop cancer!). Researchers have discovered that some persons have weakened repair systems due to certain inherited genetic disorders that interfere with the cells' ability to repair DNA damage. These persons are more likely than others without these disorders to develop certain cancers. One such condition is xeroderma pigmentosum (Figure 18-2). Persons having this hereditary disorder are unable to repair damage to their DNA caused by UV radiation, so they are unable to go into the sunlight without the risk of developing skin cancer. In fact, many persons having this disease die before the age of 30.

Promotion

For cancer to occur, initiated cells must undergo *promotion*. Promotion is a process by which the DNA of initiated cells is damaged further, eventually stimulating these cells to grow and divide. It is a gradual process and happens over a long period of time as opposed to the short-term nature of initiation. Research suggests that if the promoter (the substance causing promotion) is withdrawn in the early stages, cancer development can be reversed. For example, if a smoker stops smoking, that person's risk of lung cancer returns eventually to that of a non-smoker (depending on how long he or she has smoked).

The same agent that caused initiation may cause promotion in the same cell or promotion may be caused by another factor. The mode of action of promoters is unclear, but evidence suggests that they, like initiators, mutate genes or damage chromosomes. Those agents that can both ini-

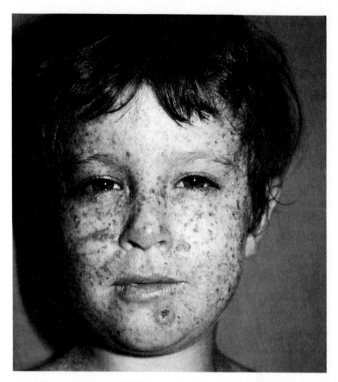

FIGURE 18-2 Xeroderma pigmentosum.
Persons with this inherited disorder easily develop multiple skin cancers when they are exposed to the UV radiation of the sun.

tiate and promote cancer are called complete **carcinogens**, or cancer-causing substances. Most substances linked with the development of cancer are complete carcinogens. A few, however, act only as an initiator or as a promoter. Heredity, for example, acts only as an initiator. Conversely, asbestos acts only as a promoter. Asbestos promotes cells initiated by other agents such as cigarette smoke or air pollution.

As promotion proceeds, damage to the DNA accumulates and the expression of oncogenes begins. That is, the oncogenes begin to be transcribed, resulting in the production of polypeptides. These polypeptides affect specific cells in specific ways, causing cells to grow and divide when normal cells would not, and causing a variety of other changes such as modifications in cells' shapes and structures, cell-to-cell interactions, membrane properties, cytoskeletal structure, protein secretion, and gene expression. The mechanisms by which a particular polypeptide interacts with a particular cell to produce one or more of the above effects vary also. One way in which oncogene-transcribed polypeptides affect cell growth, for example, is that they mimic growth factors. This type of polypeptide binds to receptor sites on the surfaces of certain cells, activating specific enzymes within them. The activated enzymes cause these cells to grow and divide when they would normally *not* be growing and dividing.

When damage to the DNA of a cell is not drastic, most of the normal components of the cell are produced and it

Many people are confused when they hear scientists refer to cancer as a genetic disease. We tend to think of genetic diseases as those inherited from our parents. However, cancers are not directly inherited, although we can inherit our individual tendencies to develop various types of cancer. Although the popular press may report the discovery of, for example, the "colon cancer gene," the common forms of cancer, such as colon and breast cancer, require the interaction of multiple and varied genes. Because the term "cancer" includes such a variety of different diseases, there is a tremendous diversity of genetic elements involved in the process of carcinogenesis, which is basically the result of accumulating specific types of genetic changes over a period of time. Some individuals inherit one or more of these changes, which increases the possibility that the required amount of additional genetic damage will occur during that individual's lifetime, leading to cancer. Although only 5% of all cancer cases appear to involve a strong hereditary predisposition, understanding the mechanisms involved in cancer genetics can be helpful in understanding the development of all cancers.

Doctors and others have long been aware that people are more likely to develop the same type of cancer that has been diagnosed in close family members, such as siblings and parents. In 1985, it was shown that children who inherited a specific genetic mutation were strongly predisposed to develop retinoblastoma, a rare type of eye cancer. Since then, many "susceptibility genes" (mutated genes that contribute to development of specific cancer types) have been studied. These forms of cancers have been documented to occur in certain families (see list above for a partial list), although it must be emphasized that the majority of cases of these cancers do not have a clear genetic pattern. For example, only about 5% of breast cancer patients have a strong family history of breast cancer (discussed later).

Identifying and studying cancer susceptibility genes offers a number of important potential benefits. It will

Examples of Cancers with Inherited Susceptibility Genes

Breast cancer
Colon cancer
Kidney cancer
Liver cancer
Lung cancer
Melanoma
Neuroblastoma
Osteosarcoma
Retinoblastoma

eventually be possible to screen individuals and predict their likelihood of developing specific cancers, which could lead to lifestyle modifications and ultimately prevention of the cancer. Individuals who know that they are predisposed to certain cancers should have regular medical checkups and cancer tests, leading to early diagnosis if cancer does develop. Ultimately, scientists hope to be able to counteract cancer predisposition genes, either by reversing the biochemical effects of these genes or by modifying or replacing the genes themselves. However, we will need a great deal of knowledge about these genes before we can reach these goals. In the meantime, research continues on the genetics of many specific cancers.

RETINOBLASTOMA

Retinoblastoma is a widely studied model for human cancer genetics, in part because it has the most simple genetic mechanism yet identified. This rare form of childhood eye cancer occurs in two main disease patterns. In one type, infants and very young children develop multiple tumors, frequently in both eyes. In these cases, there is almost always a family history of retinoblastoma. In the second pattern, older children with no family history of retinoblastoma develop a single tumor in one eye. Dr. Alfred Knudson proposed, in 1971, that in all cases retinoblastoma is the result of two specific occurrences of genetic damage within a single eye cell, and that the first type of patient inherits one of these genetic events in all of their cells (see Figure 18-A). In these patients with "inherited" retinoblastoma, one mutation is already present,

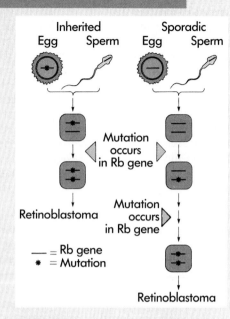

FIGURE 18-A The two-hit model for development of retinoblastema

so only one additional mutation needs to occur for a cell to become cancerous. In the second type, sporadic retinoblastoma, both mutations must occur in the same eye cell for cancer to develop. This accounts both for the later age of onset, and for the fact that usually only one tumor develops. In the 1980s, scientists discovered the site of the genetic damage responsible for retinoblastoma. Normally, the Rb tumor suppressor gene apparently prevents tumor development. When both copies of this gene in an eye cell are damaged, retinoblastoma results.

COLON CANCER

Unlike retinoblastoma, colon cancer is one of the most common forms of cancer. A significantly more complex series of genetic changes occurs during the development of colon cancer than has been found in retinoblastoma. Study of this disease has led to the exciting recent discovery of a new class of cancer gene and the hope for a predictive test to identify individuals at increased risk. An estimated 55,000 Americans die of colon cancer each year. Most of these individuals are diagnosed at a relatively late stage of the disease, after cancer has spread to other organ systems. Although colon cancer is highly curable in its early

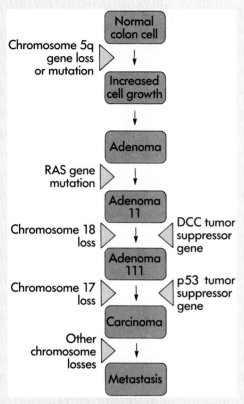

FIGURE 18-B Stages in the evolution of colon cancer.

Genes currently known to be involved in colon cancer

GENE	% OF TUMORS WITH MUTATIONS	TYPE OF GENE	GENE ACTIVITY
FCC	~15%	?	Aids accurate DNA replication
ras	~50%	Oncogene	Intracellular signals
Cyclins	4%	Oncogene	Regulates cell growth cycle
neu/Her2	2%	Oncogene	Receptor for cell growth factors
myc	2%	Oncogene	Regulates gene activity
APC	>70%	Tumor suppressor	Unknown
DCC	>70%	Tumor suppressor	Cell adhesion
p53	>70%	Tumor suppressor	Regulates gene activity

Adapted from "New Colon Cancer Gene Discovered," *Science* 260:752, 1993.

stages, some people avoid medical checkups for colon cancer because of embarrassment or fear of discomfort. Many lives could be saved if a reliable noninvasive test were available for this disease.

Cancers of the colon show a distinct set of cellular changes as normal tissue begins to overproliferate, first forming benign tumors (adenomas) that progress to malignancy and eventually spread throughout the body (Figure 18-B). These cellular changes are paralleled by genetic changes in the tumor cells. In contrast to retinoblastoma, current understanding suggests that at least five genes must be altered during the development of a colon cancer. These target genes include both oncogenes and tumor suppressor genes, as shown in the table above. Activation of the oncogenes is found in many types of cancer, as is the inactivation of the p53 tumor suppressor gene. Inactivation of the adenomatous polyposis coli (APC) tumor suppressor gene, however, is characteristic of colon cancers, where it appears to be an early event in carcinogenesis. This gene was originally identified as the heritable element in a condition called

familial adenomatous polyposis (FAP). Individuals with FAP develop large numbers of polyps (noncancerous growths) in the colon throughout their lifetimes. If these polyps are not removed, some will inevitably progress to become malignant tumors. FAP results from inherited alterations in the APC gene, although, as shown in Figure 18-B, many additional changes are needed for the progression of polyps to colon cancer in these patients.

Although FAP is the inherited precursor of approximately 1% of all colon cancers, some families have strong histories of colon cancer without the presence of FAP. Scientists have recently identified another inherited gene, FCC (for "familial colon cancer"), a susceptibility gene that occurs in about 1 out of every 200 people in the United States, and may account for as many as 15% of all colon cancer cases. Of the individuals who carry this defective gene, scientists estimate that 90% to 100% will develop some form of cancer. Most will have colon cancer, but many women with this gene will develop uterine cancers. Many other cancer types are also associated with this defect.

From a scientific standpoint, the FCC gene is an exciting discovery because it presents for study a new mechanism by which a gene can cause cancer. Instead of acting as either an oncogene or a tumor suppressor gene, the FCC gene somehow seems to encourage the occurrence or accumulation of multiple mutations in affected cells. Because colon and other cancers require a series of genetic events for progression, any cellular process that increases genetic damage would certainly speed up the carcinogenic pro-

cess. It is possible that the activity of this gene could be responsible for many of the other genetic changes seen in cancer cells with this defect.

As well as providing a new way for scientists to understand cancer, the discovery of this common cancer gene may have great public impact. A predictive test for FCC will be developed as soon as the gene itself is isolated and characterized, with the potential of identifying individuals at high risk for developing colon and other types of cancer. Because early detection is the key to curing colon cancer, this test, with appropriate follow-up, is likely to save many lives.

BREAST CANCER

At least 10% of women in the United States will develop breast cancer at some point in their lives. For some women, the risk is significantly higher because of genetic factors. Breast cancer is so common that many families include at least one member with this disease. In the vast majority of these cases, recent evidence indicates that other female family members have only a slightly increased risk of developing breast cancer. However, in some families the risk is clearly higher. A woman is considered to have a significant family history, and therefore a higher risk of developing breast cancer, if she has more than one sister with breast cancer, if her mother or sister developed breast cancer before the age of 50, or if any family member has had cancer in both breasts. Many of these families still have only moderate increases in breast cancer risk, and it is clear from the different patterns that several inherited factors may be responsible for familial breast cancer. *Continued.*

Box continued from p. 357.

About 5% of all breast cancer cases occur in families with extremely high-risk patterns. This group includes all of the above family characteristics, with women developing the disease at very young ages (teens to twenties) as well as significant numbers of males who also develop breast cancer. The mortality rate from breast cancer is so high in these families that some female members will choose to have both breasts removed surgically before cancer can develop. Progress has recently been made in discovering the gene responsible for this severe pattern of predisposition. A susceptibility gene, called BRCA1, has been located on chromosome 17. It is estimated that 1 out of every 200 women in the United States may carry this genetic defect, which confers an 80% to 90% risk of developing breast cancer. The function of this gene is not known at present, but it appears to act as a tumor suppressor gene. A screening test for this marker is already in use for members of some high-risk families. This screening test reassures those individuals who have not inherited this gene and allows those who test positive for this gene to make more informed choices about preventive measures.

THE FUTURE OF CANCER GENETICS

Cancer is such a complex genetic problem that there will undoubtedly be new and sometimes unexpected discoveries about the carcinogenic process for many years. Scientists are constantly identifying new oncogenes and tumor suppressor genes, and each discovery brings us closer to an understanding of how cancer develops. In the past two years, inherited genes that predispose individuals to develop two of the most common causes of cancer death in the United States have been identified. (Only lung cancer kills more Americans than colon and breast cancer.) The information gained from these discoveries promises not only a means of identifying high-risk individuals but also the hope of producing preventive strategies for these cancers.

Cynthia J. Moore, Ph.D.
Washington University

A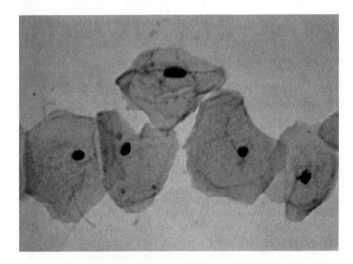

B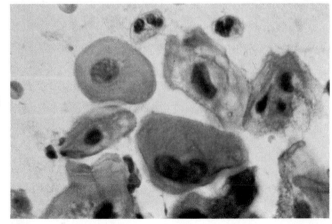

FIGURE 18-3 A comparison of normal and dysplastic cells.
A Normal cells. These cells are all approximately the same size and have nuclei that look similar.
B Dysplastic cells. These cells (stained differently from **A**) are irregular in size and the appearance of their nuclei. Both white and red blood cells can be seen at the top of this photo.

still responds to normal growth-inhibiting factors. Sometimes initiated cells or cells in the early stages of promotion grow and divide abnormally, forming a benign (noncancerous) tumor. **Benign tumors** are growths or masses of cells that are made up of partially transformed cells, are confined to one location, and are encapsulated, shielding them from surrounding tissues. Such tumors are not life-threatening. Some benign growths, although not life-threatening at the time, exhibit patterns of growth that are characteristic of the development to cancer cells. These cells are said to exhibit *dysplasia* (Figure 18-3).

⌄⌄⌄
For cancer to occur, initiated (DNA-mutated) cells must undergo promotion, a process by which the DNA is damaged further. As promotion proceeds, damage to the DNA accumulates and the expression of oncogenes begins. The polypeptides produced cause cells to grow and divide when normal cells would not, and cause a variety of other cellular changes.

Progression

As promoters damage the DNA more and more, partially transformed cells reach a point where they irreversibly become cancer cells. This point marks the beginning of the third stage in the development of cancer; it is called *progression*. During progression, the transformed cells usually become less well-differentiated than benign cells and increase their rate of growth and division without regard to the body's needs. In addition, these cells acquire the ability to (1) *invade and kill* other tissues and (2) *metastasize*, or move to other areas of the body. Tumors with these properties are **malignant**. The word "malignant" is derived from two Latin words meaning "of an evil nature," while the word "benign" means "kind-hearted."

Malignant growths, or cancers, are divided into three

groups: *carcinomas*, *sarcomas*, and *leukemias/lymphomas*. This classification is based on the tissues in which these cancers arise. The tissues themselves are grouped according to the primary germ layers that produce them. The primary germ layers (the ectoderm, endoderm, and mesoderm) are three layers of cells from which all the organs and tissues of the body develop (see Figure 22-8). Carcinomas, which make up 90% of all cancers, arise from epithelial (surface) cells of either endodermal or ectodermal origin. Therefore, carcinomas are cancers of the tissues that cover the outside of the body and line its interior, such as skin, breast, lung, and colon cancers. Sarcomas and the leukemias and lymphomas develop from cells of mesodermal origin. Therefore these are cancers of the muscles, bones, cartilage, blood and vessels, lymph tissue, and parts of the kidneys and sex organs. Cancers are further named and classified according to the specific tissue they invade (bone, lung, breast) and the pattern of growth they exhibit.

The spread of cancer during progression is a multistage process, as is the development of the cancer cells themselves. At first the cancer cells proliferate, forming tumors. These cancers are referred to as *in situ*, meaning "in place," and are small localized tumors that have not invaded the surrounding normal tissue. In the next stage of cancer progression, cancer cells invade the surrounding tissue by secreting chemicals that break down the intercellular matrix—the substances that hold cells together. Other secretions cause the cells to break apart. Figure 18-4 shows these stages in the development of a carcinoma. Once cancer cells invade surrounding tissues they can metastasize or travel to other parts of the body by entering the blood and/or lymphatic vessels.

▼▼▼ **As DNA is damaged more and more, partially transformed cells irreversibly become cancer cells. Cancer cells are malignant cells, which means that they can invade and kill other tissues and metastasize, or move to other areas of the body.**

Factors that increase the risk of cancer

Researchers suggest that 90% of all cancers are environmentally induced; that is, they are not inherited and are the result of external factors. What follows is a listing of those factors that are initiators and/or promoters of cancer. You may notice that many of these factors are implicated in other diseases or conditions that damage health. So avoiding these factors may increase your chances for a longer, healthier life in many ways. And although your heredity is not a factor you can control, knowledge about your hereditary background can help you control other factors important to your health.

Heredity

When a physician or other health care professional asks you about your family history, he or she is gathering data regarding heritable diseases or increased risks to certain conditions. Having a predisposition to a certain type of cancer

1. Initial tumor cell

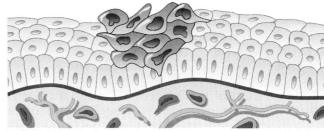
2. Epithelial dysplasia

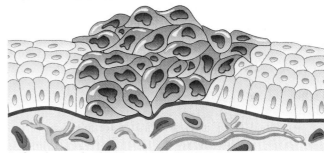
3. Carcinoma *in situ*

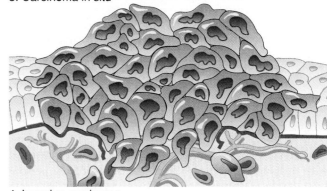
4. Invasive carcinoma

FIGURE 18-4   How cancer cells multiply and spread.
In (1) a partially transformed tumor cell is shown in the epidermis of the skin. This cell multiplies (2), forming a mass of dysplastic cells. As the DNA of these cells is further damaged, they irreversibly become cancer cells. Their growth rate increases, and they form a cancerous tumor that is localized (3). These cells then invade the underlying dermis (4), entering blood vessels and traveling throughout the body.

does not mean that you will get that cancer. It means that you are more likely to contract that cancer than other members of the general population. A generalization made by many physicians is that if one of your first-degree relatives (a sibling, parent, or offspring) has cancer, your risk of developing that type of cancer increases threefold.

Although a genetic link among family members and certain diseases can only be inferred from statistical correlations, researchers are now beginning to identify specific genes that carry certain disease traits. Such genes are concrete evidence that genetic links for certain diseases exist within certain families. In 1993, for example, researchers discovered a gene located on chromosome two (see Figure 20-1) that causes several major cancers. This gene, which leads to colon cancer and a variety of other cancers, is found in one out of every 200 people. It appears to act differently from oncogenes and tumor supressor genes in that it actually *induces* thousands of mutations in other genes. Within a few years, scientists expect to develop a test that shows whether or not a person carries this gene.

An important point to note is that most cancers are not caused by heredity alone. (A few rare cancers of this type are discussed earlier in this chapter.) The added action of one or more environmental factors is usually needed for the cancer to develop. Persons having predispositions or family histories of certain cancers should follow their physicians' recommendations to avoid environmental factors that would increase their risks of developing those cancers. In addition, physicians may recommend regular screening procedures to detect and treat any developing cancers early.

Tumor viruses

As mentioned previously, five viruses are initiators of human cancer: hepatitis B virus, human T lymphotropic/leukemia virus, human papillomavirus, human cytomegalovirus, and the Epstein-Barr virus (Table 18-1).

The *hepatitis B virus* (HBV) is transmitted in blood or blood products (such as blood serum or plasma), and by contaminated needles or syringes. Therefore the persons most likely to contract this virus are health care workers (although their precautions are strict), intravenous drug users who share contaminated needles, and persons having sexual contact with infected persons. In addition, an infected pregnant woman can pass this virus on to her developing fetus.

HBV causes a serious infection of the liver. Persons with prolonged hepatitis B liver disease, especially persons who develop cirrhosis, are at risk for developing liver cancer. (Cirrhosis is a condition in which liver tissue is destroyed and is replaced by scar tissue.) Liver cancer as a result of hepatitis B infection is relatively rare in the United States but is quite common in developing countries of Africa and Asia. This cancer is usually fatal; most patients die within 6 months to a year after diagnosis.

The *human T lymphotropic-leukemia virus, or HTLV,* causes adult T-cell leukemia-lymphoma (ATLL). This disease is rare in the United States but is common in Japan and the Caribbean. The cancers caused by HTLV are T-cell leukemias or lymphomas. *Leukemia* is a disease of the red bone marrow (the substance that produces most of the body's blood cells) resulting in the manufacture of a greater than normal number of abnormal white blood cells that are immature and unable to perform their infection-fighting roles (Figure 18-5). *Lymphoma* is a malignancy of the lymphoid tissue — the fluid or tissues of the lymphatic system

TABLE 18-1	Tumor Viruses

VIRUS	CANCER TYPE
Hepatitis B virus (HBV)	Primary liver cancer
Human T lymphotropic/ leukemia virus (HTLV)	Leukemias and lymphomas
Cytomegalovirus (CMV)	Kaposi's sarcoma
Human papillomavirus (HPV)	Vaginal/vulval cancer Penile cancer
Epstein-Barr virus (EBV)	Burkitt's lymphoma Nasopharyngeal cancer

A

B

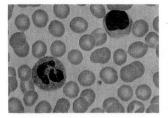
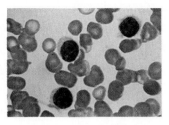

FIGURE 18-5 A normal blood smear contrasted with a hairy cell leukemia blood smear.
A This micrograph of a normal blood smear shows one neutrophil and one monocyte, both types of white blood cells, among red blood cells.
B This micrograph of a hairy cell leukemia blood smear shows three abnormal white blood cells among red blood cells.

(see Chapter 9). T lymphocytes, or T cells, are a type of white blood cell that develops in the bone marrow but matures in the thymus, an organ of the lymphatic system. T cells are integral in the immune response — your defense against disease (see Chapter 16).

ATLL spreads quickly in its victims and often results in an enlarged liver, spleen, and lymph nodes. Researchers are still uncertain how the HTLV is transmitted, but they think possible routes may involve sexual activity, the sharing of needles and syringes among IV drug users, and transfusion with contaminated blood. These pathways of infection are the same as those of HBV and the human immunodeficiency virus (HIV), which causes acquired immunodeficiency syndrome, or AIDS.

Although HIV is a "cousin" to HTLV (it was previously known as HTLV-III), the AIDS virus is not a tumor virus itself; however it causes a breakdown of immunity that leaves its victims susceptible to other infections and cancers. The most common of the "AIDS cancers" is Kaposi's sarcoma, a skin cancer characterized by flat or raised red or purplish lesions (Figure 18-6). The cytomegalovirus, or CMV, is thought to be the initiator of this cancer.

Over 60 types of *human papillomaviruses* (HPVs) have been isolated in humans. Some of these viruses initiate only benign tumors, such as warts of the hands and feet. (Warts on the soles of the feet are called plantar warts.) Other human papillomaviruses cause a sexually transmitted disease commonly known as venereal warts; at least two types of

these papillomaviruses (referred to as #16 and #18) are strongly linked to the development of cancer, particularly cervical carcinoma. (The cervix is the tissue surrounding the opening to the uterus, or womb.) Although venereal warts may appear on the cervix, within the vagina, or on the labial tissues in women, researchers think that the cervix has an area of tissue that is particularly vulnerable to viral infection. Researchers also suggest that the development of cancers of the cervix linked to HPV infection may be due to an interaction of factors, and speculate that infection with other viruses and smoking may act as tumor initiators with HPV types 16 or 18 acting as promoters.

Women contract the papillomavirus during sexual intercourse with an infected partner. The risks of infection with the virus and the development of cervical cancer rise as a woman's number of sexual partners rises. Also, women who become sexually active at an early age are at a greater risk than women who become sexually active at an older age. Scientists are unsure whether the tissues of a young woman are simply more vulnerable, or whether women who are sexually active at an early age are more likely to have a greater number of partners than other women.

Cancers caused by the *Epstein-Barr virus* (EBV) are rare in the United States. Americans are most familiar with the noncancerous condition it causes: mononucleosis. The virus is found in saliva because it is shed from cells lining the nose and throat. For this reason, mononucleosis is often called the "kissing disease," but the virus can also be transmitted on contaminated cups, glasses, eating utensils, and similar objects.

The cancer-causing effects of the Epstein-Barr virus are most frequently seen in people living in Africa and China. In fact, cancers of the nose and upper throat linked to this virus are one of the leading causes of cancer deaths in China. In Africa the more common cancer in which the EBV is implicated is Burkitt's lymphoma, a cancer of the lymph system (Figure 18-7).

Cigarette smoke

In the United States, cigarette smoking is responsible for approximately one third of all cancers and causes about 85% of all lung cancer deaths. In fact, smoking is the leading cause of preventable death in the United States and is the reason for one out of every seven deaths. Clearly, cigarette smoking is a highly risky behavior.

Cigarette smoke is made up of both gases and particles, which together contain about 4000 different chemicals. Although scientists are unsure exactly how many cancer-causing substances are in this mixture, a few have been identified. Most of these substances, which initiate and/or promote cancer, are in the tars (particles that are black and sticky like road tar), although a few are in the gases. Among these chemicals are nitrosamines (similar to the preservatives found in foods such as bacon, hot dogs, and salami), polycyclic aromatic hydrocarbons (PAHs) such as benzo(a)pyrene (also found in smoked foods), and various metals (including arsenic). All are potent carcinogens.

The chemicals in the gases affect the cells they pass by when cigarette smoke is inhaled. The tars continually affect

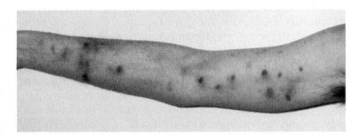

FIGURE 18-6 Kaposi's sarcoma.
This photograph shows the multiple lesions of the skin cancer, Kaposi's sarcoma, on the arm of an AIDS patient.

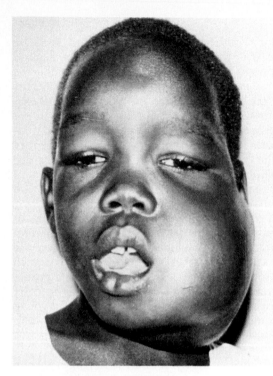

FIGURE 18-7 Burkitt's lymphoma.
Burkitt's lymphoma is a cancer of the lymphatic system and is usually manifested as a large mass in the jaw or abdomen.

cells of the respiratory system, however, because they stick to the membranes of the trachea, bronchi, and lungs. The cells lining the air passageways as well as the lung tissue may eventually begin to transform because of this exposure to the variety of carcinogens in the gases and tars. The Chapter 8 opener photo shows the tar deposits within the lung of a smoker who died from lung cancer.

Smokers not only risk developing lung cancer, they also risk developing cancers of the larynx, mouth, lip, tongue, throat, and esophagus (Figure 18-8). Smoking also leads

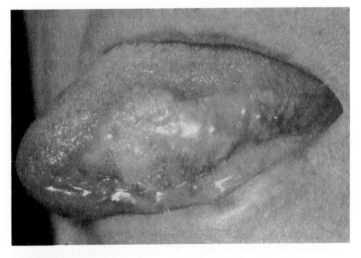

FIGURE 18-8
A cancer of the tongue.

to the presence of chemicals in the urine that may contribute to the development of cancers of the bladder and kidney. In addition, the incidence of cancer of the pancreas is more than twice as high for smokers as for nonsmokers.

The risk for developing a smoking-related cancer rises proportionately with the number of cigarettes (or cigars or pipes) a person smokes, the number of years he or she smokes, the age at which the smoker started, and how deeply the smoker inhales. Those who smoke filtered, low-tar cigarettes have a lower lung cancer risk than those who smoke nonfiltered, high-tar cigarettes. However, the cancer risk for any smoker is still far higher than for nonsmokers — about 6 1/2 times greater.

Unfortunately, nonsmokers also have an increased risk for smoking-related cancers if they regularly breathe in sidestream smoke. Sidestream smoke comes from the tip of a burning cigarette. The Environmental Protection Agency (EPA) estimates that 500 to 5000 nonsmokers die each year from lung cancer caused by sidestream smoke.

The combination of smoking and certain other behaviors additionally increases a smoker's cancer risk. For example, chewing tobacco and smoking cigarettes greatly increases the risk of a person developing mouth and throat cancers. Likewise, uranium miners and asbestos workers, already at risk for lung cancer, substantially increase their risk by smoking. Heavy drinking of alcoholic beverages combined with smoking greatly increases the risk of cancers of the mouth, throat, larynx, and esophagus. Alcohol itself is not a carcinogen, but it enhances the effects of other carcinogens, particularly tobacco smoke, and *multiplies* the risk of developing cancer.

Industrial Hazards

Although we are all concerned about industrial pollution and the possibility of industrial wastes tainting our water and air supplies, the persons at greatest risk for developing cancers from industrial sources are industrial workers (Figure 18-9). The industries that pose the highest cancer risk for their workers are those in which carcinogenic agents are either produced or used in the manufacturing process. These agents are certain types of fibers, chemicals, or dusts.

Asbestos, a filamentous, silicate (glass-like) mineral, is the principal fiber posing a cancer risk to industrial workers. Figure 18-10 shows what happens when a macrophage attempts to digest an asbestos fiber. Asbestos does not conduct heat or burn, so it is useful in the construction and shipbuilding industries as a fireproofing and insulating material. It is also used in the manufacture of ceiling and floor tiles and, in the automobile industry, in the manufacture of clutch and brake linings.

Workers in these industries who are exposed to asbestos as well as those workers who mine or mill asbestos must protect themselves from breathing in asbestos fibers. The presence of these fibers in the lungs increases the risk of lung cancer and mesothelioma, a relatively rare cancer of the membranes that line the chest and abdominal cavities. Airborne asbestos fibers are so dangerous, in fact, that the federal Environmental Protection Agency recently called for a ten-year phase-out of all manufacturing uses of asbestos.

FIGURE 18-9 Potential carcinogens in the workplace.
A A worker exposed to dangerous fumes in a coke plant.
B A carpenter wearing a mask as protection against inhaling wood dust.

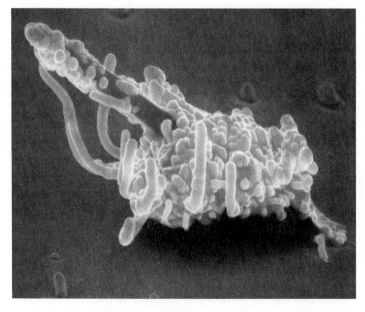
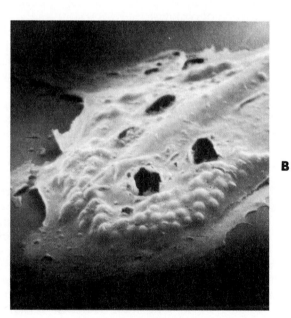

FIGURE 18-10 Why asbestos fibers can be deadly.
A A macrophage engulfs an asbestos fiber. These cells protect the lungs by engulfing and digesting unwanted material.
B Asbestos fibers are undigestible. The macrophage collapses and dies, and the toxic fiber is released into the lung once more.

Workers in some industries are exposed to certain carcinogenic chemicals. For example, *acrylonitrile* is a carcinogenic substance used in the manufacture of synthetic fibers, plastics, and rubber. *Benzene* is a carcinogenic solvent used in the chemical and drug industries. In addition, it is used in the manufacture of pesticides, inks, paints, and shoes. It is also used as an additive in some gasolines and is a by-product of oil refining. (Benzo(a)pyrene, one of the carcinogens in cigarette smoke, is chemically related to benzene.) Also, those who work with tar, soot, oil, coal gas, pitch, and coke, which contain other cancer-causing polycyclic aromatic hydrocarbons (PAHs) in addition to benzo(a)pyrene, should protect themselves.

Many different types of metals are used in manufacturing, especially in the smelting and metallurgic industries. In these industries, metals are liquified; dangerous fumes result. Examples of carcinogenic metals used in industry are *arsenic* (used in the manufacture of pesticides, glass, ceramics, paints, dyes, and wood preservatives), *cadmium* (used in the processing and manufacture of rubber, plastics, paints, and batteries), *chromium* (used in the manufacture of stainless steel, glass, bricks, and ceramics), and *nickel* (used in the shipbuilding and aerospace industries, in electroplating, and in the manufacture of paints).

Dust also poses a cancer risk for certain workers. For example, studies show higher cancer rates among woodworkers, carpenters, furniture makers and refinishers, and paper mill workers. Although not conclusive, studies indicate that the inhalation of wood dust increases the risk of lung cancer. Coal miners are also at risk for lung cancer from the inhalation of coal dust.

In addition to the risks already mentioned for asbestos miners and coal miners, those who mine uranium and other minerals such as hematite (an important iron ore) face an increased risk of lung cancer. *Uranium*, the main source of nuclear energy, is a radioactive element and produces a colorless, odorless, carcinogenic gas called *radon* as it decays. Radon is present in uranium mines as well as in the rocks and soils of other mines. Recent concern has focused on radon exposures in homes, because this gas can leak through cracks in basement walls and become trapped in well-insulated homes. This topic will be discussed later.

All workers in industry exposed to these workplace hazards should protect themselves by wearing protective clothing and masks or ventilators as well as by ventilating the work area. In addition, those persons who work with the above products, such as paints, dyes, pesticides, oils, wood preservatives, and ceramics, should use them only in well-ventilated areas when indoors. In addition, they should wear a protective mask or respirator and possibly protective clothing when using these products. Persons who smoke should keep in mind that their risk of cancer multiplies when they are exposed regularly to the carcinogenic substances mentioned above.

Ultraviolet radiation

Ultraviolet (UV) radiation from the sun is the primary cause of skin cancer, resulting in approximately 600,000 new cases each year. There are two types of UV radiation: UV-A and UV-B. UV-B radiation has a shorter wavelength (see p. 246), penetrates the skin less deeply, and causes the skin to burn more quickly than UV-A; it is the type known to cause skin cancer. UV-A radiation may also cause skin cancer, but researchers are unsure at this time. Because of this uncertainty, most physicians recommend avoiding exposure to UV-A radiation in tanning parlors even though this method of tanning is touted as risk-free.

Those at greatest risk for skin cancer are fair-skinned individuals who sunburn easily. These individuals have less melanin, a black pigment found in specialized skin cells called *melanocytes*. Melanocytes are located in the basal layer of the skin, the deepest portion of the epidermis (see Figure 15-1). Melanin absorbs UV radiation, thereby protecting the surrounding cells against cancer.

The risk of developing skin cancer from exposure to UV radiation is cumulative. Therefore the older you are, the more likely you are to develop skin cancer. Also, your risk of skin cancer increases as your exposure to UV radiation increases. Exposure to UV radiation is highest at increased altitudes, at midday, in low humidity, and near the equator. To protect yourself against skin cancer, avoid lengthy exposure to the sun under these conditions. Wear protective clothing and apply sunscreen to exposed body parts, especially to the face and hands. Most UV-induced skin cancers develop on the face and hands because these body parts are most frequently exposed to the sun. Some evidence also suggests that infrequent, intense exposure to the sun, such as when an office worker spends a vacation sunning at the beach, may be worse than constant exposure, such as that of a construction worker. Similarly, severe sunburns in childhood appear to greatly increase the risk of melanoma (see below) in adulthood.

The two most common types of skin cancer are *basal cell carcinoma* and *squamous cell carcinoma*. The basal cell type makes up 90% of all skin cancers in the United States. This cancer, which looks like a sore that has scabbed over (Figure 18-11, *A*), begins in the basal layer of the skin (the deepest layer of the epidermis) and extends upward to the surface. It is slow-growing and rarely spreads to other parts of the body. The squamous cell type begins in the layer of tissue just above the basal layer, from cells that produce a substance called *keratin*. Keratin is a tough protein found in hair and nails; it gives squamous cell lesions a "warty" or "horny" look (Figure 18-11, *B*). Squamous cell carcinoma occasionally invades the deeper tissues of the skin and is therefore more likely to spread than the basal cell type. However, it is rarely fatal but can be fatal if it is not treated.

The most dangerous type of skin cancer caused by UV radiation is *malignant melanoma*, which comprises about 5% of skin cancers. This type of cancer originates in the melanocytes and spreads rapidly to other parts of the body. It is usually recognized by its asymmetry, irregular border, uneven but deeply colored pigmentation, and size (greater than 6 mm — about the width of your smallest fingernail) (Figure 18-11, *C*). Because of its ability to quickly invade tissues and spread to other parts of the body, it is usually fatal unless caught very early. To protect yourself, see your physician if you develop any skin lesion that persists; do not self-diagnose.

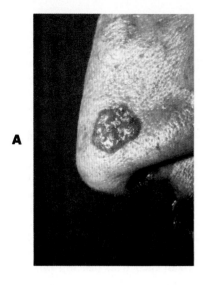

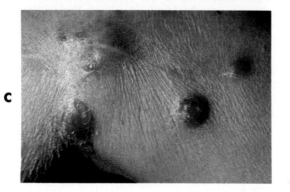

FIGURE 18-11   Types of skin cancers.
A Basal cell carcinoma.
B Squamous cell carcinoma.
C Malignant melanoma.

Ionizing radiation

Although ionizing radiation can cause a variety of cancers such as leukemia, bone cancer, breast cancer, and lung cancer, it accounts for only 3% of all cancers. Some ionizing radiation comes to us from natural sources, such as *cosmic rays* in the atmosphere and *uranium* and *radon* in the earth's crust. Other types of ionizing radiation, such as *x-rays*, are used for medical diagnosis and treatment. A third type of ionizing radiation is *particulate radiation*, or radioactive fallout, which consists of radioactive particles that fall to the ground after a nuclear explosion.

There are various hypotheses regarding the role of ionizing radiation in the development of cancer. One current hypothesis holds that there is no safe dose of ionizing radiation. Researchers who hold this view think that the risk of developing radiation-related cancers is directly proportional to the amount of radiation a person receives; any dose of ionizing radiation, no matter how small, is carcinogenic. Another hypothesis holds that the risk of developing radiation-related cancer from a dose lower than a certain threshold amount is zero. According to this view, there are safe (noncarcinogenic) doses of ionizing radiation. Unfortunately, no one knows what this dose might be.

There is no doubt, however, that ionizing radiation causes cancer. One of the first pieces of evidence came from a study of women who, around the 1930s, painted numerals on the dials of "glow in the dark" clocks. The numerals glowed because the paint included a radioactive element. The women swallowed this radioactive element when they licked their brush tips to make them finely pointed. In later years, this population of women exhibited high rates of bone sarcomas and head cancers. Another study looked at patients who, before 1954, received radiation therapy for spinal disorders. Researchers noticed that these patients had more leukemia and cancers of the stomach, pancreas, lung, and other highly irradiated organs than would be expected in a healthy population. In addition, a study of the survivors of the atomic bomb detonations in Hiroshima and Nagasaki, Japan during World War II revealed a tenfold to twentyfold increase in leukemias in this population compared to a control population. This study also pointed out, however, that the susceptibility to radiation-induced leukemia varies from one individual to another. Not all exposed persons developed cancer.

The types of radiation to which most persons are commonly exposed are diagnostic x-rays and radon. X-rays, a type of radiation with a slightly shorter wavelength than UV radiation, pass through soft body tissues such as skin and muscle but cannot pass through denser tissues such as bones. This property makes x-rays useful for visualizing interior parts of the body. As the x-rays pass through the soft tissues, however, this radiation is absorbed by the cells, possibly damaging the DNA and creating a cancer risk.

The best way to lower your cancer risk due to x-ray exposure is to eliminate unnecessary medical x-rays. Today, however, diagnostic x-rays are safer than in the past; most medical and dental x-rays are adjusted to deliver the lowest dose possible. In addition, x-ray technicians use lead shields and aprons to protect parts of the body not being irradiated. Decide with your physician whether the benefits of a particular x-ray procedure outweigh its risks, especially in the case of infants and young children, who are particularly susceptible to the damaging effects of ionizing radiation. If you are female and are being screened for breast cancer, ask if your physician's office has a dedicated, low-dose mammogram (breast x-ray) machine that is approved by the American Cancer Society.

The other type of ionizing radiation to which we are exposed is radon. Radon is a colorless, odorless, radioactive gas that is a product of the radioactive decay of uranium. In some parts of the United States, the earth contains dangerous levels of radon contamination. Presently, areas of the United States known to have high radon levels are Maryland, eastern Pennsylvania, New York, New Jersey, and certain communities in Montana, North Dakota, Colorado, and Washington. This gas can become trapped within homes, increasing the risk of lung cancer for those who live there, particularly cigarette smokers. Inexpensive measuring devices are now available to assess radon levels in your home. If the levels are found to be high, many methods are available to channel this gas away from your home and prevent its buildup.

Hormones

The hormones implicated in cancer are estrogen (in women) and androgens (in men). Estrogen is produced by the ovaries and adrenal cortex (see Chapter 14). It helps regulate menstruation and pregnancy, and regulates the growth and development of secondary sexual characteristics, such as breasts. Testosterone is the major androgen in males. This hormone, secreted by the testes, is necessary for the normal functioning of the accessory sex organs (such as the prostate gland). It also regulates the growth and development of male secondary sexual characteristics such as facial hair. Under certain conditions, estrogen causes cells within the ovaries, uterus, or breasts to grow and divide when they normally would not, forming cancerous tumors. Similarly, testosterone may trigger prostate cells to proliferate abnormally, but this connection is unclear.

Estrogen appears to be implicated in the development of cancer in a few instances. Women who have long menstrual histories (began menstruating early and/or experienced menopause, the cessation of menstruation, late), and have therefore been exposed to estrogen for a longer than average time span, have an increased risk of developing cancer of the breast and endometrium (lining of the uterus). Synthetic estrogens can also increase a woman's chance of developing these cancers, such as when it is taken alone in a regimen of estrogen replacement therapy (ERT) during menopause. However, ERT that includes the female hormone progesterone confers less risk of breast cancer and actually *lowers* a woman's risk of developing endometrial cancer. Sequential birth control pills, which were taken in sequence — first the estrogen and then the progesterone, were found to increase the risk of cancer of the endometrium. Consequently, they were taken off the market in the late 1970s. Combination birth control pills, those containing both estrogen and progesterone in the same pill, pose no increased cancer risk and are the type used today. In fact, they appear to *decrease* a woman's risk of ovarian or endo-

metrial cancers. This observation is consistent with the lowered risk for these cancers in women who have borne children; the combination pill provides a woman with a pattern of estrogen and progesterone that mimics, somewhat, the hormonal pattern of pregnancy. Progestin-only pills, called "minipills," and progestin implants (Norplant) also appear safe and may also decrease the risk of developing these cancers.

The role of testosterone in the development of prostate cancer is unclear at this time. Two types of studies show that it probably plays a role in the development of prostate cancer but these studies do not define that role. One study shows that boys who have their testicles removed before puberty do not develop prostate cancer. Other studies using animals show that prostate cancer can be induced in rats by long-term administration of testosterone. Researchers are currently probing the differences in testosterone production and metabolism in men who develop prostate cancer and those who do not.

Diet

Every day the news seems to contain information regarding yet another dietary cancer threat. The following discussion focuses on dietary factors that research consistently shows increase the risk of developing certain cancers.

The primary dietary factor that increases the risk of cancer is the consumption of *fat*. Diets high in fat — those in which fat accounts for substantially more than 30% of the daily caloric intake — increase the risk of breast, prostate, and colon cancers. These types of cancers are the second, third, and fourth (respectively) causes of cancer deaths in the United States, as Figure 18-12 shows. Together, these cancers account for approximately one-third of all cancers. In addition, some evidence exists that high-fat diets add to the risk of ovarian, endometrial, and pancreatic cancers.

Research shows that dietary fat is a promoter of cancer, encouraging the development of cancer in initiated cells. Excess fat also encourages the growth of breast cancers by another mechanism: it affects the production of estrogen. High-fat diets cause women to produce more estrogen than they normally would produce. In addition, women who are overweight (a condition fostered by a high-fat diet) produce more estrogen than women who are not overweight. High estrogen levels in women consuming high-fat diets and in women who are overweight have been linked to the development of breast cancer. A similar connection may exist between fat and the development of ovarian and endometrial cancers, but this link is not as well-supported as is the link with breast cancer. Prostate cancer may also be influenced by fat intake; scientists think that male hormone levels are probably affected by high-fat diets in a way that can promote changes in prostate cells.

A diet high in fat also promotes cancer of the colon (large intestine). The intake of fats, especially saturated fats, increases the production of bile. Bile is produced in the liver, stored in the gallbladder, and released into the small intestine to aid in the digestion and absorption of fats. As the digestive wastes move to the large intestine, components of the bile that have not been reabsorbed in the small intes-

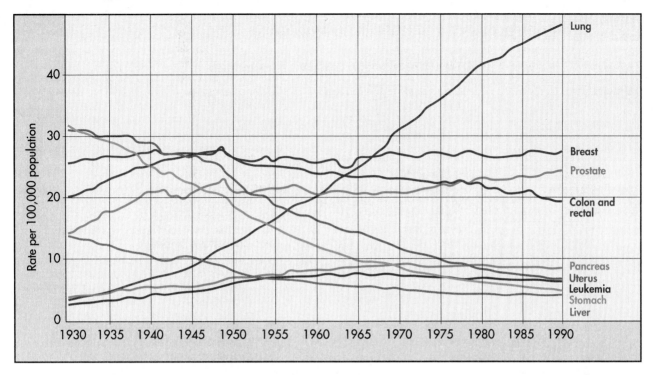

FIGURE 18-12 Cancer death rates in the United States, 1930 to 1988. (Rates are adjusted to the age distribution of the 1970 population. Rates are for both sexes, except breast and uterus [female only] and prostate [male only].) (Data from National Center for Health Statistics and Bureau of the Census, United States.)

tine move along with the wastes. One component of the bile implicated in colon cancer is substances called *bile acids*. High amounts of these acids can damage the colon wall. In addition, the colon bacteria chemically convert bile acids to free radicals and lipid peroxidases by oxidation: removing electrons from their molecules. The lipid peroxides are then oxidized to form more free radicals.

Polyunsaturated fats (see p. 40) are the most likely to produce free radicals that can damage cell structures and promote cancer. With respect to heart disease, however, polyunsaturated fats are preferable to saturated fats because they lower blood cholesterol and, therefore, the risk of heart disease. But with *both* heart disease and cancer prevention in mind, it is preferable to lower your intake of both saturated fats (primarily fats from animal sources) and polyunsaturated fats and oils (primarily fats from vegetable sources). Instead, use fats that contain a high percentage of monounsaturated fats such as olive oil.

Nitrites are food additives that have been implicated as a major cause of stomach cancer and cancer of the esophagus. Nitrites are used in salt-cured meats such as bacon, ham, hot dogs, and sausages, and in some luncheon meats such as liverwurst and salami. They are also found in smoked foods such as smoked turkey and smoked salmon, in salt-pickled foods such as pickles and pickled pigs feet, and in some baked goods. Nitrites are dangerous because they can combine with amines (protein breakdown products) in the stomach to form cancer-causing compounds called nitrosamines. These compounds, mentioned previously, are also found in cigarette smoke. These foods should be kept to a minimum in the diet.

Aflatoxins are cancer-causing compounds produced by the fungus *Aspergillus flavus*. These compounds are not found in fresh foods, but are produced when foods such as nuts, grains, seeds, and rice become moldy. To avoid this cancer risk you should avoid eating any food that has become moldy, especially molding, damp, or shriveled nuts, grains, or seeds.

At this time, there are many other food questions regarding possible cancer risks. There is controversy over the use of pesticides on foods, the use of certain food additives and dyes, and the use of the artificial sweetener saccharin. Teas contain tannins, which are mutagens but have not been shown to cause cancer. Some decaffeinated coffees use methylene chloride, a proven carcinogen, to remove the caffeine. Charcoal broiling foods produces mutagens and possibly carcinogenic agents. Do we need to be wary of everything we eat? To address these questions and concerns, some persons choose to buy fruits and vegetables that have not been exposed to pesticides; cut down on sodas containing saccharin; only drink decaffeinated coffees that have been processed without chemicals; avoid foods with preservatives, additives, and dyes; and avoid burning or overly browning foods. The choice is yours. The list of factors that increase the risk of cancer is lengthy but worth remembering, so that where possible you can avoid unhealthy choices. These factors are summarized in Table 18-2.

Factors that decrease the risk of cancer

One way to decrease your risk of cancer is to determine which of the above cancer risks applies to you and to change your behavior accordingly. Another way to decrease your

TABLE 18-2 Major factors that increase the risk of cancer

FACTOR	EXAMPLES OF IMPLICATED CANCERS	COMMENTS
Heredity	Retinoblastoma (childhood eye cancer) Osteosarcoma (childhood bone cancer)	Most cancers are not caused by heredity alone. Persons having family histories of certain cancers should follow physicians' recommendations.
Tumor viruses	Liver cancer Adult T cell leukemia/lymphoma Cervical cancer	Five viruses are initiators of certain cancers. See Table 18-1.
Cigarette smoke	Lung cancer Cancers of the oral cavity and throat Cancers of the kidney and bladder	Cigarette smoking is responsible for approximately one-third of all cancers. Nonsmokers have an increased risk of smoking-related cancers if they regularly breathe in sidestream smoke.
Industrial hazards	Lung cancer	Certain fibers, such as asbestos; chemicals such as benzene, PAHs, and arsenic; and wood and coal dust are prominent industrial hazards.
Ultraviolet radiation from the sun	Skin cancers	Those at greatest risk are fair-skinned persons who burn easily. However, everyone is at risk and should wear sunscreens and protective clothing when in the sun for extended periods of time.
Ionizing radiation	Related to location and type of exposure	Eliminate unnecessary medical x-rays to lower cancer risk. Infants and children are particularly susceptible to the damaging effects of ionizing radiation. Check your home to detect high levels of radon gas.
Hormones (estrogen and possibly testosterone)	Breast, endometrial, ovarian, and prostate cancers	When estrogen is used with progesterone in birth control pills and hormone replacement therapy, the risk of cancer from this hormone is lowered and may become *less* than normal. The role of testosterone in prostate cancer is unclear.
Diet	Colon, breast, and prostate cancers (fat) Stomach and esophageal cancers (nitrites)	The primary dietary factor that increases the risk of cancer is the consumption of fat, particularly polyunsaturated fats. Nitrites found in salt-cured, salt-pickled, and smoked foods also increase the risk of cancer.

cancer risk is to follow the recommendations of the American Cancer Society (ACS) regarding diagnostic tests, which are described below. The box on the top left of p. 369 lists the danger signs of cancer; if you notice any of these signs, see your doctor immediately. Otherwise, the ACS recommends a cancer-related checkup by a physician every 3 years for persons age 20 to 39 years and annually for those age 40 and over. Persons at risk for particular cancers may need to see their physician more often.

Diagnostic tests

Widely available tests exist to detect cancers of the breast, cervix, and colon and rectum. Women should perform breast self-examinations, and men should perform testicular self-examinations, monthly.

The American Cancer Society recommends one baseline *mammogram* (see opener photo) for women between 35 and 39; one mammogram every 1 to 2 years between the ages of 40 and 49; and annual exams after age 50. The benefit of these diagnostic exams outweighs the cancer risk from exposure to x-rays, since the dose of radiation received is low and the incidence of breast cancer in the United States is so high. At this time, one out of every nine women develops breast cancer. The ACS also recommends that women over the age of 19 examine their own breasts monthly, receive a clinical examination every 3 years between ages 20 and 40, and receive a clinical examination every year after the age of 40. Breast self-examination is usually taught as a part of the clinical exam.

Women who are or who have been sexually active, or who have reached the age of 18 should have an annual pelvic exam and Papanicolaou (Pap) smear. During the pelvic examination, the physician checks for any visible or palpable (able to be felt) abnormal growths. The Pap smear is used to detect any abnormal cells at the cervix or the body of the uterus. During this test, the physician swabs these areas, transfers the swabbing to a microscope slide (see opener photo), and a trained technician examines the slide under a microscope.

The American Cancer Society recommends three tests for the early detection of colon and rectum cancer. Everyone should receive a *digital rectal exam* every year after the age of 40. This test should be accompanied by a *stool blood test* every year after the age of 50. This test, prepared at home using special materials (see opener photo) and sent in to a medical lab or the doctor's office, detects hidden blood in the feces. In addition, a *proctosigmoidoscopy* (literally, "to view [scopy] the rectum [procto] and s-shaped colon [sigmoid]") should be performed every 3 to 5 years after the age of 50. In this test, the physician uses a hollow, lighted tube to inspect the rectum and lower colon.

Men should perform a testicular self-examination each month. The best time to perform the exam is after a warm shower or bath when the skin in this area is relaxed. To perform the exam, a man should hold the testicle with both hands and then press lightly on the testicular surface. If any lumps are felt (other than the epididymis, which extends up and down on the back side of the testicle), a physician should be consulted immediately.

Diet

Consuming sufficient fiber in the diet has been shown to reduce the risk of colorectal cancer. Conversely, diets low in fiber appear to increase the risk of colon and rectal cancers. Fiber is commonly referred to as "bulk" or "roughage;" it appears to lower cancer risk by binding to bile acids and carcinogens and moving them quickly out of the intestine before they can do any damage. The presence of fiber in the colon may also affect the type of bacteria present there and their chemical interactions with food wastes and bile acids. Low fiber combined with a high-fat diet multiplies this risk.

Bran is the most highly recommended dietary source of fiber for cancer prevention. Other rich sources of fiber are beans, whole-grain breads and cereals, and most fruits and vegetables. Pastas are generally *not* high in fiber, nor are certain vegetables such as lettuce, mushrooms, and peppers; certain fruits such as grapes and watermelons; and fruit juices.

Other nutrients that may lower the risk of cancer are the antioxidants: beta-carotene, vitamin C, and vitamin E. These nutrients help block the oxidation of polyunsaturated fats in the colon as well as stop or reverse the genetic damage done by free radicals in various parts of the body.

Beta-carotene is a substance that is converted to vitamin A in the body. Vitamin A and precursors such as beta-carotene appear to lower the risk of lung cancer, gastrointestinal cancer, and cancer of the esophagus. They may (although evidence is scanty at this time) reduce the risk of other cancers also, such as colon, rectal, bladder, prostate, and breast cancers. Vitamin A and beta-carotene are found in green and yellow fruits and vegetables.

Some studies show that vitamin C may protect against stomach cancer. It is found in dark, leafy green vegetables and citrus fruits as well as many other sources. Although vitamin E is an antioxidant and blocks free radical formation, there is no evidence as yet regarding its ability to reduce the risk of specific cancers. Vitamin E is also found in dark, leafy green vegetables and in whole grain breads and cereals.

In addition to the antioxidant roles played by some fruits and vegetables, scientists have evidence that vegetables of the cabbage family (such as broccoli, brussel sprouts, and cauliflower) may play a role in cancer prevention. These vegetables contain substances called *indoles*, which appear to deactivate initiators and promoters. At this time, the American Cancer Society does not recommend eating any specific fruits and vegetables over any other but suggests that a variety of fruits and vegetables be included in the diet each day. The box above lists the American Cancer Society's dietary guidelines for the prevention of cancer.

Cancer and the future

A new field of study has emerged in the fight against cancer: *chemoprevention*. Chemoprevention focuses on ways to stop cancer development during progression by specific uses of a variety of foods and vitamins. For example, a soybean derivative is currently being tested to see if applying it to precancerous growths can reverse the progression of the tumor cells. Synthetic forms of vitamin A are being used in a similar way. Likewise, a plant oil extracted from orange peels is being used to battle breast cancer. Such products are highly concentrated; medical researchers warn that eating large quantities of these foods is not effective.

The key to future progress in dealing with the collection of diseases called cancer is research in multiple areas, such as in chemoprevention and in those described in the boxed essay (p. 356-358). Since cancer is not a single entity, the road to a "cure" is elusive. In fact, a single cure may be an unrealistic expectation of a way to fight cancer. Instead, we must all learn about cancer prevention and detection, and incorporate this information into our lifestyles to help curb the number of cancer-related deaths. Research in cancer treatments as well as in early detection has already helped in this regard, resulting in a survival rate today of nearly one out of two cancer victims, in comparison to one out of four 30 years ago, and one out of five 60 years ago. So although we are still losing the war against cancer in terms of increasing numbers of cases (as the chapter opener points out), we are making progress in winning the war against cancer in terms of survival.

Summary

1. Cancer is not a single disease but is a cluster of over 200 diseases. All cancers have four characteristics: (a) uncontrolled cell growth, (b) loss of cell differentiation (specialization), (c) invasion of normal tissues, and (d) metastasis, or spread, to multiple sites.

2. Cancer cells arise through a series of step-wise, progressive mutations, or changes, to the DNA of normal body cells. The first set of changes involves proto-oncogenes (dormant forms of cancer-causing genes), and/or tumor suppressor genes (genes that can be thought of as "off" switches in the development of cancer). These first mutations result in precancerous cells, which are termed initiated or transformed cells.

3. Some types of initiated cells are inherited, such as the cells that make up moles. In addition, certain viruses have been shown to cause initiation: the hepatitis B virus (cancer of the liver), human T lymphotropic/leukemia virus (cancer of white blood cells), human papillomavirus (cancers of the cervix and skin), human cytomegalovirus (Kaposi's sarcoma, a cancer of the skin), and the Epstein-Barr virus (cancers of the lymph nodes and nasopharynx). These viruses are called tumor viruses.

4. For cancer to occur, initiated cells must undergo promotion, a process by which the DNA of initiated cells is damaged further, eventually stimulating these cells to grow and divide. Research suggests that if the promoter (the substance causing promotion) is withdrawn in the early stages, cancer development can be reversed.

5. A wide array of chemicals are initiators and/or promoters, such as certain chemicals used in the manufacture and processing of various products as well as the chemicals found in cigarette smoke. Cigarette smoking is related to approximately one third of all cancers.

6. Two types of radiation are especially dangerous because they can modify DNA: ultraviolet (UV) radiation (which comes to us in sunlight) and the ionizing radiation (primarily x-rays and radon gas).

7. The hormones implicated in cancer are estrogen (in women) and testosterone (in men). Synthetic estrogens can increase a woman's chance of developing cancers of the breast and endometrium (lining of the uterus) when it is taken alone in a regimen of estrogen replacement therapy (ERT) during menopause. However, ERT that includes the female hormone progesterone confers less risk of breast cancer and actually *lowers* a woman's risk of developing endometrial cancer. The role of testosterone in the development of prostate cancer is unclear at this time.

8. Diets high in fat increase the risk of colon, breast, and prostate cancers. Nitrites, food additives found in salt-cured meats, and smoked and pickled foods, have been implicated as a major cause of stomach cancer and cancer of the esophagus.

9. One way to decrease your risk of cancer is to determine which cancer risks apply to you and to change your behavior accordingly. Other ways are to follow the recommendations of the American Cancer Society (ACS) regarding diagnostic tests and diet, watch out for the cancer danger signs, and have regular cancer-related checkups.

1. What common factors must exist for a disease to be labeled as a form of cancer?

2. In what manner does mutation affect proto-oncogenes? In What manner does mutation affect tumor-suppressor genes? What are the clinical results?

3. Explain how cigarette smoke can act as a "complete" carcinogen.

4. Lynn's doctor informs her that her pathology report on her cyst indicates a benign growth. What does this mean?

5. Using your knowledge of initiators, can you construct a theory as to why most cancers (90%) are carcinomas?

6. Design a family medical tree identifying known cancers in your medical history. Go back as many generations as possible and include aunts, uncles, and cousins. What cancers emerge as hereditary or potentially a health trend in your family?

7. What factors in your life and environment predispose you towards cancer (excluding heredity)? How many of these can you personally restrict or eliminate? Have you done so?

8. Why must children be especially protected from exposure to excessive ultraviolet radiation?

9. Some health advocates are concerned about the high doses of hormones used in modern dairy, beef, and poultry farming. Can you determine the cause of their alarm? What do you think of this issue?

10. Discuss the ways in which a high-fat diet may increase your personal cancer risk.

11. What factors can you address to reduce your personal cancer risk? Have you taken advantage of any of these in your lifestyle?

12. Terry has developed venereal warts. Does this pose any cancer threat to her?

13. Ellen has had three children and breast-fed all of them for periods of up to a year. Do these facts increase or decrease her risk of breast or ovarian cancers?

1. As a class, list the various agents known to act as carcinogens. Which are naturally occurring? Which are created by human activity? In what ways can such agents be restricted or protected against? Do you think that cancer is, to some degree, a natural response to a fluctuating environment or totally avoidable?

2. Divide the class into smaller groups. In each group, discuss the known risks of cigarette smoking as regards to cancer development. Discuss the issue of passive smoking where a non-smoker is exposed to the exhalation of a smoker. Does this offer possible risks also?

Hooper, (1992, February). Unconventional cancer treatments. *Discover,* pp. 59-61. *Many cancer patients are turning to native or holistic medicines in order to treat their diseases.*

Joyce, C. (1193, March). Taxol: search for a cancer drug. *Bioscience,* pp. 133-136. *The use of taxol, a natural chemical found in yew trees, for treatment of ovarian cancer reflects the expanding trend of natural cancer treatments.*

Miller, JA (1990, September). Genes that protect against cancer. *Bioscience,* pp 563-566. *A new focus in cancer research is on tumor suppressor genes, normally present in our bodies, which may be used in new therapeutic approaches to cancer.*

Murray, L. (1993, February). The cancer war: stories from the front. *Omni,* pp. 50-58. *This article explores the most innovative new treatments being used in cancer therapy.*

Radetsky, P. (1991, May). The roots of cancer. *Discover,* pp. 60-65. *Using colon cancer as a model, a scientist details the process by which a normal cell becomes cancerous.*

19 Patterns of Inheritance

▼ Over the centuries, the nature of heredity was misunderstood by scientists and philosophers until the work of Mendel, Sutton, Morgan, and others in the late 1800s began to uncover its mechanisms.

▼ Working with pea plants that exhibited alternative forms of various characteristics (traits), Mendel established that traits are inherited as discrete packets of information, which scientists today call genes.

▼ Through his experiments with pea plants, Mendel also discovered that alternative forms of genes (alleles) separate from one another during the formation of gametes and are distributed independently of other traits..

▼ Mendel and other early geneticists took the first real steps toward solving the puzzles of inheritance and laid the foundation for one of the great revolutions in thinking of the twentieth century: an understanding of the nature of genetic material and how it is transmitted from generation to generation.

The same yet different—How often have you heard that phrase? And what does it really mean? Scientists would answer the last question with a single word: variation.

Variation can be seen in the group of flamingos in the photo. Although the flamingos are all the same—with long legs and beaks and pink feathers covering their bodies—they are all different. Look closely at the same characteristic in each. One has longer legs than the others. Another has a slightly different shade of pink. What other differences do you see?

Clearly, each species of living things exhibits variation. Humans, for example, all have characteristics you recognize as human, but each person (except for identical twins) looks different from all others. What is the source of this variation? And how are these differences distributed among populations of living things that are all the same?

Inheritance and variation within species

Today, it is common knowledge that organisms inherit characteristics from their parents. During sexual reproduction, parents pass on traits to their offspring by means of genetic material within the eggs of the mother and sperm of the father. The intermingling of parental genes that takes place at fertilization, the union of the egg and sperm, is the material of variation. Organisms produced by asexual reproduction do not exhibit variation for just this reason. Their genetic makeup is derived from one parent only, so offspring are genetically identical to that parent. For example, a plant produced asexually by rooting a cutting will have the same genes as the "mother" plant, but a plant produced by cross-pollination—a type of sexual reproduction—will have certain characteristics of both its parents.

▼
▼

Sexual reproduction introduces variation within a species because offspring inherit characteristics from both their parents. Asexual reproduction does not introduce variation because the offspring is an exact duplicate of its parent.

Historical views of inheritance

Although genetic inheritance seems obvious today, this fact was not always obvious to scientists and philosophers. Hippocrates (460-377BC) believed that a child inherited traits from "particles" given off by all parts of the bodies of the father and mother. These particles, he suggested, travel to the sex organs. During intercourse, the father's particles merge with the mother's particles to form the child. This idea of inheritance was held by many until the mid-1800s. Most theories of the direct transmission of hereditary material assumed that the male and female traits blended in the offspring. Thus a parent with red hair and a parent with brown hair would be expected to produce children with reddish brown hair, and a tall parent and a short parent would produce children of intermediate height. However, taken to its logical conclusion, this theory suggests that all individuals within a species would eventually look like one another as their traits continually blended together.

Other ideas regarding inheritance were formulated after the invention of a simple, hand-held microscope. Anton van Leeuwenhoek (1632-1723) observed sperm for the first time with the microscope, drew pictures of them, and developed hypotheses regarding inheritance based on his observations. A widely held notion at the time was that each sperm contained a tiny but whole human being (Figure 19-1). *Preformationists* (as this group was called) were separated into two camps. The spermists thought that sperm encased microscopic humans. Because the human was fully formed, the body contained sperm that each encased another preformed individual, and so forth . . . ad infinitum! Ovists, on the other hand, held that it was the eggs of the mother that contained minute humans.

Not until the mid-1800s with the work of Schleiden, Schwann, and Virchow (see Chapter 3) did scientists real-

ize that new life arose from old life in the form of new cells arising from old cells. By means of the growth and division of these cells, new organisms developed from individual cells of parent organisms. Scientists of the late 1800s studied the nuclei of cells to uncover the mysteries of cell growth and division. They observed the complex process of mitosis (see Chapter 17) and wondered why cells went through this intricate process. Wouldn't it be more efficient for a cell to simply pinch in two along its middle? By 1883, scientists knew that the complex process of cell division ensured an equal distribution of the nuclear material to two daughter cells. And not only did each daughter cell receive the same amount of nuclear material, they each received a complete amount of the nuclear material.

At this same time, scientists also observed that an even more complex series of nuclear events (now known as *meiosis* [see Chapter 17]) preceded the formation of eggs and sperm. By 1885, several scientists independently concluded that this nuclear material was the physical bond that linked generations of organisms. But how nuclear material regulated the development of fertilized eggs and how it was related to heredity and variation was still a mystery. About 1900, scientists began to answer this question by piecing together research of the day with research that had long been ignored: the work of Gregor Mendel. Mendel was an Austrian monk trained in botany and mathematics at the University of Vienna.

FIGURE 19-1 Drawing of a homunculus.
A widely held belief before the nineteenth century was that sperm contained a fully formed, miniature human being called a *homunculus.* It was supposedly implanted in the uterus during fertilization, where it grew into maturity.

The birth of the study of inheritance

Approximately 25 years before scientists had discovered a link between heredity and the complex processes of mitosis and meiosis, Mendel began his work with the garden pea. Mendel chose the pea plant because it was an annual plant that was small and easy to grow and had a short generation time. Therefore he could conduct experiments involving numerous plants and obtain results relatively quickly.

Pea plants are well suited to studies of inheritance because each pea flower contains both female parts (stigma, style, and ovary) and male parts (filaments that support anthers). Both are enclosed and protected by the petals (Figure 19-2). The gametes produced within each flower—pollen grains within the anthers and eggs within the ovary—are able to fuse and develop into seeds of new plants. Fertilization of this sort, called **self-fertilization,** takes place naturally within individual pea flowers if they are not disturbed. As a result, the offspring of self-fertilizing garden peas are derived from one pea plant, not two. After generations of self-fertilization, some plants produce offspring consistently identical to the parent with respect to certain defined characteristics; these plants are said to be **true-breeding.**

Mendel selected a number of different true-breeding **varieties** of pea plants with which to work. Differing varieties, or strains, of an organism each belong to the same species, but each has one or more distinctive characteristics that are passed from parent to offspring. To study the inheritance patterns of these characteristics, Mendel took true-breeding plants and artificially cross-fertilized them. **Cross-fertilization** occurs when the pollen of one plant fertilizes the egg cells of another plant. To do this, Mendel removed the anthers of a flower before they shed pollen and then dusted this flower with pollen from another plant. In this way, Mendel was able to perform experimental crosses between two different true-breeding varieties of pea plants

that exhibited differences regarding particular traits. The offspring, or progeny, of the cross between two different varieties of plants of the same species are called **hybrids.** (In other contexts, the word *hybrid* may also refer to the cross between two different species of organisms. A mule, for example, is the hybrid offspring of a horse and a donkey.)

Gregor Mendel's experiments to determine inheritance patterns

Mendel first designed a set of experiments that involved crossing varieties of pea plants that differed from one another in a single characteristic. Mendel chose seven different characteristics, or **traits,** to study (Figure 19-3). Although various other varieties of pea plants exist, Mendel chose only those varieties that differed from one another clearly and distinctly.

The purpose of Mendel's experiments was to observe the offspring from the crossing of each pair of plants and to look for patterns in the transmission of single traits. Although he was not the first to perform such experiments, he was the first to count and classify the peas that resulted from his crosses and compare the proportions with mathematical models. Mendel planned to use these data to try to deduce the laws by which these traits are passed on from generation to generation. First, Mendel crossed plants having contrasting forms of the single traits listed in Figure 19-3 by artificially fertilizing one with the other. Mendel called these plants the **parental (P) generation** and called their hybrid offspring the **first filial (F_1) generation.** (The word *filial* is from Latin words meaning "son" and "daughter.") These progeny are called **monohybrids** because they are the product of two plants that differ from one another in a single trait.

When Mendel crossed two contrasting varieties, such as purple-flowered plants with white-flowered plants, the hybrid offspring that he obtained were not intermediate in flower color, as the theory of blending inheritance predicted. Instead, all hybrid offspring in each case resembled *only one* of their parents. Thus in a cross of white-flowered plants with purple-flowered plants, *all* the F_1 offspring had purple flowers. In a cross of tall plants and short plants, *all* the F_1 offspring were tall plants. Mendel referred to the form of a trait that was expressed in the F_1 plants as *dominating,* or **dominant,** and to the alternative form, which was not expressed in the F_1 plants, as **recessive.** He chose the word *recessive* because this form of the trait receded, or disappeared entirely, in the hybrids. For each of the seven contrasting pairs of traits that Mendel examined, one member of each pair was dominant; the other was recessive. Figure 19-3 shows which traits Mendel found to be dominant and which traits he found to be recessive.

Then Mendel went a step further. He allowed each F_1 plant to mature and self-pollinate. He collected and planted seeds from each plant, which produced the **second filial (F_2) generation.** He found that most of the F_2 plants exhibited the dominating form of the trait and looked like the F_1 plants, but some exhibited the recessive form. None of the plants had blended characteristics. Therefore Mendel

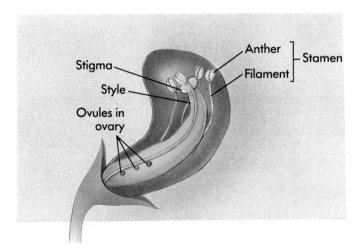

FIGURE 19-2 Anatomy of a pea plant.
In the flower of a pea plant the petals enclose the male (anther) and female (stigma) parts, ensuring that self-fertilization will take place.

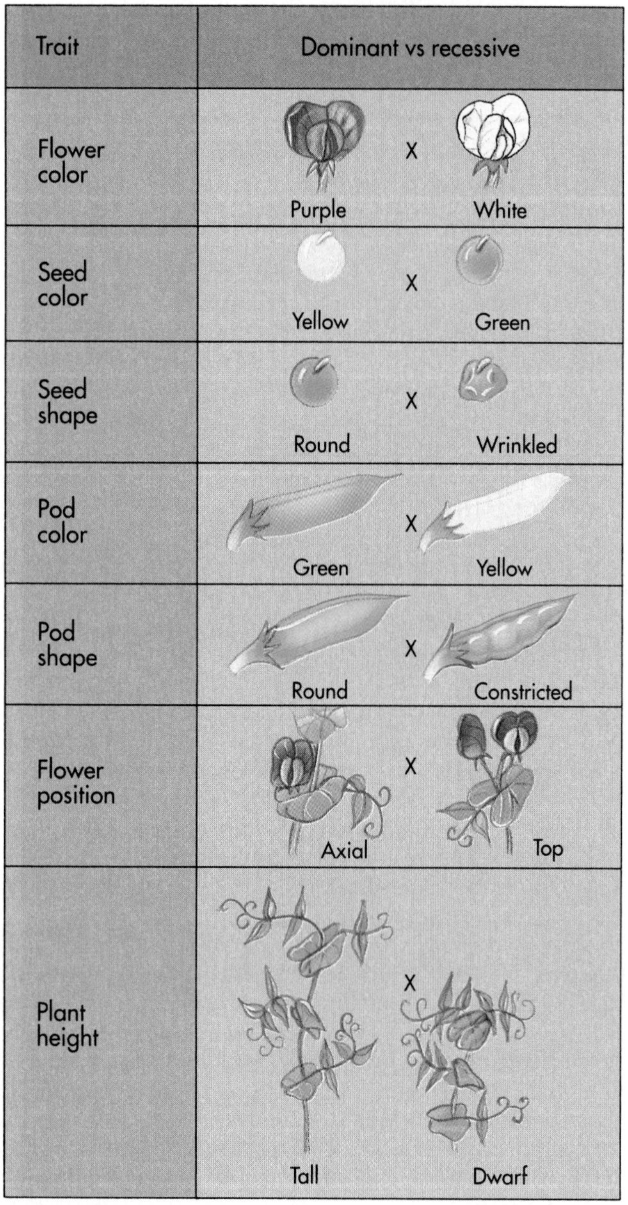

Trait	Dominant vs recessive	
Flower color	Purple	X	White
Seed color	Yellow	X	Green
Seed shape	Round	X	Wrinkled
Pod color	Green	X	Yellow
Pod shape	Round	X	Constricted
Flower position	Axial	X	Top
Plant height	Tall	X	Dwarf

FIGURE 19-3 The seven pairs of contrasting traits in the garden pea studied by Mendel.
To determine inheritance patterns, Mendel crossed plants with contrasting forms of each of seven traits. The parent plants were the P (parental) generation, and their offspring were the F_1 (first filial) generation. Among the progeny of these crossing experiments, Mendel found that some traits dominated over other traits.

was able to count the numbers of each of the two contrasting varieties of F_2 progeny and compare these results.

Earlier in history, scientists had carried out hybridization experiments. However, the plants these scientists chose often produced hybrids that differed in appearance from both their parents because they exhibited blended traits. Scientists had also not quantified the results of their experiments. Mendel's change in experimental design—counting the progeny—was a key component of his ability to unravel the mystery of certain inheritance patterns.

When Mendel quantified the traits he observed in the F_2 generation, he discovered that for every three plants exhibiting the dominant form of the trait, one exhibited the recessive trait. Put another way, both contrasting forms of the parental characteristics reappeared in the F_2 generation in an approximate 3:1 ratio: three fourths of the plants exhibited the dominant form (determined in the F_1 generation), and one fourth exhibited the recessive form. Figure 19-4, A illustrates Mendel's experiments using the trait of flower color; Figure 19-4, B lists the results Mendel obtained in the F_2 generation for each of the contrasting forms of the seven traits. Notice that these numbers reflect a 3:1 ratio of dominant to recessive forms for each trait. Notice also that in his experiments Mendel used hundreds and sometimes thousands of plants. Why do you think that such a procedure is part of a good experimental design?

Mendel went on to examine what happened when each F_2 plant was allowed to self-pollinate. He found that the recessive one fourth were always true-breeding. For example, self-fertilizing white-flowered F_2 plants reliably produced only white-flowered offspring. By contrast, only one third of the dominant purple-flowered F_2 individuals (one fourth of the total offspring) proved true-breeding, whereas two thirds were not true-breeding. This last class of plants produced dominant and recessive F_3 individuals in a ratio of 3:1. The ratio of individuals in the entire F_2 population was the following (Figure 19-5):

1 true-breeding dominant:
2 not true-breeding dominant:
1 true-breeding recessive

Conclusions Mendel drew from his experiments

From his experimental data, Mendel drew conclusions regarding the nature of heredity—conclusions that have withstood tests of time and further experimentation. In fact, Mendel's work is historically looked upon as the birth of **genetics,** the branch of biology dealing with the principles of heredity and variation in organisms. The statements that follow regarding Mendel's conclusions are considered to be the first established principles of genetics.

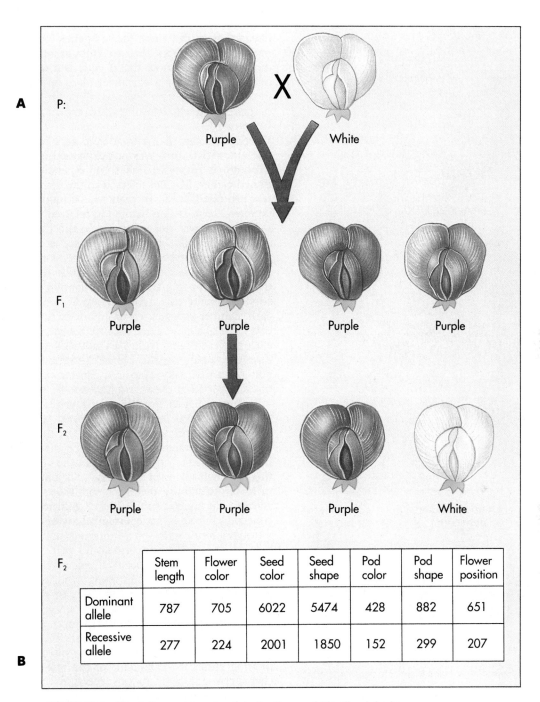

	Stem length	Flower color	Seed color	Seed shape	Pod color	Pod shape	Flower position
Dominant allele	787	705	6022	5474	428	882	651
Recessive allele	277	224	2001	1850	152	299	207

FIGURE 19-4 Mendel's experiments refute the theory of blending inheritance.
A When crossing a purple flower with a white flower, Mendel observed that all the F_1 generation flowers were purple. When the F_1 plants were allowed to self-pollinate, three quarters of the F_2 generation exhibited the dominant trait (purple) and one quarter the recessive trait (white). There were no intermediate or blended flowers.
B Mendel found the approximate 3:1 ratio of dominant to recessive forms to be exhibited in each of the seven traits he studied.

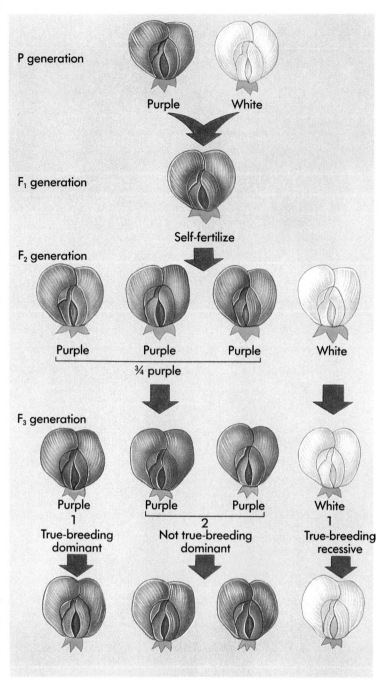

FIGURE 19-5 The F₃ generation allowed Mendel to determine which of the F₂ plants were true-breeding.
By allowing the F₂ generation to self-pollinate, Mendel reasoned from the F₃ offspring that the F₂ generation exhibited the ratio of one true-breeding dominant, to two not-true-breeding dominant, to one true-breeding recessive.

First, as mentioned previously, Mendel observed that the plants exhibiting the traits he studied did not produce progeny of intermediate appearance when crossed. These observations did not uphold the theory of blending inheritance but suggested instead that traits are inherited as discrete "packets" of information that are either present or ab-

sent in a particular generation. Mendel called these discrete bits of information *factors*. These factors, hypothesized Mendel, act later in the offspring to produce the trait. Today, scientists call these factors **genes,** the units of transmission of hereditary characteristics in an organism. In addition, scientists know that a gene is a segment, or piece, of DNA occupying a particular place on a particular chromosome. (These concepts regarding the molecular nature of genes and chromosomes are explained more fully in Chapter 17.)

Second, for each pair of traits that Mendel examined, one alternative form was not expressed in the F₁ hybrids, although it reappeared in some F₂ individuals. As mentioned earlier, Mendel referred to the form of the trait that was expressed in the F₁ plants as "dominating;" today the preferred term is dominant. He referred to the alternative form, which was not expressed in the F₁ plants, as recessive. He inferred from these observations that each individual, with respect to each trait, contains two factors. Each pair of factors may contain information for (be a code for) the same form of a trait, or each member of the pair may code for an alternative form of a trait. Today, scientists call each member of a factor pair an **allele.** An allele is a particular form of a gene. Each human, for example, receives one allele for each gene from the mother's egg and one allele from the father's sperm. The 46 chromosomes of each human cell are actually 23 paired chromosomes, one member of each pair from the sperm and one from the egg.

Third, Mendel hypothesized that (1) because the two alleles that coded for a trait remained "uncontaminated," not blending with one another as the theory of blending inheritance predicted, and (2) since the results obtained from experiments on various traits showed similar results, then pea hybrids must form egg cells and pollen cells (gametes) in which the alleles for each trait separate from one another "in equal shares" during gamete formation. This concept is referred to as **Mendel's Law of Segregation.** Put in today's terms with today's understandings: Each gamete receives only one of an organism's pair of alleles. Chance determines which member of a pair of alleles becomes included in a gamete. This random segregating process takes place during the process of meiosis, or reduction division of the nuclei of cells destined to be sex cells.

Fourth, Mendel realized that plants exhibiting the dominant trait in his monohybrid crosses of pea plants, when self-fertilized, would breed true or would produce plants exhibiting either the dominant or the recessive form of the characteristic in a 3:1 ratio, respectively. He observed that plants exhibiting the recessive trait, when self-fertilized, would always breed true. These data suggested to Mendel that true-breeding plants receive *only* the dominant factors or the recessive factors from each of their parents and that non-true-breeding plants were hybrids, which received the dominant and the recessive factors in equal shares. Today, scientists call an individual having two identical alleles for a trait **homozygous** for that trait. The prefix *homo* means "the same"; the suffix *zygous* refers to the zygote, or fertilized egg. An individual having two different alleles for a trait is said to be **heterozygous** (*hetero* means "different") for that trait.

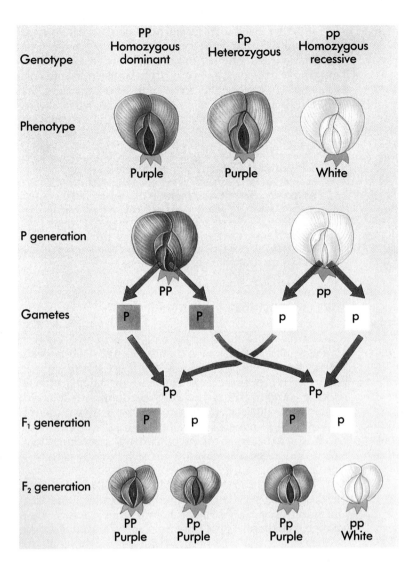

Genotype	PP Homozygous dominant	Pp Heterozygous	pp Homozygous recessive

Phenotype — Purple — Purple — White

P generation

Gametes — PP → P, P — pp → p, p

F₁ generation — Pp — P, p — Pp — P, p

F₂ generation — PP Purple — Pp Purple — Pp Purple — pp White

FIGURE 19-6 Analysis of Mendel's experiments.
Mendel determined that the physical characteristics of his plants were a reflection of alleles, which he represented with letters. In this diagram, P represents purple flower color, and p represents white flower color. Because true-breeding purple flowers can produce only P gametes and white flowers only p gametes, a cross between these two types of flowers (the P generation) can yield only purple flowers (Pp) in the F_1 generation. The p allele is recessive and thus is not expressed in the F_1 generation. The P and p alleles segregate randomly during gamete formation and randomly recombine in the F_2 generation to produce plants in an approximate ratio of 1 PP : 2 Pp : 1 pp.

Analyzing Mendel's experiments

Looking back to Mendel's experiments, you can use the information from the conclusions he drew to further analyze and understand his experiments and data. Mendel used letters to represent alleles, with the dominant allele commonly denoted by an uppercase letter, and the recessive allele by the lowercase of the same letter. In the parental generation the cross of true-breeding (therefore homozygous) pea plants with purple flowers (the dominant trait) and true-breeding pea plants with white flowers (the recessive trait) can be represented as PP × pp (Figure 19-6). The × denotes a cross between two plants. Because the purple-flowered parent can produce only P gametes and the white-flowered parent can produce only p gametes, the union of an egg and a pollen grain from these parents can produce only heterozygous Pp offspring in the F_1 generation. But because the P allele is dominant, all of the F_1 individuals

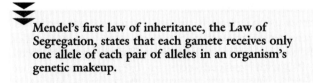

Mendel's first law of inheritance, the Law of Segregation, states that each gamete receives only one allele of each pair of alleles in an organism's genetic makeup.

Scientists understand that Mendel's results were well-defined because he was studying traits that exhibited complete dominance. This is not always the case. Incomplete dominance is a situation in which neither member of a pair of alleles exhibits dominance over the other. In fact, the "blending" of genes observed by some early investigators may have been visible expressions of incomplete dominance. Since Mendel's time, many examples of incomplete dominance have been found for various traits in both plants and animals (see Chapter 20).

have purple flowers. The p allele, although present, is not visibly expressed.

To distinguish between the presence of an allele and its expression, scientists use the term **genotype** to refer to an organism's allelic makeup and the term **phenotype** to refer to the expression of those genes. The phenotype—the organism's outward appearance—is the end result of the functioning of the enzymes and the proteins coded by an organism's genotype.

The genotype of the F₁ generation of pea plants from the cross of true-breeding plants with purple flowers (PP) and true-breeding plants with white flowers (pp) is Pp, but the phenotype of the flowers of the hybrids is purple because P is the dominant allele. When these F₁ plants are allowed to self-fertilize, the P and p alleles segregate randomly during gamete formation. Their subsequent union at fertilization to form F₂ individuals is also random. Figure 19-6 shows the possible combinations of the gametes formed by the F₁ plants. Their random combination produces plants in an approximate ratio of 1 PP:2 Pp:1 pp. From these genotypes, can you determine the phenotypes of these plants?

Using a simple diagram called a **Punnett square** is another way to visualize the possible combinations of genes in a cross. Named after its originator, the English geneticist Sir Reginald Punnett, the Punnett square is used to align possible female gametes with possible male gametes in an orderly way. The male gametes are shown along one side of the square; the female gametes are shown along the other. As in Figure 19-7, the square is divided into smaller squares as columns are drawn vertically and rows are drawn horizontally, providing a "cell" for each possible combination of gene pair.

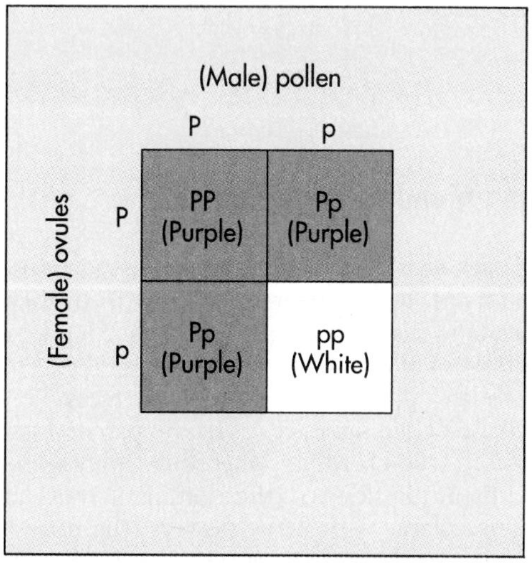

Whether using a Punnett square or visualizing the gametes and their recombinations as in Figure 19-6, you can see the expected ratios of the three kinds of F₂ plants: one fourth are true-breeding pp white-flowered plants, two fourths are heterozygous Pp purple-flowered plants, and one fourth are pure-breeding PP purple-flowered individuals. The 3:1 phenotypic ratio is really a 1:2:1 genotypic ratio.

The outward appearance of an individual (the expression of the genes) is referred to as its phenotype. The genetic makeup of an individual is referred to as its genotype. The genotype represents the alleles for given genes that are present. Using a Punnett square is one way to visualize the genotypes of progeny in simple Mendelian crosses and to illustrate their expected ratios.

How Mendel tested his conclusions

To test his conclusions further and to distinguish between homozygous dominant and heterozygous phenotypes, Mendel devised two procedures. The first test, already mentioned, was to self-fertilize the plant having a dominant phenotype. If the plant is homozygous dominant, it breeds true: purple-flowered plants produce progeny with purple flowers, tall plants produce tall plants, and so forth. If the plant is heterozygous, on the other hand, it produces dominant and recessive offspring in a 3:1 ratio when self-fertilized.

The other procedure Mendel used is called a **testcross**. In this procedure, Mendel crossed the phenotypically dominant test plant with a known homozygous recessive plant. He predicted that (1) if the test plant is homozygous for the dominant trait, the progeny will all be hybrids, Pp for example, and will therefore look like the test plant and that (2) if the test plant is heterozygous, then *half* the progeny will be heterozygous and look like the test plant, but half the progeny will be homozygous recessive and therefore will exhibit the recessive characteristic. Figure 19-8 shows the two possible testcross scenarios, using the characteristics that Mendel actually used in his first testcross experiments.

What did Mendel's data reveal? When he performed the testcross using hybrid F₁ plants having smooth seeds (Ss) and crossed them with a variety of plant having wrinkled seeds (ss), he obtained 208 plants: 106 with smooth seeds, and 102 with wrinkled seeds—a 1:1 ratio just as he had predicted. These data confirmed the primary conclusion Mendel drew from his earlier work: alternative alleles segregate from one another in the formation of gametes, coming together in the progeny in a random manner.

Further questions Mendel asked

Expanding on his Law of Segregation, Mendel asked a new question: Do the pairs of factors (alleles) that determine particular traits segregate independently of factor pairs that determine other traits? In other words, does the segregation of one factor pair influence the segregation of another?

FIGURE 19-7 Punnett square analysis of Mendel's F₁ generation. Each smaller cell within the square contains the possible F₂ phenotypic combinations from this cross. The phenotypic ratio is 3:1, but the genotypic ratio is 1:2:1. Look back at Figure 19-5 and see that the genotypic ratio matches the expected F₂ ratio of true-breeding dominant to non-true-breeding dominant to true-breeding recessive.

To answer his question, Mendel first developed a series of true-breeding lines of peas that differed from one another with respect to two of the seven pairs of characteristics with which he had worked in his monohybrid studies. He then crossed pairs of plants that exhibited contrasting forms of the two characteristics and that bred true. For example, he crossed plants having smooth, yellow seeds with plants having wrinkled, green seeds. From his monohybrid studies, Mendel knew that the traits "smooth seeds" (S) and "yellow seeds" (Y) are dominant to "wrinkled seeds" (s) and "green seeds" (y) Therefore the genotypes of the true-breeding parental (P) plants were SSYY and ssyy.

Mendel's F_1 progeny are **dihybrids**—the product of two plants that differ from one another in two traits. As in his monohybrid crosses, all the F_1 progeny had smooth, yellow seeds—the dominant phenotype. Mendel then allowed the F_1 dihybrids to self-fertilize. The seeds from these self-crosses grew into 315 plants having smooth, yellow seeds; 101 plants having wrinkled, yellow seeds; 108 plants having smooth, green seeds; and 32 plants having wrinkled, green seeds—an approximate ratio of 9:3:3:1. Other dihybrid crosses also produced offspring having the same approximate ratio.

Analyzing the results of Mendel's dihybrid crosses

Mendel reasoned that if the alleles for seed color and seed shape segregated into gametes independently of one another and were therefore inherited independently of one another, then the outcome for each trait would exhibit the 3:1 ratio of a monohybrid cross. Looking at Mendel's results, 315 + 108 (423) plants had smooth seeds and 101 + 32 (133) plants had wrinkled seeds. Put simply, *three times* as many plants had smooth seeds as had wrinkled seeds—a 3:1 ratio. Study these figures for the trait "seed color." How many plants produced yellow seeds? How many produced green seeds? What is the approximate ratio of plants having yellow seeds to plants having green seeds?

The contrasting alleles for the genes of seed shape and seed color assort independently from one another during gamete formation. This concept is referred to as **Mendel's Law of Independent Assortment.** Put in today's terms with today's understandings: The distribution of alleles for one trait into the gametes does not affect the distribution of alleles for other traits.

Even though you may understand the concept of the

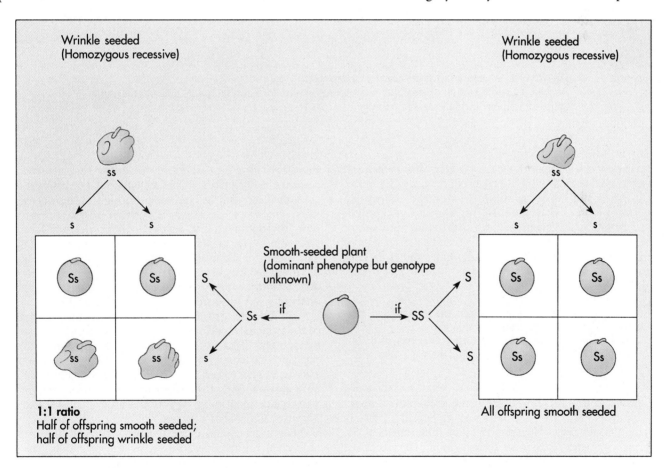

FIGURE 19-8 A testcross.
The phenotypically dominant test plant, which has smooth seeds but an unknown genotype, is in the center, crossed with a known homozygous recessive plant having wrinkled seeds. The Punnett square *(left)* shows the expected genotypes and phenotypes if the test plant is heterozygous dominant. The Punnett square on the right shows the expected genotypes and phenotypes if the test plant is homozygous dominant.

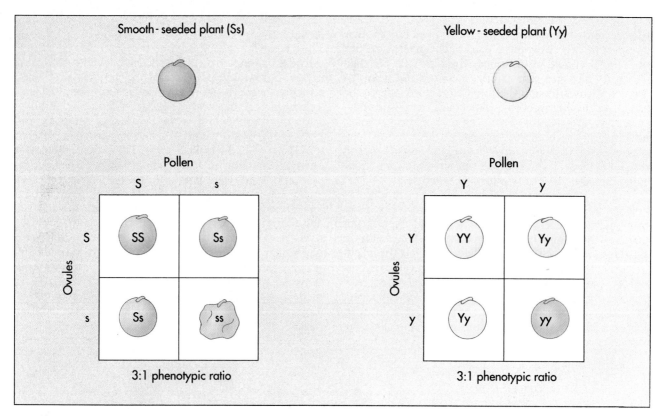

FIGURE 19-9   Mendel's law of independent assortment.
As this diagram demonstrates, the contrasting alleles for seed shape (S and s) and color
(Y and y) assort independently from one another during gamete formation.

independent assortment of alleles, you may not understand how two 3:1 ratios combine to produce a 9:3:3:1 ratio. These ratios and the relationship between these ratios are governed by the laws of **probability,** or chance. Each ratio is not simply a statement of the comparative numbers of plants Mendel found but is also a predictive statement of events that could occur in the future under the same conditions.

▼
▼
Mendel's second law of inheritance, the Law of Independent Assortment, states that the distribution of alleles for one trait into the gametes does not affect the distribution of alleles for other traits.

Analysis of a dihybrid cross using probability theory

Figure 19-9 shows the self-cross of hybrid F_1 plants having smooth seeds. The genotype of these plants is Ss. The male gametes S and s are shown along one side of the Punnett square, and the female gametes S and s are shown along the other. These four gametes can combine in four ways. What is the probability that this cross will produce a plant having wrinkled seeds? Because there are only four possible combinations of gametes and the alleles segregate randomly as the gametes are formed, there is only a one in four possibility that the ss gametes will combine. Likewise,

there is a three out of four probability that gametes can combine in such a way that they will produce plants having smooth seeds: SS, Ss, and sS. Although Ss and sS are the same genotypes, the reversed position of the alleles represents the dominant and recessive alleles as contributed by each of two parent plants. Hence the 3:1 phenotypic ratio. The alleles for the trait seed color, when looked at independently of seed shape, segregate in the same manner to produce plants having yellow seeds and plants having green seeds in a 3:1 ratio, respectively (see Figure 19-9).

To illustrate further, you can simulate the combination of the gametes S and s of two parents by performing a simple activity. Take two pennies and tape the letter "S" on one side of each and "s" on the other. Flip the two pennies 100 times and record your results. The probability of flipping an S on one of the pennies is one out of two, or 1/2. The chance of flipping an S on the other penny is also 1/2. The probability that an event will occur at the same time as another independent event is simply the product of their individual probabilities. Therefore the probability of flipping SS with the two pennies is $1/2 \times 1/2$, or 1/4. (Did you flip SS approximately 25 times out of 100?) Likewise, the probability of flipping ss is 1/4, flipping Ss is 1/4, and flipping sS is 1/4. (Do your data match?) If the pennies were in fact gametes, 3/4 would produce plants having smooth seeds and 1/4 would produce plants having wrinkled seeds—a 3:1 ratio.

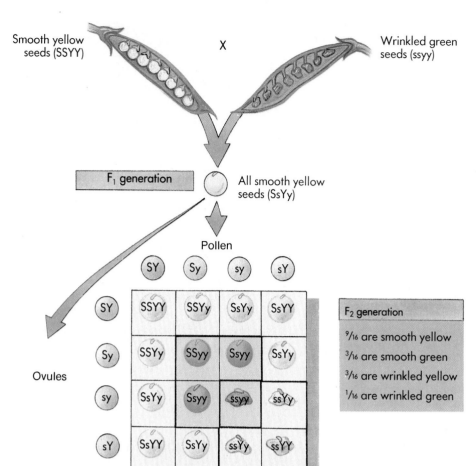

Smooth yellow seeds (SSYY)   X   Wrinkled green seeds (ssyy)

F₁ generation   All smooth yellow seeds (SsYy)

Pollen

Ovules

F₂ generation

9/16 are smooth yellow

3/16 are smooth green

3/16 are wrinkled yellow

1/16 are wrinkled green

FIGURE 19-10   A Punnett square showing the results of Mendel's self-cross of dihybrid smooth yellow-seeded plants. The approximate ratio of the four possible combinations of phenotypes is predicted to be 9:3:3:1, the ratio that Mendel found.

Now look at these traits as they occur together in a dihybrid cross. The probability that a plant with wrinkled, green seeds will appear in the F₂ generation is equal to the probability of observing a plant with wrinkled seeds (1/4) times the probability of observing a plant with green seeds (1/4), or 1/16. The probability that a plant with smooth, green seeds will appear in the F₂ is equal to the probability that the F₁ parents will produce a plant with smooth seeds (3/4) times the probability that they will produce a plant with green seeds (1/4), or 3/16. Can you figure out the probability that a plant with wrinkled, yellow seeds will appear in the F₂ or that a plant with smooth, yellow seeds will appear?

Analysis of a dihybrid cross using a Punnett square

Figure 19-10 shows the self-cross of hybrid F₁ plants having smooth seeds and yellow seeds, showing how the gametes segregate to produce the F₂ plants. The eight gametes of the two parents can combine in 16 different ways. What is the probability that this cross will produce a plant having wrinkled, green seeds? Because there are only 16 possible combinations of gametes and if you assume that the alleles segregate randomly and assort independently as the gametes are formed, there is only a 1 in 16 possibility that an sy egg will combine with an sy sperm (producing ssyy offspring). Likewise, there are only 3 combinations of gametes out of 16 possible combinations that will produce

plants having wrinkled, yellow seeds: ssYY, ssYy, and ssyY. Following the same reasoning and using the Punnett square, notice that there are 3 possible combinations of gametes that will form plants producing smooth, green seeds and 9 possible combinations of gametes that will form plants producing smooth, yellow seeds. So whether you calculate the expected offspring in a dihybrid cross by using a Punnett square or whether you do this analysis by using the probability theory, the ratio of the F₂ progeny is predicted to be 9:3:3:1.

The connection between Mendel's factors and chromosomes

During the years Mendel was experimenting with pea plants to determine the principles of heredity, other scientists were studying the structure of cells. Although Mendel published his theories of inheritance in 1866, few scientists read his work or understood its significance. In the late 1870s, scientists had described the process of nuclear division now known as mitosis and the process of nuclear reduction-division that occurs as gametes are formed now known as meiosis (see Chapter 17). In fact, in 1888, scientists gave the name *chromosomes* to the discrete, threadlike bodies that form as the nuclear material condenses during these processes of cell division. But they still had no idea of the link between Mendel's *factors* of inheritance and the newly named chromosomes—both important keys to unlocking the mysteries of heredity.

In 1900, three biologists, Carl Correns, Hugo de Vries, and Eric von Tschermak, independently worked out Mendel's principles of heredity. However, they knew nothing of Mendel's work until they searched the literature before publishing their results. The rediscovery of Mendel's work—his hypotheses supported by the independent work of others—helped scientists begin to make connections between Mendel's ideas and chromosomes.

By the late 1800s, scientists had observed the process of fertilization and knew that sexual reproduction required the union of an egg and a sperm. However, they did not know how each contributed to the development of a new individual. Many scientists hypothesized that the sperm merely stimulated the egg to develop. An American graduate student, Walter Sutton, suggested that if Mendel's hypotheses were correct, then each gamete must make equal hereditary contributions. Sutton also suggested that because sperm contain little cytoplasm, the hereditary material must reside within the nuclei of the gametes. He noted that chromosomes are in pairs and segregate during meiosis, as did Mendel's factors. In fact, the behavior of chromosomes during the meiotic process paralleled the behavior of the hereditary factors. Using this line of reasoning, Sutton suggested that Mendel's factors were located on the chromosomes. However, Sutton had no experimental evidence to support his hypothesis. Years later, various scientists worked on this problem, but the most conclusive evidence to uphold Sutton's chromosomal theory of inheritance was provided by a single, small fly.

Sex linkage

In 1910, Thomas Hunt Morgan, studying the fruit fly *Drosophila melanogaster,* detected a male fly that differed strikingly from normal flies of the same species. This fly had white eyes (Figure 19-11) instead of the normal red eyes. Morgan quickly designed experiments to determine if this new trait was inherited in a Mendelian fashion.

Morgan first crossed the white-eyed male fly to a normal female to see if red or white eyes were dominant. All F_1 progeny had red eyes, and Morgan therefore concluded that red eye color was dominant over white. Following the experimental procedure that Mendel had established long ago, Morgan then crossed flies from the F_1 generation with each other. Eye color did indeed segregate among the F_2 progeny as predicted by Mendel's theory. Of 4252 F_2 progeny that Morgan examined, 782 had white eyes—an imperfect 3:1 ratio but one that nevertheless provided clear evidence of segregation. Something was strange about Morgan's result, however—something totally unpredicted by Mendel's theory: all of the white-eyed F_2 flies were males!

How could this strange result be explained? The solution to this puzzle involves gender. In drosophila (as in most animals), the gender of the fly is determined by specific chromosomes called X and Y chromosomes. Female flies have four pairs of chromosomes, with one of those pairs being two X chromosomes. Male flies, on the other-

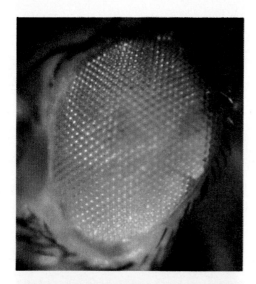

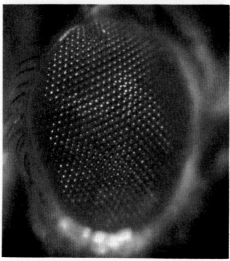

FIGURE 19-11 Red-eyed and white-eyed *Drosophila melanogaster*. The white-eyed defect in eye color is hereditary, the result of a mutation in a gene located on the sex-determining X chromosome. It was by studying this mutation that Morgan first demonstrated that genes are on chromosomes.

hand, have three pairs plus an X and a Y chromosome. To explain his results, Morgan deduced that the white-eyed trait is located on the X chromosome but is absent from the Y chromosome. (Scientists now know that the Y chromosome carries relatively few functional genes.) Because the white-eye trait is recessive to the red-eye trait, Morgan's result was a natural consequence of the Mendelian segregation of alleles (Figure 19-12). Morgan's experiment is one of the most important in the history of genetics because it presented the first clear evidence upholding Sutton's theory that the factors determining Mendelian traits are located on the chromosomes. When Mendel observed the segregation of alternative traits in pea plants, he was observing the out-

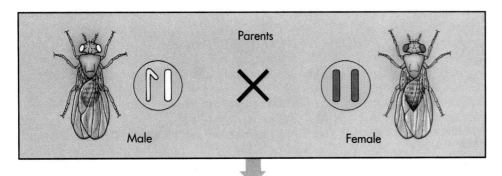

Parents

Male × Female

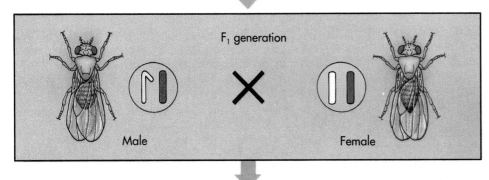

F₁ generation

Male × Female

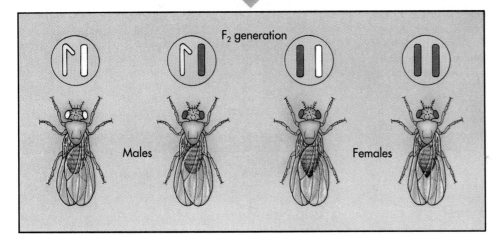

F₂ generation

Males Females

FIGURE 19-12 Morgan's experiment demonstrating the chromosomal basis of sex-linkage in *Drosophila melanogaster*. White-eyed mutant male flies were crossed with normal red-eyed females. The F₁ generation flies all exhibited red eyes. The male flies carried the normal red-eyed allele along with a Y chromosome that contains no allele for eye color, whereas the female flies carried one red-eyed allele and one white-eyed allele. Therefore in the F₂ generation, all female progeny were red eyed, being either homozygous or heterozygous for this dominant trait. The F₂ male flies, however, exhibited the trait inherited on their single X chromosome. Because half of them bear the white allele (the F₁ mother is heterozygous), half the male progeny will exhibit white eyes. This is exactly the result that Morgan observed: All of the white-eyed generation flies were male.

ward reflection of the meiotic segregation of homologous chromosomes.

From his observation of chromosomes during meiosis and his knowledge of Mendel's work, Walter Sutton hypothesized that the hereditary factors were on the chromosomes. Thomas Hunt Morgan provided experimental evidence to uphold this hypothesis, also revealing that certain traits may be located on the chromosomes that determine the gender of an organism. Such traits are said to be sex-linked.

Solving the mysteries of inheritance

Throughout human history, an understanding of the nature of heredity was highly speculative until the work of Mendel, Sutton, and Morgan. These early geneticists took the first real steps toward solving the puzzles of inheritance and laid the foundation for one of the great scientific advancements of the twentieth century: an understanding of the nature of genetic material and how it is transmitted from generation to generation. This basic outline of heredity led to a long chain of questions and was to be modified and refined as scientists provided additional experimental data and evidence. In one line of questioning described in Chapter 17, scientists such as Beadle and Tatum probed the structure and function of genes at the molecular level. Another line of questioning regards inheritance in humans and is the topic of Chapter 20.

Summary

1. Scientists and philosophers hypothesized about the nature of inheritance over many centuries. Some suggested that parents gave off particles from their bodies that traveled to their sex organs during reproduction. Many assumed that the male and female contribution blended in the offspring. Others held that either sperm or eggs carried tiny preformed beings within them. Not until the mid-1800s did scientists realize that new life arose from old life in the form of new cells arising from old cells.

2. In the mid-1800s, Gregor Mendel, an Austrian monk trained in botany and mathematics, studied patterns of inheritance using garden pea plants. Using true-breeding varieties of pea plants that exhibited alternative forms of seven different traits, Mendel artificially cross-fertilized them. The purpose of his experiments was to observe the offspring from the crossing of each pair of plants and to look for patterns in the transmission of traits.

3. Mendel found that alternative traits segregate in crosses and may mask each other's presence. From counting progeny types, Mendel learned that the alternatives that were masked in hybrids appeared only 25% of the time when the hybrids were self-crossed. This finding, which led directly to Mendel's model of heredity, is usually referred to as the Mendelian ratio of 3:1 dominant to recessive traits.

4. Mendel deduced from the 3:1 ratio that traits are specified by discrete factors that do not blend in the offspring. Today, scientists refer to Mendel's factors as genes and to alternative forms of his factors as alleles.

5. Because Mendel observed that traits did not blend in the offspring and because the results he obtained from experiments on various traits showed similar results, Mendel hypothesized that alleles separate from one another during gamete formation. This concept is called *Mendel's Law of Segregation*.

6. Working with pea plants that differed from one another in two characteristics, Mendel discovered that alleles of different genes assort independently during gamete formation. This concept is referred to as *Mendel's Law of Independent Assortment*.

7. The first clear evidence that genes reside on chromosomes was provided by Thomas Hunt Morgan. Morgan demonstrated that the segregation of the white-eye trait in *Drosophila melanogaster* was associated with the segregation of the X chromosome, the one responsible for sex determination.

REVIEW QUESTIONS

1. How do offspring of sexual reproduction differ from those produced by asexual reproduction? Compare the amount of variation introduced within a species that reproduces sexually with a species that reproduces asexually.

2. Distinguish between self-fertilization and cross-fertilization.

3. If you are told that an individual is heterozygous for a particular trait (brown eyes, for example), what information do you know? Will one of the alleles be dominant over the other in all cases?

4. What is Mendel's Law of Segregation? When does this segregation occur?

5. Was Mendel, in your opinion, able to successfully assess the phenotype of his plant crosses? Was he able to assess genotype with complete accuracy? What may affect the assessment of a genotype?

6. Assume that "L" represents the dominant trait of having long leaves, and "l" represents the recessive short-leaved trait in a plant. In the parental generation, you cross a homozygous long-leaved plant with a homozygous short-leaved plant. Draw a Punnett square illustrating this cross, and give the genotypes and phenotypes of the F_1 generation.

7. Using a Punnett square, show the genotypes and phenotypes of the F_2 generation if the F_1 plants in question 6 are self-fertilized.

8. What was Mendel testing when he used a testcross? What procedure did he use, and what was the outcome?

9. What is Mendel's Law of Independent Assortment?

10. In question 7, what is the probability that the F_2 plants will have short leaves?

11. In a dihybrid cross between organisms that are heterozygous for both traits, what is the probability that their offspring will exhibit the phenotype for (a) both recessive traits? (b) both dominant traits?

12. How did the work of Walter Sutton and Thomas Hunt Morgan change the way scientists viewed the role of sperm in heredity and reproduction?

1. Can you think of a distinctive human trait that is *not* inherited? How would you test this hypothesis?

2. In small groups, gather and discuss data concerning dominant and recessive traits that you have traced in your own family. Some areas may include eye color, hair color, color blindness, diseases such as diabetes or high blood pressure, height, etc. Are there traits that you theorize may be genetically transferred although science has not strictly determined the origin? (For example, there is evidence, although little proof, that the tendency toward alcoholism or schizophrenia may be familial.)

Blixt, S. (1975). Why didn't Gregor Mendel find linkage? *Nature, 256,* 206.
This is an interesting examination of the pea strains first studied by Mendel.

Diamond, J. (1991, March). Curse and blessing of the ghetto. *Discover,* pp. 60-65.
A balanced look at Tay-Sachs disease, a fatal genetic disorder that occurs primarily among people of Jewish Eastern European ancestry.

Grady, D. (1993, January). Gay genes. *Discover,* pp. 55-56.
A short look at the possibility of an X chromosome-linked gene that may encode for homosexuality.

Morgan, T.H. (1910). Sex-limited inheritance in *Drosophila. Science, 32,* 120-122.
This article describes Morgan's original account of his famous analysis of the inheritance of the white-eye trait.

Sutton, W.S. (1903). The chromosomes of heredity. *Biological Bulletin, 4,* 213-251.
This is the original statement of the chromosomal theory of heredity.

1. Among Hereford cattle there is a dominant allele called *polled;* the individuals that have this allele lack horns. After college, you become a cattle baron and stock your spread entirely with polled cattle. You have many cows and few bulls. You personally make sure that each cow has no horns. Among the calves that year, however, some grow horns. Angrily you dispose of them and make certain that no horned adult has gotten into your pasture. The next year, however, more horned calves are born. What is the source of your problem? What should you do to rectify it?

2. Many animals and plants bear recessive alleles for albinism, a condition in which homozygous individuals completely lack any pigments. An albino plant lacks chlorophyll and is white. An albino person lacks any melanin pigment. If two normally pigmented persons heterozygous for the same albinism allele have children, what proportion of their children would be expected to be albino?

3. Your uncle dies and leaves you his race horse, Dingleberry. To obtain some money from your inheritance, you decide to put the horse out to stud. In looking over the stud book, however, you discover that Dingleberry's grandfather exhibited a rare clinical disorder that leads to brittle bones. The disorder is hereditary and results from homozygosity for a recessive allele. If Dingleberry is heterozygous for the allele, it will not be possible to use him for stud because the genetic defect may be passed on. How would you go about determining whether Dingleberry carries this allele?

4. In *Drosophila,* the allele for dumpy wings (d) is recessive to the normal long-wing allele (D). The allele for white eye (w) is recessive to the normal red-eye allele (W). In a cross of DDWw × Ddww, what proportion of the offspring are expected to be "normal" (long wing, red eye)? What proportion "dumpy, white"?

5. Your instructor presents you with a drosophila named Oscar. Oscar has red eyes, the same color that normal flies possess. You add Oscar to your fly collection, which also contains Heidi and Siegfried, flies with white eyes, and Dominique and Ronald, which are from a long line of red-eyed flies. Your previous work has shown that the white-eyed trait exhibited by Heidi and Siegfried is caused by their being homozygous for a recessive allele. How would you determine whether Oscar was heterozygous for this allele?

6. In some families, children are born who exhibit recessive traits (and therefore must be homozygous for the recessive allele specifying the trait), even though one or both of the parents do not exhibit the trait. What can account for this occurrence?

20 Human Genetics

HIGHLIGHTS

- Genetic disorders can occur when a person inherits a fewer or greater number of chromosomes than is normal, chromosomes with pieces that have been added or removed, or chromosomes having changes in the molecular structure of their DNA.

- Geneticists use pictures of chromosomes arranged in pairs according to size, and pedigrees, diagrams of genetic relationships among family members over several generations, to study the inheritance of genetic disorders.

- Inherited traits do not always exhibit clear-cut dominance and recessiveness; certain traits exhibit incomplete dominance or codominance or may be coded by multiple alleles.

- Although most genetic disorders cannot yet be cured, research scientists are making continual progress in developing gene therapies that may, in the future, have a drastic impact on a physician's ability to treat genetic disorders before birth.

About 100 years ago, this is what family photos looked like. But this family is not just any family—it is a royal family. Queen Victoria of England, matriarch of this family, is sitting in the center and is wearing a crown. Queen Victoria affected many of her descendants because of a single allele—a mutant, or changed gene, which coded for a disorder known as *hemophilia.*

Hemophilia is a hereditary condition in which the blood clots slowly or not at all. It is a recessive disorder, expressed only when an individual does not have a normal blood-clotting allele that masks the mutant's appearance. In addition to being recessive, the allele for this type of hemophilia is sex-linked: it is located on the X chromosome, one of the chromosomes that determines gender. This mutant gene probably arose in one of the sex cells from which Queen Victoria developed because the disease was not manifested in earlier generations.

Genetically normal females have two X chromosomes; normal males have one X and one Y chromosome. A male who inherits an X chromosome with a mutant clotting allele will develop hemophilia because his Y chromosome does not have a corresponding allele to mask the allele on the X chromosome. A woman who inherits a mutant allele on one X chromosome and a normal allele on the other will not have the disorder but can pass the mutant allele along to her offspring. Such women are called *carriers.* Of Queen Victoria's four daughters who lived to bear children, two daughters—Alice and Beatrice—were carriers of hemophilia. Two of Alice's daughters, Princess Irene of Prussia and Czarina Alexandra of Russia, were also carriers of hemophilia.

Studying inheritance patterns in humans using karyotypes

In addition to a pair of **sex chromosomes,** each human body cell also contains 22 pairs of **autosomes.** Unlike sex chromosomes, autosomes (or "body" chromosomes) are the same in both sexes. The 23 pairs of human chromosomes are shown in Figure 20-1. Arranged in this manner according to size, shape, and other characteristics, the chromosome pairs make up a **karyotype.**

Looking at a karyotype can often help researchers see genetic disorders if they are caused by the loss of all or part of a chromosome or by the addition of extra chromosomes

or chromosome fragments. Changes in single genes *cannot* be seen. The differences between alleles that code for alternate forms of a trait lie in the chemical structure of the DNA, so they are invisible in a karyotype. Permanent changes in the genetic material, whether they affect single genes, pieces of chromosomes, whole chromosomes, or entire sets of chromosomes, are called **mutations.**

Each human cell contains 23 pairs of chromosomes. A karyotype is a picture of these chromosome pairs and shows whether a person has inherited a fewer or greater number of chromosomes than is normal or has lost or gained pieces of chromosomes.

The inheritance of abnormal numbers of autosomes

Look at the karyotype in Figure 20-2, *A* and compare it with that in Figure 20-1. What differences do you see? Carefully examine chromosome 21. One karyotype contains an extra copy of this chromosome, a situation called *trisomy 21*. The developmental defect produced by trisomy 21 was first described in 1866 by J. Langdon Down. For this reason, it is called **Down syndrome.** In these individuals the maturation of the skeletal system is delayed, so persons having Down syndrome are generally short and have poor muscle tone. In addition, they are mentally retarded.

Down syndrome is only one genetic disorder caused by the inheritance of an abnormal number of autosomal or sex chromosomes. How does such a situation arise? In humans, it comes about almost exclusively as a result of errors during the process of meiosis. Meiosis is the process of nuclear division in which the number of chromosomes in cells is halved during gamete formation (see Chapter 17).

Early in meiosis, pairs of chromosomes called *homologues* (the pairs of chromosomes shown in the karyotype) line up side by side in a process called *synapsis*. Because, at

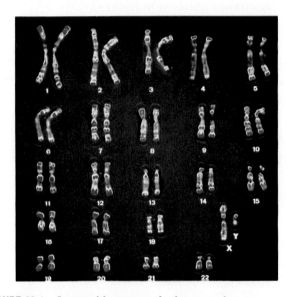

FIGURE 20-1   A normal karyotype of a human male.
Humans have 23 pairs of chromosomes, including the two sex chromosomes. Notice the small Y chromosome in pair 23 that is characteristic of males.

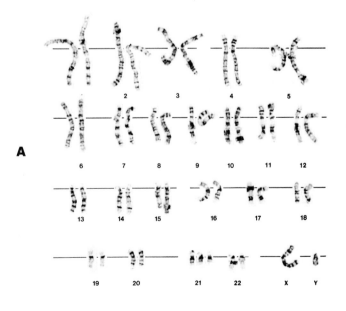

FIGURE 20-2   Down syndrome.
A As shown in this karyotype of a male, Down syndrome is usually associated with trisomy of chromosome 21.
B Down syndrome child sitting on his father's knee.

this time, each chromosome is made up of two sister chromatids, the paired homologous chromosomes together have four chromatids. Gametes can gain or lose chromosomes at this point in the meiotic process if two homologous chromosomes fail to separate, or disjoin. If **nondisjunction** occurs, two of the resulting gametes carry a double of the chromosome; the other two gametes lack the chromosome entirely. Nondisjunction can occur later in the meiotic process as well, when two sister chromatids fail to separate (Figure 20-3).

The cause of nondisjunction is not known. However, the occurrence of nondisjunction of chromosome 21, which results in Down syndrome, increases as a woman's age increases (Figure 20-4). In mothers less than 20 years of age, the occurrence of Down syndrome children is only about 1 per 1700 births. In mothers 20 to 30 years old, the incidence is only slightly greater—about 1 per 1400. However, in mothers 30 to 35 years old, the incidence almost doubles to 1 per 750. And in mothers over 45, the incidence of Down syndrome babies is as high as 1 in 16 births.

During gamete formation, homologous chromosomes occasionally fail to separate after synapsis. This occurrence, called nondisjunction, results in gametes with abnormal numbers of chromosomes. Down syndrome is a genetic disorder produced when an individual receives three (instead of two) 21 chromosomes.

The incidence of nondisjunction of other chromosomes also rises as a woman's age rises. Babies with other serious autosomal chromosome abnormalities are rare. Fertilized eggs with the improper number of chromosomes are almost always inviable; that is, they are unable to survive. These eggs do not begin normal development and implantation but are cast out of the body with the menstrual flow—a process called *spontaneous abortion*. This increase in the incidence of nondisjunction and its negative impact on the viability of zygotes is one reason older women often have a harder time conceiving than younger women.

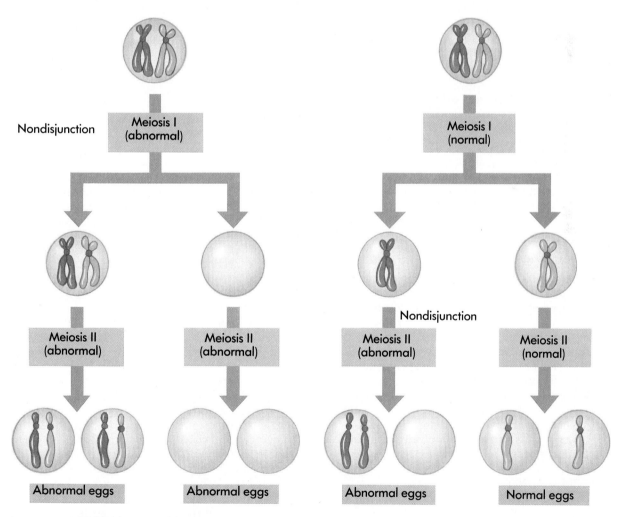

FIGURE 20-3 Nondisjunction.
Nondisjunction results from an error in meiosis in which homologous chromosomes fail to separate during meiosis I. Nondisjunction can also occur during meiosis II when two sister chromatids fail to separate.

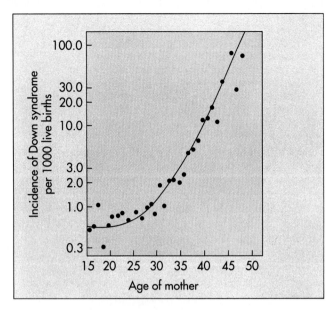

FIGURE 20-4 Incidence of Down syndrome vs. maternal age.
The occurrence of this nondisjunction increases sharply as a woman grows older, thus the Y axis uses an exponential scale. The 10-fold increase from 1 to 10 is graphed using the same scale as the 10-fold increase from 10 to 100.

The inheritance of abnormal numbers of sex chromosomes

Nondisjunction can also occur with the sex chromosomes. However, persons inheriting an extra X chromosome or inheriting one X too few do not have the severe developmental abnormalities that persons with too many or too few autosomes do. However, persons who inherit abnormal numbers of sex chromosomes often have abnormal physical features.

Triple X females

When X chromosomes fail to separate in meiosis, some gametes are produced that possess both of the X chromosomes; the other gametes have no sex chromosome and are designated O. If an XX gamete joins an X gamete during fertilization, the result is an XXX (triple X) zygote. Even though, triple X females usually have underdeveloped breasts and genital organs, they can often bear children. In addition, a small number of XXX people have lower-than-average intelligence. Although rare, a few individuals have been discovered to have tetra X (XXXX) and penta X (XXXXX) genotypes. Individuals having these genotypes are similar phenotypically to triple X individuals but are usually mentally retarded.

Klinefelter syndrome

If the XX gamete joins a Y gamete, the result is quite serious. The XXY zygote develops into a sterile male who has, in addition to male genitalia and characteristics, some female characteristics, such as breasts (Figure 20-5) and a high-pitched voice. In some cases, XXY individuals have lower-than-average intelligence. This condition, called

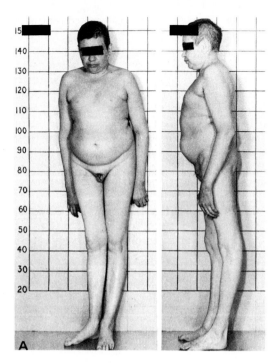

FIGURE 20-5 Klinefelter syndrome.
A male with Klinefelter syndrome (XXY) exhibits some female characteristics, such as enlarged breasts and a high-pitched voice.

Klinefelter syndrome, occurs in about 1 out of every 600 male births.

Turner syndrome

If an O gamete (no X) from the mother fuses with a Y gamete, the resulting OY zygote is nonviable and fails to develop further. If, on the other hand, an O gamete from either the mother or the father fuses with an X gamete to form an XO zygote, the result is a sterile female of short stature, a "webbed" neck, low-set ears, a broad chest, and immature sex organs that do not undergo puberty changes (Figure 20-6). The mental abilities of an XO individual are slightly below normal. This condition, called **Turner syndrome,** occurs roughly once in every 3000 female births. The ways in which nondisjunction can result in abnormal numbers of sex chromosomes are shown in Figure 20-7.

XYY males

The Y chromosome occasionally fails to separate from its sister chromatid in meiosis II (see Chapter 17). Failure of the Y chromosome to separate leads to the formation of YY gametes and viable XYY zygotes that develop into males who are unusually tall but have normal fertility. The frequency of XYY among newborn males is about 1 per 1000. The XYY syndrome has some interesting history associated with it. In the 1960s, the frequency of XYY males in penal and mental institutions was reported to be approximately 2% (that is, 20 per 1000)—20 times higher than in the general population. This observation led to the suggestion that XYY males are inherently antisocial and violent. Further studies revealed that XYY males have a higher probability

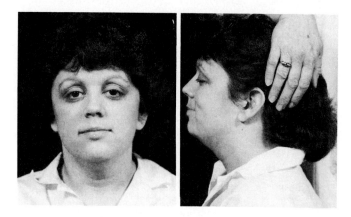

FIGURE 20-6   Turner syndrome.
A female with Turner syndrome (XO) exhibits short stature, webbed neck, low-set ears, broad chest, and immature sex organs.

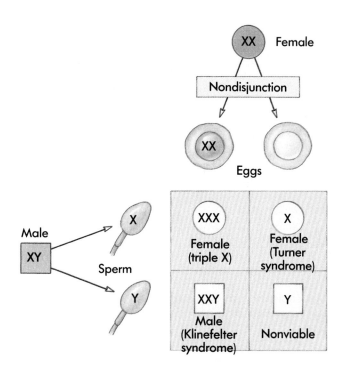

FIGURE 20-7   How nondisjunction can result in abnormalities in the number of sex chromosomes.
Both Klinefelter syndrome and Turner syndrome result from nondisjunction of either the male or female gamete. This diagram shows how these genetic disorders occur when nondisjunction takes place in female gametes. It also shows how nondisjunction in female gametes can result in a triple X female.

of coming into conflict with the law than XY (normal) males, but their crimes are usually nonviolent. Most XYY males, however, lead normal lives and cannot be distinguished from other males.

> Persons inheriting abnormal numbers of sex chromosomes often have abnormal features and may be mentally retarded. Zygotes without an X chromosome are not viable.

Changes in chromosome structure

Although a person may have inherited the proper number of chromosomes, a chromosome that is structurally defective may occur if a chromosome breaks and the cell repairs the break incorrectly or does not repair the break at all. These broken and misrepaired chromosomes can then be passed on in the gametes of the parents to produce disorders in the offspring.

Chromosomes may break naturally or may be caused by outside agents, such as ionizing radiation and chemicals. **Ionizing radiation,** such as x-rays and nuclear radiation, is a form of energy known as *electromagnetic energy*. Sunlight is also a type of electromagnetic energy. Ionizing radiation, however, has a higher level of energy than ordinary light does. When ionizing radiation reaches a cell, it transfers energy to electrons in the outer shells of the atoms it encounters, raising them to a still higher energy level and ejecting them from their orbitals. The result is the breaking of covalent bonds and the formation of charged fragments of molecules with unpaired electrons. The charged molecular fragments, or **free radicals,** are highly reactive. They may interact with DNA, producing chromosomal breaks or changes in the nucleotide structure.

When chromosomes break and are improperly repaired by the cell, some chromosomal information may be added, lost, or moved from one location on the chromosome to another. Chromosomal rearrangement changes the way that the genetic message is organized, interpreted, and expressed. Newly added chromosomal information can be caused by a **duplication** of a section of a chromosome. Seen in a karyotype, a chromosome having a duplication appears longer than its homologue. A **translocation** could also produce an abnormally long chromosome. In this situation, a section of a chromosome breaks off and then reattaches to another chromosome. The chromosome losing a section would then appear shorter because of this **deletion** of information. As gametes form, the progeny could receive one or both of these defective chromosomes. If a chromosomal **inversion** occurs, the broken piece of chromosome reattaches to the same chromosome but in a reversed direction (Figure 20-8).

A well-known disorder associated with a chromosomal deletion in humans is the **cri du chat syndrome.** Described in 1963 by a French geneticist, cri du chat means "cat cry" and describes the cat-like cry made by cri du chat babies. Other symptoms of this disorder include severe mental retardation and a round "moon face." (Table 20-1 summarizes the chromosomal aberrations discussed.)

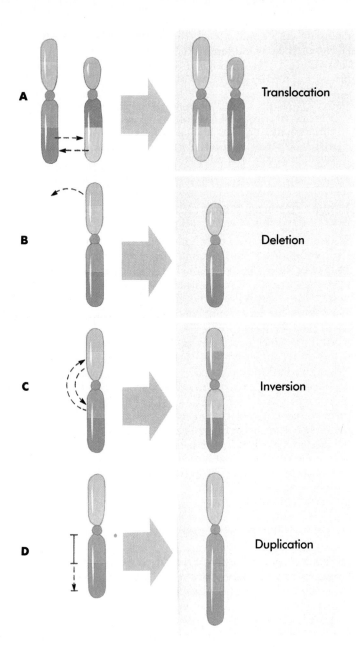

TABLE 20-1	Summary of chromosomal aberrations	
CONDITION	**CHARACTERISTICS**	**ABERRATION**
Trisomy 13	Multiple defects, including severe mental retardation and deafness Death before 6 months of age for 90% of those who survive birth	3 13 auto-somes
Trisomy 18	Facial deformities Heart defects Death before 1 year of age for 90% of those who survive birth	3 18 auto-somes
Down syndrome (trisomy 21)	Developmental delay of skeletal system Mental retardation	3 21 auto-somes
Trisomy 22	Similar features to Down syndrome More severe skeletal deformities	3 22 auto-somes
Cri du chat	Moon face Severe mental retardation	Deletion on 5
Triple X female	Underdeveloped female characteristics	XXX XXXX XXXXX
Turner syndrome	Sterile female Webbed neck Broad chest	XO
Klinefelter syndrome	Sterile male Male and female characteristics	XXY
XYY male	Fertile male Usually quite tall	XYY

FIGURE 20-8 Types of chromosomal rearrangement.
A Translocation occurs when a section of a chromosome breaks off and attaches to another chromosome.
B A deletion occurs when a chromosome loses a section.
C Inversion occurs when a broken piece of a chromosome reattaches to the same chromosome but in a reversed direction.
D A duplication occurs when chromosomal information is duplicated within the chromosome.

Gene mutations

Sometimes changes take place in a single allele rather than entire sections of chromosomes. A change in the genetic message of a chromosome caused by alterations of molecules within the structure of the chromosomal DNA is called a **point mutation** or **gene mutation.** Through mutation, a new allele of a gene is produced. Mutations may occur spontaneously (although their occurrence is rare) or may be caused by ionizing radiation, UV radiation, or chemicals.

Ultraviolet (UV) radiation, the component of sunlight that leads to suntan (and sunburn), is much lower in energy than x-rays but still higher in energy than ordinary light. Certain molecules within the structure of chromosomes absorb UV radiation, developing chemical bonds among them that are not normally present. These unusual bonds produce a kink in the molecular structure of the DNA of chromosomes. Normally, a chromosome is able to repair itself by removing the affected molecules and synthesizing new, undamaged molecules. Sometimes, however, mistakes can take place in some part of the repair process and a change may occur in a gene.

Sometimes chemicals damage DNA directly. LSD (the hallucinogenic compound lysergide), marijuana (leaves of

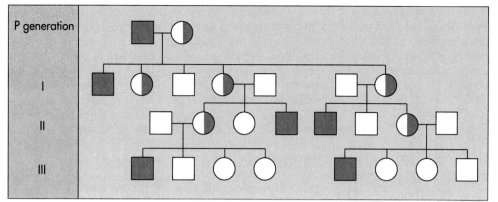

P generation

I

II

III

FIGURE 20-9 A pedigree showing red-green color blindness. *Squares* indicate males, *circles* indicate females. From this pedigree, it can be determined that the carriers of the color blindness gene are the female in the P generation, the three females in generation I, and the first and third females in generation II. The status of the other females is unknown.

the *Cannabis sativa* plant), cyclamates (compounds widely used as nonnutritive sugar substitutes), and certain pesticides (compounds used to kill insects on crops and other plants) are a few examples of chemicals known to damage DNA. In general, chemicals alter the molecular structure of nucleotides resulting in a mispairing of bases. As with UV radiation, mistakes can take place as the cell works to repair the DNA and changes may then occur in a gene.

> Three major sources of environmental damage to chromosomes are (1) high-energy radiation, such as x-rays; (2) low-energy radiation, such as UV light; and (3) chemicals, such as LSD, marijuana, cyclamates, and certain pesticides.

Studying inheritance patterns in humans using pedigrees

Karyotypes are useful in studying diseases or disorders caused by an abnormal number of chromosomes or the addition or deletion of chromosome pieces. However, most inherited disorders, such as the type of hemophilia discussed in the chapter opener, are caused by point mutations, which cannot be seen in a karyotype.

To study how this and other human traits are inherited, scientists study family histories—the records of relevant genetic features—to draw pedigrees. **Pedigrees** are diagrams of genetic relationships among family members over several generations. By studying which relatives exhibit a trait, it is often possible to say if the gene producing the trait is sex-linked (occurs on one of the sex-determining chromosomes) or autosomal (occurs on a non-sex-determining chromosome). Pedigree analysis also helps a geneticist determine whether the trait is a dominant or a recessive characteristic. In many cases, it is also possible to infer which individuals are homozygous or heterozygous for the allele carrying the trait.

Figure 20-9 is a pedigree that shows the history of red-green color blindness in a family. The circles in the diagram represent females, and the squares represent males. Solid-colored symbols stand for individuals that exhibit the trait being studied. In this case, those individuals would be color

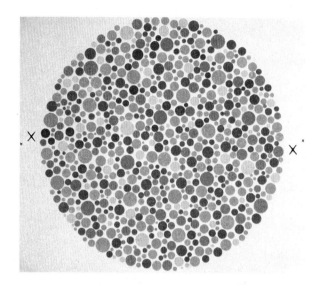

FIGURE 20-10 A test for red-green color blindness.
About 8% of Caucasian males and 0.5% of Caucasian females have some loss of color vision, which is almost always caused by an X-linked recessive allele. This recessive allele causes a defect in one of three groups of color-sensitive cells in the eye. The most common form of color blindness is dichromatic vision, in which affected individuals cannot distinguish red from green or yellow from blue. The pattern tests for an inability to distinguish red from green. Those with normal vision will see a path of green dots between the points marked X. Those with red-green color blindness will not be able to distinguish the green dots from red and so will not see the green path.

blind (Figure 20-10). Parents are represented by horizontal lines connecting a circle and a square. Vertical lines coming from two parents indicate their children, arranged along a horizontal line in order of their birth.

First, to determine whether a trait is sex-linked or autosomal, notice whether the trait is expressed more frequently in males than in females. If so, the trait is most likely a sex-linked trait. In addition, the trait would then likely be recessive because few dominant sex-linked traits are known. An autosomal trait (whether dominant or recessive) is expressed equally in both males and females. A sex-linked trait, however, is always expressed in a male, because the relatively inert Y chromosome lacks alleles that correspond to alleles on the X chromosome; one deleterious gene on a male's X chromosome results in its phenotypic expression. Is red-green color blindness a sex-linked trait?

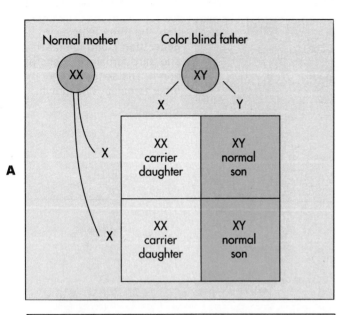

A

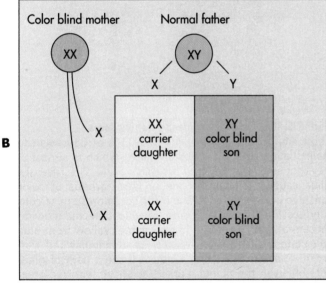

B

FIGURE 20-11 Punnett squares depicting the outcomes for the sex-linked disorder color blindness.
A shows a Punnett square for a normal mother and color-blind father. **B** shows a Punnett square for a color-blind mother and normal father.

Second, to determine whether a trait is dominant or recessive, notice whether each person expressing the trait has a parent who expressed the trait. In this case, if color blindness is dominant to normal color vision, then each color-blind person will have a color-blind parent. However, if the trait is recessive, a person expressing the trait can have parents who do not express the trait. Both parents may be heterozygous (may carry the trait). If each parent passes on the recessive gene to a child, the child is then homozygous recessive and the trait will be expressed. Is color blindness a dominant or a recessive characteristic?

Next, determine which individuals are carriers of the color blindness gene. By now you probably realize that color blindness is a sex-linked recessive trait. A color-blind male always contributes an X chromosome with the defective allele to his daughters; it is the only X he can contribute. His sons, however, get a Y chromosome from him and an unaffected X chromosome from their (normal) mother. A color-blind female can only contribute a chromosome with the defective allele to her children because both her X chromosomes are affected. Women who are carriers of the trait, however, may contribute either a normal or a defective X. The Punnett square in Figure 20-11 illustrates the contributions of genes by a normal mother and a color-blind father (20-11, *A*) and a color-blind mother and normal father (20-11, *B*). Can you determine which individuals are carriers of color blindness in the pedigree?

> **Pedigrees, diagrams of genetic relationships among families over several generations, are useful in determining whether traits are sex-linked or autosomal and dominant or recessive. Carriers of recessive genes can also be identified.**

Queen Victoria's family pedigree is shown in Figure 20-12. Persons carrying a mutant allele but not having the disorder are shown by partially colored symbols. Using the strategy outlined above, analyze the pedigree to determine whether hemophilia is sex-linked or autosomal and whether it is a dominant or recessive trait. Look back to the chapter opener to confirm your results.

As shown in the royal pedigree, in the six generations since Queen Victoria, 10 of her male descendants have had hemophilia. The British royal family escaped the disorder because Queen Victoria's son King Edward VII did not inherit the defective allele. Three of Victoria's nine children did receive the defective allele, however, and carried it by marriage into many of the royal families of Europe. It is still being transmitted to future generations among these family lines, except in Russia, where the five children of Alexandra, Victoria's granddaughter, were killed soon after the Russian revolution (Figure 20-13).

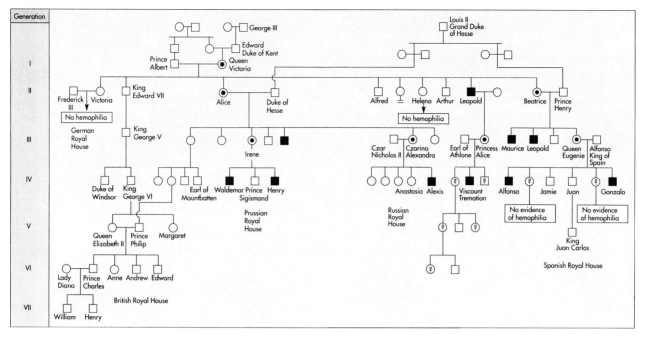

FIGURE 20-12 The royal hemophilia pedigree.
From Queen Victoria's daughter, Alice, the disorder was introduced into the Prussian and Russian royal houses, and from her daughter Beatrice, it was introduced into the Spanish royal house. Victoria's son Leopold, himself a victim, also transmitted the disorder in a third line of descent.

FIGURE 20-13 The last Russian royal family.
Shown here are Czar Nicholas II of Russia, the last Russian czar, and his wife Alexandra, with their five children: Olga, Tatiana, Maria, Anastasia, and Alexis. Alexandra, Queen Victoria's granddaughter, was a carrier of hemophilia and passed it on to her son Alexis. Because the kind of hemophilia they had is caused by a recessive mutant allele located on the X chromosome, it is not expressed in the heterozygous condition in women because women have two X chromosomes. It is not known which of Alexandra's four daughters might have received the hemophilia allele from her; none of the four daughters lived to bear children.

Dominant and recessive genetic disorders

Most genetic disorders are recessive; these mutant genes are able to persist in the population among carriers. Unfortunately, persons receiving a mutant allele from each of their parents are affected with the disease and, in the case of some diseases, may die before reaching adulthood. Likewise, persons having certain dominant disorders may die before reaching reproductive age, so lethal dominant disorders are less likely to persist in the population.

Huntington's disease, the disorder that killed folksinger and songwriter Woody Guthrie, is caused by a mutant dominant allele that does not show up until individuals are more than 30 years old—after they may have had children. This disorder causes progressive deterioration of brain cells. Other dominant genetic disorders include the following:

- **Marfan's syndrome,** which results in skeletal, eye, and cardiovascular defects
- **Polydactyly,** which results in extra fingers or toes
- **Achondroplasia,** which results in a form of dwarfism
- **Hypercholesterolemia,** which results in high blood cholesterol levels and a higher likelihood of developing coronary artery disease

Recessive genetic disorders are often seen primarily within specific populations or races of people unless many members of the population marry and have children outside of their population or race. Among the Caucasian population, for example, the most common fatal genetic disorder is **cystic fibrosis.** Affected individuals secrete a thick mucus that clogs the airways of their lungs and the passages of their pancreas and liver. Among Caucasians, about 1 in 20 individuals has a copy of the defective gene but shows no symptoms. Approximately 1 in 1800 has two copies of the gene and therefore has the disease. These individuals inevitably die from complications that result from their disease. It was learned only recently that the cause of cystic fibrosis is a defect in the way cells regulate the transport of chloride ions across their membranes.

Sickle-cell anemia is a recessive disorder most common among African blacks and their descendants. In the United States, for example, about 9% of African Americans are heterozygous for this allele; about 0.2% are homozygous and therefore have sickle-cell anemia. In some groups of people in Africa, up to 45% of the individuals are heterozygous for this allele. Heterozygous carriers of the sickle-cell gene do not have the disease but can pass the gene along to their children.

Individuals afflicted with sickle-cell anemia are unable to transport oxygen to their tissues properly because the molecules within red blood cells that carry oxygen—molecules of the protein hemoglobin—are defective. Red blood cells that contain large proportions of such defective molecules become sickle shaped and stiff; normal red blood cells are disk shaped and much more flexible (Figure 20-14). As a result of their stiffness and irregular shape, the sickle-shaped red blood cells are unable to move easily through capillaries. Therefore they tend to accumulate in blood vessels, reducing the blood supply to the organs they serve, causing pain, tissue destruction, and an early death.

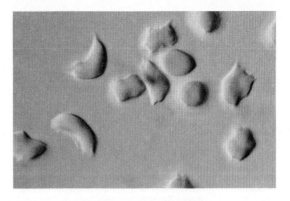

FIGURE 20-14 Sickle-shaped red blood cells.
In individuals who are homozygous for the recessive sickle cell trait, many of their red blood cells are sickle shaped and stiff. These irregularities are caused by defective hemoglobin molecules within the red blood cells. Because of their irregular shape, sickle-shaped red blood cells are unable to move easily through capillaries and become lodged in these blood vessels.

Interestingly, the gene for sickle-cell anemia is most prevalent in the regions of Africa where malaria is prevalent. Malaria is a disease caused by microorganisms that live in a person's red blood cells. These microbes are injected into a person's bloodstream by the bite of a female *Anopheles* mosquito. A long-lasting disease, malaria affects the physical and mental development of its victims, causing damage to many body organs. Scientists have discovered that the defective hemoglobin molecules of the person with sickle-cell anemia produce conditions that are unfavorable to the growth of the malaria organism. However, these persons eventually die from their anemia. But persons heterozygous for the sickle-cell gene, although not afflicted with the disease, are more resistant to malaria. Heterozygotes, then, have a survival advantage with respect to malaria and sickle-cell anemia (although their offspring may be afflicted with sickle-cell anemia if they reproduce with persons also carrying the defective gene).

> **Most genetic disorders are recessive because mutant genes are able to persist in the population among carriers. Some more common recessive genetic disorders among humans are color blindness, hemophilia, cystic fibrosis, and sickle-cell anemia.**

Tay-Sachs disease is an incurable, fatal recessive hereditary disorder. Although rare in most human populations, Tay-Sachs has a high incidence among Jews of Eastern and Central Europe and among American Jews (90% of whom are descendants of Eastern and Central European ancestors). In fact, geneticists estimate that 1 in 28 individuals in these Jewish populations carries the allele for this disease, and that approximately 1 in 3600 infants within this population is born with this genetic disorder. Affected children appear normal at birth but begin to show signs of mental deterioration at about 8 months of age. As the brain be-

TABLE 20-2	Dominant and recessive disorders

NAME	CHARACTERISTICS
DOMINANT DISORDERS	
Huntington's disease	Progressive deterioration of brain cells
Marfan's syndrome	Skeletal, eye, and cardiovascular defects
Polydactyly	Extra fingers or toes
Achondroplasia	Dwarfism
Hypercholesterolemia	High blood cholesterol levels
RECESSIVE DISORDERS	
Cystic fibrosis	Production of thick mucus that clogs airways
Sickle-cell anemia	Defective hemoglobin in red blood cells, effect on oxygen transport
	Misshapen red blood cells, tendency to form clots in vessels
Tay-Sachs disease	Brain deterioration beginning at 8 months of age
SEX-LINKED RECESSIVE DISORDERS	
Color-blindness	Inability to discern certain colors
Hemophilia	Improper clotting of blood
Albinism	Lack of pigment in skin, hair, and eyes
Duchenne muscular dystrophy	Degeneration of muscle
Fragile X syndrome	Easy breakage of tip of X chromosome
	Long face, squared forehead, large ears
	Mental retardation

TABLE 20-3	Common dominant and recessive human traits

DOMINANT TRAITS
Widow's peak
Hair on middle segment of fingers
Short fingers
Inability to straighten little finger
Brown eyes
A or B blood factor

RECESSIVE TRAITS
Common baldness
Blue or gray eyes
O blood factor
Attached ear lobes

gins to deteriorate, affected children become blind; they usually die by the age of 5 years.

Table 20-2 summarizes the dominant and recessive disorders discussed. Many common human traits are also coded by either dominant or recessive genes. Table 20-3 lists some of these characteristics.

Incomplete dominance and codominance

Alleles do not always exhibit clear-cut dominance or recessiveness. The pea plants that Gregor Mendel worked with exhibited complete dominance, and for this reason his work disputed the concept of blended inheritance (see Chapter 19). However, since Mendel's time, researchers have discovered many cases of **incomplete dominance** in which alternative alleles are *not* dominant over or recessive to other alleles governing a particular trait. Instead, heterozygotes are phenotypic "intermediates."

Incomplete dominance is found in various plant and animal traits. For example, a cross between snapdragons having red flowers and those having white flowers yields plants having pink flowers. Crossing black Andalusian chickens with white Andalusian chickens yields an intermediate hybrid that is slate blue. In humans, a curly haired Caucasian and a straight haired Caucasian will have children with wavy hair. And persons with wavy hair will have children that are either straight haired, wavy haired, or curly haired. Figure 20-15 shows a cross between two wavy haired people. Notice that an upper case H denotes the "hair" allele. No lower case letters are used because neither allele (curly or straight) is recessive. Instead, one allele is designated as *H* and the other as *H'*.

A slightly different situation occurs with alleles that are codominant. **Codominant** alleles are *both* dominant; both characteristics are exhibited in the phenotype. In humans the alleles that code the A, B, or AB blood types are a good example of codominance. For example, a person having allele A and allele B has blood type AB. In addition to being coded by codominant alleles, blood types are coded by more than two alleles. So far, genes that consist of only two—a pair of—alleles have been discussed. But a gene may be represented by more than two alleles within the population. Some genes, such as the ABO blood type genes, consist of a system of alleles, or **multiple alleles.** In this system of multiple alleles, the alleles A and B exhibit codominance, and the O allele is recessive.

▼▼

In traits exhibiting incomplete dominance, alternative forms of an allele are neither dominant nor recessive; heterozygotes are phenotypic intermediates. In traits exhibiting codominance, alternative forms of an allele are both dominant; heterozygotes exhibit both phenotypes.

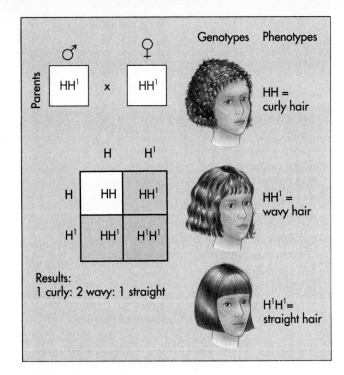

FIGURE 20-15 Incomplete dominance.
Sometimes alternative alleles are not dominant or recessive. For example, neither straight nor curly hair is dominant in Caucasians. The predicted ratio of the offspring of two wavy haired people will be one curly haired individual, one straight haired individual, and two wavy haired individuals. Wavy hair is the phenotypic intermediate.

Multiple alleles

As mentioned, human ABO blood types are coded by multiple alleles. In fact, four phenotypes (A, B, AB, and O blood types) are determined by the presence of two of three possible alleles (A, B, or O) in an individual. The A and B alleles each code for the production of different enzymes. These enzymes add certain sugar molecules to lipids on the surface of red blood cells. These sugars act as recognition markers for the immune system and are called *cell surface antigens*. The enzyme produced by allele A results in the addition of one type of sugar; allele B adds a different sugar. Allele O adds no sugar. Different combinations of the three possible alleles occur in different individuals, with each individual having *one pair* of alleles. Therefore a person having an AA genotype produces only the A sugar. A person having an AB genotype produces both A and B sugars. (The A and B alleles are codominant and both are expressed.) A person having an AO phenotype will produce the A sugar (so is said to have type A blood). The A allele is expressed because it is dominant to the O allele.

> Some genes consist of a system of alleles, or multiple alleles, which are usually codominant to one another. The ABO system of human blood types is an example of codominant multiple alleles.

Using Blood Typing to Test for Paternity

Paternity testing is not just the stuff of soap operas. Disputes involving adoption, divorce, and legal heirs can require a determination of a person's true father. Although no test can definitely state that a suspect is the true father of a child, the paternity tests being performed today can yield a probability of paternity in excess of 99%.

Paternity testing involves the analysis of genetic information inherited by a child from his or her mother and true father. Certain antigens (see Chapter 16) are attached to the surface of each person's red blood cells. The type of antigens present on your red blood cells is inherited from your parents. Testing a child's mother and suspected father for these antigens and then using the principles of genetics to determine whether the child has received its complement of antigens from the hypothetical parents is the basis of paternity testing.

There are several types of antigens that are analyzed in paternity testing. The most familiar are the antigens associated with the ABO system. Each person is a particular blood type: A, B, AB, or O. Type A persons make antibodies against the B antigen. If an A person needed a blood transfusion and was given B blood, the B antibodies in the recipient's blood would attack the B antigen in the transfused blood. The blood cells would clump together, and death could occur. Similarly, B individuals have A antibodies, AB individuals have no antibodies (and both A and B antigens), and O individuals have both antibodies (and neither antigen). The presence or absence of these antigens is governed by alleles inherited from one's parents. The alleles for each blood type are shown in Figure 20-A, *1*.

How can you rule out a suspected father using ABO blood groups? Say a child's mother is type O, and the suspected father is AB. The child is type AB. Is the suspect the true father? Examine the Punnett square in Figure 20-A, *2*. The only blood types possible from O and AB parents are types A and B. An AB child could not be born to such parents, and thus the suspect is not the true father.

Paternity testing, however, is based on more than ABO blood groups. DNA analysis is now used in conjunction with antigen analysis to test paternity. It is this combination of tests that contributes to the high accuracy of the results.

FIGURE 20-A
1 The alleles for the ABO blood group system.
2 A Punnett square showing the possible offspring from a type **O** mother and a type **AB** father.

Type	Possible alleles
A	$I^A I^A$, $I^A i$
B	$I^B I^B$, $I^B i$
AB	$I^A I^B$
O	ii

AB father

O mother	I^A	I^B
i	$I^A i$	$I^B i$
i	$I^A i$	$I^B i$

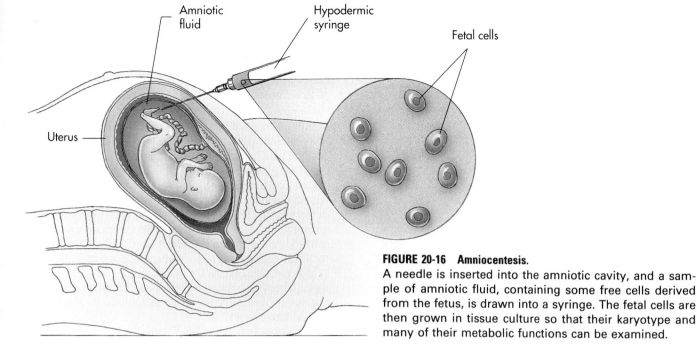

Amniotic fluid

Hypodermic syringe

Fetal cells

Uterus

FIGURE 20-16 Amniocentesis.
A needle is inserted into the amniotic cavity, and a sample of amniotic fluid, containing some free cells derived from the fetus, is drawn into a syringe. The fetal cells are then grown in tissue culture so that their karyotype and many of their metabolic functions can be examined.

Genetic counseling

Although most genetic disorders cannot yet be cured, research scientists and physicians are continually learning a great deal about them. Exciting methods of genetic therapy are being studied. Geneticists can identify couples at risk of having children with genetic defects and can help them have healthy children. This process is called **genetic counseling.**

By analyzing family pedigrees and applying the laws of statistical probability, genetic counselors can often determine the probability that a person is a carrier of a recessive disorder. When a couple is expecting a child and both parents have a significant probability of being carriers of a serious recessive genetic disorder, the pregnancy is said to be a high-risk pregnancy. In such a pregnancy, there is a significant probability that the child will exhibit the clinical disorder. Another class of high-risk pregnancies occurs with mothers who are more than 35 years old. Remember, the frequency of birth of infants with Down syndrome increases dramatically among the pregnancies of older women (see Figure 20-4).

When a pregnancy is diagnosed as being high risk, many women elect to undergo **amniocentesis,** a procedure that permits the prenatal diagnosis of many genetic disorders (Figure 20-16). In the fourth month of pregnancy, a small sample of amniotic fluid is taken from the mother using a sterile hypodermic needle. The amniotic fluid, which bathes the fetus, contains free-floating cells derived from the fetus. Once removed, these cells can be grown as tissue cultures in the laboratory. Studying these tissue cultures, genetic counselors can test for many of the most common genetic disorders.

During amniocentesis, the position of the needle in relationship to the fetus is observed by means of a technique called **ultrasound.** The term *ultrasound* refers to high-frequency sound waves. Pulses of these waves are sent into the body and are reflected back in various patterns depending on the tissues or fluids the waves hit. These patterns of sound-wave reflections are then mapped to produce a picture of inner tissues as in Figure 20-17. Because ultrasound allows the position of the fetus to be determined, the person performing the amniocentesis can avoid damaging the fetus. Ultrasound also allows the fetus to be examined for the presence of major abnormalities.

At this time, most of the problems that can be diagnosed by pedigree analysis, amniocentesis, chorionic villus sampling (see p. 437), and ultrasound techniques cannot be treated. Sometimes the only options available to a couple are to continue the pregnancy and deal with the problems after birth or to have a therapeutic abortion. However, continual progress in developing gene therapies may, in the future, have a drastic impact on a physician's ability to treat genetic disorders before birth.

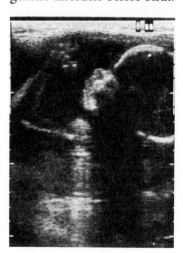

FIGURE 20-17 Ultrasound.
Before amniocentesis, the fetus is observed with ultrasound to determine its position. Imaging the fetus using ultrasound before amniocentesis is important, since the amniocentesis needle must be inserted precisely without damaging the fetus.

Summary

1. Human cells contain 46 chromosomes: 44 autosomes and 2 sex chromosomes. The autosomes form 22 pairs of homologous (matched) chromosomes. In females, the two sex chromosomes are similar in size and appearance and are designated XX. In males, the two sex chromosomes are not similar in size and appearance. The smaller of the two is designated Y and the larger X. The genes that determine male characteristics are located on the Y chromosome.

2. Researchers often use karyotypes to study the inheritance of genetic disorders caused by the loss of all or part of a chromosome or by the addition of extra chromosomes or chromosome fragments. A karyotype is a picture of chromosomes paired with their homologues and arranged according to size.

3. In humans the inheritance of one autosome too few usually results in a nonviable zygote. The inheritance of one autosome too many, or a trisomy, also results in a nonviable zygote with the exception of chromosome 21. Individuals with an extra copy of this chromosome are retarded and have Down syndrome. Down syndrome is much more frequent among pregnant mothers over 35 years of age, and it occurs when two sister chromatids fail to separate, or disjoin, during the meiotic process.

4. Nondisjunction can occur with the sex chromosomes. Persons who inherit abnormal numbers of sex chromosomes often have abnormal features and may be mentally retarded. Examples of genetic disorders caused by abnormal numbers of sex chromosomes are poly-X females, XXY males (Klinefelter syndrome), XO females (Turner syndrome), and XYY males.

5. Persons may inherit chromosomes that are structurally defective due to chromosomal breaks and misrepairs or changes that may take place in the molecular structure of the chromosomal DNA. The three major sources of environmental damage to chromosomes are (1) high-energy radiation, such as x-rays; (2) low-energy radiation, such as UV light; and (3) chemicals, such as LSD, marijuana, cyclamates, and certain pesticides.

6. Patterns of inheritance observed in family histories, or pedigrees, can be used to determine the mode of inheritance of a particular trait. By such analysis, it can often be determined whether a trait is associated with a dominant or a recessive allele and whether the gene determining the trait is sex linked.

7. Some genetic disorders are relatively common in human populations, whereas others are rare. Many of the most common genetic disorders are associated with recessive alleles, the functioning of which may lead to the production of defective versions of enzymes that normally perform critical functions. Because such traits are determined by recessive alleles and therefore expressed only in homozygotes, the alleles are not eliminated from the human population. Dominant alleles that lead to severe genetic disorders are less common; in some of the more frequent ones, the expression of the alleles does not occur until after the individuals have reached their reproductive years.

8. Alleles do not always exhibit clear-cut dominance or recessiveness but may instead exhibit incomplete dominance or codominance. In traits exhibiting incomplete dominance, alternative forms of a trait are neither dominant nor recessive; heterozygotes are phenotypic intermediates. In traits exhibiting codominance, alternative forms of an allele are both dominant; heterozygotes exhibit both phenotypes. Some genes consist of a system of alleles, or multiple alleles, which are usually codominant to one another. The ABO system of human blood types is an example of multiple alleles with two of the alleles (A and B) codominant to one another and one allele (O) recessive to the other two.

9. Although most genetic disorders cannot yet be cured, research scientists are making progress in developing gene therapies that may, in the future, have an important impact on a physician's ability to treat genetic disorders before birth.

REVIEW QUESTIONS

1. To produce a karyotype for a specific individual, must the chromosomes be gathered from the patient's gonads (ovaries or testes)?

2. The extra chromosome 21 that is found in person with Down syndrome is the cause of multiple developmental defects. What might this tell you about the interaction of genes on a particular chromosome?

3. What is Down syndrome and what causes it? Give another term for this condition, and summarize its symptoms.

4. What happens when human offspring inherit abnormal numbers of sex chromosomes? Summarize the four examples discussed in the chapter and give the genotype of each.

5. Which sex chromosome is necessary for the survival of the developing zygote?

6. What are the three major sources of damage to chromosomes?

7. Describe how heavy use of drugs could affect a woman's ova or a man's sperm.

8. What would you conclude about the inheritance pattern of each human trait in each of the following situations?:
   a. The trait is expressed more frequently in males than in females.
   b. Offspring who exhibit this trait have at least one parent who exhibits the same trait.
   c. Offspring can exhibit this trait even though the parents do not.
   d. The trait is expressed equally in both males and females.

9. Why do most genetic disorders in humans result from recessive genes? Name several examples.

10. Distinguish between incomplete dominance and codominance. Describe the phenotype of a heterozygote in each case.

11. A woman whose blood type is AB marries a man with the same blood type. Draw a Punnett square to illustrate the possible genotypes of their children. What blood type will each genotype have?

12. If a couple wants to have a child but suspects that they may be at risk for a genetic disorder, what can they do? If a pregnancy turns out to be high risk, what options are available?

DISCUSSION QUESTIONS

1. Women are advised to have babies before they are 35 years old if possible, but no such advice is usually offered to men. Why the difference?

2. Some people smoke all their lives and never develop lung cancer. Do you think the propensity to develop lung cancer on exposure to the mutagens in cigarette smoke is hereditary? Discuss.

3. Gather in small groups to discuss the effectiveness, role, and problems related to genetic counseling. Do you think most parents would benefit from such counseling? Are most people aware of genetic determinants in disease? Might such counseling aid in prenatal treatment of disorders?

FOR FURTHER READING

Anderson, W.F. (1992, May). Human gene therapy. *Science, pp.808-813.*
The author of this article supervised the first use of gene therapy to treat human patients. Here he summarizes 11 new uses for gene therapy currently underway. The author also discusses the safety, social, and ethical concerns that gene therapy poses.

Collins, F.S. (1992, May). Cystic fibrosis: molecular biology and therapeutic implications. *Science, pp. 774-779.*
This challenging article presents the latest information revealed since the identification of the defective gene in patients with cystic fibrosis. Prospects for gene therapy are also discussed.

Diamond, J. (1989, February). Blood, genes, and malaria. *Natural History.*
This is a lucid account of the evolutionary history of sickle-cell anemia.

Kinochita, J. (1991, January). Master of sex. *Discover,* p. 47.
A short article on the recent discovery of the gene which may code for male secondary sex characteristics and possible therapeutic use in XXY male patients.

Lewis, R. (1991, May). Genetic imprecision. *Bioscience,* pp. 288-293.
A thorough and clear article on the use and effectiveness of human genetic counseling written by a genetic counselor. The author particularly focuses on how diagnosis does not predict prognosis of disease.

HUMAN GENETICS PROBLEMS

1. George has Royal hemophilia and marries his mother's sister's daughter Patricia. His maternal grandfather also had hemophilia. George and Patricia have five children: two daughters are normal, and two sons and one daughter develop hemophilia. Draw the pedigree.

2. A couple with a newborn baby are troubled that the child does not appear to resemble either of them. Suspecting that a mix-up occurred at the hospital, they check the blood type of the infant. It is type O. Because the father is type A, and the mother is type B, they conclude that a mistake must have been made. Are they correct?

3. How many chromosomes would you expect to find in the karyotype of a person with Turner syndrome?

4. A woman is married for the second time. Her first husband was ABO blood type A, and her child by that marriage was type O. Her new husband is type B, and their child is type AB. What is the woman's ABO genotype and blood type?

5. Total color blindness is a rare hereditary disorder among humans in which no color is seen, only shades of gray. It occurs in individuals homozygous for a recessive allele and is not sex linked. A man whose father is totally color blind intends to marry a woman whose mother was totally color blind. What are the chances that they will produce offspring who are totally color blind?

6. This pedigree is of a rare trait in which children have extra fingers and toes. Which if any of the following patterns of inheritance is consistent with this pedigree?
   a. Autosomal recessive
   b. Autosomal dominant
   c. Sex-linked recessive
   d. Sex-linked dominant
   e. Y-linkage

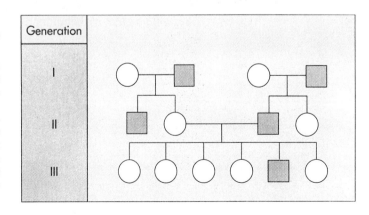

BIOETHICAL DECISIONMAKING FRAMEWORK
Nuturing a Newborn with a Genetic Aberration

Consider the following questions as you think about the bioethical dilemma presented on page 321:

1. What are the bioethical issues in this case?
   - What has to be decided?
   - Who are the decisionmakers?
   - Outline the decisionmaking process in this case as you understand it.

2. What factual information do the decisionmakers need? Consider the effects of the answers to the following questions on the decisionmaking process.
   - What is trisomy 18? What are its causes? Will a complete understanding of trisomy 18 aid the decisionmakers? If so, in what ways?
   - If the parents decide that every effort (medication, respiratory assistance, surgery) should be made to keep this baby alive, what kinds of costs will be incurred? Who will pay these costs?
   - What other questions should the decisionmakers ask?
   - What additional factual information do the decisionmakers need?

3. Who are the "stakeholders" in this decision—those who stand to gain or lose as a result of the decision?
   - Are the parents stakeholders? The infant? What other persons or groups are stakeholders?
   - Which stakeholders are decisionmakers? Which are not decisionmakers? Will individuals in the latter group be able to influence the decisionmaking process? Should they have influence?
   - In what ways would each stakeholder be affected by the decision?

4. What are the values at stake in the decision? As you list and describe them, consider the following questions:
   - What treatments and medications should be given to an infant whose future quality of life is in jeopardy?
   - If treatments such as resuscitation and correction of the arterial abnormality are rejected by the parents, what other kinds of measures should be taken to ease the infant's suffering?
   - Would parental nurturing of an infant such as this baby fulfill a need for the parents, or is it a moral obligation that goes hand in hand with basic care such as feeding? Keep in mind that the baby will receive nurturing attention from the staff of the intensive care unit.

5. What options are available to the decisionmakers? As you list these options, consider the following questions:
   - Which of these alternatives seem ethically feasible? Which seem administratively possible?
   - How would each alternative decision affect each of the stakeholders?
   - Is there a compromise solution that might give all parties the sense that they have come out the "winner" in the decision?

6. What are the values inherent to the decisionmaking process?
   - Is the decisionmaking process fair?
   - If the parents decide to nurture (touch and hold) their child, will this activity influence their decision to continue resuscitative efforts and treatment to correct the arterial defect? If so, is such an influential activity useful to the decisionmaking process?
   - Do all stakeholders have equal resources to advocate their position?
   - What further steps might each group of stakeholders take if their views are disallowed?

PART SIX

How Humans Reproduce

21 Sex and Reproduction

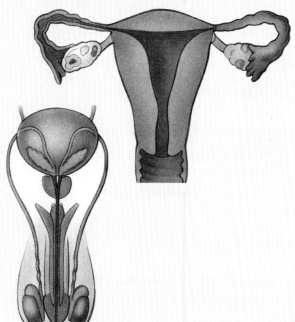

22 Development Before Birth

23 Sexually Transmitted Diseases

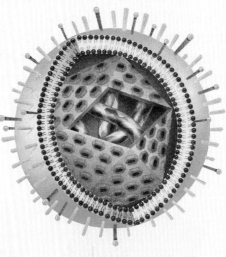

BIOETHICAL DECISIONMAKING
Conceiving One Life to Help Sustain Another

A 28-year-old married man has been on dialysis for 3 years and is growing desperate because of symptoms he experiences during this procedure and the restrictions it places on his life. Dialysis is necessary because he is in renal failure: his kidneys are not functioning properly to remove the wastes that build up in his blood as a result of the normal activities of his cells.

Dialysis mimics the work of the kidneys by cleansing the blood in a filtration process. Unfortunately, the process is very slow; an average session of dialysis takes 4 hours. In severe cases of renal failure such as this patient's, dialysis must be repeated every other day. Consequently, this man cannot work regularly because of the time he must spend in the dialysis center. He also suffers unpleasant symptoms during many of his dialysis treatments: a decrease in blood pressure, dizziness, muscle cramps, nausea, vomiting, and headaches. In addition, he must follow strict dietary guidelines. A kidney transplant is unfeasible for this man because finding a suitable donor kidney would be nearly impossible. He was adopted as an infant and does not know his natural family, eliminating the possibility of a sibling or parent as a donor.

In addition, tests show that he has a rare tissue type.

As his physical and mental state continues to deteriorate, the man tells his wife that life under these conditions is intolerable. He begins to consider suicide as his only viable option. His wife then suggests a solution to the transplant surgeon. She will become pregnant and bear a child that would likely be a suitable donor. When the child is a few years old and its kidneys have matured sufficiently, the child's tissues could be crossmatched with its father's. If the match is close, the transplantation could be performed.

The surgeon knows that, technically, such a transplant could work. Young transplanted kidneys have been shown to grow with time. However, kidneys from donors under the age of six do not survive transplantation as well as those from adolescents or adults. The surgeon also knows that this patient has threatened to commit suicide if he has to remain on dialysis indefinitely.

Should the surgeon agree to transplant the kidney of a child that was conceived specifically to be an organ donor for its parent?

21 Sex and Reproduction

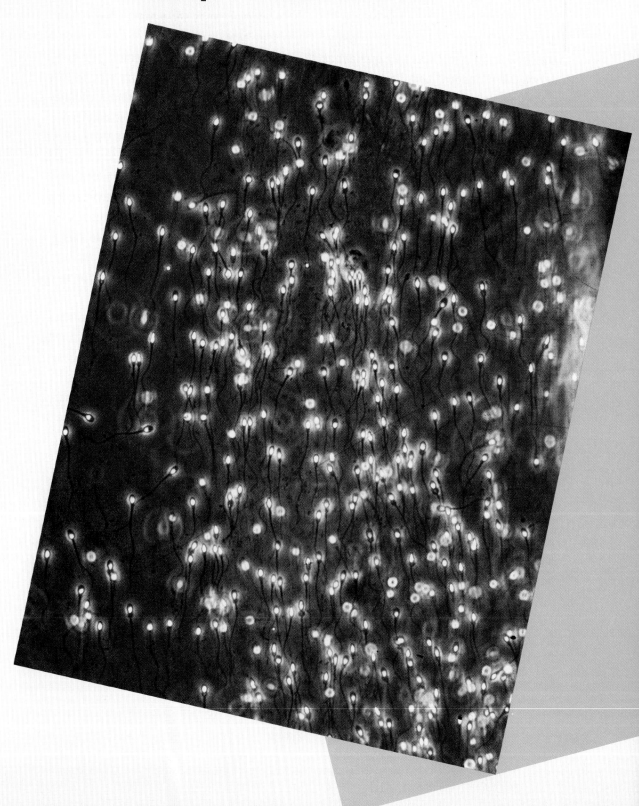

▾ Sexual reproduction in humans, as well as in most sexually reproducing organisms, is a process in which a male and female sex cell unite to form the first cell of a new individual.

▾ The male reproductive system produces male sex cells called sperm and deposits them in the female reproductive tract during sexual intercourse.

▾ The female reproductive system receives the male sex cells, produces female sex cells called eggs, and provides an environment for a fertilized egg to grow and develop into a new individual.

▾ The human sexual response promotes sexual reproduction; techniques to avoid conception during sexual activity vary in their methods and success rates.

Their nuclei glowing with a special fluorescent dye, these sperm are all moving in the same direction, propelled by their whip-like flagella. Only one of the hundreds of millions introduced into the vagina will be the first to encounter the female gamete—a developing egg. Enzymes in the sperm head will dissolve the jelly-like covering of the egg and pierce its membrane. Once the union of egg and sperm takes place, changes on the surface of the egg block the entry of additional sperm, ensuring that the fertilized egg will have only one complete set of hereditary material. Having more than one complete set could be fatal to a new embryo's existence. But with a set of genes from each of its parents and with conditions right for survival, a single human embryo has the potential to develop into the complex network of 100 trillion cells that make up the human body.

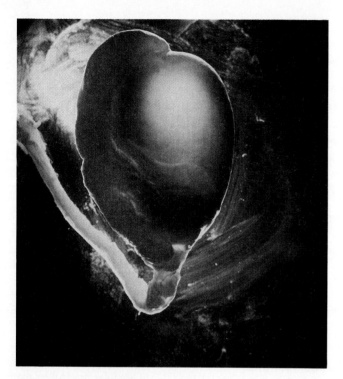

FIGURE 21-1 Human testis.
The testis is the ovoid structure in the center of the photograph; sperm are formed within it. Cupped along the side of the testis is the epididymis, a highly coiled passageway within which sperm complete their maturation. Extending away from the epididymis is a long tube, the vas deferens.

Reproduction

Each male sex cell, or **spermatozoon** (sperm), is a highly motile cell that can penetrate the membrane of a secondary oocyte (potential egg). After penetration, a sperm joins its half of the hereditary message—the "blueprints" for the development of a new individual—with the hereditary material of the oocyte. This process, whereby a male and a female sex cell combine to form the first cell of a new individual, is called *sexual reproduction*. The organs of the human male and female reproductive systems are the organs of sexual reproduction. Both the male and female reproductive systems have organs called **gonads** that produce the sex cells, or **gametes** (eggs and sperm). Other organs and ducts store, transport, and receive the sex cells. Accessory glands help nourish the sex cells.

The male reproductive system

The function of the male reproductive system is to produce sperm cells and transport them to the female reproductive tract. Sperm are produced in the male gonads, which are called the **testes.**

The production of sperm: The testes

The testes, or testicles (Figure 21-1), are located outside of the lower pelvic area of the male, housed within a sac of skin called the **scrotum** (Figure 21-2). The placement of

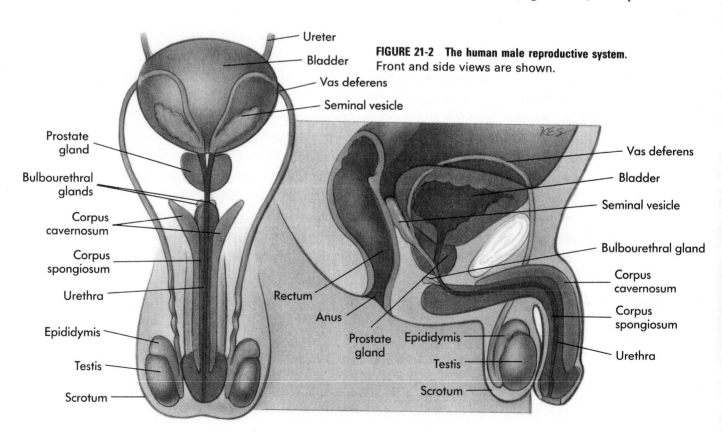

Ureter

Bladder

Vas deferens

Seminal vesicle

Prostate gland

Bulbourethral glands

Corpus cavernosum

Corpus spongiosum

Urethra

Epididymis

Testis

Scrotum

Rectum

Anus

Prostate gland

FIGURE 21-2 The human male reproductive system.
Front and side views are shown.

Vas deferens

Bladder

Seminal vesicle

Bulbourethral gland

Corpus cavernosum

Corpus spongiosum

Urethra

Epididymis

Testis

Scrotum

this organ allows the sperm to successfully complete their development at a temperature slightly lower than the 37° C (98.6° F) internal temperature of the human body. Tight jeans or other clothing that press the testes close to the body can have a detrimental effect on sperm development, lowering the number of viable sperm that a man produces.

Each testis is packed with approximately 750 feet of tightly coiled tubes called **seminiferous tubules** (Figure 21-3, *A*). Male gametes, or sperm cells, develop within the tissue lining these tubules during a process of meiosis (see Chapter 17) and development called **spermatogenesis** (literally, "the making of sperm"). Hundreds of millions of sperm are produced by this process each day! Spermatogenesis usually begins during the teenage years when a boy reaches sexual maturity, or **puberty,** and continues throughout his life. Sperm production is triggered by follicle-stimulating hormone, or FSH.

Luteinizing hormone, or LH, regulates the testes' secretion of testosterone, a sex hormone responsible for the development and maintenance of male secondary sexual characteristics. These characteristics, such as a deepening of the voice and the growth of facial hair, begin to develop at puberty and are signs that sexual maturation is taking place.

Both FSH and LH are secreted by the pituitary, a tiny gland that hangs from the underside of the brain (see Chapter 14). The secretion of these hormones is regulated by means of a negative feedback loop involving the hypothalamus, a tiny portion of the brain that controls the pituitary. A high level of testosterone in the blood inhibits the hypothalamus from triggering the pituitary to release FSH and LH. Without stimulation by these hormones, the testes produce fewer sperm and less testosterone. When the testos-

terone level drops too low, the hypothalamus once again triggers the release of FSH and LH from the pituitary, causing the testes to step up their production of sperm and testosterone.

Sperm production, or spermatogenesis, takes place within the coiled tubules of the testes and is triggered by the hormone FSH. The development of functionally mature sperm also requires LH and testosterone.

Packed within the walls of the seminiferous tubules are cells called **spermatogonia,** the cells that give rise to sperm (Figure 21-3, *B*). These cells have a full complement (diploid amount) of hereditary material and constantly produce new cells by the process of mitosis (see Chapter 17). Some of the new (daughter) cells produced by mitotic cell division move inward toward the interior of the tubule and undergo meiosis. The reduction-division of meiotic cell division produces four cells from each original cell, each one having *half* the normal amount (or haploid amount) of hereditary material. These haploid cells are now called **spermatids.** Each spermatid contains one member from each pair of the 23 chromosome pairs present in the cells of the human body. Included in these 23 chromosomes is either an X sex chromosome or a Y sex chromosome, which will determine the gender of the new individual (Figure 21-4).

The spermatids then undergo a process of development, producing sperm cells, or spermatozoa. Spermatozoa are relatively simple cells (Figure 21-3, *C* and *D*). Each has an anterior portion, or head, that consists primarily of a cell

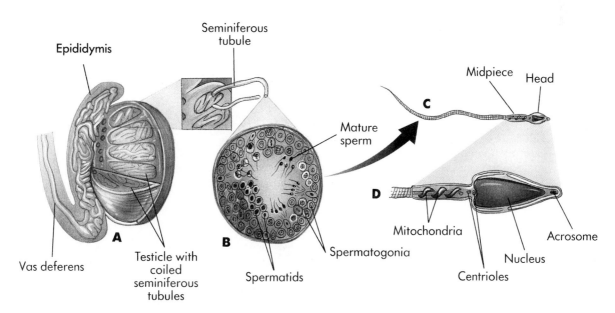

FIGURE 21-3 The interior of the testis, site of spermatogenesis.
Within the seminiferous tubules of the testis (A), cells called *spermatogonia* (B) develop into sperm, passing through the spermatocyte and spermatid stages. Each sperm (C) possesses a long tail attached to a head (D), which contains a haploid nucleus.

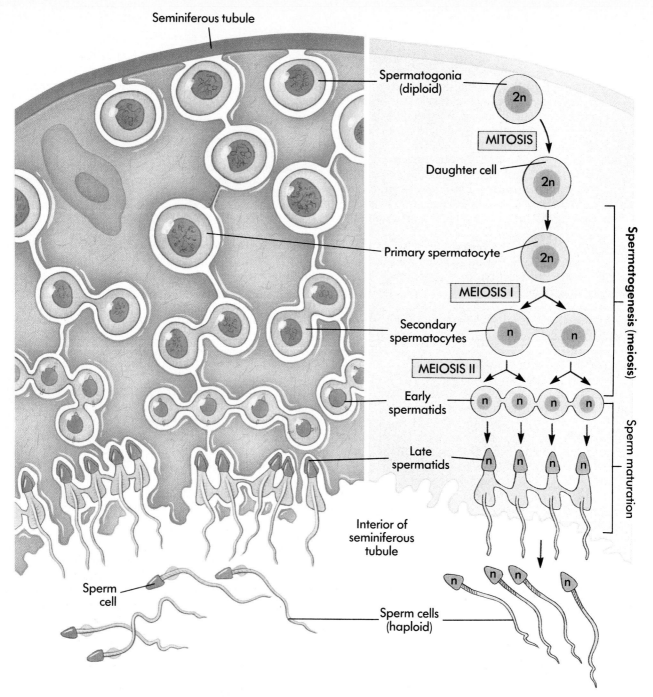

FIGURE 21-4 Spermatogenesis.
Spermatogonia undergo mitosis to produce more spermatogonia. Some of the spermatogonia, however, move to the interior of the seminiferous tubule to undergo meiosis. Meiotic cell division produces four haploid spermatids that will eventually develop into spermatozoa.

membrane encasing hereditary material. A vesicle called an **acrosome,** derived from the Golgi body, is located at the leading tip of the sperm cell. It contains enzymes that aid in the penetration of the protective layers surrounding the egg. In addition, each spermatozoon has a whip-like tail, or flagellum, that propels the cell and mitochondria, which produce ATP from which a sperm derives energy that powers its flagellum. Sperm development takes about 2 months from spermatogonia to mature spermatozoa. On average, 300 million mature sperm are produced per day.

In the testes, diploid cells called spermatogonia give rise to haploid cells called spermatids. These haploid cells contain half the normal amount of hereditary material of body cells. The spermatids then develop into sperm cells, or spermatozoa, which have a head containing the hereditary material, a vesicle containing enzymes to penetrate an egg, and a whip-like tail.

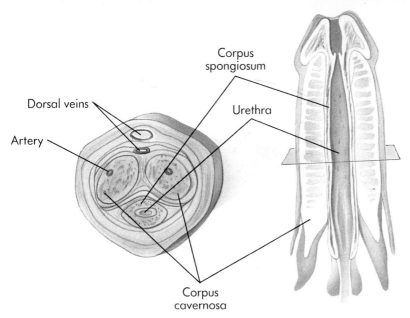

Dorsal veins

Artery

Corpus
spongiosum

Urethra

Corpus
cavernosa

FIGURE 21-5   A penis in cross section.
The three cylinders of spongy tissue are the corpus spongiosum in the middle and the two corpora cavernosa, one on each side.

Maturation and storage: The epididymis and vas deferens

After formation within the testes, the sperm move through its tubules to a nearby long, coiled tube called the **epididymis** (see Figure 21-3, *A*) that sits on the back side of the testes. Here the sperm undergo further development and may be stored for about 18 hours to 10 days, becoming capable of propelling themselves and penetrating an oocyte. The sperm then move toward a connecting tube, the **vas deferens,** a long tube that ascends from the epididymis into the pelvic cavity, looping over the side of the urinary bladder (see Figure 21-2). Stored in the epididymis and the very beginning of the vas deferens, sperm retain their ability to fertilize an oocyte for a short while. If they are not ejaculated, "old" sperm are reabsorbed by the body to make room for "new" sperm.

⬇⬇
Spermatozoa mature in the epididymis, a long, coiled tube that sits on the back side of the testes and leads to the long ascending vas deferens.

Nourishment of the sperm: The accessory glands

When a male ejaculates (see p. 410), the sperm are propelled through the vas deferens to the **urethra,** where the reproductive and urinary tracts join. On the way, accessory glands add fluid to the sperm, producing an ejaculate called **semen.** The semen leaves the body through the urethral opening at the tip of the penis.

The first accessory glands to add fluid to the traveling sperm are the **seminal vesicles.** This pair of glands has short ducts that empty a thick, clear fluid into each vas deferens just before they join and flow into the urethra. The fluid secreted by the seminal vesicles is primarily composed of the sugar fructose, which serves as a source of energy for the sperm.

Near its beginning, the urethra is surrounded by a gland called the **prostate.** About the size of a chestnut, the prostate adds a milky alkaline fluid to the semen. This fluid neutralizes the acidity of any traces of urine left in the urethra and also neutralizes the acidity of the female vagina. Sperm are unable to swim in an acid environment, so the secretion of the prostate ensures their motility.

Just beneath the prostate lies a set of tiny, round accessory glands called the **bulbourethral glands.** The purpose of these glands is somewhat a mystery. Like the prostate, the bulbourethral glands secrete an alkaline fluid into the semen. However, they secrete only a drop or two, which precedes the ejaculate. It does carry sperm to the outside before ejaculation, making the withdrawal method of birth control highly unreliable (see p. 422). Scientists think that the purpose of this secretion may be to neutralize the acidity of the urethra just before ejaculation as a further protection for sperm.

⬇⬇
During ejaculation, sperm are propelled through the vas deferens to the urethra and out the penis. Fluid is added to the sperm from various accessory glands along the way. This fluid contains substances that nourish the sperm and neutralize the acidity of the vagina.

The penis

The scrotum (which encloses the testes and epididymi) and the penis are the two male external sexual organs, or **external genitals.** The **penis** is a cylindrical organ that transfers sperm from the male reproductive tract to the female reproductive tract. As shown in the cross-sectional view of the penis in Figure 21-5, this organ is composed of three cylinders of spongy erectile tissue. Two veins run along the top surface of the penis. Beneath these veins, two of the cylinders of erectile tissue sit side by side. And beneath them lies a third cylinder, surrounding the urethra.

The tissue that makes up the three erectile cylinders is riddled with spaces between its cells. These spaces normally contain a small amount of blood and are lined by a layer of flattened cells similar to the inner lining of blood vessels. During sexual stimulation, nerve impulses from the central nervous system cause the arterioles leading into this tissue to widen, causing additional blood to collect within the spaces. Pressure from the increased volume of blood within the spaces causes the erectile tissue to become distended and compresses the veins that normally drain blood from the penis, causing it to become erect and rigid. Continued stimulation by the central nervous system is required for this erection to be maintained.

Erection can be achieved without any physical stimulation of the penis. However, physical stimulation usually is required for the ejaculation of semen, which corresponds to the culmination of sexual excitement, or orgasm. Prolonged stimulation of the penis, as by repeated thrusts into the female's vagina, leads first to the mobilization of the sperm. In this process, muscles encircling the vas deferens contract, moving the sperm into the urethra. Then ejaculation takes place: muscles at the base of the penis and within the walls of the urethra contract repeatedly, ejecting approximately a teaspoon of semen containing about 200 million sperm out of the penis.

The female reproductive system

The part of the female reproductive tract that receives the sperm is called the **vagina,** a muscular tube 9 to 10 centi-meters (3 1/2 inches) long (Figure 21-6). But the female reproductive tract does more than receive sperm. It usually produces one secondary oocyte (potential egg) each month and transports it to where it can be fertilized and the resultant zygote nourished as it develops into an embryo and then a fetus (see Chapter 22).

The production of eggs: The ovaries

Secondary oocytes are produced in the female gonads, or **ovaries** (Figure 21-6). These two almond-shaped organs are about 3 centimeters long, slightly larger than the distance from the last knuckle on your thumb to the thumb's tip. They are located in the lower portion of the abdominal cavity in an area called the *pelvic cavity*. The ovaries contain **primary oocytes,** cells that have the potential to develop into eggs, surrounded by supporting cells called **follicular cells.** Together the follicular cells and the oocyte are called a **follicle,** a word derived from a Latin word meaning "bag" or "sac."

The process of meiosis and development that produces mature female sex cells, or eggs, is called **oogenesis** (literally, "the making of eggs"). Unlike males, whose spermatogonia are constantly dividing to produce new spermatocytes, females have all of the primary oocytes at birth that they will ever produce—about 1 to 2 million of them! (By the age of puberty, more than half these oocytes have degenerated, leaving about 400,000 viable oocytes.) These primary oocytes were produced during fetal development from diploid cells called **oogonia.** The oocytes in the ovaries of a female began the process of meiosis before birth,

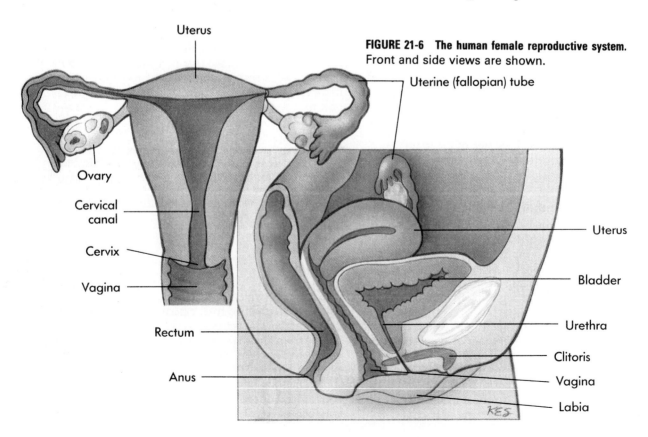

FIGURE 21-6 The human female reproductive system. Front and side views are shown.

Uterus

Uterine (fallopian) tube

Ovary

Cervical canal

Cervix

Vagina

Rectum

Anus

Uterus

Bladder

Urethra

Clitoris

Vagina

Labia

KES

but the process stopped during the first meiotic division (Figure 21-7). In other words, a female's primary oocytes are in a developmental holding pattern during her lifetime. As a woman ages, her oocytes age. The oocytes are continually exposed to chromosomal mutation, or change, throughout life. After 35 years, the odds of a harmful mutation having occurred are appreciable. This is one reason that developmental abnormalities occur with increasing frequency in pregnancies of women who are over 35 years old.

With the onset of puberty, one oocyte completes the first meiotic division approximately every 28 days. (The ovaries alternate in the production of oocytes.) As a result of this division, two cells of unequal size are produced. One is called the **secondary oocyte** and contains most of the cytoplasm of the primary oocyte. The other cell, called a **polar body,** contains little cytoplasm and soon dies. The secondary oocyte breaks away from the ovary during **ovulation** and continues with the second meiotic division only if it is fertilized by a sperm. After the completion of the second meiotic division, the second polar body dies, and the egg, or **ovum,** is mature. The haploid nuclei of the sperm and the egg fuse, producing a **zygote,** the first cell of a new individual.

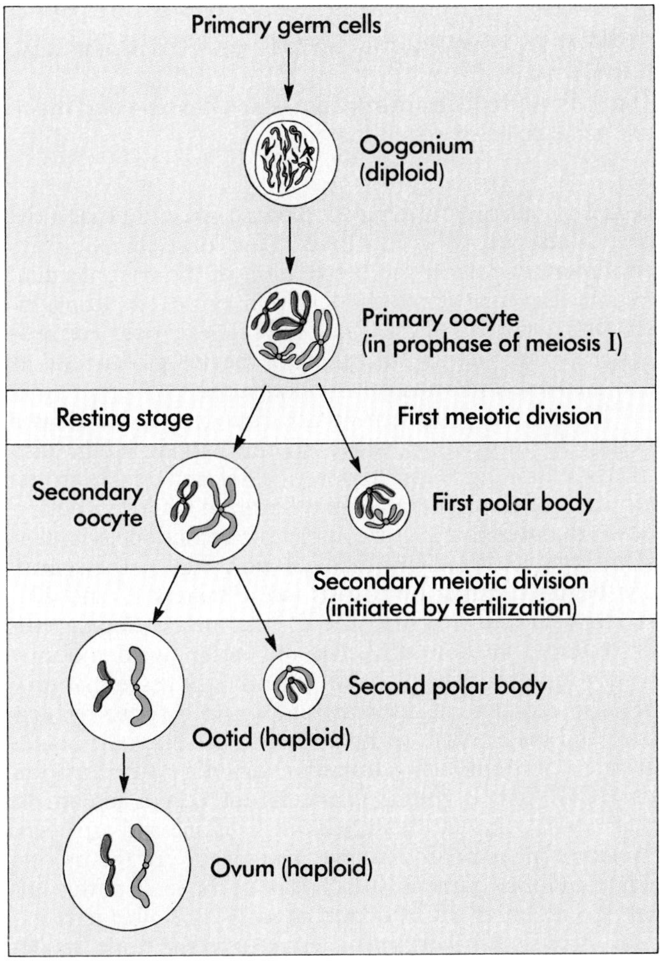

The ovaries are made up of primary oocytes—cells that have the potential to develop into eggs—surrounded by supporting cells called follicular cells. At birth, females have all of the primary oocytes that they will ever produce. With the onset of puberty, one primary oocyte matures into a secondary oocyte capable of breaking away from the ovary each month during a process called ovulation.

Passage to the uterus: The uterine tubes

At ovulation the secondary oocyte is released from the ovary. Lying close to each ovary is the entrance to a tube-like passageway that will take the egg to the **uterus,** the organ in which a fertilized egg can develop. Each passageway from an ovary to the uterus is called an *oviduct,* or **uterine tube.** In humans, the uterine tubes are commonly called the *fallopian tubes.*

Each uterine tube has an expanded, fringed end near each ovary. The tube and its fringed ends are lined with ciliated cells that beat in a synchronized manner, creating a current in the surrounding fluid that sweeps the egg into the tube. Once in the uterine tube, the egg is swept along by the beating of the ciliated cells lining the tube and by rhythmic peristaltic contractions of the muscles within its walls.

The journey from the ovary to the uterus is a slow one, taking about 3 days to complete. Because unfertilized oocytes can live for only 24 hours, a secondary oocyte must be fertilized while in the uterine tube, or it is no longer viable (able to be fertilized). In addition, sperm live for approximately 48 to 72 hours; they cannot simply wait in the uterine tubes for an egg to come along. Therefore fertilization can only take place if sexual intercourse occurs within three days before to one day after ovulation. (However, knowing exactly when ovulation will occur is usually a difficult task unless specific testing procedures are used; see p. 421.) If fertilization occurs, the egg completes its development, its hereditary material joins with that of the sperm's, and development of the zygote begins as it moves along the uterine tube. By the time the new embryo reaches the uterus, it is a tiny ball of cells. After a few days, it implants in the lining of the uterus to receive nourishment. (Further development of the embryo is discussed in the next chapter.)

The secondary oocyte journeys to the uterus, or womb, by means of a ciliated muscular tube called a uterine tube. One uterine tube extends from near each ovary to the uterus. If fertilized while in the tube, an oocyte will complete its maturation, join its hereditary material with that of a sperm, and begin its development as an embryo. A few days after reaching the uterus, the embryo will implant in the uterine lining to continue development.

Primary germ cells

↓

Oogonium (diploid)

↓

Primary oocyte (in prophase of meiosis I)

Resting stage | First meiotic division

Secondary oocyte | First polar body

Secondary meiotic division (initiated by fertilization)

Ootid (haploid) | Second polar body

↓

Ovum (haploid)

FIGURE 21-7 Oogenesis.
Notice that the oocytes have already completed part of the first meiotic division and are in a holding pattern until puberty, when one oocyte completes the first meiotic division approximately every 28 days.

The site of prenatal development: The uterus

As shown in Figure 21-6, the uterine tubes lead directly to the uterus. The uterus (from a Latin word meaning "womb") sits above the urinary bladder and in front of the rectum and directly connects with the vagina. Its walls are made up of thick layers of muscle that contract during the birth process and during menstruation (see p. 418). The interior of the uterus is hollow and provides a cavity for the development of a fertilized egg. Amazingly, the uterus of a woman who has never been pregnant is only 7.5 centimeters (3 inches) long and 5 centimeters (2 inches) wide, yet it can stretch to accommodate the size of a newborn infant!

The inner lining of the uterus is called the **endometrium.** This lining has two layers: one functional, transient layer that is in contact with the uterine cavity and an underlying permanent layer. The functional layer grows and thickens each month, readying itself for the implantation of an embryo. If an embryo is not present, the functional layer is shed. The monthly development and shedding of the functional layer of the endometrium (called the *menstrual cycle*) and the monthly maturation of an egg and its release (called the *ovarian cycle*) are both governed by levels of various female sex hormones. Together, these two cycles are commonly referred to as the *reproductive cycle.*

The reproductive cycle

Each month, a small number of primary oocytes (20 to 25) begin to develop within an ovary. This initial development is triggered by follicle-stimulating hormone (FSH) released by the pituitary gland in the brain (see Chapter 14). After they are stimulated, these follicles start producing very low levels of a group of hormones called **estrogens.** Estrogens develop and maintain the female reproductive structures such as the ovarian follicles as well as the lining of the uterus and the breasts. Therefore as the follicles develop in the ovaries and secrete estrogens, the lining of the uterus begins to thicken, preparing for the implantation of a fertilized egg. As the developing follicles mature, a membrane forms around each potential egg, fluid builds up within each follicle (Figure 21-8), and each follicle's cells produce increasing amounts of estrogens. During the second week of the reproductive cycle, most of the developing follicles die; usually only one follicle continues to mature. The hypothalamus senses the rise in blood level of estrogens and triggers the pituitary to secrete a surge of luteinizing hormone, or LH. A smaller surge of FSH occurs also. The surge in LH triggers ovulation. During ovulation the follicle breaks open and releases its immature egg into the abdominal cavity. This rise in LH can be detected by home test kits, informing a woman 1 day before ovulation occurs. A couple can then use this information to help them conceive a child.

Ovulation usually (but not always) occurs at the midpoint of the reproductive (menstrual) cycle—around day 14 in a 28-day cycle (Figure 21-9). After ovulation the movement of the ciliated cells at the fringes of the nearby uterine tube sweep the egg into the tube. The egg then begins its 3- to 4-day journey to the uterus. The ruptured follicle collapses and, under the continued influence of LH, it

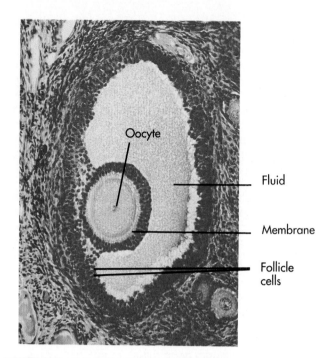

FIGURE 21-8   A mature oocyte (potential egg) within an ovarian follicle of a cat.
The follicle produces estrogens, which develop and maintain other follicles within the ovary.

begins to enlarge, forming a yellowish structure called the **corpus luteum,** or "yellow body." The corpus luteum plays an important role in the preparation of the endometrium for the implantation of the fertilized egg by secreting increasing quantities of estrogens and progesterone. The progesterone steps up the thickening of the lining of the uterus and dramatically increases its blood supply.

The rise in progesterone and estrogens also acts as a negative feedback mechanism to the hypothalamus, ultimately inhibiting the secretion of FSH and LH from the pituitary. If the immature egg is fertilized while journeying down the uterine tube, it completes a second meiotic division, joins its hereditary material with that of the sperm, and begins dividing by mitosis (see Chapters 17 and 22). A few days after reaching the uterus, the developing embryo nestles into the thickened uterine lining to continue its development. The placenta, a flat disk of tissue that provides an exchange of nutrients and wastes between the embryo and the mother, begins to form. Its embryonic tissues secrete a hormone called **human chorionic gonadotropin, or HCG.** This hormone maintains the corpus luteum so that it will continue to secrete progesterone and estrogen. Progesterone is needed for the maintenance of the uterine lining and the continued attachment of the fetus to this lining. Secretion of HCG occurs about 8 days after fertilization. Because this hormone is excreted in the urine, its detection is the basis for both laboratory and home pregnancy tests.

If the egg is not fertilized while in the uterine tube, it dies and cannot implant in the uterus and develop. Therefore no placenta develops and no HCG is produced. The corpus luteum begins degenerating on approximately day

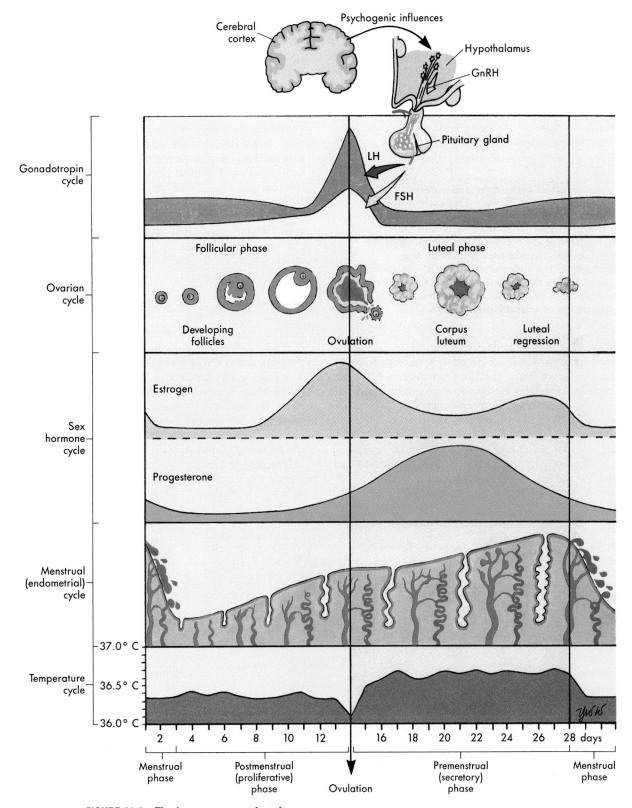

FIGURE 21-9 The human menstrual cycle.
The growth and thickening of the uterine lining is governed by increasing levels of estrogen and progesterone; menstruation, the sloughing off of the blood-rich tissue, is initiated by decreasing levels of these hormones.

24 of the cycle. As it degenerates, it stops producing estrogens and progesterone, hormones necessary to maintain the buildup of the lining of the uterus. As the blood level of these hormones falls, the endometrial lining sloughs off in a process known as **menstruation,** or the menses. The lining degenerates over a period of approximately 5 days, causing a somewhat steady flow of blood, tissue, and mucus from the uterus and out through the vagina, usually heaviest during the first three days of the menses. The process of menstruation is traditionally considered to mark the *beginning* of the reproductive cycle.

The reproductive cycle of females occurs approximately every 28 days. This cycle includes the maturation of the primary oocyte, its release from the ovary, its journey to the uterus, and the development of the former follicular cells into the corpus luteum. In addition, it includes the thickening of the endometrial lining of the uterus in preparation for the implantation of a new embryo. The hormones FSH, LH, estrogen, and progesterone orchestrate these events.

Before the onset of a menstrual period, many women experience symptoms that are collectively referred to as *premenstrual tension syndrome,* or *PMS.* Premenstrual symptoms are thought to be related to the cutoff of progesterone and the retention of water. Symptoms vary from woman to woman and include breast swelling and tenderness, bloating, weight gain, headaches, fatigue, and backache. Physicians suggest that a diet high in protein and low in salt, alcohol, and carbohydrates can reduce water retention during this time and lessen the symptoms of PMS.

The reproductive cycle of women generally begins during adolescence and ends between the ages of 50 and 55 years. This cessation of the menses is termed **menopause.** As a woman ages, changes take place in the reproductive cycle that lead to menopause. These changes usually begin between the ages of 40 and 50 years. The menstrual cycles may become irregular, varying in length. Generally they become less frequent. These changes result from the failure of the ovaries to respond to stimulation by FSH and LH secreted by the pituitary. As a result of these changes, follicles do not develop; the ovaries therefore produce less estrogen. The drop in estrogen causes the two major symptoms associated with menopause: flushes, the reddening of the face and a feeling of warmth, and flashes, short periods of intense flushing. Although some people think that depression often accompanies menopause, this link does not exist. Recent psychiatric studies show that depression occurs no more often during this time of a woman's life than at any other.

The vagina

The uterus is shaped somewhat like an upside-down pear: wider at its top and narrower at its bottom. The narrower portion, called the **cervix** (or neck), opens into the vagina. The vagina, a muscular tube-like passageway to the exterior of the body, is an organ with three functions: it accepts the penis during sexual intercourse and is the place where sperm are deposited, it is the lower portion of the birth canal during childbirth, and it provides a passageway for the exit of the menstrual flow. Although only about 9 centimeters (3 1/2 inches) in length, the vagina can stretch considerably during intercourse and childbirth because its walls are com-

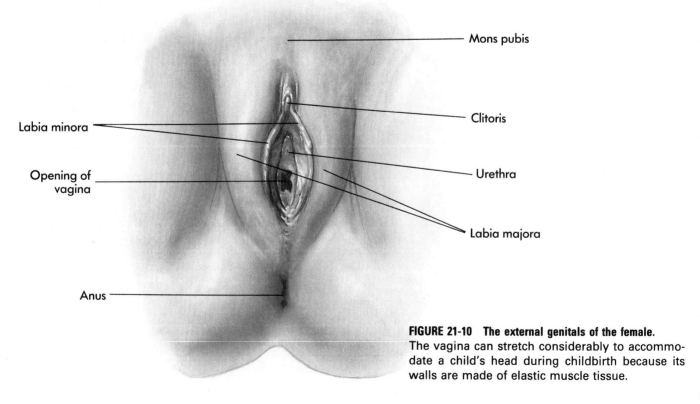

Mons pubis

Clitoris

Labia minora

Opening of vagina

Urethra

Labia majora

Anus

FIGURE 21-10 The external genitals of the female. The vagina can stretch considerably to accommodate a child's head during childbirth because its walls are made of elastic muscle tissue.

posed of elastic-like smooth muscle tissue. The mucous membrane that lines the inside of the vagina produces a viscous fluid that keeps the vagina moist and provides lubrication during intercourse.

Bacteria that normally reside in the vagina use the large amounts of glycogen in the vaginal secretion as a food source. As a by-product of the digestion of this glycogen, these normal vaginal bacteria produce acid, which accounts for the acidity of the vagina so harmful to sperm. However, the ejaculate contains substances that neutralize this acidity (see p. 413). These bacteria have a positive effect in that they discourage the growth of unwanted bacteria and yeasts. Often, when a woman takes antibiotics to kill bacteria infecting another part of her body, the antibiotic also kills the bacteria residing in the vagina. If these bacteria die, yeast cells or other bacteria can begin to grow. A vaginal infection can be a troublesome side effect of antibiotic therapy in women, since it can produce itching, discomfort, and discharges from the vagina.

The external genitals

The external genitals of a female are collectively called the **vulva.** Interestingly, parts of the vulva are homologous to the external genitals of the male, which means that the organs have a similar structure and anatomical position and originated from the same tissues during embryonic development. The most anterior structure is the **mons pubis** (Figure 21-10). The word *mons* comes from a Latin word meaning "prominence" and refers to the mound of fatty tissue that lies over the place of attachment of the two pubic bones. Two longitudinal folds of skin called the **labia majora** (*labia* means "lips") run posteriorly from the mons. These folds are homologous to the scrotum in the male. Covered by the labia majora are additional folds of skin called the **labia minora.** Both sets of skin folds protect the vaginal and urethral openings beneath. Figure 21-10 shows that the urethra opens to the outside slightly in front of the vagina and is not connected to the reproductive system as in males. In addition to the vaginal and urethral openings, the labia minora also covers the openings of several tiny ducts that produce a mucus-like secretion during sexual stimulation. This secretion helps lubricate the vagina and penis during sexual intercourse. Slightly anterior to the convergence of the labia minora is the **clitoris,** a small mass of

erectile and nervous tissue that responds to sexual stimulation. The clitoris is homologous to the tip of the penis in males.

The mammary glands

The **mammary glands,** or milk-producing glands, lie over the chest muscles. Each mammary gland is made up of 15 to 20 lobes that are separated by fat. The amount of fat determines the size of the breast and is not an indicator of a woman's ability to produce milk. Ducts extend from the glands to the nipple of the breast.

The mammary glands are secondary sexual characteristics that begin to develop in adolescent girls as the hormonal changes of puberty take place. These changes are initiated as the ovary begins to produce estrogens and accelerate as the menstrual cycle begins and the ovaries produce even higher blood levels of estrogens.

The function of the mammary glands is lactation, the production and secretion of milk. Prolactin, a hormone secreted by the anterior pituitary during pregnancy, is the hormone primarily responsible for stimulating the production of milk. As an infant nurses, its sucking sends nervous impulses to the hypothalamus. These messages stimulate the continued production of prolactin and therefore of milk. In addition, the nervous impulses trigger the hypothalamus to produce oxytocin, a hormone that is released by the posterior pituitary and that causes milk to be ejected into the ducts of the mammary glands. This process is called *milk letdown.*

The sexual response

The sexual act is referred to by a variety of names, including *intercourse, copulation,* and *coitus,* as well as a host of more informal ones. The physiological events associated with sexual intercourse can be described as having four phases, although the division of the sexual response into phases is somewhat arbitrary. These phases are excitement, plateau, orgasm, and resolution (Figure 21-11).

The *excitement phase* refers to the sexual activity that precedes intercourse. This phase therefore varies in length depending on the needs and desires of the sexual partners. During excitement the heartbeat, blood pressure, and rate

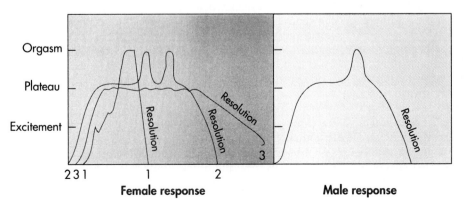

FIGURE 21-11 The human orgasmic response.
Among females, the response is highly variable. It may be typified by one of the three patterns illustrated here. Among males, the response is not as variable.

TABLE 21-1 | **Methods of birth control***

DEVICE	ACTION	FAILURE RATES (%)	ADVANTAGES	DISADVANTAGES
Rhythm method	Avoidance of sexual intercourse during woman's fertile period	13-21	Contraceptive devices unnecessary; agreeable to some religious groups	High failure rate due to difficulty of predicting ovulation; no protection against sexually transmitted diseases
Withdrawal	Removal of penis from vagina before ejaculation	9-25	Contraceptive devices unnecessary	High failure rate attributed to the secretion of sperm before ejaculation; self-control necessary
Condom	Thin rubber sheath for penis that collects semen	3-15	Easy to use, effective, and inexpensive; the most reliable protection against some sexually transmitted diseases with the exception of abstinence	Possible decrease in spontaneity; possible deterioration on the shelf
Diaphragm	Soft rubber cup that covers entrance to uterus, prevents sperm from reaching egg, and holds spermicide	4-25	No dangerous side effects, reliable if used properly; some protection against cervical cancer	Careful fitting required; some inconvenience associated with insertion and removal; possible dislodgment during sex
Cervical cap	Miniature diaphragm that covers cervix closely, prevents sperm from reaching egg, and holds spermicide	Probably comparable to diaphragm	No dangerous side effects; fairly effective; able to remain in place longer than diaphragm	Problems with fitting and insertion; limited number of sizes; not available in the United States
Sponge	Device acting as sperm barrier and releasing spermicide	15-30	Safe and easy to insert; possible to leave in place for 24 hours; no fitting needed	Relatively unreliable; only one size available; some sensitivity and removal problems; no use during menstruation

*Approximate effectiveness of these reversible methods of birth control is measured in pregnancies per 100 actual users per year.
†Due to lawsuits, no longer widely used in the United States.

of breathing increase. In addition, the blood vessels of the face, breasts, and genitals widen, producing a reddening of the skin in these areas called the *sex flush.* The nipples commonly harden and become more sensitive. In the genital area, increased circulation leads to an erection in the male and a swelling and parting of the labia in females. The vaginal walls become moister and the muscles of the vagina relax.

The act of sexual intercourse signals the beginning of the *plateau phase,* a period of intensifying physiological changes initiated in the excitement phase. During sexual intercourse the penetration of the vagina by the thrusting penis results in the repeated stimulation of nerve endings both in the tip of the penis and in the clitoris. The clitoris, which is now swollen, becomes very sensitive and withdraws up into a sheath, or hood. Once it has withdrawn, the stimulation of the clitoris is indirect, with the thrusting movements of the penis rubbing the clitoral hood against the clitoris. This type of stimulation of the clitoris is insufficient

for many women, however, who require a more direct stimulation of this organ.

The climax of intercourse (*orgasm*) is reached when the stimulation is sufficient to initiate a series of reflexive muscular contractions. The nerve signals producing these contractions are associated with other nervous activity within the central nervous system, activity that you experience as sexual pleasure. In females the contractions are initiated by impulses in the hypothalamus that cause the pituitary to release large amounts of the hormone oxytocin. This hormone, in turn, causes the muscles in the uterus and around the vaginal opening to contract and the cervix to be pulled upward. There may be one or several intense peaks of contractions (orgasm) or the peaks may be more numerous but less intense (see Figure 21-11).

Analogous contractions occur in the male, initiated by nerve signals from the brain. These signals first cause emission, in which rhythmic peristaltic contractions of the vas deferens and the prostate gland cause the sperm and semi-

TABLE 21-1   Methods of birth control—cont'd

DEVICE	ACTION	FAILURE RATES (%)	ADVANTAGES	DISADVANTAGES
Foams, creams, jellies, vaginal suppositories	Chemical spermicides inserted in vagina before intercourse that also prevent sperm from entering uterus	10-25	Possible use by anyone who is not allergic, no known side effects	Relatively unreliable, sometimes messy; necessary to use 5 to 10 minutes before each act of intercourse
Oral contraceptives (birth control pills)	Hormones, either in combination or progestin only, that primarily prevent release of egg	1-5, depending on type	Convenient and highly effective; significant noncontraceptive health benefits, such as protection against ovarian and endometrial cancers	Necessary to take regularly; possible minor side effects, which new formulations have reduced; not for women with cardiovascular risks, mostly those over 35 who smoke
Implant (Norplant)	Capsules surgically implanted under skin that slowly release a hormone that blocks release of eggs	0.3	Very safe, convenient and effective; very long lasting (5 years); possible nonreproductive health benefits like those of oral contraceptives	Irregular or absent periods; necessity of minor surgical procedure to insert and remove
Intrauterine devices	Small plastic or metal devices placed in the uterus that somehow prevent fertilization or implantation; some contain copper, others release hormones	1-5	Convenient, highly effective, infrequent replacement	Possible excess menstrual bleeding and pain; danger of perforation, infection, and expulsion; not recommended for those who are childless or not monogamous; risk of pelvic inflammatory disease or infertility; dangerous in pregnancy†

nal fluid to move to the base of the penis. Shortly after, nerve signals from the brain induce contractions of the muscles at the base of the penis, resulting in the ejaculation of the semen from the penis.

The *resolution phase* begins after orgasm. The bodies of both men and women return slowly over a period of several minutes to their normal physiological states. After ejaculation, males rapidly lose their erection and enter a period lasting 20 minutes or longer in which sexual arousal is difficult to achieve and ejaculation is almost impossible. By contrast, women can be aroused again almost immediately.

Contraception and birth control

In most vertebrates, sexual intercourse is associated solely with reproduction. In humans, however, sexual behavior serves a second important function—the reinforcement of pair bonding, the emotional relationship between two individuals. Couples who wish to limit the pregnancies resulting from sexual intercourse may use one of many methods of family planning, or birth control (Table 21-1). Several different approaches are commonly taken to achieve birth

control. These methods differ from one another in their effectiveness and in their acceptability to different couples. Some of them are shown in Figure 21-12. In addition, some methods of birth control also protect against sexually transmitted diseases.

Abstinence

The most reliable way to avoid pregnancy and sexually transmitted diseases is not to have sex at all. A variant of this approach (for birth control purposes only) is to avoid sexual relations on the three days preceding and the day after ovulation, since this is the only time during which fertilization can occur. This approach, called the **rhythm method,** is satisfactory in principle but difficult in application, since ovulation is not easy to predict and may occur unexpectedly. The effectiveness of the rhythm method is low. However, a woman can use techniques that involve taking her basal body temperature or analyzing her cervical mucus to help determine when ovulation takes place. Home test kits are also available that detect the time of ovulation. (These methods can be used to help a couple conceive a

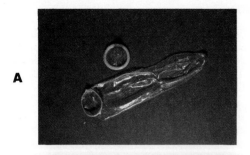

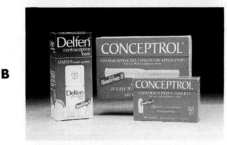

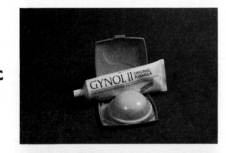

FIGURE 21-12 Five common methods of birth control.
A Condom.
B Foams.
C Diaphragm and spermicide.
D Oral contraceptives.
E Contraceptive sponge.

child as well as to avoid conception.) As an added birth control measure, some couples using the rhythm method of birth control conservatively avoid sexual intercourse many days before and a few days after ovulation. The failure rate of the rhythm method is estimated to be 13% to 21% (13 to 21 pregnancies per 100 women practicing the rhythm method, per year).

Another variant of this approach is to withdraw the penis before ejaculation. This method is as unreliable as the rhythm method, with a failure rate estimated between 9% and 25%. The reason for this high failure rate is that the penis can secrete prematurely released sperm within its lubricating fluid and a second sexual act may transfer sperm ejaculated earlier.

Sperm blockage

If sperm do not reach the uterine tubes, fertilization cannot take place. One way to prevent sperm from reaching the uterine tubes is for the male partner to use a **condom.** A condom is a sheath for the penis, constructed of thin rubber or other natural or synthetic materials. In principle, this method is easy to use and should be highly successful. However, in practice the failure rate of condoms is from 3% to 15%, primarily due to improper use or failure to use a condom consistently. Nevertheless, it is the most commonly used form of birth control in the United States. The use of latex condoms is also an excellent way to reduce the risk of contracting sexually transmitted diseases, including AIDS.

A second way to prevent the entry of sperm into the uterine tubes is to place a cover over the cervix. The cover may be a relatively tight-fitting **cervical cap** (not available in the United States at this time), which is worn for days at a time, or a rubber dome called a **diaphragm,** which is inserted immediately before intercourse. In addition, the vaginal side of a diaphragm is covered with a spermicide before insertion and is then kept in place for a minimum of six hours after intercourse. Because the dimensions of individual cervices vary, a cervical cap or diaphragm must be fitted by a physician. Failure rates average from 4% to 25% for diaphragms and are somewhat lower for cervical caps. These high failure rates are due, in part, to incorrect use of these birth control devices. Neither form of birth control is effective against sexually transmitted diseases.

Sperm destruction

The spermicidal (sperm-killing) sponge is inserted and used much like a diaphragm, but it is composed of a sponge-like material impregnated with a spermicide. The sponge provides somewhat of a barrier to the uterus but also absorbs the sperm into the sponge to be killed there. Sperm can also be destroyed in the vagina by the use of spermicidal jellies, creams, or foams applied immediately before intercourse. The failure rate of these methods varies widely from 10% to 25%, and they are not useful in the prevention of sexually transmitted diseases.

Prevention of egg maturation

Since about 1960, a widespread form of birth control has been the use of **birth control pills** by women. These pills contain estrogen and progesterone, either taken together in the same pill or in separate pills taken sequentially. In the normal reproductive cycle of a female, these hormones act to shut down the production of the pituitary hormones FSH and LH. The artificial maintenance of high levels of estrogen and progesterone in a woman's bloodstream cause the body to act as if ovulation had already occurred, when in fact it has not. The ovarian follicles do not mature in the absence of FSH, and ovulation does not occur in the absence of LH. For these reasons, birth control pills provide a very effective means of birth control, with a failure rate of 0% to 5%. They play no role in the prevention of sexually transmitted diseases, but research shows that the synthetic progesterone (progestin) in the pill helps ward off cancer of the uterus and ovaries. Scientists are concerned, however, that the estrogen in the pill may increase the risk of breast cancer. Medical researchers are now experimenting with a pill that includes LH-releasing hormone. This pill is currently undergoing clinical trials. Another, more highly experimental pill substitutes melatonin for the estrogen but is not yet approved for testing.

In 1990 a product that works in a manner similar to the pill but that prevents pregnancy for up to 5 years was introduced in the United States. This product is called Norplant (Figure 21-13). In a 15-minute operation in the doctor's office, the six matchstick-sized tubes are surgically implanted under the skin of the upper arm. These tubes contain the synthetic hormone progestin, the active ingredient in most birth control pills. Norplant prevents pregnancy by inhibiting ovulation as the pill does, but it also thickens the cervical mucus so that sperm cannot move through the female reproductive tract. Although 99.8% reliable, Norplant causes irregular menstrual bleeding in 75% of its users.

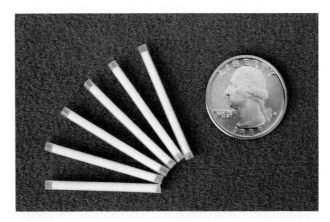

FIGURE 21-13 The contraceptive implant: a new method of birth control for women.
The tubes shown here are implanted in a woman's upper arm in a simple surgical procedure. Once implanted, the tubes release a constant, low-level flow of progestin that prevents ovulation. The implant is effective for about 5 years.

A Male Birth Control Pill

New birth control methods such as Norplant are now on the market; several more should be available within the next ten years. Research in birth control once focused on the female reproductive system, but that focus is changing. One new method now being investigated is a male birth control pill: a contraceptive that prevents sperm maturation.

Researchers are testing a substance that blocks sperm production by mimicking an important "releasing hormone," so named because it affects the release of other hormones from the anterior pituitary (see p.261). This releasing hormone, gonadotropic releasing hormone or GnRH, controls secretion of follicle-stimulating hormone (FSH) and luteinizing hormone (LH) in both men and women. In men, FSH triggers sperm production and LH controls the release of testosterone from the testes. Researchers have found that injecting men with a modified, inactive form of GnRH stops sperm production. This inactive GnRH binds to receptors on the membranes of cells in the anterior pituitary, preventing secretion of both FSH and LH.

A major side effect discovered during testing has already been overcome. When the modified form of GnRh binds to receptors in the anterior pituitary, it prevents secretion of LH. When LH secretion is blocked, testosterone levels fall, causing impotence. This effect can be avoided by accompanying injections of the modified GnRH with injections of testosterone. The combination seems to be working in clinical trials, and the next step is to develop an oral form of the two substances. If this step is successful, a male birth control pill may soon be a reality.

Surgical intervention

A completely effective means of birth control is the surgical removal of a portion of the tube through which gametes move from one reproductive structure to another (Figure 21-14). In males such an operation involves the removal of a portion of the vas deferens, the tube through which spermtravel to the penis. This procedure, called a **vasectomy,** can be carried out in a physician's office. Reversing a vasectomy is difficult but can sometimes be done. In females the comparable operation involves the removal of a section of each of the two uterine tubes through which the oocyte travels to the uterus. Since these tubes are located within the abdomen, the operation, called a **tubal ligation,** is more difficult to perform than a vasectomy and is even more difficult to reverse.

Among methods of birth control, the rhythm method and withdrawal are not highly reliable. Condoms and diaphragms are effective when used correctly, but mistakes are common. Birth control pills and implanted hormonal tubes are very effective. Vasectomies and tubal ligations are completely effective, although usually permanent.

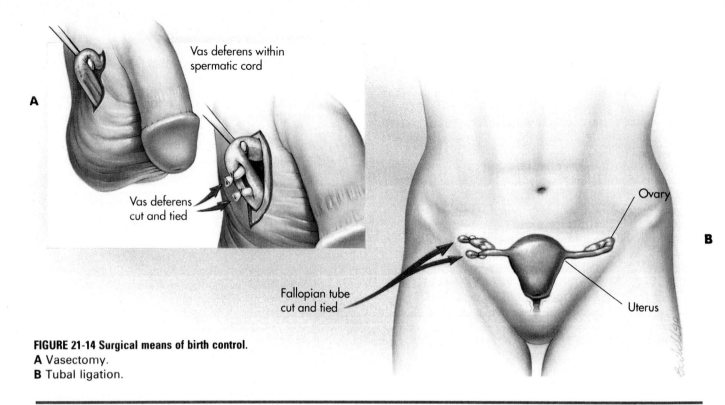

FIGURE 21-14 Surgical means of birth control.
A Vasectomy.
B Tubal ligation.

Summary

1. Sexual reproduction is the process whereby a male and a female sex cell combine to form the first cell of a new individual. The male and female reproductive systems are made up of organs and ducts that produce, store, transport, and receive the sex cells. Accessory glands help nourish the sex cells.

2. The male reproductive system produces male sex cells called *sperm* and transports them to the female reproductive tract. Sperm cells develop in the tightly packed tubules of the testes, which are covered with a pouch of skin called the *scrotum* and hang from the lower pelvic area of the male. Sperm production is triggered by follicle-stimulating hormone (FSH).

3. During the development of sperm, diploid cells called *spermatogonia* give rise to haploid cells called *spermatids*. These haploid cells contain half the normal amount of hereditary material of body cells. The spermatids then develop into sperm cells, or spermatozoa, which have a head containing the hereditary material, a vesicle containing enzymes to penetrate the oocyte membrane, and a whip-like tail. They mature in the epididymis, a long, coiled tube that sits on the back side of the testes.

4. The accessory glands of the male reproductive system secrete a fluid that combines with the sperm during ejaculation. This alkaline fluid nourishes the sperm and neutralizes the acidity of the female vagina. During ejaculation, sperm are propelled through the vas deferens to the urethra and out the penis.

5. The female reproductive tract produces one potential egg (secondary oocyte) each month. Each potential egg develops in the ovaries, travels to the uterus via one of the two uterine tubes, and implants in the inner lining of the uterus if fertilized while journeying down the tube.

6. The reproductive cycle of the female encompasses the events of the maturation of each potential egg, or primary oocyte, its release from the ovary as a secondary oocyte, its journey to the uterus, and the "healing" of its follicle. Certain primary oocytes in the ovaries continue the development they began before birth when stimulated by the hormone FSH. Their surrounding cells start producing estrogens, which promote the thickening of the endometrial lining of the uterus. Of the developing oocytes, one matures into a secondary oocyte that bursts from the ovary as a surge of LH occurs midcycle. The ruptured follicular cells that surrounded the oocyte secrete estrogens and progesterone. If fertilization of the oocyte does not take place, the progesterone and estrogens maintain the endometrial lining until diminished levels of these hormones cause it to degenerate. A sloughing off of the endometrial lining follows, which is referred to as *menstruation*.

7. The human sexual response has four physiological periods: excitement, plateau, orgasm, and resolution. Orgasm in women is variable and may be prolonged. Orgasm in men is more uniform and abrupt; it coincides with the ejaculation of sperm.

8. Humans practice a variety of birth control procedures; men using condoms and women using birth control pills are the most common.

1. What is sexual reproduction?

2. Discuss the roles of the hormones involved in the development of male gametes and secondary sexual characteristics.

3. Relate the structure of a spermatozoon to its function.

4. What are the seminal vesicles, prostate gland, and bulbourethral glands? Describe the contribution made by each during ejaculation.

5. Explain why women over 35 years of age are more likely to bear children with developmental abnormalities.

6. Helen has had one of her ovaries surgically removed. Can she still conceive a child? What restrictions might there be to conception?

7. Two monthly cycles are involved in a woman's reproductive cycle. What are they, and what happens in each one?

8. Summarize the reproductive cycle of a human female when fertilization does not occur. What hormones are involved?

9. Summarize what happens during the reproductive cycle of the human female if fertilization occurs. What hormone is secreted?

10. John and Mary have had difficulty conceiving a child, so their doctor recommend that they use in an in-home ovulation test to determine the day of Mary's ovulation. Given this information, during what window of time could fertilization take place?

11. Which methods of birth control can help prevent the spread of sexually transmitted diseases?

12. Explain how birth control pills prevent conception. What hormones are involved?

13. Compare the effectiveness of the various birth control methods discussed in the chapter. Which are most effective? Least effective?

14. Can you assess why a cervical cap or diaphragm is ineffective in preventing the transfer of sexually transmitted diseases?

1. Female gametes begin their development prenatally, so at age 20, a woman's gametes are all 20 years old. A male's gametes develop all during his life, so at age 20 a man's gametes are only a few days old. What are some implications inherent in this difference?

2. Earlier in the text, the role of hormones in human body function was discussed. In human reproduction, the sex hormones play the key roles in fertilization and implantation. Discuss the roles of female and male sex hormones in the sexual response. Might hormonally based birth control affect this response? Is the sexual response affected by the varying hormone levels of the female reproductive cycle? In what ways?

Hoffman, P. (1992, June). The science of sex. *Discover,* pp. 32-89.
This entire issue is devoted to articles regarding human sexuality and reproduction.

Kline, D. (1991, February). Activation of the egg by sperm. *Bioscience,* pp. 89-95.
This article is a brief but excellent survey of the biochemistry of egg activation by sperm.

Leishman, K. (1987, February). Heterosexuals and AIDS. *The Atlantic,* pp.39-58.
This is a chilling account of the difficulty of modifying sexual behavior, despite the knowledge of the dangers associated with AIDS.

Small, M. (1991, July). Sperm wars. *Discover,* pp 48-53.
A fantastic look at the process of fertilization with splendid color electron photomicrographs.

22 Development Before Birth

The image of a mother nursing, rocking, and cuddling her baby has been portrayed in art for hundreds of years. But scientists have only recently validated that these activities are not only emotionally good for moms and babies, but they also help babies grow properly. Cuddling and caressing an infant stimulates respiration, blood flow, and growth rate. The baby is healthier and cries less. For these reasons, volunteers at Duke University Medical Center cuddle hospital-bound premature infants whose parents must work and are unable to be with them continually. Interestingly, gentle rocking of an infant stimulates the baby's cerebellum—the part of the brain that controls coordination. Rocking hastens the maturation of this control center. And while a baby is being cuddled, rocked, and nursed by its mother, her breast milk is providing nourishment and antibodies that will help stave off disease until the baby's own defenses are produced. In fact, this peaceful nurturing provides the baby with medical benefits that even the most high-tech pediatric unit would find hard to match.

Development

What happens after the birth of an infant is crucial to its survival. However, what happens before birth may be even more crucial. In fact, if an infant does not develop properly before birth, normal growth after birth becomes difficult and sometimes impossible. This chapter focuses on life before birth, or **prenatal development,** the gradual growth and progressive changes in a developing human from conception until the time the fetus leaves the mother's womb. This time of development is also called **gestation** and lasts approximately 8 1/2 months. (The 9-month pregnancy calculation is computed from the first day of a woman's last menstrual period, but conception usually takes place in the middle of her cycle.) The gestation period is commonly referred to as *pregnancy.*

Fertilization

The union of a male gamete (sperm) and a female gamete (egg) is called **fertilization,** or conception. In the human, fertilization usually takes place in the uterine tube of the female (see Chapter 21 for a discussion of gamete formation and the events leading up to fertilization). Therefore development begins in the uterine tube.

Figure 22-1 shows that a human egg, or **ovum,** is a relatively large cell. In fact, ova are among the largest cells within an animal's body. Making up most of the substance of an ovum is the **yolk,** the nutrient material that the developing individual lives on until nutrients can be derived from the mother. In humans, the yolk granules provide nutrition for a week or so. In the case of birds, however, the young develop totally within the egg. Therefore the yolk of these eggs must be substantial enough to maintain the animal throughout its entire course of development. The yolk of an ostrich egg, for example, is so large that it is approximately the size of a baseball!

As mentioned in Chapter 21, the secondary oocyte breaks away from the ovary during ovulation in placental mammals (which includes people) and is swept into the uterine tube. This cell is not yet a mature ovum, or egg. Only after penetration of the oocyte by a sperm will the second meiotic division be completed, yielding the mature ovum and a second polar body. And, although fertilization may sound like an easy job for sperm, only 50 to 100 sperm make it to the egg from an ejaculate that contains approximately 200 to 300 million!

Many things can go wrong from the time the sperm are manufactured in the testes, stored in the epididymis, and travel out of the man's body and into the vagina of a woman. For example, up to 20% of sperm are deformed in some way. A common abnormality is having two flagella instead of one. Sperm with this abnormality do not have normal motility and cannot make the lengthy journey from the vagina, through the constricted cervix, up through the uterus, and along the uterine tube.

Although the acid environment of the female vagina is treacherous territory for sperm and although they constantly swim upstream against the downward currents of fe-

male secretions, they are also aided by the female body. During the time of ovulation, a female produces strands of a special protein called **mucin.** This substance becomes a part of the cervical mucus her body produces and provides thread-like highways along which the sperm can travel. The sperm make their way up these strands of mucin to the uterus. As they move along, enzyme inhibitors located at the tips of their heads are slowly worn away, gradually uncovering enzymes that are capable of penetrating the egg's outer protective layers and its membrane. Figure 22-2, *A* pictures a sperm that has penetrated an egg's jelly-like covering, the **zona pellucida.**

The moment of penetration of a human oocyte by a sperm is an event only recently captured on film. On entry of the cytoplasm of the oocyte, the sperm sheds its tail, and

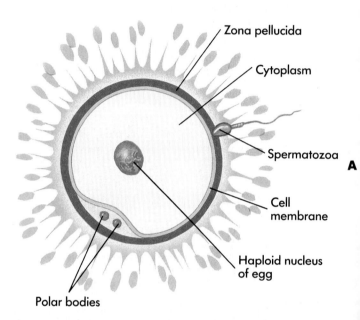

A

B

FIGURE 22-1 The egg.
A A human egg is surrounded by a membrane, is nourished briefly by yolk, and contains a haploid nucleus.
B The membrane of this sea urchin egg has been penetrated by a sperm cell. Once the sperm cell enters the egg and reaches the nucleus, the fused cells begin to divide.

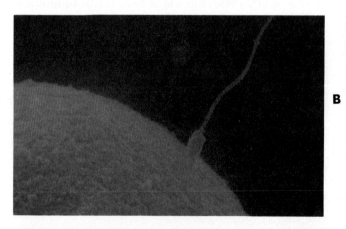

428   PART SIX   How Humans Reproduce

its head swells. Immediate changes in the surface of the egg allow no other sperm to penetrate, and oocyte meiosis is completed. Finally, the sperm and ovum nuclei, clearly seen as separate from one another in Figure 22-3, *A,* fuse to form the nucleus of the first cell of a new individual (Figure 22-3, *B*). This new cell, which contains intermingling genetic material from both the mother and the father, is called a **zygote.**

> The penetration of the secondary oocyte by the sperm is called fertilization. This penetration causes changes in the surface of the egg that allow no other sperm to enter and triggers the completion of meiosis. After the sperm sheds its tail, the nuclei of the egg and sperm fuse to form a zygote, the first cell of a new individual.

With the union of the chromosomal material of both gametes, the zygote begins to divide by mitotic cell division. As division proceeds during the next 2 weeks, the developing cell mass is referred to as a **pre-embryo.**

The first and second weeks of development: The pre-embryo

Within 30 hours, the one-celled zygote begins to divide rapidly: one cell into two, two into four, four into eight, and so forth, producing a cluster of cells. This process of cell division occurs without cell growth and is called **cleavage.** Occasionally, a single, fertilized ovum splits into two cell clusters during cleavage, and each cluster continues developing on its own. Since both cell clusters arose from the same cell, they have identical genetic information and will

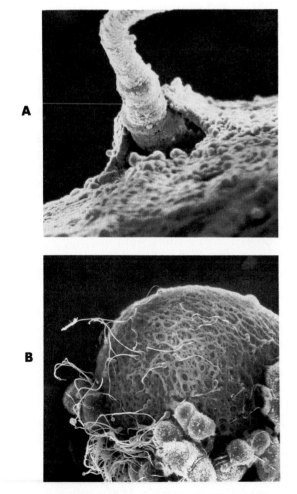

FIGURE 22-2 Fertilization.
The moment of penetration of a human egg by a sperm cell **(A)** initiates changes in the surface of the egg that prevent other sperm from entering **(B).**

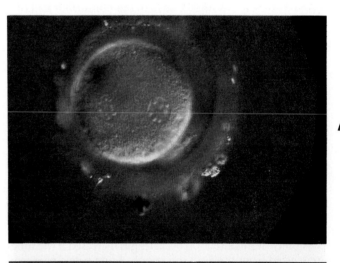
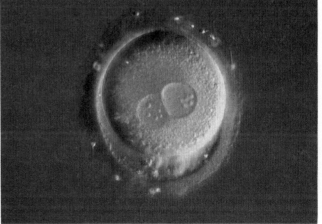

FIGURE 22-3 The fusion of nuclei.
A The nuclei of the sperm and ovum are clearly separate.
B The nuclei have merged to form the nucleus of the first cell of a new individual.

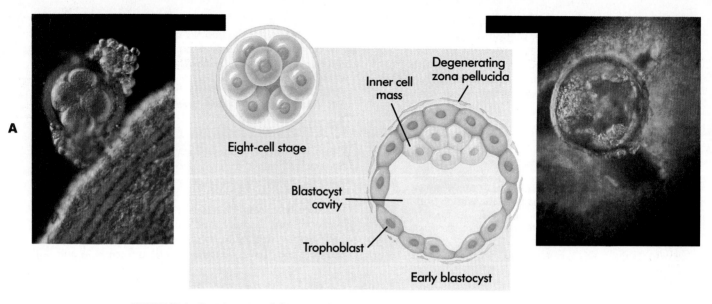

FIGURE 22-4 Development of the pre-embryo.
A View of the pre-embryo at the eight-cell stage. At this stage, the pre-embryo is floating free in the uterus as its cells continue to divide.
B After 2 days in the uterus, the ball of cells has developed into a blastocyst. The inner cell mass contains cells that will develop into the different body tissues of the new individual.

result in the development of identical twins. Identical twins are always the same sex. Fraternal twins arise from the release of two secondary oocytes and the fertilization of both. Fraternal twins are genetically different from one another because they are two separate oocytes fertilized by two different sperm cells. Therefore they may be different sexes.

As the cell cluster (pre-embryo) divides, it journeys along the remaining two thirds of the uterine tube. This trip takes approximately 3 days. Occasionally, a pre-embryo gets caught in the folded inner lining of the uterine tube and implants there, creating an **ectopic pregnancy.** The possibility of this situation occurring is increased if the tubes are scarred from previous infections. Acute pelvic pain usually signals this problem, which requires immediate medical attention. Normally, however, the pre-embryo reaches the uterus, or womb. Still the same size as a newly fertilized ovum, the pre-embryo now consists of about 16 densely clustered cells and is called a **morula,** from a Latin word meaning "mulberry." This stage of development is common to all vertebrates and even invertebrates. In fact, the processes of development in all vertebrates are very similar to the course of human development before birth.

▼▼
Cleavage, or cell division of the zygote without cell growth, is the first stage in the development of humans as well as other multicellular animals. It results in the formation of a mass of cells known as a morula approximately 3 days after fertilization.

The pre-embryo floats free in the uterus as its cells continue to divide. After 2 days in the uterus, the morula has developed into the **blastocyst,** a stage of development in

which the pre-embryo is a hollow ball of cells. The center is filled with fluid from the uterine cavity. Like the term *morula,* the term *blastocyst* is descriptive, derived from two Greek words meaning "germ (germinal) sac."

One portion of the blastocyst contains a concentrated mass of cells destined to differentiate into the various body tissues of the new individual. It is referred to as the *inner cell mass.* Interestingly, each cell in this mass has the ability to develop into a complete individual. In fact, scientists have been able to produce test-tube mice using transplanted nuclei from inner cell mass cells. The outer ring of cells, called the **trophoblast** from a Greek word meaning "nutrition," will give rise to most of the extraembryonic membranes, including much of the placenta, an organ that helps maintain the developing embryo (Figure 22-4).

The general term **blastula** is used to describe the saclike blastocyst of mammals and, in other animals, the stage that develops a similar fluid-filled cavity. This stage of development is significant for all vertebrates; it is the first time that cells begin to move, or migrate, to shape the new individual in a process called **morphogenesis.** However, the major morphogenetic events occur during the third to eighth weeks.

▼▼
Cell migration, which begins to shape the pre-embryo, is the process that begins approximately 4 days after fertilization. Cell migration helps shape the developing individual in a process called morphogenesis. At this early stage, cell movement results in the formation of a hollow ball of cells known as a blastocyst in humans and in other mammals a stage more generally called the blastula.

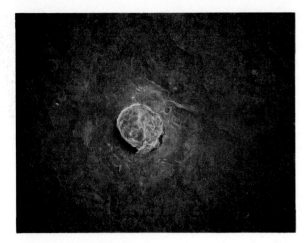

FIGURE 22-5   Implantation.
About 7 to 8 days after fertilization, the blastocyst imbeds itself into the wall of the uterus.

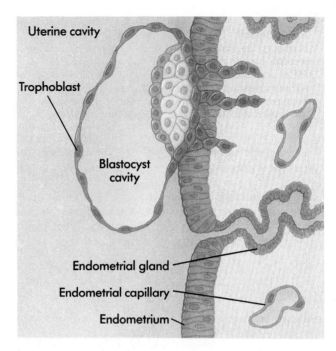

FIGURE 22-6   A detailed view of implantation.
Special finger-like projections produced by the trophoblast anchor the blastocyst to the wall of the uterus, or endometrium.

Approximately 1 week after fertilization, the blastocyst secretes enzymes that digest a microscopic portion of the uterus. It then nestles into this site, nourished by the digested uterine cells, in a process called **implantation** (Figure 22-5). Barely visible to the naked eye, the blastocyst most often attaches to the posterior wall of the uterus (Figure 22-6). Figure 22-7 summarizes the events that take place from fertilization to implantation.

By this time, a woman is nearing the end of her menstrual cycle (see Chapter 21), and the blastocyst is in danger of being swept away during menstruation. However, the blastocyst secretes a hormone called **human chorionic gonadotropin,** or **HCG,** which maintains the corpus luteum. The corpus luteum is a structure derived from the ruptured follicle from which the egg was cast out of the ovary. Sustained by HCG, the corpus luteum continues to secrete progesterone and estrogen, hormones that maintain the uterine lining and allow the development of the pre-embryo to proceed. After the first 3 months of development, the placenta (see p. 433) begins to secrete the estrogens and progesterone that maintain the pregnancy.

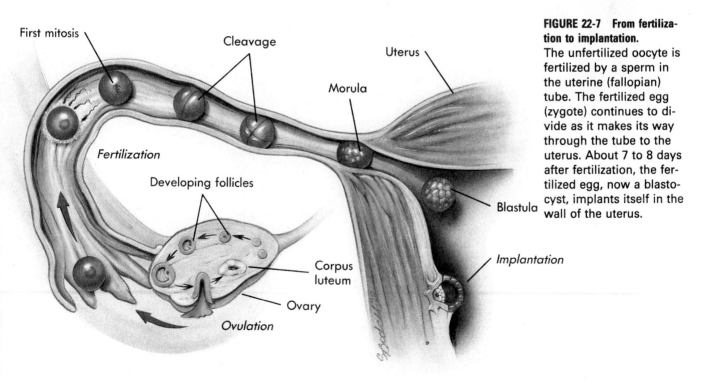

FIGURE 22-7   From fertilization to implantation.
The unfertilized oocyte is fertilized by a sperm in the uterine (fallopian) tube. The fertilized egg (zygote) continues to divide as it makes its way through the tube to the uterus. About 7 to 8 days after fertilization, the fertilized egg, now a blastocyst, implants itself in the wall of the uterus.

▼▼▼ **Approximately 1 week after fertilization, the blastocyst implants in the lining of the uterus and secretes human chorionic gonadotropin (HCG). HCG acts on the corpus luteum in the ovary. The corpus luteum responds by continuing to produce estrogens and progesterone, hormones that sustain the implanted blastocyst as the placenta develops.**

During its second week of development, the pre-embryo completes its implantation within the uterine wall, two of its three **primary germ layers** develop, and the extraembryonic membranes begin to form. The primary germ layers are three layers of cells that develop from the inner cell mass of the blastocyst and from which all the organs and tissues of the body develop. These three layers are called the *ectoderm* ("outside skin"), *endoderm* ("inside skin"), and the *mesoderm* ("middle skin"). The **ectoderm** forms the outer layer of skin, the nervous system, and portions of the sense organs. The **endoderm** gives rise to the lining of the digestive tract, the digestive organs, the respiratory tract, and the lungs; the urinary bladder; and the urethra. The **mesoderm** differentiates into the skeleton, muscles, blood, reproductive organs, connective tissue, and the innermost layer of the skin (Figure 22-8). Figure 22-9, *A* shows the completely implanted pre-embryo buried within the uterine lining. Figure 22-9, *B* diagrams this pre-embryo, visualizing two of the germ layers and the beginnings of the third. At the beginning of the second week only the endoderm and the ectoderm have formed.

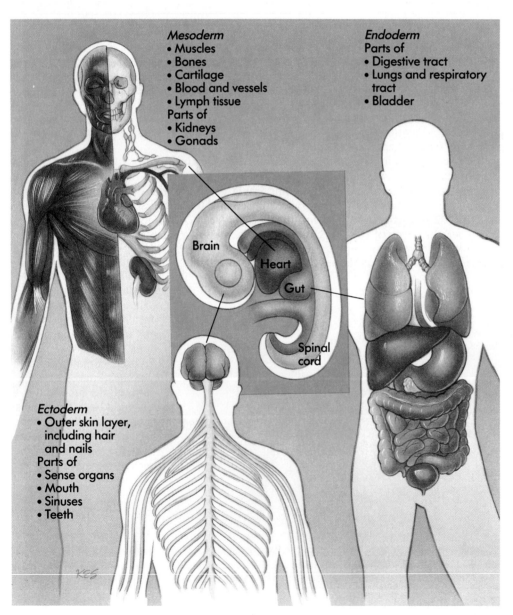

Mesoderm
• Muscles
• Bones
• Cartilage
• Blood and vessels
• Lymph tissue
Parts of
• Kidneys
• Gonads

Endoderm
Parts of
• Digestive tract
• Lungs and respiratory tract
• Bladder

Brain
Heart
Gut
Spinal cord

Ectoderm
• Outer skin layer, including hair and nails
Parts of
• Sense organs
• Mouth
• Sinuses
• Teeth

FIGURE 22-8 Structures produced by the three primary germ layers.
The diagram shows the body systems and tissues into which the germ layers develop.

Early development of the extraembryonic membranes

In Figure 22-9, *B* the extraembryonic membranes have begun to form even at this early stage of development. The **extraembryonic membranes** all play some role in the life support of the pre-embryo, the embryo, and then the fetus. (The term **fetus** is used to describe the stage of development after 8 weeks.) Called *extraembryonic membranes* because they are not a part of the body of the embryo, these structures provide nourishment and protection. They form from the trophoblast, the ring of cells surrounding the inner cell mass. At the same time the pre-embryo is forming from the inner cell mass cells. The further development of these membranes continues into the fetal period.

The **amnion** is a thin, protective membrane that grows down around the embryo during the third and fourth weeks, fully enclosing the embryo in a membranous sac. The amniotic sac can be thought of as a shock absorber for the embryo. This thin membrane encloses a cavity that is filled with a fluid—**amniotic fluid**—in which the fetus floats and moves. This fluid also helps keep the temperature of the embryonic and fetal environment constant. The amniotic cavity is first seen at about 8 days as a slit-like space that appears between the inner cell mass and the underlying trophoblast cells that are invading the uterine wall. It can be seen as a better-developed structure in Figure 22-9, *B* at the end of 2 weeks of development.

Notice also in Figure 22-9, *B* that a structure called the **chorion** is beginning to develop as tissue outside of and including the trophoblast cells that ring the developing embryo and extraembryonic tissue. The chorion is highly specialized to facilitate the transfer of nutrients, gases, and wastes between the embryo and the mother's body. It is a primary part of an organ called the **placenta**, a flat disc of tissue about the size (at birth) of a large, thick pancake that grows into the uterine wall. The placenta is made up of both chorionic and maternal tissues. Digging deeply into the uterine lining, finger-like extensions of the chorion come into close contact with the blood-filled uterine tissues at the placenta. When the embryo reaches a stage of development in which its heart begins to beat, oxygen-poor blood filled with wastes is sent from the embryo's body through the **umbilical arteries** to the placenta.

The two umbilical arteries and a single vein are embedded in the connective tissue of the **umbilical cord,** the developing embryo's lifeline to the mother. This "highway" joins the circulatory system of the embryo with the placenta. At the placenta, embryonic wastes are exchanged for nutrients and oxygen through a thin layer of cells that separates the embryo's blood from the mother's blood. The embryonic blood and maternal blood do not mix. The fetal blood then travels through the umbilical vein back to the embryo. The umbilical cord develops from the body stalk, the yolk sac, and the allantois during the fourth week of development.

The **allantois** (from a Greek word meaning "sausage") gives rise to the umbilical arteries and vein as the umbilical cord develops. Although this extraembryonic membrane is

FIGURE 22-9 The implanted pre-embryo showing the three primary germ layers during the third week of development.
A An implanted pre-embryo in the uterine wall.
B The endoderm and ectoderm have already formed at this stage, with the mesoderm just beginning its development.

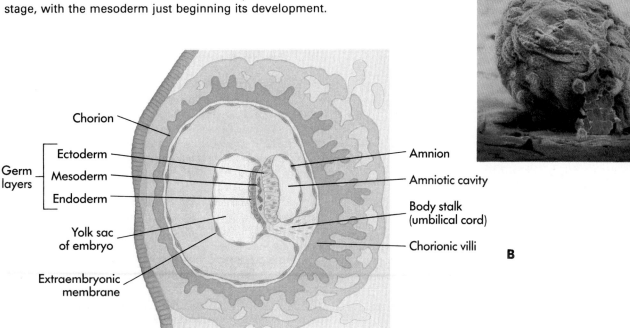

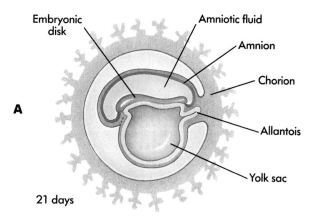

Embryonic disk
Amniotic fluid
Amnion
Chorion
Allantois
Yolk sac

A

21 days

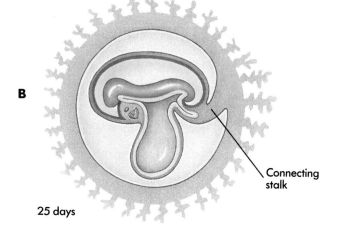

B

Connecting stalk

25 days

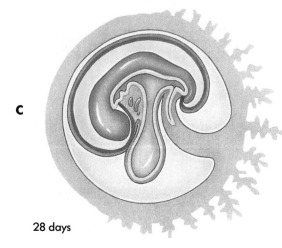

C

28 days

FIGURE 22-10 Extraembryonic membranes.
The embryo rapidly develops extraembryonic membranes during a single week. This diagram depicts the embryo and the development of these membranes at **(A)** 3 weeks, **(B)** 3½ weeks, and **(C)** 4 weeks.

small and cannot be seen in Figure 22-9, *B*, it is shown in Figure 22-10. Appearing during the third week of development as a tiny, sausage-shaped pouching on the yolk sac, the allantois is initially responsible for the formation of the embryo's blood cells, and later develops into the umbilical blood vessels. Notice that the **yolk sac,** a structure established during the end of the second week, also becomes a part of the umbilical cord. Before becoming a nonfunctional part of the cord, the yolk sac produces blood for the embryo until its liver becomes functional during the sixth week of development. In addition, part of the yolk sac becomes the lining of the developing digestive tract.

⋙

> During the second week of development, the pre-embryo completes its implantation within the uterine wall, two of the three layers of cells develop from which its organs and tissues will arise, and the extraembryonic membranes—the amnion, chorion, yolk sac, and allantois—begin to form from the trophoblast.

Development from the third to eighth weeks: The embryo

During this crucial time period, the developing individual is termed an **embryo.** Throughout the next six weeks, the embryo takes on a human shape by means of the ongoing process called *morphogenesis* mentioned earlier. During morphogenesis, cells move to shape the developing embryo. In addition, the organs are established but need further development during the third through eighth weeks in a process called **organogenesis.** Because of the incredible array of developmental processes proceeding simultaneously during this period, the embryo is particularly sensitive to **teratogens,** certain agents such as alcohol that can induce malformations in the rapidly developing tissues and organs (see the boxed essay).

The third week

At the end of the second week and continuing into the third week, various cell groups of the inner cell mass begin to divide, move, and differentiate, changing the two-layered pre-embryo into a three-layered embryo. This process is called **gastrulation.** The word *gastrulation* is derived from a Greek word *gastros* meaning "belly." In fact, the prefix *gastr-* is found in many words denoting parts of the human body, such as gastric, referring to the stomach. This term is descriptive of the fact that at this stage in many animals, a primitive gut is formed by the invagination (infolding) of the blastula, but the intestines develop differently in humans and many animals.

At the beginning of the third week, the embryo is an elongated mass of cells barely one tenth of an inch long. A streak (called the *primitive streak*) runs down the midline of what will be the back side of the embryo. Cells at the streak migrate inward, producing the mesoderm that develops during the gastrulation period. Cells at the head end of the

According to the public Health Service, as many as 86% of women drink at least once during pregnancy, and between 20% and 35% of pregnant women drink regularly; that is, drinking is not confined to special occasions but is a daily or, weekly event. These statistics are alarming because new studies now show that even moderate alcohol consumption during pregnancy can harm the unborn child.

When a pregnant woman drinks, the alcohol she consumes crosses the placenta and intoxicates the fetus. A recent study has demonstrated that women have less of a stomach enzyme to neutralize alcohol than men do, so women become intoxicated faster due higher levels of alcohol in their bloodstreams. These high blood alcohol levels also mean that more alcohol is passed along to the fetus. To cause damage, a pregnant woman must drink above a certain threshold level of danger. But experts are not sure what the alcohol levels are that will cause damage from one day of the pregnancy to the next. Having two drinks on day 39 may not harm the fetus. But having two drinks on day 40 may cause fetal brain damage.

The damage that is inflicted on the fetus can be severe, or it can be more subtle. There seems to be a rough correlation between the amount of alcohol consumed and the severity of the birth defects that result. Full blown fetal alcohol syndrome results in a child who has a number of physical and mental handicaps. These children require special education and sometimes physical therapy to help them contend with their disabilities. More subtle is fetal alcohol effect in which a child has learning difficulties, shows poor judgement, and is impulsive, unable to learn from mistakes, and undisciplined. These children are often placed in "regular" classrooms that are unsuited to their special needs. Often, these are the students that are doomed to fail in school and who may drop out of school.

Experts agree that the surest way to protect the unborn child from alcohol-related effects is not to drink at all during pregnancy. Some researchers believe that a woman even contemplating pregnancy should not drink. This position makes sense, since many women do not know they are pregnant until weeks after conception, and unwitting alcohol consumption may have already wreaked its damage on the fetus. Given the uncontrollable factors influencing the birth of a healthy baby (such as heredity), it makes sense to control those factors within our reach. Not drinking is one of the factors pregnant women can control that will contribute to a health baby.

FIGURE 22-A Drinking during pregnancy has been shown to cause harm to the unborn child.

streak grow forward to form the beginnings of the **notochord.** The notochord is a structure that forms the midline axis along which the vertebral column (backbone) develops. An embryonic notochord forms in all vertebrate animals. However, in humans and in most other vertebrates it degenerates and disappears long before birth. Gastrulation ends with the completion of the notochord, midway through the third week. By the end of gastrulation, a layer of ectoderm covers over the notochord tissue. Figure 22-11 diagrams the events of gastrulation.

▼▼
Gastrulation is a process by which groups of the inner cell mass migrate, divide, and differentiate into three primary germ layers from which all the organs and tissues of the body will develop. This process, in humans as well as all vertebrates, results in a developmental stage called the gastrula.

In the photo of the embryo at 4 1/2 weeks (Figure 22-12), its head can be seen to have the beginnings of eyes, a sign that **neurulation** has taken place. Neurulation is the development of a hollow nerve cord, which later develops into the brain, spinal cord, and related structures such as the eyes.

Neurulation begins in the third week with the folding of the ectoderm lying above the notochord, forming an indentation along the back of the embryo. This indentation is called the **neural groove.** On either side of the groove are areas of tissue called *neural folds*. In Figure 22-13 the neural folds of the 3-week embryo have come together at one spot and have fused. This spot is destined to be the neck region of the developing individual. The tissue above the fused region, looking somewhat like a pair of lips, will develop into the brain. The less broad area of tissue below the fused region will develop into the spinal cord. Eventually the edges of the groove will fuse along its length, forming a neural tube, the precursor to these structures.

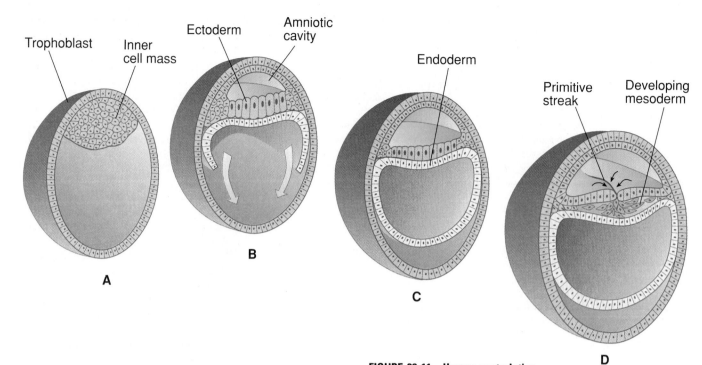

FIGURE 22-11 Human gastrulation.
The amniotic cavity forms within the inner cell mass (**A**), and in its base, layers of ectoderm and endoderm differentiate (**B** and **C**). A primitive streak develops, through which cells destined to become mesoderm migrate into the interior (**D**).

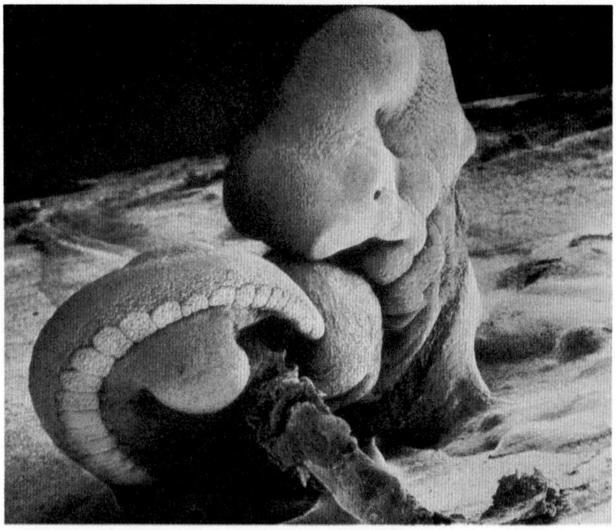

FIGURE 22-12 A human embryo at 4½ weeks.
Note that the eyes have begun to develop.

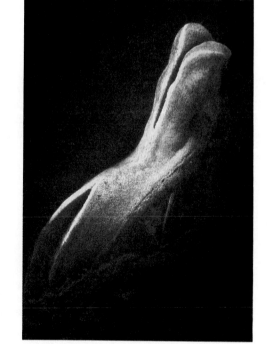

FIGURE 22-13 Neurulation.
The ectoderm folds inward to form the neural groove and, at 3 weeks gestation, fuses. The spot at which the fusion occurs will become the neck, and the tissue above this spot will become the brain. The area below the fused region will become the spinal cord.

During neurulation, the mass of ectodermal cells lying over the notochord curls up, forming a groove. The edges of the groove move together, eventually forming a tube that will develop into the brain and spinal cord—the central nervous system.

Neurulation results in an embryo called a *neurula* and signals the developmental process of **tissue differentiation.** During tissue differentiation, groups of cells become distinguished from other groups of cells by the jobs they will perform in the body. This differentiation appears to be accomplished by the interaction of cytoplasmic stimulators and inhibitors of certain cells with various genes of other cells. Put simply, some cells act like on and off switches for the genes of neighboring cells. This process is **induction.**

Important processes of pre-embryonic and embryonic development are cleavage, cell migration, morphogenesis, and tissue differentiation. The four stages of development of the pre-embryo and the embryo are the morula, the blastula, the gastrula, and the neurula.

The embryo's heart also begins its development during the third week as a pair of microscopic tubes. In fact, the cardiovascular system is the very first system to become functional in the embryo. At the end of the third week of development, the heart tubes have fused and have linked with blood vessels in the embryo, body stalk, chorion, and yolk sac to provide a primitive circulation of blood (Figure 22-14), and the heart actually begins to beat! At the same time, finger-like structures called **villi** begin to protrude from the chorion. These blood-filled projections dig into the uterine tissues of the mother, increasing the surface area over which gases, nutrients, and wastes can be exchanged. At 8 to 10 weeks of development, doctors can take some of this tissue to detect whether genetic abnormalities exist in the embryo. Termed *chorionic villus sampling,* or *CVS,* this procedure is performed by inserting a suction tube through the vagina, into the uterus, and to the chorionic villi. Because chorion cells and fetal cells contain identical genetic information, doctors can use these cells for genetic studies.

Colorized with a blue-gray tint, paired segments of tissue are also prominent in Figure 22-12. These chunks of mesoderm are called **somites** (from a Greek word meaning "a body"). They will give rise to most of the axial skeleton (see Chapter 15) with its associated skeletal muscles and most of the dermis of the body—tissues that underlie the epidermis of the skin. The first somites appear during the third week of development and are added as the embryo grows. Eventually, 42 to 44 pairs develop by the middle of the fifth week.

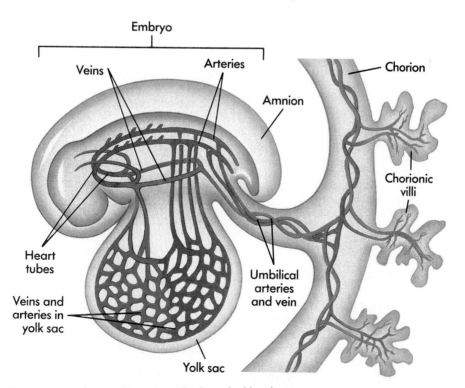

FIGURE 22-14 Cardiovascular system of a 3-week-old embryo.
At the end of the third week, the heart begins to beat. Villi extending out from the chorion dig into the uterine wall and provide a surface for the exchange of gases, nutrients, and wastes.

The fourth week

During the fourth week of development, the embryo begins to curl (see Figure 22-12). The curling occurs as folds are formed at the head and tail end of the embryo. As the embryo curls, the yolk sac becomes squeezed into a narrow stem that fuses with the body stalk connecting the embryo to the placenta (see Figure 22-10). As this fused body stalk lengthens and as its surface is tightly covered by the growing amnion membrane, it is properly called the umbilical cord. Blood cells continue to be produced by the yolk sac until the liver completely takes over this job in the sixth week. The umbilical arteries and vein, already functional, arose from the pouch of the allantois in the body stalk and have been transporting blood between the embryo and the placenta since the third week.

Four visible sets of swellings called the **branchial arches** develop on either side of the head end of the embryo during the fourth week. The word *branchial* is derived from a Greek word meaning "gill" and better describes similar structures that develop into gill supports in fish. In fact, the head end of the human embryo at this stage somewhat resembles a fish embryo.

The presence of gill arches and a tail (see Figure 22-12) in the human embryo indicates a relationship between humans and the lower vertebrates (fish and amphibians). In the nineteenth century, the German scientist Ernst Haeckel described this link as "ontogeny recapitulates phylogeny." What Haeckel meant was that the embryological development of an individual organism (ontogeny) repeats (recapitulates) the evolutionary history of its ancestors (phylogeny). This statement, however, is untrue. Embryonic stages of particular vertebrates are not a replay of the succession of its adult ancestors. Rather, the embryonic stages of an individual organism often reflect embryonic stages of its ancestors. For example, gill arches form during the embryological development of humans. These arches develop into structures such as the middle ear, eustachian tube, tonsils, thymus, and parathyroids.

The embryo's heart begins development during the third week. Somites—chunks of mesoderm—also become prominent at this time. They will give rise to most of the axial skeleton. During the fourth week, the gill arches appear, which will later develop into such structures as the middle ear and the tonsils.

The fifth through eighth weeks

During the fifth week, the embryo doubles in length from 4 millimeters (3/16 inch) to about 8 millimeters (3/8 inch). A nose begins to take shape as tiny pits. Although **limb buds** were first visible during the fourth week, first the arms and then the legs, at this stage of development the limbs look like microscopic flippers. The brain grows rapidly this week, resulting in an embryo with a large head in proportion to the rest of the developing body.

Seen floating within the fluid-filled amniotic sac in Figure 22-15, the 6-week-old embryo now has arm buds with

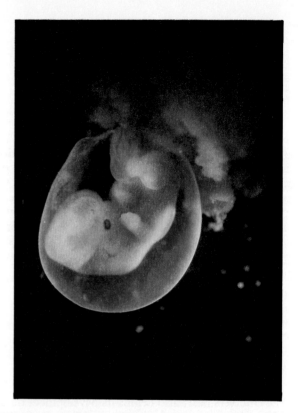

FIGURE 22-15 Embryo at 6 weeks of age. At this stage, the arms and legs are beginning to form. No bones have formed in the skull, so the brain can be clearly seen above the eye.

distinct wrists. Fingers are just beginning to form, as are the ears. The retina of the eyes is now darkly pigmented. Although the trunk of the body straightens out somewhat as the liver and digestive system grow, the neck area remains bent, forcing the head to rest on the chest above the red protruding heart, which now beats 150 times per minute. At the end of 6 weeks, the embryo is little more than half an inch long.

During the seventh week of development, eyelids begin to partially cover the eyes, and the ears develop more fully. The face begins to take on a human appearance. Each arm develops an elbow. Individual fingers can be distinguished, but they are connected with webs of skin that disappear during the eighth week. The legs, slower in their development than the arms, develop ankles and the suggestion of toes. During the eighth week—the last week as an embryo—the developing individual grows to 30 millimeters (slightly over an inch) in length.

From the fourth to eighth weeks of development, dramatic changes take place in the embryo. The embryo grows from a length of 2 millimeters to approximately 30 millimeters (slightly longer than an inch). A primitive circulation is established within the embryo, and a maternal-fetal exchange of nutrients, gases, and wastes begins. The central nervous system and its associated structures begin to develop. The body form is established, including the appendages.

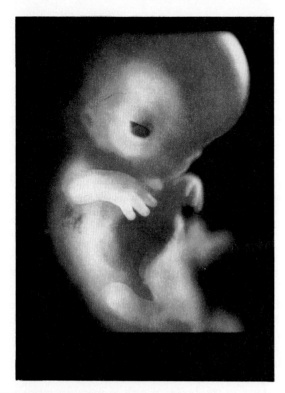

FIGURE 22-16   Fetus at 11 weeks of age.
Fingers have begun to develop at this stage. The eyes are
well formed and are covered with eyelids.

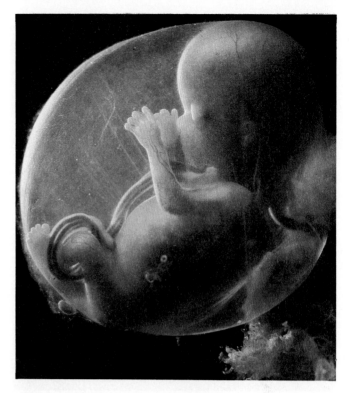

FIGURE 22-17   Fetus at 12 weeks of age.
Ears can be seen, as well as the fingers and toes.

Development from the ninth to thirty-eighth weeks: The fetus

The embryonic period is primarily one of development. By
the ninth week, most of the body systems are functional.
The primary job of the fetal period is the refinement, maturation, and growth of these organ systems and of the body
form of the developing individual.

The third month

The **first trimester** ends with the completion of the third
month of pregnancy. During the third month, the fetus
grows rapidly, tripling its length to approximately 85 millimeters (3 1/3 inches). Fine hair called **lanugo,** meaning
"down," appears over its body, but this downy coat is lost
before birth. Changes in the shape of the face cause the eyes
to face forward and appear closer together, although the
forehead remains prominent (Figure 22-16). The eyes also
become well developed during this month. The eyelids have
continued their development and now fuse shut. They will
not open until the fetus is 7 months old. A suggestion of
an ear can be seen on the side of the head in line with the
jaw bone in the 12-week-old fetus in Figure 22-17.

During the embryonic period, male babies cannot be
distinguished from female babies in their outward appearance. During early fetal development, outward differences
between the sexes begin to take shape. The differentiation

of male or female sex organs depends, of course, on the genetic makeup of the fetus but also on a complex interplay
between hormones and tissues in the developing fetus. This
interplay of factors results in the development of strikingly
different reproductive systems by the end of the third
month, with the penis in the male and the clitoris in the
female arising from the same embryonic tissues. Likewise,
the scrotum in the male is homologous to the labia majora
in the female.

**During the third month the fetus grows to 3 1/3
inches in length. Eyes become well-developed, and
ears begin to form.**

The fourth through sixth months

During the **second trimester,** the fetus grows to about 3/5
kilogram (about 1 1/2 pounds) and 3/10 meter (1 foot)
long. The 4-month-old fetus in Figure 22-18 looks quite
human. Halfway through the fourth month, it can bring its
hands together and suck its thumb. By 15 weeks, the sensory organs are almost completely developed, and by 16
weeks the fetus is actively turning inside the mother. Many
of the bones are forming, replacing areas of cartilage. The
process of bone formation, termed **ossification,** began at
approximately 8 weeks of development and will continue
beyond birth to the age of 18 or 19 years. By the end of
the fifth month, the heartbeat of the fetus can be heard

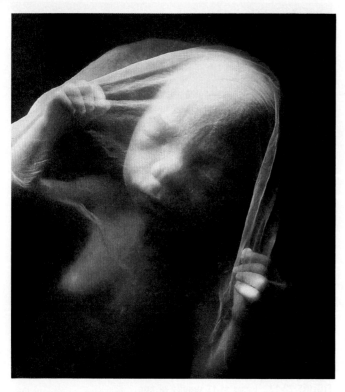

FIGURE 22-18 Fetus at 4 months of age.
The fetus at this point has a human appearance and can even bring its hands together and suck its thumb.

through a stethoscope. Although the body systems have been rapidly continuing their development, the fetus is still unable to survive outside of the mother's womb. At the end of the sixth month, the head is no longer quite as large compared to the rest of the body, the eyelids have separated, and the eyelashes have formed. The fetus is capable of independent survival at the sixth month but only with special medical intervention.

> During the fourth through sixth months, the fetus grows to 30 centimeters (12 inches) in length and begins to look human. The sensory organs become well developed, and the bones begin to form, replacing cartilage.

The seventh through ninth months

The **third trimester** is predominantly a period of growth rather than one of development. In the seventh, eighth, and ninth months of pregnancy, the weight of the fetus doubles several times because of growth but also because of fat that is laid down under its skin. This increase in bulk is not the only kind of growth that occurs. Most of the major nerve tracts in the brain, as well as many new brain cells, are formed during this period. The mother's bloodstream fuels all of this growth by the nutrients it provides. Within the placenta these nutrients pass into the fetal blood supply (Figure 22-19). If the fetus is malnourished because its mother is malnourished, this growth can be adversely affected. The result is is a severely retarded infant. Retarda-

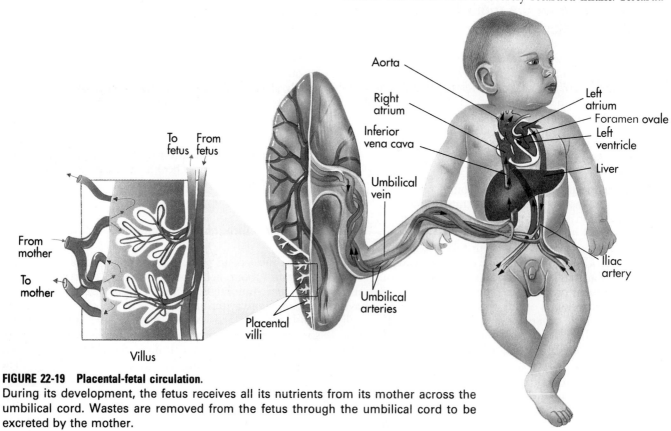

FIGURE 22-19 Placental-fetal circulation.
During its development, the fetus receives all its nutrients from its mother across the umbilical cord. Wastes are removed from the fetus through the umbilical cord to be excreted by the mother.

tion resulting from fetal malnourishment is a serious problem in many underdeveloped countries where poverty is common.

By the end of the third trimester, the neurological growth of the fetus is far from complete and, in fact, continues long after birth. By this time, however, the fetus is able to exist on its own.

▼▼
▼ **The critical stages of human development take place quite early. All the major organs of the body have been established by the end of the third month. The following 6 months are essentially a period of growth.**

Birth

Birth takes place at the end of the third trimester, 38 weeks from conception (40 weeks from the start of the last menstrual period). Although the exact mechanism of the onset of **labor,** the sequence of events that leads to birth, is not

well understood, scientists know that changing hormone levels in the developing fetus initiates this process. These hormones induce placental cells of the mother to manufacture **prostaglandins** (see p. 273), hormone-like substances that cause the smooth muscle of the uterine wall to contract. In addition, the pressure of the baby's head against the cervix sends nerve impulses to the mother's brain that trigger the hypothalamus to release the hormone oxytocin from her pituitary. Working together, oxytocin and prostaglandins stimulate waves of contractions in the walls of the uterus, forcing the fetus downward (Figure 22-20). Initially, only a few contractions occur each hour, later increasing to one every 2 to 3 minutes. Eventually, strong contractions, aided by the mother's pushing, expel the fetus through the vagina, or **birth canal.** The fetus is now a newborn baby.

After birth, uterine contractions continue and expel the placenta and associated membranes, called the *afterbirth*. The umbilical cord is still attached to the baby, and to free the newborn, a doctor or midwife ties and cuts it; blood clots in the cord and contraction of its muscles prevent excessive bleeding.

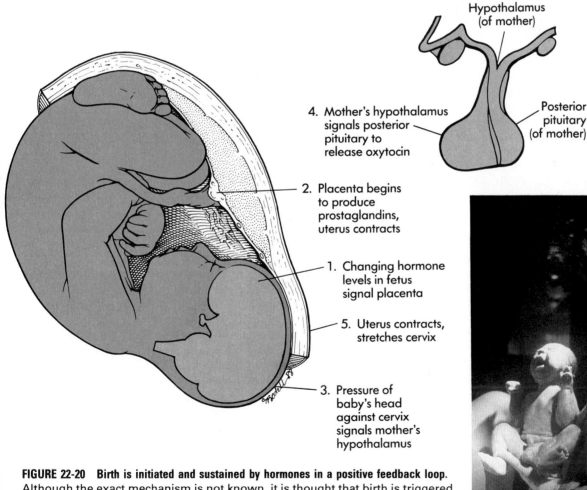
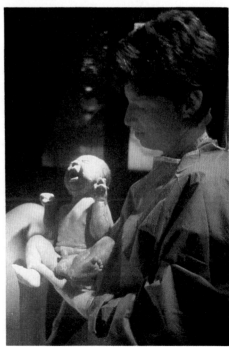

4. Mother's hypothalamus signals posterior pituitary to release oxytocin

Hypothalamus (of mother)

Posterior pituitary (of mother)

2. Placenta begins to produce prostaglandins, uterus contracts

1. Changing hormone levels in fetus signal placenta

5. Uterus contracts, stretches cervix

3. Pressure of baby's head against cervix signals mother's hypothalamus

FIGURE 22-20 Birth is initiated and sustained by hormones in a positive feedback loop. Although the exact mechanism is not known, it is thought that birth is triggered by the following mechanism: changing hormone levels in the fetus (1) signal the placenta to produce prostaglandins, causing the uterus to contract (2). In addition, the fetus' head pushing against the cervix (3) signals the hypothalamus to release oxytocin from the pituitary (4), which causes the uterus to contract even harder (5). This feedback loop, in which the pressure of the fetus' head causes the release of oxytocin, continues until the baby is born.

Physiological adjustments of the newborn

At birth, the baby's lungs are not filled with air. Its first breath is therefore unusually deep. For the first time, its lungs are inflated; the baby cries. Because the baby is now obtaining its oxygen from its lungs rather than from the placenta, several major changes must take place in the circulation of the blood.

Until birth, the placenta was the source of nutrients and oxygen for the fetus; in addition, it was the site for the removal of waste products from the fetal circulation. The lungs were not functional as organs of gas exchange. The fetal body had two major adaptations to limit the flow of blood to the lungs. First, a hole between the two atria called the *foramen ovale* shunted most right atrial blood directly

into the left atrium, thus avoiding the right ventricle and the pulmonary circulation (see Figure 22-19). In addition, the right ventricular blood that is pumped into the pulmonary artery was mostly shunted into the aorta rather than through the lungs by the *ductus arteriosus,* a direct connection between the pulmonary artery and the aorta. At birth, the foramen ovale is closed by two flaps of heart tissue that fold together and fuse. The ductus arteriosus is shut off by contractions of muscles in its walls. Complete closure may take several months. The umbilical arteries and vein also must close off.

At birth, the circulation of the newborn changes as the lungs rather than the placenta become the organ of gas exchange.

Summary

1. Human development before birth, or gestation, lasts approximately 8 1/2 months. Conception takes place when a sperm, or male sex cell, penetrates a secondary oocyte, or female sex cell. This penetration, or fertilization, usually takes place in the uterine tube.

2. The fertilized egg, or zygote, begins to divide after the genetic material of the egg and sperm unite. This process of cleavage is the first stage in the development of humans as well as other multicellular animals. Cleavage results in a ball of cells, or morula.

3. After 2 days in the uterus, the morula has developed into the blastocyst, a stage of development in which the embryo is a hollow ball of cells. This stage of development is significant; it is the first time that cells begin to move, or migrate, to shape the new individual. This process of cell movement to shape the developing individual is morphogenesis.

4. At approximately 1 week after fertilization, the blastocyst nestles into the lining of the uterine wall, which is the process of implantation. It also secretes a hormone that acts on the corpus luteum in the ovary, stimulating the body to produce estrogens and progesterone to maintain the uterine lining rather than having it slough off during a menstrual period.

5. During the first 2 weeks of development, the developing mass of cells is generally referred to as a pre-embryo; from 3 to 8 weeks, an embryo; and from 9 to 38 weeks, a fetus. Structures also develop that are not a part of the growing individual but that help sustain the pre-embryo, embryo, and fetus through development. These extraembryonic membranes are the amnion, chorion, yolk sac, and allantois.

6. At the end of the second week and continuing into the third week, various cell groups of the blastula begin to divide, move, and differentiate in a process called *gastrulation*. During this time a three-layered embryo is formed. Each of these three layers will give rise to specific tissues and organs of the developing individual.

7. Neurulation, the development of a hollow nerve cord that becomes the central nervous system, begins in the third week. However, the development of the nervous system continues even after birth.

8. Dramatic changes take place in the embryo from the fourth to the eighth weeks of development. Limb buds become visible in the fourth week and are quite well developed by the seventh week. A primitive circulation is established, and a maternal-fetal exchange of nutrients, gases, and wastes begins. By the eighth week of development, the embryo is about an inch long, and most of the body systems are functional.

9. The fetal period, from 9 to 38 weeks, is a time of refinement, maturation, and growth.

10. Changing hormone levels in the fetus at about the thirty-eighth week trigger the onset of labor, the sequence of events that leads to birth. Waves of contractions in the walls of the uterus force the fetus downward and out the birth canal.

11. At birth, the circulation of the newborn changes as the lungs rather than the placenta become the organ of gas exchange.

1. At what point in the prenatal development of a human does the zygote exhibit a new genetic makeup different from that of either parent?

2. What happens to a sperm and a secondary oocyte immediately after fertilization occurs?

3. Does the development of the zygote during the first 2 weeks after fertilization involve meiotic or mitotic cell division?

4. Some birth control methods involve the prevention of implantation of the blastocyst in the uterine wall. What would result if this were the case? What does an implanted blastocyst secrete to prevent such an event?

5. Identify the three primary germ layers, and describe the structures into which they will develop.

6. What are the extraembryonic membranes? Explain their significance.

7. Summarize the events that occur during gastrulation.

8. Define neurulation, and explain its significance.

9. What is a notochord, and what role does it play in humans?

10. Maternal nutrition is a key element in normal development of the fetus. What specific fetal systems would be affected either adversely or positively by maternal nutritional habits during the first 3 weeks of development?

11. Summarize the changes that occur in the embryo between the fourth and eighth weeks of development.

12. Summarize the changes that occur in the embryo/fetus during the first, second, and third trimesters. When do most body systems become functional?

13. Explain why good nutrition is so important during pregnancy.

14. Describe the physiological adjustments that a newborn baby must undergo to survive.

1. What physical changes occur in a fertilized egg that prevent the penetration of a second sperm? What might be the consequences of a second sperm gaining entry?

2. Assess the three trimesters involved in pregnancy. What are the key developments of each trimester? How might different behaviors (drinking alcohol, smoking cigarettes, drug use, trauma) affect the developing fetus at different times? What key systems would be affected by maternal malnutrition in each specific trimester?

Bogin, B. (1990, January). The evolution of human childhood. *Bioscience,* pp. '6-25.
A fascinating study of the extensive childhood period experienced by humans and its role in development and evolution.

Ohlendorf-Moffat, L. (1991, February). Surgery before birth. *Discover,* pp. 58-65.
An encouraging look at prenatal treatment of genetic disorders and anatomical defects in the human fetus.

Steinmetz, G. (1992, February). Fetal alcohol syndrome. *National Geographic,* pp. 36-39.
A short, clear article with effective photographs outlining the dangers of alcohol consumption during pregnancy.

23 Sexually Transmitted Diseases

▼ Sexually transmitted diseases (STDs) are caused by the transmission of certain agents of infection from one person to another during sexual activity.

▼ The most common causative agents of sexually transmitted diseases are viruses and bacteria.

▼ Other organisms such as certain fungi, protozoans, mites, and lice can be transferred from person to person by sexual contact, but are regularly transferred in other ways as well.

▼ The best protection against the transmission of sexually transmitted diseases, other than abstinence from sexual activity, is the proper and consistent use of latex condoms.

This scene may have been viewed as unthinkable or outrageous only 10 years ago. Yet today, it is repeated frequently on college campuses and in a variety of other settings. For example, the New York City School District entered the debate regarding condom handouts early in 1991 when Chancellor Joseph Fernandez proposed to make condoms freely available in the city's 120 public high schools as part of an AIDS education program. Opponents of the plan argued that passing out condoms told students that it was all right to have sex. They felt that abstinence should be suggested instead. Backers of the plan cited the statistics: New York City has 3% of the nation's 13- to 21-year-olds, yet has 20% of all reported AIDS cases in that age group. Students were having sex and were becoming infected. They needed protection from disease. By the end of that year the plan was approved and New York City became the first school district in the country to distribute condoms to its students.

The debate regarding condom hand-outs is still not over — feelings run deep on both sides. Yet no matter how you feel about the distribution of condoms in public or private places, one fact remains: latex condoms are the best protection sexually active persons have against the spread of sexually transmitted diseases.

The causes of sexually transmitted diseases

Sexually transmitted diseases (STDs) are caused by the transmission of certain agents of infection from one person to another during sexual activity. STDs are *not* caused by poor personal hygiene and are *not* transmitted only by persons of low socioeconomic status. These ideas are misconceptions. Statistics show that the incidence of sexually transmitted diseases crosses all boundaries of race, gender, ethnicity, social class, and economic status. Although the incidence of STDs crosses boundaries of age, too, young people are hardest hit. Today, 12 million new sexually transmitted infections occur each year; two thirds of these cases are in persons under the age of 25.

All sexually transmitted diseases are **communicable,** or **contagious**; that is, they can spread from one person to another. The most common causative agents of sexually transmitted diseases are viruses and bacteria, which cause **infection**. They enter the tissues, multiply, and cause damage. The most common sexually transmitted diseases in the United States are gonorrhea and chlamydial infection, which are both caused by bacteria, and genital herpes, which is caused by a virus. Taken together, these three diseases make up about 10 million of the 12 million annual cases of STDs.

Other organisms such as certain *fungi, protozoans, mites,*

and lice can be transferred from person to person by sexual contact, but are regularly transferred in other ways as well. Fungi, organisms that feed on dead or decaying material, and protozoans, animal-like protists, can cause infections of the genital area as do viruses and bacteria. Mites and lice, which are members of a diverse phylum of animals called arthropods, cause **infestation**. They live and/or feed on the skin and underlying tissues.

Viruses

Viruses invade organisms and cause their cells to make more viruses. However, viruses themselves are not living. They do not have a cellular structure, which is the basis of all life. They are nonliving **obligate parasites,** which means that viruses cannot reproduce outside of a living system. They must exist in association with and at the expense of other organisms.

Viruses primarily infect plants, animals, and bacteria. A specific virus can only infect a certain species of organisms. So you cannot be infected by a bacterial virus, nor can your dog catch your cold. Some viruses, however, can infect more than a single species of organism; for example, the human immunodeficiency virus (HIV virus that causes acquired immunodeficiency syndrome [AIDS]) is thought to have been introduced to humans from African monkeys.

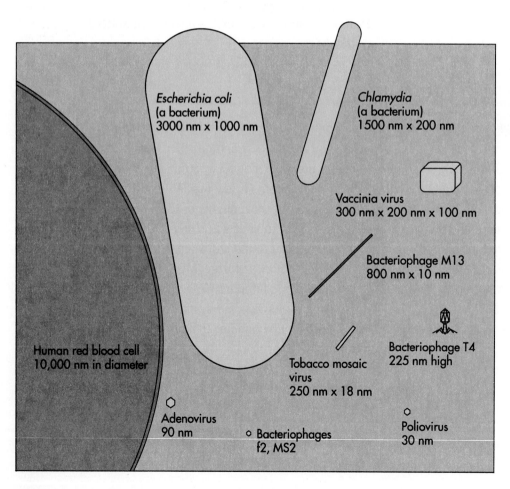

FIGURE 23-1 The shapes and sizes of viruses.
The size of various viruses are shown here in relation to a bacterium and a human red blood cell. Dimensions are given in nanometers.

Escherichia coli (a bacterium) 3000 nm x 1000 nm

Chlamydia (a bacterium) 1500 nm x 200 nm

Vaccinia virus 300 nm x 200 nm x 100 nm

Bacteriophage M13 800 nm x 10 nm

Tobacco mosaic virus 250 nm x 18 nm

Bacteriophage T4 225 nm high

Human red blood cell 10,000 nm in diameter

Adenovirus 90 nm

Bacteriophages f2, MS2

Poliovirus 30 nm

Viral structure

Each virus has its own unique shape (Figure 23-1), but all contain the same basic parts: a nucleic acid **core** (either DNA or RNA) and a protein "overcoat" called a **capsid**. The structure of the tobacco mosaic virus (TMV), which causes a disease of tobacco plants, is shown in Figure 23-2, *B* and illustrates one way that a virus is put together. This virus is helical, with its single strand of RNA coiled like a spring, surrounded by a spiraling capsid of protein molecules. Many viruses have another chemical layer over the capsid called the **envelope,** which is rich in proteins, lipids, and carbohydrate molecules. Figure 23-3, *A* is an electron micrograph of a typical enveloped virus, a herpesvirus. Its structure is illustrated in Figure 23-3, *B*. One type of herpesvirus causes genital herpes, an STD that will be described later in this chapter.

It is hard to conceptualize how small viruses are, but Figure 23-1 helps by showing the size of a few viruses relative to the size of a bacterium and a human red blood cell. Some viruses, such as the poliovirus, are as small as the width of the plasma membrane on a human cell. The largest viruses are barely visible with a light microscope. Most viruses can be seen only by using an electron microscope.

> Viruses are made up of a nucleic acid core surrounded by a protein covering called a capsid. Some viruses also have an additional covering, or envelope.

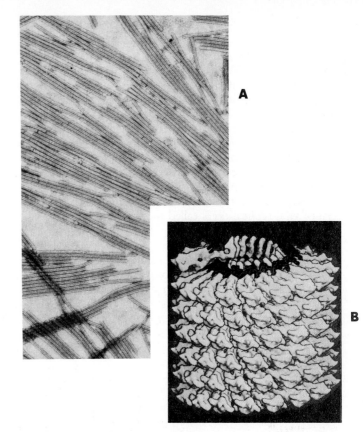

FIGURE 23-2 Tobacco mosaic virus.
A An electron micrograph of purified tobacco mosaic virus. **B** Computer-generated model of a portion of tobacco mosaic virus. An entire virus consists of 2130 identical protein molecules—the yellow knobs—which form a cylindrical coat around a single strand of RNA (colored *red*).

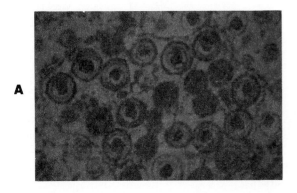

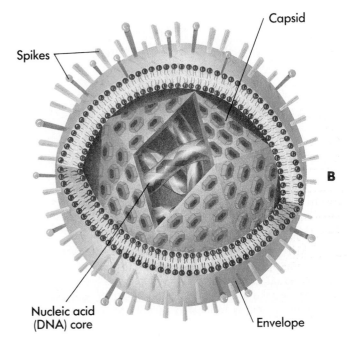

FIGURE 23-3 Structure of a typical virus.
A Electron micrograph of the herpesvirus.
B Structure of the herpesvirus.

Viral replication

Viruses cannot multiply on their own. They must enter a cell and use the cell's enzymes and ribosomes to make more viruses. This process of viral multiplication within cells is called **replication.** Various patterns of viral replication exist. Some viruses enter a cell, replicate, and then cause the cell to burst, releasing new viruses. This pattern of viral replication is called the **lytic cycle.** Other types of viruses enter into a long-term relationship with the cells they infect, their nucleic acid replicating as the cells multiply. This pattern of viral replication is called the **lysogenic cycle.**

The lytic cycle

The process of viral replication has been studied most extensively in bacteria because bacteria are easier to grow in the laboratory and infect with viruses than plant or animal cells. Many bacterial viruses (usually called **bacteriophages** or simply **phages**) follow a lytic cycle pattern of rep-

lication. As shown in Figure 23-4, a bacteriophage first attaches to a receptor site on a bacterium. The virus then injects its nucleic acid into the host cell, while its protein capsid is left outside the cell. Next, the viral genes take over cellular processes and direct the bacterium to produce viral components that will be used to assemble whole viruses. After their manufacture, these strands of nucleic acid and proteins are assembled into mature viruses that **lyse,** or break open, the host cell. Each bacterium releases many virus particles. Each "new" virus is capable of infecting another bacterial cell.

Some animal viruses infect cells in a manner similar to bacterial virus infection, but they enter animal cells by endocytosis (see Chapter 3) and must be uncoated before they can cause the cell to manufacture viruses. These cells may die as new virus particles are released in a lytic infection, or they may survive if virus particles are slowly budded from the cell by a process similar to exocytosis. This slow budding causes a persistent infection.

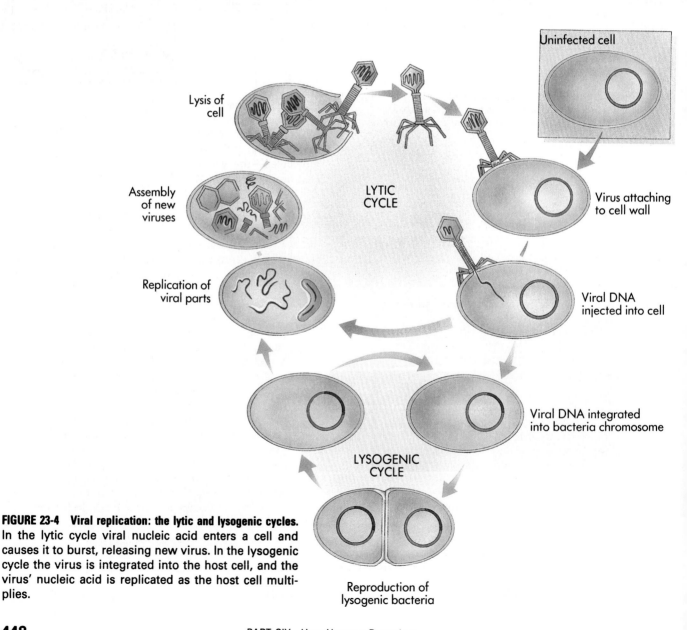

Uninfected cell

Lysis of cell

Assembly of new viruses

LYTIC CYCLE

Virus attaching to cell wall

Replication of viral parts

Viral DNA injected into cell

Viral DNA integrated into bacteria chromosome

LYSOGENIC CYCLE

Reproduction of lysogenic bacteria

FIGURE 23-4 Viral replication: the lytic and lysogenic cycles. In the lytic cycle viral nucleic acid enters a cell and causes it to burst, releasing new virus. In the lysogenic cycle the virus is integrated into the host cell, and the virus' nucleic acid is replicated as the host cell multiplies.

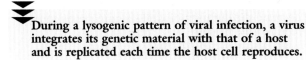

During a lytic pattern of viral infection, a bacterial virus injects its nucleic acid into a host cell, whereas an animal virus enters by endocytosis. The viral nucleic acid directs the cell to produce "new" viral nucleic acid and protein coats. After assembly of these parts, the bacterial virus particles cause the cell to burst open, releasing them. Animal viruses often leave the cell by slow budding.

The lysogenic cycle

Some viruses, instead of killing host cells, integrate their genetic material with that of the host. Then, each time the host cell reproduces, the viral nucleic acid is replicated as if it were a part of the cell's genetic makeup (see Figure 23-4). In this way, the virus is passed on from cell to cell. Infection of this sort is called a **latent infection.** These integrated latent genes may not cause any change in the host for a long time. Then, triggered by an appropriate stimulus, the virus may enter a lytic cycle and produce symptoms.

The herpes simplex virus causes latent infections of the skin. Herpes nucleic acid remains in nerve tissue (sensory ganglia) without damaging the host until a cold, a fever, or another factor such as ultraviolet radiation from the sun acts as a trigger, and the cycle of cell damage begins. When infection is with herpes simplex virus 1, this "damage" is usually manifested as cold sores or fever blisters. The herpes zoster virus (the chickenpox virus) can also act in the same way. This virus may remain latent in the nerve tissue of a person having had chickenpox, only to be triggered at a later time to cause the painful nerve disorder shingles.

During a lysogenic pattern of viral infection, a virus integrates its genetic material with that of a host and is replicated each time the host cell reproduces.

Viral sexually transmitted diseases

Three sexually transmitted diseases caused by viruses are **genital herpes, genital warts,** and **acquired immune deficiency syndrome (AIDS).**

Acquired immune deficiency syndrome (AIDS)

Acquired immune deficiency syndrome is discussed extensively in Chapter 16. The causative agent of AIDS, the human immunodeficiency virus (HIV), is present in the blood, semen, and vaginal secretions of infected individuals. Therefore the virus is spread by sexual contact as well as by the sharing of needles and syringes contaminated with blood from an infected person. In addition, the human immunodeficiency virus can be transmitted by mothers to their babies before or during delivery.

Hepatitis B, a disease of the liver caused by the hepatitis B virus (HBV), can also be spread by sexual contact but is not usually classified as a sexually transmitted disease. Like HIV, this virus is present in the blood, semen, and vaginal secretions of infected individuals. Therefore it is spread by sexual contact as well as by other means, such as the sharing of contaminated needles and syringes. Like HIV and most of the sexually transmitted diseases, HBV can be spread to newborns by their mothers at the time of delivery. (The role of the hepatitis B virus in primary liver cancer is discussed in Chapter 18.)

Genital herpes

Genital herpes is an STD caused most often by the **herpes simplex virus (HSV) 2.** However, HSV 1, which is associated primarily with the development of cold sores and fever blisters, is found to be the causative agent of genital herpes approximately 10% to 15% of the time. This situation arises from transmission through oral sex.

Genital herpes develops within a few days after sexual contact with an infected person. The first symptoms are an itching or throbbing in the genital area. Blister-like, painful, itchy lesions and swollen lymph nodes in the groin area develop soon after. In women, lesions develop in the vagina and on the cervix, vulva, and/or thighs. In men, lesions develop primarily on the penis (Figure 23-5). The virus also causes an inflammation of the urethra in men, resulting in a watery discharge from the urethral opening.

The herpes viruses cause latent infections. In genital herpes, the virus particles travel via sensory nerve fibers to ganglia in the sacral region of the spinal cord after the initial infection appears to subside. There, the virus remains dormant or slowly replicates. As is typical with a latent infection, the virus is reactivated by one of a variety of stimuli such as stress, fever, or menstruation. Once reactivated, the virus moves along the nerve fibers back to the genital area where it replicates, causing lesions once again. This cycle of dormancy followed by a recurrence of lesions continues, but successive recurrences usually become milder. Eventually the recurrences may cease, but the viruses remain latent in the ganglia and can be reactivated by severe emotional or physical stress even a long time later. Along with the pain and suffering this disease causes both genders, women face additional problems. Women infected with HSV have a higher rate of miscarriage than uninfected women. Also, pregnant women infected with HSV must have their babies delivered by Caesarean section because the baby becomes infected as it travels down the birth canal.

A person with genital herpes (or oral herpes) can pass the virus on to another person any time viruses are being shed, or cast off. Unfortunately, it is impossible to know when a person is *not* shedding virus. Scientists know that shedding occurs when lesions are present and usually starts a few days before lesions appear, but shedding may *never* cease. In addition, there is no way of knowing if a person is infected unless lesions are present and observable, or unless the person says he or she is infected. Unfortunately, there is no way to completely protect yourself from infection if you have sex with an infected person. Using latex condoms only reduces the chance of transmission of the virus.

Genital herpes is an incurable disease. The antiviral drug acyclovir, which interferes with the replication of HSV, is usually used to treat the symptoms. The topical

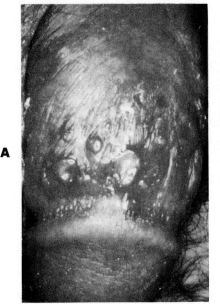
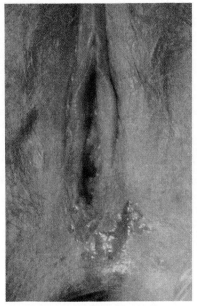

FIGURE 23-5 A genital herpes lesion on the penis (A) and on the female genitalia (B).

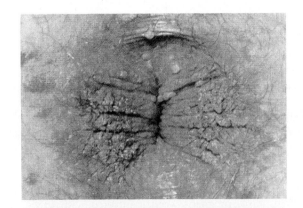

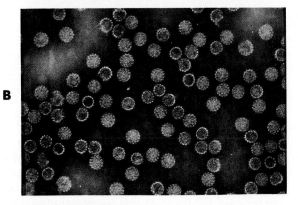

FIGURE 23-6 Genital warts.
A Perianal genital warts.
B An electron micrograph of the causative agent of genital warts, the human papilloma virus, or HPV.

form is used directly on lesions and helps reduce the pain and itching they cause and the length of time they are present. Oral acyclovir is also available. Both forms of the drug decrease the duration of viral shedding and reduce the time required for healing.

Genital warts

Genital warts are soft, pink, flat or raised growths that appear singly or in clusters on the external genitals and rectum (Figure 23-6,A). In women, these irritating and itchy growths can also appear on the vaginal walls and on the cervix. In men, they can invade the urethra. Caused by the human papillomavirus, or HPV, shown in Figure 23-6,B, genital warts is becoming an increasingly prevalent sexually transmitted disease in the United States. Although the warty growths, or papillomas, caused by HPV are usually benign (noncancerous), genital warts that persist for many years can transform into malignant growths. In addition, HPV types 16 and 18 are tumor viruses that can initiate cancers of the cervix (see Chapter 18). Women infected with these virus types are at a higher risk for cervical cancer than uninfected women; they should have a Pap smear to detect this type of cancer once every 6 months.

At this time, genital warts are treated with electrocauterization (burning the infected tissue by means of electric current) or cryotherapy (freezing the infected tissue with liquid carbon dioxide and then removing it surgically). Sometimes, surgery alone is used. This virus can also infect babies during delivery, as does the herpes simplex virus and most sexually transmitted disease organisms.

Bacteria

Bacteria are present on and in virtually everything you eat and touch. They are the only organisms with a prokaryotic cellular organization. Smaller than eukaryotic cells, the tiniest bacteria have a diameter about 100 times smaller than one of the cells in your body. The largest bacteria are about two and one-half times smaller. Figure 23-7 shows how bacteria compare in size to a eukaryotic cell. Along with being smaller than eukaryotic cells, bacteria also have a much simpler internal organization containing no organelles other than ribosomes. It differs from eukaryotic cellular organization in primarily two ways: (1) the prokaryotic cell has no membrane-bounded nucleus, and (2) it contains no membrane-bounded organelles that compartmentalize the cell. This structural uniqueness places bacteria in a kingdom all their own: **Monera,** meaning "alone."

Bacterial structure

Although bacteria are single-celled organisms, you may be fooled if you observed them under a microscope. Notice the bacteria in Figure 23-8. Some types form long chains of spherical cells, whereas other bacteria characteristically form arrangements that look like bunches of grapes. However,

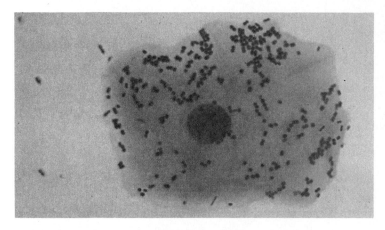

FIGURE 23-7 Bacteria are smaller than eukaryotic cells.
The small dots that you see in this photo are bacteria. The large, somewhat rectangular shape in the background is a human cheek cell. As you can see, the eukaryotic cell dwarfs the tiny bacteria that are on it.

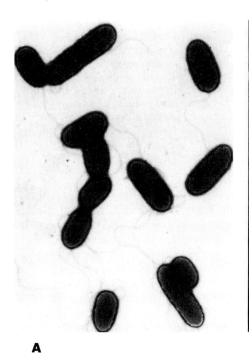

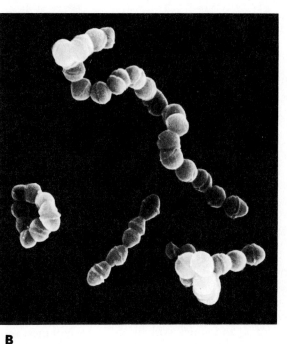

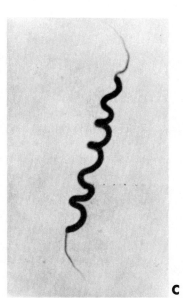

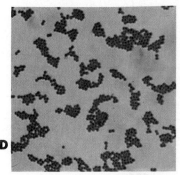

A

B

C

D

FIGURE 23-8 Bacterial cells have several different shapes.
A A rod-shaped bacterium, *Pseudomonas* species, a type associated with many plant diseases.
B *Streptococcus* species, a relatively spherical bacterium in which the individuals adhere in chains.
C *Spirillum* species, a spiral bacterium. This large bacterium has a tuft of flagella at each end.
D *Staphylococcus* species, a spherical bacterium in which the individuals form grape-like clusters.

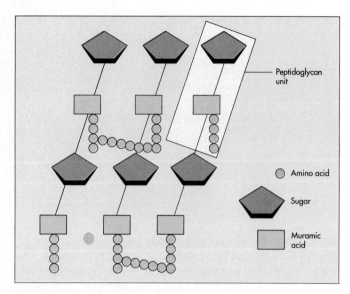

Peptidoglycan unit

● Amino acid

⬠ Sugar

▭ Muramic acid

FIGURE 23-9 Peptidoglycan gives structural strength to the bacterial cell wall.
The structural strength of the bacterial cell wall is due to a network of sugar derivatives and unusual amino acids called *peptidoglycan*. The backbone of the wall is alternating molecules of an acidic sugar and an amino sugar, and extending down as pillars off of each acidic sugar is a chain of four or five amino acids. The backbones are united and stabilized against osmotic pressure by crosslinking bridges of amino acids.

each member of a group of bacteria is an individual organism. Bacterial shapes vary, too. Some bacteria are rod shaped; others look like corkscrews. Still others are minute spheres.

With the exception of only one group, all bacteria are enclosed by a rigid cell wall. But this cell wall is unlike that of plants, fungi, or protists. The cell wall of bacteria is made up of a network of large molecules called *peptidoglycan*. This network is shown in Figure 23-9. Notice that two types of molecules make up the network: sugars and amino acids. This network of molecules performs many jobs for the cell, such as keeping out many harmful substances and keeping the cell from bursting.

Certain antibiotics such as penicillin kill bacteria (and not your body cells) because they interfere with the synthesis of the bacterial cell wall. Other antibiotics interfere with the functioning of the bacterial plasma membrane or block certain metabolic processes. Because antibiotics work by attacking bacterial structures or metabolic processes, they are ineffective against viruses or other agents of disease.

The bacterial plasma membrane lies beneath the bacterial cell wall. Similar in structure to that of eukaryotic cells, this thin, fragile membrane surrounds the cytoplasm of the cell. The cytoplasm of prokaryotic cells is made up of about 80% water, an assortment of molecules involved in the chemical reactions of the cell, DNA, ribosomes, and several kinds of reserve materials known as *inclusions*. Types of inclusions vary from one kind of bacterium to another.

The cytoplasm of prokaryotes does not contain the varied organelles of eukaryotes. Ribosomes, however, are packed into the cytoplasm of bacteria in great numbers, giving it a "grainy" appearance. These ribosomes are smaller than eukaryotic ribosomes. The single, circular strand of DNA found in bacteria is not surrounded with a membrane as in eukaryotes and is not a "true nucleus." In fact, the word *prokaryote* means "before the nucleus." Therefore this area of the cell is termed a **nucleoid,** rather than a nucleus. In addition, bacteria often contain small "rings" of DNA called **plasmids.**

Although motile bacteria have flagella like some eukaryotic cells, flagellar structure is different. Bacterial flagella (and bacterial cytoplasm) do not contain microtubules. Instead, bacterial flagella are composed of several chains of protein that wrap in corkscrew fashion around a hollow core. These proteins are attached to others that anchor the flagellum to the cell wall and membrane, and are covered by a flexible tube. Bacteria swim by rotating their flagella rather than by "whipping" them as eukaryotes do (Figure 23-10).

Most bacteria contain infoldings of the plasma membrane known as *mesosomes*. Mesosomes are connected to the plasma membrane and play a role in reproduction. In addition, enzymes needed for certain chemical reactions of the cell to take place are often bound to the mesosome and plasma membrane.

⬗⬗

Bacteria have a cell structure different from other organisms: the cytoplasm contains no internal compartments or organelles, the hereditary material is not enclosed by a membrane to form a nucleus, and the cell is bounded by a membrane encased within a cell wall. For these reasons, bacteria are classified as a separate kingdom of organisms, Monera.

Bacterial reproduction

Reproduction among bacteria is asexual; one cell divides into two with no exchange of genetic material among cells. This process is called **binary fission.** Before fission, or division of the cell, the genetic material replicates and divides.

Bacterial DNA exists as a single, circular molecule that is attached at one point to the interior surface of the cell membrane. As eukaryotic cells do, bacteria make a copy of their genetic material before cell division. The bacterium also grows in size and manufactures sufficient ribosomes, membranes, and macromolecules for two cells before dividing. When the cell reaches an appropriate size and the synthesis of cellular components is complete, binary fission begins.

The first step of binary fission is the formation of a new cell membrane and cell wall between the attachment sites of the two DNA molecules (Figure 23-11). As the new membrane and wall are added, the cell is progressively constricted in two. Eventually the invaginating membrane and wall reach all the way into the cell center, forming two cells from one.

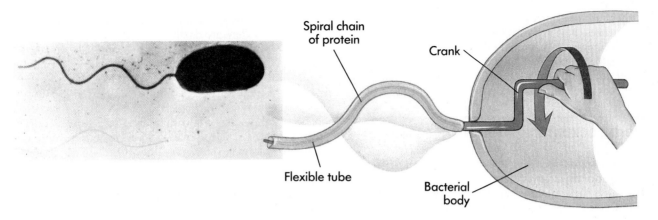

Spiral chain
of protein

Crank

Flexible tube

Bacterial
body

FIGURE 23-10   Bacteria move by rotating their flagella.
The photograph is of *Vibrio cholerae,* the microbe that causes the serious intestinal disease cholera. Imagine that you are inside a *Vibrio* cell, turning the flagellum like a crank. You would create a spiral wave that travels down the flagellum. The bacterium uses this kind of rotary motion when it moves.

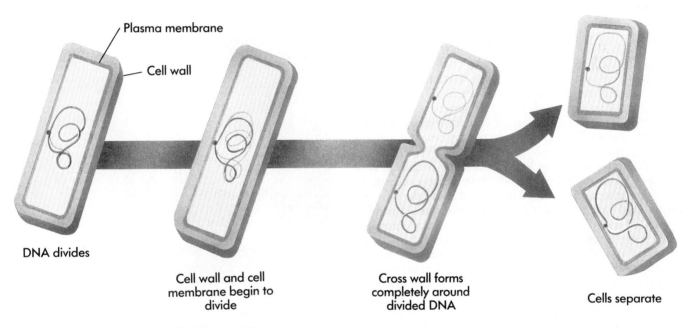

Plasma membrane

Cell wall

DNA divides

Cell wall and cell
membrane begin to
divide

Cross wall forms
completely around
divided DNA

Cells separate

FIGURE 23-11   Binary fission in bacteria.
During binary fission, one bacterium divides into two bacteria.

Most bacteria reproduce every 1 to 3 hours. Some bacteria take a great deal longer. However, bacteria having conditions favoring their growth could produce a population of billions in little more than a day! This type of growth is referred to as **exponential growth,** a period of rapid doubling of cells. However, the population cannot grow unchecked indefinitely. Many cells compete for food and other growth factors they need to survive. With resources limited, the entire population cannot be maintained, and cells begin to die. Wastes also accumulate, poisoning some of the cells. The growth of the population levels out. Eventually, if the growth requirements of the bacterial population are no longer met, the population may begin to die as rapidly as it once grew.

Bacteria reproduce asexually by binary fission. First, they produce sufficient cell parts for two cells and replicate their single, circular molecule of DNA. Then the cell wall and membrane grow inward, between the attachment sites of the two DNA molecules, and literally split the cell in two.

Most disease-producing bacteria use their hosts for food, but some poison their hosts. To cause disease, bacteria or the poisons they produce must first get into the body; bacterial species each have their own, specific entry routes. Some bacteria enter the body in contaminated food or water. Others are present in the air, such as after an infected person sneezes, and are inhaled. Some species can survive on objects and are transmitted when the object is touched. Sometimes bacteria enter the body through broken skin as the result of an injury or injection with a contaminated needle. Yet others are transmitted by sexual contact.

Bacterial sexually transmitted diseases

The sexually transmitted diseases caused by bacteria include **syphilis**, **gonorrhea**, and **chlamydial infection**. The bacteria that cause these diseases enter the body via the mucous membranes of the genitals. Persons harboring these organisms transmit them to other individuals during sexual acts. After entering the body, bacteria attach to body cells and cause various types of tissue damage. The chemicals bacteria produce digest the tissues so that the breakdown products can be taken into the bacteria and metabolized.

Syphilis

Syphilis is caused by a spiral bacterium, *Treponema pallidum* (Figure 23-12). Although it is curable if treated with penicillin, medical researchers estimate that approximately 400,000 persons in the United States have this disease. If left untreated, syphilis can result in death.

The disease progresses through a variety of stages. Approximately 3 weeks after sexual contact with an infected partner, the newly infected person usually develops a lesion on either the cervix (in women) or the penis (in men) where the organism entered the body. This lesion is called a *hard chancre*, and is the hallmark of the *primary stage* of syphilis. At first the lesion is painless. It is raised above the skin and has a hard base. However, it soon develops into a painful, ulcerated sore. During this time, the bacterium enters the lymphatic system, and the lymph nodes closest to the lesion enlarge. Once in the lymph, the organisms quickly travel to the bloodstream and throughout the body, infecting other tissues. Within 4 to 12 weeks the sore heals and the primary phase is over.

The *secondary stage* of syphilis begins from 6 weeks to several months after infection. Because the organisms are now dispersed throughout the body, lesions of the skin and mucous membranes develop away from the site of the original infection — usually on the trunk, arms, and legs. Some-

times the lesions appear as discolored, flat spots on the skin. Other times they are small, solid, raised bumps. A person with syphilis is highly contagious during the primary stage and through the secondary stage, until these secondary lesions heal.

During the next stage, an infected person has no symptoms and may think that his or her body has successfully battled the disease. Unfortunately, the disease is only in a *latent stage*. This stage may last a lifetime but, more often, leads to the final, or *tertiary stage*. Once again, lesions develop, but the disease is no longer communicable. The most typical type of tertiary lesions are *gummas*. These lesions are tumor-like masses that can invade the skin, tissues beneath the skin, mucous membranes, bones, and/or internal organs. When gummas develop in the cardiovascular and central nervous systems, paralysis and death often result. Figure 23-13 shows lesions typical of the primary, secondary, and tertiary stages of syphilis.

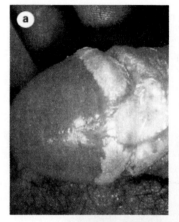
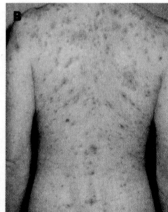
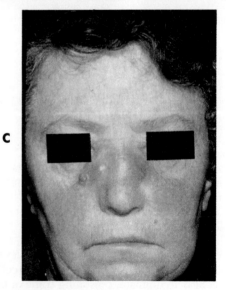

FIGURE 23-13 **The three stages of syphilis.**
A Genital lesions of the primary stage.
B Skin lesions of the secondary stage.
C Gumma, or tertiary stage.

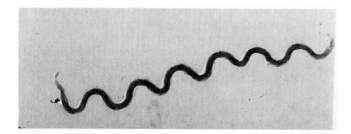

FIGURE 23-12 **Causative agent of syphilis.**
This photomicrograph shows the spiral bacterium, *Treponema pallidum*, which is the cause of syphilis.

Gonorrhea

Gonorrhea is caused by *Neisseria gonorrhoeae,* a paired, coffee-bean-shaped bacterium (Figure 23-14, *A*). The word "gonorrhea" is derived from two Greek words meaning "a flow of semen." This name was given to the disease in 130 AD by the Greek physician Galen when he mistook the genital discharge caused by gonorrhea for seminal fluid. This discharge, a fluid composed of mucus intermingled with pus, is a result of infection of tissues of the urogenital system by *N. gonorrhoeae* Figure 23-14, *B* shows this typical symptom of gonorrheal infection in the male.

Men who become infected usually develop an inflammation of the urethra, with initial symptoms of discomfort and pain. Within 2 to 5 days, a discharge like that shown in Figure 23-14,B becomes evident. The infection then passes up the urethra. Although urination becomes more difficult at this stage of the disease, the urge to urinate becomes more frequent. Occasionally these symptoms are accompanied by a headache and fever. If the infection remains untreated, other urogenital structures may become infected. Infection of the epididymis (ducts within which sperm are stored) and/or vas deferens (ducts that conduct sperm away from the testes) is serious; scar tissue may develop and block these passageways, resulting in sterility.

Women who become infected can develop an inflammation of the urethra, vagina (and nearby glands), cervix, and rectum. The initial symptoms of infection are abdominal or pelvic pain, vaginal discharge, and painful or difficult urination. If the infection remains untreated, a chronic (persistent) infection develops with symptoms such as tenderness of the lower abdomen, backaches, inflammations of the urethra or other urogenital structures, and profuse menstrual bleeding. Both women and men may have no symptoms and so may not seek treatment, which puts them at risk for chronic infection and puts their partners at risk for contracting this disease.

Chronic infections in women can lead to pelvic inflammatory disease (PID) if the bacteria migrate up through the uterus and to the uterine (fallopian) tubes. PID is also caused by *C. trachomatis* (see below) and a variety of other bacteria, but a large portion of the cases are caused by *N. gonorrhoeae.* PID can cause sterility if scar tissue develops and blocks the uterine tubes, which are passageways that lead from the ovaries to the uterus. If the tubes become constricted rather than blocked, sperm may be able to reach and fertilize an egg, but the developing embryo may become stuck in the tube as it travels to the uterus. An ectopic pregnancy results, in which the egg embeds in the wall of the tube. Such a pregnancy is fatal to the developing fetus and may cause the tube to rupture. In addition, pregnant women with gonorrhea can infect the eyes of their newborns as they pass through the birth canal; blindness can result. Babies' eyes are treated with a solution of silver nitrate or the antibiotic erythromycin to avoid such infection.

In addition to causing infection of the urogenital tract, *N. gonorrhoeae* can cause infections of the joints, skin, and blood if it invades the bloodstream. It commonly infects the rectum due to its proximity to the site of initial infection. In addition, the organism can infect the throat as a result of oral-genital contact. Although gonorrhea is most often transmitted by sexual contact, the bacteria can survive for several hours on objects such as bed linens. Therefore unsanitary conditions can sometimes be a route of transmission. Most infections respond to penicillin; other antibiotics are sometimes used as well.

Chlamydial infection

Chlamydial sexually transmitted infection is caused by an unusual bacterium, *Chlamydia trachomatis.* These organisms, among the smallest of the bacteria, grow only within other cells and obtain ATP (see Chapter 5) from their host cells.

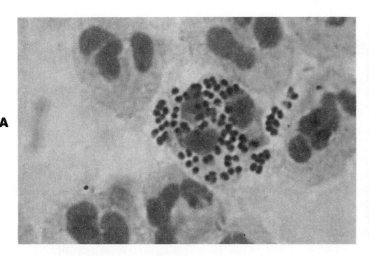
A

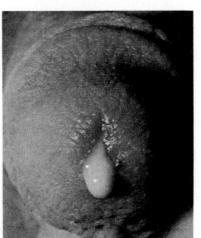
B

FIGURE 23-14 Gonorrhea.
A *Neisseria gonorrhoea,* the causative agent of gonorrhea, appears as pairs of coffee bean-shaped cells.
B The mucus-like discharge of gonorrhea from the urethra of a male.

For this reason, scientists call the chlamydiae "energy parasites." Another unusual feature of the chlamydiae is that they exhibit two different forms depending on whether they are inside or outside host cells. The chlamydia capable of infecting cells are metabolically inactive, small, dense bodies having rigid cell walls. These infective forms of chlamydiae are called **elementary bodies**. They attach to host cells and are taken into these cells by phagocytosis. Once inside their hosts, the elementary bodies transform into **reticulate bodies** (Figure 23-15): relatively large, metabolically active cells having flexible cell walls. The reticulate bodies then multiply, condense to form elementary bodies, and cause the host cell to burst, releasing them. Each new elementary body is capable of infecting a new host cell.

Chlamydia trachomatis is the primary causative agent of nongonococcal urethritis (NGU), a disease similar to gonorrhea but caused by organisms other than *N. gonorrhoeae*. In addition, one highly invasive strain, or group, of *C. trachomatis* causes *lymphogranuloma venereum*, a sexually transmitted disease that is rare in the United States. However, chlamydial NGU infections are extremely common; this realization is relatively recent due to the development of new diagnostic techniques that can detect this organism.

After infection with *Chlamydia trachomatis*, mild, gonorrhea-like symptoms appear within 1 to 3 weeks. A discharge is present, but it is more watery than the discharge of gonorrhea. Unfortunately, many persons with chlamydial NGU have no symptoms, so do not seek treatment and pass the organism on to other partners. As with gonorrhea, chronic infection with *Chlamydia* can lead to PID and sterility in women, and inflammation of the epididymis and sterility in men. Infants passing through the birth canal can also become infected. Erythromycin is used to treat the eyes of infants. Tetracycline and sulfa drugs (anti-bacterial chemical compounds containing the element sulfur) are used to treat chlamydial NGU.

Other organisms that can be transmitted by sexual contact

Candidiasis (yeast infection)

Vaginal yeast infections, superficial infections of the mucous membranes of the vagina, are common occurrences in women and are most often caused by *Candida albicans*. Candida is normally found in small numbers in the vagina, but the acid environment of the vagina and the proliferation of normal vaginal bacteria limit its growth. When the environment of the vagina changes, this organism often flourishes, producing raised gray or white patches on the vaginal walls, a scanty but thick whitish discharge, and itching. Situations that change the environment of the vagina are pregnancy or the use of birth control pills, which often change the vaginal pH, or taking broad-spectrum antibiotics such as tetracycline, which kills the normal vaginal bacteria. In addition, patients with AIDS or uncontrolled diabetes often develop yeast infections. Candidiasis can also occur in other areas of the body, such as the mouth, hands, feet, skin, and nails.

Yeasts are a type of **fungi**, a separate kingdom of mostly multicellular eukaryotic organisms that are *saprophytic*; that is, they feed on dead or decaying organic material. To do this, fungi secrete enzymes onto a food source to break it down and then absorb the breakdown products. Some fungi, such as Candida, are *parasites* and feed off living organisms in the same way. (Other examples of fungal parasites are the organisms that cause ringworm and athlete's foot.) Most fungi are composed of slender filaments called **hyphae** that form cottony masses like those seen on moldy bread or fruit. Sometimes the filaments (hyphae) are packed together to form complex structures, such as mushrooms.

Some fungi, such as Candida, are single-celled and do not have a true hyphal structure. These fungi are called *yeasts*. As yeasts like Candida invade tissue, however, they develop elongated structures termed *pseudohyphae*, as shown in the photo of a vaginal smear from an infected patient (Figure 23-16).

Although candidiasis is not considered a sexually transmitted disease because it is usually contracted without sexual contact, a vaginal yeast infection can spread to a partner during sexual activity. The infection in the male is characterized by the growth of small, elevated yeast colonies on the penis. In addition, like most sexually transmitted diseases, a vaginal yeast infection can be transmitted to a newborn as it passes through the birth canal. A number of antifungal drugs are available that can be applied locally to treat infections caused by Candida.

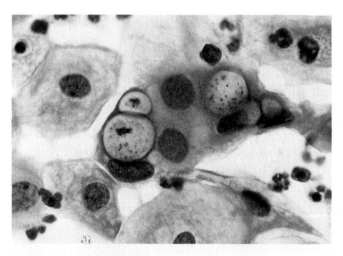

FIGURE 23-15 Chlamydial reticulate and elementary bodies in a host cell.
This micrograph shows a Pap smear of cells taken from the cervix. The cytoplasm of the cells is stained blue, with nuclei stained dark pink. Normal cells surround a cell infected with Chlamydia. The infected cell has a thin ring of cytoplasm surrounding the Chlamydial cells, which appear as various shades of pink and take up the rest of the cell. The reticulate bodies are dark pink cells without red centers. These cells are the metabolically active, reproductive form of Chlamydia. The light pink cells with red centers are in the process of condensing to form elementary bodies: the infective, dormant form of Chlamydia.

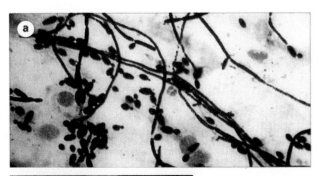

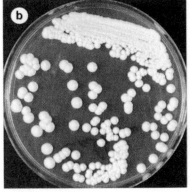

FIGURE 23-16 Candidiasis.
These photomicrographs show the pseudohyphae of *Candida albicans* in a vaginal smear. **(A)**, and the colonial form **(B)**.

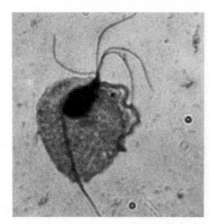

FIGURE 23-17 The causative agent of trichomoniasis.
The flagella of the protozoan *Trichomonas vaginalis* can be clearly seen in this photomicrograph.

Trichomoniasis

Trichomonas vaginalis causes genital infections in both women and men (despite its name). This organism is a *protozoan*, or animal-like protist. The **protists** are a varied group of eukaryotic organisms. Many are single celled, although some phyla of protists include multicellular or colonial forms (single cells that live together as a unit). Within this kingdom are animal-like, plant-like, and fungus-like organisms. The animal-like protists (protozoans) are heterotrophs: they take in and use organic matter for energy.

The protozoans are grouped into phyla according to the way they move and obtain their food. *Trichomonas vaginalis* is a *flagellate*, a member of a phyla of protozoans having long, whip-like organelles of motility called flagella. The flagella of *T. vaginalis* can easily be seen in Figure 23-17. All flagellates have a relatively simple cell structure and have no cell walls or protective outer shells as some protists do. Therefore, a protozoan easily absorbs food through its cell membrane, sometimes using its flagella to ensnare food particles. *T. vaginalis* feeds on bacteria and cell secretions in the urogenital structures it infects.

Like Candida, Trichomonas cannot survive in the normally acidic environment of the vagina; it causes infection only when the pH of the vagina is higher than normal. Usually limited to the vagina, cervix, and vulva, a Trichomonas infection is characterized by itching, burning, and a profuse discharge that may be bloody or frothy. This organism can survive on objects for some time, so an infection can be contracted from a toilet seat or garments that are contaminated with the organism. Transmission is usually by sexual intercourse, however.

In males, Trichomonas usually causes an inflammation of the urethra, but the epididymis, prostate gland, and seminal vesicles can also become infected. An infected man may have no symptoms or may experience a slight discharge from the urethra, painful urination, or increased urination. Infection with *Trichomonas vaginalis* is treated with antiparasitic drugs.

Scabies and pubic lice

Scabies and pubic lice (commonly known as crabs) are two common, contagious parasitic skin infestations. Both of these organisms are transmitted by close physical contact and are often spread by sexual contact. Although they do not cause serious disease, both mites and lice can be vectors, or carriers, of other diseases. Both respond promptly to treatment with antiparasitic medications applied to the skin.

Scabies is caused by the itch mite, *Sarcoptes scabiei* (Figure 23-18). Mites are arachnids, organisms closely related to spiders. Female mites bore into the top layers of skin of their host to lay their eggs. Burrows are formed that look like fine, wavy, dark lines on the surface of the skin. The eggs hatch in a few days, increasing the level of infestation. Itching becomes intense, but scratching abrades the skin surface, which creates an environment in which a secondary bacterial infection can take hold. The common sites of infestation on the body are the base of the fingers, the wrists, the armpits, the skin around nipples, and the skin around the belt line.

Lice are insects that are closely related to fleas. The pubic (crab) louse, *Phthirius pubis* (Figure 23-19), is the most common louse to infect humans. It lives in the hairs of the anal and genital area and the females lay their eggs there, attaching the eggs to the hairs. Infestation causes intense itching.

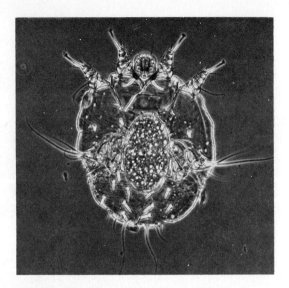

FIGURE 23-18 The itch mite, *Sarcoptes scabiei.*

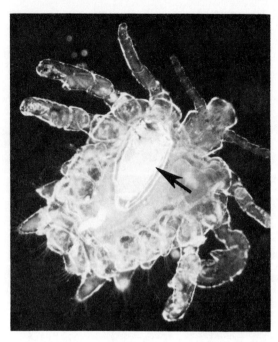

FIGURE 23-19 The pubic louse, *Phthirius pubis.* The *arrow* shows a developing egg.

Protecting yourself against sexually transmitted diseases

The only way to totally protect yourself against contracting STDs is to abstain from sexual activity. If you do engage in sexual activity, your risk of contracting a sexually transmitted disease rises as your number of partners rises. A monogamous relationship between two partners is the safest situation in terms of disease transmission.

How else can you protect yourself from STDs? The best protection is the proper and consistent use of latex condoms. The condom puts a barrier between you and any disease-producing organisms, but *condoms are no guarantee against contracting disease.* The use of the spermicide nonoxynol-9 in addition to a condom can provide further protection because it inactivates viruses. In addition, observe your partner, if possible, for the presence of any of the signs or symptoms of disease described in this chapter. (Table 23-1 summarizes these diseases.) However, absence of symptoms does not mean that a person is free of disease. You may choose to ask your partner if he or she is currently infected with an STD so that you can make an informed choice regarding your behavior. Finally, if you observe any of the signs or symptoms of an STD in yourself, see your physician immediately.

TABLE 23-1 Sexually transmitted diseases and infestations

DISEASE	CAUSATIVE AGENT	TYPE OF AGENT	BRIEF DESCRIPTION OF DISEASE	TREATMENT
Genital herpes	Herpes simplex virus (HSV)	Virus	Painful sores in genital area. Virus causes latent infection so recurrences common.	Acyclovir and other antiviral drugs (no cure)
Genital warts	Human papilloma-virus (HPV)	Virus	Soft, pink, flat or raised growths on external genitals, rectum, vagina, cervix.	Electrocauterization, cryotherapy, surgery (no cure)
Acquired immune deficiency syndrome (AIDS)	Human immuno-deficiency virus (HIV)	Virus	Virus attacks and destroys T cells, a key component in the body's immune system.	Various anti-viral drugs (no cure)
Syphilis	*Treponema pallidum*	Bacterium	Disease progresses through stages of localized infection to widespread infection. If untreated, can result in death.	Penicillin
Gonorrhea	*Neisseria gonorrhoeae*	Bacterium	Primary infection is of urethra (in men and women) and vagina and cervix (in women). Other urogenital structures may become infected. Disease often causes pus-like discharge. Can result in sterility and/or damage to other organs.	Penicillin and other antibiotics
Chlamydial infection (nongonococcal urethritis)	*Chlamydia trachomatis*	Bacterium	Infection similar to gonorrhea but usually has milder symptoms.	Tetracycline and sulfa drugs
Candidiasis (yeast infection)	*Candida albicans*	Yeast	Vaginal infection results in raised gray or white patches on the vaginal walls, a thick whitish discharge, and itching. Penile infection results in the growth of small, raised yeast colonies on the penis.	Topical antifungal drugs
Trichomoniasis	*Trichomonas vaginalis*	Protozoan	Infection in women results in vaginal itching, burning, and a profuse discharge that may be bloody or frothy. Infection in men results in a slight discharge from the urethra, painful urination, or increased urination.	Antiparasitic drugs
Scabies	*Sarcoptes scabiei*	Itch mite	Common sites of infestation are the base of the fingers, the wrists, the armpits, the skin around nipples, and the skin around belt line. Female mites bore into the top layers of skin of an infected person to lay their eggs. Symptoms are dark, wavy lines in the skin and itching.	Topical antiparasitic medications
Pubic lice (crabs)	*Phthirius pubis*	Pubic louse	Females lay eggs in pubic hairs. Causes intense itching.	Topical antiparasitic medications

Summary

1. Sexually transmitted diseases (STDs) are caused by the transmission of certain agents of infection from one person to another during sexual activity. The most common sexually transmitted diseases are caused by bacteria and viruses. Other organisms such as certain fungi, protozoans, mites, and lice can be transferred from person to person by sexual contact, but are regularly transferred in other ways as well.

2. Three sexually transmitted diseases caused by viruses are genital herpes, genital warts, and acquired immune deficiency syndrome (AIDS). Viruses are not living cells; they are protein-coated nucleic acids that replicate (multiply) within living cells.

3. Various patterns of viral replication exist. In the lytic cycle a virus enters a cell and causes it to produce viral nucleic acid and protein coats. After these viral parts are asembled, the new virus particles may burst from the host cell or may leave the host cell by budding. In the lysogenic cycle, viruses enter into a long-term relationship with the cells they infect, their nucleic acid replicating as the cells multiply.

4. The sexually transmitted diseases caused by bacteria include syphilis, gonorrhea, and chlamydial infection. The bacteria that cause these diseases enter the body via the mucous membranes of the genitals, usually during sexual activity. After entering the body, bacteria attach to body cells and cause various types of tissue damage. The chemicals bacteria produce digest the tissues so that the breakdown products can be taken into the bacteria and metabolized.

5. Bacteria (kingdom Monera) have a prokaryotic cell structure. They differ from eukaryotic cells in many ways but primarily in that they have no membrane-bounded nucleus or membrane-bounded organelles.

6. Bacteria reproduce asexually by binary fission, a splitting in two, after replication of the genetic material takes place. The numbers of bacteria within a population increase rapidly when growth conditions are favorable.

7. Other infections and infestations that can be transmitted by sexual contact are candidiasis, which is caused by a yeast; trichomoniasis, which is caused by a flagellated protozoan; and scabies and pubic lice, which are caused by parasitic arthropods.

8. The best protection against the transmission of sexually transmitted diseases, other than abstention from sexual activity, is the consistent and proper use of latex condoms.

1. Are high standards of personal hygiene sufficient protection against sexually transmitted diseases?

2. What are viruses? What do scientists mean when they say that viruses are not alive?

3. Distinguish between the lytic cycle and the lysogenic cycle.

4. One of your friends usually develops a cold sore on his mouth when he gets a cold. Why? What pattern of viral replication is involved?

5. What danger is posed by the act of oral sex if one partner has an actively open cold sore or fever blister?

6. What health risks are problematic to women who have developed genital herpes?

7. Are genital warts cancerous?

8. Many scientists think that bacteria are the most primitive biological organisms and probably evolved long before eukaryotes. Can you support this theory?

9. What are gummas? What damage can they cause to internal organs and systems?

10. Describe how gonorrhea may cause sterility in both men and women.

11. Explain how persons with chlamydial NGU, gonorrhea, or syphilis may unknowingly pass on these sexually transmitted diseases.

12. Which sexually transmitted diseases are caused by protozoans?

13. Are condoms a completely adequate barrier to sexually-transmitted diseases? Is there still a risk factor present if condoms are used correctly?

1. One of the greatest obstacles to AIDS research is the fact that viruses are more difficult to research, immunize against, and treat than bacterial infections. Often a virus may mutate randomly into a newer and more virulent form. Discuss these and other obstacles to present AIDS research.

2. One of the greatest obstacles to successful research on sexually transmitted diseases is the lack of data available. Personal rights in our country prevent access to medical files by many parties. Gather in small groups and discuss the following issues: (1) Did open information and government involvement play a role in the extermination or reduction of many dread diseases (polio, smallpox, measles etc.)? (2) What are the restrictions placed on research of sexually transmitted diseases? (3) What are the biological complexities of this research (i.e. viral vs. bacterial research)?

Baskin, Yvonne. (1991, December) Intimate enemies. *Discover*, pp. 16-17. *An interview with Flossie Wong-Staal about her approaches to AIDS research.*

Campbell Susan Miller. (1992, September) Women, men, and condoms: attitudes and experiences of heterosexual college students. *Psychology of Women Quarterly.* pp. 273-288. *A clinical study of the effectiveness of condom use to prevent sexually transmitted diseases as it relates to user attitude.*

Hoffman, Paul. (1992, June) The science of sex. *Discover* pp. 32-89. *This entire issue is focused on sexuality, human reproduction, and includes material on sexually transmitted diseases.*

Press, Michell. (1989, July) Interview with Nancy Padian on the heterosexual transmission of aids. *An open and interesting interview with a leading AIDS researcher on the increase of heterosexually transmitted AIDS.*

BIOETHICAL DECISIONMAKING FRAMEWORK
Conceiving One Life to Help Sustain Another

Consider the following questions as you think about the bioethical dilemma presented on page 407.

1. What are the bioethical issues in this case?
   - What has to be decided?
   - Who are the decisionmakers?
   - Outline the decisionmaking process in this case as you understand it.

2. What factual information do the decisionmakers need? Consider the effects of the answers to the following questions on the decisionmaking process.
   - What is the probability of success of such a transplant? Has the transplant of an organ from a young child to an adult ever been done before? Was the transplant successful?
   - What are the medical risks involved in transplantation? ...in dialysis? Is one alternative less risky than the other?
   - Has the patient received counseling about his condition and help in accepting his dialysis?
   - Given the severity of this patient's condition, will he be "cured" if he receives a transplant, or will another transplant be required in the future?
   - What other questions should the decisionmakers ask?
   - What additional factual information do the decisionmakers need?

3. Who are the "stakeholders" in this decision—those who stand to gain or lose as a result of the decision?
   - Are the husband and wife stakeholders? The surgeon? The unborn child? (Can a child that is not yet conceived be a stakeholder?) What other persons or groups are stakeholders?
   - Which stakeholders are decisionmakers? Which are not decisionmakers? Will individuals in the latter group be able to influence the decisionmaking process? Should they have influence?
   - In what ways would each stakeholder be affected by the decision?

4. What are the values at stake in the decision? As you list and describe them, consider the following questions:
   - Do parents have the right to decide whether a child should be an organ donor? Does anyone?
   - Under what circumstances could deliberately conceiving a child and using one of its organs to save another life be acceptable? If you agree that the wife's suggestion is ethical, can you think of any circumstances that would not be acceptable?
   - What differences exist between conceiving a child for the expressed purpose of organ donation and using tissue from previously aborted fetuses for medical purposes?
   - It is possible to determine the tissue type of the fetus in utero. What if the fetus that is conceived were not a suitable match to donate a kidney to its father? Would it be acceptable for the couple to have the fetus aborted and then conceive another fetus?
   - Examine how you feel about using fetal tissue transplants as a treatment for Parkinson's disease, a degenerative brain disorder. In this situation, tissue from aborted fetuses is gathered from medical facilities and is transplanted into the brains of Parkinson's patients. Do you agree or disagree with this procedure? How does it differ from the situation presented in the Part Opener?

5. What options are available to the decisionmakers? As you list these options, consider the following questions:
   - Which of these alternatives seem ethically feasible? Which seem administratively possible?
   - How would each alternative decision affect each of the stakeholders?
   - Is there a compromise solution that might give all parties the sense that they have come out the "winner" in the decision?

6. What are the values inherent to the decisionmaking process?
   - Is the decisionmaking process fair?
   - Do all stakeholders have equal resources to advocate their position?
   - What further steps might each group of stakeholders take if their views are disallowed?

PART SEVEN

Human Evolution and Ecology

24
Human Evolution

25
Human Population Concerns

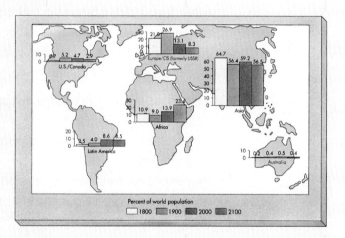

Percent of world population
☐ 1800 ▨ 1900 ▨ 2000 ▨ 2100

U.S./Canada   0.7   5.2   4.7   2.9

Europe/CIS (formerly USSR)   21.8   26.9   13.1   8.3

Africa   10.9   9.0   13.9   23.4

Latin America   2.5   4.0   8.6   8.5

Asia   64.7   56.4   59.2   56.5

Australia   0.2   0.4   0.5   0.4

26
The Human Impact on the Environment

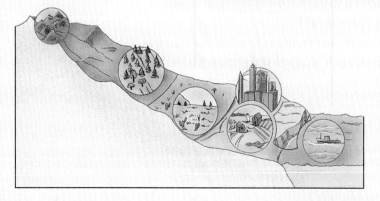

BIOETHICAL DECISIONMAKING
National Family Planning Programs and Cultural Values

In a developing (unindustrialized) nation, both government-sponsored and private family planning association programs dispense contraceptives to all who seek them, regardless of age or marital status. These family planning programs were instituted in an effort to reduce the country's extremely high birth rate, to encourage people to limit the size of their families, and to provide a way to space the births of their children. In addition to providing contraceptives, the programs also advocate improvement in education, aid to families with dependent children, and other measures to raise the country's standard of living.

Current statistics show that 40% of the people in this country are under the age of 15. The government fears that such a large proportion of people who will soon reach reproductive age could lead to a population explosion that would stretch already scarce resources to their limits.

These family planning programs have generated criticism within the nation. Married women who receive contraceptives are not asked whether their husbands consent to their actions; the programs also do not question the marital status of younger women. Some cultural leaders maintain that dispensing contraceptives to young unmarried women contributes to moral breakdown in the nation. In their opinion, the availability of contraceptives at the clinics is directly responsible for a rising "moral looseness" and a breakdown of traditional controls on sexual promiscuity among the unmarried. Some other observers charge that making contraceptives available to married women without the knowledge or consent of their husbands is, in this society, an open invitation to infidelity. Although they can cite no statistics, several of these observers maintain that there has been a notable rise in adultery since the programs were initiated.

Spokespersons for the family planning programs defend their policies on the ground that it is their task to prevent unwanted births among both unmarried and married women, and that they are not the moral judges for the nation. The representatives of the government-sponsored program also point out that the World Population Plan of Action of the United Nations states that individuals have the right to the means for controlling the number and spacing of their children.

Should freedom of contraceptive choice and the availability of contraceptives have a higher priority than local social or religious traditions and beliefs about sexual behavior?

24 Human Evolution

A parent and child walking hand in hand on the wet edge of a beach might leave an imprint of their presence. But the trail of footprints in this photograph is more permanent than it appears. Although these footprints were made near a lake, they are not embedded in sand but in volcanic ash that has preserved them for over 3 1/2 million years. Even though they are human in appearance, these footprints are not human. They were made by nonhuman ancestors, *Australopithecus afarensis,* and give scientists important clues to our heritage. One clue, for example, is the size of the footprints. Some scientists suspect that they were made by a male and a female rather than by a parent and child and therefore may reflect our ancestors' sexual dimorphism, or size difference with gender. Another clue to our heritage is that these organisms are walking erect on two legs instead of four, a characteristic called *bipedalism*. Bipedalism is only one of the many evolutionary changes that led to the appearance of modern humans.

The development of the theory of evolution

Evolution is the genetic change in a population of organisms over generations. The development of the theory of evolution begins in 1831 with English naturalist Charles Darwin, who had the chance to study plants and animals during an ocean voyage from 1831 to 1836. He was able to experience firsthand the remarkable diversity of living things on the Galapagos Islands off the west coast of South America. After years of reflection on his observations, Darwin began to formulate a theory integrating his observations with current thinking and understanding of geology, population biology, and the fossil record. Beginning in 1842, Darwin began to write his explanation of the diversity of life on earth and the ways in which living things are related to one another. In 1859, he presented his work at a seminar with another English naturalist, Alfred Russel Wallace, who had independently developed a similar theory.

During his 5 years on the ship, *Beagle,* Darwin observed many phenomena that were of central importance to the development of his theory of evolution. While in southern South America, for example, Darwin observed fossils (the preserved remains) of extinct armadillos that were similar to armadillos still living in that area (Figure 24-1). This observation suggested to Darwin that the fossilized armadillos were related to the present-day armadillos.

Another observation made by Darwin was that geographical areas having similar climates, such as Australia, South Africa, California, and Chile, are each populated by different species of plants and animals. (A **species** is a group of related organisms that share common characteristics and are able to interbreed and produce viable offspring.) These differences suggested to Darwin that factors other than or in addition to climate must play a role in the diversity (variation) of plants and animals. Otherwise, all lands having the same climate would have the same species of animals and plants.

On the Galapagos Islands, Darwin encountered giant land tortoises. The tortoises on the various islands were similar yet different from one another. Their patterns of physical variation suggested that all of the tortoises were related, but that they had changed slightly in appearance after becoming isolated on the different islands.

As Darwin studied the data he collected during his voyage and made inferences from his observations, he also reflected on their significance in the context of what was known about geology, the breeding of domesticated animals, and population biology. Scientists studying the rock layers of the Earth in the late eighteenth and early nineteenth centuries saw evidence that the Earth had changed over time, acted on by natural forces such as the winds, rain, heat, cold, and volcanic eruptions. In addition, they noticed that the fossils found within the Earth's rock layers were similar to but different in many ways from living organisms—an observation Darwin himself had made on his voyage. Not only had the Earth changed, thought scientists, but evidence existed that the organisms living on its surface had changed also.

As he pondered the concepts that the earth and its organisms may have changed over time, Darwin also reflected on the results of a process called **artificial selection.** In artificial selection a breeder selects for desired characteristics, such as those of the pigeons shown in Figure 24-2. At one time these pigeons came from the same stock, but through artificial breeding over successive generations, their offspring have changed dramatically. Artificial selection is based on the *natural variation* all organisms exhibit. By choosing organisms that exhibit a particular trait and then breeding that organism with another exhibiting the same trait, breeders are able (over successive breedings) to produce animals or plants having a desired, inherited trait.

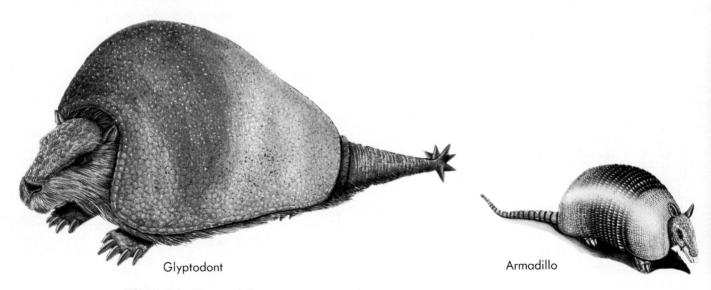

Glyptodont

Armadillo

FIGURE 24-1 Distant relatives.
Reconstruction of a glyptodont, a 2-ton fossil of a South American armadillo, compared with a modern armadillo, which averages about 10 pounds.

Darwin also studied Thomas Malthus' *Essay on the Principles of Population*. Malthus, an economist who lived from 1766 to 1834, pointed out that populations of plants and animals (including human beings) tend to increase geometrically. In a geometric progression, a population (for example) increases as its number is multiplied by a constant. In the geometric progression 2, 6, 18, 54, and so forth, each number is three times the preceding one. Malthus suggested that although populations grow geometrically, food supplies increase only arithmetically. An arithmetic progression, in contrast, is one in which the elements increase by a constant difference, as the progression 2, 6, 10, 14, and so forth. Food, therefore, was a factor that limited geometric population growth. Darwin realized that similar factors must also act to limit plant and animal populations in nature.

Natural selection: A mechanism of evolution

Darwin realized that environmental factors could influence which organisms in a population lived and which ones died. Individuals that possess physical, behavioral, or other attributes well-suited to their environment are more likely to survive than those that possess physical, behavioral, or other attributes less suited to their environment. The survivors have the opportunity to pass on their favorable characteristics to their offspring. These characteristics are naturally occurring inheritable traits found within populations and are called **adaptations**. (Populations are individuals of a particular species inhabiting a locale or region.) Notice that the term *adaptation* is used differently than in its everyday sense. Here, it refers to naturally occurring *inheritable* traits present *in a population* of organisms rather than *noninheritable* traits *in individuals*. Adaptive traits are inherited characteristics that confer a reproductive advantage to the portion of the population possessing them.

As reproductively advantageous (adaptive) traits are passed on from surviving individuals to their offspring, the individuals carrying these traits increase in numbers within the population, and *the nature of the population as a whole gradually changes*. Darwin called this process, in which organisms having adaptive traits survive in greater numbers than those without such traits, **natural selection**. Change in populations of organisms therefore occurs over time because of natural selection: the environment imposes conditions that determine the results of the selection and thus the direction of change. The driving force of change—natural selection—is often referred to as *survival of the fittest*. Again, the term *fittest* does not have the everyday meaning of the healthiest, strongest, or most intelligent. Fitness in the context of natural selection refers to reproductive fitness—the ability of an organism to survive to reproductive age in a particular environment and produce viable offspring.

Natural selection provides a simple and direct explanation of biological diversity—why organisms are different in different places. Environments differ, so organisms are "favored" by natural selection differently in different places. The nature of a population gradually changes as more individuals are born that possess the selected traits. **Evolution** by means of natural selection is this process of change over time by which existing populations of organisms develop from ancestral forms through modification of their characteristics.

FIGURE 24-2   Artificial selection: another clue in the natural selection puzzle
The differences that have been obtained by artificial selection of the wild European rock pigeon **(A)** and domestic races such as the red fantail **(B)** and the fairy swallow **(C)** are so great that birds probably would, if wild, be classified in entirely different major groups. In a way similar to that in which these races were derived, widely different species have originated in nature by means of natural selection.

The scientific evidence for evolution

More than a century has elapsed since Darwin's time. During this period the evidence supporting this theory has grown progressively stronger. In fact, evolution is no longer considered a theory but is accepted as a **scientific law**, a theory that has been upheld countless times as it is tested and retested. By convention, the phrase *the theory of evolution* is still used, but its use does not suggest that evolution by means of natural selection is a highly tentative concept. Evolution is, rather, a scientific observation that is as well accepted in the scientific community as is the theory that the Earth revolves around the sun. Scientists are continuously learning more, however, about the intricacies of the mechanism of natural selection and the history of the evolution of life on Earth.

What is the scientific evidence that upholds the theory of evolution? Scientists find evidence in the fossil record,

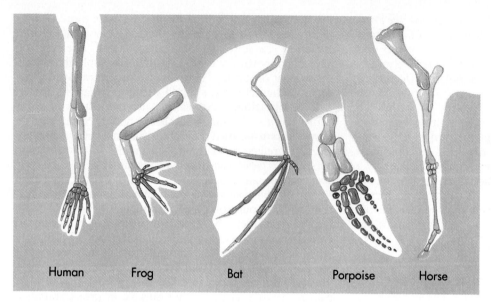

FIGURE 24-3 Homology among vertebrate limbs.
Homologies among the forelimbs of four mammals and a frog show the ways that the proportions of the bones have changed in relation to the particular way of life of the organism and that the forelimb of each animal has the same basic bone structure.

Human   Frog   Bat   Porpoise   Horse

using widely accepted techniques to assess the age of the rocks in which fossils are often found, while gathering a picture of the history of the earth and its organisms. In addition, the tools of comparative anatomy help researchers understand relationships among organisms alive today. Significant scientific advances, such as those in genetics and molecular biology, have given scientists tools Darwin did not have, so today scientists understand more fully than Darwin ever could how organisms change over time.

A **fossil** is a record of a dead organism. Fossils may be nearly complete impressions of organisms or merely burrows, tracks, molecules, or other traces of their existence (see Figure 24-13). Fossils provide an actual record of organisms that once lived, an accurate understanding of where and when they lived, and some appreciation of the environment in which they lived. Direct methods of dating rocks and fossils first became available in the late 1940s. Some methods give scientists information about the age of rocks; others measure the length of time since the death of an organism. The oldest rocks on Earth that have been dated include rocks from South Africa, southwestern Greenland, and Minnesota that are approximately 3.9 billion years old. Recently, rocks brought back to Earth from the moon have been dated as being 3.3 to 4.6 billion years old. These pieces of evidence and others suggest that the Earth and the moon, most likely formed from the same processes at the same time, are about 4.6 billion years old.

Fossils, impressions of organisms that once lived, provide a record of the past. Scientists can determine the age of fossils and use this information to establish patterns of life's progression.

Comparative studies of animal anatomy also provide strong evidence for evolution. If derived from the same ancestor, organisms should possess similar structures with modifications reflecting adaptations to their environments.

Such relationships have been shown most clearly in vertebrate animals. Within the subphylum Vertebrata, the classes of organisms (such as birds, mammals, and amphibians) have the same basic anatomical plan of groups of bones (as well as nerves, muscles, and other organs and systems), but these bones are put to different uses among the classes. For example, the forelimbs seen in Figure 24-3 are all constructed from the same basic array of bones, modified in one way in a bat's wing, in another way in a porpoise's fin, and in yet another way in a horse's leg. The bones are said to be **homologous** in the different vertebrates — that is, of the same evolutionary origin, now differing in structure and function. In some cases, homologous structures exist among related organisms but are no longer useful. These structures, called **vestigial organs**, have diminished in size over time. Humans have a tiny pouch called the appendix that hangs at the junction of the small and large intestines. It serves no useful purpose in humans, but helps in digestion of plant material in organisms that are evolutionarily related to humans.

In contrast to homologous structures, similar structures often evolve within organisms that have developed from different ancestors. Such body parts or organs, called **analogous** structures, have a similar form and function but different evolutionary origins. The eyes of vertebrates and octopuses, which evolved independently but are similar in design, are analogous structures, as well as the wings of birds and insects.

Embryologists, scientists who study the development of organisms from conception to birth, noticed as early as the nineteenth century (around the time of Darwin) that various groups of organisms, although different as adults, possess early developmental stages that are quite similar. These similar developmental forms tell scientists that similar genes are at work during the early developmental stages of related organisms. The genes active during development have been passed on to distantly related organisms from a common ancestor. Over time, new genetic instructions are added to the old; the instructions are expressed at different times, re-

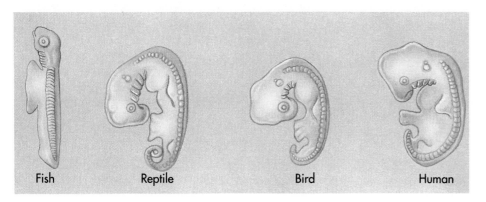

FIGURE 24-4 Embryos show our evolutionary relatedness.
The embryos of various groups of vertebrate animals show the primitive features that all vertebrate animals share early in development, such as gill arches and a tail.

Fish   Reptile   Bird   Human

sulting in similar embryos that develop into organisms quite different from one another. For example, the embryological development of vertebrate animals is similar in that all vertebrate embryos have a similar number of gill arches, seen as pouches below the head (Figure 24-4). Only fish, however, actually develop gills.

Comparative studies of animal anatomy show that many organisms have groups of bones, nerves, muscles, and organs with the same anatomical plan but with different functions. These homologous structures provide evidence of evolutionary relatedness. Comparative embryological studies show that many organisms have early developmental stages that are quite similar. These similar developmental forms provide evidence of evolutionary relatedness.

Today, biochemical tools provide additional evidence for evolution and give scientists new insights into the evolutionary relationships among organisms. Molecular biologists study the progressive evolution of organisms by looking at their hereditary material, DNA. According to evolutionary theory, every evolutionary change involves the formation of new alleles from the old by mutation; favorable new alleles persist because of natural selection. In this way, a series of evolutionary changes in a species involves a progressive accumulation of genetic change in its DNA. Organisms that are more distantly related will therefore have accumulated a greater number of changes in their DNA than organisms that more recently evolved from a common ancestor. Within the last decade, molecular biologists have learned to study and compare these changes in DNA. By comparing the sequences of nitrogenous bases in the DNA (see Chapter 17) of different groups of animals or plants, scientists can show the degree of relatedness among groups of organisms and develop detailed "family trees," called **phylogenetic trees** (Figure 24-5). By studying and interpreting the evidence from the fossil record, comparative anatomy, and genetic studies, it is often possible for scien-

tists to estimate the rates at which evolution is occurring in different groups of organisms.

The pattern of progressive change seen in the molecular record supports other scientific evidence for evolution and provides strong, direct evidence for change over time.

The history of early life

When discussing the history of life on Earth, scientists divide the time from the formation of the Earth until the present day into five major time periods or **eras** shown in the table of geological time (Table 24-1).

Before the Archean Era, the Earth was coalescing from an original cloud of dust formed as the Earth was "born" 4.6 billion years ago. Approximately 800 million (0.8 billion) years passed before the first rocks were formed. Approximately 3.8 billion years ago, chemical evolution began, resulting in the formation of the first cells 3.5 billion years ago. Scientists speculate that the first cells to evolve fed on organic materials in the environment. Because there would have been a very limited amount of suitable organic food available, a type of nutrition must have soon evolved in which cells were able to capture energy from inorganic chemicals. A pigment system that could capture the energy from sunlight and store it in chemical bonds most likely evolved after that. Then oxygen-producing bacteria evolved. Probably similar to present-day **cyanobacteria** (formerly called blue-green algae), these single-celled organisms became key figures in the evolution of life as it is known today. Their photosynthesis gradually oxygenated the atmosphere and the oceans around 2 billion years ago, as evidenced by Archean and Proterozoic sediments and fossils of cyanobacteria.

The beginning of Proterozoic time extends from 2.5 billion to 590 million years ago. During the Proterozoic Era, the first eukaryotic organisms appeared on Earth. How did the eukaryotes arise? The most widely accepted hypoth-

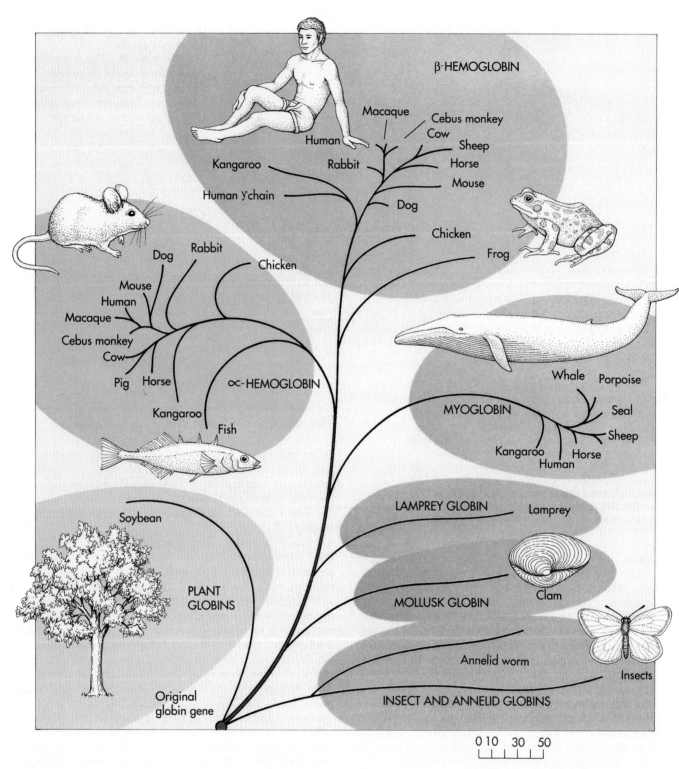

FIGURE 24-5 Evolution of the globin gene.
The length of the various lines is proportional to the number of nucleotide substitutions in the gene and measures the relatedness of the species.

TABLE 24-1

Table of geological time (Read up from bottom)

ERA	PERIOD	EPOCH	(MYA)*	MAJOR BIOLOGICAL AND GEOLOGICAL EVENTS
Cenozoic	Quaternary	Pleistocene		
Cenozoic	Tertiary	Pliocene	1-2	First humans.
Cenozoic	Tertiary	Miocene	7	Origin of first human-like forms.
Cenozoic	Tertiary	Oligocene	26	Monkey-like primates appear.
Cenozoic	Tertiary	Eocene	38	Origin of *Eohippus*.
Cenozoic	Tertiary	Paleocene	54	Small mammals undergo adaptive radiation.
Mesozoic	Cretaceous		65	Major extinction of the dinosaurs and many marine organisms. Flowering plants appear, insects become more diverse.
Mesozoic	Jurassic		130	Large dinosaurs dominant. First birds, mammals.
Mesozoic	Triassic		210	Small dinosaurs appear.
Paleozoic	Permian		250	Major extinction occurs. Most species disappear. Conifers appear.
Paleozoic	Carboniferous		285	First reptiles and arthropods, coal deposits formed, horsetails, ferns, and seed-bearing plants abundant. Fungi appear.
Paleozoic	Devonian		370	"Age of the fishes." Fishes with internal bones and jaws appear. Amphibians also appear. Major extinction of marine invertebrates and fishes.
Paleozoic	Silurian		410	Notochord becomes flexible as single rod is replaced with separate pieces, as seen in the Ostracoderms, the first vertebrates (cartilaginous fish with bony armor, an extinct subclass of the Agnatha).
Paleozoic	Ordovician		430	First chordates appear. Major extinction of marine species.
Paleozoic	Cambrian		500	Major extinction of the trilobites. Origin of the main invertebrate phyla.
Proterozoic			590	Multicellular eukaryotic animals appear. First eukaryotic cells appear. Oxygen-producing bacteria present; atmosphere and oceans oxygenated.
Archean			2500	Chemical evolution resulting in formation of first cells (3500 MYA). Stromatolites formed. Earth is born (4600 MYA).

*MYA; millions of years ago.

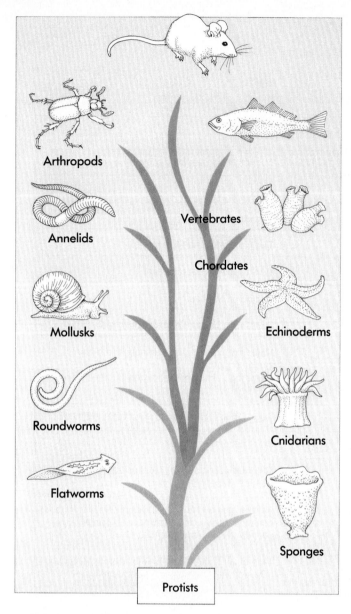

Arthropods

Annelids

Vertebrates

Chordates

Mollusks

Echinoderms

Roundworms

Cnidarians

Flatworms

Sponges

Protists

FIGURE 24-6 Evolution of the major phyla.
During the Precambrian and Cambrian periods, an explosion of animal diversity took place, resulting in the origination of all the major phyla with the exception of the chordates. The different colors denote differences in body cavity structure and embryological development among groups.

esis at this time is called the **endosymbiotic theory.** The term *symbiosis* refers to a relationship between two different organisms in which both organisms benefit. According to this theory, bacteria became attached to or were engulfed by "pre-eukaryotic" (host prokaryotic) cells. The cell membranes of the pre-eukaryotes are thought to have pouched inward during these symbiotic relationships, loosely surrounding the bacteria. These membranous invaginations are thought to have been precursors to nuclear envelopes and endoplasmic reticula. The bacteria are thought to be early mitochondria. Chloroplasts are thought to be derived from symbiotic photosynthetic bacteria.

The Paleozoic Era is divided into six shorter time spans called *periods*. The **Cambrian Period,** the oldest period within the Paleozoic Era, represents an important point in the evolution of life. Multicellular eukaryotic animals arose prior to this time, approximately 630 million years ago. Then all of the main phyla and divisions of organisms that exist today (except for the chordates and land plants) evolved by the end of the Cambrian Period (Figure 24-6).

The evolution of Cambrian organisms took place in the sea. Figure 24-7 shows fossils of the organisms that lived on the seafloor during the Cambrian Period—quite unusual organisms by today's standards. As multicellular organisms arose that were capable of moving from place to place, the forces of natural selection resulted in an array of organisms capable of filling previously unoccupied ecological niches, or roles, within their communities. These possibilities led to diversification along new evolutionary pathways; some resulted in dead ends, and others ultimately led to the contemporary phyla of organisms.

Scientists speculate that the first cells to evolve fed on organic materials in the environment. Then oxygen-producing bacteria evolved, gradually oxygenating the atmosphere. The first eukaryotes appeared, then during the Cambrian Period of the early Paleozoic Era, an array of species of multicellular eukaryotes evolved in the sea. Some of these species still exist today.

The evolution of the vertebrates

As the Paleozoic Era continued into the **Ordovician Period** (500 to 430 million years ago), worm-like aquatic animals similar to lancelets and lampreys began to evolve. These organisms were the first **chordates.** The defining characteristics of chordates are as follows: (1) a single hollow **nerve cord** located along the back; (2) a rod-shaped **notochord,** which forms between the nerve cord and the developing gut (stomach and intestines); and (3) **pharyngeal (gill) arches and slits,** which are located at the throat (pharynx). (These three features are shown in Figure 24-8 as they appear in the embryo.)

The beginning of the story of human evolution can be traced back to the appearance of these first chordates. One of the earliest known chordate fossils is shown in Figure 24-9, *A*. This photo is of *Pikaia*, a small fish-like organism that resembles today's lancelets, shown in Figure 24-9, *B*. The approximately 42,500 species of chordates living today include fishes, amphibians, reptiles, birds, and mammals (and therefore humans). All the features of chordates are evident in their embryos, even if they are not present in the adult form of the organism.

Each of the three chordate characteristics played an important role in the evolution of the chordates and the vertebrates. The dorsal nerve cord increased the animals' responsiveness to the environment. In the more advanced vertebrates, it became differentiated into the brain and spinal cord. The notochord was the starting point for the development of an internal stabilizing framework, the backbone and skeleton, which provided support for locomotion. The

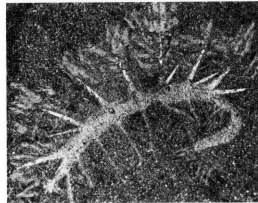

C

E

FIGURE 24-7 Cambrian period fossils from the Burgess Shale, British Columbia, Canada, about 530 million years old.
A and **B** *Sidneyia inexpectans* and a model of the organism. This creature was an arthropod.
C *Hallucigenia sparsa.* This specimen is 12.5 millimeters (approximately ½ inch) long. This animal seems to have been supported on seven pairs of spines; its trunk bore seven long tentacles and an additional group of tentacles near the rear end. *H. sparsa* may have been a scavenger on the bottom of the sea.
D *Wiwaxis corrugata.* The body of this animal was covered with scales and also bore spines. This specimen is 30.5 millimeters (approximately 1¼ inches) across, excluding the spines. It may have been a distant relative of the mollusks.
E *Burgessochaeta setigera,* a segmented worm. The photograph shows the front end of the worm, which had a pair of tentacles. Foot-like structures are attached to the worm in pairs along the sides of the body. The specimen is 16.5 millimeters (approximately ⅝ inch) long.

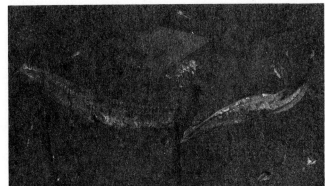

A

B

Pharyngeal slits

Hollow dorsal nerve cord

FIGURE 24-8 Chordate features.
Embryos reveal the three principal features of the chordates: a nerve cord, a notochord, and pharyngeal (gill) arches and slits.

Notochord

FIGURE 24-9 The earliest known chordate.
A *Pikaia gracilens* is a small fish-like animal, and it is one of the first organisms with a notochord. This particular fossil was found in the Burgess Shale.
B A lancelet. Note the resemblance to *Pikaia.*

CHAPTER 24 Human Evolution

475

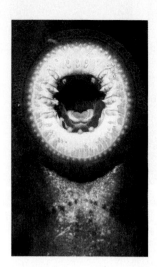

FIGURE 24-10 A lamprey, member of class Agnatha. Lampreys attach themselves to fish by means of their sucker-like mouths, rasp a hole in the epidermis, and suck out blood and other fluids from within. Lampreys do not have a distinct jaw.

Human evolution can be traced back to the appearance of the first chordates, which were small, fish-like organisms. Today, chordates include fishes, amphibians, reptiles, birds, and mammals. The vertebrates evolved from chordates and are characterized by a vertebral column surrounding a nerve cord located along the back. In addition, most vertebrates have a distinct head and a bony skeleton.

The first vertebrates to evolve were jawless fishes (Agnatha), about 500 million years ago (see Figure 24-10). Jaws first developed among fishes that lived about 410 million years ago, toward the end of the Silurian and beginning of the Devonian Periods. During the Devonian Period, fishes having a bony skeleton appeared. One group of fishes, the lobe-finned fishes, is believed to be the ancestor of the land-living **tetrapods,** or four-limbed vertebrates.

The first land vertebrates were **amphibians,** animals able to live both on land and in the water. The moist climate of the Carboniferous Period fostered the dominance of the amphibians during this time. However, the climate then changed dramatically as the Permian Period began. The amphibians, the dominant land vertebrates for about 100 million years, were gradually replaced by the reptiles.

Reptiles had adaptations to dry climates that gave them a survival advantage over the amphibians. In addition, reptiles developed a reproductive advantage—the amniotic egg. An **amniotic egg** has a thick shell that encloses the developing embryo and a nutrient source within a watery sac (Figure 24-11). This type of egg protects the embryo from drying out, nourishes it, and enables it to develop away from water. Birds, too, have amniotic eggs. In contrast, amphibians have shell-less eggs that are shed, fertilized, and develop in water.

bony structures that support the pharyngeal arches evolved into jaws with teeth, allowing these organisms to feed differently than their ancestors.

With the exception of two groups of relatively small marine animals, the tunicates and lancelets (see Figure 24-9, B), all chordates are vertebrates. Vertebrates (a subphylum of the chordates) differ from these two chordate groups in that the adult organisms have a **vertebral column,** or backbone, that develops around and replaces the embryological notochord. In addition, most vertebrates have a distinct head and a bony skeleton, although the living members of two classes of fishes, Agnatha (lampreys and hagfishes) (Figure 24-10) and Chondrichthyes (sharks and rays), have a cartilaginous skeleton.

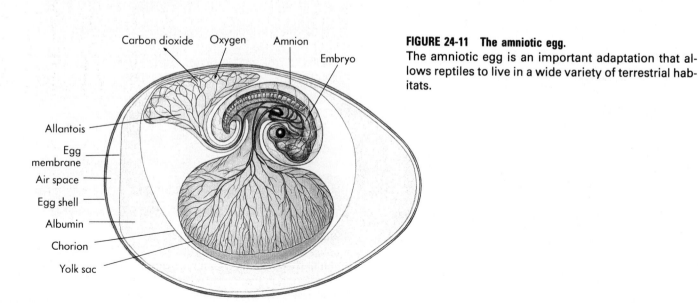

Carbon dioxide   Oxygen   Amnion

Embryo

Allantois

Egg membrane

Air space

Egg shell

Albumin

Chorion

Yolk sac

FIGURE 24-11 The amniotic egg. The amniotic egg is an important adaptation that allows reptiles to live in a wide variety of terrestrial habitats.

One group of jawed, bony fishes, the lobe-finned fishes, are thought to be the ancestors of the amphibians. Amphibians, animals that live on land but return to water to breed, became dominant during the warm, moist climate of the Carboniferous Period. As the climate changed during the Permian Period, however, reptiles took over the land.

Birds (class Aves) evolved from reptiles during the Mesozoic Era, although the entire story of the evolution of birds is somewhat of a mystery due to gaps in the fossil record. Scientists have fossils of *Archaeopteryx* and *Protoavis* (Figure 24-12 A and B) two of the earliest known birds. No fossils have been found of birds that lived after *Archaeopteryx* until about 10 million years later in the Cretaceous Period. However, scientists think that all modern birds evolved from animals like *Archaeopteryx*.

The evolution of the mammals

The fossil record clearly shows that **mammals,** too, evolved from reptiles. Mammals are warm-blooded vertebrates that have hair and whose females secrete milk from mammary glands to feed their young. Organisms having *both* mammalian and reptilian characteristics, called **transitional forms,** first appear in the fossil record approximately 245 million years ago. Then, about 200 million years ago in the early Mesozoic Era, the first known mammals appear. About 65 million years ago, following the extinction of the dinosaurs, mammals became abundant.

Various natural selection pressures led a number of significant anatomical and physiological changes in the mammals as they evolved from their reptilian ancestors. These changes resulted in a class of organisms that not only sur-

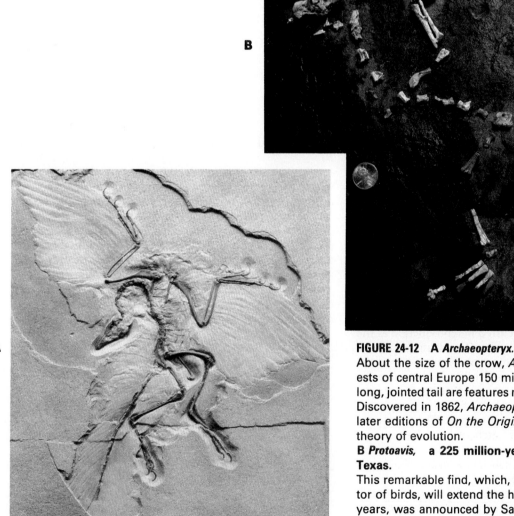

FIGURE 24-12 A *Archaeopteryx.*
About the size of the crow, *Archaeopteryx* lived in the forests of central Europe 150 million years ago. The teeth and long, jointed tail are features not found in any modern birds. Discovered in 1862, *Archaeopteryx* was cited by Darwin in later editions of *On the Origin of Species* in support of his theory of evolution.
B *Protoavis,*   **a 225 million-year-old fossil bird, from West Texas.**
This remarkable find, which, if it proves to be a true ancestor of birds, will extend the history of birds back 75 million years, was announced by Sarkar Chaterjee of Texas Technological University in 1986.

FIGURE 24-13 Monotremes and marsupials (class Mammalia)
A Duckbilled platypus at the edge of a stream in Australia.
B Kangaroo with young in its pouch.

vived but flourished in a wide variety of habitats. Changes occurred in the reptilian arrangement of limbs as the mammals evolved, raising them high off the ground and allowing them to walk quickly and to run. A hinge developed between the lower jaw and the skull, and the teeth became differentiated, allowing mammals to eat a wide variety of food. The reptilian heart, having two ventricles with an incomplete separation, developed a complete wall in the mammals, preventing the mixing of oxygenated and deoxygenated blood. Mammals had also developed **warm bloodedness,** a constant internal body temperature. Their ancestors were **cold blooded,** having internal body temperatures that followed the temperature of their environments.

Important changes also occurred in reproduction as the mammals evolved from the reptiles. The most "reptilian" type of reproduction is seen in the **monotremes,** one of the three subclasses of mammals living today. Monotremes lay eggs with leathery shells and incubate these eggs in a nest. The underdeveloped young that hatch from these eggs feed on their mother's milk until they mature. The platypuses (Figure 24-13, *A*) and spiny anteaters of Australia are some present-day monotremes.

The **marsupials,** a second subclass of mammals, do not lay eggs but give birth to immature young. These blind, embryonic-looking creatures crawl to the mother's pouch and nurse until they are mature enough to venture out on their own. Today most marsupials, such as kangaroos,

wombats, and koalas, are found in Australia (Figure 24-13, *B*).

In **placental mammals,** the young develop to maturity within the mother. They are named for an organ formed during the course of their embryonic development, the placenta. The placenta is located within the walls of the uterus, or womb. Composed of both maternal and fetal tissues, the placenta is connected to the fetus by the umbilical cord. At the placenta, fetal wastes pass into the bloodstream of the mother, and oxygen and nutrients in the mother's bloodstream pass into the bloodstream of the fetus, a mechanism that allows the fetus to develop within the mother until it reaches a certain stage of maturity.

Mammals evolved from the reptiles approximately 200 million years ago. Changes in the structure and placement of their limbs, the structure of the heart, and reproductive strategies resulted in their ability to survive in a variety of climates and to eventually become abundant.

The evolution of the primates

There are 14 orders of placental mammals, which include many animals familiar to you, such as dogs, cats, horses,

Primate Characteristics

- Ability to spread toes and fingers apart
- Opposable thumb (thumb can touch the tip of each finger)
- Nails instead of claws

- Omnivorous diet (teeth and digestive tract adapted to eating both plant and animal food)
- A semi-erect to an erect posture
- Binocular vision (overlap of visual fields of both eyes) resulting in depth perception

- Well-developed eye-hand coordination
- Bony sockets protecting eyes
- Flattened face without a snout
- A complex brain that is large in relation to body size

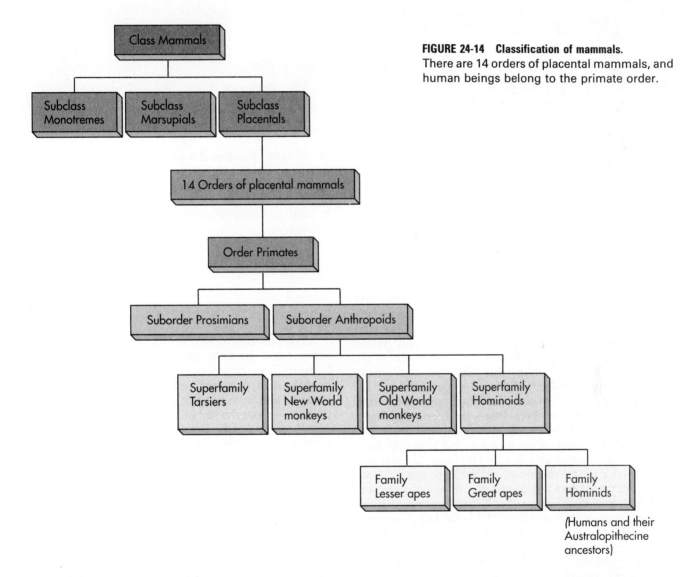

FIGURE 24-14 Classification of mammals.
There are 14 orders of placental mammals, and human beings belong to the primate order.

whales, squirrels, rabbits, bats, and a variety of others. The order of placental mammals that humans belong to is the **primates.** Primates are mammals that have characteristics reflecting an arboreal, or tree-dwelling, lifestyle. Among these characteristics are hands and feet that are able to grasp objects (such as tree branches), flexible limbs, and a flexible spine. The box at the top of the page lists primate characteristics. (Figure 24-14 diagrammatically represents the taxonomic relationships of organisms living today.)

The earliest fossils that resemble any living primates be-

long to a group of organisms that look very much like today's insect-eating shrews (Figure 24-15). (Once classified as primates, today's tree shrews are now considered a separate order of placental mammals.) These primate ancestors are thought to have evolved in the late Mesozoic Era, about 75 million years ago, filling new habitats created by the appearance of the flowering plants, shrubs, trees, and the insects that fed on these plants. These early primates lived in the underbrush, hiding as they competed with the dinosaurs and other reptiles that were dominant at that time. As thou-

CHAPTER 24 Human Evolution   **479**

FIGURE 24-15 A shrew.
Shrews are small nocturnal animals that feed on insects. They resemble the first known primates that appeared about 75 million years ago.

FIGURE 24-16 Evolution of depth perception.
As primates evolved, their eyes moved closer together from their placement on either side of the head. Because the eyes are closer together, each eye focuses on the same object but with a slightly different angle, resulting in greater depth perception.

sands of years passed, humans' shrew-like ancestors probably moved into the trees, eating insects that fed on the fruits and flowers growing on tree branches.

Selection pressures must have been great for these arboreal creatures. Those that survived in this habitat developed excellent **depth perception,** the ability to see in more than one plane as they moved from tree to tree. Depth perception is a function of **stereoscopic vision,** vision created by two eyes focusing on the same object. As primates evolved from their shrew-like ancestors, the eyes moved closer together from their placement on either side of the head (Figure 24-16). With this new placement, each eye can focus on the same object but from a slightly different angle. The brain puts both sets of messages together, resulting in the perception of three-dimensional form and shape.

The primates also developed long limbs with flexible hands and feet adapted to grasping and swinging from branch to branch. Primates have two bones in the lower part of a limb that enable the wrists and ankles to rotate. In addition, the hands and feet of primates have digits that can be spread apart from one another, helping primates balance themselves when walking or running or helping them grasp objects. An **opposable thumb,** one that can touch the tip of each finger, helps in grasping. Most primates also developed flattened nails at the end of the digits, replacing the claws of their mammalian relatives.

⏷⏷
The primates, an order of mammals that humans belong to, reflect an arboreal heritage. The earliest primates arose about 75 million years ago and lived on the ground, feeding on plants and insects. Over time, the primates moved into the trees, developing excellent depth perception and flexible, grasping hands.

The primates are divided into two suborders: the **prosimians** and the **anthropoids** (the suborder that includes humans). The prosimians (meaning "before ape") are small animals, such as lemurs, indris, aye-ayes, and lorises; they range in size from less than a pound to approximately 14 pounds—about the size of a cat or a small dog (Figure 24-17). By the end of the Eocene Epoch (38 million years ago), prosimians were abundant in North America, Europe, and Asia and were probably present in Africa. Their descendants now live only in tropical areas of Asia and Africa, and on Madagascar.

The *anthropoids* (meaning "human-like") include the monkeys, apes, gorillas, chimpanzees, and humans. These primates differ from the prosimians in the structure of the teeth, brain, skull, and limbs. The prosimians have pointed molars and horizontal lower front teeth that are used to comb the coat or to get at food. The anthropoids have more rounded molars and no horizontal lower front teeth. The brain of the prosimian is much smaller in relation to body size than the brain of an anthropoid. The face of an anthropoid is somewhat flat. In addition, the eyes of an anthropoid are closer together than those of a prosimian. Finally, a prosimian's front limbs are short in relation to its long hind limbs, whereas both the front and hind limbs of an anthropoid are long. Compare these features in the prosimians (see Figure 24-17) and the anthropoids (see Figures 24-19 and 24-20).

FIGURE 24-17   Prosimians.
A Ringtail lemur, *Lemur catta.* All living lemurs are restricted to the island of Madagascar, and all are in danger of extinction as the rain forests are destroyed.

FIGURE 24-18   The anthropoids: Tarsiers.
Tarsius syrichta, tropical Asia. Note the large eyes of the tarsier, an adaptation to nocturnal living.

FIGURE 24-19   The anthropoids: Facial differences between an Old World monkey and a New World monkey.
A This macaque has a nose in which the nostrils are next to each other and point downward. Such noses are typical of Old World monkeys.
B This marmoset has a nose in which the nostrils face outward. This trait is characteristic of New World monkeys.

FIGURE 24-20 The anthropoids: Hominoids (the apes).
A Gorilla, *Gorilla gorilla*.
B Mueller gibbon, *Hylobates muelleri*.
C Chimpanzee, *Pan troglodytes*.
D Orangutan, *Pongo pygmaeus*.

In addition to these structural differences, prosimians and anthropoids also exhibit behavioral differences. Anthropoids are **diurnal,** that is, active during the day, whereas the prosimians are nocturnal. The anthropoids have evolved color vision, probably in relationship to their diurnal existence. Also, the anthropoids live in groups in which complex social interaction occurs. In addition, they tend to care for their young for prolonged periods.

The **hominoids** (also meaning "human-like") are one of four superfamilies of the anthropoid suborder. This su-

perfamily includes apes and humans. The other three anthropoid superfamilies include (1) tarsiers (formerly classified with the prosimians, see Figure 24-18), (2) New World monkeys, and (3) Old World monkeys. In general, New World monkeys are found in the New World—South and Central America—and they have flat noses whose nostrils face outward (Figure 24-19, *B*). Old World monkeys have noses similar to humans in which the nostrils are next to each other and point downward (Figure 24-19, *A*); these monkeys are found in the Old World—Africa, southern

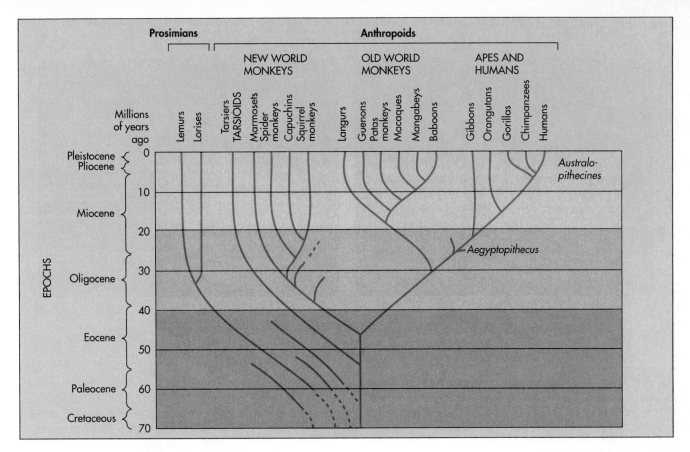

FIGURE 24-21 The primate family tree.
This tree is based on DNA comparisons between living species. The dating of the branches is based on the ages of fossils.

Asia, Japan, and Indonesia.

The hominoid superfamily is divided into three families: the lesser apes, the great apes, and the hominids, or humans. A variety of characteristics put the apes in a different superfamily from the monkeys: most apes are bigger than monkeys, have larger brains than monkeys, and lack tails.

The **lesser apes** include the gibbons, which are the smallest hominoids and closest in size to monkeys. They are about the size of a small dog, weighing 4 to 8 kilograms (9 to 18 pounds). As all monkeys and apes do, they live in tropical rain forests. Here, they leap and swing from tree to tree with their long arms.

The **great apes** include the orangutans, gorillas, and chimpanzees. These apes are much larger than the gibbons (Figure 24-20). The orangutans are about the size of humans, weighing between 50 and 100 kilograms (110 to 220 pounds). These apes exhibit sexual dimorphism; the females weigh about half what the males weigh. Like the gibbons, the orangutans have long arms, but they walk—they do not swing—from branch to branch amoung the rain forest trees. The gorillas are the largest of the apes; they weigh about 160 kilograms, or 350 pounds. The females are smaller, ranging in weight from 165 to 240 pounds. The gorillas spend most of their time on the ground. The smallest of the great apes are the chimpanzees—humans' closest relatives. These animals weigh between 40 and 50 kilograms, or 90 to 110 pounds; females are slightly lighter. Like the other apes (except the gorillas), they spend their time in the trees.

The **hominids,** the family that includes humans of today, are the most intelligent of the hominoids. They are distinguished from the other families of hominoids in that they walk upright on two legs; they are said to be **bipedal.** In addition, hominids communicate by language and exhibit culture—a way of life that is passed on from one generation to another. The only living hominids are humans—**Homo sapiens.**

The evolution of the anthropoids

Scientists have found jaw fragments that suggest that the ancestors of monkeys, apes, and humans began their evolution approximately 50 million years ago. The tarsioids may have begun their evolution even earlier—about 54 million years ago. Scientists do not know what adaptive pressures resulted in the appearance of these early anthropoid primates, nor do they know which prosimian was their ancestor.

Although the only fossil evidence of the emergence of the anthropoids consists of pieces of jaw, biochemical studies complement the knowledge gained from the fossil record. Together, these techniques tell scientists a great deal about the evolution of the anthropoids and the relationships among humans, apes, and monkeys. The phylogenetic tree of the anthropoids is shown in Figure 24-21. Fossils and biochemical studies show that the New World monkeys

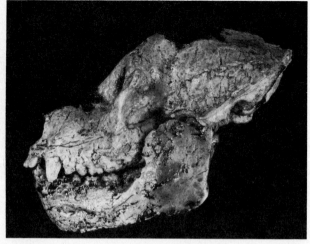

FIGURE 24-22 *Aegyptopithecus zeuxis.*
This primate fossil dates to the late Oligocene Era and is thought to be the ancestor of the hominoids that lived in Africa during the early Miocene Era.

branched from the line leading to the Old World monkeys and the hominoids about 45 million years ago, in the mid-Eocene Epoch. In addition, scientists have discovered many fossils in North Africa that date from 25 to 30 million years ago, in the Oligocene Epoch. One of the earliest of these fossils, which scientists have named *Parapithecus,* probably led to the line of Old World monkeys, splitting from the hominoids approximately 30 million years ago. The others, scientists think, are probably members of the evolutionary line that leads to the hominoids.

The most well-known of the Oligocene fossils found in North Africa is called *Aegyptopithecus.* This fossil is from the late Oligocene Epoch and is thought to be the ancestor to the early Miocene hominoids of Africa. Looking at the partially restored skull in Figure 24-22, you can see that *Aegyptopithecus* had some prosimian characteristics. It had a pronounced snout, leading scientists to believe that its sense of smell was still highly specialized, much like that of the prosimians. In addition, like the prosimians, *Aegyptopithecus* lived singly rather than in social groups.

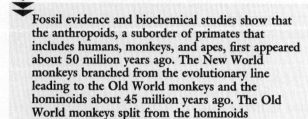

Fossil evidence and biochemical studies show that the anthropoids, a suborder of primates that includes humans, monkeys, and apes, first appeared about 50 million years ago. The New World monkeys branched from the evolutionary line leading to the Old World monkeys and the hominoids about 45 million years ago. The Old World monkeys split from the hominoids approximately 30 million years ago.

Fossil evidence is still being accumulated that will help tell the story of hominoid evolution. From mid-Miocene times on, the hominoid fossil record is quite extensive but consists primarily of skull and teeth fragments. Investigators have calculated that the evolutionary line leading to gibbons diverged from the line leading to the other apes about 18 to 22 million years ago, the line leading to

orangutans split off roughly 13 to 16 million years ago, the line leading to gorillas diverged 8 to 10 million years ago, and the split between hominids and chimps occurred approximately 5 to 8 million years ago. This last statement suggests that chimpanzees and gorillas are humans' closest relatives, with a common relative alive 5 to 8 million years ago.

The evolution of the hominids

The first hominids: *Australopithecus*

The two critical steps in the evolution of humans were the evolution of bipedalism (walking on two feet) and the enlargement of the brain. Scientists think that bipedalism arose as a *preadaptation* because of the way humans' arboreal, ape-like ancestors moved through the trees. In other words, the skeletons and muscles of human ancestors were structured in a way that these hominoids were able to walk bipedally even though they lived in the trees. These structural adaptations developed as a part of their arboreal life and the types of locomotion they exhibited in the trees. Figure 24-23 shows the movements of gibbons and other related brachiators — those hominoids that move through trees by hanging from the branches with their arms, "walking" themselves along. As the weather in Africa cooled somewhat and became seasonal, patches of savannah grasslands began to invade former areas of tropical forest. The hominoids best able to walk efficiently on the ground survived, and bipedalism evolved.

Although hominids may have first appeared as long ago as 5 million years, the oldest undisputed evidence of the hominids is 3.6 to 3.8 million years old. This find was made relatively recently, in 1976, by Mary D. Leakey and an international team of scientists. The team discovered the fossil footprints shown on p. 466. Anthropologists think that the individuals who made the footprints are, or are very closely related to, human ancestors. Fossil bones discovered

FIGURE 24-23 Brachiation and bipedalism.
Brachiators, such as gibbons and siamangs, locomote by hanging from branches with their arms and reaching from hold to hold. Brachiation has preadapted these animals to bipedal walking, which they do on broad branches (as the siamang in the illustration is doing) or on the ground.

a few years earlier, at a site in Ethiopia about 2000 kilometers (1250 miles) north of the footprints, support this hypothesis. At 3.5 million years old, these hominid bones are somewhat younger than the footprints but are the oldest hominid bones ever found. These fossils were named *Australopithecus afarensis,* meaning "southern ape of Afar," by Donald C. Johanson and an international team of scientists who found them in the Afar region of Ethiopia. In 1974, this team also found and pieced together one of the most complete fossil skeletons of *A. afarensis,* which has since become famous (Figure 24-24). This "first" hominid was named Lucy after the Beatles song "Lucy in the Sky with Diamonds," which was popular at that time.

Although the australopithecines are considered to be the first hominids, they are not humans (members of the genus *Homo*). Their brains were still small in comparison to present-day human brains, and they had long, monkey-like arms. In addition, their faces were ape-like, as shown in the photo of a reconstruction of Lucy. Lucy probably weighed about 25 kilograms (55 to 60 pounds) and was about 1 meter tall (slightly over 3 feet). Males were larger than females, however; they stood up to 1.2 meters tall (4 feet) and weighed as much as 45 kilograms (100 pounds).

A. afarensis evolved into two (and possibly more) lineages, including the species *A. africanus, A. robustus,* and *A. boisei.* These australopithecines lived on the ground in the open savannah of eastern and southern Africa. Their diets consisted primarily of plants. At night they probably slept in the few trees that existed in these grasslands, much like the savannah baboons do today to protect themselves from predators.

The oldest evidence of the first appearance of the hominids is 3.6 to 3.8 million-year-old footprints. The oldest hominid fossil skeleton, nicknamed Lucy, is 3.5 million years old and is not classified as human.

The phylogenetic relationships among these australopithecines is not clear; a family tree that is widely accepted at this time is shown in Figure 24-25. Notice from the diagram that no australopithecines are alive today; the last ones disappeared about 1 million years ago.

The first humans: *Homo habilis*

Climatic changes during the Pleistocene Epoch (2 million to 10,000 years ago) may have contributed to the disappearance of the australopithecines and the evolution of a new, more intelligent genus of hominids: the human (ge-

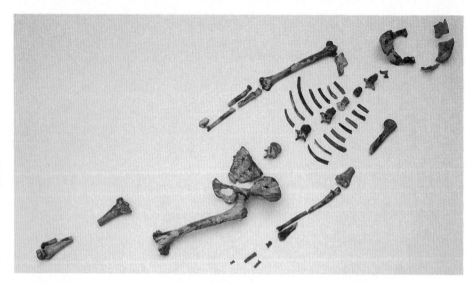

FIGURE 24-24 Lucy, from Ethiopia, is the most complete skeleton of *Australopithecus* discovered so far.
The reconstruction was made by a careful study of muscle attachments to the skull.

nus *Homo*). During the Pleistocene Epoch, the earth cooled, repeatedly undergoing **ice ages** during which vast regions (from the poles to a latitude of about 40 degrees) were covered by massive glaciers. Organisms such as the australopithecines had a low level of intelligence and no innate cold weather survival behaviors, and they died. Apparently, however, a species of hominid more intelligent than the australopithecines was evolving from (most likely) *A. afarensis.* These hominids protected themselves from the cold by building shelters and wearing clothes. They are thought to have been the first humans and were given a name to emphasize their intelligence—*Homo habilis,* or "skillful human." Scientists have fossil bones and tools of *H. habilis* dating back about 2 million years. The first *H. habilis* fossils were discovered in 1964 by Louis Leakey, Philip Tobias, and John Napier in the Olduvai Gorge of eastern Africa.

Judging from the structure of the hands, *H. habilis* regularly climbed trees as did their australopithecine ancestors, although the *H. habilis* people spent much of their time on the ground and walked erect on two legs. Skeletons found in 1987 indicate that the *H. habilis* people were small in stature like the australopithecines, but fossil skulls and teeth reveal that the diet of *H. habilis* was more diverse than that of the australopithecines, including meat as well as plants. The tools found with *H. habilis* were made from stones fashioned into implements for chopping, cutting, and pounding food. The use of stone tools by these early humans

marks the beginning of the **Stone Age,** a time which spans approximately 2 million to 35,000 years ago.

> The first human fossils date back about 2 million years and are of the extinct species *H. habilis,* meaning "skillful human." This species is considered human because its members exhibited an intelligence far greater than their ancestors by making tools and clothing.

Human evolution continues: *Homo erectus*

All of the early evolution of the genus *Homo* seems to have taken place in Africa. There fossils belonging to the second, also extinct species of *Homo*—*Homo erectus*—are widespread and abundant from 1.6 million to about 300,000 years ago. By 1 million years ago, however, *H. erectus* had migrated into Asia and Europe.

The *H. erectus* people were about the size of modern-day humans, were fully adapted to upright walking, and had brains that were roughly twice as large as those of their ancestors. However, they still retained prominent brow ridges, rounded jaws, and large teeth. The tools of *H. erectus* were much more sophisticated than those of *H. habilis* and were used for hunting, skinning, and butchering animals. These

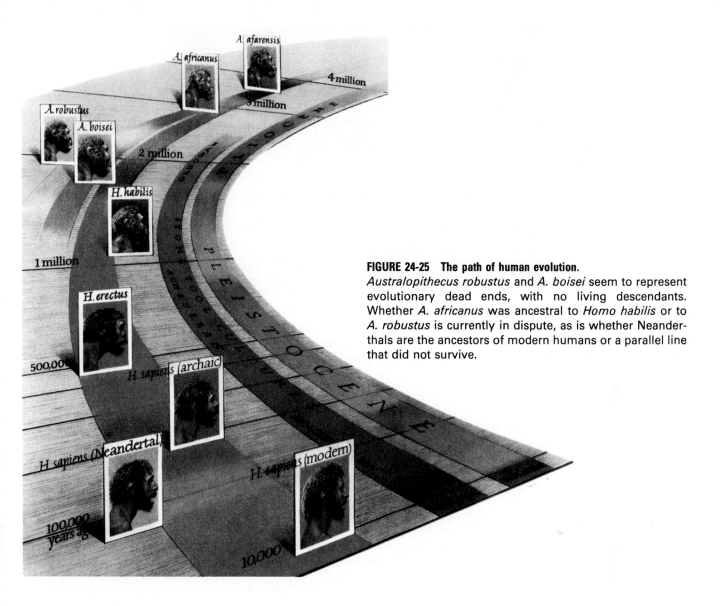

FIGURE 24-25   The path of human evolution.
Australopithecus robustus and *A. boisei* seem to represent evolutionary dead ends, with no living descendants. Whether *A. africanus* was ancestral to *Homo habilis* or to *A. robustus* is currently in dispute, as is whether Neanderthals are the ancestors of modern humans or a parallel line that did not survive.

people were hunter gatherers, which means that they collected plants, small animals, and insects for food, while occasionally hunting large mammals. Researchers have found the first evidence of the use of fire by humans at 1.4 million-year-old campsites of *H. erectus* in the Rift Valley of Kenya, Africa. Fire is characteristically associated with populations of this species from that time onward. All of these activities: tool making, hunting, using fire, and building shelters are signs of **culture,** or a way of life that depends on intelligence and the ability to communicate knowledge of the culture to succeeding generations. Inherent in the concept of culture, then, is the concept of language. The ability to communicate enhances the ability of a species to survive, especially in harsh conditions, such as an ice age, by sharing survival tactics and warning each other of danger. Anthropologists think that the development of language was probably one of the most important factors in the appearance of *Homo sapiens*.

Fossils of a second extinct species of human, *H. erectus,* date back to 1.6 million years ago. These humans made sophisticated tools, built shelters, used fire, and probably communicated using language.

Modern humans: *Homo sapiens*

The earliest fossils of *Homo sapiens* (meaning "wise humans") are dated to be about 200,000 years old and most likely evolved from the *H. erectus* species in Africa. The oldest *H. sapiens,* however, are not considered to be anatomically modern, that is, to have the same anatomical features of today's humans. This species is therefore referred to as an early or archaic form (see Figure 24-25). In general, these early *H. sapiens* had larger brains, flatter heads, more

FIGURE 24-26 Cave painting.
Cave paintings, almost always showing animals and sometimes hunters, were made by Cro-Magnon people, our immediate ancestors. These paintings are found primarily in Europe and were made for about 20,000 years, until 8000 to 10,000 years ago.

sloping foreheads, and more protruding brow ridges and faces than today's humans.

The fossil record shows gradual change of the species *H. sapiens,* with the early form evolving over a 75,000 year span to a subspecies of *H. sapiens* called **Neanderthal.** This subspecies was named after the Neander Valley in Germany where their fossils were first found. The Neanderthals lived from about 125,000 to 35,000 years ago in Europe and the Middle East.

Compared with modern humans, the Neanderthal people were powerfully built, short, and stocky. Their skulls were massive, with protruding faces, projecting noses, and rather heavy bony ridges over the brows. Their brains were even larger than those of modern humans, a fact that may have been related to their heavy, large bodies. The Neanderthals made diverse tools, including scrapers, borers, spearheads, and hand axes. Some of these tools were used for scraping hides, which they used for clothing. They lived

in hutlike structures or in caves. Neanderthals took care of their injured and sick and commonly buried their dead, often placing food and weapons and perhaps even flowers with the bodies. Such attention to the dead strongly suggests that they believed in a life after death. For the first time, the kinds of thought processes characteristic of modern *H. sapiens,* including symbolic thought, are evident in these acts.

Approximately 10,000 years before the Neanderthal subspecies died out, modern *H. sapiens* made their appearance. This "modern" subspecies (our subspecies) is called *Homo sapiens sapiens.* The early members of this subspecies are the Cro-Magnons and are named after a cave in southwestern France where scientists found some of their fossils.

The **Cro-Magnons** had a stocky build, much like the Neanderthals, but their heads, brow ridges, teeth, jaws, and faces were much smaller than the Neanderthals and were

FIGURE 24-27 The beginnings of civilization.
This photo shows the remains of a house in Jericho, which dates to about 7000 BC.
The ruins of Jericho also contain the remnants of city walls and towers, demonstrating
that by about 9000 years ago, many of our ancestors had moved away from the hunting-
gathering life-style into an agricultural life-style.

more similar to today's humans. However, just as modern humans show variation among races, so, too, did the Cro-Magnons. The Cro-Magnons used sophisticated tools that were made not only from stone but also from bone, ivory, and antler—materials that were not used by earlier peoples. Hunting was an important activity for the Cro-Magnons, evidenced by the abundance of animal bones found with human bones and elaborate cave paintings of animals and hunt scenes (Figure 24-26). The paintings appear to have been part of a ritual to ensure the success of the hunt.

The subspecies of *H. sapiens* that preceded us showed a gradual development of culture and society, which was the foundation for the development of "modern" culture and society. About 10,000 years ago, the last ice age came to a close, the global climate began to warm, and various groups of *H. sapiens sapiens* began to cultivate crops and breed animals for food. Archeologists have uncovered the remains of small, ancient cities, such as those of Jericho shown in

Figure 24-27, which give evidence that by 9000 years ago humans had developed complex social structures. By 5000 years ago the first large cities and great civilizations appeared, such as those in Egypt (3100-1090 BC) and Mesopotamia (3100-1200 BC), and the final break occurred with the hunter-gatherer way of life.

The rest of the story of human development is one of history and is best left to the historians, anthropologists, and sociologists to tell. From a biologist's perspective, however, the spread of modern humans throughout the world has a dark side. As people inhabited new lands and increased their numbers, they destroyed many populations of animals and plants. Today, the growing human population is hastening global pollution, destruction, and devastation. Although humans have made incredible progress in the ability to survive, they still need to make progress in living in harmony with the rest of the living world and its resources.

Summary

1. A central theory of biology is Darwin's theory of evolution, which states that living things change over time by means of natural selection: some individuals have traits that make them better-suited to a particular environment, allowing more of them to survive to reproductive age and produce more offspring than other individuals lacking these traits. These characteristics, or adaptations, are naturally occurring inherited traits found within populations. The adaptations allowing greater reproduction increase in frequency over time.

2. Two direct lines of evidence uphold the theory of evolution: (1) the fossil record, which exhibits a record of progressive change correlated with age, and (2) the molecular record, which exhibits a record of accumulated changes, the amount of change correlated with age as determined in the fossil record. Several indirect lines of evidence uphold the theory of evolution, including progressive changes in homologous structures, the existence of vestigial structures, and changes in DNA sequences.

3. Scientists speculate that the first cells to evolve fed on organic materials in the environment. Then oxygen-producing bacteria evolved, gradually oxygenating the atmosphere. The first unicellular eukaryotes appeared about 1.4 billion years ago. Eukaryotic cells likely arose as "pre-eukaryotic" cells became hosts to endosymbiotic prokaryotes. Multicellular organisms first appeared about 630 million years ago.

4. The story of human evolution can be traced back to the appearance of the first chordates about 500 million years ago. Chordates are characterized by a single, dorsal, hollow nerve cord; a flexible rod, the notochord, which forms between the nerve cord and the developing gut in the early embryo; and pharyngeal (gill) arches located at the throat.

5. The vertebrates evolved from the chordates. The first vertebrates to evolve were the jawless fishes. Jaws first developed among vertebrates that lived about 410 million years ago. One ancient group of bony fishes is believed to be the ancestors of the first land vertebrates, the amphibians. Amphibians depend on water and lay their eggs in moist places. The amphibians gave rise to the reptiles.

6. The reptiles were the first vertebrates that were fully adapted to life on land. Amniotic eggs, which evolved in this group but are also characteristic of the birds and the few egg-laying mammals, represent a significant adaptation to the dry conditions that are widespread on land. The birds and mammals evolved from the reptiles.

7. Mammals, vertebrates that have hair and whose females secrete milk from mammary glands to feed their young, evolved from the reptiles approximately 200 million years ago. Primates, one of the 14 orders of mammals, first appeared 75 million years ago. Primates have large brains in proportion to their bodies, binocular vision, and five digits, including an opposable thumb; they also exhibit complex social interactions.

8. The primates are divided into two suborders: the prosimians (small animals such as lemurs, indris, and aye-ayes) and the anthropoids (a group that includes monkeys, apes, and humans). The hominoids (meaning "human-like") are one of four superfamilies of the anthropoid suborder. This superfamily includes apes and humans. The other three anthropoid superfamilies include tarsiers, New World monkeys, and Old World monkeys. Ancestors to the apes gave rise to the gibbons, orangutans, chimpanzees, gorillas, and hominids.

9. The two critical steps in the evolution of humans were the evolution of bipedalism (walking on two feet) and the enlargement of the brain. The earliest hominids and the direct ancestors of humans belong to the genus *Australopithecus*. They appeared in Africa about 5 million years ago. They were small hominids, standing 3 to 4 feet tall and weighing 50 to 100 pounds.

10. The genus *Australopithecus* gave rise to humans belonging to the genus *Homo*. The first species of this genus, *H. habilis*, appeared in Africa about 2 million years ago. Now extinct, the people of this species are considered human because they exhibited an intelligence far greater than their ancestors by making tools and clothing.

11. The second species of *Homo*, *H. erectus*, appeared in Africa approximately 1.6 million years ago. These people used fire, built shelters, fashioned sophisticated tools, and exhibited culture. *H. sapiens* probably evolved from *H. erectus* about 200,000 years ago.

1. Before the nineteenth century and Darwin's work, science supported the view that plants and animals have remained unchanged, as they are now, since the beginning of life on earth. How did Darwin's work challenge this view?

2. Distinguish between a geometric progression and an arithmetic progression. Which increases more quickly? Relate these concepts to the development of Darwin's theory of evolution.

3. Suppose a species of fish has many individuals in the population which have inherited a high tolerance to fluctuation in water temperature. If the climate should change, causing an increased range of temperatures annually, what might result? Which fish are best adapted to survive? What is acting as the mechanism for evolution here?

4. Explain the phrase *survival of the fittest*. What does "fit" mean in this context?

5. Most species of bears are black or brown. Why are polar bears white?

6. What is a phylogenetic tree? How does it support the concept of evolution?

7. A human embryo, in its early stages may exhibit gill arches and a dorsal nerve cord. Are we chordates? What does this embryological data indicate about human evolution?

8. Recent scientific debate has caused many people to reconsider the premise that all dinosaurs were cold-blooded reptiles. Some smaller dinosaurs exhibited speed of movement and posture indicative of warm-bloodedness. What might you call such species? Why do you suppose such hypotheses are difficult to support with evidence?

9. What do monotremes, placental mammals, and marsupials have in common? How do they differ?

10. What are primates? What two characteristics have helped them to be successful?

11. Distinguish between the prosimians and the anthropoids. Give an example of each.

12. Explain the development of hominid bipedalism in terms of evolutionary adaptation.

13. Explain the significance of each of the following: *Australopithecus afarensis, Homo habilis,* and *Homo erectus.* Which is most like you?

14. How did *Homo sapiens sapiens* differ from earlier *Homo* species?

15. As members of the only existent branch of the *Homo sapiens* species, humans have a tendency to classify the Neanderthals as a lesser, more brutish strain. On what information do we base our assessment?

1. The most diverse time in the history of life was the pre-Cambrian era, when creatures with many different body plans lived. Only a few of these basic body plans survived into the post-Cambrian era; the other body plans were weeded out by evolution. Stephen Gould has speculated that evolution does not foster ever-greater complexity, more complex forms evolving from simpler primitive ones, but rather acts in the opposite fashion, tending to eliminate more and more options. Discuss his suggestion in light of what you have learned about evolution.

Carson H. The process whereby species originate. *Bioscience, 37,* 715-720.

Gould S. (1987, January) Darwinism defined: The difference between fact and theory. *Discover,* pp. 64-60.

Thorne A., & Wolpoff, M. (1992, April). The multiregional evolution of humans. *Scientific American,* pp. 66-83.

Wilson A., & Cann, R. (1992, April). The recent African genesis of humans. *Scientific American,* pp. 66-83.

The last two articles outline polar positions on the origins of humans: Are humans descended from a single African ancestor, as postulated by researchers investigating DNA, or are modern humans related to a number of interconnected lineages scattered throughout the world, as suggested by fossil remains?

25 Human Population Concerns

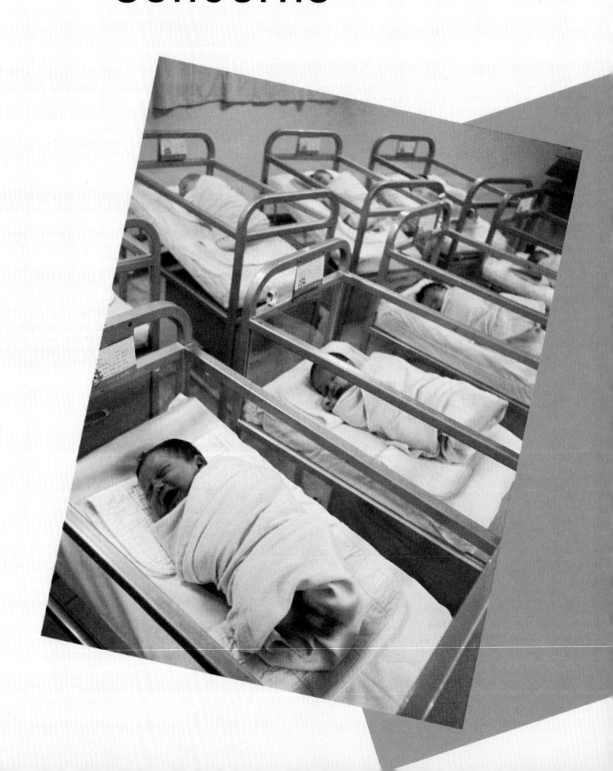

▼ Under ideal conditions, populations grow at an exponential rate, leveling off at the carrying capacity of the environment.

▼ Very small populations are less able to survive than large populations; in addition, inbreeding in small populations leads to a loss of genetic diversity and increases the probability of the extinction of that species

▼ Large populations face threats to survival because of competition for resources such as food, light, and shelter and predation by other organisms.

▼ In 1992, the global human population of more than 5.3 billion people was growing at approximately 1.8% per year; at that rate, the human population will reach well over 10 billion people by 2029.

Approximately 75 babies will be born worldwide in the time it takes to read this paragraph. At this rate, the world's population will reach an astonishing 11 to 13 billion people by the year 2100. This rising population will place an increasing demand on the use of the Earth's natural resources. Adequate food and housing for many people will continue to be only a dream. Pollution of the air and water will worsen. Poverty, crime, and infant mortality will increase. The stability of populations of various plants and animals, which are all interdependent, will collapse, resulting in the the ever-increasing loss of species. Is this apocalyptic nightmare a true vision of the future? Many scientists think so, unless the Earth's peoples curb their own staggering population growth.

A **population** consists of the individuals of a given species that occur together at one place and at one time. This flexible definition allows the use of this term in many contexts, such as the world's human population, the population of protozoans in the gut of an individual termite, or the population of blood-sucking swallow bugs living in the feathers of a cliff swallow. The growth of any population is governed by similar principles; factors resulting from the growth of a population regulate its subsequent growth. Many scientists agree that "nature" will regulate the size of the human population by means of starvation and disease if we humans don't curb our own growth. What do you think will happen? What do you think should be done? Reading this chapter and the next one may help you understand many of the factors involved in world population growth and its impact on the environment so that you can answer these crucial questions.

Population growth

Most populations will grow rapidly if the ideal conditions for growth and reproduction of their individuals exist. But why, then, is the Earth not completely covered in bacteria, cockroaches, or houseflies? Why do some populations change from season to season or year to year?

To answer these questions, you need to understand how the size of a population is determined. The size of a population at any given time is the result of additions to the population from births and from **immigration,** the movement of organisms into a population, and deletions from the population from deaths and **emigration,** movement of organisms out of a population. Put simply, (births + immigrants) − (deaths + emigrants) = population change.

These statistics (births and deaths) are often expressed as a *rate:* numbers of individuals per thousand per year. For example, the population of the United States at the beginning of 1989 was approximately 250 million people. During 1989 there were the following:

- 3,975,000 live births: The birth rate was 3,975,000 per 250,000,000 people, or 15.9 births per 1000.
- 570,009 immigrations: The immigration rate was 570,009 per 250,000,000 people, or 2.3 immigrants per 1000.
- 2,175,000 deaths: The death rate was 2,175,000 per 250,000,000 people, or 8.7 deaths per 1000.
- 177,600 emigrations: The emigration rate was 177,600 per 250,000,000 people, or 0.7 emigrants per 1000.

The population change in the United States in 1989 can be calculated as follows: (15.9 births/1000/year + 2.3 immigrants/1000/year) − (8.7 deaths/1000/year + 0.7 emigrants/1000/year) = 8.8 people/1000/year. This figure can also be expressed as a population change of 0.88%—an increase of nearly 1%.

> The size of a population is the result of additions to the base population because of births and immigrations, and deletions from the population because of deaths and emigrations.

In natural populations of plants and animals, immigration and emigration are often minimal. Therefore a determination of the **growth rate** of a population does not include these two factors. Growth rate (r) is determined by subtracting the death rate (d) from the birth rate (b):

$$r = b - d$$

Using the figures from our previous example:

$$r = 15.9 \text{ births/1000/year} - 8.7 \text{ deaths/1000/year}$$
$$r = 7.2/1000 \text{ or } 0.0072$$

To calculate the number of individuals added to a population of a specific size (N) in a given time *without* regard to immigration and emigration, r is multiplied by N:

$$\text{population growth} = rN$$

Therefore the population growth in the United States in 1989 solely from births and deaths was 0.0072 x 250,000,000 people = 1,800,000 people.

> The determination of the growth rate of a population does not include the factors of immigration and emigration. It is determined by subtracting the death rate from the birth rate.

Exponential growth

Although the *rate* of increase in population size *may stay the same,* the *actual increase* in the number of individuals *grows.* This sort of growth pattern is similar to the growth pattern of money in the bank as interest is earned and compounded. If you put $1000 in the bank at 8% per year, the first year you will earn $80. The second year you will earn 8% interest on $1080, or $86.40. Although your interest rate has stayed the same, the amount of money you earn grows as your money grows. Actually, in a bank your earnings would grow even more quickly because interest would be posted and compounded more often than once a year.

Figure 25-1 illustrates this principle with a population of bacteria in which each individual divides into two every half hour. The rate of increase remains constant, but the actual increase in the number of individuals accelerates rapidly as the size of the population grows. This type of mathematical progression found in the growth pattern of bacteria is termed **exponential growth.** (For example, 2 cells split to form 2^2 or 4, 4 become 2^3 or 8, and so on. The number, or power, to which 2 is raised is called an *exponent.*) Exponential growth refers to the rapid growth in numbers of a population of any species of organism, even though most organisms reproduce sexually and one organism does not split into two "new" organisms.

A period of exponential growth can occur only as long as the conditions for growth are ideal. In nature, exponential growth often takes place when an organism begins to grow in a new location having abundant resources. Such a situation occurred when the prickly pear cactus was introduced into Australia from Latin America. The species flourished, overrunning the ranges. In fact, the cactus became so abundant that cattle were unable to graze (Figure 25-2, *A*). Scientists regulated the population by introducing a cactus-eating moth to the area. The larvae of the moth fed on the pads of the cactus and rapidly destroyed the plants. Within relatively few years, the moth had reduced the population; the prickly pear cactus became rare in many regions where it was formerly abundant (Figure 25-2, *B*).

Time (Hours)	Number of bacteria	Growth curve
10	1,048,576	
$9\frac{1}{2}$	524,288	
9	262,144	
$8\frac{1}{2}$	131,072	
8	65,536	
$7\frac{1}{2}$	32,768	
7	16,384	
$6\frac{1}{2}$	8,192	
6	4,096	
$5\frac{1}{2}$	2,048	
5	1,024	
$4\frac{1}{2}$	512	
4	256	
$3\frac{1}{2}$	128	
3	64	
$2\frac{1}{2}$	32	
2	16	
$1\frac{1}{2}$	8	
1	4	
$\frac{1}{2}$	2	
0	1	

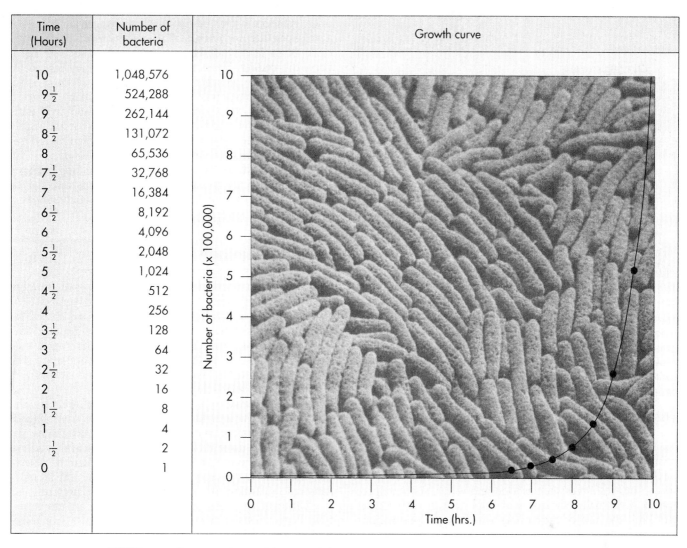

FIGURE 25-1 Exponential growth in a population of bacteria.
This period of rapid exponential growth can only be sustained as long as resources are abundant.

FIGURE 25-2 A cactus takes over Australia.
After an initial period in which prickly pear cacti, introduced from Latin America, choked many of the pastures of Australia with their rampant growth, they were controlled by the introduction of a cactus-feeding moth from the areas where the cacti were native. **A** An infestation of prickly pear cacti in scrub in Queensland, Australia, in October 1926. **B** The same view in October 1929, after the introduction of the cactus-feeding moth.

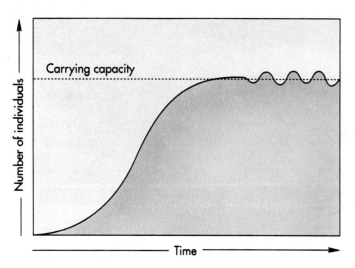

FIGURE 25-3 The sigmoid growth curve.
The sigmoid growth curve, characteristic of biological populations, begins with a slow period of growth quickly followed by a period of exponential growth. When the population approaches its environmental limits, the growth begins to slow down, and it finally stabilizes, fluctuating around the maximum number of individuals that the environment will hold. This maximum number is the carrying capacity.

Carrying capacity

No matter how rapidly a population may grow under ideal conditions, it cannot grow at an exponential rate indefinitely. As a population grows, each individual takes up space, uses resources such as food and water, and produces wastes. Eventually, shortages of important growth factors will limit the size of the population. In some populations such as bacteria, a buildup of toxic wastes may also limit population growth. Ultimately, a population stabilizes at a certain size, called the **carrying capacity** of the particular place where it lives. The carrying capacity is the number of individuals within a population that can be supported within a particular environment for an indefinite period. A population actually rises and falls in numbers at the level of the carrying capacity but tends to be maintained at an average number of individuals (Figure 25-3). The exponential growth of a population and its subsequent stabilization at the level of the carrying capacity is represented by an S-shaped **sigmoid growth curve** (after the Greek letter *sigma*).

> **Under ideal conditions, populations grow at an exponential rate and show some stability in size at the carrying capacity of that place for that species.**

Population size

The size of a population has a direct bearing on its ability to survive. Very small populations are less able to survive than large populations and are more likely to become ex-

tinct. Random events or natural disturbances can wipe out a small population, whereas a large population—simply because of its larger numbers—is more likely to have survivors. Inbreeding, reproduction between closely related individuals, is also a negative factor in the survival of small populations. Inbreeding tends to produce many homozygous offspring (see Chapter 19), which results in the expression of many recessive deleterious traits that are usually masked by dominant genes. In addition, inbreeding reduces the level of variability in the gene pool (the genes of all breeding individuals) of the population, detracting from the population's ability to adjust to changing conditions. Loss of genetic diversity therefore increases the probability of extinction of that species.

Population density and dispersion

In addition to a population's size, its **density**—the number of organisms per unit of area—influences its survival. For example, if the individuals of a population are spaced far from one another, they may rarely come into contact. Sexually reproducing animals cannot produce offspring if they do not mate. Therefore the future of such a population may be limited even if the absolute numbers of individuals over a wide area are relatively high.

A factor related to population density is **dispersion,** the way in which the individuals of a population are arranged. In nature, organisms within a population may be distributed in one of three different patterns: uniform, random, and clumped (Figure 25-4). Each of these patterns reflects the interactions between a given population and its environment, including the other species that are present.

Uniform, or evenly spaced, distributions are rare in nature. Populations of plants exhibiting allelopathy, the secretion of toxic chemicals that harm other plants, often show a uniform distribution. For example, the creosote bush, often the dominant vegetation covering wide areas of the deserts of Mexico and the southwestern United States, grows well spaced and evenly dispersed. This uniform pattern of distribution is probably caused by chemicals secreted by the bush that retard the establishment of other individuals near existing ones.

Random distributions occur if individuals within a population do not influence each other's growth and if environmental conditions are uniform—that is, if the resources necessary for growth are distributed equally throughout the area. Random distributions are often seen in plants as the result of certain types of seed dispersal, such as scattering by the wind.

Clumped distributions are by far the most frequent in nature. Organisms that show a clumped distribution are close to one another but far from others within the population. Clumping occurs as a result of the interactions among animals, plants, microorganisms, and unevenly distributed resources in an environment. Organisms are found grouped in areas of the environment that have the resources they need. Furthermore, animals often congregate for a variety of other reasons, such as for hunting, mating, or caring for their young.

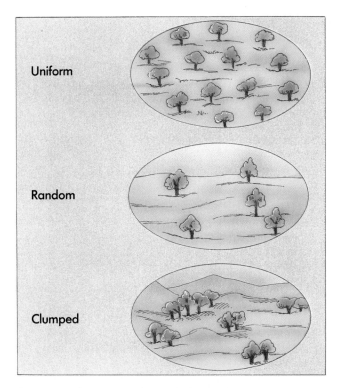

FIGURE 25-4   Distribution patterns in populations.
Uniform distribution patterns are rare in nature but are sometimes caused by allelopathy, in which plants secrete toxic chemicals that discourage the growth of other plants near them. Random patterns in plants are often caused by random seed dispersal, such as by wind. Clumped patterns, the most common type, result in an environment in which resources are unevenly distributed.

Regulation of population size

As a population grows and its density increases, competition among organisms for resources such as food, shelter, light, and mating sites increases and toxic waste products accumulate. Factors resulting from the growth of a population *regulate its subsequent growth* and are "nature's way" of keeping the population size of every species in check. Such factors increase in effectiveness as population density increases and are appropriately termed **density-dependent limiting factors.** Other factors such as the weather, availability of soil nutrients, and physical disruptions of an area (such as volcanoes or earthquakes) can also limit the growth of a population. Because these factors operate regardless of the density of a population, they are called **density-independent limiting factors.**

⩔ Density-dependent limiting factors come into play when a population size increases in a given area; density-independent limiting factors operate regardless of population size.

Density-independent limiting factors

A variety of environmental conditions can limit populations. For example, freak snowstorms in the Rocky Mountains of Colorado in the summer can kill butterfly populations there. The size of insect populations that feed on pollen and flower tissues varies seasonally with the blooming of flowering plants. Humans, too, can affect the sizes of populations. Poachers have killed so many African elephants for their ivory, for example, that the species may become extinct.

Density-dependent limiting factors

Individuals within a species and individuals of differing species **compete** for the same limited resources. Competition among different species of organisms is often greatest between those that obtain their food in similar ways. In fact, if two species are competing with one another for the same limited resource in a specific location, the species able to use that resource most efficiently will eventually eliminate the other species in that location. This concept is called the principle of **competitive exclusion.** In fact, competition among organisms of the same and differing species was described by Charles Darwin as resulting in natural selection and survival of the fittest or most well-adapted organisms. Competition, therefore, not only limits the sizes of populations but is one of the driving forces of evolutionary change.

Predation is another factor that limits the size of populations and works more effectively as the density of a population increases. Predators are organisms of one species that kill and eat organisms of another—their prey. The intricate interactions between predators and prey are an essential factor in the maintenance of diverse species living in the same area. By controlling the levels of some species, the predators make the continued existence of other species in that same community possible. In other words, by keeping the numbers of individuals of some of the competing species low, the predators prevent or greatly reduce competitive exclusion. In fact, a given predator may very often feed on two or more different kinds of plants or animals, switching from one to the other as their relative abundance changes. Similarly, a given prey species may be a primary source of food for increasing species of predators as it becomes more abundant, a factor that will limit the size of its population automatically.

Parasitism also limits the size of populations by weakening or killing host organisms. Parasites live on or in larger species of organisms and derive nourishment from them. As a population increases in density, parasites such as bacteria, viruses, and a variety of invertebrates can more easily move from one organism to another, infecting an increasing proportion of a population. Once again, this limiting factor to population size acts in negative feedback fashion, becoming more effective as the density of the population increases.

⩔ Three density-dependent limiting factors are competition, predation, and parasitism.

Cities are a relatively new phenomenon. Villages and towns were first organized only about 9000 years ago, long after the development of agriculture. The first great cities of Mesopotamia date soon after that, but relative to a modern metropolis, the cities of ancient times were small. Only in the last thousand years have people lived in cities containing hundreds of thousands of people. Until the Industrial Revolution, only one person in five lived in a town of over 10,000 people. In the past hundred years, however, there has been a mass influx of people into cities; 14% of the world's population was urbanized in 1900. Starting in the industrial north, this mass migration has since spread to the less developed nations of the tropics. The cities of the Third World have swollen to hold one third of its total population. In 1920 the world's urban population was 360 million. By the year 2000, it will be near 3 billion—over 50% of the world's population will be urbanized. Two thirds of all people will be in cities of 100,000 or more, and over 20% in cities with more than a million people.

This massive movement of people is alarming because it is difficult to manage so many people crowded together. Mexico City, the largest city in the world today, is plagued by smog, traffic, waste disposal, and other prob-

lems, all worsened by the incredible congestion of over 20 million inhabitants (Figure 25-A). The prospects of supplying adequate food, water, and sanitation to these people, in a city whose population will increase to over 30 million by the end of the century, are almost unimaginable.

Nor is Mexico City's astonishing urban growth unique. Only 7 cities had a population larger than 5 million in 1950; by 2000 there will be 57 such megacities, 42 of them in the Third World. New York City has almost 16 million inhabitants, and Tokyo and São Paulo are bigger than New York! These four cities alone contain over 70 million inhabitants—half as many as the entire human population in the year 1 AD. In 1992 there were 16 cities with populations greater than 10 million. By 2000 there will be 25 such cities—and all but 3 of these will be in the northern hemisphere.

Most major Third World cities are really two cities: Shanty towns ring the outskirts of most megacities—in Calcutta they house 67% of the city's population. What draws the people to the city? Urban incomes in the northern hemisphere average three times rural incomes, and modern services such as doctors, teachers, sanitation, clean water, and electricity are at least within reach. Appalling though conditions are, they can be even worse in the countryside. As population numbers

FIGURE 25-A Mexico City, the world's largest city.

swell and resources become even more stretched, the difference between urban and rural becomes greater and the mass movement to the cities intensifies even more.

Management of cities will be a priority for governments in the twenty-first century. Environmentally sound ways of disposing of waste, provision of livable housing, and the supply of safe food and water to the multitudes living in large urban areas are just some of the concerns that will be at the forefront of city management.

Mortality and survivorship

A population's growth rate depends not only on the availability of needed resources and on the ability of its individuals to survive and compete effectively for those resources but also on the ages of the organisms in it. Interestingly, when a population lives in a constant environment for a few generations, its **age distribution**—the proportion of individuals in the different age categories—becomes stable. This distribution, however, differs greatly from species to species and even to some extent within a given species from place to place.

Scientists express the age distribution characteristics of a population by means of a survivorship curve. **Survivorship** refers to the proportion of an original population that survives to a certain age. The curve is developed by graph-

ing the number of individuals within a population that survive through various stages of the life span. Samples of survivorship curves that represent certain types of populations are shown in Figure 25-5.

In the hydra, individuals are equally likely to die at any age, as indicated by the straight survivorship curve (type II). This type of survivorship curve is characteristic of organisms that reproduce asexually, such as hydra, bacteria, and asexually reproducing protists. Oysters, on the other hand, produce vast numbers of offspring, but few of these offspring live to reproduce. The rate of death, or **mortality,** of organisms that reach reproductive age is extremely low (type III survivorship curve). This type of survivorship curve is characteristic of organisms producing offspring that must survive on their own and therefore die in large numbers when young because of predation or their inability to acquire the resources they need. The survivorship curve for

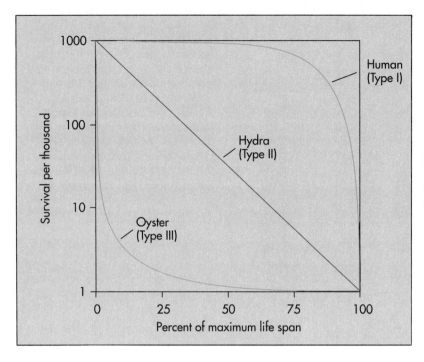

FIGURE 25-5 Survivorship curves.
The shapes of the respective curves are determined by the percentages of individuals in populations that die at different ages.

humans and other large vertebrates is much different from that for hydra and oysters. Humans, for example, produce few offspring but protect and nurture them; therefore most humans (except in areas of great poverty, hunger, and disease) survive past their reproductive years (type I survivorship curve).

Many animal and protist populations in nature have survivorship curves that lie somewhere between those characteristic of type II and type III. Many plant populations, with high mortality at the seed and seedling stages, have survivorship curves close to type III. Humans have probably approached type I more and more closely through the years, with the life span being extended because of better health care and new medical technology.

When a population lives in a constant environment for a few generations, the proportion of individuals in various age categories becomes stable. Characteristic age distributions occur among species and are closely linked in animal populations to parental care for offspring.

Demography

Demography is the statistical study of populations. The term comes from two Greek words: *demos,* "the people" (the same root in the word *democracy*), and *graphos,* "to write." It therefore means the description of peoples and the characteristics of populations. Demographers predict the ways in which the sizes of populations will alter in the future, taking into account the age distribution of the population and its changing size through time.

A population whose size remains the same through time is called a **stable population.** In such a population, births plus immigration exactly balance deaths plus emigration. In addition, the number of females of each age group within the population is similar. If this were not the case, the population would not remain stable. For example, if there were many more females entering their reproductive years than older females leaving the population, the population would grow.

The age distribution of males and females in human populations of Kenya, the United States, and Austria is shown in Figure 25-6. A **population pyramid** is a bar graph that shows the composition of a population by age and sex. Males are conventionally enumerated to the left of the vertical age axis and females to the right. By using population pyramids, scientists can predict the future size of a population. First, the number of females in each age group is multiplied by the average number of female babies women in that age group bear. These numbers are added for each age group to see whether the new number will exceed, equal, or be less than the number of females in the population being studied. By such means the future growth trends of the human population as a whole and of individual countries and regions can be determined.

The population pyramids in Figure 25-6 show the differences in the pattern of a rapidly growing population (Kenya), a slowly growing population (the United States), and a country experiencing negative growth (Austria). The population pyramid of Kenya is characteristic of **developing countries,** those that have not yet become industrialized, such as countries in Africa, Asia, and Latin America. Each of these countries has a population pyramid with a broad base, reflecting the large numbers of individuals yet to enter their reproductive years. In Kenya, for example, 50% of the population is under the age of 15. These children will reach reproductive age in the near future, leading to a population explosion in Kenya over the next decade.

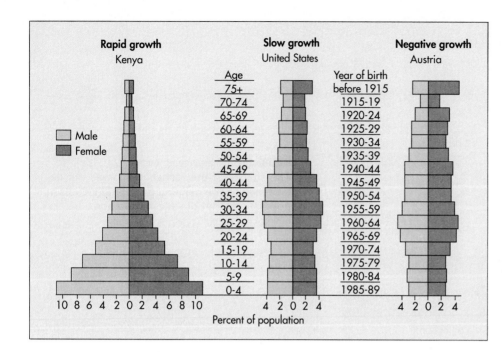

FIGURE 25-6 Three patterns of population change.
Kenya shows a rapid growth pattern—its pyramid has a broad base because of high fertility. The United States and Austria both show declining fertility and mortality, but the United States' "baby boom" has resulted in higher fertility rates than Austria, whose population is declining.

In the United States, birth rates are higher than death rates at present, producing a growth rate of approximately 0.7%. The high birth rate is not caused by couples having large families but by the large size of the "baby boom" generation who are at the peak of their reproductive years. Individuals in this age group were born within the 20 years or so following World War II. The large number of women in this group causes the births to still outnumber the deaths. Austria and the United States are both experiencing a decline in fertility and mortality. However, Austria's population does not include as high a percentage of women in their child-bearing years as does that of the United States, so that deaths are outnumbering births.

▼▼

Developing countries, those that have not yet become industrialized, have proportionately young populations and are experiencing rapid growth. Developed countries have populations with similar proportions of their populations in each age group, and are growing very slowly or not at all.

The human population explosion

Although some countries have populations that are no longer growing, such as Denmark, West Germany, Hungary, and Italy, and some countries such as Austria are declining in numbers, the population of the world as a whole is growing at the rate of 1.8% a year. This growth rate may sound low, but with the world population numbering over 5.3 billion, it adds over 95 *million* people to the population each year. Scientists estimate that the world population will double between 1990 and 2029!

How did the human population reach its present-day size? With the development of agriculture 11,000 years ago

FIGURE 25-7 The development of agriculture was a key step in the growth of human populations.
By producing abundant supplies of food, agriculture made the growth of cities and the future development of human culture possible. These workers are using a primitive method to thresh sorghum in southern India.

(Figure 25-7), human populations began to grow steadily (Figure 25-8). Villages and towns were first organized about 9000 years ago, and human effects on the environment began to intensify. In these centers of civilization, however, the specialization of professions such as metallurgy became possible; technology advanced. By 1650, the world population totaled approximately 500 million peo-

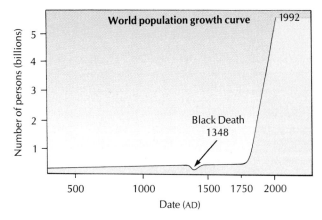

FIGURE 25-8 World population growth through history.
Except for the blip caused by the Black Death (25 to 35 million people died in Europe alone), the human population has grown steadily since the Stone Age.

ple. The Renaissance in Europe, with its renewed interest in science, ultimately led to the establishment of industry in the seventeenth century and to the Industrial Revolution of the late eighteenth and early nineteenth centuries. By the mid-nineteenth century, Louis Pasteur put forth the germ theory of disease, the understanding that microbes caused infection. With this understanding came new medical technology and discoveries. In the 1920s, Alexander Fleming accidentally discovered penicillin and opened the door to antibiotic therapy—medicine's "magic bullets" against bacterial infection. These medical advancements decreased the death rate by increasing the number of individuals surviving infection.

The Industrial Revolution also created new farming and transportation technology, which helped provide better nutrition for many people, especially those in industrialized countries. With better nutrition and increased medical understanding and technology, the death rate fell steadily and dramatically from the mid-nineteenth century on (Figure 25-9, *A*). In developing countries, international foreign aid imported this new technology along with food aid after World War II. The mortality plunged in a matter of years (Figure 25-9, *B*). Although birth rates declined dramatically in developed countries, they declined very little in developing countries. Taken together, the world's population growth rate soared. In fact, at their present rates of growth, the population of tropical South America will double in 31 years and that of tropical Africa will double in only 24 years. By the year 2000, about 60% of the people in the world will be living in countries that are at least partly tropical or subtropical, 20% will be living in China, and the remaining 20% will be in the developed countries of Europe, the countries of the former Soviet Union, Japan, the United States, Canada, Australia, and New Zealand together (Figure 25-10). Putting it another way, for every person living in an industrialized country like the United States in 1950, there were two people living elsewhere; by 2020, just 70 years later, there will be five.

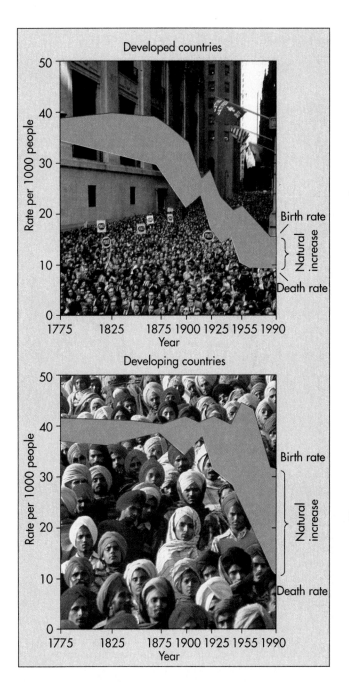

FIGURE 25-9 Population growth from 1775 to 1990.
In developed countries, the Industrial Revolution caused mortality (death) to drop. Birth rates also began to drop at the turn of the century.
A In developing countries, mortality began to decline after World War II, but birth rates remained high.
B Taken together, these changes caused human population growth rates to soar, especially in developing countries.

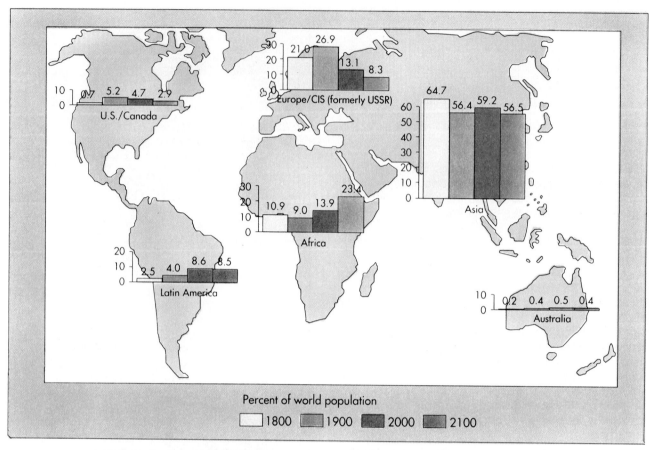

FIGURE 25-10 World population distribution by region, 1880 to 2100.
If current trends continue, Asia will have 57% of the total world population in 2100, Africa nearly a quarter, and Europe's share will drop to less than 10%.

▼▼▼
The world population rose sharply and dramatically after the Industrial Revolution because of new technology in agriculture, transportation, industry, and medicine.

Of the estimated 2.8 billion people living in the tropics in the late 1980s, the World Bank estimated that about 1.2 billion people were living in absolute poverty. (The World Bank is an international bank that provides loans and technical assistance for economic development projects in developing member countries.) These people cannot reasonably expect to consistently provide adequate food for themselves and their children. Even though experts estimate that enough food is produced in the world to provide an adequate diet for everyone in it, the distribution is so unequal that large numbers of people live in hunger. The United Nations Children's Fund (UNICEF) estimates that

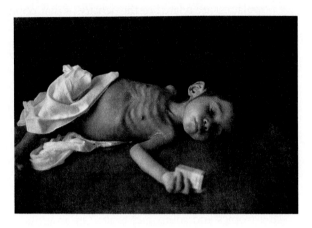

FIGURE 25-11 The face of starvation.
This Colombian child suffers from malnutrition. UNICEF estimates that 14 million children die each year as a consequence of malnutrition.

in the developing world, about 14 million children under the age of 5—40,000 per day—starve to death each year, mainly of malnutrition and the complications associated with it (Figure 25-11).

The size of human populations, like those of other organisms, is or will be controlled by the environment. Early in their history, human populations were regulated by both density-dependent and density-independent limiting factors, including food supply, disease, and predators; there was also ample room on Earth for migration to new areas to relieve overcrowding in specific regions. In the past century, however, humans have been able to expand the carrying capacity of the Earth because of their ability to develop technological innovations. Gradually, changes in technology have given humans more control over their food supply and enabled them to develop superior weapons to ward off predators, as well as the means to cure diseases. Improvements in transportation and housing have increased the efficiency of migration. At the same time, improvements in shelter and storage capabilities have made humans less vulnerable to climatic uncertainties.

As a result of the ability to manipulate these factors, the human population has been able to grow explosively to its present level of more than 5.3 billion people. However,

both the current human population level and the projected rate of growth have potentially grave consequences for the future. Pressures are placed on the land, water, forests, and other natural resources. Industrialization, although raising the standard of living by increasing the availability of goods and services, adds to air and water pollution. In the developed countries, nations of consumers have developed into "throwaway" societies, adding billions of tons of solid waste to landfills every year.

The most effective means of dealing with the population explosion has been the support of governments to encourage small families, the establishment of family planning clinics, improvement in education, and socioeconomic development. The developed countries of Western Europe, North America, Japan, and Australia have very low birth rates at this time. Mexico, Indonesia, Thailand, South Korea, Hong Kong, and Singapore have had considerable success with lowering their birth rates. Countries such as China and India have had some success in reducing their birth rates but are still striving toward this goal. The countries in sub-Sahara Africa have the highest birth rate of any countries in the world—some as high as 4.1%. Family planning programs are now being implemented across the continent.

Summary

1. Populations consist of the individuals of a given species that occur together at one place and at one time. They may be dispersed in an evenly spaced, clumped, or random manner. Clumped patterns are the most frequent.

2. The rate of growth of any population is the difference between the birth rate and the death rate per individual per unit of time. The actual rate is affected by emigration from the population and immigration into it.

3. Most populations exhibit a sigmoid growth curve, which implies a relatively slow start in growth, a rapid increase, and then a leveling off when the carrying capacity of the species' environment is reached.

4. Survivorship curves are used to describe the characteristics of growth in different kinds of populations. Type I populations are those in which a large proportion of the individuals approach their physiologically determined limits of age. Type II populations have a constant mortality throughout their lives. Type III populations have very high mortality in their early stages of growth, but an individual surviving beyond that point is likely to live a very long time.

5. Each population grows in size until it eventually reaches the limits of its environment to support it; resources are always limiting. Some of the limits to the growth of a population are related to the density of that population, but others are not. Competition within the populations and between populations of any two species limits their coexistence. Predation and other forms of interaction among populations also play an important role in limiting population size.

6. Agriculture was developed in several centers about 11,000 years ago when about 5 million people lived throughout the world. By 1990, the global population was more than 5.3 billion people and was growing at a rate of 1.8% per year, a rate that will double the population in approximately 39 years.

7. In the 1980s, the World Bank estimated that about 1.2 billion of the more than 2.75 billion people living in the tropics and subtropics existed in absolute poverty. Some 4 million children under 5 years of age were starving to death each year. With the populations of tropical countries growing from 1.8% to 4.1% per year, the task of feeding these people will be extraordinarily difficult.

1. How is the work of population ecologists similar to that of demographers? How does it differ?

2. In the early twentieth century, the United States experienced a large influx of immigrants from many European nations. Does immigration affect the size or growth rate of the U.S. population?

3. Do you think that humans are able to artificially increase the carrying capacity of a place because of our increasing technology? Give an example.

4. Which is more likely to survive, a small population or a large one? Why?

5. Distinguish between density and dispersion. How does each affect a population's chances for survival?

6. Identify the three patterns of population dispersion found in nature. Into which pattern do human populations fall?

7. Distinguish between density-dependent and density-independent limiting factors. Give an example of each.

8. Draw type I, type II, and type III survivorship curves. Summarize the types of organisms that are characteristic of each curve, and give an example of each.

9. Compare the typical population pyramids of a developing country and industrialized country.

10. Is the present human population growth uniform among all countries? What areas are experiencing the greatest population growth?

11. At this point in history, are the most effective means of limiting population growth based on natural forces or human intervention? Explain your answer.

12. Both the current human population growth and the projected rate of growth worldwide have potential consequences for the future that are extremely grave. Explain why.

13. Suppose that you were given the political power to deal with the world's population explosion. What steps would you take?

1. Divide into groups to facilitate discussion of the problem of human overpopulation. Have each group select a different viewpoint to study and represent to the class. Some groups, for example, may represent:
   (a) A farm family in a developing nation dependent on children as laborers in the fields
   (b) Consumers in an industrialized nation
   (c) A medical agency concerned with the high disease and death rates in overpopulated areas
   (d) A sociologist concerned with the psychological impact of overpopulation.
   There are many more possibilities; propose as many positions as possible.

2. No other primate species has undergone a population explosion like humans. Why do you think humans alone have not controlled their population growth?

Berreby, D. (1990, April). The numbers game. *Discover,* pp. 42-49.
This article presents a balanced look at the issues involved in the problem of human overpopulation.
Daily, G. and Erlich, P. (1992, November). Population, sustainability, and earth's carrying capacity. *BioScience,* pp. 761-771.
A thorough scientific discussion of the many aspects involved in predicting the effects of human population size on life style.
Population Reference Bureau. (Annual). *World population data sheet.* Washington, DC: Population Reference Bureau.
This annual data sheet provides the latest population statistics from around the world.

26 The Human Impact on the Environment

- ▾ The biosphere, often spoken of as the environment, extends from the tops of the mountains to the depths of the seas; it is all the parts of the Earth where biological activity occurs.

- ▾ Humans need to work toward a sustainable society that uses nonfinite and renewable sources of fuel, recycles resources to the fullest extent, and manages forests to meet global needs while not compromising the ability of future generations to survive.

- ▾ Water is being polluted by multiple sources, causing physical or chemical changes that harm living and nonliving things; prevention of this contamination is essential to ensure a safe water supply.

- ▾ A primary cause of air pollution is the combustion of fossil fuels; energy conservation measures and new energy technology are needed.

The biosphere: The global environment
The land
    Diminishing natural resources
    Species extinction
    Solid waste
The water
    Surface water pollution
    Groundwater pollution
    Acid rain
The atmosphere
    Air pollution
    Ozone depletion
Overpopulation and environmental problems

Just imagine, as in this photograph, that you hold the world. What you do now will affect its future. Will you handle it carefully, or toss it away? Well, imagining isn't even necessary. All people do hold the world in their hands in a figurative way. Each person's actions directly affect the Earth and the quality of life that you and others will experience for generations to come.

However, you must ask yourself some crucial questions. How are you affecting the Earth? What environmental problems do people face today? And what can you do to deal with those problems to be sure that the quality of life on Earth will be enhanced for yourself and your children? The answers to these questions are the focus of this chapter and will help you understand more about how you shape this fragile planet on which you live.

The biosphere: The global environment

Life on Earth is confined to a region called the **biosphere,** the global ecosystem in which all others exist. (An *ecosystem* is a community of organisms that interact with one another and with the nonliving things around them.) The biosphere extends from approximately 9000 meters (30,000 feet) above sea level to about 11,000 meters (36,000 feet) below sea level. You can think of it as extending from the tops of the highest mountains (such as Mount Everest or some of the Himalayas) to the depths of the deepest oceans (such as the Mariana Trench of the Pacific Ocean)—the part of our Earth in which the land, air, and water come together to help sustain life (Figure 26-1).

The biosphere is often spoken of as the **environment.** This general term refers to everything around you—not only the land, air, and water but other living things as well. You can speak, for example, of the environment of an ant, a water lily, or all the peoples of the world. Your particular environment can change during the day from a home environment, to a classroom environment, and then to an office environment. The environment can include a great deal—or very little—of the total biosphere and its living things.

The land

Humans interact with the land and its inhabitants in a myriad of ways. Humans use its natural resources. Humans produce wastes that are filling and in some cases polluting the land. Humans cut down forests, stripping many species of their *habitats*, the areas in which organisms survive, including the living and nonliving things on which they depend. When organisms lose their habitats, they die. And humans continue to procreate at a rate that will result in the doubling of the world's population by the year 2030. What can people do to stop using the land in destructive ways? What can people do to help heal the Earth?

Diminishing natural resources

Humans get many things froms the land: fossil fuels, timber, food, and minerals. Water, too, is an important natu-

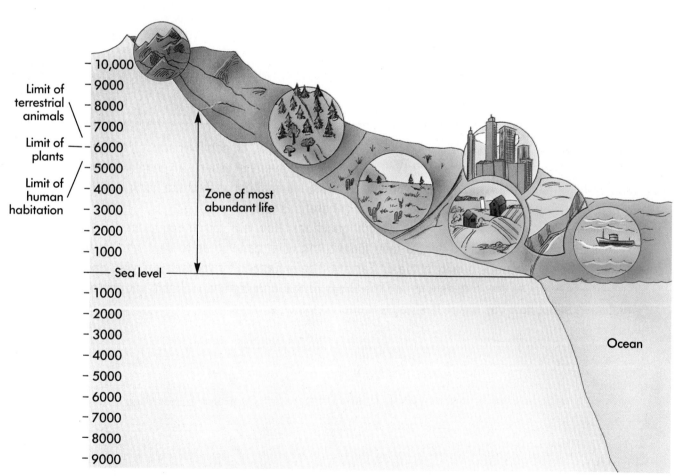

FIGURE 26-1   The biosphere.
The biosphere is that part of the Earth where life can be found, from the highest mountain peaks to the depths of the ocean. Most life, however, is found in the areas indicated by the arrows.

ral resource. Some of these resources—fossil fuels and minerals—are finite; that is, they cannot be replaced. Forests *can* be used and replaced *if managed wisely*. However, when whole sections of forest are cut and burned and their soil depleted, they cannot be replaced . . . nor can the wildlife that once lived there.

Fossil fuels

Many of the fuels used to heat homes and run cars are **fossil fuels.** These substances—coal, oil, and natural gas—are formed over time (acted on by heat and pressure) from the undecomposed carbon compounds of organisms that died millions of years ago. Environmental scientists suggest that instead of depending on these fuels for energy—fuels that are finite—people should work toward a **sustainable society** that uses nonfinite and renewable sources of fuel. In a sustainable society, the needs of the society can be satisfied without compromising the ability of future generations to survive and without diminishing the available natural resources.

The primary renewable and nonfinite sources of power that are available are the sun, the wind, moving water, geothermal energy, and bioenergy. Technologies available now to harness these energies are not yet in widespread use. **Nuclear power,** once considered a viable alternative energy source, will probably contribute only 6% to 8% of the world's energy by the year 2000. Although nuclear power depends on uranium, a finite but abundant natural resource, its problems lie primarily with the cost of building nuclear power plants, disposal of highly radioactive wastes, and public fears regarding safety. The waste disposal problem would be virtually eliminated if nuclear fusion reactors could be developed to replace today's reactors, all of which use nuclear fission (splitting) reactions. Nuclear power could then become a primary source for generating electricity.

Solar power is not a new technology; panels mounted on rooftops, for example, heat water that can be used for bathing, cooking, and space heating (Figure 26-2, *A*). In addition, homes and businesses can be built using the strategies of passive solar architecture (Figure 26-2, *B*). The technology is also available to use solar power to produce electricity by converting the sun's energy to electricity after it has been captured within a fluid such as oil or by the use of photovoltaic solar cells that can convert sunlight directly into electricity.

Water has been used as an energy source for centuries (Figure 26-2, *C*) and is currently supplying 20% of the world's electricity. A new form of hydropower called **wave power** is now being tested. Wave power uses the vertical motion of sea waves to produce electricity. In addition, **tidal power,** the use of the movement of the tides of the oceans to generate electricity, is currently under study in France and England (Figure 26-2, *D*). The wind, too, has been used for centuries as a source of energy. Today, windmills are being used in developing countries (those not yet industrialized) for pumping water to livestock and to irrigate the land. In developed countries, however, windmills are being used in an entirely new way—to generate electricity. This "new breed" of windmill has rigid blades fashioned from lightweight materials (Figure 26-2, *E*), and

looks unlike the picturesque windmills of Holland and Cape Cod, Massachusetts. Currently, the United States and China are the two countries that lead in the use of **wind power** to generate electricity. In fact, some scientists predict that the United States will be generating 10% to 20% of its electricity from wind power by the year 2030.

Geothermal energy refers to the use of heat deep within the Earth. In some places, reservoirs of hot water exist that can be extracted from the Earth using drilling procedures much like those used to tap into the Earth's oil and natural gas reserves. Alternatively, dry, hot rock can be drilled and water flushed through it. After the water is heated within the Earth, it can be used directly for heating purposes or as part of a process to produce electricity. Currently, this technology is being used and further developed in the United States, England, Italy, New Zealand, and Japan.

Bioenergy refers to the use of living plants to produce energy. The most obvious type of bioenergy, the burning of wood, was first used by our ancestors approximately 1 million years ago. In fact, until the Industrial Revolution of the 1800s, wood, not coal, supplied most of the world's energy. Today, wood supplies 12% of the world's energy, primarily in Latin America, Asia, India, and Africa. Unfortunately, however, the world is experiencing a fuel wood crisis—demand is exceeding the supply. The reasons for this crisis are complex but include the high world population and therefore high demand for wood, the degradation of woodlands without proper reforestation (replanting) techniques, and the cutting and burning of huge areas of tropical rain forests. In developing countries, the use of **bio-gas machines** is helping ease the shortage of fuel wood. These stoves use microorganisms to decompose animal or human excrement or other organic wastes in a closed container. This process yields a methane-rich gas that can be used to fuel stoves, light lamps, and produce electricity.

Environmental scientists suggest that humans use renewable and nonfinite energy sources such as solar, wind, and water power, as well as tap the Earth's geothermal energy. The use of such fuels rather than the extensive use of fossil fuels will help satisfy people's needs without diminishing the available natural resources.

A newer form of bioenergy is the use of plants such as corn and sugar cane to produce carbohydrates that are fermented, producing liquid fuels like ethanol. This technology, however, produces a product that appears to be an expensive alternative to fossil fuels. In addition, many cars do not function well on gasoline with ethanol additives.

Mineral resources

Minerals are inorganic substances that occur naturally within the Earth's crust. Zinc, lead, copper, aluminum, and iron are the minerals that humans use in the greatest quantities. However, other minerals are also mined, such as gold, silver, copper, and mercury. These minerals are present in the Earth in fixed amounts; once they are used, they are

A

B

C

D

E

FIGURE 26-2 Alternative energy sources.
To decrease reliance on fossil fuels, many individuals and nations are experimenting with alternative energy sources.
A Solar power. These panels collect the energy from sunlight and use this energy to heat homes and water.
B A passive solar home, with solar panels mounted on the roof.
C Hoover Dam in Arizona. Water power has been used for many centuries.
D Tidal power plant in the Bay of Fundy. Using the ocean's tides to generate power is still in the experimental stages.
E Modern windmills in southern California.

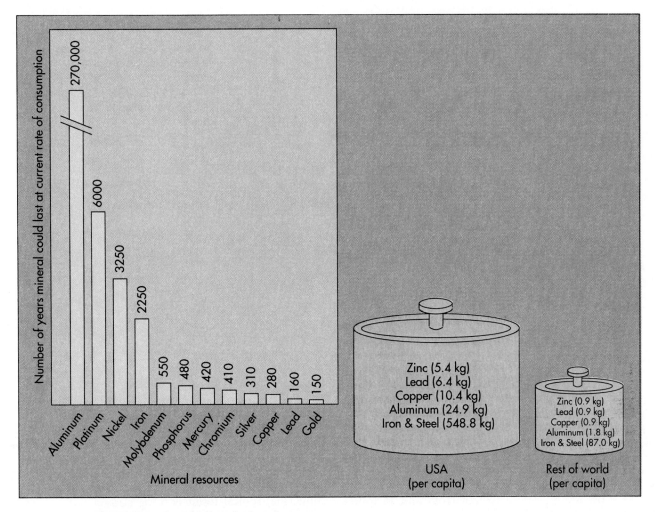

FIGURE 26-3 Consumption of mineral resources.
According to *The Earth Report,* modern industrialized societies require large amounts of minerals to sustain their high standard of living. The left shows a number of major minerals and the years they could last at the current rates of consumption. The right compares the consumption of major minerals by the United States with the rest of the world.

gone. Figure 26-3 shows the number of years the world's reserves of various minerals will last based on the rate of current consumption.

What can be done to avert a mineral shortage in years to come? First of all, people can cut down on their consumption. An American uses, on the average, 6 times more zinc, lead, and iron than a person living outside of the United States. In addition, an American uses 11 times more copper and 14 times more aluminum! Researchers agree that increased use of plastics and technology such as microelectronics will lower the demand for certain minerals. Plastics, however, are derived from petroleum products, so their manufacture increases consumption of fossil fuels.

Recycling is another way to help avert a mineral shortage in the coming years. Aluminum soda cans are produced from the clay-like mineral bauxite. Producing cans from recycled aluminum uses 95% less energy than producing them

from bauxite, saves mineral resources, and saves waste disposal costs and problems. Plastics are not easily recycled and are not truly recyclable. That is, plastics cannot be refashioned into the product from which they were claimed; plastic milk jugs cannot be made into plastic milk jugs but must be made into park benches or parking lot curbs. Grocery store plastic bags are the closest truly recycled plastic products, being made from used plastic bags and other additives. Therefore purchasing goods in recyclable containers such as paper, glass, and aluminum *and recycling those containers* is a wise choice. Scrap metal and old automobiles are also recyclable, as are automobile tires and batteries.

▼▼▼
Recycling paper, glass, and various metals will help preserve mineral resources as well as other natural resources.

FIGURE 26-4 Deforestation.
Farmers in this settlement in the rain-forests of South America have cleared trees to be able to plant crops. However, because this land is poor, with few nutrients, after a year or two the people will have to move on to clear new land.

Deforestation

Paper makes up 40% of the garbage in the typical American household. Recycling just your daily newspaper will save four trees every year. Buying products made from recycled paper will save even more. But recycling is not enough. The forests of the world are in severe crisis and will be lost if steps are not taken to stop their destruction.

The most severe crisis is that of **tropical rain forest deforestation.** Tropical rain forests are located in Central and South America, tropical Asia, and central Africa, forming a belt around the equatorial "waist" of the Earth in regions having both high temperature and high rainfall. Although this belt of forest covers only 2% of the Earth's surface, it is home to over *half* the world's species of plants, animals and insects. These organisms contribute 25% of medicines, along with fuel wood, charcoal, oils, and nuts. In addition, the tropical rain forests play an important role in the world climate.

Population and poverty are both high in rain forest countries. People with few resources move from towns and cities to the rain forest and cut the trees for sale as lumber or burn them to clear a patch of land to grow crops and raise cattle to sustain themselves and their families (Figure 26-4). Commercial ranchers also cut and burn the forests to make way for pastureland to feed beef-producing cattle. Unfortunately, the soil of the rain forests is poor, with few nutrients, and does not support crops. Before it is cut, the forest sustains itself because of symbiotic relationships between the trees and microorganisms that quickly decompose dead and dying material on the forest floor. These processed nutrients are quickly reabsorbed by the tree roots. Few nutrients stay in the soil; most of the nutrients are in the vegetation. Cutting these trees down and burning them releases the nutrients from the trees. Crops grow poorly on this land after it is stripped. After a year or two, crops will not grow

at all. Then the people move on, cutting yet another portion of the forest.

Commercial logging also takes its toll on the tropical rain forests. Many of the trees are cut to supply fuel wood, paper, wood panels such as plywood, and charcoal and to supply furniture manufacturers with mahogany and other woods demanded by consumers around the world. At this time, the tropical forest is being slashed and burned at a devastating rate. By 1950, two thirds of the forests of Central America had been cleared. Madagascar, an island off the southwestern coast of Africa, had lost about half its rain forest by 1950, but as Figure 26-5 shows, has lost half again since then! The United Nations Food and Agriculture Organization estimates that 100,000 square kilometers (62,000 square miles) of rain forest are now being lost each year worldwide—about the size of New England. At the present rate, scientists estimate, nearly all the tropical rain forests will be gone—including their rich diversity of animal life—within the next 50 years.

In addition to losing a rich natural resource, many scientists agree that the burning of the tropical forests is adding tremendous quantities of carbon dioxide (CO_2) to the air. CO_2 acts like the glass in a greenhouse (or the windows in your car), allowing heat to enter the Earth's atmosphere but preventing it from leaving. This selective energy absorption by CO_2 in the atmosphere is called the **greenhouse effect.** Rising levels of atmospheric CO_2 may therefore result in a worldwide temperature increase, a situation called **global warming.** Global warming could melt the Arctic and Antarctic ice packs, causing a rise in the sea level and the flooding of one fifth of the world's land area. In addition, a rise in global temperatures could affect rain patterns and agricultural lands.

To help stop rain forest destruction, individuals can join and support organizations involved in rain forest conserva-

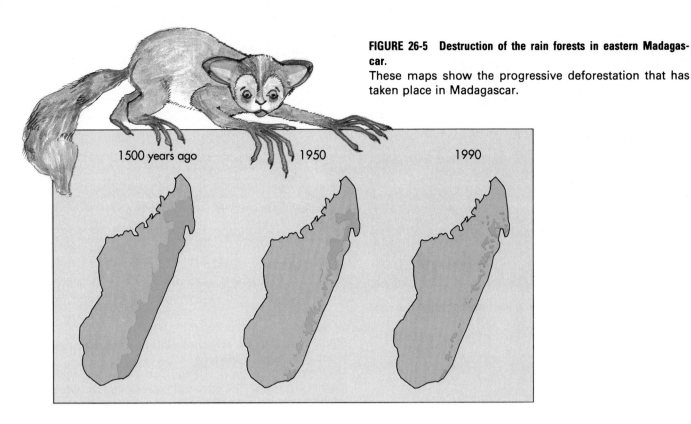

FIGURE 26-5 Destruction of the rain forests in eastern Madagascar.
These maps show the progressive deforestation that has taken place in Madagascar.

1500 years ago   1950   1990

FIGURE 26-6 A rain forest reserve.
In 1979, the World Wildlife Fund established a research program—the Biological Dynamics of Forest Fragments Project. The program isolates "islands" of rain forests out of the larger forest during conversion to pastureland. Scientists can study these islands to determine what their optimum size and shape should be if they are to provide a suitable habitat for various species.

tion, as well as avoid buying furniture constructed from tropical hardwoods. Research programs are currently being conducted that are exploring the concept of conserving fragments of the rain forest as reserves that will provide suitable habitats for species (Figure 26-6).

The world's forests are being destroyed at an alarming rate, resulting in the loss not only of this precious resource but of the habitats of thousands of species of organisms. In addition, the burning of the forests adds tremendous quantities of carbon dioxide to the air, a situation that may result in a worldwide temperature increase, or global warming.

Species extinction

Although scientists have classified approximately 1,700,000 species of organisms, they estimate that approximately 40,000,000 exist. But many of these species are becoming extinct—dying out—and will never be seen again. An estimated 1000 extinctions are taking place each year, a number that translates into more than two species per day. Although such mass extinctions have occurred in the past, as with the dying out of the dinosaurs, these former extinctions were caused by climatic and geophysical factors. The extinctions today are caused by human activity.

One way in which humans destroy species is by destroying their habitats. Widespread habitat destruction is taking place as the tropical rain forests are cut down. This one factor alone will cause the extinction of one third of the world's species.

Humans are also destroying coral reefs at an alarming rate. Because the base of the coral reef food chain is algae, the reef ecosystem depends on sunlight for its existence. (A food chain is a series of organisms that feed on one another.) In areas where soil erosion muddies the water, the reef dies from insufficient sunlight. In some cases the water may become polluted with fertilizer runoff or with sewage, which causes the algae to overgrow, smothering the corals. In some cases, humans use dynamite to kill and harvest fish,

FIGURE 26-7 A germ plasm bank at the United States Department of Agriculture.
Researchers are in a cold storage room that contains seeds from around the world.

FIGURE 26-8 Zoos are now responsible for preserving genetic diversity in endangered species.
These workers at the San Diego Zoo are helping this baby elephant to nurse. The efforts of zoos around the world will be instrumental in saving some endangered species from extinction.

a practice that obviously destroys the coral reef. In addition, coral is often harvested to sell to tourists.

Although habitat destruction and pollution pose the most serious threat to the existence of certain species, exploitation of commercially valuable species threatens them as well. The Convention on International Trade in Endangered Species of Wild Fauna and Flora (CITES) regulates trade in live wildlife and products. However, illegal trade still takes place because of smuggling and the inability of law enforcement inspectors to check all shipments of goods. Certain types of alligator, crocodile, sea turtle, snake, and lizard trade are illegal and endanger the existence of various species. Buying other products such as coral and ivory endangers the existence of coral reefs and African elephants. Even certain plants such as cacti and succulents should be purchased only if cultivated in greenhouses; they should not be taken from the wild. Organizations such as the World Wildlife Fund are valuable sources of information regarding which products should be avoided by consumers so that they can help stop trade that threatens certain species.

⯆⯆
Humans are destroying species by destroying their habitats, polluting their habitats, and illegally trading endangered species.

The extinction of many species leads to a reduction in **biological diversity,** a loss of richness of species. This loss is certainly regrettable; each species is not only the result of millions of years of evolution and can *never* be reproduced once it is gone but also is an intricate part of the interwoven relationships among organisms within the ecosystems of the world. The extinction of just one species can affect ecosystems in many unforeseen ways. In addition, many people feel that humans have no right to influence the world in such a devastating way. And looking at the issue from a

utilitarian standpoint, humans rely on the other species of the world as sources of food, medicine, and other substances.

Recently, for example, the genetic diversity in crop plants has declined as scientists have used selective breeding techniques to produce plants with specific characteristics, such as resistance to particular diseases or pests, hardiness, and other characteristics considered important. However, when only a few species or varieties of a species are cultivated or survive, the genetic diversity of the organism declines. Populations of species that have little diversity are more vulnerable to being wiped out by new diseases or climatic changes.

In the 1960s, the United Nations Food and Agricultural Organization (FAO) made recommendations that have led to the establishment of "banks" that store plant seeds and genetic material, or germ plasm (Figure 26-7). Zoos around the world are making similar efforts to preserve genetic diversity among animals by establishing and carrying out sophisticated breeding programs to increase genetic diversity among endangered species (Figure 26-8).

Solid waste

The average American produces about 19 pounds of garbage and trash—referred to as **solid waste**—per week. If that does not sound like very much, multiply that number by 52, and you will realize that each person produces approximately a *half ton* of solid waste per year. In 1992, the population of the United States was over 250 million—a population that produced approximately 125 million tons

FIGURE 26-9   Sanitary landfill, New York City.
Sanitary landfills around the country are filling up rapidly. Communities must quickly find new ways to dispose of their trash. One of the most popular and efficient methods is recycling.

of waste per year, not including the waste produced by schools, stores, and manufacturing. Americans, often described as having a "disposable society," are beginning to realize much of the wastes produced should be viewed as resources that must be reclaimed rather than as substances to throw away and clog the landscapes.

What happens to your trash when you put it out for collection? The burial site for your throwaways is the **sanitary landfill,** an enormous depression in the ground where trash and garbage is dumped, compacted, and then covered with dirt (Figure 26-9). In 1983, the Federal Resource Conservation and Recovery Act forced the closing of all **open dumps** or required them to be converted to landfill sites. At an open dump, solid waste is heaped on the ground, periodically burned, and left uncovered. Landfills are considered superior to dumps because landfill wastes are covered, reducing the number of flying insects and rodents that are attracted to the site and reducing the odor produced by open, rotting organic material. In addition, wastes are not burned at landfills, decreasing the problem of air pollution. Additionally, when the capacity of a landfill site is reached, it may be used as a building site or recreational area. Examples of landfill reuse are Mount Trashmore recreational complex in Evanston, Illinois, and Mile High Stadium in Denver, Colorado.

Problems do exist with landfills, however. First of all, space is running out. In just 1 year, the population of New York City alone produces enough trash to cover over 700 acres of land 10 feet deep. Another problem with landfills is that liquid wastes can trickle down through a landfill, reaching and contaminating ground water below. Liquids leaching from landfills can also pollute nearby streams, lakes, and wells (therefore *never* put batteries, paint solvents, drain cleaners, and pesticides in with your trash). In addition, as the organic material compacted in landfills is decomposed in the absence of oxygen, methane gas is produced. This

highly explosive gas rises from landfills and can seep into buildings constructed on or near reclaimed sites.

To reduce solid waste and landfill problems, everyone should recycle paper, glass, aluminum cans, and even clothing. An important part of recycling is buying recycled goods so that a market is maintained for them. In addition, people should purchase products in recyclable containers, avoid purchasing overpackaged products, and compost yard waste. Composting involves piling (and periodically turning to aerate) grass clippings, wood shavings, and similar yard wastes. Bacteria will degrade these substances, and they can be used to fertilize flower beds and vegetable gardens. By composting, you will be eliminating the second largest waste by volume in landfills.

In the future, careful planning will be necessary to ensure that landfill sites are located away from streams, lakes, and wells and that they have proper drainage and venting systems. Most likely, landfills will be only a portion of a solid waste disposal system that incorporates recycling, safe incineration, and waste-to-energy reclamation.

Solid waste is disposed of in sanitary landfills, depressions in the ground where trash and garbage is dumped, compacted, and covered with dirt. Solid waste management could be improved with increased and better-organized recycling efforts, safe incineration, better-engineered landfill sites, and waste-to-energy reclamation.

The water

The water, or hydrosphere, of this planet lies mainly in the oceans but is also found in freshwater lakes and ponds, in the atmosphere as water vapor, and as subsurface reservoirs called **groundwater.** Heated by the sun, water continually cycles from the land to the air, condenses, and falls back to the Earth. As this cycling of water repeats continually, contaminants may mix with the water, **polluting** it—causing physical or chemical changes in the water that harm living and nonliving things.

Surface water pollution

Surface water can be polluted by factories, power plants, and sewage treatment plants that dump waste chemicals, heated water, or human sewage into a lake, stream, or river. These sources of pollutants are called **point sources** because they enter the water at one or a few distinct places. Other types of pollutants may enter surface water at a variety of places and are called **nonpoint sources.** Examples of nonpoint sources of pollution are (1) sediments in land runoff caused by erosion from poor agricultural practices (a major type of water pollution), (2) metals and acids draining from mines, (3) poisons leaching from hazardous waste dumps (Figure 26-10), and (4) pesticides, herbicides, and fertilizers washing into surface waters after a rain. These pollutants affect aquatic organisms and also affect terrestrial organisms that drink the water. The manner in which a pollutant affects living things depends on its type: nutrient, in-

FIGURE 26-10 A toxic chemical dump in northern New Jersey. Toxic chemical dumps are serious threats to groundwater and surface water. Pollution occurs when the drums rust through and release their contents, which then enter the surface water and may eventually percolate down to the groundwater.

fectious agent, toxin (poison), sediment, or thermal pollutant.

Organic nutrients are sometimes discharged into rivers or streams by sewage treatment plants, paper mills, and meat-packing plants. These "organics" are food for bacteria. If high amounts of organic nutrients are available to bacteria, their populations will grow exponentially. As they grow and reproduce, they use oxygen—oxygen that fish need. Therefore as the bacterial populations rise, the only organisms that survive are those that can live on little oxygen. So-called trash fish such as carp can outsurvive other species such as trout and bass, but if oxygen levels become extremely low, all the fish die, survived only by various worms and insects.

The accumulation of **inorganic nutrients** in a lake is called **eutrophication,** meaning "good feeding." Certain inorganics such as nitrogen and phosphorus, which come from croplands or laundry detergents, stimulate plant growth. Although heavy plant growth makes swimming, fishing, or boating difficult, it does not cause most of its problems until the autumn (in most regions of the United States), when the plants die. At that time, bacteria decompose the dead plant material, and problems similar to those of organic nutrient pollution arise. In addition, the decomposed materials begin to fill the bottom of the lake. Eventually, the lake may become transformed into a marsh and then into a terrestrial community. **Sediment** that flows into lakes from erosion of the land caused by certain agricultural practices, mining, and road construction also fills in lakes. An example of eutrophication that led to the filling in and "death" of a lake occurred in Lake Washington near Seattle. The problem stemmed from local communities dump-

ing their wastes into the lake. In 1968 the dumping was halted, and Lake Washington is now fully recovered.

Surface waters are rarely polluted with **infectious agents,** or disease-causing microbes, in the United States. However, in areas such as Africa, Asia, and Latin America, waterborne diseases are common. Surface waters become polluted from untreated human wastes and from animal wastes, causing diseases such as hepatitis, polio, amebic dysentery, and cholera.

An array of **toxic substances** pollutes surface waters worldwide. Toxic substances include both organic compounds such as PCBs (polychlorinated biphenyls) and phenols and inorganic substances such as metals, acids, and salts. These toxic, or poisonous, substances come from a diverse array of sources such as industrial discharge, mining, air pollution, soil erosion, old lead pipes, and many natural sources. The effects on humans from drinking these substances in water range from numbness, deafness, vision problems, and digestive problems to the development of cancers.

Unfortunately, most toxic pollutants do not **degrade,** or break down, and are therefore present in bottom sediments of surface waters for decades or more. In fact, some organisms accumulate certain chemicals (often deadly ones) within their bodies, a process called **biological concentration.** Oysters, for example, accumulate heavy metals such as mercury, so these organisms might be highly toxic when living in waters with relatively low concentrations of this metal. Also, as organisms higher on the food chain eat organisms lower on the food chain, toxins accumulate in the predators in a high concentration, a concept called **biological magnification.** The relationships between the feeding levels of food chains are pyramidal; a smaller number of organisms eat a larger number of organisms as you progress up the chain. (Figure 26-11 illustrates this concept.) Scientists estimate that the concentration of a toxin in polluted water may be magnified from 75,000 to 150,000 times in humans consuming tainted fish.

The electric power industry and various other industries such as steel mills, refineries, and paper mills use river water for cooling purposes, discharging the subsequently heated water back into the river (Figure 26-12). Small levels of **thermal pollution** do not cause serious problems in aquatic ecosystems, but sudden, large temperature changes kill heat-intolerant plants and animals. Interestingly, ecosystems adjust to artificially heated waters and are damaged if the heat source is shut down, as when a power plant closes.

Surface water can be polluted by waste chemicals, heated water, or human sewage put into the water by factories, power plants, and sewage treatment plants or by silt and chemicals that can leach into the water from surrounding sites. These substances all affect the aquatic ecosystem in different ways.

Groundwater pollution

The surface water and rainwater that trickles through the soil to underground reservoirs is groundwater. This water can be contaminated with some of the same substances as

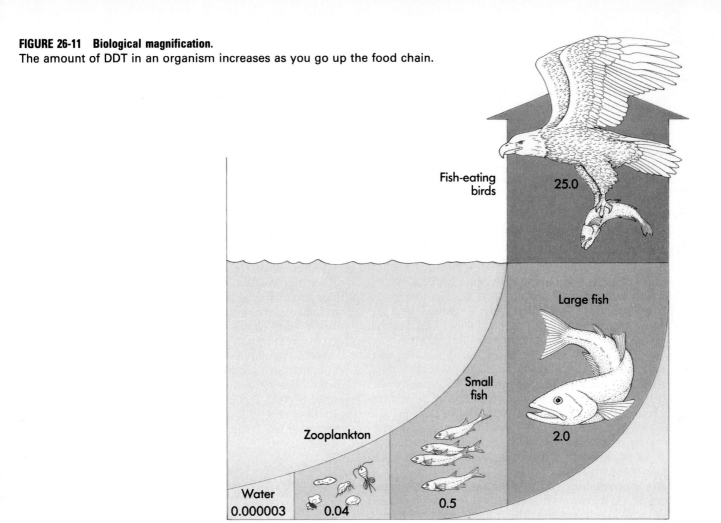

FIGURE 26-11 Biological magnification.
The amount of DDT in an organism increases as you go up the food chain.

Fish-eating birds 25.0

Large fish 2.0

Small fish 0.5

Zooplankton 0.04

Water 0.000003

Amount of DDT (ppm)

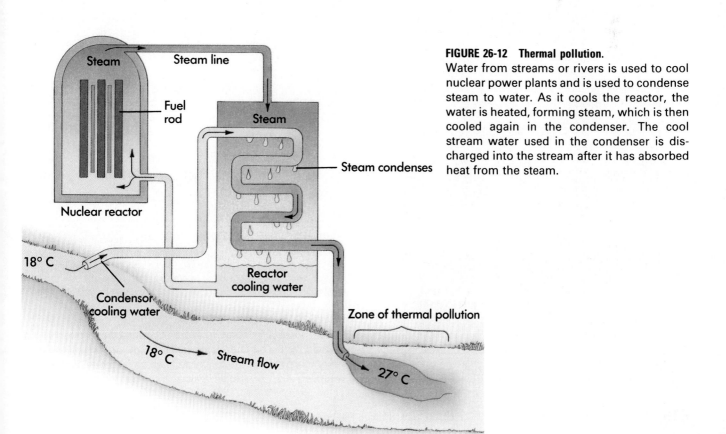

Steam

Steam line

Fuel rod

Steam

Steam condenses

Nuclear reactor

Reactor cooling water

18° C

Condensor cooling water

18° C → Stream flow

Zone of thermal pollution

27° C

FIGURE 26-12 Thermal pollution.
Water from streams or rivers is used to cool nuclear power plants and is used to condense steam to water. As it cools the reactor, the water is heated, forming steam, which is then cooled again in the condenser. The cool stream water used in the condenser is discharged into the stream after it has absorbed heat from the steam.

surface water. The primary groundwater contaminants are toxic chemicals that seep into the ground from hazardous waste dump sites and chemicals such as pesticides used in agriculture. Although groundwater does get filtered and cleansed of some substances as it trickles through the soil, toxic chemicals consist of molecules too small to be filtered in this manner. At this time, prevention of contamination is the cheapest and most feasible way to end groundwater contamination. Pumping contaminated water from underground sources to the surface, purifying it, and returning it to the ground is extremely costly.

Acid rain

In recent years, the water in the atmosphere has become polluted with sulfur dioxide and nitrogen dioxide, two chemical compounds that form acids when combined with water. As this water vapor condenses and falls to the ground, it is commonly referred to as **acid rain,** although acid precipitation also falls as snow or as dry micro particles, mixing with water when it reaches surfaces on the ground. "Normal" rain has a pH of approximately 5.7, primarily because of dissolved carbon dioxide (see Chapter 2 for a discussion of pH). The pH of acid rain is lower than 5.7 and usually falls between 3.5 and 5.5. However, rainfall samples taken in the eastern United States have measured as low as 1.5—a pH lower than that of lemon juice and approaching that of battery acid!

Acid rain results in many devastating effects on the environment. As it mixes with surface water, it acidifies lakes and streams, killing fish and other aquatic life. It seeps into ground water, causing heavy metals to leach out of the soil.

The result is that these heavy metals enter the groundwater and surface water, posing health problems for humans as well as fish. Acid rain also eats away stone buildings and monuments as well as metal and painted surfaces (Figure 26-13).

The effect of acid rain falling on plant life has been hypothesized but undocumented until recently. Botanists realized that acid rain not only leached many of the minerals essential to plant growth from the soil but also liberated toxic minerals such as aluminum. Recent research suggests that acid rain also kills or damages microorganisms that live in symbiotic associations with forest trees, helping them extract water and needed minerals from the soil. Without these organisms, the trees die (Figure 26-14).

Although sulfur and nitrous oxides are produced naturally during volcanic eruptions and forest fires, humans produce more than half these chemicals by burning coal in electricity-generating plants, industrial boilers, and large smelters that obtain metals from ores. In addition, nitrogen oxides are emitted by cars and trucks. The situation also becomes complicated because countries pollute their own air as well as the air of other countries. Emissions produced in the Midwest and eastern portions of the United States not only affect those areas, for example, but are carried by the wind into Canada. Emissions produced in England move into the Scandinavian countries.

Sulfur dioxide and nitrogen dioxide, gases emitted primarily by coal-fired power plants, combine with water in the atmosphere to produce acid rain, a precipitation that harms both living and nonliving things.

FIGURE 26-14 Effects of acid rain.
These balsam fir trees in North Carolina have been killed by acid rain. The chemicals in the acid rain, which are carried on prevailing winds, come from as far away as the Midwest.

FIGURE 26-13 Acid rain damage.
This statue has been eroded by acid precipitation.

As the human population grows, the amount of resources available to sustain our population shrinks. In addition, humans create wastes and pollute the environment. One result of these increases in population, pollution, and wastes and the decrease in natural resources is that global ecological stability becomes difficult to maintain. Are we on the brink of disaster? Some think the picture may not be as gloomy as it looks. Humans have made astonishing technological advances in a variety of areas while their numbers were "exploding." Can technology be an answer to our problems? Can technology help avert an ecological crisis resulting from the human population explosion and all its ramifications?

In recent years, advances in gene technology have allowed scientists to genetically alter bacteria, producing new strains that can break down hazardous pollutants such as oil from coastal oil spills. Other bacteria have been "gene-spliced" to consume potentially harmful medical refuse such as waste blood. Although solutions like these are important in that they alleviate serious ecological damage that would otherwise occur, they respond to immediate problems only. To assure a bright ecological future for all organisms living on the Earth, scientists must develop structured strategies that allow for economic development and ensure *sustainability* of the environment. To approach sustainability, we must meet human needs without continuing to degrade our environment and diminish our resource base, while concurrently using technologies that help our human ecosystem imitate biological ecosystems.

In biological ecosystems, plants produce their own food using carbon dioxide from the atmosphere, nutrients from the soil, and energy from the sun. This food allows plants to grow but also provides food for plant-eating organisms, the herbivores. Herbivore populations grow, and in turn, feed meat-eating organisms, the carnivores. Wastes from these organisms and their remains cycle through yet another group of organisms, the decomposers (fungi and bacteria), serving eventually as nutrients for plants.

Learning from this process of cycling by-products and degraded materials in natural systems, individuals and organizations are finding ways to reduce waste products or reclaim them. For example, one industrial manufacturing leader recovers hydrochloric acid, a hazardous waste product of their manufacturing process, which was formerly discarded. Now this company either reuses the acid or sells it to others who use it. Another company, which disposed of its used (and hazardous) alumina catalysts in the past, now sells them to cement makers for use in their manufacturing processes. And fly ash, previously a problematic waste product for energy companies, is being used to build roads.

Similarly in agriculture, with the help of new technologies and the resurgence of ancient methods, wastes are being minimized or reclaimed, providing more ecologically sound agricultural systems. One new irrigation method, called trickle irrigation, involves carrying water to plants by tubing and delivering it through nozzles rather than spraying it into the air to fall on the plants. In standard irrigation systems nearly two thirds of the water sprayed into the air is lost by evaporation; trickle irrigation decreases this amount dramatically. Additionally, as water evaporates using standard methods, the salts dissolved in the water become concentrated. With trickle irrigation, salt concentrations increase only slightly and the soil suffers less salt buildup. An additional technology also helps trickle irrigation systems trap runoff water and re-use it, thereby further reducing water use and reducing the pollution of nearby lakes and streams by herbicides and pesticides in the runoff.

Another agricultural management system is multiple cropping. This ancient method, in which several crops are planted together, results in a decrease in the growth of crop pests such as weeds, insects, and fungi because the multiple-crop environment is more diverse than that of a single-crop environment. For example, if a particular fungus normally attacks one type of crop, it can spread less easily if other crop plants are growing between the fungus and its host. This type of diverse environment also allows predators from one crop to inhibit pests from another crop. Thus, even the use of pesticides and herbicides, sources of serious groundwater pollution, can be minimized or eliminated. In one multiple cropping system in the tropics, family gardens are created by collecting soil from unprofitable swamp land and building raised gardens on which several crops are grown. While the garden is established in such a way as to recycle nutrients from the garden, it also makes previously undervalued swamp forests more valuable, decreasing the possibility that these forests will be destroyed.

In our households, many Americans have focused on reclaiming and recycling materials to prevent the by-products of our daily lives from being discarded as waste products. Aluminum recycling not only maintains the use of the aluminum involved, but also conserves nearly 20 times the energy it would cost to manufacture the same amount of aluminum from ore. Similarly, recycling plastic bottles and jugs into other plastic products such as polyester fiber and synthetic lumber substantially reduces the cost of fuel to create the products from "scratch" and conserves natural resources.

A sustainable society is indeed a future possibility if we can integrate the ecosystem concept into our farming, industrial, business, and home activities, recycling by-products and spent products repeatedly through our human ecosystem. There are two major challenges to actualizing such a system, however. The first challenge is developing more technologies that can be based on the use of by-products and reused products. The second challenge is more difficult and is where the analogy of biological ecosystems to human-centered ecosystems breaks down. The source of energy for natural ecosystems is almost entirely from solar energy, whereas the source of energy for human-centered ecosystems arises mostly from fossil fuels such as coal and oil—fuels that will someday be depleted. Until this problem is rectified, the maintenance of a sustainable human ecosystem will not be possible. And even then—as we approach the "biological model" of a human ecosystem—can the Earth support a continually growing human population? Although recycling and re-use technologies, and the use of resources that are infinite, such as solar power, may help increase our carrying capacity, we cannot raise the carrying capacity of the Earth past the levels of the amount of food we can produce, the techologies we can provide, amid the space that is necessary for humans to enjoy civilized, healthy lives.

Solving the problem of acid rain and curtailing these emissions is not easy or inexpensive. One technique used to reduce sulfur dioxide is to put **scrubbers** on coal-burning power plants. This technology can remove up to 95% of the sulfur dioxide emissions produced. Unfortunately, the United States lags behind most sulfur-emitting countries of the world in implementing this technology. A solution to this problem depends on international agreements to reduce emissions, energy conservation measures, and the increased use of public transportation.

The atmosphere

The Earth's atmosphere actually extends much higher than the portion within the biosphere, a part of the atmosphere more technically called the **troposphere.** The troposphere extends approximately 11 kilometers (36,000 feet) into the atmosphere but slopes downward toward the poles and upward toward the equator. The word *troposphere* literally means "turning over," a name extremely descriptive of the atmosphere. As the Earth is heated by the sun, air rises from its surface, cooling as it ascends. Cooler air then falls, resulting in a constant turnover of the air, aided by the prevailing winds.

Air pollution

About 99% of the clouds, dust, and other substances in the atmosphere are located in the troposphere. Some of these "other substances" are nitrogen and sulfur oxide pollutants. Other major air pollutants are carbon monoxide, hydrocarbons, and tiny particles, or particulates. As Figure 26-15 shows, sulfur oxides and particulates are produced primarily by the burning of coal in electricity-generating plants. Carbon monoxide and hydrocarbons are emitted primarily by cars, buses, and trucks; all these sources spew out nitrogen oxides.

The type of air pollution in a city depends not only on which of the pollutants are in the air, but also on the climate of the city. **Gray-air cities,** such as New York, Philadelphia, and Pittsburgh, are located in relatively cold but moist climates and have an abundance of sulfur oxides and particulates in the air. The haze, or **smog,** that can be seen in the air is the result of the burning of fossil fuels in power plants, other industries, and homes. **Brown-air cities,** such as Los Angeles, Denver, and Albuquerque, have an abundance of hydrocarbons and nitrogen oxides in the air. In these sun-drenched cities the hydrocarbons and nitrogen oxides undergo photochemical reactions that produce new pollutants called **secondary pollutants.** The principal secondary pollutant formed is **ozone** (O_3), a chemical that is extremely irritating to the eyes and the upper respiratory tract. Smog caused by pollutants reacting in the presence of sunlight is called **photochemical smog** (Figure 26-16).

The solutions to cutting down on smog are the same solutions to problems of acid rain formation and fossil fuel depletion: the use of coal-fired power plant scrubbers, energy conservation, and the recycling of resources leading to a reduction in energy use for manufacturing.

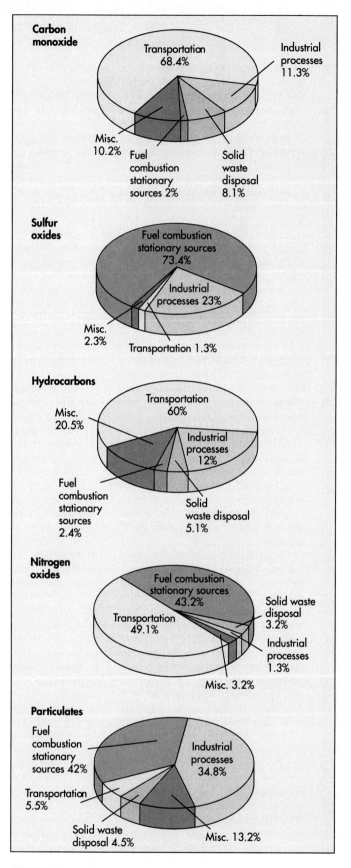

FIGURE 26-15 Major air pollutants and their sources. Transportation and fuel combustion at stationary sources are the main contributors to pollution.

A

B

FIGURE 26-16 Air pollution.
A "Brown air" in Los Angeles. Sunlight heats the chemicals spewed from automobiles to create ozone, which in the upper atmosphere protects you from the sun's harmful rays but in the lower atmosphere is poisonous.
B "Gray air" in New York City is caused by fossil fuel pollutants from power plants.

The primary type of air pollution in the first 11 kilometers of the atmosphere consists of smoke and fog, or smog. Smog is caused by sulfur oxides, nitrogen oxides, hydrocarbons, and particulates in the air as a result of the combustion of fossil fuels.

Ozone depletion

Ironically, humans are producing ozone in the troposphere that is polluting the environment but destroying it in the **stratosphere** where it is needed. The stratosphere is the layer of the atmosphere directly above the biosphere. It contains a layer of ozone that is formed when sunlight reacts with oxygen. Although ozone is harmful in air that is breathed, it is helpful in the stratosphere, acting as a shield against the sun's powerful ultraviolet (UV) rays. Excess exposure to UV rays can cause serious burns and skin cancers and can harm or kill bacteria and plants.

Scientists have measured "holes" in the ozone layer where it is thinnest, over the polar ice caps. The chemical chlorofluorocarbon, or CFC, is the main culprit. The spray-can propellant and refrigerant used in air conditioners, freon, is a CFC. In addition, CFCs are used in the manufacture of styrofoam and foam insulation. To protect the ozone layer, people should have their air conditioners serviced by persons who use equipment that does not allow the escape of freon. In addition, they should not use aerosol products containing CFC and should avoid the use of styrofoam products.

Overpopulation and environmental problems

Some scientists hold that the enormous world population is the source of the problems of pollution and diminishing natural resources. Others state that **technology,** the application of science to industrial use, is the culprit. Most, however, would agree that neither factor alone is the cause of these complex problems. Many factors interact to affect population size and the health of the environment.

The size of the human population influences the environment because it puts a demand on resources. However, the social, economic, and technological development of a country affects the demand its population places on resources. A person living in a rural area of Kenya, for example, does not use the same amount and kind of environmental resources as a person living in a large city in the United States. The life-style and per capita consumption of a population make a big difference on the impact of that population on the environment.

Other factors involved in the impact of a population on the environment are how a population uses its resources and the effects of that use. Using resources and disposing of wastes in certain ways pollute the environment. The pollution of one aspect of the environment (such as the air) can lead to pollution of other aspects of the environment (such as the water through acid rain). Pollution, in turn, can limit population size by increasing the death rate. However, living with pollution can lead to attitudinal changes among members of a population, which may result in the development of laws to better manage the use of resources and to curb the pollution resulting from their use.

The impact of the human population on the environment is extremely complex and has multiple causes and effects. Many factors, such as population size, per capita consumption, technology, and politics, interact in complex ways, resulting not only in the problems faced today but in solutions for the future. Through research, environmental scientists will help everyone understand how each person can live on this planet without harming it and everyone's future existence.

Summary

1. All life on Earth exists in the biosphere. The biosphere is the interface of the land, air, and water, extending from approximately 9 kilometers (30,000 feet) above sea level to 11 kilometers (36,000 feet) below.

2. Many of the natural resources of the Earth are finite or nonrenewable; that is, they cannot be replaced. Coal, oil, and natural gas are fossil fuels, nonrenewable resources formed over time from the remains of organisms that lived long ago. To curb the use of these resources, scientists are testing and refining alternative renewable energy sources, such as solar, wind, water, and geothermal power.

3. The most severe crisis of natural resource destruction is occurring today in the tropical rain forests. Approximately 100,000 square kilometers (62,000 square miles) of rain forest are being lost each year because of slashing and burning for agriculture and logging and to create pastures for cattle. Scientists estimate that at the present rate, nearly all the tropical rain forest will be gone within the next 50 years.

4. The atmospheric rise in carbon dioxide levels, which is caused by the burning of the tropical forests and the combustion of fossil fuels, is acting as a barrier against the escape of heat from the surface of the Earth. This greenhouse effect could affect global temperatures, rainfall patterns, and agricultural lands.

5. Species are dying out at a rate of 1000 extinctions per year. A major cause of species extinction is habitat loss, which occurs when the tropical rain forests are cut. The extinction of many species leads to a reduction in biological diversity, a loss of species richness. In addition, the loss of species affects ecosystems and diminishes future sources of food, medicine, and other substances.

6. The populations of the world are literally drowning in their trash and garbage, running out of room in which to put it. Solutions to this problem lie in recycling, lowering consumption, composting yard waste, and implementing landfill technology that incorporates recycling, safe incineration, and energy reclamation.

7. Surface water is contaminated by factories, power plants, and sewage treatment plants that dump waste chemicals, heated water, and human sewage into lakes, streams, and rivers. Other sources of surface water pollution are sediment runoff during erosion and the leaching of chemicals from mines, hazardous waste dumps, and croplands. These pollutants affect aquatic organisms in different ways and can become concentrated in their bodies.

8. Underground reservoirs of water can be contaminated by the same sources as surface water when the contaminants trickle through the earth; however, the primary groundwater contaminants are toxic chemicals. At this time, prevention of contamination is the cheapest and most feasible way to end groundwater contamination.

9. The atmosphere has become polluted with sulfur and nitrogen oxides, carbon monoxide, hydrocarbons, and particulates. The primary source of these pollutants is the combustion of fossil fuels in automobiles and electricity-generating plants. As the sulfur and nitrogen oxides mix with water vapor in the atmosphere, they form acid rain, which harms both living and nonliving things. As the nitrogen oxides and hydrocarbons react with sunlight, they form photochemical smog, an upper respiratory irritant that is a health hazard.

10. The environmental problems of this and the next century are the result of many interacting factors. Through research, environmental scientists will help people understand how they can live on this planet without harming it and their future existence.

1. What is the biosphere?

2. Many scientists feel people should work toward creating a "sustainable society." What does this mean?

3. Discuss several energy sources that could be used to help create a sustainable society.

4. What can be done to help prevent a mineral shortage in the future? Why are preventive measures important?

5. Why is the destruction of tropical rain forests a serious problem for everyone—not just the people living in tropical countries?

6. What is meant by global warming? Why is it dangerous?

7. Define *biological diversity*. How are humans affecting the biological diversity of the world's species? Why is this serious?

8. How can the amount of solid waste thrown away be reduced and waste management improved?

9. Distinguish between point and nonpoint sources of surface water pollution. Give an example of each.

10. Describe the different effects of pollution by organic nutrients, inorganic nutrients, infectious agents, and toxic substances in surface water.

11. How is acid rain produced? What are its effects?

12. Explain the terms *gray-air cities* and *brown-air cities*. What pollutants are involved?

13. Ozone is a dangerous pollutant in air that is breathed. Why should people be concerned that the ozone layer of the stratosphere is being depleted?

14. Suppose the President of the United States asked you to put together a plan of action for addressing environmental problems. What steps would you recommend?

1. Rainforest destruction is a complex issue with global impact and many parties involved. Divide into groups that represent the following positions:
   (a) Scientists concerned about the thermal and ecological impact of rain forest destruction
   (b) Native tribes dependent on rain forest ecology for traditional life-styles
   (c) Poor farmers desperate for new crop sites to feed growing population
   (d) Politicians torn between populations of ever-increasing poverty in the cities and protection of national natural resources
   (e) Small logging companies trying to provide jobs for loggers and sell valuable wood to world markets
   Add any other positions that you deem important. After discussing your small group position, present it to the class and allow intergroup debate on the topic.

2. The most tragic of environmental injuries are those that needlessly consume or destroy irreplaceable resources. In the United States, two of the most important resources that are being seriously compromised today are ground water and topsoil. List potential sources of damage to these resources. What might be done to limit the damage?

3. Many environmentalists believe that the economic system of the United States subsidizes pollution of the environment. Consumption is kept higher than it should be, they claim, because the price a consumer pays for a manufactured item does not include the entire cost—the costs of injury to the environment are instead passed on to a third party (the future). As a result, consumers buy more of the item that they would if it were priced at its true cost. What might realistically be done to address this problem?

Brown, L., editor. (1990). *State of the world, 1990*, New York: W. W. Norton & Co.
This is a highly recommended, easily read summary of the ecological problems faced by an overcrowded and hungry world, with an excellent chapter on suggested solutions. A new edition appears every year.

Dyer, M.I. and Holland, M.M. (1991, May). The biosphere reserve concept: needs for a network design. *Bioscience*, pp. 319-325.
A scientific analysis of the need for biosphere reserves of native plants and animals in order to preserve vanishing species.

Hoffman, P. (1990, April). The struggle to save our planet. *Discover*, pp. 36-88.
This entire issue focuses on the human impact on the environment, ecological problems, and possible solutions. An excellent overview.

National Wildlife. (1990). What on Earth are we doing? *28*(2).
An excellent issue of this outstanding magazine is entirely devoted to the state of the environment and presents many actions that you can take to help solve the problems discussed in this chapter.

National Wildlife. (1992, April-May). Endangered species: preserving pieces of the puzzle. *30*(5).
This entire issue is devoted to the fight to protect plants and animals from extinction. In-depth features include the endangered species in the tropical rain forest, the effects of poaching on certain species, and the success stories of bald eagles, gray whales, and alligators.

Rathje, W. (1991, May). Once and future landfills. *National Geographic*, pp. 116-134.
A clear discussion and excellent illustrations support this study of the problem of solid waste disposal.

BIOETHICAL DECISIONMAKING FRAMEWORK
National Family Planning Programs and Cultural Values

Consider the following questions as you think about the bioethical dilemma presented on page 465.

1. What are the bioethical issues in this case?
   - What has to be decided?
   - Who are the decisionmakers?
   - Outline the decisionmaking process in this case as you understand it.

2. What factual information do the decisionmakers need? Consider the effects of the answers to the following questions on the decisionmaking process.
   - How have the contraceptive programs been publicized? Has the type of publicity used offended those who uphold traditional cultural values?
   - Do studies show (statistically) a rise in adultery as a result of the contraceptive distribution?
   - Are the clinics patronized by women only?
   - What other questions should the decisionmakers ask?
   - What additional factual information do the decisionmakers need?

3. Who are the "stakeholders" in this decision—those who stand to gain or lose as a result of the decision?
   - Are the programs' leaders stakeholders? The men and women of the country? What other persons or groups are stakeholders?
   - Which stakeholders are decisionmakers? Which are not decisionmakers? Will individuals in the latter group be able to influence the decisionmaking process? Should they have influence?
   - In what ways would each stakeholder be affected by the decision?

4. What are the values at stake in the decision? As you list and describe them, consider the following questions:
   - How should the world population problem affect decisions to be made in this country?
   - Based on the information in this case, what values are important to this society?
   - Is one group of individuals ethically justified in replacing the values of another group with differing social, religious, economic, or cultural orientations?
   - Should the cultural leaders' belief that fear of pregnancy is a deterrent to premarital or extramarital sexual activity be recognized and upheld by the personnel of the family planning programs?
   - Do the programs' goals for the future well-being of the citizens outweigh the importance of local cultural beliefs?

5. What options are available to the decisionmakers? As you list these options, consider the following questions:
   - Which of these alternatives seem ethically feasible? Which seem administratively possible?
   - How would each alternative decision affect each of the stakeholders?
   - Is there a compromise solution that might give all parties the sense that they have come out the "winner" in the decision?

6. What are the values inherent to the decisionmaking process?
   - Is the decisionmaking process fair?
   - Do all stakeholders have equal resources to advocate their position?
   - What further steps might each group of stakeholders take if their views are disallowed?

Appendix: Answers to Review Questions

1. All scientists, regardless of their special area of study, use a common scientific method to understand more fully the world around us. This process includes hypotheses, experimentation, and producing results that are verifiable by other researchers. This common method allows scientists to build on and incorporate others' work into their own and make scientific research globally relevant.

2. Inductive reasoning develops generalizations from specific instances (for instance, the large number of dying fish in a particular river could be due to rising pollution from factories in the area). Deductive reasoning begins with a general statement and proceeds to a specific statement (pollution from factories could kill wildlife; we will measure the effects of pollution on fish in a specific river).

3. Scientists cannot actually prove hypotheses; they can only disprove them or support them with evidence. However, there is no guarantee that further evidence might not disprove a hypothesis.

4. A theory is a synthesis of hypotheses that are supported by so much evidence they are commonly accepted as "true." However, scientists cannot state with certainty that they are true, since future evidence could disprove any theory.

5. An organ is a higher level of organization and function than cells themselves, and therefore damage to an organ is more threatening to an organism. Interactions in an organism take place along levels of organization, and the higher levels affect more activities than the less inclusive, lower levels, such as cells and tissues.

6. As with all forms of life, human beings display both diversity from other organisms and unity with other organisms. Humans are composed of cells, interact with each other and our environment, transform energy, and maintain a steady internal environment. Humans exhibit form that fits function in our design. Humans reproduce and have exhibited evolution over time.

7. Unlike all other organisms, people use many nonrenewable resources and fill the biosphere with wastes. In addition, people are overpopulating the land, destroying habitats, and killing off various species.

8. Ultimately, all energy comes from the sun. Solar energy is captured by producers, which use photosynthesis to convert it into chemical energy. Other organisms (consumers) feed on the producers and on each other, passing the energy along. When you eat plants or animals, you are harvesting their stored energy.

9. The theory of evolution states that organisms alive today are descendants of organisms that lived long ago and that organisms have changed and diverged from one another over time. Fossils are remains of earlier cells and organisms that have been preserved in rocks; they provide a record of how living things have changed over billions of years.

10. Animals in the same class are probably closely related with regard to evolutionary history and also probably resemble one another in many ways.

1. a. See Figure 2-1, A. Because hydrogen has an atomic number of 1, your atom would have one proton and one electron, although not necessarily one neutron.
   b. The atom would still have one proton and one electron, but it would have a different number of neutrons.

2. The three chemical forces that influence how an atom interacts with other atoms are (1) the tendency of electrons to occur in pairs, (2) the tendency of atoms to balance positive and negative charges, and (3) the tendency of the outer shell (energy level) of electrons to be full. The third point is known as the *octet rule*, because an atom with an unfilled outer shell tends to interact with other atoms to gain a complete set of eight electrons in this outer shell.

3. Nitrogen gas exhibits triple bonds. Like water, nitrogen gas is bound by covalent bonds, although the triple bond of the latter is stronger. Both involve the sharing of electrons or electron pairs between molecules.

4. Water is unusual because it is the only common molecule on Earth that exists as a liquid in the natural environment. This liquid enables other molecules to move and interact; life evolved as a result. A second important characteristic is its ability to form hydrogen bonds because of its polar molecule. Water molecules are strongly attracted to ions and other polar molecules, giving water another important trait: it is an excellent solvent. Chemical interactions readily take place in water because so many molecules are water soluble.

5. Oil is a nonpolar molecule, which means that it cannot form hydrogen bonds with water and therefore does not dissolve.

6. Organic molecules tend to be large, contain carbon, and interact with each other via covalent bonding. Inorganic molecules tend to be small, do not usually contain carbon, and interact by means of ionic bonding. If you wanted to study living things—such as human beings—you would learn about organic molecules.

7. This environment would be described as slightly basic. Like all basic environments, the intestinal environment would have a relatively low level of free H^+ ions available.

8. Both water and carbon are essential to all living organisms. Water is a very polar molecule. It quickly and easily forms hydrogen bonds, which, although not very strong, allow water to react with many other molecules.

9. Monosaccharides, disaccharides, and polysaccharides are all carbohydrates. Most organisms use carbohydrates as an important fuel. Monosaccharides are among the least complex carbohydrates. Many organisms link monosaccharides to form disaccharides that are less readily broken down as they are transported within the organism. To store the energy from carbohydrates, organisms convert monosaccharides and disaccharides into polysaccharides, long polymers of soluble sugars.

10. Plants and animals must store energy as insoluble polysaccharide compounds, and glucose is a very soluble sugar in either blood or water. Plants generally store sugars as starch, whereas animals store it as glycogen.

11. The human body contains cells that have a phospholipid membrane. The steroids of male and female sex hormones are also types of lipids. Human diets high in saturated fats upset the balance of fatty acids in the body, leading to circulatory disease.

12. Saturated fats are fatty acids that carry as many hydrogen atoms as possible because they have only single bonds between their component carbon atoms. Polyunsaturated fats are fatty acids that carry fewer hydrogen atoms because they have more than one double bond between their carbon atoms. This product contains lipids (fats).

13. Proteins can be distinguished from one another by the amino acid sequence that is unique to each protein and the shape determined by the different properties of the amino acids involved. The sequence of amino acids in a protein is its primary structure. These amino acids interact to form coils or sheets called the secondary structure. The three-dimensional shape of the protein is its tertiary structure, and the quaternary structure results from a clustering or aggregation of proteins.

14. Both DNA and RNA are nucleic acids composed of a five-carbon sugar, a phosphate group, and a nitrogenous base. Human cells store and use hereditary information by means of these nucleic acids. They vary in that RNA contains the base uracil and is responsible for directing protein synthesis, whereas DNA contains thymine and stores the hereditary information of the cell.

15. The three classes of macromolecules taken in as food energy by humans are carbohydrates, fats, and proteins. All three are made up of smaller units that, when disassembled, release energy. Because these molecules were all put together by dehydration synthesis, breaking them apart (digesting them) entails hydrolysis, an opposite process.

CHAPTER 3

1. The human body is composed of millions of cells that interact and work together for the good of the entire organism. Cells are specialized for different tasks, yet all cells take in nutrients, maintain homeostasis, react to stimuli, and are composed of smaller units called organelles.

2. Large, complex cells that are active often have many nuclei. A single nucleus could not control the activities of such a large cell.

3. A nutrient outside of a cell would come in contact with the cell plasma membrane and pass into the cell via proteins in the lipid bilayer that act as channels. It would pass into the cell's interior.

4. The cell would have produced the protein product within a ribosome located in rough endoplasmic reticulum. The protein would then enter the inner space of the ER, and eventually be encased in a vesicle. This vesicle would fuse with the membrane of the Golgi body and possibly be modified. The vesicle then passes to the plasma membrane and leaves the cell. The smooth ER plays no role in protein production but rather builds carbohydrates and lipids.

5. Cilia in the respiratory tract of humans sweep invading bacteria and particles up the trachea and away from the lungs. If this effectiveness is reduced because of smoking, these invading organisms or particles could damage the delicate lung tissue and cause disease.

6. If the lysosomes stopped working, your cells would soon fill up with old cell parts and foreign substances such as bacteria. In short, they would die.

7. See Table 3-1.

8. See Table 3-2 for a summary of the differences. For example, the cell with chloroplasts would be the plant, the cell with mitochondria but no chloroplasts would be the animal, and the one with neither mitochondria nor chloroplasts would be the bacterium.

9. No. The ancient bacteria that were endosymbionts to other cells and developed into chloroplasts or mitochondria appeared millions of years ago. Today mitochondria and chloroplasts are functioning organelles that are part of the organism itself, as are other cell parts.

10. a. Facilitated diffusion (passive).
    b. Osmosis (passive).
    c. Diffusion (passive).
    d. Active transport (active).

11. The solute is the instant coffee crystals, the solvent is water, and the solution is the liquid coffee.

12. If a hypertonic solution is added to blood, the red blood cells will shrink as water exits the red blood cells. If a hypotonic solution is created, the red blood cells will absorb water until they eventually lyse. To maintain red blood cells an isotonic solution must therefore be used.

13. Both diffusion and facilitated diffusion occur along the concentration gradient and do not cause energy expenditure. However, unlike diffusion, facilitated diffusion involves the movement of selected specific molecules by specific transport proteins.

14. Sodium and potassium are necessary because nearly a third of a nondividing cell's energy is used to drive the sodium-potassium pump necessary for normal cell function and particularly essential in human muscle and nerve cells.

15. See Figure 3-25. White blood cells use endocytosis to engulf bacteria and other foreign substances.

CHAPTER 4

1. Free energy of activation destabilizes existing chemical bonds in the substrates of a reaction, allowing the reaction to continue.

2. The reactions involved in building complex molecules, such as blood cells, from simpler substrates would be anabolic reactions. Energy is used to build the chemical bonds, and the product contains more energy than the substrates. The pro-

cess of breaking down monosaccharides, such as glucose, is a catabolic reaction, which releases energy.

3. Both glycogen and lipid storage are examples of potential energy, as the energy within the chemical bonds of these substances is capable of performing work but is presently stored.

4. The first law of thermodynamics states that energy cannot be created or destroyed, it can only be changed from one form to another. The second law states that as disorder in the universe constantly increases, energy spontaneously converts to less organized forms.

5. Entropy is the energy lost to disorder. Your friend is restating the second law of thermodynamics, which states that disorder in the universe constantly increases.

6. The Earth constantly receives energy from the sun. Photosynthetic organisms change this energy to other forms of energy that drive life processes.

7. Metabolic pathways are the chains of reactions within your body that move, store, and free energy. By means of metabolic pathways, people obtain energy from food, repair damaged tissues, and in general, avoid increasing entropy.

8. A catalyst increases the rate and often the probability of a chemical reaction while remaining unchanged itself. It may reduce the free energy of activation needed by placing stress on the bonds of a substrate and bringing substrates together. The cells of your body require such a high number of enzymes because there is a high degree of specificity in enzymatic reactions.

9. Most human enzymes work best within a fairly narrow temperature range. If your body temperature became too high, this could affect the bonds between the amino acids that are responsible for the enzymes' three-dimensional shapes. Eventually this could stop chemical reactions from occurring.

10. Both activators and inhibitors bind to specific sites on the enzyme and affect enzymatic activity. However, activators stimulate catalysis whereas inhibitors restrict it. Inhibitors play a key role in negative feedback loops. As end products are produced in catalysis, they may serve as inhibitors by binding to the first enzyme of the metabolic pathway and cause the catalysis to stop when sufficient product has been produced.

11. Cofactors are special nonprotein molecules that help enzymes catalyze chemical reactions; one example is a zinc ion that helps digestive enzymes break down proteins in food. Coenzymes are cofactors that are nonprotein organic molecules. Many vitamins are synthesized into coenzymes in your body.

12. Your body can store energy for later use by converting it to fat, glycogen, or ATP (adenosine triphosphate). This is important because otherwise you would expend your available energy too quickly.

13. ATP is a high-energy compound that can be broken down easily to release energy for use by cells. It is called "energy currency" because cells can save energy released in exergonic reactions by storing it as ATP; cells can also spend ATP to provide necessary energy for endergonic reactions.

14. The universality and speed of the ATP recycling process allows the cell to fuel a large variety of cell processes as quickly as possible. The process also has endergonic and exergonic aspects so that it can make full use of the cell's nutrient supply as it varies.

15. Most enzymes function best within a narrow range of pH. If an environment becomes too acidic, enzymes could be affected, causing chemical reactions to stop and ultimately affecting the metabolic pathways of organisms.

CHAPTER 5

1. ATP, created by chemical energy, is the energy currency of cells. The splitting of ATP is coupled to endergonic reactions that provide the energy necessary to keep cells alive and functioning.

2. Cellular respiration is the process by which living things make the ATP that powers cellular operations. During respiration, fuel molecules are broken down in the presence of oxygen to release energy. Fermentation is the process by which organisms that do not breathe oxygen make ATP.

3. This simplified formula summarizes the process of cellular respiration. It shows that the net effect is to break down one molecule of glucose in the presence of six oxygen molecules to yield six molecules of carbon dioxide and six molecules of water.

4. The breakdown of glucose during cellular respiration is exergonic in that energy is released from the glucose being cleaved. The energy is then used endergonically to produce molecules of ATP.

5. No. Oxidation describes the process in which an atom or molecules gives up an electron. The atom or molecule gaining the electron is "reduced." The term *oxidation* is used because in biological systems oxygen is most often the electron acceptor.

6. Both NAD^+ and FAD are key parts of the electron transport chain of cellular respiration. They serve as electron carriers and pass electrons and protons in a series of redox reactions causing a flow of energy in the process. NAD^+ can accept 2 electrons and 1 proton to be reduced to NADH, whereas FAD can accept 2 electrons and 2 protons to be reduced to $FADH_2$.

7. Your body metabolizes foods by breaking down complex molecules into simple ones. These simple molecules are then broken apart through metabolic pathways (the primary pathways are glycolysis, the Krebs cycle, and the electron transport chain) to release their stored energy and capture it as ATP.

8. Three changes occur during glycolysis: (1) glucose is converted to pyruvate, (2) ADP + P, is converted to ATP, and (3) NAD^+ is converted to NADH.

9. Glycolysis is inefficient because it captures only about 2% of the available chemical energy of glucose. However, cells continue to do it, probably because it was one of the first biochemical processes to evolve. As cells evolved, they retained glycolysis as the first step in catabolic metabolism but added additional steps that were more efficient.

10. The Krebs cycle consists of nine reactions. The first three reactions are preparation reactions in which acetyl-CoA joins a four-carbon molecule from the previous cycle to form citric acid, and the chemical groups are rearranged. The last six reactions are energy extraction reactions. At every turn of the cycle, acetyl-CoA enters and is oxidized to CO_2 and H_2O, and the hydrogen ions and electrons are donated to electron carriers.

11. See Figure 5-14.

12. Water is the electron acceptor (thus, it is reduced) for both the electrons and protons of the electron transport chain. It is an important end product of cellular respiration; 1 H_2O molecule is produced for each NAD or $FADH_2$ produces in the process.

13. See diagram to right.

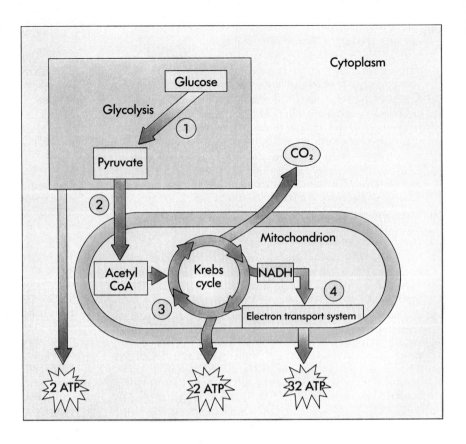

CHAPTER 6

1. A cell is the smallest structure in an organism that is capable of performing all the functions necessary for life. An example is a cardiac muscle cell. The cells of the body are organized into tissues (groups of similar cells that work together to perform a function, such as cardiac muscle tissue). Several different tissues group together to form a structural and functional unit—an organ (the heart.) An organ system is a group of organs that works together to carry out the body's principal activities (such as the circulatory system).

2. The four types of tissue in the body are (1) epithelial (skin cells), (2) connective (chondrocytes), (3) muscle (skeletal muscles such as leg muscles), and (4) nervous (neurons in your brain).

3. See Table 6-2. Squamous cells are found in the air sacs of the lungs, cuboidal cells line ducts in glands, and columnar cells line much of the digestive tract.

4. Lymphocytes, erythrocytes, and fibroblasts are all cells found in connective tissue, but they have different functions. Lymphocytes defend the body against infection, erythrocytes pick up and deliver gases in the blood, and fibroblasts produce fibers that are found in various types of connective tissue.

5. This is part of the body's inflammation response to injury. Mast cells produce histamine, which dilates blood vessels and increases blood flow to the area. This makes the area turn red and feel warm.

6. The connective tissue matrix may provide a nutrient pool for connective tissue cells, allow for waste removal, and provide an environment enhancing cell mobility. Proteins secreted into the matrix may provide a fibrous, stronger structure to matrix, such as that found in bone and cartilage.

7. Oxygen delivery by means of red blood cells is necessary for cells to use the aerobic process of cellular respiration. This process is the primary means of ATP (hence, energy) production in our bodies.

8. Like most body tissues, bone is constantly renewing itself, and the blood vessels and osteocytes in bone allow for new bone to be laid down when a break has occurred. Spongy bone in the interior of the femur aids in this process.

9. Yes, fat cells have their uses. In addition to storing fuel, fat tissue helps shape and pad the body and insulate it against heat loss.

10. Striated skeletal muscle; cardiac muscle.

11. Nerve fiber is specialized to carry electrical impulses that are transmitted almost instantly. This system of homeostatic communication is far quicker than hormone release and response.

12. See Table 6-1.

13. Homeostasis is the maintenance of a stable environment inside your body despite conditions in the external environment. The molecules, cells, tissues, organs, and organ systems in your body must all work together to maintain this internal equilibrium.

CHAPTER 7

1. The six classes of nutrients are carbohydrates, fats, proteins, vitamins, minerals, and water. The first three are organic compounds that your body uses as a source of energy; they are also used as building blocks for growth and repair and to produce other important substances. Vitamins, minerals, and water help body processes take place. Some minerals are also part of body structures.

2. Three types of enzymes help to digest the energy nutrients. Proteases break down proteins into peptides and amino acids. Amylases break down carbohydrates (starches and glycogen) to sugars. Lipases break down the triglycerides in lipids to fatty acids and glycerol.

3. The process of digestion begins as soon as the saliva in the mouth lubricates food and the salivary amylase breaks down starches into maltose.

4. The shape of the teeth on the skull would indicate the type of food eaten by the animal. Herbivores (plant-eaters) have flat, grinding teeth that look like human molars.

5. You would bite off the mouthful with your incisors, your canines would help you tear the food away, and your premolars and molars would allow you to crush and grind the food thoroughly.

6. Peristalsis is a series of involuntary muscular contractions. No, the esophagus transports the food from mouth to stomach, but no digestive processes occur here.

7. The hydrochloric acid in the stomach converts pepsinogen to the active form of pepsin, softens connective tissue in food, denatures large proteins, and kills bacteria. The stomach wall is protected by thick mucus.

8. The duodenum is the first part of the small intestine; digestion is completed there. Starch and glycogen are broken down to disaccharides and then to monosaccharides. Proteins and polypeptides are broken down to shorter peptides and then to amino acids. Triglycerides are digested to fatty acids and glycerol.

9. The liver and pancreas are not organs in which the digestive products are altered and pass on and so are called accessory organs. They are not a stop in the digestive tract itself.

10. These are hormones that help regulate digestion. Gastrin controls the release of hydrochloric acid in the stomach. Secretion stimulates the release of sodium bicarbonate to neutralize acid in the chyme and increases bile secretion in the liver. Cholecystokinin stimulates the gallbladder to release bile into the small intestine and stimulates the pancreas to release digestive enzymes.

11. Sodium bicarbonate neutralizes the acid in chyme. Thus it can help reduce the uncomfortable symptoms of acid indigestion.

12. Increasing the internal surface area of the small intestine helps absorb more nutrients from the same amount of food. Three features accomplish this: inner folds, projections (villi) on the folds, and additional projections on the projections (microvilli).

13. Glucose is broken down by glycolysis, the Krebs cycle, and the electron transport chain. Amino acids and triglycerides are converted to substances that can be metabolized by two of these pathways. Fatty acids are metabolized by another pathway.

14. Answers will vary. See Figure 7-13.

CHAPTER 8

1. Respiration is the uptake of oxygen and the release of carbon dioxide by the body. Cellular respiration is the process at the cellular level that uses the oxygen you breathe in and produces the carbon dioxide you breathe out. Internal respiration is the exchange of oxygen and carbon dioxide between the blood and tissue fluid; the exchange of the two gases between the blood and alveoli is external respiration.

2. Your vocal cords produced the sound for speech as air rushed by and made them vibrate. Your lungs served as a power supply and volume control for your voice, and your lips and tongue formed the sounds into words.

3. The sound of the hiccup is produced as the sudden inhaled air of the spasm causes the glottis at the back of the throat to close suddenly. The opening of the vocal cords and quick closing produce a loud gasp.

4. You can increase air intake by practicing deep breathing techniques and consciously increasing your rate of breathing.

5. As the volume of the thoracic cavity increases, the air pressure within it decreases. Outside air is pulled in, equalizing the pressures inside and outside the thoracic cavity. As the volume of the thoracic cavity decreases, the air pressure inside it increases and forces air out, equalizing the pressures.

6. The circulatory system provides a transport system that distributes gases throughout the body. Without it you would not survive because it would take too long for oxygen to diffuse from the lungs to the rest of the body.

7. At high altitudes the pressure of the oxygen molecules in the air is lower than at sea level. This means that the pressure gradient is lower at the alveoli and less oxygen diffuses into the blood. This can cause you to feel dizzy and short of breath.

8. At the alveoli, carbon dioxide diffuses out of the blood into the alveoli because it moves down the pressure gradient (its pressure in the blood is greater than its pressure within the alveoli.) Meanwhile, oxygen diffuses from the alveoli into the blood because its pressure within the lungs is greater than in the blood.

9. Hemoglobin is known as the oxygen-carrying molecule, but it also carries almost 25% of circulating carbon dioxide in the bloodstream.

10. The hemoglobin in the deoxygenated blood of your veins absorbs oxygen in the air as soon as it leaves the body. Thus, wounds appear to bleed bright red blood even when a vein is involved.

11. At the capillaries, oxygen moves down a pressure gradient to diffuse from the blood into the tissue fluid. Meanwhile, carbon dioxide moves down its own pressure gradient and diffuses from the tissue fluid into the blood.

12. You apply the Heimlich maneuver when a victim cannot seem to cough or talk and is unable to breathe.

13. One of the primary symptoms of respiratory diseases is that patients tire easily. This is because their decreased lung capacity does not allow for sufficient reoxygenation of blood and produces an overall effect of less oxygen reaching the brain and other organ systems.

CHAPTER 9

1. The circulatory system has four main functions: (1) nutrient and waste transport, (2) oxygen and carbon dioxide transport, (3) temperature maintenance, and (4) hormone circulation.

2. The blood carries sugars, amino acids, and fatty acids to the liver, where some of the molecules are converted to glucose and released into the bloodstream. Excess energy molecules are stored in the liver for later use. Essential amino acids and vitamins pass through the liver into the bloodstream. The cells release their metabolic waste products into the blood, which carries them to the kidneys.

3. A regulatory center in your brain constantly monitors your body temperature. If your temperature gets too high, signals from this center dilate your surface blood vessels and increase blood flow to the surface of your skin. This increases heat loss and lowers your body temperature.

4. The circulatory system has three components: the heart, the blood vessels, and the blood. The term *cardiovascular system* refers to the "plumbing" (heart and blood vessels) of the circulatory system.

5. As blood flows through tissue, from capillaries to venules, it loses gases (primarily oxygen) to the tissue and nutrients. The blood in the venule is deoxygenated and carries waste products from the tissue bed.

6. When people are scared (or cold), the walls of the arterioles can contract and the blood flow decreases, routing more blood to other areas of the body. This can cause light-skinned people to "turn pale."

7. The entry to a capillary is guarded by a ring of muscle, which can constrict to block blood flow into that vessel. This is an important means of limiting heat loss. It also permits adjustments in blood flow, allowing more blood to go to areas where it is needed, such as to the intestines after a meal.

8. The walls of arteries have more elastic tissue and smooth muscle than those of veins; this helps arteries accommodate the pulses and high pressures of blood pumped from the heart. The lumen of veins is larger because blood flows through them at lower pressures; a larger diameter offers less resistance. The walls of capillaries are only one cell thick, which permits the exchange of substances between the cells and the blood.

9. The heart has left and right sides, which both serve as pumps yet are not directly connected with one another. Oxygenated blood from the lungs enters and is pumped from the left side, while deoxygenated systemic blood passes through the right side into the lungs. These two types of blood must be separated—hence the two-pump system.

10. The heart is composed of cardiac muscle. Like skeletal muscle, cardiac muscle may be voluntarily strengthened by means of aerobic exercise.

11. The heart valves prevent backflow during the strong contractions of the heart. They shut in response to backflow allowing pressure to push blood in one direction only.

12. The SA node is the pacemaker of the heart; this cluster of cells initiates the excitatory impulse that causes the atria to contract and the impulse to be passed along to other cardiac cells. The AV node conducts the impulse from the SA node to other cardiac cells, initiating the contraction of the ventricles.

13. Normal blood pressure is 110 to 130 mm Hg systolic and 70 to 90 mm Hg diastolic. Answers may vary.

14. A high-fat diet can encourage the development of fatty deposits (plaque) on the inner walls of arteries, making the vessels narrower and less elastic. This can lead to atherosclerosis, heart attacks, and strokes.

CHAPTER 10

1. Excretion is the removal of metabolic wastes and excess water from the body. Without excretion, your body would soon become poisoned by the buildup of metabolic waste products.

The process also helps maintain the balance of water and ions that is necessary for life.

2. The primary metabolic waste products are carbon dioxide, water, salts, and nitrogen-containing molecules.

3. Urea, urine, and uric acid are all forms of metabolic waste products (nitrogenous wastes). Urea consists of ammonia and carbon dioxide. Uric acid forms from the breakdown of nucleic acids you eat and from the metabolic replacement of your nucleic acids and ATP. Urine is the excretion product consisting of water, urea, creatinine, uric acid, and other substances.

4. Carbon dioxide is a waste product of cellular respiration and is used by the liver to form urea. Other excess carbon dioxide is excreted by the lungs.

5. The kidneys help maintain the fluid balance and isotonicity of the blood plasma.

6. The kidneys control the ion concentration and pH of the blood as well as ion balances necessary for the electrical activity in muscle responsible for muscle movement.

7. See Figures 10-4 and 10-5.

8. Kidneys help conserve water by reabsorbing it from the filtrate. By changing the concentrations of salts and urea in the filtrate, the kidneys create an osmotic gradient that results in water moving from the filtrate into the surrounding tissue fluid.

9. Urine can reveal the presence of certain substances in the body because the kidney detoxifies the blood. When these substances, such as drugs, are removed from the blood, they become part of the filtrate.

10. There is no right or wrong answer. Be sure to back up your opinion with reasons, however.

11. Urine is formed when the blood that flows through the kidneys is filtered, removing most of its water and all but its largest molecules and cells. The kidneys then selectively reabsorb certain substances.

12. Homeostasis is the maintenance of constant physiological conditions in the body. ADH and aldosterone are two hormones that help regulate the water and ion balance necessary for homeostasis. ADH regulates that amount of water reabsorbed at the collecting ducts; aldosterone promotes the retention of sodium (and therefore water), while promoting the excretion of potassium.

13. Two problems with kidney function are kidney stones and renal failure. Kidney stones are crystals of certain salts that can block urine flow. Renal failure is a reduction in the rate of filtration of blood in the glomerulus.

14. The process of donor rejection involves the immune system of the recipient.

CHAPTER 11

1. Neurons and hormones are both forms of communication that integrate and coordinate body functions. They differ in that neurons transmit rapid signals that report information or initiate quick responses in specific tissues. Hormones are chemical messengers that trigger widespread prolonged responses, often in a variety of tissues.

2. A sensory neuron in your hand would transmit the sensation of heat immediately when the coffee contacted you. Usually

in such a case an interneuron in your spinal cord would stimulate a motor neuron, causing your hand to move almost instantaneously.

3. A nerve impulse is an electrical signal, not chemical, which is transmitted on nerve cells and may stimulate a chemical response in a receptor cell.

4. *Resting potential* refers to the difference in electrical charge along the membrane of the resting neuron. The action of sodium-potassium transmembrane pumps and ion-specific membrane channels separates positive and negative ions along the inside and outside of the membrane, which creates the resting potential. The difference in electrical charges is the basis for the transmission of nerve impulses.

5. A nerve impulse travels because nearby transmembrane proteins respond to the electrical changes that accompany depolarization of the nerve cell membrane. The adjacent section of membrane depolarizes, followed by another section, leading to a wave of depolarization.

6. Saltatory conduction occurs along myelinated neurons when impulses jump to unmyelinated areas and skip over myelinated portions. Impulses travel much more quickly by this method than by continuous waves of depolarization that occur along continuous portions of the membrane.

7. Synapses between neurons and skeletal muscle cells are neuromuscular junctions. At a neuromuscular junction, acetylcholine released from an axon tip depolarizes the muscle cell membrane, releasing calcium ions that trigger muscle contraction.

8. The enzyme acetylcholinesterase breaks down acetylcholine. If the neurotransmitter were not broken down, it would continue to signal the muscles to contract.

9. The postsynaptic neuron integrates the information it receives from presynaptic neurons. The summed effect of excitatory and inhibitory signals either facilitates or inhibits depolarization.

10. All drugs, whether stimulatory or inhibitory, act by interfering with the normal activity of neurotransmitters.

11. Psychoactive drugs, by affecting neurotransmitter transmission in certain parts of the brain, can produce emotional and physical states that are, at least temporarily, extremely exciting or pleasant to the drug abuser. This effect often outweighs the person's intellectual considerations of the drug's potential for harm if abused. Drug addiction may occur quickly, and withdrawal symptoms make it very difficult to stop the drug use without professional help.

12. Drug tolerance develops over time, causing an addict to require not only increased drug doses for the desired effect but also increased drug side effects and swifter degradation in the body. These higher doses may become financially unmanageable and lead to criminal behavior or cause side effects that are antisocial and harder for an addict to hide. Heavy drug use also may interfere with judgment and assessment of situations and interactions between people.

13. Although a few alcoholic drinks or sleeping pills (barbiturates) are not themselves dangerous, the combination may be deadly. Barbiturates and alcohol enhance the sedative activities of each other, leading to a potentially dangerous combination.

14. These stimulants actually block the breakdown and recycling of neurotransmitters, causing a depletion of the former. At this point, the drug abuser needs consistently higher doses of stimulant (tolerance has developed).

15. Drug addiction, as defined in the text, is the compulsive urge to continue drug use, a tendency to increase drug dosage, and either physical or psychological (or both) dependence on the drug. Marijuana abuse meets all of these criteria for drug addiction.

CHAPTER 12

1. The nervous system is a complex network of neurons that gathers information about the internal and external environment and processes and responds to this information. The central nervous system (brain and spinal cord) is the site of information processing. The peripheral nervous system (nerves) brings messages to and from the central nervous system.

2. The somatic nervous system consists of motor neurons that control voluntary responses (for example, moving your leg to take a step). The autonomic nervous system consists of motor neurons that control involuntary activities (for example, digesting a meal.)

3. Integration would occur in the spinal cord for such a simple reflex.

4. Integration would occur in the cerebellum.

5. As animals rise on the evolutionary scale, primates in particular, the area of cerebral cortex devoted to associative activities increases. Therefore the chimpanzee would have a higher percentage of associative cortex than the dog.

6. The areas of the hands and face are associated with the primary senses (touch, taste, sight) and, as such, require more of the cortex area to interpret and react to increased input from sensory and motor neurons.

7. Infants and toddlers are quickly developing nervous system connections and expanding motor skills. The myelin sheath of many nerve fibers, particularly in the cerebral white matter and motor neurons, is critical for nerve signal transmission and normal development.

8. The limbic systems of both a lion and a human respond to similar stimuli (pain, sexual drive, hunger, thirst) and would be somewhat similar, while their associative cortexes would be quite dissimilar in function.

9. The brainstem (midbrain, pons, medulla) contains tracts of nerve fibers that carry messages to and from the spinal cord. Nuclei located there control important body reflexes.

10. As the spinal cord extends from the brain, many sensory and nerve tracts enter it. The higher the point of injury, the higher the number of sensory and motor nerve tracts that are no longer connected to the brain itself.

11. Sensory receptors change stimuli into nerve impulses. The nerve fibers of sensory neurons carry this information to the central nervous system, where interneurons interpret them and direct a response (in this case, turning your head). The axons of motor neurons conduct these impulses to the appropriate muscles.

12. How you perceive stimuli depends on which receptors are stimulated. You registered this stimulus as a sound because it stimulated your auditory nerve.

13. These systems act in opposition to each other to maintain homeostasis and help you respond to environmental changes. The sympathetic nervous system generally mobilizes the body for greater activity (faster heart rate, increased respiration),

whereas the parasympathetic nervous system stimulates normal body functions such as digestion.

CHAPTER 13

1. Pain is, for the most part, a subjective experience. Although a doctor may assess potential for pain given a situation, the individual response and sensitivity vary widely among people. This makes pain a very difficult medical management problem.

2. For you to sense a stimulus, it must be of sufficient magnitude to open ion channels within the membrane of the receptor cell. This depolarizes the membrane, creating a generator potential that leads to an action potential (nerve impulse) in the sensory neurons with which the receptor synapses. Nerve fibers conduct the impulse to the central nervous system.

3. A roller coaster ride would most probably include an extreme rise in proprioception stimuli as the person's spatial orientation changes quickly.

4. Satiation is a sensation involving the body's information about the internal environment, particularly those receptors in the digestive system.

5. Nasal congestion would most probably affect the special senses of both smell and taste by reducing sensory input in these areas.

6. Olfactory receptors detect different smells because of specific binding of airborne gases with the receptor chemicals located in the cilia of the nasal epithelium.

7. On its way to the olfactory area of the cerebral cortex, the nerve impulse travels through the limbic system, the area of the brain that is responsible for many of your drives and emotions. Thus, certain odors become linked in your memory with emotions and events.

8. Taste buds are taste receptors concentrated on the tongue. They detect chemicals in food and register an overall taste that consists of different combinations of sweet, salty, sour, and bitter. The sense of taste interacts with the sense of smell to produce a taste sensation.

9. Color vision is caused by cone cells. There are three types of cones, each of which absorbs a specific wavelength of light. The color you perceive depends on how strongly each group of cones is stimulated by a light source.

10. You see objects because light enters the eye through the pupil and the lens focuses it on the fovea, which is rich in cone cells. These cells, along with surrounding rods and cones, initiate nervous impulses that travel to the cerebrum via the optic nerve.

11. See Figure 13-9.

12. Rod cells, which can detect low light levels, are the primary cell type stimulated in a dark room, but in a well-lit setting the cone cells (which sense color) would be equally activated.

13. You have depth perception because of the positioning of your two eyes on either side of the head, which sends slightly different images to the brain. Covering one eye makes it more difficult to judge distance.

14. Your outer ear funnels sound waves toward the eardrum, which changes these waves into mechanical energy. This energy is then transmitted to the bones of the middle ear, which increases its force. Receptor cells in the inner ear change the mechanical energy into nerve impulses.

15. You can detect movements of your head because of the otoliths embedded in the jelly-like layer that covers the cilia in your inner ear. When you move your head, the otoliths slide and bend the underlying cilia. This generates signals to the brain, which interprets the type and degree of movement.

CHAPTER 14

1. Hormones are chemical messages secreted by cells that affect other cells. They are an important method the body uses to integrate the functioning of various tissues, organs, and organ systems.

2. The nervous system sends messages to glands and muscles, regulating glandular secretion and muscular contraction. Endocrine hormones carry messages to virtually any type of cell in the body.

3. Peptide hormones are not lipid soluble and so do not pass easily through lipid bilayers of cell membranes. Cyclic AMP acts as the second messenger to complete the hormonal activity begun by the binding of the hormone to a membrane-bound hormone receptor.

4. The sexual and physiological changes in puberty are primarily triggered by high steroid hormone levels.

5. A feedback loop controls hormone production by initially stimulating a gland to produce the hormone. After the hormone has exerted its effect on the target cell, the body feeds back information to the endocrine gland. In a positive feedback loop, the feedback causes the gland to produce more hormone; in a negative feedback loop, it causes the gland to slow down or stop hormone production.

6. ADH levels would be monitored and controlled by the hypothalamus. This structure produces "releasing hormones" that trigger ADH production and release from the posterior pituitary.

7. Tropic hormones stimulate other endocrine glands. The four are the following: (1) Follicle-stimulating hormone (FSH): In women, FSH triggers the maturation of eggs in the ovaries and stimulates the secretion of estrogens. In men, it triggers the production of sperm. (2) Luteinizing hormone (LH): In women, LH stimulates the release of an egg from the ovary and fosters the development of progesterone. In men, it stimulates the production of testosterone. (3) Adrenocorticotropic hormone (ACTH): ACTH stimulates the adrenal cortex to produce steroid hormones. (4) Thyroid-stimulating hormone (TSH): TSH triggers the thyroid gland to produce the thyroid hormones.

8. People living far from the ocean faced little chance of receiving their iodine from seafood, a primary source of iodine. Until this century, iodized salt was not freely available. This lack of dietary iodine caused goiter.

9. No. Alcohol suppresses the release of ADH (antidiuretic hormone), which means that it encourages more water to leave your body in your urine. If you are already hot and thirsty, this will only dehydrate you further.

10. Parathyroid hormone (PTH) and calcitonin (CT) work antagonistically to maintain appropriate calcium levels. If the level becomes too low, PTH stimulates osteoclasts to liberate calcium from the bones and stimulates the kidneys and intestines to reabsorb more calcium. When levels grow too high, more CT is secreted, which inhibits the release of calcium from bones and speeds up its absorption.

11. Over a prolonged period of stress, the body reacts in three stages: (1) alarm reaction (quickened metabolism triggered by

adrenaline and noradrenaline), (2) resistance (glucose production and blood pressure rise; hormones involved are ACTH, GH, TSH, mineralocorticoids and glucocorticoids, and (3) exhaustion (loss of potassium and glucose; organs become weak and may stop functioning).

12. Vitamin B_6 may enhance the functions of the adrenal cortex. Answers will vary as to personal experience.

13. Chronic stress leads to long-term stimulation by the autonomic nervous system, which heightens metabolism, raises blood pressure, and speeds up internal chemical reactions. Over time, this can physically stress the body and lead to health problems.

14. The pancreatic islets of Langerhans secrete two hormones that act antagonistically to one another to regulate glucose levels. Glucagon raises the glucose level by stimulating the liver to convert glycogen and other nutrients into glucose, whereas insulin decreases glucose levels in the blood by helping cells transport it across their membranes.

C H A P T E R 1 5

1. Your movement resulted from the contraction of your skeletal muscles, which are anchored to bones. The muscles use bones like levers to direct force against an object. When you raised your hand, your skin stretched to accommodate the change in position.

2. Hair aids the role of skin as a protective barrier by providing reduced access to the skin surface and helps control the body's internal temperature by its protection.

3. The role of skin as a sensory surface is of great use to small children. As we age, we tend to rely less heavily on such input and more on visual perception.

4. Bone is a type of connective tissue consisting of living cells that secrete collagen fibers into the surrounding matrix. The bones of the skeletal system support the body and permit movement by serving as points of attachment and acting as levers against which muscles can pull. They also protect delicate internal structures, store important minerals, and produce red and white blood cells.

5. Bone marrow transplants entail the removal and transfer of red bone marrow from spongy bone in the end of long bones.

6. Spongy bone makes up most of the tissue of the smaller bones of the axial skeleton.

7. Excess calcium taken in by the body and not needed at the moment in cellular activities is stored in bone tissue until a later time.

8. A "slipped disk" refers to one of the intervertebral disks of fibrocartilage that separate the vertebrae from each other (except in the sacrum and coccyx). These disks act as shock absorbers, provide the means of attachment between vertebra, and allow the vertebral column to move.

9. An articulation is a joint—a place where bones, or bones and cartilage, come together. Joints are classified according to the degree to which they permit movement: immovable joints (the sutures in your skull), slightly movable joints (joints between your vertebra), and synovial (freely movable) joints (wrists).

10. These are all types of synovial (freely movable) joints. They differ in the type of movement they allow. A hinge joint allows movement in one plane only, a ball-and-socket joint al-

lows rotation, and a pivot joint permits side-to-side movement.

11. Tendons connect muscle to bone. Ligaments connect muscles together.

12. Osteoarthritis generally strikes most severely in synovial joint tissue.

13. Actin is a protein that makes up the thin myofilaments of muscle; the protein myosin makes up the thick myofilaments. Myofilaments are the microfilaments of muscle cells. Muscle cells contract when the actin and myosin filaments slide past each other. Changes in the shape of the ends of the myosin molecules (located between adjacent actin filaments) cause the myosin molecule to move along the actin, causing the myofilament to contract.

14. When depolarization from a nerve impulse reaches a neuromuscular junction, it triggers the release of the neurotransmitter acetylcholine. The acetylcholine crosses over to the muscle fiber membrane and opens the ion channels of that membrane, depolarizing it. This sets off a series of reactions that release calcium ions; the calcium ions initiate the chemical reactions of contraction.

15. Answers may vary. People generally exhibit less elasticity; wrinkling, and stretching or sagging skin with age; as well as lower touch sensation. Bones often become brittle, causing more fractures and breaking more easily. Joints often stiffen, and mosteoarthritis is common.

C H A P T E R 1 6

1. Nonspecific defenses act against any foreign invader, whereas specific defenses work against particular types of microbes. Nonspecific defenses are the first line of defense because they are the first barriers that a microorganism must bypass to enter your body.

2. The nonspecific defenses include (1) the skin (which if unbroken provides a barrier against invasion), (2) mucous membranes (mucus can trap particles and move them away from delicate areas), (3) chemicals that kill bacteria (many membranes are washed by fluids deadly to bacteria or have an acidic environment), (4) the inflammatory process (a series of events that remove the irritation, repair the damage, and protect the body from further damage).

3. In this case, the immune response (specific resistance) is not involved. Nonspecific resistance includes cases where foreign matter is trapped by mucous membranes and expelled from the body, probably via tears or eye watering.

4. The immune system differs from other body systems because it is not a system of organs and it lacks a single "controlling" organ. Instead, it consists of cells scattered throughout the body that have a common function: reacting to specific foreign molecules.

5. The transplanted cell would be identified as "non-self"; therefore it would act as an antigen and probably produce an immune response in the new environment.

6. These phagocytes serve to sound the alarm for an immune response if the body is being invaded by foreign microbes. They offer a quick response by engulfing the invader, stimulating the maturation of large numbers of monocytes into macrophages, and inducing an inflammation or fever to resist microbial growth.

7. The four principal types of T cells are (1) helper T cells (which initiate the immune response), (2) cytotoxic T cells (which

break apart infected and foreign cells), (3) inducer T cells (which oversee the development of T cells in the thymus), and (4) suppressor T cells (which limit the immune response).

8. During the cell-mediated immune response, cytotoxic T cells recognize and destroy infected body cells in addition to destroying transplanted and cancer cells. Helper T cells initiate the response, activating cytotoxic T cells, macrophages, inducer T cells, and finally, suppressor T cells.

9. When you had measles, B cell clones that did not become plasma cells became circulating lymphocytes—memory B cells. These cells give you an accelerated response during subsequent exposures to measles, promptly defending you against infection.

10. During the humoral response, B cells recognize foreign antigens and, if activated by helper T cells, produce antibodies. The antibodies bind to the antigens and mark them for destruction.

11. Antibodies have highly specific binding sites that fit only one specific antigen with the exact amino acid composition necessary for complete binding.

12. This is a case of passive immunity, where an organism is protected not by its own cell-mediated immune response but by short-term protection from another source (in this case, the maternal immune system).

13. Injection with antigens causes an antibody (B cell) response, with the production of memory cells. A booster shot induces these memory cells to differentiate into antibody-producing cells and form still more memory cells.

14. The human immunodeficiency virus (HIV), which is responsible for AIDS, is dangerous because it destroys helper T cells, thus destroying the immune system's ability to mount a defense against any infection.

15. An allergic reaction occurs when the immune system mounts a defense against a harmless antigen. When class E antibodies are involved and bind to the antigens, they cause a strong inflammatory response that can dilate blood vessels and lead to symptoms ranging from uncomfortable to life-threatening.

CHAPTER 17

1. The chemical instructions that determine our specific personal characteristics are located within chromosomes. The DNA within our chromosomes directs the millions of complex chemical reactions that govern our growth and development.

2. The two types of nucleic acids are DNA (deoxyribonucleic acid) and RNA (ribonucleic acid). Both consist of nucleotides that are made up of three molecular parts: a sugar, a phosphate group, and a base. The sugar in RNA is ribose, whereas the sugar in DNA is deoxyribose. DNA contains the bases thymine and cytosine; RNA contains uracil instead of thymine.

3. *Double helix* refers to the DNA molecule, which is shaped like a double-stranded helical ladder. The bases of each strand together form rungs of uniform length, and alternating sugar-phosphate units form the ladder uprights.

4. Chargaff's experiments showed that the proportion of bases varied in the DNA of different types of organisms but that the amount of adenine always equaled the amount of thymine, and guanine always equaled cytosine. This suggested that DNA was the hereditary material that encoded the information used by cells for growth, development, and repair.

5. There are many answers, and student responses may vary. Possible answers may include: a nonviable DNA strand is produced, an error causes the chemical message to vary and results in genetic mutation of some sort, or the change does not directly affect instruction because of repetition of the instruction elsewhere on the strand.

6. According to the one gene–one enzyme theory, a single genetic mutation may lead to lack of a particular enzyme product.

7. The type of RNA found in ribosomes, along with the proteins also found there, is ribosomal RNA (rRNA). Transfer RNA (tRNA) is in the cytoplasm; during polypeptide synthesis, tRNA molecules transport amino acids to the ribosomes and position each amino acid at the correct place on the elongating polypeptide chain. Messenger RNA (mRNA) brings information from the DNA in the nucleus to the ribosomes in the cytoplasm to direct which polypeptide is assembled.

8. Sexual reproduction, whereby a new human is formed by the fusion of egg and sperm meiotically produced, leads to tremendous variation. The alternative, mitosis, produces identical daughter cells and is responsible for human growth during the life cycle.

9. The correct sequence is c (prophase), a (metaphase), d (anaphase), b (telophase). This is the process of mitosis.

10. The correct sequence is c (prophase I), d (metaphase I), a (anaphase I), b (telophase I), e (interphase). This is the process of meiosis I.

11. Mitosis produces two daughter cells from one parent cell; the daughter cells are identical with each other and with the parent. Meiosis produces four sex cells, each of which contains half the amount of the parent cell's hereditary material.

12. Genetic recombination during meiosis allows the hereditary material to be recombined during sexual reproduction. It is the principal factor that has made the evolution of eukaryotic organisms possible.

13. Meiosis II produces four haploid cells that may function as gametes (animals) or spores (plants).

14. There may be only one gene coding for a particular enzyme, and many enzymes are individually essential to the viability of an organism. A "back-up" system of repetition may ensure enzyme production despite a single mutation or alteration in genetic code.

CHAPTER 18

1. All cancers exhibit uncontrolled cell growth, loss of cell differentiation, invasion of normal tissues, and metastasis to other sites.

2. Mutation of the DNA of proto-oncogenes causes them to become active oncogenes. These act as the "on" switches in the development of cancer. Mutation of the DNA of tumor-suppressor cells causes them to be inactivated and they cannot stop the development of cancerous tissue. As a result of these mutations, cancer will develop in a patient.

3. Cigarette smoke is a "complete" carcinogen in that it both initiates and promotes cancer. It initiates by mutating the DNA of a cell leading to stimulation of proto-oncogenes and inactivation of tumor suppressor genes. It acts as a promoter by continuing to damage the DNA of affected tissue over long periods of time and encouraging the expression of oncogenes.

4. If a cyst or tumor is benign it indicates that the growth of this cell mass is confined and encapsulated and poses no serious health threat.

5. It is possible that most cancers are carcinomas involving the tissues that cover the outside of the body or line the interior, because these tissues would be most exposed to initiating agents during normal living. Student theories may vary among the group.

6. Answers will vary.

7. Answers will vary.

8. Severe sunburns in childhood, due to overexposure to UV radiation, have been found to greatly increase the risk of melanoma in adulthood.

9. Health advocates concerned about high hormone doses given to domestic cattle and poultry are concerned that these hormones may enter our bodies via meat consumption and act as either cancer initiators or promoters in our bodies. The effect of these agents is still unknown. Student reaction may vary.

10. A high-fat diet acts as a promoter in initiated cancer cells. It may affect estrogen production in women, leading to ovarian or breast cancers. It may affect prostrate cancer development in men. A fat diet promotes colon cancer by its chemical action on bile and increased bile acids in the colon. Polyunsaturated fats, though more "heart healthy" may promote cancer by means of high free radical production.

11. To reduce cancer risk, a person may make use of available diagnostic tests, adjust personal diet to include more bran fiber and anti oxidants (such as beta-carotene, vitamin C, and vitamin E), and reduce environmental exposure to carcinogens.

12. Yes, venereal warts are caused by human papilloma virus, which has been linked to vaginal and vulval cancer.

13. Childbirth has been found to decrease later risk of breast and ovarian cancers in women. This may be due to the fluctuating progesterone levels found in pregnancy.

CHAPTER 19

1. Offspring of sexual reproduction inherit characteristics from both parents; those of asexual reproduction are exact duplicates of one parent. Sexual reproduction introduces variation within a species; the asexual variety does not.

2. Self-fertilization occurs when the gametes of one plant fertilize each other so that the offspring derive from one organism. Cross-fertilization occurs when the male gametes of one plant fertilize the female gametes of another.

3. An individual who is heterozygous for a particular trait has two different alleles for that trait. Often alleles express dominance or recessiveness in relation to one another, but there are also many instances where incomplete dominance occurs.

4. Mendel's Law of Segregation states that each gamete receives only one of an organism's pair of alleles. Random segregation occurs during meiosis.

5. Phenotype assessment, since it involves the outward appearance of an individual, is relatively easy and accurate. However, genotype determination is far more complex, especially in the era in which Mendel lived. Genotype may be complicated by cases of incomplete dominance, more than one gene coding of the same trait, genetic linkage, and other complex relationships between individual genes or chromosomes.

6. All of the F_1 offspring would have an Ll genotype and the phenotype of long leaves.

	L	L
l	Ll	Ll
l	Ll	Ll

7. The F_2 genotype would be 1:2:1 (LL:Ll:ll); the phenotype would be 3:1 (long-leaved:short-leaved).

	L	l
l	LL	Ll
l	Ll	ll

8. Mendel used a testcross to determine whether a phenotypically dominant plant was homozygous or heterozygous for the dominant trait. He crossed the plant with a homozygous recessive plant. When the test plant was homozygous, the offspring were hybrids and phenotypically dominant. When it was heterozygous, half the progeny were heterozygous and looked like the test plant, and half were homozygous recessive and resembled the recessive parent.

9. Mendel's Law of Independent Assortment states that the distribution of alleles for one trait into the gametes does not affect the distribution of alleles for other traits, unless they are on the same chromosome.

10. The probability is ¼.

11. a. ¹⁄₁₆.
    b. ⁹⁄₁₆.

12. Sutton and Morgan provided a framework that explained the equal genetic role of both egg and sperm in the hereditary material of offspring. Sutton suggested the presence of hereditary material within the nuclei of the gametes. While Morgan gave the first clear evidence that genes reside on chromosomes.

Genetics problems

1. Somewhere in your herd you have cows and bulls that are not homozygous for the dominant gene "polled." Because you have many cows and probably only one or some small number of bulls, it would make sense to concentrate on the bulls. If you have only homozygous "polled" bulls, you could never produce a horned offspring regardless of the genotype of the mother. The most efficient thing to do would be to keep track of the matings and the phenotype of the offspring resulting from these matings and prevent any bull found to produce horned offspring from mating again.

2. Albinism, *a*, is a recessive gene. If heterozygotes mated, you would have the following:

	A	a
A	AA	Aa
a	Aa	aa

   One-fourth would be expected to be albinos.

3. The best thing to do would be to mate Dingleberry to several dames homozygous for the recessive gene that causes the brittle bones. Half of the offspring would be expected to have brit-

tle bones if Dingleberry were a heterozygous carrier of the disease gene. Although you could never be 100% certain Dingleberry was not a carrier, you could reduce the probability to a reasonable level.

4. Your mating of DDWw and Ddww individuals would look like the following:

	Dw	Dw	dw	dw
DW	DDWw	DDWw	DdWw	DdWw
Dw	DDww	DDww	Ddww	Ddww
DW	DDWw	DDWw	DdWw	DdWw
Dw	DDww	DDww	Ddww	Ddww

Long-wing, red-eyed individuals would result from 8 of the possible 16 combinations, and dumpy, white-eyed individuals would never be produced.

5. Breed Oscar to Heidi. If half of the offspring are white eyed, Oscar is a heterozygote.

6. Both parents carry at least one of the recessive genes. Because it is recessive, the trait is not manifested until they produce an offspring who is homozygous.

CHAPTER 20

1. No. Each human cell contains the full complement of 23 pairs of chromosomes.

2. The fact that a genetic abnormality such as trisomy 21 can exist shows that there are often groups of genes located near each other on a chromosome that may be transferred or altered as a group and cause multiple alterations that occur as a discrete group.

3. Down syndrome (trisomy 21) is a genetic disorder caused by having three 21 chromosomes. Individuals who inherit this condition show delayed maturation of the skeletal system and are often mentally retarded.

4. People who inherit abnormal numbers of sex chromosomes often have abnormal features and may be mentally retarded. Examples are (1) triple X females (XXX zygote), underdeveloped females who may have lower-than-average intelligence; (2) Klinefelter syndrome (XXY zygote), sterile males with some female characteristics; (3) Turner syndrome (XO zygote), sterile females with immature sex organs; and (4) XYY males, fertile males of normal appearance.

5. An X chromosome is necessary for zygote viability.

6. The three major sources of damage to chromosomes are high-energy radiation (such as x-rays), low-energy radiation (such as UV light), and chemicals (such as certain legal and illegal drugs).

7. Heavy use of drugs could affect ova and sperm by damaging the DNA. In general, chemicals add or delete molecules from the structure of DNA. This can result in chromosomal breaks or changes as the cell works to repair the damage.

8. a. Sex-linked.
   b. Dominant.
   c. Recessive.
   d. Autosomal.

9. Most human genetic disorders are recessive because those genes are able to persist in the population among carriers; people carrying lethal dominant disorders are more likely to die before reproducing. Recessive disorders include cystic fibrosis, sickle-cell anemia, and Tay-Sachs disease.

10. In incomplete dominance, alternative forms of an allele are neither dominant nor recessive; heterozygotes are phenotypic intermediates. In codominance, alternative forms of an allele are both dominant, so heterozygotes exhibit both phenotypes.

11. Their children's genotypes would be 1:2:1 (AA [type A], AB [type AB], BB [type B]).

	A	B
A	AA	AB
B	AB	BB

12. Couples who suspect they may be at risk for genetic disorders can undergo genetic counseling to determine the probability of this risk. When a pregnancy is diagnosed as high risk, a woman can undergo amniocentesis (analysis of a sample of amniotic fluid) to test for many common genetic disorders.

Genetics problems

1.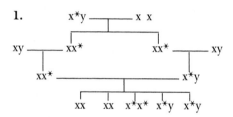

2. $I^A I^O \times I^B I^O \rightarrow I^O I^O$

3. 45 (44 autosomes + one X)

4. AO (blood type A)

5.

rr ——— RR   rr ——— RR

rR ——————————— rR

¼rr

6. c—Y-linkage

CHAPTER 21

1. Sexual reproduction is the process in which a male and a female sex cell combine to form the first cell of a new individual.

2. Follicle-stimulating hormone (FSH) triggers sperm production. Luteinizing hormone (LH) regulates the testes' secretion of testosterone, a hormone responsible for the development of male secondary sexual characteristics.

3. A spermatozoon has a head that contains the hereditary material. Located at its leading tip is an acrosome that contains enzymes helping the sperm penetrate the egg's membrane. The sperm also has a flagellum that propels it and mitochon-

dria that produce the ATP from which sperm derive the energy to power the flagellum.

4. These are accessory glands that add fluid to the sperm to produce semen. The seminal vesicles supply a fluid containing fructose, which serves as a source of energy for the sperm. The prostate gland adds an alkaline fluid that neutralizes the acidity of any urine in the urethra and the acidity of the female vagina. The bulbourethral glands also contribute an alkaline fluid.

5. At birth, females have all of the oocytes that they will ever produce. As the woman ages, so do her oocytes, and the odds of a harmful mutation increase appreciably after age 35.

6. Yes, she could still conceive with oocytes from her remaining ovary. However, she may only ovulate every other month and hence be fertile on alternate months.

7. The reproductive cycle of a woman consists of both her menstrual cycle (monthly development and shedding of the functional layer of the endometrium) and her ovarian cycle (monthly maturation of her egg and its release).

8. The reproductive cycle of females occurs roughly every 28 days. The primary oocyte matures, is released from the ovary during ovulation, and journeys through the uterine tube to the uterus. The endometrial lining of the uterus has thickened to prepare for implantation; if fertilization does not occur, it sloughs off during menstruation. The hormones FSH, LH, estrogen, and progesterone orchestrate these events.

9. Fertilization occurs in the uterine tube. After the egg is fertilized, it completes a second meiotic division, joins its hereditary material with that of the sperm, begins dividing by mitosis, and implants itself on the thickened uterine wall. The placenta begins to form and human chorionic gonadotropin (HCG) is secreted.

10. Once the date of ovulation is determined, a couple must have intercourse within 48 hours to fertilize the egg. The egg is only viable up to 1 day after ovulation.

11. The only methods of birth control that may prevent the transmission of sexually transmitted diseases are abstinence and condoms.

12. Birth control pills contain estrogen and progesterone, which shut down the production of FSH and LH. By maintaining high levels of estrogen and progesterone, the pills cause the body to act as if ovulation has already occurred; the ovarian follicles do not mature, and ovulation does not occur.

13. The most effective birth control methods are vasectomies and tubal ligation. Birth control pills are very effective. Condoms and diaphragms are effective when used correctly, but mistakes are common. Least reliable are the rhythm method and withdrawal, which have high failure rates.

14. When a cervical cap or diaphragm is used, there is still blood-to-blood contact between sexual partners as the penis contacts the vaginal walls. This contact permits the transfer of sexually transmitted diseases.

CHAPTER 22

1. At the instant of union and fertilization between a male and female gamete, the zygote formed has a unique genetic composition.

2. After fertilization, the oocyte's surface changes so that no other sperm can penetrate, and oocyte meiosis is completed. The sperm sheds its tail, and the sperm and egg nuclei fuse.

3. This period consists of mitotic cell division.

4. If the blastocyst does not successfully implant in the uterine wall, it will be swept away in the consequent menstruation. If implanted, the blastocyst secretes human chorionic gonadotropin, which maintains the corpus luteum and prevents menstruation.

5. The three primary germ layers are the (1) ectoderm (outer layer of skin, the nervous system, and portions of sense organs), (2) endoderm (lining of the digestive tract and digestive organs, respiratory tract and lungs, and urinary bladder and urethra), and (3) mesoderm (skeleton, muscles, blood, reproductive organs, connective tissues, and innermost layer of skin).

6. The extraembryonic membranes play a role in the life support of the preembryo/embryo/fetus. They are the (1) amnion (cushions the embryo in amniotic fluid and keeps the temperature constant), (2) chorion (facilitates the exchange of nutrients, gases, and wastes between the embryo and mother), (3) yolk sac (produces blood for the embryo before its liver is functional and becomes the lining of the digestive tract), and (4) allantois (responsible for formation of the embryo's blood cells and vessels).

7. During gastrulation, groups of inner mass cells differentiate into the three primary germ layers from which all the organs and tissues will develop.

8. During neurulation, cells lying over the notochord curl upward to form a tube that will develop into the central nervous system.

9. The notochord is a structure that forms the midline axis of an embryo. In humans and in most other vertebrates, it develops into the vertebral column.

10. Along with general systemic development, neural development is a key aspect of the first 3 weeks of fetal development, and the fate of the central nervous system is dependent on good maternal nutrition.

11. Between the fourth and eighth weeks, the embryo grows much longer, establishes a primitive circulation, and begins to exchange gases, nutrients, and wastes with the mother. The central nervous system and body form begin to develop.

12. The first trimester is primarily a time of development; by the ninth week, most body systems are functional. During the second trimester the fetus grows, ossification is well underway, and the fetus has a heartbeat. The third trimester is primarily a period of growth; by birth the fetus is able to exist on its own.

13. During pregnancy the fetus obtains all of its nutrients from the mother. Poor nutrition in the mother can damage the child, possibly resulting in retardation and stunted growth.

14. At birth the circulation of the newborn changes as the lungs, rather than the placenta, become the organ of gas exchange.

CHAPTER 23

1. No. Sexually transmitted diseases are not caused by poor personal hygiene or socioeconomic class. They are communicable illnesses transmitted between persons during sexual contact.

2. Viruses are infectious agents that lack a cellular structure, so they are not living. Instead, they are nonliving obligate parasites that must exist in association with and at the expense of other organisms.

3. Both cycles are patterns of viral replication. In the lytic cycle, viruses enter a cell, replicate, and cause the cell to burst and release new viruses. In the lysogenic cycle, viruses enter into a long-term relationship with the host cells, their nucleic acid replicating as the cells multiply.

4. A cold sore results from the lysogenic cycle of cell damage caused by the herpes simplex virus. The virus remains latent in nervous tissues until something triggers it, such as a cold.

5. Herpes simplex virus 1 (HSV1) is the agent causing cold sores and fever blisters. It can cause genital herpes (and does 10% to 15% of the time) if oral sex is practiced.

6. Women infected with HSV have a higher rate of miscarriage that uninfected women. Their children must be delivered via Caesarean section to prevent possible infection of the baby as it passes through the birth canal. Women may experience a recurrence of lesions during menstruation.

7. No. The human papilloma virus causing genital warts has various types; types 16 and 18 are tumor viruses that may cause cervical cancer in women. These women should have Pap smears every 6 months.

8. The extreme simplicity of bacterial design; small size, lack of discrete organelles, lack of a membrane-bound nucleus, seems to support the theory that they evolved before eukaryotes.

9. Gummas are tumor-like masses exhibited during the tertiary stage of syphilitc infection. These lesions are not communicable but may develop in the cardiovascular or central nervous systems causing paralysis or death.

10. In men, gonorrheal infection, if untreated, may spread to other urogenital structures from the urethra. Infection of the epididymis or vas deferens may result in scar tissue causing male sterility. Chronic gonorrheal infections in women may lead to pelvic inflammatory disease (PID) and if uterine tubes are involved, scar tissue may develop causing sterility.

11. These diseases may be acquired without the knowledge of the person or partner. Occasionally, patients do not have extreme or even normal symptoms of infection and may unwittingly pass on these diseases.

12. Protozoans cause Trichomonas vaginalis which is found in both men and women.

13. The only completely effective protection against sexually transmitted diseases is abstinence. There is decreased risk if latex condoms are used correctly along with the spermicide nonoxynol-9.

CHAPTER 24

1. Darwin's theory of evolution, through the mechanism of natural selection, provided a scientific framework to explain how species diversify over time. It was supported by the discoveries of fossils and dinosaur remains being unearthed at the time. His theory seemed substantiated by evidence of extinct and adapted animals found throughout the world.

2. A geometric progression increases more rapidly because it involves multiplying a number by a constant factor; an arithmetic progression is one in which the elements increase by a constant difference. Malthus theorized that populations grow geometrically, but certain factors limit this growth. Darwin realized that nature acts to limit population numbers.

3. Those fish which are genetically able to tolerate heat and cold will survive due to this adaptation. They will be the individuals most likely to reproduce and then the nature of the population as a whole will change. Natural selection is the mechanism whereby this is accomplished.

4. *Survival of the fittest* refers to the fact that natural selection tends to favor those organisms that are most fit to survive to reproductive age in a particular environment and produce offspring.

5. Polar bears are white because they live in the Arctic where there is snow year round. Thus their white color is an adaptation that camouflages them and has made them more fit to survive in this environment.

6. A phylogenetic tree diagrams the degree of relatedness among groups of organisms. Phylogenetic trees support evolution by showing the same evolutionary relationships revealed by anatomical studies.

7. Yes, humans are in the phylum Chordata. As with all chordates, our embryos exhibit a dorsal nerve cord, notocord, and bony gill arches. This indicates that genes used in the development of different species probably originated in a common ancestor. At some point in the distant past, our evolutionary paths diverged yet we retain some genes in common.

8. A warm blooded reptile may be seen as a "transitional form" in the evolution of mammals. Since such animals are extinct and fossil evidence remains of only a tiny fraction of species, the theory of dinosaur variation is difficult to approach. What we know must be extrapolated from very little empirical data on fossil remains.

9. These are all subclasses of mammals that are living today. Monotremes lay eggs with leathery shells and incubate them in a nest. Marsupials bear immature young and nurse them in a pouch until they are old enough to be on their own. In placental mammals, the young develop to maturity inside the mother.

10. Primates are the order of mammals with characteristics reflecting an arboreal life-style. They have developed two especially helpful characteristics: depth perception resulting from stereoscopic vision and flexible, grasping hands with opposable thumbs.

11. These are both suborders of the primates. Prosimians (lower primates such as lemurs) are small animals, usually nocturnal, with a well-developed sense of smell. Anthropoids (higher primates such as apes and humans) have larger brains, flatter faces, eyes that are closer together, and relatively long front and hind limbs. Anthropoids are also diurnal and possess color vision.

12. Early hominoid ancestors were arboreal and scientists think that some exhibited a preadaptation that enabled them to walk on two lower limbs while hanging onto three limbs with their arms. As the climate cooled and became more arid, those species exhibiting bipedalism would have been better able to survive and reproduce and hence were naturally selected for by climatic change.

13. *Australopithecus afarensis* is the oldest hominid fossil skeleton that has yet been found; it is not considered human. The first human fossils belong to the extinct species *Homo habilis,* which was more intelligent than its ancestors and able to make tools and clothing. The extinct species *Homo erectus* was close to modern human size, walked upright, and had a larger brain than its ancestors. Of the three, it is most like modern humans.

14. Early members of the species had smaller heads, brow ridges, teeth, jaws, and faces than earlier species did. They also fashioned sophisticated tools from stone and from other substances such as bone and ivory. Over time, groups of *Homo*

sapiens sapiens moved away from the hunter-gatherer life-style to develop agriculture, complex social structures, and civilization.

15. We know little about Neanderthal culture, but what we have found indicates a large-brained people capable of tool-making, community life, medical care, and ceremony indicative of belief in an afterlife. Their lack of evolutionary survival cannot yet be explained yet does not indicate a superiority or sophistication of the part of their contemporaries, the Cro-Magnons.

CHAPTER 25

1. Population ecologists study how populations grow and interact and demographers do statistical studies of such populations. The work of a population ecologist would probably include more variable data sources and subjective data than that of a demographer. The former studies interactions among populations whereas the latter mathematically assesses existing objective data concerning a population.

2. The population size is affected by immigration. The growth rate does not include factors of emigration and immigration.

3. Answers may vary. A possible scenario might be one that states that people live in desert areas, such as in Southern California, normally unable to support large human populations, because of technology that permits water storage and transport from outlying areas.

4. A large population is more likely to survive because it is less vulnerable to random events and natural disasters and because its size promotes genetic diversity.

5. Density refers to the number of organisms per unit of area; dispersion refers to the way in which the individuals of a population are arranged. If individuals are too far apart, they may not be able to reproduce. If population becomes too dense, however, factors can arise that limit the population's size (disease, predation, starvation).

6. The three patterns are (1) uniform (evenly spaced), (2) random, and (3) clumped (organisms are grouped in areas of the environment that have the necessary resources). Human populations are distributed in the clumped pattern.

7. Density-dependent limiting factors (such as competition) come into play when a population size is large, whereas density-independent factors (such as weather) operate regardless of population size.

8. See Figure 25-5. Type I is typical of organisms that tend to survive past their reproductive years (such as humans). Type II characterizes organisms that reproduce asexually and are equally likely to die at any age (such as the hydra). Type III is characteristic of organisms that produce offspring that must survive on their own and therefore die in large numbers when young (oysters).

9. Developing countries tend to have a population pyramid with a broad base, reflecting a rapidly growing population with large numbers of individuals entering their reproductive years. Industrialized countries tend to have populations with similar proportions of their populations in each age group and are growing slowly or not at all.

10. The human population is increasing much more steadily and dramatically among nations in tropical and subtropical regions such as Africa, South America, and Asia. The world population distribution is being dramatically altered.

11. The most effective means of limiting population growth has been human intervention as represented by encouraging smaller families, establishing family planning clinics, improving education, and aiding countries with low socioeconomic status in their development.

12. People are already putting pressure on our natural resources (land, water, forests, atmosphere). Increasing industrialization leads to rising levels of pollution and solid waste. Even though it is estimated that there is enough food produced to feed the world's population, many people live—and die—in poverty and hunger.

13. Answers will vary.

CHAPTER 26

1. The biosphere is the global ecosystem in which all other ecosystems on the Earth exist.

2. A sustainable society uses nonfinite, renewable sources of energy. Society's needs are satisfied without compromising future generations and natural resources.

3. People could use solar, wind, and water power, as well as the Earth's geothermal energy.

4. People can recycle glass and metal products to help preserve mineral resources. This is important because mineral supplies are finite; once used up, they are gone forever.

5. Tropical rainforests are home to over half the world's species of plants, animals, and insects from which people get many medicines as well as wood, charcoal, oils, and nuts. Burning the forests adds carbon dioxide to the air, which may raise temperatures worldwide. Destroying the forests also destroys the habitat for many species and leads to extinctions.

6. Global warming refers to a worldwide increase in temperature. Even a small increase in temperature could melt ice at the poles, raising the sea level, and flooding one fifth of the world's land area. Higher temperatures also affect rain patterns and agriculture.

7. Biological diversity refers to the richness of species. Humans are reducing the world's biological diversity through extinctions and selective breeding. Reducing diversity makes species more vulnerable to being wiped out by disease or environmental changes.

8. Humans can improve solid waste management by increasing and improving recycling, using safe incineration, engineering better landfill sites, and practicing waste-to-energy reclamation.

9. Point sources are sources of pollutants that enter the water at one or a few distinct places (industrial waste dumped by a specific factory). Nonpoint sources refer to pollutants that enter water at a variety of places (metals and acids draining from mines).

10. Organic nutrients are food for bacteria; as the bacteria multiply, they use up the oxygen in the water, killing the fish. Inorganic nutrients can stimulate plant growth in the water. Bacteria decompose the plants after they die; again, when the bacteria multiply, they consume the water's oxygen. The decomposed materials also begin to fill in the body of water, eventually turning it into a terrestrial community. Pollution with infectious agents can cause serious diseases. Toxic substances in water can poison the organisms that take in this water; sometimes organisms accumulate these substances in their bodies.

11. Acid rain results from gases such as sulfur dioxide and nitro-

gen dioxide that combine with water in the atmosphere. When this acidic rain falls, it kills aquatic life, pollutes groundwater, damages plants, and eats away at stone, metal, and painted surfaces.

12. Gray-air cities are those with relatively cold, moist climates. They develop a layer of smog because of the burning of fossil fuels and the abundance of sulfur oxides and particulates in the air. The air over brown-air cities contains hydrocarbons and nitrogen oxides that react with the sunny climate to produce secondary pollutants such as ozone.

13. Ozone in the stratosphere helps shield you from the sun's ultraviolet rays. Depletion of this layer can damage bacteria and plants and cause burns and skin cancers.

14. Answers will vary.

Glossary

acetyl-CoA
(ə sēt′ əl kō′ā) A compound combining the two-carbon acetyl fragment removed during the oxidation of pyruvate with the carrier molecule coenzyme A (CoA). p. 96

acetylcholine
(ə sēt′əl kō′lēn′) The neurotransmitter found at neuromuscular junctions that depolarizes the muscle cell membrane, releasing calcium ions that trigger muscle contraction. p. 214

acetylcholinesterase
(ə sēt′əl kō′lə nes′ +ə rās′) The enzyme that stops the action of acetylcholine; it is one of the fastest-acting enzymes in the blood. p. 214

acid
(as′əd) Any substance that dissociates to form H+ ions when it is dissolves in water. p. 33

acid rain
(as′əd rān) An acid precipitation that falls to the ground as rain, caused primarily by coal-fired plants' emission of sulfur dioxide and nitrogen dioxide, which then combines with water in the atmosphere; results in many devastating environmental effects. p. 518

acrosome
(ak′rə sōm) (Gr. akron, extremity + soma, body) A vesicle located at the tip of a sperm cell. p. 412

ACTH
(ā′sē′tē′āch′) See adrenocorticotropic hormone.

actin
(ak′tən) (Gr. actis, ray) A protein that makes up the thin myofilaments in a muscle fiber; provides support and helps determine cell shape and movement. p. 293

action potential
(ak′shən pəten′chəl) The rapid change in a membrane's electrical potential caused by the depolarization of a neuron to a certain threshold. p. 211

active immunity
(ak′tiv i myōon′ətē) A type of immunity conferred by vaccination, which causes your body to build up antibodies against a particular disease without getting the disease. p. 311

active site
(ak′tiv sīt) The grooved or furrowed location on the surface of an enzyme where catalysis occurs. p. 80

active transport
(ak′tiv trans′pôrt) The movement of a solute across a membrane against the concentration gradient with the expenditure of chemical energy. This process required the use of a transport protein specific to the molecule(s) being transported. p. 69

activator
(ak′tə vāt′ər) A chemical that binds to an enzyme and changes its shape so that catalysis can occur. p. 83

adaptation
(ad ap tā′ shən) (L. adaptare, to fit) A naturally occurring inherited trait found within a population that makes an individual better suited to a particular environment and produce more offspring than an individual lacking this trait. p. 469

adenine
(ad′ən ēn′) An organic compound that is one of the two purine bases of RNA and DNA. p. 47

adenosine diphosphate (ADP)
(ə den′ə sēn′ dī fos′fāt) The molecule remaining from the breaking off of a phosphate group when adenosine triphosphate is used to drive an endergonic reaction. p. 85

adenosine triphosphate (ATP)
(ə den′ə sēn′ trī fos′fāt) A molecule composed of three subunits: ribose, adenine, and a triphosphate group; ATP captures energy in its high-energy bonds and later releases this energy. ATP is used to fuel a variety of cell processes and is the universal energy currency of all cells. p. 84

ADP
(ā′ dē′ pē′) See adenosine diphosphate.

adrenal cortex
(ə drē′ nəl kôr′teks) (L. near, + ren, kidney; L. rind) The outer, yellowish portion of each adrenal gland that secretes a group of hormones known as corticosteroids in response to ACTH. p. 268

adrenal gland
(ə drē′nəl gland) (L. near, + ren, kidney) Either of two triangular glands, named for their position in the body, having two parts with two different functions, the adrenal cortex and the adrenal medulla. p. 268

adrenal medulla
(ə drē′nəl mə dul′ə) (L. near, + ren, kidney; L. marrow) The inner, reddish portion of each adrenal gland surrounded by the cortex that secretes the hormone adrenaline and noradrenaline, p. 268

adrenaline
(ə dren′əl ən) See epinephrine. p. 269

adrenocorticotropic hormone (ACTH)
(ə drē′ nō kôrt′ə kō träp′ik hôr′ mōn) (L. near, + ren, kidney + cortex, bark + Gr. tropikos, turning) A tropic hormone secreted by the anterior pituitary that triggers the adrenal cortex to produce certain steroid hormones. p. 263

aerobic
(er rō′bik) (Gr. aer, air + bios. life) Oxygen dependent. p. 90

aerobic respiration
(er rō′bik res′pə rā′shən) The process in which the original glucose molecule has been consumed entirely by the combined actions of glycolysis and the Krebs cycle. p. 100

afferent neuron
(af′ər ənt nōōr′on) See sensory neuron. p. 224

agranulocyte
(ā gran′yə lō sīt′) (Gr. a-, not + L. granulum, granule + Gr. kytos, cell) One of the two major groups of leukocytes; they have neither a cytoplasmic granule nor a lobed nuclei. p. 177

AIDS (acquired immune deficiency syndrome)
A disease transmitted by the exchange of body fluids (such as blood or semen) that are infected with the human immunodeficiency verus (HIV). This virus attacks and destroys T cells, a key component of the body's immune system. p. 449 The causative agent of genital herpes. p. 449

albumin
(al byōo′mən) (L. albumen, white of egg) A protein found in blood that serves to elevate the solute concentration of the blood to match that of the tissues so that the movement of water molecules is regulated. p. 69

aldosterone

(al dôs′tə rōn) A mineralocorticoid hormone produced by the adrenal cortex that regulates the level of sodium and potassium ions in the blood, thereby promoting the conservation of sodium and water and the excretion of potassium. p. 195

allantois

(ə lan′tō əs) (Gr. allas, sausage + eidos, form) An extraembryonic membrane that gives rise to the umbilical arteries and vein as the umbilical cord develops. p. 433

allele

(ə lēl′) (Gr. allelon, of one another) Each member of a factor pair containing information for an alternative form of a trait that occupy corresponding positions on paired chromosomes. p. 378

allergen

(al′ər jən) (Gr. allos, other + ergon, work) Any substance that causes manifestations of allergy. p. 313

all-or-nothing response

(ôl′ ôr′ nuth′ing) Refers to the nerve impulse response; the amount of stimulation applied to the receptor or neuron must always be sufficient to open enough sodium channels to generate an action potential; otherwise, the cell membrane will simply return to the resting potential. p. 211

alveolus, pl. alveoli

(al vē′ə ləs, al vē′ əlī). (L. a small cavity) Microscopic air sacs in the lungs where oxygen enters the blood and carbon dioxide leaves. p. 150

amino acid

(ə mē′ nō as′əd) (Gr. Ammon, referring to the Egyptian sun god, near whose temple ammonium salts were first prepared from camel dung) A molecule containing an amino acid group ($-NH_2$), a carboxyl group ($-COOH$), a hydrogen atom, a carbon atom, and a functional group that differs among amino acids; an extremely diverse array of proteins is made from the 20 common amino acids. p. 42

amniocentesis

(am′nē ō sen tē′səs) (Gr. amnion, membrane around the fetus + centes, puncture) A prenatal diagnostic procedure in which a sampling of amniotic fluid is obtained by insertion of a needle into the amniotic cavity and withdrawn into a syringe; the removed fetal cells are then grown in tissue culture and tests are performed to determine if genetic abnormalities are present. p. 401

amnion

(am′nē ən) (Gr. membrane around the fetus) A thin, protective membrane that grows around the embryo during the third and fourth weeks, fully enclosing the embryo in the membranous sac. p. 433

amniotic egg

(am′nē ot′ik eg) (Gr. membrane around the fetus) An egg, characteristic of reptiles, birds, and monotremes, which protects the embryo from drying out, nourishes it, and enables it to develop outside of water. p. 476

amniotic fluid

(am′nē ot′ik floo′əd) (Gr. membrane around the fetus) A fluid in which the fetus floats and moves; it also helps keep the temperature constant for fetal development. p. 433

amphibian

(am fib′ē ən) (Gr. amphibios, double life) An animal capable of living on land and in the water. p. 476

amylase

(am′ə lās) (Gr. amylon, starch + asis, colloid enzyme) An enzyme that breaks down starches and glycogen to sugars. p. 132

anaerobic

(an′er ō′bik) (Gr. an, without + aer, air + bios, life) Literally, without oxygen; any process that can occur without oxygen; includes glycolysis and fermentation. p. 91

analogous

(ə nal′ə gəs) (Gr. proportional) Describes a part or organ of an organism that has a similar form and function but possess different evolutionary origins. p. 470

anaphase

(an′ə fāz) (Gr. ana, up + phasis, form) The stage of mitosis characterized by the physical separation of sister chromatids and their movement to opposite poles of the cell. p. 343

antagonists

(an tag′ə nəsts) (Gr. antagonizesthai, to struggle against) An opposing pair of skeletal muscles. p. 291

anthropoid

(an′thrə poid) (Gr. anthropos, man + eidos, form) A suborder of mammals that includes monkeys, apes, gorillas, chimpanzees, and humans; they differ from prosimians in the structure of the teeth, brain, skull, and limbs; they are diurnal, live in groups with complex social interactions, and care for their young for prolonged periods. p. 480

antibody

(ant′i bäd′ē) (Gr. anti, against) A protein produced in the blood by a B lymphocyte that specifically binds circulating antigen and marks cells or viruses bearing antigens for destruction. p. 304

anticodon

(ant′i kō′don) (Gr. anti, against + L. code) A portion of a tRNA molecule with a sequence of three base pairs complementary to a specific mRNA codon. p. 337

antidiuretic hormone (ADH)

(ant′i dī yoo ret′ik hôr′mōn) (Gr. anti, against + dia, intensive +o ouresis, urination) A hormone produced by the hypothalamus but stored and released by the posterior lobe of the pituitary that helps control the volume of the blood by regulating the amount of water reabsorbed by the kidneys. p. 195

antigen

(ant′i jən) (Gr. anti, against + genos, origin) A foreign substance inducing the formation of antibodies that specifically bind to the foreign substance, marking it for destruction. p. 304

anus

(ā′nəs) The opening of the rectum for the elimination of feces. p. 143

aorta

(ā ôrt′ə) (Gr. aeirein, to lift) The largest artery in the body, it carries the blood from the left side of the heart throughout the body except the lungs. p. 171

aortic semilunar valve

(ā ôrt′ik sem′i loo′nər valv′) A one-way valve that permits blood flow from the left side of the heart and then snaps shut, preventing a backflow from the aorta to the heart. p. 171

appendicular skeleton

(ap′ən dik′yə lər skel′ə tən) (L. appendicula, a small appendage) The portion of the human skeleton, containing 126 bones, that consists of the bones of the appendages (arms and legs) and the bones that help attach the appendages to the axial skeleton. p. 285

appendix

(ə pen′diks) (L. appendere, to hang) A pouch that hangs from the beginning of the large intestine and serves no essential purpose in humans. p. 143

aqueous humor

(ăk′wē əs hyoo′mər) (L. aqua, water + humor, fluid) A watery fluid filling a chamber behind the cornea that nourishes the cornea and the lens and, together with vitreous, creates a pressure within the eyeball maintaining the eyeball's shape. p. 248

arteriole

(är tir′ē ōl) A smaller artery that leads from an artery to a capillary. p. 167

artery, pl. arteries

(ärt′ə rē, ärt′ə rēz) (Gr. arteria, artery) A blood vessel that carries blood away from the heart and through the body. p. 167

articulation
(är tik′yə lā′shən) *See* joint.

artificial selection
(ärt′ə fish′əl sə lek′shən) The process of selecting organisms for a desirable characteristic and then breeding that organism with another organism exhibiting the same trait. p. 468

asexual reproduction
(ā′seksh′ə wəl *or* ā′sek′shəl rē′prə duk′shən) A type of reproduction in which a parent organism divides by mitosis and produces two identical organisms; does not introduce variation. p. 340

association area
(ə sō′sē ā′shən er′ē ə) The area in the brain that connects all parts of the cerebral cortex and appears to be the site of higher cognitive activities such as memory, reasoning, intelligence, and personality. p. 228

aster
(as′tər) In animal mitosis, an array of microtubules that radiates outward from the centrioles when the centrioles reach the poles of the cell. p. 343

atherosclerosis
(ath′ə rō sklə rō′səs) (Gr. athere, porridge + sklerosis, hardness) A disease in which the inner walls of the arteries accumulate fat deposits, narrowing the passageways and leading to elevated systolic blood pressure. p. 175

atom
(at′əm) (Gr. atomos, indivisible) A core (nucleus) of protons and neutrons surrounded by orbiting electrons. The electrons largely determine the chemical properties of an atom. p. 24

atomic mass
(ə täm′ik mas) The combined mass of all the protons and neutrons of an atom without regard to its electrons. p. 24

atomic number
(ə täm′ik num′bər) The number of protons in an atom; the atomic number is also the same as the number of electrons in that atom. p. 24

ATP
(ā′tē′pē′) *See* adenosine triphosphate.

atrioventricular (AV) node
(ā′trē ō ven trik′yə lər nōd) A group of specialized cardiac muscle cells that receives the impulse initiated by the sinoatrial node and conducts them by way of the bundle of His. p. 174

atrium, pl. atria
(ā′trē əm, ā′trē ə) (L. main room) The upper chamber of each half of the heart; the right atrium receives deoxygenated blood from the body (except the lungs), and the left atrium receives oxygenated blood from the lungs through the pulmonary veins. p. 171

auditory canal
(ôd′ə tōr′ē kə nal′) (L. audire, to hear) A 1-inch long canal that receives sound waves and leads directly to the eardrum. p. 280

autonomic nervous system
(ô′tə nom′ik nurv′əs sis′təm) (Gr. autos, self + nomos, law) A branch of the peripheral nervous system consisting of motor neurons that control the involuntary and automatic responses of the glands and the nonskeletal muscles of the body. p. 225

autosome
(ô′tə sōm′) (Gr. autos, self + soma, body) Any of the 22 pairs of human chromosomes that carry the majority of the genetic information but have no genes that determine gender. p. 390

AV node
(ā′vē′ nōd′) *See* atrioventricular (AV) node.

axial skeleton
(ak′sē əl skel′ə tən) The central axis of the human skeleton, consisting of 80 bones, that includes the skull, vertebral column, and rib cage. p. 285

axon
(ak′son) (Gr. axle) A single projection extending from a neuron that conducts impulses away from the cell body. p. 118

B lymphocyte (B cell)
(bē′ lim′fə sīt′) A type of lymphocyte that matures in human bone marrow and secretes antibodies during the humoral immune response; named after a digestive organ in birds (the bursa of Fabricius) in which these lymphocytes were discovered. p. 308

bacteriophage (phage)
(bak tir′ē o fāj) (Gr. baktereion, little rod + phagein, to eat) A virus that infects a bacterial cell. p. 448

bacterium, pl. bacteria
(bak tir′ē əm, bak tir′ē ə) (Gr. bakterion, a little rod) The oldest, simplest, and most abundant organism; it is the only organism with a prokaryotic cellular organization. p. 52

basal body
(bā′ səl bäd′ē) A structure composed of microtubules that serves to anchor a cilium or flagellum to the cell. p. 65

basal ganglion, pl. ganglia or ganglions
(bā′səl gang′ glē ən, gang′glē ə *or* gang′glē ənz) Groups of nerve cell bodies located at the base of the cerebrum that control large, subconscious movements of the skeletal muscles, p. 229

base
(bās) Any substance that combines with H+ ions; a substance that has a pH value higher than water's neutral value of 7. p. 33

basophil
(bā′sə fil) (Gr. basis, base + philein, to love) A type of granulocyte containing granules that rupture and release chemicals enhancing the body's response to injury or infection; they also play a role in causing allergic responses. p. 178

benign tumor
(bē′ nīn) (L. benignus, favorable) Masses of cells that are made up of partially transformed cells, are confined to one location, and are encapsulated. p. 358

bile
(bīl) (L. bilis) A collection of molecules secreted by the liver than helps in the digestion of lipids. p. 138

binomial nomenclature
(bī nō′mē əl nməno′ klā′chər or nō men′klə chər) (L. bi, twice, + Gr. nomos, law; L. nomen, name + calare, to call) The system of using the last two categories in the hierarchy of classification, genus and species, to provide the scientific name of an organism, usually written in Latin. p. 15

biosphere
(bī′ə sfir) (Gr. bios, life + sphaira, ball) The global ecosystem of life on Earth that extends from the tops of the tallest mountains to the depths of the deepest seas. p. 508

blastocyst
(blas′tə sist) (Gr. blastos, germ + kytos, cell) The stage of development following the morula in which the embryo is a hollow ball of cells. p. 430

blastula
(blas′chə lə) (Gr. a little sprout) The general term used to describe the sac-like blastocyst of mammals and, in other animals, the stage that develops a similar fluid-filled cavity. p. 430

blood pressure
(blud presh′ər) The pressure, determined indirectly, existing in the large arteries at the height of the pulse wave; the systolic intraarterial pressure; normal blood pressures values are 70 to 90 (mm of Hg) diastolic and 110 to 130 systolic. p. 175

bone
(bōn) (A.S. ban, bone) A hard material that forms the vertebrate skeleton; composed of collagen fibers that contribute flexibility and needle-shaped crystals of calcium that impart rigidity. p. 283

Bowman's capsule
(bō′mənz kap′səl *or* kap′sool) (after Sir William Bowman, British physician) An apparatus at the front end of each nephron tube in a kidney that functions

as a filter in the formation of urine. p. 188

brain
(brān) That part of the central nervous system comprised of four main parts: the cerebrum, the cerebellum, the diencephalon, and the brainstem. p. 206

brainstem
(brān'stem) The part of the brain consisting of the midbrain, pons, and medulla that brings messages to and from the spinal cord and controls important body reflexes such as the rhythm of the heartbeat and rate of breathing. p. 226

bronchiole
(brong'kē ōl) L. bronchiolus, air passage) The last division of bronchi, having thousands of tiny air passageways, whose walls have clusters of tiny pouches, or alveoli. p. 152

bronchus, pl. bronchi
(brong'kəs, brong'kī) (Gr. bronchos, windpipe) One of a pair of airway structures that branches from the lower end of the trachea into each lung. p. 152

bulbourethral glands
(bul'bō yoo rē'thrəl glandz) (L. bulbus, bulbous root + Gr. ourethra, urethra) A set of tiny accessory glands lying beneath the prostate that secretes an alkaline fluid into the semen. p. 413

bundle of His
(bun'dəl uv his) (after Wilhelm His, Jr, German physician) A strand of impulse-conducting muscle that conducts heartbeat impulses from the right atrium to the ventricles of the heart. p. 174

calcitonin (CT)
(kal'sə tō'nən) (L. calcem, lime) A hormone secreted by the thyroid that works with parathyroid hormone to regulate the concentration of calcium in the bloodstream. p. 265

calorie
(kal'ə rē) (L. calor, heat) The measurement of the unit of energy in food. p. 130

capillary
(kap'ə ler'ē) (L. capillaris, hair-like) A microscopic blood vessel with a wall only one cell thick that connects the end of an arteriole with the beginning of a venule; the site where gases are exchanged between the blood and tissues, nutrients delivered, and wastes picked up. p. 167

capsid
(kap' sid) (L. capsa, box) A protein covering over the nucleic acid core of a virus. p. 447

carbohydrate
(kär'bō hī'drāt) (L. carbo, charcoal + hydro, water) A molecule that contains carbon, hydrogen, and oxygen, with the concentration of hydrogen and oxygen atoms in a 2:1 ratio. p. 37

carcinogen
(kär sin'ə jən) (Gr. karkinos, cancer + -gen) Any cancer-causing agent. p. 355

cardiac muscle
(kärd'ē ak' mus'əl) A type of striated muscle fiber arranged in a special way critical for cardiac function; cardiac muscle makes up the heart, acting as a pump for the circulatory system. p. 117

carnivore
(kär'nə vôr) (L. carnivorous, flesh eating) An animal that eats meat. p. 133

carpal
(kär'pəl) (Gr. karpos, wrist) Any of the eight short bones, lined up in two rows of four, that make up the wrist. p. 287

carrying capacity
(ker'ē'ing kə pas'ət ē) The number of individuals within a population that can be supported within a particular environment for an indefinite period. p. 496

cartilage
(kärt'əl ij or kärt'lij) (L. cartilago, gristle) A specialized connective tissue that is hard and strong; composed of chondrocytes that secret a matrix consisting of a semisolid gel and fibers. Laid down in long parallel arrays, the result is a firm and flexible tissue that does not stretch. p. 114

catabolic
(kat'ə bäl'ik) (Gr. katabole, throwing down) Referring to a process in which complex molecules are broken down into simpler ones. p. 76

catalyst
(kat'əl əst) (Gr. kata, down + lysis, a loosening) A substance that increases the rate of a chemical reaction but is not chemically changed by the reaction; an enzyme is a catalyst. p. 80

cell
(sel') (L. cella, a chamber or small room) A membrane-bounded unit containing hereditary material, cytoplasm, and organelles; a cell can release energy from fuel and use that energy to grow and reproduce. p. 54

cell body
(sel bäd'ē) The body of a nerve cell or neuron, which contains a nucleus and other cell organelles and two types of cellular projections, axons and dendrites. p. 207

cell cycle
(sel sī'kəl) The life of a cell; the major portion concerned with the activities of interphase and the minority portion with mitosis. p. 341

cell-mediated immune response
(sel' mēd'ē āt'əd ri spons') A chain of events unleashed by T cells during which cytotoxic T cells attack infected body cells. p. 307

cell membrane
(sel' mem'brān') A bilayer of phospholipid molecules studded with proteins to which carbohydrates are attached. The membrane proteins allow the cell to interact with the environment and perform various cellular functions. p. 56

cell theory
(sel' thē'ə rē or thir'ē) A statement first formulated in the mid-1800s, which states that all living things are made up of cells, that cells are the smallest living units of life, and that all cells arise from preexisting cells. p. 52

cell wall
(sel' wôl) The structure that surrounds the plasma membrane in cells. In many plants, algae, and fungi the wall is rigid and composed of cellulose and imparts a stiffness to the tissues; in single-celled organisms, cell walls give shape to the organisms and help protect them. p. 66

cellular respiration
(sel'yə lər res'pə rā'shən) The complex series of chemical reactions—glycolysis, the Krebs cycle, and the electron transport chain—by which cells break down fuel molecules to release energy, using oxygen and producing carbon dioxide. p. 63

central nervous system
(sen'trəl nur'vəs sis'təm) The site of information processing within the nervous system, comprising the brain and spinal cord. p. 224

centriole
(sen'trē ōl) (Gr. kentron, center of a circle + L. olus, little one) An organelle surrounded by microtubule-organizing centers that play a key role in the mitotic process; most plants and fungi lack centrioles. p. 341

centromere
(sen'trə mir) (Gr. kentron, center + meros, a part) A constricted region of the chromosome where two identical structures (sister chromatids) are joined. p. 345

cerebellum
(ser'ə bel'əm) (L. little brain) The part of the brain located below the occipital lobes of the cerebrum that coordinates subconscious movements of the skeletal muscles. p.226

cerebral cortex
(sə rē'brəl kôr'teks) The thin layer of tissue, gray matter, that forms the outer layer of the cerebrum; the major site of higher cognitive processes such as sense perception, thinking, learning, and memory. p. 226

cerebrospinal fluid
(sə rē′brō spī′nəl floo′əd) A liquid that cushions the brain and the spinal cord, acting like a shock absorber. p. 232

cerebrum
(sə rē′brəm) (L. brain) The largest and most dominant part of the human brain, divided into two hemispheres connected by the corpus callosum. p. 226

cervix
(sur′viks) (L. neck) The narrower part of the uterus that opens into the vagina. p. 418

chiasma, pl. chiasmata
(kī az′mə, kī az′mə tə) (Gr. a cross) In meiosis, the point of crossing over where parts of chromosomes have been exchanged during synapsis; under a light microscope, a chiasma appears as an X-shaped structure. p. 345

chitin
(kīt′ən) (Gr. chiton, tunic) A modified form of cellulose, relatively indigestible, that is the structural material in insects and many fungi. p. 39

chlamydial sexually transmitted infection
(klah mid′ē al) (Gr. cloak) An infection caused by the bacterium *Chlamydia trachomatis* that has gonorrhea-like symptoms. p. 454

chloroplast
(klôr′ə plast) Gr. chloros, green + plastos, molded) An energy-producing organelle found in the cells of plants and algae; the site of photosynthesis in plants. p. 64

cholecystokinin (CCK)
(kol′ə sis′tə kī′nən) (Gr. chole, bile + kystis, bladder + kinein, to move) A hormone that helps control digestion in the small intestine. p. 140

chondrocyte
(kon′drə sīt) (Gr. chondros, cartilage + kytos, cell) A cell that produces cartilage, a specialized connective tissue that is hard and strong. p. 111

chordate
(kôr′dāt) (Gr. chorde, cord) An organism distinguished by three principal features: a nerve cord, a notochord, and pharyngeal slits; includes fishes, amphibians, reptiles, birds, mammals, and humans. p. 474

chorion
(kôr′ə on) A extraembryonic membrane that facilitates the transfer of nutrients, gases, and wastes between the embryo and the mother's body. p. 433

choroid
(kôr′oid′) (Gr. chorioeides, skin-like) A thin, dark-brown membrane that lines the sclera, containing blood-carrying vessels that nourish the retina and a dark pigment that absorbs light rays so that

they will not be reflected within the eyeball. p. 249

chromatin
(krō′mə tən) (Gr. chroma, color) The complex of proteins and the hereditary material, DNA, which make up the chromosomes of eukaryotes. p. 324

chromosome
(krō′mə sōm′) (Gr. chroma, color + soma, body) A discrete, thread-like body that forms as the nuclear material condenses during meiosis and that carries genetic information. p. 62

chyme
(kīm) (Gr. chymos, juice) The mixture of partly digested food, gastric juice, and mucus, having the consistency of pea soup, found in the stomach during digestion. p. 138

ciliary muscle
(sil′ē er′ē mus′əl) (L. ciliaris, pert. to eyelid) A tiny circular muscle that slightly changes the shape of the lens by contracting or relaxing. p. 248

cilium, pl. cilia
(sil′ē əm, sil′ē ə) (L. eyelash) A whip-like organelle of motility that protrudes from some eukaryotic cells. p. 64

citric acid cycle
(sit′rək as′əd sī′kəl) *See* Krebs cycle. p. 92

cleavage
(klē′vij) The process of cell division that occurs without cell growth. p. 95

cleavage furrow
(klē′vij fur′ō) During cytokinesis in animal cells, the area where a belt of microfilaments pinches the cell at the metaphase plate. p. 344

clitoris
(klit′ə rəs) (Gr. kleitoris) A small mass of erectile and nervous tissue in the female genitalia that responds to sexual stimulation; it is homologous to the tip of the penis in males. p. 419

clone
(klōn) (Gr. klon, a cutting used for propagation) A group of identical cells that arises by repeated mitotic divisions from one original cell. p. 308

cochlea
(kok′lē ə) (Gr. kokhlos, land snail) A winding, cone-shaped tube forming a portion of the inner ear that contains the organ of Corti, the organ of hearing. p. 250

cochlear duct
(kok′lē ər dukt) The inner tube of the cochlea containing specialized cells that are the receptors of hearing. p. 251

codominant
(kō′ däm′ə nənt) Refers to traits in

which the alternative forms of an allele are both dominant. p. 399

codon
(kōdän) (L. code) A sequence of three nucleotide bases in transcribed mRNA that code for an amino acid, which is the building block of a polypeptide. p. 335

coelom
(sē′ləm) (Gr. koilos, a hollow) A body cavity that is a fluid-filled enclosure within a bilaterally symmetrical organism. p. 108

coenzyme
(kō′en′zīm) (L. co-, together + Gr. en, in + zyme, leaven) A cofactor that is a nonprotein organic (carbon-containing) molecule helping an enzyme catalyze a chemical reaction. p. 84

cofactor
(kō′fak′tər) A special nonprotein molecule that helps an enzyme catalyze a chemical reaction. p. 84

collagen
(käl′ə jən) (Gr. kolla, glue + gennan, to produce) The most abundant protein in the human body, whose fibers are strong and wavy; found in the connective tissue of skin, bone, and cartilage. p. 42

collecting duct
(kə lek′ting dukt) A small duct that receives urine from the kidney nephrons. p. 188

colon
(kō′lən) (Gr. kolon) The large intestine from the small intestine to the rectum; its function is to absorb sodium and water, to eliminate wastes, and to provide a home for friendly bacteria. p. 142

communicable
(kom yun′i kabl) Able to be spread from one individual to another. p. 446

compact bone
(käm′pakt′ bōn) A type of bone in the human skeleton that runs the length of long bones and has no spaces within its structure visible to the naked eye; it is hard and dense, which gives the bone the strength to withstand mechanical stress. p. 114

competition
(käm′pə tish′ən) The striving by organisms of different species that live near one another to obtain the same limited resources. p. 497

complement
(käm′plə mənt) A group of proteins that kill foreign cells by creating a hole in their membranes. p. 309

compound
(käm′pound′) A molecule made up of the atoms of two or more elements. p. 26

cone
(kōn) A light receptor located within the retina at the back of the eye that functions in bright light and detects color. p. 246

connective tissue
(kə nek′tiv tish′ōō) A collection of tissues and its cells that provides a framework for the body, joins its tissues, helps defend it from foreign invaders, and acts as storage sites for specific substances. p. 110

consumer
(kən sōōm′ər) An organism in an ecosystem that feeds on producers and other consumers, passing energy along that was once captured from the sun. p. 12

contagious
(kon tā′jus) Able to be spread from one person to another; communicable. p. 446

control
(kən trōl′) In a scientific experiment, a standard against which observations or conclusions may be checked to establish their validity. p. 5

cornea
(kôr′nē ə) (L. corneus, horny) The transparent portion of the eye's outer layer that permits light to enter the eye. p. 248

corpus callosum
(kôr′pəs kə lō′sm̄) (N.L. callous body) The single, thick bundle of nerve fibers that connects the two hemispheres of the cerebrum in humans and primates. p. 226

corpus luteum
(kôr′pəs lōō′tē əm) (N.L. yellow body) A structure that emerges from a ruptured follicle in the ovary after ovulation; it secretes increased estrogen and progesterone, preparing the endometrium for the implantation of the fertilized egg. p. 416

cortex
(kôr′teks) (L. rind, bark) (1) The outer layer of an organ as distinguished from the inner, as in the cerebral cortex. (2) The outer superficial portion of the root of a vascular plant. p. 188

coupled channel
(kup′əld chan′əl) A type of channel that has binding sites on one membrane transport protein for both sodium (Na+) and potassium (K+) ions, which are transported across the cell membrane in opposite directions. p. 70

coupled reaction
(kup′əld rē ak′shən) A reaction in which the energy released in an exergonic reaction is used to drive an endergonic reaction. p. 76

covalent bond
(kō vā′lənt bänd) (L. co-, together + valare, to be strong) A chemical bond created by atoms sharing one or more pairs of electrons. p. 26

cranial nerves
(krā′nē əl nurvz) (Gr. kranion, skull) Any of the twelve pairs of nerves that enter the brain through the holes in the skull. p. 234

creatinine
(krē at′ə nēn) (Gr. kreas, flesh) A nitrogenous waste found in urine, derived primarily from creatinine found in muscle cells. p. 187

cri du chat syndrome
(krē dōō shä sin′drōm) A congenital disorder so named because the infant's cry resembles that of a cat; other symptoms include severe mental retardation and a moon face; caused by a deletion located on one of the 5 chromosomes. p. 393

crista, pl. cristae
(kris′tə, kris′tē) (L. crest) The enfoldings of the inner membrane of a mitochondrion. p. 63

Cro-Magnon
(krō mag′nən) (after a cave in southwestern France) An early member of *H. sapiens sapiens* whose anatomical features were more similar to modern humans; they used sophisticated tools, hunted, and made elaborate cave paintings of animals and hunt scenes. p. 488

crossing over
(krôs′ing ō′vər) An essential element of meiosis, which produces sister chromatids that are not identical with each other, resulting in new combinations of genes. p. 345

cuboidal
(kyōō boid′əl) (Gr. kubos, cube, + eidos, form) One of the main shapes of epithelial cells. Cuboidal cells have complex shapes but look like cubes when the tissue is cut at right angles to the surface; found lining tubules in the kidney and the ducts of glands. p. 109

cyclic adenosine monophosphate
(sī′klik *or* sik′lik əden′ə sēn′ mon′ə fos′fāt) A cousin of ATP that triggers enzymes causing a cell to alter its functioning in response to a hormone. p. 260

cystic fibrosis
(sis′tik fī brō′səs) (Gr. kystis, bladder + L. fibra, fiber + osis, condition) The most common fatal genetic disease of Caucasians in which affected individuals secrete a thick mucus that clogs the airways of the lungs and the passages of the pancreas and liver. p. 398

cytokinesis
(sī′tō kə nē′səs) (Gr. kytos, hollow vessel + kinesis, movement) The physical division of the cytoplasm of a eukaryotic cell into two daughter cells. p. 344

cytoplasm
(sī′tə plaz′əm) (Gr. kytos, hollow vessel + plasma, anything molded) The viscous or gel-like fluid within a cell that contains storage substances, a network of interconnected filaments and fibers, and cell organelles. p 56

cytoskeleton
(sī′tō skel′ə tən) (Gr. kytos, hollow vessel + skeleton, a dried body) A network of filaments and fibers within the cytoplasm that helps maintain the shape of the cell, move substances within cells, and anchor various structures in place. p. 55

cytotoxic T cell
(sī′tə tôk′sik tē sel) (Gr. kytos, cell + toxikon, poison) A type of T cell that breaks apart cells infected by viruses and foreign cells such as incompatible organ transplants. p. 222

deamination
(dē am′ə nā′shən) The process in which an amino compound loses a (−NH₂) group; takes place in the human liver. p. 187

decomposer
(dē′kəm pō′zər) An organism in an ecosystem that breaks down organic molecules of dead organisms and contributes to the recycling of nutrients to the environment. p. 12

dehydration synthesis
(dē′hī drā′shən sin′thə səs) The process by which monomers are put together to form polymers. p. 35

deletion
(dē lē′shən) Refers to an abnormally short chromosome that has lost a chromosomal section. p. 393

dendrite
(den′drīt) (Gr. dendron, tree) A projection extending from a neuron that acts as an antenna for the reception of nerve impulses and conducts these impulses toward the cell body. p. 118

density
(den′sə tē) The number of organisms or individuals in a population per unit of area. p. 496

deoxyribonucleic acid (DNA)
(de ok′sə rī′bō nōō klē′ik as′əd) A nucleic acid present in the chromosomes that is the chemical basis of heredity and the carrier of genetic information; arranged as two long chains that twist around each other to form a double helix. p. 61

depolarization
(dē pō′lə rə zā′shən) The change in electrical potential of a receptor cell or nerve cell membrane. p. 210

diabetes
(dī′ə bēt′ēz *or* dī′ə bēt′əs) (Gr. passing through) A set of disorders characterized by a high level of glucose in the blood, the underlying cause being the lack or partial lack of insulin; in type I or juvenile onset diabetes, a person has no effective insulin; in type II or maturity onset diabetes, a person has some effective insulin but not enough to meet body needs. p. 270

dialysis
(dī al′ə səs) (Gr. dia, through + lysis, dissolution) The filtering of blood through a selectively permeable membrane to remove toxic wastes, regulate blood pH, and regulate ion concentration; used in renal failure. p. 197

diastolic period
(dīə stol′ik pir′ē əd) (Gr. diastole, expansion) The period during the first part of a heartbeat when the atria are filling; at this time the pressure in the arteries leading from the left side of the heart to the tissues of the body decreases slightly as the blood moves out of the arteries, through the vascular system, and into the atria. p. 174

diatomic molecule
(dī′ə tom′ik môl′ə kyōol′) A molecule having two atoms. p. 28

diencephalon
(dī′ən sef′ə lôn) (Gr. dia, between + enkephalon, within the head) The part of the brain consisting of the thalamus and hypothalamus. p. 226

diffusion
(di fyōo′zhən) (L. diffundere, to pour out) The net movement of molecules from a region of higher concentration to a region of lower concentration, eventually resulting in a uniform distribution of the molecules. This movement is the result of random, spontaneous molecular motions. p. 67

dihybrid
(dī hī′brəd) (Gr. dis, twice + L. hybrida, mongrel) The product of two plants that differ from one another in two traits. p. 381

diploid
(dip′loid) (Gr. diploos, double + eidos, form) A cell that contains double the haploid amount; a double set of the genetic information. p. 339

disaccharide
(dī sak′ə rīd) (Gr. dis, twice + sakcharon, sugar) Two monosaccharides linked together; sucrose (table sugar) is a disaccharide formed by linking a

molecule of glucose to a molecule of fructose. p. 37

distal convoluted tubule
(dis′təl kôn′və lōo′təd tōo′byōol) The portion of the kidney tubule whose walls are permeable to water. p. 192

DNA
(dē′ en′ ā) *See* deoxyribonucleic acid.

dominant
(dôm′ə nənt) The form of a trait that will be expressed in a hybrid offspring. p. 375

Down syndrome
(doun sin′drōm) (after J. Langdon Down, British physician) A genetic disorder produced when an individual receives three (instead of two) 21 chromosomes; also called trisomy 21. p. 390

duodenum
(dōo′ə dē′nəm *or* dōo äd′ən əm) (L. duodeni, twelve each; with reference to its length, about twelve finger breadths) The initial, short segment of the small intestine that is actively involved in digestion. p. 138

duplication
(dōo′ pli kā′shən) A chromosomal abnormality in which a section of a chromosome has been duplicated; in a karyotype, the duplicated chromosome appears longer than its homologue. p. 393

ectoderm
(ek′tə durm′) (Gr. ectos, outside + derma, skin) The outer layer of cells formed during the development of embryos; forms the outer layer of skin, the nervous system, and portions of the sense organs. p. 432

effector
(i fek′tər) A muscle or gland that effects (or causes) responses when stimulated by nerves. p. 213

efferent neuron
(ef′ər ənt nōor′on) *See* motor neuron. p. 224

electrocardiogram (ECG)
(i lek′trō kärd′ē əgram′) (Gr. elektron, amber + kardia, heart + -gram, written) A recording of the electrical impulses initiated at the SA node as they pass throughout the heart as an electric current and then as a wave throughout the body. p. 175

electron
(i lek′tron) A subatomic particle, having very little mass and carrying a negative charge, that orbits the nucleus of an atom. p. 24

electron-transport chain
(i lek′tron trans′pōrt chān) A term that describes the membrane-associated electron carriers produced by the citric

acid cycle; the electrons gleaned from the oxidation of glucose then work as proton pumps. p. 91

element
(el′ə mənt) A pure substance that is made up of a single kind of atom and that cannot be separated into different substances by ordinary chemical methods. p. 26

elementary bodies
The infective form of chlamydiae, which are metabolically inactive, small, dense bodies with rigid cell walls. p. 456

elimination
(i lim′ə nā′shən) A process that takes place as digestive wastes leave the body during defecation. p. 186

embryo
(em′brē ō′) (Gr. embryon, something that swells in the body) The early stage of development in humans between the second and eighth weeks. p. 434

endergonic
(en′dər gôn′ik) (Gr. endon, within + ergos, work) Used to describe a reaction in which the products of the reaction contain more energy than the reactants, so the extra energy must be supplied for the reaction to proceed. p. 76

endocrine gland
(en′də krən gland) (Gr. endon, within + krinein, to separate) A ductless gland that secretes hormones and spills these chemicals directly into the bloodstream. p. 206

endocrine system
(en′də krən sis′təm) (Gr. endon, within + krinein, to separate) The collective term for the 10 different endocrine glands that secrete 30 different hormones. p. 259

endocytosis
(en′dō sī tō′ səs) (Gr. endon, within + kytos, cell) A process in which cells engulf large molecules or particles and bring these substances into the cell packaged within vesicles. p. 70

endoderm
(en′dō durm′) (Gr. endon, within + derma, skin) The inner layer of cells formed during the early development of embryos; it gives rise to the digestive tract lining, the digestive organs, the respiratory tract, the lungs, the urinary bladder, and the urethra. p. 432

endometrium
(en′dō mē′trē əm) (Gr. endon, within + metrios, of the womb) The inner lining of the uterus, which has two layers. p. 416

endoplasmic reticulum
(en′dō plaz′mik ri tik′yə ləm) (Gr. endon, within + plasma, from cytoplasm; L. reticulum, network) An

extensive system of membranes that divides the interior of eukaryotic cells into compartments and channels. p. 59

endosymbiont
(en′dō sim′bī änt) (Gr. endon, within + bios, life) An organism that is symbiotic within another; the major endosymbionts that occur in eukaryotic cells are mitochondria and chloroplasts. p. 55

endosymbiotic theory
(en′dō sim′bē ôt′ik thir′ē). (Gr. endon, within + bios, life) The idea that mitochondria and chloroplasts originated symbiotically, mitochondria from aerobic bacteria and chloroplasts from anaerobic bacteria. p. 474

end-product inhibition
(end prôd′ə kt in′ə bish′ən) The process in which the enzyme catalyzing the first step in a series of chemical reactions has an inhibitor binding site to which the end product of the pathway binds. As the concentration of the end product builds up in the cell, it begins to bind to the first enzyme in the metabolic pathway, shutting off that enzyme. In this way, the end product is feeding information back to the first enzyme in the pathway, shutting the pathway down when additional end product is not needed. p. 84

energy level
(en′ər jē lev′əl) An electron shell that surrounds the nucleus of an atom. p. 26

entropy
(en′trə pē) (Gr. en, in + tropos, change in manner) The energy lost to disorder; it is a measure of the disorder of a system p. 79

environment
(in vī′rən mənt) (M.E. environen, encircle) A general term for the biosphere; the land, air, water, and every living thing on the Earth. p. 508

enzyme
(en′zīm) (Gr. enzymos, leavened, from en, in + zyme, leaven) A protein that lowers the free energy of activation, thus allowing chemical reactions to take place. p. 42

eosinophil
(ē′ə sin′ə fil) (Gr. eos, dawn (rose-colored) + philein, to love) A kind of granulocyte believed to be involved in allergic reactions; they also act against certain parasitic worms. p. 178

epididymis
(ep′ə did′ə məs) (Gr epi, upon + didymos, testis) A long, coiled tube that sits on the back side of the testes where sperm undergo further development after their formation within the testes. p. 413

epiglottis
(ep′ə glot′əs) (Gr. epi, upon + glotta, tongue) A flap of tissue that folds back over the opening to the larynx, thus preventing food or liquids from entering the airway. p. 135

epinephrine
(ep′ə nef′rən) (Gr. epi, on, over + nephros, kidney) A hormone produced by the adrenal medulla that readies the body to react to stress p. 326

epithelial tissue
(ep′ə thē′lē əl tish′oo) A collection of tissues that cover and line internal and external surfaces of the body and compose the glands. p. 108

epithelium
(ep′ə thē′lē əm) (Gr. epi, on + thele, nipple) The collective term for all epithelial cells, which have six different functions in the body: protection, absorption, sensation, secretion, excretion, and surface transport. p. 108

erythrocyte
(i rith′rō sīt) (Gr. erythros, red + kytos, hollow vessel) A red blood cell, packed with hemoglobin, which acts as a mobile transport unit, picking up and delivering gases. p. 115

esophagus
i sof′ə gəs) (Gr. oiso, carry + phagein, to eat) The food tube that connects the pharynx to the stomach. p. 135

essential amino acids
(i sen′chəl əmēn′ō as′ədz) The eight amino acids that humans cannot manufacture and therefore must be obtained from proteins in the food they eat. p. 145

estrogen
(es′trə jən) (Gr. oistros, frenzy + genos, origin) Any of various hormones that develop and maintain the female reproductive structures such as the ovarian follicles, the lining of the uterus, and the breasts. p. 416

eukaryotic cell
(yoo kar′ē ôt′ik sel′) (Gr. eu, good + karyon, kernel) A type of cell more complex than a prokaryote that makes up the bodies of plants, animals, protists, and fungi; a plasma membrane encloses the cytoplasm, which contains organelles and the nucleoid. p. 14

eustachian tube
(yoo stā′kē ən or yoo stā′shən toob) (after Bartolomeo Eustachio, Italian anatomist) A structure that connects the middle ear with the nasopharynx; it equalizes air pressure on both sides of the eardrum when the outside air pressure is not the same. p. 250

evolution
(ev′ə loo′shən) (L. evolvere, to unfold) Genetic change in a population of

organisms over generations; Darwin proposed that natural selection was the mechanism behind evolutionary change. p. 13

excitatory synapse
(ik sīt′ə tōr′ē sin′aps) A type of synapse in which a neurotransmitter depolarizes the postsynaptic membrane, resulting in the continuation of the nerve impulse. p. 215

excretion
(ik skrē′shən) A process whereby metabolic wastes, excess water, and excess salts are removed from the blood and passed out of the body. p. 108

exergonic
(ek′sər gon′ik) (L. ex, out + Gr. ergon, work) Used to describe a reaction in which the products contain less energy than the reactants and the excess energy is released; exergonic reactions take place spontaneously. p. 76

exocrine gland
(ek′sə krən gland) (Gr. exo, outside + krinein, to separate) A term applied to a gland whose secretion reaches its destination by means of ducts. p. 258

exocytosis
(ek′sō sī tō′səs) (Gr. ex, out of + kytos, cell) The reverse of endocytosis; the discharge of material by a cell by packaging it in a vesicle and moving the vesicle to the cell surface. p. 72

exon
(ek′son) (Gr. exo, outside) A nucleotide sequence that encodes the amino-acid sequence of a polypeptide. p. 334

expiration
(ek′spə rā′shən) (Gr. ex, out + L. spirare, to breathe) The expelling of the air from the lungs in breathing; it occurs when the volume of the thoracic cavity is decreased and the resulting positive pressure forces air out of the lungs. p. 151

exponential growth
(ek′spō nen′shəl grōth) A growth rate in which although the rate of increase in population size may stay the same, the actual increase in the number of individuals grows. p. 453

external respiration
(ek sturn′əl res′pə rā′shən) The exchange of carbon dioxide and oxygen gases by the red blood cells and alveoli in the lungs. p. 150

extraembryonic membrane
(ek′strə em′brē on′ik mem′brān) A structure that forms from the the trophoblast and provides nourishment and protection; so named because it is not a part of the embryo. p. 433

facilitated diffusion
(fə sil′ə tā′təd di fyoo′shən) The movement of selected molecules across

the cell membrane by specific transport proteins along the concentration gradient and without an expenditure of energy. p. 69

fatty acid
(fat'ē as'əd) A long hydrocarbon chain ending in a carboxyl ($-COOH$) group; a fatty acid can be saturated, unsaturated, or polyunsaturated. p. 33

feces
(fē'sēz) (L. faeces) Body waste discharged by way of the anus. p. 141

feedback loop
(fēd'bak' lo͞op) A mechanism by which information regarding the status of a physiologic situation or system is fed back to the system so that appropriate adjustments can be made. p. 120

femur
(fē'mur) The thigh bone in the appendicular skeleton of a human. p. 287

fermentation
(fur'mən tā'shən) (L. fermentum, ferment) An anaerobic process by which certain organisms make ATP. p. 90

fertilization
(furt'ə lə zā'shən) (L. ferre, to bear) The union of a male gamete (sperm) and a female gamete (egg). p. 339

fibroblast
(fī'brə blast') (L. fibra, fiber + Gr. blastos, sprout) The most numerous of the connective tissue cells, they are flat, irregular, branching cells that secrete fibers into the matrix between them. p. 111

fibrocartilage
(fī'brə kärt'əl ij or fī'brə kärt'lij) (L. fibra, fiber + cartilago, gristle) A type of cartilage that has collagen fibers embedded in its matrix; used by the body as a "shock absorber" in the knee joint and as disks between the vertebrae. p. 114

filtrate
(fil'trāt) The water and dissolved substances that are first filtered out of the blood during the formation of urine. p. 187

filtration
(fil'trā'shən) The process by which the blood is passed through nephron membranes that separate blood cells and proteins from the water and small molecules of the blood. p. 188

flagellum, pl. flagella
(flə jel'əm, flə jel'ə) (L. flagellum, whip) A long, whip-like organelle of motility that protrudes from some cells. p. 65

fluid mosaic model
(flo͞o'əd mō zā'ik mod'əl) The model of the cell membrane that describes the fluid nature of a lipid bilayer studded with a mosaic of proteins. p. 56

follicle
(fol'e kəl) (L. folliculus, little bag) A term for the follicular cells and the oocyte in the ovary. p. 414

follicle-stimulating hormone (FSH)
(fol'ə kəl-stim'yə lāt'ing hôr'mōn) A gonadotropic hormone secreted by the anterior pituitary that triggers the maturation of one egg each month in females; it triggers sperm production in males. p. 263

foramen, pl. foramina
(fə rā'mən, fə ram'ən ə) The inner space or tunnel in the vertebral column in which the spinal cord runs down the neck and back; this body casing protects the spinal cord from injury. p. 232

formed elements
(fôrmd el'ə məntz) The solid portion of blood plasma composed principally of erythrocytes, leukocytes, and platelets. p. 175

fossil
(fos'əl) (L. fodere, to dig) Any record of a dead organism; any trace or impression of an animal or plant that has been preserved in the Earth's crust. p. 470

fovea
(fō'vē ə) (L. a pit) The area of sharpest vision within the retina due to its high concentration of cones. p. 249

free energy of activation
(frē en'ər jē uv ak'tə vā'shən) The energy needed to initiate a chemical reaction. p. 74

free radical
(frē rad'ə kəl) A charged molecule fragment with an unpaired electron that is highly reactive. p. 393

frontal lobe
(frunt'əl lōb) A section on both hemispheres of the cerebral cortex dealing with the motor activity movement of the body. p. 227

functional group
(fungk'shən əl gro͞op) Special groups of atoms attached to an organic molecule; important because most chemical reactions that occur within organisms involve the transfer of a functional group from one molecule to another. p. 35

fungus, pl. fungi
(fung'ges, fun'ji) (L. mushroom) A multicellular, eukaryotic organism that feeds on dead or decaying organic material. p. 456

gall bladder
(gôl blad'ər) In human beings, a sac attached to the underside of the liver, where excess bile is stored and concentrated. p. 139

gamete
(gam'ēt or mēt') (Gr. wife) A sex cell; the female gamete is the egg, and the male gamete is the sperm. p. 339

ganglion, pl. ganglia
(gang' glē ən, gang'glē ə) A nerve cell body located within the peripheral nervous system. p. 229

gastric glands
(gas'trik glandz) Glands dotting the inner surface of the stomach that secrete a gastric juice of hydrochloric acid and pepsinogen. p. 137

gastrin
(gas'trən) A digestive hormone of the stomach that controls the production of acid. p. 137

gastrulation
(gas'trə lā'shən) (L. little belly) The process by which groups of inner cells mass, migrate, divide, and differentiate into three primary germ layers from which all the organs and tissues of the body develop. p. 434

gene
(jēn) (Gr. genos, birth, race) A piece of hereditary information carried on the X and Y sex chromosomes. p. 333

gene families
(gēn fam'lēz or fam'ə lēz) Multiple copies of genes in eukaryotes, which are derived from a common ancestral gene and are a reflection of the evolutionary process. p. 339

gene mutation
(jēn myo͞o tā'shən) A change in the genetic message of a chromosome due to alterations of molecules within the structure of the chromosomal DNA. p. 394

gene transfer therapy
(jēn ther'ə pē) The technique in which scientists try to cure inherited genetic disorders by inserting genes with the proper genetic message into patients having defective genes. p. 332

general adaptation syndrome
(jen'ə rəl ad ap tā shən sin'drōm) the three stages of reaction by the body to stress: the alarm reaction, resistance, and exhaustion. p. 268

genetic counseling
(jə net'ik coun'səl ing) The process in which geneticists identify couples at risk of having children with genetic defects and help them have healthy children. p. 401

genetics
(jə net'iks) (Gr. genos, birth, race) The branch of biology dealing with the principles of hereditary and variation in organisms. p. 376

genital herpes
(hur'pēz) (Gr. spreading skin infection) Asexually transmitted disease caused by the herpes simplex virus (HSV)2, and occasionlly by HSV1, that produces blister-like sores on the genitals. p.449

genital warts
A sexually transmitted disease caused by

the human papillomavirus (HPV) that produces warty growths on the genitals. p. 449

genotype
(jēn′ə tīp) (Gr. genos, offspring + typos, form) The total set of genes that constitutes an organisms's genetic makeup. p. 380

gestation
(jes tā′shən) (L. gestare, to bear) The time of a developing human from conception until birth, approximately 8½ months. p. 428

gland
(gland) (L. glans, acorn) An epithelial cell specialized to produce and discharge substances. p. 108

glial cell
(glē′əl *or* glī′əl sel) (Gr. glia, glue) A supporting nerve cell of the brain and spinal cord. p. 118

glomerulus
(glə mer′ə ləs) (L. a little ball) A tuft of capillaries surrounded by Bowman's capsule that acts as filtration devices in the formation of urine. p. 190

glucagon
(glōō′kə gon) A hormone produced in the islets of Langerhans that raises blood glucose level by converting glycogen into glucose. p. 270

glycogen
(glī′kə jən) (Gr. glykys, sweet + gen, of a kind) Animal starch; a storage form of glucose within animals. p. 37

glycolysis
(glī kol′ə səs) (Gr. glykys, sweet + lyein, to loosen) The first of three series of chemical reactions in cellular respiration, which results in the formation of two ATP molecules and two molecules of pyruvate. p. 91

Golgi complex
(gol′jē käm+pleks) (after Camillo Golgi, Italian physician) The delivery system of the eukaryotic cell; it collects, modifies, packages, and distributes molecules that are made at one location within the cell and used at another. p. 60

gonad
(gō′nad) (Gr. gone, seed) A male or female reproductive sex organ that produces sex cells, or gametes. p. 410

gonorrhea
(gon′orē ah) (Gr. gonē, seed + Gr. rhein, to flow) A sexually transmitted disease caused by the bacterium *Neisseria gonorrhoeae* that causes a primary infection of the urethra (in men and women) and vagina and cervix (in women). p. 454

gradient
(grā′dē ənt) Describing the differences in concentration, pressure, or electrical charge in the random motion of

molecules, which often results in a net movement of molecules in a particular direction. p. 67

granulocyte
(gran′yə lō sīt) (L. granulum, little grain + Gr. kytos, cell) A circulating leukocyte that gets its name from the tiny granules in its cytoplasm; granulocytes are classified into three groups by their staining properties. p. 177

greenhouse effect
(grēn′hous′ əfekt′) The selective energy absorption of carbon dioxide (CO_2), which allows heat to enter the Earth's atmosphere but prevents it from leaving; may be contributing factor to global warming. p. 512

growth hormone (GH)
(grōth hôr′mōn) A hormone secreted by the anterior pituitary that works with the thyroid hormones to control normal growth. p. 263

haploid
(hap′loid) (Gr. haploos, single + eidos, form) A sex cell that contains half the amount of hereditary material of the original parent cell. p. 339

haversian canal
(həvur′shən kə nal′) (after Clopton Havers, British physician and anatomist) A narrow channel that runs parallel to the length of the bone that contains blood vessels and nerve cells. p. 283

heart
(härt) (A.S. heorte) The muscular pump that is the center of the cardiovascular or circulatory system. p. 166

helper T cell
(help′ər tē′ sel) A kind of T lymphocyte that initiates the immune response by identifying foreign invaders and stimulating the production of other cells to fight an infection. p. 307

hemoglobin
(hē′mə glō′bən) (Gr. haima, blood + L. globus, a ball) The iron-containing pigment that imparts the color to red blood cells; hemoglobin is produced within the red bone marrow and carries oxygen in the blood. p. 157

hemophilia
(hē′mə fil′ē ə) (Gr. haima, blood + philein, to love) A hereditary condition in which the blood is slow to clot or does not clot at all. p. 389

herpes simplex virus
(hur pēz) (Gr. spreading skin infection) The causative agent of genital herpes. p. 449

hetereozygous
(het′ər əzī′gəs) (Gr. heteros, other + zygotos, a pair) Refers to a individual having two different alleles for a trait. p. 378

homeostasis
(hō′mē əstā′səs) (Gr. homeos, similar + stasis, standing) The maintenance of a stable internal environment in spite of a possibly very different external environment. p. 120

hominid
(hom′ə nid) (L. homo, man) The family of hominoids consisting of human beings; the only living hominid is *Homo sapiens sapiens*. p. 483

hominoid
(hom′ə noid) (L. homo, man) A superfamily of the anthropoid suborder that includes apes and humans. p. 482

Homo erectus
(hō′mō i rek′təs) (L. homo, man + erectus, upright) An extinct species of hominids whose fossil record dates back to 1.6 million years ago; *H. erectus* was fully adapted to upright walking, made sophisticated tools, built shelters, used fire, and probably communicated with language. p. 486

Homo habilis
(hō′mō hab′ə ləs) (L. homo, man + habilis, skillful) An extinct species of hominids whose fossil record dates back about 2 million years; considered human because they exhibited a far greater intelligence than their ancestors by making tools and clothing. p. 486

Homo sapiens
(hō′ mō sā′pē ənz *or* sap′ē ənz) (L. homo, man + sapiens, wise) A hominid whose fossil record dates back about 200,000 years and most likely evolved from *H. erectus;* their anatomy featured larger brains, flatter heads, more sloping foreheads, and more protruding brow ridges than modern humans. p. 486

Homo sapiens sapiens
(hō′ mō sā′pē ənz sā′pē ənz) (L. homo, man + sapiens, wise) Modern man; the subspecies of hominids who made their appearance 10,000 years before the Neanderthal subspecies died out and whose early members are called Cro-Magnons. p. 488

homologous
(hō mol′ə gəs) (Gr. homologia, agreement) Said of the bones of different vertebrates that now differ in structure and function, although having the same evolutionary origin. p. 470

homozygous
(hō′ mə zī′gəs) (Gr. homos, same or similar + zygotos, a pair) Refers to an individual having two identical alleles for a trait. p. 378

hormone
(hôr′ mōn) (Gr. hormaien, to excite) A chemical messenger secreted and sent by a gland to other cells of the body. p. 195

human chorionic gonadotropin (HCG)
(hyoo′ mən kōr′ēän′ik gō′ nad ətrō′pik) (Gr. chorion, chorion + gonos, genitals + trope, turning) A hormone secreted by embryonic placental tissue that maintains the corpus luteum so that it will continue to secrete progesterone and estrogen; the detection of this hormone in the urine is the basis for home pregnancy tests. p. 416

human genome project
(hyoo′mən jē′ nōm proj′ekt) A monumental, worldwide scientific project, the goal of which is to decipher the DNA code of all 46 human chromosomes. p. 332

human immunodeficiency virus (HIV)
(hyoo′ mən im yoo′ nō dē fish′ən sē vī′rəs) The virus that causes AIDS, especially deadly because it destroys the ability of the immune system to mount a defense against any infection because it attacks and destroys helper T cells. p. 311

humerus
(hyoo′ mər əs) (L. upper arm) The upper arm bone in the appendicular skeleton of a human. p. 287

humoral immune response
(hyoo′ mər əl i myoon ri spons′) A second, longer-range defense than the cell-mediated immune response, in which B cells are converted to plasma cells that secrete the proteins antibodies. p. 307

Huntington's disease
(hunt′ing tənz diz ēz′) (after G. Huntington, U.S. physician) A fatal genetic disorder caused by a mutant dominant allele that causes progressive deterioration of brain cells. p. 398

hyaline cartilage
(hī′ə lən or hī′ə līn kärt′əl ij or kärt′lij) (Gr. hyalos, glass + L. cartilago, gristle) A type of cargilage that has very fine collagen fibers in its matrix; it is found on the ends of long bones, ringing the windpipe, and in the ribs and nose. p. 114

hybrid
(hī′brəd) (L. hybrida, mongrel) The offspring of the cross between two different varieties of plants of the same species; also the cross between two different species of organisms. p. 375

hydrogen bond
(hī′drə jən bänd) A molecule formed when the partial negative charge at one end of a polar molecule is attracted to the partial positive charge of another polar molecule. p. 30

hydrolysis
(hī drōl′ə səs) (Gr. hydro, water + lyse, to break) The process by which a polymer is disassembled by adding a molecule of water. p. 35

hydrolyzing enzyme
(hī′drə līz′ing en′zīm) (Gr. hydro, water + lyse, to break) An enzyme that breaks down substances by hydrolysis. p. 133

hydrophobic
(hī′drə fō′bik) (Gr. hydor, water + phobos, hating) Refers to nonpolar molecules like oil that cannot form hydrogen bonds with water; this is why oil and water do not mix. p. 32

hyperpolarization
(hī′pər pō′lər əzā′shən) (Gr. hyper, above + polaris, pole) The resulting state in the interior of a rod cell when it becomes even more negatively charged than before because sodium channels have closed because of stimulation. p. 247

hypertonic
(hī′pər ton′ik) (Gr. hyper, above + tonos, tension) Refers to a solution with a solute concentration higher than that of another fluid. p. 68

hyphae
(hī′fā) (Gr. web) Slender filaments that make up much of the structure of most fungi. p. 456

hypothalamus
(hī′pō thal′ə məs) (Gr. hypo. under + thalamos, inner room) A mass of gray matter lying at the base of the cerebrum that produces two hormones and controls the secretion of hormones by the pituitary gland. p. 230

hypothesis
(hī poth′ə səs) (Gr. hypo, under + tithenai, to put) A plausible answer to a scientific question, based on available knowledge and generalizations made from observations. p. 4

hypotonic
(hī′ pə ton′ik) (Gr. hypo, under + tonos, tension) Refers to a solution with a solute concentration lower than that of another fluid. p. 68

ileum
(il′ē əm) (L. groin, flank) The third and final part of the small intestine, following the jejunum. p. 138

immune system
(i myoon′ sis′təm) The collective term for populations of white blood cells that resist disease. p. 303

immunity
(i myoon′ə tē) (L. immunitas, safe) The specific defense of a human body that consists of cellular and molecular responses to particular foreign invaders. p. 302

implantation
(im′plan tā′shən) (L. in, into + plantare, to plant) The embedding of the developing blastocyst into the posterior wall of the uterus approximately 1 week after fertilization. p. 431

incomplete dominance
(in′kəm plēt′ däm′ə nəns) A situation in which neither member of a pair of alleles exhibits dominance over the other. p. 399

induction
(in duk′shən) (L. inductio, leading in) The process by which some cells turn "off and on" switches for the genes of neighboring cells. p. 437

infection
(in fek′ shun) The invasion and multiplication of agents of infection, such as bacteria and viruses, in body tissues. p. 446

infestation
(in fəs tā′ shun) The subsistence and growth of parasites on the skin or within underlying tissues. p. 446

inflammation
(in′flə mā′shən) (L. inflammare, to flame) A reaction when cells are damaged by microbes, chemicals, or physical substances. p. 302

inhibitory synapse
(in hib′ə tôr′ē sin′aps) A type of neurotransmitter that reduces the ability of the postsynaptic membrane to depolarize. p. 215

inner ear
(in′ər ir) A complex of fluid-filled canals in the ear where hearing actually takes place; receptor cells of this organ change the mechanical "sound" energy into nerve impulses. p. 250

insertion
(in sur′shən) The attachment of one end of skeletal muscle to a bone that will move. p. 291

inspiration
(in′spə rā′shən) (L. in, in + spirare, to breathe) Drawing air into the lungs; it occurs when the volume of the thoracic cavity is increased and the resulting negative pressure causes air to be sucked into the lungs; opposite of expiration. p. 151

insulin
(in′sə lən) (L. insula, island) A hormone produced in the islets of Langerhans of the pancreas that promotes the regulation of glucose metabolism by the cells. p. 270

integration
(int′ə grā′shən) A function of the central nervous system in which the brain and spinal cord make sense of incoming sensory information and then produce outgoing motor impulses. p. 226

integument
(in teg′yə mənt) (L. integumentum,

covering) The skin, hair, and nails of the human body. p. 283

interneuron
(int′ər nŏŏr′on) (L. inter, between + Gr. neuron, nerve) A nerve cell found in the spinal cord and brain situated between other neurons that receives incoming messages and sends outgoing messages in response. p. 206

interphase
(int′ər fāz′) The portion of the cell cycle preceding mitosis in which the cell grows and carries out normal life functions. During this time the cell also produces an exact copy of the hereditary material, DNA, as it prepares for cell division. p. 341

intron
(in′tron) (L. intra, within) A segment of DNA transcribed into mRNA but removed before translation. p. 334

inversion
(in vur′zhən) Refers to the process in which a broken piece of chromosome reattaches to the same chromosome but in a reversed direction. p. 393

ion
(ī′ən or ī′on) (Gr. going) An electrically charged particle that results from an exchange of electrons in an atom. p. 27

ionic bond
(ī on′ik bänd) An attraction between ions of opposite charge. p. 26

iris
(ī′rəs) (L. rainbow) A diaphragm lying between the cornea and the lens that controls the amount of light entering the eye. p. 249

islets of Langerhans
(ī′ləts uv läng′ər hänz′) (after Paul Langerhans, German anatomist) The separate types of cells within the exocrine cells of the pancreas that produce the hormones insulin and glucagon. p. 270

isomer
(ī′sə mər) (Gr. isos, equal + meros, part) One of two or more molecules that have the same molecular formula but are arranged slightly differently; fructose is an isomer of glucose. p. 37

isotonic
(ī′sə ton′ik) (Gr. isos, equal + tonos, tension) Refers to solutions having equal solute concentrations to one another. p. 68

isotope
(ī′sə tōp) (Gr. isos, equal, + topos, place) An atom of an element that has the same number of protons but different numbers of neutrons in its nuclei. p. 24

jejunum
(ji jŏŏ′ nəm) (L. empty) The second portion of the small intestine extending from the duodenum to the ileum. p. 138

joint
(joint) An articulation; a place where bones or bones and cartilage come together. p. 288

karyotype
(kar′ē ətīp′) Gr. karyon, kernel + typos, stamp or print) The particular array of chromosomes that belongs to an individual. p. 324

kidney
(kid′nē) The organ in all vertebrates that carries out the processes of filtration, reabsorption, and excretion. p. 187

kidney stone
(kid′nē stōn) Crystals of certain salts that develop in the kidney and block urine flow. p. 196

kinetic energy
(kə net′ik en′ər jē) The energy of motion. p. 78

Klinefelter syndrome
(klīn′felt ər sin′drōm) (After Harry F. Klinefelter, Jr, U.S. physician) A genetic condition resulting from an XXY zygote that develops into a human male who is sterile, has many female body characteristics, and in some cases, has diminished mental capacity. p. 392

Krebs cycle
(krebz sī′kəl) (after Hans A, Krebs, German-born English biochemist) The series of nine reactions during which pyruvate, the end product of glycolysis, enters the cycle to form citric acid and is finally oxidized to carbon dioxide. Also called citric acid cycle. p. 91

lacteal
(lak′tē əl) (L. lacteus, of milk) A lymphatic vessel within a villus that helps pass nutrients into the lymph and blood. p. 141

lacuna, pl. lacunae
(lə kyŏŏ′nə, lə kyŏŏ′nē) (L. a pit) The tiny chambers where cartilage cells lie. p. 114

lanugo
(lə gŏŏ′nə) A fine body hair that appears over the body of a fetus toward the end of the third month of pregnancy but that is lost before birth. p. 439

larynx
(lar′ingks) (Gr.) The voice box located at the upper end of the human windpipe. p. 135

latent infection
Infection in which a virus integrates its genetic material with that of the host. p. 449

lens
(lenz) (L. lentil) A body in the eye lying just behind the aqueous humor that plays a major role in focusing the light entering the eye. p. 248

leukocyte
(lŏŏ′kə sīt) (Gr. leukos, white + kytos, hollow vessel) Any of several kinds of white blood cells including macrophages and lymphocytes, all functioning to defend the body against invading microorganisms and foreign substances. p. 115

ligament
(lig′ə mənt) (L. ligare, to bind) A bundle or strip of dense connective tissue that holds a bone to a bone. p. 288

limb bud
(lim bud) The appearance of arms and legs that appear as microscopic flippers during the fourth week in an embryo. p. 438

limbic system
(lim′bik sis′təm) (L. limbus, border) A network of neurons, which together with the hypothalamus, forms a ring-like border around the top of the brainstem; responsible for many of the most deep-seated drives and emotions of vertebrates. p. 230

lipase
(lī′pās or lip′ās) (Gr. lipos, fat + -ase, enzyme) An enzyme that breaks down the triglycerides in lipids to fatty acids and glycerol. p. 132

lipid
(lip′id) (Gr. lipos, fat) Any of a wide variety of molecules, all of which are soluble in oil but insoluble in water; important categories of lipids are oils, fats, and waxes; phospholipids; and steroids. p. 40

lipid bilayer
(lip′id bī′lā′ər) The basic foundation of biological membranes; it forms a fluid, flexible covering for a cell and keeps the watery contents of the cell on one side of the membrane and the water environment on the other. p. 56

liver
(liv′ər) A large complex, organ weighing over 3 pounds, lying just under the diaphragm, that performs over 500 functions in the body, including aiding in the digestion of lipids. p. 138

loop of Henle
(lŏŏp uv hen′lē) (after F.G.J. Henle, German anatomist) The descending and ascending loops of the renal tubule. p. 190

lumen, pl. lumina
(lŏŏ′ mən, lŏŏ′mə nə) (L. light) The hollow core in the three layers of tissue that makes up the walls of the arteries through which blood flows. p. 168

luteinizing hormone (LH)
(loo'tē ən īz'ing hôr'mōn) A gonadotropic hormone secreted by the anterior pituitary that stimulates the release of an egg in females and stimulating the production of testosterone in males. p. 261

lymph
(limf) (L. lympha, clear water) A tissue fluid diffused out of the blood through the capillaries. p. 178

lymph node
(limf nōd) A small, ovoid "spongy" structure located in various places of the body along the route of the lymphatic vessels filtering the lymph as it passes through. p. 180

lymphatic system
(lim fat'ik sis'təm) The system of one-way, blind-ended vessels that collects and returns to the blood the approximately 10% of the fluid that does not return to the blood directly. p. 178

lyse
(līz) (Gr. lysis, dissolution) To break open. p. 448

lysogenic cycle
(lī sə jən ik sī kl) (Gr. lysis, dissolution + gennan, to produce) A pattern of viral replication in which a virus integrates its genetic material with that of a host and is replicated each time the host cell replicates. p. 448

lysosome
(lī'sə sōm) (Gr. lysis, a loosening + soma, a body) A membrane-bounded vesicle containing digestive enzymes that break down old cell parts or materials brought into the cell from the environment and are extremely important to the health of a cell. p. 61

lytic cycle
(līt'ik sī kl) (Gr. lysis, dissolution) A pattern of viral replication in which a virus enters a cell, replicates, and then causes the cell to burst, releasing new viruses. p. 448

macromolecule
(mak'rə mol'ə kyool) (Gr. makros, large + L. moliculus, a little mass) A large organic molecule having many functional groups. p. 35

macrophage
(mak'rō fāj) (Gr. makros, long + -phage, eat) A phagocytic cell in the bloodstream that engulfs foreign bacteria and antibody-coated cells or particles in the process of phagocytosis; macrophages act as the body's scavengers. p. 111

mammal
(mam'əl) (L. mamma, breast) A warm-blooded vertebrate that has hair in which the female secretes milk from mammary glands to feed her young. p. 477

marsupial
(mär soo'pē əl) (L. marsupium, pouch) A subclass of mammals that give birth to immature young that are carried in a pouch; a kangaroo is a marsupial. p. 478

medulla
(mə dul'ə) (L. marrow) The lowest portion of the brainstem, continuous with the spinal cord below; the site of neuron tracts, which cross over one another deliverying sensory information from the right side of the body to the left side of the brain and vice versa. p. 188

megakaryocyte
(meg'ə kar'ē əsīt) (Gr. megas, large + karyon, nucleus + kytos, cell) A large bone marrow cell that pinches off bits of its cytoplasm, resulting in a cell fragment, or platelet. p. 178

meiosis
(mī ō' səs) (Gr. meioun, to make smaller) The two-staged process of nuclear division in which the number of chromosomes in cells is halved during gamete formation. p. 339

meninges, sing. meninx
(mə nin'jēz, mē'ningks) (Gr. membrane) Any of the three layers of membranes covering both the brain and spinal cord. p. 233

menopause
(men'ə pôz) (L. mens, month + pausis, cessation) The period that marks the permanent cessation of menstrual activity in a woman, usually between the ages of 50 and 55; the end of the menses. p. 418

menstruation
(men'strooā'shən) (L. mens, month) The monthly sloughing off of the blood-enriched lining of the uterus when pregnancy does not occur; the lining degenerates and causes a flow of blood, tissue, and mucus from the uterus out the vagina. p. 418

mesoderm
(mez'ə durm') (Gr. mesos, middle + derma, skin) The layer of cells in the developing embryo that differentiates into the skeleton, muscles, blood, reproductive organs, connective tissue, and the innermost layer of the skin. p. 432

messenger RNA (mRNA)
(mes'ən jər är'en'ā') A type of RNA that brings information from the DNA within the nucleus to the ribosomes in the cytoplasm to direct which polypeptide is assembled. p. 333

metabolism
(mə tab'ə liz'əm) (Gr. metabole, change) All the chemical reactions that take place within a living organism. p. 94

metaphase
(met'ə fāz) (Gr. meta, middle + phasis, form) The stage of mitosis characterized by the alignment of the chromosomes in a ring, equidistant from the two poles of the cell. p. 343

metastasis
(mə tas'tah sis) (Gr. meta, after, beyond, over + Gr. stasis, stand) Transfer of disease from one part of the body to another. p. 354

microfilament
(mī'krō fil'ə mənt) (Gr. mikros, small + L. filum, a thread) A thin, twisted double-chain fiber of protein within the cytoskeleton that helps support and shape eukaryotic cells. p. 56

microtubule
(mī'krō too'byool) (Gr. mikros, small + tubulus, little pipe) A spiral array composed of protein subunits within the cytoskeleton that provide intracellular support in the nondividing cell. p. 56

microvillus, pl. microvilli
(mī'krō vil'əs, mī krō vil'ī) (Gr. mikros, small + L. villus, tuft of hair) A microscopic, cytoplasmic projection that covers the epithelial cells of the villi on their exposed surfaces. p. 141

midbrain
(mid'brān') The top part of the brainstem; it contains nerve tracts connecting the upper and lower parts of the brain and nuclei that acts as reflex centers for movement. p. 231

middle ear
(mid'əl ir) The middle portion of the ear containing three bones that act together like an amplifier to increase the force of sound vibrations. p. 250

mineral
(min'ə rəl) (L. minerale) An inorganic substance transported around the ions dissolved in blood and other body fluids; a variety of minerals perform a variety of functions in the human body. p. 130

mitochondrion, pl. mitochondria
(mīt'ə kon'drē ən, mīt'ə kon'drē ə) (Gr. mitos, thread + chondrion, small grain) An oval, sausage-shaped, or thread-like organelle about the size of a bacterium, bounded by a double membrane whose function is to break down fuel molecules, thus releasing energy for cell work. p. 63

mitosis
(mī tō'səs or mi tō'səs) (Gr. mitos, thread) A process of cell division that produces two identical cells from an original parent cell. p. 340

molecule
(môl'ə kyool') (L. molecula, little mass) A combination of tightly bound atoms. p. 26

monohybrid
(mon′əhī′brəd) (Gr. monos, single + L. hybrida, mongrel) The progeny or product of two plants that differ from one another in a single trait. p. 375

monosaccharide
(mon′ə sak′ə rīd) (Gr. monos, one + sakcharon, sugar) A simple sugar. p. 37

monotreme
(mon′ə trēm) (Gr. mono. single + treme, hole) A mammal that lays eggs having leathery shells similar to those of a reptile; the only extant monotremes are the duckbilled platypus and two genera of spiny anteaters. p. 478

morphogenesis
(môr′fə jen′ə səs) (Gr. morphe, form + genesis, origin) The early stage of development in a vertebrate when cells begin to move, or migrate, thus shaping the new individual. p. 416

motor area
(mōt′ər er′ē ə) The part of the brain straddling the rearmost portion of the frontal lobe that sends messages to move the skeletal muscles. p. 227

motor neuron
(mōt′ər nōōr′on) A neuron of the peripheral nervous system that transmits commands away from the central nervous system. p. 206

multiple alleles
(mul′tə pəl a lēlz′) A system of alleles in a gene that exhibits either complete dominance or codominance. p. 399

muscle fiber
(mus′əl fī′bər) A long, multinucleated cell packed with organized arrangements of microfilaments capable of contraction. p. 293

muscle tissue
(mus′əl tish′ōō) Any of three different kinds of muscle cells—smooth, skeletal, or cardiac—that are the workhorses of the body; characterized by an abundance of special thick and thin microfilaments. p. 106

mutation
(myōō tā′shən) (L. mutare, to change) A permanent change in the genetic material. p. 390

myelin sheath
(mī′ə lən shēth) (Gr. myelinos, full of marrow) The fatty wrapping created by multiple layers of Schwann cell membranes; the myelin sheath insulates the axon. p. 207

myofibril
(mī′ə fī′brəl) (Gr. myos, muscle + L. fibrilla, little fiber) A cylindrical, organized arrangement of special thick and thin microfilaments capable of shortening a muscle fiber. p. 116

myosin
(mī′ə sin) (Gr. mys, muscle + in, belonging to) One of the two protein components of myofilaments in a muscle fiber; actin is the other. p. 293

natural selection
(nach′ə rəl sə lek′shən) The process in which organisms having adaptive traits survive in greater numbers than organisms without such traits. p. 469

Neanderthal
(nē an′dər thôl′ or nē an′dər täl′) (Neander, valley in western Germany) A subspecies of *H. sapiens* that lived from 125,000 to 35,000 years ago in Europe and the Middle East; Neanderthals were short and powerfully built, with large brains; they made diverse tools, took care of the sick and injured, and buried their dead. p. 488

negative feedback
(neg′ ət iv fēd′bak′) The process by which enzyme activity is regulated by inhibitors. p. 83

nephron
(nef′ron) (Gr. nephros, kidney) Any of the millions of microscopic tubular units of the kidney where urine is formed. p. 187

nerve
(nurv) A cluster of axons and dendrites surrounded by numerous supporting cells. p. 118

nerve cord
(nurv kôrd) A single, hollow cord along the back that is a principal feature of chordates; in vertebrates, the nerve cord differentiates into a brain and spinal cord. p. 474

nerve impulse
(nurv im′pəls) A rapid electrical signal of a neuron that reports information or initiates a quick repsonse in specific tissues. p. 206

neuromuscular junction
(nyōōr′ō mus′kyə lər jungk′shən) A synapse between a neuron and a skeletal muscle cell. p. 214

neuron
(nōōr′on) (Gr. nerve) A nerve cell specialized to conduct an electric current. p. 118

neurotransmitter
(nōōr′ō trans′mit ər) (Gr. neuron, nerve + L. trans, across + mitere, to send) A chemical released when a nerve impulse reaches the axon tip of a nerve cell. p. 214

neurulation
(nōōr′ə lā′shən) (Gr. neuron, nerve) The development of a hollow nerve cord, which later develops into the central nervous system. p. 435

neutron
(nōō′tron) (L. neuter, neither) A subatomic particle found at the nucleus of an atom, similar to a proton in mass but neutral and carrying no charge. p. 24

neutrophil
(nōō′trə fil) (L. neuter, neither + Gr. philein, to love) A type of granulocyte that migrates to the site of an injury and sticks to the interior walls of blood vessels, where it forms projections and phagocytizes microorganisms and other foreign particles. p. 177

node of Ranvier
(nōd uv räN vyā′) (after L. A. Ranvier, French histologist) An uninsulated spot between two Schwann cells. p. 207

nondisjunction
(non dis jungk′shən) The failure of homologous chromosomes to separate after synapsis, resulting in gametes with abnormal numbers of chromosomes. p. 391

nonspecific defense
(non spə sif′ik di fens′) A set of defenses that the body uses to act against foreign invaders; they include the skin and mucous membranes, chemicals that kill bacteria, and the inflammatory process. p. 302

notochord
(nō′tə kôrd) (Gr. noto, back + L. chorda, cord) A structure that forms the midline axis along which the vertebral column (backbone) develops in all vertebrate animals. p. 435

nuclear envelope
(nōō′klē ər en′və lōp) The outer, double membrane surrounding the surface of the nucleus of the eukaryotic cell. p. 61

nucleic acid
(nōō klē′ik or nōō klā′ik as′əd) A long polymer of repeating subunits called nucleotides; the two types of nucleic acid within cells are deoxyribonucleic acid (DNA) and ribonucleic acid (RNA). p. 47

nucleic acid core
(noo klē′ik) (L. little nut) The hereditary material of a virus. p. 447

nucleoid
(noo′klē oyd) (Gr like a nut) The non-membrane bounded area of DNA in a bacterium. p. 452

nucleolus, pl. nucleoli
(nōō klē′ə ləs, nōō klē′ə lī′) (L. a small nucleus) The site within the nucleus of ribosomal RNA synthesis; consists of ribosomal RNA plus some ribosomal proteins. p. 62

nucleotide
(nōō′klē ə tīd) A single unit of nucleic acid consisting of a five-carbon sugar, a phosphage group, and an organic

nitrogen-containing molecule, or base. p. 47

nucleus
(noo'klē əs) (L. a kernal, dim. fr. nux, nut) (1) The central core of an atom containing protons and neutrons. (2) The double membrane vesicle of a eukaryotic cell that contains the hereditary material, or DNA. p. 61

nutrient
(noo'trē ənt) (L. nutritio, nourish) A raw material of food; the six classes of nutrients are carbohydrates, fats, proteins, vitamins, minerals, and water. p. 130

obligate parasite
(ob'li gāt) (L. obligatus, necessary) Parasite able to survive only by living in association with and at the expense of other organisms. p. 446

occipital lobe
(ok sip'ə təl lōb) The section of the cerebral cortex in each hemisphere of the brain having to do with vision, with different sites corresponding to different positions on the retina. p. 227

omnivore
(om'nə vôr) (L. omnis, all + vorare, to eat) An organism that eats both plant and animal foods; human beings are omnivores. p. 133

oncogene
(ong'ko jen) (Gr. onos, mass + Gr. gennan, to produce) Cancer-causing gene. p. 354

oogenesis
(ō'ə jen'ə səs) (Gr. oon, egg + genesis, generation, birth) The process of meiosis and development that produces mature female sex cells, or eggs. p. 414

optic nerve
(op'tik nurv) The nerve carrying impulses for the sense of sight. p. 249

organ
(ôr'gən) (L. organon, tool) Grouped tissues that form a structural and functional unit. p. 106

organ of Corti
(ôr'gən uv kôrt'ē) (after Alfonso Corti, Italian anatomist) The organ of hearing; the collective term for the hair cells, the supporting cells of the basilar membrane, and the overhanging tectorial membrane. p. 251

organ system
(ôr'gən sis'təm) A group of organs that function together to carry out the principal activities of the organism. p. 106

organelle
(ôr'gə nel') (Gr. organella, little tool) Any of a number of highly specialized, membrane-bound, intracellular structures within a cell that perform specific cellular

functions; a feature common to most eukaryotes but lacking in bacteria. p. 13

origin
(ôr'ə jən) (L. oriri, to arise) The attachment of one end of a skeletal muscle to a stationary bone. p. 291

osmosis
(oz mō'səs *or* os mō'səs) (Gr. osmos, impulse + osis, condition) A special form of diffusion in which water molecules move from an area of higher concentration to an area of lower concentration across a differentially permeable membrane. p. 67

osmotic pressure
(oz mot'ik *or* os mot'ik presh'ər) The increase that water pressure exerts on a cell as water molecules continue to diffuse into a cell. p. 68

osteoblast
(os'tē əblast) (Gr. osteon, bone + blastos, cell) A cell that forms new bone. p. 283

osteocyte
(os'tē əsīt) (Gr. osteon, bone + kytos, hollow vessel) A cell that produces bone. p. 111

otolith
(ō'tə lith) (Gr. otos, ear + lithos, stone) Small pebbles of calcium carbonate embedded in a layer of jelly-like material that is spread over the surface of ciliated and nonciliated cells within the saccule. p. 252

outer ear
(out'ər ir) The part of the ear that funnels sound waves in toward the eardrum; includes the flaps of skin on the outside of the head called ears. p. 250

oval window
(ō'vəl win'dō) The entrance to the inner ear. p. 250

ovary
(ōv'ə rē) (L. ovum, egg) *(1)* A female gonad, located in the pelvic cavity of an animal, where egg production occurs. *(2)* In flowering plants, a chamber at the base of the female pistil that completely encloses and protects the ovules. p. 414

ovulation
(ov'yə lā'shən) (L. ovulum, little egg) The monthly process by which an egg is produced and released by the ovary. p. 415

ovule
(ōₒ'vyool) (L. ovulum, little egg) A protective structure in which egg cells grow in a naked seed plant. p. 375

ovum, pl. ova
(ō' vəm, ō'və) (L. egg) A mature egg cell, p. 415

oxidation
(ok'sə dā'shən) (Fr. oxider, to oxidize) The loss of an electron by an atom or a molecule. p. 28

oxidation-reduction
(ok'sə dā'shən ri duk'shən) In some chemical reactions, the passing of electrons from one atom or molecule to another; critically important to the flow of energy through living systems and essential to the flow of energy in cellular respiration. p. 92

oxygen debt
(ok'si jən det) A term used to describe the oxygen needed to break down the lactic acid in the liver, delivered by the bloodstream from the muscles during strenuous exercise. p. 101

oxytocin
(ok'si tō'sən) (Gr. oxys, sharp + tokos, birth) A hormone produced by the hypothalamus but stored and released in the posterior lobe of the pituitary that affects the contraction of the uterus during childbirth and stimulates the mammary glands, allowing a new mother to nurse her child. p. 264

ozone
(ō'zōn) (Gr. ozein, to smell) A principal chemical air pollutant, (O_3), formed by photochemical reactions on hydrocarbons and nitrogen oxides in the air, that is extremely irritating to the eyes and upper respiratory tract. p. 520

pancreas
(pang'krē əs *or* pan'krē əs) (Gr. pan, all + kreas, flesh) A long gland that lies beneath the stomach and is surrounded on one side by the curve of the duodenum; it secretes a number of digestive enzymes and the hormones insulin and glucagon. p. 138

parasympathetic system
(par'ə sim'pə thet'ik sis'təm) (Gr. para, beside + syn, with + pathos, feeling) A subdivision of the autonomic nervous system that generally stimulates the activities of normal internal body functions and inhibits alarm responses; opposite of sympathetic nervous system. p. 236

parathyroid gland
(par'ə thī'roid gland) (Gr. para, beside + thyreos, shield + eidos, form, shape) One of four small glands embedded in the posterior side of the thyroid that produces parathyroed hormone. p. 266

parathyroid hormone (PTH)
(par'ə thī'roid hôr'mōn) (Gr. para, beside + thyreos, shield + eidos, form, shape) A hormone secreted by the parathyroid glands that works antagonistically to calcitonin to help maintain the proper blood levels of various ions, primarily calcium. p. 265

parietal lobe
(pə rī'ə təl lōb) The section of the cerebral cortex of each hemisphere of the brain containing sensory receptors from different parts of the body. p. 227

passive immunity

(pas′iv i myo͞on′ə tē) The type of immunity produced by injection of antibodies into the subject to be protected or acquired by the fetus through the placenta. p. 311

passive transport

(pas′iv trans′pôrt) Molecular movement down a gradient but across a cell membrane; the three types of passive transport are diffusion, osmosis, and facilitated diffusion. p. 67

pectoral girdle

(pek′tə rəl gurd′əl) (L. pectus, chest) The part of the appendicular skeleton made up of two pairs of bones: the clavicles, or collarbones, and the scapulae, or shoulder blades. p. 287

pelvic girdle

(pel′vik gurd′əl) (L. pelvis, basin) The part of the appendicular skeleton made up of the two bones called coxal bones, pelvic bones or hip bones. p. 287

penis

(pē′nəs) A cylindrical organ that transfers sperm from the male reproductive tract to the female reproductive tract; the male urinary organ. p. 413

pepsin

(pep′sən) (Gr. pepsis, digestion) An enzyme of the stomach that digests only proteins, breaking them down into short peptides. p. 137

peptide bond

(pep′tīd bänd) A covalent bond that links two amino acids formed during dehydration synthesis when the amino group at one end and the carboxyl group at the other end lose a molecular of water between them. p. 42

peripheral nervous system

(pə rif′ə rəl nurv′əs sis′təm) (Gr. peripherein, to carry around) The part of the nervous system made up of the nerves of the body that bring messages to and from the brain and spinal cord. p. 224

peristalsis

(per′ə stôl′səs) (Gr. peri, around + stellein, to wrap) The rhythmic wave of contractions by the muscles of the esophagus that moves food down toward the stomach. p. 135

pH scale

(pē′āch′ skāl) A scale that indicates the relative concentration of H+ ions in a solution. Low pH values indicate high concentrations of H+ ions (acids), and high pH values indicate low concentrations. p. 33

phagocytosis

(fag′ə sī tō′səs) (Gr. phagein, to eat + kytos, hollow vessel) A type of endocytosis in which a cell ingests an organism or some other fragment of organic matter; macrophages and neutrophils are phagocytes. p. 70

pharyngeal (gill) slit

(fə rin′jē əl *or* far′in jē′əl) (Gr. pharynx, gullet) A principal feature of chordates that develops into the gill structure of a fish and into the ear, jaw, and throat structures of a terrestrial vertebrate. p. 474

pharynx

(far′inkgs) (Gr. gullet) The upper part of the throat that extends from behind the nasal cavities to the openings of the esophagus and larynx. p. 135

phenotype

(fē′nə tīp) (Gr. phainein, to show + typos, print) The outward appearance or expression of an organism's genes. p. 380

phospholipid

(fos′fō lip′id) (Gr. phosphoros, light-bearer + lipos, fat) A molecule made up of a portion of a fat molecule with a phosphate functional group attached. Because these molecules have polar and nonpolar parts, they form a double layer of molecules (a bilayer) when a in a watery environment. A phospholipid bilayer is the foundation of cell membranes. p. 40

photochemical

(fōt′ō kem′i kəl smôg) (Gr. photos, light + chemeia, chemistry) Smog that is caused by pollutants reacting in the presence of sunlight. p. 520

photon

(fō′ton) (Gr. photos, light) A discrete packet of energy from sunlight. p. 246

photosynthesis

(fōt′ō sin′thə səs) (Gr. photos, light -syn, together + tithenai, to place) The process whereby energy from the sun is captured by living organisms and used to produce molecules of food; it takes place in the chloroplasts of photosynthetic eukaryotic cells. p. 12

phylum, pl. phyla

(fī′ləm, fī′lə) (Gr. phylon, race, tribe) A major taxonomic group, ranking about a class. p. 14

pineal gland

(pin′ē əl gland) (L. pinus, pine tree) A tiny gland lying deep within the brain whose exact function remains a mystery; it is the possible site of an individual's biological clock. p. 271

pinna

(pin′ə) (L. feather) The projected part of the outer ear, the ear flap. p. 250

pinocytosis

(pi′nō sī tō′səs) (Gr. pinein, to drink + kytos, vessel) A type of endocytosis in which a cell ingests liquid material containing dissolved molecules. p. 70

pituitary

(pə to͞o′ə ter′ē) (L. pituita, phlegm) A tiny gland hanging from the underside of the brain, under the control of the hypothalamus, that secretes nine different major hormones. p. 261

placenta

(plə sen′tə) (L. a flat cake) A flat disk of tissue that grows into the uterine wall, through which the mother supplies the offspring with food, water, and oxygen and through which she removes wastes. p. 433

placental mammal

(plə sent′əl mam′əl) (L. a flat cake) A mammal that nourishes its developing embryo with the body of the mother by means of a placenta until development is almost complete. p. 478

plasma

(plaz′mə) (Gr. form) The fluid intercellular matrix within which blood cells float; contains practically every substance used and discarded by cells as well as nutrients, hormones, proteins, salts, ions, and albumin. p. 175

plasma cell

(plaz′mə sel) Any of several different kinds of cells and cell parts suspended within plasma, including erythrocytes, leukocytes, and platelets. p. 308

plasma membrane

(plaz′mə mem′brān) A thin, nonrigid structure that encloses the cell and regulates interactions between the cell and its environment. p. 55

plasmid

(plaz′mid) (Gr. plasma, form) A small fragment of DNA that replicates independently of the main chromosome. p. 452

platelet

(plāt′lət) (Gr. dim of plattus, flat) A cell fragment present in blood that plays an important role in the clotting of blood. p. 178

pleura, pl. pleurae

(plo͞or′ə, plo͞or′ē) (Gr. side) A thin, delicate, sheet-like membrane that lines the interior walls of the thoracic cavity and folds back on itself to cover each lung; covered by a thin film of liquid, the pleura reduces friction during respiratory movements of the lungs. p. 155

pollution

(pə lo͞o′shən) (L. polluere, to pollute) Contamination of the water sources and air of the Earth, causing physical and chemical changes that harm living and nonliving things. p. 515

polymer

(pol′ə mər) (Gr. polus, many + meris, part) A giant molecule formed of long chains of similar molecules. p. 35

polypeptide
(pol′ē pep′tīd) (Gr. polys, many + peptein, to digest) A long chain of amino acids linked end to end by peptide bonds; proteins are long, complex polypeptides, p. 42

polysaccharide
(pol′ē sak′ə rīd) (Gr. polys, many + sakcharon, sugar) A long polymer composed of insoluble sugar. p. 37

polyunsaturated
(pol′ē un sach′ə rā′təd) Referring to a fat composed of fatty acids that has more than one double bond; polyunsaturated fats have low melting points and are therefore liquid fats, or oils. p. 40

pons
(ponz) (L. bridge) The part of the brainstem consisting of a band of nerve fibers that acts as "bridges" and connects various parts of the brain to one another; it also brings messages to and from the spinal cord. p. 232

population
(pop′yə lā′shən) (L. populus, the people) A group that consists of the individuals of a given species that occur together at one place and at one time. p. 493

positive feedback loop
(poz′ət iv fēd′ bak′ lōōp) A feedback loop in which the response of the regulating mechanism is positive with respect to the outcome. p. 122

postsynaptic membrane
(pōst′sə nap′tik mem′brān) The membrane of the target cell of the synaptic cleft. p. 214

potential energy
(pə ten′chəl en′ər jē) Stored energy; energy not actively doing work but having the capacity to do so. p. 78

predation
(pri dā′shən) (L. praeda, prey) The killing and eating of an organism of one species by an organism of another species; an animal that kills and eats members of its own species is a cannibal. p. 497

primate
(prī′māt or prī′mət) (L. primus, first) A mammal that has characteristics reflecting a tree-dwelling life-style, such as hands and feet able to grasp things, flexible limbs, and a flexible spine. p. 479

producer
(prə dōōs′ər) An organism in an ecosystem capable of capturing energy from the sun and converting it to chemical energy usable to themselves and consumers. p. 12

prokaryotic cell
(prō kar′ē ot′ik sel) (Gr. pro, before + karyon, kernel) A cell smaller than a eukaryote, it has a simple interior organization with a single, circular strand of hereditary material that is not enclosed with a membrane; bacteria and the blue-green bacteria are prokaryotes. p. 14

prolactin
(prō lak′tən) (L. pro, before + lac, milk) A hormone secreted by the anterior pituitary that in association with estrogen, progesterone, and other hormones, stimulates the mammary glands in the breasts to secrete milk after a woman has given birth to a child. p. 263

prophase
(prō fāz′) (Gr. pro, before + phasis, form) The stage of mitosis characterized by the appearance of visible chromosomes. p. 341

proprioceptor
(prō′ prē əsep′tər) (L. proprius, one's own + ceptor, a receiver) A receptor located within the skeletal muscles, tendons, and inner ear that gives the body information about the position of its parts relative to each other and to the pull of gravity. p. 243

prosimian
(prō sim′ē ən) (Gr. pro, before + L. simia, an ape) A suborder of primates that includes lemurs, indris, aye-ayes, and lorises; they are small animals, mostly nocturnal, with large ears and eyes, elongated snouts, and rear limbs. p. 480

prostaglandin
(pros′tə glan′dən) (from prosta[te] gland ± -in) A hormone secreted by cell stimulates throughout the body that stimulates smooth muscle contraction and the dilation and constriction of blood vessels. p. 273

prostate
(pros′tāt) (Gr. prostates, one standing in front) A gland surrounded by the male urethra that adds a milky alkaline fluid to semen, neutralizing the acidity of the female vagina. p. 413

protein
(prō′tēn or prō′tē ən) (Gr. proteios, primary) A linear polymer of amino acids. p. 42

protist
(prōt′ tist) (Gr. protos, first) A member of the kingdom Protista, which includes unicellular eukaryotes as well as some multicellular forms. p. 457

proton
(prō′tôn) A subatomic particle in the nucleus of an atom that has mass and carries a positive charge. p. 24

proximal convoluted tubule
(prôk′sə məl kän′və lōō′təd tōō′byōōl)

A coiled portion of the nephron closest to Bowman's capsule lying in the cortex of the kidney; the site where reabsorption begins as the filtrate passes through the proximal tubule. p. 190

pseudostratified
(sōōdǒ′ō strat′ə fid′) (Gr. pseudos, false + L. stratificare, to arrange in layers) Refers to a type of epithelial tissue that gives the false appearance of being stratified. p. 110

pulmonary circulation
(pul′mə ner′ē sur′kyə lā′shən) The part of the human circulatory system that circulates blood to and from the lungs. p. 171

Punnett square
(pun′ət skwar) (after Reginald C. Punnett, English geneticist) A diagram that visualizes the genotypes of progeny in simple Mendelian crosses and illustrates their expected ratios. p. 380

pupil
(pyōō′pəl) (L. pupilla, little doll) The opening in the center of the iris through which light passes. p. 249

pyruvate
(pī rōō′vāt) The three-carbon molecule left when glycolysis is completed and the beginning material of the citric acid cycle. p. 91

receptor
(ri sep′tər) A specialized cell component that detects stimuli; it provides the body with information about the internal environment, the position in space, and the external environment. p. 210

recessive
(ri ses′iv) The form of a trait that recedes or disappears entirely in a hybrid offspring. p. 375

rectum
(rek′təm) (L. straight) The lower part of the large intestine, which terminates at the anus. p. 143

red blood cell
(red blud sel) *See* erythrocyte.

red bone marrow
(red bōn mar ′ō) The soft tissue that fills the spaces within the bony latticework of spongy bone; it is the place where most of the body's blood cells are formed. p. 284

reduction
(ri duk′shən) (L. reduction, a bringing back: originally "bringing back" a metal from its oxide) The gain of an electron by an atom or a molecule. p. 28

reflex
(rē′fleks) (L. reflectare, to bend back) An automatic response to a nerve stimulation. p. 225

reflex arc

(rē′fleks ärk) The pathway of nervous activity in a reflex. p. 232.

refractory period

(ri frak′tə rē pir′ē əd) The recovery period after membrane depolarization during which the membrane is unable to respond to additional stimulation. p. 211

releasing hormone

(ri lēs′ing hôr′mōn) A hormone produced by the hypothalamus that affects the secretion of specific hormones from the anterior pituitary p. 261

replication fork

(rep′lə kā′shən fôrk) The split in a DNA molecule where the double-stranded DNA molecule separates during DNA replication. p. 331

respiration

(res′pə rā′shən) (L. respirare, to breathe) The uptake of oxygen and the release of carbon dioxide by the body. Cellular, internal, and external respiration are all part of the general process of respiration. p. 150

respiratory assembly

(res′pə rə tôr′ē əsemb′blē) A special channel that allows protons to pass back from the outer compartment of a mitochondrion into the inner compartment; each passage of a proton back into the inner compartment through a respiratory assembly is coupled to the synthesis of an ATP molecule. p. 98

response

(ri spons′) (L. respondere, to reply) The reply or reaction of an individual organism to a stimulus; it can be an innate or inborn reflex or a learned response such as by operant or classical conditioning. p. 225

resting potential

(rest′ing pə ten′chəl) An electrical potential difference, or electrical charge, along the membrane of the resting neuron. p. 210

reticulate bodies

(rə tik′ yoo lāt) (L. net) The metabolically active forms of chlamydae that multiply and spread within the body, causing disease. p. 456

retina

(ret′ən ə) (L. a small net) The structure in the eye, composed of rod and cone cells, that is sensitive to light. p. 247

rhodopsin

(rō dop′sən) (Gr. rhodon, rose + opsis, vision) A complex in the retina formed by the coupling of retinal and opsin. p. 247

ribonucleic acid (RNA)

(rī′bō nōō klē′ik as′əd) One of two types of nucleic acid found in cells; differs from DNA in that its sugar is ribose and uracil is present rather than thymine. p. 326

ribosomal RNA (rRNA)

(rī′bə sō′məl är′en′ā′) The type of RNA found in ribosomes that plays a role in the manufacture of polypeptides. p. 62

ribosome

(rī′bə sōm′) A minute, round structure found in endoplasmic reticulum; ribosomes are the places where proteins are manufactured. p. 59

RNA polymerase

(är′en′ā′ pol′ə mə rās′) The special enzyme that transcribes RNA from DNA. p. 333

rod

(räd) A light receptor located within the retina at the back of the eye that functions in dim light and detects white light only. p. 246

rough endoplasmic reticulum

(ruf en′dō plaz′mik ri tik′yə ləm) (Gr. endon, within +plasma, from cytoplasm; L. reticulum, network) The type of endoplasmic reticulum that makes and transports proteins destined to leave the cell; rough refers to the minute, round structures called ribosomes covering the surface where proteins are made. p. 59

round window

(round win′dō) A membrane-covered hole at the wider end of the cochlea. p. 250

SA node

(es′ā′ nōd) See sinoatrial (SA) node.

saccule

(sak′yōōl) (N.L. sacculus, small bag) A sac inside a bulge in the vestibule of the inner ear containing both ciliated and nonciliated cells. p. 252

saliva

(sə lī′və) (L. spittle) The secretion of the salivary glands; a solution consisting primarily of water, mucus, and the digestive enzyme salivary amylase. p. 133

salivary amylase

(sal′ə ver′ē am′ə lās) (L. salivarius, slimy + Gr. amylon, starch -asis, coloid enzyme) A digestive enzyme that breaks down starch into molecules of the disaccharide maltose. p. 133

salivary glands

(sal′ə ver′ē glandz) (L. salivarius, slimy + glans, acorn) The paired glands of the mouth that secrete saliva. p. 133

saltatory conduction

(sal′tətôr′ē kən duk′shən) (L. saltatio, leaping) A very fast form of nerve impulse conduction in which impulses "jump" along myelinated neurons. p. 213

sarcimere

(sär′kə mir′) (Gr. sarx, flesh + meris, part of) The repeating bands of actin and myosin myofilaments that appear between two Z lines in a muscle fiber. p. 294

sarcoplasmic reticulum

(sär′kō plaz′mik ri tik′yə ləm) (Gr. sarx, flesh + plassein, to form, mold; L. reticulum, network) A tubular, branching latticework of endoplasmic reticulum that wraps around each myofibril like a sleeve. p. 296

Schwann cells

(shwän or shvän selz) (after Theodor Schwann, German anatomist) The supporting cells associated with nerve fibers of all the other cells that make up the peripheral nervous system. p. 118

scientific method

(sī′ən tif′ik meth′əd) A set of procedures used to answer questions that is common among the various scientific disciplines. p. 4

sclera

(sklir′ə) (Gr. skleros, hard) The tough outer layer of connective tissue that covers and protects the eye. p. 248

scrotum

(skrō′təm) (L. a bag) A sac of skin, located outside the lower pelvic area of the male, which houses the testicles, or testes. p. 410

selective reabsorption

(sə lek′tiv rē′əb sôrp′shən) The process in which the kidneys select specific substances according to the body's needs from the filtrate. p. 188

semen

(sē′mən) (L. seed) Fluid produced by the accessory glands of the male reproductive system combined with sperm. p. 413

semicircular canal

(sem′i sur′kyə lər kə nal′) Any of three fluid-filled canals in the inner ear that detect the direction of an individual's movement. p. 252

seminal vesicle

(sem′ ən əl ves′ə kəl) One of two accessory glands that secrete a thick, clear fluid forming a part of the semen. p. 413

seminiferous tubule

(sem′əmf′ər əs tōō′byōōl) (L. semen, seed + ferre, to produce) A tightly coiled tube within a testis where sperm cells develop. p. 411

sensory neuron

(sens′ə rē nōōr′on) A neuron of the peripheral nervous system that transmits information to the central nervous system. p. 206

septum, pl. septa

(sep′təm, sep′tə) (L. saeptum, a fence)

The tissue that separates the two sides of the heart. p. 174

sex chromosome
(seks krō'mə sōm') The X and Y chromosomes that determine the gender of an individual as well as certain other characteristics. p. 390

sexual reproduction
(seksh'ə wəl *or* sek'shəl ē prə duk'shən) The type of reproduction that involves the fusion of gametes to produce the first cell of a new individual. p. 339

sickle-cell anemia
(sik'əl sel' ənē'mē ə) (A.S. sicol, curved + L. cella, chamber + Gr. a, not + haima, blood) A recessive genetic disorder common to African blacks and their descendants in which affected individuals cannot transport oxygen to their tissues properly because the molecules within the red blood cells that carry oxygen, hemoglobin proteins, are defective. p. 398

sinoatrial (SA) node
(sī' nō ā' trē əl nōd) A small cluster of specialized cardiac muscle cells embedded in the upper wall of the right atrium of the heart that automatically and rhythmically sends out impulses initiating each heartbeat. p. 174

sister chromatid
(sis'tər krō'mə tid) Either of two identical sturcutres held together at the centromere, composed of chromatin material that coils and condenses just before and during cell division to form chromosomes. p. 343

skeletal muscle
(skel'ət əl mus'əl) A type of muscle that is voluntary because of conscious control over its action; skeletal muscle is connected to bones and allows for body movement. p. 116

small intestine
(smôl in tes'∂tən) The tube-like portion of the digestive tract that begins at the pyloric sphincter and ends at its T-shaped junction with the large intestine. p. 138

smooth endoplasmic reticulum
(smōōth en'dō plaz'mik ri tik'yə ləm) (Gr. endon, within + plasma, from cytoplasm; L. reticulum, network) The type of endoplasmic reticulum that helps build carbohydrates and lipids within the cytoplasm; it does not have ribosomes attached to its surface and does not manufacture proteins. p. 59

smooth muscle
(smōōth mus'əl) A type of muscle that contracts involuntarily and is located in the walls of certain internal structures such as blood vessels and the stomach. p. 116

sodium-potassium pump
(sōd'ē əm pə tas'ē əm pump) The term given to the coupled channel that uses energy to move sodium (Na^+) and potassium (K^+) ions across the cell membrane. p. 70

soft palate
(sôft pal'ət) (L. palatum, palate) The tissue at the back of the roof of the mouth p. 135

solute
(sol'yōōt) The other kinds of molecules dissolved in water. *See* solution, solvent. p. 68

solution
(s lōō'shən) A mixture of molecules and ions dissolved in water. p. 68

solvent
(solv'ənt) The most common of the molecules in a solution, usually water. p. 68

somatic nervous system
(sō mat'ik nurv'əs sis'təm) (Gr. soma, body) The branch of the peripheral nervous system consisting of motor neurons that send messages to the skeletal muscles and control voluntary responses. p. 225

somite
(sō'mīt) (Gr. soma, body) A chunk of mesoderm that gives rise to most of the axial skeleton and most of the dermis of the body. p. 437

species
(spē'shēz *or* spē'sēz) A group of related organisms that shares common characteristics and is able to interbreed and produce viable offspring. p. 9

specific defense
(spə sif'ik di fens') The immune response of the body. p. 302

spermatid
(spur'mə tid) A haploid cell in the testes arising from a diploid cell called a spermatogonium. p. 411

spermatogenesis
(spur'mə tō jen'ə səs) (Gr. sperma, sperm, seed + gignesthai, to be born) The development of sperm cells within the coiled tubules of the testis triggered by follicle-stimulating hormones. p. 411

spinal cord
(spīn'əl kôrd) The part of the central nervous system that runs down the neck and back, receives information from the body, carries this information to the brain, and sends information from the brain to the body. p. 224

spinal nerve
(spīn'əl nurv) A nerve by which the spinal cord receives information from the body; includes sensory and motor nerves. p. 232

spindle fibers
(spin'dəl fi'bərz) Special microtubules that are assembled from a pair of related centrioles during the prophase stage of mitosis. p. 343

spleen
(splēn) (Gr. splen) An organ of the lymphatic system that stores an emergency blood supply and also contains white blood cells. p. 180

spongy bone
(spun'jē bōn) A type of bone in the human skeleton that is composed of an open latticework of thin plates of bone; spongy bone is found at the ends of long bones and within short, flat, and irregularly shaped bones. p. 114

squamous
(skwā'məs) (L. squama, scale) One of the main shapes of epithelial cells. Squamous cells are thin and flat and are found in the air sacs of the lungs, the lining of blood vessels, and the skin. p. 109

starch
(stärch) (A.S. stercan) Stored energy in plants formed by using glucose to form polysaccharides. p. 37

stereoscopic vision
(ster'ē ō skôp'ik vizh'ən) (Gr. stereos, solid + skopein, to view) Vision created by two eyes focusing on the same object. p. 480

stomach
(stum'ək) (Gr. stomachos, mouth) A muscular sac in which food is collected and partially digested by hydrochloric acid and proteases. p. 137

stratified
(strat'ə fid') (L. stratificare, to arrange in layers) Refers to epithelium that is made up of two or more layers. p. 110

stretch receptor
(strech ri sep'tər) A special nerve that is sensitive to any stretching in its tissue. p. 243

suppressor T cell
(sə pres'ər tē sel) A kind of T cell that limits the immune response. p. 307

symbiosis
(sim'bē ō'səs *or* sim'bī ō'səs) (Gr. a living together) The living together of two or more organisms in a close association. p. 55

sympathetic nervous system
(sim'pə thet'ik nurv'əs sis'təm) A subdivision of the autonomic nervous system that generally mobilizes the body for greater activity; produces responses that are the opposite of the parasympathetic nervous system. p. 236

synapse
(sin'aps *or* sə naps') (Gr. synapsis, a union) A junction between an axon tip and another cell, usually including a

narrow gap separating the two cells. p. 213

synapsis
(sə nap'səs) (Gr. union) The lining up of homologous chromosomes during prophase I of meiosis, initiating the process of crossing over. p. 345

synaptic cleft
(sə nap'tik kleft) The space or gap between two adjacent neurons. p. 213

synovial joint
(sənō'vē əl joint) (L. synovia, joint fluid) A freely movable joint in which a space exists between articulating bones. p. 288

syphilis
(sif'i lis) A sexually transmitted disease caused by the bacterium *Treponema pallidum* that produces stages oflocalized infection to widespread infection. p. 454

systemic circulation
(sis tem'ik sur'kyə lā'shən) The pathway of blood vessels to the body regions and organs other than the lung. p. 173

systolic period
(sis tol'ik pir'ē əd) (Gr. systole, contraction) The pushing period of heart contraction, which ends with the closing of the aortic valve, during which a pulse of blood is forced into the systemic arterial system, immediately raising the blood pressure within these vessels. p. 174

T cell (T lymphocyte)
(tē sel) A type of lymphocyte that carries out the cell-mediated immune response. p. 307

T lymphocyte
(tē lim'fə sīt) *See* T cell.

tarsal
(tär'səl) (Gr. tarsos, a broad, flat surface) Any of the seven short bones that make up the ankle in the appendicular skeleton of a human. p. 287

taste bud
(tāst bud) A microscopic chemoreceptor embedded within the papillae of the tongue that works with the olfactory receptors to produce the taste sensation. p. 245

taxonomy
(tak sän'ə mē) (Gr. taxis, arrangement + nomos, law) The classification of the diverse array of species by categorizing organisms based on their common ancestry. p. 13

Tay-Sachs disease
(tā'saks' diz ēz') (after Warren Tay, British physician, and Bernard Sachs, U.S. neurologist) An incurable, fatal, recessive, hereditary disorder in which brain deterioration causes death by the age of 5 years; has a high incidence of occurrence among Jews of Eastern and

Central Europe and among American Jews. p. 398

tectorial membrane
(tek tôr'ē əl mem'brān) (L. tectum, roof) The membrane that covers the hairs that stick up from the cochlear duct. p. 251

telophase
(tel'ə fāz) (Gr. telos, end + phasis, form) The stage of mitosis during which the mitotic apparatus assembled during prophase is disassembled, the nuclear envelope is reestablished, and the normal use of the genes present in the chromosomes is reinitiated. p. 344

temporal lobe
(tem'pə rəl lōb) (L. temporalis, the temples) The section of the cerebral cortex in each hemisphere of the brain dealing with hearing; different surface areas correspond to different tones and rhythms. p. 227

tendon
(ten'dən) (Gr. tenon, stretch) A tissue that connects muscle to bones. p. 291

teratogen
(tə rat'ə jən) (Gr. teratos, monster + gennan, to produce) An agent, such as alcohol, that can induce malformations in rapidly developing tissues and organs. p. 434

testcross
(test'krôs') A cross between a phenotypically dominant test plant with a known homozygous recessive plant; devices by Mendel to further test his conclusions. p. 380

testis, pl. testes
(tes'təs, tes'tēz') (L. witness) The male gonads where sperm production occurs. p. 410

testosterone
(tes'tos'tə rōn) (Gr. testis, testicle + steiras, barren) A sex hormone secreted by the testes responsible for the development and maintenance of male secondary sexual characteristics. p. 263

tetrad
(te'trad') (Gr. tetras, four) During prophase I of meiosis I, the name given to the paired homologous chromosomes that together have four chromatids. p. 345

thalamus
(thal'ə məs) (Gr. thalamos, chamber) A mass of gray matter lying at the base of the cerebrum that receives sensory stimuli, interprets some of these stimuli, and sends the remaining sensory messages to appropriate locations in the cerebrum. p. 229

theory
(thē'ə rē or thir'ē) A synthesis of hypotheses that has withstood the test of

time and is therefore a powerful concept that helps scientists made dependable predictions about the world. p. 8

thrombus
(throm'bəs) (Gr. clot) A blood clot that forms in a blood vessel and interferes with the flow of blood. p. 180

thymus
(thī'məs) (Gr. thymos) A small gland located in the neck that plays an important role in the maturation of certain lymphocytes called T cells, which are an essential part of the immune system. p. 180

thyroid gland
(thī'roid gland) An important gland located in the neck near the voice box that produces hormones regulating the body's metabolism. p. 264

thyroid-stimulating hormone (TSH)
(thī'roid stim'yə lāt ing hôr'mōn) A tropic hormone produced by the anterior pituitary that triggers the thyroid gland to produce the three thyroid hormones. p. 263

thyroxine (T_4)
(thī rok'sēn *or* thī rok'sən) A hormone produced by the thyroid gland that helps regulate the body's metabolism. p. 264

tidal volume
(tīd'əl väl' yəm *or* väl'yum) The amount or volume of air inspired or expired with each breath. p. 157

tissue
(tish'oo) (L. texere, to weave) A member of a group of similar cells that works together to perform a function. p. 10

trachea
(trā'kē ə) (L. windpipe) The windpipe; the air passageway that runs down the neck in front of the esophagus and brings air to the lungs. p. 151

trait
(trāt) A distinguishing feature or characteristic of a plant or person due to the transmission of genes. p. 373

transcription
(trans krip'shən) (L. trans, across + scribere, to write) The first step in the process of polypeptide synthesis in which a gene is copied into a strand of messenger RNA. p. 333

transfer RNA (tRNA)
(trans'fur är'en'ā') A type of RNA that transports amino acids, used to build polypeptides, to the ribosomes; they also align each amino acid at the correct place on the elongating chain. p. 333

translation
(trans lā'shən) (L. trans, across + locare, to put or place) The second step of gene expression in which mRNA, using its

copied DNA code, directs the synthesis of a polypeptide. p. 335

translocation
(trans'lō kā'shən) (L. trans, across + locare, to put or place) A situation in which a section of a chromosome breaks off and then reattaches to another chromosome, producing an abnormally long chromosome. p. 393

tropomyosin
(trō'pə mī'ə sən *or* trop'ə mī'ə sən) (Gr. tropos, turn + myos, muscle) A muscle protein that is involved in the formation of cross-bridges during muscle contraction. p. 296

troponin
(trō'pə nən *or* trop'ə nən) (Gr. tropos, turn) A muscle protein that attaches to both actin and tropomyosin; it is concerned with calcium binding and inhibiting cross-bridge formation. p. 296

true breeding
(trōō brēd'ing) Said of plants that produce offspring consistently identical to the parent with respect to certain defined characteristics after generations of self-fertilization. p. 375

trypsin
(trip'sən) (Gr. tripsis, friction) An enzyme produced by the pancreas, which together with chymotrypsin and carboxypeptidase, completes the digestion of proteins. p. 139

tubular secretion
(tōō'byōō lər sə krē'shən) The process by which the kidneys excrete a variety of potentially harmful substances from the blood. p. 188

tumor
(tōō' mər) (L. swollen) An uncontrolled growth of a large mass of cells. p. 354

Turner syndrome
(tur' nər sin' drōm) (after H.H. Turner, U.S. physician) A genetic condition resulting from an XO zygote that develops into a human female who is sterile, of short stature, with a webbed neck, low-set ears, a broad chest, infantile sex organs, and low-normal mental abilities. p. 392

tympanic membrane
(tim pan'ik mem'brān) (Gr. tympanon, drum) The thin piece of fibrous connective tissue stretched over the opening to the middle ear; the eardrum. p. 250.

ultrasound
(ul'trə sound') A noninvasive procedure that uses sound waves to produce an image of the fetus but that harms neither the mother nor the fetus; allows the fetus to be examined for major abnormalities. p. 401

umbilical arteries
(um bil'ə kəl ärt'ə rē and văn) (L. umbilicus, navel) The blood lines of the umbilical cord; the artery provides nourishment and sends wastes from the embryo to the placenta; the fetal blood then travels through the umbilical vein back to the embryo. p. 433

umbilical cord
(um bil'ə kəl körd) (L. umbilicus, navel) The attachment connecting the fetus with the placenta. p. 433

unsaturated
(un sach'ə rā'təd) Referring to a fat composed of fatty acids with double bonds that replace some of the hydrogen atoms. p. 40

urea
(yōō rē' ə *or* yōōr' ē ə) (Gr. ouron, urine) The primary excretion produce from the deamination of amino acids. p. 187

ureter
(yōō rē'tər *or* yōōr'ə tər) (Gr. oureter) The tube that carries urine from the kidney to the bladder. p. 188

urethra
(yōō rē'thrə) (Gr. ourein, to urinate) A muscular tube that brings urine from the urinary bladder to the outside; in men, the urethra also carries semen to the outside of the body during ejaculation. p. 194

uric acid
(yōōr'ik as'əd) A nitrogenous waste in the urine formed from the breakdown of nucleic acids (DNA and RNA) found in the cells of ingested food and from the metabolic turnover of bodily nucleic acids and ATP. p. 187

urinary bladder
(yōō'ə ner'ē blad'ər) A hollow muscular organ that acts as a storage pouch for urine. p. 195

urine
(yōōr'ən) (Gr. ouron, urine) The fluid produced by the kidneys made up of water and dissolved waste products. p. 187

uterus
(yōō'tər əs) (L. womb) The organ in females in which a fertilized ovum can develop; the womb. p. 415

vaccination
(vak'sə nā'shən) (L. vaccinus, pert. to cows) An injection with disease-causing microbes or toxins that have been killed or changed in some way so as to be harmless; it causes the body to build up antibodies against a particular disease. p. 303

vagina
(və jīn'ə) (L. sheath) An organ in the body of a female whose muscular, tubelike passageway to the exterior has

three functions; it accepts the penis during intercourse; it is the lower portion of the birth canal, and it provides an exit for the menstrual flow. p. 414

valve
(valv) (L. valva, leaf of a folding door) Any of the one-way valves found in the heart and blood vessels, similarly constructed, that prevent the backflow of blood. p. 173

vas deferens
(vas def'ə rəenz) A long connecting tube that ascends from the epididymis into the pelvic cavity, looping over the side of the urinary bladder. p. 413

vein
(vān) (L. vena, a blood vessel) A small vein that collects blood from the capillary beds and brings it to larger veins. p. 167

ventricle
(ven'trə kəl) (L. ventriculus. belly) Either of two lower chambers of the heart; the right ventricle pumps blood into the pulmonary artery and then the lungs, whereas the left ventricle pumps blood through the aorta into the arteries. p. 232

venule
(ven'yōōl) (L. vena, vein) A small vein that starts at a capillary and connects it to a larger vein. p. 167

vertebral column
(ver'tə brəl kol'əm) The collection of 26 bones in the middle of the back, stacked one on top of the other, that acts like a strong, flexible rod and supports the head in a human skeleton; the spine or backbone. p. 286

villus, pl. villi
(vil'əs, vil'ī) (L. a tuft of hair) Fine, finger-like projections that increase the surface absorption capability of the small intestine. p. 141

viral envelope
Chemical layer over the protein capsid found on some viruses. p. 447

viral replication
The process of viral multiplication within cells. p. 448

vitamin
(vīt'ə mən) (L. vita, life + amine, of chemical origin) An organic molecule that performs functions such as helping the body use the energy of carbohydrates, fats, and proteins; 13 different vitamins play a vital role in the human body. p. 130

vocal cord
(vō'kəl kôrd) Two pieces of elastic tissue covered with a mucous membrane stretched across the larynx that are involved in the production of sound. p. 151

vulva
(vul'və) (L. covering) The collective term for the external genitalis of a female. p. 419

white blood cell
(hwīt *or* wīt blud sel) *See* leukocyte.

yellow marrow
(yel'ō mar◊'ō) A soft, fatty connective tissue that fills the hollow cylindrical core of long bones. p. 284

yolk
(yōk) (O.E. geolu, yellow) The nutrient material of an ovum that the developing individual can liver on until nutrients can be derived from the mother. p. 428

yolk sac
(yōk sak) A membranous sac surrounding the food yolk in the embryo. p. 434

zona pellucida
(zō'nə pə lōō'sə də) (L. zona, girdle + pellucidus, transparent) A jelly-like membranous covering of the ovum. p. 428

zygote
(zī'gōt) (Gr. zygotos, paired together) A cell produced by the haploid nuclei of the sperm and egg; the fertilized ovum. p. 415

Credits

Chapter 1
Opener, © James H. Karales/Peter Arnold, Inc.; © Jerry Jacka; Visuals Unlimited
1-1 Dr. Betsy Dresser, The Cincinnati Zoo
Laura J. Edwards
Russell Kaye © 1992/Discover Magazine
Ed Kashi © 1991/Discover Magazine
1-2, 1-5, 1-7, Nadine Sokol
1-3, *A* Stephen Dalton/Natural History Photographic Agency
1-3, *B* John Trager/Visuals Unlimited
1-3, *C* Richard Walters/Visuals Unlimited
1-3, *D* Cabisco/Visuals Unlimited
1-3, *E* Balkwill-D. Maratea/Visuals Unlimited
1-4, *A* Triarch/Visuals Unlimited
1-4, *B* Biophoto Associated/Photo Researchers, Inc.
1-4, *C,* **1-4,** *F* E. Rhone Rudder
1-4, *D* Raychel Ciemma
1-4, *E* Brian Milne/Animals Animals
1-4, *G* Jeft Fort/Bruce Coleman Ltd.
1-4, *H* Robert Maier/Animals Animals
1-4, *I* NASA
1-6, *A* Patti Murray/Animals Animals
1-6, *B* Wildtype Products/Bruce Coleman Ltd.
1-6, *C* Adrian Davies/Bruce Coleman Ltd.
1-8 Barbara Cousins

Chapter 2
Opener © 92 Don Mason/The Stock Market
2-1, 2-2, 2-3, *A-B,* **2-7, 2-8, 2-9, 2-17,** *B* Nadine Sokol
2-3, *C* Michael Gadomski/Tom Stack & Associates
2-4 The Bettmann Archives
2-5, *A* Jurgen Schmitt/The Image Bank
2-5, *B,* **2-5,** *D* Frank T. Awbrey/Visuals Unlimited
2-5, *C,* Nicholas Foster/The Image Bank
2-6 Michael & Patricia Figden
3-8, *A* Joseph Devenney/The Image Bank
2-8, *B,* **2-24,** *C* George Bernard/Animals Animals
2-8, *C* Eastcott/Momatiuk/The Image Works
2-10 Lilli Robins
2-15, *B* E.S. Ross
2-16, *A* Manfred Kage/Peter Arnold, Inc.
2-17, *A* J.D. Litvay/Visuals Unlimited
2-18 Scott Johnson/Animals Animals
2-23 Nadine Sokol after Bill Ober
2-24, *A* Manfred Kage/Peter Arnold
2-24, *B* Michael Pasdizor/The Image Bank
2-24, *D* Oxford Scientific Films/Animals Animals
2-24, *E* Scott Blakeman/Tom Stack & Associates
2-A Simon Fraser/Medical Phisics, RVI, Newcastle/Science Photo Library/Custom Medical Stock Photo, Inc.
2-B Tom Tracey/Photographic Resources

Chapter 3
Opener Allen, R.D.: The microtubule; Scientific American, Inc. 1987, p. 43
3-1, *A* M. Abbey/Visuals Unlimited
3-1, *B-C,* **3-23,** *B* David M. Phillips/Visuals Unlimited
3-1, *D* John D. Cunningham/Visuals Unlimited
3-1, *E* Bruce Iverson/Visuals Unlimited
3-1, *F* Triarch/Visuals Unlimited
3-1, *G* Carolina Biological Supply Co.
3-2, L. L. Sims/Visuals Unlimited
3-4, 3-5, 3-8, 3-1, *B,* **3-14,** *A,* **3-18,** *B* Bill Ober
3-6, *A* Manfred Kage/Peter Arnold
3-6, *B* J. David Roberson
3-7, *A-C* Klaus Weber & Mary Osborn, for Scientific American, vol. 153, pp. 110-121, 1985 (unpublished)
3-7 (art) Barbara Cousins
3-9, *A* Dr. A. Brody/Science Photo Library/Photo Reasearchers, Inc.
3-9, *B* Kevin Somerville after Bill Ober
3-12, *A* Richard Rodewald, University of Virginia
3-11, *A,* **3-14,** *C,* **3-17,** *A* Charles J. Flickinger
3-11, *B,* **3-12** Nadine Sokol
3-13 K. G. Murti/Visuals Unlimited
3-14, *B* Dr. Thomas W. Tillack
3-15, *C-D* Ed Reschke
3-18, *A* Kenneth R. Miller
3-21, 3-22, 3-25, *B,* **3-26,** *A* Barbara Cousins
3-24 Jack Tandy after Nadine Sokol
3-25, *A-B* Christy Krames
3-25, *C-D* Jim Person/Taurus Associates
3-26, *B* Dr. Birgit H. Satir

Chapter 4
Opener © 1983 Thomas Braise/The Stock Market
4-3, 4-5, 4-11, 4-14 Barbara Cousins
4-6 AP/Wide World Photos, Inc.
4-7 John Sohlden/Visuals Unlimited
4-9 Bill Ober
4-10 Nadine Sokol after Bill Ober

Chapter 5
Opener Tom Tracy/Stock Market
5-1, 5-6, 5-11, 5-12, *B,* **5-13** Nadine Sokol
5-2 Robert Barclay/Grant Heilman Photography
5-3 Barbara Cousins
5-4 George Klart
5-8 Grant Heilman/Grant Heilman Photography
5-12, *A* Custom Medical Stock Photo, Inc.
5-15, *B* Michael Freeman/Bruce Coleman Ltd.

Chapter 6
Opener, 6-8, 6-11, *A* Lennart Nilsson
Behold Man, Little, Brown and Co.
6-1, 6-11, *B,* **6-13** Nadine Sokol
6-2(art) Christine Oleksyk
6-2(photo) Tom Tracy/Photographic Resources
6-3 Barbara Cousins
6-4 Emma Shelton
6-5 J.V. Small & F. Rinnerthaler
6-6 *St. Louis Globe-Democrat*
6-7, *A* David J. Mascaro and Associates
6-7, *B-C* John Hagen
6-9 David M. Phillips/Visuals Unlimited
6-10 Bill Ober
6-12 Cynthia Turner Alexander/Terry Cockerham, Synapse Media Production/Christine Oleksyk
Taboe 6-2, Table 6-3 Ed Reschke
Table 6-6, *A* Triarch/Visuals Unlimited
Table 6-6, *B-C* John D. Cunningham/Visuals Unlimited

Chapter 7
Opener Chet Hanchet/Photographic Resources
7-1, 7-2, *A,* **7-5, 7-8, 7-10** Nadine Sokol
7-2, *B* G. David Brown
7-3, 7-9, *A* Barbara Cousins
7-4 Kate Sweeney
7-6 Bill Ober
7-7 Christy Krames after Bill Ober
7-9, *B* David M. Phillips/Visuals Unlimited
7-12 Lilli Robbins
7-13 Laura J. Edwards
7-A Benjamin, M.D./Custom Medical Stock Photos, Inc.

Chapter 8
Opener(top) American Cancer Society
Opener (bottom) James Stevenson/SPL/Photo Researchers, Inc.
8-1, 8-11, Kate Sweeney
8-2 Courtesy of AT&T Archives
8-3 Ellen Dirkson/Visuals Unlimited
8-4 Lennart Nilsson, *Behold Man,* Little, Brown and Co.
8-5 Art Siegel, University of Pennsylvania
8-6, 8-10 Nadine Sokol
8-7, 8-8, 8-9 Barbara Cousins
8-12 M. Moore/Visuals Unlimited

Chapter 9
Opener William Strode/Humana, Inc./Black Star
9-1, 9-13 Nadine Sokol
9-2, 9-17 Kate Sweeney
9-3 Christy Krames

9-4, 9-7, 9-18 Ed Reschke
9-5, 9-12 Bill Ober
9-6 D. W. Fawcett-T. Kuwabara/Visuals Unlimited
9-8 John D. Cunningham/Visuals Unlimited
9-9, 9-10, 9-11 Barbara Cousins
9-14 Mako Murayama/BPS/Tom Stack
9-15 Raychel Ciemma
9-16 Manfred Kage/Peter Arnold, Inc.
9-19 Harry Ransom Humanities Research Center
9-A Laura J. Edwards

Chapter 10

Opener M.P. Kahl/Photo Researcher, Inc.
10-1 Kate Sweeney
10-2 Dan Gotshall
10-2 Larry Brock/Tom Stack & Associates
10-4, 10-5, 10-6, 10-14 Barbara Cousins
10-13 Raychel Ciemma
10-16 Organon Teknika/Visuals Unlimited
10-A © 1991 Ted Horowitz/The Stock Market

Chapter 11

Opener Tom McCarthy, 1988 Discover Publications
11-1 Peter Cohen/Custom Medical Stock Photo, Inc.
11-2, 11-3 (art), 11-7, 11-8, 11-9, 11-10, 11-11, 11-14 Nadine Sokol
11-3 C.S. Raines/Visuals Unlimited
11-4 E.S. Ross
11-6 Jack Tandy after Barbara Cousins
11-11 Uniphoto Picture Agency
11-12, B, 11-13 Barbara Cousins
11-12, A Heimer L. *Human Brain and Spinal Cord,* Springer-Verlag
11-15 Dr. Michael J. Kuhar, NIDA Addiction Research Center

Chapter 12

Opener James H. Karales/Peter Arnold
12-1 Kate Sweeney
12-3, 12-4, 12-6, 12-9 Nadine Sokol
12-5 Marcus Raichle, M.D./Washington University Medical School
12-6 Bill Ober
12-7, 12-11, 12-12 Barbara Cousins
12-8, 12-10 Michael P. Schenk
12-13 Raychel Ciemma
12-A Sobel/Klonsky/The Image Bank

Chapter 13

Opener Nathan Benn/Woodfin Camp
13-1, A Martha Swope, 1990
13-1, B-C Martin/Custom Mecical Stock Photo, Inc.
13-2, 13-9, 13-12 Nadine Sokol
13-4, A Marsha A. Dohrman
13-4, B Christine Oleksyk
13-5, 13-11, 13-12, 13-15 Raychel Ciemma
13-7, A Scott Mittman and Maria T. Mag
13-8 Bill Ober

Chapter 14

Opener *U.C. Davis Magazine,* University of California, Davis
14-1 Kate Sweeney

14-2, 14-3, 14-9 Barbara Cousins
14-4, 14-5, 14-13, 14-14 Nadine Sokol
14-6 Bettina Cirone/Photo Researchers, Inc.
14-7 *American Journal of Medicine* 20 (1956) 133
14-8 NMSB/Custom Medical Stock Photo, Inc.
14-11, 14-12 Raychel Ciemma
14-15 Ed Reschke
14-A Susan Lapides/Time Magazine, Inc.

Chapter 15

Opener Vince Rodriguez
15-1, 15-13, B Raychel Ciemma
15-2 Bill Ober
15-3, 15-9 Kate Sweeney
15-4, 15-10 Nadine Sokol
15-5, 15-6, 15-7, 15-11, 15-15 Barbara Cousins
15-8 Scott Bodell
15-12 Richard Rodewald, University of Virginia
15-13 Raychel Ciemma after Bill Ober
15-14 John D. Cunningham/Visuals Unlimited
15-A Jacques Cochin/The Image Bank
Table 15-1 Nadine Sokol after Rusty Jones

Chapter 16

Opener Lennart Nilsson
16-1 Raychel Ciemma
16-2 Science VU-NLM/Visuals Unlimited
16-3, 16-12, A Bill Ober
16-5 Kate Sweeney
16-6, 16-8, 16-9, 16-15 Barbara Cousins
16-7 Dr. A. Liepins/SPL/Photo Researchers, Inc.
16-10 Secchi, LeCaque, Roussel Uclaf, CNRI/Science Source/Photo Researchers, Inc.
16-11 Manfred Kage/Peter Arnold, Inc.
16-12, B Nadine Sokol after Bill Ober
16-16 Larry G. Arlain, Wright State University
16-A M. English/Custom Medical Stock Photo, Inc.

Chapter 17

Opener CNRI/SPL/Science Source
17-1 U.K. Laemmli & J.R. Paulson
17-2, 17-24, B, 17-32 Raychel Ciemma
17-3, A Ada L. Olins/Biological Photo Service
17-3, B, 17-13, 17-22, 17-25, 17-26, 17-31 (art) Barbara Cousins
17-4, A Dennis D. Kunkel/Biological Photo Service
17-8, 17-9 Cold Springs Harbor Laboratory Archives
17-10, 17-11 Bill Ober
17-15, 17-21, A, 17-27, A, 17-28, 17-B Nadine Sokol
17-17, 17-20 Molly Babich
17-6, 17-19 Carlyn Iversen
17-21, B 1982 C. Franke, J.E. Edstrom, A.W. McDowall & O.L. Miller, Jr.
17-23 John D. Cunningham/Visuals Unlimited
17-24 Lilli Robins
17-25(photos) Carolina Biological Supply Company

17-26 Dr. A. S. Bajer
17-27, B B.A. Palevitz & E.H. Newcomb/ BPS/Tom Stack & Associates
17-29 Kevin Somerville
17-30 James Kezer, University of Oregon
17-32(photo) C.A. Hasenkampf, University of Toronto/Biological Photo Service
17-A Herb Weitman/Washington University in St. Louis

Chapter 18

Opener National Cancer Institute; American Cancer Society; Laura J. Edwards
18-2 © Kenneth E. Greer/Visuals Unlimited
18-3 VU/Cabisco
18-8 Science VU/Visuals Unlimited
18-9 Biophoto Associates/Science Source/ Photo Researchers
18-10, A Gerhard Gscheidle/Peter Arnold, Inc.
8-10, B © Uniphoto Picture Agency
18-11 Lennart Nilsson © Boehringer Ingelheim International GmbH
Table 18-1 National Cancer Institute;, Science Photo/Photo Researchers; VU/© Veronika Burmeister; Science VU/Visuals Unlimited; Howard Sochurek/The Stock Market
18, A, 18, B Jack Tandy

Chapter 19

Opener Bob Krist
19-1 E. Rhone Rudder
19-2, 19-3 Nadine Sokol after Bill Ober
19-4, 19-5, 19-6, 19-8, 19-10 Nadine Sokol
19-11 Carolina Biological Supply Company
19-12 Raychel Ciemma

Chapter 20

Opener Science VU/NLM/Visuals Unlimited
20-1 CNRI/SPL/Science Source/Photo Researchers, Inc.
20-2, A The Children's Hospital, Denver, Cytogenics Laboratory
20-2, B R. Hutchings/Photo Researcher, Inc.
20-3, 20-8 Barbara Cousins
20-5 Victor A. McCusick/Blackwell Scientific Publications
20-6 Margaret A. Davee, M.S.; David D. Weaver M.D.; Department of Medical Genetics, Indiana University School of Medicine/Blackwell Scientific Publications
20-10 Adam Hart-Davis/SPL/Custom Medical Stock Photo, Inc.
20-13 The Bettmann Archive
20-14 M. Mrayama/Biological Photo Service
20-16 Kevin Somerville after Bill Ober
20-17 Washington University School of Medicine
20-A Dr. W. French Anderson/National Institutes of Health

Chapter 21

Opener, 21-1 Lennart Nilsson, *Behold Man,* Little, Brown and Co.
21-2, 21-6 Kate Sweeney
21-3, 21-5 Nadine Sokol after Bill Ober
21-4 Barbara Cousins
21-7 Raychel Ciemma
21-8 Ed Reschke

Index

Atrioventricular (AV) node, 174
Atrium, 171
Attention deficit disorder, 219
Australopithecus, evolution of, 484-485, 486
Autonomic nervous system, 225, 236-238
Autosomes, 390
  abnormal numbers of, inheritance of, 390-391
  pedigree analysis and, 395-396, 397
AV node; *see* Atrioventricular node
Axial skeleton, 285-286, 287
Axis, 290
Axolotl, 9
Axons, 118, 206-207, 234

B

B cells, 305, 308, 310
B lymphocytes, 176, 308
Backbone, 108
  development of, in embryo, 435
  in vertebrates, 476
Bacteria, 54, 450-456
  evolution of, 474
  exponential growth of, 453
  flagella of, 452, 453
  Kingdom Monera and, 13-14
  reproduction of, 452-454
  sexually transmitted diseases and, 446, 450-456
  size of, 451
  structure of, 451-452
  symbiotic, 55
Bacterial cell wall, 452
Bacterial plasma membrane, 452
Bacterial sexually transmitted diseases, 454-456
  chlamydial infection, 455-456
  gonorrhea, 455
  syphilis, 454
Bacteria-like organelles, 63-64
Bacteriophages, lytic cycle of replication of, 448
Baker's yeast, 91
Balance, 244, 252, 253
Ball-and-socket joint, 289, 290
Barbiturates, 217
Basal body, 65
Basal body temperature, recording, birth control and, 421
Basal cell carcinoma, 364
Basal ganglia, 229
Bases, 33, 47
Basic Four food guide, 144
Basic Seven food guide, 144
Basophils, 176, 178
Beadle, George, 331, 332, 333, 385
Benign tumors, 358
Benzene, 364
Benzodiazepines, 217
Benzo(a)pyrene, 364
Beta-carotene, cancer prevention and, 369
Bicuspid valve, 171
Bile, 138-139, 186, 366-367
Bile acids, 367
Bile duct, 139
Bile pigments, 138-139, 186, 187
Bile salts, 138, 139, 140, 142
  digestion and, 132
Binary fission, bacterial reproduction and, 452, 453
Binomial nomenclature, 15
Bioenergy, 509
Bioethics of controlled experiments, 1
Bio-gas machines, 509

Biological catalysts, enzymes as, 80-84
Biological clock, 272
Biological concentration of toxic pollutants in organisms, 516
Biological diversity, species extinction and, 514
Biological Dynamics of Forest Fragments Project, 513
Biological information, passing on, to offspring by living things, 12-13, 320-405
Biological magnification, 516, 517
Biomedical researchers, human biology and, 7, 8
Biosphere, 10, 11
  human impact on, 508
Bipedal hominids, evolution of, 483
Birds, evolution of, 477
Bird's nest fungi, 9
Birth, 441
  development before, 426-443
Birth canal, labor and, 441
Birth control, 421-424
  methods of, 420-421
  withdrawal method of, 413
Birth control pills
  combination, 366
  as method of birth control, 421, 423, 424
  sequential, 366
Bivalents, 345
Blastocyst, 430-431, 432
  implantation of, 431, 432
Blastula, 430, 437
Blended inheritance, 375-376, 377, 378, 399
Blindness, color; *see* Color blindness
Blood, 113, 158, 166, 175-178
Blood cells, 176, 177-178
Blood clot, strokes and, 180
Blood clotting, 115, 178
Blood plasma, 175-177
Blood pressure, 174-175
Blood vessels, 166, 167-175
  diseases of, 180
Blue-green algae, 471
Blushing, 168
Body
  internal environment of, sensing, 243
  levels of organization in, 104-123
  position of, in space, sensing, 243-244
Body chromosomes, 390
Bohr, Niels, 24
Bolus, 135
Bone cells, 113, 114
Bones, 282, 283-290
  attachments of skeletal muscles to, 291
  compact, 114, 284
  coxal, 287
  facial, 284, 285-286
  flat, 284
  irregularly shaped, 284
  long, 284
  organization of, 283
  palatine, 286
  short, 284
  spongy, 114, 115, 284
Booster shot, vaccination and, 311
Bowman's capsule, 188-190
Brain, 108, 206, 226-232
Brainstem, 226, 231-232
Bran, cancer prevention and, 369
Branchial arches, development of, in embryo, 438
BRCA1 gene, 356-357
Breakage of chromosomes, 393
Breast cancer, 356-357

Breast self-examination, 368
Breastbone, 286
Breast-feeding, passive immunity and, 311
Breathing, 150
  deep, 156
  mechanics of, 153-157
Bronchi, 152-153
Bronchioles, respiratory, 152, 153
Bronchitis, chronic, 160
Bronchodilators in treatment of asthma, 161
Brown-air cities, air pollution and, 520, 521
Brownian movement, 67
Bulbourethral glands, 413
Bulking up, 294
Bundle of His, 174
Burkitt's lymphoma, 361
Bursa of Fabricius, 308

C

Cabbage family, cancer prevention and, 369
Cadmium, 364
Calcitonin (CT), 265, 266, 267, 272
Calcium, 131, 132
  levels of, in blood, 266, 267
Calories, 130
Cambrian Period, 473, 474, 475
Cancer, 352-371
  characteristics of, 354
  chemoprevention and, 370
  cigarette smoking and, 154, 361-362
  danger signs of, 368
  diagnostic tests for, 368-369
  diet and, 366-367, 369
  factors that decrease risk of, 367-369
  factors that increase risk of, 359-367
  genetics of, 356-357
  heredity and, 359-360
  hormones and, 366
  industrial hazards and, 362-364
  inherited susceptibility genes and, 356-357
  initiation and, 354-355, 359
  ionizing radiation and, 365-366
  metastasis and, 354
  molecular biology of, 354-359
  progression and, 358-359
  promotion and, 355-358
  tumor viruses and, 360-361
  ultraviolet radiation and, 364
Cancer susceptibility genes, 356
Candida albicans, vaginal yeast infections and, 456
Candidiasis, 456-457, 459
Canines, 134
Capillaries, 167, 168-169, 170, 173
  glomerular, 190
Capillary beds, 168-169, 170
Capsid of virus, 447
Carbohydrates, 37-39, 130, 132, 145-146
Carbon, 33-34
Carbon dioxide, 91, 157, 158-159, 166
Carboniferous Period, 473, 476, 477
Carboxypeptidase, 84, 139
Carcinogenesis, 356-357
Carcinogens, 355
Carcinomas, 358
Cardiac muscle, 116, 117, 290
Cardiac opening, 135, 136
Cardiovascular system, 166, 167-175
  development of, in embryo, 437, 438
Carnivores, 133, 519
Carotene, 264
Carotid arteries, 173
Carpals, 287
Carriers of recessive genes, 396, 397, 398-399

Carrying capacity of population, 496
Cartilage cells, 114
Catabolic process, 95
Catabolic reaction, 76
Catalysis, 80
Catalysts, biological, enzymes as, 80-84
Cave paintings, Cro-Magnons and, 488, 489
CCK; *see* Cholecystokinin
Cecum, 143
Cell cluster, fertilized ovum and, 429-430
Cell cycle, 341
Cell division, 339-340
Cell growth, 339-340
Cell membrane, 53, 57, 58, 67
Cell migration, fertilized ovum and, 430, 437
Cell reproduction, 322-351, 352-371
Cell surface antigens, 400
Cell theory, 52
Cell walls, 66
Cell-mediated immune response, 307-308
Cell-poisoning cells, 307
Cells, 106
  hierarchical organization of, in living things, 10, 11
  how biological information is passed on by, 320-405
  living things composed of, 10
  movement of, that does not require energy, 67-69
  movement of, that requires energy, 69-72
  movement of substances into and out of, 67-72
  nerve, 204-221
  protoplasm and, 10
  size of, 53-54
  structure and function of, 50-73
Cellular respiration, 63-64, 88-103, 150, 166
Cellulose, 39
Cenozoic Era, 473
Central nervous system, 224, 225-233
  development of, in embryo, 437, 438
Centrioles, 341, 343
Cerebellum, 226, 231
Cerebral cortex, 226-228
Cerebrospinal fluid, 232-233
Cerebrum, 226-229
Cervical cancer, human papillomavirus types 16 and 18 and, 361, 450
Cervical cap as method of birth control, 420, 422
Cervical mucus, analysis of, birth control and, 421
Cervical vertebrae, 286
Cervix, 418-419
CFC; *see* Chlorofluorocarbon
Chancre, hard, syphilis and, 454
Chargaff, Erwin, 328, 329
Chase, Martha, 329
Chemical bond, nature of, 26
Chemical formula, 26
Chemical reactions, 76, 77, 80-84
Chemicals
  chromosomal breakage and, 393
  mutations caused by, 394-395
Chemistry, inorganic versus organic, 33-34
Chemoprevention, cancer and, 370
Chemoreceptors, 133
Chest cavity, 153
Chiasmata, 345, 347
Chickenpox virus, 449
Chitin, 39, 66
Chlamydial infection, 91, 446, 459
Chlamydial sexually transmitted infection, 455-456

Chlorofluorocarbon (CFC), ozone and, 521
Chlorophyll, 64
Chloroplasts, 64, 65
  evolution of, 474
Choking, 160
Cholecystokinin (CCK), 138, 140
Cholesterol, 42, 138, 145-146, 180
Chondrocytes, 111, 114
Chordates, evolution of, 474-476
Chorion, 433, 434
Chorionic villus sampling (CVS), 401, 437
Choroid, 249
Chromatin, 61-62, 324, 329
Chromium, 364
Chromosome 21, nondisjunction of, 391
Chromosomes, 62, 324, 325, 345
  aberrations of, 390-395
  body, 390
  broken and misrepaired, 393
  connection between Mendel's factors and, 383-384
  crossing-over of, 345, 346, 347
  deletion of section of, 393, 394
  duplication of section of, 393, 394
  homologous, 345
  inversion of, 393, 394
  mapping of, 332
  rearrangement of, 393, 394
  sex; *see* Sex chromosomes
  structure of, changes in, 393, 394
  translocation of, 393, 394
Chronic obstructive pulmonary disease (COPD), 160-161
Chyme, 138, 140
Chymotrypsin, 139
Cigarette smoking, 219
  cancer and, 154, 355, 361-362, 364, 366, 367, 368
  chronic bronchitis and, 160-161
  heart disease and, 180
Cilia, 108
  on eukaryotic cells, 64-65
  in nasal cavities, 151
  in trachea, 152
Ciliary muscle, 248
Circulation, 164-183
  placental-fetal, 440, 442
Circulatory shock, 122
Circulatory system, 107, 119, 120
  functions of, 166-167
  hormone circulation and, 167
  nutrient and waste transport and, 166
  oxygen and carbon dioxide transport and, 166
  respiration and, 157
  temperature maintenance and, 166
CITES; *see* Convention on International Trade in Endangered Species of Wild Fauna and Flora
Cities
  air pollution and, 520, 521
  population size and, 498
Citric acid cycle, 92
Civilization, beginnings of, 489
Clavicles, 287
Cleavage, cell division and, 429, 430, 437
Cleavage furrow, cytokinesis and, 344
Clitoris, 419, 439
Clone, humoral immune response and, 308
Clumped distributions of organisms within population, 496, 497
Cocaine, 219
Coccyx, 286
Cochlea, 250, 252

Cochlear duct, 251
Code of life, DNA and, 12-13, 324
Codeine, 217
Codominance, 399, 400
Codons, DNA and, 335
Coelom, 108
Coenzymes, enzyme activity and, 84
Cofactors, enzyme activity and, 84
Coitus, 419-421
Cold blooded animals, evolution of, 478
Cold receptors, 245
Cold sores, herpes simplex virus and, 449
Collagen, 42
Collagen fibers, 111, 114, 283
Collecting ducts of kidney, 188, 192, 194
Colon, 142-143
Colon cancer, 356-357, 366, 369
Colon cancer gene, 356-357
Colonial organism, 10
Color blindness, 398, 399
  Punnett square and, 396
  red-green, pedigree showing, 395
Colorectal cancer, 369
Columnar epithelium, 109, 110
Communication
  and regulatory systems, 202-277
  sensory, 242-243
Communication systems of body, 206
Community of organisms, mutualistic relationships within, 10
Compact bone, 114, 284
Competition among organisms, population size and, 497
Competitive exclusion, population size and, 497
Complement, antibodies and, 309
Complete dominance, 379
Composite molecules, 35
Compounds, 26
Conception, 428-429
  of one life to help sustain another, 407
Condensation, mitosis and, 341
Condom
  latex
    in protection from sexually transmitted diseases, 458
    reduction of risk of contracting sexually transmitted diseases and, 422
  as method of birth control, 420, 422, 424
Cones, 246-250
Connective tissues, 106, 110-116
Constipation, 143
Consumers, transformation of energy by, 12
Contraception, 421-424
Control, hypothesis and, 5, 6
Controlled experiment in testing of hypothesis, 5
Convention on International Trade in Endangered Species of Wild Fauna and Flora (CITES), 514
Convolutions, 226
COPD; *see* Chronic obstructive pulmonary disease
Copulation, 419-421
Coral reefs, destruction of, 513-514
Cornea, 248
Coronary arteries, 173
Corpus callosum, 226
Corpus luteum, 416
  human chorionic gonadotropin and, 416, 431, 432
Correns, Carl, 384
Cortex of kidney, 188
Corticosteroids, 268, 269

Food Wheel—A Daily Pattern for Food
    Choices, 144
Foramen ovale, placental-fetal circulation and,
    442
Foramina, 232
Forest ecosystem, energy pyramid in, 12
Fossil fuels, diminishing, 509
Fossils
    of single-celled organisms, 13
    theory of evolution and, 468, 470
Fovea, 249
Fragile X syndrome, 399
Franklin, Rosalind, 329
Fraternal twins, 430
Free energy of activation, 76
Free radicals, 355, 367, 369, 393
Freely movable joints, 288, 290
Frontal lobe, 227
Fructose, 37
Fruit fly, studies of sex linkage and, 384-385
FSH; *see* Follicle-stimulating hormone
Functional groups of organic molecules, 35,
    36
Fungi
    bird's nest, 9
    sexually transmitted diseases and, 446, 456-
        457

G

G_1 stage of interphase, cell cycle and, 341
G_2 stage of interphase, cell cycle and, 341
GABA; *see* Gamma-aminobutyric acid
Galactose, 37
Gallbladder, 139, 140
Gametes, 339, 375, 410-412
Gamma-aminobutyric acid (GABA), 217
Ganglia, basal, 229
Gas transport and exchange, 157-159
Gases, noble, 26
Gastric glands, 137
Gastrin, 137-138, 140
Gastrula, 435, 437
Gastrulation, 434-435, 436
Gene, 331-333, 378
    deoxyribonucleic acid and, 12-13
    dominant; *see* Dominant genes
    globin, evolution of, 472
    recessive; *see* Recessive genes
    reproduction and, 12
    tumor suppressor; *see* Tumor suppressor
        gene
Gene expression, 322-351
Gene families, 339
Gene switches, 339
Gene transfer therapy, 332
General adaptation syndrome, 268
General senses, 244-245
Generator potential, 234, 242
Genetic aberrations, infants with, 321
Genetic code, 335, 336
Genetic counseling, 401
Genetic disorders, dominant and recessive,
    398-399
Genetic engineering of vaccines, 311
Genetics, 375-383
    human, 388-403
        dominant and recessive disorders and,
            398-399
        gene mutations and, 394-395
        genetic counseling and, 401
        incomplete dominance and codominance
            and, 399, 400
        inheritance of abnormal numbers of auto-
            somes and, 390-391, 392

Genetics—cont'd
    human—cont'd
        inheritance of abnormal numbers of sex
            chromosomes and, 392-393
        multiple alleles and, 400
        studying inheritance patterns in humans
            using pedigrees in, 395-397
        studying inheritance patterns using karyo-
            types in, 390-395
Genital herpes, 446, 447, 449-450, 459
Genital warts, 450, 459
Genotype, 380, 392
Genus, 15
Geological time, table of, 471, 473
Geometric progression, population increase
    and, 469
Geothermal energy, 509
Germ layers, primary, of pre-embryo, 432
Germ plasm banks, species extinction and, 514
Germ theory of disease, 501
Gestation, 426-443
GH; *see* Growth hormone
Giantism, 263
Gill arches
    in chordates, 474
    development of, in embryo, 438
Glands, 108, 258
Glial cells, 118
Gliding joint, 289
Global warming, 512
Globin gene, evolution of, 472
Glomerular capillaries, 190
Glomerulus, 190
Glottis, 135, 152
Glucagon, 270, 271, 273
Glucocorticoids, 268, 270, 273
Glucose, 37
Glycerol, 40
Glycogen, 37, 38
Glycolysis, 91, 94-96, 100
Goiter, 264
Golgi, Camillo, 60
Golgi body, 59, 60
Gonadotropins, 261, 263
Gonads, 263, 410, 414-415
Gonorrhea, 446, 459
Gradient, 67
Grana, 64
Granulocytes, 177
Gravity, theory of, 8
Gravity receptors, 244, 252
Gray matter, 226, 229
Gray-air cities, air pollution and, 520, 521
Greenhouse effect, 512
Groundwater, 515
    pollution of, 516
Growth
    cell, 339-340
    exponential, of population, 494, 495
Growth hormone (GH), 263, 270, 272
Growth rate of population, 494-496
Guanine, DNA and, 328, 329, 334
Gumma, syphilis and, 454

H

H zone, 294
Habitats
    destruction of, 513-514
    human impact on, 508
Haeckel, Ernst, 438
Hair cells, 251
Hallucinogens, 216, 219
Hammer, 250
Hammerling, Joachim, 326, 327

Haploid cells, 339, 340, 344, 347
Hard chancre, syphilis and, 454
Hassle-Free Guide to a Better Diet in 1979,
    144
Haversian canal, 283
Hay fever, 312
HBV; *see* Hepatitis B virus
HCG; *see* Human chorionic gonadotropin
Hearing, sense of, 250-251
Heart, 166, 167-175
    contraction of, 174
    development of, in embryo, 437, 438
    diseases of, 180
Heart attacks, 180, 181
Heart disease, avoidance of, 173
Heart murmur, 174
Heartbeat, 174-175
Heartburn, 135, 136
Heat, 78, 79
Heat receptors, 245
Heavy chains, antibodies and, 310
Heimlich, Henry, 160
Heimlich maneuver, 160
Helium, 26
Helper T cells, 307, 308, 311-312
Hemoglobin, 116, 157, 158, 159, 177
Hemophilia, 396, 397, 398, 399
Hepatitis B, 449
Hepatitis B virus (HBV), 360, 449-450
Herbivores, 133, 519
Heredity
    cancer and, 355, 359-360, 368
    heart disease and, 180
Hernia, hiatal, 135
Herpes
    genital, 446, 447, 449-450, 459
    oral, 449, 450
Herpes simplex virus (HSV), 449
Herpes zoster virus, 449
Herpesvirus, 447, 449
Hershey, Alfred, 329
Heterotrophs, 130, 457
Heterozygotes, incomplete dominance and,
    399
Heterozygous individual, 378, 379, 380, 396
Hiatal hernia, 135
Hiatus, esophageal, 135
Hierarchical organization of cells in living
    things, 10, 11
High altitude sickness, 157
High-energy bonds, adenosine triphosphate
    and, 84-85
High-risk pregnancy, genetic counseling and,
    401
Hinge joint, 288, 289
Hip bones, 287
Histamine, 111
Histones, DNA wrapped around, 324, 325
Homeostasis, 120-122, 194, 195-196, 225,
    230, 236
Hominids, evolution of, 483, 484-489
Homo erectus, evolution of, 486-487
Homo habilis, evolution of, 485-486
Homo sapiens, evolution of, 483, 487-489
Homologous chromosomes, 345
Homologous structures in evidence for evolu-
    tion, 470
Homologues, 345, 390-391
Homonoids, evolution of, 483, 484
Homozygous individual, 378, 379, 380, 396
Homunculus, 374
Hormones, 120-122, 140, 167, 195, 196,
    256-275
    cancer and, 366, 368

Hormones—cont'd
  communication by, 206
  digestive, 137, 138
  endocrine, 259-260
  local, 259, 272-273
  nonendocrine, 272-273
  peptide, 259-260
  releasing, 260, 261, 272
  steroid, 259-260
  tropic, 261, 263
HPV; *see* Human papillomavirus
HSV; *see* Herpes simplex virus
HTLV; *see* Human T lymphotropic-leukemia
      virus
Human chorionic gonadotropin (HCG), cor-
      pus luteum and, 416, 430, 432
Human evolution and ecology, 464-525
Human genetics; *see* Genetics, human
Human Genome Project, 332
Human immunodeficiency virus (HIV), 311-
      312, 314-315, 360-361, 446, 449
  impact of, 314
  prevention of, 315
  spectrum of, 314
  transmission of, 315
Human impact on environment, 506-523
Human papillomavirus (HPV), 360, 361, 450
Human population concerns, 492-505
Human subjects, medical research using, 8
Human T lymphotropic-leukemia virus
      (HTLV), 360, 361
Humerus, 287
Humoral immune response, 307, 308-310
Humoral response, 308
Huntington's disease, 398, 399
Hyaline cartilage, 112, 114, 288
Hybrids, 375
Hydra, asexual reproduction and, 340, 341
Hydrochloric acid, 140
  digestion and, 132
  recycling of, 519
Hydrogen bonds, 30-31
Hydrolysis, 35-37, 132, 133
Hydrolyzing enzymes, 133
Hydrophobic bonding, 32
Hydrosphere, human impact on, 515-520
Hyoid bone, 286
Hypercholesterolemia, 398, 399
Hyperpolarization, 247
Hyperthyroidism, 265, 266
Hypertonic solution, 68, 69
Hyphae, fungi and, 456
Hypopituitary dwarfism, 263
Hypothalamus, 122, 166, 229-230, 243, 261,
      264, 269, 272
Hypothesis
  control and, 5, 6
  scientific method and, 4-7
Hypothyroid goiter, 264
Hypothyroidism, 265
Hypotonic solution, 68, 69

I

I band, 294
Ice Ages, 486
Identical twins, 430
Ileum, 138
Imipramine, 216
Immigration, population growth and, 494
Immovable joints, 288
Immune response, 303-310
  cell-mediated, 307-308
  humoral, 307, 308-310
  two branches of, 307-310

Immune system, 107, 119, 120, 303, 305
Immunity, 302, 303, 311
Immunization, 311
Immunoglobulins, humoral immune response
      and, 308-310, 311
Immunology, 303-304
Immunosuppressive drugs, kidney transplants
      and, 198
Implantation of blastocyst, 431, 432
Inbreeding, population size and, 496
Incisors, 134
Inclusions, bacteria and, 452
Incomplete dominance, 379, 399, 400
Incubator Earth, 13
Incus, 250
Independent variable, hypothesis and, 5, 6, 7
Indoles, 369
Inducer T cells, 307, 308
Induction, tissue differentiation and, 437
Inductive reasoning, scientific method and,
      4-5
Industrial hazards, cancer and, 362-364, 368
Industrial Revolution
  effect of, on population size, 501, 502
  energy supplies and, 509
Inert gases, 26
Infants
  with genetic aberrations, 321
  passive immunity of, 311
  physiological adjustments of, 440, 442
Infection
  latent, 449
  nonspecific versus specific resistance to, 302-
      304
  sexually transmitted diseases and, 446
  yeast, vaginal, 419
Inferior vena cava, 173
Infestation, sexually transmitted diseases and,
      446
Inflammation, 302
Inheritance
  blended, 375-376, 377, 378, 399
  historical views of, 374
  patterns of, 372-387
  solving mysteries of, 385
  study of, 375
  and variation within species, 374-375
Inheritance patterns
  Gregor Mendel's experiments to determine,
      375-383
  in humans, studying
    using karyotypes, 390-395
    using pedigrees, 395-397
Inhibitor, enzyme activity and, 83
Inhibitory synapse, 215
Initiation, cancer and, 354-355, 359
Inner cell mass of blastocyst, 430
Inner ear, 250, 251, 252
Inorganic nutrients, accumulation of, in lakes,
      516
Inorganic versus organic chemistry, 33-34
Insertion of skeletal muscle, 291
Inspiration, 151, 155, 156
Insulator, feather as, 12, 13
Insulin, 194, 259, 270, 271, 273
Integration, central nervous system and, 226
Integration, peripheral nervous system and,
      234
Integrator, 215
Integument, 283
Integumentary system, 107, 119, 120, 283
Interaction of living things with each other
      and with their environments, 10, 11
Intercellular fluid, 150

Intercostal muscles, 153
Intercourse, 419-421
Interleukin-1, 306, 307
Internal environment, steady, maintenance of,
      by living things, 12
Internal respiration, 150, 158-159
Interneurons, 206-207, 234
Interphase
  cell cycle and, 341
  meiosis and, 345, 347
Interstitial fluid, 150
Intervention, hypothesis and, 7
Intervertebral disks, 286
Intrauterine devices as method of birth con-
      trol, 421
Introns, DNA and, 334, 335
Inversion, chromosomal, 393, 394
Involuntary responses, motor neurons and,
      225
Ionic bonds, 26-28
Ionization, 32-33
Ionizing radiation
  cancer and, 355, 365-366, 368
  chromosomal breakage and, 393
  mutations caused by, 394-395
Ions, 26-28, 67, 209
Iris, 249
Irrigation, trickle, 519
Islets of Langerhans, 270, 273
Isolating connective tissue, 115-116
Isoleucine, 84
Isomers, 37
Isotonic solution, 68, 69
Isotopes, 24, 25

J

Jawless fishes, evolution of, 476
Jejunum, 138
Jellies, spermicidal, as method of birth control,
      421, 422
Jenner, Edward, 303, 311
Johanson, Donald C., 485
Joints, 288-290
Juvenile onset diabetes, 270

K

Kaposi's sarcoma, 361
Karyotypes, 324
  changes in chromosome structure and, 393,
      394
  gene mutations and, 394-395
  inheritance of abnormal numbers of auto-
      somes, 390-391, 392
  inheritance of abnormal numbers of sex
      chromosomes and, 392-393
  studying inheritance patterns in humans us-
      ing, 390-395
kcal; *see* Kilocalories
Keratin, 364
Ketones, 271
Kidney stones, 196-197, 266
Kidney transplants, renal failure and, 198
Kidneys, 187-194
  anatomy of, 188
  homeostasis and, 194, 195-196
  major blood vessels in, 188, 189
  problems with function of, 196-198
  selective reabsorption by, 190-192
  structure of, 188, 189
Killer cells, 307
Kilocalories (kcal), 130
Kinetic energy, 78, 79, 80, 209
Kinetochore, 343
Kingdom Animalia, 13-14

Mouth, 133-134
mRNA; *see* Messenger RNA
MS; *see* Multiple sclerosis
MSH; *see* Melanocyte-stimulating hormone
MTOC; *see* Microtubule organizing center
Mucin, 60, 428
Mucosa lining stomach, 137
Mucous membranes as nonspecific defense of body, 303
Multicellular organism, 10
Multiple alleles, 399, 400
Multiple cropping, 519
Multiple sclerosis (MS), 213
Muscle fibers, 117, 293, 294
Muscle spindles, 243-244
Muscle tissues, 106, 116-117
Muscles, 282, 290-297
Muscular system, 107, 118, 291-297
Mushrooms, 456
Mutations, 331, 354, 390, 394-395
    caused by ionizing radiation, 394-395
    point, 394-395
Mutualistic relationships within community, 10
Myelin sheath, 207, 212
Myofibrils, 116-117, 293-296
Myofilaments, 293-296
Myosin, 293-296

N

Napier, John, 486
Narcosis, 217
Narcotic analgesics, 217
Nasal cavities, 151, 152
Nasal conchae, 286
National Institutes of Health (NIH), medical research and, 8
Natural history, scientific method and, 4
Natural killer (NK) cells, 305, 306
Natural resources, diminishing, human impact on, 508-513
Natural selection, theory of evolution and, 347, 469, 474
Natural variation, theory of evolution and, 468
Naturalists, scientific method and, 4
Neanderthals, evolution of, 488
Nearsightedness, 248
Negative feedback loop, 120-122, 260, 261
Neisseria gonorrhoeae, gonorrhea and, 455
Nephrons, 187, 188-194
Nerve cells, transmitting information between, 204-221
Nerve cord, 108, 474, 475
Nerve fibers, 118
Nerve gases, 214
Nerve impulse, 206, 208-213
    all-or-nothing response and, 211
    conduction of, 210-211
    muscle fiber contraction and, 296
    transmission of, 211
Nerves, 118
    cranial, 234
    in peripheral nervous system, 229
    spinal, 232
    structure of, 235
Nervous system, 107, 120, 204-221, 222-239
    autonomic, 225, 236-238
    central; *see* Central nervous system
    organization of, 224-225
    parasympathetic, 225, 236, 237
    peripheral, 224, 225, 233-238
    somatic, 225, 234-236
    sympathetic, 225, 236, 237

Nervous tissues, 106, 118
Neural folds, development of, in embryo, 435
Neural groove, development of, in embryo, 435, 437
Neural tube, development of, in embryo, 435
Neurofibromatosis, cancer and, 354
Neuroglia, 207, 226
Neuromuscular junction, 214-215, 296
Neurons, 118, 206-207
    afferent, 224
    efferent, 224
    insulation of, 207, 208
    motor, 206-207, 224
    sensory, 206-207, 224
Neuron-to-muscle cell connections, 214-215
Neuron-to-neuron connections, 215
Neurotransmitters, 214-215
Neurula, 437
Neurulation in embryo, 435, 436, 437
Neutrons, 24
Neutrophils, 176, 177, 302, 306
New World monkeys, evolution of, 481, 482, 484
Newborns; *see* Infants
NGU; *see* Nongonococcal urethritis
Nickel, 364
Nicotinamide adenine dinucleotide, 93
Nicotine, 219
NIH; *see* National Institutes of Health
Nitrites, 367
Nitrogen, 26
Nitrogen dioxide, acid rain and, 518-520
Nitrogen-containing molecules, 187
Nitrogenous wastes, 187
Nitrosamines, 367
NK cells; *see* Natural killer cells
Noble gases, 26
Nocturnal mammals, evolution of, 477
Nocturnal prosimians, 482
Nodes of Ranvier, 207, 213
Nondisjunction
    of autosomes, meiosis and, 391
    of chromosome 21, 391
    of sex chromosomes, 392-393
Nonendocrine hormones, 272-273
Nongonococcal urethritis (NGU), 91, 456, 459
Nonoxynol-9 in protection from sexually transmitted diseases, 458
Nonpoint sources of pollutants, 515
Nonspecific versus specific resistance to infection, 302-304
Noradrenaline, 215, 269, 273
Norepinephrine, 215, 219, 269
Norplant as method of birth control, 366, 421, 423, 424
Nose, development of, in embryo, 438
Nostrils, 151
Notochord
    in chordates, 474
    embryonic, development of, in embryo, 435
Nuclear envelope, 61
Nuclear fission reactors, 509
Nuclear fusion reactors, 509
Nuclear pores, 61
Nuclear power, 509
Nuclear radiation, chromosomal breakage and, 393
Nuclei, 54, 61-62, 229, 327
Nucleic acid core of virus, 447
Nucleic acids, 47, 327-329
Nucleoid, 54, 452
Nucleolus, 62, 63, 341
Nucleotides, 12-13, 47, 327, 329

Nutrients, 130, 132
    inorganic, accumulation of, in lakes, 516
    transport of, circulatory system and, 166
Nutrition
    diet and, 143-146
    digestion and, 130-132

O

Obesity, 143
Obligate parasites, viruses as, 446
Observation, scientific method and, 4
Observational studies, hypothesis and, 7
Occipital lobe, 227
Octet rule, 26
Office of Women's Health, medical research and, 8
Offspring, passing on biological information to, by living things, 12-13
Oils, 40
Old World monkeys, evolution of, 481, 482-483, 484
Olfactory receptors, 245, 246
Omnivores, 133
Oncogenes, 354, 356-357
Oncogene-transcribed polypeptides, 355
One gene–one enzyme theory, 332, 333
Oocyte, secondary, 410, 414-415, 428
Oogenesis, 414-415
Oogonia, 414-415
Open dumps, solid waste and, 515
Opiates, 216, 217, 218
Opium, 217
Opposable thumb, development of, 480
Opsin, 247
Optic nerve, 249
Oral contraceptives as method of birth control, 421, 422, 423, 424
Oral herpes, 449, 450
Orbital of electron, 24
Order, laws of thermodynamics and, 79
Ordovician Period, 473, 474
Organ, 10
    of Corti, 251
Organ donations and consent, 279
Organ systems, 10, 106, 118-122
Organelles
    bacteria-like, 63-64
    Kingdom Monera and, 13-14
Organic molecules, 33-34, 35
Organic versus inorganic chemistry, 33-34
Organisms
    classification of, 13-15
    community of, 10
    flow of energy within, 74-87
Organogenesis, 434
Organs, 106, 118
Orgasm, 414, 419, 420-421
Osmosis, 67-69
Osmotic pressure, 68
Ossification, development of, in fetus, 439
Osteoblasts, 283
Osteocytes, 111, 114
Osteoporosis, 266
Osteosarcoma, tumor suppressor genes and, 354
Otoliths, 252
Outer ear, 250, 251
Oval window, 250
Ovarian cycle, 416
Ovaries, 263, 272, 273, 414-415
Overpopulation, environmental problems and, 521
Oviduct, 415
Ovists, historical views of inheritance and, 374

Proprioceptors, 243-244
Prosimians, evolution of, 480, 481, 482
Prostaglandins, 273, 441
Prostate cancer, 366
Prostate gland, 413
Proteases, 132
Protective connective tissue cells, 111
Protein synthesis, 337, 338, 339
Proteins, 42-46, 130, 132, 145-146
  muscle building and, 294
Proterozoic Era, 471-474
Prothrombin activator, 178
Protists, 457
Protons, 24, 26
Proto-oncogenes, 354
Protoplasm, 10, 54
Protozoans, 446, 457
Proximal convoluted tubule, 190
Pseudohyphae, yeasts and, 456
Pseudomonas species, 451
Pseudostratified epithelium, 110
Psychedelic drugs, 219
Psychoactive drugs, 216, 217-219
PTH; *see* Parathyroid hormone
Puberty, spermatogenesis and, 411-412
Pubic lice, 457-458, 459
Public Health Service (PHS), United States,
  medical research and, 8
Pulmonary arteries, 173
Pulmonary circulation, 171, 172
Pulmonary semilunar valve, 173
Pulmonary veins, 171
Pulp of tooth, 134
Punnett square, 380, 383, 396
Pupil of eye, 249
Purines, DNA and, 328, 329
Purkinje fibers, 174
Pyloric sphincter, 138
Pyrimidines, DNA and, 328, 329
Pyrocystis, 9
Pyruvate, 91, 92
Pyruvic acid, 91

Q

Qualitative data, hypothesis and, 5
Quantitative data, hypothesis and, 5

R

Radiation
  ionizing; *see* Ionizing radiation
  nuclear, 393
  particulate, 365
  ultraviolet; *see* Ultraviolet radiation
Radicals, free, 355, 367, 369, 393
Radioactive fallout, 365
Radius, 287
Radon, 26, 364, 365-366
Rain, pH of, 518
Random distributions of organisms within
  population, 496, 497
Random motion of molecules, 79
Reasoning
  deductive, hypothesis and, 5
  inductive, scientific method and, 4-5
Receptors, 233
  nerve impulse and, 210-211
  sensory, 242-243
Recessive genes, 375-383
  pedigree analysis and, 396, 397
Recessive genes, carriers of, 396, 397, 398-
  399
Rectal examination, digital, 369
Rectum, 143

Recycling
  aluminum, 511, 519
  of hydrochloric acid, 519
  paper, 512
  solid waste, 515
Red blood cells, 115-116, 177, 178, 285
Red bone marrow, 284, 285
Red-green color blindness, pedigree showing,
  395
Redox reactions, 28, 93
Reduction, 28, 92-93
Reduction-division, 344, 383
Reflex, 236
Reflex arcs, 232, 236
Refractory period, nerve impulse and, 211
Regulatory sites, transcription of genes and,
  339
Releasing hormones, 260, 261, 272
Renal arteries, 188
Renal failure, 197-198
Renal pelvis, 188, 195
Renal pyramids, 188
Repeated trials of hypothesis, 7
Replication, viral, 448-449
Replication fork, DNA and, 331
Representative samples, medical research and,
  8
Reproduction
  asexual, 12, 340, 341, 374
  cell, 322-351, 352-371
  genes and, 12
  hormones and, 259
  human, 406-463
  by living things, 12-13
  sexual; *see* Sexual reproduction
Reproductive system, 119, 120
  female; *[i]see* Female reproductive system
  male; *see* Male reproductive system
Reptiles, evolution of, 476, 477
Research
  in human biology, 7, 8
  medical, representative samples and, 8
Reserpine, 215
Residual air, 157
Resistance
  to disease, 303
  stress and, 268, 270
Resolution phase of sexual intercourse, 419,
  421
Respiration, 148-163
  cellular, 63-64, 88-103, 150, 166
  external, 150, 157-158, 159
  internal, 150, 158-159
Respiratory assemblies, electron transport
  chain and, 98, 99
Respiratory bronchioles, 152, 153
Respiratory system, 107, 119, 120
Responding variable, hypothesis and, 5, 6
Resting potential, 208-210
Resting stage, cell cycle and, 341
Restriction site, 332
Reticular connective tissue, 112, 114
Reticular formation, 232
Reticulate bodies, chlamydiae and, 455
Reticulin fibers, 111, 114
Retina, 247, 249, 250, 438
Retinal, 247
Retinoblastoma, 354, 356-357
Rhodopsin, 247
Rhythm method of birth control, 420, 421,
  422, 424
Rib cage, 285
Ribonucleic acid (RNA), 47, 61, 327-329
Ribose, 84, 327

Ribosomal ribonucleic acid (rRNA), 62, 333,
  334, 341
Ribosomes, 59, 333, 337, 339, 452
Ribs, 286
Right atrium, 171, 173
Right ventricle, 171, 173
Ringworm, 456
Ritalin, 219
RNA; *see* Ribonucleic acid
RNA polymerase, 333
Rods, 246-250
Root of tooth, 134
Rough endoplasmic reticulum, 59
Round window, 250
rRNA; *see* Ribosomal RNA
Runner's high, 273

S

S stage of interphase; *see* Synthesis stage of
  interphase
SA node; *see* Sinoatrial node
Saccharin, 367
Saccule, 252, 253
Sacrum, 286
Saddle joint, 289
Saliva, 133, 134
Salivary amylase, 133
Salivary glands, 133
Saltatory conduction, nerve impulse and, 212-
  213
Sample, representative, medical research and, 8
Sanitary landfills, solid waste and, 515
Saprophytic organisms, 456
Sarcoma, 358
  Kaposi's, 361
Sarcomere, 293, 294
Sarcoplasmic reticulum, 296
Saturated fats, 40, 367
Scabies, 457-458, 459
Scapulae, 287
Schleiden, Matthias, 52
Schwann, Theodor, 52
Schwann cells, 118, 207, 212
Scientific law, evolution as, 469-471
Scientific method, pathway of thinking in, 4-7
Scientific process, 4-8
Sclera, 248
Scrotum, 410-412, 413-414, 439
Second filial (F_2) generation of traits, 375
Secondary oocyte, 410, 414-415, 428
Secondary pollutants, air pollution and, 520,
  521
Secretin, 138, 140
Sedative-hypnotics, 217
Sediment, accumulation of, in lakes, 516
Selection
  artificial, theory of evolution and, 468, 469
  natural, theory of evolution and, 347, 469,
  474
Selectively permeable membranes, 67
Self-fertilization, 375
Selye, Hans, 268
Semen, 413
Semicircular canals, 252, 253
Seminal vesicles, 413
Seminiferous tubules, 411
Semipermeable membranes, 67
Senses, 240-255
  general, 244-245
  special, 245-253
Sensory area of cerebral cortex, 227, 228
Sensory communication, nature of, 242-243
Sensory neurons, 206-207, 224

Wheezing, asthma and, 161
White blood cells, 115, 116, 177, 285, 305
White matter, cerebral, 229
White matter tracts of spinal cord, 232
Wilkins, Maurice, 329
Windmills as energy source, 509, 510
Windpipe, 135, 152
Withdrawal method of birth control, 413, 420, 422, 424
Withdrawal symptoms, drug addiction and, 216
Women of child-bearing age, medical research and, 8
World Bank, 502

World population distribution by region, 502
World Wildlife Fund, 513, 514
Wrists, development of, in embryo, 438

X

Xeroderma pigmentosa, 355
X-rays, 365-366, 393
XYY male, 394
XYY syndrome, 392-393

Y

Yeast artificial chromosomes (YAKs), 332
Yeast infections, vaginal, 419, 456-457, 459

Yeasts, 456-457
Yellow body, 416
Yellow marrow, 284
Yolk sac, 434

Z

Z line, 296
Zona pellucida, 428
Zoos, breeding programs in, species extinction and, 514
Zygote, 414, 415, 429